# Educational Administration

**∎**

## Concepts and Practices

### Fifth Edition

# Educational Administration

■

## Concepts and Practices

### Fifth Edition

Fred C. Lunenburg
Sam Houston State University

Allan C. Ornstein
St. John's University

**WADSWORTH**
CENGAGE Learning™

Australia • Brazil • Japan • Korea • Mexico • Singapore • Spain • United Kingdom • United States

WADSWORTH
CENGAGE Learning

**Educational Administration: Concepts and Practices, Fifth Edition**
Fred C. Lunenburg, Allan C. Ornstein

Social Work Editor: Dan Alpert

Development Editor: Tangelique Williams

Assistant Editor: Ann Lee Richards

Editorial Assistant: Stephanie Rue

Technology Project Manager: Julie Aguilar

Marketing Manager: Karin Sandberg

Marketing Assistant: Teresa Marino

Marketing Communications Manager: Shemika Britt

Project Manager, Editorial Production: Tanya Nigh

Creative Director: Rob Hugel

Art Director: Vernon Boes

Print Buyer: Linda Hsu

Permissions Editor: Bob Kauser

Production Service: Newgen–Austin

Copy Editor: Carolyn Haley

Cover Designer: Bartay Studio

Cover Image: Design Pics Inc. / Alamy

Compositor: Newgen

For product information and technology assistance, contact us at **Cengage Learning Customer & Sales Support, 1-800-354-9706**
For permission to use material from this text or product, submit all requests online at **www.cengage.com/permissions**
Further permissions questions can be emailed to **permissionrequest@cengage.com**

Library of Congress Control Number: 2007923794

ISBN-13: 978-0-495-11585-4

ISBN-10: 0-495-11585-1

**Wadsworth**
10 Davis Drive
Belmont, CA 94002-3098
USA

Cengage Learning is a leading provider of customized learning solutions with office locations around the globe, including Singapore, the United Kingdom, Australia, Mexico, Brazil, and Japan. Locate your local office at:
**international.cengage.com/region**

Cengage Learning products are represented in Canada by Nelson Education, Ltd.

For your course and learning solutions, visit
**academic.cengage.com**

Purchase any of our products at your local college store or at our preferred online store **www.ichapters.com**

Printed in the United States of America
2  3  4  5  6  7  11  10  09  08

# Contents

## 12 ■ Legal Considerations and Education 366

# Part IV
# Administration of Programs and Services    404

## 13 ■ Curriculum Development and Implementation    404

## 14 ■ Analyzing and Improving Teaching    446

## 15 ■ Human Resources Administration    485

# Administrative Advice

# PRO/CON Debates

# Administrator Profiles

# ■ Foreword

During the past decade, the nation's attention has again been riveted on education. Numerous publications offer a myriad of recommendations focused on what must be done to improve the quality of education in America. This intense desire for a new and restructured education process offers many windows of opportunity for positive change.

When school reform efforts have been directed to and given a sense of direction by those local leaders who are responsible for effective change in our nation's schools, the results have been favorable. *Educational Administration: Concepts and Practices*, Fifth Edition, will serve as a valuable primer for prospective school leaders as they work toward effecting change in an orderly, efficient, and effective manner.

Its authors, Fred Lunenburg and Allan Ornstein, have addressed both the concepts surrounding educational change and the processes they feel are essential for improvement, and they have done it in a forthright and interesting manner. In addition, the authors have discussed the fundamental principles of effective administrative leadership, including the need to effectively manage the process of collaboration and coordinate improvement efforts.

Creative, high quality leadership is essential to the reform and restructuring of American education, as our schools strive to meet the needs and challenges of our society.

Richard D. Miller
*Former Executive Director*
*American Association of*
*School Administrators*

# Preface

Educational administrators face a challenging and changing climate in our nation's schools. In the past, textbooks in educational administration have focused mainly on theory and research as a way of providing a knowledge base and preparation for students and professionals. In *Educational Administration: Concepts and Practices*, Fifth Edition, we have attempted to go beyond this tradition by including, in addition to comprehensive coverage of theory and research, a third component: practical applications that help educational administrators make use of the knowledge base they acquire. This practical, applied component makes our book a unique entry to the literature and a resource that we believe will enhance the abilities of future and current educational administrators to become effective leaders in our changing educational climate.

The practical and applied component of *Educational Administration: Concepts and Practices* can be found in many aspects of this text.

- New and unique coverage of topics such as the post–behavioral science era—school improvement, democratic community, and social justice; ethics and values; gender, race/ethnicity, and class; critical theory and postmodernism; instructional leadership; site-based decision making; change; curriculum development and implementation; improving teaching; technology; human resources administration; and emergent perspectives are included.

- Chapter openings begin with five to eight focusing questions designed to focus the reader's attention on the major issues within the chapter.

- Administrative Advice sections (about three or four per chapter) demonstrate how significant concepts can be applied to administrative practice.

- PRO/CON Debates (one per chapter) illustrate opposing perspectives on major issues facing educational administrators.

- Summaries at the ends of chapters highlight critical points and especially salient issues in theory, research, and applications.

- Lists of key terms and discussion questions at the end of each chapter stimulate application of concepts and enhance understanding of the chapter.

- Extensive documentation throughout and suggestions for additional readings at the end of each chapter encourage readers to pursue further exploration of significant subject matter.

- Full-page Exemplary Educational Administrator boxes are included in each chapter.

The chapters on federal and state government, local school districts, school finance and productivity, legal constraints, curriculum development and implementation, and improving teaching have been extensively revised.

## Organization of the Text

This book contains fifteen chapters in four major parts. The introductory chapter defines the field, looks at how it came into existence, and presents a conceptual model that provides a framework for the remainder of the book. The next chapter focuses on several alternative approaches to organizational structure. The last chapter in this opening part provides a cultural context for the study and application of educational administration.

After this foundation is provided, Part II examines the basic administrative processes with chapters on motivation, leadership, decision making, communication, and organizational change. Part III focuses on the structural framework for education. The chapter on the federal and state role in education is followed by chapters on the local school district, school finance and productivity, and legal considerations in education. Part IV explores the administration of programs and services. Specific chapters deal with curriculum development, teaching strategies, and human resources management.

The four parts and fifteen chapters of the book are relatively self-contained. Thus, an entire part, selected chapters, or even portions of chapters, could be skipped, or studied in a different sequence, without damaging the flow or content of the book.

We have developed a robust companion website for the new edition of this book. The website includes a series of original cases for each chapter based on real-life scenarios in school administration. In addition, we have included a full chapter on careers in educational administration (formerly Chapter 16) as well as additional resources on careers in educational administration, all of which can be downloaded free of charge. The website can be accessed as follows: academic.cengage.com/education/lunenburg.

## Acknowledgments

This book has been a cooperative effort between scholars and experienced editors and publishers. We wish to express our appreciation to the reviewers and others whose suggestions led to improvements in this and in earlier editions:

| | |
|---|---|
| Judy A. Alston | Bowling Green State University |
| Paul Baker | Illinois State University |
| Edwin D. Bell | East Carolina University |
| Dale L. Bolton | University of Washington |
| James Boothe | Xavier University |
| Norman Boyles | Iowa State University |
| Fred E. Bradley | University of Missouri, St. Louis |
| Dennis C. Brennan | University of the Pacific |
| Jerry Cicchelli | Fordham University |
| James A. Conway | State University of New York, Buffalo |
| Philip A. Cusick | Michigan State University |
| Andrew E. Dubin | San Francisco State University |
| Janet Fredericks | Northeastern Illinois University |
| Lloyd E. Frohreich | University of Wisconsin, Madison |
| Jits Furusawa | California State University, Dominguez Hills |
| Patricia Hoehner | University of Nebraska, Kearney |
| Ernest Johnson | University of Texas, Arlington |
| Franklin B. Jones | Tennessee State University |
| Lawrence Kajs | University of Houston, Clear Lake |
| Frank Keane | Fayetteville State University |
| Donald Layton | State University of New York, Albany |
| Arthur Lehr | University of Illinois, Urbana-Champaign |
| Robert B. Lowe | Angelo State University |
| Steve Nowlin | Troy State University |
| Anita M. Pankake | University of Texas, Pan American |
| Albert Pautler | State University of New York, Buffalo |
| Lorrie C. Reed | Chicago State University |
| Glenn B. Schroeder | University of Northern Colorado |
| Linda T. Sheive | State University of New York, Oswego |
| Donald W. Smitley | Eastern Illinois University |
| Carl Steinhoff | University of Nevada, Las Vegas |
| Clark Webb | Brigham Young University |

We also wish to gratefully acknowledge the following individuals who contributed Exemplary Administrators in Action boxes for this edition: Henry S. Bangser, Superintendent, New Trier Township High School District, Winnetka/Northfield, IL; Mirabelle Baptiste, Principal, Clifton Middle School, Houston Independent School District, Houston, TX; Richard (Rick) Earl Berry, Superintendent, Cypress-Fairbanks Independent School District, Houston, TX; James F. Causby, Superintendent, Johnson County Schools, Smithfield, NC; Craig L. Elliott, Superintendent, Maize Unified School District, Maize, KS; Pascal Forgione, Superintendent, Austin Independent School District, Austin, TX; Barry Fried, Principal, John Dewey High School, Brooklyn, NY; Carlos A. Garcia, Superintendent, Clark County School District, Las Vegas, NV; Joe A. Hairston, Superintendent, Baltimore County Public Schools, Towson, MD: David Kazakoff, Principal, Terra Nova High School, Pacifica, CA; William G. Meuer, Principal, Norwood Park School, Chicago Public Schools, Chicago, IL; Joanna Miller, Principal, E. M. Baker Elementary School, Great Neck, NY; Lonnie E. Palmer, Superintendent, City School District of Albany, Albany, NY; Art Rainwater, Superintendent, Madison Metropolitan School District, Madison, WI; Ron Saunders,

Superintendent, Barrow County Schools, Winder, GA; Paul Vance, Superintendent, District of Columbia Public Schools, Washington, DC. Your willingness to share your experiences will help to guide and inspire future generations of school administrators.

We wish to thank Marion Czaja for conducting and writing the cases for each chapter of the text that appear on the Wadsworth companion website. We also wish to thank Paula Lester, Long Island University, for her contribution to Chapter 10 of the book and William Owings, Old Dominion University, and Leslie Kaplan, Newport News Public Schools, for their contribution to Chapter 11.

We want to thank the people at Wadsworth whose contributions made this a much better book: Dan Alpert, Acquisitions Editor; Tangelique Williams, Development Editor; Stephanie Rue, Editorial Assistant; Tanya Nigh, Senior Project Manager; Karin Sandberg, Marketing Manager; Shemika Brett, Marketing Communications Manager; and Teresa Marino, Marketing Assistant.

We are grateful to our respective deans Genevieve Brown and Jerry Ross for creating an environment and contributing the resources necessary to complete this book. Special thanks is also extended to Alicia Raley and Michael Russo, each of whom typed portions of the fifth edition.

Fred C. Lunenburg
Allan C. Ornstein

# The Authors

**Fred C. Lunenburg** is the Jimmy N. Merchant Professor of Education at Sam Houston State University. Prior to moving to the university, he served as a teacher, principal, and superintendent of schools. He has authored or co-authored more than 100 articles and 20 books, including *The Principalship: Vision to Action* (Thomson/Wadsworth, 2006), *Shaping the Future* (Rowman & Littlefield, 2003), *The Changing World of School Administration* (with George Perreault) (Scarecrow Press, 2002), and *High Expectations: An Action Plan for Implementing Goals 2000* (Corwin, 2000). He received the Phi Delta Kappa Research Award in 1986 and was The Distinguished Visiting Professor at the University of Utrecht (The Netherlands) in 1995.

**Allan C. Ornstein** is Professor of Administrative and Instructional Leadership at St. Johns University. He is the author of 54 books and some 400 articles on education, and has been a consultant for more than 75 government and educational agencies, including the Chicago and New York City school districts. He is a former Fulbright-Hayes Scholar and member of the Fulbright-Hayes screening committee. Among Dr. Ornstein's most recent books are *Foundations of Education,* 10th ed. (Houghton Mifflin, 2008), *Contemporary Issues in Education,* 4th ed. (Allyn and Bacon, 2007), *Pushing the Envelope* (Merrill, 2003), and *Teaching and Schooling in America: Pre and Post September 11* (Allyn and Bacon, 2003). His most recent book, *Class Counts: Education, Inequality and the Shrinking Middle Class* (Rowman and Littlefield, 2007), examines growing inequality, the shrinking middle class, the slow decline of the nation, and the waning influence of education.

# 1.

# Development of Administrative Theory

## FOCUSING QUESTIONS

1  To what extent is educational administration characterized by the use of theory?

2  What is theory?

3  How do theories function in educational administration?

4  What are the major components of classical organizational theory, the human relations approach, the behavioral science approach, and the post–behavioral science era?

5  Why is contingency theory popular today in administering schools?

6  Why is systems theory important for preventing organizational failures?

7  How have emergent nontraditional perspectives influenced the study and practice of educational administration?

In this chapter, we attempt to answer these questions concerning theoretical and historical developments in administration. We begin our discussion by exploring the nature of theory in administration and discuss six functions of theory in educational administration. Then we identify and explain major developments in the history of administrative thought: classical, human relations, behavioral science, and post–behavioral science approaches to administration. Finally, we examine contingency theory and open systems theory, and we conclude the chapter with a discussion of emergent perspectives in educational administration.

## Theory

Educational administrators are professionals who have a code of ethics and are licensed by state boards of education.[1] Thus, their behavior is guided by acceptable standards of practice. One of the best criteria of a profession, however, is that it has matured as a science; that is, it has developed a solid theoretical base—a body of organized and tested knowledge. Such is the case with educational administration as a social science.[2] Theory in educational

---

[1] American Association of School Administrators, *Code of Ethics for School Administrators* (Arlington, VA: The Association, 2008).

[2] It may be more accurate to refer to educational administration as an *applied* science.

administration has been evolving since the 1950s. To an increasing degree, educational administration is characterized by using theory to explain and predict phenomena in educational organizations.[3]

What are theories? Fred Kerlinger defines **theory** as "a set of interrelated constructs (concepts), definitions, and propositions that present a systematic view of phenomena by specifying relations among variables with the purpose of explaining and predicting phenomena."[4] Daniel Griffiths includes many of the same ideas in his discussion of theory. He adds that a theory is a deductively connected set of empirical laws and that all statements in a theory are generalizations that explain the empirical laws and unify the areas of subject matter.[5]

A theory, then, is a statement (generalization) that explains some phenomena in a systematic way. Theories may range from a simple generalization to a complex set of laws, from philosophical to scientific. Some theories deal with simple generalizations such as results of educational polls or school surveys undertaken by state accrediting associations. Such studies involve measures of the nature of some condition at a particular time. They explain what is. More sophisticated theories may seek to explain why particular phenomena occur; examples are Einstein's theory of relativity and Newton's theory of universal gravitation. Most theories in the social sciences require a process of refinement through revision and extension.[6]

Several such efforts to refine and extend the scientific theory movement deserve mention. To begin with, Griffiths proposes "theoretical pluralism" that is linked to problems of practice.[7] Willower suggests philosoph-

ical naturalism and pragmatism, variously called scientific methods, inquiry, or reflective methods.[8] These philosophies rely on logic and evidence, consistent with such definitions of truth as Dewey's warranted assertibility.[9] Hoy provides a pragmatic perspective on science and theory in the practice of educational administration. He suggests the heuristic value of social science research and theory. He argues that research and theory building can serve as useful frames of reference for practitioners as they engage in real-world problem solving.[10] Evers and Lakomski provide a postpositivist conception of science in educational administration that they call "naturalistic coherentism." This view contends that knowledge generation should be assessed on the basis of its testability, simplicity, consistency, comprehensiveness, fecundity, familiarity of principle, and explanatory power.[11] Bridges and Hallinger espouse a problem-based learning model, which simulates the world of practice. Educational administration trainees focus on a problem likely to be encountered by practitioners. Self-directed teams of trainees define the problem, gather data from a variety of disciplines, and apply new knowledge as they solve the problem. The teams present their solutions in the form of a final project.[12] Donmoyer introduces the concept of "utilitarianism" as a potential way to bridge the theory–practice gap. This approach takes the form of expanding the definition of knowledge to include nontraditional along with traditional methods of inquiry. He sees the resulting fusion of quantitative and qualitative methods of inquiry as valuable to both the researcher and the

[3]See, for example, Daniel E. Griffiths, "Administrative Theory," in N. J. Boyan (ed.), *Handbook of Research on Educational Administration* (New York: Longman, 1988), pp. 27–51.

[4]Fred N. Kerlinger, *Foundations of Behavioral Research*, 3rd ed. (San Diego, CA: Harcourt Brace, 1986), p. 9.

[5]Griffiths, "Administrative Theory."

[6]William Wiersma et al., *Research Methods in Education*, 8th ed. (Boston: Allyn and Bacon, 2004).

[7]Daniel E. Griffiths, "Theoretical Pluralism in Educational Administration," in R. Donmoyer, M. Imber, & J. J. Scheurich (eds.), *The Knowledge Base in Educational Administration: Multiple Perspectives* (Albany: State University of New York Press, 1995), pp. 300–309; Daniel E. Griffiths, "The Case for Theoretical Pluralism," *Educational Management and Administration*, 25 (1997): 371–380.

[8]Donald J. Willower, "Fighting the Fog: A Criticism of Postmodernism," *Journal of School Leadership*, 8 (1998): 448–463.

[9]John Dewey, *Logic: The Theory of Inquiry* (New York: Henry Holt, 1938).

[10]Wayne K. Hoy, "Science and Theory in the Practice of Educational Administration: A Pragmatic Perspective," *Educational Administration Quarterly*, 32 (1996): 366–378.

[11]Colin W. Evers and Gabriele Lakomski, "Science in Educational Administration: A Postpositivist Conception," *Educational Administration Quarterly*, 32 (1996): 379–402.

[12]Edwin M. Bridges and Philip Hallinger, *Problem-Based Learning for Administrators* (Eugene: University of Oregon, ERIC Clearinghouse on Educational Management, 1992); Edwin M. Bridges and Philip Hallinger, *Implementing Problem-Based Learning in Leadership Development* (Eugene: University of Oregon, ERIC Clearinghouse on Educational Management, 1995).

practitioner.[13] Finally, Murphy discusses a "dialectic" strategy to bridge the theory–practice gap[14] and later offers some unifying concepts—a "synthesizing paradigm"—to aid in the preparation and practice of school administrators.[15]

## Functions of Theories

Many school administrators feel uncomfortable with theories. They prefer that social scientists provide them with practical prescriptions for administering their schools. Upon closer examination, however, almost every action a school administrator takes is based to some degree on a theory. For example, a school administrator may include others in a decision involving an issue that is relevant to them and that they have the expertise to make, instead of making the decision unilaterally. Such action is referred to in the research literature as participatory decision making. Participatory decision making, also referred to as shared, collaborative, or group decision making, focuses on decision processes that involve others.

In education, participatory decision making is based on the idea that active involvement of teachers, parents, or community members in school decisions will lead to improved school performance.[16] It is believed that those closest to teaching and learning, namely teachers, and those with the most knowledge about the children, namely parents, should be involved in decisions because they have expertise that is crucial to improving school performance. Furthermore, it is believed that when teachers and parents are involved in decision making, they will be more committed to implementing and sup-

porting the decision, and a sense of ownership in the school will result.[17] Without knowing it, the school administrator made the choice to involve others in the decision-making process on the basis of a theory.

Educational administrators would most likely flounder without theories to guide them in making choices. Thus, theories provide a guiding framework for understanding, predicting, and controlling behavior in organizations. Theories also contribute to the advancement of knowledge in the field.[18] Deobold Van Dalen has suggested six functions of theories, and we follow his categorization in this discussion.[19]

**Identifying Relevant Phenomena** Theories determine the number and kinds of phenomena that are relevant to a study. A theory tells a social scientist what to observe and to ignore. For example, social scientists may study school administration from the open systems perspective. (Open systems theory is discussed later in this chapter.) A relevant component in the open systems approach is the external environment that impacts the organization. Several subsystems exist within this environment. Among the more important are economic, political, productive, distributive, and resource systems. Social scientists may study the external environment from within all these frameworks. Multiple phenomena are associated with each subsystem. Social scientists will not know precisely what phenomena to observe until they construct theoretical solutions for each problem area under investigation.

**Classifying Phenomena** Scientists rarely work efficiently with masses of phenomena; therefore, they construct theoretical frameworks for classification. The physical sciences have been successful in developing such conceptual schemes. Geologists have developed schemes for classifying rocks, and botanists have devised systems for classifying plants.

---

[13]Robert Donmoyer, "The Continuing Quest for a Knowledge Base: 1976–1998," in J. Murphy and K. S. Louis (eds.), *Handbook of Research on Educational Administration*, 2nd ed. (San Francisco: Jossey-Bass, 1999), pp. 25–43.

[14]Joseph Murphy, *The Landscape of Leadership Preparation: Reframing the Education of School Administrators* (Newbury Park, CA: Corwin Press, 1992).

[15]Joseph Murphy, "Reculturing the Profession of Educational Leadership: New Blueprints," *Educational Administration Quarterly*, 39 (2002): 176–191.

[16]Kenneth Leithwood and Daniel L. Duke, "A Century's Quest to Understand School Leadership," in J. Murphy and K. S. Louis (eds.), *Handbook of Research on Educational Administration*, 2nd ed. (San Francisco: Jossey-Bass, 1999), pp. 45–72.

[17]Ellen Goldring and William Greenfield, "Understanding the Involving Concept of Leadership in Education: Roles, Expectations, and Dilemmas," in J. Murphy (ed.), *The Educational Leadership Challenge: Redefining Leadership for the 21st Century* (Chicago: University of Chicago Press, 2002), pp. 1–19.

[18]Donmoyer, "The Continuing Quest for a Knowledge Base."

[19]Deobold B. Van Dalen, *Understanding Educational Research*, 4th ed. (New York: McGraw-Hill, 1979).

An example of a classification scheme in educational administration is the study of organizational climate by Andrew Halpin and Don Croft.[20] Using factor analysis, they developed eight dimensions of organizational climate and classified them into six categories: open, autonomous, controlled, familiar, paternal, and closed. Another example comes from the work of Henry Mintzberg. After extensive, structured observation of five executives (one a school superintendent), Mintzberg classified managerial activities into ten administrative roles: figurehead, leader, liaison (interpersonal); monitor, disseminator, spokesperson (informational); and entrepreneur, disturbance-handler, resource-allocator, negotiator (decisional).[21] If educational administrators fail to develop theoretical frameworks for classifying phenomena, they will limit the advancement of knowledge in the field.

**Formulating Constructs**    Reliable information can be obtained through direct observation and measurement. However, many aspects of behavior cannot be directly observed. Intelligence is not an observable entity; it is inferred from using instruments that sample subject behavior. Affective predispositions such as attitudes, interests, and opinions cannot be observed directly; they are observed indirectly as they manifest themselves in behavior. Consequently, social scientists have developed constructs to explain why certain types of behavior occur. These constructs are often referred to as *hypothetical constructs* to imply that they are a construction of the social scientist's imagination. Kurt Lewin's force-field analysis is an example of a theoretical construct.[22]

**Summarizing Phenomena**    Theories summarize isolated lists of data into a broader conceptual scheme of wider applicability. These summaries can be stated with varying degrees of comprehensiveness and precision. They may range from simple generalizations to complex theoretical relationships. A school superintendent making a generalization about granting certificates of achievement to outstanding teachers in the school district is an example of low-level summarizing. This type of summary is not usually referred to as a theory. But the superintendent might construct a more complex generalization, one that describes the relationship between phenomena. For example, after observing the granting of certificates of achievement to deserving teachers, the superintendent may note a relationship: Public recognition is a means of motivating teachers. Summarizing and explaining phenomena permit deeper understanding of data and translate empirical findings into a more comprehensive, theoretical framework.

In the natural sciences, for instance, the theory of oxidation brings many of the chemical reactions common to everyday life into focus. The more comprehensive the theory, which is supported by verified observations, the more mature the science becomes.

**Predicting Phenomena**    A theory permits social scientists to predict the existence of unobserved instances conforming to it. For example, Abraham Maslow made the following generalization: People at work seek to satisfy sequentially five levels of needs arranged in a prepotency hierarchy.[23] A deprived need dominates the person's attention and determines behavior. Once this deficit is satisfied, the next higher-level need is activated, and the individual progesses up the hierarchy. When the level of self-actualization is reached, progression ceases. The more this need is satisfied, the stronger it grows. On the basis of this theory, one can expect to find a similar pattern of behavior in a variety of work settings where no statistics have been generated. That is, theory enables one to predict what should be observable where no data are available.

**Revealing Needed Research**    Theories generalize about phenomena and predict phenomena. They also pinpoint crucial areas to be investigated and crucial questions to be answered. Earlier we noted that theories in the social sciences may lack supporting evidence and therefore require a refining process. Such refinement through revision and extension is necessary to provide the maturity required for continually expanding the knowledge base in educational administration.

## Classical Organizational Theory

**Classical organizational theory** emerged during the early years of the twentieth century. It includes two different **management perspectives:** scientific management

[20]Andrew W. Halpin and Don B. Croft, *The Organizational Climate of Schools* (Chicago: University of Chicago Press, 1963).

[21]Henry Mintzberg, *The Nature of Managerial Work* (New York: HarperCollins, 1990).

[22]Kurt Lewin, *Field Theory in Social Science* (New York: Harper & Row, 1951).

[23]Abraham Maslow, *Motivation and Personality*, rev. ed. (Reading, MA: Addison-Wesley, 1970).

and administrative management. Historically, scientific management focused on the management of work and workers. Administrative management addressed issues concerning how an overall organization should be structured.

## Scientific Management

Prior to the turn of the twentieth century, there was almost no systematic study of management. The practice of management was based on experience and common sense. Frederick W. Taylor tried to change that view. An engineer, he pursued the idea that through careful scientific analysis the efficiency of work could be improved. His basic theme was that managers should study work scientifically to identify the "one best way" to perform a task.

Taylor's **scientific management** consists of four principles:[24]

1. *Scientific Job Analysis.* Through observation, data gathering, and careful measurement, management determines the "one best way" of performing each job. Such job analysis replaces the old rule-of-thumb method.

2. *Selection of Personnel.* Once the job is analyzed, the next step is to scientifically select and then train, teach, and develop workers. In the past, workers chose their own work and trained themselves.

3. *Management Cooperation.* Managers should cooperate with workers to ensure that all work being done is in accordance with the principles of the science that has been developed.

4. *Functional Supervising.* Managers assume planning, organizing, and decision-making activities, whereas workers perform their jobs. In the past, almost all work and the greater part of the responsibility were thrust on workers.

Taylor's four principles of scientific management were designed to maximize worker productivity. In his early career as a laborer in the steel industry, he observed firsthand how workers performed well below their capacities. He referred to this activity as *soldiering.* Taylor felt that scientific management—time study

for setting standards, separation of managerial and employee duties, and incentive systems—would correct the problem. Rather than relying on past practice or rules of thumb, he provided managers with explicit guidelines for improving production management, based on proven research and experimentation.

## Administrative Management

Whereas scientific management focuses on jobs of individual workers, **administrative management** concentrates on the management of an entire organization. The primary contributors to administrative management were Henri Fayol, Luther Gulick, and Max Weber.

Henri Fayol was an engineer and French industrialist. For many years, he served as managing director of a large coal-mining firm in France. He attributed his success as a manager not to any personal qualities he may have possessed but, rather, to a set of management principles that he used. Fayol claimed that all managers perform five basic functions: planning, organizing, commanding, coordinating, and controlling.

Besides the five basic management functions, Fayol identified fourteen principles that he felt should guide the management of organizations and that he found useful during his experience as a manager (Table 1–1).

Fayol's fourteen principles of management emphasize chain of command, allocation of authority, order, efficiency, equity, and stability. Max Weber also recognized the importance of these factors. But Fayol was the first to recognize management as a continuous process.

Luther Gulick, another classical theorist, augmented Fayol's five basic management functions while serving on Franklin D. Roosevelt's Committee on Government Administration. He coined the acronym POSDCoRB, which identified seven functions of management: planning, organizing, staffing, directing, coordinating, reporting, and budgeting.[25]

1. *Planning* involves developing an outline of the things that must be accomplished and the methods for accomplishing them. It attempts to forecast future actions and directions of the organization.

2. *Organizing* establishes the formal structure of authority through which work subdivisions are

---

[24]Frederick W. Taylor, *Principles of Scientific Management* (New York: Harper, 1911).

[25]Luther Gulick and Lyndall Urwick (eds.), *Papers on the Science of Administration* (New York: Columbia University Press, 1937).

**Table 1–1    Fayol's Fourteen Principles of Management**

| Component | Description |
|---|---|
| Division of work | The object of division of work is improved efficiency through a reduction of waste, increased output, and a simplification of job training. |
| Authority | Authority is the right to give orders and the power to extract obedience. Responsibility, a corollary of authority, is the obligation to carry out assigned duties. |
| Discipline | Discipline implies respect for the rules that govern the organization. Clear statements of agreements between the organization and its employees are necessary, and the state of discipline of any group depends on the quality of leadership. |
| Unity of command | An employee should receive orders from only one superior. Adherence to this principle avoids breakdowns in authority and discipline. |
| Unity of direction | Similar activities that are directed toward a singular goal should be grouped together under one manager. |
| Subordination of individual interest | The interests of individuals and groups within an organization should not take precedence over the interests of the organization as a whole. |
| Remuneration | Compensation should be fair and satisfactory to both employees and the organization. |
| Centralization | Managers must retain final responsibility, but they should give subordinates enough authority to do the task successfully. The appropriate degree of centralization will vary depending on circumstances. It becomes a question of the proper amount of centralizing to use in each case. |
| Scalar chain | The scalar chain, or chain of command, is the chain of supervisors ranging from the ultimate authority to the lowest ranks. The exact lines of authority should be clear and followed at all times. |
| Order | Human and material resources should be coordinated to be in the right place at the right time. |
| Equity | A desire for equity and equality of treatment are aspirations managers should take into account in dealing with employees. |
| Stability of personnel | Successful organizations need a stable workforce. Managerial practices should encourage long-term commitment of employees to the organization. |
| Initiative | Employees should be encouraged to develop and carry out plans for improvement. |
| Esprit de corps | Managers should foster and maintain teamwork, team spirit, and a sense of unity and togetherness among employees. |

Source: Adapted from Henri Fayol, *General and Industrial Administration* (New York: Pitman, 1949), pp. 20–41. (Originally published in French in 1916 with the title *Administration Industrielle et Generale.*)

arranged, defined, and coordinated to implement the plan.

3. *Staffing* involves the whole personnel function of selecting, training, and developing the staff and maintaining favorable working conditions.

4. *Directing,* closely related to leading, includes the continuous task of making decisions, communicating and implementing decisions, and evaluating subordinates properly.

5. *Coordinating* involves all activities and efforts needed to bind together the organization in order to achieve a common goal.

6. *Reporting* verifies progress through records, research, and inspection; ensures that things happen according to plan; takes any corrective action when necessary; and keeps those to whom the chief executive is responsible informed.

7. *Budgeting* concerns all activities that accompany budgeting, including fiscal planning, accounting, and control.

One of the most influential contributors to classical organizational theory was German sociologist Max Weber, who first described the concept of bureaucracy. Weber's contributions were not recognized until years after his death.[26] Weber's concept of bureaucracy is based on a comprehensive set of rational guidelines. Similar in concept to many of Fayol's fourteen principles, Weber's guidelines were believed to constitute an ideal structure for organizational effectiveness. Weber's ideal bureaucracy and Fayol's fourteen principles of

---

[26]Max Weber, *The Theory of Social and Economic Organization,* trans. Talcott Parsons (New York: Oxford University Press, 1947).

management laid the foundation for contemporary organizational theory.[27]

Classical organizational theories and their derived principles have many critics. An emphasis on efficiency characterized the classical approach to management. To these theorists, an efficiently designed job and organization were of prime importance. Psychological and social factors in the workplace were ignored. The critics claim that when managers ignore the social and psychological needs of workers, organizations do not provide adequate motivation to their employees. The classicists assumed that financial incentives would ensure worker motivation. In short, the focus of classical organizational theory was on the task, with little attention given to the individual or group in the workplace. This flaw was primarily responsible for the emergence of the second approach to management thought: the human relations approach.

## Human Relations Approach

The **human relations approach** is considered to have started with a series of studies conducted at the Hawthorne Plant of Western Electric near Chicago by Elton Mayo and his associates between 1927 and 1933.[28] These studies, widely known as the **Hawthorne studies**, have strongly influenced administrative theory.

### The Hawthorne Studies

The Hawthorne studies consisted of several experiments. They included the first Relay Assembly Test Room, the second Relay Assembly Group, the Mica-Splitting Group, the Typewriting Group, and the Bank Wiring Observation Room experiments. In addition, an interview program involving 21,126 employees was conducted to learn what workers liked and disliked about their work environment.

[27]Kenneth Leithwood and Daniel L. Duke, "A Century's Quest to Understand School Leadership," in J. Murphy and K. Seashore Louis (eds.), *Handbook of Research on Educational Administration,* 2nd ed. (San Francisco: Jossey-Bass, 1999), pp. 45–72.

[28]Elton Mayo, *The Human Problems of an Industrial Civilization* (New York: Macmillan, 1933); and Fritz J. Roethlisberger and William J. Dickson, *Management and the Worker* (Cambridge, MA: Harvard University Press, 1939).

Two experiments in particular are noteworthy. In the Relay Assembly Test Room experiments, the research began with the designation of two groups of female workers. Each group performed the same task, and the groups were located in two separate rooms, each of which was equally lighted. One group, designated the control group, was to have no changes made in lighting or other work-environment factors. The other was the experimental group in which lighting and other environmental factors were varied. Changes in the productivity of the two groups was subsequently measured and analyzed. Regardless of the light level or various changes in rest periods and lengths of workdays and workweeks, productivity in both the control and the experimental groups improved; in fact, the worse things got, the higher the productivity rose.

In the Bank Wiring Observation Room experiments, a group of nine men were paid on a piecework incentives pay system. That is, their pay increased as their productivity increased. Researchers expected that worker productivity would rise over time. As in the Relay Assembly Test Room experiments, researchers found an unexpected pattern of results. They discovered that the group informally established an acceptable level of output for its members. Most workers, the "regulars," ignored the incentive system and voluntarily conformed to the group's standard level of acceptable output, called a *group norm.* Those who did not conform, the "deviants," were disciplined by the group to bring their output in line with the group's standard output. Workers who produced too much were called "rate-busters" and sometimes were physically threatened to make them conform with the rest of the group. On the other hand, employees who underproduced were labeled "chislers" and were pressured by the group to increase their productivity.

To understand the complex and baffling pattern of results, Mayo and his associates interviewed over 20,000 employees who had participated in the experiments during the six-year study. The interviews and observations during the experiments suggested that a human-social element operated in the workplace. Increases in productivity were more of an outgrowth of group dynamics and effective management than any set of employer demands or physical factors. In the lighting experiment, for example, the results were attributed to the fact that the test group began to be noticed and to feel important. Researchers discovered that the improvement in productivity was due to such human-social factors as morale, a feeling of belongingness, and effective management in which such interpersonal skills as motivating, leading, participative decision making, and effective communications were used. Researchers concluded, from the results of the incentive pay-system experiment, that informal work groups emerged with their own norms for appropriate behavior of group members. In short, the importance of understanding human behavior, especially group behavior, from the perspective of management was firmly established.

## Other Contributors to the Human Relations Approach

Mayo and his associates were not the only contributors to the human relations approach. There were several strong intellectual currents, which influenced the human relations movement, during this period. Kurt Lewin emphasized field theory and research known as group dynamics.[29] Noteworthy is his work on *democratic* and *authoritarian* groups. Lewin and his associates generally concluded that democratic groups, in which members actively participate in decisions, are more productive in terms of both human satisfaction and the achievement of group goals than are authoritarian groups.[30] Furthermore, much of the current work on individual and organizational approaches to change through group dynamics (sensitivity training, team building, Alcoholics Anonymous, and Weight Watchers) and the action-research approach to organizational development is based on Lewin's pioneering work.

Carl Rogers deserves mention here as well. Not only did he develop a procedure for industrial counseling[31] while working with Mayo and his associates at Western Electric, but the metapsychological assumptions on which his client-centered therapy[32] is based also provide the skeletal framework on which the human relations approach is built. For example, according to Rogers, the best vantage point for understanding behavior is from the internal frame of reference of the individual, who exists in a continually changing world of experience; who perceives the field of experience as real-ity for her; and who strives to actualize, maintain, and enhance her own human condition.[33]

The writings of Jacob Moreno made a substantial contribution to the human relations movement. Like Lewin, Moreno was interested in interpersonal relations within groups. He developed a sociometric technique: People develop selective affinities for other people. Groups composed of individuals with similar affinities for one another will likely perform better than groups lacking such affective preferences.[34]

Additional contributors to the human relations school of thought include William Whyte and George Homans. Using a field study methodology similar to the one used by Mayo, Whyte studied the nature and functioning of work group behavior in the restaurant industry. He examined intergroup conflict, status within groups, workflow, and the like. Consistent with Moreno's sociometric theory, Whyte found that selective preferences among group members are associated with such factors as similarities in age, sex, and outside interests.[35] His study is significant because the findings are based on observations of real-life situations rather than isolated laboratory conditions. George Homans's general theory of small groups was a major landmark. Homans conceptualized the totality of group structure and functioning that has received wide attention among organizational theorists and practitioners alike.[36]

The major assumptions of the human relations approach include the following ideas:

1. Employees are motivated by social and psychological needs and by economic incentives.

2. These needs, including but not limited to recognition, belongingness, and security, are more important in determining worker morale and productivity than the physical conditions of the work environment.

3. An individual's perceptions, beliefs, motivations, cognition, responses to frustration, values, and similar factors may affect behavior in the work setting.

---

[29] Kurt Lewin, *Field Theory in Social Science.*

[30] Kurt Lewin, Ronald Lippitt, and Robert White, "Patterns of Aggressive Behavior in Experimentally Created 'Social Climates,'" *Journal of Social Psychology,* 10 (1939): 271–299.

[31] Carl R. Rogers, *Counseling and Psychotherapy* (Boston: Houghton Mifflin, 1942).

[32] Carl R. Rogers, *Client-Centered Therapy* (Boston: Houghton Mifflin, 1951).

[33] Ibid., pp. 483–494.

[34] Jacob L. Moreno, *Who Shall Survive?* rev. ed. (New York: Beacon House, 1953).

[35] William F. Whyte, *Human Relations in the Restaurant Industry* (London: Pittman, 1949).

[36] George C. Homans, *The Human Group* (New York: Harcourt, Brace & World, 1950).

4. People in all types of organizations tend to develop informal social organizations that work along with the formal organization and can help or hinder management.

5. Informal social groups within the workplace create and enforce their own norms and codes of behavior. Team effort, conflict between groups, social conformity, group loyalty, communication patterns, and emergent leadership are important concepts for determining individual and group behavior.

6. Employees have higher morale and work harder under supportive management. Increased morale results in increased productivity.

7. Communication, power, influence, authority, motivation, and manipulation are all important relationships within an organization, especially between superior and subordinate. Effective communication channels should be developed between the various levels in the hierarchy, emphasizing democratic rather than authoritarian leadership.

The human relationists used field study methods extensively as well as laboratory experiments to study the work environment. These social scientists made important contributions to our understanding of employee behavior in the workplace.

## Behavioral Science Approach

Behavioral scientists considered both the classicists' rational-economic model and the human relationists' social model to be incomplete representations of employees in the work setting. A number of authors attempted to reconcile or show points of conflict between classical and human relations theory; thus, the **behavioral science approach** was born.

### The Individual and the Organization

Behavioral scientists fueled a new interest in individuals and the way in which they relate to the organization.

**Effectiveness/Efficiency** Although a contemporary of many human relationists, Chester Barnard was one of the first authors to take the behavioral science approach. For many years, Barnard served as president of the New Jersey Bell Telephone Company. His executive experience and extensive readings in sociology and organizational psychology resulted in one of management's few classic textbooks.[37]

His best-known idea is the **cooperative system,** an attempt to integrate, in a single framework, human relations and classical management principles. Barnard argues that the executive must meet two conditions if cooperation and financial success are to be attained. First, the executive must emphasize the importance of *effectiveness,* which is the degree to which the common purpose of the organization is achieved. Second, the executive must be aware of *efficiency,* which is the satisfaction of "individual motives" of employees.[38] His major point is that an organization can operate and survive only when both the organization's goals and the goals of the individuals working for it are kept in equilibrium. Thus, managers must have both human and technical skills.

**Fusion Process** Another major contributor to the behavioral science approach was E. Wight Bakke of the Yale University Labor and Management Center. He views the organization as embodying a **fusion process.**[39] The individual, he argues, attempts to use the organization to further his own goals, whereas the organization uses the individual to further its own goals. In the fusion process, the organization to some degree remakes the individual and the individual to some degree remakes the organization. The fusion of the *personalizing process* of the individual and the *socializing process* of the organization is accomplished through the *bonds of organization,* such as the formal organization, the informal organization, the workflow, the task(s) to be completed, and the system of rewards and punishments.

**Individual/Organization Conflict** Having views similar to Bakke's, Chris Argyris argues that there is an inherent conflict between the individual and the organization.[40] This conflict results from the incompatibility between the growth and development of the individual's maturing personality and the repressive nature of the formal organization. Argyris believes that people

[37] Chester I. Barnard, *The Functions of the Executive* (Cambridge, MA: Harvard University Press, 1938).

[38] Ibid.

[39] E. Wight Bakke, *The Fusion Process* (New Haven, CT: Yale University Press, 1955).

[40] Chris Argyris, *The Individual and the Organization* (New York: Irvington, 1993).

progress from a state of psychological immaturity and dependence to maturity and independence and that many modern organizations keep their employees in a dependent state, preventing them from achieving their full potential. Further, Argyris believes that some of the basic principles of management are inconsistent with the mature adult personality. The resulting incongruence between individual personality and the organization causes conflict, frustration, and failure for people at work. People learn to adapt to the failure, frustration, and conflict resulting from the incongruency by ascending the organizational hierarchy, by using defense mechanisms, or by developing apathy toward their work that ultimately leads to the dysfunction of the organization's goals. This trend to conformity has been espoused in such popular books as *The Organization Man*[41] and *Life in the Crystal Palace*.[42]

**Nomothetic/Idiographic**   A useful theoretical formulation for studying administrative behavior is the social systems analysis developed for educators by Jacob Getzels and Egon Guba.[43] Getzels and Guba conceive of the social system as involving two classes of phenomena that are independent and interactive. First are institutions with certain roles and expectations that together constitute the **nomothetic dimension** of activity in the social system. Second are the individuals with certain personalities and need-dispositions inhabiting the system who together constitute the **idiographic dimension** of activity in the social system. Behavior then in any social system can be seen as a function of the interaction between personal needs and institutional goals. Conformity to the institution, its roles, and its expectations results in organizational effectiveness, whereas conformity to individuals, their personalities, and their need-dispositions results in individual efficiency. (Note the similarity between Getzels and Guba's framework and those of Barnard, Bakke, and Argyris.)

**Need Hierarchy**   The behavioral science approach has drawn heavily on the work of Abraham Maslow, who developed a **need hierarchy** that an individual attempts

to satisfy.[44] Maslow's theory suggests that an administrator's job is to provide avenues for the satisfaction of an employee's needs that also support organizational goals and to remove impediments that block need satisfaction and cause frustration, negative attitudes, or dysfunctional behavior.

**Theory X and Theory Y**   Based on the work of Maslow, Douglas McGregor formulated two contrasting sets of assumptions about people and the management strategies suggested by each. He called these **Theory X** and **Theory Y**.[45] McGregor believed that the classical approach was based on Theory X assumptions about people. He also thought that a modified version of Theory X was consistent with the human relations perspective. That is, human relations concepts did not go far enough in explaining people's needs and management's strategies to accommodate them. McGregor viewed Theory Y as a more appropriate foundation for guiding management thinking.

**Hygiene–Motivation**   Extending the work of Maslow, Frederick Herzberg developed a two-factor theory of motivation.[46] Herzberg makes a distinction between factors that cause or prevent job dissatisfaction (**hygiene factors**) and factors that cause job satisfaction (**motivation factors**). Only the latter group of factors can lead to motivation. Herzberg's hygiene factors relate closely to Maslow's lower-level needs: physiological, safety, and social; his motivation factors relate to the needs at the top of Maslow's hierarchy: esteem and self-actualization. Recognition of motivation factors calls for a different style of management from that proposed by the classical or human relations advocates.

**Systems 1–4**   Another writer concerned with the way in which the goals of individuals and those of the organization can coincide is Rensis Likert. Likert conducted extensive empirical research at the Institute for Social Research—University of Michigan to examine the effect of management systems on employees' attitudes and behavior. He developed four management systems, ranging from **System 1**, Exploitive Authoritative, to

[41]William H. Whyte, *The Organization Man* (New York: Simon & Schuster, 1956).

[42]Allan Harrington, *Life in the Crystal Palace* (London: Jonathan Cape, 1960).

[43]Jacob W. Getzels and Egon G. Guba, "Social Behavior and the Administrative Process," *School Review,* 65 (1957): 423–441.

[44]Abraham Maslow, *Motivation and Personality,* rev. ed. (Reading, MA: Addison-Wesley, 1970).

[45]Douglas McGregor, *The Human Side of Enterprise* (New York: McGraw-Hill, 1960).

[46]Frederick Herzberg, *The Motivation to Work* (New Brunswick, NJ: Transaction, 1993).

System 4, Participative Group.[47] Each system characterizes an organizational climate based on several key dimensions of effectiveness, including leadership, motivation, communications, interaction/influence, decision making, goal setting, control, and performance goals. Likert posits the participative group system (System 4) as coming closest to the ideal. The essence of System 4 theory is based on three key propositions: supportive relationships, group decision making in an overlapping group structure, which he calls *linking-pins*,[48] and high-performance goals of the leader. (Note the parallel here to McGregor's Theory X and Theory Y dichotomy.) Likert, however, provides more categories and more specificity. His Systems 1–4 represent four different leadership styles.

**Managerial Grid** In the area of leadership, Robert Blake and Jane Mouton assess managerial behavior on two dimensions: concern for production and concern for people. Managers can plot their scores on an eighty-one-celled **managerial grid**.[49] The grid is designed to help managers identify their own leadership styles, to understand how subordinates are affected by their leadership style, and to explore the use of alternative leadership styles consistent with employees' needs.

**Contingency Theory** Contingency theories of leadership have come into vogue in recent years. Fred Fiedler developed a contingency theory of leadership effectiveness.[50] The basic premise is that in some situations relationship-motivated leaders perform better, while other conditions make it more likely that task-motivated leaders will be most effective. Three variables determine the situations under which one or the other type of leader will be most effective: leader–member relations (the degree to which leaders feel accepted by their followers), task structure (the degree to which the work to be done is clearly outlined), and position power (the extent to which the leader has control over rewards and punishments the followers receive).

**Situational Leadership** Another popular leadership theory is situational leadership developed by Paul Hersey and Kenneth Blanchard.[51] **Situational leadership theory** is based primarily on the relationship between follower maturity, leader task behavior, and leader relationship behavior. In general terms, the theory suggests that the style of leadership will be effective only if it is appropriate for the maturity level of the followers. Hersey and Blanchard see two types of maturity as particularly important: job maturity (a person's maturity to perform the job) and psychological maturity (the person's level of motivation as reflected in achievement needs and willingness to accept responsibility).

**Other Important Contributors** The great diversity of perspectives in the behavioral science school makes it impossible to discuss all of its contributors here. Social scientists like Victor Vroom,[52] William Reddin,[53] and Amitai Etzioni[54] did much to assist its development. Warren Bennis, in his best-selling book on leadership, identifies bureaucracy and other classical management principles as the "unconscious conspiracy" that prevents leaders from leading.[55]

A key contribution of the contingency perspective may best be summarized in the observation that there is no one best way to administer an organization. There are no motivation strategies, organizational structures, decision-making patterns, communication techniques, change approaches, or leadership styles that will fit all situations. Rather, school administrators must find different ways that fit different situations.

## Post–Behavioral Science Era

The behavioral science approach influenced the preparation and practice of school administrators for some time, but it has lost much of its original appeal recently

[47]Rensis Likert, "From Production and Employee-Centeredness to Systems 1–4," *Journal of Management,* 5 (1979): 147–156.

[48]Rensis Likert, *New Patterns of Management* (New York: Garland, 1987).

[49]Robert R. Blake and Jane S. Mouton, *The Managerial Grid: Leadership Styles for Achieving Production Through People* (Houston: Gulf, 1994).

[50]Fred E. Fiedler and Martin M. Chemers, *Improving Leadership Effectiveness,* 2nd ed. (New York: Wiley, 1984).

[51]Paul Hersey and Kenneth Blanchard, *Management of Organizational Behavior,* 8th ed. (Paramus, NJ: Prentice Hall, 2007).

[52]Victor Vroom and Arthur Jago, *The New Leadership: Managing Participation in Organizations* (Englewood Cliffs, NJ: Prentice Hall, 1988).

[53]William J. Reddin, *Managerial Effectiveness* (New York: McGraw-Hill, 1970).

[54]Amitai Etzioni, *A Comparative Analysis of Complex Organizations,* rev. ed. (New York: Free Press, 1975).

[55]Warren G. Bennis, *Why Leaders Can't Lead: The Unconscious Conspiracy Continues* (San Francisco: Jossey-Bass, 1990).

with challenges to modernist views of organizations and leadership. Building on the strengths and shortcomings of the past, three powerful, interrelated concepts of school improvement, democratic community, and social justice emerge, which form the development of the next era of the profession: the **post–behavioral science era.** Joseph Murphy reminds us that "persons wishing to affect society as school leaders must be directed by a powerful portfolio of beliefs and values anchored in issues such as justice, community, and schools that function for all children and youth."[56]

## School Improvement

Accountability for school improvement is a central theme of state policies. The No Child Left Behind Act of 2001 (Public Law 107-110) sets demanding accountability standards for schools, school districts, and states, including new state testing requirements designed to improve education. For example, the law requires that states develop both content standards in reading and mathematics and tests that are linked to the standards for grades 3 through 8, with science standards and assessments to follow. States must identify adequate yearly progress (AYP) objectives and disaggregate test results for all students and subgroups of students based on socioeconomic status, race/ethnicity, English language proficiency, and disability. Moreover, the law mandates that 100 percent of students must score at the proficient level on state tests by 2014. Furthermore, the No Child Left Behind Act requires states to participate every other year in the National Assessment of Educational Progress (NAEP) in reading and mathematics.

Will schools, school districts, and states be able to respond to the demand? In an ideal system, school improvement efforts focus educational policy, administration, and practices directly on teaching and learning. This will require districtwide leadership focused directly on learning. School leaders can accomplish this by (1) clarifying purpose, (2) encouraging collective learning, (3) aligning with state standards, (4) providing support, and (5) making data-driven decisions. Taken together, these five dimensions provide a compelling framework for accomplishing sustained districtwide success for all children.

**Clarifying Purpose**    The school district and the administrators and teachers who work in it are accountable for student learning. This assertion has strong economic, political, and social appeal; its logic is clear. What teachers teach and students learn is a matter of public inspection and subject to direct measurement.[57] Superintendents need to develop a practical rationale for school improvement. Clearly and jointly held purposes help give teachers and administrators an increased sense of certainty, security, coherence, and accountability.[58] Purposes cannot remain static for all time, however. They must be constantly adapted to changing circumstances and the needs of the system. Few really successful schools lack purpose.[59]

In their studies of "successful school restructuring" in over 1500 schools, Newmann and Wehlage found that successful schools focused on "authentic" pedagogy (teaching that requires students to think, to develop an in-depth understanding, and to apply academic learning to important realistic problems) and student learning.[60] They achieved this in two ways: greater organizational capacity and greater external support. The most successful schools, according to Newmann and Wehlage, were those that functioned as professional communities. That is, they found a way to channel staff and student efforts toward a clear, commonly shared purpose for learning. Moreover, they found that external agencies helped schools to focus on student learning and to enhance organizational capacity through three strategies: setting standards for learning of high intellectual quality; providing sustained schoolwide professional development; and using deregulation to increase school autonomy. In short, dynamic internal learning communities and their relationships with external networks made the difference. Evidence on the critical combination of internal and external learning is mounting.[61]

---

[56]Joseph Murphy, "Reculturing the Profession of Educational Leadership: New Blueprints," *Educational Administration Quarterly*, 38 (2002): 186.

[57]Richard F. Elmore, *School Reform from the Inside Out: Policy, Practice, and Performance* (Cambridge, MA: Harvard Education Publishing Group, 2004).

[58]Roland Barth, *Learning by Heart* (New York: John Wiley, 2004).

[59]Fred C. Lunenburg and Beverly J. Irby, *The Principalship: Vision to Action* (Belmont, CA: Wadsworth/ Thompson, 2006).

[60]Fred Newmann and George Wehlage, *Successful School Restructuring* (Madison, WI: Center on Organization and Restructuring of Schools, 1995).

[61]Michael G. Fullan, *Learning Places: A Field Guide for Improving the Context of Schooling* (Thousand Oaks, CA: Corwin Press, 2006).

There are instructional strategies that can help teachers increase student learning. In research recently completed at the Mid-continent Research for Education and Learning (McREL) Institute, Marzano and others[62] identified classroom practices that generally increase student achievement: identifying similarities and differences; summarizing and note taking; receiving reinforcement for effort and recognition for achievement; doing homework and practicing; using nonlinguistic representations; learning cooperatively; setting objectives and testing hypotheses; and using cues, questions, and advance organizers. Regardless of whether or not teachers teach to standards, these classroom practices work well.

**Encouraging Collective Learning**   A key task for school administrators is to create a collective expectation among teachers concerning the state's accountability criteria. That is, administrators need to raise teachers' collective sense about state standards. Then administrators must work to ensure that teacher expectations are aligned with the state's accountability criteria.[63] Furthermore, administrators need to eliminate teacher isolation, so that discussions about state standards become a collective mission of the school and school district.

"The key to student growth is educator growth."[64] In a collective learning environment, teachers become generators of professional knowledge rather than simply consumers of innovations. Innovations are built around the system rather than using prepackaged school improvement models. Changing mental models replaces training educators in new behaviors.[65] Continuous instruction-embedded staff development replaces one-shot non-instruction-specific professional development events.[66] Single-loop, linear learning that monitors whether a system is reaching its goals is replaced by double-loop learning where systems are able to revisit whether goals are still appropriate and then recycle as needed.[67]

School administrators must develop and sustain school structures and cultures that foster individual and group learning. That is, administrators must stimulate an environment in which new information and practices are eagerly incorporated into the system. Teachers are more likely to pursue their group and individual learning when there are supportive conditions in the school and school district, such as particularly effective leadership.[68] Schools where teachers collaborate in discussing issues related to their school improvement efforts are more likely to be able to take advantage of internally and externally generated information.[69] Teachers can become willing recipients of research information if they are embedded in a setting where meaningful and sustained interaction with researchers occurs in an egalitarian context.

**Aligning with State Standards**   Most states are attempting to align their tests with their standards. Gandal and Vranek[70] encourage states to consider three principles in this endeavor. First, tests not based on the standards are neither fair nor helpful to parents or students. States that have developed their own tests have done a good job of ensuring that the content of the test can be found in the standards. That is, children will not be tested on knowledge and skills they have not been taught. This is what Fenwick English and Betty Steffy refer to as "the doctrine of no surprises."[71] However, the same is not true when states use generic, off-the-shelf standardized tests. Such tests cannot measure

---

[62]Robert J. Marzano, Debra J. Pickering, and Jane E. Pollock, *Classroom Instruction That Works* (Baltimore: Association for Supervision and Curriculum Development, 2001).

[63]Carl Glickman, *Leadership for Learning: How to Help Teachers Succeed* (Baltimore: Association for Supervision and Curriculum Development, 2005).

[64]Bruce Joyce and Beverly Showers, *Student Achievement Through Staff Development,* 3rd ed. (Baltimore: ASCD, 2002), p. XV.

[65]Peter Senge, *Schools That Learn* (New York: Doubleday, 2001).

[66]Gene E. Hall and Shirley M. Hord, *Implementing Change: Patterns, Principles, Potholes* (Boston: Allyn and Bacon, 2005).

[67]Chris Argyris, *Reasons and Rationalizations: The Limits to Organizational Knowledge* (New York: Oxford University Press, 2006).

[68]Kenneth Leithwood and Karen Seashore Louis, *The Learning School and School Improvement: Linkages and Strategies* (Lisse, NL: Swets and Zeitlinger, 2000).

[69]Karen Seashore Louis and Sandra Kruse, "Creating Community in Reform: Images of Organizational Learning in Urban Schools," in K. Leithwood and K. Seashore Louis (eds.), *Organizational Learning and Strategies* (Lisse, NL: Swets and Zeitlander, 2000).

[70]Matthew Gandal and Jennifer Vranek, "Standards: Here Today, Here Tomorrow," *Educational Leadership,* 59 (2001): 7–13.

[71]Fenwick English and Betty Steffy, *Deep Curriculum Alignment* (Lanham, MD: Scarecrow Press, 2001).

the breadth and depth of each state's standards. Second, when the standards are rich and rigorous, the tests must be as well. Tests must tap both the breadth and depth of the content and skills in the standards. Third, tests must become more challenging in each successive grade. The solid foundation of knowledge and skills developed in the early grades should evolve into more complex skills in the later grades.

If one accepts the premise that tests drive curriculum and instruction, perhaps the easiest way to improve instruction and increase student achievement is to construct better tests. Critics argue that many state-mandated tests require students to recall obscure factual knowledge, which limits the time teachers have available to focus on critical thinking skill.[72] However, according to Yeh, it is possible to design force-choice items (multiple-choice test items) that test reasoning and critical thinking.[73] Such tests could require students to *use* facts, rather than *recall* them. And test questions could elicit content knowledge that is worth learning.

Yeh argues that to prepare students to think critically, teachers could teach children to identify what is significant. Teachers could model the critical thinking process in the classroom, during instruction, through assignments, in preparing for tests, and in the content of the test itself. By aligning test content with worthwhile questions in core subject areas, it may be possible to rescue testing and instruction from the current focus on the recall of trivial factual knowledge. Test items could be created for a range of subjects and levels of difficulty. Then there would be little incentive for teachers to drill students on factual knowledge.

**Providing Support**   One of the biggest challenges in advancing state standards and tests, and the accountability provisions tied to them, is providing teachers with the training, teaching tools, and support they need to help all students reach high standards. Specifically, teachers need access to curriculum guides, textbooks, or specific training connected to state standards. They need access to lessons or teaching units that match state standards. They need training on using state test results

to diagnose learning gaps.[74] Teachers must know how each student performed on every multiple-choice item and other questions on the state test. And training must be in the teachers' subject areas. Only then can teachers be prepared to help students achieve at high levels on state-mandated tests.

In addition to professional development for teachers, all schools need an intervention and support system for students who lag behind in learning the curriculum. Schools need to provide additional help to students who lag behind in core subjects, either in school, after school, on weekends, or during the summer. School administrators need to supply the financial resources to fulfill this mandate. This involves acquiring materials, information, or technology; manipulating schedules or release time to create opportunities for teachers to learn; facilitating professional networks; or creating an environment that supports school improvement efforts.[75]

Higher state standards usually mean changes in curriculum, instruction, and assessment—that is, changes in teaching and learning. The history of school reform indicates that innovations in teaching and learning seldom penetrate more than a few schools and seldom endure when they do.[76] Innovations frequently fail because the individuals who make them happen—classroom teachers—may not be committed to the effort or may not have the skills to grapple with the basic challenge being posed.[77] Teachers are motivated to change when their personal goals are aligned with change, when they are confident in their ability to change, and when they feel supported in attempting the change.[78] To gain commitment of teachers and students to pursue school improvement efforts, school administrators must promote school cultures that reward achievement.

**Making Data-Driven Decisions**   How can school districts gauge their progress in achieving high state standards? Three factors can increase a school district's

---

[72]Linda McNeil, *Curriculum of School Reform: Educational Costs of Standardized Testing* (New York: Routledge, 2000).

[73]Stuart S. Yeh, "Tests Worth Teaching To: Constructing State Mandated Tests That Emphasize Critical Thinking," *Educational Researcher*, 30 (2001): 12–17.

[74]Fred C. Lunenburg and Beverly J. Irby, *High Expectations: An Action Plan for Implementing Goals 2000* (Thousand Oaks, CA: Corwin Press, 1999).

[75]Fred C. Lunenburg, *The Principalship: Concepts and Applications* (Englewood Cliffs, NJ: Merrill/Prentice Hall, 1995).

[76]Elmore, *School Reform from the Inside Out.*

[77]Fullan, *Learning Places.*

[78]Lunenburg and Irby, *The Principalship.*

## ■ Exemplary Educational Administrators in Action

**HENRY S. BANGSER** Superintendent, New Trier Township High School District, Winnetka/Northfield, Illinois.

**Previous Positions:** Superintendent of Schools, St. Charles Community Unit School District, Illinois; Superintendent of Schools, Pelham Union Free School District, New York; Principal, Lake Forest High School—East Campus, Illinois.

**Latest Degree and Affiliation:** Ph.D., Educational Administration, Northwestern University.

**Number One Influence on Career:** Certainly, it was the first district in which I taught and served as an administrator. New Trier was and is one of the finest high schools in the nation. Thus, I learned early where the bar could be set for first-rate, public suburban high school education.

**Number One Achievement:** In different ways, facilitating the work among the school board, staff, community, students, and parents in four school districts where expectations were and are extremely high.

**Number One Regret:** Leaving my first two superintendencies after four and three years, respectively; therefore, not having the opportunity to see several important initiatives come to fruition.

**Favorite Education-Related Book or Text:** *Leadership Jazz* by Max DePree.

**Additional Interests:** Spending time with my children as they grew up in the schools and communities which I served as superintendent. Learning the unique challenges which golf brings to the human spirit, through caddying as a youngster and playing golf competitively during college and adulthood.

**Leadership Style:** Ask tough questions during the process of resolving of an issue. Give others credit where their work was critical in the successful completion of a project. Take responsibility for the decisions that are made within the organization.

**Professional Vision:** Hire the best people you can find as leaders and other staff members. Support them in their job in a way that will allow them to flourish. Ultimately, the organization will benefit as a result of their combined efforts.

**Words of Advice:** As early in your career as possible, hopefully well before you become a superintendent, develop a baseline philosophy and a set of principles around which you will build your management and leadership style. These are standards from which you will not vary. In my opinion, these must embody respect for all individuals within the organization: student to student, student to adult, adult to student, and adult to adult.

**Example of How an Issue Could Have Been Handled Better:** When I entered my first superintendency, I inherited a committee which had been formed to address the issue of a gifted program for the elementary grades. My predecessor, an interim superintendent, had appointed twenty passionate advocates for a self-contained program (i.e., a system in which the brightest students in the district would be educated in classes together, thus leaving behind those students who needed them as role models). As an educator who had spent my whole career in high school education, I knew very little about this matter. However, my gut feeling was that it was unfair and inappropriate. I allowed the committee to deliberate longer than I should have. Finally, close to the date when the committee report that was designed to create the self-contained program was scheduled to be made public, I pulled the plug on it. I did this by meeting individually with each person on the committee before I announced my decision to the board of education and the community. What I learned from this experience—and what I have told superintendent aspirants often—is that many more leadership errors are made by *omission* than *commission*. Develop a philosophy, trust your basic principles, and act on them.

progress in meeting state standards.[79] The primary factor is the availability of performance data connected to

each student, broken down by specific objectives and target levels in the state standards. Then schools across the district and across the state are able to connect what is taught to what is learned. The state standards should be clear enough to specify what each teacher should teach. And a state-mandated test, aligned with state standards, will indicate what students have learned.

[79]Susan Sclafani, "Using an Aligned System to Make Real Progress in Texas Students," *Education and Urban Society*, 33 (2001): 305–312.

Also, teachers need access to longitudinal data on each student in their classroom. With such data, teachers are able to develop individual and small-group education plans to ensure mastery of areas of weakness from previous years while also moving students forward in the state-mandated curriculum.

The second factor is the public nature of the measurement system. Assuming the school district has a system of rating schools, the district should publish annually a matrix of schools and honor those schools that have performed at high levels. This provides an impetus for low-performing schools to improve their performance. It also provides role models for other schools to emulate. At the school and classroom levels, it provides a blueprint of those areas where teachers should focus their individual education plans and where grade levels or schools should focus the school's professional development plans. The public nature of the data from the accountability system makes clear where schools are. Assuming the state disaggregates its data by race/ethnicity and socioeconomic status, performance of each subgroup of students on state-mandated tests makes the school community aware of which students are well served and which students are not well served by the school district's curriculum and instruction.

The third factor is the specifically targeted assistance provided to schools that are performing at low levels. Before the advent of state accountability systems, it was not evident which schools needed help. The first step is to target the schools in need of help based on student performance data. Each targeted school is paired with a team of principals, curriculum specialists/instructional coaches, and researchers to observe current practices, discuss student performance data with the staff, and assist in the development and implementation of an improvement plan. The targeted schools learn how to align their program of professional development to the weaknesses identified by the data. They learn how to develop an improvement plan to guide their activities and monitor the outcomes of the activities, all of which are designed to raise student performance levels.

In sum, the new framework for school improvement that we have described here provides a powerful and useful model for achieving school success. Sustained districtwide school improvement is not possible without a strong connection across levels of organization (school, school district, community, and state). Internal school development is necessary from principals, teachers, and parents; but school improvement cannot occur unless each school is supported by a strong external infrastructure; stable political environments; and resources outside the school, including leadership from the superintendent and school board as well as leadership from the state.

## Democratic Community

The concept of democratic community is not new. Much of the current work is grounded in Dewey's ideas promulgated more than 100 years ago.[80] For example, at the turn of the twentieth century, John Dewey argued that schools should embody the kind of community that combined the best aspects of classic liberalism and communitarianism or, in Dewey's words, of "individualism and socialism"[81]—a place that could prepare people to live within and to maintain a healthy, democratic society. However, Dewey's vision was relatively uninfluential throughout much of the twentieth century. A resurgence of interest in Dewey and his concept of a democratic community as it relates to schooling has emerged in education in recent years.[82]

At mid-twentieth century, James Contant suggested that the basic tenets of American democracy should be taught in schools, along with language, history, economics, science, mathematics, and the arts.[83] More recently, Wood expanded this theme by suggesting that democratic citizenship should be taught in schools. These include traits such as commitment to community and a desire to participate; values such as justice, liberty, and equality; skills of interpretation, debate, and compromise; and habits of study and reflection.[84] Others concur. Hargreaves suggests that the cultivation of "openness, informality, care, attentiveness, lateral working relationships, reciprocal collaboration, candid

---

[80] John Dewey, *The School and Society* (Chicago: University of Chicago Press, 1900).

[81] Dewey, *The School and Society*, p. 7.

[82] See, for example, Carol Rogers, "Defining Reflection: Another Look at John Dewey and Reflective Thinking," *Teachers College Record*, 104 (2002): 842–866; Aaron Schutz, "John Dewey's Conundrum: Can Democratic Schools Empower?" *Teachers College Record*, 103 (2001): 267–302; Julie Webber, "Why Can't We Be Dewey on Citizens?" *Educational Theory*, 51 (2001): 178–189.

[83] James B. Contant, *Education and Liberty: The Role of the Schools in a Modern Democracy* (New York: Vintage Books, 1953).

[84] George H. Wood, *Schools That Work: America's Most Innovative Public Education Programs* (New York: Dutton, 1992).

and vibrant dialogue, and the willingness to face uncertainty together"[85] is a central purpose of schooling, not merely the production of employable workers.

Critiques concerning the meaning of democracy in our time have proliferated over the last two decades. And a number of publications have addressed the various meanings of community. For example, community is described in multiple ways in the education literature.[86] Community is referred to as "professional community" among educators, "learning community" among students, "school–community" addressing school–community relations, and "community of difference" in multicultural settings. Furman and Starratt advocate the definition of community of difference as more compatible with contemporary postmodernism.[87] Thinking about a community of difference requires a reconceptualization of the concept of community itself, moving away from homogeneity toward a new center in which diverse groups negotiate a commitment to the common good. According to Shields, "a *community of difference* begins, not with an assumption of shared norms, beliefs, and values; but with the need for respect, dialogue, and understanding."[88] Educational leaders who want to move toward a community of difference will be informed by research on race and ethnicity.

Similarly, democracy is subject to many interpretations in education. Its most common meaning is usually tied to the idea of the nation-state and the American version of democracy. According to Mitchell, democratic community cannot be limited to such a narrow view of democracy in a world characterized by diversity, fragmentation, and globalization.[89] National boundaries are permeated by regional and global alliances. Children should be educated within an increasingly global context.

Our version of democratic community resembles more the ideas promulgated by Gail Furman and Robert Starratt.[90] They extend the emerging work on democratic community through a deeper analysis of the linkages between democratic community and leadership in schools. And Furman and Starratt's model places democratic community in a context of postmodernism, characterized by inclusiveness, interdependence, and transnationalism. In their view and ours, professional community, learning community, school–community, and community of difference, and the American version of democracy, along with Dewey's progressivism, laid much of the groundwork for the concept of democratic community. But the model requires some modifications in a contemporary, postmodern context of diversity, fragmentation, and globalization.

Some common themes are beginning to emerge regarding the concept of democratic community derived from Dewey's progressivism and its more contemporary, postmodern interpretations. Furman and Starratt discuss the nature and character of democratic community and how it might be enacted in schools.[91] The central tenets of democratic schools include the following:

1. Democratic community is based on the open flow of ideas that enables people to be as fully informed as possible.

2. Democratic community involves the use of critical reflection and analysis to evaluate ideas, problems, and policies.

3. Democratic community places responsibility on individuals to participate in open inquiry, collective choices, and actions in the interest of the common good.

---

[85]Andy Hargreaves, "Rethinking Educational Change: Going Deeper and Wider in the Quest for Success," in A. Hargreaves (ed.), *Rethinking Educational Change with Heart and Mind* (Alexandria, VA: Association for Supervision and Curriculum Development, 1997), p. 22.

[86]Patricia E. Calderwood, *Learning Community: Finding Common Ground in Difference* (New York: Teachers College Press, 2000); Gail C. Furman, *School as Community: From Promise to Practice* (Albany: State University of New York Press, 2003); Karen F. Osterman, "Students' Need for Belonging in the School Community," *Review of Educational Research*, 70 (2001): 323–367; Carolyn M. Shields, "Thinking about Community from a Student Perspective," in G. Furman (ed.), *School as Community: From Promise to Practice* (Albany: State University of New York Press, 2003).

[87]Gail C. Furman and Robert J. Starratt, "Leadership for Democratic Community in Schools," in J. Murphy (ed.), *The Educational Leadership Challenge: Redefining Leadership for the 21st Century* (Chicago: University of Chicago Press, 2002), pp. 105–133.

[88]Carolyn M. Shields, Linda J. Larocque, and Steven L. Oberg, "A Dialogue about Race and Ethnicity in Education: Struggling to Understand Issues in Cross-Cultural Leadership," *Journal of School Leadership*, 12 (2002): 132.

[89]Katheryne Mitchell, "Education for Democratic Citizenship: Transnationalism, Multiculturalism, and the Limits of Liberalism," *Harvard Educational Review*, 71 (2001): 51–78.

[90]Furman and Starratt, "Leadership for Democratic Community in Schools."

[91]Furman and Starratt, "Leadership for Democratic Community in Schools."

4. Democratic community involves acting for others as well as with others in the interest of the common good.

5. Democratic community is based on the acceptance and celebration of difference, and focuses on the integral linkages between the school, the surrounding community, and the larger global community.

6. Creating democratic community in schools involves systematic attention to structure, process, curriculum, and instruction.

**Family and Community Involvement**   Schools alone cannot adequately provide children and youth with the necessary resources and support they need to become successful students, productive workers, and responsible citizens in a democratic society. Family and community involvement in schools is viewed as so critical for the success of students, especially poor and minority students, that many reform programs include a family and community involvement component in their school improvement strategies.[92]

Epstein's parent involvement strategies,[93] Henry Levin's Accelerated Schools,[94] Robert Slavin's Success for All schools,[95] and James Comer's School Development Program[96] are grounded in developing inclusive and democratic connections with families and communities. The programs emphasize family and community support processes. They provide the school's faculty with strategies for increasing parent involvement, raising attendance rates, improving classroom management, preventing behavior problems, integrating social and health services, and solving other nonacademic problems. The programs structure the school in ways that fundamentally change the notion of school as merely an academic institution.

Levin's Accelerated Schools, Slavin's Success for All schools, and Comer's School Development Program have been shown to result in student success in school, including positive attitudes toward school, better attendance and behavior in school, higher rates of homework completion, and better achievement in academic subjects. This research has been supplemented by studies that have shown that well-planned activities, such as Epsein's parent involvement strategies, can increase parent and community involvement even among families traditionally considered hard to reach, including low-income, minority, and single-parent families.[97]

**National and State Education Policies**   Research on the benefits of family and community involvement has had a positive effect on national policies during the past decade. The Goals 2000: Educate America Act of 1994, for example, identified eight national goals for public schools. Goal 8 states:

> Every school will promote partnerships that will increase parental involvement and participation in promoting the social, emotional, and academic growth of children.[98]

Linked to Goals 2000 was the Improving America's Schools Act (IASA) of 1994, a reauthorization of the Elementary and Secondary Education Act of 1965. Among other things, this reauthorization strengthened the family involvement component of Title I, which seeks to improve the educational opportunities for and outcomes of poor children. The reauthorization of Title I mandated that school-level family involvement policies include parent-school agreements designed to clarify the goals, expectations, and shared responsibilities of schools and parents as partners in students' education. Such agreements were intended to be helpful frameworks for discussions between schools and parents about how to encourage better student performance in school. And, recently, "Title V: Promoting Informed Parental Choice and Innovative Programs" of the No Child Left Behind Act of 2001 contains numerous provisions for school, family, and community involvement in students' learning.

[92]Mavis G. Sanders, Glenda L. Allen-Jones, and Yolanda Abel, "Involving Families and Communities in Educating Children and Youth," in S. Stringfield and D. Land (eds.), *Educating At-Risk Students* (Chicago: Univeristy of Chicago Press, 2002), pp. 171–188.

[93]Joyce L. Epstein, *School, Family, and Community Partnerships: Preparing Educators and Improving Schools* (Boulder, CO: Westview Press, 2001).

[94]Henry M. Levin, *Accelerated Schools for At-Risk Students* (CPRHE Research Report RR-010), (New Brunswick, NJ: Rutgers University, Center for Policy Research in Education, 1987).

[95]Robert E. Slavin and Nancy A. Madden (eds.), *One Million Children: Success for All* (Mahwah, NJ: Erlbaum, 2001).

[96]James Comer, *School Power: Implications for an Intervention Project* (New York: Free Press, 1980); James Comer et al. (eds.), *Rallying the Whole Village* (New York: Teachers College Press, 1996).

[97]Epstein, *School, Family, and Community Partnerships.*

[98]Goals 2000: Educate America Act of 1994, Sec. 102 (www.ed.gov/legislation/GOALS2000/TheAct/).

States have developed standards to encourage greater family and community involvement in schools. Key educational reform groups, such as the Interstate School Leaders Licensure Consortium (ISLLC), the Interstate New Teacher Assessment and Support Consortium (INTASC), and the National Council for Accreditation of Teacher Education (NCATE), have developed standards pertaining to parent and community involvement in schools. Created in 1994, ISLLC is a consortium of thirty-two education agencies and thirteen educational administration associations that have established an education policy framework for school leadership. In 1996, the consortium adopted ISLLC Standards for School Leaders. Currently, thirty-eight states have either adopted or adapted the ISLLC Standards and are in different stages of implementing the standards in reforming educational leadership within their state. Standard 4 of the six standards states:

> A school administrator is an educational leader who promotes the success of all students by collaborating with families and community members, responding to diverse community interests and needs, and mobilizing community resources.[99]

In 1992, INTASC (a consortium of state education agencies, higher education institutions, and national education organizations) developed ten principles that all teachers should master. According to Principle 10, teachers are expected to foster relationships with school colleagues, parents, and community agencies to support students' learning. The NCATE emphasized in its standard for content knowledge that teacher candidates should understand principles and strategies for school, family, and community partnerships to support students' learning.

**Curriculum and Instruction**    A resurgence of interest in democratic community in recent years has implications for schools and schooling, particularly as it relates to curriculum and instruction. To be sure, the enactment of democratic community in schools would require changes in curriculum and instruction. These modifications would be compatible with some components found in Theodore Sizer's Coalition of Essential

Schools (CES)[100] and Mortimer Adler's Paideia Proposal (PP).[101] More specifically, two powerful strategies that are grounded in the tenets of democratic community and found in Sizer's CES and Adler's PP are critical thinking and constructivism.

***Critical Thinking***    The Center for Critical Thinking provides an excellent treatise on **critical thinking** applied to instruction.[102] Critical thinking shifts classroom design from a model that largely ignores thinking to one that renders it pervasive and necessary. Critical teaching views content as something alive only in minds, modes of thinking driven by questions, existing in textbooks only to be regenerated in the minds of students.

Once we understand content as inseparable from the thinking that generates, organizes, analyzes, synthesizes, evaluates, and transforms it, we recognize that content cannot in principle ever be "completed" because thinking is never completed. To understand content, therefore, is to understand its implications. But to understand its implications, one must understand that those implications in turn have further implications, and hence must be thoughtfully explored.

The problem with didactic teaching is that content is inadvertently treated as static, as virtually dead. Content is treated as something to be mimicked, to be parroted. And because students only rarely process content deeply when they play the role of passive listeners in lecture-centered instruction, little is learned in the long term. Furthermore, because students are taught content in a way that renders them unlikely to think it through, they retreat into rote memorization, abandoning any attempt to grasp the logic of what they are committing to memory.

Those who teach critically emphasize that only those who can think through content truly learn it. Content "dies" when one tries to learn it mechanically. Content has to take root in the thinking of students and, when properly learned, transforms the way they think. Hence,

---

[99]Council of Chief State School Officers, *Interstate School Officers, Interstate School Leaders Licensure Consortium: Standards for School Leaders* (Washington, DC: Council of Chief State School Officers, 1996), p. 16.

[100]Theodore R. Sizer, *Horace's Compromise: The Dilemma of the American High School* (Boston: Houghton Mifflin, 1984); *Horace's School: Redesigning the American High School* (Boston: Houghton Mifflin, 1992); *Horace's Hope* (Boston: Houghton Mifflin, 1997).

[101]Mortimer J. Adler, *The Paideia Proposal: An Educational Manifesto* (New York: Macmillan, 1982).

[102]Center for Critical Thinking, *Critical Thinking and the Redesign of Instruction* (Santa Rosa, CA: Center for Critical Thinking, 2003).

when students study a subject in a critical way, they take possession of a new mode of thinking that, so internalized, generates new thoughts, understandings, and beliefs. Their thinking, now driven by a set of new questions, becomes an instrument of insight and a new point of view.

History texts become, in the minds of students thinking critically, a stimulus to historical thinking. Geography texts are internalized as geographical thinking. Mathematical content is transformed into mathematical thinking. As a result of being taught to think critically, students study biology and become biological thinkers. They study sociology and begin to notice the permissions, injunctions, and taboos of the groups in which they participate. They study literature and begin to notice the way in which all humans tend to define their lives in the stories they tell. They study economics and begin to notice how much of their behavior is intertwined with economic forces and needs.

There are ways, indeed almost an unlimited number, to stimulate critical thinking at every educational level and in every teaching setting. When considering technology for this stimulation, the World Wide Web (WWW) is important to instructional design; it contains three keys to educational value: hypertext, the delivery of multimedia, and true interactivity. These values are operant and alive in the classroom through such applications as graphics, audio, and video, which bring to life world events, museum tours, library visits, world visits, and up-to-date weather maps. Through these WWW mechanisms, a constructivist instructional model advances higher-level instruction, such as problem solving and increased learner control. The WWW becomes a necessary tool for student-centered discovery and research. Of course, it can also be used for lower-level drill and practice.

At every level and in all subjects, students need to learn how to ask questions precisely, define contexts and purposes, pursue relevant information, analyze key concepts, derive sound inferences, generate good reasons, recognize questionable assumptions, trace important implications, and think empathetically within different points of view. The WWW enables learners and teachers in each area by providing information for good reasoners to figure things out. Critical thinking may be a key organizing concept for curriculum reform and for improving teaching and learning.[103]

***Constructivism***   Constructivism may be the most significant recent trend in education relative to the dynamic relationship between how teachers teach and how children learn. One foundational premise of constructivism is that children actively construct their knowledge, rather than simply absorbing ideas spoken to them by teachers. For example, more than thirty years ago, Jean Piaget proposed that children make sense in ways very different from adults, and that they learn through the process of trying to make things happen, trying to manipulate their environment. Theories such as these, which assert that "people are not recorders of information, but builders of knowledge structures," have been grouped under the heading of *constructivism*.[104] Thus, students are ultimately responsible for their own learning within a learning atmosphere in which teachers value student thinking, initiate lessons that foster cooperative learning, provide opportunities for students to be exposed to interdisciplinary curriculum, structure learning around primary concepts, and facilitate authentic assessment of student understanding.

In constructivist theory, it is assumed that learners have to construct their own knowledge—individually and collectively. Each learner has a repertoire of conceptions and skills with which she or he must construct knowledge to solve problems presented by the environment. The role of the teacher and other learners is to provide the setting, pose the challenges, and offer the support that will encourage cognitive construction. Because students lack the experience of experts in the field, teachers bear a great responsibility for guiding student activity, modeling behavior, and providing examples that will transform student group discussions into meaningful communication about subject matter.

Constructivism emphasizes the processes by which children create and develop their ideas. Applications lie in creating curricula that not only match but also challenge children's understanding, fostering further growth and development of the mind. Furthermore, when children collaborate in cooperative learning groups, they share the process of constructing their ideas with others. This collective effort provides the opportunity for children to reflect on and elaborate not only their own ideas but also those of their peers. With improvement of and access to the WWW, the children's cooperative classroom becomes the world. In this cooperative learning setting, children view their peers as resources rather

---

[103] Center for Critical Thinking, *Critical Thinking and the Redesign of Instruction.*

[104] Jean Piaget, "Piaget's Theory," in P. Mussen (ed.), *Carmichael's Manual of Child Psychology,* Vol. I (New York: Wiley, 1970), pp. 703–732.

than as competitors. A feeling of teamwork ensues. These processes have resulted in substantial advances in student learning.[105]

Constructivism is serving as the basis for many of the current reforms in several subject matter disciplines. The National Council of Teachers of Mathematics published *Curriculum and Evaluation Standards for School Mathematics,* which calls for mathematics classrooms where problem solving, concept development, and the construction of learner-generated solutions and algorithms are stressed rather than drill and practice on correct procedures and facts to get the "right" answer.[106] The National Committee on Science Education Standards and Assessment similarly issued *National Science Education Standards,* which calls for science education reform based on experimentation and learner-generated inquiry, investigations, hypotheses, and models.[107] The National Council of Teachers of English has called for emergent literacy as an important thrust in language arts reform. Interdisciplinary curricula is the theme of social studies reform being advocated by the National Council of Social Studies. In sum, in Sizer's Coalition of Essential Schools and Adler's Paideia Proposal, critical thinking and constructivism are compatible with the principles of democratic community, particularly the open flow of ideas, critical reflection and analysis to evaluate ideas, and dialogue.

## Social Justice

A concern for social justice is at the core of democracy. The United States prides itself on being a fair and just democracy, a nation in which every citizen is to be treated equally in social, economic, political, and educational arenas. According to its Constitution, the United States seeks to establish "liberty and justice for all." In spite of these goals, U.S. society is composed of many inequities: rich and poor, educated and illiterate, powerful and powerless. Now in the first decade of the twenty-first century, educational leaders must continue

to question whether they have an obligation to create a nation whose words are supported by the experiences of its citizens.

The Fourteenth Amendment to the U.S. Constitution addressed the question of equal opportunity, declaring that "no state shall deny to any person within its jurisdiction the equal protection of the laws." The mandate that people receive equal protection extends to equal educational opportunity. While this fundamental affirmation of equal opportunity has been part of American discourse since the inception of this nation and is found in the Declaration of Independence and other documents, inequities in the major social, economic, political, and educational institutions continue to exist in American society.

Inequities in schooling are among the social injustices with which educational leaders need to be most concerned. Although it has been a stated goal in the United States that all youngsters, regardless of family background, should benefit from their education, many students do not. Most schools do not teach all students at the same academic level. The U.S. educational system to this day is beset with inequities that exacerbate racial and class-based challenges. Differential levels of success in school distributed along race and social-class lines continues to be the most pernicious and prevailing dilemma of schooling. Furthermore, there is considerable empirical evidence that children of color experience negative and inequitable treatment in typical public schools.[108]

Many children of color find themselves marginalized in toxic schools that offer inferior education. These schools affect the opportunities and experiences of students of color in several immediate ways: They tend to have limited resources; textbooks and curricula are outdated; and computers are few and obsolete. Many of the teachers do not have credentials in the subjects they teach. Tracking systems block minority students' access to the more rigorous and challenging classes, which retain these students in non-college-bound destinations. These schools generally offer few (if any) Advanced Placement courses, which are critical for entry into many of the more competitive colleges. Furthermore, African American students are overrepresented in special education programs, compared with the overall student population. More than a third of African

[105]Jacqueline Grennon Brooks and Martin G. Brooks, *In Search of Understanding: The Case for Constructivist Classrooms* (Baltimore: Association for Supervision and Curriculum Development, 2003).

[106]National Council of Teachers of Mathematics, *Curriculum and Evaluation Standards for School Mathematics* (Reston, VA: Author, 1989).

[107]National Committee on Science Education Standards and Assessment, *National Science Education Standards* (Washington, DC: National Academy Press, 1996).

[108]Linda Skrla, James J. Scheurich, Joseph F. Johnson, and James W. Koschoreck, "Accountability for Equity: Can State Policy Leverage Social Justice?" *International Journal of Leadership in Education,* 4 (2001): 237–260.

American students (as compared with fewer than a fifth of white students) in special education are labeled with the more stigmatizing labels of "mentally retarded" and "emotionally disturbed." Conversely, four-fifths of the white students (as compared with two-thirds of the African American students) in special education are much more likely to be labeled "learning disabled" or "speech impaired." African American males are more than twice as likely as white males to be suspended or expelled from school or to receive corporal punishment.[109] Jonathan Kozol, in *Savage Inequalities*, described the inferior education received by minority students (particularly African Americans and Hispanic Americans)— fewer resources, inequities in funding, inadequate facilities, tracking systems, low expectations, segregated schools, and hostile learning environments.[110]

These related inequities, the persistent and disproportionate academic underachievement of children of color and their injurious treatment in our schools, are compelling evidence that the United States public education system remains systemically racist.[111] This is not to suggest that racism is consciously intended or even recognized by educators; it is institutional racism that is systemically embedded in assumptions, policies and procedures, practices, and structures of schooling. Nevertheless, every day more than 17 million African American, Hispanic American, Native American, and Asian American children experience the effects of systemic racism in U.S. public schools.[112]

**Systemic Racism in Schools** Racism in the United States includes a broad spectrum (individual, institutional, white racism, racial prejudice, interethnic and intraethnic hostility, and cultural racism to name a few).[113] African American, Asian American, European American, Hispanic American, Native American, and mixed racial categories all play a part within these subtle racist systems. However, the targets of racism in our schools and in society are people of color through both institutional and individual racism. Racial prejudice, individual bigotry, and institutional racism have devastating effects on students and society at large.

The disproportionate academic underachievement by children of color has been the driving force behind the current accountability policy in the United States. However, a shift in U.S. demographics would seem to exacerbate the problem of achieving educational equity and its attendant impact on social justice. The student population grows increasingly diverse, the teaching force remains predominantly white, and achievement of children of color continues to lag significantly behind their white counterparts.[114]

Demographic trends indicate that growth in the nation's minority population will have significant implications for public schools. In 1990, the total population of the United States was 248.7 million and increased to 281.4 million in 2000, an increase of 32.7 million people.[115] A significant proportion of individuals making up this increase are people of color. Demographic projections indicate that the nation's population will grow to 294 million by the year 2020. At that time, more than 98 million Americans, one-third of the nation, will be nonwhite.[116] Moreover, students of color are the fastest-growing segment of the school population and have been the least well served by the schools. The U.S. Census in 2000 reported that of the nation's 49 million elementary and secondary school students, 38 million were white; 8 million were African American; 7.3 million were Hispanic American, and 2.1 million were Asian or Pacific Islanders. Experts project that the percentage of students of color in elementary and secondary schools will increase steadily during the coming decades from 30 percent in 1990 to 36 percent in 2000 and will reach 50 percent of the public school population in the twenty-five major cities in the United States.[117]

---

[109]Carola Suárez-Orozco and Marcelo M. Suárez-Orozco, *Children of Immigration* (Cambridge, MA: Harvard University Press, 2001).

[110]Jonathan Kozol, *Savage Inequalities: Children in America's Schools* (New York: Crown, 1991).

[111]Skrla, Scheurich, Johnson, and Koschoreck, "Accountability for Equity: Can State Policy Leverage Social Justice?"

[112]Linda Skrla, "Accountability, Equity, and Complexity," *Educational Researcher*, 30 (2001): 15–21.

[113]Karen B. McLean Donaldson, *Shattering the Denial: Protocols for the Classroom and Beyond* (Westport, CT: Greenwood, 2000).

[114]Kathy Hytten and Amee Adkins, "Thinking Through a Pedagogy of Whiteness," *Educational Theory*, 51 (2001): 432–449.

[115]U.S. Census Bureau, United States Department of Commerce, *School Enrollment* (Washington, DC: U.S. Census Bureau, 2000).

[116]Harold Hodgkinson, *Demographics of Education: Kindergarten through Graduate School* (Washington, DC: Institute for Educational Leadership, 2001).

[117]National Center for Education Statistics, *Characteristics of the 100 Largest Public Elementary and Secondary School Districts in the United States: 2000–2001* (Washington, DC: Author, 2004).

In general, similar demographic shifts have not occurred in the teaching ranks. Despite the changing racial makeup of public school students in the United States, 87.7 percent of the teaching force is white, 9.3 percent is African American, and 3.0 percent is classified as "other."[118] This often results in considerable cultural and social distance between middle-class white teachers and students of color. Young and Laible suggest that white educators and educational leaders do not have a thorough enough understanding of racism in its many manifestations, nor do they comprehend the ways in which they are perpetuating white racism in their schools.[119] Short further summarizes the consequences of this mismatch between white middle-class teachers and students of color. She cites how teacher preparation programs rarely train teacher candidates in strategies for teaching culturally diverse students. The lack of familiarity with their students' cultures, learning styles, and communication patterns translates into teachers holding negative expectations for students, what some theorists refer to as *deficit thinking*.[120] And often, inappropriate curricula, instructional materials, and assessments are used with these students.[121]

Murray and Clark found eight forms of racism operating in U.S. schools at all grade levels: (1) hostile and insensitive acts; (2) bias in the use of harsh sanctions; (3) inequalities in the amount of teacher attention given to students; (4) bias in the selection of curriculum materials; (5) inequalities in the amount of instructional time provided; (6) biased attitudes toward students; (7) failure to hire educators and other personnel of color; and (8) denial of racist actions.[122] These subtle forms of racism that exist in schools threaten the academic success of students of color. For example, denial of racist actions and attitudes, and biased education, policies, and hiring practices, are present in schools at all levels and adversely affect students' success in school. For example, Donaldson found that racist treatments affect the learning and development of students of color. The study confirmed that, as a result of racist treatment, students felt low self-esteem, causing diminished interest in school; a perceived need to overachieve academically; and guilt and embarrassment at seeing other students victimized.[123]

Thomas Good reviewed the research on teachers' differential treatment of high-achieving students and at-risk students. He identified seventeen teaching behaviors that are used with different frequencies with the two groups of students. These behaviors define a pattern of diminished expectations for at-risk students' ability to learn, and perhaps a lower regard for their personal worth as learners. The teaching practices are as follows: (1) wait less time for at-risk students to answer questions, (2) give at-risk students the answer or call on someone else rather than try to improve their responses by giving clues or using other teaching techniques, (3) reward inappropriate behavior or incorrect answers by at-risk students, (4) criticize at-risk students more often for failure, (5) praise at-risk students less frequently than high-achieving students for success, (6) fail to give feedback to the public responses of at-risk students, (7) pay less attention to at-risk students or interact with them less frequently, (8) call on at-risk students less often to respond to questions, or ask them only easier, nonanalytical questions, (9) seat at-risk students farther away from the teacher, (10) demand less from at-risk students, (11) interact with at-risk students more privately than publicly and monitor and structure their activities more closely, (12) grade tests or assignments in a differential manner, so that high-achieving but not at-risk students are given the benefit of the doubt in borderline cases, (13) have less friendly interaction with at-risk students including less smiling and less warm or more anxious voice tones, (14) provide briefer and less informative feedback to the questions of at-risk students, (15) provide less eye contact and other nonverbal communication of attention and responsiveness when interacting with at-risk students, (16) make less use of effective but time-consuming instructional methods with at-risk students when time is limited, and (17) evidence less acceptance and use of ideas given by at-risk students. According to Good, academic achievement is highly correlated with race and social class,

[118]National Education Association, *Status of the American Public School Teacher, 2000–2001* (Washington, DC: Author, 2004).

[119]Michelle Young and Julie Laible, "White Racism, Antiracism, and School Leadership Preparation," *Journal of School Leadership,* 10 (2000): 374–415.

[120]Richard R. Valencia, *The Evolution of Deficit Thinking: Educational Thought and Practice* (London: Falmer, 1997).

[121]Donna J. Short, "Integrating Language and Content for Effective Sheltered Instruction Programs," in C. J. Faltis and P. M. Wolfe (eds.), *So Much to Say: Adolescents, Bilingualism, and ESL in the Secondary School* (New York: Teachers College Press, 1999).

[122]Carolyn Murray and Reginald Clark, "Targets of Racism," *American School Board Journal,* 177 (1990): 22–24.

[123]Karen B. Donaldson, *Through Students' Eyes: Combating Racism in United States Schools* (London: Praeger, 1996).

which means that at-risk students are more likely to come from disadvantaged home backgrounds, whereas high-achieving students are likely to come from advantaged home backgrounds. Therefore, the differential teaching behaviors found by Good suggest a pattern of discrimination based on students' race and social class as well as their achievement level.[124]

A recent Education Trust document concluded, "We take students who have less to begin with and give them less in school too."[125] Darling-Hammond confirmed this data, making explicit reference to teachers in the schools. Being poor, being of color, being an inner-city resident do not cause differences in educational achievement. Rather, the lack of resources put into the education of some students and the inequitable treatment of children of color and low-income children are the major causes of difference and social injustice. And teachers are the most important educational resource available to students.[126]

In its simplest form, social justice is linked to redressing institutionalized inequality and systemic racism. Rawls argues that social justice is defined by four principles.[127] The first is based on equality of treatment of all members of society (equal rights and liberties). The second is based on all people being regarded as individuals. The third involves giving everyone a fair chance (equal opportunity). The fourth involves giving the greatest social and economic benefits to those least advantaged. The application of these four principles of social justice to education would mean that more resources should be allocated to improve circumstances of those historically least served by the system rather than treating all individuals equally. The notion of social justice suggests that treating all people equally may be inherently unequal. Rawls argues that all education stakeholders are obligated not only to safeguard individuals' rights, but also to actively redress inequality of opportunity in education. This notion posits that educational leaders are obligated to examine the circumstances in which children of color and poverty are educated. Social justice in schooling, then, would mean equal treatment, access, and outcomes for children from oppressed groups. It would mean closing the achievement gap between children from low-income communities and communities of color and their mainstream peers so they are successful in school so that school success would be equitable across such differences as race and socioeconomic status. It would mean working toward such a vision of social justice in school by engaging the powerful force of accountability policy, that is, excellence and equity for all children.

***Excellence and Equity***    Educational leadership for social justice is founded on the belief that schooling must be democratic, and an understanding that schooling is not democratic "unless its practices are excellent and equitable."[128] Skrtic asserts that educational equity "is a precondition for excellence."[129] Gordon linked social justice to excellence and equity by arguing:

> The failure to achieve universally effective education in our society is known to be a correlate of our failure to achieve social justice. By almost any measure, there continue to be serious differences between the level and quality of educational achievement for children coming from rich or from poor families, and from ethnic-majority or from some ethnic-minority group families. Low status ethnic-minority groups continue to be overrepresented in the low achievement groups in our schools and are correspondingly underrepresented in high academic achievement groups.[130]

We must achieve equal educational results for all children. Failure to do so will hamper specific groups from attaining the fundamental, primary goods and services distributed by society—rights, liberties, self-respect, power, opportunities, income, and wealth. Education is a social institution, controlling access to important opportunities and resources.

Education policy in the United States is dominated by accountability concerns. Public education issues are a top priority of national and state political agendas. The Goals 2000: Educate America Act of 1994, the Improving America's Schools Act (IASA) of 1994, a reau-

---

[124]Thomas L. Good, "Two Decades of Research on Teacher Expectations: Findings and Future Directions," *Journal of Teacher Education*, 38 (1987): 32–47.

[125]Education Trust, *Education Watch: The 2001 Education Trust State and National Data Book* (Washington, DC: Author, 2002).

[126]Linda Darling-Hammond, *Doing What Matters Most: Investing in Quality Teaching* (New York: National Commission on Teaching and America's Future, 1997).

[127]James Rawls, *A Theory of Justice* (London: Oxford University Press, 1971).

[128]Thomas M. Skrtic, *Behind Special Education: A Critical Analysis of Professional Culture and School Organization* (Denver, CO: Love, 1991), p. 199.

[129]Thomas M. Skrtic, "The Special Education Paradox: Equity as a Way to Excellence," *Harvard Educational Review*, 61 (1991): 181.

[130]Edmund W. Gordon, *Education and Justice: A View from the Back of the Bus* (New York: Teachers College Press, 1999), p. XII.

thorization of the Elementary and Secondary Education Act of 1965, and the No Child Left Behind Act of 2001 call for equal treatment, access, and outcomes for all children.

There are numerous reports that demonstrate that it is possible to find effective public schools where administrators, teachers, and parents collaborate to produce high achievement for all students. But these successes occur in only a small number of schools. We still cannot account for the fact that some students master academic content and many others do not. And there is little research on organizational design and practice in exceptionally high-performing school districts.[131] The available documentation does point to some common themes that high-performing school districts possess, but the knowledge base on which to offer advice to school districts and administrators on the design of sustained districtwide improvement processes is limited.

Government officials, academic scholars, business leaders, and the educational community have begun to look at state accountability systems to realize the vision that "equity and excellence need not be mutually exclusive goals."[132] Within the past ten years a few examples of sustained districtwide academic success of children have begun to emerge in the research literature. These examples have appeared in states that have highly developed, stable accountability systems, such as Connecticut, Kentucky, New York, North Carolina, and Texas. There is evidence from these states and others that their accountability systems driven by state policy initiatives have improved student performance for all students (as measured by state achievement tests, National Assessment of Educational Progress (NAEP), Advanced Placement (AP) exams, and ACT and SAT tests. In addition, there is evidence of narrowing of the achievement gap between the performance of children of color and low-income children and that of their white and more economically advantaged counterparts.[133]

Preliminary research in some of these districts found evidence of common strategic elements in the way these districts managed themselves. Superintendents in high-performing districts exhibited a much greater clarity of purpose, along with a much greater willingness to exercise tighter controls over evidence of performance. They used data on student performance to focus attention on problems and successes; they built

district accountability systems that complemented their own state's system; and they forged strong relationships with their school boards around improvement goals. They created a climate in which teachers and principals were collectively responsible for student learning and in which the improvement of instruction was the central task. Incentive structures in these districts focused on the performance of *all* students, not just on average school performance. Superintendents realigned district offices in these school districts to focus on direct relationships with schools around instructional issues; and they focused more energy and resources on content-specific professional development.[134] The success of these school districts confirms the findings of Valencia that it is critically important for school leaders to reject assumptions of deficit thinking.[135] Leaders who reject deficit thinking about students and their parents engage in what many theorists call *capacity building*, helping people to acquire skills and dispositions to learn new ways of thinking and acting.[136] Darling-Hammond underscores the fundamental importance of capacity-building skills on the part of educators when she states that the capacity to "achieve associations beyond those of any narrow group — to live and learn heterogeneously together"[137] undergirds our ability to live in a diverse democratic society.[138]

## Leadership in Schools

We will examine several leadership frameworks in Chapter 5. A few deserve brief mention here for their contributions to the post–behavioral science era. In addition, we mention briefly here attempts by some scholars to expand the traditional knowledge domains that define educational leadership.

In his examination of the concept of transformational leadership, Bernard Bass contrasts two types of leadership behavior: transactional and transformational.[139] According to Bass, transactional leaders determine what subordinates need to do to achieve their own and organizational goals, classify those require-

[131]Elmore, *School Reform from the Inside Out.*

[132]Debra Viadero, "Setting the Bar: How High?" *Education Week,* 17 (1999): 24.

[133]Skrla, Scheurich, Johnson, and Koschoreck, "Accountability for Equity: Can State Policy Leverage Social Justice?"

[134]Elmore, *School Reform from the Inside Out.*

[135]Richard R. Valencia, *The Evolution of Deficit Thinking.*

[136]Fullan, *Learning Places.*

[137]Darling-Hammond, *Doing What Matters Most.*

[138]Shields, Larocque, and Oberg, "A Dialogue about Race and Ethnicity in Education: Struggling to Understand Issues in Cross-Cultural Leadership."

[139]Bernard M. Bass et al., *Transformation Leadership* (Mahwah, NJ: Lawrence Erlbaum, 2005).

ments, help subordinates become confident that they can reach their goals by expending the necessary efforts, and reward them according to their accomplishments. Transformational leaders, in contrast, motivate their subordinates to do more than they originally expected to do. They accomplish this in three ways: by raising followers' levels of consciousness about the importance and value of designated outcomes and ways of reaching them; by getting followers to transcend their own self-interest for the sake of the team, organization, or larger polity; and by raising followers' need levels to the higher-order needs, such as self-actualization, or by expanding their portfolio of needs.

One of the most comprehensive models of transformational leadership in schools has been provided by Leithwood. The model conceptualizes transformational leadership along eight dimensions: building school vision, establishing school goals, providing intellectual stimulation, offering individualized support, modeling best practices and important educational values, demonstrating high performance expectations, creating a productive school culture, and developing structures to foster participation in school decisions.[140]

Peter Senge provides important insight into how educators can transform schools into "learning organizations" that renew themselves.[141] A number of observers have suggested that the increasing complexity of modern organizations puts a greater premium on leaders' possession of a repertoire of styles and strategies. Bolman and Deal,[142] for example, argue that the ability to *reframe*—to reconceptualize the same situation using multiple perspectives—is a central capacity for leaders of the twenty-first century. W. Edwards Deming's Total Quality Management (TQM) principles are revitalizing businesses, service organizations, universities, and elementary and secondary schools.[143]

Irby and her colleagues have developed a new theory of leadership sensitive to the feminine perspective called the *synergistic leadership theory*. Six aspects par-

ticular to the synergistic leadership theory influence the ideas and include issues concerning diversity and the inclusion of the female voice in the theory. Four factors are key to the relational and interactive nature of the theory, which provides a useful framework for building and understanding the interdependent relationships. In a tetrahedron model, the theory uses four factors, including leadership behavior, organizational structure, external forces, and attitudes, beliefs, and values to demonstrate aspects not only of leadership but its effects on various institutions and positions. Developed through a qualitative approach, the theory has been validated qualitatively and quantitatively nationwide and is currently being validated internationally.[144]

Subjectivist and interpretivist approaches to the study of educational administration (variously labeled neo-Marxist/critical theory and post-modernism) emerged in the late 1970s and have continued to the present. The scholars in this tradition have attempted to expand the traditional knowledge domains that define educational administration. These alternative, nontraditional perspectives have spawned scholarship on ethics and values by researchers such as Christopher Hodgkinson, Jackie Stefkovich, Joan Shapiro, Lynn Beck, and Jerry Starratt; gender, race/ethnicity, and class by scholars such as Carol Gilligan, Sonia Nieto, Lisa Delpit, Charol Shakeshaft, Margaret Grogan, Cryss Brunner, Marilyn Tallerico, Beverly Irby, Genevieve Brown, Linda Skrla, Joseph F. Johnson, Flora Ida Ortiz, Catherine Marshall, Kofi Lomotey, Barbara Jackson, Diana Pounder, Norma Mertz, Cynthia Dillard, and Gretchen Rossman; and critical theory and postmodernism by analysts such as T. B. Greenfield, Henry Giroux, Richard Bates, Peter McLaren, William Foster, Fenwick English, Colleen Capper, Spencer Maxcy, James Scheurich, Michael Dantley, Cornel West, Michelle Young, Colleen Larson, Gail Furman, Gary Anderson, Carolyn Shields, Patti Lather, and Paulo Freire.

## Development of Administrative Thought

We have attempted to place the development of administrative thought into a loose historical framework. In general, four models emerge: classical organizational theory, the human relations approach, the behavioral science approach, and the post–behavioral science ap-

---

[140]Kenneth Leithwood, "Leadership for School Restructuring," *Educational Administration Quarterly*, 35 (1994): 498–518.

[141]Peter Senge, *The Fifth Discipline: The Art and Practice of the Learning Organization* (New York: Doubleday, 1990, 2006).

[142]Lee G. Bolman and Terrence E. Deal, *Reframing Organizations: Artistry, Choice, and Leadership*, 3rd ed. (San Francisco: Jossey-Bass, 2003).

[143]W. Edwards Deming, *Out of the Crisis* (Cambridge, MA: MIT Press, 1988).

[144]Beverly J. Irby, Genevieve Brown, JoAnn Duffy, and Diane Trautman, "The Synergistic Leadership Theory," *Journal of Educational Administration*, 40 (2002): 304–322.

proach. The classical "rational" model evolved around the ideas of scientific and administrative management, including the study of administrative processes and managerial functions. The human relations "social" model was spurred by some early seminal social science research, including experimentation and analysis of the social and psychological aspects of people in the workplace and the study of group behavior. The behavioral science approach was an attempt to reconcile the basic incongruency between the rational-economic model and the social model. The more recent post–behavioral science approach includes the interrelated concepts of school improvement, democratic community, and social justice, as well as postmodernism. Table 1–2 briefly summarizes the major differences among the four approaches to administrative thought.

**Table 1–2   Overview of the Four Major Developments in Administrative Thought**

| Period | Management Elements | Procedures | Contributors and Basic Concepts |
|---|---|---|---|
| Classical organizational theory | Leadership Organization Production Process  Authority Administration Reward Structure | Top to bottom Machine Individual Anticipated consequences Rules; coercive Leader separate Economic Formal | Time-and-motion study, functional supervisor, piece rate (Taylor); five basic functions, fourteen principles of management (Fayol); POSDCoRB (Gulick); ideal bureaucracy (Weber) |
| Human relations approach | Leadership Organization Production Process  Authority Administration Reward  Structure | All directions Organism Group Unanticipated consequences Group norms Participative Social and psychological Informal | Hawthorne studies (Mayo, Roethlisberger, and Dickson); intellectual undercurrents: group dynamics leadership studies (Lewin, Lippitt, and White); client-centered therapy (Rogers); sociometric technique (Moreno); human relations in the restaurant industry (Whyte); small groups (Homans) |
| Behavioral science approach | Consideration of all major elements with heavy emphasis on contingency leadership, culture, transformational leadership, and systems theory | | Cooperative systems (Barnard); fusion process (Bakke); optimal actualization—organization and individual (Argyris); social systems theory—nomothetic and idiographic (Getzels and Guba); need hierarchy (Maslow); Theory X and Y (McGregor); hygiene–motivation (Herzberg); Systems 1–4 (Likert); open–closed climates (Halpin and Croft); managerial grid (Blake and Mouton); contingency theory (Fiedler); situational leadership (Hersey and Blanchard); expectancy theory (Vroom); 3–D leadership (Reddin); compliance theory (Etzioni); structure of organizations (Mintzberg); leadership–unconscious conspiracy (Bennis) |
| Post–behavioral science approach | Interrelated concepts of school improvement, democratic community, and social justice with heavy emphasis on leadership; and emergent nontraditional perspectives | | School improvement, democratic community, and social justice (Murphy); transformational leadership (Bass, Leithwood); learning organization (Senge); reframing organizations (Bolman and Deal); TQM (Deming); synergistic leadership theory (Irby, Brown, Duffy, and Trautman); instructional leadership, tranformational leadership, managerial leadership, moral leadership, participative leadership, reflective/craft leadership (Leithwood and Duke); values and ethics (Hodgkinson, Stefkovich, Shapiro, Beck, and Starratt); gender, race/ethnicity, and class (Gilligan, Nieto, Delpit, Shakeshaft, Grogan, Brunner, Tallerico, Irby, Brown, Skrla, Johnson, Ortiz, Marshall, Lomotey, Jackson, Pounder, Mertz, Dillard, Rossman); critical theory and postmodernism (T. B. Greenfield, Derrida, Foucault, Lyotard, Giroux, Bates, Williams, Habermas, McLaren, Foster, English, Capper, Maxcy, Scheurich, Dantley, West, Young, Larson, Furman, Anderson, Shields, Lather, Freire, and Murtadha) |

As shown in Table 1–2, differences in leadership, organization, production, process, power, administration, reward, and structure are important distinguishing characteristics of the four approaches. We can see how organization and administrative theory have evolved from a concern for efficiency and the basic principles of management to an emphasis on human and psychological factors, to social systems and contingency theory, and finally, to a concern for school improvement, democratic community, social justice, and postmodernism. While we have not included all people who have made contributions in the evolution of administrative thought, we have highlighted major contributors and basic concepts and primary eras in the evolution. Furthermore, no attempt is made to date the eras precisely. In fact, if we view the sequence of developments in organizational and administrative theory, we notice a correlational rather than a compensatory tendency.

Traces of the past coexist with modern approaches to administration. For example, while the classical "rational" model has been modified somewhat since its emergence during the 1900s, views of the school as a rational-technical system remain firmly embedded in the minds of policymakers and pervade most educational reforms proposed since the publication of *A Nation at Risk* in 1983[145] and the many reports that followed. Indeed, this view of schooling is in place today with current accountability policy to assess student, teacher, and school performance. Implicit in the No Child Left Behind Act of 2001[146] is the concomitant expectation that school administrators and teachers will adjust instructional strategies to yield more effective learning outcomes for all children.

## Systems Theory

One of the more useful concepts in understanding organizations is the idea that an organization is a system. A system can be defined as a set of interrelated elements that function as a unit for a specific purpose. **Systems theory** is a way of viewing schools as learning organizations.[147] Senge suggests that an organization must be studied as a whole, taking into consideration the interrelationships among its parts and its relationship with the external environment.

The learning organization concept has received much attention since the initial publication of Peter Senge's book *The Fifth Discipline* in 1990, now in its second edition. A **learning organization** is a strategic commitment to capture and share learning in the organization for the benefit of individuals, teams, and the organization. It does this through alignment and the collective capacity to sense and interpret a changing environment; to input new knowledge through continuous learning and change; to imbed this knowledge in systems and practices; and to transform this knowledge into outputs.

Senge defines the learning organization as "organizations where people continually expand their capacity to create the results they truly desire, where new and expansive patterns of thinking are nurtured, where collective aspiration is set free and where people are continually learning how to learn together."[148] Senge describes a model of five interdependent disciplines necessary for an organization to seriously pursue learning. He identifies systems thinking as the "fifth discipline" because he believes that thinking systemically is the pivotal lever in the learning and change process. Brief definitions of Senge's principles follow.

- *Systems thinking:* A conceptual framework that sees all parts as interrelated and affecting each other.

- *Personal mastery:* A process of personal commitment to vision, excellence, and lifelong learning.

- *Shared vision:* Sharing an image of the future you want to realize together.

- *Team learning:* The process of learning collectively; the idea that two brains are smarter than one.

- *Mental models:* Deeply ingrained assumptions that influence personal and organizational views and behaviors.

The five disciplines work together to create the learning organization. A metaphor to describe this systems theory–based model would be DNA or a hologram. Each is a complex system of patterns, and the whole is greater than the sum of its parts.

Senge, author of the best-selling book, *The Fifth Discipline,* has written a companion book directly fo-

[145] National Commission on Excellence in Education, *A Nation at Risk* (Washington, DC: U.S. Government Printing Office, 1983).

[146] No Child Left Behind Act of 2001 (www.ed.gov/nclb/landing.jhtml?src=pb).

[147] Senge, *The Fifth Discipline.*

[148] Senge, *The Fifth Discipline*, p. 3.

cused on education. In *Schools That Learn*,[149] Senge argues that teachers, administrators, and other school stakeholders must learn how to build their own capacity; that is, they must develop the capacity to learn. From Senge's perspective, real improvement will occur only if people responsible for implementation design the change itself. He argues that schools can be re-created, made vital, and renewed not by fiat or command, and not by regulation, but by embracing the principles of the learning organization.

Senge makes a powerful argument regarding the need for a systems approach and learning orientation. He provides a historical perspective on educational systems. Specifically, he details "industrial age" assumptions about learning: that children are deficient and schools should fix them, that learning is strictly an intellectual enterprise, that everyone should learn in the same way, that classroom learning is distinctly different from that occurring outside of school, and that some kids are smart while others are not. He further asserts that schools are run by specialists who maintain control, that knowledge is inherently fragmented, that schools teach some kind of objective truth, and that learning is primarily individualistic and competition accelerates learning. Senge suggests that these assumptions about learning and the nature and purpose of schooling reflect deeply embedded cultural beliefs that must be considered, and in many cases directly confronted, if schools are to develop the learning orientation necessary for improvement.

Through learning, people make meaning of their experience and of information. Learning helps people to create and manage knowledge that builds a system's intellectual capital. Karen Watkins and Victoria Marsick have developed a model of the learning organization around seven action imperatives that speak to the kind of initiatives that are implemented in learning organizations. (See Administrative Advice 1–1.)

## Basic Systems Model

Figure 1–1 depicts the basic systems theory of organizations, which has five parts: inputs, a transformation process, outputs, feedback, and the environment. *Inputs* are the human, material, financial, or information resources used to produce a product or service.

Through technology and administrative functions, the inputs undergo a *transformation process*. In schools the interaction between students and teachers is part of the transformation or learning process by which students become educated citizens capable of contributing to society. *Outputs* include the organization's products and services. An educational organization generates and distributes knowledge. *Feedback* is information concerning the outputs or the process of the organization that influences the selection of inputs during the next cycle. Such information may lead to changes in both the transformation process and future outputs. The *environment* surrounding the organization includes the social, political, and economic forces that impinge on the organization.

The environment in the systems model takes on added significance today in a climate of policy accountability. The social, political, and economic contexts in which school administrators work are marked by pressures at the local, state, and national levels. Thus, school administrators today find it necessary to manage and develop "internal" operations while concurrently monitoring the environment and anticipating and responding to "external" demands.

Since the publication of *A Nation at Risk* in 1983,[150] education has been near the top of the national political agenda. The report nationalized the discussion concerning the well-being of public schooling in America. It linked the health of the economy to the performance of the public school system. Furthermore, at the time the report was released, the United States was in a severe recession, and there was concern regarding our economic competitiveness with other nations. In particular, comparisons were made between Japanese industrial performance and that of the United States. These economic comparisons led to corresponding educational comparisons, and many people concluded that the U.S. public school system was underperforming.[151]

While there was little change at the national level concerning educational reform, the scope of state involvement greatly expanded, including intrusion into the technical core of schooling (teaching and learning). Issues addressed were what should be taught, how it should be taught, how students should be grouped for

[149] Peter Senge, *Schools That Learn* (New York: Doubleday, 2001).

[150] National Commission on Excellence in Education, *A Nation at Risk*.

[151] David C. Berliner and Bruce J. Biddle, *The Manufactured Crisis: Myths, Fraud and the Attack on America's Public Schools* (Reading, MA: Addison-Wesley, 1995).

## Administrative Advice 1–1

### The Seven Action Imperatives of a Learning Organization

The seven action imperatives can be interpreted in terms of what must change to help schools become learning organizations.

- *Create Continuous Learning Opportunities.* This means that learning is ongoing, strategically used, and grows out of the work itself. Administrators and teachers have many opportunities to consciously look at what they are learning from new initiatives. They can look at results as opportunities to learn why an initiative was not successful; and they can initiate projects to experiment with change. They can make it attractive for faculty members to serve as mentors. They can find ways to use technology better to help faculty gain new skills. Schools might also find ways to provide time, money, and other incentives for professional development.

- *Promote Inquiry and Dialogue.* The key to this imperative is a culture in which people ask questions freely, are willing to put difficult issues on the table for discussion, and are open to giving and receiving feedback at all levels. Strategies to implement this action imperative include the use of dialogue and questioning in meetings and learning sessions.

- *Encourage Collaboration and Team Learning.* The relevant action imperative for this level focuses on the spirit of collaboration and the skills that undergird the effective use of teams. People in schools frequently form groups, but they are not always encouraged to bring what they know to the table. Strategies to implement this action imperative might include support for the effective functioning of teams that cross levels and groups (students, faculty, administrators, and parents). A step in this direction is to extend training that is commonly given to a few key people, and to focus instead on team building for intact site-based decision-making teams that include teaching everyone needed skills of dialogue, negotiation, consensus, and meeting management.

- *Create Systems to Capture and Share Learning.* Technology-based strategies that are used for this purpose focus on the use of software such as Lotus Notes or Microsoft Access to capture ideas across dispersed teams and divisions, and computerized documentation of changes in a particular area. Options for sharing knowledge include keeping journals of lessons learned and processes for collaborative development of new ideas so all are involved in co-creating knowledge before using it. Celebration events can be used to bring people together, recognize accomplishments, and share ideas across geographical, functional, time, and experience levels.

- *Empower People toward a Collective Vision.* The primary criteria for success with this action imperative are the degree of alignment throughout the organization around the vision, and the degree to which everyone in the organization actively participates in creating and implementing the changes that follow from the vision. To gain acceptance of a shared vision, schools could ask task forces to identify and change elements that are inconsistent with the vision. They could engage people in ceremonies to mourn the passing of the old culture and skits to depict the new. They could ask community artists to render a new vision. They could invite stakeholders to physically modify the creative product to represent their ideas.

- *Connect the Organization to Its Environment.* Schools must function at both global and local levels. Schools can use benchmarking to see what other schools are doing to achieve excellence and to solve similar problems, and can scan their environment for new trends by using computer databases. Technology enables people in schools to move beyond their walls. Schools often initiate Internet projects whereby students and teachers from one school can communicate with other students around the globe; or design programs that bring school faculty and staff members, students, and community groups together around special interests.

- *Provide Strategic Leadership for Learning.* Leaders who model learning are key to the learning organization. They think strategically about how to use learning to move the organization in new directions. School leaders can routinely discuss development plans and opportunities with faculty and staff members, can make information available regarding opportunities for learning, and can seek resources to support faculty development.

Source: Adapted from Karen E. Watkins and Victoria J. Marsick, "Sculpting the Learning Community: New Forms of Working and Organizing," *NASSP Bulletin*, 83, no. 604 (1999): 78–87. Copyright © 1999 National Association of Secondary School Principals. www.principals.org. Reprinted with permission.

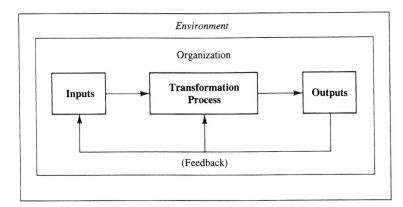

**Figure 1–1**

Basic Systems Model

instruction, and how instruction should be evaluated. The increased involvement of the state in the technical core of teaching and learning led to a change in policy focus. Prior to the *A Nation at Risk* report, state education policy tended to focus on inputs and processes, not on outputs such as student academic achievement. With the rise of international economic and educational comparisons, states began to focus their policy on standards, accountability, and the improvement of student academic achievement. Statewide assessment systems were implemented nationwide. Thus was born an era of high-stakes testing complete with rewards and sanctions for low-performing schools.

The social, political, and economic forces that impinge on the school organization are not all state and national, however. Local school administrators also face a number of challenges that are exclusively local in nature, such as bond referenda, difficult school boards, and teacher unions. These local political issues can at times confound state-mandated policies. For example, principals often face mandated programs that do not meet the changing demographics of their student population. Teachers are often bound by union contracts that conflict with the norms of their particular school. Superintendents are expected to respond to federal mandates even though resources are scarce. Zero-tolerance policies may require expelling a student, even though it may not be in the best interest of the student to miss school for an extended period of time. And educational leaders are faced with ongoing pressures to show good school results on standardized achievement tests, while at the same time dealing with a growing number of management duties, such as budgeting, hiring personnel, labor relations, and site committees resulting from School-Based Management initiatives.

## A Systems View of School Administration

It is useful to analyze the operation of an educational organization and the role of school administrators within that operation from an **open systems framework**. The dimensions of a school district's operation can be grouped into the three broad categories of inputs, transformation process, and outputs. This framework aids in the analysis of school district operations and, more specifically, in the organization's system of operational management. It contributes greatly to the quick and accurate diagnosis of problems, and it can focus the school administrator's efforts on the key areas to introduce change in the system.

The basic systems model is expanded to focus on the role of the school administrator in operating a school or school district. Figure 1–2 shows the interrelationships among the dimensions of the operational management system. (Many of the topics will be discussed in subsequent chapters.) This figure, although oversimplifying the relationships, helps make clear the pattern of interrelationships in operating a school district or other educational institution.

**Inputs**   The school district's environment provides it with personnel, financing, and theory/knowledge. In addition, federal, state, and local governments enact laws that regulate school district operations. Other groups make demands on the school district as well. Students, for example, want relevant and useful curriculum content to prepare them for the world of work or higher education. Teachers want higher salaries, better working conditions, fringe benefits, and job security. School board members want a high return on their investment, that is, quality education within an operating budget.

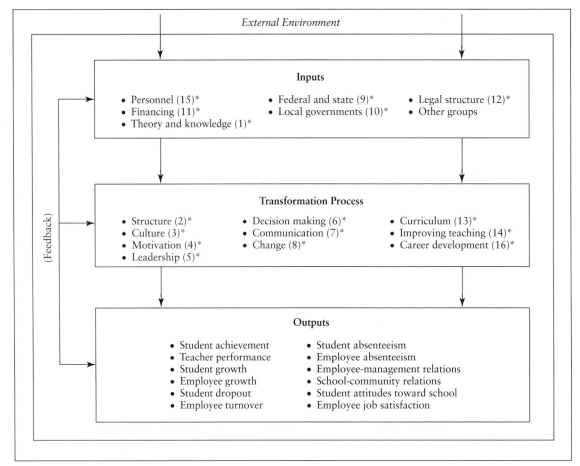

**Figure 1–2**

A Systems View of School Administration
(*The numbers indicate chapters in this book.)

Similarly, the community expects the schools to provide quality education to all the district's clients without an increase in taxes. And special interest groups have a variety of agendas. Each group has its own goals, which often conflict. The job of the school administrator is to integrate these diverse goals into a viable plan of action.

**Transformation Process** Organizations convert the inputs from the external environment into some form of output. Work of some kind is done in the system to produce output. The system adds a *value added* to the work in process. This transformation process includes the internal operation of the organization and its system of operational management. Some components

of the system of operational management include the technical competence of school administrators, including their decision-making and communication skills, their plans of operation, and their ability to cope with change. Activities performed by school administrators within the organization's structure will affect the school district's outputs.

**Outputs** The school administrator's job is to secure and use inputs from the external environment, transform them through administrative activities such as providing a structure, developing a culture, motivating, leading, decision making, communicating, implementing change, developing curriculum, administering personnel, and financing the institution to produce outputs. In school organizations, outputs include student achievement, teacher performance, growth levels of students and employees, student dropout, employee turnover, student and employee absenteeism, employee–management relations, school–community relations, student attitudes toward school, and employee job satisfaction (see Figure 1–2).

Finally, the external environment reacts to these outputs and provides feedback to the system. Feedback is crucial to the success of the school district operation. Negative feedback, for example, can be used to correct deficiencies in the school administrator's operational plan of action, which in turn will have an effect on the school district's outputs.

Most schools were not designed in the systems approach as conceptualized by Peter Senge. They just evolved from earlier versions, adding and subtracting programs as they moved from decade to decade. Most schools are loosely coupled systems in which the whole is often less important than its parts.

## The Malcolm Baldrige Framework

The Baldrige Framework is a systems perspective for achieving continuous education quality improvement. The core values and concepts of the framework are embodied in seven categories:

1. Leadership.
2. Strategic Planning.
3. Student, Stakeholder, and Market Focus.
4. Measurement, Analysis, and Knowledge Management.
5. Faculty and Staff Focus.
6. Process Management.
7. Results.

Figure 1–3 provides the framework connecting and integrating the seven categories. From top to bottom, the framework has the following basic elements.

### Organizational Profile

The Organizational Profile (top of figure) sets the context for the way the organization operates. The environment, key working relationships, and strategic challenges serve as an overarching guide for the organizational performance management system.

### System Operations

The system operations are composed of the six Baldrige categories in the center of the figure that define the operations and the results achieved.

Leadership (Category 1), Strategic Planning (Category 2), and Student, Stakeholder, and Market Focus (Category 3) represent the leadership triad. These categories are placed together to emphasize the importance of a leadership focus on strategy and on students and stakeholders. Senior leaders (superintendent and associates) set the organizational direction and seek future opportunities for organizational direction and future opportunities for the organization.

Faculty and Staff Focus (Category 5), Process Management (Category 6), and Results (Category 7) represent the results triad. The organization's faculty and staff and key processes accomplish the work of the organization that yields the overall performance results.

All actions point toward Results (Category 7)—a composite of student, stakeholder, market, budgetary, financial, and operational performance results including faculty and staff, governance, and social responsibility results.

The horizontal arrow in the center of the framework links the leadership triad to the results triad, a linkage critical to organizational success. Furthermore, the arrow indicates the central relationship between Leadership (Category 1) and Results (Category 7). The two-headed arrows indicate the importance of feedback in an effective performance management system.

### System Foundation

Measurement, Analysis, and Knowledge Management (Category 4) are critical to the effective management of the organization and to a fact-based, knowledge-driven system for improving performance. Measurement, analysis, and knowledge management serve as a foundation for the performance management system.

## Emergent Perspectives

Positivism was the dominant orthodoxy in educational administration until the late 1970s. Positivism is a view of knowledge as objective, absolutely true, and independent of other conditions such as time, circumstances, societies, cultures, communities, and geography. Another tradition of positivism is *empiricism*, which maintains that knowledge of the world can only be acquired

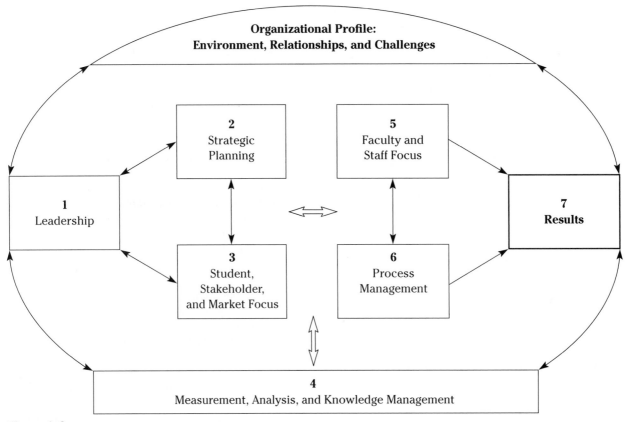

**Figure 1–3**

Baldrige Education Criteria for Performance Excellence Framework: A Systems Perspective

Source: Adapted from Baldrige National Quality Program, National Institute of Standard and Technology, Technology Administration, U.S. Department of Commerce, Administration Building, Room A600, 100 Bureau Drive, Stop 1020, Gaithersburg, MD 20899–1020.

through the senses and through experience. This view of science came to be known as *logical empiricism* or *logical positivism*. From these philosophies there developed *positivism*—the view that any investigation in the natural or social sciences must be derived from empiricist postulates in order to be considered academically acceptable. Simply stated, **positivism** is a worldview that all knowledge of the world comes to us from sense experience and observation.

The positivist approach to research consists of several functions: (a) the observation and description of perceptual data coming to us from the world through our senses, (b) the development of theories inferred from such observations and descriptions of perceptual data, (c) the testing of hypotheses derived from the theories,

and (d) the verification of hypotheses that are then used to verify the theories derived from the observation and description of perceptual data. The approach evolved from an empiricist model of science that involves observation and description, theory building, and hypothesis testing and verification. Quantitative methods using large samples with the objective of statistical inferences was the predominant tool used. The positivist approach to the generation of knowledge dominated research in educational administration until the late 1970s.

At the time, objections began to surface regarding the dominant (positivist) orthodoxy. Alternative paradigms began to appear and continued to be refined through the 1980s. These emerging nontraditional perspectives came under the general heading of *subjectivist* and *in-*

## PRO/CON Debate

### Training School Leaders

Xerox's CEO David Kearns said that schools "are admirably suited to the economy and culture of the 1950s and spectacularly unsuited to the high-tech future of the next century." He believes that education is big business and the same theories that guide industrial executives are the ones school leaders need to solve education's problems.

**Question:** Is the management training provided by business and industry for their leaders the best source of information and skill development for principals and superintendents?

**Arguments PRO**

1. Organizational theory is generic. Its essential concepts are applicable in all organizations.

2. Most organizational theory taught in educational administration courses was generated by researchers in the industrial setting. Industrial management thought leads the way. Why not do away with intermediaries?

3. Business and school leaders need to work more closely together. If they share the same training, think about the same ideas, and speak the same language, it will improve the collegial relationship between schools and the communities they serve.

4. Management training is current and tested. Industry has invested heavily in the development of management-training programs. If that resource is being offered to schools, it would be foolish not to take advantage of the offer.

5. Management trainers understand organizational theory well and can teach adult learners in all types of organizations to apply theory to their settings.

**Arguments CON**

1. Business is private enterprise; schools are public service agencies. It would be a dangerous mistake to borrow management theory wholesale.

2. Many aspects of management theory do not apply in educational settings. It takes several years to adapt management theory into educational administrative theory. Educational researchers play an important role in sifting and applying organizational theory.

3. The scions of industry are one consumer group for schools. Educators' relationship to them is important but no more important than the relationship with the leaders of other consumer groups such as parents, colleges, and civic agencies. While educators should be open to feedback from clients, they should not be co-opted by them.

4. Management training is behaviorist and outcome-driven. It does not consider the social and psychological needs of the teacher as much as the profits of the organization.

5. Management trainers understand profit-driven organizations but do not understand the norms and values of educators.

terpretivist approaches. Subjectivist and interpretivist views refer to perspectives that look inward to the mind rather than outward to experience and that connect to philosophical idealism and, more recently, to phenomenology and existentialism. Subjectivist and interpretivist perspectives are illustrated by the early work of scholars such as T. B. Greenfield in Canada; by the work of neo-Marxist and critical theorists such as Bates and others; and by the early work of postmodernists such as Derrida, Foucault, and Lyotard. These alternate nontraditional approaches spawned scholarship on ethics and values; gender, race/ethnicity, and class; and critical theory and postmodernism as mentioned previously.

The subjectivist and interpretivist perspectives led to the increased popularity of qualitative research methods under various labels: qualitative methods, ethnography, participant observation, case studies, fieldwork, and naturalistic inquiry. These approaches are attempts to understand educational processes within local situations. Societies; cultures; communities; unique circumstances; gender, race, and class; and geography serve as important analytical categories in such inquiry. There seems to be an increasing interest in bringing together positivist and interpretive paradigms that may prove valuable to both the researcher and the practitioner.

## Summary

1. The practice of educational administration has changed in response to historical conditions and theoretical developments.

2. To an increasing degree, educational administration is characterized by using theory to explain and predict phenomena in educational organizations.

3. The functions of theories include identification of relevant phenomena, classification of phenomena, formulation of constructs, summarization of phenomena, prediction of phenomena, and revelation of needed research.

4. Since the early 1900s, four major perspectives on administration have evolved: classical organization theory, the human relations approach, the behavioral science approach, and the post–behavioral science approach.

5. Three contemporary extensions of administrative perspectives are contingency theory, systems theory, and emergent nontraditional perspectives. Contingency theories suggest that numerous factors or situations affect leadership, many of which cannot be predetermined or perfectly controlled. Systems theory is usually discussed in terms of inputs, a transformation process, outputs, feedback, and environment.

6. Emergent nontraditional perspectives have spawned research in ethics and values; gender, race/ethnicity, and class; and critical theory and postmodernism.

7. The major dimensions of leadership may be divided into two categories—task dimensions and human relations skills.

## Key Terms

theory
classical organizational theory
management perspectives
scientific management
administrative management
human relations approach
Hawthorne studies
behavioral science approach
cooperative system
fusion process
nomothetic dimension
idiographic dimension
need hierarchy
Theory X and Theory Y
hygiene factors
motivation factors
Systems 1–4
managerial grid
contingency theories
situational leadership theory
post–behavioral science approach
critical thinking
constructivism
systems theory
learning organization
open systems framework
positivism

## Discussion Questions

1. What are the functions of theories in educational administration?

2. Why is it important to understand the different approaches to administrative theory that have evolved throughout the history of organizations?

3. What is the post–behavioral science approach? How does it differ from earlier approaches to administration?

4. Discuss the basic concepts underlying school improvement, democratic community, and social justice.

5. What are the major components of systems theory?

6. What contributions do the emergent perspectives have on the study and practice of educational administration?

## Suggested Readings

Blankstein, Alan M. *Failure Is Not an Option: Six Principles That Guide Student Achievement in High-Performing Schools* (Thousand Oaks, CA: Corwin Press, 2004). Covering theory into practice, applications that include case studies and vignettes, and techniques for addressing difficult issues, this state-of-the-art resource provides practical approaches to perplexing problems. The author identifies the professional learning community as the center of effective school reform and offers six guiding principles for creating and sustaining high-performing schools.

Conyers, John G., and Robert Ewy. *Charting Your Course: Lessons Learned during the Journey toward Performance Excellence* (Milwaukee: ASQ Press, 2004). Conyers and Ewy have chosen to entitle this book *Charting Your Course* because the Malcolm Baldrige criteria are nonprescriptive. The criteria do not tell you what to do—you have the leeway to chart your own course. What Baldrige does is give you a systematic framework for organizational excellence. How you bring it about is dependent on your leadership.

English, Fenwick W. (ed.). *The SAGE Handbook of Educational Leadership* (Thousand Oaks, CA: Sage Publications, 2005). A landmark work with contributions from 37 internationally renowned scholars covering an extensive range of issues confronting the field of educational leadership and administration. The *Handbook* reviews how leadership was redefined by management and organizational theory in its quest to become scientific, then looks forward to promising theories, concepts, and practices that show potential for development and application.

Firestone, William A., and Carolyn Riehl (eds.). *A New Agenda for Research in Educational Leadership* (New York: Teachers College Press, 2006). This book, the product of the task force on research co-sponsored by the American Educational Research Association Division A and the University Council for Educational Administration, sets an ambitious agenda for research in educational leadership. Prominent scholars cover a broad range of topics.

Fullan, Michael. *Leadership & Sustainability: System Thinkers in Action* (Thousand Oaks, CA: Corwin Press, 2005). Pursue long-term sustainability without jeopardizing short-term results. Provide an examination of what leaders at all levels of the educational system can do to pave the way for large-scale, sustainable reform. Fullan asks the question: How do you develop and sustain a greater number of system thinkers in action, or new theoreticians? This groundbreaking work defines an agenda for the new theoretician, including crucial elements of sustainability.

Marion, Russ. *Leadership in Education: Organizational Theory for the Practitioner* (Long Grove, IL: Waveland Press, 2006). Marion writes in the preface, "Theories are little more than ivory tower artifacts if they cannot be translated into guides for actual leadership behavior." This idea permeates *Leadership in Education*. Bridging the gap between the theoretical and the practical, Marion places organizational theory in broad historical and philosophical contexts to help students see patterns in the material. Each major paradigm shift the field has undergone is examined in detail, along with the background shifts that accompanied them. All major organizational theories are covered: machine theory, human relations, structuralism, open systems, and finally anti-positivist theories.

Marzano, Robert J., Timothy Waters, and Brian A. McNulty. *School Leadership That Works: From Research to Results* (Alexandria, VA: Association for Supervision and Curriculum Development, 2005). What can school leaders really do to increase student achievement, and which leadership practices have the biggest impact on school effectiveness? This book answers these questions definitively and gives you a list of leadership competencies that are research based. Drawing from 35 years of studies, the authors explain critical leadership principles that every administrator needs to know.

# 2. Organizational Structure

## FOCUSING QUESTIONS

1 How do the basic dimensions of organizational structure function?

2 Why is it usually necessary to have equal authority and responsibility?

3 What are the advantages of a decentralized (centralized) organization?

4 Are there differences between line and staff authority?

5 How does bureaucracy influence approaches to organizational structure?

6 How does participatory management influence organizational structure?

7 In what ways do schools represent machine bureaucracies? Professional bureaucracies?

8 How can instructional roles conflict (coincide) with individual needs?

In this chapter, we attempt to answer these questions concerning organizational structure in schools. Our primary emphasis is on formal rather than informal relationships concerning organizational structure. We begin our discussion by examining the basic concepts of organizational structure. We then discuss the bureaucratic model of organizational structure. Next, we present the participatory management model and compare the two approaches to organizing schools. We then describe three alternative models of organizational structure: organic and mechanistic organizations, compliance theory, and strategy-structure typology. Finally, we discuss the school as a social system using several of Getzels's models.

## Basic Concepts of Organizational Structure

Basic concepts of organizational structure provide a framework for vertical control and horizontal coordination of the organization. We discuss some of these concepts to provide the background for a more thorough analysis of the bureaucratic, participatory management, and alternative models of organizational structure. These important dimensions include job specialization, departmentalization, chain of command, authority and responsibility, centralization/decentralization, line and staff authority, and span of management.

### Job Specialization

A basic concept of organizational structure is to divide the work to be accomplished into specialized tasks and to organize them into distinct units. Examples of **job specialization** are the division of the school into elementary, middle, and high school units; the distinction between administrative and teaching functions; and the variety of position certificates required by the fifty state departments of education, including superintendent, business manager, principal, supervisor, teaching specialties, and the like.

The three most common alternatives to job specialization are job rotation, job enlargement, and job enrichment.[1] *Job rotation* involves systematically moving employees from one job to another. In large school districts, principals are often rotated between schools every five years. *Job enlargement* adds breadth to a job by increasing the number and variety of activities performed by an employee. *Job enrichment* adds depth to a job by adding "administrative" activities (decision making, staffing, budgeting, reporting) to an employee's responsibilities. The latter two alternatives were recommended by the Carnegie Task Force on Teaching as a Profession and the Holmes Group as a way to restructure schools through shared governance, participatory management, and site-based decision making, whereby teachers play a more active role in the operation of the school.[2]

## Departmentalization

**Departmentalization**, the organizationwide division of work, permits the organization to realize the benefits of job specialization and to coordinate the activities of the component parts. School districts may be broadly divided into divisions of instruction, business, personnel, and research and development. Further subdividing of a division such as instruction may produce departments responsible for specific subjects, such as English, social studies, mathematics, and science. Departments—frequently labeled divisions, building units, departments, or teams—often indicate hierarchical relationships. Thus, an assistant superintendent may lead a division; a principal, a building unit; a department head, an academic department within a building unit; and a teacher, a grade-level team in a school.

The most common grouping in schools is by function. Functional departmentalization offers a number of advantages. Because people who perform similar functions work together, each department can be staffed by experts in that functional area. Decision making and coordination are easier, because division administrators or department heads need to be familiar with only a relatively narrow set of skills. Functional departments at the central office can use a school district's resources more efficiently because a department's activity does not have to be repeated across several school district divisions. On the other hand, functional departmentalization has certain disadvantages. Personnel can develop overly narrow and technical viewpoints that lose sight of the total system perspective, communication and coordination across departments can be difficult, and conflicts often emerge as each department or unit attempts to protect its own area of authority and responsibility.

## Chain of Command

**Chain of command**, concerned with the flow of authority and responsibility within an organization, is associated with two underlying principles. *Unity of command* means that a subordinate is accountable to only one person—the person from whom he receives authority and responsibility. The *scalar principle* means that authority and responsibility should flow in a direct line vertically from top management to the lowest level. It establishes the division of work in the organization in hierarchical form.

Although organizations differ in the degree of their vertical divisions of work and the extent to which it is formalized, they all exhibit aspects of this characteristic. For example, in the military, the vertical specialization is established by specific definitions of roles for the various positions, and there are definite status differences among levels. Within the officer ranks in the Navy, there is a distinct difference of role and status in the hierarchy from ensign to admiral. In the university, there is a hierarchy within the professional ranks: instructor, assistant, associate, and full professor. In the school district organization, there are vertical differentiations of positions ranging from teachers to department heads, principals, directors, and superintendents. These levels are typically well defined, with differences in role and status for the various positions.

## Authority and Responsibility

**Authority** is the right to make decisions and direct the work of others. It is an important concept in organizational structure because administrators and other per-

---

[1]Frederick Herzberg, "One More Time: How Do You Motivate Employees?" *Harvard Business Review*, 65 (1987): 109–120.

[2]Carnegie Task Force on Teaching as a Profession, *A Nation Prepared: Teachers for the 21st Century* (Washington, DC: Carnegie Task Force, 1986); Holmes Group, *Tomorrow's Teachers: A Report of the Holmes Group* (East Lansing, MI: The Holmes Group, 1986).

sonnel must be authorized to carry out jobs to which they are assigned. Furthermore, authority and responsibility should be linked; that is, **responsibility** for the execution of work must be accompanied by the authority to accomplish the job.

In a school district, authority stems from the board of education. This body then delegates to the superintendent of schools the authority necessary to administer the district. As authority is delegated further, it becomes narrower in scope. Each succeedingly lower-level occupant has narrower limits on her areas of legitimate authority. This view of authority and responsibility provides the framework for legitimizing organizational hierarchy and provides the basis for direction and control.

## Centralization/Decentralization

Delegation of authority between a superior and a subordinate is a way of sharing power. The cumulative effect of all these superordinate-subordinate empowerment practices can have a dramatic impact on the overall organization. If administrators in a school district tend to delegate considerable authority and responsibility, more decisions are made at lower levels in the organization. Subordinates in such districts possess considerable influence in the overall operation of the school district. In these cases, the organization follows an administrative philosophy of **decentralization**. On the other hand, when school administrators retain most of the authority, depending on subordinates to implement decisions only, the organization is practicing **centralization**. Centralization and decentralization represent opposite ends of a continuum. That is, authority is delegated to a relatively small or large degree in the organization.

Should organizations centralize or decentralize? In the United States and Canada, the trend over the last thirty years has been toward greater decentralization of organizations.[3] Decentralization is said to have the following advantages: It makes greater use of human resources, unburdens top-level administrators, ensures that decisions are made close to the firing line by personnel with technical knowledge, and permits more rapid response to external changes.[4]

## Line and Staff Authority

Another way to view organizational structure is as line and staff authority. **Line authority** is that relationship in which a superior exercises direct supervision over a subordinate—an authority relationship in a direct line in the chain of command. Line authority relates specifically to the unity of command principle and the scalar principle. For example, line administrators such as the superintendent, assistant superintendent, directors of elementary and secondary education, and principals have authority to issue orders to their subordinates. Thus, the superintendent can order the assistant superintendent of instruction to implement a curriculum change, and the assistant superintendent in turn can order the directors of elementary and secondary education to do the same, and so on down the chain of command.

**Staff authority** is advisory in nature. The function of personnel in a staff position is to create, develop, collect, and analyze information, which flows to line personnel in the form of advice. Staff personnel do not possess the legitimate authority to implement this advice. One familiar example of staff is the "assistant to" in which the person assists the superintendent or other superior in a variety of ways. Another example is the legal counsel who advises the superintendent in legal matters affecting the schools.

## Span of Management

**Span of management** refers to the number of subordinates reporting directly to a supervisor. Is there an ideal span of management? There is no agreement regarding what is the best span of management. The most widely used criteria on this point suggest that spans can be larger at lower levels in an organization than at higher levels.[5] Because subordinates in lower-level positions typically perform much more routine activities, subordinates can be effectively supervised at lower levels. In practice, larger spans are often found at lower levels in organizations. Elementary schools, for example, are characterized by very large spans, as many as fifty or more teachers reporting to one principal. In such organizations, there is a tendency to assign team leaders within a school. These team leaders (teachers) report to the school principal. They may not be officially legitimized as a layer of administration within the

[3]Richard L. Daft, *Organizational Theory and Design* (Belmont, CA: Thomson South-Western, 2006).

[4]Samuel C. Certo, *Modern Management* (Englewood Cliffs, NJ: Prentice Hall, 2005).

[5]Robert P. Vecchio, *Organizational Behavior: Core Concepts* (Belmont, CA: Thomson South-Western, 2006).

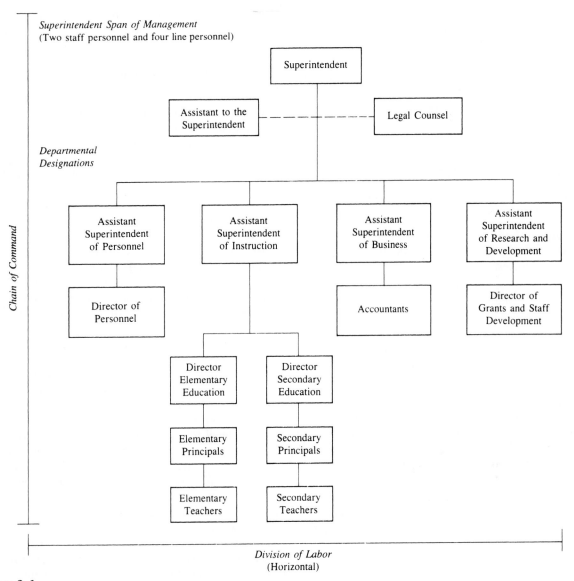

*Superintendent Span of Management*
(Two staff personnel and four line personnel)

Superintendent

Assistant to the Superintendent - - - - - - - Legal Counsel

*Departmental Designations*

*Chain of Command*

Assistant Superintendent of Personnel

Assistant Superintendent of Instruction

Assistant Superintendent of Business

Assistant Superintendent of Research and Development

Director of Personnel

Accountants

Director of Grants and Staff Development

Director Elementary Education

Director Secondary Education

Elementary Principals

Secondary Principals

Elementary Teachers

Secondary Teachers

*Division of Labor*
(Horizontal)

**Figure 2–1**

An Organizational Structure for a Hypothetical School District

school. The "informal" team leader approach permits a principal to expand the number of teachers he can effectively supervise. At the same time, this unofficial position does not result in another cumbersome layer of administration.

Figure 2–1, highlighting each basic concept of organizational structure, illustrates how these key concepts function in a school setting and are the foundation for most structure decisions. In practice, one can observe these structural dimensions in most organizations. In

theory, most scholars recommend a flattening pyramid, but unfortunately, this is not happening in practice in most school districts.

## The Bureaucratic Model

Today the term **bureaucracy** has a negative connotation. We tend to associate bureaucracy with rigidity, meaningless rules, red tape, paperwork, and inefficiency. In fact, there is almost no evil that has not, at some point, been attributed to bureaucracy.

The pioneering work on bureaucracy is credited to the famous German sociologist Max Weber, who made a comparative study of many organizations existing at the turn of the twentieth century. From his study, Weber evolved the concept of bureaucracy as an ideal form of organizational structure.

## Bureaucratic Characteristics

According to Weber, the ideal bureaucracy possesses the following characteristics.[6]

- *Division of Labor.* Divide all tasks into highly specialized jobs. Give each jobholder the authority necessary to perform these duties.

- *Rules.* Perform each task according to a consistent system of abstract rules. This practice helps ensure that task performance is uniform.

- *Hierarchy of Authority.* Arrange all positions according to the principle of hierarchy. Each lower office is under the control of a higher one, and there is a clear chain of command from the top of the organization to the bottom.

- *Impersonality.* Maintain an impersonal attitude toward subordinates. This social distance between managers and subordinates helps ensure that rational considerations are the basis for decision making, rather than favoritism or prejudices.

- *Competence.* Base employment on qualifications and give promotions based on job-related performance. As a corollary, protect employees from arbitrary dismissal, which should result in a high level of loyalty.

Weber's characteristics of bureaucracy apply to many large-sized organizations today. General Motors, Xerox, the U.S. military system, the Vatican, most universities, and boards of education are bureaucracies. However, not all characteristics outlined by Weber appear in practice as they were originally intended.[7] Numerous misconceptions in the literature exist regarding Weber's concept of the ideal bureaucracy. Although few "pure"

bureaucracies exist today, almost all organizations have some elements of bureaucracy within their structure.

## Bureaucratic Dysfunctions

Although Weber's intention was based on rational behavior, the bureaucratic characteristics he formulated have some built-in dysfunctions. First, a high degree of division of labor may reduce the challenge and novelty of many jobs, which can eventually result in reduced performance, absenteeism, or turnover. Second, heavy reliance on bureaucratic rules can cause inefficiency or inertia. For example, rules often become ends in themselves rather than the means toward an end. Rules can also lead to excessive red tape and rigidity. Third, Weber advocated that hierarchy of authority helps coordinate activities, maintains authority, and serves a communication function. In theory, the hierarchy has a downward and an upward communication flow. In practice, however, it typically has only a downward orientation. Many subordinates withhold information from superiors and are frustrated because they do not have an opportunity to participate in decision making. Fourth, Weber proposed that employment and promotion be based on qualifications and performance. This he felt would reduce favoritism and personal prejudices. Because performance is difficult to measure in many professional jobs, the tendency is to base promotions more on seniority and loyalty than on competence and merit. Finally, the impersonal nature of bureaucracy is probably its most serious shortcoming. Recent critics of bureaucracy attack it as emphasizing rigid, control-oriented structures over people.

New viewpoints are leading to a decline in the use of bureaucratic structure in modern organizations.[8] School administrators in the twenty-first century will see a change in some of their duties. One change will be a shift away from simply supervising the work of others to that of contributing directly to the school district's objectives. Instead of shuffling papers and writing reports, the modern administrator may be practicing a craft.[9]

The renowned organization theorist Warren Bennis represents one of the extreme critics of bureaucratic

---

[6]Max Weber, *The Theory of Social and Economic Organization,* trans. T. Parsons (New York: Oxford University Press, 1947).

[7]Charles Heckscher, *Working Changes: The New Dynamics of Organizational Intervention* (New York: Oxford University Press, 2003).

[8]Camilla Stivers, *Democracy, Bureaucracy, and the Study of Administration* (Boulder, CO: Westview Press, 2001).

[9]Carl D. Glickman, *Leadership for Learning: How to Help Teachers Succeed* (Alexandria, VA: Association for Supervision and Curriculum Development, 2006).

---

### Administrative Advice 2–1

#### Restructuring Schools: Changing How the Bureaucracy Works

The wholesale change involved in restructuring the bureaucracy of a school raises a number of questions:

- Can union contracts, board policies, administrative procedures, state mandates, and federal regulations be waived if necessary to support restructuring?
- Will there still be school system goals, standards, and expectations?
- What will change mean for the least—and most—successful students?
- What is the role of the school principal, as well as the central office administrators and staff?
- Who will be held accountable for the students' learning, and how will the results be assessed?

- How will the reward and incentive system be changed?
- Will each school develop its own budget?
- Is there a danger that teachers and students in every school will be tempted to be different simply for the sake of being different?
- Are these changes really for the best, and do teachers and parents want them?

Source: Adapted from Thomas W. Payzant, "To Restructure Schools, We've Changed the Way the Bureaucracy Works," *American School Board Journal*, 176 (1989): 19–20. Copyright 1989, the National School Boards Association. Used by permission.

---

structuring in organizations. Over two decades ago, he forecasted the demise of bureaucracy.[10] In a more recent book, *Reinventing Leadership*,[11] he exposes the hidden obstacles in our organizations—and in society at large—that conspire against good leadership. According to Bennis, within any organization an entrenched bureaucracy with a commitment to the status quo undermines the unwary leader. This creates an unconscious conspiracy in contemporary society, one that prevents leaders—no matter what their original vision—from taking charge and making changes.

In recent years, popular writers have expressed increasing dissatisfaction with bureaucratic structures. This is reflected in the phenomenal appeal of numerous best-selling books such as *In Search of Excellence, The Fifth Discipline, Principle-Centered Leadership,* and *Schools That Learn*.[12] The basic theme permeating these books is that there are viable alternatives to the bureaucratic model. There is a strong implication that warm, nurturing, caring, trusting, challenging organizations produce high productivity in people.

On the surface, school restructuring appears to be worthwhile. It makes good sense to give teachers the power to make important decisions about how their school is run and how teaching occurs—and then hold them accountable for the results. But in practice, giving teachers greater authority is not a simple matter. Most educators embrace stability and accept change cautiously. When we talk about restructuring schools, we're really talking about changing the way the present bureaucracy works—the way we organize, structure, and allocate resources in the schools. (See Administrative Advice 2–1.)

## The Participatory Management Model

Participatory management represents an extension of the bureaucratic model. The excessive rigidity and inherent impersonality of the bureaucratic approach stimulated interest in participatory management. These new theories of organization place greater emphasis on employee morale and job satisfaction. Participatory management stresses the importance of motivating employees and building an organization for that purpose. The organization is structured to satisfy employees' needs, which will in turn result in high worker productivity.

---

[10]Warren G. Bennis, *Changing Organizations* (New York: McGraw-Hill, 1966).

[11]Warren G. Bennis, *Reinventing Leadership: Strategies to Empower the Organization* (New York: HarperCollins, 2006).

[12]Thomas J. Peters and Robert H. Waterman, *In Search of Excellence,* rev. ed. (New York: Warner Books, 2006). Peter M. Senge, *The Fifth Discipline,* rev. ed. (New York: Doubleday, 2006); Stephen R. Covey, *Principle-Centered Leadership* (New York: Simon & Schuster, 1992); Peter M. Senge, *Schools That Learn* (New York: Doubleday, 2001).

## Theory X and Theory Y

In 1960 Douglas McGregor presented a convincing argument that most managerial actions flow directly from the assumptions managers hold about their subordinates.[13] The idea is that management's views of people control operating practices as well as organizational structure. McGregor referred to these contrasting sets of assumptions as **Theory X** and **Theory Y**.

Managers with Theory X assumptions have the following views of people:

- The average person dislikes work and will avoid it if possible.
- Because people dislike work, they must be coerced, controlled, directed, and threatened.
- The average person prefers to be directed and controlled by someone in authority.

The opposite assumptions characterize the Theory Y manager.

- Work is as natural as play or rest.
- Commitment to objectives is a function of rewards for achievement.
- Under proper conditions, people accept and seek responsibility.

McGregor considers Theory X to be incompatible with democratic or participatory organizations because it conflicts with individual need fulfillment on the job. Therefore, McGregor espouses Theory Y because people's behavior in modern organizations more nearly matches its set of assumptions.

Theory Y does not concentrate on organizational structure as much as it argues for a general management philosophy that would force reconsideration of structural dimensions. For example, job enrichment would replace highly specialized jobs and departments. Span of control would be wide, not narrow, in order to provide greater freedom and opportunities for growth and fulfillment of employees' needs. Emphasis on hierarchy would be replaced by emphasis on decentralization and delegation of decisions. Formal, rational authority would give way to "empowerment" of subordinates.

## Individual versus Organization

The school administrator's job is to contribute to the achievement of organizational effectiveness. An important part of this effort is to enlist the support of sub-

### Table 2–1  The Immaturity–Maturity Continuum

| Immaturity Characteristics | Maturity Characteristics |
| --- | --- |
| Passivity | Activity |
| Dependence | Independence |
| Few ways of behaving | Many ways of behaving |
| Shallow interests | Deeper interests |
| Short time perspective | Long time perspective |
| Subordinate position | Superordinate position |
| Lack of self-awareness | Self-awareness and control |

Source: Adapted from Chris Argyris, *The Individual and the Organization: Some Problems of Mutual Adjustment* (New York: Irvington, 1993).

ordinates to this same end. In a school setting, this includes teachers and all other professionals who work with students. Chris Argyris suggests that rigid, impersonal organizations such as those prescribed by the bureaucratic perspective hinder employees from using their full potential. He describes the growth or development of human personality and advocates the premise that organizational structure is often incongruent with the fulfillment of human needs. Argyris asserts that an analysis of the basic properties of relatively mature human beings and the formal organization results in the conclusion that there is an inherent incongruency between the self-actualization of each one.[14] This basic incongruency creates conflict and frustration for the participants.

Argyris proposes that the human personality progresses along an **immaturity–maturity continuum**—from immaturity as an infant to maturity as an adult. He views this progression in psychological rather than in purely physiological terms. That is, at any age, people can have their degree of growth or development plotted according to seven dimensions (see Table 2–1).

According to Argyris's continuum, as individuals mature, they have increasing needs for more activity, a state of relative independence, behaving in many different ways, deeper interests, a long time perspective, occupying a superordinate position in reference to their peers, and more awareness of and control over themselves.

Argyris believes that teachers and other professionals want to be treated as mature people, but modern

---

[13] Douglas McGregor, *The Human Side of Enterprise* (New York: McGraw-Hill, 1960).

[14] Chris Argyris, *The Individual and the Organization: Some Problems of Mutual Adjustment* (New York: Irvington, 1993).

bureaucratic organizations often treat people as if they fit the immature personality type. Teachers and other professionals react to this treatment by becoming either aggressive or apathetic, which starts a chain reaction. School administrators then impose further restrictions, which turn out to be counterproductive. This hinders optimum organizational effectiveness.

The restraining effects of bureaucratic organizational structure can be alleviated by less rigid rules and operating procedures, a decrease in the division of labor, greater delegation of authority, more participation in decision making, and a more fluid structure throughout the organization. Argyris believes that a more participatory management structure can result in the growth and development of human personality and hence eliminate the incongruency between the individual and the organization.[15]

## System 4 Organization

Like McGregor and Argyris, Rensis Likert opposes the kinds of organizations that hew to the bureaucratic model. Likert's theory treats the structural prescriptions for organizational effectiveness more explicitly and completely. He builds his structural recommendations around three key elements that undergird four systems of organization.

Based on many years of research conducted in various organizational settings—industrial, government, health care, and educational—Likert proposed four basic systems of organization.[16] System 1, which Likert originally labeled exploitive authoritative, follows the bureaucratic or classical structure of organization. Characteristics of the classical structure include limited supportive leadership, motivation based on fear and superordinate status, one-way downward communication, centralized decision making, close over-the-shoulder supervision, no cooperative teamwork, and low performance goals of managers.

The **System 4 organization,** which Likert calls participative group, is more team oriented. There is a high level of trust and confidence in the superior; communication flows freely in all directions; decision making occurs throughout the organization; cooperative teamwork is encouraged; and managers actively seek high

performance goals. System 2 is less classical than System 1, and System 3 is less supportive than System 4 while coming closer to Likert's ideal model of organization. Table 2–2 shows the characteristics of System 1 and System 4, the extreme ends of Likert's systems continuum.

**Key Elements of System 4**   According to Likert, System 4 has three key elements: the manager's use of the principle of supportive relationships, the use of group decision making in an overlapping group structure, and the manager's high performance goals for the organization.[17] The underlying theory is that if an organization is to be effective, the leadership and other processes of the organization must ensure that in all interactions between superordinates and subordinates, subordinates will perceive the relationship as enhancing their own sense of personal worth and importance in the organization. Furthermore, Likert argues that "an organization will function best when its personnel function not as individuals but as members of highly effective work groups with high performance goals."[18] In this way, decisions are group decisions, not simply orders from above. And the leader is seen as a "linking-pin"; that is, the leader is the head of one group but a member of another group at the next higher level. For example, the high school principal is the leader of school staff but also a subordinate to an administrator at the central office in another group at the next level in the organization. Thus, the principal serves as an important communication link between two levels of organization—school and school district.

**System 4 Variables**   Likert identifies System 4 as the ideal model of organization. The object of this approach is to move an organization as far as possible toward System 4. To analyze an organization's present system and move it toward System 4, Likert uses an organizational paradigm consisting of three broad classes of variables.

*Causal variables* are independent variables that affect both the intervening and end-result variables. They include the administrator's assumptions about subordinates, the organization's objectives and how they emerge, administrative behavior and practices, the nature of the authority system that prevails, the union contract, the administrator's view of change, and the needs and desires of members of the organization. Causal variables are within the control of administration, and

[15] Chris Argyris, *Integrating the Individual and the Organization* (New Brunswick, NJ: Transaction Publications, 1990).

[16] Rensis Likert, "From Production and Employee-Centeredness to Systems 1–4," *Journal of Management,* 5 (1979): 147–156.

[17] Rensis Likert, *New Patterns of Management* (New York: Garland, 1987).

[18] Likert, *New Patterns of Management.*

**Table 2–2   Characteristics of System 1 and System 4**

| Organizational Characteristics | System 1 Organization | System 4 Organization |
| --- | --- | --- |
| Leadership | Little confidence and trust between administrators and subordinates | Subordinate ideas are solicited and used by administrators |
| Motivation | Taps fear, status, and economic motives exclusively | Taps all major motives except fear |
| Communication | One-way, downward communication | Communication flows freely in all directions |
| Interaction–influence | Little upward influence; downward influence overestimated | Substantial influence upward, downward, and horizontally |
| Decision making | Centralized; decisions made at the top | Decentralized; decisions made throughout the organization |
| Goal setting | Established by top-level administrators and communicated downward | Established by group participation |
| Control | Close over-the-shoulder supervision | Emphasis on self-control |
| Performance goals | Low and passively sought by administrators; little commitment to developing human resources | High and actively sought by administrators; full commitment to developing human resources |

Source: Adapted from Rensis Likert, *The Human Organization* (New York: McGraw-Hill, 1967), pp. 197–211.

the value that administration places on these variables will determine the organization's management system. Causal variables, then, are the ones administrators should attempt to change in order to move the organization to System 4.

*Intervening variables*, representing the internal state and health of the organization, are those variables that are subsequently affected by causal variables. They include the attitudes that subordinates have toward their jobs, their superiors, peers, and subordinates; their commitment to organizational goals; their levels of performance goals; their levels of group loyalty and group commitment to the organization; their confidence and trust in themselves and their superiors; their feeling of upward influence in the organization; their motivational forces; and the extent to which communications flow freely and in all directions within the organization.

*End-result variables* are dependent variables that represent the achievements of the organization. In schools they include performance and growth levels of teachers and students, absence and turnover or dropout rates of employees and students, union-management relations, school-community relations, students' attitudes

toward school, and levels of intrinsic job satisfaction of school employees. Figure 2–2 shows the relationship among the variables.

To move an organization to System 4, Likert recommends using the survey-feedback method and leadership training. Using his Profile of Organizational Characteristics instrument, the organization can determine the management system that is currently in place.[19] The survey instrument measures the eight characteristics of organizational systems (see Table 2–2). Respondents are given a range of choices for each item on the questionnaire through which they indicate whether the organization tends to be exploitive authoritative (System 1), benevolent authoritative (System 2), consultative (System 3), or participative group (System 4). Respondents are also asked where they would like the organization to be on the continuum. Then an organization–systems profile chart is plotted, which visually conveys the organization's present management system and the desired system. Another instrument, the Profile of a School,

---

[19]Likert, *New Patterns of Management.*

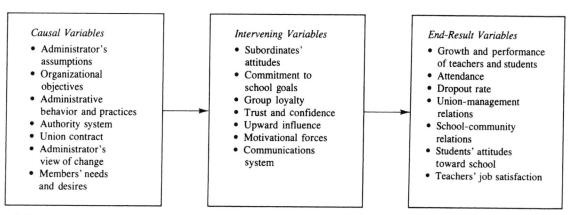

**Figure 2–2**

Relationships Among Causal, Intervening, and
End-Result Variables in a System 4 Organization

also measures the organizational systems of schools.[20] It has several versions that can be used with students, teachers, counselors, principals, superintendents, central office administrators, school board members, and parents. By comparing the perceptions of several subgroups within the organization, it is possible to measure the management system of a school or an entire school district.

The profile charts become a basis for discussing and analyzing an organization's management system so that plans for improving it can be made. Because effectiveness and System 4 go together in Likert's theory, the implications for organizational improvement are straightforward: Move the present management style of the organization to System 4 and keep it there. This is accomplished by training all administrators throughout the organization to acquire the skills needed for achieving a System 4 structure: manifesting supportive leadership, focusing on high performance goals, and building intact work groups into more effective teams.

### Shaping School Culture

Terrence Deal and Kent Peterson contend that the movement toward participatory management involves transforming the basic character, or **culture,** of schools.[21]

They contend that culture is concerned with shared values, rituals, and symbols and suggest that the core problems of schools, for the most part, are not technical but social.

Previous efforts to improve schools have concentrated on correcting visible structural flaws such as the organizational hierarchy, centralization/decentralization, or decision-making authority. Such changes overlook more durable cultural values and mindscapes that underlie everyday behavior. These deeper patterns provide meaning and continuity. Modifying them involves another level of changes that most reform efforts have ignored.

Deal and Peterson contend that symbolic structures and patterns cannot be reformed; they must be transformed. To transform an organization is to change its basic character. Examples are Lee Iaccoca's transformation of Chrysler or AT&T's struggle to compete in a deregulated communications industry. Such basic structural changes, however, are the exception rather than the rule.

### Moral Leadership

In a groundbreaking examination of **moral leadership,** Amitai Etzioni provides a case for moral authority as a basis for management.[22] Etzioni acknowledges the importance of basic, extrinsic motivation and higher-order, intrinsic motivation (see Maslow and Herzberg,

---

[20]Additional information on the Profile of a School instrument can be obtained from Rensis Likert Associates, 630 City Center Building, Ann Arbor, Michigan 48104.

[21]Terrence E. Deal and Kent D. Peterson, *Shaping School Culture: The Heart of Leadership* (New York: Wiley, 2003).

[22]Amitai Etzioni, *The Moral Dimension* (New York: Macmillan, 1990).

Chapter 4). But Etzioni goes further. He contends that what means most to people is what they believe, how they feel, and the shared norms, values, and cultural symbols that emerge from the groups with which they identify. He maintains that morality and shared values and commitments are far more important motivators than the basic, extrinsic needs and motives and even some intrinsic concerns. (Note the similarity between Etzioni and Deal's concept of culture.)

Thomas Sergiovanni further specifies the concept of moral leadership.[23] He contends that when moral authority transcends bureaucratic leadership in a school, the outcomes in terms of commitment and performance far exceed expectations. His four stages of value-added leadership are the following:

1. *Leadership by Bartering.* The leader and led strike a bargain within which the leader gives to the led something they want in exchange for something the leader wants.

2. *Leadership by Building.* The leader provides the climate and the interpersonal support that enhances the led's opportunities for fulfillment of needs for achievement, responsibility, competence, and esteem.

3. *Leadership by Bonding.* The leader and led develop a set of shared values and commitments that bond them together in a common cause.

4. *Leadership by Banking.* The leader institutionalizes the improvement initiatives as part of the everyday life of the school. This conserves human energy and effort for new projects and initiatives.[24]

A new kind of hierarchy then emerges in the school—one that places purposes, values, and commitments at the apex and teachers, principals, parents, and students below, in service to these purposes. According to Sergiovanni, moral authority is a means to add value to an administrator's leadership practice, and this added value results in extraordinary commitment and performance in schools.

To implement this new kind of hierarchy, Roland Barth views restructuring as learning by heart.[25] In his best-selling book, he examines the adults—parents, teachers, principals, and central office administrators—who help children learn. He describes how these stakeholders can assume responsibility for shaping their own school system. He stresses the importance of collaboration among these stakeholders in promoting learning and promoting schools. He sees transformation as focusing on the fact that the different roles of the major stakeholders serve a common purpose—to improve the education of all children in the school system. According to Barth, change in the classroom is the only change that really matters.

Participatory management proponents have high concern for people in structuring organizations. They view people as the most important resource of the organization. Supportiveness, participation, shared decision making, empowerment, flexibility, and employee growth and development are the keys to participatory management.

### School-Based Management

**School-based management** (SBM) represents a change in how a school district is structured, that is, how authority and responsibility are shared between the district and its schools. It changes roles and responsibilities of staff within schools and how the school district's central office staff is organized with respect to its size, roles, and responsibilities.[26] Professional responsibility replaces bureaucratic regulation. School districts accomplish this new structure in two ways: (1) increasing autonomy through some type of relief from constraining rules and regulations and (2) sharing the authority to make decisions with the school's major stakeholder groups, including teachers, parents, students, and other community members.[27]

In practice, authority to make changes at the building level is typically granted by some type of waiver

---

[23]Thomas J. Sergiovanni, *Strengthening the Heartbeat: Leading and Learning Together in Schools* (New York: John Wiley, 2005).

[24]Thomas J. Sergiovanni, *Value-Added Leadership: How to Get Extraordinary Leadership in Schools,* 2nd ed. (New York: Harcourt Brace, 1997).

[25]Roland Barth, *Learning by Heart* (New York: John Wiley, 2005).

[26]Richard F. Elmore, *School Reform from the Inside Out: Policy, Practice, and Performance* (Cambridge, MA: Harvard Education Publishing Group, 2004).

[27]Joseph Murphy and Amanda Datnow, *Leadership Lessons from Comprehensive School Reforms* (Thousand Oaks, CA: Corwin Press, 2002).

process. Usually, a waiver process is the result of agreements between the school district and teachers' union that expand the scope of authority granted individual school sites. In a few cases, districts may also have agreements with their states that permit waivers from state regulations or laws that mandate school-based decision making.[28]

To increase shared decision making, a school typically forms a school-site council with representatives from the school's major stakeholder groups. The composition of this council, how members are selected, and what their responsibilities are vary considerably between and within school districts. Some councils are composed of teachers elected from the entire faculty or by grade level or department. Others are composed of members from preexisting committees such as the curriculum, staffing, or budget committees. In some schools, the entire faculty constitutes the council.[29]

Numerous states and districts have instituted a variety of school-based management provisions.[30] In Texas, Senate Bill 1 of 1990 and House Bill 2885 of 1991 introduced the term *school-based management* to schools throughout the state of Texas by establishing a legislative decree for school-based management. In the Kentucky Education Reform Act of 1990, House Bill 940 mandated, with few minor exceptions, that all schools in the state employ an SBM model of governance by July 1, 1996. Signed into law in 1989, Act 266 of the Hawaii State Legislature was a major initiative designed to facilitate improved student performance in the public school system through School/Community-Based Management. In Oregon, legislation was passed in 1991 to establish school-based decision-making committees in all public schools in the state by 1995. Related events have unfolded in New York, South Carolina, Tennessee, Washington, and other states.

At the district level, especially in urban areas such as Dade County (FL), Chicago, Los Angeles, and Rochester (NY), similar efforts to move decision-making authority to the school level have been initiated. For example, a provision for the establishment of SBM councils, composed of parents, teachers, citizens, and principals

at each school site, was at the heart of legislation passed by the Illinois General Assembly to improve schooling in Chicago.[31] Power was to shift from a large central office to each school site, and a bureaucratic, command-oriented system was to yield to a decentralized and democratic model. The traditional pyramid-shaped organizational structure was to be inverted. The existing insiders, particularly the central administration and the Chicago Teachers Union, found their traditional sources of influence circumscribed.[32] Similar reforms have occurred in Memphis, Detroit, Dallas, Cincinnati, Los Angeles, White Plains (NY), and other school districts.

## Total Quality Management

**Total Quality Management (TQM)** is based on the assumption that people want to do their best and that it is management's job to enable them to do so by constantly improving the *system* in which they work.[33] TQM is not new. It resembles Douglas McGregor's Theory Y[34] and William Ouchi's Theory Z.[35] What is new is that large corporations are taking Theory Y and Theory Z seriously by assigning more authority and responsibility to frontline workers. However, like Theory Y and Theory Z, TQM is more than delegation. It requires teamwork, training, and extensive collection and analysis of data.

When educators look at TQM principles they assume that the model applies only to profit-making organizations. Actually, Total Quality Management applies as well to corporations, service organizations, universities, and elementary and secondary schools.

Indeed, the concepts formulated by TQM founder, W. Edwards Deming, have proved so powerful that educators want to apply TQM to schools. Deming's philosophy provides a framework that can integrate many positive developments in education, such as team teaching, site-based management, cooperative learning, and outcomes-based education.

---

[28] Ibid.

[29] Murphy and Datnow, *Leadership Lessons from Comprehensive School Reforms.*

[30] Joseph Murphy and Lynn G. Beck, *School-Based Management as School Reform* (Thousand Oaks, CA: Corwin Press, 1995).

[31] Chicago School Reform Act of 1988; reenacted in 1991.

[32] G. Alfred Hess, *Restructuring Urban Schools: A Chicago Perspective* (Newbury Park, CA: Corwin Press, 1995).

[33] W. Edwards Deming, *Out of the Crisis* (Cambridge, MA: MIT Press, 1988).

[34] Douglas McGregor, *The Human Side of Enterprise* (New York: McGraw-Hill, 1960).

[35] William G. Ouchi, *Theory Z: How American Business Can Meet the Japanese Challenge* (New York: Avon Books, 1993).

## ■ Exemplary Educational Administrators in Action

**MIRABELLE BAPTISTE** Principal, Clifton Middle School, Houston Independent School District, Texas.

**Previous Positions:** Executive Director Staff Development, Houston Independent School District; Principal, Janowski Elementary School, Houston Independent School District; University of Houston, Curriculum and Instruction, College of Education, Instructor for Math Methods; Assistant Director of the Displaced Teacher Program; Assistant Director of the Teachers Institute Program; Instructional Coordinator, Doctoral Program for Developing Competencies in Multicultural Education; Supervisor, Reading Program, Title I, Houston Independent School District; Curriculum Coordinator, Houston Independent School District; Fifth-Grade Teacher, High School History Teacher, South San Antonio Independent School District, Texas.

**Latest Degree and Affiliation:** M.Ed., University of Houston.

**Number One Influence on Career:** Exceptional work experiences in the Houston Independent School District with fellow administrators and teachers who live their belief in the public schools for our nation.

**Number One Achievement:** Having led a middle school to the highest academic rating within an urban school system has been the ultimate reward. Knowing that students can and do learn every day has been my guiding light.

**Number One Regret:** I did not leave central office administration sooner to return to the campus as a middle school administrator.

**Favorite Education-Related Book or Text:** *Alice in Wonderland* by Lewis Carroll.

**Additional Interests:** My love for frogs has served me well with the middle school students. They are all princes.

**Leadership Style:** A clear direction toward excellence provides the pathway that is active and engaging. I believe my job is to offer support for all the members of my community.

**Professional Vision:** I believe the public school is the hope for our nation to succeed. Educated citizens will lead us forward. The public school's leaders must establish the standards, expectations, and accountability to erase the achievement gap for students.

**Words of Advice:** To the entering student in educational administration, my wisdom word is *believe*. Say it often. The next word is *trust*. The drama of your life each day is greatly enhanced when you believe in the people of your school community and when the sense of trust is present. Your commitment to public education will serve as your guiding beacon. The students believe you can move mountains, and there will be days when you will. Knowing that your school community believes in you and trusts you is the most wonderful feeling you will enjoy each day.

---

The problem is that words like *learning* and *curriculum* are not found in Deming's fourteen points. Some of Deming's terminology needs to be translated to schools as well. For example, superintendents and principals can be considered *management*. Teachers are *employers* or *managers* of students. Students are *employees*, and the knowledge they acquire is the *product*. Parents and society are the *customers*. With these translations made, we can see many applications to schools.

The framework for transforming schools using Deming's fourteen principles follows.

1. *Create Constancy of Purpose for Improvement of Product and Service.* For schools, the purpose of the system must be clear and shared by all stakeholder groups. Customer needs must be the focus in establishing educational aims. The aims of the system must be to improve the quality of education for all students.

2. *Adopt the New Philosophy.* Implementation of Deming's second principle requires a rethinking of the school's mission and priorities, with everyone in agreement on them. Existing methods, materials, and environments may be replaced by new teaching and learning strategies where success for every student is the goal. Individual differences among students are addressed. Ultimately, what may be required is a total transformation of the American system of education as we know it.

3. *Cease Dependence on Inspection to Achieve Quality.* The field of education has recently entered an era that many American corporations have abandoned: inspection at the end of the

line.[36] In industry this was called "product inspection." According to Deming, it always costs more to fix a problem than to prevent one. Reliance on remediation can be avoided if proper intervention occurs during initial instruction. Furthermore, preventive approaches such as Head Start, Follow Through, and preschool programs can help students to avoid learning problems later.

4. *End the Practice of Awarding Business on the Basis of Price Alone.* The lowest bid is rarely the most cost efficient. Schools need to move toward a single supplier for any one time and develop long-term relationships of loyalty and trust with that supplier.

5. *Improve Constantly and Forever Every Activity in the Company, to Improve Quality and Productivity.* The focus of improvement efforts in education, under Deming's approach, are on teaching and learning processes. Based on the latest research findings, the best strategies must be attempted, evaluated, and refined as needed. And, consistent with learning style theories[37] and Howard Gardner's multiple intelligences,[38] educators must redesign the system to provide for a broad range of people— handicapped, learning-disabled, at-risk, special needs students—and find ways to make them all successful in school.

6. *Institute Training on the Job.* Training of educators is needed in three areas. First, there must be training in the new teaching and learning processes that are developed. Second, training must be provided in the use of new assessment strategies. Third, there must be training in the principles of the new management system.

7. *Institute Leadership.* Deming's seventh principle resembles Peter Senge's systems thinking.[39] According to both Senge and Deming, improve-

ment of a stable system comes from altering the system itself, and this is primarily the job of management and not those who work within the system. Deming asserts that the primary task of leadership is to narrow the amount of variation within the system, bringing everyone toward the goal of perfection. In manufacturing processes that makes sense, but in educational processes it may not.

8. *Drive Out Fear.* A basic assumption of TQM is that people want to do their best. The focus of improvement efforts then must be on the processes and on the outcomes, not on trying to blame individuals for failures. If quality is absent, the fault is in the system, says Deming. It is management's job to enable people to do their best by constantly improving the system in which they work.

9. *Break Down Barriers Among Staff Areas.* Deming's ninth principle is somewhat related to the first principle: Create constancy of purpose for improvement of product and service. In the classroom this principle applies to interdisciplinary instruction, team teaching, writing across the curriculum, and transfer of learning. Collaboration needs to exist among members of the learning organization so that total quality can be maximized.

10. *Eliminate Slogans, Exhortations, and Targets That Demand Zero Defects and New Levels of Productivity.* Implicit in most slogans, exhortations, and targets is the supposition that staff could do better if they tried harder. This offends rather than inspires the team. It creates adversarial relationships because the many causes of low quality and low productivity in schools are due to the system and not the staff. The system itself may need to be changed.

11. *Eliminate Numerical Quotas for the Staff and Goals for Management.* There are many practices in education that constrain our ability to tap intrinsic motivation and falsely assume the benefits of extrinsic rewards. They include rigorous and systematic teacher evaluation systems, merit pay, management by objectives, grades, and quantitative goals and quotas. These Deming refers to as forces of destruction. Such approaches are counterproductive for several reasons: setting goals leads to marginal performance; merit pay destroys teamwork; and appraisal of individual performance nourishes fear and increases variability in desired performance.

---

[36]John J. Bonstingl, *Schools of Quality,* 3rd ed. (Thousand Oaks, CA: Corwin Press, 2001).

[37]Rita Dunn, Kenneth Dunn, and Janet Perrin, *Teaching Young Children Through Their Individual Learning Styles: Practical Approaches for Grades K–2* (Needham Heights, MA: Allyn and Bacon, 1994); Rita Dunn and Kenneth Dunn, *Teaching Students Through Their Individual Learning Styles,* 2 vols.: *Practical Approaches for Grades 3–12* (Needham Heights, MA: Allyn and Bacon, 1992).

[38]Howard Gardner, *Frames of Mind,* rev. ed. (New York: Basic Books, 1994).

[39]Peter M. Senge, *The Fifth Discipline,* rev. ed. (New York: Doubleday, 2006).

## Administrative Advice 2–2

### The Four Pillars of Total Quality

Total Quality Management, viewed through Deming's fourteen points, can best be understood as an integral set of fundamental tenets.

▪ *The organization must focus, first and foremost, on its suppliers and customers.* In schools, the student is the teacher's customer, the recipient of educational services. The teacher and the school are suppliers of effective learning to the student, who is the school's *primary customer.* The school's stakeholders and *secondary customers*—including parents, businesses, community, taxpayers—have a legitimate right to expect progress in students' competencies. Administrators work collaboratively with *their* customers: teachers.

▪ *Everyone in the organization must be dedicated to continual improvement, personally and collectively.* The Japanese call this ethos *kaizen,* a societywide covenant of mutual help in the process of continual improvement. If schools are to be true learning organizations, they must be afforded the resources, especially time and money, needed for training, quality circles, research, and communication with the school's stakeholders.

▪ *The organization must be viewed as a system, and the work people do within the system must be seen as ongoing processes.* A system consists of the seemingly immu-

table patterns of expectations, activities, perceptions, resource allocations, power structures, values, and the traditional school culture in general. Every system is made up of processes, and improvements made in the quality of those processes in large part determine the quality of the resulting products. In the new paradigm of education, continual improvement of learning processes will replace the outdated "teach and test" mode of instruction.

▪ *The success of Total Quality Management is the responsibility of top management.* Educational leaders must provide concerted, visible, and constant dedication to making TQM principles and practices part of the culture of the organization. School leaders must focus on establishing the context in which students can best achieve their potential through the continual improvement of teachers' and students' work together.

Source: Adapted from John J. Bonstingl, "The Quality Revolution in Education," *Educational Leadership,* 50 (1992): 5–7.

12. *Remove Barriers That Rob People of Pride of Workmanship.* Most people want to do a good job. Effective communication and the elimination of "demotivators"—such as lack of involvement, poor information, the annual or merit rating, and supervisors who don't care—are critical.

13. *Institute a Vigorous Program of Education and Retraining for Everyone.* The principal and staff must be retrained in new methods of school management, including group dynamics, consensus building, and collaborative styles of decision making. All stakeholders on the school's team must realize that improvements in student productivity will create higher levels of responsibility, not less responsibility.

14. *Put Everyone in the Organization to Work to Accomplish the Transformation.* The school board and superintendent must have a clear plan of action to carry out the quality mission. The quality mission must be internalized by all mem-

bers of the school organization. The transformation is everybody's job.[40]

As educational leaders begin to adopt TQM as their operational philosophy, they are discovering that Total Quality Management cannot be successful if it is viewed as a school district's project for *this* school year. The real rewards begin to emerge when TQM ideas and practices become embedded in the culture of the organization. Its greatest benefits come about as a natural part of the evolutionary process of implementing a program of continuous improvement in a consistent manner. (See Administrative Advice 2–2.)

### Frames of Organization

Lee Bolman and Terrence Deal provide a four-frame model (see Table 2–3) with its view of organizations as factories (*structural frame*), families (*human resource*

[40]Deming, *Out of the Crisis,* pp. 23–24.

### Table 2–3  Overview of the Four-Frame Model

|  | Frame | | | |
|---|---|---|---|---|
|  | **Structural** | **Human Resource** | **Political** | **Symbolic** |
| Metaphor for organization | Factory or machine | Family | Jungle | Carnival, temple, theater |
| Central concepts | Rules, roles, goals, policies, technology, environment | Needs, skills, relationships | Power, conflict, competition, organizational politics | Culture, meaning, metaphor, ritual, ceremony, stories, heroes |
| Image of leadership | Social architecture | Empowerment | Advocacy | Inspiration |
| Basic leadership challenge | Attune structure to task, technology, environment | Align organizational and human needs | Develop agenda and power base | Create faith, beauty, meaning |

Source: Adapted from Lee G. Bolman and Terrence E. Deal, *Reframing Organizations,* 2nd ed. (San Francisco: Jossey-Bass, 1997), p. 15.

frame), jungles (*political frame*), and temples (*symbolic frame*).[41] Their distillation of ideas about how organizations work has drawn much from the social sciences—particularly from sociology, psychology, political science, and anthropology. They argue that their **four frames** or major perspectives can help leaders make sense of organizations. Bolman and Deal further assert that the ability to *reframe*—to reconceptualize the same situation using multiple perspectives—is a central capacity for leaders of the twenty-first century.[42]

■ *Structural Frame.* Drawing from sociology and management science, the structural frame emphasizes goals, specialized roles, and formal relationships. Structures—commonly depicted by organization charts—are designed to fit an organization's environment and technology. Organizations allocate responsibilities to participants ("division of labor") and create rules, policies, procedures, and hierarchies to coordinate diverse activities. Problems arise when the structure does not fit the situation. At that point,

[41]Lee G. Bolman and Terrence E. Deal, *Reframing Organizations: Artistry, Choice, and Leadership,* 3rd ed. (San Francisco: Jossey-Bass, 2003).

[42]To preserve the metaphorical content, we have quoted liberally from Bolman and Deal, *Reframing Organizations.*

some form of reframing is needed to remedy the mismatch.

■ *Human Resource Frame.* The human resource frame, based particularly on ideas from psychology, sees an organization as much like an extended family, inhabited by individuals who have needs, feelings, prejudices, skills, and limitations. They have a great capacity to learn and sometimes an even greater capacity to defend old attitudes and beliefs. From a human resource perspective, the key challenge is to tailor organizations to people—to find a way for individuals to get the job done while feeling good about what they are doing.

■ *Political Frame.* The political frame is rooted particularly in the work of political scientists. It sees organizations as arenas, contests, or jungles. Different interests compete for power and scarce resources. Conflict is rampant because of enduring differences in needs, perspectives, and lifestyles among individuals and groups. Bargaining, negotiation, coercion, and compromise are part of everyday life. Coalitions form around specific interests and change as issues come and go. Problems arise when power is concentrated in the wrong places or is so broadly dispersed that nothing gets done. Solutions arise from political skill and acumen in reframing the organization.

_Types of Power_

| | Coercive | Utilitarian | Normative |
|---|---|---|---|
| Alienative | X | | |
| Calculative | | X | |
| Moral | | | X |

_Types of Involvement_ (vertical label on left side)

**Figure 2–3**

Etzioni's Compliance Types

■ *Symbolic Frame.* The symbolic frame, drawing on social and cultural anthropology, treats organizations as tribes, theaters, or carnivals. It abandons the assumptions of rationality more prominent in the other frames. It sees organizations as cultures, propelled more by rituals, ceremonies, stories, heroes, and myths than by rules, policies, and managerial authority. Organization is also theater: Actors play their roles in the organizational drama while audiences form impressions from what they see onstage. Problems arise when actors play their parts badly, when symbols lose their meaning, when ceremonies and rituals lose their potency. Leaders reframe the expressive or spiritual side of organizations through the use of symbol, myth, and magic.

## Alternative Models of Organizational Structure

The bureaucratic and participatory management models laid the groundwork for more complex approaches to organizational structure. Top-level school administrators must consider the relative suitability of alternative approaches to organizational structure, based on the problems they face and the environment in which they work. We describe some alternative approaches to organizational structure, including Etzioni's compliance theory, Hage's mechanistic-organic organizations, and Mintzberg's strategy-structure typology.

### Compliance Theory

Etzioni developed an innovative approach to the structure of organizations that he calls **compliance theory**.[43] He classifies organizations by the type of power they use to direct the behavior of their members and the type of involvement of the participants. Etzioni identifies three

[43]Amitai Etzioni, *A Comparative Analysis of Complex Organizations,* rev. ed. (New York: Free Press, 1975).

types of organizational power: coercive, utilitarian, and normative, and relates these to three types of involvement: alienative, calculative, and moral (Figure 2–3). This figure, while grossly oversimplifying the relationships, helps to make clear the pattern among the components. It should be noted that life in organizations is much more complicated.

*Coercive power* uses force and fear to control lower-level participants. Examples of organizations that rely on coercive power include prisons, custodial mental hospitals, and basic training in the military.

*Utilitarian power* uses remuneration or extrinsic rewards to control lower-level participants. Most business firms emphasize such extrinsic rewards. These rewards include salary, merit pay, fringe benefits, working conditions, and job security. Besides many business firms, utilitarian organizations include unions, farmers' co-ops, and various government agencies.

*Normative power* controls through allocation of intrinsic rewards, for example, interesting work, identification with goals, and making a contribution to society. Management's power in this case rests on its ability to manipulate symbolic rewards, allocate esteem and prestige symbols, administer ritual, and influence the distribution of acceptance and positive response in the organization.

Many professional people work in normative organizations. Examples of such organizations are churches, political organizations, hospitals, universities, and professional associations (such as the American Association of School Administrators, National Association of Secondary School Principals, and National Education Association). Public schools probably fit this category for the most part, although there are vast differences in their use of power to gain member compliance, particularly the control of pupils.

**Types of Involvement** All three types of power can be useful in obtaining subordinates' cooperation in organizations. However, the relative effectiveness of each approach depends on the organizational participant's involvement. Involvement refers to the orientation of a person to an object, characterized in terms of intensity and direction. Accordingly, people can be placed on an involvement continuum that ranges from highly negative to highly positive. Etzioni suggests that participants' involvement can be broadly categorized as alienative, calculative, or moral.

*Alienative involvement* designates an intense, negative orientation. Inmates in prisons, patients in custodial mental hospitals, and enlisted personnel in basic training all tend to be alienated from their respective organizations.

*Calculative involvement* designates either a negative or a positive orientation of low intensity. Calculative orientations are predominant in relationships of merchants who have permanent customers in various types of business associations. Similarly, inmates in prisons ("rats") who have established contact with prison authorities often have predominantly calculative attitudes toward those in power.

*Moral involvement* designates a positive orientation of high intensity. The involvement of the parishioner in her church or synagogue, the devoted member of his political party, and the loyal follower of her leader are all moral.

**Relationship of Power to Involvement**   According to Etzioni, when an organization employs coercive power, participants usually react to the organization with hostility, which is alienative involvement. Utilitarian power usually results in calculative involvement; that is, participants desire to maximize personal gain. Finally, normative power frequently creates moral involvement; for instance, participants are committed to the socially beneficial features of their organizations.

Some organizations employ all three powers, but most tend to emphasize only one, relying less on the other two. Power specialization occurs because when two types of power are emphasized simultaneously with the same participant group, they tend to neutralize each other.

Applying force, fear, or other coercive measures, for example, usually creates such high-degree alienation that it becomes impossible to apply normative power successfully. This may be one reason why using coercive control in gaining student compliance in schools often leads to a displacement of educational goals.[44] Simi-

larly, it may be why teachers in progressive schools tend to oppose corporal punishment.

In most organizations, types of power and involvement are related in the three combinations depicted in Figure 2–3. Of course, a few organizations combine two or even all three types. For instance, some teachers' unions use both utilitarian and normative power to gain compliance from their members. Nevertheless, school officials who attempt to use types of power that are not appropriate for the environment can reduce organizational effectiveness. Schools tend to be normative organizations. According to this logic, oppressive use of coercive and utilitarian power with teachers and students can be dysfunctional.

## Mechanistic-Organic Organizations

Some writers have called attention to the incongruency between bureaucratic and professional norms. Specifically, they argue that occupants of hierarchical positions frequently do not have the technical competence to make decisions about issues that involve professional knowledge. That is, there is a basic conflict in educational organizations between authority based on bureaucracy and authority based on professional norms.[45] Others support the notion that bureaucratic orientations and professional attitudes need not conflict if teachers are provided with sufficient autonomy to carry out their jobs.[46]

We can conclude from this research that most schools have both bureaucratic and professional characteristics that are often incompatible but need not be. Jerald Hage suggests an axiomatic theory of organizations that provides a framework for defining two ideal types of organizations: **mechanistic** (bureaucratic) and **organic** (professional).[47] His theory identifies eight key variables found in schools and other organizations. These key variables are arranged in a means-ends relationship and are interrelated in seven basic propositions.

---

[44]William Glasser, *The Quality School: Managing Students Without Coercion*, 2nd ed. (New York: HarperCollins, 1992).

[45]Max G. Abbott and Francisco Caracheo, "Power, Authority, and Bureaucracy," in N. J. Boyan (ed.), *Handbook of Research on Educational Administration* (New York: Longman, 1988), pp. 239–257.

[46]Wayne K. Hoy and Scott R. Sweetland, "School Bureaucracies That Work: Enabling, Not Coercive," *Journal of School Leadership*, 10(2000): 525–541.

[47]Jerald Hage, "An Axiomatic Theory of Organizations," *Administrative Science Quarterly*, 10 (1965): 289–320.

**Eight Organizational Variables**    Complexity, central-ization, formalization, and stratification are the four variables that constitute the organizational *means* by which schools are structured to achieve objectives. Adaptiveness, production, efficiency, and job satisfac-tion are the four variables that represent categories for sorting organizational *ends*. We describe each in turn.

1. *Complexity,* or specialization, refers to the number of occupational specialities included in an organi-zation and the length of training required of each. Person specialization and task specialization distin-guish the degree of specialization. A teacher who is an expert in English literature is a person special-ist, whereas one who teaches eleventh-grade English is a task specialist. The greater the number of per-son specialists and the longer the period of training required to achieve person specialization (or degree held), the more complex the organization.

2. *Centralization,* or hierarchy of authority, refers to the number of role incumbents who participate in decision making and the number of areas in which they participate. The lower the proportion of role incumbents who participate and the fewer the deci-sion areas in which they participate, the more cen-tralized the organization.

3. *Formalization,* or standardization, refers to the proportion of codified jobs and the range of varia-tion that is tolerated within the parameters defining the jobs. The higher the proportion of codified jobs in schools and the lesser range of variation allowed, the more formalized the organization.

4. *Stratification,* or status system, refers to the differ-ence in status between higher and lower levels in the school's hierarchy. Differentials in salary, pres-tige, privileges, and mobility usually measure this status difference. The greater the disparity in re-wards between the top and bottom status levels and the lower the rates of mobility between them, the more stratified the organization.

5. *Adaptiveness,* or flexibility, refers to the use of professional knowledge and techniques in the in-struction of students and the ability of a school to respond to environmental demands. The more ad-vanced the knowledge base, instructional tech-niques, and environmental response, the more adaptive the organization.

6. *Production* refers to the quantity and quality of output. Some schools are more concerned with quantity and less concerned with quality, and vice versa. This variable is difficult to measure because

of the dichotomy between quantity and quality. For example, some universities are "degree mills"; that is, they award a large number of degrees each year with little concern for quality. Other institu-tions are less concerned about increasing the quan-tity of degrees awarded and more concerned about the quality of the product (the degree recipient). The greater the emphasis on quantity, not quality, of output, the more productive the organization.

7. *Efficiency,* or cost, refers to financial as well as human resources and the amount of idle resources. For example, class size ratios of one teacher to thirty students are more efficient than a one-to-ten ratio. The lower the cost per unit of production, the more efficient the organization.

8. *Job satisfaction,* or morale, refers to the amount of importance a school places on its human resources. Measures of job satisfaction include feelings of well-being, absenteeism, turnover, and the like. The higher the morale and the lower the absenteeism and turnover, the higher the job satisfaction in the organization.[48]

**Seven Organizational Propositions**    Central to Hage's axiomatic theory are seven propositions, which have been drawn from the classic works of Weber,[49] Barnard,[50] and Thompson.[51] The major theme perme-ating Hage's theory is the concept of functional strains, that is, maximizing one organizational-means variable minimizes another. The eight key variables are related in fairly predictable ways. For instance, high centraliza-tion results in high production and formalization, high formalization in turn results in high efficiency, high stratification results in low job satisfaction and adap-tiveness and high production, and high complexity re-sults in low centralization. These ideas are expressed in seven propositions:

▪ The higher the centralization, the higher the production.

▪ The higher the formalization, the higher the efficiency.

▪ The higher the centralization, the higher the formalization.

---

[48] Ibid.

[49] Weber, *The Theory of Social and Economic Organization.*

[50] Chester Barnard, "Functions and Pathology of Status Sys-tems in Formal Organizations," in William F. Whyte (ed.), *Industry and Society* (New York: McGraw-Hill, 1964), pp. 46–83.

[51] Victor Thompson, *Modern Organization* (New York: Knopf, 1961).

## Table 2–4 Characteristics of Mechanistic and Organic Organizational Forms

| Mechanistic Organization (Bureaucratic) | Organic Organization (Professional) |
| --- | --- |
| Low complexity | High complexity |
| High centralization | Low centralization |
| High formalization | Low formalization |
| High stratification | Low stratification |
| Low adaptiveness | High adaptiveness |
| High production | Low production |
| High efficiency | Low efficiency |
| Low job satisfaction | High job satisfaction |

Source: Adapted from Jerald Hage, "An Axiomatic Theory of Organizations," *Administrative Science Quarterly*, 10 (1965): 305. Used by permission.

■ The higher the stratification, the higher the production.

■ The higher the stratification, the lower the job satisfaction.

■ The higher the stratification, the lower the adaptiveness.

■ The higher the complexity, the lower the centralization.[52]

**Two Ideal Types** The interrelationship of the eight key variables in seven basic propositions was used to define two ideal types of organizations, as Table 2–4 shows. Mechanistic and organic concepts are organizational extremes that represent pure types not necessarily found in real life. No school is completely mechanistic (bureaucratic) nor completely organic (professional). Most schools fall somewhere between these two extremes.

Bureaucratic-type schools tend to have a hierarchical structure of control, authority, and communication with little shared decision making (high centralization). Each functional role requires precise definitions of rights and obligations and technical methods (high formalization). These schools emphasize status differences between hierarchical levels in the organization (high stratification); and an emphasis on quantity, not quality, of output at least cost is prevalent (high production, high efficiency). There is little emphasis on professional expertise in both subject-matter knowledge and instruc-

tional methodology (low complexity). As well, there is little responsiveness to changing needs of students, society, and subject matter (low adaptiveness); and human resources are of little importance (low job satisfaction).

The ideal professional-type school is characterized by high complexity, adaptiveness, and job satisfaction. That is, school administrators respect the professional knowledge of teachers, respond readily to the changing needs of the school and society, and consider the intrinsic satisfaction of teachers to be an important school outcome. Furthermore, centralization is low because administrators encourage teacher participation in decision making and delegate considerable authority and responsibility to teachers in the operation of the school. A network structure of control, authority, and communication prevails. School administrators adjust and continually redefine tasks and avoid always "going by the book." The organization deemphasizes status differences among the occupants of the many positions in the hierarchy and adopts a collegial, egalitarian orientation. Low efficiency and productivity also characterize the ideal professional school. School administrators in the professional-type school are not as concerned with the quantity of output as they are with the quality of outcomes. Professional-type schools are probably more expensive to operate than bureaucratic-type schools because professional-school administrators tend to deemphasize quantity of output at least cost. Such schools tend to be less efficient but more effective.

Each ideal type of school has advantages and disadvantages. Moreover, there are limits on how much a school administrator can emphasize one variable over another. For example, if there is no codification of jobs (formalization), then a condition of normlessness prevails, which will likely result in low job satisfaction of faculty members. If schools do not respond to the knowledge explosion, technological innovations, and the changing needs of students and society, schools are apt to fail in the face of an ever changing environment. Conversely, too high a change rate is likely to result in increased costs involved in implementing new programs and techniques. Limits exist on each of the eight variables, beyond which a school dare not move. Hage expresses it this way: "Production imposes limits on complexity, centralization, formalization, stratification, adaptiveness, efficiency, and job satisfaction."[53] In other words, extremes in any variable result in the loss of production, even in a school that has the means to maximize this end.

---

[52]Hage, "An Axiomatic Theory of Organizations."

[53]Ibid., p. 307.

**Administrative Advice 2–3**

**Strategic Questions**

In structuring a professional-school orientation, school administrators must answer the following strategic questions:

▪ *In which decisions will professional teachers become involved?* There appears to be general agreement among the major stakeholders that teachers should be more involved in making decisions. However, we need to specify the areas in which teachers will play larger roles in decision making.

▪ *Who will make what decisions in the school?* How much influence should teachers have with respect to decisions affecting other parties in the school—students, teachers, support staff, principals, central office administrators, school board members? The roles of these stakeholders may need to be clarified or redefined in a professional-school structure.

▪ *What are the basic tasks of administrators and teachers in the context of a professional-school structure?* Put another way, what is the basis of teachers' expertise and professional identity? The amount of participation in decision making probably should be contingent on whether the issue is relevant to teachers and whether teachers have the expertise to make the decision.

▪ *What is the role of teacher unions in a professional-school structure?* The involvement of teacher unions is a key strategic issue in structuring a professional-school orientation.

Source: Adapted from Sharon C. Conley and Samuel B. Bacharach, "From School-Site Management to Participatory School-Site Management," *Phi Delta Kappan*, 71 (1990): 539–544.

All the relationships specified in the seven propositions are curvilinear. For instance, if centralization becomes too high, production drops; if stratification becomes too low, job satisfaction falls. Therefore, exceeding the limits on any variable results in a reversal of the hypothesized relationships specified in the seven propositions. According to Hage, "These represent important qualifications to the axiomatic theory."[54]

The tension between the mechanistic (bureaucratic) and organic (professional) models is constantly negotiated between teachers and administrators. Sometimes it is resolved in favor of professionals, and sometimes it is resolved in favor of administrators.[55]

Because schools are fragile political coalitions, each decision must be considered strategically, examining its implications for all the major stakeholders.[56] Thus, school administrators must examine several strategic questions before a professional-school orientation can be effectively implemented. (See Administrative Advice 2–3.)

## Strategy-Structure Typology

Another alternative approach to organizational structure concerns the relationship between organizational strategy and structure. This approach began with the landmark work of Alfred Chandler, who traced the historical development of such large American corporations as DuPont, Sears, and General Motors.[57] He concluded from his study that an organization's strategy tends to influence its structure. He suggests that strategy indirectly determines such variables as the organization's tasks, technology, and environments, and each of these influences the structure of the organization.

More recently, social scientists have augmented Chandler's thesis by contending that an organization's strategy determines its environment, technology, and

[54]Ibid.

[55]Samuel B. Bacharach et al., *Advances in Research and Theories of School Management and Educational Policy* (Greenwich, CT: JAI Press, 2000).

[56]Robert O. Slater and William L. Boyd, "Schools as Polities," in J. Murphy and K. Seashore Louis (eds.), *Handbook of Research on Educational Administration,* 2nd ed. (San Francisco: Jossey-Bass, 1999), pp. 323–335.

[57]Alfred D. Chandler, *Strategy and Structure* (Cambridge, MA: MIT Press, 1962); see also Chandler, *The Dynamic Firm: The Role of Regions, Technology, Strategy and Organization* (New York: Oxford University Press, 1998).

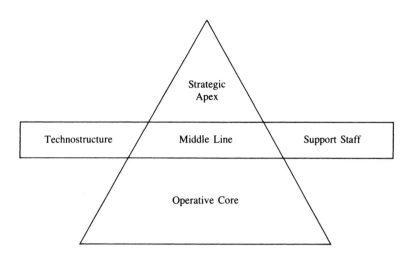

**Figure 2–4**

The Key Parts of an Organization

Source: Adapted from Henry Mintzberg, *Structure in Fives: Designing Effective Organizations,* © 1992, p. 11. Adapted by permission of Prentice Hall, Upper Saddle River, New Jersey. Used with permission.

tasks. These variables coupled with growth rates and power distribution affect organizational structure. Henry Mintzberg and James Quinn suggest that organizations can be differentiated along three basic dimensions: (1) the key part of the organization, that is, the part of the organization that plays the major role in determining its success or failure; (2) the prime coordinating mechanism, that is, the major method the organization uses to coordinate its activities; and (3) the type of decentralization used, that is, the extent to which the organization involves subordinates in the decision-making process.[58] The key parts of an organization are shown in Figure 2–4 and include the following:

- *The strategic apex* is top management and its support staff. In school districts, this is the superintendent of schools and the administrative cabinet.

- *The operative core* are the workers who actually carry out the organization's tasks. Teachers constitute the operative core in school districts.

- *The middle line* is middle- and lower-level management. Principals are the middle-level managers in school districts.

- *The technostructure* are analysts such as engineers, accountants, planners, researchers, and personnel managers. In school districts, divisions such as instruction, business, personnel, research and development, and the like constitute the technostructure.

- *The support staff* are the people who provide indirect services. In school districts, similar services include maintenance, clerical, food service, legal counsel, and consulting to provide support.[59]

The second basic dimension of an organization is its prime coordinating mechanism. This includes the following:

- *Direct supervision* means that one individual is responsible for the work of others. This concept refers to the unity of command and scalar principles discussed earlier.

- *Standardization of work process* exists when the content of work is specified or programmed. In school districts, this refers to job descriptions that govern the work performance of educators.

- *Standardization of skills* exists when the kind of training necessary to do the work is specified. In school systems, this refers to state certificates required for the various occupants of a school district's hierarchy.

- *Standardization of output* exists when the results of the work are specified. Because the "raw material" that is processed by the operative core (teachers) consists of people (students), not things, standardization of output is more difficult to measure in schools than in other nonservice organizations. Nevertheless, a movement toward the standardization of output in schools in recent years has occurred. Examples include competency testing of teachers, state-

[58]Henry Mintzberg, *The Strategy Process: Concepts, Contexts, and Cases,* 4th ed. (Englewood Cliffs, NJ: Prentice Hall, 2002).

[59]Ibid.

**Table 2–5   Mintzberg's Five Organizational Structures**

| Structural Configuration | Prime Coordinating Mechanism | Key Part of Organization | Type of Decentralization |
|---|---|---|---|
| Simple structure | Direct supervision | Strategic apex | Vertical and horizontal centralization |
| Machine bureaucracy | Standardization of work processes | Technostructure | Limited horizontal decentralization |
| Professional bureaucracy | Standardization of skills | Operating core | Vertical and horizontal decentralization |
| Divisionalized form | Standardization of outputs | Middle line | Limited vertical decentralization |
| Adhocracy | Mutual adjustment | Support staff | Selective decentralization |

Source: Adapted from Henry Mintzberg, *Structure in Fives: Designing Effective Organizations,* 2nd ed. (Upper Saddle River, NJ: Prentice Hall, 1992), p. 153.

mandated testing of students, state-mandated curriculum, prescriptive learning objectives, and other efforts toward legislated learning.

■ *Mutual adjustment* exists when work is co-ordinated through informal communication. Mutual adjustment or coordination is the major thrust of Likert's "linking-pin" concept discussed earlier.[60]

The third basic dimension of an organization is the type of decentralization it employs. The three types of decentralization are the following:

■ *Vertical decentralization* is the distribution of power down the chain of command, or shared authority between superordinates and subordinates in any organization.

■ *Horizontal decentralization* is the extent to which nonadministrators (including staff) make decisions, or shared authority between line and staff.

■ *Selective decentralization* is the extent to which decision-making power is delegated to different units within the organization. In school districts, these units might include instruction, business, personnel, and research and development divisions.[61]

Using the three basic dimensions—key part of the organization, prime coordinating mechanism, and type of decentralization—Mintzberg suggests that the strategy an organization adopts and the extent to which it

practices that strategy result in five structural configurations: simple structure, machine bureaucracy, professional bureaucracy, divisionalized form, and adhocracy. Table 2–5 summarizes the three basic dimensions associated with each of the five structural configurations. Each organizational form is discussed in turn.[62]

**Simple Structure**   The **simple structure** has as its key part the strategic apex, uses direct supervision, and employs vertical and horizontal centralization. Examples of simple structures are relatively small corporations, new government departments, medium-sized retail stores, and small elementary school districts. The organization consists of the top manager and a few workers in the operative core. There is no technostructure, and the support staff is small; workers perform overlapping tasks. For example, teachers and administrators in small elementary school districts must assume many of the duties that the technostructure and support staff perform in larger districts. Frequently, however, small elementary school districts are members of cooperatives that provide many services (i.e., counselors, social workers) to a number of small school districts in one region of the county or state.

In small school districts, the superintendent may function as both superintendent of the district and principal of a single school. Superintendents in such school

---

[60]Ibid.

[61]Ibid.

[62]Henry Mintzberg, *Structure in Fives: Designing Effective Organizations,* 2nd ed. (Upper Saddle River, NJ: Prentice Hall, 1992).

districts must be entrepreneurs. Because the organization is small, coordination is informal and maintained through direct supervision. Moreover, this organization can adapt to environmental changes rapidly. Goals stress innovation and long-term survival, although innovation may be difficult for very small rural school districts because of the lack of resources.

**Machine Bureaucracy**   Machine bureaucracy has the technostructure as its key part, uses standardization of work processes as its prime coordinating mechanism, and employs limited horizontal decentralization. Machine bureaucracy has many of the characteristics of Weber's ideal bureaucracy and resembles Hage's mechanistic organization. It has a high degree of formalization and work specialization. Decisions are centralized. The span of management is narrow, and the organization is tall—that is, many levels exist in the chain of command from top management to the bottom of the organization. Little horizontal or lateral coordination is needed. Furthermore, machine bureaucracy has a large technostructure and support staff.

Examples of machine bureaucracy are automobile manufacturers, steel companies, and large government organizations. The environment for a machine bureaucracy is typically stable, and the goal is to achieve internal efficiency. Public schools possess many characteristics of machine bureaucracy, but most schools are not machine bureaucracies in the pure sense. However, large urban school districts (New York, Los Angeles, and Chicago) are closer to machine bureaucracies than other medium-sized or small school districts.

**Professional Bureaucracy**   Professional bureaucracy has the operating core as its key part, uses standardization of skills as its prime coordinating mechanism, and employs vertical and horizontal decentralization. The organization is relatively formalized but decentralized to provide autonomy to professionals. Highly trained professionals provide nonroutine services to clients. Top management is small; there are few middle managers; and the technostructure is generally small. However, the support staff is typically large to provide clerical and maintenance support for the professional operating core. The goals of professional bureaucracies are to innovate and provide high-quality services. Existing in complex but stable environments, they are generally moderate to large in size. Coordination problems are common. Examples of this form of organization include universities, hospitals, and large law firms.

Some public school districts have many characteristics of the professional bureaucracy, particularly its aspects of professionalism, teacher autonomy, and structural looseness. For example, schools are formal organizations, which provide complex services through highly trained professionals in an atmosphere of structural looseness.[63] These characteristics tend to broaden the limits of individual discretion and performance. Like attorneys, physicians, and university professors, teachers perform in classroom settings in relative isolation from colleagues and superiors, while remaining in close contact with their students. Furthermore, teachers are highly trained professionals who provide information to their students in accordance with their own style, and they are usually flexible in the delivery of content even within the constraints of the state- and district-mandated curriculum. Moreover, like some staff administrators, teachers tend to identify more with their professions than with the organization.

**Divisionalized Form**   The divisionalized form has the middle line as its key part, uses standardization of output as its prime coordinating mechanism, and employs limited vertical decentralization. Decision making is decentralized at the divisional level. There is little coordination among the separate divisions. Corporate-level personnel provide some coordination. Thus, each division itself is relatively centralized and tends to resemble a machine bureaucracy. The technostructure is located at corporate headquarters to provide services to all divisions; support staff is located within each division. Large corporations are likely to adopt the divisionalized form.

Most school districts typically do not fit the divisionalized form. The exceptions are those very large school districts that have diversified service divisions distinctly separated into individual units or schools. For example, a school district may resemble the divisionalized form when it has separate schools for the physically handicapped, emotionally disturbed, and learning disabled; a skills center for the potential dropout; a special school for art and music students; and so on. The identifying feature of these school districts is that they have separate schools within a single school district, which have

---

[63]Charles E. Bidwell, "The School as a Formal Organization," in J. G. March (ed.), *Handbook of Organizations* (Chicago: Rand McNally, 1965), pp. 972–1022; Karl E. Weick, "Educational Organizations as Loosely Coupled Systems," *Administrative Science Quarterly*, 21 (1976): 1–19.

**Figure 2–5**

The Getzels–Guba Model

Source: From Jacob W. Getzels and Egon G. Guba, "Social Behavior and the Administrative Process," *School Review,* 65 (1957), p. 429. Used by permission of the University of Chicago Press.

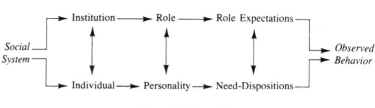

separate administrative staffs, budgets, and so on. Elementary and secondary school districts that have consolidated but retained separate administrative structures with one school board are also examples of the divisionalized form. As might be expected, the primary reason for a school district to adopt this form of structure is service diversity while retaining separate administrative structures.

**Adhocracy**   The **adhocracy** has the support staff as its key part, uses mutual adjustment as a means of coordination, and maintains selective patterns of decentralization. The structure tends to be low in formalization and decentralization. The technostructure is small because technical specialists are involved in the organization's operative core. The support staff is large to support the complex structure. Adhocracies engage in nonroutine tasks and use sophisticated technology. The primary goal is innovation and rapid adaptation to changing environments. Adhocracies typically are medium sized, must be adaptable, and use resources efficiently. Examples of adhocracies include aerospace and electronic industries, research and development firms, and very innovative school districts. No school districts are pure adhocracies, but medium-sized school districts in very wealthy communities may have some of the characteristics of an adhocracy. The adhocracy is somewhat similar to Hage's organic organization.

**Strategy and Structure**   The work begun by Chandler and extended by Mintzberg has laid the groundwork for an understanding of the relationship between an organization's strategy and its structure. The link between strategy and structure is still in its infancy stage. Further research in this area, particularly in service organizations like schools, will enhance school administrators' understanding of school organizations. In the

meantime, school leaders must recognize that organization strategy and structure are related.

## The School as a Social System

We can view the school as a social system. A **social system** refers to activities and interactions of group members brought together for a common purpose.[64] Thus, a school district, a school, and a classroom can all be viewed as social systems. A useful framework for understanding the administrative process within social systems is the Getzels-Guba model (see Figure 2–5).[65]

### Dimensions of a Social System

Jacob Getzels and Egon Guba conceive of the social system as involving two dimensions that are independent and interactive. First are institutions with certain roles and expectations that will fulfill the goals of the system. Second are individuals with certain personalities and need-dispositions inhabiting the system, whose interactions comprise observed behavior. Thus, observed behavior can be understood as a function of these major elements: institution, role, and expectations, which together constitute the *nomothetic,* or normative, dimension of activity in a social system; and individual, personality, and need-dispositions, which together con-

[64]George C. Homans, *The Human Group* (New York: Harcourt, Brace, & World, 1950).

[65]Jacob W. Getzels and Egon G. Guba, "Social Behavior and the Administrative Process," *School Review,* 65 (1957): 423–441; see also James M. Lipham, "Getzels's Models in Educational Administration," in N. J. Boyan (ed.), *Handbook of Research on Educational Administration* (New York: Longman, 1988), pp. 171–184.

stitute the *idiographic,* or personal, dimension of activity in a social system.

Translated into the school setting, this means that an organization is designed to serve one of society's needs—to educate. In this organization, there are positions, or roles, such as the roles of the student, teacher, principal, superintendent, and the like. For each individual who occupies a given role, there are role expectations. Role expectations represent not only the duties and actions expected from each role player but also the expectations concerning the quality of performance. The various roles and role expectations constitute the nomothetic dimension of the social system.

The idiographic dimension includes individuals who occupy the roles and their personal needs. Schools as social systems must be "peopled," and all kinds of individuals who have their own idiosyncrasies "people" them. Thus, individuals chosen to occupy roles are different from one another in action and in reaction, and we can analyze these differences in terms of personality. Personality is determined in part by needs, which predispose a person to behave in a certain way in a given situation. In other words, the individual who occupies a given role has needs he tries to fulfill. These are personalized needs and may not be associated with the needs of the school system.

Behavior can be stated in the form of the equation $B = f(R \times P)$, where $B$ is observed behavior, $f$ is function, $R$ is a given institutional role defined by the expectations attached to it, and $P$ is the personality of the role player defined by his need-dispositions.[66] The proportion of role and personality factors determining behavior varies with the specific act, the specific role, and the specific personality involved.

It is presumed in the military that behavior is influenced more by role than personality, whereas with the free-lance artist, behavior is influenced more by personality than by role. Many other examples can illustrate this variation in the influence exerted by role or personality on behavior. In educational organizations, we could hypothesize that the proportion of role and personality might be balanced somewhere between the two. But different educational systems are characterized by different proportions of role and personality.[67]

## Expanded Model: Cultural Dimensions

The developers of this early model recognized its oversimplification. In focusing on the sociological dimension with "role" as the central concept and on the psychological dimension with "personality" as the central concept, other dimensions had been omitted, thus giving the model a closed systems orientation. To overcome this deficiency, Getzels and Herbert Thelen expanded the basic model to describe the classroom as a unique social system.[68] According to these social system theorists, the sociological aspects of an institution are mediated by cultural factors—the ethos, mores, and values—in which the institution is embedded. The expectations of the roles must, it seems, be somehow related to the ethos or cultural values. Similarly, the individual's personality functions in a biological organism with certain potentialities and abilities, with the need-dispositions of the personality mediated in some way by these constitutional conditions.

Getzels, James Lipham, and Roald Campbell further extended the model for school administrators. They added a second cultural dimension to interact with the psychological aspects of the individual.[69] The composite model of the school as a social system depicts educational administration as a social process (see Figure 2–6). The bottom line in their model indicates that the culture, ethos, and values held by individuals in schools and school systems explain much social behavior. The model also clearly indicates that any social system (classroom, school, or school district) must operate within a larger environment. The addition of these dimensions gives Getzels's composite model a more open-systems orientation.

**Some Derivations** Getzels's models suggest three sources of potential conflicts: role conflicts, personality conflicts, and role-personality conflicts.[70] *Role conflicts* refer to situations where a role player is required to conform simultaneously to expectations that are con-

---

[66]Jacob W. Getzels, "Administration as a Social Process," in A. W. Halpin (ed.), *Administrative Theory in Education* (New York: Macmillan, 1958), pp. 150–165.

[67]Ibid.

[68]Jacob W. Getzels and Herbert A. Thelen, "The Classroom as a Social System," in N. B. Henry (ed.), *The Dynamics of Instructional Groups,* 59th Yearbook of the National Society for the Study of Education, Part II (Chicago: University of Chicago Press, 1960), pp. 53–83.

[69]Jacob W. Getzels, James M. Lipham, and Roald F. Campbell, *Educational Administration as a Social Process* (New York: Harper & Row, 1968).

[70]Getzels, "Administration as a Social Process."

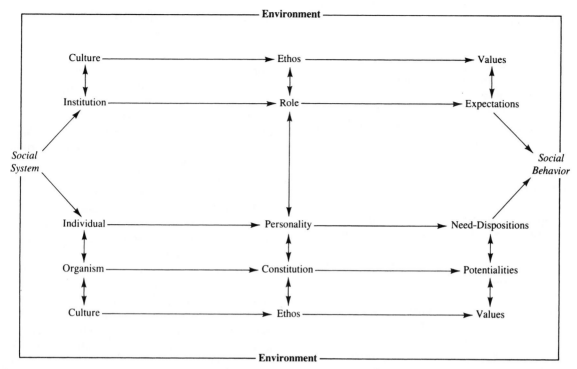

**Figure 2–6**

Composite Model of Behavior in Social Systems

Source: Adapted from Jacob W. Getzels, James M. Lipham, and Roald F. Campbell, *Educational Administration as a Social Process* (New York: Harper & Row, 1968), p. 105. Used with permission.

tradictory or inconsistent. Adjustment to one set of expectations makes adjustment to the other difficult or impossible. For example, a teacher may attempt to be a devoted mother and simultaneously a successful career woman. A university professor may be expected by the department head to emphasize teaching and service to students and the community, respectively, while the academic dean expects an emphasis on research and publication. Role conflicts represent incongruencies in the nomothetic dimension (see Figure 2–6).

*Personality conflicts* occur as a result of opposing need-dispositions within the personality of the individual role players. For example, a teacher may be expected, as a social norm, to maintain adequate social distance between self and students. However, the teacher may feel the need for more extensive interactions. Personality conflicts represent incongruencies in the idiographic dimension of the social systems model.

*Role-personality conflicts* occur as a result of discrepancies between the institution's role expectations and the individual's need-dispositions. For ex-

ample, suppose an introverted school administrator were placed in the role of superintendent in a small- to medium-sized school district. The board of education makes clear its expectation that the newly appointed administrator maintain high visibility and extensive contact with the community. The superintendent, however, has a high need for privacy and anonymity. The superintendent in this school district would experience a role-personality conflict. As shown in Figure 2–6, role-personality conflicts represent incongruencies between the nomothetic and idiographic dimensions of the social systems model.

According to Getzels, incongruencies in the nomothetic and idiographic dimensions, or in their interaction, are symptomatic of administrative failure and lead to a loss in individual and institutional productivity.[71]

Furthermore, Getzels's models suggest three leader-followership styles: normative (nomothetic), personal

---

[71]Ibid.

## PRO/CON Debate

### School-Based Management

In many school districts, the direction of school reform is away from the bureaucratic patterns of top-down control and toward more autonomy for those who are assigned to the site, that is, the school. Theoretically, the superintendent and central office staff relinquish elements of their authority to a school-based team consisting of the principal, teachers, parents, students, and community members. The expectation is that the school-based team will make better decisions because they better understand the needs of students and teachers at the school.

**Question:** Does school-based decision making enhance student learning?

**Arguments PRO**

1. Issues related to curriculum, resource allocation, and personnel assignments impact classroom instruction. When teachers serve on school-based teams, they are in a position to make decisions that enable student learning.

2. Teachers must be held more accountable. We are increasing teacher certification requirements and teacher salaries in order to secure a more professional workforce. Professionals need a wide sphere of influence. They must have the authority to change whatever needs to be changed to meet standards.

3. School-based teams ensure that everyone with a stake in a matter is consulted. Their decisions are likely to be more workable because all perspectives are considered.

**Arguments CON**

1. Teachers' expertise is in teaching and learning, not managerial decision making. When teachers serve on school-based teams, their attention and energies are deflected away from ensuring increased student learning.

2. Teachers expect administrators to make school-based decisions. If teachers wished to engage in a wider area of decision making, they would become administrators.

3. Most school-based teams have difficulty because so many different perspectives are on the table. Many points of view are mutually exclusive, so weak compromises are reached.

---

(idiographic), and transactional.[72] The *normative style* emphasizes the fulfillment of institutional role requirements and obligations rather than the personal needs of individuals. Role definition, authority vested in roles, and organizational goal achievement are stressed. The *personal style* emphasizes the personal activities and propensities of individuals. Minimum role definition, a diffusion of authority, and efforts to maximize each individual's meaningful contribution to the organization are stressed. The *transactional style* represents a balance of emphasis on the performance of the role requirements of the organization and the expression of personal needs of individuals. The school administrator moves alternately toward the normative style or the personal style depending on the situation.

### Getzels's Latest Model: Communities Dimension

In the late 1970s, Getzels expanded his social systems model still further by including a communities dimension.[73] Here Getzels makes much more manifest the cultural setting of the school as a social system and extends its usefulness as an open systems model. He identifies six communities of education and defines communities as groups of people conscious of a collective identity through common cognitive and affective norms, values, and patterns of social relationships. He defines each type of community as follows:

▪ *Local community* is established in a particular neighborhood or region. Examples include a local neighborhood or school community.

---

[72]Getzels, Lipham, and Campbell, *Educational Administration as a Social Process.*

[73]Jacob W. Getzels, "The Communities of Education," *Teachers College Record*, 79 (1978): 659–682.

▪ *Administrative community* is established in a specific, politically determined identity. A country, a city, or a school district are examples.

▪ *Social community* is established in a particular set of interpersonal relationships not restrained by local or administrative boundaries. An example would be all the people in one's community of friends.

▪ *Instrumental community* is established through direct or indirect activities and interactions with others who are brought together for a common purpose. Examples include a professional group such as teachers or professors who make up an educational community, a teachers' union, or a philanthropic community.

▪ *Ethnic community* is established through affinity with a particular national, racial, or socioeconomic group. Italian, black, or upper-class communities are examples.

▪ *Ideological community* is established in a particular historic, conceptual, or sociopolitical community that stretches across the local, administrative, social, instrumental, and ethnic communities. Examples include Christian, scholarly, or communist communities.[74]

Getzels's revised and latest models make much more explicit the cultural setting of the school as a social system. The concept of culture, the mainstay of anthropology since its beginnings, is not new. Recently, the concept of organizational culture has enjoyed tremendous appeal in both the popular and professional management literature.

Getzels's models of the school as a social system are widely treated in introductory textbooks in educational administration, textbooks that deal specifically with the school principalship, textbooks on supervision, and references on organizational behavior and theory in educational administration. In addition, the *Handbook of Research on Educational Administration,* a project of the American Educational Research Association, devotes an entire chapter to Getzels's models in educational administration.[75]

## Summary

1. Basic concepts of organizational structure provide a framework for vertical control and horizontal coordination of schools. These important dimensions include job specialization, departmentalization, chain of command, authority and responsibility, centralization/decentralization, line and staff authority, and span of management.

2. According to this view, division of labor, abstract rules, vertical hierarchy of authority, impersonality in interpersonal relations, and advancement based on competence characterize the ideal bureaucratic structure.

3. The participatory management model is the antithesis of the ideal bureaucracy. Supportiveness, shared leadership, flexibility, and employee growth and development are the keys to participatory management.

4. Compliance theory, mechanistic and organic organizations, and strategy-structure typology are alternative approaches to organizational structure. These approaches integrate several ideas from the classical and participatory management models and the fundamentals of organizational structure.

5. Getzels's models of the school as a social system have proven to have enduring appeal and widespread application in the administration of schools.

## Key Terms

job specialization
departmentalization
chain of command
authority and responsibility
centralization and decentralization
line and staff authority
span of management
bureaucracy
Theory X and Theory Y
immaturity–maturity continuum
System 4 organization
culture
moral leadership
school-based management
Total Quality Management
four frames
compliance theory
mechanistic and organic organizations
simple structure
machine bureaucracy
professional bureaucracy

---

[74]Ibid.

[75]Lipham, "Getzels's Models in Educational Administration," pp. 171–184.

divisionalized form
adhocracy
social system

## Discussion Questions

1. Which fundamentals of structuring are associated with the following organizational forms: (a) simple structure, (b) machine bureaucracy, (c) professional bureaucracy, (d) divisionalized form, and (e) adhocracy?

2. Why are many of the characteristics of Weber's ideal bureaucracy still used in schools today?

3. Likert developed a paradigm consisting of three sets of variables: causal, intervening, and end-result. Do you think that Likert's paradigm is useful in assessing the effectiveness of a school or school district? Why?

4. Using Etzioni's typology, is it possible to analyze a particular type of organization, such as a school, as representing more than one kind of organization? Explain.

5. Describe the mechanistic or organic characteristics of a school with which you are familiar.

## Suggested Readings

Bolman, Lee G., and Terrence E. Deal. *Reframing Organizations: Artistry, Choice, and Leadership,* 3rd ed. (San Francisco: Jossey-Bass, 2003). In this updated version of their best-selling classic, the authors explain how the powerful tool of "reframing"—appraising situations from diverse perspectives—can be used to build high-performing, responsive organizations.

Fullan, Michael. *Breakthrough* (Thousand Oaks, CA: Corwin Press, 2006). This groundbreaking book presents an extraordinary new framework for classroom instruction that can significantly enhance learning for both students and teachers.

Howley, Aimee, and Craig Howley. *Thinking About Schools: New Theories and Innovative Practices* (Mahwah, NJ: Lawrence Erlbaum Associates, 2006). As its title implies, this book has a deceptively simple mission: to prepare would-be school leaders to draw upon a variety of theoretical perspectives when thinking about schools and schooling. It shows how theories can function as cognitive tools to be mastered, carefully stored in one's intellectual toolbox and used to interpret and resolve real-world problems. Beneath this goal lies the belief that the most effective leaders are those who are able to construct their own well-grounded interpretations of events and their own responses to those events.

Leithwood, Kenneth, Robert Aitken, and Doris Jantzi. *Making Schools Smarter: Leading with Evidence* (Thousand Oaks, CA: Corwin Press, 2006). Achieve a workable model for effectively reshaping today's school districts for positive outcomes by addressing three of the most central challenges in district and school leadership.

Morgan, Gareth, *Images of Organization* (Thousand Oaks, CA: Sage Publications, 2007). Since its first publication over twenty years ago, *Images of Organization* has become a classic in the canon of management literature. The book is based on a simple premise—that all theories of organization and management are based on implicit images or metaphors that stretch our imagination in a way that can create powerful insights, but at the risk of distortion. Gareth Morgan provides a rich and comprehensive resource for exploring the complexity of modern organizations internationally, translating leading-edge theory into leading-edge practice.

Sarason, Seymour B. *Letters to a Serious Education President,* 2nd ed. (Thousand Oaks, CA: Corwin Press, 2006). In this new edition of his original collection of letters, education luminary Seymour B. Sarason details how school reformers still have difficulty examining the differences between contexts of productive and unproductive learning. Sarason's acute insight into why school reforms fail forces us to ask how we teach all students.

Sergiovanni, Thomas J. *Rethinking Leadership: A Collection of Articles,* 2nd ed. (Thousand Oaks, CA: Corwin Press, 2006). In this innovative approach to reframing leadership, Sergiovanni encourages school leaders to discover the craft of moral leadership while learning how to practice effective instructional leadership and build strong learning communities for today and tomorrow.

# 3. Organizational Culture

## FOCUSING QUESTIONS

1 Why is knowledge of organizational culture so important to a school administrator?

2 How is an organizational culture created?

3 How is an organizational culture maintained?

4 Can organizational culture be changed?

5 Are there similarities between organizational culture and climate?

6 What is meant by organizational climate?

7 How can organizational climate be conceptualized?

8 How do culture and climate relate to performance in schools?

In this chapter, we attempt to answer these questions concerning organizational culture in school settings. We begin our discussion by exploring the nature and characteristics of organizational culture. Next we discuss how organizational cultures are created, maintained, and changed. Then we discuss the features of corporate cultures of excellent firms and their relationship to school organizations. We examine differences between Japanese and American management styles and their implications for administering schools. We discuss the similarities between organizational culture and organizational climate. Finally, we present and analyze four well-known organizational climate constructs with implications for improving school effectiveness.

## The Nature of Organizational Culture

In recent years, organizational culture has been popularized by best-selling books such as *In Search of Excellence*,[1] *A Passion for Excellence*,[2] and *Corporate Cultures*.[3] Although much has been written about organizational culture, little research supports the concept. For ex-

[1] Thomas J. Peters and Robert H. Waterman, *In Search of Excellence: Lessons from America's Best Run Companies* (New York: DIANE Publishing Company, 2006).

[2] Thomas J. Peters, *A Passion for Excellence* (New York: Random House, 1997).

[3] Terrence E. Deal and Allan A. Kennedy, *Corporate Cultures: The Rites and Rituals of Corporate Life* (Reading, MA: Addison-Wesley, 1984).

ample, two academic journals devoted entire issues to organizational culture, but most articles were speculative in nature.[4]

## Definition and Characteristics

The culture of an organization is all the beliefs, feelings, behaviors, and symbols that are characteristic of an organization. More specifically, **organizational culture** is defined as shared philosophies, ideologies, beliefs, feelings, assumptions, expectations, attitudes, norms, and values.[5]

While there is considerable variation in the definitions of organizational culture, it appears that most contain the following characteristics:

- *Observed Behavioral Regularities.* When organizational members interact, they use common language, terminology, and rituals and ceremonies related to deference and demeanor.

- *Norms.* Standards of behavior evolve in work groups, such as "a fair day's work for a fair day's pay." The impact of work-group behavior, sanctioned by group norms, results in standards and yardsticks.

- *Dominant Values.* An organization espouses and expects its members to share major values. Typical examples in schools are high performance levels of faculty and students, low absence and dropout rates, and high efficiency.

- *Philosophy.* Policies guide an organization's beliefs about how employees and clients are to be treated. For example, most school districts have statements of philosophy or mission statements.

- *Rules.* Guidelines exist for getting along in the organization, or the "ropes" that a newcomer must learn in order to become an accepted member.

- *Feelings.* This is an overall atmosphere that is conveyed in an organization by the physical layout and the way in which members interact with clients or other outsiders.[6]

None of these characteristics by itself represents the essence of organizational culture. However, the characteristics taken collectively reflect and give meaning to the concept of organizational culture.

The culture of an organization is interrelated with most other concepts in educational administration, including organization structures, motivation, leadership, decision making, communications, and change. To better understand this concept, Figure 3–1 depicts organizational culture within the context of social systems theory and more specifically open systems theory, being characterized by inputs, a transformation process, outputs, external environments, and feedback.

Organizations import energy from the environment in the form of information, people, and materials. The imported energy undergoes a transformation designed to channel behavior toward organizational goals and fulfill members' needs. Administrative processes (e.g., motivation, leadership, decision making, communication, and change) and organizational structures (e.g., job descriptions, selection systems, evaluation systems, control systems, and reward systems) have a significant impact on organizational culture and vice versa. In turn, these administrative processes and organizational structures export a product into the external environment. In a school, the output may be students' knowledge, skills, and attitudes or attendance, dropout rates, and more precise performance criteria such as scholastic awards. Figure 3–1 also shows that the organization not only influences but also is influenced by the external environment. And the social system uses feedback in an attempt to examine its present culture or to create a new culture.

## Uniformity of Culture

Figure 3–1 shows the interrelationship of organizational culture with most other concepts in educational administration. Thus, culture represents the organization's cumulative learning, as reflected in organizational structures, people, administrative processes, and the external environment. This tends to perpetuate beliefs and behavior and specifies the goals, values, and

---

[4]Philip A. Cusick (ed.), "Organizational Culture and Schools," *Educational Administration Quarterly*, 11 (1987), whole issue; Mariann Jelinek, Linda Smircich, and Paul Hirsch (eds.), "Organizational Culture," *Administrative Science Quarterly*, 28 (1983), whole issue.

[5]Mats Alvesson, *Understanding Organizational Culture* (Thousand Oaks, CA: Sage, 2002).

[6]Edgar H. Schein, *Organizational Culture and Leadership* (New York: John Wiley, 2004).

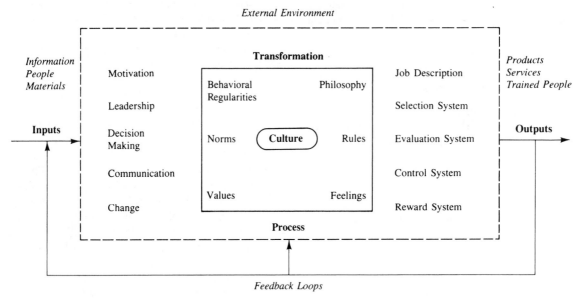

**Figure 3–1**

Dimensions of Organizational Culture

mission of the organization and the criteria by which to measure the organization's success.

**Subcultures**  Large and complex organizations do not typically manifest single homogeneous beliefs, values, and behavior patterns. In other words, there may be more than one culture in an organization. First, there are differences between the formal culture, which consists of the ideal philosophy of the organization and how organizational members should behave, and the informal culture, which consists of the actual manifestations of the ideal philosophy in the day-to-day behavior of organizational members. Second, there are likely to be different cultures in various functional groups in the organization, such as the divisions of instruction, business, personnel, and research and development in a large school district; differences between student, teacher, and administrator groups; and differences between elementary, middle school, and high school levels. Put another way, whenever the task requirements have resulted in a unique combination of people, structures, and function, the requirement to fulfill the group's goals will result in a unique culture.[7]

---

[7]Alvesson, *Understanding Organizational Culture.*

**Dominant Culture**  Besides the subcultures that exist in an organization, the larger organization may also have a culture that distinguishes it from other large systems. For example, one large school district highly favored innovation. This philosophy translated itself into a variety of practices including team teaching, flexible scheduling, teacher-advisor programs, report card conferences, use of speakers' bureaus, collaboration with business firms, and internships. It resulted in values that emphasized good interpersonal relations between students and teachers, teachers and administrators, teachers and parents, and school and community.

Thus, central office administrators created policies and made decisions that perpetuated the overall school district's philosophy of innovation. Most key administrators portrayed the same image. They demonstrated excellent interpersonal and verbal skills and strived to be accessible to students, teachers, parents, and the community. They spent a portion of their time cultivating relations with the business community through membership in the Rotary, Kiwanis, Lions Club, Chamber of Commerce, and so on. This example shows that even large and relatively heterogeneous school districts that are known to have dominant cultures can improve their educational goals.

## Developing, Maintaining, and Changing Organizational Culture

Organizational cultures are created, maintained, and changed through similar processes. But the following questions arise: How does an organizational culture develop? How is the culture of an organization maintained? Can organizational culture be changed by administrative action? In this section, we explore the answers to these questions.

### Creating Organizational Culture

The process of creating an organizational culture is complex. Organizational heroes, rites and rituals, and communication networks play key roles in creating organizational cultures.[8]

**Heroes**  Most successful organizations have their heroes. Heroes are born and created. The born hero is the visionary institution builder like Henry Ford, founder of Ford Motor company, and Mary Kay Ash, founder of Mary Kay Cosmetics. Created heroes, on the other hand, are those the institution has made by noticing and celebrating memorable moments that occur in the day-to-day life of the organization. Thomas Watson, head of IBM, is an example of a situation hero. Other well-known heroes include Lee Iacocca at Chrysler, Sam Walton at Wal-Mart, and Vince Lombardi, the legendary coach of the Green Bay Packers. Heroes perpetuate the organization's underlying values, provide role models, symbolize the organization to others, and set performance standards that motivate participant achievement.

In many schools, local heroes and heroines, exemplars of core values, provide models of what everyone should be striving for. These deeply committed staff come in early, are always willing to meet with students, and are constantly upgrading their skills.

**Rites and Rituals**  Another key aspect in creating organizational cultures are the everyday activities and celebrations that characterize the organization. Most successful organizations feel that these rituals and symbolic actions should be managed. Through rites and

rituals, recognition of achievement is possible.[9] The Teacher of the Year Award and National Merit Schools are examples. Similarly, a number of ceremonial rituals may accompany the appointment of a new superintendent of schools, including press and other announcements, banquets, meetings, and speeches.

Some organizations have even created their own reward rituals. At Hollibrook Elementary School in Spring Branch, Texas, rites and rituals reinforce student learning. Under the leadership of Suzanne Still and faculty, and supported through ties to the Accelerated Schools Model, the school developed numerous traditions to create a powerful professional culture and foster increased student success.[10] For example, faculty meetings became a hotbed of professional dialogue and discussion of practice and published research. "Fabulous Friday" was created to provide students with a wide assortment of courses and activities. A "Parent University" furnishes courses and materials while building trust between the school and the largely Hispanic community. Norms of collegiality, improvement, and connection reinforce and symbolize what the school is about.[11]

**Communication Networks**  Stories or myths of heroes are transmitted by means of the communications network. This network is characterized by various individuals who play a role in the culture of the organization. Each institution has *storytellers* who interpret what is going on in the organization. Their interpretation of the information influences the perceptions of others. *Priests* are the worriers of the organization and the guardians of the culture's values. These individuals always have time to listen and provide alternative solutions to problems. *Whisperers* are the powers behind the throne because they have the boss's ear. Anyone who wants something done will go to the whisperer. *Gossips* carry the trivial day-to-day activities of the organization through the communications network. Gossips are very important in building and maintaining heroes. They embellish the heroes' past feats and exaggerate their latest accomplishments. And, finally, *spies* are buddies in the wood-

---

[8] Much of this discussion is based on Deal and Kennedy, *Corporate Cultures.*

[9] Terrence E. Deal and Kent D. Peterson, *Shaping School Culture: The Heart of Leadership* (New York: John Wiley, 2003).

[10] Wendy S. Hopfenberg, *The Accelerated School Resource Guide* (San Francisco: Jossey-Bass, 1995).

[11] Kent D. Peterson and Terrence E. Deal, "How Leaders Influence the Culture of Schools," *Educational Leadership,* 56(1) (1998): 28–30.

## Administrative Advice 3–1

### How Leaders Influence the Culture of Schools

School leaders do several important things when creating culture. First, they *read the culture*—its history and current condition. Leaders should know the deeper meanings embedded in the school before trying to reshape it. Second, leaders *uncover and articulate core values,* looking for those that reinforce what is best for students and that support student-centered learning. It is important to identify which aspects of the culture are negative and which are positive. Finally, leaders work to *fashion a positive context,* reinforcing cultural elements that are positive and modifying those that are negative and dysfunctional. Positive school cultures are never monolithic or overly conforming, but core values and shared purpose should be pervasive and deep. Some of the specific ways school leaders shape culture follow.

- They communicate core values in what they say and do.
- They honor and recognize those who have worked to serve students and the purpose of the school.
- They observe rituals and traditions to support the school's heart and soul.
- They recognize heroes and heroines and the work these exemplars accomplish.
- They eloquently speak of the deeper mission of the school.

- They celebrate the accomplishments of the staff, the students, and the community.
- They preserve the focus on students by recounting stories of success and achievement.

Source: Adapted from Kent D. Peterson and Terrence E. Deal, "How Leaders Influence the Culture of Schools, *Educational Leadership,* 56(1) (1998): 28–30.

work. They keep everyone well informed about what is going on in the organization. Each of these individuals plays a key role in building and maintaining an organization's culture. It should be noted that the names used here are those ascribed by Deal and Kennedy to emphasize the importance of communication networks in creating an institution's organizational culture.

How do strong cultures come about? School leaders—including principals, teachers, and often parents and community members—develop and maintain positive values and a shared vision.

School leaders from every level are key to creating school culture. Principals communicate core values in their school buildings. Teachers reinforce values in their words and behavior. Parents enhance spirit when they visit school, participate in governance, and celebrate successes. In the strongest school cultures, leadership comes from many sources. (See Administrative Advice 3–1.)

## Maintaining Organizational Culture

Once an organizational culture is created, a number of mechanisms help solidify the acceptance of the values and ensure that the culture is maintained or reinforced

(**organizational socialization**). These mechanisms, illustrated in Figure 3–2, are the following steps for socializing employees:[12]

Step 1: *Selection of Entry-Level Candidates.* The socialization process starts with the careful selection of entry-level candidates. Trained recruiters use standardized procedures and focus on values that are important in the culture. Those candidates whose personal values do not fit with the underlying values of the organization are given ample opportunity to opt out (deselect).

Step 2: *Humility-Inducing Experiences.* After the chosen candidate is hired, considerable training ensues to expose the person to the culture. Humility-inducing experiences, which cause employees to question prior beliefs and values, are assigned, thereby making new employees more receptive to the values of the new culture. Many organizations give newly hired employees more work than they can reasonably handle and assign work for which

[12]Richard T. Pascale, "The Paradox of 'Corporate Culture': Reconciling Ourselves to Socialization," *California Management Review,* 27 (1985): 26–41.

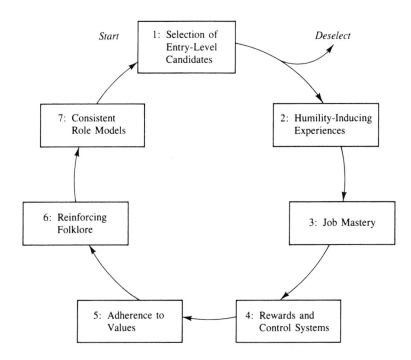

*Start* 　　　　　　　　　　　　*Deselect*

**Figure 3–2**

The Process of Organizational Socialization

Source: Adapted from Richard T. Pascale, "Paradox of 'Corporate Culture': Reconciling Ourselves to Socialization," *California Management Review,* 27 (1985): 38. Copyright 1985 by the Regents of the University of California. Used by permission of the Regents.

the individual is overqualified. For example, a new faculty member of a university may be assigned undesirable tasks, which senior professors of the department do not wish to perform: teaching the basic courses, off-campus assignments, assignment to several committees, heavy advisement loads, field work, and assignment to an inequitable number of doctoral committees. The message conveyed to the newcomer is, "You must pay your dues."

Step 3: *Job Mastery.* Whereas Step 2 is intended to foster cultural learning, Step 3 is designed to develop the employee's technological knowledge. As employees move along a career path, the organization assesses their performance and assigns other responsibilities on the basis of their progress. Frequently, organizations establish a step-by-step approach to this career plan. For example, the Holmes Group recommends a three-step career ladder process for teachers: (1) instructors, (2) professional teachers, and (3) career professionals.[13] The Carnegie Task Force on Teaching as a Profession proposes another approach consisting of four steps: (1) licensed teachers, (2) certified teachers,

(3) advanced certified teachers, and (4) lead teachers.[14]

Step 4: *Reward and Control Systems.* The organization pays meticulous attention to measuring operational results and to rewarding individual performance. Reward systems are comprehensive, consistent, and focus on those aspects of the organization that are tied to success and the values of the culture. For example, a school district will specify the factors that are considered important for success. Operational measures are used to assess these factors, and performance appraisals of employees are tied to the accomplishment of these factors. Promotions and merit pay are determined by success on each of the predetermined critical factors. For instance, those school administrators who violate the culture are often transferred or given a relatively innocuous staff position at central office. These administrators are now "off their career tracks," which can inhibit their promotion in the organization. This is the typical pattern used in large bureaucratic school districts as an alternative to firing the administrator.

---

[13]Holmes Group, *Tomorrow's Teachers: A Report of the Holmes Group* (East Lansing, MI: The Holmes Group, 1986).

[14]Carnegie Task Force on Teaching as a Profession, *A Nation Prepared: Teachers for the Twenty-First Century* (New York: Carnegie Corporation, 1986).

Step 5: *Adherence to Values.* As personnel continue to work for the organization, their behavior closely matches the underlying values of the culture. Identification with underlying values helps employees reconcile personal sacrifices caused by their membership in the organization. Personnel learn to accept the organization's values and place their trust in the organization not to hurt them. For instance, school administrators work long hours on a multiplicity of fragmented tasks for which they sometimes receive little recognition from their superiors, subordinates, and the community. They sometimes endure ineffective school board members and supervisors and job assignments that are undesirable and inconvenient. Identification with the common values of the organization allows these administrators to justify such personal sacrifices.

Step 6: *Reinforcing Folklore.* Throughout the socialization process, the organization exposes its members to rites and rituals, stories or myths, and heroes that portray and reinforce the culture. For example, in one educational institution, the story is told of an administrator who was fired because of his harsh handling of subordinates. The administrator had incorrectly believed a myth that being "tough" with his subordinates would enhance himself in the eyes of his superiors. The organization deemed such managerial behavior to be inconsistent with its organizational philosophy of cultivating good interpersonal relationships and high levels of morale and job satisfaction among all its employees.

Step 7: *Consistent Role Models.* Those individuals who have performed well in the organization serve as role models to newcomers to the organization. By identifying these employees as symbolizing success, the organization encourages others to do otherwise. Role models in strong-culture institutions can be thought of as one type of ongoing staff development for all organizational members.

## Changing Organizational Culture

To this point, we have discussed how organizational culture is created and maintained. Sometimes an organization determines that its culture needs to be changed. The **change cycle** (see Figure 3–3) has the following components.[15]

---

[15]Schein, *Organizational Culture and Leadership.*

- *External Enabling Conditions.* Enabling conditions, if they exist, indicate that the environment will be supportive of culture change. Such conditions are in the external environment and impact the organization. In a school setting, examples include scarcity or abundance of students, stability or instability of the external environment, and resource concentration or dispersion. In combination these external enabling conditions determine the degree of threat to the organization's input sources (information, people, and materials) (see Figure 3–1).

- *Internal Permitting Conditions.* To increase the likelihood of organizational culture change, four internal permitting conditions must exist: (1) a surplus of change resources (managerial time and energy, financial resources, and the like that are available to the system beyond those needed for normal operating); (2) system readiness (willingness of most members to live with the anxiety that comes with anticipated uncertainty that is characteristic of change); (3) minimal coupling (coordination and integration of system components); and (4) change-agent power and leadership (the ability of administrators to envision alternative organizational futures).

- *Precipitating Pressures.* Four factors that precipitate organizational culture change include (1) atypical performance; (2) pressure exerted by stakeholders; (3) organizational growth or decrement in size, membership heterogeneity, or structural complexity; and (4) real or perceived crises associated with environmental uncertainty.

- *Triggering Events.* Culture change usually begins in response to one or more triggering events. Examples include (1) environmental calamities or opportunities such as natural disasters, economic recession, innovations, or the discovery of new markets; (2) managerial crises such as a major shakeup of top administration, an inappropriate strategic decision, or a foolish expenditure; (3) external revolution such as mandated desegregation, PL101-476, or Title IX; and (4) internal revolution such as the installation of a new administrative team within the organization.

- *Cultural Visioning.* Creating a vision of a new, more preferred organizational culture is a necessary step toward that culture's formation. Leaders survey the beliefs, values, assumptions, and behaviors of the organization's existing culture. Then they seek to anticipate future conditions and create an image of the organization within that future.

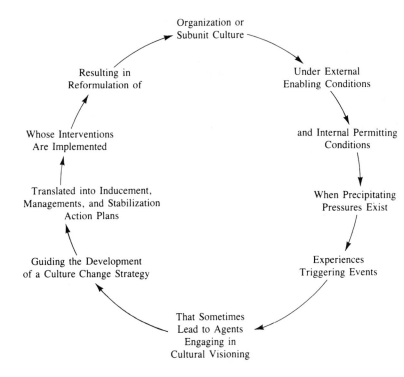

**Figure 3–3**

The Change Cycle of Organizational Culture

Source: Adapted from Peter Frost et al., *Reframing Organizational Culture* (Thousand Oaks, CA: Sage, 1991). Copyright 1991 by Sage Publications, Inc. Used by permission of the publisher.

■ *Culture Change Strategy.* Once a new cultural vision exists, an organization needs a strategy to achieve that culture. Such a strategy outlines the general process of transforming the present culture into the new one.

■ *Culture Change Action Plans.* A series of explicit action plans for the inducement, management, and stabilization of change make a change strategy known. Inducement action planning involves stimulating organizational members to a change or countering resistance to change. Management action planning involves outlining interventions and mobilizing change agents. Stabilization action planning focuses on the institutionalization of culture change, that is, establishing the existence of the new culture as an accepted fact.

■ *Implementation of Interventions.* An organization selects culture change interventions based on the ecology of a particular organization for each action-plan phase and the change agent's competencies in implementing them.

■ *Reformulation of Culture.* When implemented, the intervention plans result in a reformulated culture.

Any comprehensive program of organizational change involves an attempt to change the culture of the organization. (See Administrative Advice 3–2.)

## Effects of Organizational Culture

As noted earlier, the culture of an organization affects many administrative processes. Among these are motivation, leadership, decision making, communication, and change. Culture also affects an organization's structural processes. The selection process, evaluation system, control system, and reward system must fit with the organization's culture. In addition, culture has an influence on employee performance and organizational effectiveness. Administrators are evaluated on the basis of the results they achieve; therefore, the organization's culture is an important concept because of the results it produces.

### Views of Excellence

Thomas Peters and Robert Waterman and later Peters, in their search for excellence in America's best-run companies, found culture to be closely tied to the success of those firms.[16] From their research, they identi-

---

[16]Peters and Waterman, *In Search of Excellence*; Peters, *A Passion for Excellence.*

## Administrative Advice 3–2

### Keys to Changing an Organization's Culture

Attempting to change an organization's culture can be frustrating. Most people resist change, and when change affects the basic character of the workplace, many people will get upset. A few administrators have found some common keys to success:

- *Understand Your Old Culture First.* You can't chart a course until you know where you are.

- *Encourage Employees.* Back up those employees who are bucking the old culture and have ideas for a better one.

- *Find the Best Subculture in Your Organization.* Hold it up as an example from which others can learn.

- *Don't Attack the Culture Head On.* Help employees find their own new ways to accomplish their tasks, and a better culture will follow.

- *Allow Time.* Figure on several years for significant, organizationwide improvement.

- *Live the Culture You Want.* As always, actions speak louder than words.

Source: Adapted from Brian Dumaine, "Creating a New Culture," *Fortune,* 121 (1990): 127–131. © 1990, The Time Inc. Magazine Company. Used by permission.

---

fied the following attributes that characterize excellent companies:

- *A Bias Toward Action.* The company continually does, experiments, and tries. An example in a school setting might be implementing strategic planning to guide a school district's mission and measure its results.

- *Close to the Customer.* The company looks to the customer for direction in the formation of new products, quality, and service. School districts that remain tuned-in to their clients' (students') needs while maintaining a close professional relationship with parents remain "close to the customer." Different types of family and community involvement were found to distinguish high-achieving schools from low-achieving schools.[17]

- *Autonomy and Entrepreneurship.* The company values and fosters risk taking and innovation. School districts that encourage innovation and risk taking, while permitting some failure, have a philosophy of "autonomy and entrepreneurship." Such systems can be characterized as dynamic in that they are constantly attempting new ways of accomplishing school district objectives.

- *Productivity Through People.* The company demonstrates a belief in the organization's employees through shared decision making and encouragement of new ideas. This belief is reflected in the language used by the company. The company views the employee as extended family, and there is an absence of rigidity of command. Schools that manifest high levels of trust in subordinates, use participatory decision making, listen to and use members' ideas, and show concern for the welfare of all employees are practicing "productivity through people."

- *Hands-On, Value-Driven Effort.* The company pays explicit attention to cultural values and devotes substantial effort to promoting and clarifying core values to employees. Strong-culture schools that emphasize high achievement levels of students and high performance and growth of faculty are practicing "hands-on, value-driven effort."

- *"Sticking to the Knitting."* The company stays in businesses they know how to run. This success attribute can be applied to public schools. The public has thrust upon educators the myth that schools can correct all of society's ills: the breakdown of the family, crime, racial strife, poverty, unemployment, drug abuse, child abuse, teenage pregnancy, and the like. It may be more accurate to say that more responsibility has been thrust upon the schools than

[17]Joyce L. Epstein, *School, Family, and Community Partnerships: Preparing Educators and Improving Schools* (Boulder, CO: Westview Press, 2001).

they should accept; more results have been expected than they could possibly produce; and in too many cases, schools have assumed more than they should.[18] Put another way, schools have been programmed for failure, just as companies have failed who have expanded beyond their ability to compete in the marketplace.

■ *Simple Form, Lean Staff.* The company does not use complex matrix structures, and keeps corporate staffs small. In the educational setting, this approach resembles somewhat the concept of site-based management.[19]

■ *Simultaneous Loose-Tight Properties.* The company exhibits both tight and loose couplings.[20] It is tight about cultural values and loose or decentralized about autonomy, providing individuals throughout the organization room to perform. By following corporate world goals, schools can promote strong cultural values while providing people with the opportunity to grow and the flexibility to function within the school district's belief system.

Warren Bennis and Burt Nanus found that many organizations are overmanaged and underled. They ascertain that the leader should be concerned with the organization's basic purpose and general direction.[21] Time should be spent on doing the right thing: creating new ideas, new policies, and new methodologies. From the ninety leaders interviewed, they found the following leadership strategies: (1) attention through vision, (2) meaning through communication, (3) trust through positioning, and (4) deployment of self through positive self-regard and positive thinking. In short, effective leaders communicate their vision for the company and embody this vision by being reliable, persistent, relentless, and dedicated to the implementation of the vision. Effective leaders know their strengths and weaknesses. They build on their strengths and compensate for their

weaknesses. Their focus is on success. The word *failure* is rarely used; unsuccessful attempts are considered learning experiences.

## Theory Z

William Ouchi examined high-producing companies in order to discover what, if anything, these firms had in common. To explain the success of these companies, Ouchi developed **Theory Z**.[22] Theory Z is an extension of McGregor's Theory X and Theory Y concepts (see Chapter 2). The principal difference is that McGregor's Theory X and Theory Y formulation is an attempt to distinguish between the personal leadership styles of an individual supervisor, whereas Theory Z is concerned with the "culture of the whole organization." That is, Theory Z is not concerned with the attitudes or behavior patterns of an individual supervisor but rather with the difference the organizational culture makes in the way the whole organization is put together and managed. Theory Z culture involves long-term employment, consensual decision making, individual responsibility, slow evaluation and promotion, an informal control system with explicit measures of performance, moderately specialized career paths, and extensive commitment to all aspects of the employee's life, including family.[23]

The features of Theory Z applied to schools include trust, subtlety, and intimacy; shared control and decision making; training in planning, organizational processes, budgeting systems, and interpersonal skills; motivation through self-interest; rewards over the long run; and the importance of high-quality education.[24] Figure 3–4 depicts these concepts.

**Trust, Subtlety, and Intimacy** According to Ouchi, no institution can exist without trust, subtlety, and intimacy. Trust in a school can only exist among people who understand that their objectives are compatible in the long run. The concept is based on the assumption that if you don't understand what someone else does, if you don't understand their language, their technology, and their problems, then you can't possibly trust them.

[18]Thelbert L. Drake and William H. Roe, *The Principalship*, 6th ed. (Upper Saddle River, NJ: Merrill/Prentice Hall, 2003).

[19]Joseph Murphy and Amanda Datnow, *Leadership Lessons from Comprehensive School Reforms* (Thousand Oaks, CA: Corwin Press, 2002).

[20]Karl E. Weick, "Educational Organizations as Loosely Coupled Systems," *Administrative Science Quarterly,* 21 (1976): 1–19.

[21]Warren Bennis and Burt Nanus, *Leaders: The Strategies for Taking Charge* (New York: HarperCollins, 2007).

[22]William G. Ouchi, *Theory Z: How American Business Can Meet the Japanese Challenge* (New York: Avon Books, 1993).

[23]Ibid.

[24]William Ouchi, "Theory Z and the Schools," *School Administrator,* 39 (1982): 12–19.

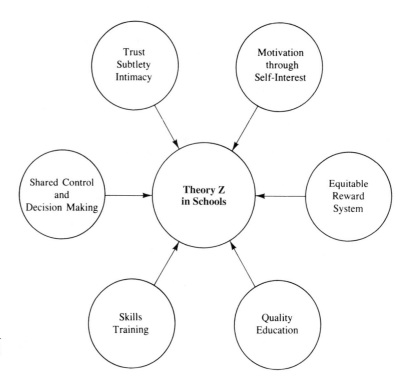

**Figure 3–4**

Major Components of Theory Z as Applied
to Schools

Trust can be developed only through intimate, professional experience with someone else, including close interpersonal relations between students and students, teachers and students, teachers and teachers, administrators and teachers, and administrators and students.

**Shared Control and Decision Making**   School administrators must spend adequate time discussing with students, teachers, parents, and the community the objectives of the schools and how the schools are run. School leaders must understand the incentive system available to personnel in their careers and help them to rationalize these incentives so that they can trust them. Then, administrators can invite subordinates to share control, which provides stakeholders with input into decisions that will affect the way they perform their responsibilities.

**Training**   The concept of *quality circles,* also called learning teams or cooperative learning groups, is advocated. Quality circles consist of small groups of employees who meet regularly to discuss the way they do their jobs and to recommend changes. The purpose is to yield a group-based suggestion system for solving problems and improving the quality of the system.[25] This

requires a period of training to increase participation, consensus in decisions, and shared control. The training is directed toward getting to know the organization: its objectives, problems, and overall resources. Specifically, teachers and other nonadministrative personnel are trained in planning, organizational processes (motivation, leadership, decision making, communication, and change), the system's budgetary process, group dynamics, and many of the school administrator's day-to-day activities to which teachers are rarely exposed. The training is designed to create a culture that lends itself to openness, trust, and employee involvement.

**Motivation Through Self-Interest**   Ouchi believes that there is only one form of interest—self-interest. If you cannot create a setting in which people are permitted to naturally do what seems desirable to them—to satisfy their self-interest—then you are always fighting, constraining, holding back, and can never have high commitment nor high productivity. In the Theory Z organization, because people have participated in shaping the goals and objectives of the system, you can say to people, "Do what comes naturally; do what you prefer to do, because we have agreed that those things you choose to do are simultaneously good for the institution."[26]

---

[25]John J. Bonstingl, *Schools of Quality* (Thousand Oaks, CA: Corwin Press, 2001).

[26]Ouchi, "Theory Z and the Schools," p. 14.

**Rewards** An organizational memory is essential. Some key person must remember who has gone the extra mile, who is committed, and who has put in extra time; this person must ensure that those efforts are recognized and rewarded. According to Ouchi, if there is that kind of organizational memory, then people will have confidence that as long as they do what is right, there will be equity in the end. They therefore lose whatever incentives they might have to be selfish, narrow-minded, or short-sighted. What does Ouchi say about the lockstep salary schedules prevalent in most school districts? Ouchi responds by saying that it is necessary that schools disassemble the currently bureaucratic approach to evaluation, promotion, and pay.

**Importance of High-Quality Education** One of the greatest assets any country has in developing its social health and its economic health is its school systems. High-quality education leads to an educated workforce, thereby increasing economic capital in the improved country. An enlightened citizenry is important to the welfare of a nation.

## A Typology of Organizational Culture

Carl Steinhoff and Robert Owens developed a framework that suggests four distinctive **culture phenotypes** likely to be found in public schools.[27] These phenotypes are clearly describable and differentiated from one another in terms of the metaphorical language elicited from school participants.

Unlike most students of organizational culture, the researchers examined the culture of schools by survey methods rather than by using the more typical ethnographic approach. To support this methodology, Owens found in conducting a long-term ethnographic study of a senior high school that a culture assessment instrument could have been valuable in that study.[28]

Consistent with survey research methods, the researchers drew upon the literature to develop a theory of organizational culture.[29] As discussed earlier, the theory posits that organizational culture is the *root metaphor* of an organization.[30] That is, "the culture of an organization does not merely describe what an organization is like, it describes the essence of the organization itself."[31] With this concept as an organizer, the researchers developed a taxonomic structure of organizational culture. The resulting taxonomy has six interlocking dimensions that define the culture of a school: (1) the history of the organization; (2) values and beliefs of the organization; (3) myths and stories that explain the organization; (4) cultural norms of the organization; (5) traditions, rituals, and ceremonies characteristic of the organization; and (6) heroes and heroines of the organization.

Based on the taxonomy of organizational culture, Steinhoff and Owens constructed the Organizational Culture Assessment Inventory (OCAI) that, when taken as a whole, represents the consensual press, that is, the root metaphor perceived by organizational participants. "Culture as root metaphor promotes a view of organizations as expressive forms, manifestations of human consciousness."[32] These metaphors serve to illuminate the perceptual reality of the respondents and therefore serve as the basis on which they set goals, make commitments, and execute plans.[33]

**School Culture Phenotypes** After several revisions of the initial form of the OCAI, the final version was validated in pilot studies of teachers, principals, and central office administrators in forty-seven elementary and secondary schools. The responses were sorted on the basis of school metaphor to establish metaphorical themes prevalent among the three groups. Data analysis produced four distinctive phenotypes of school culture, each of which can be described in terms of its metaphorical content.[34]

---

[27]Carl R. Steinhoff and Robert G. Owens, "The Organizational Culture Assessment Inventory: A Metaphorical Analysis in Educational Settings," *Journal of Educational Administration*, 27 (1989): 17–23.

[28]Robert G. Owens, "The Leadership of Educational Clans," in L. T. Sheive and M. B. Schoenheit (eds.), *Leadership: Examining the Elusive* (Alexandria, VA: Association for Supervision and Curriculum Development, 1987).

[29]Steinhoff and Owens, "The Organizational Culture Assessment Inventory."

[30]Linda Smircich, "Concepts of Culture and Organizational Analysis," *Administrative Science Quarterly*, 28 (1983): 339–358.

[31]Steinhoff and Owens, "The Organizational Culture Assessment Inventory," p. 18.

[32]Smircich, "Concepts of Culture and Organizational Analysis," p. 347.

[33]Gareth Morgan, *Images of Organization* (Thousand Oaks, CA: Sage, 2007).

[34]To preserve the metaphorical content used to describe the four culture phenotypes, we have quoted liberally from Steinhoff and Owens, "The Organizational Culture Assessment Inventory."

## ■ Exemplary Educational Administrators in Action

**RICHARD (RICK) EARL BERRY** Superintendent, Cypress-Fairbanks Independent School District, Houston, Texas.

**Previous Positions:** Superintendent, Interim Superintendent, Deputy Superintendent, Assistant Superintendent, Principal, Assistant Principal, and Counselor, Arlington Independent School District, Texas; Business Teacher, Coach, and Bus Driver, Roscoe Independent School District, Texas.

**Latest Degree and Affiliation:** Postgraduate certification, Educational Administration, East Texas State University.

**Number One Influence on Career:** The special people in my life—my wife and son, my parents, my wife's parents, colleagues and many friends—have influenced my career greatly. Each person in his or her own way has made significant contributions to my philosophy and my leadership style.

**Number One Achievement:** We have opened 17 new schools while losing millions of dollars in state funding, with only a minimal increase in taxes. Simultaneously, we built community support to pass three bond elections totaling $811,405,500. Cy-Fair is the largest district in Texas to achieve a "Recognized" rating four years in a row. Over 4,000 new students come into our district every year. These are phenomenal accomplishments.

**Number One Regret:** After being in one district for 21 years, moving up through the ranks to become superintendent and establishing many close friendships, a great opportunity came for my second superintendency. The end result of the move was positive for every member of my family, but the transition was very difficult for our son, who was just starting high school.

**Favorite Education-Related Book or Text:** *Leadership by the Book* by Ken Blanchard and *Good to Great* by Jim Collins.

**Additional Interests:** I enjoy a variety of activities including traveling, reading, listening to all kinds of music, church and community functions, exercising and spending time with my family. We often do these activities together.

**Leadership Style:** My leadership reflects several key components. First, I promote teamwork and building positive relationships not only with my staff, but with students and the community that we serve. Second, I place a strong focus on the success of all students, and all students *know* without a single doubt that their teachers and administrators want and expect their success. Third, to ensure continuous improvement and learning, I attend conferences, workshops, and regional meetings to keep abreast of current trends. I also encourage others to be active in professional organizations.

**Professional Vision:** My vision for CFISD is directly focused on the idea that all children will learn given the leadership, instruction, and care that they need. We have developed guidelines, called "The Portrait of a Cy-Fair Graduate," "The Portrait of a Cy-Fair Teacher," and "The Portrait of a Cy-Fair Administrator." To accomplish this is not only my vision; it is my expectation.

**Words of Advice:** The advice that I would like to share with others includes several ideas that have served me well:

- Practice the golden rule.
- Seek out mentors.
- Keep balance in your life.
- Build trusting relationships with those around you.
- Surround yourself with intelligent, talented, creative, and caring people.
- Work hard and work smart.
- Be a problem solver, but before there is a problem, plan ahead.
- Strive not to make permanent enemies.

*Family Culture* This school can be described using metaphors such as family, home, or team. The principal in this school can be described as a *parent* (strong or weak), *nurturer, friend, sibling,* or *coach*. In this school, "concern for each other is important as well as having a commitment to students above and beyond the call of duty." Everyone should be willing to be a part of the family and pull their own weight. The school as family then is nurturent and friendly, often cooperative and protective, to which members are alternately submissive and rebellious—leaning on the shoulders, or bosom, of someone who has their best interests at heart.

*Machine Culture*   This school can be described using the metaphor of the machine. Metaphors for the school include *well-oiled machines, political machines, beehives of activity,* or *rusty machines.* Metaphors for the principal range from *workaholic, Paul Bunyan,* and *The General* to *Charlie Brown* and the *slug.* The school as machine then is viewed purely in instrumental terms. The driving force appears to come from the structure of the organization itself, and administrators are described in terms of their varying ability to provide maintenance inputs. The social structure of these schools is tightly woven; however, unlike those of the family culture, its mission is protection rather than warmth. The school is a machine teachers *use* to accomplish work.

*Cabaret Culture*   Metaphors such as a *circus,* a *Broadway show,* a *banquet,* or a *well-choreographed ballet* performed by well-appreciated *artists* describe this school. The principal is seen as a *master of ceremonies,* a *tightrope walker,* and a *ring master.* Teachers in these schools experience many of the same group-binding social activities as do their colleagues in the family culture school. The essential difference is that, in this culture, relationships center on performances and the reactions of the audience. There is great pride in the artistic and intellectual quality of one's teaching, which is carried out under the watchful eye of the maestro. At the cabaret the show must go on!

*"Little Shop of Horrors" Culture*   This school can be described as unpredictable, tension-filled *nightmares* having the characteristics of a war zone or revolution. "One never knows whose head will roll next." Teachers report their schools as *closed boxes* or *prisons.* The principal is a *self-cleaning statue* ready to offer up a sacrifice if it will maintain his position. In general, administrators in this school are seen as individuals whose main function is to keep things smoothed over. Others have a Napoleon complex that promotes dominance and control or Jekyll-Hyde personalities that promote a *walking-on-eggs* style of adaptive behavior among faculty. Unlike the family and cabaret cultures, teachers in this school lead isolated lives; there is little social activity. For example, written requests are often needed to hold any social activity — even for special occasions like Thanksgiving. One is expected to conform and to smile when appropriate. Verbal abuse among faculty is common, and closeness seems to be melting away. This culture is cold, hostile, and paranoid. "Almost anything can get you — and it often does."

Steinhoff and Owens's school culture phenotypes resemble somewhat the cultures delineated by Peters and Waterman[35] and the human resource–orientation typology suggested by Nirmal Sethia and Mary Ann Von Glinow.[36] With increasing emphasis in the literature for school administrators to become managers of culture, typologies such as these can be useful in examining the culture of school organizations. Moreover, Steinhoff and Owens's OCAI appears to be a valid and reliable device to provide researchers and practitioners with a rich source of imagery not found in conventional instruments designed to measure organizational environments.

## Organizational Climate

**Organizational climate** is the total environmental quality within an organization. It may refer to the environment within a school department, a school building, or a school district. Organizational climate can be expressed by such adjectives as *open, bustling, warm, easygoing, informal, cold, impersonal, hostile, rigid,* and *closed.*

Theorists refer to organizational culture and climate as overlapping concepts.[37] Organizational culture has its roots in sociology and anthropology, whereas organizational climate is rooted in psychology. Recent attention to school effectiveness and organizational cultures has reemphasized the importance of organizational climate. As noted earlier, a great deal has been written about organizational culture in the popular literature, but our research-based knowledge of the concept is very limited. In contrast, organizational climate has been studied with a multitude of variables, methodologies, theories, and models, resulting in a substantial body of research.[38] Studies of organizational climate have been shown to contain elements of leadership, motivation, and job satisfaction. For example, in one

---

[35] Peters and Waterman, *In Search of Excellence.*

[36] Nirmal K. Sethia and Mary Ann Von Glinow, "Arriving at Four Cultures by Managing the Reward System," in R. Kilmann et al. (eds.), *Gaining Control of the Corporate Culture* (San Francisco: Jossey-Bass, 1985), pp. 400–420.

[37] John B. Miner, *Organizational Behavior 3: Historical Origins, Theoretical Foundations, and the Future* (New York: M. E. Sharpe, 2006).

[38] Carolyn S. Anderson, "The Search for School Climate: A Review of the Research," *Review of Educational Research,* 52 (1982), pp. 368–420.

comprehensive review of organizational climate studies, these elements have been linked with climate.[39]

We discuss four well-known constructs for conceptualizing organizational climate in schools: Halpin and Croft's concept of open and closed climates; Hoy and Tarter's organizational health construct; NASSP's Comprehensive Assessment of School Environments; and Willower, Eidell, and Hoy's concepts of pupil control ideology.

## Open and Closed Climates

Andrew Halpin and Don Croft postulate a conceptual continuum that extends from **open** to **closed climates**. Their observations of how schools differ provided the major impetus for their research into organizational climate.[40] Halpin notes: "Anyone who visits more than a few schools notes quickly how schools differ from each other in their 'feel.'" And as one moves from school to school, "one finds that each appears to have a 'personality' that we describe here as the 'organizational climate' of the school. Analogously, personality is to the individual what organizational climate is to the organization."[41]

The instrument that Halpin and Croft constructed is the Organizational Climate Description Questionnaire (OCDQ). It contains sixty-four Likert-type items that are assigned to eight subtests delineated by factor-analytic methods. Four subtests pertain primarily to characteristics of the group, as a group, and the other four to characteristics of the principal as a leader. From the scores of these eight subtests, they then constructed for each school a profile, which determines the relative position of the school on the open-to-closed continuum.[42] Table 3–1 presents the eight subtests together with the open-to-closed intensity scale.

As Table 3–1 shows, the open-climate school is low in disengagement, low in hindrance, very high in esprit, high in intimacy, low in aloofness, low in production emphasis, very high in thrust, and high in considera-

tion. The closed-climate school is depicted as very high in disengagement, high in hindrance, very low in esprit, high in intimacy, high in aloofness, high in production emphasis, low in thrust, and low in consideration.

Using this information, we can sketch a behavioral picture of each climate. Composites for the two extremes of the climate continuum, the open and closed climates, are described next.

**Open Climate** An energetic, lively organization that is moving toward its goals and that provides satisfaction for group members' social needs describes the open climate. Leadership acts emerge easily and appropriately from both the group and the leader. Members are preoccupied disproportionately with neither task-achievement nor social-needs satisfaction; satisfaction on both counts seems to be obtained easily and almost effortlessly. The main characteristic of this climate is the "authenticity" of the behavior that occurs among all members.

**Closed Climate** A high degree of apathy on the part of all members of the organization characterizes the closed climate. The organization is not "moving"; esprit is low because group members secure neither social-needs satisfaction nor task-achievement satisfaction. Members' behavior can be construed as inauthentic; indeed, the organization seems to be stagnant.

The OCDQ has had tremendous heuristic value and has promoted a broad-based interest in school climate within elementary and secondary schools.[43] Two revised versions of the OCDQ were developed recently: one for elementary schools—the OCDQ–RE—and one for secondary schools—the OCDQ–RS.[44]

The overwhelming majority of studies on school climate focus on adults in the form of teachers and principal-teacher relations. In fact, school climate has rarely been studied in relation to its effect on student achievement.[45] In recent years, the emphasis in climate has shifted from a management orientation to a focus on

[39]Wayne K. Hoy and Cecil G. Miskel, *Educational Administration: Theory, Research, and Practice*, 7th ed. (Boston: McGraw-Hill, 2005).

[40]Andrew W. Halpin and Don B. Croft, *The Organizational Climate of Schools* (Chicago: University of Chicago Press, 1963).

[41]Andrew W. Halpin, *Theory and Research in Administration* (New York: Macmillan, 1966), p. 131.

[42]Halpin and Croft, *The Organizational Climate of Schools.*

[43]Anderson, "The Search for School Climate: A Review of the Research."

[44]Wayne K. Hoy and Sharon I. Clover, "Elementary School Climate: A Revision of the OCDQ," *Educational Administration Quarterly,* 22 (1986): 93–110; Robert B. Kottkamp, John A. Mulhern, and Wayne K. Hoy, "Secondary School Climate: A Revision of the OCDQ," *Educational Administration Quarterly,* 23 (1987): 31–48.

[45]Stephen K. Miller, "School Climate," National Association of Secondary School Principals, Reston, VA, 2003.

## Table 3–1   The OCDQ Subtests

| Characteristics | Intensity Scale[a] | |
|---|---|---|
| | Open | Closed |
| **Teacher's Behavior** | | |
| *Disengagement* indicates that teachers do not work well together. They pull in different directions with respect to the task; they gripe and bicker among themselves. | − | ++ |
| *Hindrance* refers to teachers' feelings that the principal burdens them with routine duties, committee demands, and other requirements, which teachers construe as unnecessary busywork. | − | + |
| *Esprit* refers to morale. Teachers feel that their social needs are being satisfied while enjoying a sense of accomplishment in their job. | ++ | −− |
| *Intimacy* refers to teachers' enjoyment of friendly social relations with each other. | + | + |
| **Principal's Behavior** | | |
| *Aloofness* refers to formal and impersonal principal behavior; the principal goes by the book and maintains social distance from the teachers. | − | + |
| *Production emphasis* refers to behavior that is characterized by close supervision of the staff. The principal is highly directive and task oriented. | − | + |
| *Thrust* refers to behavior in which an attempt to "move the school" is made through the example that the principal sets for teachers. | ++ | − |
| *Consideration* refers to behavior that is characterized by an inclination to treat teachers "humanly," to try to do a little something extra for them in human terms. | + | − |

[a]++ Very high emphasis; + high emphasis; − low emphasis; −− very low emphasis.

Source: Adapted from Andrew W. Halpin, *Theory and Research in Administration* (New York: Macmillan, 1966), pp. 150–151.

students.[46] The three school climate constructs, which we now discuss, are examples of avenues of research in this tradition.

## Healthy and Sick Schools

Another instrument to assess the climate of the school is the Organizational Health Inventory (OHI) developed by Wayne Hoy and John Tarter.[47] Whereas the OCDQ examines the openness/closedness of teacher-teacher and principal-teacher interactions, the OHI describes the health of the interpersonal relations in schools among students, teachers, administrators, and community members.

Hoy and Tarter conceptualize organizational health at three levels: institutional, administrative, and teacher. The institutional level connects the school with its environment. The administrative level controls the internal managerial function of the organization. The teacher level is concerned with the teaching and learning process. A healthy school is one that keeps the institutional, administrative, and teacher levels in harmony, meets functional needs and successfully copes with disruptive external forces, and directs its energies toward school goals.

Three versions of the instrument were developed: one for elementary schools (the OHI–E), one for middle schools (the OHI–M), and one for secondary schools (the OHI–S). The elementary, middle, and secondary school versions of the OHI contain five, six,

---

[46]Thomas J. Sergiovanni and Robert J. Starratt, *Supervision: A Redefinition*, 8th ed. (New York: McGraw-Hill, 2006).

[47]Wayne K. Hoy and C. John Tarter, *The Road to Open and Healthy Schools: A Handbook for Change, Elementary and Middle School Edition* (Thousand Oaks, CA: Corwin Press, 1997); *The Road to Open and Healthy Schools: A Handbook for Change, Middle and Secondary School Edition* (Thousand Oaks, CA: Corwin Press, 1997).

---

## Table 3–2　The OHI–M Subtests

### Characteristics

**Institutional Level**

*Institutional integrity* is the degree to which the school can cope with its environment in a way that maintains the educational integrity of its programs. Teachers are protected from unreasonable community and parental demands.

**Administrative Level**

*Collegial leadership* is principal behavior that is friendly, supportive, open, and guided by norms of equality. At the same time, the principal sets the tone for high performance by letting people know what is expected of them.

*Principal influence* is the principal's ability to influence the actions of superiors. Influential principals are persuasive with superiors, get additional consideration, and proceed relatively unimpeded by the hierarchy.

*Resource support* is the extent to which classroom supplies and instructional materials are readily available; in fact, even extra materials are supplied if requested.

**Teacher Level**

*Teacher affiliation* is a sense of friendliness and strong affiliation with the school. Teachers feel good about each other, their job, and their students. They are committed to both their students and their colleagues and accomplish their jobs with enthusiasm.

*Academic emphasis* is the extent to which the school is driven by a quest for academic excellence. High but achievable academic goals are set for students, the learning environment is orderly and serious, teachers believe in their students' ability to achieve, and students work hard and respect those who do well academically.

---

Source: Adapted from Wayne K. Hoy and C. John Tarter, *The Road to Open and Healthy Schools: A Handbook for Change, Elementary and Middle School Edition* (Thousand Oaks, CA: Corwin Press, 1997), pp. 58–59.

---

and seven subtests and thirty-seven, forty-five, and forty-four items, respectively, in a four-point, Likert-type format.[48] The subtests of the OHI–M are summarized in Table 3–2. Brief descriptions of the healthy and sick school follow.[49]

**Healthy School**　A *healthy school* is characterized by student, teacher, and principal behavior that is harmonious and works toward instructional success. Teachers like their colleagues, their school, their job, and their students (high teacher affiliation), and they are driven by a quest for academic excellence. Teachers believe in themselves and their students; consequently, they set high but achievable goals. The learning environment is serious and orderly, and students work hard and respect others who do well academically (high academic emphasis). Principal behavior is also healthy—that is, friendly, open, egalitarian, and supportive. Such principals expect the best from teachers (high collegial leadership). Principals get teachers the resources they need to do the job (high resource support) and are also influential with superiors (high principal influence); they go to bat for their teachers. Finally, a healthy school has

high institutional integrity; teachers are protected from unreasonable and hostile outside forces.

**Sick School**　A *sick school* is vulnerable to destructive outside forces. Teachers and administrators are bombarded by unreasonable parental demands, and the school is buffeted by the whims of the public (low institutional integrity). The school lacks an effective principal. The principal provides little direction or structure, exhibits scant encouragement for teachers (low collegial leadership), and has negligible clout with superiors (low influence). Teachers don't like their colleagues or their jobs. They act aloof, suspicious, and defensive (low teacher affiliation). Instructional materials, supplies, and supplementary materials are not available when needed (low resource support). Finally, there is minimal press for academic excellence. Neither teachers nor students take academic life seriously; in fact, academically oriented students are ridiculed by their peers and viewed by their teachers as threats (low academic emphasis).

### Comprehensive Assessment of School Environments (CASE)

The National Association of Secondary School Principals (NASSP) named a task force to investigate the current literature and measures of school climate. Af-

---

[48] Ibid.

[49] Wayne K. Hoy and C. John Tarter, *The Road to Open and Healthy Schools: A Handbook for Change, Elementary and Middle School Edition* (Thousand Oaks, CA: Corwin Press, 1997).

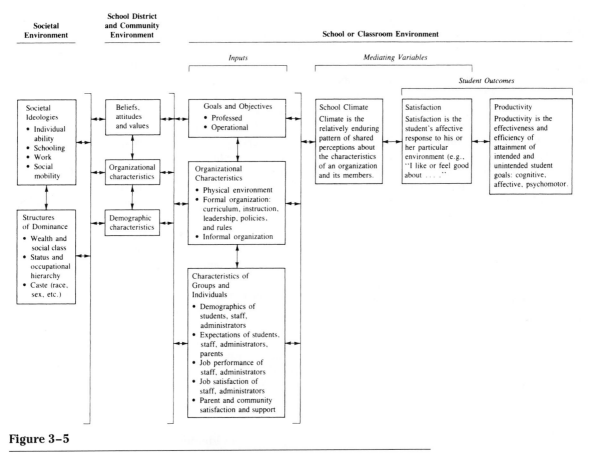

**Figure 3–5**

An Interactive Model of the School Environment

Source: James W. Keefe and Eugene R. Howard, "Redesigning Schools for the New Century: A Systems Approach," NASSP, 1997. Used by permission.

ter an extensive review of the literature, the task force found that most existing definitions of climate were unclear, that many climate studies were based on one stakeholder group (usually teachers), that climate and satisfaction measures were frequently confused, and that measures with good psychometric properties were scarce and rarely used by practitioners.

The task force formulated a general model depicting the contextual, input, mediating, and outcome variables of school environments (see Figure 3–5). Assumptions accepted in the formulation of the model were as follows:

■ Climate and satisfaction are distinct but related concepts.

■ Climate does not define effectiveness; it only predicts it.

■ Student outcomes (cognitive, affective, and psychomotor) and efficiency data (cost) are the most appropriate measures of school effectiveness.[50]

The model of the school environment developed by the NASSP task force goes beyond a simple consideration of school climate to encompass a full range of inputs and outputs to the process of school improvement. As Figure 3–5 shows, perceptions of climate held by stakeholder groups (students, teachers, parents) are mediating variables—influencing factors—not outcome mea-sures. Teacher and parent satisfaction are input variables. Student satisfaction is both a mediating variable and an outcome measure; it both influences school success and corroborates it.

---

[50]Miller, "School Climate."

**The Instruments** The Comprehensive Assessment of School Environments (CASE) battery consists of four survey instruments: the NASSP School Climate Survey, which is designed to elicit responses from all major stakeholder groups (students, teachers, parents), and three separate NASSP Satisfaction Surveys, one for each of the three major stakeholder groups.

The NASSP survey instruments were validated in national pilot and normative studies of 1500 teachers, 14,600 students, and 4400 parents. Each survey has eight to ten subscales touching on all important aspects of the school environment. Computer scoring programs provide separate climate and satisfaction profiles for each school.[51]

The NASSP School Climate Survey collects and measures data about perceptions on the following subscales:

- *Teacher-student relationships:* The quality of the interpersonal and professional relationships between teachers and students.

- *Security and maintenance:* The quality of maintenance and the degree of security people feel at the school.

- *Administration:* The degree to which school administrators are effective in communicating with different role groups and in setting high performance expectations for teachers and students.

- *Student academic orientation:* Student attention to task and concern for achievement at school.

- *Student behavioral values:* Student self-discipline and tolerance for others.

- *Guidance:* The quality of academic and career guidance and personal counseling services available to students.

- *Student-peer relationships:* Students' care and respect for one another and their mutual cooperation.

- *Parent and community school relationships:* The amount and quality of involvement in the school of parents and other community members.

- *Instructional management:* The efficiency and effectiveness of teacher classroom organization and use of classroom time.

- *Student activities:* Opportunities for and actual participation of students in school-sponsored activities.

The NASSP survey instruments have been developed as measures within a CASE battery based on the task-force model (see Figure 3–5). The instruments can be used singly or in any combination, but the task force encourages their use within the context of the entire model. The principal aim of the measures and procedures of the CASE model is to foster school improvement. The CASE data may also be useful in preparing school reports required by state or regional accrediting agencies. Outcomes-based evaluation for school accreditation is gaining support and acceptance from several accrediting bodies.[52] The CASE battery permits the organization and monitoring of outcomes-based data.

The CASE organizational climate variables imply that most schools are not as effective as they might be. Because effectiveness is a continuum, schools can always improve their performance. Unfortunately, schools are not easy to change. Schools that somehow manage to produce achievement levels higher than that predicted by the socioeconomic composition of the school and community are by definition exceptions. If becoming an effective school were easy, such schools would be the rule rather than the atypical extreme. Nevertheless, there are a number of other identifiable characteristics that can be used to measure school quality. (See Administrative Advice 3–3.)

### Pupil Control Ideology

Another method of conceptualizing organizational climate is in terms of the attitudes toward students and the behavior faculty use to control them. William Glasser has underscored the saliency of pupil control in the organizational life of public schools.[53] Moreover, according to nearly two decades of annual Gallup polls, pupil control remains a key concern of teachers, administrators, and citizens. In fact, a teacher's inability to control students effectively is a major source of dissatisfaction for many of today's teachers.

The importance of pupil control in schools is not surprising. Schools are people-developing or people-changing institutions. The objective of the school as a social institution is to achieve major changes in the child. These changes are not restricted to cognitive behavior (learning) but include a wide range of social, emotional, physical, and, in some cases, moral

---

[51]NASSP Task Force, *Comprehensive Assessment of School Environments: Examiner's Manual* (Reston, VA: National Association of Secondary School Principals, 1987).

[52]Ibid.

[53]William Glasser, *The Quality School: Managing Students Without Coercion,* 2nd ed. (New York: HarperCollins, 1992).

## Administrative Advice 3–3

### Characteristics to Measure School Quality

The quality of a school is the result of a number of factors, many of which are listed here. Any school possessing a majority of these characteristics can be called a high-quality school.

- *Heterogeneous Grouping.* Schools have ended tracking and have reduced ability grouping.

- *Cooperative Learning.* Students engage in far less competitive learning. In heterogeneous groups, they work democratically and collaboratively.

- *High Expectations for All.* The school adopts the philosophy that all students, if motivated and provided adequate opportunities, can learn important, challenging, and interesting content. Important knowledge is no longer for an elite. It is for all students, regardless of their social circumstances or career aspirations.

- *Responsiveness to Student Diversity.* Educators view the increasing cultural, linguistic, and socio-economic diversity of the student population as an opportunity as well as a challenge. Curriculum content and pedagogical approaches are built on and are respectful of the diversity.

- *Emphasis on Active Learning.* Students spend far less time passively receiving knowledge. They spend far more time — sometimes individually, often in groups — doing, experimenting, and discovering knowledge and understanding for themselves.

- *Essential Curriculum.* Schools select the most important concepts and skills to emphasize, so that they can concentrate on the quality of understanding rather than on the quantity of information presented. Stu-

dents acquire the tools to add to their knowledge independently.

- *Authentic Assessment.* The type of assessment employed is determined by the learning being measured. This means there will be increased use of performance as a means of assessment. Educators as well as students are held accountable for what students can do instead of relying solely on standardized test results.

- *Technology as a Tool.* Computers, videodiscs, satellite TV, and other state-of-the-art technologies are viewed as resources to enhance learning, not as symbols of excellence or innovation.

- *Time as a Learning Resource.* School time is organized around learning, instead of the other way around. Teacher and administrator needs are secondary to the needs of learners. The typical fifty-minute, seven-period day may need to be restructured to fit the curricula content.

- *Diverse Pedagogy.* Educators employ more diverse and more balanced kinds of teaching and learning experiences to implement curricula. This will require new kinds of teacher training and staff development for teachers and administrators.

Source: Adapted from Fred C. Lunenburg, "The Urban Superintendent's Role in School Reform," *Education and Urban Society*, 25 (1992): 37–38. Used by permission.

---

behavior.[54] Organizations that achieve or attempt to achieve the most thoroughgoing change are performing functions crucial to the maintenance of social control.

Furthermore, schools accept as conscripted clients all those who legally must attend. That is, neither the organization (school) nor the client (student) exercises choice concerning participation in the relationship.[55]

The mandatory nature of the pupil's participation suggests that schools are dealing with clients whose motivations and desires for the school's services cannot be assumed. It seems reasonable that pupil control would be a major concern.

Evidence to support the prominence of pupil control in schools is provided by a field study of a junior high school in which the researchers indicated that pupil control was the "integrative theme" that pervaded the culture of the school.[56] This study eventually led to the development of the construct of **pupil control ideology**

---

[54]Charles E. Bidwell, "The School as a Formal Organization," in J. G. March (ed.), *Handbook of Organizations* (Chicago: Rand McNally, 1965), pp. 972–1022.

[55]Richard O. Carlson, "Environmental Constraints and Organizational Consequences: The Public School and Its Clients," in D. E. Griffiths (ed.), *Behavioral Science and Educational Administration* (Chicago: University of Chicago Press, 1964), pp. 262–276.

[56]Donald Willower and Ronald Jones, "Control in an Educational Organization," in J. Raths, J. Pancella, and J. Van Ness (eds.), *Studying Teaching* (Englewood Cliffs, NJ: Prentice Hall, 1967), pp. 424–428.

as a school climate descriptor. The conceptualization of pupil control and the research initiated by Donald Willower, Terry Eidell, and Wayne Hoy at Pennsylvania State University have permitted some of the first steps toward a systematic analysis of pupil control in the school.[57]

Willower and his colleagues postulate pupil control along a humanistic to custodial continuum. These terms refer to contrasting types of individual ideology and the types of school organization that they seek to rationalize and justify. Prototypes of humanistic and custodial schools are presented next.[58]

**The Humanistic School**  The model for humanistic control orientation is an educational community in which students learn through cooperative interaction and experience. In this model, learning and behavior are viewed in psychological and sociological terms rather than moralistic ones. Learning is viewed as an engagement in worthwhile activity rather than the passive absorption of facts. The withdrawn student is seen as a problem equal to that of the troublesome one. Self-discipline is substituted for strict teacher control. The humanistic orientation leads teachers to desire a democratic atmosphere with its attendant flexibility in status and rules, sensitivity to others, open communication, and increased student self-determination. Both teachers and pupils are willing to act on their own volition and to accept responsibility for their actions.

**The Custodial School**  The prototype of custodial control orientation is the traditional school that often provides a rigid and highly controlled setting concerned with the maintenance of order. Students are generally stereotyped in terms of their appearance, their behavior, and their parents' social status. Teachers who have a custodial orientation tend to conceive of the school as an autocratic organization with a well-defined pupil–teacher status hierarchy. Furthermore, teachers are predisposed to view the flow of power and communication as unilateral and as downward where students must accept the decisions of teachers without question. Teachers do not attempt to understand student behavior but, instead, view it in moralistic terms. Student misbehavior is taken as a personal affront; students are perceived

as irresponsible and undisciplined persons who must be controlled through punitive sanctions. Impersonality, pessimism, and "watchful mistrust" imbue the atmosphere of the custodial school.

**The Pupil Control Ideology Form**  To operationalize pupil control ideology along a humanistic-custodial continuum, the Pupil Control Ideology form (PCI) was developed and field tested.[59] The PCI consists of twenty Likert-type items. Examples of items are: "Beginning teachers are not likely to maintain strict enough control over their pupils," "Pupils can be trusted to work together without supervision," and "It is often necessary to remind pupils that their status in school differs from that of teachers." Responses are made on a five-point scale in a strongly agree to strongly disagree format. The scoring range is 20 to 100; the higher the score, the more custodial the ideology of the respondent. Pooled scores represent the pupil control ideology of the school. Reliability and validity of the instrument have been reported in numerous studies.[60]

**Pupil Control Ideology: A School Climate Descriptor**  Each school appears to have a prevailing pupil control ideology that influences its members. For instance, pupil control ideology is a school characteristic that affects the values of new teachers coming into a school. They are heavily influenced by the prevailing climate. Studies show how student teachers and neophyte teachers gradually shift from very humanistic values proselytized by teacher education staffs to more prevalent values held by teachers in the schools.[61]

One study found that pupil control ideology was a fruitful measure of the climate of the school; humanism in school pupil control ideology was associated with openness in organizational climate.[62] Another study tested further the utility of the humanistic-custodial construct as a predictor of school climate. To determine

---

[57]Donald J. Willower, Terry L. Eidell, and Wayne K. Hoy, *The School and Pupil Control Ideology,* rev. ed. (University Park: Pennsylvania State University Studies Monograph No. 24, 1973).

[58]Ibid.

[59]Ibid.

[60]John S. Packard, "The Pupil Control Studies," in N. J. Boyan (ed.), *Handbook of Research on Educational Administration* (New York: Longman, 1988), pp. 185–207.

[61]Fred C. Lunenburg, "The Influence of Experience on the Student Teacher," *High School Journal,* 69 (1986): 214–217; Wayne K. Hoy and Richard Rees, "The Bureaucratic Socialization of Student Teachers," *Journal of Teacher Education,* 28 (1977): 23–26.

[62]Fred C. Lunenburg and Robert R. O'Reilly, "Personal and Organizational Influence on Pupil Control Ideology," *Journal of Experimental Education,* 42 (1974): 31–35.

the openness of the climate of the fifty-three-school sample, Fred Lunenburg used three organizational climate subtests of the OCDQ (esprit, thrust, and disengagement) to compare the most humanistic schools and the most custodial schools in terms of their climate-openness scores.[63] There were no surprises. Schools with custodial pupil control ideologies had significantly lower esprit and thrust scores and significantly higher disengagement scores. That is, custodial schools as compared to humanistic schools appear to have (1) teachers who have low morale, reflecting low job satisfaction with respect to both task achievement and social needs satisfaction; (2) principals who are ineffective in directing the activities of teachers through personal example; and (3) teachers who do not work well together, resulting in minimal group achievement.

Two researchers developed and tested hypotheses concerning relationships among pupil control ideology, pupil control behavior, and the quality of school life. The hypotheses, tested in 239 elementary and secondary school classrooms in five school districts, were confirmed.[64] Custodialism in pupil control ideology and in pupil control behavior (another climate construct) were associated with students' negative reactions to the quality of school life. In addition, differences in pupil control ideology, pupil control behavior, and the quality of school life were found among urban, suburban, and rural schools. Urban schools were significantly more custodial in both pupil control ideology and behavior and had lower quality of school life scores than did either suburban or rural schools.

In a comprehensive study of school climate and alienation of high school students, one study reported that the more custodial and closed the school climate, the greater the students' sense of alienation.[65] Another inquiry involving high school students found a relationship between a humanistic school climate and high levels of self-actualization among the student body.[66]

Moreover, humanistic pupil control ideology and pupil control behavior (a companion construct) were associated with environmental robustness (a positive school climate).[67]

Yet another study, involving nearly 3000 students in thirty-five elementary schools, found that the humanistic school, not the custodial one, was associated with high student self-concept as a learner. In addition, students' perceptions of a humanistic school climate were positively related to their motivation, task orientation, problem solving, and seriousness about learning.[68]

Do teachers' pupil control ideologies influence students' feelings toward teachers? Researchers explored this question in a comprehensive study involving over 3000 students and teachers in 131 elementary school classrooms. As predicted, custodialism in teacher pupil control ideology was directly related to students' projections of rejection and hostility toward teachers. The hypothesis was supported in the overall sample of 131 teachers ($r = .60$) and in subsamples of male ($r = .71$) and female ($r = .54$) teachers.[69] Moreover, the more custodial the pupil control ideology of the teacher, the more severe were his reported reactions to specific incidents of pupil disruptive behavior.[70] In addition, teacher burnout was related to both custodial pupil control ideology and external locus of control. Additional analysis revealed that external, custodial teachers were found more often to experience depersonalized feelings and to frequently and intensely experience a lack of personal accomplishment (or self-efficacy).[71]

In his book, William Glasser provides an analogy relating to the relationship between pupil control styles and organizational climate. Glasser makes a distinction in his book between boss management (coercive control)

[63] Fred C. Lunenburg, *Pupil Control in Schools: Individual and Organizational Correlates* (Lexington, MA: Ginn, 1984).

[64] Fred C. Lunenburg and Linda J. Schmidt, "Pupil Control Ideology, Pupil Control Behavior, and the Quality of School Life," *Journal of Research and Development in Education,* 22 (1989): 36–44.

[65] Wayne K. Hoy, "Dimensions of Student Alienation and Pupil Control Orientations of High Schools," *Interchange,* 3 (1972): 38–52.

[66] John Deibert and Wayne Hoy, "Custodial High Schools and Self-Actualization of Students," *Educational Research Quarterly,* 2 (1977): 24–31.

[67] Fred C. Lunenburg, "Pupil Control Ideology and Behavior as Predictors of Environmental Robustness: Public and Private Schools Compared," *Journal of Research and Development in Education,* 24 (1991): 15–19.

[68] Fred C. Lunenburg, "Pupil Control Ideology and Self-Concept as a Learner," *Educational Research Quarterly,* 8 (1983): 33–39.

[69] Fred C. Lunenburg and Jack W. Stouten, "Teacher Pupil Control Ideology and Pupils Projected Feelings Toward Teachers," *Psychology in the Schools,* 20 (1983): 528–533.

[70] Fred C. Lunenburg, "Educators' Pupil Control Ideology as a Predictor of Educators' Reactions to Pupil Disruptive Behavior," *High School Journal,* 74 (1991): 81–87.

[71] Fred C. Lunenburg and Victoria Cadavid, "Locus of Control, Pupil Control Ideology, and Dimensions of Teacher Burnout," *Journal of Instructional Psychology,* 19 (1992): 13–22.

## PRO/CON Debate

### Recognizing Excellent Schools

In the past decade, more and more attention has been given to informing the public about the state of the schools. Schools are rated nationally, statewide, and locally. Poor schools receive attention, and, frequently, additional resources to spur their development. Excellent schools receive recognition through such awards as the National Merit Schools, which are recognized annually at a ceremony in the Rose Garden of the White House.

**Question:** When excellent schools are recognized, is it an incentive for those schools to maintain excellence and for other schools to strive for excellence?

**Arguments PRO**

1. When an outstanding school is recognized by the President of the United States, it receives the recognition it deserves. Communities, parents, children, and educators are proud. Everyone wins.

2. The possibility of national recognition for excellence will spur mediocre schools to positive action.

3. Competition is part of the U.S. culture. We recognize outstanding athletes, actors, musicians, poets, car salespersons, and school superintendents. Why not excellent schools?

4. Although we know excellence when we see it, we have not developed yet a national image of excellent public schooling. An award will force us to identify more and better indicators of excellence. Excellence will be pursued more easily by all schools when a clearer picture of it emerges.

5. Principals are key figures in school effectiveness. Excellent schools do not happen by accident. They are led by strong leaders with clear vision. Such principals deserve rewards and career advancement.

**Arguments CON**

1. Those who are recognized as excellent are not necessarily the best. The application process is so demanding and redundant that many have chosen to put their energies into other efforts.

2. The majority of schools do not have the resources to achieve excellence. The recognition that a few receive will be a disincentive for the many.

3. Competition among schools can have negative effects. People in the winning schools develop an unrealistic sense of worth; once they are recognized, some people will rest on their laurels.

4. Principals and teachers will put their energies into meeting the criteria identified by the award rather than dealing with other areas that need improvement. The arbitrary parameters established by the award rather than the clear pursuit of excellence will guide action.

5. Superintendents will expect principals to apply for awards and receive them. Principals whose school won an award will have an advantage when they apply for new principalships. Principals, rather than schools, will be the real winners.

and lead management (noncoercive control).[72] He contends that boss management results in an adversarial relationship between teachers and students and hinders the quality of learning. The personal power struggle between teacher and pupil becomes a vicious cycle: The student learns less and resists more; the teacher coerces more and teaches less. That is, teachers who use boss management exclusively will limit the learning in their classes. And a principal who embraces boss management will make it so hard for teachers to use lead management that the whole school will be negatively affected.

Glasser proposes a philosophy of lead management that is based on the use of persuasion and problem solving to control students. The lead manager spends all of his time and energy determining how to run the system so that the students will see that it is to their benefit to produce high-quality work. Once quality becomes central to a school's coursework, students will be proud of what they do, and this pride will become as contagious as pride elsewhere. In fact, Glasser believes that schools can make quality as much a part of academics as it is now part of athletics. (Note the similarity between Glasser's boss management and custodial schools and his lead management and humanistic schools.)

[72] Glasser, *The Quality School.*

## Summary

1. Organizational culture is the pattern of beliefs and assumptions shared by organizational members. Some important characteristics of organizational culture include observed behavioral regularities, norms, dominant values, philosophy, rules, and feelings.

2. Organizational heroes, rites and rituals, and communication networks play key roles in creating organizational cultures.

3. In maintaining a culture, institutions carry out several steps including careful selection of entry-level candidates, humility-inducing experiences, mastery of one's job, implementation of reward and control systems, careful adherence to values, reinforcing folklore, and the use of role models.

4. Changing organizational culture involves the following steps: external enabling conditions; internal permitting conditions; precipitating pressures; triggering events; cultural visioning; culture-change strategy; culture-change action plans; implementation of interventions; and reformulation of the culture.

5. Organizational culture has effects on administrative processes (e.g., motivation, leadership, decision making, communication, and change) and organizational structures (e.g., the selection process, evaluation system, control system, and reward system).

6. Certain types of cultures characterize excellent enterprises. Peters and Waterman offer a generalized concept of excellence. Ouchi postulates Theory Z as an approach to excellence, with specific application to schools.

7. Organizational climate is the total environmental quality within an organization. Four climate constructs were discussed: the open-closed model, healthy and sick schools, CASE, and the humanistic-custodial model.

## Key Terms

organizational culture
heroes
rites and rituals
communications network
organizational socialization
change cycle

Theory Z
culture phenotype
family culture
machine culture
cabaret culture
"little shop of horrors" culture
organizational climate
open and closed climates
healthy and sick schools
Comprehensive Assessment of School
 Environments (CASE)
pupil control ideology

## Discussion Questions

1. Describe several important characteristics of organizational culture and give some examples of each operating in your school/school district.

2. How are organizational cultures developed, maintained, and changed?

3. Describe some of the features of the cultures of excellent firms as elaborated by Thomas Peters and Robert Waterman and apply these to your school or school district.

4. Discuss the tenets of Theory Z as described by William Ouchi. What are its applications to schools?

5. How do each of the four organizational climate constructs relate to school effectiveness? Analyze these in relation to your school or school district.

## Suggested Readings

Deal, Terrence E., and Kent D. Peterson. *Shaping School Culture: The Heart of Leadership* (New York: John Wiley, 2003). The authors draw from over twenty years of research and work to show how leaders can harness the power of school culture to build a lively, cooperative spirit and a sense of school identity. They describe the critical elements of culture—the purposes, traditions, norms, and values that guide and glue the community together—and show how a positive culture can make school reforms work.

Frost, Peter J., Larry F. Moore, Meryl Reis Lewis, Craig C. Lundberg, and Joanne Martin (eds.). *Reframing Organizational Culture* (Thousand Oaks, CA: Sage, 1991). In a thorough update and challenge to the cutting edge of their earlier classic work, *Organizational Culture,* the authors offer a thorough overview of organizational culture: its development, maintenance, and strategies for change.

Kotter, John P. *Corporate Culture and Performance* (New York: Free Press, 1992). This volume proposes a new conceptual framework for the study of organizational culture and shows how a culture is developed within an organization and how it shapes policy and performance.

Ouchi, William G. *Theory Z: How American Business Can Meet the Japanese Challenge* (New York: Avon Books, 1993). To explain the success of high-producing Japanese companies, Ouchi developed Theory Z, which becomes the basis for describing and understanding the cultural mindset of an organization and the manner in which its members think, feel, and behave.

Peters, Thomas J., and Robert H. Waterman. *In Search of Excellence,* rev. ed. (New York: DIANE Publishing Company, 2006). The authors point out that the culture of an organization affects many administrative processes (motivation, leadership, decision making, communication, and change), structural processes (selection process, evaluation system, control system, and reward system), and has an influence on employee performance and organizational effectiveness.

Sarason, Seymour B. *Revisiting the Culture of the School and the Problem of Change* (New York: Teachers College Press, 1996). Part I reproduces the second edition of Sarason's ground-breaking work, *The Culture of the School and the Problem of Change,* in which he detailed how change can affect a school's culturally diverse environment—either through the implementation of new programs or as a result of federally imposed regulations. In Part II, Sarason "revisits" the text and the issues twenty-five years after the original publication.

Sashkin, Marshall, and Herbert J. Walberg (eds.). *Educational Leadership and School Cultures* (Berkeley, CA: McCutchan, 1993). Recognized experts explore pieces of the puzzle of educational leadership and culture: the nature of educational leadership, the nature of culture in schools and school systems, and the way leaders construct high-performance cultures.

# 4. Motivation

FOCUSING QUESTIONS

1 Why are some employees highly motivated, while others lack drive and commitment?

2 Which motivation theory is most practical for school administrators: motivation-hygiene or existence relatedness growth theory? Why?

3 What can school administrators learn from expectancy theory to improve their effectiveness in motivating employees?

4 How might school administrators improve equity to avoid dysfunctional consequences?

5 What are the key elements of goal-setting theory? How do they pertain to employee motivation?

6 How can these approaches to motivation be used in your school district?

In this chapter, we attempt to answer these questions concerning work motivation in school organizations. We begin our discussion with some brief definitions of motivation, and we examine the concepts of effort, persistence, and direction of employee motives as a foundation of work motivation. Then we describe and contrast several popular content theories of motivation: need hierarchy, motivation-hygiene, and existence relatedness growth approaches. Next, we examine three of the more applied areas of motivation: expectancy, equity, and goal setting.

## Defining Motivation

School administrators widely agree that **motivation** is a critical determinant of performance in organizations, but there is less agreement on the definition of the word *motivation*. Derived from the Latin word *movere* (which means "to move"), this definition is far too narrow in scope, from an organizational perspective. Motivation has been defined as "those processes within an individual that stimulate behavior and channel it in ways that should benefit the organization as a whole";[1] "the forces acting on and coming from within a person that account, in part, for the willful direction of one's efforts toward the achievement of specific goals";[2] and "motivation means three things: The person works hard; the person keeps at his

---

[1] John B. Miner, *Organizational Behavior 3: Historical Origins, Theoretical Foundations, and the Future* (New York: M. E. Sharpe, 2006).

[2] R. Dennis Middlemist, *Experiencing Organizational Behavior* (Belmont, CA: Thomson South-Western, 2000), p. 145.

**Table 4–1   Types of Motivation Theories**

| Type | Characteristics | Theories | Examples |
|------|-----------------|----------|----------|
| Content | Concerned with identifying specific factors that motivate people | Need hierarchy Motivation-hygiene Existence relatedness growth | Satisfying people's needs for pay, promotion, recognition |
| Process | Concerned with the process by which motivational factors interact to produce motivation | Expectancy Equity Goal setting | Clarifying people's perception of work inputs, performance requirements, and rewards |

or her work; and the person directs his or her behavior toward appropriate goals."[3] In general, these definitions seem to contain three common aspects of motivation: effort, persistence, and direction.[4]

**Effort**   Effort concerns the magnitude, or intensity, of the employee's work-related behavior. For example, a superintendent of schools might manifest greater effort by implementing a districtwide program to decrease school dropouts in his school district. A building principal might exhibit greater effort by examining several strategies to increase student attendance in the school building. And a teacher might show greater effort by developing various types of media and other supplementary materials to accompany the text used in a social studies course. All are exerting effort in a manner appropriate to their specific jobs.

**Persistence**   Persistence concerns the sustained effort employees manifest in their work-related activities. For example, school superintendents who make many important contributions to the district early in their tenure and then rest on their laurels for several years prior to retirement would not be considered highly motivated. Likewise, building principals who work very hard in the morning each day and then leave the job to play golf in the afternoon would not be considered highly moti-

vated. Neither school employee has been persistent in applying effort on the job.

**Direction**   Whereas effort and persistence concern the quantity of work performed, **direction** refers to the quality of an employee's work—that is, the investment of sustained effort in a direction that benefits the employer. From an employer's perspective, a high school counselor is expected to provide sound advice, concerning available and suitable career opportunities or appropriate college placements, to her group of graduating seniors. To the extent that correct decisions are made by the counselor, persistent effort is translated into desired school outcomes.

These three aspects of motivation serve as the basis for our discussion of the most prominent theories of motivation. Most theories can be separated into two major categories, according to whether they are concerned with the content or process of motivation. Table 4–1 summarizes these approaches.

## Content Theories

**Content theories** of motivation focus on the question, What energizes human behavior? The three most popular content theories of motivation are Maslow's need hierarchy theory, Herzberg's motivation-hygiene theory, and Alderfer's existence relatedness growth theory. These theories have received considerable attention both in research exploration and in organizational application.

---

[3] Gary Johns, *Organizational Behavior: Understanding and Managing Life at Work,* 5th ed. (Reading, MA: Addison-Wesley, 2000), p. 175.

[4] Ibid.

**Table 4–2  Maslow's Need Hierarchy**

|  | General Factors | Need Levels | Organizational Factors |
|---|---|---|---|
| Complex Needs | Growth<br>Achievement<br>Advancement | Self-actualization<br>(5) | Challenging job<br>Advancement in organization<br>Achievement in work |
|  | Self-esteem<br>Esteem from others<br>Recognition | Esteem<br>(4) | Titles<br>Status symbols<br>Promotions |
|  | Affection<br>Acceptance<br>Friendship | Social<br>(3) | Quality of supervision<br>Compatible work group<br>Professional friendships |
|  | Safety<br>Security<br>Stability | Safety<br>(2) | Safe working conditions<br>Fringe benefits<br>Job security |
| Basic Needs | Water<br>Food<br>Shelter | Physiological<br>(1) | Heat and air conditioning<br>Base salary<br>Working conditions |

### Need Hierarchy Theory

Abraham Maslow's **need hierarchy theory** is probably one of the best known and most widely used theories for the study of motivation in organizations.[5] Maslow identified five basic groups of human needs that emerge in a specific sequence or pattern—that is, in a hierarchy of importance. In this scheme, once one need is satisfied, another emerges and demands satisfaction, and so on through the hierarchy. The five levels of needs, which represent the order of importance to the individual, are physiological, safety, social, esteem, and self-actualization (see Table 4–2).

1. *Physiological needs* include the need for food, water, and shelter. Once these needs are sufficiently satisfied, other levels of needs become prominent and provide motivation for an individual's behavior. Organizations might satisfy these needs by providing a base salary and basic working conditions such as heat, air conditioning, and cafeteria services.

2. *Safety needs* include protection against danger, threat, and deprivation, including avoidance of anxiety. Organizations can provide these needs with safe working conditions, fair rules and regulations, job security, pension and insurance plans, salary increases, and freedom to unionize.

3. *Social needs* include affection, affiliation, friendship, and love. People who reach this third level in the hierarchy have primarily satisfied physiological and safety needs. Organizations might meet these needs by including employee-centered supervision, providing opportunities for teamwork, following group norms, and sponsoring group activities such as-organized sports programs and school or districtwide picnics.

4. *Esteem needs* focus on self-respect and include recognition and respect from others. Fulfilling esteem needs produces feelings of self-confidence, prestige, power, and control. Organizations can satisfy this need through recognition and award programs, articles in the district newsletter, promotions, and prestigious job titles (e.g., Team Leader, Director of Computer Services, or Senior Researcher).

5. *Self-actualization needs* focus on the attainment of one's full potential for continued self-development; in Maslow's words, the desire to become "more and more what one idiosyncratically is, to become everything one is capable of becoming."[6] Unlike the other needs, self-actualization is manifested differently in different people. For example, to achieve ultimate satisfaction, a musician must create music, an artist must paint, a teacher must teach students,

---

[5] Abraham H. Maslow, *Motivation and Personality,* 2nd ed. (Reading, MA: Addison-Wesley, 1970).

[6] Ibid., p. 46.

and an administrator must lead people. Organizations might provide self-actualization by involving employees in planning job designs, making assignments that capitalize on employees' unique skills, and relaxing structure to permit employees' personal growth and self-development.

**Research on the Need Hierarchy Theory**     One of the first and most widely used measures of Maslow's need hierarchy theory, the Need Satisfaction Questionnaire (NSQ), was developed by Lyman Porter.[7] Porter modified Maslow's hierarchy by eliminating physiological needs on grounds that they are widely satisfied and thus of relatively little importance in organizational settings in North America. In addition, Porter added autonomy needs, which he inserted between Maslow's esteem and self-actualization needs.

There have been many research studies of the need hierarchy theory in educational organizations. Studies of 233 educators from a suburban Rochester, New York, school district and of 1593 secondary school teachers in thirty-six Illinois high schools reported large need deficiencies for the higher-level needs (esteem, autonomy, and self-actualization) with esteem showing the greatest need deficiency.[8] A later study of teacher need deficiencies was somewhat similar to those of the two earlier ones. The three higher-level needs were still the dominant areas of perceived need deficiency. There was, however, a significant increase in the security need in the later study. The authors attributed this increase in the security needs of teachers to a reflection of a tightening job market and pressures of reduction in force.[9] Other researchers examined the need deficiencies of teachers and administrators. The findings revealed that school administrators had fewer need deficiencies than did teachers on all five subscales of Porter's NSQ—security, social, esteem, autonomy, and self-

actualization.[10] In a study comparing female homemakers and women working in professional and managerial positions, safety and social needs emerged as more important among homemakers; esteem and autonomy needs did not differ markedly between the two groups; and self-actualization was of highest importance in both instances.[11]

Outstanding schools require leaders who have the ability to motivate people to maximize their performances, to grow professionally, and to change. To achieve these goals, school administrators must know and be able to apply the basic theories of motivation. (See Administrative Advice 4–1.)

Maslow's need hierarchy theory has a commonsense appeal that has resulted in wide discussion and application of the theory among practitioners. Despite this appeal, limited research has been done to validate the theory. The findings are mixed. A review of relevant research found little support for Maslow's framework.[12] Evidence that supports the five distinct need categories is scant, but a two-level hierarchy of lower-order and higher-order needs may exist. In addition, the idea of prepotency has been questioned.[13] In this regard, evidence—particularly at the higher-order needs level—supports the view that unless physiological needs and safety needs are satisfied, employees will not be concerned with higher-order needs. Little evidence, however, supports the view that a hierarchy exists once one moves above the security level.[14] For example, an individual can have strong social, esteem, and self-actualization needs simultaneously. In fact, Maslow's clinical studies showed that the idea of prepotency may not be relevant for all individuals.[15] Nevertheless, Maslow's theory has not been completely disproved.

[7]Lyman W. Porter, *Organizational Patterns of Managerial Job Attitudes* (New York: American Foundation for Management Research, 1964).

[8]Francis M. Trusty and Thomas J. Sergiovanni, "Perceived Need Deficiencies of Teachers and Administrators: A Proposal for Restructuring Teacher Roles," *Educational Administration Quarterly*, 2 (1966): 168–180; Fred D. Carver and Thomas J. Sergiovanni, "Complexity, Adaptability and Job Satisfaction in High Schools: An Axiomatic Theory Applied," *Journal of Educational Administration*, 9 (1971): 15–30.

[9]Mary Beth Anderson and Edward F. Iwanicki, "Teacher Motivation and Its Relationship to Burnout," *Educational Administration Quarterly*, 20 (1984): 109–132.

[10]Grace B. Chisolm, Roosevelt Washington, and Mary Thibodeaux, "Job Motivation and the Need Fulfillment Deficiencies of Educators," paper presented at the annual meeting of the American Educational Research Association, Boston, 1980.

[11]Ellen L. Betz, "Need Fulfillment in the Career Development of Women," *Journal of Vocational Behavior*, 20 (1982): 60–61.

[12]Mahmoud A. Wahba and Lawrence G. Bridwell, "Maslow Reconsidered: A Review of the Research on the Need Hierarchy Theory," *Organizational Behavior and Human Performance*, 15 (1976): 212–240.

[13]Ibid.

[14]Lyman W. Porter (ed.), *Annual Review of Psychology*, vol. 45 (Palo Alto, CA: Annual Reviews, 1994).

[15]Miner, *Organizational Behavior 3*.

---

**Administrative Advice 4–1**

### Practical Motivational Strategies

Applying the concepts of motivation theory is sometimes difficult to achieve. However, if this is done effectively, school administrators can help teachers become more effective and more fulfilled instructors. Below are some practical motivational strategies to enhance teacher performance and growth.

▪ *Personal Regard.* To show personal regard, personally follow up on all faculty concerns, affirm the inquiry, and appropriately question to determine a common understanding; each day, discuss informally — with a set number of faculty members — what can be done to assist them; and be sensitive to faculty members' feelings when implementing new policies and procedures.

▪ *Communication.* To enhance communication, develop, publish, and model clear and consistent educational goals; seek opinions and viewpoints on changes that affect the faculty; listen to understand, not to respond or to defend; and listen, listen, listen.

▪ *Recognition.* To recognize teachers, start each faculty meeting or memo with words of appreciation for a job

well done; promote teacher successes when talking to students, parents, central office personnel, the community, and other teachers; inform teachers of professional opportunities that might appeal to them; and give teachers specific praise face-to-face frequently.

▪ *Participation.* To allow participation in the decision-making process, use cooperative goal setting in formative evaluation; elect an administrative advisory committee; allow faculty to have a major voice in staff development, evaluation, and in-service programs; and create ad hoc, small groups to brainstorm problems.

Source: Adapted from Lynn E. Lehman, "Practical Motivational Strategies for Teacher Performance and Growth," *NASSP Bulletin*, 73 (1989): 76–80. Used by permission.

---

There is evidence that people do tend to think of their own needs in terms of the five categories that Maslow defined.[16] Another study empirically demonstrated the viability of both five- and two-level need categories, suggesting that the two perspectives need not be mutually exclusive.[17]

### Motivation-Hygiene Theory

Frederick Herzberg developed a unique and exciting motivation theory that builds on Maslow's earlier work. The theory has been called the **motivation-hygiene theory,** the two-factor theory, and the dual-factor theory.[18] Like Maslow's need hierarchy theory, the motivation-hygiene theory seeks to determine factors that cause mo-

tivation. Rather than looking for needs energized within the individual, Herzberg focused attention on the work environment to identify factors that arouse in people either positive or negative attitudes toward their work.

The original research used to develop the theory was conducted with 203 accountants and engineers employed in nine manufacturing firms in the Pittsburgh area. Herzberg used the critical incident technique to obtain data for analysis. The subjects in the study were asked to think of times when they felt good about their jobs. Each subject was then asked to describe the conditions that led to those feelings. Herzberg repeated this same approach with a wide variety of other employees. Results obtained from the critical incident method were fairly consistent across the various subjects. Reported good feelings were generally associated with the job itself — content, intrinsic, or psychological factors. These included achievement, recognition, the work itself, responsibility, advancement, and growth. Herzberg named these content factors "job satisfiers," or *motivators,* because they fulfill an individual's need for psychological growth. Reported bad feelings, on the other hand, were generally associated with the environment surrounding the job — context, extrinsic, or physical factors. These included company policies,

---

[16] Simcha Ronen and Allen I. Kraut, "An Experimental Examination of Work Motivation Taxonomies," *Human Relations*, 33 (1980): 505–516.

[17] Vance F. Mitchell and Pravin Moudgill, "Measurement of Maslow's Need Hierarchy," *Organizational Behavior and Human Performance*, 16 (1976): 334–339.

[18] Frederick Herzberg, Bernard Mausner, and Barbara S. Snyderman, *The Motivation to Work* (New Brunswick, NJ: Transaction, 1993).

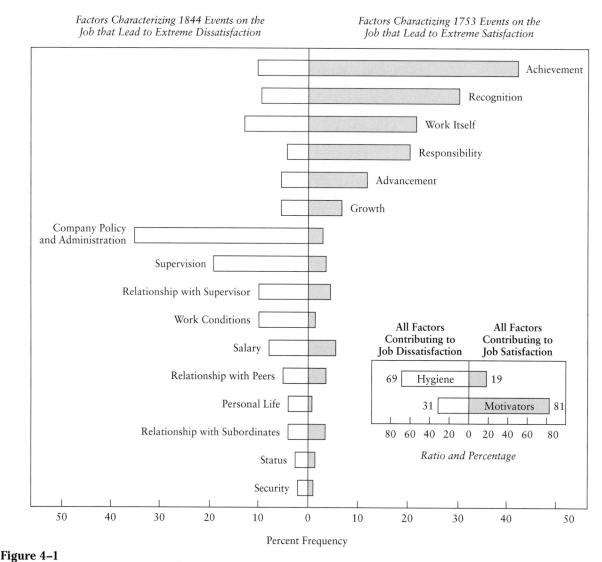

*Factors Characterizing 1844 Events on the Job that Lead to Extreme Dissatisfaction*

*Factors Charactizing 1753 Events on the Job that Lead to Extreme Satisfaction*

Achievement
Recognition
Work Itself
Responsibility
Advancement
Growth
Company Policy and Administration
Supervision
Relationship with Supervisor
Work Conditions
Salary
Relationship with Peers
Personal Life
Relationship with Subordinates
Status
Security

All Factors Contributing to Job Dissatisfaction

All Factors Contributing to Job Satisfaction

69 Hygiene 19

31 Motivators 81

80 60 40 20 0 20 40 60 80

*Ratio and Percentage*

50 40 30 20 10 0 10 20 30 40 50

Percent Frequency

**Figure 4–1**

Comparison of Satisfiers and Dissatisfiers

Source: Reprinted by permission of *Harvard Business Review.* Adapted from "One More Time: How Do You Motivate Employees?" by Frederick Herzberg, issue 65 (1987): 112. Copyright © 1987 by the Harvard Business School Publishing Corporation. All rights reserved.

supervision, interpersonal relations, working conditions, and salary. Herzberg named these context factors "job dissatisfiers," or *hygiene factors,* because they are preventative and environmental. Figure 4–1 illustrates these findings.

The motivation-hygiene theory is related to the need hierarchy theory. Herzberg has reduced Maslow's five-level need system into a two-level system—hygiene needs and motivation needs. Hygiene factors (dissatisfiers) are roughly equivalent to Maslow's lower-level needs, because they serve to reduce dissatisfaction but do not lead to satisfaction. Motivators (satisfiers) are roughly equivalent to Maslow's higher-level needs. According to Herzberg, dissatisfiers may ensure that employees will perform at minimum levels, but motivation, which contributes to superior performance, is possible only through satisfiers. That is, only the work itself and recognition, advancement, personal growth, and development stemming from this work will provide a situation for motivated behavior in the workplace.

**Research on the Motivation-Hygiene Theory** The motivation-hygiene theory has been subjected to extensive research, but little research on the theory has been done in the past 20 years. Thomas Sergiovanni replicated Herzberg's study with teachers. His study suggests that achievement, recognition, and responsibility contribute to teacher motivation. Dissatisfaction seems to result from poor interpersonal relations with students, inadequate styles of supervision, rigid and inflexible school policies and administrative practices, and poor interpersonal relations with colleagues and parents.[19]

Sergiovanni's study deviated in at least two important ways from Herzberg's study, which was conducted in an industrial setting. First, the work itself accounted for both satisfaction and dissatisfaction among teachers. In explaining this finding, Sergiovanni noted "elements of the job of teaching as we presently know it are inherently less satisfying."[20] First, routine housekeeping, attendance taking, procuring milk money, paperwork, study hall supervision, lunch duty, and so on seem to neutralize the more satisfying aspects of teaching. Second, whereas "advancement" was an important motivator for Herzberg's accountants and engineers, it was conspicuously missing from Sergiovanni's teachers. According to Sergiovanni, teaching as an occupation offers little opportunity for advancement as it is currently structured.[21]

Two other researchers using a sample of teachers in Georgia and a sample of teachers in Saskatchewan, Canada, provided additional support for the two-factor theory.[22] Each used methods similar to Herzberg's. Using the critical incident method in a mail questionnaire format, another study found support for Herzberg's theory with a sample of college and university faculty.[23] Cecil

Miskel compared teachers, principals, and central office administrators' responses using a questionnaire variation of the Herzberg method. He found that teachers have a lower tolerance for work pressure than do principals. In addition, teachers have a greater desire for security than do central office administrators, except those teachers who aspired to administrative positions. The aspiring administrators also expressed a greater desire for the motivators.[24]

In another study, Miskel found that a different conceptual framework concerning motivation, hygiene, and risk factors existed for teachers, school administrators, and industrial managers. Teachers exhibited high concern for hygiene factors with low-risk propensity; managers showed low concern for hygiene factors with high-risk propensity; and educational administrators, appearing in the middle of the continuum, were similar to teachers in their high concern for hygiene factors but resembled managers in their risk propensity.[25]

School administrators may neglect to consider that dissatisfied teachers may weaken the educational program. Basic motivational principles and techniques can help administrators meet teacher needs. (See Administrative Advice 4–2.)

**Critique of the Motivation-Hygiene Theory** Three consistent criticisms have been leveled against Herzberg's theory. First, Herzberg's theory is regarded as *methodologically bound;* that is, the method he used to measure motivation-hygiene factors determined the results. The subjects in Herzberg's studies were given the following directions by an interviewer: "Think of a time when you felt exceptionally good or exceptionally bad about your job, either your present job or any other job you have had. This can be either the 'long-range or the short-range' kind of situation, as I have just described it. Tell me what happened."[26] In response to such questions, people tend to give socially acceptable answers—that is, what they think the interviewer wants to hear. In reviewing more than twenty studies

[19]Thomas J. Sergiovanni, "Factors Which Affect Satisfaction and Dissatisfaction of Teachers," *Journal of Educational Administration,* 5 (1967): 66–82.

[20]Thomas J. Sergiovanni and Fred D. Carver, *The New School Executive* (New York: Harper & Row, 1980), p. 108.

[21]Ibid.

[22]Ralph M. Savage, "A Study of Teacher Satisfaction and Attitudes: Causes and Effects," doctoral dissertation, Auburn University, 1967; Rodney A. Wickstrom, "An Investigation into Job Satisfaction Among Teachers," doctoral dissertation, University of Oregon, 1971.

[23]L. Moxley, "Job Satisfaction of Faculty Teaching Higher Education: An Examination of Herzberg's Dual Factor Theory and Porter's Need Satisfaction Research," ERIC Document No. ED 139–349, 1977.

[24]Cecil G. Miskel, "The Motivation of Educators to Work," *Educational Administration Quarterly,* 9 (1973): 42–53.

[25]Cecil G. Miskel, "Intrinsic, Extrinsic, and Risk Propensity Factors in the Work Attitudes of Teachers, Educational Administrators, and Business Managers," *Journal of Applied Psychology,* 59 (1974): 339–343.

[26]Herzberg, Mausner, and Snyderman, *The Motivation to Work,* p. 141.

---

### Administrative Advice 4–2

#### Improving Teacher Job Satisfaction

The following are some tips that can help school administrators improve teacher job satisfaction.

■ *Use Praise to Recognize Exemplary Behavior.* Catch your faculty members doing something right and tell them. Often, the only contact teachers have with administrators is when they do something wrong, and then they are "zapped"! Moreover, tell parents about staff accomplishments through the school newsletter.

■ *Rotate Faculty Meeting Locations.* Conduct faculty meetings in different classrooms to give your teachers an opportunity to tell their colleagues about the things they are doing.

■ *Institute a "5–10 Report" from Teachers.* Promote "quick and easy" communication. A 5–10 report takes no more than five minutes to read and ten to write. Each report is divided into three parts: a quick update of job-related activities; a description of the teacher's morale; and an idea for improving the efficiency or effectiveness of the school.

■ *Empower Teachers.* Establish a school leadership team consisting of yourself, teachers you select, and teachers selected by faculty members. Have the team participate in decisions concerning budget preparations, school improvement projects, and the like.

■ *Recognize Group Accomplishments.* Work with your PTA or other support groups to recognize schoolwide accomplishments, perhaps over morning doughnuts or with a staff appreciation banquet or afternoon cake and ice cream.

■ *Don't Overlook the Little Things.* Design inexpensive birthday or holiday cards that can be produced on duplicating machines or by computer. Before the school year begins, have the school secretary preaddress and stamp each card and arrange for them to be mailed at the appropriate times.

■ *Create a "Bragging Wall" in the Faculty Lounge.* Use an area of the faculty lounge to post "smile-a-grams," articles faculty members have published, newspaper clippings, letters from parents, and other examples of good things that are going on in your school.

■ *Follow Up on Requests.* Get back quickly to faculty members who make requests for a decision or status report. Such behavior demonstrates that you are concerned about their needs.

■ *Select a Faculty Member of the Month.* Make the selection yourself or ask the staff leadership team to help with the decision.

■ *Institute a Teacher-for-a-Day Program.* Select one day a year and recruit key community members to come to your school to teach for the entire day or for a period. Teachers will benefit from a new sense of community participation (especially if the local press covers the story).

---

Source: Adapted from Terry B. Grier, "15 Ways to Keep Staff Members Happy and Productive," *Executive Educator*, 10 (1988): 26–27. Copyright 1988, the National School Boards Association. Used by permission.

---

that used a different method from Herzberg's critical incident technique, one researcher found only 3 percent that supported the theory.[27]

Second, some critics have questioned the mutual exclusiveness of the satisfaction and dissatisfaction dimensions (i.e., whether there are really two separate dimensions). For example, some researchers have found that motivators appear frequently as satisfiers as well as dissatisfiers.[28] This tendency to appear in the wrong context is also characteristic of the hygienes.[29]

Third, little research has focused on the link between satisfying job experiences and favorable performance effects and on the association between dissatisfying experiences and unfavorable performance

---

[27]Hanafi M. Solimon, "Motivator-Hygiene Theory of Job Attitudes: An Empirical Investigation and Attempt to Reconcile Both the One- and the Two-Factor Theories of Job Attitudes," *Journal of Applied Psychology*, 54 (1970): 452–461.

[28]Robert J. House and Lawrence A. Wigdor, "Herzberg's Dual-Factor Theory of Job Satisfaction and Motivation: A Review of the Evidence and a Criticism," *Personnel Psychology*, 20 (1967): 369–389.

[29]Valerie M. Bockman, "The Herzberg Controversy," *Personnel Psychology*, 24 (1971): 155–189.

effects.[30] The implications of such findings for motivational rather than merely attitudinal hypotheses of the theory are evident. Herzberg's work focused on employee satisfaction, not the actual motivation and performance of the employee.

Despite these criticisms, Herzberg has contributed substantially to school administrators' thinking about what motivates employees. He extended Maslow's need hierarchy theory and made it more applicable to the work environment. Herzberg's theory is useful because it distinguishes between extrinsic job factors and intrinsic job factors such as opportunities for achievement, responsibility, growth, and personal development. This two-factor approach concept altered school administrators' thinking about job motivation. For many years schools, which tended to focus on "hygiene" factors such as salary, job security, and working conditions, ignored intrinsic job factors. Herzberg's theory drew attention to the intrinsic job factors, and these "motivators" have been introduced in school settings. Important developments from the two-factor idea are job enrichment, or quality of work life and shared leadership, which are designed to increase job satisfaction and performance.

**Motivating Midcareer Teachers**    The teaching profession is experiencing a profound demographic change. The majority of teachers today are middle aged and immobile, according to a national study. Many have been teaching in one school for most of their professional careers, and their average age is forty-six. Seventy-five percent have been teaching for at least ten years; fifty percent, for over fifteen years. Fifty percent have taught in only one or two schools.[31]

The first wave of school reform, following the release of *A Nation at Risk*,[32] dealt with broad philosophical questions concerning the structure, mission, curriculum, and methods of schooling. It focused particular attention on the principal as leader in directing school improvement efforts. Frequently missing from these proposals was recognition of the current demography of the teaching force. Consequently, the second wave of reform, particularly the Carnegie Task Force on Teaching

as a Profession[33] and the Holmes Group,[34] expanded the focus to include teachers, emphasizing the need to enhance their motivation and participation. This approach to school improvement represents efforts to restructure schools through shared governance, participatory management, and site-based management, whereby teachers play an active role in the operation of the school.

Although the second wave of reform efforts is based on sound theories of organizational behavior and factors that foster competence, few reports have noted the importance of regarding teachers as developing adults. Any restructuring of school governance and management must include the role of the principal as a developer of professionals.

Bruce Joyce and Beverly Showers have applied career-development research to teachers, emphasizing the school as a context for adult growth and the principal's role as adult developer.[35] They suggest that midcareer teachers are prone to demotivation (boredom, complacency, and loss of challenge), which often results in a leveling off of performance.

Typically, organizations respond to this mid-career syndrome by imposing the following measures: greater central office control over planning, policy, and curriculum to compensate for a lack of initiative on the part of teachers; rigorous evaluation and clinical supervision to motivate veteran teachers; defect-based in-service retraining designed to correct performance deficiencies; and career ladders or other financial rewards to increase incentives to senior faculty members. These measures offer little stimulus to veteran teachers' performance.[36] Moreover, as Herzberg notes, they play a secondary role in motivating employees because they are hygiene factors, extrinsic to the job itself.[37]

To enhance teachers' motivation and participation, principals will need to focus on ongoing development of their human resources: match the changing needs of teachers over the course of their careers with those

---

[30] John P. Campbell et al., *Managerial Behavior, Performance, and Effectiveness* (New York: McGraw-Hill, 1970).

[31] C. Emily Feistritzer, *Profile of Teachers in the United States* (Washington, DC: National Center for Education Information, 1990).

[32] National Commission on Excellence in Education, *A Nation at Risk* (Washington, DC: U.S. Department of Education, 1983).

[33] Carnegie Task Force on Teaching as a Profession, *A Nation Prepared: Teachers for the 21st Century* (Washington, DC: Carnegie Task Force, 1986).

[34] Holmes Group, *Tomorrow's Teachers: A Report of the Holmes Group* (East Lansing, MI: The Holmes Group, 1986).

[35] Bruce Joyce and Beverly Showers, *Student Achievement Through Staff Development*, 3rd ed. (Baltimore: Association for Supervision and Curriculum Development, 2002).

[36] Ibid.

[37] Frederick Herzberg, "One More Time: How Do You Motivate Employees?" *Harvard Business Review*, 65 (1987): 109–120.

## ▪ Exemplary Educational Administrators in Action

**JAMES F. CAUSBY** Superintendent, Johnston County Schools, North Carolina.

**Previous Positions:** Superintendent, Polk County Schools, North Carolina; Superintendent, Swain County Schools, North Carolina.

**Latest Degree and Affiliation:** Ed.D., Educational Administration, University of North Carolina at Greensboro.

**Number One Influence on Career:** As a teacher my first principal, Mr. Cowan Wikle.

**Number One Achievement:** Moving the Johnston County School System's student academic achievement from the bottom third to the top 10 percent of North Carolina school systems.

**Number One Regret:** I have no regrets.

**Favorite Education-Related Book or Text:** *Closing the Achievement Gap: No Excuses* by Patricia Davenport and Gerald Anderson.

**Additional Interests:** Golfing, reading, travel.

**Leadership Style:** I hire good people, train them how I want things done, help them set their goals, let them do their jobs with minimal interference, and provide support and motivation.

**Professional Vision:** Educational leaders must first themselves serve those whom they want to serve others. They must set the example by always working harder than those who work for them. And everything they do must be directed toward high student academic achievement. They must have a constancy of purpose that is clearly evident.

**Words of Advice:** Students who aspire to become educational administrators should be aware of what a

wonderful and rewarding career they can have in educational administration if they approach it with the right attitude and the right priorities. There has never been a more exciting time in our profession than the present. There are so many changes and challenges that one is never bored, and opportunities to do good things for students come in abundance.

Career opportunities for educational administrators have never been better than they are now. As the student population in our nation grows, and as those of us who are baby boomers retire, there will be a tremendous demand for school administrators at all levels and in all parts of our nation. An individual who is a good teacher, who is willing to complete a quality school administrator program, and who enjoys working with people will find many opportunities to advance his or her career. And school administrator salaries have vastly improved over recent years.

Aspiring school administrators must understand that they will live in a glass house. They will be admired and looked up to, but they will constantly be in the public eye. They must learn, and be able to accept, the fact that their friendships and personal relations will be limited to others who share their profession because there is no one else who can truly understand their job and their concerns. Everyone in the community will either work for them or have children in their schools.

They should understand that high quality and strong leadership will enable them to achieve wonderful things for their employees and the children in their care. Educational administration is the very best career in the world!

of the school or school district. (See Administrative Advice 4–3).

### Existence Relatedness Growth Theory

Clayton Alderfer's existence relatedness growth theory is an extension of Herzberg's and Maslow's content theories of employee motivation.[38] Like Maslow and Herzberg, Alderfer feels that people do have needs, that these needs can be arranged in a hierarchy, that there is a basic distinction between lower-level needs and higher-level needs, and that needs are important determinants of employee motivation in organizations. Alderfer suggests three broad categories of needs: existence (E), relatedness (R), and growth (G)—hence, the **ERG theory:**

1. *Existence needs* comprise all forms of physiological and material desires such as food, clothing, and shelter. In organizational settings, specific examples include salary, fringe benefits, job security, and

[38]Clayton P. Alderfer, *Existence, Relatedness, and Growth* (New York: Free Press, 1972).

## Administrative Advice 4–3

### Motivating Midcareer Teachers

To combat boredom, loss of enthusiasm, and diminished job interest characteristic of some midcareer teachers, principals must redesign both jobs and organizational structures to provide experience-enhancing roles for teachers. Here are some strategies principals can use to develop and motivate teachers:

▪ *Revitalize Careers.* Measures that increase the variety of a teacher's total career experiences include job sharing, voluntary transfers to new jobs within the district, temporary released-time assignments to special projects, developing multiple specialties (becoming adept at two disciplines or two grade levels) so a teacher can move between assignments, and traditional methods that enhance job variety (team teaching, peer study and supervision groups, intraschool and interschool visiting, curriculum development workshops, attending conferences, minisabbaticals).

▪ *Enrich Jobs.* Measures that improve the quality of experience a given job provides include increasing teachers' control over budget, curriculum, schedule, class size, and so on; providing opportunities for teachers to study and develop new models of school structure and pedagogy; requiring and permitting teachers to take greater responsibility for colleagues with performance problems; and limiting the imposition of externally imposed

competency requirements and substantially increasing the role of teachers in determining appropriate outcomes to measure.

▪ *Provide Supportive Leadership.* Because many midcareer performance problems are rooted in the loss of motivation, principals must emphasize recognition, exploration, and awareness of choice among teachers whenever possible. Principals can seek ways to maximize teachers' success and experimentation and to reward faculty for their accomplishments and for willingness to explore new interests or experiment with new approaches to problems, even when they fail. Teachers need recognition not only for achievement but also for effort.

Source: Adapted from Robert Evans, "The Faculty in Midcareer: Implications for School Improvement," *Educational Leadership,* 46 (1989): 10–15.

---

work conditions. This category corresponds roughly to Maslow's physiological and safety needs.

2. *Relatedness needs* include all those that involve interpersonal relationships with others—supervisors, colleagues, subordinates, family, friends, and so on. Alderfer stresses that relatedness needs can be satisfied by expressing anger and hostility as well as by developing close, warm, and personal relationships with others. This need category corresponds approximately to Maslow's social needs and to those esteem needs involving feedback from others.

3. *Growth needs* concern the individual's intrinsic desire to grow, develop, and fulfill one's potential. In the workplace, satisfaction of growth needs results when an employee engages in tasks that involve not only the full use of his skills and abilities but also tasks that may require the creative development of new skills and abilities. This category of ERG needs corresponds to Maslow's self-actualization needs and certain aspects of his esteem needs. Figure 4–2

depicts how Alderfer's need categories are related to the Maslow and Herzberg categories.

ERG theory differs from Maslow's need hierarchy theory in two important ways. First, Maslow's theory proposes that a lower-level need must be gratified before other needs become operative. ERG theory, on the other hand, proposes that people may experience several needs simultaneously. Existence needs do not necessarily have to be satisfied before a person can become concerned about the satisfaction of his relatedness or growth needs. Hence, ERG theory is more flexible than is need hierarchy theory and accounts for a wide variety of individual differences in need structure. Second, Maslow's theory proposes that a satisfied need is no longer a motivator. According to Alderfer, however, the continual frustration of higher-order needs will lead employees to regress to a lower-need category. For example, the principal who is unable to secure a position as a superintendent (growth needs) may increase interest in fulfilling relatedness needs in order to demonstrate to

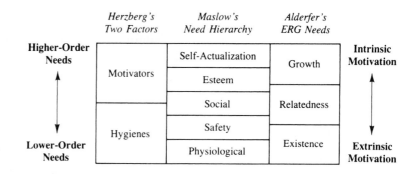

**Figure 4–2**

Relationships Among Content Motivation
Theories

the higher administration her capabilities for a promotion to superintendent.

**Research on ERG Theory**   To date, there has not been much research on ERG theory. Most research tends to support Alderfer's theory over Maslow's and Herzberg's theories.[39] For example, some evidence supports the three classifications of needs.[40] Moreover, some researchers recommend ERG theory over Maslow's theory because the latter was not aimed specifically toward the study of employee motivation in the workplace.[41] Also, there is support for several of Alderfer's basic propositions such as the idea that a satisfied need may remain a motivator—that is, the confirmation that the frustration of relatedness needs increases the strength of existence needs.[42] Overall, "many behavioral scientists tend to view ERG theory as the most current, valid, and researchable theory based on the need concept."[43]

## Process Theories

The content theories of motivation attempt to identify *what* motivates employees in the workplace (e.g., advancement, self-actualization, and growth). The **process theories,** on the other hand, are more concerned with *how* motivation occurs—in other words, they explain the process of motivation. Expectancy theory, equity theory, and goal-setting theory are the three major process theories that concern this approach to motivation in organizational settings.

### Expectancy Theory

Victor Vroom is usually credited with developing the first complete version of the **expectancy theory** with application to organizational settings.[44] Expectancy theory is based on four assumptions. One assumption is that people join organizations with expectations about their needs, motivations, and past experiences. These influence how individuals react to the organization. A second assumption is that an individual's behavior is a result of conscious choice. That is, people are free to choose those behaviors suggested by their own expectancy calculations. A third assumption is that people want different things from the organization (e.g., good salary, job security, advancement, and challenge). A fourth assumption is that people will choose among alternatives so as to optimize outcomes for them personally.

[39]Bronston T. Mayes, "Some Boundary Considerations in the Application of Motivation Models," *Academy of Management Review,* 3 (1978): 51–52.

[40]John P. Wanous and Abram Zwany, "A Cross-Sectional Test of Need Hierarchy Theory," *Organizational Behavior and Human Performance,* 18 (1977): 78–97.

[41]Benjamin Schneider and Clayton P. Alderfer, "Three Studies of Measures of Need Satisfaction in Organizations," *Administrative Science Quarterly,* 18 (1973): 489–505.

[42]Clayton P. Alderfer, Robert E. Kaplan, and Ken K. Smith, "The Effect of Relatedness Need Satisfaction on Relatedness Desires," *Administrative Science Quarterly,* 19 (1974): 507–532.

[43]Clayton P. Alderfer, "A Critique of Salancik and Pfeffer's Examination of Need Satisfaction Theories," *Administrative Science Quarterly,* 22 (1977): 658–659.

[44]Victor H. Vroom, *Work and Motivation* (San Francisco: Jossey-Bass, 1994).

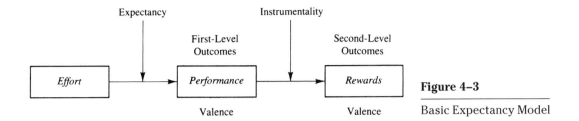

Figure 4–3

Basic Expectancy Model

**Basic Expectancy Model** The expectancy theory based on these assumptions has four key elements: outcomes, expectancy, instrumentality, and valence (see Figure 4–3).

**Outcomes,** classified as first or second level, are the end results of certain work behaviors. *First-level outcomes* refer to some aspect of performance and are the direct result of expending some effort on the job. *Second-level outcomes* are viewed as consequences to which first-level outcomes are expected to lead. That is, the end result of performance (first-level outcome) is some type of reward (second-level outcome) for work goal accomplishment. Examples include salary increases, promotion, peer acceptance, recognition by the supervisor, or a sense of accomplishment.

**Expectancy** is the strength of belief that job-related effort will result in a certain performance level. Expectancy is based on probabilities and ranges from 0 to 1. If an employee sees no chance that effort will lead to the desired performance level, the expectancy is 0. On the other hand, if the employee is completely certain that the task will be completed, the expectancy has a value of 1. Generally, employee estimates of expectancy lie somewhere between these two extremes.

**Instrumentality** is the relationship between performance (first-level outcomes) and rewards (second-level outcomes). As with expectancy, instrumentality ranges from 0 to 1. If an employee sees that a good performance rating will always result in a salary increase, the instrumentality has a value of 1. If there is no perceived relationship between the first-level outcome (good performance rating) and the second-level outcome (salary increase), then the instrumentality is 0.

**Valence** is the strength of an employee's preference for a particular outcome or reward. Thus, salary increases, promotion, peer acceptance, recognition by supervisors, or any other second-level outcome might have more or less value to individual employees. The valence of first-level outcomes is the sum of the product of the associated second-level outcomes and their instrumentalities. That is, the valence of a first-level outcome depends on the extent to which it results in valuable second-level outcomes. Unlike expectancy and instrumentality, valences can be either positive or negative. If an employee has a strong preference for attaining an outcome, valence is positive. At the other extreme, valence is negative. And if an employee is indifferent to an outcome, valence is 0. The total range is from $-1$ to $+1$. Theoretically, an outcome has a valence because it is related to an employee's needs. Valence, then, provides a link to the content theories of motivation.

In sum, the basic expectancy model shows that the motivational force that an employee exerts on the job is a function of (1) the perceived expectancy that a certain level of performance will result from expending effort and (2) the perceived instrumentality that rewards will result from a certain level of performance, both of which are moderated by the valences attached to these outcomes by the employee. The combination of these three factors that produces the strongest motivation is high positive valence, high expectancy, and high instrumentality. If any key element is low, then motivation will be moderate. If all three elements are low, weak motivation will result.

**Porter-Lawler Model** Lyman Porter and Edward Lawler have extended the concepts of the basic expectancy theory of motivation to examine the factors that influence an employee's performance and satisfaction.[45] For many years, behavioral scientists believed that satisfaction led to performance. This causal relationship can be traced to the human relations era. In recent years, Porter and Lawler have turned the human relationists' proposition around and contend that performance leads to satisfaction. They argue that the intervening variable between these two is rewards. Thus, if employees do a good job and are rewarded for doing so, satisfaction will result. In contrast to human relationists' think-

---

[45]Lyman W. Porter and Edward E. Lawler, *Managerial Attitudes and Performance* (Homewood, IL: Irwin, 1968).

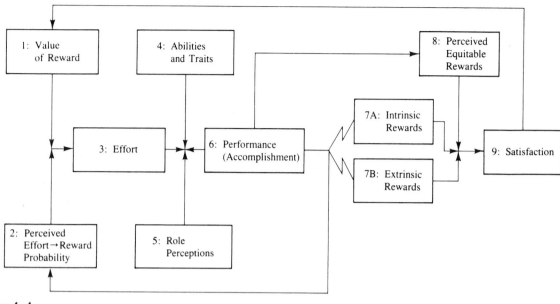

**Figure 4–4**

The Porter-Lawler Model

Source: Adapted from Lyman W. Porter and Edward E. Lawler, *Managerial Attitudes and Performance*, © 1968, p. 37. Used by permission of Irwin, Homewood, IL.

ing, performance is viewed as the independent variable and satisfaction as the dependent variable in a causal relationship.

Figure 4–4 depicts the complex relationship that exists between motivation, performance, and satisfaction. As shown in the model, Boxes 1 through 3 are simply a restatement of the basic expectancy theory of motivation. Value of reward (Box 1) refers to the valence of second-level outcomes. Perceived effort → reward probability (Box 2) refers to perceptions of expectancy and instrumentality. Note that Porter and Lawler recognize that it takes more than effort (Box 3) to produce high performance. They indicate that employees' abilities and traits (Box 4) and their role perceptions (Box 5) will have an effect on performance (Box 6). For example, consider a school principal who manifests high effort but lacks human relations skills, has no knowledge of management techniques, and is confused about the respective roles that teachers, principals, and superintendents play in the school organization. Such a person will perform poorly despite high effort. It is at the point where effort and performance intersect that supervisors make judgments about the motivation of employees. Hence, our principal might be judged by

the superintendent or other direct supervisor as having high but misdirected motivation because she is directing persistent effort that does not help the school achieve its goals.

Performance, then, is the result of effort, abilities and traits, and role perceptions. The resulting level of performance leads to intrinsic rewards (Box 7A). Intrinsic rewards are inherent in the job itself, much like the satisfiers and motivators in Herzberg's motivation-hygiene theory. For example, the school principal who assists several teachers needing help will likely feel a sense of accomplishment. Or performance may lead to extrinsic rewards (Box 7B), which are external to the task. Extrinsic rewards are not guaranteed because they are dependent on evaluations of the employee's performance by supervisors and on the willingness of the organization to reward that performance. For example, the school superintendent may or may not recommend attendance at a state or national principal's conference (an extrinsic reward) for good performance by the principal. Furthermore, employees have their own perception of the equitableness of the total reward received. The individual measures the perceived equitable rewards (Box 8) against the rewards actually received, which result in the level of satisfaction (Box 9) experienced by the employee.

The Porter-Lawler framework resembles an open systems model through its two feedback loops. The feedback loop in the lower part of the model runs from the performance rewards connection to the perceived effort → reward probability. This suggests that if performance is rewarded, the perceived effort → reward probability is strengthened. The feedback loop in the upper part of the model runs from satisfaction to the value of the reward. Porter and Lawler argue that rewards associated with higher-order needs become more attractive, the more the person is rewarded. Thus, intrinsic rewards for performance tend to result in an increased value of these rewards to employees. This is consistent with Maslow's self-actualization needs. Earlier, Maslow suggested that as a self-actualization need is satisfied, it should increase the strength of this need to the individual.[46]

**Research on Expectancy Theory**    Generally, research supports expectancy theory. It has been able to explain the relationship between salary and managerial performance.[47] Research also shows that expectancy theory is effective for predicting the occupational choices of individuals.[48] Earlier, another study supported Porter and Lawler's predictions that differential performance determines rewards and that rewards produce valence in satisfaction.[49]

The number of research efforts investigating the expectancy theory in educational organizations has grown significantly since the mid-1970s, and studies have reported the following: (1) School principals with higher expectancy motivation are more active in attempting to influence district policy than are those lower in expectancy motivation.[50] (2) Schools high in centralization and stratification are staffed with teachers having low expectancy motivation.[51] (3) A significant relationship exists between principal consideration and high expectancy motivation of teachers.[52] (4) A significant relationship exists between motivation and job satisfaction and performance for a sample of secondary and higher education teachers.[53] Expectancy motivation is positively related to student achievement, student and teacher attitudes, and communication among educators.[54]

Research evidence validates expectancy theory. Major components of the theory have been measured, and research related to the theory has been done in different organizational settings including schools. However, three major problems associated with expectancy theory have been highlighted. First, expectancy theory has become so complex that it has exceeded the measures to adequately test it.[55] More recently, however, there have been major improvements in measures.[56] Second, research does not support the notion that individuals actually engage in detailed cognitive arithmetic before deciding at what level to perform. For example, researchers report that upwardly mobile employees tend to engage in the complex multiplicative calculations required by the model, whereas less ambitious employees simply make impulsive decisions before effort

[46]Maslow, *Motivation and Personality.*

[47]Edward E. Lawler, *Strategic Pay: Aligning Organizational Strategies and Pay Systems* (San Francisco: Jossey-Bass, 1990).

[48]John P. Wanous, Thomas L. Keon, and Janina C. Latack, "Expectancy Theory and Occupational/Organizational Choices: A Review and Test," *Organizational Behavior and Human Performance*, 29 (1983): 66–86.

[49]Anthony Pecotich and Gilbert A. Churchill, "An Examination of the Anticipated Satisfaction Importance Valence Controversy," *Organizational Behavior and Human Performance*, 27 (1981): 213–226.

[50]Richard T. Mowday, "The Exercise of Upward Influence in Organizations," *Administrative Science Quarterly*, 23 (1978): 137–156.

[51]H. Scott Herrick, "The Relationship of Organizational Structure to Teacher Motivation in Multiunit and Non-Multiunit Elementary Schools" (Technical Report No. 322), Madison: Wisconsin Research and Development Center for Cognitive Learning, University of Wisconsin, 1973.

[52]C. A. F. Pulvino, "Relationship of Principal Leadership Behavior to Teacher Motivation and Innovation," doctoral dissertation, University of Wisconsin, 1979.

[53]Cecil Miskel, JoAnn DeFrain, and Kay Wilcox, "A Test of Expectancy Motivation Theory in Educational Organizations," *Educational Administration Quarterly*, 16 (1980): 70–92.

[54]Cecil Miskel, David McDonald, and Susan Bloom, "Structural and Expectancy Linkages Within Schools and Organizational Effectiveness," *Educational Administration Quarterly*, 19 (1983): 49–82.

[55]John P. Campbell and Robert D. Pritchard, "Motivation Theory in Industrial and Organizational Psychology," in M. D. Dunnette (ed.), *Handbook of Industrial and Organizational Psychology* (Chicago: Rand McNally, 1976): 63–130.

[56]Daniel R. Ilgen, Delbert M. Nebeker, and Robert D. Pritchard, "Expectancy Theory Measures: An Empirical Comparison in an Experimental Simulation," *Organizational Behavior and Human Performance*, 28 (1981): 189–223.

is exerted.[57] Finally, some researchers question whether the model is complete in its present form. For example, organizational commitment, identification with the employer, loyalty to the organization itself, and lack of job alternatives may be a function of worker beliefs in outcomes or organizational rewards.[58] Others suggest that some factors such as high energy levels of employees or strong beliefs in the work ethic may override expectancy considerations alone.[59] And still others have examined behavioral and decisions theory approaches to motivation beyond what is inherent in the expectancy formulations.[60]

It appears that expectancy theory can accurately predict an employee's work effort, satisfaction, and performance.[61] Moreover, expectancy theory has been shown to be related to a number of important managerial practices including goal setting, which will be discussed later in this chapter.

## Equity Theory

Equity concepts are inherent in the Porter-Lawler model discussed earlier. According to Porter and Lawler, perceived equitable rewards are a major input into employee satisfaction. Earlier, Herzberg found that feelings of inequity was a frequently reported source of dissatisfaction among employees. Although Herzberg did not pay much attention to this finding, a number of theorists have examined the concept of equity to explain employee motivation.[62] Among them, Stacy Adams has de-

veloped the most detailed and organizationally relevant equity theory.[63]

**Equity theory** asserts that employees hold certain beliefs about the outputs they receive from their work and the inputs they invest to obtain these outcomes. The outcomes of employment refer to all things the employee receives as a result of performing the job, such as salary, promotions, fringe benefits, job security, working conditions, job prerequisites, recognition, responsibility, and so on. **Inputs** cover all things that the employee contributes to performing the job and include education, experience, ability, training, personality traits, job efforts, attitude, and so on. Employees expect that the ratio of their outcomes to inputs will be fair or equitable. But how do employees judge fairness?

**General Model**   Simply put, equity theory argues that employees evaluate the equity, or fairness, of their outcomes by a process of social comparison. Employees compare the ratio of their outcomes to inputs with the ratio of outcomes to inputs for some comparison other. The comparison other may be a colleague or a group average (such as prevailing standards in a school, school district, or job role). For example, superintendents often use other superintendents as the comparison others rather than corporate executives. The equity relationship can be diagrammed as follows:

$$\frac{\text{Outcomes (employee)}}{\text{Inputs (employee)}} \quad \text{versus} \quad \frac{\text{Outcomes (comparison others)}}{\text{Inputs (comparison others)}}$$

When these ratios are equal, the employee should feel that a fair and equitable exchange exists with the employer. Such equitable exchange should contribute to employee–job satisfaction. Conversely, when ratios are unequal, inequity is perceived by the employee, which should contribute to job dissatisfaction. Obviously, the ideal ratio between outcomes and inputs is perfect equity. Schematically, perfect equity is

$$\frac{\text{Outcomes (employee)}}{\text{Inputs (employee)}} = \frac{\text{Outcomes (comparison others)}}{\text{Inputs (comparison others)}}$$

[57]Barry M. Staw and Larry L. Cummings (eds.), *Research in Organizational Behavior,* vol. 12 (Greenwich, CT: JAI Press, 1990).

[58]Richard W. Scholl, "Differentiating Organizational Commitment from Expectancy as a Motivating Force," *Academy of Management Review,* 6 (1981): 589–599.

[59]Lawrence R. Walker and Kenneth W. Thomas, "Beyond Expectancy Theory: An Integrative Motivational Model from Health Care," *Academy of Management Review,* 7 (1982): 187–194.

[60]John Naylor, Robert Pritchard, and Daniel Ilgen, *A Theory of Behavior in Organizations* (New York: Academic Press, 1980).

[61]Miner, *Organizational Behavior 3.*

[62]Karen S. Cook and Karen A. Hegtvedt, "Distributive Justice, Equity, and Equality," *Annual Review of Sociology,* 9 (1983): 217–241.

[63]J. Stacy Adams, "Inequity in Social Exchange," in L. Berkowitz (ed.), *Advances in Experimental Social Psychology,* vol. 2 (New York: Academic Press, 1965): 267–299.

Inequity can occur in either direction: (1) when employees feel their ratio of outcomes to inputs is less than that of the comparison other and (2) when employees feel their ratio of outcomes to inputs is greater than that of the comparison other. The first situation, in which the employee's perceived outcomes-to-inputs ratio is less than the comparison other, can be diagrammed as follows:

$$\frac{\text{Outcomes (employee)}}{\text{Inputs (employee)}} < \frac{\text{Outcomes (comparison others)}}{\text{Inputs (comparison others)}}$$

The second situation, in which the employee's perceived ratio of outcomes to inputs is greater than that of the comparison other, can be diagrammed as follows:

$$\frac{\text{Outcomes (employee)}}{\text{Inputs (employee)}} > \frac{\text{Outcomes (comparison others)}}{\text{Inputs (comparison others)}}$$

This prediction is less straightforward than the former because the employee is at an advantage vis-à-vis the comparison other. Nevertheless, the theory argues that employees will feel uncomfortable about the inequity of their outcome-to-input ratio compared to the outcome-to-input ratio of their comparison other.

Comparisons of the inputs and outputs of the employee and comparison other are similar to those judgments made by employees according to expectancy theory. They are based on the employee's perceptions, which may or may not be valid. Inequity in either direction creates discomfort and tension, and the employee is motivated to reduce the tension and restore equity.

**Methods of Restoring Equity** An employee may engage in any of the following behaviors to restore equity:[64]

1. *Alter Inputs.* An employee who feels underpaid may contribute less time and effort to the job or demand a salary increase. An employee who feels overpaid may increase the quantity and quality of his work, expend extra hours without pay, and so on.

2. *Alter Outcomes.* Unions attract members by pledging to improve salary, working conditions, and

[64]Lyman W. Porter et al. *Motivation and Work Behavior* (New York: McGraw-Hill, 2003).

hours without any increase in employee effort or input. For example, many teacher unions have managed to negotiate a decrease in calendar days while increasing teacher salaries, fringe benefits, and working conditions.

3. *Cognitively Distort Inputs or Outcomes.* According to the theory of cognitive dissonance, the individual tries to modify one of the incompatible perceptions so as to reduce the tension or dissonance. In a sense, that person engages in coping behavior to regain a condition of consonance or equilibrium. For example, if a colleague (comparison other) were receiving disproportionately high outcomes in comparison with another employee, that fact could make the employee tense. As a coping strategy, the employee could distort his perception by reasoning that the comparison other possesses more job knowledge or intelligence than the employee does. Conversely, an employee can justify the disproportionately high outcomes he receives by convincing himself that he possesses more experience or ability than the comparison other does.

4. *Change the Inputs or Outcomes of the Comparison Other.* Behaviors designed to change the actual or perceived inputs or outcomes of the comparison other can take many forms. A colleague (comparison other) may be forced to reduce his inputs, or a colleague may be pressured into leaving the organization. Or the comparison other's inputs or outputs may come to be viewed differently. For example, an employee may come to believe that the comparison other actually works harder than he does and therefore deserves greater outcomes or rewards.

5. *Change the Comparison Other.* If the input-to-outcome ratio of an employee to a comparison other results in feelings of inequity, the employee can switch his comparison other to restore equity. For example, a very ambitious superintendent, who has been comparing herself to the state's top superintendents, may decide instead to use his colleagues in smaller school districts who are paid less than he is as his comparison others.

6. *Leave the Organization.* An employee can request a transfer or leave the organization entirely.

**Research on Equity Theory** The limited research to date generally supports the theory and provides some important insights into the concept. First, overpayment (positive inequity) may motivate people to increase their performance.[65] Moreover, overpayment inequity appears to work best with those who have a strong conscience and a sense of what is ethically appropriate.[66] In contrast, underpayment (negative inequity) seems to lead to absenteeism and turnover.[67] Second, some employees seek to establish competitive edges for their supervisor's favor. When these competitive edges are created so that an employee's input-to-output ratio exceeds another's, the employee with the competitive edge may tolerate inequity for a longer period of time.[68] Some employees are more sensitive to inequity than others; consequently, equity theory becomes much more relevant to these individuals. Other employees tend to respond to performance-reward incongruencies more in terms of expectancy theory.[69] The major criticism of equity theory is the inability to predict which method(s) employees will use to restore equity.[70] Research will need to address this issue in order to increase the applicability of equity theory in the motivation of employees in schools.

## Goal-Setting Theory

Goals have a pervasive influence on behavior in school organizations and administrative practice. Nearly every modern school organization has some form of goal setting in operation. Programs such as campus improvement plans (CIP), planning programming budgeting systems (PPBS), management information systems (MIS), as well as systems thinking and strategic planning, include the development of specific goals.

There has been considerable development of **goal-setting theory** initiated primarily by the work of Edwin Locke. Locke's contributions to goal-setting theory are the following.[71]

1. Difficult goals lead to higher task performance than do easier goals.

2. Specific goals lead to higher performance than do vague goals such as "do your best."

3. The mechanisms by which goals affect performance are directing attention and action, mobilizing effort, increasing persistence, and motivating a search for appropriate performance strategies.

4. Feedback appears necessary for goal setting to work because it allows people to compare their performance against their goals.

5. Goal commitment is necessary if goals are to affect performance, and expectation of success and degree of success affect goal commitment.

6. Individual differences in factors like personality and education are not generally related to goal-setting performance.

**General Model**   Figure 4–5 depicts a simplified view of goal-setting theory. According to the theory, there appear to be two cognitive determinants of behavior: values and intentions (goals). A goal is defined simply as what the individual is consciously trying to do. Locke postulates that the form in which one experiences one's value judgments is emotional. That is, one's values create a desire to do things consistent with them. Goals also affect behavior (job performance) through other mechanisms. For Locke, goals therefore direct attention and action. Furthermore, challenging goals mobilize energy, lead to higher effort, and increase persistent effort. Goals motivate people to develop strategies that will enable them to perform at the required goal levels. Finally, accomplishing the goal can lead to satisfaction and further motivation, or frustration and lower motivation if the goal is not accomplished.[72]

[65]Jerald Greenberg and Gerald Leventhal, "Equity and the Use of Overreward to Motivate Performance," *Journal of Personality and Social Psychology*, 34 (1976): 179–190.

[66]Robert P. Vecchio, "An Individual-Differences Interpretation of the Conflict Predictions Generated by Equity Theory and Expectancy Theory," *Journal of Applied Psychology*, 66 (1981): 470–481.

[67]Michael R. Carrell and John E. Dittrich, "Employee Perceptions of Fair Treatment," *Personnel Journal*, 55 (1976): 523–524.

[68]R. Dennis Middlemist and Richard B. Peterson, "Test of Equity Theory by Controlling for Comparison Coworkers Efforts," *Organizational Behavior and Human Performance*, 15 (1976): 335–354.

[69]Richard C. Huseman, John D. Hatfield, and Edward W. Miles, "Test for Individual Perceptions of Job Equity: Some Preliminary Findings," *Perceptual and Motor Skills*, 61 (1985): 1055–1064.

[70]Porter et al., *Motivation and Work Behavior*.

[71]Edwin A. Locke and Gary P. Latham, *A Theory of Goal Setting and Task Performance*, 2nd ed. (Englewood Cliffs, NJ: Prentice Hall, 1995).

[72]Ibid.

*Satisfaction and Further Motivation*

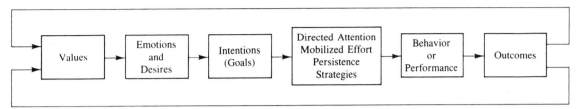

*Frustration and Lower Motivation*

**Figure 4–5**

General Model of Goal-Setting Theory

## PRO/CON Debate

### Merit Pay

In many workplaces financial incentives are offered to motivate performance. For example, sales-people frequently operate on commission—the more they sell, the more they earn. In the educational realm, many administrators receive annual salary increments based on some form of merit pay system. A merit pay system allows those whose performance is judged as superior to earn more than those whose work is deemed to be average.

**Question:** Would merit pay increase teacher performance?

**Arguments PRO**

1. Teachers receive little or no external recognition for the important work they do. Merit pay would justly reward truly superior teachers and motivate them to continue their fine work.

2. Unlike thirty years ago, we now know what good teaching is. We can ensure that it occurs in classrooms by measuring it and awarding salary proportionally.

3. With a merit pay system, average teachers would be motivated to excel. Competition works for students, why not for teachers? Our society functions on the basis of competition.

**Arguments CON**

1. Excellent teachers are born, not made. The work itself motivates them, not some external reward.

2. While we can recognize good teaching when we see it, it is difficult to develop a system that recognizes excellence in all its forms. Most attempts at merit pay in education have failed because of this measurement problem.

3. A norm of the teaching profession is cooperation, so teachers avoid situations where the actions of a few are singled out as either good or bad. Merit pay does not fit this norm of cooperation.

**Research on Goal-Setting Theory** One researcher claims that goal setting improves performance about 90 percent of the time.[73] Furthermore, Locke and his associates report that goal setting resulted in a median performance improvement of 16 percent. And when goal setting was combined with monetary rewards, the median performance increase was over 40 percent.[74] The early evidence came primarily from laboratory

---

[73]Thomas R. Chidester and W. Charles Grigsby, "A Meta-Analysis of the Goal Setting–Performance Literature," *Academy of Management Proceedings*, 44 (1984): 202–206.

[74]Edwin A. Locke et al., "The Relative Effectiveness of Four Methods of Motivating Employee Performance," in K. Duncan, M. Gruneberg, and D. Wallis (eds.), *Changes in Work Life* (New York: Wiley, 1980).

investigations; now there is evidence that goal setting works in organizational settings as well.[75]

Several important issues remain unanswered. First, according to Locke, individual differences in factors like personality are not generally related to goal-setting effectiveness. However, employees with strong achievement motivation appear to be more responsive to goal setting than do others.[76] Another unanswered question is the effect that subordinate participation in goal setting has on employee performance. Early research indicated that employee participation in goal setting led to job satisfaction but not increased performance.[77] But employee participation in goal setting can also improve performance.[78] Finally, evidence indicates that a supportive management style has a moderating effect between goal setting and performance.[79] Despite these unanswered questions, ample evidence shows that goal setting has a significant impact on the motivation and performance of employees.

## Summary

1. Motivation is the extent to which persistent effort is directed toward organizational objectives.

2. Content theories of motivation are concerned with identifying the specific factors that motivate employees. The three content theories discussed were Maslow's need hierarchy theory, Herzberg's motivation-hygiene theory, and Alderfer's ERG theory.

3. Maslow's need hierarchy theory proposes five levels of needs (physiological, safety, social, esteem, and self-actualization). These needs are arranged in a prepotency hierarchy. School administrators often use it when analyzing motivational problems in schools.

4. Herzberg's motivation-hygiene theory proposes that two distinct factors influence motivation—hygienes, which merely prevent dissatisfaction, and motivators, which are the source of satisfaction and motivation for the employee. One important application of this theory, job enrichment, is recommended by the Holmes Group, Carnegie Task Force, and the National Commission on Excellence in Educational Administration for restructuring schools.

5. Alderfer's ERG theory is similar to Maslow's need hierarchy theory, but it is not as rigid concerning prepotency of needs. Like Herzberg's motivation-hygiene theory, ERG theory makes a distinction between intrinsic and extrinsic motivation. The theory is easily understood and useful to school administrators.

6. Process theories of motivation focus on how various factors interact to affect employee motivation. The three process theories discussed were expectancy theory, equity theory, and goal-setting theory.

7. Expectancy theory helps school administrators explain how behavior is directed. It is concerned with why employees choose certain paths toward obtaining outcomes that will satisfy their needs.

8. Equity theory helps school administrators understand how employees calculate what they put into the job with what they receive for their performance and compare that with what they perceive others are contributing and receiving as rewards for performance. Inequitable relationships resulting from such calculations cause the equity-sensitive employee to restore equity.

9. Goal setting helps channel an employee's persistent effort toward organizationally relevant outcomes. Goals can be a powerful motivational device, providing they are accepted by the employee.

[75]Locke and Latham, *A Theory of Goal Setting and Task Performance*.

[76]Donald J. Campbell, "Determinants of Choice of Goal Difficulty Level: A Review of Situational and Personality Influences," *Journal of Occupational Psychology*, 55 (1982): 79–95.

[77]Edwin A. Locke and Douglas Henne, "Work Motivation Theories," in C. L. Cooper and I. Robertson (eds.), *Review of Industrial and Organizational Psychology* (Chichester, England: Wiley, 1986).

[78]Miriam Erez, P. Christopher Earley, and Charles L. Hulin, "The Impact of Participation on Goal Acceptance: A Two-Step Model," *Academy of Management Journal*, 28 (1985): 50–66.

[79]Gary P. Latham and Lise M. Saari, "Importance of Supportive Relationships in Goal Setting," *Journal of Applied Psychology*, 64 (1979): 151–156.

## Key Terms

motivation
effort
persistence
direction
content theories

need hierarchy theory
motivation-hygiene theory
ERG theory
process theories
expectancy theory
outcomes
expectancy
instrumentality
valence
Porter-Lawler model
equity theory
inputs
comparison other
goal-setting theory

## Discussion Questions

1. Describe how a school administrator would assess the individual needs of employees.

2. Once needs are assessed, discuss how the school administrator could use the needs hierarchy, the motivation-hygiene theory, and ERG concepts to motivate employees.

3. Of what practical value is the expectancy theory for school administrators? What can school administrators learn from the theory to improve their effectiveness in motivating employees at work?

4. How might a school employee's perceived inequity be dysfunctional to the school system?

5. What are the four key elements of goal-setting theory, and how do they pertain to employee motivation?

## Suggested Readings

Bredeson, Paul V. *Designs for Learning: A New Architecture for Professional Development in Schools* (Thousand Oaks, CA: Corwin Press, 2002). Using the metaphor of architecture, this landmark book outlines innovative ways to create and implement professional development, and highlights the rationale behind why these changes are so crucial. This insightful guide also offers straightforward explanations of the past, present, and future of professional development programs.

De Pree, Max. *Leading Without Power: Finding Hope in Serving Community* (New York: John Wiley,

2003). The author provides fresh wisdom on what it takes to inspire people toward their potential in business, nonprofit organizations . . . and life. With his usual warmth and wisdom, Max De Pree shows leaders how to lead without power and transform their organizations into movements that fulfill the human spirit.

Fruchter, Norm. *Urban Schools, Public Will* (New York: Teachers College Press, 2006). In this important book, Norm Fruchter argues that our national failure to carry out the *Brown* mandate has produce segregated urban school systems that fail poor students of color. Drawing on a rich array of research and personal experience, he examines why urban districts have failed and what must be done to transform our city schools. He identifies urban districts as the key actors in this transformation and profiles three school districts that have achieved significant success in closing the achievement gap. He also identifies grassroots community organizing as a critical lever for provoking and supporting meaningful change in schools.

Hoyle, John R. *Leadership and Futuring: Making Visions Happen* (Thousand Oaks, CA: Corwin Press, 2006). This updated book serves as a guide for visionary leaders striving to lead, inspire, and motivate students and team members toward positive personal visions, successful lives, and fulfilling careers. Characteristics of effective leaders and techniques for improving visionary leadership are highlighted.

Kouzes, James M., and Barry Z. Posner. *The Leadership Challenge* (New York: John Wiley, 2006). The authors explore the art of encouragement and reveal the practices and techniques that exceptional leaders use to inspire extraordinary performance in others.

Owens, Robert G. et al. *Organizational Behavior in Education: Adaptive Leadership and School Reform* (Boston, MA: Allyn and Bacon, 2006). This edition of *Organizational Behavior in Education* marks the thirty-sixth year of the publication of this popular text that synthesizes the research on such aspects of organizational behavior as organizational culture, leadership, motivation, change, conflict, and decision making.

Petri, Herbert L. *Motivation: Theory, Research, and Application.* (Belmont, CA: Thomson Wadsworth, 2003). This volume provides a comprehensive treatment of motivation and an extensive bibliography.

# 5. Leadership

FOCUSING QUESTIONS

1 What is leadership?

2 Are there traits or skills that differentiate leaders from nonleaders, or effective leaders from ineffective ones?

3 What kinds of leadership behavior are more effective than others?

4 In what situations will one leader be successful, while another will be unsuccessful?

5 What are some key situational factors that are significant in determining which leadership style to use in a given situation?

6 Why is it important for an administrator to develop the ability to diagnose a situation?

In this chapter, we attempt to answer these questions concerning leadership in school organizations. We begin our discussion by exploring the nature of leadership in organizations. Next we examine the concept of emotional intelligence as one of the essentials of leadership. Then we discuss the trait, behavioral, and contingency approaches to leadership. Finally, we present and analyze various styles of leadership. A summary of supporting research on these approaches is included.

## The Nature of Leadership

Since the beginning of the twentieth century, the topic of **leadership** has been the object of extensive study. During this time, both researchers and practitioners have sought to analyze and define leadership. Today there are almost as many different definitions of effective leadership as there are researchers who have studied the concept. More than 3000 empirical investigations have examined leadership.[1] More recently, Kenneth Leithwood and Daniel Duke reviewed the literature dealing with leadership in educational administration over approximately the past decade.[2] The results suggest that six major categories of leadership dominate contemporary writing about school leadership: instructional leadership, transformational leadership, moral leadership, participative leadership, contingency leadership, and managerial leadership.

[1] Bernard M. Bass, *Bass and Stogdill's Handbook of Leadership: Theory, Research, and Managerial Applications*, 4th ed. (New York: Simon & Schuster, 2007).

[2] Kenneth Leithwood and Daniel L. Duke, "A Century's Quest to Understand School Leadership," in J. Murphy and K. S. Lewis (eds.), *Handbook of Research on Educational Administration*, 2nd ed. (San Francisco: Jossey-Bass, 1999), pp. 45–72.

**Instructional leadership** typically focuses *"on the behaviors of teachers as they engage in activities directly affecting the growth of students"* (emphasis in original).[3] Most conceptions of instructional leadership allocate authority and influence to formal administrative roles, usually the building principal. But there is some disagreement over where instructional leadership resides. Principals alone cannot fulfill all of a school's needs for instructional leadership. Some argue for the value of teachers serving as instructional leaders. Others focus on district-level instructional leadership. Still others challenge the idea that instructional leadership can be a substitute for capable management. However, most examples of contemporary models of instructional leadership concern the effects of leadership behaviors on student achievement and other important school outcomes.

**Transformational leadership** includes a variety of terms used to define the concept: charismatic, visionary, cultural, and empowering. The focus of transformational leadership is on *"the commitments and capacities of organizational members"* (emphasis in original).[4] Transformational leaders raise organizational members' levels of personal commitment to achieve organizational goals, resulting in greater productivity. Authority and influence are not necessarily allocated to those occupying formal positions, although this perspective may be evident. Rather, power is attributed to whomever is able to inspire higher levels of personal commitment and the accomplishment of group goals. The concept of transformational leadership has varying interpretations, but the most common interpretation seems to be that "transforming leadership ultimately becomes moral in that it raises the level of ethical aspiration of both leader and led, and thus has a transforming effect on both"[5] by raising their levels of commitment to mutual purposes and by further developing their capacities for achieving those purposes.[6]

The focus of **moral leadership** is on *"the values and ethics of leadership"* (emphasis in original),[7] so authority and influence are to be derived from defensible conceptions of what is right and good. The research reviewed illustrates quite different approaches to moral leadership. However, all seem to agree that leadership in a democratic society entails a moral imperative to promote equity, democratic community, and social justice.

**Participative leadership,** variously called "group," "shared," or "teacher" leadership, stresses *"the decision-making processes of the group"* (emphasis in original).[8] A majority of the research associated participative leadership with increased organizational effectiveness. Site-based management (SBM) was seen as the vehicle for achieving such goals.

The focus of **contingency leadership** is on *"how leaders respond to the unique organizational circumstances or problems that they face"* (emphasis in original)[9] as a consequence of the preferences of coworkers, conditions of work, and the tasks to be completed. It is assumed, using this approach to leadership, that there are wide variations in the contexts for leadership and that to be effective these different contexts require different leadership styles. It is also assumed that individuals providing contingency leadership, typically those in formal administrative roles, are capable of mastering a large repertoire of leadership styles. Their influence depends, in large measure, on matching the appropriate leadership style to the situation. Leadership styles have been studied extensively in both school and nonschool settings. We will examine some of these later in the chapter.

**Managerial leadership** focuses on *"the functions, tasks, or behaviors of the leader"* (emphasis in original)[10] and assumes that if these functions are carried out competently, the work of others in the organization will be facilitated. A distinction between leadership and management is frequently made in the research literature. This distinction usually entails allocating management with responsibilities for policy implementation, maintaining organizational stability, and dealing with the day-to-day routines of the job such as providing and distributing financial and material resources, managing the school facility, managing the student body, maintaining effective communications with education stakeholders, reducing disruptions to the instructional program, mediating conflicts, and attending to political demands of the school or school district. Leadership, in contrast, entails responsibilities for policymaking, organizational change, and other more dynamic processes of work.

---

[3] Ibid., p. 47.

[4] Ibid., p. 48.

[5] James M. Burns, *Leadership* (New York: Harper & Row, 1978), p. 20.

[6] Leithwood and Duke, "A Century's Quest to Understand School Leadership," p. 49.

[7] Ibid., p. 50.

[8] Ibid., p. 51.

[9] Ibid., p. 54.

[10] Ibid., p. 53.

Warren Bennis and Burt Nanus offer a clever distinction, however, between a **manager** and a **leader**: A manager does the *thing right;* a leader does the *right thing.*[11] The first person is concerned about carrying out policy; the second person formulates policy. The first person thinks in terms of trees; the second person has a larger view of life and deals with the forest.

To be sure, an organization needs good management, not necessarily good leadership, to survive—that is, people who can deal with the day-to-day functions, activities, and routines. Otherwise, the organization falls apart from the bottom up. Very quickly, poor management catches up with the organization. But the person on top need not always be a leader in the sense that she has vision or direction or can cope with the future. It's only after many years that poor leadership takes a toll on the organization—that is, when trends or events catch up to the organization.

Effective leaders, according to Peter Drucker, do not make many decisions. They focus on important ones and ones that have impact on the larger aspects of the organization. They try to think through what is generic and strategic, rather than solve daily problems or "put out fires." They try to make few important decisions on the highest level of conceptual understanding.[12] Effective leaders in organizations engage in decentralized decision making—that is, responsibility and authority are given to middle management—and shared decision making—that is, decisions are made in a committee or by a group. Thus, effective leaders bring in people inside and outside the organization as part of the team. In school contexts, justifying a distinction between management and leadership is difficult. Deal and Peterson adopt a "bifocal" perspective.[13]

The six major categories of leadership contain three important concepts. First, there is no clear, agreed-on definition of leadership in schools. Second, although the six major categories of leadership were presented as distinct leadership models, they are not pure types. They differ with respect to their basic foci and the premises on which the foci are based. Differences also exist with respect to the sources of leadership influence. Sometimes leadership influence resides in those occupying formal positions. At other times, the nature and locus of leadership influence is attributed to whomever is able to inspire their commitments to collective aspirations and the desire to accomplish collective goals. Third, there are many aspects of the six leadership models that are similar. Each leadership approach is concerned with student achievement, ethics and values, democratic principles, and social justice.

## What Makes a Good Leader?

With respect to the nature and locus of leadership influence, Daniel Goleman and colleagues provide an interesting perspective.[14] They argue that leadership is not about who's smarter or tougher but about qualities we all have or can develop. They relate how just after the World Trade Center towers collapsed on September 11, a stunned nation was glued to a press conference with New York City Mayor Rudy Giuliani. Asked by a reporter how many people died in the collapse, Giuliani replied, "We don't know the exact number yet, but whatever the number, it will be more than we can bear."

In that moment, Giuliani performed a masterful act of leadership according to Daniel Goleman. He spoke with conviction, from the depths of his own heart, in a way that resonated with our own unspoken feelings. Like Giuliani, great leaders move us deeply. They inspire us by touching our feelings. Leadership works through the emotions. That's true whether they head a large urban school district, a rural elementary classroom, or a local PTA meeting.

Research conducted by Daniel Goleman and colleagues is bringing scientific data to the question of leadership. They have been tracking the science of outstanding performance for the last two decades. In order to identify the essential ingredients of outstanding leadership, they reviewed data ranging from neurology to measures of the emotional climate that the leader creates. Hundreds of studies in organizations of all kinds—from small family businesses to the largest companies, from religious groups to schools and hospitals—have yielded a dozen or so abilities that distinguish the best leaders. (See Table 5–1 to rate yourself on some of these essentials of leadership.)

---

[11] Warren Bennis and Burt Nanus, *Leaders: The Strategies for Taking Charge* (New York: HarperCollins, 2007).

[12] Peter F. Drucker, *Management: Tasks, Responsibilities, Practices* (New York: Transaction Publishers, 2007).

[13] Terrance E. Deal and Kent D. Peterson, *The Leadership Paradox: Balancing Logic and Artistry in Schools* (San Francisco: Jossey-Bass, 2000).

[14] Daniel Goleman, Richard Boyzatzis, and Annie McKee, *Primal Leadership: Realizing the Power of Emotional Intelligence* (Boston: Harvard University Press, 2002).

## Table 5–1 Leadership Skills: Rate Yourself

*The best leaders have strengths in at least a half-dozen key emotional-intelligence competencies out of 20 or so. To see how you rate on some of these abilities, assess how the statements below apply to you. While getting a precise profile of your strengths and weaknesses requires a more rigorous assessment, this quiz can give you a rough rating. More important, we hope it will get you thinking about how well you use leadership skills—and how you might get better at it.*

| Statement | Seldom | Occasionally | Often | Frequently |
|---|---|---|---|---|
| 1. I am aware of what I am feeling. | ☐ | ☐ | ☐ | ☐ |
| 2. I know my strengths and weaknesses. | ☐ | ☐ | ☐ | ☐ |
| 3. I deal calmly with stress. | ☐ | ☐ | ☐ | ☐ |
| 4. I believe the future will be better than the past. | ☐ | ☐ | ☐ | ☐ |
| 5. I deal with changes easily. | ☐ | ☐ | ☐ | ☐ |
| 6. I set measurable goals when I have a project. | ☐ | ☐ | ☐ | ☐ |
| 7. Others say I understand and am sensitive to them. | ☐ | ☐ | ☐ | ☐ |
| 8. Others say I resolve conflicts. | ☐ | ☐ | ☐ | ☐ |
| 9. Others say I build and maintain relationships. | ☐ | ☐ | ☐ | ☐ |
| 10. Others say I inspire them. | ☐ | ☐ | ☐ | ☐ |
| 11. Others say I am a team player. | ☐ | ☐ | ☐ | ☐ |
| 12. Others say I helped to develop their abilities. | ☐ | ☐ | ☐ | ☐ |

Total the number of checks in each column: ___ ___ ___ ___
Multiply this number by: ×1 ×2 ×3 ×4
To get your score, add these four numbers: = ___ + ___ + ___ + ___

**Interpretation:** Total: ___

**36 +:** An overall score of 36 or higher suggests you are using key leadership abilities well—but ask a coworker or partner for his opinions, to be more certain. **30–35:** Suggests some strengths but also some underused leadership abilities. **29 or less:** Suggests unused leadership abilities and room for improvement.

Leaders are unique, and they can show their talent in different ways. To further explore your leadership strengths, you might ask people whose opinions you value: "When you have seen me do really well as a leader, which of these abilities am I using?" If a number of people tell you that you use the same quality when doing well, you have likely identified a leadership strength that should be appreciated and nurtured.

Source: Daniel Goleman, "Could You Be a Leader?" Sunday Star Ledger, *Parade Magazine,* June 16, 2002, p. 5.

Just what are the essentials of leadership? Goleman's work and that of hundreds of other researchers make clear that what sets the beloved leaders apart from those we hate is excellence at things like "motivating power," "empathy," "integrity," and "intuitive ability." These abilities fall within the domain of **emotional intelligence**—an adeptness at managing ourselves and our interactions with others—not school smarts. For instance, why do Phil Jackson, Oprah Winfrey, the Dalai Lama, and Colin Powell have what it takes to be effective leaders? Phil Jackson, LA Lakers coach, winner of nine NBA championships, has "motivating power." His skill in bringing out the best from his players helps to make the team a winner. Oprah Winfrey has "empathy." Her capacity to listen, to relate, and to communicate the pain and resolve of millions has given her enormous authority. The Dalai Lama has "integrity." His consistent stance of tolerance, nonviolence, and humility has made him a great moral leader and a voice of conscience. Former Secretary of State Colin Powell has "intuitive ability." His ability to connect with others makes him a superior diplomat.

According to Daniel Goleman and colleagues, new findings in brain science reveal that this kind of intelligence uses different parts of the brain than does the academic kind. Cognitive abilities such as verbal fluency or mathematics skills reside in the neocortex, the wrinkled topmost layers, which are the most recent evolutionary addition to the human brain. But emotional intelligence relies largely on the ancient emotional centers deep in the midbrain between the ears, with links to the prefrontal cortex—the brain's executive center, just behind the forehead.[15]

According to Goleman and colleagues, this may explain the fact that IQ and emotional intelligence are surprisingly independent. Of course, to be a great leader, you need enough intelligence to understand the issues at hand, but you need not be supersmart. By the same token, people who are intellectually gifted can be disasters as leaders. Such situations are all too common in organizations everywhere. It happens when people are promoted for the wrong set of skills: IQ abilities rather than the emotional intelligence abilities that good leaders display.

## Can You Learn to Lead?

According to Goleman and colleagues, the aptitudes of leadership, unlike academic or technical skills, are learned in life. That's good news for all of us. If you are weak in leadership, you can get better at virtually any point in life with the right effort. But it takes motivation, a clear idea of what you need to improve, and consistent practice. For example, good leaders are excellent listeners. Let's assume that you need to become a better listener. Perhaps you cut people off and take over the conversation without hearing them out. The first step: Become aware of the moments you do this and stop yourself. Instead, let the other people speak their minds. Ask questions to be sure you understand their viewpoints. Then—and only then—give your own opinion. With practice, you can become a better listener.[16]

Another skill that good leaders possess is helping others stay in a positive emotional state. Research shows that leaders who achieve the best results get people to laugh three times more often than do mediocre leaders.[17] Laughter signals that people are not caught up in, say, anger or fear but rather are relaxed and enjoying

what they do—and so they are more likely to be creative, focused, and productive. In sum, leaders are made, not born.

## Leader Traits

Popular literature supports the view that leaders are different from other people. If they were not different, neither researchers nor practitioners would have devoted so much attention to the study of leadership. We have noted that leaders can influence others in accomplishing goals. It seems natural to inquire whether the secret of leadership lies in the characteristics, or traits, of leaders. Are leaders different from nonleaders in terms of personality traits, physical characteristics, motives, and needs? Are there certain **traits** and **skills** that distinguish successful leaders from unsuccessful ones? We will attempt to answer these questions in the following sections.

### Traits of Leaders Compared with Nonleaders

Early studies of leadership attempted to isolate traits that would reliably differentiate leaders from nonleaders. Ralph Stogdill reviewed 124 empirical studies conducted between 1904 and 1947.[18] Low-level relationships, ranging between 0.09 and 0.26, were found in many different areas. The research suggested that leaders possessed a number of traits and skills that were not observed in nonleaders. However, the presence of a given trait seemed to vary across situations. Stogdill classified five traits and skills under the following general headings:[19]

1. *Capacity* (intelligence, alertness, verbal facility, originality, judgment).

2. *Achievement* (scholarship, knowledge, athletic accomplishments).

3. *Responsibility* (dependability, initiative, persistence, aggressiveness, self-confidence, desire to excel).

4. *Participation* (activity, sociability, cooperation, adaptability, humor).

5. *Status* (socioeconomic position, popularity).

---

[15]Ibid.

[16]Bruce Benward and Timothy J. Kolosick, *Ear Training: A Technique for Listening* (Madison, WI: Brown and Benchmark, 1995); Larry Barker, *Listening Behavior* (New Orleans: Spectra, 1991).

[17]Goleman, Boyzatzis, and McKee, *Primal Leadership: Realizing the Power of Emotional Intelligence.*

[18]Ralph M. Stogdill, "Personal Factors Associated with Leadership: A Survey of the Literature," *Journal of Psychology,* 25 (1948): 35–71.

[19]Bass, *Bass and Stogdill's Handbook of Leadership.*

Several years after Stogdill's widely quoted survey of leadership studies, other research concluded that the numerous studies of personalities of leaders have failed to find any consistent patterns of traits that characterize leaders.[20] Disappointing results such as these are partly attributable to combining leadership studies from varying situations, each of which may have different leadership demands. For example, combining a study assessing the personal traits of football coaches with a study examining the personal characteristics of corporate executives will probably result in inconclusive findings. Leadership studies that examine leaders in comparable situations are more likely to reveal traits that differentiate between more effective and less effective leaders.

## Traits of Effective Leaders

More recent trait research is being conducted in a different way. Rather than comparing leaders and nonleaders across a number of situations, researchers are comparing effective with ineffective leaders in the same situation, or they are comparing the relationship between traits and leadership effectiveness. The results of these studies are stronger and more consistent than the earlier trait studies.

The literature on traits of effective leaders can be organized into three categories of studies. In the first category, leaders are evaluated in terms of the actual performance of their organizational units. Because effectiveness is influenced by so many factors, there are only a handful of studies evaluating the impact of leadership on organizational performance. Some of the best evidence we have concerns the performance of flight crews and U.S. presidents. These studies show that certain leadership traits correlate with enhanced unit performance, when appropriate components of effectiveness are examined.

Research on the performance of commercial airline flight crews is important because breakdowns in team performance are the primary cause of airline accidents. Researchers showed that flight crew performance—defined in terms of the number and severity of errors made by the crew—correlates significantly with the leadership traits of the captain. Crews with captains who were warm, friendly, self-confident, and able to stand up to pressure made the fewest errors. Conversely, crews with captains who were arrogant, hostile, boastful, egotistical, passive-aggressive, or dictatorial made the most errors.[21] With respect to U.S. presidents, researchers reported that effective presidents—labeled charismatic—have strong needs for power and high energy levels, and they are socially assertive, achievement oriented, self-confident, emotionally stable, nurturant, and have a high need for change.[22]

In the second category, subordinates', supervisors', and self ratings are used to evaluate leader effectiveness. What leadership traits do subordinates feel are most important? Research indicates that credibility or trustworthiness may be the single most important factor in subordinates' judgments of a leader's effectiveness.[23] Subordinates' and supervisors' evaluations of a target leader's performance were found to be reasonably congruent ($r = 0.50$). However, supervisors' ratings of a leader's overall effectiveness were largely influenced by judgments of technical competence (e.g., "The leader is a flexible and far-sighted problem solver"), whereas subordinates' ratings of a leader's overall effectiveness were largely influenced by judgments of integrity (e.g., "My leader has earned my trust"). In addition, leaders' self-ratings were uncorrelated with the ratings of the other groups.[24] But there is a type of leader who routinely overevaluates self-performance, and that tendency is associated with poor leadership.[25]

[20]Cecil A. Gibb, "Leadership," in G. Lindzey (ed.), *Handbook of Social Psychology*, vol. 2 (Reading, MA: Addison-Wesley, 1954), pp. 877–920.

[21]Thomas R. Chidester et al., "Pilot Personality and Crew Coordination," *International Journal of Aviation Psychology*, 1 (1991): 25–44.

[22]Robert J. House, William D. Spangler, and John Waycke, "Personality and Charisma in the U.S. Presidency: A Psychological Theory of Leadership Effectiveness," *Administrative Science Quarterly*, 36 (1991): 364–396.

[23]George Harris and Joyce Hogan, "Perceptions and Personality Correlates of Managerial Effectiveness," paper presented at the 13th Annual Psychology in the Department of Defense Symposium, Colorado Springs, CO, April 1992.

[24]Jing-Lih Farh and Gregory H. Dobbins, "Effects of Self-Esteem on Leniency Bias in Self-Reports of Performance: A Structural Equation Model," *Personnel Psychology*, 42 (1989): 835–850.

[25]Dianne Nilsen and David P. Campbell, "Self-Observer Rating Discrepancies: Once an Overrater, Always an Overrater?" *Human Resource Management*, 32 (1993): 265–281.

A recent study of personality traits and leadership effectiveness in education reached similar conclusions.[26] The purpose of the study was to examine the validity of the Sixteen Personality Factor Questionnaire (16PF) as a predictor of principal performance. Seventy-nine elementary and secondary school principals from one large, urban school district were administered the 16PF. Four independent criteria were used to measure principal effectiveness: supervisors' ratings, paired comparison ratings, peer nomination ratings, and teacher ratings, resulting in an overall effectiveness score. The results of the study revealed that Factors E (dominant), M (imaginative), Q2 (self-sufficient), and A (warm) were consistent predictors of superior performance.

Popular books on leadership[27] portray superior leaders as possessing Factor E characteristics such as assertiveness, self-confidence, and independence. Factor M individuals prefer to deal with dynamic, essential matters rather than with superfluous, marginal issues. Moreover, persons high in this factor are more open to interaction with those different from themselves, not necessarily out of friendliness but because of curiosity coupled with self-confidence, which reduces fear and suspicion of the unfamiliar. Factor Q2 characterizes individuals who prefer their own decisions, are self-sufficient, and show resourcefulness. And finally, those individuals high in Factor A are good natured, easygoing, emotionally expressive, ready to cooperate, attentive to people, softhearted, kindly, and adaptable.[28] These personality traits appear to fit the demands of an urban principal to deal with essentials and to interact with a diverse school population in a collaborative manner.

In the third category of research, effectiveness is defined by low performance ratings—that is, ratings given to persons who have been fired or passed over for promotion. This line of research is usually after the fact and uses a wide variety of assessment techniques, such as

---

### Table 5–2   Traits and Skills Associated with Successful Leaders

| Traits | Skills |
|---|---|
| Adaptable to situations | Intelligent |
| Alert to social environment | Conceptually skilled |
| Ambitious and achievement oriented | Creative |
| Assertive | Diplomatic and tactful |
| Cooperative | Fluent in speaking |
| Decisive | Knowledgeable about group task |
| Dependable | Organized |
| Dominant (desire to influence others) | Persuasive |
| Energetic (high activity level) | Socially skilled |
| Persistent | |
| Self-confident | |
| Tolerant of stress | |
| Willing to assume responsibility | |

Source: Adapted from Gary A. Yukl, *Leadership in Organizations*, 2nd ed., © 1989, p. 176. Used by permission of Prentice Hall, Inc., Englewood Cliffs, NJ. Used with permission.

---

multi-rater assessment instruments and psychological tests, to identify the traits of ineffective leaders. Perhaps most important is subordinates' reactions to inept leadership: high turnover, insubordination, sabotage, and malingering. This research reveals that leadership incompetence is associated with arrogance, untrustworthiness, overcontrol, exploitation, micromanagement, emotional instability, aloofness, and an inability to delegate or make good decisions.[29]

In 1990, Bernard Bass and Ralph Stogdill updated Stogdill's earlier research by reporting the results of a review of nearly 300 trait studies that had been conducted between 1949 and 1990,[30] and Gary Yukl reviewed and reassessed their findings.[31] Many of the traits and skills presented in Table 5–2 are representative of those found in other trait studies.

[26]Fred C. Lunenburg and Lynn Columba, "The 16PF as a Predictor of Principal Performance: An Integration of Quantitative and Qualitative Research Methods," *Education*, 113 (1992): 68–73.

[27]Thomas J. Peters and Robert H. Waterman, *In Search of Excellence* (New York: DIANE Publishing Company, 2006); Bernard M. Bass et al., *Transformation Leadership* (Mahwah, NJ: Lawrence Erlbaum, 2005).

[28]Robert R. Cattell, Harold Eber, and Michael Tatsuoka, *Handbook for the Sixteen Personality Factor Questionnaire (16PF)* (Champaign, IL: Institute for Personality and Ability Testing, 1986).

[29]Lowell W. Hellervik, Jeffrey F. Hazucha, and Robert J. Schneider, "Behavior Change: Models, Methods, and a Review of the Evidence," in M. D. Dunnette and Lawrence M. Hough (eds.), *Handbook of Industrial and Organizational Psychology*, vol. 3, 2nd ed. (Palo Alto: Consulting Psychologists Press, 1992).

[30]Bass, *Bass and Stogdill's Handbook of Leadership*.

[31]Gary A. Yukl, *Leadership in Organizations*, (Paramus, NJ: Prentice Hall, 2005).

## Administrative Advice 5–1

### The Big Five Dimensions of Personality Traits

The Big Five model of personality structure can provide a common vocabulary for interpreting the results of leadership trait research.

■ *Surgency.* Surgency measures the degree to which an individual is sociable, gregarious, assertive, and leader-like, versus quiet, reserved, mannerly, and withdrawn. Some of the more common personality traits associated with this dimension include dominance, capacity for status or social presence, the need for power, sociability, or assertiveness.

■ *Agreeableness.* Agreeableness measures the degree to which individuals are sympathetic, cooperative, good natured, and warm, versus grumpy, unpleasant, disagreeable, and cold. Personality traits associated with this dimension include likeability, friendly compliance, need for affiliation, and openness to love.

■ *Conscientiousness.* Conscientiousness differentiates individuals who are hardworking, persevering, organized, and responsible from those who are impulsive, irresponsive, undependable, and lazy. Personality traits categorized under this dimension include prudence and ambition, will to achieve, need for achievement, dependability, constraint, and willingness to work.

■ *Emotional Stability.* This dimension of personality concerns the extent to which individuals are calm, steady, cool, and self-confident, versus anxious, insecure, worried, and emotional. Some of the personality traits associated with emotional stability include composure, self-awareness and acceptance, and affect.

■ *Intellectance.* This dimension of personality concerns the extent to which an individual is imaginative, cultured, broad minded, and curious, versus concrete minded, practical, and having narrow interests. Personality traits associated with this dimension include curiosity, broad-mindedness, tolerance, and openness to experience.

Adapted from Robert Hogan, Gordon J. Curphy, and Joyce Hogan, "What We Know About Leadership: Effectiveness and Personality," *American Psychologist*, 49 (1994): 503–504. Copyright © 1994 by the American Psychological Association. Reprinted by permission.

The leadership traits identified in Bass and Stogdill's review[32] easily map onto the Big Five model of personality structure endorsed by many modern psychologists.[33] This model holds that leadership traits as perceived by supervisors and subordinates can be described in terms of five broad dimensions: surgency, agreeableness, conscientiousness, emotional stability, and intellect. (See Administrative Advice 5–1.)

Educators have known for some time that measures of normal personality, cognitive ability, simulations, and assessment centers can predict leadership success relatively well.[34] Yet many organizations are either

unaware of or reluctant to take advantage of these selection devices.

## Assessment Centers: Using Traits and Skills to Identify and Develop Leaders

One method that has been used to identify and develop leaders is the **assessment center,** a technique that uses a number of traits and skills to assess a person's suitability for being hired or promoted.[35] The exact methods of assessment centers have been somewhat unclear. Guidelines and ethical considerations for assessment center operations were developed by the International Task

[32]Bass, *Bass and Stogdill's Handbook of Leadership.*

[33]John M. Digman, "Personality Structure: Emergence of the Five-Factor Model," *Annual Review of Psychology*, vol. 41 (Palo Alto: Annual Reviews, 1990), pp. 417–440.

[34]Robert L. Hughes, Richard A. Ginnett, and Gordon J. Curphy, *Leadership: Enhancing the Lessons of Experience* (New York: McGraw-Hill, 2005).

[35]George C. Thornton, *Assessment Centers in Human Resource Management: Strategies for Prediction, Diagnosis, and Development* (Mahwah, NJ: Lawrence Erlbaum Associates, 2005).

Force on Assessment Center Guidelines. A brief summary of these standards is as follows:[36]

1. Multiple assessment techniques, including at least one simulation exercise, must be used.

2. Multiple assessors with prior training must be used.

3. Selection or development judgments/decisions must be based on pooled information from assessors and techniques.

4. Overall evaluations must be made by assessors at a time other than the time of actual observation.

5. Simulation exercises must be tested prior to use to ensure that they provide reliable, objective, and relevant information for the organization in question.

6. The various dimensions, attributes, characteristics, and qualities that are evaluated must be derived from an analysis of relevant job behaviors.

7. The purpose of the technique used is to provide information for evaluating the dimensions, attributes, or qualities previously determined.

8. A physical location (called an *assessment center*) conforms to the prescribed site and space requirements specified in the center design and recommended by the National Association of Secondary School Principals (NASSP).

9. The assessment center has a director assigned (in addition to the required assessors) to administer the center in a professional manner with concern for the treatment of individuals, accuracy of results, and overall quality of the operation. The director is a trained assessor.

10. Full documentation of each assessment center is maintained on file for a minimum of seven years for use in follow-up counseling of candidates and for research purposes.

Defining standards as these should help ensure that using only a test battery, only one simulation exercise, or only panel interviews is not considered an assessment center. Specifically, the most frequently used techniques include leaderless group exercises, in-basket exercises, oral presentations, case analysis, and letter-writing exercises.

**History of the Assessment Center**    The assessment center idea is not new. First developed in the early 1900s by German psychologists, it was adopted later by the German military high command in the 1930s for use in choosing officers; subsequently, the British War Office used it for the same purpose. The U.S. Office of Strategic Services (OSS), forerunner of the CIA, was the U.S. pioneer of the assessment method. The OSS specified the personality traits and behavioral skills it thought an effective secret agent needed. To test for them, the renowned Harvard psychologist Henry Murray (and his colleagues) designed a series of simulated situations. One required prospective spies to assume quickly and use convincingly a false identity even under intense interrogation.[37]

For all practical purposes, the assessment method was abandoned at the end of World War II until 1956, when American Telephone and Telegraph (AT&T) launched its ambitious Management Progress Study of the careers of over 400 young executives. AT&T used a factor analysis of the assessment dimensions, which produced the following factors together with the variables loading most highly on each, to select potential managers:[38]

1. *General Effectiveness.* Overall staff prediction, decision making, organization and planning, creativity, need for advancement, resistance to stress, and human relations skills.

2. *Administrative Skills.* Organization and planning and decision making.

3. *Interpersonal Skills.* Human relations skills, behavior flexibility, and personal impact.

4. *Control of Feelings.* Tolerance of uncertainty and resistance to stress.

5. *Intellectual Ability.* Scholastic aptitude and range of interests.

6. *Work-Oriented Motivation.* Primacy of work and inner work standards.

7. *Passivity.* Ability to delay gratification, need for security, and need for advancement (scored negatively).

8. *Dependency.* Need for superior's approval, need for peer approval, and goal flexibility.

---

[36]Endorsed by the 28th International Congress on Assessment Center Methods, May 4, 2000, San Francisco, California.

[37]Berkeley Rice, "Measuring Executive Muscle," *Psychology Today*, 12 (1978): 99.

[38]Thornton, *Assessment Center's in Human Resource Management.*

This study has become the basis for most, if not all, of the subsequent development work related to assessment centers. It should be noted that the eight dimensions used by AT&T to identify leadership potential are closely related to the traits and skills found to be predictive of leadership effectiveness in the earlier trait studies of Stogdill and others.

**The NASSP Assessment Center**   Good examples of the assessment center concept in the selection and development of aspiring and practicing school leaders are the three assessment centers developed by the National Association of Secondary School Principals. The purpose of these Assessment Centers is twofold: accurately diagnosing the presence and strength of skills to assist in selection and development; and forming skill awareness for effective practice and serving as a baseline diagnosis for individual development.

The original NASSP Assessment Center was initiated in 1975. This model operated in more than fifty centers nationally and internationally. More than 10,000 assessors were trained and accredited, and 21,000 participants have gone through this assessment center. At one time five states required participation in this assessment model for licensure or appointment. Those states are South Carolina, New Jersey, Kentucky, Missouri, and Maryland.[39]

In 1998, NASSP released a newly developed assessment center model to replace the previous one. The new model, called *Selecting and Developing the 21st Century Principal,* was created to reflect the changes in the principalship. Building on the successes and validity of the original model and eliminating many of the liabilities, this assessment center model effectively provides an accurate diagnosis for the development of aspiring principals as well as data for making decisions that help to ensure best-fit placement and selection. NASSP used the services of Applied Research Incorporated, a leading international developer of assessment instruments, to conduct a job analysis, establish the behavioral classifications, and develop the assessment techniques and simulations.

*Selecting and Developing the 21st Century Principal* provides a realistic job preview of the principalship. Participants engage in a one-day simulation consisting of six interrelated activities. The activities require participants to deal with accumulated paperwork, meet with an angry parent, conference with a teacher having performance problems, participate in a group meeting, prepare and deliver a formal oral presentation, and prepare a formal writing sample. In addition, participants complete a biographical information form prior to their participation in the assessment center. A group of trained and certified assessors observe participants while they are completing the simulations. Assessors using computer software record the participant's behavior, describe the behavior, and classify the behavior into the appropriate skill. Behavior is recorded on ten skill dimensions that correlate with the Interstate School Leaders Licensure Consortium (ISLLC) standards. Table 5–3 presents the ten skill dimensions and their definitions.

After participants complete the one-day simulation, the assessor team builds a composite report of the participant's performance, describing the presence of strengths and weaknesses and identifying developmental needs. A final report is delivered to the participant in a one-on-one feedback session a week to ten days after the simulation.

A three-year validation project, conducted by a team of researchers from Michigan State University, confirmed the content and predictive validity of the original NASSP Assessment Center. This study indicated that the assessment center has substantial utility for the selection of school administrators.[40]

In addition to *Selecting and Developing the 21st Century Principal Assessment Center,* the *Developmental Assessment Center* is a one-day skills assessment program designed specifically for development with emphasis on establishing or revising an individual development plan. This assessment center model is frequently used with aspiring school leaders. The *Advanced Leaders Developmental Assessment Center* is a one-day assessment program specifically designed for the advanced school leader who is very experienced but is looking for an objective assessment of strengths and weaknesses.

NASSP also offers skills development programs that provide development tools for aspiring and practicing school leaders. *The 21st Century School Administrators Skills Program* is a revision of the *Springfield* program. This program is a long-term skills development program utilizing the ISLLC-related skills from *Selecting and Developing the 21st Century Principal.*

---

[39]National Association of Secondary School Principals, *Leaders for the Future: Assessment and Development Programs* (Reston, VA: NASSP, n.d.).

[40]Neal Schmitt and Scott A. Cohen, *Criterion-Related and Content Validity of the NASSP Assessment Center* (Reston, VA: National Association of Secondary School Principals, 1990).

---

**Table 5–3   Selecting and Developing the 21st Century Principal**

---

### Educational Leadership

---

1. *Setting Instructional Direction.* Implementing strategies for improving teaching and learning including putting programs and improvement efforts into action. Developing a vision and establishing clear goals; providing direction in achieving stated goals; encouraging others to contribute to goal achievement; securing commitment to a course of action from individuals and groups.

2. *Teamwork.* Seeking and encouraging involvement of team members. Modeling and encouraging the behaviors that move the group to task completion. Supporting group accomplishment.

3. *Sensitivity.* Perceiving the needs and concerns of others; dealing tactfully with others in emotionally stressful situations or in conflict. Knowing what information to communicate and to whom. Relating to people of varying ethnic, cultural, and religious backgrounds.

### Resolving Complex Problems

---

4. *Judgment.* Reaching logical conclusions and making high-quality decisions based on available information. Giving priority and caution to significant issues. Seeking out relevant data, facts, and impressions. Analyzing and interpreting complex information.

5. *Results Orientation.* Assuming responsibility. Recognizing when a decision is required. Taking prompt action as issues emerge. Resolving short-term issues while balancing them against long-term objectives.

6. *Organizational Ability.* Planning and scheduling one's own and the work of others so that resources are used appropriately. Scheduling flow of activities; establishing procedures to monitor projects. Practicing time and task management; knowing what to delegate and to whom.

### Communication

---

7. *Oral Communication.* Clearly communicating. Making oral presentations that are clear and easy to understand.

8. *Written Communication.* Expressing ideas clearly in writing; demonstrating technical proficiency. Writing appropriately for different audiences.

### Developing Self and Others

---

9. *Development of Others.* Teaching, coaching, and helping others. Providing specific feedback based on observations and data.

10. *Understanding Own Strengths and Weaknesses.* Understanding personal strengths and weaknesses. Taking responsibility for improvement by actively pursuing developmental activities. Striving for continuous learning.

---

Source: National Association of Secondary School Principals, *Selecting and Developing the 21st Century Principal* © 2002, p. 3. Used by permission of National Association of Secondary School Principals, Reston, VA.

---

NASSP delivers this three-day program at a location determined by the sponsoring organization. By training local facilitators, an organization can conduct this program as local need dictates. *Leader 123* is an instructional leadership development program designed for school leaders that have responsibility for instructional leadership. This three-day program is structured to provide long-term follow-up with the development and implementation of an instructional leadership project. *Mentoring and Coaching* provides training for the development and implementation of a mentoring program with an additional capacity for training mentors to assist less experienced school leaders.[41]

---

[41]National Association of Secondary School Principals, *Professional Development and Assessment Programs* (Reston, VA: NASSP, 2002).

## Leadership Behavior

Another way of understanding leadership is to compare the behaviors of effective and ineffective leaders to see how successful leaders behave. The focus shifts from trying to determine what effective leaders *are* to trying to determine what effective leaders *do*. The issues to be explored include, In what way do leaders lead? How hard do leaders push their subordinates? How much do they listen and use their subordinates' ideas? The dichotomy between the trait and behavioral approach is not as sharp a division as one might suspect. A leader's personal traits and characteristics probably influence his leadership behavior or style. For example, an individual who feels adequate and feels comfortable with people will ordinarily adopt a people-oriented behavior style. On the contrary, a person who feels inadequate

**Table 5–4**  **Differences in Leader Behavior Style as Identified by the Iowa Researchers**

| Behavior | Authoritarian | Democratic | Laissez-Faire |
|---|---|---|---|
| Policy determination | Solely by leader | By group's decision | No policy— complete freedom for group or individual decision |
| Establishment of job techniques and activities | Solely by leader | Leader suggests— group chooses | Up to individual |
| Planning | Solely by leader | Group receives sufficient information to obtain perspective needed to plan | No systematic planning |
| Establishment of division of labor and job assignments | Dictated by leader | Left to group decision | Leader uninvolved |
| Evaluation | Leader personal in praise and criticism | Evaluation against objective standards | No appraisal— spontaneous evaluation by other group members |

Source: Adapted from Kurt Lewin, Ronald Lippitt, and Robert K. White, "Patterns of Aggressive Behavior in Experimentally Created 'Social Climates,'" *Journal of Social Psychology*, 10 (1939): 271–299. Copyright 1939 by Heldref Publications. Used by permission of the Helen Dwight Reid Educational Foundation.

and feels threatened by people will probably adopt a production-oriented behavior style.

Three widely known studies of classic behavioral theories of leadership were conducted at the University of Iowa, Ohio State University, and the University of Michigan. Each theory is closely identified with the sponsoring university. We examine each theory by describing and classifying the leader behavior constructs developed in each theory. Then we examine some of the subsequent research associated with each theory; that is, the effects of leader behaviors on organizational outcomes such as job satisfaction, morale, and productivity.

## The Iowa Studies: Authoritarian, Democratic, and Laissez-Faire Leadership

An early attempt to classify and study the effects of different styles of leader behavior on the group was conducted at the University of Iowa.[42] In a series of ex-

[42]Kurt Lewin, Ronald Lippitt, and Robert K. White, "Patterns of Aggressive Behavior in Experimentally Created 'Social Climates,'" *Journal of Social Psychology*, 10 (1939): 271–299.

periments, the Iowa researchers manipulated three leadership styles to determine their effects on the attitudes and productivity of subordinates. Leadership was classified into three different types according to the leader's style of handling several decision-making situations during the experiments:

■ **Authoritarian Leadership.** Leaders were very directive and allowed no participation in decisions. They structured the complete work situation for their subordinates. Leaders took full authority and assumed full responsibility from initiation to task completion.

■ **Democratic Leadership.** Leaders encouraged group discussion and decision making. Subordinates were informed about conditions affecting their jobs and encouraged to express their ideas and make suggestions.

■ **Laissez-faire Leadership.** Leaders gave complete freedom to the group and left it up to subordinates to make individual decisions on their own. Essentially, leaders provided no leadership.

Table 5–4 describes the three leadership styles. The table summarizes typical behaviors exhibited by leaders using the three different leadership styles in a variety of dimensions of leadership behavior.

Some of the results of the Iowa leadership studies include the following:[43]

1. Of the three styles of leadership, subordinates preferred the democratic style the best, which makes intuitive sense. The general trend today is toward wider use of participatory management practices because they are consistent with the supportive and collegial models of modern organization.

2. Subordinates preferred the laissez-faire leadership style over the authoritarian one. For subordinates, even chaos was preferable to rigidity.

3. Authoritarian leaders elicited either aggressive or apathetic behavior that was deemed to be reactions to the frustration caused by the authoritarian leader.

4. Apathetic behavior changed to aggressive behavior when the leadership style changed from authoritarian to laissez-faire; the laissez-faire leader produced the greatest amount of aggressive behavior.

5. Productivity was slightly higher under the authoritarian leader than under the democratic one, but it was lowest under the laissez-faire leader.

Later studies done at the University of Michigan, however, indicate a sharp increase in productivity initially under authoritarian leadership, but this was followed by drastic decreases in productivity over the long run for authoritarian-led groups; and these groups ultimately reached levels well below democratically led groups in productivity.[44]

**Status of the Iowa Studies**   Other behavioral science researchers have subjected the Iowa leadership studies to a great deal of criticism. The main concern has been with the methodology: Many variables in the Iowa studies were not controlled. Nevertheless, these leadership studies stand as a landmark in their attempt to determine the effects of leader behaviors on a group's attitude and productivity. Like the early trait studies, the Iowa leadership studies are often too quickly dismissed because they were experimentally crude.

The Iowa studies were important in that they helped focus attention on the investigation of leadership *behavior*. Furthermore, they provided a useful basis for describing and classifying alternative leader behavior

styles. In fact, today the three styles identified by the Iowa researchers seventy years ago are commonplace in the literature and in parlance among practitioners in the field of educational administration.

## The Ohio State Studies: Initiating Structure and Consideration

The research at Ohio State University aimed at identifying leader behaviors that were important for the attainment of group and organizational goals. Specifically, researchers sought to answer the following questions: What types of behavior do leaders display? What effect do these leader behaviors have on work group performance and satisfaction?

During these studies, researchers from the disciplines of psychology, sociology, and economics developed and used the Leader Behavior Description Questionnaire (LBDQ) to study leadership in different types of groups and situations.[45] Studies were made of Air Force commanders and members of bomber crews; officers, noncommissioned personnel, and civilian administrators in the Department of the Navy; executives of regional cooperatives; manufacturing supervisors; leaders of various student and civilian groups; and teachers, principals, and school superintendents.

Group responses to the LBDQ were then subjected to factor analysis, a mathematical technique that permits identification of a smaller set of common dimensions undergirding a large set of questionnaire responses. From the factor analysis came two dimensions that characterized the behavior of leaders in the numerous groups and situations investigated: initiating structure and consideration.

**Initiating Structure**   **Initiating structure** refers to the extent to which a leader focuses directly on organizational performance goals, organizes and defines tasks, assigns work, establishes channels of communication, delineates relationships with subordinates, and evaluates work group performance. Leaders who initiate structure assign staff members to particular tasks, maintain definite standards of performance, emphasize meeting deadlines, encourage the use of uniform procedures, let staff members know what is expected of them, and see to it that staff members are working up to capacity.

[43]Ibid.

[44]David G. Bowers, *Systems of Organization: Management of Human Resource* (Ann Arbor: University of Michigan Press, 1977).

[45]Ralph M. Stogdill and Alvin E. Coons (eds.), *Leader Behavior: Its Description and Measurement* (Columbus: Bureau of Business Research, Ohio State University, 1957).

**Consideration** Consideration refers to the extent to which a leader exhibits trust, respect, warmth, support, and concern for the welfare of subordinates. Leaders who manifest consideration listen to staff members' ideas, are friendly and approachable, treat all staff members as equals, and frequently use employee ideas. A high consideration score indicates psychological closeness between leader and subordinate; a low consideration score indicates a more psychologically distant and impersonal approach on the part of the leader.

The result was a two-dimensional leadership model. These dimensions are seen as being independent, thus resulting in four leadership behaviors as depicted in Figure 5–1.

### Studies on Initiating Structure and Consideration

Researchers have conducted numerous studies to determine the effects of these four styles on subordinate performance and satisfaction. It is not within the scope of this text to provide an exhaustive review of these myriad studies. Instead, we will briefly review a few of the more important studies in education: encompassing the roles of superintendents, principals, and teachers.

Superintendents who were rated as effective leaders by both staff and school board members were described as high on both initiating structure and consideration.[46] Another researcher reported that effective principals had higher scores on initiating structure and consideration than did ineffective principals.[47] Performance evaluations of school principals' leadership were positively related to consideration and negatively related to domination and social distance, which provided support for the theory.[48]

In a study of the relationship of principals' leadership to pupil performance in Canadian public schools, both initiating structure and consideration by the principals, as described by teachers, were significantly and positively related to pupils' examination scores on a provincewide exam.[49] Another Canadian study found that pupil performance was associated with principals'

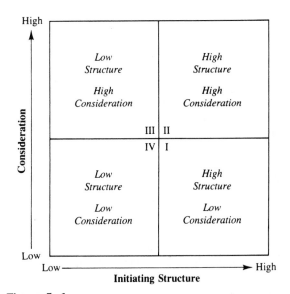

**Figure 5–1**

Ohio State Leadership Grid

LBDQ scores.[50] And in another large-scale Canadian study, results indicated that initiating structure and consideration by teachers were positively and significantly related to the scores of pupils on tests of school achievement.[51] Using 872 teacher descriptions of fifty-three principals, another researcher found that both initiating structure and consideration were highly correlated with two representative functions: (1) representing teachers' interests to superordinates and (2) representing teachers' interests to the schools' clientele. The report concluded that initiating structure and consideration were not solely concerned with internal leadership but were reflected in the manner with which leaders dealt with outsiders and higher authority.[52]

In sum, the two-dimensional theory of leader behavior that evolved from the Ohio State leadership studies represents a widely accepted research-based approach to the study and practice of leadership. The major value

[46]Andrew W. Halpin, *The Leader Behavior of School Superintendents* (Columbus: Ohio State University, 1956).

[47]Alan F. Brown, "Reactions to Leadership," *Educational Administration Quarterly*, 3 (1967): 62–73.

[48]M. Seeman, "A Comparison of General and Specific Leader Behavior Descriptions," in Stogdill and Coons, *Leader Behavior: Its Description and Measurement.*

[49]Betty T. Keeler and John H. M. Andrews, "Leader Behavior of Principals, Staff Morale, and Productivity," *Alberta Journal of Educational Research*, 9 (1963): 179–191.

[50]Thomas B. Greenfield, "Research on the Behavior of Educational Leaders: Critique of a Tradition," *Alberta Journal of Educational Research*, 14 (1968): 55–76.

[51]Thomas B. Greenfield and John H. M. Andrews, "Teacher Leader Behavior," *Alberta Journal of Educational Research*, 7 (1961): 92–102.

[52]R. Jean Hills, "The Representative Function: Neglected Dimension of Leadership Behavior," *Administrative Science Quarterly*, 8 (1963): 83–101.

## ■ Exemplary Educational Administrators in Action

**CRAIG L. ELLIOTT** Superintendent, Maize Unified School District, Kansas.

**Previous Positions:** Activities Director, Conway Springs, Kansas; Administrative Assistant, Assistant Superintendent, Deputy Superintendent, Maize Unified School District, Kansas.

**Latest Degree and Affiliation:** Ed.D., Educational Administration, Oklahoma State University.

**Number One Influence on Career:** Family—wife, parents, children, and many other relatives who are involved in public education.

**Number One Achievement:** Creating a staff development program that focuses on school improvement and student achievement.

**Number One Regret:** Not spending enough time with my own children when they were attending school.

**Favorite Education-Related Book or Text:** *Gung HO!* by Ken Blanchard and Sheldon Bowles.

**Additional Interests:** Boating, golf, spectator sports.

**Leadership Style:** Participatory—I believe that decisions must be made by the person who has the best knowledge and is closest to a particular situation. It is also important that one support the person making the decisions.

**Professional Vision:** "Building the one-room schoolhouse for 10,000 young people": In these days of high-stakes testing and electronic communication, we must continue to make efforts to develop interpersonal relationships. "Soft" skills will continue to be critical in every facet of our personal and professional lives.

**Words of Advice:** I believe there are two words that are very important to our profession, and to the superintendency. The words are *patience* and *compassion*, and both are necessary for survival as a superintendent. As I have watched and mentored building principals that move into central office positions, I have observed that the aspect of the job they have the most difficult time with is understanding that many decisions do not need to be made quickly. As a building principal, one often needs to make quick decisions. The fear is being known as a leader who cannot make a decision. As a central office administrator, we often are not the ones to be making the decision in the first place; rather, we should facilitate the process of decision making. And we should do this by asking questions.

When moving into central office work, one must adjust to a larger environment (arena may be the more fitting term, because we all know that we have many publics to please). I have witnessed all too often the quicker a decision, the sooner the decision has to be "adjusted." Many times, inexperienced central office administrators have to correct a situation because they were making their decision as an administrator responsible for a select group of children and adults, not as an administrator whose decision affects all of the district's children and adults.

Compassion, I've found, is necessary in understanding others. Teaching requires a deep understanding of why certain things are not understood by select individuals. Our natural instinct as educators is to try to help. Compassion means that you have put yourself in the other person's shoes, whether that be an employee, parent, or student. In so doing, you are understanding all points of view and, therefore, have an opportunity to look at the big picture rather than have a narrow focus. Knowing when to use patience and how to use compassion is the key to an effective and successful administration.

---

of this approach is the clear demonstration that these two dimensions of leadership behavior are real and observable and account for a great proportion of actual leader behavior. Research finds that the high initiating structure–high consideration leader behaviors (quadrant 2, Figure 5–1) result in higher satisfaction and performance among school administrators than do any of the other three leader behaviors. The implications of these findings are that they provide a framework for solving problems in school organizations. That is, we can treat initiating structure and consideration as dependent variables in leadership development and training programs. Our assumption is that we can shift leadership behavior in the desired direction; for example, from low initiating structure to high initiating structure and from low consideration to high consideration.

## The Michigan Studies: Production Centered and Employee Centered

Around the time that the Ohio State leadership studies were being conducted, a series of leadership studies were in progress at the University of Michigan's In-

## Table 5–5  Overview of Leadership Behavior Theories

| Source | Leadership Behaviors | Research Method | Summary of Results |
|---|---|---|---|
| University of Iowa studies | Authoritarian Democratic Laissez-faire | Experimental: manipulated several decision-making situations and tested different leadership styles to measure the effects of style on outcomes | Overall, democratic leadership is best. Authoritarian leadership created aggression and apathy and lower subordinate satisfaction. Laissez-faire leadership produced the most aggression. Authoritarian leadership increased productivity initially, but productivity decreased drastically over the long run. |
| Ohio State studies | Initiating structure Consideration | Survey: questionnaires completed by leaders, supervisors, subordinates, and peers | Generally, high initiating structure and consideration increased productivity and satisfaction, but findings were inconsistent. |
| University of Michigan studies | Production-centered Employee-centered | Survey: questionnaires completed by leaders, supervisors, subordinates, and peers | Initial studies found employee-centered leadership best, but later studies found a mix of employee- and production-centered leadership increased productivity and satisfaction. |

stitute for Social Research. The Michigan researchers used an approach to identify leaders who were rated as either effective or ineffective and then studied the behavior of these leaders in an attempt to develop consistent patterns of behavior that differentiated effective from ineffective leaders.

The Michigan studies identified two distinct leadership behaviors that were very similar to the initiating structure and consideration dimensions, which evolved from the Ohio State studies. The two dimensions identified were called production-centered leadership and employee-centered leadership. A description of each concept and the leader behaviors associated with each are presented next.

Production-centered leader behavior is very similar to high initiating structure leader behavior. The **production-centered leader** emphasizes employee tasks and the methods used to accomplish them. Leaders who are production centered set tight work standards, organize tasks carefully, prescribe work methods to be followed, and closely supervise their subordinates' work.

Employee-centered leader behavior is very similar to high consideration leader behavior. An **employee-centered leader** emphasizes the employee's personal needs and the development of interpersonal relationships. Leaders who are employee centered tend to be supportive of their subordinates, use group rather than individual decision making, encourage subordinates to set and achieve high performance goals, and endeavor to treat subordinates in a sensitive, considerate way.

Hundreds of studies in a wide variety of business, hospital, government, and other organizations were conducted. Thousands of employees, performing unskilled to highly professional and scientific tasks, completed a variety of questionnaires developed by the Michigan researchers. The initial research indicated that the most productive work groups tended to have leaders who were employee centered rather than production centered.[53] Subsequent research, however, concluded that leaders with the best production records were both production centered and employee centered.[54] However, the Michigan research findings have not been totally consistent. In comparison, the Ohio State leadership studies appear to have become more famous, at least in the educational setting, because of the number of studies that were generated by the initiating structure and consideration dimensions. And many of these studies were done in school organizations.

### Leadership Behavior Theories: Similarities and Conclusions

A review of the leader behavior theories reveals a number of similarities and conclusions. Table 5–5 presents a few of these points. First, the three theories attempted to explain leadership in terms of the behav-

---

[53]Rensis Likert, *The Human Organization: Its Management and Value* (New York: McGraw-Hill, 1967); Likert, *New Patterns of Management* (New York: Garland, 1987).

[54]Bowers, *Systems of Organization: Management of Human Resource.*

ior of the leader—that is, what the leader *does,* not the leader's personal traits and skills. Once leader behavior was identified, researchers measured the effects of leader behavior on productivity and satisfaction. The Iowa studies uncovered three leader behaviors, and the Ohio State and Michigan studies isolated two dimensions of leadership behavior that related to task orientation and people orientation. Second, the research we have discussed thus far has not considered the effects of situational factors on leadership—that is, differences in tasks completed, differences in the makeup of the group to be led, and differences in the external environment. All these factors have a bearing on the functions that must be performed by the leader and consequently on the appropriate leadership behavior to use in a given situation.

In an era of school reform, one trend is emerging: Efforts to improve education are now national in scope. This movement toward national standards began in the late 1980s and accelerated with the No Child Left Behind Act of 2001.[55] Meanwhile, the National Council of Teachers of Mathematics and the American Association for the Advancement of Science responded to this challenge with their respective national mathematics and science standards outlining the broad curriculum goals that our nation's schools should be striving to achieve. The National Board for Professional Teaching Standards has now completed national standards for the licensure of teachers. The National Policy Board for Educational Administration has developed national performance standards for the preparation of school principals. And the Goals 2000: Educate America Act is now law. With national standards in curriculum, teacher certification, and principal preparation—and with America committed to national goals—principals must provide local leadership for implementation of these national initiatives. (See Administrative Advice 5–2.)

## Contingency Leadership

Efforts to discover the one best set of leader traits and the one best set of leader behaviors in *all situations* have failed. Contemporary researchers and school administrators are more likely to believe that the practice of leadership is too complex to be represented by a single set of traits or behaviors. Instead, the idea that ef-

fective leadership behavior is "contingent" on the situation is more prevalent today.

The contingency approach to leadership is considerably more complex than either the trait or the behavioral approach. According to **contingency theory,** effective leadership depends on the interaction of the leader's personal traits, the leader's behavior, and factors in the leadership situation. At the same time, the contingency approach is based on the proposition that effective leadership cannot be explained by any one factor. Instead, it proposes that all factors must be considered in the context of the situation in which the leader must lead. We discuss two contingency theories of leadership that have received a great deal of attention. The questions we ask regarding contingency leadership shift from: "Is authoritarian, initiating structure, production-centered leadership more effective than democratic, consideration, employee-centered leadership?" to a different question: "In what situations will production-centered leadership be effective, and under what set of circumstances will employee-centered leadership be effective?"

### Fiedler's Contingency Theory

Fred Fiedler and his associates have spent two decades developing and refining a contingency theory of leadership.[56] According to the theory, the effectiveness of a leader in achieving high group performance is contingent on the leader's motivational system and the degree to which the leader controls and influences the situation. The three situational factors include leader-member relations, task structure, and the leader's position power. Figure 5–2 depicts the interrelationship among these variables. We discuss the three components of Fiedler's theory—leadership style, situational favorableness, and the contingency model—and the empirical evidence concerning the validity of the theory.

**Leadership Style** Fiedler developed a unique technique to measure leadership style. Measurement is obtained from scores on the *least preferred co-worker* (LPC) scale. Table 5–6 presents an example of an LPC scale. The scale usually contains twenty-four pairs of adjectives, written as a bipolar list, each of which could

---

[55]*No Child Left Behind Act of 2001* (www.ed.gov/nclb/).

[56]Fred E. Fiedler and Martin M. Chemers, *Improving Leadership Effectiveness: The Leader Match Concept,* 2nd ed. (New York: Wiley, 1984).

## Administrative Advice 5–2

## Connecting Leadership to Education's National Agenda

Administrative action is necessary in four areas of professional practice.

■ *Connect Leadership to School Outcomes.* School administrators must focus on improved student outcomes for several reasons:

—New national quality standards have been developed by organizations in the various content fields.

—The National Board for Professional Teaching Standards developed national standards for teacher licensure.

—The National Policy Board for Educational Administration developed national performance standards for the preparation of school principals.

—The Goals 2000: Educate America Act provides national goals for education.

■ *Apply a Data-Driven Change Process.* Every possible contributor to pupil learning (community, family, social services, motivational systems) must be utilized to foster cognitive achievement and growth. We must:

—Analyze the skill base of contributors.

—Develop an organizational structure that focuses on outcomes.

—Engage the institutional culture in support of outcomes.

—Develop an information management system to provide data flow to analyze problems and suggest solutions.

■ *Demonstrate an Ethical Orientation.* All school leaders, by virtue of their position, bear an ethical responsibility to:

—Help all students reach their potential.

—Promote the development of everyone within the organization.

—Ensure that the school is involved in the major national movements that seek to improve professional practice and student learning.

■ *Create Common and High Standards for Licensure.* Raising standards of practice for entry-level school leaders fulfills the need for common professional standards. We must:

—Explore the notion that common and higher standards for licensing principals will benefit schools.

—Discuss current licensing activity among the participating states.

—Consider selected documents as baseline materials to generate generic and role-specific outcomes to qualify for state licensure.

—Organize a coordinating committee of state officials interested in developing common and higher standards and examination systems for state licensure.

Adapted from Scott D. Thompson, "Connecting Leadership to Education's National Agenda," *High School Magazine*, 1 (1993): 12–13. Used by permission of NASSP. Copyright © 1993 National Association of Secondary School Principals. www.principals.org. Reprinted with permission.

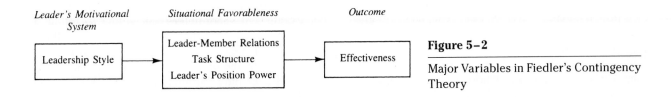

Figure 5–2

Major Variables in Fiedler's Contingency Theory

be used to describe a person. The leader completing the LPC scale is asked to describe the person with whom he worked least well in accomplishing some task, by placing Xs at the appropriate points between each of the adjective pairs. The most positive response for each pair of adjectives is assigned a score of 8 and the least positive response a score of 1. Summing all item scores on the instrument gives a leader's LPC score. A high score indicates that the leader views the least preferred co-worker in relatively favorable terms. A low score

**Table 5–6    Sample of Items from the LPC Scale**

|  |  |  |  |  |  |  |  |  |  | Scoring |
|---|---|---|---|---|---|---|---|---|---|---|
| Pleasant | — | — | — | — | — | — | — | — | Unpleasant | _____ |
|  | 8 | 7 | 6 | 5 | 4 | 3 | 2 | 1 |  |  |
| Friendly | — | — | — | — | — | — | — | — | Unfriendly | _____ |
|  | 8 | 7 | 6 | 5 | 4 | 3 | 2 | 1 |  |  |
| Rejecting | — | — | — | — | — | — | — | — | Accepting | _____ |
|  | 8 | 7 | 6 | 5 | 4 | 3 | 2 | 1 |  |  |
| Tense | — | — | — | — | — | — | — | — | Relaxed | _____ |
|  | 8 | 7 | 6 | 5 | 4 | 3 | 2 | 1 |  |  |
| Distant | — | — | — | — | — | — | — | — | Close | _____ |
|  | 8 | 7 | 6 | 5 | 4 | 3 | 2 | 1 |  |  |
| Cold | — | — | — | — | — | — | — | — | Warm | _____ |
|  | 8 | 7 | 6 | 5 | 4 | 3 | 2 | 1 |  |  |
| Supportive | — | — | — | — | — | — | — | — | Hostile | _____ |
|  | 8 | 7 | 6 | 5 | 4 | 3 | 2 | 1 |  |  |
| Boring | — | — | — | — | — | — | — | — | Interesting | _____ |
|  | 8 | 7 | 6 | 5 | 4 | 3 | 2 | 1 |  |  |

Source: Adapted from Fred E. Fiedler and Martin M. Chemers, *Improving Leadership Effectiveness: The Leader Match Concept*, 2nd ed., © 1984, p. 19. Used by permission of John Wiley & Sons, Inc., New York.

means that the least preferred co-worker is described in a very negative, rejecting manner.

How can the leader's LPC score be interpreted? Fiedler interprets a leader's LPC score to be a personality trait that reflects the leader's motivational system or behavioral preferences. High LPC leaders (those who perceive their least preferred co-workers positively) have as their basic goal the desire to maintain close interpersonal relationships with subordinates and behave in a considerate and supportive manner toward them. If the leader reaches this goal, he will be able to attain such secondary goals as status and esteem. In return, these leaders want their subordinates to admire and recognize them. Low LPC leaders have a different motivational structure: Task accomplishment is their primary goal. Needs such as esteem and status are fulfilled through the accomplishment of tasks, not directly through relationships with subordinates. Hence, a high LPC score indicates a relationship-motivated (employee-centered) leader whose interpersonal relationship needs have first priority, and a low LPC score indicates a task-motivated (production-centered) leader whose task achievement needs have first priority.

**Situational Favorableness**    After classifying leaders according to their LPC scores, Fiedler set out to discover what type of leader is most effective. The basic premise of his contingency theory is that in some sit-

uations high LPC (relationship-motivated) leaders will be more effective, whereas other circumstances make it more likely that low LPC (task-motivated) leaders will be most effective. Fiedler concludes therefore that the relationship between leadership style and effectiveness depends on several factors in the situation. He identified three: leader-member relations, task structure, and position power.

*Leader-member relations* refer to the quality of the relationship between the leader and the group. The degree of confidence, trust, and respect subordinates have in the leader assesses it. Good or bad classifies leader-member relations. The assumption is that if subordinates respect and trust the leader, it will be easier for the leader to exercise *influence* in accomplishing tasks. For example, if subordinates are willing to follow a leader because of her referent power, they are following the leader because of personality, trustworthiness, and so on. On the other hand, when the relationship between leader and subordinates is not good, the leader may have to resort to special favors (reward power) to get good performance from subordinates.

*Task structure* refers to the nature of the subordinate's task—whether it is routine (structured) or complex (unstructured). Task structure can be operationally defined by (1) the extent of goal clarity (i.e., the degree to which the task requirements are known by subordinates), (2) the multiplicity of goal paths (i.e.,

| Leader Member Relations | Good | | | | Poor | | | |
|---|---|---|---|---|---|---|---|---|
| Task Structure | Structured | | Unstructured | | Structured | | Unstructured | |
| Position Power | Strong | Weak | Strong | Weak | Strong | Weak | Strong | Weak |
| Situations | I | II | III | IV | V | VI | VII | VIII |

Favorable ◄————————————————► Unfavorable

**Figure 5–3**

Fiedler's Contingency Model

Source: Adapted from Fred E. Fiedler, *A Theory of Leadership Effectiveness,* © 1967, p. 37. Used by permission.

whether there are many or few procedures for solving the problem), (3) the extent of decision verifiability (i.e., whether performance can be easily evaluated), and (4) the solution specificity (i.e., whether there are one or many correct solutions). When the task to be performed is highly structured, the leader should be able to exert considerable influence on subordinates. Clear goals, clear procedures to achieve goals, and objective performance measures enable the leader to set performance standards and hold subordinates accountable (for example, "Type ten error-free manuscript pages per hour"). On the other hand, when the task is unstructured, the leader may be in a poor position to evaluate subordinate performance because the goals are unclear, there are multiple paths to achieve them, and the leader may possess no more knowledge about the task than the subordinates (for example, "Devise a plan to improve the quality of life in our school").

*Position power* refers to the extent to which the leader possesses the ability to influence the behavior of subordinates through legitimate, reward, and coercive powers. Examples are the power to hire and fire, to give pay raises and promotions, and to direct subordinates to task completion. The more position power held by the leader, the more favorable the leadership situation. In general, committee chairpersons and leaders in voluntary organizations have weak position power. School boards, superintendents, and principals of school organizations have strong position power.

**Contingency Model** Leader-member relations, task structure, and position power determine the situational favorableness for the leader. To combine these factors in the simplest way, Fiedler simply split each into two categories and thus produced eight possible combinations (see Figure 5–3). The eight situations vary in terms of their overall favorableness for the exercise of leadership. As Figure 5–3 shows, the most favorable situation (greater leader influence) is one in which leader-member relations are good, the task is highly

structured, and the leader has strong position power. The least favorable situation (least leader influence) is one in which leader-member relations are poor, tasks are unstructured, and leader position power is weak.

Fiedler hypothesized that the favorableness of the situation with the leadership style determines effectiveness. He reviewed studies conducted in over 800 groups to investigate which type of leader was most effective in each situation.[57] Among the groups studied were Air Force bomber crews, combat tank crews, basketball teams, fraternity members, surveying teams, open-hearth steel employees, form-supply service employees, and educational administrators. The general conclusion reached, as shown in Figure 5–4, is that task-motivated leaders were most effective in extreme situations where the leader either had a great deal of influence or very little power and influence. Relationship-motivated (high LPC) leaders were most effective where the leader had moderate power and influence.

Why is the task-motivated leader successful in very favorable situations? Fiedler provided the following explanation:

> In the very favorable conditions in which the leader has power, informal backing, and a relatively well-structured task, the group is ready to be directed and the group expects to be told what to do. Consider the captain of an airliner in its final landing approach. We would hardly want him to turn to his crew for a discussion on how to land.[58]

To explain why the task-motivated leader is successful in a highly unfavorable situation, Fiedler cites the following example:

> . . . [T]he disliked chairman of a volunteer committee . . . is asked to plan the office picnic on a beautiful Sunday. If

[57]Fred E. Fiedler, *A Theory of Leadership Effectiveness* (New York: McGraw-Hill, 1967).

[58]Ibid., p. 147.

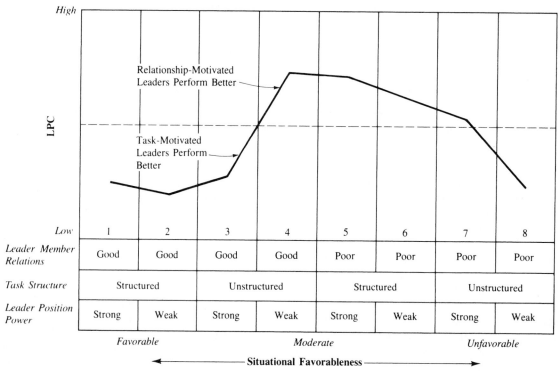

**Figure 5–4**

Summary of Contingency Model Research

Source: Adapted from Fred E. Fiedler and Martin M. Chemers, *Leadership and Effective Management,* © 1974, p. 80. Used by permission of Fred E. Fiedler.

the leader asks too many questions about what the group ought to do or how he should proceed, he is likely to be told that "we ought to go home."[59]

As Figure 5–4 shows, the relationship-motivated (high LPC) leader is effective in the intermediate range of favorableness (octants 4, 5, 6, and 7). An example of such situations is the typical university committee staffed by professionals. In these situations, the leader may not be completely accepted by the group, the task may be ambiguous, and little power may be vested in the leader. Under such circumstances, Fiedler's theory predicts that relationship-motivated leaders will be most effective.

**Research on the Contingency Model** Fiedler's contingency model has stimulated a considerable amount of research; the results are mixed. Most research has

been supportive of the theory.[60] However, the model has been criticized on several counts. Critics have argued that Fiedler's preference for a task-motivated style (in four of eight situations) is diametrically opposed to the findings of Likert,[61] and Fiedler fails to explain the effectiveness of high LPC leaders in the middle four octants. At least one study shows that middle LPC leaders perform over the entire situational range.[62] The LPC measure itself has been criticized in terms of its practical application in an organizational setting.[63] Other

---

[59]Ibid.

[60]Robert W. Rice, "Leader LPC and Follower Satisfaction: A Review," *Organizational Behavior and Human Performance,* 28 (1981): 288–294.

[61]Likert, *New Patterns of Management.*

[62]John K. Kennedy, "Middle LPC Leaders and Contingency Model of Leader Effectiveness," *Organizational Behavior and Human Performance,* 30 (1982): 1–14.

[63]Samuel Shiflett, "Is There a Problem with the LPC Score in Leader Match?" *Personnel Psychology,* 34 (1981): 765–769.

research suggests that the LPC may be a measure of cognitive complexity rather than leadership style.[64] Nevertheless, evidence supports the LPC measure of leadership style[65] and Fiedler has replied to most of the criticisms of his contingency theory.[66]

Despite these criticisms, Fiedler's contingency model has made a major contribution to the study of leadership for several reasons. First, the contingency model was one of the first approaches to leadership to examine the situation—the people, the task, and the organization. In addition, much research supports the model, and researchers continue to investigate, refine, and extend the theory. Second, the theory implies that leadership should not be thought of as either good or bad. Instead, a more realistic approach is to view an administrator's leadership style as effective in one set of circumstances but ineffective in another. Finally, leadership is a function of the interaction of leadership style and situational dimensions within the organization. There are at least two implications of such a relationship. Leaders can improve their effectiveness by modifying the situation so that it better fits with their own leadership style, or they can change their leadership style to obtain a better match with the situation. Now let's examine another contingency theory.

## Path-Goal Theory

Another widely known contingency theory of leadership is the path-goal theory of leadership effectiveness. **Path-goal theory** is based on the expectancy theory of motivation and emphasizes the leader's effect on subordinates' goals and the paths to achieve the goals. Leaders have influence over subordinates' ability to reach goals, the rewards associated with reaching goals, and the importance of the goals.

The modern development of path-goal theory is usually attributed to Martin Evans and to Robert House

and his colleagues.[67] Essentially, the path-goal theory attempts to explain the impact of leadership behavior on subordinate motivation, satisfaction, effort, and performance as moderated by situational factors of the subordinates and the work environment. House's general model and each of its parts are examined in the following sections.

**Leader Behavior**  Four distinct types of leader behavior comprise House's path-goal model:

- *Directive Leadership.* A **directive leader** lets subordinates know what is expected of them, provides specific guidance concerning what is to be done and how to do it, sets performance standards, requests that subordinates follow standard rules and regulations, schedules and coordinates work, and explains his role as leader of the group. Directive leadership is similar to the Ohio State researchers' initiating structure.

- *Supportive Leadership.* A **supportive leader** is friendly, approachable, and concerned with the needs, status, and well-being of subordinates. A supportive leader treats subordinates as equals and frequently goes out of his way to make the work environment more pleasant and enjoyable. This leadership style is similar to what the Ohio State researchers call consideration.

- *Participative Leadership.* A **participative leader** consults with subordinates concerning work-related matters, solicits their opinions, and frequently attempts to use subordinates' ideas in making decisions.

- *Achievement-Oriented Leadership.* An **achievement-oriented leader** sets challenging goals for subordinates, emphasizes excellence in performance, and shows confidence in subordinates' ability to achieve high standards of performance.

Numerous research studies in path-goal theory suggest that the same leader can manifest these four styles of leadership in various situations. Unlike Fiedler's

---

[64]Ramadhar Singh, "Leadership Style and Reward Allocation: Does the Least Preferred Coworker Scale Measure Task and Relation Orientation?" *Organizational Behavior and Human Performance*, 32 (1983): 178–197.

[65]Michael J. Strube and Joseph E. Garcia, "A Meta-Analytic Investigation of Fiedler's Contingency Model of Leadership Effectiveness," *Psychological Bulletin*, 90 (1981): 307–321.

[66]Fred E. Fiedler, "A Rejoiner to Schriesheim and Kerr's Premature Obituary of the Contingency Model," in J. G. Hunt and L. L. Larson (eds.), *Leadership: The Cutting Edge* (Carbondale: Southern Illinois University Press, 1977).

[67]Martin G. Evans, "The Effects of Supervisory Behavior on the Path-Goal Relationship," *Organizational Behavior and Human Performance,* 5 (1970): 277–298; Robert J. House, "A Path-Goal Theory of Leader Effectiveness," *Administrative Science Quarterly,* 16 (1971): 321–339; Robert J. House and Gary Dessler, "The Path-Goal Theory of Leadership: Some Post Hoc and A Priori Tests," in J. G. Hunt and L. L. Larson (eds.), *Contingency Approaches to Leadership* (Carbondale: Southern Illinois University Press, 1974).

contingency model, which considers leadership behavior as unidimensional, path-goal theory views leadership behavior as relatively adaptable.

**Situational Factors**    Each type of leader behavior works well in some situations but not in others. Two situational factors moderate the relationship between leader behavior and subordinate outcomes. The two situational variables are subordinate characteristics and environmental forces.

With respect to subordinate characteristics, the theory asserts that leadership behavior will be acceptable to subordinates to the extent that subordinates see such behavior as either an immediate source of satisfaction or as instrumental to future satisfaction.[68] Subordinate characteristics are seen to partially determine the extent to which subordinates perceive a leader's behavior as acceptable and satisfying. House and Baetz identified three subordinate characteristics:

- *Ability.* An important personal characteristic of subordinates is their perception of their ability to perform a task. For example, subordinates who feel they have low task ability should appreciate directive leadership, whereas subordinates who feel quite capable of performing the task will find directive leadership unnecessary and perhaps irritating.

- *Locus of Control.* Locus of control refers to the degree to which an individual sees the environment as systematically responding to his behavior.[69] Individuals with an internal locus of control believe outcomes are a function of their own behavior. Individuals with an external locus of control believe outcomes are a function of luck or chance. Research suggests that "internals" are more satisfied with participative leadership and "externals" are more satisfied with a directive leadership style.[70]

- *Needs and Motives.* The dominant needs, motives, and personality characteristics of subordinates may influence their acceptance of and satisfaction with

alternative leadership styles. For example, subordinates who have a high need for esteem and affiliation should be more satisfied with a supportive leader. Those with a high need for security will be more satisfied with a directive leader. Furthermore, subordinates with a high need for autonomy, responsibility, and self-actualization will probably be more motivated by a participative leader, and those who are high-need achievers should be more satisfied with achievement-oriented leaders.

With respect to the second situational factor, environmental forces, path-goal theory states: Leadership behavior will be motivational to the extent that (1) it makes satisfaction of subordinate needs contingent on effective performance, and (2) it complements the environment of subordinates by providing the coaching, guidance, support, and rewards that are necessary for effective performance and that may otherwise be lacking in subordinates or in their environment.[71] Environmental forces include three broad aspects of situational factors: subordinates' tasks, the primary work group, and the formal authority system.

- *Tasks.* An important environmental force that moderates the effects of leader behavior on subordinate outcomes is subordinates' tasks. Generally, researchers have classified tasks as highly structured or highly unstructured. Research has provided some evidence that supportive and participative leadership is more likely to increase subordinate satisfaction on highly structured tasks. This is because the tasks are routine and no further direction is necessary. Subordinates should be more satisfied with directive leadership on unstructured tasks because directive behavior can help clarify an ambiguous task.[72]

- *Work Group.* The characteristics of work groups may also influence subordinate acceptance of a particular leadership style. For example, the path-goal theory asserts that "when goals and paths to desired goals are apparent because of . . . clear group norms . . . , attempts by the leader to clarify paths and goals would be redundant and would be seen by subordinates as an imposition of unnecessarily close control."[73]

---

[68]Robert House and Mary L. Baetz, "Leadership: Some Empirical Generalizations and New Research Directions," *Research in Organizational Behavior*, vol. 12 (Greenwich, CT: JAI Press, 1990).

[69]J. B. Rotter, "Generalized Expectancies for Internal versus External Control of Reinforcement," *Psychological Monographs*, 80 (1966), whole issue.

[70]Avis L. Johnson, Fred Luthans, and Harry W. Hennessey, "The Role of Locus of Control in Leader Influence Behavior," *Personnel Psychology*, 37 (1984): 61–75.

---

[71]House and Baetz, "Leadership: Some Empirical Generalizations and New Research Directions."

[72]House and Dessler, "The Path-Goal Theory of Leadership."

[73]Ibid., pp. 29–62.

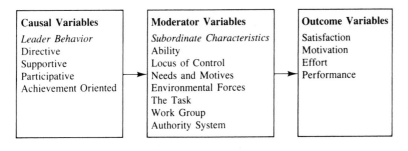

**Figure 5–5**

Relationship of Variables in the Path-Goal Theory

■ *Formal Authority System.* The final environmental force concerns such matters as (1) the degree of emphasis on rules, regulations, policies, and procedures governing the performance of tasks; (2) situations of high stress; and (3) situations of great uncertainty. Some examples follow: With tasks (e.g., typing manuscripts) that are self-evident due to mechanization, standards, and procedures, directive leadership may lead to subordinate dissatisfaction. Research suggests that directive and supportive leadership will increase subordinate satisfaction in some stressful situations.[74] In environments of uncertainty, leaders may initially use a participatory leadership style to solicit ideas in reaching a decision but later may resort to directive leadership once the final decision is made.

Figure 5–5 summarizes the path-goal theory of leadership effectiveness. As the figure shows, leader behavior moderated by subordinate characteristics and environmental forces results in subordinate motivation, satisfaction, effort, and performance.

**Research on Path-Goal Theory**   Some research evidence is available concerning path-goal theory. Because many variables in the model exist, simultaneously testing all possible relationships is difficult. Directive, supportive, participative, and achievement-oriented styles of leadership, as well as the situational factors of the model, seem to make intuitive sense. However, research to date has focused on a limited set of leader behaviors and has tested them in only one or a few situations.[75] In

particular, there is substantial evidence that directive leader behavior is most effective in supervising ambiguous, unstructured tasks and that supportive leader behavior is most beneficial in routine, structured tasks.[76] Considerable evidence also indicates that supportive leader behavior will increase motivation and satisfaction for subordinates working on stressful, frustrating, or dissatisfying tasks.[77] Furthermore, path-goal theory appears to work better in predicting subordinate motivation and satisfaction than in predicting performance.[78] Overall, the path-goal theory is important to both school leaders and researchers, for it may provide the road to a better understanding of leadership.

## Leadership Styles

The classic leadership studies (trait and behavioral approaches) and the contingency theories of leadership all have direct implications for what style the leader uses in managing human resources. The term *style* is roughly equivalent to the manner in which the leader *influences* subordinates.

In the following sections, we present the most recent approaches that deal directly with style. Before proceeding, however, Table 5–7 presents a summary of

[74]Andrew D. Szilagyi and Henry P. Sims, "An Exploration of the Path-Goal Theory of Leadership in Health Care Environments," *Academy of Management Journal,* 17 (1974): 622–634.

[75]John B. Miner, *Organizational Behavior 3: Historical Origins, Theoretical Foundations, and the Future* (New York: M. E. Sharpe, 2006).

[76]Chester A. Schriescheim and Angelo S. DeNisi, "Task Dimensions as Moderators of the Effects of Instrumental Leadership: A Two-Sample Replicated Test of Path-Goal Leadership Theory," *Journal of Applied Psychology,* 66 (1981): 589–597.

[77]H. Kirk Downey, John E. Sheridan, and John W. Slocum, "Analysis of Relationships Among Leader Behavior, Subordinate Job Performance, and Satisfaction: A Path-Goal Approach," *Academy of Management Journal,* 18 (1975): 253–262.

[78]Ricky W. Griffin, "Relationships Among Individual, Task Design, and Leader Behavior Variables," *Academy of Management Journal,* 23 (1980): 665–683.

**Table 5–7    Summary of Leadership Styles Extracted from Classic Studies and Contingency Theories**

| Studies/Theories | Task Oriented | Employee Oriented |
|---|---|---|
| Iowa studies | Authoritarian | Democratic |
| Ohio State studies | Initiating structure | Consideration |
| Michigan studies | Job centered | Employee centered |
| Contingency theory | Task motivated | Relationship motivated |
| Path-goal theory | Directive | Supportive |

Source: Reprinted by permission of Harvard Business Review. Adapted from "How to Choose a Leadership Pattern?" by Robert Tannenbaum and Warren Schmidt, issue 51 (1973): 167. Copyright © 1973 by the Harvard Business School Publishing Corporation. All rights reserved.

the leadership styles extracted from the classic leadership studies and the contingency studies. For ease of presentation, we list the styles under two headings labeled task oriented and employee oriented. This classification can serve as a background for a more detailed discussion of leadership styles to come.

## Leadership Style Continuum

Robert Tannenbaum and Warren Schmidt[79] elaborated on two styles identified in the earlier trait and behavioral studies of leadership. They conceive of a continuum that runs between *boss-centered leadership* at one extreme and *subordinate-centered leadership* at the other. Between these extremes are five points representing various combinations of managerial authority and subordinate freedom. Figure 5–6 depicts their concept of a **leadership style continuum**.

**Leadership Behaviors**    The authors identify five typical patterns of leadership behavior from their model:

1. *Telling.* The leader identifies a problem, considers alternative solutions, chooses one of them, and then tells subordinates what they are to do. They may be considered but do not participate directly in the decision making. Coercion may or may not be used or implied.

2. *Selling.* The leader makes the decision but tries to persuade the group members to accept it. The leader points out how she has considered organizational

goals and the interests of group members, and she states how the members will benefit from carrying out the decision.

3. *Testing.* The leader identifies a problem and proposes a tentative solution, asking for the reaction of those who will implement it, but making the final decision.

4. *Consulting.* The group members have a chance to influence the decision from the beginning. The leader presents a problem and relevant background information. The group is invited to increase the number of alternative actions to be considered. The leader then selects the solution she regards as most promising.

5. *Joining.* The leader participates in the discussion as a member and agrees in advance to carry out whatever decision the group makes.

**Influences on the Leader**    Tannenbaum and Schmidt assert that a wide range of factors determines whether superordinate-centered leadership, subordinate-centered leadership, or something in between is best. These factors fall into four broad categories: forces in the leader, forces in the group, forces in the situation, and long-run objectives and strategy.

1. *Forces in the Leader.*

   (a) Value system: How strongly does the leader feel that individuals should have a share in making the decisions that affect them? Or, how convinced is the leader that the official who is paid or chosen to assume responsibility should personally carry the burden of decision making? Also, what is the relative importance that the leader attaches to organizational efficiency and personal growth of subordinates?

---

[79]Robert Tannenbaum and Warren Schmidt, "How to Choose a Leadership Pattern," *Harvard Business Review,* 51 (1973): 162–180.

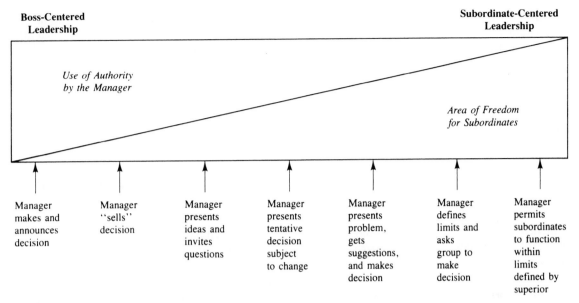

**Boss-Centered Leadership**

**Subordinate-Centered Leadership**

*Use of Authority by the Manager*

*Area of Freedom for Subordinates*

| Manager makes and announces decision | Manager "sells" decision | Manager presents ideas and invites questions | Manager presents tentative decision subject to change | Manager presents problem, gets suggestions, and makes decision | Manager defines limits and asks group to make decision | Manager permits subordinates to function within limits defined by superior |

**Figure 5–6**

Leadership Style Continuum

Source: Adapted from Robert Tannenbaum and Warren Schmidt, "How to Choose a Leadership Pattern," *Harvard Business Review*, 51 (1973): 167. Copyright © 1973 by the President and Fellows of Harvard College. Used by permission.

(b) Confidence in the group members: Leaders differ in the amount of trust they have in other people. After considering the knowledge and competence of a group with respect to a problem, a leader may (justifiably or not) have more confidence in his own capabilities than in those of the group members.

(c) Personal leadership inclinations: Leaders differ in the manner (e.g., telling or team role) in which they seem to function more comfortably and naturally.

(d) Feelings of security in an uncertain situation: The leader who releases control over the decision-making process reduces the predictability of the outcome. Leaders who have a greater need than others for predictability and stability are more likely to "tell" or "sell" than to "join."

2. *Forces in the Group Members.* Before deciding how to lead a certain group, the leader will also want to remember that each member is influenced by many personality variables and expectations. Generally speaking, the leader can permit the group greater freedom if the following essential conditions exist:

(a) Members have relatively high needs for independence.

(b) Members have readiness to assume responsibility.

(c) Members have a relatively high tolerance for ambiguity.

(d) Members are interested in the problem and feel that it is important.

(e) Members understand and identify with the goals of the organization.

(f) Members have the necessary knowledge and experience to deal with the problem.

(g) Members expect to share in decision making.

3. *Forces in the Situation.* Some of the critical environmental pressures on the leader are as follows:

(a) The problem itself: Do the members have the kind of knowledge that is needed? Does the complexity of the problem require special experience or a one-person solution?

(b) The pressure of time: The more the leader feels the need for an immediate decision, the more difficult it is to involve other people.

4. *Long-Run Objectives and Strategy.* As leaders work on daily problems, their choice of a leadership pattern is usually limited. But they may also begin to regard some of the forces mentioned as variables over which they have some control and to consider such long-range objectives as

(a) Raising the level of member motivation.

(b) Improving the quality of all decisions.

(c) Developing teamwork and morale.

(d) Furthering the individual development of members.

(e) Increasing the readiness to accept change.

Generally, a high degree of member-centered behavior is more likely to achieve these long-range purposes. But the successful administrator can be characterized as neither a strong leader nor a permissive one. Rather, a successful leader is sensitive to the forces that influence her in a given situation and can accurately assess those forces.

**Status of the Model**   The Tannenbaum-Schmidt model has not generated any empirical research probably because there are no instruments associated with the formulation. However, the model makes intuitive sense and can be used to identify alternative leadership behaviors available to a school administrator and the general classes of factors (influences on the leader) that are relevant in selecting an appropriate leadership style to fit a given situation.

## Leadership Grid® Styles

A popular approach to identifying leadership styles of practicing administrators is Robert Blake and Jane Mouton's **Leadership Grid** (formerly *Managerial Grid*).[80] They define two dimensions of leader orientation as concern for production and concern for people. These dimensions are similar to the task-oriented and employee-oriented concepts depicted in Table 5–7.

The Grid portrays five key leadership styles. Concern for production is rated on a 1 to 9 scale on the horizontal axis, while concern for people is rated similarly on the vertical axis (see Figure 5–7). The Grid identifies a range of leader orientations based on the various ways in which task-oriented and people-oriented styles can interact with each other.

**Leadership Styles**   Although there are eighty-one possible styles in the Grid, the five styles noted in Figure 5–7 and discussed below are treated as benchmarks in the theory. Blake and Mouton view leaders as capable of selecting from among them.

- *9,1 Authority-Obedience.* Leaders concentrate on maximizing production through the use of power, authority, and control.

- *1,9 Country Club Management.* Leaders place primary emphasis on good feelings among colleagues and subordinates even if production suffers as a result.

- *1,1 Impoverished Management.* Leaders do the minimum required to remain employed in the organization.

- *5,5 Organization Man Management.* Leaders concentrate on conforming to the status quo and maintaining middle-of-the-road or "go-along-to-get-along" assumptions.

- *9,9 Team Management.* Leaders use a goal-centered approach to gain high-quantity and high-quality results through broad involvement of group members: participation, commitment, and conflict resolution.

**Research on the Leadership Grid**   The authors of the Grid indicate there is evidence regarding the effectiveness of the 9,9 team management style as judged by groups of administrators from different organizational contexts.[81] Further, the authors provide empirical evidence that their Leadership Grid has more predictive validity than additive situational approaches.[82] Finally, Blake and Mouton have developed instruments that are designed to stimulate feedback from colleagues, associates, subordinates, and the like, which enable the targeted person to learn from others how they experience his or her leadership, that is, as 1,9-oriented, 9,1-oriented, 9,9-oriented, and so on. Therefore, the

---

[80] Robert R. Blake and Jane S. Mouton, *The Managerial Grid: Leadership Styles for Achieving Production Through People* (Houston: Gulf, 1994).

[81] Robert R. Blake and Jane S. Mouton, "Theory and Research for Developing a Science of Leadership," *Journal of Applied Behavioral Science,* 18 (1982): 275–291.

[82] Robert R. Blake and Jane S. Mouton, "Management by Grid Principles or Situationalism: Which?" *Group and Organization Studies,* 6 (1981): 439–455.

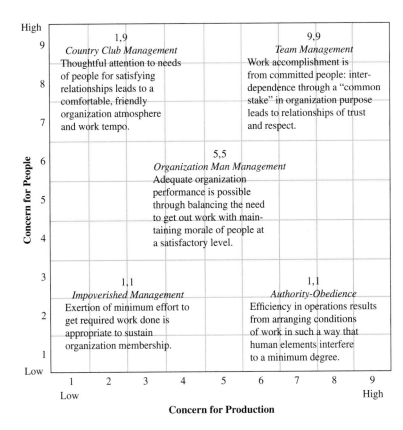

High
9  1,9  9,9
*Country Club Management*  *Team Management*
Thoughtful attention to needs  Work accomplishment is
8  of people for satisfying  from committed people: interrelationships leads to a  dependence through a "common
comfortable, friendly  stake" in organization purpose
organization atmosphere  leads to relationships of trust
7  and work tempo.  and respect.

6  5,5
*Organization Man Management*
Adequate organization
performance is possible
5  through balancing the need
to get out work with maintaining morale of people at
4  a satisfactory level.

3  1,1  1,1
*Impoverished Management*  *Authority-Obedience*
Exertion of minimum effort to  Efficiency in operations results
2  get required work done is  from arranging conditions
appropriate to sustain  of work in such a way that
organization membership.  human elements interfere
1  to a minimum degree.
Low

1    2    3    4    5    6    7    8    9
Low                              High

**Concern for Production**

Concern for People (vertical axis label)

**Figure 5–7**

The Leadership Grid® Figure

Source: The Leadership Grid® figure, Paternalism Figure and Opportunism, from *Leadership Dilemmas — Grid Solutions*, by Robert R. Blake and Anne Adams McCanse (formerly the Managerial Grid by Robert R. Blake and Jane S. Mouton). Houston: Gulf Publishing Company, p. 29. Copyright © 1991 by Scientific Methods, Inc. Reproduced by permission of the owners.

Grid is used to help people analyze the different possibilities and likely results to be achieved by each of the Grid styles and select the one they believe most effective.

### Three-Dimensional Leadership Styles

William Reddin developed another useful model for identifying the leadership styles of practicing school administrators.[83] Figure 5–8 shows his **three-dimensional model of leadership effectiveness.** By adding an effectiveness dimension to the task behavior and relationship behavior dimensions of the earlier Ohio State leadership models, Reddin has attempted to integrate the concepts of leadership style with situational demands of a specific environment. As Figure 5–8 shows, when the style of a leader is appropriate to a given situation, it is termed *effective*; when the style is inappropriate to a given situation, it is termed *ineffective*. In the center

grid, the four basic leadership styles in the model are related, integrated, separated, and dedicated. Reddin proposes that any of the four basic leadership styles may be effective or ineffective depending on the situation. These effective and ineffective equivalents result in eight operational leadership styles, which we briefly summarize.

### Effective Styles

1. *Developer.* A leader using this style gives maximum concern to relationships and minimum concern to tasks. The leader is seen as having implicit trust in people and concerned mainly with developing them as individuals.

2. *Executive.* A leader using this style gives a great deal of concern to both tasks and relationships. The leader is seen as a good motivator, setting high standards, recognizing individual differences, and using team management.

3. *Bureaucrat.* A leader using this style gives minimum concern to both tasks and relationships. The leader is seen as conscientious and is interested

---

[83]William J. Reddin, *Managerial Effectiveness* (New York: McGraw-Hill, 1970).

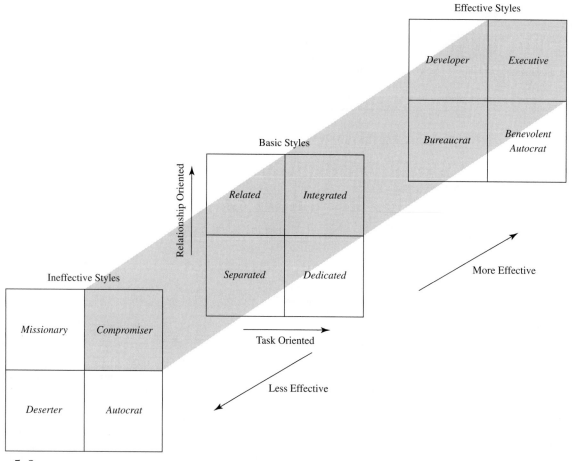

**Figure 5–8**

Reddin's Three-Dimensional Model of Leadership Effectiveness

Source: Adapted from William J. Reddin, *Managerial Effectiveness*, © 1970, p. 230.

mainly in rules and wants to maintain and control the situation by the use of rules.

4. *Benevolent Autocrat.* A leader using this style gives maximum concern to tasks and minimum concern to relationships. The leader is seen as knowing exactly what she wants and how to get it without causing resentment.

**Ineffective Styles**

1. *Missionary.* A leader using this style gives maximum concern to people and relationships and minimum concern to tasks in a situation in which such behavior is inappropriate. The leader is seen as a "do-gooder" who values harmony as an end in itself.

2. *Compromiser.* A leader using this style gives a great deal of concern to both tasks and relationships in a situation that requires emphasis on only one or on neither. The leader is seen as a poor decision maker, easily affected by pressure.

3. *Deserter.* A leader using this style gives minimum concern to tasks and relationships in a situation where such behavior is inappropriate. The leader is seen as uninvolved and passive.

4. *Autocrat.* A leader using this style gives minimum concern to tasks and minimum concern to relationships in a situation in which such behavior is inappropriate. The leader is seen as having no confidence in others, as unpleasant, and as interested only in the immediate job.

**Status of the Three-Dimensional Model**　Reddin's model incorporates three theoretical bases discussed previously, namely, leader traits and behaviors, groups, and situational factors. Reddin's model has not been the object of much empirical research. Instead, it has become a popular technique for use in training administrators in numerous organizational contexts. Using Reddin's sixty-four-item questionnaire, administrators can identify their leadership styles. Primarily, executive development seminars conducted by Reddin and his colleagues are designed to make participants cognizant of a variety of leadership styles and train leaders to adapt styles to particular situations in order to achieve maximum effectiveness.

## Situational Leadership Styles

Another well-known and useful framework for analyzing leadership behavior is Paul Hersey and Kenneth Blanchard's **situational leadership theory.**[84] It is an extension of Tannenbaum and Schmidt's leadership-style continuum, Blake and Mouton's managerial grid, and Reddin's three-dimensional leadership styles. Following the lead of the earlier Ohio State leadership studies, and like the leadership-style continuum, the grid, and the three-dimensional frameworks, situational leadership theory identifies two key leader-ship behaviors: task behavior and relationship behavior.

■ *Task Behavior.* The leader engages in one-way communication by explaining what each subordinate is to do, as well as when, where, and how tasks are to be performed.

■ *Relationship Behavior.* The leader engages in two-way communication by providing socio-emotional support, "psychological strokes," and "facilitating behaviors."

**Situational Factor: Maturity of Followers**　Taking the lead from Fiedler's contingency factors, Hersey and Blanchard incorporated the maturity of followers as a key situational variable in their model. Hersey and Blanchard see two types of maturity as particularly important: job maturity and psychological maturity.

---

[84]Paul Hersey and Kenneth H. Blanchard, *Management of Organizational Behavior* (Englewood Cliffs, NJ: Prentice Hall, 2007).

■ *Job Maturity.* This refers to a person's maturity to perform the job as influenced by education and experience. For example, a teacher or counselor in a public school who has been on the job for many years and is thoroughly competent in all areas of the job would be rated high on job maturity.

■ *Psychological Maturity.* This refers to the person's level of motivation as reflected in achievement needs and willingness to accept responsibility. An example would be a university professor who works independently on research and course preparations for publication and teaching.

Hersey and Blanchard caution that maturity of followers is task specific. For example, a principal might be a mature follower in a school district situation but be immature as a forward on the school district's basketball team. The two types combine to produce four levels of maturity, which create situations that call for four leadership styles combining task and relationship behavior.

**Leadership Styles**　The key for leadership effectiveness in Hersey and Blanchard's model is to match the situation with the appropriate leadership style. Four basic leadership styles are in the model: directing, coaching, supporting, and delegating.

■ *Directing Style.* This is a high-task, low-relationship style and is effective when subordinates are low in motivation and ability.

■ *Coaching Style.* This is a high-task, high-relationship style and is effective when subordinates have adequate motivation but low ability.

■ *Supporting Style.* This is a low-task, high-relationship style and is effective when subordinates have adequate ability but low motivation.

■ *Delegating Style.* This is a low-task, low-relationship style and is effective when subordinates are very high in ability and motivation.

Figure 5–9 summarizes the situational leadership theory.

As Figure 5–9 shows, when subordinates have low motivation (M1), leaders should define roles and direct the behavior of group members (Q1). When subordinates have moderately low motivation (M2), leaders should provide some direction, but they can attempt to persuade subordinates to accept decisions and directions (Q2). When subordinates have moderately high motivation (M3), initial direction is not needed, but

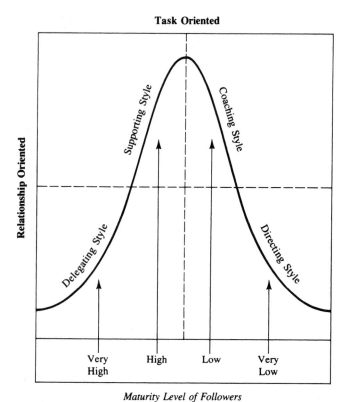

**Task Oriented**

Supporting Style

Coaching Style

Relationship Oriented

Delegating Style

Directing Style

*Subordinates*
M1 = Low motivation and ability
M2 = Adequate motivation but low ability
M3 = Adequate ability but low motivation
M4 = Needed ability and motivation are
        present

*Leader*
Q1 = High task behavior
        and low relationship behavior
Q2 = High task behavior
        and high relationship behavior
Q3 = Low task behavior
        and high relationship behavior
Q4 = Low task behavior
        and low relationship behavior

| Very<br>High | High | Low | Very<br>Low |
|---|---|---|---|

*Maturity Level of Followers*

**Figure 5–9**

Hersey and Blanchard's Situational Leadership Model

Source: Adapted from Paul Hersey and Kenneth H. Blanchard, *Management of Organizational Behavior*, 1988, p. 171. Copyrighted materials from Leadership Studies, Inc. Used by permission.

group members should share in decision making (Q3). Finally, when subordinates have high motivation (M4), leaders should demonstrate confidence in group members by delegating tasks to them (Q4). The key to the success of situational leadership theory is matching leadership styles to the appropriate people and situations. (See Administrative Advice 5–3.)

**Research on Situational Leadership Theory**    Until recently, there was almost no empirical research evidence to support the validity of the Hersey-Blanchard model. However, two industrial studies have yielded some data that support the theory, and a third educational study provides partial support for Hersey and Blanchard's model. The first industrial study, in a large division of the Xerox Corporation, found that managers who could correctly apply the Hersey-Blanchard theory got

better performance from their subordinates, as compared with their counterparts who could not correctly apply the model.[85] The second industrial study found that managers who received training during seminars in which situational leadership theory was applied scored significantly higher on a final examination than did managers who were taught using traditional methods of instruction.[86]

---

[85] Ronald K. Hambleton and Ray Gumpert, "The Validity of Hersey and Blanchard's Theory of Leadership Effectiveness," *Group and Organization Studies*, 7 (1982): 225–242.

[86] Paul Hersey, Arrigo L. Angelini, and Sofia Carakushansky, "The Impact of Situational Leadership and Classroom Structure on Learning Effectiveness," *Group and Organization Studies*, 7 (1982): 216–224.

## Administrative Advice 5–3

### Applying Situational Leadership

School administrators should consider situational leadership styles systematically, and decide under what circumstances each is appropriate. School administrators can apply the four leadership styles in the following manner:

■ *Directing Style.* Give specific instructions and supervise staff members closely. This leadership style is primarily for first-year teachers who need a lot of instruction and supervision.

■ *Coaching Style.* Explain decisions and solicit suggestions from followers but continue to direct tasks. This leadership style works especially well with nontenured teachers, who are in their second or third year on the job. They're gaining confidence and competence, but they're still getting their feet on the ground.

■ *Supporting Style.* Make decisions together with staff members and support their efforts toward performing tasks. This leadership style works with highly creative teachers. Applying this style can take the form of supporting teachers when they come up with excellent ideas and helping them to bring those ideas to fruition.

■ *Delegating Style.* Turn over decisions and responsibility for implementing them to staff members. This leadership style works with people who go above and beyond their instructions.

Source: Adapted from Bob Webb, "Situational Leadership: The Key Is Knowing When to Do What," *Executive Educator,* 12 (1990): 29–30. Copyright 1990, the National School Boards Association. Used by permission.

---

The third study was a field test of Hersey and Blanchard's situational leadership theory in a school setting. Elementary school principals received training using Hersey and Blanchard's framework. Pretests and posttests were administered to the principals and a sample of their teachers before and after training to determine the effects of training on principals' leadership effectiveness and style range. The study provided only partial support for the Hersey-Blanchard theory. Principals were perceived as more effective three years after training than before training. However, no significant differences were found in principals' effectiveness immediately following training, nor in principals' leadership style range before and after training.[87]

### Synergistic Leadership Theory

Modernist theories in leadership were traditionally dominated by masculine incorporation and lacked feminine presence in development and language. The **synergistic leadership theory** (SLT), developed by Irby and colleagues, seeks to explicate the need for a postmodernist leadership theory by providing an alternative to, and not a replacement for, traditional theories.[88] The SLT includes issues concerning diversity and the inclusion of the female voice in the theory. In a tetrahedron model, the theory uses four factors to demonstrate aspects not only of leadership but its effects on various institutions and positions (see Figure 5–10). The factors are attitudes, beliefs, and values; leadership behavior; external forces; and organizational structure.

**Factor 1: Attitudes, Beliefs, and Values**   As shown in Figure 5–10, attitudes, beliefs, and values are depicted as dichotomous, as an individual or group would either adhere or not adhere to specific attitudes, beliefs, or values at a certain point in time. Some dichotomous examples include the following: (a) believes in the importance of professional growth for all individuals including self; does not believe that professional development is important; (b) has an openness to change; does not have an openness to change; (c) values diversity; does not value diversity; or (d) believes that integrity is important for all involved in schooling; does not value integrity.

[87] Salvatore V. Pascarella and Fred C. Lunenburg, "A Field Test of Hersey and Blanchard's Situational Leadership Theory in a School Setting," *College Student Journal*, 21 (1988): 33–37.

[88] Beverly J. Irby, Genevieve Brown, Jo Ann Duffy, and Diane Trautman, "The Synergistic Leadership Theory," *Journal of Educational Administration*, 40 (2002): 304–322.

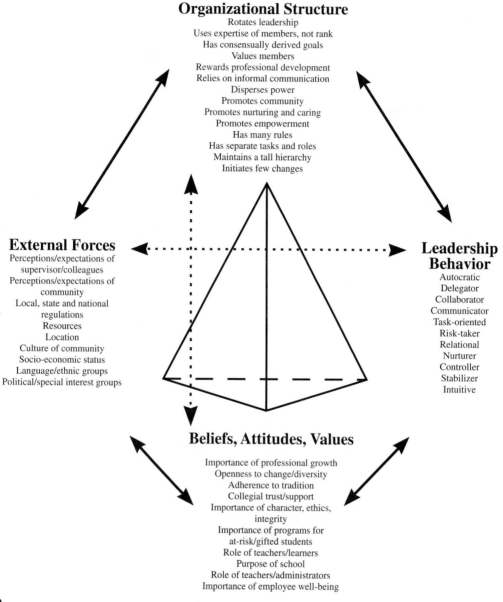

**Organizational Structure**
Rotates leadership
Uses expertise of members, not rank
Has consensually derived goals
Values members
Rewards professional development
Relies on informal communication
Disperses power
Promotes community
Promotes nurturing and caring
Promotes empowerment
Has many rules
Has separate tasks and roles
Maintains a tall hierarchy
Initiates few changes

**External Forces**
Perceptions/expectations of
supervisor/colleagues
Perceptions/expectations of
community
Local, state and national
regulations
Resources
Location
Culture of community
Socio-economic status
Language/ethnic groups
Political/special interest groups

**Leadership
Behavior**
Autocratic
Delegator
Collaborator
Communicator
Task-oriented
Risk-taker
Relational
Nurturer
Controller
Stabilizer
Intuitive

**Beliefs, Attitudes, Values**
Importance of professional growth
Openness to change/diversity
Adherence to tradition
Collegial trust/support
Importance of character, ethics,
integrity
Importance of programs for
at-risk/gifted students
Role of teachers/learners
Purpose of school
Role of teachers/administrators
Importance of employee well-being

**Figure 5–10**

Irby, Brown, Duffy, and Trautman's Synergistic Leadership Model

Source: Adapted from Beverly J. Irby, Genevieve Brown, Jo Ann Duffy, and Diane Trautman, "The Synergistic Leadership Theory," *Journal of Educational Administration,* 40 (2002): 313.

**Factor 2: Leadership Behavior**   The second factor of the theory, leadership behavior, derives directly from the literature on male and female leadership behaviors and is depicted as a range of behaviors from autocratic to nurturer. The range of behaviors includes those as-cribed to female leaders, such as interdependence, co-operation, receptivity, merging acceptance, and being aware of patterns, wholes, and context; as well as those ascribed to male leaders, including self-assertion, separation, independence, control, and competition.

**Factor 3: External Forces**  External forces, as depicted in the model, are those influencers outside the control of the organization or the leader that interact with the organization and the leader and that inherently embody a set of values, attitudes, and beliefs. Significant external influencers or forces relate to local, national, and international community and conditions, governmental regulations, laws, demographics, cultural climate, technological advances, economic situations, political climate, family conditions, and geography. These examples of external forces, as well as others, including those listed in the model, interact in significant ways with the other factors in the synergistic leadership theory.

**Factor 4: Organizational Structure**  Organizational structure refers to characteristics of the organizations and how they operate. The synergistic leadership theory model (Figure 5–10) depicts organizational structures as ranging from open, feminist organizations to tightly bureaucratic ones. Bureaucratic organizations include division of labor, rules, hierarchy of authority, impersonality, and competence, whereas feminist organizations are characterized by practices such as participative decision making, systems of rotating leadership, promotion of community and cooperation, and power sharing.

In sum, the synergistic leadership theory provides a framework for describing interactions and dynamic tensions among attitudes, beliefs, and values; leadership behaviors; external forces; and organizational structure. As a result, a leader can analyze and describe particular interactions that may account for tension, conflict, or harmony at specific points in time or over time. If it is discovered that tension exists between even two of the factors, then the effectiveness of the leader or the organization itself can be negatively impacted. Not only is the SLT beneficial in determining "fit" while a leader is employed in an organization, but also it can be of assistance in job selection. Moreover, the SLT can serve to build an understanding of the environment to aid in decisions made by the leader. And SLT fosters a reflective practice approach, as it encourages the leader to engage in self-assessment.

## Other Contemporary Perspectives

Given the importance of leadership, researchers devote attention to studying new and insightful perspectives. Four other contemporary perspectives of recent interest are the vertical dyad linkage model, reciprocal influence theory, substitutes for leadership, and transformational leadership.

### Vertical Dyad Linkage Model

Many theories of leadership assume that the superior behaves in essentially the same manner toward all members of his work group. In fact, however, leaders often act very differently toward different subordinates, and develop contrasting kinds of relationships with them. This perspective on the leadership process is provided by the **vertical dyad linkage (VDL) model**.[89]

The VDL theory focuses on a dyad, that is, the relationship between a leader and each subordinate considered independently, rather than on the relationship between the superior and the group. Each linkage, or relationship, is likely to differ in quality. Thus, the same administrator may have poor interpersonal relations with some subordinates and open and trusting relations with others. The relationships within these pairings, or dyads, may be of a predominantly in-group or out-group nature.

A leader initiates either an in-group or an out-group exchange with a member of the organization early in the life of the dyadic relationship. Members of the in-group are invited to participate in decision making and are given added responsibility. The leader allows these members some latitude in their roles; in effect, the leader and key subordinates negotiate the latter's responsibilities in a noncontractual exchange relationship. In essence, an in-group member is elevated to the unofficial role of "trusted lieutenant." In-group members, in many respects, enjoy the benefits of job latitude (influence in decision making, open communications, and confidence in and consideration for the member). The subordinate typically reciprocates with greater than required expenditures of time and effort, the assumption of greater responsibility, and commitment to the success of the organization.

In contrast, members of the out-group are supervised within the narrow limits of their formal employment contract. Authority is legitimated by the implicit contract between the member and the organization. The leader will provide the support, consideration, and as-

[89]Fred Dansereau, George Graen, and William J. Haga, "A Vertical Dyad Linkage Approach to Leadership within Formal Organizations: A Longitudinal Investigation of the Role Making Process," *Organizational Behavior and Human Performance*, 13 (1975): 46–78.

sistance mandated by duty but will not go beyond such limits. In effect, the leader is practicing a contractual exchange with such members; they are "hired hands," who are being influenced by legitimate authority rather than true leadership. In return, out-group members will do what they have to do and little beyond that.

Vertical linkage dyad theory suggests that individual superior-subordinate relationships affect leadership style and have an impact on job satisfaction, performance, and commitment. It is hypothesized that in-group members will display greater job satisfaction, superior performance, higher commitment, and lower turnover. Although the VDL theory is not without criticism,[90] in general the research continues to be relatively supportive and seems to have potential for predicting important dimensions of the leader-subordinate exchange.[91]

## Reciprocal Influence Theory

The trait theories of leadership, leadership behavior approaches, and contingency theories of leadership share one underlying assumption: Leader behavior affects subordinate behavior. Particularly in correlational studies, any association between leader behavior and group effectiveness has been interpreted as measuring the impact of the leader's action on subordinate satisfaction, motivation, or performance. More recently, however, it has been recognized that in any complex organization the flow of influence or authority is not unilateral and downward—from leader to subordinate—but also upward from subordinate to leader. **Reciprocal influence theory** states that certain leader behaviors cause subordinate behaviors, and certain acts of subordinates (for example, low performance) can cause the leader to modify behavior.[92]

The reciprocal influence theory is a reality in most organizations. For example, consider the principal of a school who is dedicated to the mission of improving student achievement scores in the building. How is this principal's behavior influenced by subordinates? One obvious response is that the leader will closely su-

pervise teachers who are not performing well and will loosely supervise others who are fulfilling their mission of improving instruction. Thus, by their performance, subordinates are influencing the leader. Of course, the leader is influencing them as well. As another example, consider a university dean who has a tenured professor who is very hot tempered. Although the dean has authority over this faculty member and can order the individual to perform many job-related activities, the dean may be fearful of the subordinate's temper and will modify her leadership style to accommodate this individual. In this case, the professor is probably exerting more influence on the university dean than the leader is influencing the subordinate.

Several studies support the notion of reciprocal influence between leaders and subordinates. The results to date suggest the following:

1. Leader consideration or employee-centered behavior and leader positive reinforcement both can lead to employee job satisfaction.

2. High initiating structure or production-centered leadership sometimes leads to lower employee job satisfaction.

3. Low-performing subordinates tend to cause leaders to use more initiating structure/production-centered leadership and punitive reward behavior (that is, punishment).

4. High leader positive reward behavior tends to lead to improved subordinate performance. However, few studies have shown any direct evidence that leader initiating structure or leader consideration causes increases or decreases in subordinate performance. These findings emphasize the importance of rewards as an influence factor in determining subordinate behavior.[93]

In short, it is realistic to view organizations as places where leaders and subordinates interact in a complex way, each exerting reciprocal influence on the other. Research efforts examining the reciprocal influence process will continue to be of interest to school administrators and researchers and will be used to emphasize the dynamics of leadership in schools.

[90]Miner, *Organizational Behavior 3.*

[91]Fred Luthans, *Organizational Behavior* (New York: McGraw-Hill, 2006).

[92]Jerry L. Gray and Frederick A. Starke, *Organizational Behavior: Concepts and Applications,* 5th ed. (Columbus, OH: Merrill/Macmillan, 1991).

[93]Andrew D. Szilagyi and Marc J. Wallace, *Organizational Behavior and Performance,* 6th ed. (New York: HarperCollins, 1994).

**Table 5-8** **Substitutes and Neutralizers for Supportive and Instrumental Leadership**

| Factor | Supportive Leadership* | Instrumental Leadership* |
|---|---|---|
| **Subordinate Characteristics** | | |
| 1. Experience, ability, training | | Substitute |
| 2. "Professional" orientation | Substitute | Substitute |
| 3. Indifference toward organizational rewards | Neutralizer | Neutralizer |
| **Task Characteristics** | | |
| 1. Structured, routine task | | Substitute |
| 2. Task feedback | | Substitute |
| 3. Intrinsically satisfying task | Substitute | |
| **Organizational Characteristics** | | |
| 1. Cohesive work group | Substitute | Substitute |
| 2. Leader lacks position power | Neutralizer | Neutralizer |
| 3. Formalization of goals and plans | | Substitute |
| 4. Rigid rules and procedures | | Neutralizer |
| 5. Physical distance between leader and subordinates | Neutralizer | Neutralizer |

*Supportive and instrumental leadership are analogous to leader consideration and leader initiating structuring.
Source: Gary A. Yukl, *Leadership in Organizations*, 2nd ed. (Englewood Cliffs, NJ: Prentice Hall, 1989), p. 109. © 1989. Reprinted by permission of Prentice Hall, Englewood Cliffs, NJ.

## Substitutes for Leadership

The concept of substitutes for leadership has evolved in response to dissatisfaction with the progress of leadership theory in explaining the effects of leader behavior on performance outcomes. Research studies demonstrate that, in many situations, leadership may be unimportant or redundant. Certain subordinate, task, and organizational factors can act as **substitutes for leadership** or neutralize the leader's influence on subordinates.[94] Table 5-8 lists some possible leadership substitutes and neutralizers for supportive/relationship leadership and instrumental/task leadership.

As shown in Table 5-8, subordinate experience, ability, and training may substitute for instrumental leadership. For example, professionals such as teach-

ers may have so much experience, ability, and training that they do not need instrumental leadership to perform well and be satisfied. Such leadership acts would be redundant and might be resented, and could even lead to reduced performance. Similarly, subordinates who have a strong professional orientation (like teachers) might not require instrumental or supportive leadership. When subordinates do not desire the rewards a leader can provide, this would neutralize almost any behavior on the part of the leader.

Certain types of work (for example, teaching) are highly structured and automatically provide feedback (through students' oral and written responses) and, therefore, substitute for instrumental leadership. Furthermore, when the task is intrinsically satisfying (like teaching), there will be little need for supportive behavior on the part of the leader to make up for poor design. Finally, when the organization is structured in a way that makes clear the paths to goals—for example, through plans, rules, policies, and standard operating procedures—such structure reduces the need for instrumental leadership. This is particularly apparent in sociotechnical and autonomous work groups found in schools. Sometimes a strong union has the same effect,

[94]Steven Kerr and John M. Jermier, "Substitutes for Leadership: Their Meaning and Measurement," *Organizational Behavior and Human Performance*, 22 (1978): 375–403; John P. Hovell and Peter W. Dorfman, "Leadership and Substitutes for Leadership among Professional and Nonprofessional Workers," *Journal of Applied Behavioral Science*, 22 (1986): 29–46.

## PRO/CON Debate

### Leadership Style

The contemporary heroes of education are people like Joe Clark who revitalized an inner-city high school, Jaime Escalante who taught calculus to Hispanic youth, and Madeline Hunter who brought research to classroom teachers. These are people with common characteristics: a vision and the perseverance to actualize it. Their styles of interaction with others as they pursue their visions are relatively constant although different.

**Question:**   Is a person's leadership style really important?

#### Arguments PRO

1. Leaders have followers. The ways leaders work with their followers is important. In the worst possible scenario, followers rebel or withdraw, and the leader's vision remains a dream.

2. An understanding of leadership style and the ability to flex one's style are important for school administrators. The context of administration changes, and situations differ. Able leaders are always open to new ways of thinking about how to work better with people in a variety of situations.

3. Researchers investigating leadership style have identified several models that practicing administrators find useful. The value of this work is evident: Journal articles on the topic are widely read; conference sessions on leadership style are well attended; and books on leadership are on nonfiction best-seller lists.

4. Principals and superintendents lose their jobs because their styles are incompatible with the values and/or norms of organizations. When the loss of high-visibility leaders is analyzed in the popular press, leadership style invariably surfaces as the problem.

#### Arguments CON

1. Style is a means to achieve an end. Time spent thinking about style is better invested in the development of good substantial ideas. People will follow leaders with good ideas.

2. School administrators are identified because they have effective styles of working with people to accomplish organizational goals. In most instances, their styles remain the same over their careers.

3. The research on leadership style has not made the impact on education that other areas of inquiry have made. Research and development funds are better spent on areas such as effective schools where the impact is clear or ethics where the impact is needed.

4. There is an old adage about success in administration: the right person in the right job at the right time. As contexts change, career administrators change their jobs but not their styles.

---

if it has a collective bargaining agreement that severely constrains the administrator's position power.

It appears that leadership matters most when substitutes are not present in subordinates' skills, task design, or the organization's structure. When substitutes are present, the impact of leadership is neutralized.

### Transformational Leadership

**Transformational leadership** focuses on leaders who have exceptional impact on their organizations. This view of leadership is extremely rare as contrasted with

other leadership approaches we have examined thus far. Although the number of leaders involved is minimal, the impact these leaders have on their institutions is significant.

In his examination of transformational leadership, Bernard Bass contrasts two types of leadership behaviors: transactional and transformational.[95] According to Bass, *transactional leaders* determine what subordinates need to do to achieve their own and organizational objectives, classify those requirements, help sub-

---

[95]Bernard M. Bass, *Transformation Leadership* (Mahwah, NJ: Lawrence Erlbaum, 2005).

ordinates become confident that they can reach their objectives by expending the necessary efforts, and reward them according to their accomplishments. *Transformational leaders,* in contrast, motivate their subordinates to do more than they originally expected to do. They accomplish this by (1) raising followers' levels of consciousness about the importance and value of designated outcomes and about ways of reaching them; (2) getting followers to transcend their own self-interest for the sake of the team, organization, or larger polity;[96] and (3) raising followers' need levels to the higher-order needs, such as self-actualization, or by expanding their portfolio of needs.

Alfred Sloan reformed General Motors into its divisional profit centers. Henry Ford revolutionized the Ford Motor Company by introducing the assembly line for the production of automobiles. More recently, John Welch of General Electric, Steven Jobs of Apple Computer, Bill Gates of Microsoft, and Roberto Goizueta of Coca-Cola guided the metamorphosis of their companies. And Lee Iacocca saved Chrysler Corporation from bankruptcy and brought it to profitability. All have become transformational leaders by creating a vision of a desired future for their companies, by instilling that vision in their followers, and by transforming their vision into reality.

## Summary

1. The literature reviewed over the past decade revealed six major categories of leadership: instructional leadership, transformational leadership, moral leadership, participative leadership, contingency leadership, and managerial leadership.

2. Leadership is not about who's smarter or tougher but about qualities such as motivating power, empathy, integrity, and intuitive abilities, which fall within the domain of "emotional intelligence."

3. Leadership theories can be classified as trait, behavioral, or contingency.

4. Early trait studies, which compared leaders and nonleaders, led to few consistent findings. Later research on traits of effective leaders has been more fruitful.

5. Recent use of assessment centers to identify potential leaders has led to a revitalization of the trait approach. Now the trait approach has been extended to include job-related skills as well as traits in the identification of potential leaders.

6. The Iowa studies, Ohio State studies, and Michigan studies identified distinct leader behaviors. Although no conclusive results emerged concerning leadership effectiveness, these behaviors have been incorporated into the more recent contingency theories of leadership.

7. The contingency theories of leadership are more complex than the trait and behavioral theories. The complexity arises from the need to consider several moderator variables in the process of leadership, such as leader-member relations, task structure, leader position power, subordinate motivation, and path-goal clarity.

8. The contingency theories are based on two different assumptions about leader adaptability. One approach assumes that leaders must change their behavior to fit the situation (House's path-goal theory); the other approach assumes that the leader must change the situation to fit the leader's behavior, which is assumed to be immutable (Fiedler's contingency theory).

9. As outgrowths of and concurrent with the contingency theories, the various leadership styles are Tannenbaum and Schmidt's leadership-style continuum, Blake and Mouton's managerial grid, Reddin's three-dimensional leadership styles, and Hersey and Blanchard's situational leadership model.

10. Other contemporary leadership perspectives include the vertical dyad linkage model, the reciprocal influence theory, substitutes for leadership, and transformational leadership.

11. The most important conclusion from leadership theory is that the traits or skills of a leader, leader behaviors, and various situational factors interacting together may ultimately determine a leader's effectiveness.

## Key Terms

leadership
instructional leadership
transformational leadership

---

[96]See, for, example, Peter Block, *Stewardship: Choosing Service over Self-Interest* (San Francisco: Berrett-Koehler, 1993).

moral leadership
participative leadership
contingency leadership
managerial leadership
manager
leader
emotional intelligence
traits
skills
assessment center
authoritarian leadership
democratic leadership
laissez-faire leadership
initiating structure
consideration
production-centered leader
employee-centered leader
contingency theory
path-goal theory
directive leader
supportive leader
participative leader
achievement-oriented leader
leadership style continuum
Leadership Grid®
three-dimensional model of leadership effectiveness
situational leadership theory
synergistic leadership theory
vertical dyad linkage model
reciprocal influence theory
substitutes for leadership
transformational leadership

## Discussion Questions

1. How many of the six categories of leadership are functioning in your school/school district? Explain.

2. Describe some leadership acts that you performed that fall under the "emotional intelligence" domain.

3. What traits or skills appear to be associated with effective leaders? Support your position.

4. Discuss several different leadership styles and the leadership models associated with each. Be specific.

5. Why is it so important for an administrator to develop the ability to diagnose and evaluate a situation? Explain.

## Suggested Readings

Collins, Jim. *Good to Great: Why Some Companies Make the Leap . . . and Others Don't* (New York: HarperCollins, 2001). Although *Good to Great* is geared more toward business, its concepts can be applied to any field. The research identified seven characteristics of companies that successfully moved from mediocrity to greatness and sustained that level of performance for fifteen years. Those characteristics included the involvement of "level 5" leaders; the importance of getting the right people "on the bus"; confronting the brutal facts as a basis for improvement; identification of what an organization does better than any other organization; the existence of a culture of discipline; and the understanding that technology is an accelerator, not a cause, of improvement. All these qualities of good-to-great companies were undergirded by what is called the flywheel concept—the idea that there is no single defining action that leads to success. Rather, the study showed that consistent, day-to-day actions aligned with the organization's basic and unifying idea—its hedgehog concept—guided it to success. With each push of the flywheel, the organization gathered momentum on its journey toward greatness.

Covey, Stephen R. *The 7 Habits of Highly Effective People: Powerful Lessons in Personal Change* (New York: Simon & Schuster, 2004). This book conveys a "principle-centered, character-based, inside-out approach to personal and interpersonal effectiveness." Covey's habits are based on principles—deep, fundamental truths that become guidelines for behavior. His discussion of behavior is almost biblical as he speaks to the importance of honesty, integrity, courage and compassion. One of the most influential segments of his book addresses the value of a personal mission statement. He entices the reader to "begin with the end in mind" and to live life accordingly.

Freiberg, Kevin, and Jackie Freiberg. *Nuts! Southwest Airlines' Crazy Recipe for Business and Personal Success* (Belmont, CA: Thomson South-Western, 2001). As you read the book, you begin to get a sense of the learning community that exists within the company. This is built upon a system of trust, risk taking, passion for the work, and celebration of individual and team contributions. It is easy to make the connection to the work in public education in which we are engaged. For strong believers in the power of relationships in our work, this book reinforces the conviction that it is the people in the organization that make the difference.

Gladwell, Malcolm. *The Tipping Point: How Little Things Can Make a Difference* (New York: Little, Brown, 2006). Gladwell begins by introducing the concept of "The Law of the Few," or (more specifically) how social epidemics are often driven by a few exceptional people—people with unique and powerful communications skills, people with a rare set of social gifts. In his treatise on "tipping points," Gladwell identifies three specific types of exceptional people or messengers who make "The Law of the Few" work: Connectors, Mavens, and Persuaders. He also notes that in creating epidemics, the messenger is critical; it is only through outstanding messengers that an epidemic spreads. Identifying and cultivating those who are not only Mavens and Connectors but also Persuaders can be of amazing value in moving forward the agenda of a district.

Gladwell, Malcolm. *Blink: The Power of Thinking without Thinking* (New York: Little, Brown, 2007). In *Blink*, Malcolm Gladwell proposes a new name for an old concept of decision making—intuition—and provides psychological explanations for how it happens and why it often works, even in high-stakes decisions. "Blinking" occurs when a person filters out all but the most critical information related to an issue and reaches a split-second conclusion or impression, instead of applying a logical thinking process. Gladwell calls this "thin slicing": a rapid cognition process that draws upon a person's alternate consciousness and can occur as quickly as within two seconds of being confronted with a dilemma. The "blink" ability is not a gift but rather is developed through storing the associated outcomes and consequences of past experiences and then generalizing the lessons learned in a new but similar context; it is related to Thorndike's theory of transfer and is a product of *wisdom*—the synergy of education and experience.

Lencioni, Patrick M. *The Five Temptations of a CEO: A Leadership Fable* (New York: John Wiley, 1998). According to Lencioni, the secret to success comes down to resisting the following five temptations: (1) choosing status over results, (2) choosing popularity over accountability, (3) choosing certainty over clarity, (4) choosing harmony over conflict, and (5) choosing invulnerability over trust. The underlying premise of the book, which resonates throughout, is that chief executives who fail have given in to one or more of the five temptations. This concept is hard for us to accept. Knowing that these temptations are ever-present, we must be willing to engage in ongoing behavioral self-examination. If life at the top of an organization is to be productive, we must be true to ourselves, morally and ethically.

Phillips, Donald T. *Lincoln on Leadership: Executive Strategies for Tough Times* (New York: Warner Books, 2001). Phillips has compiled an impressive body of research, quotations, and stories that serve as parables for how a person can provide truly great leadership. He examines leadership through Abraham Lincoln's interactions, both oral and written, as an aspiring country attorney, a senate candidate, and ultimately president and commander in chief during the Civil War. "Lincoln Principles" appear at the end of each chapter, serving as practical tips to be used by leaders at all levels. Leadership attributes are divided into four broad categories: people, character, endeavor, and communication. Within each category, Phillips provides several chapters that explore "modern management theory," which (in his opinion) Lincoln mastered long ago. The discussion includes management by walking around, alliance building, use of persuasion, need for integrity in all dealings, and the power of a clear and well-communicated vision.

# 6. Decision Making

FOCUSING QUESTIONS

1 Why is decision making an important activity in school administration?

2 What is rational decision making?

3 How do administrators make decisions?

4 What factors prevent school administrators from making optimal decisions?

5 What are the benefits and problems of site-based decision making?

6 How can site-based decision making be improved?

In this chapter, we attempt to answer these questions concerning decision making in school organizations. We begin our discussion by exploring the importance of decision making in schools. Then we provide some general decision-making models, describe the major steps in the decision-making process, and identify factors that limit rational decision making. We explore the advantages and disadvantages of site-based decision making and, finally, we examine techniques commonly used to improve site-based decision making.

## The Nature of Decision Making

**Decision making,** universally defined as the process of choosing from among alternatives, is important to an understanding of educational administration because choice processes play a key role in motivation, leadership, communication, and organizational change. Decision making pervades all other administrative functions as well. Planning, organizing, staffing, directing, coordinating, and controlling all involve decision making.

School administrators at all levels make decisions. These decisions may ultimately influence the school's clients—the students. All decisions, however, have some influence, whether large or small, on the performance of both faculty and students. Therefore, school administrators must develop decision-making skills because they make many decisions that will affect the organization. Furthermore, because school administrators are evaluated on the results of their decisions, the quality of the decisions is one criterion in judging administrators' effectiveness. Consider the following scenarios:

1. You are the principal of a small, rural high school, and it is one week away from the beginning of the state basketball tournament. The basketball team has a record of 18–2 for the season and is the favorite to win the Class A State Championship. You have just caught the star player of the basketball team, an all-state candidate, drinking an alcoholic beverage at a local restaurant. This is the player's second offense. According to board of

education policy, a second offense carries a penalty of a four-week suspension from the team. The policy has not been consistently enforced by the various athletic coaches.

2. You are the assistant superintendent for business of a large, urban school district. The district operates its budgetary procedures on a variation of program planning budgeting systems (PPBS). There is a $100,000 surplus in this year's research and development account that you must spend before the end of the fiscal year. Three program priorities for the current school year are expansion of the vocational education facilities and curriculum, initiation of a new special education curriculum for the hearing impaired, and a districtwide remediation program for students who fall below the national average on the state-administered standardized tests in the basic skills.

3. You are the superintendent of a wealthy, suburban school district. Student enrollment, increased by 20 percent during the past five years, has occurred primarily in grades 1–5. The current facilities of the school district can no longer accommodate the increased student population. The board of education has discussed several options: Merge with an adjacent urban school district, which has experienced a decline in enrollment; change the grade structure in the district from (K–5, 6–8, 9–12) to (K–4, 5–8, 9–12); build another elementary school; go on double sessions in the elementary schools; or rent one of the buildings from the nearby parochial school.

School administrators at different hierarchical levels and career stages face these problems or variations thereof every day. The elements of each problem differ—for example, athletic disciplinary action, allocation of funds from the research and development unit, and expansion of school facilities. Nevertheless, there is similarity among the scenarios; all require that a decision be made. The quality of the decision reached not only will have an impact on the school's clients but also will determine the school administrator's perceived value to the school district.

## Models of Decision Making

Decision making is one type of activity that has been studied extensively through the use of models. Models attempt to describe theoretically and practically how school administrators make decisions. All models characteristically include the concept of decision making as rational behavior. That is, a decision maker will go through a logical sequence of decision-making steps.

Herbert Simon, the Nobel Prize–winning decision theorist, describes the decision-making process in three stages:[1]

1. *Intelligence Activity.* The decision maker searches the environment for conditions calling for decision making. (The term is borrowed from the military meaning of intelligence.)

2. *Design Activity.* The decision maker invents, develops, and analyzes possible courses of action to take.

3. *Choice Activity.* The decision maker selects a particular course of action from among those available.

After analyzing the actual decisions of executives across a spectrum of organizational types and administrative levels, including a school superintendent, Henry Mintzberg and his associates identify three phases in the decision-making process:[2]

1. *Identification Phase.* The decision maker recognizes a problem or opportunity and makes a diagnosis. It was found that severe, immediate problems did not have a very systematic, extensive diagnosis, but mild problems did.

2. *Development Phase.* The decision maker searches for existing standard procedures or solutions already in place or designs a new, tailor-made solution. It was found that the design process was a groping, trial-and-error process in which decision makers had only a vague idea of the ideal solution.

3. *Selection Phase.* The decision maker chooses a solution. There are three ways of making this selection: by the *judgment* of the decision maker; by *analysis* of the alternatives on a logical, systematic basis; and by *bargaining* when the selection involves a group of decision makers and all the political maneuvering that this entails. Once the decision is formally accepted, an authorization is made.

Peter Drucker, another leading organizational theorist, contends there are six steps in the decision-making

---

[1] Herbert A. Simon, *Administrative Behavior: A Study of Decision-Making Processes in Administrative Organizations,* 4th ed. (New York: Free Press, 1997).

[2] Henry Mintzberg, Duru Raisinghani, and André Theoret, "The Structure of 'Unstructured' Decision Processes," *Administrative Science Quarterly,* 21 (1976): 246–275.

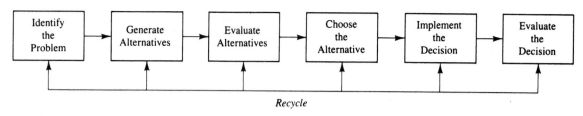

**Figure 6–1**

The Decision-Making Process

process: (1) define the problem; (2) analyze the problem; (3) develop alternative solutions to the problem; (4) decide on the best solution; (5) convert decisions into effective actions; and (6) monitor and assess the results.[3]

Every decision-making model has as its basis some more general model of decision making. Decision-making models can be classified broadly as classical and behavioral. As noted, all models include the concept of decision making as a rational activity. Decision-making models then can be thought of as ranging from complete rationality to complete irrationality.

## The Classical Decision-Making Model

The **classical model** of decision making assumes that decision making is a rational process whereby decision makers seek to maximize the chances of achieving their desired objectives by considering all possible alternatives, exploring all conceivable consequences from among the alternatives, and then making a decision. The classical model of decision making then is based on the concept of complete **rationality**. According to the classical model, the decision-making process can be broken down into logical steps. Numerous authors have provided their models of the decision-making process, but most include versions of the six steps we have included in our model: identifying problems, generating alternatives, evaluating alternatives, choosing alternatives, implementing decisions, and evaluating decisions (see Figure 6–1).

**Identifying the Problem**   The first step in the decision-making process is **identifying the problem.** If there is no problem, there is no need to make a decision. A warning

of a possible problem is a discrepancy between existing and desired conditions. For example, if a school district establishes an objective that 70 percent of the students will be reading on grade level and if only 30 percent of students are reading on grade level at the end of the period, there is a gap between actual performance and the desired level of achievement. If the student dropout rate increases 25 percent over the preceding year, if students and parents file numerous complaints about the schools, if faculty grievances significantly increase, if new book and classroom supply deliveries are twelve months past due, and if the local newspaper runs a series of articles about deficiencies in school district operations, there are problems that require decisions.

Identifying problems is more difficult than one might suspect. One writer proposes four steps in problem identification: measure results, compare results to objectives, determine the significance of the difference, and communicate threshold differences to administration.[4] Another acknowledges similar steps in problem formulation: An administrator (1) must be alert to recognize a problem, (2) must determine a level of performance so that actual performance can be measured against it, (3) must divide complex problems into subproblems and set priorities based on the seriousness of the problem, and (4) must specify the problem in terms of what, where, when, and how big the deviations are from the performance standards previously set.[5]

**Generating Alternatives**   After identifying and defining the problem, the school administrator should **generate** but not evaluate a list of **alternatives.** That is, all possible alternatives should be included no matter how

---

[3]Peter F. Drucker, *The Effective Executive: The Definitive Guide to Getting the Right Things Done* (New York: HarperCollins, 2006).

[4]Jonathan Rosenhead et al., *Rational Analysis for a Problematic World: Problem Structuring Methods for Complexity, Uncertainty and Conflict* (New York: Wiley, 2001).

[5]Zur Shapira, *Organizational Decision Making* (New York: Cambridge University Press, 2002).

ridiculous they may first appear; a choice will be made later. Eliminating alternatives from the list too early decreases the options for the best solution. The administrator must then seek information regarding each alternative and its various consequences that will contribute to solving the problem.

**Evaluating Alternatives** In evaluating alternatives, an additional search for information should be done. John Miner recommends three steps in the process:[6]

1. The decision maker must recognize all possible outcomes from each alternative solution, both positive and negative.

2. The decision maker must assess the value of each outcome, both positive and negative.

3. The decision maker must assess the likelihood of each possible outcome to each alternative.

Estimating the likelihood of each outcome prepares the decision maker to evaluate and compare alternatives, which is done under one of three conditions: certainty, risk, or uncertainty. These conditions force the school administrator into the area of quantitative decision making. An in-depth quantitative analysis of alternatives and their outcomes is beyond the scope of this book. However, we give a brief definition of each term, to clarify the process.

*Certainty* exists when the decision maker knows exactly what the probabilities of the outcome of each alternative will be. Thus, he must estimate the probabilities of the occurrence of the various outcomes.[7] *Risk* exists when the decision maker estimates the probabilities of the outcome of each alternative and determines that success is not 100 percent assured. Thus, predictions can be made, but risk is associated with the various alternatives.[8] *Uncertainty* exists when the decision maker does not know what the probabilities of the outcome of each alternative will be; that is, the likelihood of success or failure associated with alternatives is not clear.[9] In working through the three conditions of cer-

tainty, risk, and uncertainty, the decision maker should rank all alternatives from best to worst according to their likelihood of providing the greatest payoffs to the school district.

**Choosing an Alternative** The next step in the decision-making process involves **choosing an alternative** that the school administrator considers most effective, that is, the one that allows the administrator to solve the problem and accomplish the school district's objectives. The choice can be difficult even when outcomes have been evaluated based on some comparable criteria. James March and Herbert Simon, two leading decision theorists, have proposed five types of alternatives:[10]

1. A *good alternative* has a high probability of positively valued outcomes and a low probability of negatively valued outcomes.

2. A *bland alternative* has a low probability of both positively and negatively valued outcomes.

3. A *mixed alternative* has a high probability of both positively and negatively valued outcomes.

4. A *poor alternative* has a low probability of positively valued outcomes and a high probability of negatively valued outcomes.

5. An *uncertain alternative* is one for which the decision maker cannot assess the relative probabilities of outcomes. (This alternative was discussed earlier.)

Some combinations of these types of alternatives will result in more difficult choices than will other combinations. Consider a school administrator who is faced with two alternatives. If one alternative is good and the other is bland, mixed, poor, or uncertain, then choosing an alternative is easy. Now consider the choice between any other combination of two alternatives, excluding the good alternative. It is difficult to choose between a bland and a mixed alternative, a bland and a poor alternative, and so on.

For instance, consider the decision of an athletic director of a major university to hire an interim basketball coach to complete the season because the existing coach suddenly died just prior to the opening of the season. One alternative (uncertain) is to hire a former high school basketball coach with an outstanding record but no experience at the college level. Thus, the coach is virtually untested at the university level.

[6] John Miner, *Organizational Behavior 3: Historical Origins, Theoretical Foundations, and the Future* (New York: M. E. Sharpe, 2006).

[7] Max H. Bazerman, *Judgment in Managerial Decision Making* (New York: Wiley, 2005).

[8] Paul Goodwin, *Decision Analysis for Management Judgment* (New York: John Wiley, 2004).

[9] Donald G. Saari, *Decision Making* (New York: Cambridge University Press, 2001).

[10] James G. March and Herbert A. Simon, *Organizations*, 2nd ed. (Cambridge, MA: Blackwell, 2004).

Another alternative (poor) is to hire a mediocre coach from a nearby small college or junior college. A third alternative (mixed) is to hire an outstanding coach who won several NCAA championships but who was fired by his school administration for manifesting erratic and irrational behavior during games and for striking a player. While one would expect a good season, there is also the chance of alienating the school administration and a repeat of the irrational behavior and player abuse. The final alternative (bland) is to select one of the assistant coaches to assume the head coaching position. Though skilled in other areas, neither assistant coach possesses the technical court skills nor the personality to motivate players. Such a decision is likely to produce an average season in terms of record and relations with the school's administration and players.

**Implementing the Decision**   Once a decision is made to choose a solution, it must be **implemented.** The decision maker will have already considered all conceivable problems that may be associated with the implementation of the solution during the previous step in the decision-making process. However, in school organizations, administrators depend on others to implement decisions, so they must have skills not only for problem solving but also for "selling" the decision to those affected by it.[11]

**Evaluating the Decision**   The decision-making process does not end when the decision is implemented. The school administrator must **evaluate the decision**—that is, determine the extent to which the solution achieved the school district's objectives. Measuring actual performance against performance specified in the objectives is one way of evaluating success. If a discrepancy exists between actual and expected results, then the decision-making process must be recycled. Changes in the alternative that was chosen, how it was implemented, or the determination of objectives are necessary.

For example, it is possible that the objectives established are unrealistic and that no reasonable alternative could result in a successful decision. Such a situation stresses the importance of determining measurable objectives. Unless specific objectives are set, mutually agreed on, and met at all levels of operation, there will be relatively little value or basis for measuring the effectiveness of the school district's decisions.

## The Behavioral Decision-Making Model

The classical decision-making model, discussed earlier, characterizes the decision maker as completely rational. More specifically, he is assumed to (1) recognize all possible alternative solutions to the problem, (2) be aware of all possible consequences of each alternative, (3) be able to evaluate the consequences against his value system, (4) be able to rank the alternatives in the order in which they are likely to meet his objectives, and (5) select the alternative that maximizes his objectives.[12] The classical model assumes that the decision maker has perfect information (i.e., is aware of a problem, knows all alternatives and their possible consequences, and possesses a criterion for making the decision) and seeks to maximize some expected objective.

Frequently, school administrators are not aware that problems exist. Even when they are, they do not systematically search for all possible alternative solutions. They are limited by time constraints, cost, and the ability to process information. So they generate a partial list of alternative solutions to the problem based on their experience, intuition, advice from others, and perhaps even some creative thought. Rationality is, therefore, limited. Simon coined the term **bounded rationality** to describe the perspective of the decision maker who would like to make the best decisions but normally settles for less than the optimal.[13]

In contrast to the completely rational model of decision making (classical decision-making model), Mary Zey summarizes the **behavioral model** as follows:[14]

1. Decisions will always be based on an incomplete and, to some degree, inadequate comprehension of the true nature of the problem being faced.

2. Decision makers will never succeed in generating all possible alternative solutions for consideration.

3. Alternatives are always evaluated incompletely because it is impossible to predict accurately all consequences associated with each alternative.

4. The ultimate decision regarding which alternative to choose must be based on some criterion other than

---

[11]Bobby R. Patton et al., *Decision-Making Group Interaction: Achieving Quality* (Boston: Allyn and Bacon, 2004).

[12]Miner, *Organizational Behavior 3.*

[13]Herbert A. Simon, *Models of Bounded Rationality: Empirically Grounded Economic Reason* (Cambridge, MA: MIT Press, 1997).

[14]Mary Zey, *Decision Making: Alternatives to Rational Choice Models* (Thousand Oaks, CA: Sage, 1992).

## ■ Exemplary Educational Administrators in Action

**PASCAL D. FORGIONE, JR.** Superintendent, Austin Independent School District, Austin, Texas, and Adjunct Professor, Department of Educational Administration, College of Education, University of Texas at Austin.

**Previous Positions:** United States Commissioner of Education Statistics, National Center for Education Statistics; State Superintendent of Public Instruction, Department of Public Instruction, Delaware; Executive Director, National Education Goals Panel; Division Director, Division of Research, Evaluation and Assessment, Connecticut State Department of Education; Office Chief, Office of Research and Evaluation, Connecticut State Department of Education.

**Latest Degree and Affiliation:** Ph.D., Administration and Policy Analysis, Stanford University.

**Number One Influence on Career:** Exceptional training and stimulating course work at Stanford University and a deep belief in the efficacy and importance of public schools for our democracy.

**Number One Achievement:** Improved the performance and capacity of each institution I have led at the federal, national, state, and local levels.

**Number One Regret:** I did not return to public school leadership at the local district level earlier.

**Favorite Education-Related Book or Text:** Graham Allison's *Essence of Decision Making* and David Tyack's *One Best System.*

**Additional Interests:** Serving on boards of major non-profit community organizations, including the Austin Area Urban League, the Boys and Girls Clubs of Austin, and the Austin Symphony.

**Leadership Style:** An active, passionate, and engaging style that builds a strong and clear sense of purpose and direction and motivates professional colleagues and clients by an extraordinary personal commitment and dedication.

**Professional Vision:** The heart and soul of a good public school education is quality teaching and learning that provides clear expectations, high standards, rigorous content in a thinking curriculum, and shared accountability. I am a firm believer in a standards-based and an effort-based approach to education that ensures high performance for all students and closes the gap in achievement.

**Words of Advice:** I believe that one of the greatest inventions of American democracy is the American public school. Today, we must recommit ourselves to the efficacy and centrality of its mission and recruit a new generation of skillful and dedicated leaders who can build the education systems that will produce positive academic success for all students and manage the complex urban systems with efficiency and effectiveness.

---

maximization or optimization because it is impossible ever to determine which alternative is optimal.

**Satisficing** One version of bounded rationality is the principle of **satisficing.** This approach to decision making involves choosing the first alternative that satisfies minimal standards of acceptability without exploring all possibilities. This is the usual approach taken by decision makers. James March and Simon express it this way: "Most human decision making, whether individual or organizational, is concerned with the discovery and selection of satisfactory alternatives; only in exceptional cases is it concerned with the discovery and selection of optimal alternatives." [15]

---

[15] March and Simon, *Organizations*, pp. 140–141.

**Contextual Rationality and Procedural Rationality** March and Simon later proposed two other forms of bounded rationality: contextual rationality and procedural rationality. **Contextual rationality** suggests that a decision maker is embedded in a network of environmental influences that constrain purely rational decision making. [16] Although the school administrator wants to make optimal decisions, "these are mediated by such realities of organizational life as internal and external politics, conflict resolution requirements, distribution of power and authority, and limits of human

---

[16] James G. March, "Bounded Rationality, Ambiguity, and the Engineering of Choice," *Bell Journal of Economics*, 9 (1978): 587–608.

rationality."[17] Furthermore, schools have vague and ambiguous goals. This, coupled with the lack of a clearly defined success criterion, leads to policies and procedures designed to maintain stability and control, and the objectives of the school as a social institution are to achieve major changes in the student. These changes are not restricted to cognitive behavior (learning) but include a wide range of social, emotional, physical, and, in some cases, moral behavior. Thus, school administrators must pursue multiple and often conflicting goals, within a network of environmental constraints, that restrict the maximization of goal achievement.[18]

We noted that bounded rationality, satisficing, and contextual rationality limit perfectly rational decision making. This results in the inability of decision makers to "maximize" outcomes. What, then, can school administrators do to improve their decisions in view of the constraints on complete rationality implied by the classical decision-making model? Simon proposes the principle of **procedural rationality**.[19] Instead of focusing on generating and evaluating all possible **alternative solutions** to a problem and their consequences, decision makers focus on the procedures used in making decisions. Thus, techniques are perfected and used to make the best possible decisions, including operations research, systems analysis, strategic planning, program planning budgeting systems (PPBS), management information systems (MIS), and so on, each prescribed to improve the reliability of decisions. Rational procedures are not designed to focus on generating and evaluating all available information to solve problems, but they are aimed at adequate acquisition and processing of relevant information.

**Retrospective Rationality** Retrospective rationality is another major form of decision making.[20] By this we mean that decision makers devote considerable energy to justifying the rationality of decisions they have already made. One author puts it this way: "Now that I have made my choice, I need to find good reasons for it."[21]

Evidence supports the notion that decision makers tend to be defensive about their decisions.[22] Substantial dissonance occurs when a decision turns out to be unsuccessful. For this reason, many organizations do not conduct thorough evaluations of expensive programs that are implemented, for fear of exposing faulty decisions. Another aspect of retrospective rationality is the tendency for decision makers to take personal responsibility for successful decision outcomes while denying responsibility for unsuccessful ones.[23] For example, students are willing to take full responsibility for good grades, while bad grades are attributed to poor teaching.

**Incrementalizing**    Another approach to decision making, sometimes referred to as "muddling through," involves making small changes (increments) in the existing situation. Charles Lindblom, its author, distinguishes between completely rational decision making based on the classical model and **incrementalizing,** which is based on successive limited comparisons.[24] The rational approach to decision making involves determining objectives, considering all possible alternative solutions, exploring all conceivable consequences of the alternative solutions, and finally choosing the optimal alternative solution that will maximize the achievement of the agreed-on objectives. Incrementalizing, on the other hand, does not require agreement on objectives, an exhaustive search of all possible alternatives and their consequences, or selection of the optimal alternative. Instead, Lindblom argues that no more than small or incremental steps—no more than muddling through—is ordinarily possible. In other words, incrementalizing is a process of successive limited comparisons of alterna-

[17]Thomas J. Sergiovanni et al., *Educational Governance and Administration*, 3rd ed. (Needham Heights, MA: Allyn and Bacon, 1992), p. 192.

[18]Karen S. Cook and Margaret Levi (eds.), *The Limit of Rationality* (Chicago: University of Chicago Press, 1990).

[19]Herbert A. Simon, "Rationality as a Process and as a Product of Thought," *American Economic Review,* 68 (1978): 1–16.

[20]Barry M. Staw, "Rationality and Justification in Organizational Life," in B. M. Staw and L. L. Cummings (eds.), *Research in Organizational Behavior,* vol. 2. (Greenwich, CT: JAI Press, 1980), pp. 45–80.

[21]Bernard M. Bass, *Organizational Decision Making* (Homewood, IL: Irwin, 1983), p. 142.

[22]Gary Johns, *Organizational Behavior: Understanding and Managing Life at Work* (Englewood Cliffs, NJ: Prentice Hall, 2004).

[23]Anthony G. Greenwald, "The Totalitarianism Ego: Fabrication and Revision of Personal History," *American Psychologist,* 35 (1980): 603–618.

[24]Charles E. Lindblom, *The Science of "Muddling Through"* (New York: Irvington, 1993).

tive courses of action with one another until decision makers arrive at an alternative on which they agree.

**The Garbage Can Model**   Earlier we noted that while the school administrator wants to make optimal decisions, the realities of organizational life—including politics, time constraints, finances, and the inability to process information—limit purely rational decision making. Applying the classical decision-making model (rational decision making) is particularly troublesome for schools. The technologies of teaching are varied and not well understood. Moreover, schools have multiple and conflicting goals that are vague and ambiguous. And schools lack clearly defined success criteria. Thus, problems and solutions cannot be translated easily into a logical sequence of steps (classical decision-making model).[25] In accordance with this view, David Cohen and his associates conceptualized this decision-making process as a **garbage can model.**[26] As members of a school or school district generate problems and alternative solutions to problems, they deposit them into the garbage can. The mixture is seen as a collection of solutions that must be matched to problems. Participants are also deposited into the garbage can. Mixing problems, solutions, and decision participants results in interaction patterns leading to decisions that often do not follow the classical decision-making model sequence.

A number of studies in educational administration have specified and tested comparative models of decision making, using the classical and behavioral models as one of several. For example, one study found that high schools were more likely to resemble the behavioral model (bounded rationality) than were elementary schools, which more closely resembled the classical model.[27] According to the researchers, because high schools were typically departmentalized and had more diverse goals, they could be characterized as more loosely coupled than elementary schools.

Several other studies address some of the assumptions of bounded rationality. Research on administrative behavior in schools is consistent in identifying the demands on the administrator as fragmented, rapid fire, and difficult to prioritize. For example, one study noted that the fragmented and unpredictable workday of principals was not conducive to rational decision making.[28] (See Administrative Advice 6–1.)

### The Vroom-Yetton Normative Model

Victor Vroom and Philip Yetton have devised a sophisticated model of decision making that involves a clear statement of what the leader is supposed to accomplish: (1) decision quality, (2) decision acceptance, and (3) timeliness.[29] The model first identifies five decision-making styles. Second, it identifies criteria for choosing among the decision-making styles. Third, it describes attributes of decision problems that determine which levels of subordinate participation are feasible. Finally, it offers the school administrator rules for making the final choice from among an array of feasible alternatives.

**Decision Effectiveness**   As noted, three critical aspects influence overall effectiveness, or **decision feasibility:** quality, acceptance, and timeliness.

*Decision Quality*   Decision quality refers to the extent to which a decision is effective. Different problems have different quality requirements. For example, decisions such as a technique to evaluate teacher competence, the assignment of teachers to specific tasks, the selection of textbooks and other instructional materials, and the development of policies and procedures for operating a school require high decision quality. Conversely, a decision on what brand of milk to place in the school cafeteria or which teacher to put on a school committee when all are equally qualified requires low decision quality. Generally, when decision quality is important and subordinates have the expertise to make the decision, a participatory decision-making style leads to more effective decisions than does a more autocratic style.

[25]Maurice J. Elias and John F. Clabby, *Building Social Problem-Solving Skills: Guidelines for a School-Based Program* (San Francisco: Jossey-Bass, 1992).

[26]David M. Cohen, James G. March, and Johan D. Olsen, "A Garbage Can Model of Organizational Choice," *Administrative Science Quarterly,* 17 (1972): 1–25.

[27]William A. Firestone and Robert E. Herriott, "Images of Organization and the Promotion of Change," in R. G. Corwin (ed.), *Research in Sociology of Education and Socialization,* vol. 2 (Greenwich, CT: JAI Press, 1981), pp. 221–260.

[28]Van Cleve Morris et al., *Urban Principal: Discretionary Decision Making in a Large Educational Organization,* Research Report (Chicago: University of Illinois at Chicago Circle, 1981).

[29]Victor H. Vroom and Philip W. Yetton, *Leadership and Decision Making* (Pittsburgh: University of Pittsburgh Press, 1974).

## Administrative Advice 6-1

### Time Management Tips

If you are like many harried school administrators, get control of your time by using the following management techniques:

- *Use a Notebook with an Agenda and Calendar and Carry It with You.* If properly implemented, this notebook should evolve into a portable administrative resource center.

- *Start Each Day with a Five-Minute Meeting with Your Secretary.* You can increase your secretarial staff's efficiency greatly by outlining your priorities and goals daily.

- *Go through Your Mail and In-Box, Handling Any Piece of Paper Only Once.* No communication that comes across your desk should require more than one reading. After you have read it, route it, file it, act on it, or toss it.

- *Delegate.* Give your staff opportunity for growth and involvement by delegating as many tasks as possible.

- *Learn to Say No.* Don't get stuck on tasks and responsibilities that don't correspond to your priorities.

- *Control Visitors, Especially the "Drop-In" Kind.* Instruct your secretary to answer as many questions as possible, refer calls to other appropriate staff, take information from callers, and pass on to you only those calls you need to take.

- *Put a Large Wastebasket to Use.* It usually takes more time to locate vaguely recalled "old treasures" than they are worth. If you can't act on it and it isn't worth filing, throw it out.

- *Streamline Meetings.* Provide each person with an agenda prior to the meeting. Note whether each item is intended as information or requires action.

- *Use Your Subconscious Time to Your Advantage.* Research shows that many creative decisions can result from subconscious processing of conscious concerns. Try submitting pending matters to your subconscious at bedtime and let it work on them all night.

- *Clean Off Your Desk Every Night Before You Leave.* A cluttered desk wastes time and is a sure sign of disorganization to anyone who enters your office. Starting the day with a desk piled with yesterday's concerns is demoralizing.

Source: Adapted from Jack J. Bimrose, "Try These Time Management Tips," *School Administrator*, 44 (1987): 22–23. Used by permission.

*Decision Acceptance*  Decision acceptance refers to the extent to which decisions are accepted by those subordinates who must implement them. Even if a leader's decision is high in decision quality, the decision will not be effective if it is not implemented. Thus, school administrators need to consider acceptance just as important as quality in arriving at effective decisions. Research demonstrates that subordinate involvement in decision making is advantageous for arriving at better-quality decisions and for promoting acceptance. House's path-goal model (see Chapter 5) also shows that if subordinates have influence in decision making, they tend to perceive decisions as their own and are motivated to implement them successfully.

*Timeliness*  Timeliness refers to the amount of time available to the decision maker to arrive at a decision. Participatory decision making is very costly in terms of time. If time is an important factor, the leader may need to choose a more autocratic leadership style. If, however,

a long-term development of the skills and competencies of the group is the most important criterion, then choosing a more participative style may be more productive.

**Decision-Making Styles**  Vroom and Yetton identify and describe five alternative decision-making styles that can be placed on a continuum from highly autocratic to highly participatory (see Table 6-1). The styles labeled A are basically autocratic, those labeled C are consultative, and those labeled G are group styles. Roman numerals identify variants of each style. As you study each style in Table 6-1, try to determine which of these styles you used in a given situation. Test this by thinking of leadership situations you have encountered on your job and see if you can classify your styles in terms of the Vroom-Yetton taxonomy.

**Choosing the Correct Decision-Making Style**  According to Vroom and Yetton, one leader can use all five styles as listed in Table 6-1, depending on the situ-

**Table 6–1  Five Decision-Making Styles of the Vroom-Yetton Model**

| Style | Method |
|---|---|
| **Autocratic** | |
| AI | Solve the problem or make the decision yourself using the information available to you at the present time. |
| AII | Obtain any necessary information from subordinates, then decide on a solution to the problem yourself. You may or may not tell subordinates the purpose of your questions or give information about the problem or decision on which you are working. The input provided by them is clearly in response to your request for specific information. They do not play a role in the definition of the problem or in generating or evaluating alternative solutions. |
| **Consultative** | |
| CI | Share the problem with the relevant subordinates individually, getting their ideas and suggestions without bringing them together as a group. Then *you* make the decision. This decision may or may not reflect your subordinates' influence. |
| CII | Share the problem with your subordinates in a group meeting where you obtain their ideas and suggestions. Then, *you* make the decision, which may or may not reflect your subordinates' influence. |
| **Group** | |
| GII | Share the problem with your subordinates as a group. Together you generate and evaluate alternatives and attempt to reach agreement (consensus) on a solution. Your role is much like that of chairman, coordinating the discussion, keeping it focused on the problem, and ensuring that the critical issues are discussed. You can provide the group with information or ideas that you have but you do not try to press them to adopt your solution and are willing to accept and implement any solution that has the support of the entire group. |

Source: Adapted and reprinted from Victor H. Vroom and Philip W. Yetton, *Leadership and Decision Making,* by permission of the University of Pittsburgh Press. © 1973, The University of Pittsburgh Press.

ation. As a decision maker, the leader may be autocratic in one situation and participatory in the next. Thus, different types of situations require different styles. The key to effective administration is the ability to correctly diagnose the situation and then choose an appropriate decision-making style.

The Vroom-Yetton normative model contains a set of seven diagnostic questions that an administrator can use in determining which decision-making style to choose in any given situation. These diagnostic questions are based on a set of seven rules aimed at simplifying the selection of the appropriate decision-making style. The first three rules focus on the quality of the decision, and the remaining four deal with decision acceptance (see Table 6–2).

Vroom and Yetton use a decision tree to relate the seven diagnostic questions, listed at the bottom of the decision tree, to the appropriate decision-making style (see Figure 6–2). Starting at the left, the administrator answers each question along the path. At the end of each path is a list of acceptable decision-making styles. Some paths end with one acceptable style; others end with five acceptable styles. To be acceptable, the style must meet the criteria of the seven decision rules that protect quality and acceptance. If more than one style remains after the test of both quality and acceptance, the

third most important aspect of a decision—timeliness—determines the single, best style that should be used in a given situation.

**Training Administrators in Decision Making**  The rationale of the Vroom-Yetton model is that administrators should ask themselves a series of diagnostic questions when they confront a problem situation and select an approach to solving the problem based on their responses to the diagnostic questions. However, the number of questions and alternative decision-making styles make their problem-solving process complex. Therefore, Vroom has introduced a training program to help administrators learn the prescriptions of his theory.[30] The TELOS Program (marketed by the Kepner Tregoe organization) is a version of this training.[31]

In consultation with Vroom, the TELOS training explains the theory and provides administrators with practice in examining their own decision-making styles.

---

[30]Victor H. Vroom, "Can Leaders Learn How to Lead?" *Organizational Dynamics,* 4 (1976): 17–28.

[31]Blanchard B. Smith, "The TELOS Program and the Vroom-Yetton Model," in J. G. Hunt and L. L. Larson (eds.), *Crosscurrents in Leadership* (Carbondale: Southern Illinois University Press, 1979), pp. 39–60.

## Table 6–2   Rules for Decision-Making Selection

### Rules to protect the quality of the decision

1. *Leader information rule.* If decision quality is important and the leader does not possess enough information or expertise to solve the problem by himself, then eliminate AI from the feasible set.

2. *Goal congruence rule.* If decision quality is important and subordinates are not likely to pursue the organization goals in their efforts to solve this problem, then eliminate GII from the feasible set.

3. *Unstructured problem rule.* In decisions in which decision quality is important, if the leader lacks the necessary information or expertise to solve the problem alone, and if the problem is unstructured, the problem-solving method should provide for interaction among subordinates likely to possess relevant information. Accordingly, eliminate AI, AII, and CI from the feasible set.

### Rules to protect the acceptance of the decision

4. *Acceptance rule.* If decision acceptance by subordinates is critical to effective implementation and if it is not certain that an autocratic decision will be accepted, eliminate AI and AII from the feasible set.

5. *Conflict rule.* If decision acceptance is critical and if an autocratic decision is not certain to be accepted and disagreement among subordinates in methods of attaining the organizational goal is likely, the problem-solving methods should enable those in disagreement to resolve their differences with full knowledge of the problem. Accordingly, under these conditions, eliminate AI, AII, and CI, which permit no interaction among subordinates and therefore provide no opportunity for those in conflict to resolve their differences, from the feasible set. Their use runs the risk of leaving some of the subordinates with less than the needed commitment to the final decision.

6. *Fairness rule.* If decision quality is unimportant but acceptance of the decision is critical and not certain to result from an autocratic decision, the decision process must generate the needed acceptance. The decision process should permit subordinates to interact with one another and negotiate over the fair method of resolving any differences with the full responsibility on them for determining what is fair and equitable. Accordingly, under these circumstances, eliminate AI, AII, CI, and CII from the feasible set.

7. *Acceptance priority rule.* If acceptance is critical, but not certain to result from an autocratic decision, and if subordinates are motivated to pursue the organizational goals represented in the problem, then methods that provide equal partnership in the decision-making process can provide greater acceptance without risking decision quality. Accordingly, eliminate AI, AII, CI, and CII from the feasible set.

Source: Adapted and reprinted from Victor H. Vroom and Philip W. Yetton, *Leadership and Decision Making,* by permission of the University of Pittsburgh Press. © 1973, The University of Pittsburgh Press.

Essentially, the program exposes administrators to a standardized set of cases and allows them to make a choice among responses. A computer, which generates a detailed analysis of decision-making styles, processes the responses. Administrators receive printouts showing how their decision-making style compares with other trainees in the workshop. They are also able to form profiles of the extent to which they vary their styles. Subsequently, cases are reanalyzed, and small group discussions take place, where trainees may feel considerable peer pressure to shift their decision-making style. Generally, this pressure causes trainees to adopt new decision-making styles that are congruent with the Vroom-Yetton theory.

## Benefits of Site-Based Decision Making

Up to this point, we have been discussing decision making as an individual activity. We pictured a school administrator working at a hectic pace and making decisions under pressure with little time for reflective planning. But more often than not, a number of people participate in important decisions in schools, and they come together to solve school problems. Whether decision making involves individual or group activity, the process requires the individual or group to go through the typical decision-making steps: identifying the problem, generating alternatives, evaluating alternatives, choosing an alternative, implementing the decision, and evaluating the decision. We pointed out, however, that this description of decision making is limited by various forms of bounded rationality and thus misrepresents how decisions are actually made in school organizations.

In the group decision-making process, decisions are the product of interpersonal decision processes and group dynamics.[32] Thus, the school administrator must be concerned with leading the group from a collection of individuals to a collaborative decision-making unit.

[32]Patton et al., *Decision-Making Group Interaction.*

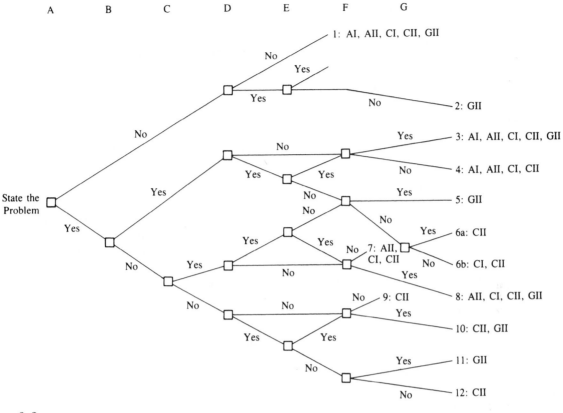

**Figure 6–2**

The Decision Tree

Source: Adapted and reprinted from Victor H. Vroom and Philip W. Yetton, *Leadership and Decision Making*, by permission of the University of Pittsburgh Press. © 1973, The University of Pittsburgh Press.

This implies that school administrators must develop group decision-making skills as well as skills in individual decision making.

School administrators and faculty alike spend large amounts of time participating in committees that are attempting to make decisions. Superintendents are usually chosen by boards of education. Principals are selected by committees consisting of a variety of organizational participants including administrators, teachers, students, and sometimes community members. Faculty committees usually decide on which textbooks to adopt. Formal review committees normally process curriculum modifications. These activities are intended to bring school participants into the organization's decision-making process.

It is believed that shared decision making results in a number of benefits over individual decision making,

including increased decision quality, creativity, acceptance, understanding, judgment, and accuracy. Experts advise school districts that a proven method to increase school effectiveness is to involve school employees in the decision-making process.[33] With these generalizations in mind, the benefits of participative decision making include the following:[34]

1. *Decision Quality.* A greater sum of knowledge and information is accessible in a group than in any of its members. Members can often fill in each other's information gaps. Groups are more vigilant, can

---

[33]Byron M. Roth, *Decision Making: Its Logic and Practice* (Blue Ridge Summit, PA: Roman and Littlefield, 2002).

[34]Andrew J. DuBrin, *Essentials of Management*, (Belmont, CA: Thomson South-Western, 2005).

generate more ideas, and can evaluate ideas better than individuals.

2. *Decision Creativity.* Groups provide a greater number of approaches to a problem because individuals are more likely to be close minded in their thinking. Because group members do not have identical approaches, each can contribute by getting people to become more open minded in their thinking. Group participation increases performance. More participation leads to more creative thinking, which often results in more feasible solutions to problems.

3. *Decision Acceptance.* Participation in decision making increases acceptance of the decision or the solution to the problem. This idea is exemplified in the movement toward site-based decision making.[35] Site-based decision making, however, is not viable in school districts that are highly centralized.

4. *Decision Understanding.* Group participation increases understanding of the decision. When group members have been involved in the decision-making process, further information about the decision does not have to be provided to them. Moreover, members comprehend the decision better because they were involved in the developmental stages of the decision process.

5. *Decision Judgment.* Groups are more effective at establishing objectives, identifying alternatives, and evaluating alternatives because of the increased knowledge and viewpoints available to them.

6. *Decision Accuracy.* Because group members evaluate each other's thinking, major errors, bloopers, and glitches tend to be avoided. Poor or nonfeasible alternatives are more likely to be spotted.

Do groups actually make better decisions than individuals? The discussion here suggests that they do. Reviews of research on the benefits of shared decision making, however, are inconsistent. Research related specifically to the relationship between participative decision making and decision outcomes reveals ambiguity or nonsupport for the relationship.[36] Most research in this area assumes the benefits of teacher participation as a given.[37] The benefits of shared decision making are probably not directly related to decision outcomes but instead are more associated with morale and job satisfaction.[38] One review of research concludes that groups usually produce more and better solutions to problems than do individuals working alone.[39] And two prominent consultants claim the benefits of participatory decision making over individual decision making.[40] The conclusions of the latter three works are qualified by the exact nature of the problem being solved and the composition of the group making the decision. More specifically, groups should perform better than individuals when (1) group members differ in relevant skills and abilities, as long as they don't differ so much that conflict occurs; (2) some division of labor can occur; (3) memory of facts is an important issue; and (4) individual judgments can be averaged to arrive at a group position.[41]

Site-based decision making (SBDM) seems destined to be one of the major reforms of the twenty-first century. The American Association of School Administrators and the National Education Association are pushing for adoption of SBDM. And some states and school districts have mandated SBDM. Therefore, school administrators need to learn as much as possible about SBDM. One of the first steps to success with SBDM is understanding what it is. (See Administrative Advice 6–2.)

## Problems in Site-Based Decision Making

We have pointed out the potential benefits of shared decision making over individual decisions; however, the social nature of group processes can negatively affect performance. More specifically, three tendencies in particular can damage group decision processes: groupthink, risky shift, and escalation of commitment.[42]

[35] Joseph Murphy and Amanda Datnow, *Leadership Lessons from Comprehensive School Reforms* (Thousand Oaks, CA: Corwin Press, 2002).

[36] James A. Conway, "The Myth, Mystery and Mastery of Participative Decision Making in Education," *Educational Administration Quarterly,* 20 (1984): 11–40.

[37] Murphy and Datnow, *Leadership Lessons from Comprehensive School Reforms.*

[38] Wayne K. Hoy and Cecil G. Miskel, *Educational Administration: Theory, Research and Practice,* 7th ed. (New York: McGraw-Hill, 2005).

[39] Bodo Glaser, *Efficiency Versus Sustainability in Dynamic Decision Making: Advances in Intertemporal Compromising* (New York: Springer-Verlag, 2002).

[40] David Currie, *Integrating Management Decision Making* (Upper Saddle River, NJ: Pearson Books, 2002).

[41] Johns, *Organizational Behavior.*

[42] Miner, *Organizational Behavior 3.*

---

## Administrative Advice 6–2

### Premises of Site-Based Decision Making

While SBDM takes many forms, it emphasizes several common beliefs or premises.

■ Those closest to the students and "where the action is" will make the best decisions about the students' education.

■ Teachers, parents, and school staff should have more to say about policies and programs affecting their schools and children.

■ Those responsible for carrying out decisions should have a voice in determining those decisions.

■ Change is most likely to be effective and lasting when those who implement it feel a sense of ownership and responsibility for the process.

Source: Adapted from Lynn Balster Liontos, "Shared Decision Making," *ERIC Digest*, 87 (1994) (ED 368034), p. 1.

---

## Groupthink

Irving Janis coined the term **groupthink,** which happens when in-group pressures lead to a deterioration in mental efficiency, poor testing of reality, and lax moral judgments.[43] It tends to occur in highly cohesive groups in which the group members' desire for consensus becomes more important than evaluating problems and solutions realistically. An example would be the top administrative cabinet (the superintendent and associate superintendents) of a school district who have worked together for many years. They know each other well and think as a cohesive unit rather than as a collection of individuals. Similarly, when a group of teachers collectively decides to go on strike, the decision may be a product of groupthink. Janis identifies eight symptoms of groupthink:[44]

1. *Invulnerability.* Most or all group members develop an illusion of invulnerability, which causes them to become overly optimistic and take extreme risks.

2. *Rationalization.* Group members collectively rationalize in order to discount warnings that might lead them to reconcile their assumptions before they recommit themselves to their past policy decisions.

3. *Morality.* Group members develop an unquestioned belief in the group's inherent morality, inclining the members to ignore ethical or moral consequences of their decisions.

4. *Stereotyping.* Group members develop stereotyped views of opposition leaders as too evil to warrant genuine attempts to negotiate or as too weak and stupid to counter whatever risky attempts are made to defeat their purposes.

5. *Pressure.* Group members apply direct pressure on any member who expresses strong arguments against any of the group's stereotypes, illusions, or commitments, making clear that this type of dissent is contrary to what is expected of all loyal members.

6. *Self-Censorship.* Group members censor themselves from any deviations from the apparent group consensus, reflecting each member's inclination to minimize the importance of his doubts and counterarguments.

7. *Unanimity.* Group members perceive a shared illusion of unanimity concerning judgments conforming to the majority view (partly resulting from self-censorship of deviations, augmented by the false assumption that silence means consent).

8. *Mindguards.* Some group members appoint themselves to protect the group from adverse information that might shatter their shared complacency about the effectiveness and morality of their decisions.

The likelihood that groupthink will emerge is greatest when: (1) the group is cohesive, (2) the group becomes insulated from qualified outsiders, and (3) the leader promotes his own favored solution.[45] In suggest-

---

[43]Irving L. Janis, *Groupthink: Psychological Studies of Policy Decisions and Fiascoes,* 2nd ed. (Boston: Houghton Mifflin, 1982).

[44]Ibid.

[45]Ibid.

ing ways of avoiding groupthink, Janis hopes to reduce cohesiveness and open up decision activity in various ways. One way is to select ad hoc groups to solve problems; in this way, the members do not already belong to a cohesive group. Another approach is to have higher-level administrators set the parameters of the decision. Still another method is to assign different groups to work on the same problem.[46] And, finally, different group decision-making techniques can be used to limit the effects of groupthink and other problems inherent in shared decision making. Nine suggestions for avoiding groupthink are as follows:[47]

1. The leader of a policy-forming group should assign the role of critical evaluator to each member, encouraging the group to give high priority to airing objections and doubts.

2. The leaders in an organization's hierarchy, when assigning a policy-planning mission to a group, should be impartial instead of stating their preferences and expectations at the outset.

3. The organization should routinely follow the administrative practice of setting up several independent policy-planning and evaluation groups to work on the same policy question, each carrying out its deliberations under a different leader.

4. Through the period when the feasibility and effectiveness of policy alternatives are being surveyed, the policy-making group should from time to time divide into two or more subgroups to meet separately, under different chairpersons, and then come together to reconcile their differences.

5. Each member of the policy-making group should periodically discuss the group's deliberations with trusted associates in her own unit of the organization and report their transactions back to the group.

6. One or more outside experts or qualified colleagues within the organization who are not core members of the policy-making group should be invited to each meeting on a staggered basis and should be encouraged to challenge the views of the core members.

7. At each meeting devoted to evaluating policy alternatives, at least one member should be assigned the role of devil's advocate, expressing as many objections to each policy alternative as possible.

8. Whenever the policy issue involves relations with a rival organization, a sizable block of time should be spent surveying all warning signals from the rivals and constructing alternative scenarios of the rivals' intentions.

9. After reaching a preliminary consensus about what seems to be the best policy alternative, the policy-making group should hold a second-chance meeting at which the members are expected to express as vividly as they can all their residual doubts and to rethink the entire issue before making a definitive choice.

## Risky Shift

Problem solving in groups always involves some degree of risk. One can never be certain whether a decision made in a group would be the same as a decision made by an individual. This raises an interesting question: Do groups make decisions that are more or less risky than individual decisions? Or is a group decision simply the average of the individuals in the group?

In the 1960s, James Stoner initiated research on the amount of risk taken by groups in making decisions. Stoner tested the hypothesis that group decisions would be more cautious than individual decisions. He compared individual and group decisions using a series of hypothetical cases developed to measure an individual's propensity for risk taking. The alternative choices provided in each case ranged from relatively cautious with moderate payoffs to relatively risky with higher payoffs. For example, situations ranged from a football team playing cautiously for a tie or riskily for a win to a graduate student choosing to pursue a Ph.D. degree in chemistry at one of two universities. Contrary to Stoner's prediction, the group decisions were consistently riskier than individual decisions.[48] This finding has been called the **risky shift** in group decision making.

Several explanations have been proposed for this risky shift phenomenon:

---

[46]R. Dennis Middlemist, *Experiencing Organizational Behavior* (Belmont, CA: Thomson South-Western Learning, 2000).

[47]Janis, *Groupthink: Psychological Studies of Policy Decisions and Fiascoes.*

[48]James A. Stoner, "Risky and Cautious Shifts in Group Decisions: The Influence of Widely Held Values," *Journal of Experimental Social Psychology*, 4 (1968): 442–459.

■ Making a decision in a group produces a diffusion of responsibility. Because no single person is held accountable for a bad decision, the group takes greater risks. Blame for a bad decision can then be shared with others; in fact, individuals may shift the blame entirely to others.

■ Leaders of groups are greater risk takers than other members and so are more likely to persuade others to become more risky.

■ Group discussion leads to a more thorough examination of the pros and cons of a particular decision than individual decision making. Consequently, greater familiarization with all aspects of a problem leads to higher risk levels.

■ Risk taking is socially desirable in our culture, and socially desirable qualities are likely to be expressed in a group rather than individually.[49]

Subsequent research refutes the conclusion that groups consistently take greater risk than individuals. For some groups and some decisions, cautious shifts were observed; that is, groups arrived at decisions that were less risky than those of individuals. Thus, both risky and cautious decisions are possible in groups. A key factor in determining which kind of shift occurs—more risky or more cautious—is the position assumed by the members before group interaction occurs. If the members lean initially toward risk, group discussion results in a shift toward greater risk; and if members lean initially toward caution, discussion leads to a cautious shift. Group discussion tends to polarize the initial position of the group.[50] This phenomenon, called *group polarization*, is a reality in shared decision making, but risky shift is more prevalent. Risky shift and group polarization are aspects of SBDM worth the attention of school administrators. In both cases, variance in individual decisions is reduced in groups.

### Escalation of Commitment

**Escalation of commitment** is closely related to retrospective rationality. Whereas retrospective rationality occurs in individuals exclusively, escalation of commit-

ment can occur among individuals as well as among groups.[51] This phenomenon deals with the tendency of groups to escalate commitment to a course of action in order to justify their original decision. For example, a board of education makes a decision to renovate a high school building rather than build a new one. As the project progresses, the board soon becomes aware that the renovation will cost considerably more money than it would cost to build an entirely new structure. The decision makers continue to commit additional resources into what obviously was a poor decision. It is important for school administrators to recognize that groups making decisions face problems similar to those faced by individuals making decisions.

Site-based decision making (SBDM) offers one of the most promising strategies for genuine school improvement, but SBDM practices are not without risks. By anticipating the risks and viewing them as challenges rather than as barriers, school leaders can preempt the risks and the discouragement that could lead to the abandonment of this initiative. (See Administrative Advice 6–3.)

## Site-Based Decision-Making Techniques

Because decision making in schools is frequently based on group participation, several techniques have been developed to improve the process. Five important techniques for shared decision making are brainstorming, nominal group technique, the Delphi technique, devil's advocacy, and dialectical inquiry.

### Brainstorming

**Brainstorming,** developed by Alex Osborn more than fifty years ago, is a technique for creatively generating alternative solutions to a problem.[52] The unique feature of brainstorming is the separation of ideas from evaluation. Earlier, we noted the importance of generat-

---

[49]Richard M. Hodgetts, *Modern Human Relations at Work* (Orlando, FL: Dryden Press, 2001).

[50]Robert F. Bordley, "A Bayesian Model of Group Polarization," *Organizational Behavior and Human Performance*, 32 (1983): 262–274.

[51]Max H. Bazerman, Toni Giulano, and Alan Appelman, "Escalation of Commitment in Individual and Group Decision Making," *Organizational Behavior and Human Performance*, 33 (1984): 141–152.

[52]Alex Osborn, *Applied Imagination* (New York: Scribner, 1957).

---

## Administrative Advice 6–3

### A Few Suggestions on Site-Based Decision Making

Here are some suggestions for the successful implementation of SBDM.

■ *Persuading Staff.* Your staff needs to be convinced that everyone has a vested interest in contributing to good decisions. SBDM cannot succeed if it becomes a spectator sport in which nonparticipants frolic when the players stumble.

■ *Relieving the Threats.* Principals held accountable for building level success may feel threatened by site-based decision making for fear of losing authority. Principals lose nothing by embracing SBDM, because it has the potential to enhance, not limit, their effectiveness.

■ *Tackling the Important.* Problem-solving teams sometimes focus on issues that are perceived to be trivial. While teams should not be directed from the top, they should be trained to use prioritization techniques to achieve maximum impact by aligning their activity with the strategic goals of the school district.

■ *Defining the Limits.* Site-based decision making works most effectively when the parameters of team authority are addressed and people develop firm relationships based on mutual respect and trust.

■ *Watch Your Size.* The size of the groups should be limited to ten members. Once groups exceed ten, you end up with a town meeting, not a problem-solving team.

■ *Understanding Consensus.* The commitment of team-members is critically important to success; commitment alone is no substitute for effective problem-solving and consensus-building techniques. Consensus is difficult to understand, difficult to achieve, and essential for success.

■ *Securing Top Support.* Site-based decision making cannot succeed without the participation of the superintendent. The superintendent and building principals must be fully informed and enthusiastic participants and champions of the process.

■ *Broadening participation.* The definition of staff should not be limited to professionals. Classified staff members, including secretaries, custodians, cooks, and bus drivers, should be viewed as potential SBDM team participants.

■ *Defining the Roles.* Define and articulate at the outset a mechanism for selecting team members, a succession plan, and a way of communication with the entire building and district staff. Involve union officials in the process.

Adapted from Joseph Baim and Joseph C. Dimperio, *School Administrator,* 6 (1994): 42. Used by permission of AASA.

---

ing a wide variety of new ideas during the generating alternatives step of the decision-making process (see Figure 6–1). This increases the number of alternatives from which school administrators can choose when evaluating alternatives and making their decisions. People tend to evaluate solutions to problems when they are proposed, which often eliminates many creative and feasible ideas from further consideration. The following rules are central to brainstorming:[53]

1. *Do Not Evaluate or Discuss Alternatives.* Evaluation comes later. Avoid criticism of your own or others' ideas.

2. *Encourage "Freewheeling."* Do not consider any idea outlandish. An unusual idea may point the way to a truly creative decision.

3. *Encourage and Welcome Quantities of Ideas.* The greater the number of ideas generated, the greater the number of useful ideas will remain after evaluation.

4. *Encourage "Piggybacking."* Group members should try to combine, embellish, or improve on an idea. Consequently, most of the ideas produced will belong to the group and not to a single individual.

As an idea-generating technique, group brainstorming may not be any more effective than individual brainstorming. However, the technique is in widespread use today in all types of organizations, including schools.

---

[53]Ronald N. Taylor, *Behavioral Decision Making* (Glenview, IL: Scott, Foresman, 1984).

## Nominal Group Technique

Another technique that can be used in SBDM, which incorporates some of the features of brainstorming, is the **nominal group technique**.[54] As in brainstorming, individuals are brought together to develop a solution to a problem. Unlike brainstorming, the nominal group technique is concerned with both the generation of ideas and the evaluation of these ideas. The process of decision making in nominal groups has six steps:[55]

1. *Silent Generation of Ideas.* Allow five to ten minutes for this phase. The problem should be posted on a flip chart in the front of the room. Group members are asked to solve the problem on the chart. They are cautioned not to talk to or look at the worksheets of other participants.

2. *Round-Robin Recording of Ideas.* The leader circulates around the room eliciting one idea from each group member and recording it on the flip chart. This continues, round-robin fashion, until all ideas are exhausted. The chief objective of this step is to get before the group an accurate list of ideas that can serve as a compilation of group ideas.

3. *Discussion of Ideas.* Each idea on the flip chart is discussed in the order it appears on the chart. The leader reads each item and asks the group if there are any questions, needs for clarification, agreement, or disagreement.

4. *Preliminary Vote on Item Importance.* Each participant makes an independent judgment about the alternatives by rank ordering them secretly on $3 \times 5$ inch cards. The average of these judgments is used as the group's decision. The nominal group process may end here, or the decision may be further refined through discussion and revoting.

5. *Additional Discussion.* The voting patterns are analyzed and reasons examined to determine if a more accurate decision can be made.

6. *Final Vote.* The final voting occurs in the same manner as the preliminary vote, by secret rankings. This action completes the decision process and provides closure.

As noted, the nominal group technique separates ideation from evaluation. Ideas are generated nominally (without verbal communication). This prevents inhibition and conformity, which we noted in the phenomenon of groupthink. Evaluation occurs in a structured manner that allows each idea to get adequate attention.

The research on the effectiveness of the nominal group technique is encouraging. In terms of the number and quality of ideas generated, studies indicate that nominal group technique is superior to both ordinary group decision making and brainstorming.[56] Furthermore, nominal group techniques often facilitate the implementation of decisions.[57] In any event, the nominal group technique provides for both greater expression and evaluation of creative ideas by group members than either brainstorming or ordinary group decisions. Despite the research support for the nominal group technique, many school administrators still do not take advantage of its benefits in group decisions.

## Delphi Technique

Researchers at the Rand Corporation developed the **Delphi technique** in the 1960s.[58] Unlike brainstorming and the nominal group technique, the Delphi approach relies completely on a nominal group; that is, participants do not engage in face-to-face discussions. Instead their input is solicited by mail at their various home bases, thus allowing the polling of large numbers of experts, clients, administrators, or constituencies who are removed from the organization by distance and scheduling problems. For example, suppose the superintendent of schools of a large urban school district wishes to evaluate the curriculum in the basic skills areas. Selected members of the student body, administration, faculty, community, and nationally renowned experts could participate in the various phases of the Delphi process.

---

[54]André L. Delbecq, Andrew H. Van de Ven, and David H. Gustafsen, *Group Techniques for Program Planning: A Guide to Nominal Group and Delphi Processes* (Middleton, WI: Green Briar Press, 1986).

[55]Ibid.

[56]J. Keith Murnighan, "Group Decision Making: What Strategies Should You Use?" *Management Review,* 70 (1981): 55–64.

[57]Sam E. White, John E. Dittrich, and James R. Lang, "The Effects of Group Decision-Making Process and Problem Solving–Situation Complexity on Implementation Attempts," *Administrative Science Quarterly,* 25 (1980): 428–440.

[58]Norman Dalkey, *The Delphi Method: An Experimental Study of Group Opinion* (Santa Monica, CA: Rand Corporation, 1969).

The Delphi technique has many variations, but generally it works as follows:[59]

1. The organization identifies a panel of experts, both inside and outside the organization, and solicits their cooperation.
2. Each member of the panel receives the basic problem.
3. Each individual expert independently and anonymously writes comments, suggestions, and solutions to the problem.
4. A central location compiles, transcribes, and reproduces the experts' comments.
5. Each panelist receives a copy of all the other experts' comments and solutions.
6. Each expert provides feedback on the others' comments, writes new ideas stimulated by their comments, and forwards these to the central location.
7. The organization repeats Steps 5 and 6 as often as necessary until consensus is reached or until some kind of voting procedure is imposed to reach a decision.

Success of the Delphi technique depends on the expertise, communication skills, and motivation of the participants and the amount of time the organization has available to make a decision.

There are several benefits of the Delphi approach. First, it eliminates many of the interpersonal problems associated with other group decision-making approaches. Second, it enlists the assistance of experts and provides for the efficient use of their time. Third, it allows adequate time for reflection and analysis of a problem. Fourth, it provides for a wide diversity and quantity of ideas. And, finally, it facilitates the accurate prediction and forecasting of future events.[60] The major objectives of the Delphi technique include the following:[61]

■ To determine or develop a range of possible program alternatives.

■ To explore or expose underlying assumptions or information leading to different judgments.

■ To seek out information that may generate a consensus among the group members.

■ To correlate informed judgments on a subject that spans a wide range of disciplines.

■ To educate group members concerning the diverse and interrelated aspects of the subject.

Today, numerous organizations in business, government, the military, health care agencies, and schools are using the Delphi technique. Research shows that the technique is superior to ordinary group decision making in terms of the number and quality of ideas generated and group members' overall satisfaction.[62] The major disadvantage of the Delphi technique is the amount of time involved in going through the questionnaire phases of the process. Variations of the Delphi technique have been used to overcome this problem.

One special type of Delphi approach is a procedure called *ringi* used by the Japanese. This version of the Delphi technique involves the circulation of a written document from member to member, in nominal group fashion, for sequential editing until no more changes are required and each participant has signed off the final document. Another Japanese variation of the Delphi technique is assigning parts of the problem to each of several subgroups who prepare responses for their assignments. This version differs from the pure Delphi approach in that the written minireports are then circulated among the group members before face-to-face discussion starts. In essence, the latter Japanese version of the Delphi technique combines with simple group decision making.

## Devil's Advocacy

**Devil's advocacy,** another technique for improving the quality of group decisions, introduces conflict into the decision-making process. Janis suggests that this concept is an antidote for groupthink. Earlier, we noted that groupthink results in inhibitions and premature conformity to group norms. Devil's advocacy can nullify these and other group phenomena to which group

---

[59]Linda N. Jewell and H. Joseph Reitz, *Group Effectiveness in Organizations* (Glenview, IL: Scott, Foresman, 1981).

[60]Gustave Rath and Karen Stoyanoff, "The Delphi Technique," in F. L. Ulshak (ed.), *Human Resource Development: The Theory and Practice of Needs Assessment* (Reston, VA: Reston Publishing, 1983), pp. 111–131.

[61]Delbecq, Van de Ven, and Gustafsen, *Group Techniques for Program Planning.*

[62]Murnighan, "Group Decision Making: What Strategies Should You Use?"; Rath and Stoyanoff, "The Delphi Technique."

---

## PRO/CON Debate

### Principal Power

With the introduction of collective negotiations into most educational workplaces in the late 1960s, principals' roles changed. For over forty years, principals have administered the negotiated contract in their buildings. Many principals who have served both before and after collective negotiations indicate that their decision-making discretion was limited by the constraints of union contracts. In the 2000s, the school as a workplace will be altered again in the area of principal decision making. Employee participation in decision making is evident in the most innovative recent contracts.

**Question:** Does teacher participation in decision making enhance principals' power?

**Arguments PRO**

1. Power increases when it is shared. When principals share decisions with other stakeholders in the system (teachers, parents, students), all become more responsible for outcomes.

2. By becoming facilitators of the decision-making process, principals enhance their personal power as well as their role power.

3. Principals who are experienced in shared decision making point out that, like the students who participate in establishing rules of behavior in the classroom, teachers are tougher on themselves than are principals.

4. As teachers assume greater responsibility for improving the educational environment of the school, principals become the leaders of leaders. The principal leads rather than manages.

5. Principals' roles will change for the better. For example, most articles in professional journals on shared decision making are written by administrators or administrator-teacher teams.

6. The national reform literature is filled with recommendations that teachers assume more responsibility and accountability for schooling. Principals who accommodate this call will increase their stature in the community.

**Arguments CON**

1. If principals are accountable for everything that happens in their buildings, they should have the power to control people, resources, events, and plans.

2. Principals can only effect desired outcomes if they have the role power to do so.

3. Teacher tenure puts serious limits on principals' power to deal with weak teachers. If principals' power to supervise teachers diminishes, the quality of classroom instruction will decrease.

4. If teachers are responsible for school decisions, principals will act less as instructional leaders and more as managers.

5. Few teachers are willing to make school decisions. They expect principals to support their work in the classroom by dealing with the traditional tasks of budgeting, hiring, firing, disciplining, and monitoring.

6. Parents expect someone to be in charge of the school. When they have concerns about their children, they want someone to make immediate decisions. Parents will view principals as weak if principals must share in decision making.

---

members are subjected. After a planning group has developed alternative solutions to a problem, the plan is given to one or more staff members, with instructions to find fault with it. "If the plan withstands the scrutiny of the devil's advocates, it can be presumed to be free of the effects of groupthink . . . and thus viable."[63] Although devil's advocacy can be used as a critiquing technique after alternative solutions to a problem have been developed, it can also be used dur-

---

[63]Miner, *Organizational Behavior*, pp. 307–308.

ing the early stages of the decision-making process. For example, during a decision-making session one member could be assigned the role of devil's advocate, expressing as many objections to each alternative solution to a problem as possible.[64]

### Dialectical Inquiry

Like devil's advocacy, **dialectical inquiry** is an alternative approach for controlling group phenomena such as groupthink in decision making. The process can be described as follows:[65]

1. The process begins with the formation of two or more divergent groups to represent the full range of views on a specific problem. Each group is made as internally homogeneous as possible; the groups, however, are as different from one another as possible. Collectively they cover all positions that might have an impact on the ultimate solution to a problem.

2. Each group meets separately, identifies the assumptions behind its position, and rates them on their importance and feasibility. Each group then presents a "for" and an "against" position to the other groups.

3. Each group debates the other groups' position and defends its own. The goal is not to convince others but to confirm that what each group expresses as its position is not necessarily accepted by others.

4. Information, provided by all groups, is analyzed. This results in the identification of information gaps and establishes guidelines for further research on the problem.

5. An attempt to achieve consensus among the positions occurs. Strategies are sought that will best meet the requirements of all positions that remain viable. This final step permits further refinement of information needed to solve the problem.

Although agreement on an administrative plan is a goal of this approach, a full consensus does not always follow. Nevertheless, the procedure can produce useful indicators of the organization's planning needs.

## Summary

1. Decision making is a process of choosing from among alternatives. All decision-making models include the concept of rational activity. Decision-making models can be thought of as ranging on a continuum from perfect rationality (classical model) to nonrationality (behavioral model).

2. Rational decision making consists of several steps: identifying problems, generating alternatives, evaluating alternatives, choosing the optimum alternative, implementing the decision, and evaluating the decision.

3. Although school administrators want to make the best decisions, the realities of school life affect rational decision making. These include internal and external politics, conflict resolution techniques, distribution of power and authority, time constraints, cost, the inability to process information, and other limits of human rationality.

4. There are advantages of site-based decision making in schools. Groups have the potential to generate and evaluate more ideas, and once a decision is made, acceptance will be easier.

5. The disadvantages of site-based decision making include groupthink, risky shift, and escalation of commitment.

6. Techniques to improve site-based decision making include brainstorming, the nominal group technique, the Delphi technique, devil's advocacy, and dialectical inquiry.

[64]David M. Schweiger and Phyllis A. Finger, "The Comparative Effectiveness of Dialectical Inquiry and Devil's Advocacy: The Impact of Task Biases on Previous Research Findings," *Strategic Management Journal*, 5 (1984): 335–350.

[65]Vincent P. Barabba, "Making Use of Methodologies Developed in Academia: Lessons from One Practitioner's Experience," in R. H. Kilmann et al. (eds.), *Producing Useful Knowledge for Organizations* (New York: Praeger, 1983), pp. 147–166.

## Key Terms

decision making
classical model
rationality
identifying the problem
generating alternatives
evaluating alternatives
choosing an alternative
implementing the decision

evaluating the decision
bounded rationality
behavioral model
satisficing
contextual rationality
procedural rationality
retrospective rationality
incrementalizing
garbage can model
decision feasibility
groupthink
risky shift
escalation of commitment
brainstorming
nominal group technique
Delphi technique
devil's advocacy
dialectical inquiry

## Discussion Questions

1. Give an example of a decision-making situation with which you are familiar and illustrate how the problem was solved.

2. What are the basic assumptions of the classical model of decision making? Describe the steps that occur in the decision-making process.

3. Should school administrators attempt to make decisions according to the classical model? Why or why not?

4. What are the major benefits and problems of site-based decision making?

5. What group techniques can be used to improve site-based decision making?

## Suggested Readings

Conzemius, Anne, and Jan O'Neill. *Building Shared Responsibility for Student Learning* (Baltimore: Association for Supervision and Curriculum Development, 2001). Learn how schools reach "success" by creating shared responsibility for student learning among educators, administrators, students, and parents. Examples from winning schools and numerous tools and strategies help you focus diverse constituents on common goals, encourage reflection, and promote collaboration.

Epstein, Joyce L., Mavis G. Sanders, Beth S. Simon, Karen Clark Salinas, Natalie Rodriguez Jansorn, and Frances L. Van Voorhis. *School, Family, and Community Partnerships: Your Handbook for Action,* 2nd ed. (Thousand Oaks, CA: Corwin Press, 2002). This book offers a research-based framework that guides state and district leaders, school principals, teachers, parents, and community partners to form Action Teams for Partnerships, and to plan, implement, evaluate, and continually improve family and community involvement.

Glickman, Carl D. *Leadership for Learning: How to Help Teachers Succeed* (Baltimore: Association for Supervision and Curriculum Development, 2002). School leaders can't improve education all by themselves. In fact, they don't have to. Because with the right plans and systems in place, you can get your entire faculty focused on continuous improvement and committed to advancing student learning. Distinguished educator and author Carl D. Glickman explains how and provides all of the guidelines and components you need.

Hargreaves, Andy, Lorna Earl, Shawn Moore, and Susan Manning. *Learning to Change: Teaching Beyond Subjects and Standards* (San Francisco: Jossey-Bass, 2001). "In a compelling highly readable book the reader learns what supports and hinders teachers' struggle to create higher standards for their students. The authors go beyond the technical and intellectual work of teaching recognizing the highly emotional cultural aspects of change."— Ann Lieberman, senior scholar, The Carnegie Foundation for the Advancement of Teaching.

Murphy, Joseph, and Amanda Datnow. *Leadership Lessons from Comprehensive School Reforms* (Thousand Oaks, CA: Corwin Press, 2002). Comprehensive School Reform (CSR) is proving to be one of the most promising avenues for improving student achievement. The authors have found that leadership is frequently acknowledged to be a prime factor in the successful implementation of comprehensive school reform. Murphy and Datnow have gathered together a group of CSR insiders and researchers to examine the issue of leadership in CSR for the first time.

Rubin, Hank. *Collaborative Leadership: Developing Effective Partnerships in Communities and Schools* (Thousand Oaks, CA: Corwin Press, 2002). In his provocative book, visionary Hank Rubin empowers school, community, and government leaders with usable, successful models of collaboration that can boost their performance and capacity to propel their missions forward. He illustrates how to cultivate mutually beneficial relationships, including 24 specific attributes that foster successful collaboration, 12 phases of collaboration, and the 7 essential characteristics of effective collaborative leaders.

Sergiovanni, Thomas J. *The Lifeworld of Leadership: Creating Culture, Community, and Personal Meaning in Our Schools* (San Francisco: Jossey-Bass, 2000). Sergiovanni gets to the heart of school reform and renewal in this book. He shows how local school communities can construct standards that support serious learning and effective caring for students.

# 7. Communication

In this chapter, we attempt to answer these questions concerning communication in school organizations. We begin our discussion with a brief treatment of the importance of communication in schools. Then we examine the process and patterns of verbal and nonverbal communication. Next, we identify and describe some common barriers to communication. Finally, we discuss some useful techniques for overcoming these communication barriers.

## The Importance of Communication

Anyone who walks through a school will observe numerous communication activities taking place. Secretaries type letters, memoranda, and reports; others talk on the telephone; a parent conference is under way in the assistant principal's office; the principal is in an evaluation conference with a teacher; other meetings are in session; teachers and students exchange information in classrooms; other students use the computer terminals in another part of the building; the library buzzes with activity; and a number of other communication activities, using a variety of media, can be observed.

Communication, the lifeblood of every school organization, is a process that links the individual, the group, and the organization. To be sure, communication mediates inputs to the organization from the environment and outputs from the organization to the environment. As Chester Barnard asserted, communication occupies a central place in organizations "because the structure, extensiveness, and scope of organizations are almost entirely determined

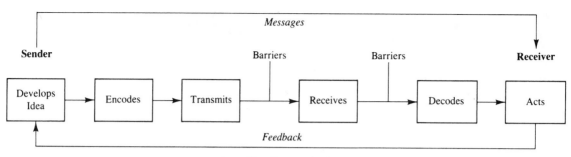

**Figure 7–1**

The Communication Process

by communication techniques."[1] Or as Daniel Katz and Robert Kahn put it, communication is the "essence of organizations."[2]

The administrator of today's school organization has a multifaceted job, which includes setting objectives, organizing tasks, motivating employees, reviewing results, and making decisions. School administrators plan, organize, staff, direct, coordinate, and review. Tasks cannot be accomplished, objectives cannot be met, and decisions cannot be implemented without adequate communication.

The centrality of communication to the overall job of the administrator is evident when we consider how much time administrators spend communicating in organizations. The results of two separate studies of executives across a spectrum of organizational types and administrative levels indicate that administrators spend 80 percent of their time in interpersonal communication.[3] Similar findings ranging from 70 to 80 percent have been reported for elementary school principals, high school principals, and school superintendents.[4] School administrators therefore need a clear understanding of the process of communication.

[1]Chester I. Barnard, *The Functions of the Executive* (Cambridge, MA: Harvard University Press, 1938), p. 91.

[2]Daniel Katz and Robert L. Kahn, *The Social Psychology of Organizations*, 2nd ed. (New York: Wiley, 1978), p. 223.

[3]Henry Mintzberg, *The Nature of Managerial Work* (Reading, MA: Addison-Wesley, 1997).

[4]Fred C. Lunenburg and Beverly J. Irby, *The Principalship: Vision to Action* (Belmont, CA: Thomson Wadsworth, 2006).

## The Communication Process

The **communication process** involves the exchange of information between a sender and a receiver. Figure 7–1 shows the key components of the communication process, which involves a sequence of steps: ideating, encoding, transmitting, receiving, decoding, and acting. In simple terms, the sender encodes an idea into a message and transmits the message to a receiver who decodes the message and acts.[5] Barriers to communication can occur at any step in the process but most frequently occur between transmission and reception and between receiving and decoding. Barriers to communication and techniques for overcoming them are discussed later in the chapter. Although feedback is not present in all cases, it is necessary to ensure effective communication.

### Ideating

Senders in a school district can be central office administrators, building administrators, faculty members, departments within a school, a school, or the school district itself. Administrators communicate with other administrators, subordinates, students, the board of education, and members of the community. Faculty members communicate with administrators, staff, students, parents, and the community. Communications within the school district are important ways of coordinating the tasks of superintendents, assistant superintendents, directors, coordinators, supervisors, principals, and

[5]Michael Dues et al., *The Process of Organizational Communication* (New York: McGraw-Hill, 2001).

teachers. Communications within school buildings help coordinate the work of faculty and staff. School districts communicate with employees at all levels: unions, the community, the school board and local, state, and federal governments. The first step is **ideating**—developing an idea, message, or information to transmit to some individual or group.

## Encoding

**Encoding** symbolizes the ideas that the sender wishes to transmit. Symbols (words, nonverbal cues, or even pictures and diagrams) are designed to communicate only messages. Meaning cannot be transmitted because it lies in the significance that the encoder attributes to the symbol. The receiver of the message will also assign meaning to that symbol. The greater the agreement between the sender and the receiver regarding the meaning of the symbols, the greater the probability of understanding between the two parties. It is important, therefore, that school administrators select symbols that have mutual meaning for them and their intended receivers.

## Transmitting

Once the message is developed, **transmitting** is the next step by one of several methods including memoranda, telephone, closed-circuit television, computers, board policy statements, and face-to-face communication. Unintended messages such as silence or inaction on particular issues are not as obvious. And such nonverbal cues as hand gestures, body position, facial expression, and voice intonation also communicate messages.

## Receiving

**Receiving** is the next step, which requires that the receiver be a good listener if the message is oral. If the message is written, the receiver must be attentive to its stated and implied meaning.

## Decoding

**Decoding** is the translation of a received message into a perceived or interpreted meaning. Because meaning cannot be transmitted, it cannot be received. Therefore, receivers must take transmitted messages and give meaning to them. Barriers to communication can occur at any stage of the communication process, but they are most prevalent during the decoding step.

## Acting

**Acting** is the final step in the communication process. The receiver can ignore the communication, store it for possible action later, or do something else with it. The receiver, however, should give feedback to the sender that the message was received and understood.

The effectiveness of communication with staff is influenced by information processing preferences (cognitive style) of both the senders and receivers of the communication. Understanding and accommodating these cognitive styles can lead to communication that reduces misunderstanding and conflict.

Although several models are available for describing cognitive style, Carl Jung's *Psychological Types*[6] is a basic reference point for a majority of currently available models. Jung's model presents four dimensions of cognitive style, two of which are significant in sending and receiving messages. (See Administrative Advice 7–1.)

# Nonverbal Communication

We communicate as many messages nonverbally as we do verbally. **Nonverbal communication**—the way we stand, the distance we maintain from another person, the way we walk, the way we fold our arms and wrinkle our brow, our eye contact, being late for a meeting—conveys messages to others. However, we need not perform an act for nonverbal communication to occur. We communicate by our manner of dress and appearance, the automobile we drive, and the office we occupy.[7]

Nonverbal communication comes in many forms: *kinesis* (body movements and position), *paralanguage* (voice qualities), *proxemics* (space and proximity), and *chronemics* (determination and definition of time).

Kinesis applies to ways in which facial expressions, the use of hands, arms, and legs, and posture affect communication.[8] What is your facial expression when

---

[6]Carl G. Jung, *Psychological Types* (New York: Harcourt Brace, 1923).

[7]Mark L. Hickson, *Nonverbal Communication: Studies and Applications* (New York: Roxbury, 2003).

[8]Lewis Hedwig, *Body Language: A Guide for Professionals* (Thousand Oaks, CA: Sage, 2000).

## Administrative Advice 7–1

### The Impact of Cognitive Style on Communication

Jung's two dimensions and four cognitive styles are explained below.

#### Two Dimensions

The two dimensions are labelled *perception* and *decision making*. Perception—variations in the way one sees the world—is a bipolar continuum of *intuition* and *sensing*. Decision making, alternative ways of processing information, is a bipolar continuum of *thinking* and *feeling*.

#### Four Cognitive Styles

Each individual will have a dominant preference on each of the two dimensions. These preferences interact to form four distinctly different cognitive styles that view, interpret, and act upon communications in their own unique way.

- *Sensor-thinker.* This individual responds well to detailed, factual, and sequentially ordered information that is based on a logical and rational database. The sensor-thinker expresses self in factual, pragmatic, concrete-reality terms.

- *Sensor-feeler.* This individual responds well to communication that attends to individual feelings, demonstrates warmth and empathy, and includes a personal touch.

The sensor-feeler expresses self in specific, humanistic, biographical terms.

- *Intuitor-feeler.* This individual responds to warmth and empathy characteristic of the feeling dimension, while the intuitor preference leads to a personal interpretation of the communication. The intuitor-feeler values personal growth, self-development, self-concept, values clarification, and expresses self with creative emotion.

- *Intuitor-thinker.* This individual is also less attracted to detail and prefers the theoretical, logical, and rational database of the thinker. The intuitor-thinker expresses self in rational, scientific, and general terms.

The Jungian *definition* of cognitive style is by far the most widely used and thoroughly researched, while the Myers-Briggs Type Indicator (MBTI) is the most frequently used *instrument* for identifying style.

Source: Adapted from Donald Nasca, "The Impact of Cognitive Style on Communication," *NASSP Bulletin,* 78 (1994): 99–103. Used by permission. Copyright © 1994 National Association of Secondary School Principals. www.principals.org. Reprinted with permission.

---

you talk to others? What are your body gestures? Even a person's clothing can be important. For instance, John Molloy points out that the most authoritative pattern is the pinstripe, followed in descending order by the solid, the chalk stripe, and the plaid. If you need to be more authoritative, says Molloy, stick with dark pinstripes.[9]

Besides the truly silent aspects of kinesis, people say things in ways that are important aspects of nonverbal communication. Sometimes referred to as paralanguage, these include voice quality, volume, speech rate, pitch, nonfluences (*ah, um,* or *uh*), laughing, yawning, and the like. Also, *who* says a word (e.g., whether the boss or a colleague asks for "volunteers") and in what *environmental context* it is said (e.g., in the boss's office or out on the golf course) make a difference.[10]

Proxemics refers to the physical environment of communication and deals with space, including location. For example, how close do you stand to someone in normal conversation?

Edward Hall, an anthropologist, suggests that in the United States there are definable *personal space zones.*[11]

1. *Intimate Zone (0 to 2 Feet).* To be this close, we must have an intimate association with the other person or be socially domineering.

2. *Personal Zone (2 to 4 Feet).* Within this zone, we should be fairly well acquainted with the other individual.

3. *Social Zone (4 to 12 Feet).* In this zone, we are at least minimally acquainted with the other person and have a definite purpose for seeking to communicate. Most behavior in the business world occurs in this zone.

---

[9]John T. Molloy, *John T. Molloy's Dress for Success* (New York: Warner, 1993); see also *New Women's Dress for Success* (New York: Warner, 1996).

[10]Fred Luthans, *Organizational Behavior*, 9th ed. (New York: McGraw-Hill, 2001).

[11]Karen Price Hassell, *Body Language* (Portsmouth, NH: Heinemann, 2002).

4. *Public Zone (Beyond 12 Feet).* When people are more than 12 feet away, we treat them as if they did not exist. We may look at others from this distance, provided our gaze does not develop into a stare.

Related to the notion of personal space zones is the concept of physical space. For example, employees of higher status have better offices (more spacious, finer carpets and furniture, and more windows) than do employees of lower status. Furthermore, the offices of higher-status employees are better protected than those of lower-status employees. Top executive areas are typically sealed off from intruders by several doors, assistants, and secretaries. Moreover, the higher the employee's status, the easier they find it to invade the physical space of lower-status employees. A superior typically feels free to walk right in on subordinates, whereas subordinates are more cautious and ask permission or make an appointment before visiting a superior.[12]

Chronemics, or the use of time, is another form of nonverbal communication.[13] For example, being late for a meeting may convey any number of different messages including carelessness, lack of involvement, and lack of ambition. Yet, at the same time, the late arrival of high-status persons reaffirms their superiority relative to subordinates. Their tardiness symbolizes power or having a busy schedule.[14]

*You cannot not communicate.* Everything that you do is a form of communication, verbal and nonverbal. The way you walk, your facial expression, and your silence are interpreted by others, so you might as well do it right. (See Administrative Advice 7–1.)

## Direction of Communication

Communication is interlinked with most of the processes that take place in school districts, such as planning, organizing, staffing, directing, coordinating, and reporting. The purpose of organizational communication is to provide the means for transmitting information essential to goal achievement. Much of this **communication flow** is carried in four distinct directions (see Figure 7–2): downward, upward, horizontally, and diagonally.[15] The other major communication flow is the grapevine.

### Downward Communication

Hierarchical systems like large school districts tend to use downward communication, in which people at higher levels transmit information to people at lower levels. The communication can take place among different groups of senders and receivers, including superintendent to assistant superintendents, assistant superintendents to principals, principals to department heads, department heads to teachers, or any other combination of superior to subordinate.

For example, the school district's superintendent might instruct the assistant superintendent of instruction to prepare for a new personnel evaluation system mandated by the state. In turn, the assistant superintendent would provide specific instructions to the principals, who would inform the teachers accordingly. Downward communication is necessary to help clarify the school district's goals, provide a sense of mission, assist in indoctrinating new employees into the system, inform employees about educational changes impacting the district, and provide subordinates with data concerning their performance.

*Downward communication* occurs easily, but it is frequently deficient. One problem is that subordinates select from among the various directives transmitted from above those most in keeping with their perceptions of their boss's character, personality, motivation, and style and give them priority. Another problem is that not enough time and effort are devoted to learning whether messages sent from above have been received and understood. A third problem is that those at the top of the hierarchy may shut off this channel at times and on certain subjects, that is, withhold information on a need-to-know basis.[16] And, finally, downward communication tends to dominate in mechanistic organizations as op-

---

[12]Don Hellriegel, John W. Slocum, and Richard W. Woodman, *Organizational Behavior,* 9th ed. (Belmont, CA: Thomson South-Western, 2006).

[13]Mark L. Knapp and Judith Hall, *Nonverbal Behavior in Human Interaction* (Belmont, CA: Thomson Wadsworth, 2005).

[14]Robert P. Vecchio, *Organizational Behavior: Core Concepts* (Belmont, CA: Thomson South-Western, 2005).

[15]John B. Miner, *Organizational Behavior 3: Historical Origins, Theoretical Foundations, and the Future* (New York: M. E. Sharpe, 2006).

[16]Thomas E. Harris, *Applied Organizational Communication: Principles and Pragmatics for Future Practice* (Mahwah, NJ: Erlbaum, 2002).

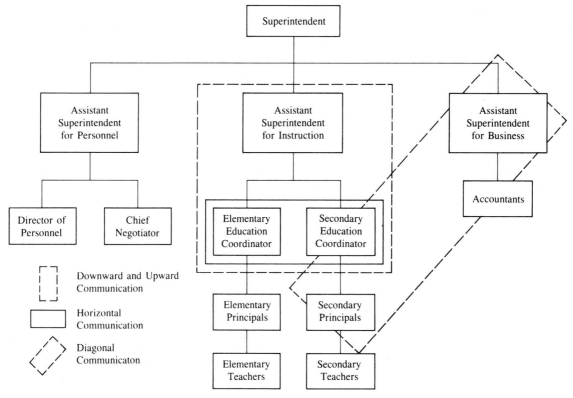

**Figure 7–2**

School District Communication Flows

posed to organic systems, which are characterized by more open and unidirectional flows of information.[17]

One author has identified three ways for administrators to improve downward communication.[18]

1. School districts should adopt communication training programs for all administrative personnel. Most school administrators could benefit greatly from learning better ways of communicating, as well as developing more effective listening skills.

2. School administrators should get out of their offices and talk to employees on the "firing line." Two authors refer to this technique as management by wandering around (MBWA).[19] It allows adminis-

trators to become more aware of the needs of their subordinates.

3. School administrators should conduct regular supervisory-subordinate discussions. Such participative interactions will help administrators identify, analyze, and solve problems collaboratively with subordinates.

**Upward Communication**

*Upward communication* also follows the hierarchical chart and transmits information from lower to higher levels in the organization. For example, a teacher might conceive of a new course in social studies. The teacher would pass this information upward to the department head, who would in turn pass the information to her immediate supervisor, who would then inform the superintendent. Upward communication is necessary to provide administrators with feedback on downward communication, monitor decision-making effectiveness, gauge

---

[17] Samuel B. Bacharach et al., *Advances in Research and Theories of School Management and Educational Policy* (Greenwich, CT: JAI Press, 2000).

[18] Pamela Shockley-Zalabak, *Fundamentals of Organizational Communication* (Boston: Allyn and Bacon, 2005).

[19] Larry Frase et al., *School Management by Wandering Around* (Lanham, MD: Scarecrow Press, 2003).

organizational climate, deal with problem areas quickly, and provide needed information to administrators.

For several reasons, upward communication is difficult to achieve. Upward communication is usually subject to filtering and distortion because subordinates do not want their superiors to learn anything that may be potentially damaging to subordinates' careers.[20] This tendency is likely to increase when subordinates do not trust supervisors. Furthermore, highly cohesive groups tend to withhold information from superiors that might be damaging to the group as a whole.[21] However, all subordinates tend to distort upward communication somewhat less under a participatory management system than under an authoritative system.[22] Other research shows that lower-level subordinates perceive much less openness to upward communication than is perceived at higher levels in the organization. In fact, "higher-level managers involve their subordinates more in the decision-making process and thus expect upward communication more than do lower-level managers."[23] Similar findings have been reported in educational settings.[24]

Other research recommends four practices to improve upward communication: employee meetings, open door policy, employee letters, and participation in social groups.[25]

[20]Daniel P. Modaff et al., *Organizational Communication: Foundations, Challenges, and Misunderstandings* (New York: Roxbury, 2005).

[21]Rebecca Blair, Karlene H. Roberts, and Pamela McKechnie, "Vertical and Network Communication in Organizations: The Present and the Future," in R. D. McPhee and P. Thompkins (eds.), *Organizational Communication: Traditional Themes and New Directions* (Beverly Hills, CA: Sage, 1985), pp. 55–77.

[22]Kanika T. Bhal et al., *Managing Dyadic Interactions in Organizational Leadership* (Thousand Oaks, CA: Sage, 2000).

[23]R. Dennis Middlemist, *Experiencing Organizational Behavior* (Belmont, CA: Thomson South-Western Learning, 2000), p. 323.

[24]Edwin M. Bridges and Maureen T. Hallinan, "Subunit Size, Work System Interdependence, and Employee Absenteeism," *Educational Administration Quarterly,* 14 (1978): 24–42; Cecil Miskel, David McDonald, and Susan Bloom, "Structural and Expectancy Linkages Within Schools and Organizational Effectiveness," *Educational Administration Quarterly,* 19 (1983): 49–82.

[25]John W. Newstrom and Keith Davis, *Human Behavior at Work: Organizational Behavior,* 12th ed. (New York: McGraw-Hill, 2006).

**Employee Meetings**   These meetings attempt to probe job problems, needs, and administrative practices that help and hinder subordinate job performance. These meetings, sometimes referred to as *quality circles,* provide feedback to administrators and encourage subordinates to submit ideas to supervisors. As a consequence, subordinates feel a sense of personal worth and importance because administrators listen to them. By opening channels upward, administrators help the flow and acceptance of communication downward. Also, subordinates' attitudes improve, and turnover declines.

**Open Door Policy**   An open door policy is a statement that encourages subordinates to walk in and talk to administrators many levels up the hierarchy. Generally, however, subordinates are encouraged to see their immediate supervisors first. Then, if their problem is not resolved at that level, they are free to approach higher-level administrators. Bringing a problem to one's immediate supervisor first should alleviate resentment among administrators who are bypassed when subordinates skip several administrative levels in the hierarchy. The goal of an open door policy—to facilitate upward communication—has merit but is often difficult to implement because psychological barriers often exist between superiors and subordinates. Some subordinates do not want to be identified as having a problem or lacking information. A more effective open door procedure is for administrators to get out of their offices and observe firsthand what is happening in the organization. This was referred to earlier as "management by wandering around."

**Employee Letters**   Programs that use employee letters or suggestions serve as a type of written open door policy. This direct and personal method provides subordinates with the opportunity to present their ideas to administrators. To increase the effectiveness of this procedure, submissions can be anonymous, all submissions must be answered, and replies must be delivered without delay. Replies can be directed to the appropriate lower-level administrator or, in cases where the communicator is anonymous, responses can be deposited in an "answer box," similar to a suggestion box in which employees communicate with superiors.

**Participation in Social Groups**   This method provides excellent opportunities for unplanned upward communication. Information at these activities is shared informally between subordinates and superiors. Examples include departmental parties, sports events, picnics, golf outings, and other employer-sponsored activities. The major barrier to such activities is lack of attendance; that is, those who need to share information the most may not attend the activities. Although upward communication is not the primary goal of these activities, it is certainly an important by-product. It is also a means of enhancing employee morale. Other approaches are job satisfaction surveys, grievance or complaint procedures, counseling programs, exit interviews, discussions with union representatives, consultative supervision, and suggestion systems.

## Horizontal Communication

*Horizontal communication* takes place between employees at the same hierarchical level. This type of communication is frequently overlooked in the design of most organizations. Integration and coordination between units in an organization is facilitated by horizontal communication. At the upper levels of a school district, for example, the assistant superintendents for instruction, business, and personnel will coordinate their efforts in arriving at an integrated strategic plan for the district. In a high school, meanwhile, the department chairpersons will work together in developing a curriculum for the entire school. Likewise, in a school of education of a large university, it is common to observe departments coordinating their efforts for the purpose of ensuring that all units of the school are working toward the same general goals. This horizontal communication is frequently achieved through cross-functional committees or council meetings, groups or liaison positions that tie together units horizontally, and informal interpersonal communication.

Besides providing task coordination, horizontal communication furnishes emotional and social support among peers. In effect, it serves as a socialization process for the organization. The more interdependent the various functions in the organization, the greater the need to formalize horizontal communication.

## Diagonal Communication

*Diagonal communication* is important in situations in which participants cannot communicate effectively through other channels. For example, the assistant superintendent for business of a large, urban school district may wish to conduct an instructional program cost analysis for each high school. One part of the analysis involves having each high school principal send a spe-

cial report directly to the assistant superintendent for business, rather than go through the traditional circuitous channels of assistant superintendent for instruction to the coordinator of secondary education to the high school principals and back again. Thus, the flow of communication would be diagonal rather than vertical (downward and upward). In this instance, diagonal communication minimizes the time lag in securing the needed data. The four directions of organizational communication flows are shown in Figure 7–2.

## The Grapevine

When the shortcomings of the four types of organizational communication become apparent, employees build their own channels of communication, **grapevines.** Grapevines exist in all large organizations regardless of communication flow. This type of communication flow does not appear on any organizational chart, but it carries much of the communication in the organization. The term *grapevine* applies to all informal communication including institutional information that is communicated verbally between employees and people in the community. It coexists with the administration's formal communication system. Therefore, school administrators should learn to integrate grapevine communication with formal communication.

Because the grapevine is flexible and usually involves face-to-face communication, it transmits information rapidly. Moreover, nearly five out of every six messages are carried by the grapevine rather than through official channels.[26] And in normal work situations, well over 75 percent of grapevine information is accurate.[27]

The grapevine has both positive and negative features. According to Deal and Kennedy and others, its positive features include the following:[28]

■ Keeps subordinates informed about important organizational matters.

■ Gives school administrators insights into subordinates' attitudes.

[26]John M. Ivancevich and Michael T. Matteson, *Organizational Behavior and Management,* 7th ed. (New York: McGraw-Hill, 2008).

[27]Newstrom and Davis, *Human Behavior at Work: Organizational Behavior.*

[28]Terrence Deal and Allan Kennedy, *Corporate Cultures* (Reading, MA: Addison-Wesley, 1982); Terrence E. Deal and Kent D. Peterson, *Shaping School Culture: The Heart of Leadership* (New York: John Wiley, 2003).

## ■ Exemplary Educational Administrators in Action

**BARRY FRIED** Principal, John Dewey High School, Brooklyn, New York.

**Previous Positions:** Assistant Principal, Supervision Science and Technology, Canarsie High School, Brooklyn, New York.

**Latest Degree and Affiliation:** Professional diploma, Educational Administration, St. John's University, New York.

**Number One Influence on Career:** My son, Nicholas, who has taught me that all students, in spite of having special needs, can draw upon their strengths in the learning and social curve. These students display skills and talents that, if stimulated, channeled, and nurtured, can lead to rewarding and productive educational experiences.

**Number One Achievement:** Taking applied learning in meteorology and technology to practical levels by implementing NASA-sponsored activities, remote sensing, and hurricane tracking. This led to my involvement at New York City and National Science conferences as a presenter, as a committee member for national and regional organizations, as a curriculum writer and staff developer, and as an author of various publications.

**Number One Regret:** Early on in my administrative career, many of my experienced teachers found it difficult to adjust to the changing climate in education. I often found myself at crossroads with staff who could not or would not make the important paradigm shifts in pedagogical methodologies, classroom technologies, and varied student learning styles. I could have been more assertive in directing these teachers to comply with my visions at that time, and not allow them to "ride it out" until retirement.

**Favorite Education-Related Book or Text:** *Dealing with Difficult Teachers* by Todd Whitaker.

**Additional Interests:** Hockey, baseball, music (guitar), The Beatles, gardening, astronomy.

**Leadership Style:** Listen, formulate a course of action, and respond to the needs of the school community and its constituents, without creating "knee-jerk" reactions. Show respect, be consistent, maintain your composure (never lose control) and your sense of humor. Lead by example!

**Professional Vision:** As the educational leader of a public high school, working with staff, students, and parents is paramount in establishing the tone of a sound school environment. Student choices in the selection of courses, in compliance with state educational requirements, empowers them in the educational process and stimulates their interest in learning.

**Words of Advice:** An effective leader must set clearly defined goals and expectations for all staff and students. Resources and support systems are integral attributes for any successful organization, primarily when student achievement is the benchmark for success. Employ the experiences of your personnel to help in effective management of a school. You cannot do it alone! Accepting this responsibility and accountability is inherent for all members of the school community (administrators, teachers, support staff, students, and parents) to be able to succeed. You need to be accessible and involved in all facets of the learning and management process. Objective observation, monitoring, evaluation and reevaluation of programs, instructional strategies and performance are crucial to improve the quality of education in addressing individual student needs. Take risks, encourage teachers to explore, experiment, and experience new programs and methodologies. Support these experiences and prepare leaders of tomorrow. Offering gestures of "thank-you" and "signs of appreciation" bolsters self-esteem and encourages staff to continue these efforts. Speak with your students. Let them know who you are, and listen to their concerns. They are attuned to the school and can provide valuable insights. Establish meaningful relationships among all constituencies of the school community. It is essential to shape, foster, and nurture the students through "experiential learning."

- Provides subordinates with a safety valve for their emotions.
- Provides a test of subordinates' reactions to a new policy or procedural change without making formal commitments. (School administrators have been known to "feed" ideas into the grapevine in order to probe their potential acceptance by subordinates.)
- Helps build morale by carrying the positive comments people make about the school district.

One of the negative features of the grapevine, the one that gives the grapevine its poor reputation, is rumor. A rumor is an unverified belief that is in general circulation. Because the information cannot be verified,

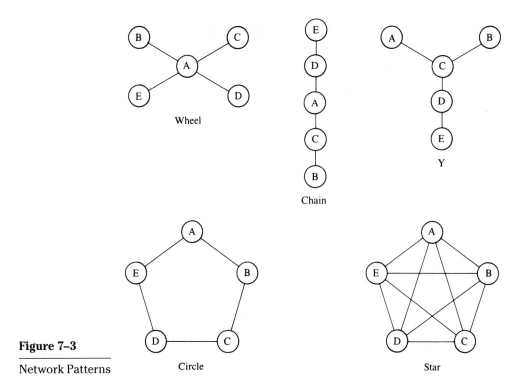

**Figure 7–3**

Network Patterns

rumors are susceptible to severe distortion as they are passed from person to person within the organization. One way to minimize the spread of rumors is to improve other forms of communication. If school administrators provide information on issues relevant to subordinates, then damaging rumors are less likely to develop.

Joseph Licata and Walter Hack examined grapevine structures among principals and report that grapevine linkages differed between elementary and secondary school principals. In elementary schools, where relationships are closer, principals tended to communicate informally; in high schools, where the structure is more formal, principals built the grapevine around professional survival and development.[29]

## Communication Networks

As noted, organizational communication can be transmitted in a number of directions: downward, upward, horizontally, diagonally, and through the grapevine. These communications can be formal or informal; whether formal or informal, the actual pattern and flow of communication connecting senders and receivers are called communication networks. Because this system contains all the communication of the organization, these networks have a pervasive influence on the behavior of individuals functioning within them.

## Network Patterns

**Network patterns** are derived from laboratory experiments in which the structure of the groupings can be manipulated by the experimenter. Figure 7–3 depicts five of the more frequently used networks (wheel, chain, Y, circle, and star). The major difference among the networks is the degree to which they are centralized or decentralized.[30] Each network pattern is discussed in turn.[31]

The *wheel network*, a two-level hierarchy, is the most structured and centralized of the patterns because each member can communicate with only one other person. For example, a superintendent of schools and those who are his immediate subordinates (assistant superintendent for business, instruction, personnel, and

[29] Joseph W. Licata and Walter G. Hack, "School Administrator Grapevine Structure," *Educational Administration Quarterly*, 16 (1980): 82–99.

[30] Miner, *Organizational Behavior 3.*

[31] Shockley-Zalabak, *Fundamentals of Organizational Communication.*

## Table 7–1  Summary of Research on Communication Networks

| Characteristic | Circle | Chain | Wheel | Star |
|---|---|---|---|---|
| Speed | Slow | Fast | Very fast | Slow/fast |
| Accuracy | Poor | Good | Good | Poor/excellent |
| Morale | High | Low | Very low | Very high |
| Leadership stability | None | Marked | Very pronounced | None |
| Organization | Unstable | Emerging stability | Very stable | Unstable |
| Flexibility | High | Low | Low | High |

Source: Adapted from Phillip V. Lewis, *Organizational Communication: The Essence of Effective Management,* © 1987, p. 53. Used by permission of John Wiley & Sons, New York.

assistant to the superintendent), probably form a wheel network. The superintendent is A and his assistant superintendents are B, C, D, and E, respectively. The four subordinates send information to the superintendent, and the superintendent sends that information back to them, usually in the form of decisions.

The *chain network* ranks next highest in centralization. Only two people communicate with one another, and they in turn have only one person to whom they communicate. Information is generally sent through such a network in relay fashion. A typical chain network would be one in which a teacher (B) reports to the department head (C), who in turn reports to the principal (A), who reports to the assistant superintendent for instruction (D), who reports to the superintendent (E). Another example is the grapevine through which information passes throughout a school building or district between different departments and organizational levels.

The *Y network* is similar to the chain except that two members fall outside the chain. In the Y network, for example, members A and B can send information to C, but they can receive information from no one. C and D can exchange information; E can receive information from D but cannot send any information. For example, two assistant principals (A and B) report to the principal (C). The principal, in turn, reports to the assistant superintendent (D), who reports to the superintendent (E).

The *circle network*, a three-level hierarchy, is very different from the wheel, chain, and Y networks. It is symbolic of horizontal and decentralized communication. The circle gives every member equal communication opportunities. Each member can communicate with persons to their right and left. Members have identical restrictions, but the circle is a less restricted condition than the wheel, chain, or Y networks. For example,

the circle network has more two-way channels open for problem solving (i.e., five) than the four channels of the aforementioned networks. In the circle network, everyone becomes a decision maker.

The *star network* is an extension of the circle network. By connecting everyone in the circle network, the result is a star, or all-channel, network. The star network permits each member to communicate freely with all other persons (decentralized communication). The star network has no central position, and no communication restrictions are placed on any member. A committee in which no member either formally or informally assumes a leadership position is a good example of a star network.

**Effectiveness of Different Networks**   The importance of a communication network lies in its potential effects on such variables as speed, accuracy, morale, leadership, stability, organization, and flexibility. Table 7–1 summarizes the findings of most research that has been done on communication networks.

Studies in communication networks show that the network effectiveness depends on situational factors.[32] For example, centralized networks are more effective in accomplishing simple tasks, whereas decentralized patterns are more effective on complex tasks. In addition, the overall morale of members of decentralized networks is higher than those of centralized networks. This finding makes sense in view of the research indicating that employees are most satisfied with their jobs when they have participated in decision making about them. Moreover, research shows that a member's position in the network can affect personal satisfaction. Members

[32] Emory Griffin, *A First Look at Communication Theory,* 4th ed. (New York: McGraw-Hill, 2002).

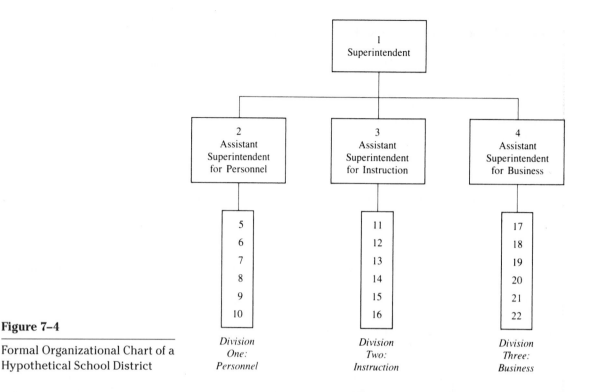

**Figure 7–4**

Formal Organizational Chart of a
Hypothetical School District

in more central positions in the network tend to be more
satisfied.[33]


## Network Analysis

Besides network patterns, another method to help school
administrators analyze communication flows and patterns is network analysis. In **network analysis,** communication flows and patterns are analyzed between
units and across hierarchical positions. Network analysis uses survey sociometry rather than controlled laboratory experiments to identify cliques and certain specialized roles of members in the communication structure
of real-life organizations.

To illustrate, consider the communication network
for a hypothetical school district.[34] Figure 7–4 presents
a formal organizational chart showing the hierarchical

positions occupied by twenty-two people in three divisions of the school district. The numbers within the
boxes represent individuals in the school district. Person 1 at the top of the hierarchy is the superintendent
of schools. The three people immediately below him
are the assistant superintendents of the three divisions:
personnel, instruction, and business. The remaining
individuals are employees in each division. This chart
represents the formal structure of communications
within the school district. Through network analysis,
Figure 7–5 shows a communication network and contrasts it with the school district's formal structure (Figure 7–4). As Figure 7–5 shows, Person 1 (the superintendent) frequently communicates with Persons 2, 3,
and 4, the assistant superintendents for personnel, instruction, and business, respectively. His communications with other lower-level members are less frequent
or nonexistent. Figure 7–5 also identifies cliques in the
communication network of the twenty-two members
on the basis of intercommunication patterns among
them. The lines indicate patterned communication contacts. Some communication contacts are two way (↔),
and some are one-way (→). Two-way arrows connect
Persons 1 and 4, 1 and 2, 1 and 3, and 2 and 4, while
one-way communications exist between Persons 2 and
3, 4 and 17, and so on.

[33]Daniel J. Brass, "Being in the Right Place: A Structural
Analysis of Individual Influence in an Organization," *Administrative Science Quarterly,* 29 (1984): 518–539.

[34]Our hypothetical illustration is similar to the data provided
in the description of the network analysis by Everett M. Rogers and Rekha Agarwala Rogers, *Communication in Organizations* (New York: Free Press, 1976).

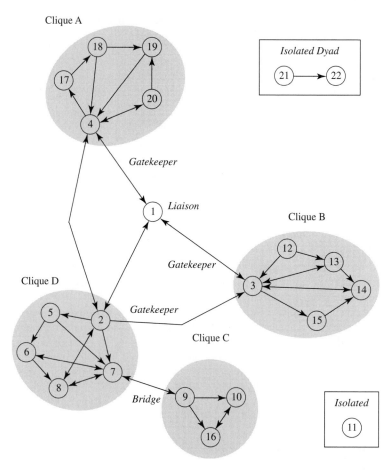

**Figure 7–5**

Communication Network of a Hypothetical School District

There are four cliques in the school district: A, B, C, and D. "A clique is a subsystem whose elements interact with each other relatively more frequently than with other members of the communication system."[35] Clique A is composed of Persons 4, 17, 18, 19, 20; Clique B is composed of Persons 3, 12, 13, 14, and 15; and so on. Most clique members in a network are usually relatively close to each other in the formal hierarchy of the organization. However, a school district's actual communication network can be very different from the pattern of communication established by its formal organizational structure. Four main communication roles have emerged in network analysis: gatekeepers, liaisons, bridges, and isolates.

Person 1, the superintendent, is dependent on Persons 2, 3, and 4, the three assistant superintendents, for access to communication flows. The three superinten-

dents are also *gatekeepers,* having the capacity to control information moving in either direction between the superintendent and the rest of the school district. Person 1 also serves as a *liaison* (an individual who interpersonally connects two or more cliques within the system without himself belonging to any clique) who connects Clique A, Clique B, and Clique D. If this liaison were removed from the network, it would be a much less interconnected system. Person 7 is a *bridge,* a person who is a member of one communication clique and links it, via a communication dyad, with another clique. Thus, Person 7 is a member of Clique D and communicates with Person 9, who is a member of Clique C. Person 11 is an *isolate* (an individual who has few communication contacts with the rest of the system) and is virtually cut off from communication. Person 21 has an in-group relationship in an isolated dyad with Person 22.

Patrick Forsyth and Wayne Hoy studied communication isolates in five secondary schools. Results indicated that communication isolates tend to be separated

[35]Ibid., p. 130.

from perceived control, the school's control structure, respected colleagues, and sometimes friends.[36] A subsequent study of communication isolates in elementary schools reports similar findings, except that isolation from friends was not related to isolation from formal authority.[37] In another study of communication networks in one high school and five elementary schools, using sociometry and frequency surveys of communication, results indicate more frequent communication contacts in elementary schools as compared with high schools. According to this study, three factors affect horizontal communication patterns in schools: level and size of school, specialization, and proximity.[38]

In sum, we have identified and described individuals who have potential influence in the informal communication network and their roles in interpersonal communication in school districts. School administrators entering a school district would be well advised to establish good interpersonal relationships with gatekeepers, liaisons, and bridges. Furthermore, it is vital to be cognizant of the potentially destructive aspect of isolates who often become alienated and exhibit detrimental behaviors dysfunctional to the school district. Knowledge of communication networks can serve as useful interpersonal communication sources. More important, such knowledge can determine the success or failure of a school administrator on the job.

Today, it is more important than ever for school districts to have a well-planned communications program. Until recently, only large-city school districts focused on communications and employed communications experts to plan how to reach their communities. Today all school districts need expertise in this area. (See Administrative Advice 7–2.)

## Barriers to Communication

Effective communication plays a vital role in accomplishing the goals of the school district. However, barriers may interfere with effective communication and include frames of reference, filtering, structure, information overload, semantics, and status differences.

### Frames of Reference

People can interpret the same communication differently, depending on their learning, culture, and experience. This type of communication barrier is related to the encoding and decoding components of the communication process discussed earlier. If the sender and receiver have a common **frame of reference** — that is, when the encoding and decoding of a message are similar — communication is likely to be effective. If, on the other hand, the communicators have different frames of reference, communication is likely to become distorted.[39] For example, people raised in different cultures may react quite differently to the same message. Other examples of different frames of reference in a school district may include those of superintendent and principal, principal and teacher, teacher and student, and management and union. While neither of these groups is right or wrong, each group has unique experiences, and each plays a different role, which often results in unintentional distortions of the communication between them, in the school district.

### Filtering

Another barrier to effective communication is **filtering,** a process that occurs as information is transmitted from one level to another. It involves the transmittal of partial information by the sender. Filtering can occur in either downward or upward flows of communication.

During downward communication flows, unintentional filtering can occur because of errors in encoding and decoding messages. Differences in learning, culture, and experiences may account for unintentional filtering. Intentional filtering occurs when a sender assumes that parts of a message are not needed by the receiver. This can result in distortions of the original meaning of the message. Research shows that administrators may be reluctant to transmit negative information downward. For example, subordinates who had good performance ratings were more likely to be informed of those ratings

[36] Patrick B. Forsyth and Wayne K. Hoy, "Isolation and Alienation in Educational Organizations," *Educational Administration Quarterly,* 14 (1978): 80–96.

[37] Arlene E. Zielinski and Wayne K. Hoy, "Isolation and Alienation in Elementary Schools," *Educational Administration Quarterly,* 19 (1983): 27–45.

[38] W. W. Charters, "Stability and Change in the Communication Structure of School Facilities," *Educational Administration Quarterly,* 3 (1967): 15–38.

[39] John D. Hatfield and Richard C. Huseman, "Perceptual Congruence About Communication as Related to Satisfaction: Moderating Effects of Individual Characteristics," *Academy of Management Journal,* 25 (1982): 349–358.

## Administrative Advice 7–2

### Communication Tips for School Leaders

The potential payoff of effective communication is enormous in terms of the productivity and attitudes of parents, faculty, and students. School administrators can promote effective communication by:

▪ *Small Talk.* In *In Search of Excellence,* Peters and Waterman describe the concept of "inconveniencing oneself." This concept may take many forms, including Management by Wandering Around (MBWA). A walk around the school once in the morning and once in the afternoon helps to increase communications between you and individual students and teachers.

▪ *Written Communications.* For individuals and groups, inside and outside the school, written communication is critical. A school administrator can use the following written communication tools: commendation memoranda; notes; birthday cards; daily bulletins; monthly newsletters to community partners and power brokers; articles and announcements in community newspapers, church bulletins, the local press; memoranda in response to departments'/teams' minutes; handbook/calendar; and a booklet for parents of students at each grade level.

▪ *Faculty and Staff Groups.* Establishing committees and recognizing existing groups are powerful tools for strengthening communication. These groups are also vehicles for sharing power. Some examples of such groups are: instructional council, team leaders' cabinet, faculty and administrative committee, and special committees.

▪ *Communicating with Students.* Communications with students should not be limited to the public address system. Organized student groups should have access to the principal and they should influence some decisions made by the principal. Examples of groups principals should communicate with include: student council representatives, honor society, selected student clubs, newspaper staff, and focus grade-level groups.

▪ *Communicating with Parents.* It's easy to communicate with parents who sit on the school site council, the PTA/PTO, special projects, and the Chapter I Council. The challenge then becomes reaching out to the "less active" parents and residents who do not have children in school. The latter group tend to form their opinions based on what they see and hear in the mass media. Strategies include the following: report card conferences, a targeted newsletter, tours of the school(s), special packets for real estate agents, business-school partnerships, a parent-community involvement plan, active recruitment of volunteers, and meetings at community sites other than the school(s).

Source: Adapted from Gwendolyn J. Cooke, "Communications Tips for School Leaders," *High School Magazine,* 1 (1994): 12–14. Used by permission of NASSP. Copyright © 1994 National Association of Secondary School Principals. www.principals.org. Reprinted with permission.

---

than subordinates who had poor ratings.[40] Administrators may also be reluctant to communicate positive information if they feel the subordinate will use it one day to support a claim against the organization or to oppose the administration sometime in the future.

Given this finding, it is not surprising that administrators and their subordinates sometimes have differing perceptions concerning subordinate performance ratings. Filtering by school administrators can also be a constructive means of uncertainty absorption, according to James March and Herbert Simon.[41] Administrators may intentionally withhold information that they feel might create anxiety in subordinates and thus result in a decrease in subordinates' productivity.

In school districts, filtering problems occur more often in upward communication than in downward communication. Because administrators are in a position to withhold rewards, subordinates manipulate unfavorable information flowing upward in the school district. The reason for such filtering should be obvious. Administrators make merit evaluations, give salary increases, and promote employees based on information they re-

---

[40] Gary Johns, *Organizational Behavior: Understanding and Managing Life at Work* (Englewood Cliffs, NJ: Prentice Hall, 2004).

[41] James G. March and Herbert A. Simon, *Organizations,* 3rd ed. (Cambridge, MA: Blackwell, 2004).

ceive from subordinates. Research indicates that subordinates with strong aspirations for upward mobility are especially likely to filter information in upward communication. Moreover, subordinates who distrust their superiors and lack security will filter their messages. And those who desire to impress their superiors to achieve a promotion will manipulate unfavorable information about themselves.[42]

## Structure

The **structure** of the school district can affect the quality of communications within it. A tall structure is one in which there are many hierarchical levels of authority. Generally, communication efficiency decreases with the number of levels through which information must pass before reaching its intended receiver. The reason is fairly simple: The more levels of administration through which a message must be transmitted, the greater the danger that it will be changed, modified, shortened, amended, or misinterpreted or will totally fail to reach its receiver.[43] The tall structure is very useful for horizontal communication flow. Individuals tend to communicate more at their own level than to attempt to circumvent levels and converse with others at the top and bottom of the hierarchy. Thus, communication among colleagues is good, but upward and downward communication is frequently poor and distorted.[44]

A flat structure, which has few levels between the top and bottom of the hierarchy, has many people at the bottom. It is relatively easy to get a message from the bottom to the top of the hierarchy in a flat structure. This provides a partial explanation of why face-to-face communication works more effectively in small rather than in large school districts. Direct channels can be used more readily because fewer levels of administration have to be penetrated.[45] For example, in very small school districts, board members often speak directly to building principals or teachers, bypassing the superintendent. Similarly, in small school districts, teachers often communicate directly with board members, violating the formal hierarchy. Furthermore, in a flat structure, there is less gatekeeping, and vertical (upward and

downward) communication between superior and subordinate is better.

An example of a tall structure might be the New York City public schools, and an example of a flat structure might be a small, rural elementary school. The New York City public school system has many levels of authority, with smaller units under each; the typical small, rural elementary school has a principal and several teachers. One disadvantage of the flat structure is that the head administrator might suffer from information overload because the span of control in a flat structure is generally greater than in a tall structure.[46]

## Information Overload

In today's complex school organizations, school administrators are frequently overloaded with more information than they can handle effectively. This **information overload** occurs for several reasons. First, school districts face higher levels of uncertainty today because of increasing turbulence in the external environment.[47] School districts respond by obtaining more information to reduce the uncertainty. Second, increased role specialization and task complexity create a need for more information. For example, school districts employ counselors, social workers, school psychologists, business managers, personnel directors, professional negotiators, and curriculum directors, to name only a few. In the curriculum area of special education alone, there are teacher specialists in emotionally disturbed (ED), learning disabilities (LD), educable mentally handicapped (EMH), physically handicapped and other health impairments (PHOHI), multiply handicapped (MH), orthopedically handicapped (OH), and severely and profoundly handicapped (SPH).[48] The wide variety of specialists provide needed information to accomplish a complexity of tasks. This specialization results in additional demands to process the increased amount of information. Third, advances in communication technology, such as the use of computers, increases the quantity

---

[42] Shockley-Zalabak, *Fundamentals of Communication.*

[43] Dues et al., *The Process of Organizational Communication.*

[44] Ibid.

[45] Andrew J. DuBrin, *Essentials of Management* (Belmont, CA: Thomson South-Western, 2005).

[46] David D. Van Fleet, "Span of Management Research and Issues," *Academy of Management Journal,* 26 (1983): 546–552.

[47] Catherine A. Lugg et al., "The Contextual Terrain Facing Educational Leaders," in J. Murphy (ed.), *The Leadership Challenge: Redefining Leadership for the 21st Century* (Chicago: University of Chicago Press, 2002), pp. 20–41.

[48] Special education nomenclature varies from state to state.

of information and data available. As a result, administrators are deluged with information; they cannot absorb or adequately respond to all of it. Thus, they select parts of it, which often results in incomplete or inaccurate information on which to make decisions. The problem today is not a scarcity but an overabundance of information that can be processed effectively.

One research team identifies seven categories of response to communication overload: *omitting* (failing to process some of the information); *erroring* (processing information incorrectly); *queueing* (leveling the peak loads by delaying until a lull occurs); *filtering* (separating out less relevant information); *approximating* (categorizing input and using a general response for each category); *employing multiple channels* (introducing alternative channels for information flow); and *escaping* (avoiding the information).[49]

## Semantics

The same words may have different meanings to different people. Thus, it is possible for a school administrator and subordinates to speak the same language but still not transmit understanding. As defined previously, communication is the transmission of information from a sender to a receiver through the use of common symbols. However, one cannot transmit understanding; one can only transmit information in the form of words, which are the common symbols conveying ideas, facts, and feelings. **Semantics** can be a communication barrier because of the misinterpretation of words. Meanings are not in the words but in the minds of the people who receive them.

Meanings of concrete words do not differ much from sender to receiver. Little misunderstanding arises when we speak of typewriter, computer, paper, or book. Because words such as love, happiness, and virtue are more abstract, more misunderstandings are likely to occur. Similarly, words that evoke emotional responses, like liberal and conservative, are prime candidates for greater misunderstandings.

One reason for semantic differences relates to the use of numerous specialists who tend to develop their own professional jargon. This special language can provide in-group members with feelings of belongingness, cohesiveness, and even self-esteem. And it can enhance ef-

fective communication within the group. However, the use of in-group language can often result in barriers to communication for outsiders. For example, special education teachers use abbreviations like LD (learning disabilities), ED (emotionally disturbed), EMH (educable mentally handicapped), and IEP (individualized education plan), which is common terminology among these professionals. Such abbreviations or terms will probably have little meaning to people outside this specialized group.

## Status Differences

Another barrier to communication is **status difference,** which exists within every school district. School districts create status differences through titles, size of office, carpeting, office furnishings, stationery, private secretary, a reserved parking space, salary, and the formal organizational chart. Regardless of the symbols, status interferes with effective communication between personnel at different levels of the hierarchy. The status of superordinate-subordinate relationships, for example, inhibits the free flow of information vertically (upward and downward).

The higher one's status in the school district, the less likely the person will have effective communications with personnel a few levels removed. In general, individuals who have higher status also receive more communication demands on them. Out of necessity, they must limit their communications to those who have direct influence on them—that is, their direct supervisors and subordinates. For example, the superintendent needs to be concerned with establishing communications with the assistant superintendents directly under him as well as with the board of education, who is directly above the superintendent. Such a communication pattern was outlined previously. Recall that the superintendent communicated frequently with the assistant superintendents. However, the superintendent's communication with other lower-level personnel was less frequent or nonexistent (see Figure 7–5).

Thus, as shown in network analysis, communication between higher-status personnel and lower-status personnel tends to be limited, and the messages that subordinates send upward in the hierarchy tend to be positive (filtering). Moreover, subordinates may be reluctant to express an opinion that is contrary to their supervisor's. One reason for this behavior is that the administration has the power to grant and withhold rewards such as merit evaluations, salary increases, promotions,

[49]Robert E. Callahan, C. Patrick Fleenor, and Harry R. Knudson, *Understanding Organizational Behavior: A Managerial Viewpoint* (New York: Macmillan, 1990).

and better work assignments. School administrators, because of time constraints, indifference, or arrogance, may actually strengthen status differentials by not being open to feedback or other forms of upward communication. However, when the status differences become too great, communications decrease, and subordinates initiate less communication with superiors.

# Overcoming Barriers to Communication

Effective communication requires a sustained effort by both school administrators and employees to overcome communication barriers and arrive at mutual understandings. Although there should be some responsibilities on both sides, successful communication seems to lie primarily with school administrators because they are the ones to develop a two-way communicative climate. In an attempt to overcome some of the communication barriers, we examine five communication skills—repetition, empathy, understanding, feedback, and listening—that are a means of improving school district communications.

## Repetition

One of the most frequently used techniques of effective communication is repetition. **Repetition** involves sending the same message over and over again, using multiple channels (e.g., telephone call, face-to-face discussion, memorandum, or letter). Most communication is subject to some distortion. By using two or more channels to transmit a message, communication failure is less likely to occur. For example, a personal discussion can be followed up with a memorandum or letter. Here both written and oral channels are used. The sender has gained the attention of the receiver as a result of face-to-face communication. The sender and receiver also have written records of the conversation for future reference and to stipulate all details of the conversation. Similarly, sending minutes of a meeting to participants is using repetition and multiple channels of communication to ensure understanding. It is customary in large school districts for school administrators to use multiple channels to communicate the results of a subordinate's performance evaluation. The subordinate first receives a verbal explanation of the results that is accompanied or followed by a written statement, which the superior and subordinate sign as an indication that each has read and understands its content.

## Empathy

Effective communication means that the sender can make predictions about how the receiver will respond to a message. The sender can accomplish this by visualizing the receiver's frame of reference into the transmission of the message. In other words, a school administrator should figuratively walk in the shoes of the subordinate and attempt to anticipate personal and situational factors that might influence the subordinate's interpretation of the message. For superintendents to communicate effectively with assistant superintendents, for assistant superintendents to communicate effectively with principals, for principals to communicate effectively with faculty, and for faculty to communicate effectively with students, empathy is an important ingredient and can reduce many of the aforementioned barriers to communication. **Empathy** is a technique for understanding the other person's frame of reference. The greater the gap between the learning, the culture, and the experiences of the sender and the receiver, the greater the effort that must be made to find a common ground of understanding.

## Understanding

Earlier we said that communication is effective to the extent that both the sender and the receiver have high agreement in their understanding of a transmitted message. School administrators must remember that effective communication involves transmitting **understanding** as well as messages. Regardless of the communication channel used, messages should contain simple, understandable language. School administrators must encode messages in words and symbols that are understandable to the receiver.

As noted, understanding cannot be communicated; only messages can. This is the idea behind the concept of readability popularized by Rudolf Flesch.[50] Readability seeks to make writing and speech more understandable. Flesch and others developed readability formulas that can be applied to written and oral communication alike. Some research has found that much written communication that is transmitted to employees is rated as beyond the level of satisfactory reading for typical adults.[51]

---

[50]Rudolf Flesch, *The Art of Readable Writing,* rev. ed. (New York: Macmillan, 1994).

[51]Richard L. Enos (ed.), *Oral and Written Communication* (Newbury Park, CA: Sage, 1990).

## Feedback

**Feedback** ensures effective communication and determines the degree to which a message has been received and understood. This two-way communication, in which the sender and the receiver arrive at mutual understanding, contrasts with one-way communication of the kind that occurs in most downward communication. In downward communication, for example, distortions often occur because of insufficient opportunity for feedback from receivers. For example, when the superintendent distributes a memorandum on an important board policy to all professional personnel in the school district, this act alone does not guarantee that communication has taken place. One might expect feedback in the form of upward communication to be encouraged more in school districts that use participatory management, site-based management, and site-based decision-making practices. School districts need effective upward communications if their downward communications are to be effective. Some studies report numerous benefits of two-way communication (feedback) over one-way communication. For example, although two-way communication is more time-consuming than is one-way communication, it provides increased satisfaction and is recommended in all but the simplest and routine transmission of information.[52]

Written messages provide much less opportunity for feedback than does face-to-face communication. When possible, school administrators should use face-to-face communication because this approach allows the individuals communicating with each other to receive both verbal and nonverbal feedback. Brief, straightforward questions such as the following can be helpful in eliciting feedback from subordinates about the reception of a message: How do you feel about my statement? What do you think? What did you hear me say? Do you see any problems with what we have talked about?[53] Such attempts to elicit feedback from a receiver of a message can avoid misunderstandings between a sender and a receiver.

Some guidelines that school administrators can use to elicit feedback from subordinates include the following:[54]

- Promote and cultivate feedback, but don't try to force it.

- Reward those who provide feedback and use feedback received.
- Whenever possible, go straight to the source and observe the results—don't wait for feedback.
- Give feedback to subordinates on the outcome of the feedback received. Thus, the school administrator elicits feedback, uses it, and feeds back its results to subordinates.

## Listening

Earlier, we noted that school administrators spend over 70 percent of their time communicating. Moreover, estimates indicate that over 30 percent of an administrator's day is devoted to listening. More important, tests of listening comprehension suggest that these individuals listen at only 25 percent efficiency.[55] Listening skills affect the quality of colleague and superordinate-subordinate relationships in schools. (See Administrative Advice 7–3).

Successful communication therefore requires effective **listening** on the part of both the sender and the receiver. The receiver must listen to receive and understand the sender's messages; and the sender must listen to receive and understand the receiver's feedback. Often listening is the weak link in the chain of two-way communication. Many people do not work actively at listening well. One author emphasizes that listening is an active process that demands a great deal of concentration and effort.[56] Recently, some organizations have designed training programs that explore techniques for improving listening skills.[57] For example, the following guidelines can be helpful to school administrators:[58]

- *Stop talking.*
- Put the talker at ease.
- Show the talker you want to listen.
- Remove distractions.
- Empathize with the talker.

[52]Eric M. Eisenberg et al., *Organizational Communication: Balancing Creativity and Constraint* (New York: Bedford/St. Martin's Press, 2006).

[53]DuBrin, *Essentials of Management.*

[54]Middlemist, *Experiencing Organizational Behavior.*

[55]Steven R. Corman et al., *Perspectives on Organizational Communication* (New York: Guilford Publications, Incorporated, 2000).

[56]Bruce Benward and Timothy J. Kolosick, *Ear Training: A Technique for Listening* (New York: McGraw-Hill, 2004).

[57]Larry Barker, *Listen Up: How to Improve Relationships, Reduce Stress and Be More Productive by Using the Power* (New York: St. Martin's Press, 2000).

[58]Kay Dans, *Human Behavior at Work* (New York: McGraw-Hill, 1972).

---

### Administrative Advice 7–3

#### Listening Styles

One way of viewing listening is to look at listening styles. Six listening styles, which have been developed by Performax Systems International, can help school administrators improve their listening skills.

- *Leisure Listener.* This listener is very relaxed and tunes in primarily to what is pleasant. To be more effective, a leisure listener needs to avoid wandering off on tangents and to focus on the task at hand. This listener should also be willing to listen to important information, even if it is unpleasant and makes her uncomfortable.

- *Inclusive Listener.* This listener takes in everything, wanting to understand the main ideas of the speaker in order to be comfortable. To be more effective, an inclusive listener needs to avoid getting impatient with ramblers, to stop trying to take in everything, and to concentrate more on analyzing and evaluating the message.

- *Stylistic Listener.* This listener tunes in to the mannerisms and dress of the speaker and wants to know the speaker's background and credentials. This listener also tends to place the speaker in a favorable or unfavorable category. To be more effective, a stylistic listener needs to avoid stereotyping and to pay more attention to the content that is being presented.

- *Technical Listener.* This listener is very tuned in to processing information and is listening or gathering specific data within a narrow but in-depth listening range. To be more effective, a technical listener needs to avoid tunnel listening and to become more inclusive. This

listener would also profit by paying more attention to nonverbal cues and being more open to the emotions of the speaker.

- *Empathic Listener.* This listener is looking for the unstated message and needs to understand the emotions of the speaker before becoming comfortable with the interpersonal communications. To be more effective, an empathic listener needs to focus on the task at hand, realizing that the content of the message is important as well as the emotions.

- *Nonconforming Listener.* This listener analyzes, evaluates, and has a tendency to agree or disagree quickly. This listener also tends to challenge the speaker and listens for supporting data to use in agreement or disagreement. (This is different from the technical listener who gathers supporting data to apply to a specific task situation.) To be more effective, a nonconforming listener needs to avoid hasty judgments and to look for points of agreement early in the speaker's message. This person also has a tendency to overprotect stimuli and assign a deeper meaning than was intended.

---

Source: Adapted from Frank W. Freshour, "Listening Power: Key to Effective Leadership," *Illinois School Research and Development*, 26 (1989): 17–23.

---

- Be patient.
- Hold your temper.
- Go easy on argument and criticism.
- Ask questions.
- *Stop talking.*

Note that the first and last rule for good listening is to "stop talking." Some researchers estimate that administrators spend as much as 85 percent of time devoted to communicating—in talking.[59] This does not leave much time for listening and feedback. School administrators must realize that effective communication involves understanding as well as being understood.

Lee Iacocca stresses the importance of listening, Tom Peters and Robert Waterman suggest that service to clients is the foundation of listening, and Paul Hersey and Kenneth Blanchard make numerous references to listening in their situational leadership theory.[60] And numerous reform reports—including *A Nation at Risk*, the Holmes Group, the Carnegie Task Force on Teaching as a Profession, and the Governor's Report—all recommend formal instruction in listening skills in schools.

---

[59] Middlemist, *Experiencing Organizational Behavior.*

[60] Lee Iacocca and William Novak, *Iacocca: An Autobiography* (New York: Bantam Books, 1988); Thomas J. Peters and Robert H. Waterman, *In Search of Excellence* (New York: Warner, 2004); Paul Hersey and Kenneth Blanchard, *Management of Organizational Behavior*, 8th ed. (Mahwah, NJ: Prentice Hall, 2007).

## PRO/CON Debate

### Parent Involvement

Parent-teacher organizations and booster clubs provide many schools with volunteer assistance in classrooms, school libraries, and school offices. In some communities, their fundraising abilities supply instructional, athletic, and musical equipment beyond the scope of the school budget. These resources provide visible support for schools, but they are not intended to impact directly on school policy or curriculum. Recently, the literature recommends parent involvement on school and district committees so that parents can influence decisions about schooling.

**Question:** When parents sit on district and school committees, does this communication channel enhance the relationship between school and community?

### Arguments PRO

1. Parents and educators are partners in the child's development. A partnership suggests separate but equal contributions and shared responsibility. Parents deserve greater access to the inner workings of schools. The relationship between school and community will only improve when schools provide vehicles for access.

2. Parents, especially the urban poor who were themselves not successful in school, are disenfranchised stakeholders in the educational system. They have a vested interest in the welfare of their own children but are intimidated by school policies and procedures. These parents need nonthreatening interactions with educators. Service on committees provides an arena for work on mutual goals and the development of positive attitudes.

3. Through involvement on district and school committees, parents provide the client's view of the educational system. Traditionally, this viewpoint has been sought only rarely. The relationship between school and community is enhanced because the client's perspective is valued.

4. When parents are oriented to their role in governance, they develop the knowledge and skills they need to operate well in committee structures. A period of orientation and training increases mutual understanding between parents and teachers.

5. Parents have too few opportunities to interact with schools in a positive, professional manner. Through involvement such as service on committees, parents will observe that teachers are skilled problem solvers.

### Arguments CON

1. The school acts *in loco parentis,* in place of the parent. School personnel have the responsibility for providing educational service and are certified to do so by the state. Frequently, parents are the problem, not the solution. Their access to school matters should be limited.

2. Most parents are concerned about their child's education, but, with changes in families (mothers working outside the home, single parents, etc.), many are too busy. In some settings, parents ignore or are hostile toward educators. They do not participate voluntarily in school-sponsored events such as open house. Those who need to volunteer won't.

3. Most of what parents know about the school they learn from their own children. They overgeneralize on the basis of that limited data. Their motivation is to improve conditions for only their child. They have little interest in supporting procedures that benefit the general welfare. Because committees act for the general good, parents are thwarted in their efforts. In the long run, the school-community relationship worsens.

4. Parents lack the educational expertise to understand the complex issues raised on committees. School-community relations will worsen because parents cannot participate on an equal footing with professional educators.

5. Parents have ample opportunity to observe and interact with teachers on matters related to their children's instruction. However, parents are often intimidated by teachers' knowledge. In working together on committees, they will see teachers as formal and distant.

## Summary

1. Communication is an important skill because school administrators spend over 70 percent of their time communicating.

2. The communication process is continuous and involves six steps: ideating, encoding, transmitting, receiving, decoding, and acting. Nonverbal communication involves encoding and decoding body language, vocal cues, use of time, and spatial relationships to more effectively understand verbal messages.

3. Communications within school organizations flow in four primary directions: downward, upward, horizontally, and diagonally. These communication flows are more likely to occur in open than in closed organizational climates.

4. The major informal communication flow in school organizations is called the grapevine. The grapevine carries both accurate information and rumors.

5. Whether formal or informal, the actual pattern of communication connecting people within school organizations is called a network. A school organization's network is often quite different from the pattern of relationships established by its formal structure.

6. The barriers to effective communication include differing frames of reference, filtering, structure, information overload, semantics, and status differences. Techniques for overcoming barriers to effective communication include repetition, empathy, understanding, feedback, and listening.

## Key Terms

communication process
ideating
encoding
transmitting
receiving
decoding
acting
nonverbal communication
communication flow
grapevine
network pattern
network analysis
frame of reference
filtering
structure
information overload
semantics
status differences
repetition
empathy
understanding
feedback
listening

## Discussion Questions

1. Select a communication you have had recently and analyze it using the model shown in Figure 7–1.

2. Using network analysis, develop a communication network for your school. Compare your communication network with the formal structure of the school.

3. Why is it difficult to obtain accurate information from upward and downward communication flows?

4. What are six barriers to effective communication in school organizations? And what are some techniques for overcoming these barriers?

5. Observe the nonverbal communication behavior of organizational participants for fifteen minutes. Explain the nonverbal behavior you observe. Is there any inconsistency between nonverbal and verbal behaviors?

## Suggested Readings

Bagin, Don, Donald R. Gallagher, and Leslie W. Kindred. *The School and Community Relations* (Needham Heights, MA: Allyn and Bacon, 1994). The authors clarify the present situation of the field and combine both theory and practice in charting a course toward the steady improvement of public education with programs for better school-community communication.

Brislin, Richard, and Tomoko Yoshida. *Intercultural Communication Training: An Introduction* (Thousand Oaks, CA: Sage, 1994). The approaches this volume covers—such as assessing needs, establishing goals, and building positive attitudes—apply to any situation where good personal relations and effective communication need to be established with people from different cultural backgrounds.

Burleson, Brant, Terrance L. Albrecht, and Irwin G. Sarason (eds.). *Communication of Social Support: Messages, Interactions, Relationships, and Community* (Thousand Oaks, CA: Sage, 1994). Chapters examine functional and dysfunctional patterns involved in the communication of support, and offer both scholarly and applied audiences an understanding of social support as a communication process grounded in ongoing relationships.

Gudykunst, William B. *Bridging Differences: Effective Intergroup Communication,* 3rd ed. (Thousand Oaks, CA: Sage, 1999). This volume includes culture and ethnicity; intergroup attitudes and stereotyping; managing intergroup attitudes; community building; exchanging messages with other groups; and the knowledge, motivation, and skills necessary for intergroup communication.

Gumbrecht, Hans U., and Ludwig K. Pfeiffer (eds.). *Materialities of Communication* (Stanford, CA: Stanford University Press, 1994). This volume describes the whole process of communication from ideation to activity, including barriers and methods of overcoming them.

Knapp, Mark L., and Gerald R. Miller (eds.). *Handbook of Interpersonal Communication*, 3rd ed. (Thousand Oaks, CA: Sage, 1998). The handbook lays out the key theoretical and methodological issues; focuses on component parts or growth processes, verbal and nonverbal behavior, situational and cultural influences, the characteristics each communicator brings to an encounter; and examines mutual influence and temporal processes and interpersonal processes in four important relational contexts.

Warner, Carolyn. *Promoting Your School: Going Beyond PR* (Thousand Oaks, CA: Corwin, Press, 1994). Smart school leaders have learned from corporate America that marketing is a potent tool that can help forge a partnership among educators, parents, community, and the private sector to meet the ever-increasing demands on schools.

# 8. Organizational Change

FOCUSING QUESTIONS

1  Why is the open systems model useful for understanding the characteristics of organizational change?

2  What are the major pressures for change facing schools?

3  Why do school employees resist change?

4  What methods can school administrators use to reduce resistance to change?

5  How can force-field analysis help administrators understand the change process?

6  What approaches can be used to improve school functioning?

---

In this chapter, we attempt to answer these questions concerning change in school organizations. We begin our discussion by examining the open systems model, which provides a useful framework for understanding the change process in schools. We examine internal and external pressures for change in schools. We examine the major sources of resistance to change and how to overcome them. Force-field analysis serves as a useful model in exploring the complex nature of change. Finally, we present and analyze various approaches to change, including individual and group strategies.

During the last decade, the prominent approach in organizational theory has moved from an emphasis on innovation in organizations to frameworks for change based on an organization's strategy in human resource management and on the determinism experienced by external and internal environments. This new approach stems in part from contemporary thinking about organizational management. Education is beginning to incorporate the principles of Theory Z leadership.[1] Such leadership is likely to concern itself with such issues as the empowerment of teachers, the improvement of the quality of work life, and the forging of strong linkages between school and community. When such principles are introduced in schools, they probably represent a change from existing practice. But what causes such changes to take place?

Previously, we used the term *social system* to refer to aggregates of human relationships such as schools, school districts, and communities. We pointed out the impact of the external environment on each of these social systems. Put another way, nearly all social systems are open systems. We will elaborate on the concept of **open systems** because it has considerable utility in understanding organizational change in school organizations.

---

[1]William G. Ouchi, *Theory Z: How American Business Can Meet the Japanese Challenge* (New York: Avon Books, 1993).

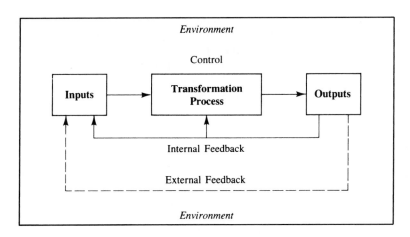

**Figure 8–1**

Open Systems Model

## Schools as Open Systems

We can view social systems, such as school organizations, as a linkage of inputs (materials, information, or people) from sources in the external environment, a transformation process (a technical-human organization), and outputs (products and services). The system may include one or more feedback loops for control. For example, feedback from the internal and external environments that the output is substandard could lead to change in either the transformation process or the inputs, or both. Effectiveness of the organization is thus based on adaptation to both internal and external forces (see Figure 8–1).

Daniel Katz and Robert Kahn provide one of the most comprehensive descriptions of the open systems perspective. They suggest nine common characteristics shared by all open systems:[2]

1. *Importation of Energy.* Open systems take in energy from the outside environment in the form of people, materials, and information.

2. *The Throughput.* Open systems transform the imported energy. The organization builds a product, trains people, provides a service, or processes materials.

3. *The Output.* Open systems export a product into the outside environment. In a school, the output may be students' knowledge, skills, abilities, and attitudes.

4. *Cycles of Events.* In open systems, the pattern of activities is recycled. The export of a product furnishes energy for the cycle to repeat. In a school system, the importation of resources (people, materials, and information) is used to teach students who are then exported into the outside environment. These graduates continue to contribute energy to the school system in the form of resources (financial, human, or material). The importation of new energy into the system triggers a new cycle.

5. *Negative Entropy.* Entropy, a law of nature, stipulates that all forms of organization move toward death or disorganization. Because the open system can import more energy than it uses, it can survive and expand. However, not all organizations continue to import more energy than they expend. Consequently, many organizations go out of business each year.

Public schools are a special type of organization, which have been classified as "domesticated" organizations.[3] Put another way, public schools are protected and secure in many ways. For example, their clients (students) must participate in the organization, and the organization will be protected regardless of its performance.[4] Furthermore, although public schools must compete for public funds, they are virtually assured by law that they will not go

---

[2]Daniel Katz and Robert L. Kahn, *The Social Psychology of Organizations* (New York: Wiley, 1978).

[3]Richard O. Carlson, "Environmental Constraints and Organizational Consequences: The Public School and Its Clients," in D. E. Griffiths (ed.), *Behavioral Science and Educational Administration* (Chicago: University of Chicago Press, 1964), pp. 262–276.

[4]There is a trend under way for state departments of education to seize control of academically deficient school systems.

out of business. Charter schools, private and parochial schools, the expansion of home schooling, and vouchers provide some competition to public schools but not enough to put public schools out of business.

6. *Feedback.* The information coming into an organization is coded and selected so that the organization does not receive more information than it can process. Information provides signals from the environment, and negative feedback indicates deviations from what the environment desires. This is a control mechanism.

7. *Dynamic Homeostasis.* There is a continuous inflow from the environment, but the ratio tends to remain relatively equal. This process serves to preserve the character of the system and to maintain it in equilibrium. However, the equilibrium is not stationary. For example, as the goals of the organization change, a new character may develop that will serve as a new homeostatic basis.

8. *Differentiation.* Open systems tend toward elaboration of roles and specialization of function. Roles in schools—including those of superintendents, principals, teachers, and other specialists—illustrate this tendency.

9. *Equifinality.* Multiple means to the same ends exist within open systems.

Figure 8–1 depicts an open system interacting with the external environment and highlights open system characteristics. The figure shows that, as open systems, organizations possess aspects of interdependency and interaction of components within an identifiable whole.

Each component (inputs, transformation process, outputs, and the external and internal environments) must be successfully managed and linked if the organization is to be effective. For example, to focus more attention on the technical-human organization (transformation process) and to ignore how the external environment is reacting to the product and services provided by the organization can result in serious consequences. Similarly, to focus on inputs or to concentrate on outputs while ignoring the effectiveness of the technical-human organization can also lead to serious consequences.

We have all seen school administrators jeopardize a school district by spending all their energies on inputs or outputs while paying little attention to employee motivation, the quality of leadership, methods of decision making, and internal communications. As a result,

school faculty exhibits low morale and job satisfaction, interpersonal conflict, and disillusionment with the leadership of the school or school district. These are examples of not providing adequate attention to feedback and managing the interrelationships of the component parts of the social system.[5]

## Pressures for Organizational Change

What causes changes to take place in school organizations? Generally, pressures on schools to change emanate from the external and internal environment. These include accountability, changing demographics, staffing shortages, changing technology and knowledge explosion, and processes and people.

### Accountability

School administrators have always had to deal with bureaucratic accountability, that is, accountability with respect to superordinate-subordinate relationships. For example, the teacher is accountable to the principal; the principal is accountable to the superintendent; the superintendent is accountable to the school board. However, accountability to constituencies external to the local school board increasingly drives accountability frameworks today. The business community pressures schools to graduate skilled workers for today's economy. Governors and state legislators play key roles in designing accountability plans. The national education plan, titled *No Child Left Behind,* stipulates specific requirements that states must follow regarding student accountability.

As accountability has become more prominent at the state and national levels, the focus has shifted from accountability for inputs or transformation processes to outputs. This is reflected in state standards and testing. Presently, 49 out of 50 states have statewide assessment systems in place, and in nearly half of the states the stakes attached to these outcomes have been gradually increased.[6] Furthermore, with the reauthorization of

---

[5] Wendell L. French, *Organization Development and Transformation: Managing Effective Change* (New York: McGraw-Hill, 2005).

[6] George J. Cizek, "Conjectures on the Rise and Fall of Standard Setting: An Introduction to Context and Practice," in G. J. Cizek (ed.), *Setting Performance Standards* (Mahwah, NJ: Erlbaum, 2002), pp. 3–17.

the Elementary and Secondary Education Act (ESEA) of 1965, each state will be required to implement a state-wide system of assessment in reading and mathematics for grades 3 through 8.[7]

Another new form of accountability is market accountability. Open enrollment policies, which allow students to choose public schools within and outside their home districts, have become popular. In addition, there has been growing political support for non-traditional methods of funding public schools, such as the expansion of home schooling, charter schools, and school vouchers. Such an expansion of public school choice frameworks has forced some school administrators to reallocate their time from internal to external functions, such as marketing and fundraising.

### Changing Demographics

Currently, enrollment in public schools is growing. Higher enrollment is generally associated with greater ethnic, racial, and linguistic diversity, a school population that has the greatest level of needs. The United States Census in 2000 reported that out of the nation's 49 million students, 62.9 percent were white, 17.1 percent were African American, 15 percent were Hispanic, 3.9 percent were Asian or Pacific Islander, and 1.1 percent were American Indian or Alaskan Native.[8] Ethnicity is closely related to poverty and the dropout rate. For example, 36.5 percent of African American and 33.6 percent of Hispanic families with children lived in poverty in 2000 compared to only 14.5 percent of white families.[9] And African American and Hispanic students are much more likely to drop out of school than white students.[10]

Immigration is also creating demographic changes in public schools. According to estimates, nearly one million legal and illegal immigrants come to the United States every year. Many of these immigrants and their children are poor and have limited English proficiency, which places greater demands on educating these students and has increased political debates about bilingual education and testing.[11]

### Staffing Shortages

After many years of having a steady stream of qualified teachers and principals, many school districts are facing severe shortages.[12] Shortages of teachers and administrators are due largely to retirements, an expanding student population, career changes, and increasing teacher and administrator turnover. Expanding student enrollment in general and a growing population of students with special needs may further exacerbate these shortages, especially in areas such as special education and bilingual education.

Another issue facing school administrators is increasing the racial and ethnic diversity of personnel. Although the student population is growing racially and ethnically more diverse, similar demographic shifts have not occurred in the teaching ranks. The teaching force is predominantly white (87.2%), with the remainder coming from minority groups (12.8%).[13] This student-teacher mismatch often results in considerable cultural and social distance between middle-class white teachers and students of color. Young and Laible suggest that white educators and school administrators do not have a thorough enough understanding of how to deal with students from different cultural backgrounds.[14] Short further summarizes the consequences of the mismatch between white middle-class teachers and students of color. She cites how teacher preparation programs rarely train teacher candidates in strategies for teaching culturally diverse students. The lack of familiarity with students' cultures, learning styles, and communication

[7]*No Child Left Behind Act of 2001.*

[8]U.S. Census Bureau, United States Department of Commerce, *School Enrollment* (Washington, DC: U.S. Census Bureau, 2000).

[9]National Center for Education Statistics, *School-Age Children Living in Poverty in the United States: 2000–2001* (Washington, DC: Author, 2003).

[10]National Center for Education Statistics, *Dropouts in Public Schools in the United States: 2000–2002* (Washington, DC: Author, 2003).

[11]Carola Suárez-Orozco and Marcelo Suárez-Orozco, *Children of Immigration* (Cambridge, MA: Harvard University Press, 2001).

[12]National Center for Education Statistics, *Digest of Educational Statistics, 2002* (Washington, DC: Author, 2003).

[13]National Education Association, *Status of the American Public School Teacher, 2000–2001* (Washington, DC: Author, 2004).

[14]Michelle Young and Julie Laible, "White Racism, Antiracism, and School Leadership Preparation," *Journal of School Leadership,* 10 (2000): 374–415.

patterns translates into some teachers holding negative expectations for students. And, often, inappropriate curricula, instructional materials, and assessments are used with these students.[15]

## Technological Change and Knowledge Explosion

Another source of external pressure for change is the technological explosion all organizations are experiencing. This pressure is due in part to research and development efforts within organizations. For example, many large, urban school districts now have research and development departments as part of their organizational structures. However, a great deal of technological development occurs outside the organization. This development is the result of government-sponsored research efforts and the efforts of numerous educational organizations including the American Association of School Administrators (AASA), National Association of Secondary School Principals (NASSP), National Association of Elementary School Principals (NAESP), Cooperative Program in Educational Administration (CPEA), University Council for Educational Administration (UCEA), National Council of Professors of Educational Administration (NCPEA), National Academy for School Executives (NASE), Association for Supervision and Curriculum Development (ASCD), National Society for the Study of Education (NSSE), and the American Educational Research Association (AERA).

Concurrent with the development of new technologies is an explosion of knowledge. More people than ever before are attending college, and a large percentage of the population is receiving graduate degrees. Higher education is no longer reserved for the elite few. There is also a growing emphasis on continuing education courses offered on university campuses across the country, and nontraditional students (older students) are returning to junior colleges and four-year institutions. New technologies require the development of knowledge to implement the technology. Thus, the interaction of new technology and the knowledge required to gener-

ate the technology into the organization compounds the rate of technological change exponentially.

## Processes and People

Pressures in the internal environment of the organization can also stimulate change. The two most significant internal pressures come from processes and people. Processes that act as pressures for change include communications, decision making, leadership, and motivational strategies, to name only a few. Breakdowns or problems in any of these processes can create pressures for change. Communications may be inadequate; decisions may be of poor quality; leadership may be inappropriate for the situation; and employee motivation may be nonexistent. Such processes reflect breakdowns or problems in the transformation process of the open systems model (see Figure 8–1) and may reflect the need for change.

Some symptoms of people problems are poor performance levels of teachers and students, high absenteeism of teachers or students, high dropout rates of students, high teacher turnover, poor school-community relations, poor management-union relations, and low levels of teacher morale and job satisfaction. A teachers' strike, numerous employee complaints, and the filing of grievances are some tangible signs of problems in the internal environment. These factors provide a signal to school administrators that change is necessary. In addition, internal pressures for change occur in response to organizational changes that are designed to deal with pressures for change exerted by the external environment.

Today, planning for change is essential as many school administrators move to one of the forms of site-based decision making (SBDM) or seek improvements in curriculum and instruction. Drawing from the related research, we can identify the primary conditions that greatly enhance the success of any change effort. (See Administrative Advice 8–1.)

## Resistance to Change

Pressures on school organizations to change demand some response from their members. But, many of the problems associated with change concern the forces resisting it—that is, the forces for maintaining the status quo or equilibrium. Two major issues concern the resistance to change: the causes of resistance and ways of reducing resistance.

[15]Donna J. Short, "Integrating Language and Content for Effective Sheltered Instruction Programs," in C. J. Faltis and P. M. Wolfe (eds.), *So Much to Say: Adolescents, Bilingualism, and ESL in Secondary School* (New York: Teachers College Press, 1999).

---

## Administrative Advice 8–1

### Making Change Work

Four conditions that help facilitate change are the following:

- *Condition 1: Participant Involvement.* Recent management theory, including W. Edwards Deming's popular Total Quality Management (TQM) model, speaks directly to involvement of participants in decisions that affect their work life. Many authors make a strong case for using consensus when introducing changes in the schools.

- *Condition 2: Senior Administrator Support.* The superintendent is not typically the change agent at the local level, but her or his support is critical to the success of a change effort. Financial support, comment about the initiative at school board meetings, and visits to the school will have a positive influence on staff members.

- *Condition 3: No Escalation of Teacher Workload.* Teachers typically have overburdened work schedules and

have little time for extra duties. Ideally, a change should not add to an already overburdened work assignment. Changes that require greater time commitment should include a plan to lighten other responsibilities.

- *Condition 4: Change Agent's Active Involvement.* The change agent may be anyone in the school or school district. The person with direct line responsibility for the change must take an active and supportive role in overseeing the change at the local level. This will assure the day-to-day progress of change and provide an informational resource for those involved.

---

Source: Adapted from Richard L. Bucko, "Making Change Work," *School Administrator*, 6 (1994): 32.

---

## Causes of Resistance to Change

Organizational change is an attempt by school executives to improve the effectiveness of schools. Such attempts result in different responses from organizational members. One typical response to any change is resistance. School administrators need to understand the common causes of resistance to change.[16] These include interference with need fulfillment, fear of the unknown, threats to power and influence, knowledge and skill obsolescence, organizational structure, limited resources, and collective bargaining agreements.

**Interference with Need Fulfillment**   Changes that interfere with a person's economic, social, esteem, or other needs are likely to meet with resistance. People usually resist changes that could lower their income or job status, such as termination or a demotion. Besides the fulfillment of economic and esteem needs, people work for social reasons. The social relationships that develop in the organization are often more important to its members than is commonly realized. For example, even

such seemingly minor changes as relocating employees within the same building or school district may affect social-status relationships and result in resistance.

**Fear of the Unknown**   People like stability. They may have invested a great deal of time and effort in the current system. They have established a normal routine in performing their jobs. They have learned their range of duties and what their supervisor's expectations are for performing these duties. They have some idea of the routine problems that may surface in the performance of their jobs. In other words, they have learned how to perform their jobs successfully, how to get good performance ratings from their supervisors, how to interact with their work group, and so on. Put another way, the present system offers a high degree of certainty.

Changes in established work routines or job duties create potential unknowns. For example, employees may fear that they will not be able to perform up to their previous standards. They may have to learn a new job. They may have to learn to adjust to a new supervisor's expectations. They may have to adjust to a new work group. They may have to make new friends. When a change occurs, the normal routine is disrupted, and the employee must begin to find new and different ways to function within the environment.

---

[16]Robert Evans, *The Human Side of School Change: Reform, Resistance, and the Real Life Problems of Innovation* (San Francisco: Jossey-Bass, 1996).

**Threats to Power and Influence**    Resistance can also occur because the proposed changes may reduce one's power and influence in the organization. One source of power in organizations is the control of something that other people need, such as information or resources. Individuals or groups who have established a power position in an organization will resist changes that are felt to reduce their power and influence. For example, a superintendent of schools whose school district is threatened with consolidation with another school district will resist the merger in order to maintain his current position. Similarly, the trend toward management information systems (MIS) in today's school districts, which makes more information available to more school district members, is likely to be resisted by top-level administrators. These administrators would lose this source of influence and power if MIS were implemented.

**Knowledge and Skill Obsolescence**    Somewhat related to threats to power and influence is knowledge and skill obsolescence. While the former usually applies to management, the latter can apply to any member of the organization's hierarchy. Employees will resist organizational changes that make their knowledge and skills obsolete. For example, consider the school bookkeeper who has mastered a complex accounting system over a long period of time. The superintendent of schools announces the implementation of a new computerized accounting system that is reputed to be easier and more efficient. The bookkeeper is threatened by a change to a new computerized system and will likely resist the change because her identity is based on the mastery of the old and more complex accounting system.

**Organizational Structure**    In Chapter 2, we characterized the school district as a bureaucratic organizational structure. Like all modern organizations, schools have many of the characteristics of an ideal bureaucracy—a hierarchy of authority, a division of labor and specialization, rules and regulations, impersonality in interpersonal relationships, and a career orientation. In fact, the very meaning of organization implies that some degree of structure must be given to groups so that they can fulfill the organization's goals. However, this legitimate need for structure can be dysfunctional to the organization and serve as a major resistance to change. For example, schools typically have narrowly defined roles; clearly spelled out lines of authority, responsibility, and accountability; and limited flows of information from the top to the bottom of the hierarchy.

Recall from Chapter 7 that an emphasis on the hierarchy of authority causes employees to feed back only positive information to superiors concerning their jobs. The avoidance of negative feedback by subordinates hampers school administrators from identifying subordinates' concerns and needed changes in the organization. Also recall that the taller the organizational structure is, the more numerous the levels through which a message must travel. This increases the probability that any new idea will be filtered as it travels upward through the hierarchy because it violates the status quo in the school or school district.

**Limited Resources**    Some school districts prefer to maintain the status quo, whereas others would change if they had the available resources. Generally, change requires resources: capital and people with the appropriate skills and time. A school district may have identified a number of innovations that could improve the effectiveness of the district operation. However, the district may have to abandon the desired changes because of inadequate resources. We are certain that you can identify a number of local school district innovations, as well as those initiated by the federal and state governments, that have been deferred or completely abandoned due to resource limitations.

**Collective Bargaining Agreements**    The most pervasive changes in educational policy matters have been brought about by the practice of negotiating formally with the teachers' union and other employee unions in a school district. Agreements between management and union usually impose obligations on participants that can restrain their behaviors. Collective bargaining agreements are a good example. That is, ways of doing things that were once considered management prerogatives may become subject to negotiation and be fixed in the collective bargaining agreement. Some examples include salaries, cost-of-living adjustments (COLA), class size, teacher transfer, school calendar, class hours, evaluations, and promotions. Such agreements restrain the behavior of school administrators from implementing desired changes in the system.

### Reducing Resistance to Change

Earlier, we focused on change as it relates to social systems, more specifically to open systems. Change must involve attention to several interacting linkages that

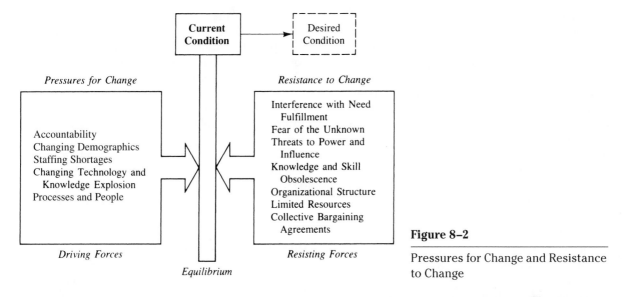

Figure 8–2

Pressures for Change and Resistance to Change

constitute an entire social system, a whole or gestalt (see Figure 8–1). Moreover, an open system is in a state of quasi-stationary equilibrium; that is, as the goals of a social system change, the equilibrium will change.

To better understand resistance to change, Kurt Lewin developed the concept of **force-field analysis**.[17] He looks upon a level of behavior within an organization not as a static custom but as a dynamic balance of forces working in opposite directions within the organization. He believes that we should think about any change situation in terms of driving forces or factors acting to change the current condition (pressures for change) and resisting forces or factors acting to inhibit change (resistance to change). These forces may originate in the internal or external environment of the organization or in the behavior of the change agent.

School administrators must play an active role in initiating change and in attempting to reduce resistance to change. School administrators can think of the current condition in an organization as an equilibrium that is the result of driving forces and resisting forces working against each other. Change agents must assess the change potential and resistance and attempt to change the balance of forces so that there will be movement toward a desired condition. There are three ways of doing this: increasing the driving forces, reducing the resisting forces, or considering new driving forces.

Lewin points out that increasing one set of forces without decreasing the other set of forces will increase tension and conflict in the organization. Reducing the other set of forces may reduce the amount of tension. While increasing driving forces is sometimes effective, it is usually better to reduce the resisting forces because increasing driving forces often tend to be offset by increased resistance. Put another way, when we push people, they are likely to push back. Figure 8–2 illustrates the two sets of forces—pressures for change and resistance to change. This is the type of situation that school administrators face and must work with on a daily basis when attempting to effect change.

As Figure 8–2 shows, change results when an imbalance occurs between the ratio of driving forces and resisting forces. Such an imbalance alters the existing condition—one hopes in the direction planned by the school administrator—into a new and desired condition. Once the new, desired condition is reached, the opposing forces are again brought into equilibrium. An imbalance may occur through a change in the velocity of any force, a change in the direction of a force, or the introduction of a new force.

Moreover, change involves a sequence of organizational processes that occurs over time. Lewin suggests this process typically requires three steps: unfreezing, moving, and refreezing.[18]

1. *Unfreezing.* This step usually means reducing the forces acting to keep the organization in its cur-

[17]Kurt Lewin, *Field Theory in Social Sciences* (New York: Harper & Row, 1951).

[18]Kurt Lewin, *Resolving Social Conflicts and Field Theory in Social Science* (Washington, DC: American Psychological Association, 1997).

rent condition. Unfreezing might be accomplished by introducing new information that points out inadequacies in the current state or by decreasing the strength of current values, attitudes, and behaviors. Crises often stimulate unfreezing. Examples of crises are significant increases in the student dropout rate, dramatic enrollment declines, shifts in population within a school district, a sudden increase in teacher or middle management turnover, a costly lawsuit, and an unexpected teacher strike. Unfreezing may occur without crises as well. Climate surveys, financial data, and enrollment projections can be used to determine problem areas in a school district and initiate change to alleviate problems before crises erupt.

2. *Moving.* Once the organization is unfrozen, it can be changed. This step usually involves the development of new values, attitudes, and behaviors through internalization, identification, or change in structure. Some changes may be minor and involve a few members—such as changes in recruitment and selection procedures—and others may be major, involving many participants. Examples of the latter include a new evaluation system, restructuring of jobs and duties performed by employees, or restructuring the school district, which necessitates relocating faculty to different school sites within the system.

3. *Refreezing.* The final step in the change process involves stabilizing the change at a new quasi-stationary equilibrium. Changes in organizational culture, changes in group norms, changes in organizational policy, or modifications in organizational structure often accomplish this.

Figure 8–2 illustrates force-field analysis that shows both the pressures for change and resistance to change within a school setting. School administrators can use six specific methods to reduce resistance to change: participation, communication, support, rewards, planning, and coercion.

**Participation** One of the best methods for reducing resistance to change is to invite those who will be affected by the change to participate in planning, design, and implementation. There are at least three explanations for the effect of participation in reducing resistance to change: (1) As those affected by the change plan, design, and implement it, new ideas and information can be generated. The increased information is likely to result in a more effective change; (2) participation builds

ownership for the change, thus leading to a commitment to see the change successfully implemented; and (3) by providing information about the nature and consequences of the change, anxiety about the unknown is reduced, and rumors are stifled.[19]

**Communication** Another method for reducing resistance to change involves communicating and explaining to employees the nature of and need for the change. In explaining the need, administrators are advised to explain the effects the change will have on employees. This too will lessen employees' fear of the unknown. Employees who are informed about the logic behind administrative decisions are more likely to support new ideas.[20]

**Support** Effective implementation of a change requires support from top-level administrators such as the superintendent of schools and his cabinet. Support from the superintendent usually means that administrators lower in the organization's hierarchy, such as building principals, will be committed to the change. It is particularly important for building principals to manifest *supportive* and *considerate* leadership behaviors when change is being implemented. This type of leader behavior includes listening to subordinates' ideas, being approachable, and using employee ideas that have merit. Supportive leaders go out of their way to make the work environment more pleasant and enjoyable. For example, difficult changes may require training to acquire new skills necessary to implement the change. Administrators need to provide such training.[21] In short, when procedures are established to implement changes smoothly, less resistance is likely to be encountered.

**Rewards** When change is imminent, most people say, "What's in it for me?" Subordinates are less likely to resist changes that will benefit them directly.[22] For example, during collective bargaining between the board of education and the teachers' union, certain concessions can be given to teachers in exchange for support of a new

[19]Chris Argyris, *Knowledge for Action: A Guide to Overcoming Barriers to Organizational Change* (San Francisco: Jossey-Bass, 1993).

[20]Jerry W. Gilley et al., *Philosophy and Practice of Organizational Learning, Performance, and Change* (Cambridge, MA: Perseus, 2001).

[21]Richard A. Schmuck, *Practical Action Research for Change* (Thousand Oaks, CA: Corwin Press, 2006).

[22]Jay Conger, *Winning 'em Over* (New York: Simon and Schuster, 2001).

## ■ Exemplary Educational Administrators in Action

**CARLOS A. GARCIA** Superintendent, Clark County School District, Nevada.

**Previous Positions:** Superintendent, Fresno Unified School District, California; Superintendent, Sanger Unified School District, California; Principal, Pajaro Valley Unified School District and San Francisco Unified School District, California; Teacher, Rowland Unified School District and Chaffey Joint Union High School District, California.

**Latest Degree and Affiliation:** Administrative credential, Educational Administration, California State University at Fullerton.

**Number One Influence on Career:** Rita Steele, my seventh-grade government teacher, was my influence for going into the field of education.

**Number One Achievement:** Working toward bringing adequate funding to public education, as well as creating equal access to education through literacy and math initiatives for all Clark County School District students.

**Number One Regret:** I regret not spending more time as a classroom teacher, because that is where education happens, as well as the real excitement and action. I also regret that progress takes so much time to happen— I wish I could speed up the process of putting policies into place, enacting legislation, and so forth.

**Favorite Education-Related Book or Text:** *Frames of Mind* by Howard Gardner or *Savage Inequalities* by Jonathan Kozol.

**Additional Interests:** I enjoy water-related sports, such as snorkeling and jet skiing, and risky sports like skydiving and racing cars. Enjoying art, listening to music, and building sandcastles are also some of my favorite pastimes.

**Leadership Style:** My style is very collaborative, rather futuristic, and almost always involves risk taking. I believe a leader's role is to encourage people to believe in themselves and help them achieve things they never thought they could achieve. I like to think I am a good coach and cheerleader.

**Professional Vision:** The vision of every educator should be to educate children, no matter how challenging the situation may be. Too many times public education tries to serve adults, when it should be serving children. As educators, we must constantly reevaluate and question the system so that public education can meet the changing needs of our children. Public education should be viewed as dynamic and always changing.

**Words of Advice:** The current trend that allows norm-referenced tests to guide educational standards is very misleading. To improve education in the United States, school districts should be able to use and emphasize diagnostic testing to improve student achievement. Norm-referenced testing does little to improve student achievement because it does not allow us to pinpoint exactly where educational weaknesses exist. Because of the politics that surround norm-referenced testing in public education, I am not sure the United States will ever be bold enough to change the way we test our students.

Another trend I find disturbing is the criticism of public education. Public education is the greatest invention of all time—where would our country be without public education? One way we can stop this trend is for educators to take the lead in problem solving and not wait for others to fix the problems within the system.

---

program desired by management. Such concessions may include salary increases, bonuses, or more union representation in decision making. Administrators can also use standard rewards such as recognition, increased responsibility, praise, and status symbols. Thus, building in rewards may help reduce subordinates' resistance to change.

**Planning** Prospective changes should be well planned in advance. Change inevitably leads to subordinate anxiety about new expectations and fear of the unknown. The proposed change may require new performance lev-

els. Therefore, performance levels need to be given careful consideration by administrators when planning a change. Performance levels that are set too low can negatively affect performance. Conversely, performance levels that are set too high can result in frustration and low performance.[23] Moreover, introducing change incrementally can lessen the impact of change on subordi-

---

[23]Marshall S. Poole, *Organizational Change Processes: Theory and Methods of Research* (New York: Oxford University Press, 2003).

---

**Administrative Advice 8–2**

**Addressing Resistance to Change**

▪ *Adhere to the following principles when initiating change.*

—Make key teachers, parents, board members, and community leaders feel that the project is their own.

—Get support for the change effort from the top.

—Engage in site-based management. Encourage consensual decision making.

—Be willing to delegate leadership of the change effort. As a change facilitator, you may not always be the most effective leader in all change efforts.

▪ *Adhere to the following principles when implementing change.*

—Let participants in the change effort see that it reduces rather than increases workloads.

—Reassure participants that the change is in accordance with longstanding values.

—Present the change effort as attractive and interesting to those who will be most involved.

—Be flexible. Be open to different ways of handling the issue to be addressed by the change effort.

—Clarify any misconceptions about the change as soon as they occur. Help participants understand that change is a process, not an event.

—Build trust and rapport among participants.

Source: Adapted from John Chamley, Ellen Caprio, and Russell Young, "The Principal as a Catalyst and Facilitator of Planned Change," *NASSP Bulletin*, 78 (1994): 1–7. Used by permission.

---

nates and allow them time to adjust to new expectations and conditions.[24]

**Coercion** When other methods have failed, coercion can be used as a last resort. Some changes require immediate implementation. And top-level administrators may have considerable power. Such instances lend themselves more readily to administrators using coercion to gain compliance to changes. Subordinates can be threatened with job loss, decreased promotional opportunities, no salary increases (this technique is used infrequently in public schools), or a job transfer to achieve compliance with a change. There are, however, negative effects of using coercion, including frustration, fear, revenge, and alienation. This in turn may lead to poor performance, dissatisfaction, and turnover.[25]

Two questions should be asked in preparing to manage staff resistance to change: Who is initiating the change? How will the change be implemented? These questions will help change agents identify the source, type, and method of change. (See Administrative Advice 8–2.)

## Individual Approaches to Change

One way to improve an organization's effectiveness is to enhance an individual's functioning within the organization. This involves two basic types of approaches. The first type is aimed at changing the job or the person's perception of the job. The objective is to make the job more intrinsically satisfying to the employee. The second type is aimed at changing the person. The approaches we discuss are job enrichment, laboratory training, behavior modification, and transactional analysis. These change strategies are important, but not all of them might be used in a specific change program. Change agents need to understand the strategies and when to use them.

### Job Enrichment

Frederick Herzberg's motivation-hygiene theory has stimulated programs in job enrichment in many organizations. Herzberg feels that the challenge to organi-

---

[24]Robert E. Hoskisson and Craig S. Galbraith, "The Effect of Quantum versus Incremental M-Form Reorganization on Performance: A Time-Series Exploration of Intervention Dynamics," *Journal of Management*, 11 (1985): 55–70.

[25]William A. Pasmore, *Research in Organizational Change and Development* (Cambridge, MA: Elsevier Science & Technology Books, 2007).

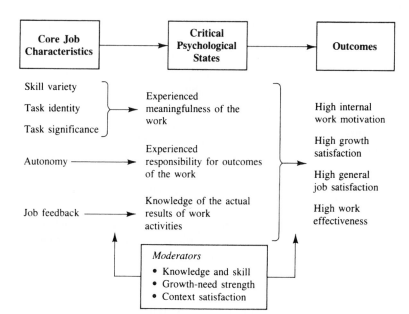

**Figure 8–3**

Job Enrichment Model

Source: Adapted from J. Richard Hackman and Greg R. Oldham, *Work Redesign,* © 1980, p. 90. Reprinted by permission of Pearson Education, Inc., Upper Saddle River, N. J.

zations is to emphasize motivation factors while ensuring that the hygiene factors are present. He refers to job enrichment as the method for achieving such a condition.[26] **Job enrichment** focuses on achieving organizational change by making jobs more meaningful, interesting, and challenging.

Expanding on the earlier work of Herzberg, Richard Hackman and Greg Oldham provide an explicit framework for enriching jobs.[27] Based on their own research and the work of others, they developed a job-characteristics model (see Figure 8–3). As the figure shows, five core job characteristics create three critical psychological states that in turn lead to a number of employee outcomes. The employee's knowledge and skills, growth-need strength, and satisfaction with context factors moderate the linkage among the job characteristics, the psychological states, and the outcomes.

The five job characteristics that are essential to job enrichment are the following:

1. *Skill variety* is the degree to which a job requires a variety of different activities in carrying out the work, which involves the use of a number of different skills and talents of the employee.

2. *Task identity* is the degree to which a job requires completion of a "whole" and identifiable piece of work—that is, doing a job from beginning to end with a visible outcome.

3. *Task significance* is the degree to which the job has a substantial impact on the lives of other people, whether those people are in the immediate organization or in the external environment.

4. *Autonomy* is the degree to which the job provides substantial freedom, independence, and discretion to the individual in scheduling the work and in determining the procedures to be used in doing the work.

5. *Job feedback* is the degree to which carrying out the work activities required by the job provides the individual with direction and clear information about the effectiveness of his performance.[28]

As shown in Figure 8–3, skill variety, task identity, and task significance together affect "experienced meaningfulness of the work." Autonomy and feedback independently affect the other two psychological states, respectively, "experienced responsibility for outcomes of the work" and "knowledge of the actual results of the work activities." And according to Hackman and Oldham, only employees who have job-related knowledge and skills, high growth-need strength, and high satisfac-

---

[26]Frederick Herzberg, "One More Time: How Do You Motivate Employees?" *Harvard Business Review,* 65 (1987): 109–120.

[27]J. Richard Hackman and Greg R. Oldham, *Work Redesign* (Reading, MA: Addison-Wesley, 1980).

[28]Ibid.

tion with context factors (Herzberg's hygienes) are likely to be affected in the manner specified in the model.

Hackman and Oldham have developed the job diagnostic survey (JDS) to diagnose the job dimensions in their model (see Figure 8–3) and to determine the effect of job changes on employees.[29] Thus, the job dimensions in the job enrichment model can be combined into the following mathematic expression, which explains the relative impact of change in each dimension of the Hackman-Oldham model:

$$MPS = \frac{\text{Skill variety} + \text{Task identity} + \text{Task significance}}{3} \times \text{Autonomy} \times \text{Feedback}$$

The motivation potential score (MPS) formula sums the scores for skill variety, task identity, and task significance and divides the total by three. The combination of these three job characteristics is equally weighted, with autonomy and feedback considered separately. The result is an overall measure of job enrichment.

## Laboratory Training

Lewin was instrumental in the development of **laboratory training**, also known as sensitivity training or T-groups.[30] The National Training Laboratories (NTL) developed and refined laboratory training in 1946. From this beginning, training has emerged as a widely used organizational strategy aimed at individual change, which generally takes place in small groups.

**Goals of Laboratory Training**    Based on an extensive review of the literature, two researchers have outlined six basic objectives common to most laboratory training sessions:

1. To increase understanding, insight, and self-awareness about one's own behavior and its impact on others, including the ways in which others interpret one's behavior.

2. To increase understanding and sensitivity about the behavior of others, including better interpretation of both verbal and nonverbal cues, which increases

awareness and understanding of what the other person is thinking and feeling.

3. To improve understanding and awareness of group and intergroup processes, both those that facilitate and those that inhibit group functioning.

4. To improve diagnostic skills in interpersonal and intergroup situations, which is attained by accomplishing the first three objectives.

5. To increase the ability to transform learning into action, so that real-life interventions will be more successful in increasing member effectiveness, satisfaction, or output.

6. To improve an individual's ability to analyze her own interpersonal behavior, as well as to learn how to help self and others with whom she comes in contact to achieve more satisfying, rewarding, and effective interpersonal relationships.[31]

These objectives point out that laboratory training can be a useful strategy for bringing about organizational change. School districts that are experiencing problems with communications, coordination, or excessive and continuing conflict in interpersonal relationships may benefit from laboratory training as a means of improving individual and organizational effectiveness.

**Design of Laboratory Training**    Laboratory training groups (T-groups) typically consist of ten to fifteen members and a professional trainer. The duration of T-group sessions ranges from a few days to several weeks. The sessions are usually conducted away from the organization, but some occur on university campuses or on the premises of large business organizations. Laboratory training stresses the process rather than the context of training and focuses on attitudinal rather than conceptual training.

The four basic types of training groups are stranger, cousin, brother, and family laboratories. In *stranger* T-groups, members are from different organizations and therefore are unknown to each other before training. An example would be several superintendents from different districts. *Cousin* laboratories consist of members taken from a diagonal slice of an organization, which cuts across two or three vertical hierarchical levels without a superior and subordinate being in the same group. An example would be the coordinator of second-

[29]J. Richard Hackman and Greg R. Oldham, "Development of the Job Diagnostic Survey," *Journal of Applied Psychology*, 60 (1975): 159–170.

[30]For a discussion of laboratory training, see Robert T. Golembiewski, *Handbook of Organizational Consultation* (New York: Marcel Dekker, 2000).

[31]John P. Campbell and Marvin D. Dunnette, "Effectiveness of T-Group Experience in Managerial Training and Development," *Psychological Bulletin*, 70 (1968): 73–104.

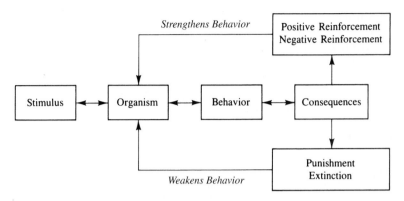

**Figure 8–4**

S-O-B-C Model

Source: Adapted from Fred Luthans, *Organizational Behavior*, 5th ed., © 1989, p. 15. Used by permission of McGraw-Hill, Inc., New York.

ary education and elementary school principals from the same district. *Brother* laboratories include members who occupy similar horizontal roles in an organization but without superiors and subordinates in the same group. For example, a group of principals from the same district would be brothers. In the *family* laboratory, all members belong to the same subunit of an organization. The superintendent of a school district and his administrative cabinet or the principal of a school and its department heads are examples of a family training group.

The trainer may structure the content of the laboratory training by using a number of exercises or management games or follow an unstructured format in which the group develops its own agenda. Robert Blake and Jane Mouton were among the first trainers to modify the unstructured format into an instrumental one.[32]

Stranger laboratory groups with an unstructured format were the classic form of T-groups used during the early beginnings of laboratory training. However, the difficulty encountered in applying interpersonal skills acquired away from the organization to the home-base organization when participants returned has led to the use of cousin and family groups in recent years. In fact, there has been a movement recently away from laboratory training groups and toward team building. This more recent application of T-groups has been exemplified in the work of Chris Argyris, an early proponent of laboratory training.[33] Thus, laboratory training is often used today as part of more complex organizational change strategies.

## Behavior Modification

**Behavior modification** has its roots in B. F. Skinner's theory of operant conditioning, which emphasizes the effect of environmental influences on behavior.[34] More recently, a social learning approach has been suggested as a more comprehensive theoretical foundation for applying behavior modification in organizations.[35] Thus, organizational behavior modification is the process of changing the behavior of an employee by managing the consequences that follow his work behavior.

Fred Luthans's S-O-B-C model provides a useful way of viewing the behavior modification process.[36] Based on a social learning approach, the behavior modification process recognizes the interaction of four parts: S (stimulus), O (organism or employee), B (behavior), and C (consequences) (see Figure 8–4).

**Stimulus**  The S in the model refers to stimulus, which includes internal and external factors, mediated by learning, that determine employee behavior. External factors include organizational structure and organizational and administrative processes interacting with the structure: decision making, control, communication, power, and goal setting. Internal factors include planning, personal goals, self-observation data, stimulus removal, selective stimulus exposure, and self-contracts.[37]

---

[32]Robert R. Blake and Jane S. Mouton, *The Managerial Grid: Leadership Styles for Achieving Production Through People* (Houston: Gulf, 1994).

[33]Chris Argyris, *On Organizational Learning,* 2nd ed. (Cambridge, MA: Blackwell, 1999).

[34]B. F. Skinner, *About Behaviorism* (New York: Knopf, 1974).

[35]Fred Luthans and Robert Kreitner, *Organizational Behavior Modification and Beyond: An Operant and Social Learning Approach* (Glenview, IL: Scott, Foresman, 1985).

[36]Fred Luthans, *Organizational Behavior,* 10th ed. (New York: McGraw-Hill, 2006).

[37]Luthans and Kreitner, *Organizational Behavior Modification and Beyond.*

**Organism**   The *O* in the model refers to the organism, or school employee. The internal and external factors in the situation constitute the organizational environment in which the school employee operates. School employees can be thought of as consisting of cognitive and psychological processes. For example, much of what we discussed about motivating behavior with need theories, expectancy theory, equity theory, goal setting, and management by objectives applies to this part of the model.

**Behavior**   The *B* in the model represents employee behavior. The study of the organizational environment (*S*) and the school employee (*O*) leads to a better understanding of the school employee's behavior — the overt and covert responses to the organizational environment. Behavior includes verbal and nonverbal communication, actions, and the like. In schools we are specifically interested in work behaviors such as performance, attendance, promptness, participation in committees, superordinate-subordinate relations, interaction among colleagues, or leaving the organization.

**Consequences**   The *C* part of the model represents the consequences that result from employee behavior. The study of behavioral consequences can help improve the prediction and control of employee behavior, but this is a very simplified generalization. Social learning theorists place more emphasis on internal states and processes when explaining job behavior than the so-called radical behaviorists.[38] However, approaches such as self-management are insufficient in producing a coordinated organizational behavior modification effort. As shown in the model, behavior is a function of internal and external cues and consequences that follow a given behavior. Some types of consequences strengthen behavior while others weaken it.

**Contingencies of Reinforcement**   Changing the interrelationships among organizational environment (*S*), employee (*O*), behavior (*B*), and consequences (*C*) is referred to as managing the *contingencies of reinforcement*.[39] As Figure 8–4 shows, the consequences that strengthen behavior are positive reinforcement and negative reinforcement. The consequences that weaken behavior are extinction and punishment.

*Positive reinforcement* involves following a desired behavior with the application of a pleasant stimulus, which should increase the probability of the desired behavior. Examples of positive reinforcement in a school setting include promotions, salary increases, merit raises, praise, more desirable work assignments, awards, or simply smiles. All reinforcement strategies, however, are specific to a given individual or situation.

*Negative reinforcement* involves the removal of an unpleasant stimulus on the appearance of a desired behavior, which should increase the probability of that behavior. For example, a football coach of a major university requires all football players to attend an early Sunday morning practice whenever their performance in a game falls below a minimum level. The players strive for a high performance level in the next game to avoid the unpleasant, early Sunday morning practice.

*Extinction* involves removing a reinforcer that is maintaining some undesired behavior. If the behavior is not reinforced, it should gradually be extinguished. For instance, suppose you have an assistant who enjoys talking about her personal life for fifteen or twenty minutes every time you come into the office. In the past, you have been polite and have listened attentively as she related her personal experiences. In essence, you have been positively reinforcing her behavior. To stop her undesired behavior, you must ignore all conversations after exchanging some brief courtesies, turn around, and walk out of the office. This should dissipate the undesired behavior that is interfering with the performance of her work.

*Punishment* involves following an unwanted behavior with the application of some unpleasant stimulus. In theory, this should reduce the probability of the undesired behavior. Examples of punishment include oral reprimands, written warnings, suspensions, demotions, and discharge. While punishment may eliminate undesirable employee behavior in the short run, long-term, sustained use of punishment is dysfunctional to the organization.[40]

**Steps in Organizational Behavior Modification**   Luthans and Kreitner suggest five steps for using organizational behavior modification to change employee-behavior patterns:[41]

---

[38]Robert Kreitner and Fred Luthans, "A Social Learning Approach to Behavioral Management: Radical Behaviorists' Mellowing Out," *Organizational Dynamics*, 13 (1984): 47–65.

[39]B. F. Skinner, *The Behavior of Organisms* (Acton, MA: Copley, 1991).

[40]Janice M. Beyer and Harrison M. Trice, "A Field Study of the Use and Perceived Effects of Discipline in Controlling Work Performance," *Academy of Management Journal*, 27 (1984): 743–764.

[41]Luthans and Kreitner, *Organizational Behavior Modification and Beyond*.

Step 1. *Identify Significant Performance-Related Behaviors.* The principal and the teachers begin by identifying and describing the changes they desire to make. The analysis includes identification of significant performance-related behaviors that can be observed, counted, and specified precisely. The teacher or the principal can do the identification process. In either case, it requires training to identify behaviors for which reinforcement strategies can be used.

Step 2. *Measure Performance-Related Behaviors.* Obtain, prior to learning, baseline measurements of the frequency of the desired target behaviors. Use tally sheets and time sampling to gather the data. In a school setting, select for assessment observed classroom performance, work-assignment completions, participation in committees, student achievement, advisement, publications, absences, service to the community, curriculum writing, and complaints. Establish some preliminary period of assessment as a baseline.

Step 3. *Analyze the Antecedents and Consequences of Behaviors.* The behavior to be changed is often influenced by prior occurrences (antecedents) and has some identifiable consequences. For example, a particularly ineffective teacher may be a case for study. The teacher lacks effective instructional techniques, has poor rapport with students, complains incessantly about administrative policies and procedures, and adversely affects the performance and attitudes of colleagues. During this step, the principal identifies existing contingencies of reinforcement to determine when the behaviors occur, what causes them, and what their consequences are. Effective behavior change in the teacher requires replacement or removal of these reinforcing consequences.

Step 4. *Implement the Change Approach.* Use positive reinforcement, negative reinforcement, extinction, and punishment to change significant performance-related behaviors of teachers or other employees. In other words, develop an intervention strategy, then apply the strategy using suitable contingencies of reinforcement. Finally, maintain the behaviors with appropriate schedules of reinforcement, including variable ratio, fixed ratio, variable interval, and fixed interval.[42]

Step 5. *Evaluate Behavior Change.* Evaluate the effectiveness of behavior modification in four areas:

reaction of the teachers to the approach, learning of the concepts programmed, degree of behavior change that occurs, and impact of behavior change on actual performance. In evaluating the success or failure of the behavior modification program, compare the original baseline measurements with outcome measurements of behavior. If it becomes apparent at Step 5 that the intervention strategy implemented in Step 4 has not resulted in the desired impact, start the process over again at Step 1.

### Transactional Analysis

Eric Berne developed **transactional analysis** for use in psychotherapy.[43] It was further popularized in the best-selling books *Games People Play* and *I'm OK—You're OK.*[44] More recently, managers have used transactional analysis as an organizational change technique.[45]

Transactional analysis is concerned with three areas of analysis: *structural analysis* (the analysis of individual personality); *time structuring* (the analysis of the way people structure their time); and *life scripts* (the analysis of the roles that people learn to play in life). The focus in organizational change has been on structural analysis and time structuring.

**Structural Analysis** The personality of each person is made up of ego states. Berne defines an ego state as a consistent pattern of feeling and experience directly related to a corresponding consistent pattern of behavior.[46] Although school administrators cannot direct ego states, they can observe behavior and from this infer which of the three ego states is operating at any given time. This should help them better understand others in the workplace and the reasons for their behavior.

The three ego states—the Parent, the Adult, and the Child—are common to all people, but the content of each is unique to each individual, based on background and experiences.

■ *The Parent ego state* derives from one's parents or other powerful figures in one's childhood. It is

---

[42]For more information on schedules of reinforcement, see Luthans, *Organizational Behavior.*

[43]Eric Berne, *Transactional Analysis in Psychotherapy* (New York: Ballantine, 1986).

[44]Eric Berne, *Games People Play,* rev. ed. (New York: Ballantine, 1996); Thomas A. Harris, *I'm OK—You're OK* (New York: Avon, 1993).

[45]Charles Albano, *Transactional Analysis on the Job and Communicating with Subordinates* (Ann Arbor, MI: University Microfilms International, 1993).

[46]Eric Berne, *Transactional Analysis in Psychotherapy.*

expressed toward others as nurturing, critical, or standard-setting behavior. A school administrator exhibiting a Parent ego state tends to talk down to subordinates and to treat them like children.

- *The Adult ego state* reflects maturity, objectivity, problem analysis, logic, and rationality. It is oriented toward objective information gathering, careful analysis, generating alternatives, and making logical choices. A school administrator who behaves fairly and objectively in dealing with subordinates is exhibiting an Adult ego state.

- *The Child ego state* derives from one's experiences as a child. This ego state can range from being submissive and conforming to being insubordinate, rebellious, emotional, or perhaps inadequate.

**Time Structuring**    Another focus of transactional analysis is the way in which people structure their time. There are six basic ways to structure time: withdrawal, rituals, pastimes, activities, games, and authenticity.[47]

1. *Withdrawal* can be either physical or psychological. Examples include walking away from an argument (physical), withdrawing to avoid pain and punishment (physical), withdrawing to think through a problem and examine alternatives (psychological), or daydreaming (psychological).

2. *Rituals* are stylized transactions, such as "Good morning, how are you?" Such a rhetorical question suggests the response, "Fine, how are you?" Such interchanges have little meaning except to recognize the other person. Should the receiver of the message actually respond to the question, the sender would be distressed because no answer is expected.

3. *Pastimes* are nonstylized transactions that have a repetitive quality. Discussing the weather or politics during social occasions are examples.

4. *Activities* consist of transactions centered on getting work done. Work fulfills various needs in people, such as recognition and accomplishment. We all know of cases where people die shortly after retirement. Explanations for this phenomenon include people's loss of a constructive way of structuring time and feeling worthwhile and important to society.

5. *Games* are sets of ulterior transactions, repetitive in nature, with well-defined psychological payoff.[48] People use games to avoid authenticity or intimacy. Other books provide several descriptions of games.[49] Therefore, we describe only a few of the more well-known games used in organizations. Superior and subordinate frequently play "Blemish." For example, a principal brings a report to the superintendent, who quickly skims it. Regardless of how good the report is, the superintendent finds one or more "blemishes" in it and points these out to the principal. In this way, the superintendent maintains his power position. This game can be played at any level along the hierarchy (principal–department head, department head–teacher, teacher-student). Another game in which the superior maintains a power position is called, "Yes, but. . . ." For example, the superintendent asks the principals for input in solving a problem. Each suggestion from the principals is followed with a "Yes, but . . ." response from the superintendent. Finally, there is the game of NIGYYSOB (Now I've Got You, You SOB). In this game, one employee lures another into a work situation (for example, a superintendent and principal) in which the victim, the subordinate, is programmed for failure. When the mistake occurs, the superintendent pounces on the principal, which results in embarrassment, a reprimand, or even dismissal.

6. *Authenticity* refers to transactions that are devoid of game playing and exploitation of people.

Andrew Halpin and Don Croft are two early researchers who recognized the significance of authenticity in organizational behavior.[50] The chief consequence of their research on organizational climate was identifying the pivotal importance of authenticity in schools.[51] Later, James Henderson and Wayne Hoy, after an extensive review of the literature, identified three basic aspects of leader authenticity in schools: accountability, nonmanipulation, and salience of self over role.[52]

---

[47]Muriel James, *Perspectives in Transactional Analysis* (San Francisco: International Transactional Association, 1998).

[48]Berne, *Transactional Analysis in Psychotherapy.*

[49]Berne, *Games People Play;* Harris, *I'm OK—You're OK.*

[50]Andrew W. Halpin and Don B. Croft, *The Organizational Climate of Schools* (Chicago: University of Chicago Press, 1963).

[51]Andrew W. Halpin, *Theory and Research in Administration* (New York: Macmillan, 1966).

[52]James E. Henderson and Wayne K. Hoy, "Leader Authenticity: The Development and Test of an Operational Measure," *Educational and Psychological Measurement,* 3 (1983): 63–75.

*Accountability* is the aspect of authenticity that describes the leader as accepting responsibility and admitting errors. The authentic leader accepts responsibility for his own actions as well as those of subordinates and admits mistakes when they are made. On the other hand, inauthentic leaders are unwilling to accept responsibility and admit mistakes; they blame others and circumstances for their shortcomings and failures.

*Nonmanipulation* of subordinates reflects the perception of subordinates that their leader avoids exploiting them. Authentic leaders are seen as those who avoid manipulating others as if they were objects, whereas inauthentic leaders are perceived as dealing with subordinates as if they were things.

*Salience of self over role* refers to the ability to break through the barriers of role stereotyping and behave in congruence with personal and situational needs. Authentic leader behavior is relatively unconstrained by traditional role requirements. Inauthentic leaders, in contrast, adhere to the narrow behavior of their job description, never allowing self to override the routinized behavior of the office.

In a follow-up study, Hoy and William Kupersmith report that perceived leader authenticity was related to commanding trust and loyalty from teachers.[53] They conclude that an atmosphere of trust facilitates organizational change in schools. They reason that one of the major impediments to change in schools is the fear that administration-proposed changes have a hidden agenda and will result in negative consequences for subordinates. "An atmosphere of trust in schools can . . . produce a climate conducive to change." Open and authentic behaviors foster trust, which in turn is likely to reduce resistance to change.[54]

How does transactional analysis relate to organizational change? People are trained in seminars to identify dysfunctional aspects of transactional analysis: time structuring, analysis of transactions, and structural analysis. The assumption is that this knowledge will make school administrators more effective in their relationships with faculty and in collegial relationships among the faculty. Increased effectiveness in interpersonal relations in schools should help to reduce resistance to change efforts proposed by school administrators.

**Redefining the Principalship in Restructuring Schools**  The principal's role is changing as a result of major attempts at school restructuring. Studies document that, while expectations are being added, little has been deleted from the principal's role. (See Administrative Advice 8–3.)

## Group Approaches to Change

In the discussion of individual approaches to change, we focused on improving a department, school, or school district by making its members more effective individually. However, educational institutions are more than an aggregate of individuals. Effective school performance depends on the ability of individual members to operate as effective groups.

Now we focus on approaches to change that aim at improving the performance of groups: role analysis technique, intergroup problem solving, process consultation, survey feedback, and strategic planning.

### Role Analysis Technique

Ishwar Dayal and John Thomas are usually credited with the development of the **role analysis technique** over thirty years ago.[55] The technique clarifies role expectations and obligations of team members. In schools people fill different specialized roles: for example, board of education, superintendent, principals, teachers, and other specialists. This division of labor brings about the school district's goals. In many school districts, people lack a clear understanding of what is expected of them and the types of support they can expect from other personnel, which can hinder performance. The role analysis technique can be used in new teams in which initial roles need to be analyzed, as well as in established teams in which role ambiguity exists. In a series of steps, role incumbents and team members define and delineate their roles.

**Step 1: Defining Roles**  Each person in succession defines his role, its place in the school district, the rationale for its existence, and its place in achieving the

[53]Wayne K. Hoy and William Kupersmith, "Principal Authenticity and Faculty Trust: Key Elements in Organizational Behavior," *Planning and Changing*, 15 (1984): 80–88.

[54]Ibid., p. 87.

[55]Ishwar Dayal and John M. Thomas, "Operation KPE: Developing a New Organization," *Journal of Applied Behavioral Science*, 4 (1968): 473–506.

## Administrative Advice 8–3

### Redefining the Role of the Principal in Restructuring Schools

The role changes of principals in restructuring schools can be grouped under three headings: leading from the center, enabling teacher success, and extending the school community.

■ *Leading from the Center.* Attempts to reshape power relationships is at the core of a redefinition of the principalship in restructuring schools. Two tasks are involved in these redesigned power relationships: delegating responsibilities and developing collaborative decision-making processes. Studies indicate the difficulty with empowerment of faculty experienced by both the organization and the community. Another difficulty for principals is their willingness to become a facilitator or equal participant in shared decision making.

■ *Enabling Teacher Success.* Principals in schools undergoing fundamental reform initiatives perform five functions: helping formulate a shared vision; developing a network of relationships both internally and externally; allocating resources consistent with the vision; providing information needed to implement change effectively; and promoting teacher development in preparation for and throughout the change effort.

■ *Extending the School Community.* Research indicates that the boundary-spanning function of the principal is enhanced as a result of school change efforts. Two tasks form the foundation of this boundary-spanning function: promoting the school and working with school site councils. More of the principal's time in restructuring schools is being directed toward public relations and promoting the school's image. Principals in restructuring schools are involved to a greater degree in working with site-based councils: providing resources, maintaining ongoing communication, consulting with them before decisions are made, and fostering cohesion among council members.

Source: Adapted from Joseph Murphy, "Redefining the Principalship in Restructuring Schools," *NASSP Bulletin*, 78 (1994): 94–99. Used by permission.

---

overall goals of the district. The entire team openly discusses these specifications, which are listed on a board. Behaviors are added and deleted until everyone is satisfied with their defined roles.

**Step 2: Examining Expectations** Each role incumbent lists her expectations of the other roles in the group that most affect the incumbent's own role performance. The entire group then discusses, modifies, and agrees on these expectations.

Then the group discusses what it expects from each role incumbent. Finally, the group and each role incumbent discuss, modify, and agree on these expectations of others.

**Step 3: Summarizing Roles** Each role incumbent makes a summary of the job as it has been defined. This role profile represents a compilation of the discussions in Steps 1 and 2. According to Dayal and Thomas, the role profile "consists of (a) a set of activities classified as to the prescribed and discretionary elements of the role, (b) the obligation of the role to each role in its set,

and (c) the expectations of this role from others in its set . . . [and] provides a comprehensive understanding of each individual's 'role space.' "[56]

Many consultants have had success with the role analysis technique because it constitutes a nonthreatening activity with high payoff for team members. Team members like the technique because it allows them to know what other people in the school district are doing and how that relates to their own roles. Furthermore, because of the public exposure and scrutiny of each role in the school district, role analysis ensures commitment to these roles.

### Intergroup Problem Solving

A school is a composite of various units or groups. In a high school, there are several academic departments: English, social studies, mathematics, science, and so on. In an elementary school, there may be grade-level divi-

---

[56]Ibid., p. 488.

sions, teams, or departments. It is important that these groups perceive their goals as being congruent with the goals of the school. Occasionally, groups or units of the school come into conflict. Similar conflicts often develop in school districts between line and staff, central office and school buildings, and union and management.

Research has identified the dynamics of intergroup conflict.[57] The competitive nature of groups can affect the total productivity of a school or school district. During competition each group becomes more cohesive. Internal differences are set aside, and members strengthen their loyalty and identification with their group. Group members view each other as more and more similar and other groups as more and more different. Each group becomes more structured and places demand for conformity on its members in order to present a united front against the other group(s). Distortions in perception of the other group(s) come into play to justify attitudes concerning other group(s). In other words, each group views the other as the enemy, and hostility increases while communication decreases.

The negative consequences of intergroup conflict cause school administrators to seek resolution. One method for resolving such intergroup conflict is **intergroup problem solving**.[58] The following represent the general pattern of activities.

**Step 1: Meeting Jointly**   The administrators of the two groups (or the total membership) meet with a consultant, who asks if the relations between them are hostile and can be improved. If the groups confirm this, the intergroup problem-solving process begins. (The use of an outside change agent is highly recommended because in these situations a mediating influence may be necessary to create a common ground between the groups.)

**Step 2: Identifying the Problem(s)**   The two groups meet in separate rooms and develop two lists. In one list, they provide their perceptions, attitudes, feelings, and opinions of the other group. The list includes answers to questions such as: What is the other group like? What do they do that upsets us? In the second list, the group attempts to predict what the other group is saying about them. The list includes answers to questions such

as: What does the other group dislike about us? How does the other group see us?

**Step 3: Sharing Information**   The two groups come together to share the information on their respective lists. Group A reads its list of how it sees Group B and what it dislikes about Group B. Then Group B does the same. The change agent does not permit discussion to take place during this step; the two groups can pose and respond to only questions of clarification. Next, Group A reads its list of what it expected Group B would say about it, and Group B reads its list of what it expected Group A would say.

**Step 4: Analyzing Information**   The two groups return to their separate rooms to discuss what they have learned about themselves and the other group. Frequently, the groups discover that the hostility and friction between them rests on misperceptions and miscommunication, as revealed by the lists. The problems between the two groups are seen to be fewer than perceived initially. After this discussion, each group is given the task of preparing a list of priority issues that remain unresolved between the two groups.

**Step 5: Resolving the Problem(s)**   The two groups meet together again to share and discuss their lists with each other. After this discussion, both groups work together to prepare one list of the unresolved issues and problems. Also, together they generate action steps for resolving the issues and assign responsibilities for the actions. These steps indicate who will do what and when.

**Step 6: Following Through**   As a follow-up to the intergroup problem-solving strategy, it is usually desirable to have a meeting of the two groups or their leaders to determine whether the action steps have occurred.

## Process Consultation

**Process consultation** is a set of activities, provided by a consultant, that helps members of an organization to perceive, understand, and act on process events that occur in their work environment.[59] The process consultant helps the organization's participants obtain insight into

---

[57]Pasmore, *Research in Organizational Change and Development.*

[58]Robert R. Blake and Jane S. Mouton, *Solving Costly Organizational Conflicts: Achieving Intergroup Trust, Cooperation, and Teamwork* (San Francisco: Jossey-Bass, 1984).

[59]Edgar H. Schein, *Process Consultation*, vol. 1, *Its Role in Organization Development*, 3rd ed. (Reading, MA: Addison Wesley Longman, 1999).

the organizational processes, of the consequences of these processes, and of the mechanisms by which they can be changed. The ultimate goal is to help the organization diagnose its problems and generate a solution. The consultant may be a competent member of the organization skilled in process activities or a professionally trained outside consultant.

Process consultation is aimed primarily at five important organizational processes: communication, functional roles of group members, decision making, group norms and growth, and leadership. The process consultant observes organizational processes firsthand, by sitting in on meetings, observing negotiations between employees or groups, and observing daily activities.

**Communication** School administrators must understand the nature and style of the communication process in the organization. The process consultant can help the administrator understand the organization's communication system. In observing a communication pattern, the process consultant examines who communicates with whom, for how long and how often, what is communicated, and how messages are transmitted. The examination of the nature and style of communication, at both the overt and covert levels and nonverbal communication patterns, can be informative. The process consultant records this information in a log. In this way, the consultant provides nonevaluative-descriptive feedback to the school district concerning possible communication problems, thereby helping the district find solutions.

**Functional Roles of Group Members** School administrators need to understand role functioning among group members. Three functional roles that need to be performed if a group is to be effective are self-related activities such as self-identity, influence and power; task-related activities such as obtaining and providing information, coordinating, setting standards, and evaluating; and group-maintenance activities, which include encouraging, supporting, harmonizing, and compromising.

The process consultant observes the different roles that organizational members assume when they are interacting in a group. For example, preoccupation with self-interests or power struggles can be dysfunctional to school district effectiveness. And an overemphasis on task-related activities to the exclusion of sufficient group maintenance activities can result in organizational goal suffering as well. The process consultant can help

the school district identify and diagnose these group dysfunctions.

**Decision Making** An important component of effective groups is decision making. Effective groups identify problems, examine alternatives, make decisions, and implement decisions. There are several methods of making decisions. One method is to ignore a suggestion made by a group member, that is, refuse to discuss it. This approach has dysfunctional consequences for the organization. Another is to place decision-making power in the hands of the person in authority. Such decisions are made by minority rule; for example, the leader makes a decision and turns to subordinates who willingly comply. A third method is by majority rule or consensus. The process consultant can help school districts understand how decisions are made, the consequences of different decision-making methods, and how to diagnose which method may be most effective in a given situation.

**Group Norms and Growth** School administrators need to understand the process of group norms and how these norms affect group functioning. Groups of people who work together develop group norms or standards of behavior. For instance, there may be an explicit norm that group members can express their ideas freely, but the implicit norm also suggests that a member does not contradict the ideas of certain other (powerful) group members. The process consultant can help the school district understand the group's norms and the effect of these norms on group functioning.

**Leadership** The process consultant can help the group understand different leadership styles and help school administrators adjust their style to better fit the situation. The idea is to enable the administrator to get a better understanding of her own behavior and the group's reaction to that behavior. Such knowledge can help the administrator change behavior to fit the situation.[60]

Process consultation, then, is aimed at facilitating organizational change by helping educational administrators to become aware of the processes of change, the consequences of these processes, and the mechanisms by which they can be changed.

---

[60]Jean Holms Mills, *Making Sense of Organizational Change* (London: Routledge, 2002).

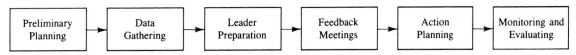

**Figure 8–5**

Steps Involved in Survey Feedback

## Survey Feedback

**Survey feedback** is an organizational approach to change that involves collecting data (usually by means of a survey questionnaire) from members of a work group or whole organization, analyzing and summarizing the data into an understandable form, feeding back the data to those who generated it, and using the data to diagnose problems and develop action plans for problem solving.[61]

Similar to process consultation in some respects, survey feedback places greater emphasis on the collection of valid data and less emphasis on the interpersonal processes of individual work groups. Instead, survey feedback focuses on the relationships between administrative personnel and their subordinates at all levels of hierarchy.

If used properly, attitude surveys can be a powerful tool in school-improvement efforts. Change agents who use survey feedback point out that most attitude surveys are not used properly. At best, most give higher-level administrators some data for changing practices or provide a benchmark against which to compare trends. At worst, they are filed away with little consequence for school improvement.

Survey feedback has two major phases. Collecting data is only part of the process; providing appropriate feedback to the organization's members is equally significant. Figure 8–5 outlines the six steps involved in survey feedback, which are described next.[62]

**Step 1: Preliminary Planning** Organizational members at the top of the hierarchy are involved in the preliminary planning. Surveys used in organizational change efforts are usually constructed around a theoretical model. This allows the user to rate himself or the organization in terms of the theory. When the approach involves a theoretical model, commitment to the model must be obtained. If top management does not accept the theoretical model undergirding the survey, the approach will likely fail no matter how effective the effort is toward gathering data.

**Step 2: Data Gathering** A questionnaire is administered to all organizational members. The best-known survey-feedback instrument is the one developed by the Institute for Social Research (ISR) at the University of Michigan.[63] The questionnaire generally asks the respondents' perceptions on such organizational areas as communications, goal emphasis, leadership styles, decision making, coordination between departments, and employee attitudes. The ISR instrument, a standardized questionnaire, permits the additions of questions that may be of interest to the organization under study. However, many organizations, including schools, develop their own questionnaires that are specific to their individual needs rather than relying on a standardized instrument.

**Step 3: Leader Preparation** Once the data have been obtained from the questionnaire, an external or internal change agent helps school administrators understand the data and instructs them on how to present the data to the work group. Data are then fed back to the top administrative team and down through the hierarchy in functional teams.

**Step 4: Feedback Meetings** Each superior conducts group feedback meetings with his subordinates in which the data are discussed and in which subordinates are asked to help interpret the data, plans are made for making constructive changes, and plans are made for introducing the information at the next lower level of subordinates.

[61]Edward J. Conlon and Lawrence O. Short, "Survey Feedback as a Large-Scale Change Device: An Empirical Examination," *Group and Organization Studies*, 9 (1984): 399–416.

[62]David G. Bowers and Jerome L. Franklin, *Survey-Guided Development: Data-Based Organizational Change* (La Jolla, CA: University Associates, 1977).

[63]James C. Taylor and David G. Bowers, *Survey of Organizations: A Machine Scored Standardized Questionnaire Instrument* (Ann Arbor: Institute for Social Research, University of Michigan, 1972).

**Table 8–1    Comparison of Strategic Planning and Long-Range Planning**

| Strategic Planning | Long-Range Planning |
|---|---|
| 1. Assumes an open system in which organizations must constantly change as the needs of the larger society change. | 1. Assumes a closed system within which short-range plans or blueprints are developed. |
| 2. Focuses on the process of planning, building a vision, external environment, organizational capacity, staff and community education. | 2. Focuses on the final blueprint of a plan, internal analysis. |
| 3. Is done by a small group of planners with widespread involvement of stakeholders. | 3. Is done by a planning department or professionals. |
| 4. Uses current and projected trends to make current decisions. | 4. Uses existing data on which to project future plans. |
| 5. Emphasizes changes outside the organization, organizational values, and proactive action. | 5. Emphasizes internal changes, planning methods, and inside-out planning. |
| 6. Focuses on what decision is appropriate today, based on an understanding of the situation five years from now. | 6. Focuses on organizational goals and objectives five years from now. |
| 7. Depends upon intuitive and creative decision making as to how to guide the organization over time in an ever-changing environment and an organization-wide process that anticipates the future, makes decisions, and behaves in light of an agreed-on vision. | 7. Depends on detailed and interrelated data sets, agency plans, and extrapolations of current budgets. |

Source: Adapted from Shirley D. McCune and Ronald Brandt, *Guide to Strategic Planning for Educators* © 1986, p. 35. Used by permission of Association for Supervision and Curriculum Development, Alexandria, VA.

For example, the superintendent of schools and the major divisional assistant superintendents meet and compare the survey findings for each of the district's functional areas — such as personnel, business, instruction, and research and development. Each assistant superintendent can see the summary data for her division and for the total school district. Problems unique to each division, the implications of the findings, and themes common to the total organization are discussed.

The next feedback meetings occur as each assistant superintendent meets with building principals or other subordinates to discuss survey data specific to each. The process continues until department heads discuss with teachers or other school personnel the issues raised in each work group by the survey data.

**Step 5: Action Planning**    The fact that a discrepancy exists between the actual state of the organization and the ideal theoretical model does not in and of itself provide sufficient motivation to change. Organizational members must be made aware of how the change can be effected. Thus, resources are allocated to implement

the changes in accordance with the needs indicated by the group feedback meetings and the systematic diagnosis of the data by the change agent and top-level administrators.

**Step 6: Monitoring and Evaluating**    The change agent helps organizational members develop skills that are necessary to move the organization toward their goals. Some of these skills include listening, giving and receiving personal feedback, general leadership techniques, problem solving, goal setting, and diagnosing group processes. Additional questionnaires are administered and analyzed to monitor the change process. Finally, the school district is formally reassessed to evaluate change, again using questionnaire data.

### Strategic Planning

Constantly changing social and economic conditions affect organizations, necessitating the imperative to plan ahead. Organizations must anticipate the turbulence of future years and plan processes for achieving their ob-

---

## PRO/CON Debate

### Mandated Staff Development

Staff development proponents argue that change begins with people. Many planned change efforts include provisions for intense, long-term staff development. In some states, practicing educators must participate in ongoing professional development to earn and/or keep their licenses to teach or administer.

**Question:** Does mandated staff development enhance organizational change?

### Arguments PRO

1. Mandates are the best way to cause change to occur because the power of the legal system is harnessed. New laws or regulations guarantee that people conform to changes that they might not like.

2. Teachers may not choose to learn what they need to learn. A teacher's knowledge base, like that of all professionals, eventually becomes obsolete. The organization must guarantee that teachers' professional knowledge is current if appropriate change is to occur.

3. In a factory, it is cost-effective to maintain equipment. In a home, it is cost-effective to make repairs. In education, which is labor-intensive, it is cost-effective to require ongoing, continual professional development just to maintain the basic unit, the teacher.

### Arguments CON

1. Mandates are only as strong as the compliance system behind them. While people can be forced to attend staff development sessions, there is no cost-effective way to insist that the people perform differently when they return to their classrooms or schools.

2. Educators are highly trained professionals. Most have many degrees and licenses. When teachers need more professional knowledge, they will identify and address that need. Teachers are lifelong learners who model learning for their students.

3. Staff development is expensive. Not only must districts bear the training costs, they must also pay for substitute teachers who replace teachers in classrooms and administrators in offices. The government should not mandate unreimbursed expenses.

---

jectives. Implicit in these processes is environmental scanning.[64]

**Strategic planning** involves identifying the mission of an organization; recognizing internal and external forces that impact the organization; analyzing those forces to determine the effects they have on the organization's ability to accomplish its mission; developing strategies for dealing with them, including a framework for improvement and restructuring of programs, management, participation, and evaluation; and instituting action plans to carry out those strategies and achieve the organization's mission.[65]

Many authors do not discriminate between long-range planning and strategic planning. Strategic planning goes beyond a mechanistic series of planning procedures. Its power lies in its capacity to create dissonance

in people, upset traditional views, identify new possibilities, and pose new questions. In this sense, "strategic planning is a management process for changing and transforming organizations."[66]

Shirley McCune outlines the structural differences between strategic planning and long-range planning. Although both types of planning are concerned with the future, long-range planning typically begins with an assumption that an organization will remain comparatively stable; it seeks to develop internal goals and projections based on that assumption. Strategic planning, on the other hand, begins with a recognition of the external environment as an important consideration of the planning process, and the actions initiated to effect plans are based on an analysis, synthesis, and evaluation of this environment. Table 8–1 shows other differences between strategic planning and long-range planning.

---

[64]Peter F. Drucker, *Leading in a Time of Change: What Will It Take to Lead Tomorrow?* (New York: Wiley, 2001).

[65]William J. Cook, *Bill Cook's Strategic Planning for America's Schools,* 3rd ed. (Arlington, VA: American Association of School Administrators, 1995).

[66]Shirley D. McCune and Ronald Brandt, *Guide to Strategic Planning for Educators* (Alexandria, VA: Association for Supervision and Curriculum Development, 1986), p. 32.

Business has devoted a great deal of attention to strategic planning.[67] Only recently has any emphasis been placed on the study of strategic planning in school settings. In a study of 127 school districts in Kentucky, researchers found relationships between strategic planning and student achievement in reading, language arts, and mathematics at several grade levels. None of the relationships was strong, however. In addition, the researchers found a direct relationship between strategic planning and both school district wealth and per-pupil expenditures. That is, the higher the assessed property value per child and the greater the percentage of revenue from local sources supporting education, the more likely the school district is engaged in strategic planning efforts.[68]

## Summary

1. We have described the change process in schools using an open systems framework. An open system has three basic, recurring cycles: inputs, a transformation process, and outputs. The internal and external environment both have an impact on the three basic cycles of the open systems model.

2. Schools face pressures for change, including accountability, changing demographics, staffing shortages, changing technology and knowledge explosion, and processes and people.

3. Schools also resist change. Resistance can stem from several sources, including interference with need fulfillment, fear of the unknown, threats to power and influence, knowledge and skill obsolescence, organizational structure, limited resources, and collective bargaining agreements.

4. Methods that schools can use to reduce resistance to change include participation, communication, support, rewards, planning, and coercion.

5. The major approaches to change can be classified as individual and group. Individual approaches to change include job enrichment, laboratory training, behavior modification, and transactional analysis. Group approaches to change include role analysis

technique, intergroup problem solving, process consultation, survey feedback, and strategic planning.

6. In practice, the approaches are generally used in combination to effect organizational change in schools.

## Key Terms

open systems
force-field analysis
job enrichment
laboratory training
behavior modification
transactional analysis
role analysis technique
intergroup problem solving
process consultation
survey feedback
strategic planning

## Discussion Questions

1. Explain why the change agent must consider the open systems framework when considering organizational change efforts.

2. Using force-field analysis, diagnose your school district, university, or other educational institution. Describe the pressures for change and the forces resisting change. Which forces would lend themselves to change? Which would make your organization more effective?

3. Discuss several methods that organizations can use to overcome resistance to change.

4. Based on your own experience, describe an educational institution that needs change. Which of the approaches to change presented in this chapter would you use to make the organization more effective?

5. Explain why schools normally need to use a combination of approaches (i.e., individual and group) in order to effect change. Cite examples where appropriate.

## Suggested Readings

Bartunek, Jean M. *Organizational and Educational Change: The Life and Role of a Change Agent Group* (Mahwah, NJ: Erlbaum, 2003). Jean M.

---

[67] Roger A. Kaufman, *Strategic Planning for Success: Aligning People, Performance, and Payoff* (New York: Wiley, 2003).

[68] Vickie Basham and Fred C. Lunenburg, "Strategic Planning, Student Achievement, and School District Financial and Demographic Factors," *Planning and Changing*, 20 (1989): 158–171.

Bartunek has written an excellent scholarly book on organizational and educational change. Using a joint insider/outsider approach, she tells the story of a change agent group—a group of teachers—that was creating change in its organization setting, a Network of Independent Schools. The group's focus was on empowerment and professional development for teachers in the Network. The book describes virtually everything that happened in the group over its first seven years and summarizes what happened during its final two years. It explores the identity, work, and evolution of change agent groups in organizations, with particular emphasis on teachers and educational change. Through the book's extensive quotations and narrative account, the reader enters into the world of the teacher group studied over the course of its nine-year history.

Darling-Hammond, Linda, Amy M. Hightower, Jennifer L. Husbands, Jeanette R. LaFors, Viki M. Young, and Carl Christopher. *Instructional Leadership for Systemic Change* (Lanham, MD: Rowman & Littlefield, 2005). This book provides a comprehensive description of how a major urban school reform initiative was undertaken and describes potential political conflicts and implementation issues.

Fullan, Michael, and Clif St. Germain. *Learning Places: A Field Guide for Improving the Context of Schooling* (Thousand Oaks, CA: Corwin Press, 2006). This inspiring approach to school change provides readers with practical and proven practices for giving staying power to school improvement initiatives. Organized to make learning contagious, this user-friendly guide helps create a culture of learning that promotes the simultaneous development of students, teachers, and parents—addressing specific ways to maximize study groups, student data, classroom walk-throughs, and more.

Kimmelman, Paul L. *Implementing NCLB: Creating a Knowledge Framework to Support School Improvement* (Thousand Oaks, CA: Corwin Press, 2006). Meeting the requirements of NCLB is a monumental task. In a concise, straightforward manner, author Paul L. Kimmelman shows readers how to overcome this challenge by building organizational capacity through a knowledge model. This model provides a simple but effective framework for evidence-based continuous improvement that complies with the fundamental underpinnings of NCLB.

Sirotnik, Kenneth A. *Holding Accountability Accountable: What Ought to Matter in Public Education* (New York: Teachers College Press, 2004). Kenneth Sirotnik asserts that however well-intentioned, past and current accountability practices in public education are "miseducative, misdirected, and misanthropic." In this provocative book, well-respected educators join Sirotnik to provide critical analyses and sophisticated perspectives on prevailing high-stakes testing practices.

Strike, Kenneth A. *Ethical Leadership in Schools: Creating Community in an Environment of Accountability* (Thousand Oaks, CA: Corwin Press, 2006). *Ethical Leadership in Schools* teaches principals and aspiring principals the concepts that inform ethical choices in leadership roles. Using brief vignettes, Strike explores common situations that principals are likely to encounter and presents questions and issues to help them determine the ethical path.

Sunderman, Gail L., James S. Kim, and Gary Orfield. *NCLB Meets School Realities: Lessons from the Field* (Thousand Oaks, CA: Corwin Press, 2005). Based on original research by The Civil Rights Project at Harvard University, this text details how NCLB is put into practice, the issues it raises, how it affects minority youth, and how teachers view NCLB's efficacy. This book uses data from the field on the implementation of NCLB to recommend policy changes that will help achieve the law's goal—ensuring that all students learn.

# 9. The Federal and State Government and Education

## FOCUSING QUESTIONS

1 How has the federal role in education changed in recent years?

2 What are the differences among dual federalism, national federalism, and the new federalism?

3 In what way did national policy become more closely linked to education after Sputnik?

4 How has the national reform movement in education affected local schools?

5 What are the different roles and responsibilities of the governor, state legislature, and state courts in deciding school policy?

6 What are the major functions of the state board of education, state department of education, and chief state school officer?

7 How can the state reform movement be improved?

8 How do the federal and state roles in education differ?

---

We attempt to answer these questions by first exploring the relationship between the federal government and education, and then that between state government and education. We examine congressional influence on education and the various federal programs designed to enhance learning. We consider the role of the federal courts and also discuss the national reform movement in education. We discuss the roles that state officials — the governor, legislature, and courts — have in determining policy. Next we examine the structure of state boards, departments of education, and chief executive officers. Finally, we explore the state reform movement in education.

---

## The Federal Role in Education

A national system of education does not exist in the United States in the same sense that it does in England, France, Germany, Japan, India, or Russia. Education in the United States is considered both a state and a local function; there are fifty different state systems, and many differences exist among local school systems within the same state. In total, there are some 15,000 different local school districts — each with its own philosophy and goals.

The U.S. Constitution makes no mention of public education, but the Tenth Amendment to the Constitution reserves to the states all powers not specifically delegated to the federal government or prohibited to the states by the Constitution. This amendment is the basis for allocating primary legal responsibility for public education to the states. However, the states have delegated to the local districts the responsibility of the practical day-to-day operation of school districts.

The schools have always been a provincial domain of the towns and cities of the United States, rooted in the colonial tradition of the nation, but the federal government has always had some say in public education. Beginning with the land grants that antedated the U.S. Constitution and highlighted by the welfare clause of the Constitution (Article I, Section 8), which gives Congress the power to tax for the general good and for broad social purposes, education has always been the federal government's concern. Although education is not specifically identified in Article I, the language is general enough for the government to use public tax monies to support the nation's schools and school programs and to enact educational laws for the welfare of the people.

## Changing Roles in the Federal Government and Education

To fully understand the federal government and its relations with the schools, one must understand that there has been a gradual shift from the historical **separation of powers** between the federal government and states toward the federal government's playing a greater role in education and social areas. Recently, there has been a trend toward greater decentralization at the federal level and sharing of educational responsibilities and functions between the federal government and states. At the same time, there is a countertrend to develop national goals, standards, and high-stake testing—a shift toward greater nationalization of the curriculum, as part of the reform movement to upgrade education.[1]

The first 150 years of U.S. education can be considered the period of **dual federalism,** whereby the founding fathers' majority view to limit the federal government at all levels and most functions prevailed. During this period, federal programs and activities in education were passive and uncoordinated. Sometime around the Great Depression and the Roosevelt administration the next period, called **national federalism,**[2] evolved. Economic and social circumstances of the day called for greater federal intervention, first in the area of labor legislation and relief acts in education and public works; followed by educational legislation for the Cold War and Sputnik period of the late 1940s and 1950s; and then the War on Poverty and civil rights movement that affected schools and society in the 1960s and 1970s. What became apparent during this national federalism period was that national action and national coordination of programs and activities were needed to resolve many problems that extended beyond the boundaries of state and local governments. National identity and national welfare were at stake, and there were dramatic increases in federal commitment to education.

### Current Period: 1980s to 2000+

Starting in the 1980s under President Ronald Reagan and continued by President George Bush, a **new federalism** evolved, which called for a dramatic shift in federal policy and programs. Driven by a belief that the federal government was too meddlesome and involved in too many activities and regulations, Reagan and Bush reduced federal funds (vis-à-vis inflation), activities, and regulations in education as well as in other social sectors of the economy.[3] In addition, monetary and program responsibilities were shifted to state (and local) agencies. Federal rules and regulations governing education were revoked or more loosely enforced. President Bill Clinton acknowledged, at least implicitly, the limits of federal

---

[1]Phillip C. Schlechty, *Inventing Better Schools* (San Francisco: Jossey-Bass, 2001); Marc S. Tucker and Judy B. Codding, *Standards for Our Schools* (San Francisco: Jossey-Bass, 1998).

[2]Roald F. Campbell et al., *The Organization of American Schools,* 6th ed. (Columbus, OH: Merrill, 1990). (It should be noted, however, that Campbell and his associates put the beginning of this second period at the time of the Civil War and the "due process" clause of the Fourteenth Amendment.) Also see Kenneth Leithwood et al., *Making Schools Smarter,* 3rd ed. (Thousand Oaks, CA: Corwin, 2006); Kenneth A. Strike et al., *The Ethics of School Administration* (New York: Teachers College Press, Columbia University, 2005).

[3]Norman Amaker, "Reagan Record on Civil Rights," *Urban Institute Policy and Research Report,* 18 (1988): 15–16; Dennis P. Doyle, "The White House and School House," *Phi Delta Kappan,* 74 (1992): 129; Allan C. Ornstein, "The Changing Federal Role in Education," *Kappa Delta Pi Record,* 21 (1985): 85–88.

activity in education, although he believed that government could solve social and economic problems.[4]

The new federalism showed up in the Reagan-Bush I and II administrations despite the rhetoric about the need to bolster education and human capital. First, there was a shift in priorities from human, social, and educational concerns to big business and military interests. This shift showed up in their lack of formal policy regarding education and in the belief that the federal government should be involved less, not more, in the education of the nation's children and youth. It also showed up in the Clinton administration with Clinton's support of choice and voucher programs, in his belief as well as his predecessor's belief in the private sector to improve education.

During the Clinton administration, new philanthropists and donors—corporate leaders such as Jim Barksdale, Michael Dell, Bill Gates, Mike Milken, and the Walton family—began to fill a vacuum in federal funding and provided discretionary money for school reform. Under the Bush II administration, the private donor trend was accelerated. By 2002 the top two education givers were Bill Gates and Walton foundations—replacing the traditional foundations such as Ford, Kellogg, Packard, and Rockefeller—all of which fell off the top fifty private donor list.[5]

Although the Clinton administration instilled the concept of higher standards for *all* children, many educators objected to the standards movement. The administration also sought to align federal programs with state reform and accountability plans, and to enhance the idea of a federal–state partnership,[6] opposite to the thinking of the Reagan and Bush I administrations, which sought to *deregulate* or reduce the federal enforcement of rules and regulations and *decentralize* or reduce federal intrusion into what should be a state or local responsibility.

Clinton's second term reflected a national consensus or demand to increase the national role in education.

Education would remain a local and state responsibility, but there was now a sense of a national priority in education and increased acceptance of a federal-state partnership. During the Clinton administration, the emphasis was on accountability and testing, smaller class sizes, improving teaching and increasing the teaching force, connecting classrooms to the Internet, preparing teachers to use technology, improving reading programs, and upgrading science and math programs. By the time the Clinton administration came to an end, forty-nine states had established state standards and/or testing programs.[7]

During the Reagan and Bush I administrations the big-city school districts were shortchanged. Federal monies were shifted to the states to dispense to the local schools, under the guise of *deemphasizing* the federal role in education and shifting more responsibility to the states. For example, by the mid-1990s only 20 percent of block grant monies (funds earmarked by the federal government for the states) were being dedicated to compensatory and basic skills programs.[8] The Clinton administration was unable to change this shift in federal funding, and Title I schools continued to be underfunded. Despite the huge growth in the economy during the 1990s, millions of low-income and minority families were left behind, trapped by poverty. Similarly, the children of the poor were systematically left behind in obtaining a quality education, as evidenced by achievement gaps between white and minority students and between middle-class and lower-class students.[9]

---

[4]Evans Clinchy, "The Educationally Challenged American School District," *Phi Delta Kappan*, 80 (1998): 272–277; Dorothy Rich, "What Educators Need to Explain to the Public," *Phi Delta Kappan*, 87 (2005): 154.

[5]Frederick M. Hess, "Inside the Gift Horse's Mouth: Philanthropy and School Reform," *Phi Delta Kappan*, 87 (2005): 131–137.

[6]Richard W. Riley, "Education Reform Through Standards and Partnerships, 1993–2000," *Phi Delta Kappan*, 83 (2002): 700–707.

[7]Riley, "Education Reform Through Standards and Partnerships, 1993–2000"; Michael S. Trevisan, "The States' Role in Ensuring Assessment Competence," *Phi Delta Kappan*, 83 (2002): 766–771.

[8]*Digest of Education Statistics 1998* (Washington, DC: U.S. Government Printing Office, 1999), table 365, p. 416. Also see John F. Jennings, "Title I: Its Legislative History and Its Promise," *Phi Delta Kappan*, 81 (2000): 516–522. Also see Richard Rothstein, *Class and Schools: Using Social, Economic, and Educational Reform to Close the Black–White Achievement Gap* (New York: Teachers College Press, Columbia University, 2004).

[9]John E. Chubb and Tom Loveless (eds.), *Bridging the Achievement Gap* (Washington, DC: Brookings Institution, 2002); Christopher Jencks and Meredith Phillips (eds.), *The Black and White Test Score Gap* (Washington, DC: Brookings Institution, 1998); Gary Orfield and Mindy Kornhaber (eds.), *Raising Standards or Raising Barriers: Inequality and High Stakes Testing in Public Education* (Washington, DC: Brookings Institution, 2001).

The Bush II administration adopted a national accountability and testing program. As a result, the reauthorization in 2001 of the Elementary and Secondary School Act required a series of annual tests for each state in grades 3 through 8, with timetables for improvement. Federal funding now comes with some leverage to expect improvement, along with penalties for not achieving target benchmarks (see Table 9–4).

Whereas partisan politics reduced Clinton's ability to implement certain education policies that would have increased the federal role in education, George W. Bush was able to get passed the No Child Left Behind Act, ushering in a new era of federal involvement in education. To what extent Rod Paige (the former head of the Department of Education) played a role in passing the act is impossible to determine, and only a few people including Bush and Paige really know. But Paige was a key player because of his ability to communicate with liberal senators (such as Kennedy, Kohl, Shermer, and Feinstein), and therefore he managed to enhance the role of the Department of Education.

As a part of this new federalism, beginning with the Clinton administration and accelerated by the Bush II administration, the **national standards movement** has been gaining momentum. This movement shows a deepening concern for declining student scores on national and international achievement tests and for the declining quality of the teaching workforce as evidenced by the difficulty of a large percentage of entry teachers in passing basic skill tests.[10] There is also concern for investment in human capital and the nation's lack of academic international competitiveness. A new consensus is developing—one that promotes national needs and goals as more important than local or pluralistic needs and goals, supports more rigorous teacher training and national testing and professional standards for teachers, and seeks a common and traditional core of subjects, content, and values in the traditional mode of the arts and sciences.

George W. Bush continued the idea by requiring statewide goals and adequate improvement over time, along with corrective action for school districts that are unable to meet state standards. Teachers and principals are able to use test data to make informed decisions for improving student performance under the new federal guidelines. Schools identified for improvement or corrective action must provide parents with the option of enrolling their children in another public school, including an alternative or charter school, and the school district must provide transportation funds, as well as funds for tutoring low-income students who fail to meet standards.[11]

Within the context of nationalization of standards, some critics are asking: Why raise standards if students cannot meet them? Why talk about a nationalized set of goals or curriculum when the focus has always been on local control of the schools and when there is little agreement on goals, standards, or requirements among the fifty states and more than 15,000 school districts? Why talk about a national commitment to educational reform when the federal government is reducing educational spending in real dollars?

### Clarifying the Federal Role in Education

The federal government's role in education is compelling because how we educate our children and youth will determine the kind of nation we become. The issue is not whether we do or do not reduce the federal role or nationalize standards in education; the issue is to clarify and determine how the federal government can and should use its resources and dollars to effectively promote schools and other social institutions. Federal leadership should support and work with state and local agencies, not for the purpose of promoting the needs of one group versus another group but for the priorities of all of us—as a people or nation.

Federal leadership can work hand in hand with local school districts, and the focus should be on enhancing academic achievement for all students and ensuring that students with special needs have equal opportunity to succeed. In no way should our goals or priorities suggest that schools be nationalized or that the federal government establish national standards of educational performance.

---

[10]Linda Darling-Hammond, *Professional Development Schools* (New York: Teachers College Press, Columbia University, 2005); James H. Stronge, *Teacher Pay and Teacher Quality* (Thousand Oaks, CA: Corwin, 2006); and Tucker and Codding, *Standards for Our Schools*.

[11]Daniel L. Duke, "What We Know and Don't Know About Improving Low-Performing Schools," *Phi Delta Kappan*, 87 (2006): 728–734; Margaret E. Goertz, "Redefining Government Roles in an Era of Standards-Based Reform," *Phi Delta Kappan*, 83 (2001): 62. Also see James P. Comer et al., *Six Pathways to Healthy Child Development and Academic Success* (Thousand Oaks, CA: Corwin, 2004).

**Table 9–1**    **Federal Funds (in billions) from Department of Education, and All Federal Departments, 1970–2000**

|  | 1970 | 1980 | 1990 | 2000 |
|---|---|---|---|---|
| Department Education |  |  |  |  |
|   K–12 | $2,719 | $6,629 | $9,681 | $20,758 |
|     Higher education | 1,187 | 5,682 | 11,175 | 15,834 |
| All other programs, all departments | 12,526 | 13,137 | 23,198 | 33,985 |

Source: *Digest of Education Statistics, 1993* (Washington, DC: U.S. Government Printing Office, 1993), tables 348, 349, 350, pp. 363–368; *Digest of Education Statistics 2000* (Washington, DC: U.S. Government Printing Office, 2001), tables 364–365, pp. 416–417.

The federal role in education should be based on helping local schools and school districts build consensus and confidence in educating their clients. Many educational problems are both national and local. The problem is national because it occurs in many parts of the country and because world and national events help construct it. It is also local in the sense that the composition and needs of the student population differ from place to place and that local efforts and resources are needed to resolve the problem. If local efforts and resources are not funded, then the services or personnel will not be provided. A federal strategy is needed—one that stimulates state and local school planning and reform and supplements state and local efforts and resources.

## The Department of Education

Although many different federal agencies (thirteen departments and about fifteen other agencies or units) are involved in some type of educational program or activity, the U.S. Department of Education is the major agency through which the federal government demonstrates its commitment to education. Of the thirteen departments, it receives 45 percent of all federal funds for education.

Table 9–1 shows an increase in federal funding in actual and real dollars (after inflation) for the Department of Education since 1980, reflecting its new role with full department status (starting in 1979) alongside thirteen other federal departments. However, federal funding for all programs (K–college) and federal departments decreased in real dollars in the 1980s, when the new federalism movement first surfaced. After increasing 30 percent in real dollars between 1970 and 1980, it declined 5 percent between 1980 and 1990. Elemen-

tary and secondary education slightly declined in real dollars between 1980 and 1990, whereas higher education increased in real dollars (almost 25 percent). Many educators have criticized this shift in federal education priorities—from K–12 schooling to higher education—given the fact that the eventual outcomes of human capital are rooted or primarily formed in the children's early years of schooling. As a result of the criticism, since 1995 the DOE has funded more money for K–12 programs than for higher education.[12] Whereas the public often criticizes public schools for being inefficient or wasteful, perhaps there is greater need to scrutinize the budgets of colleges and universities since they are receiving increased federal dollars.

When the Department of Education was formed in 1867, its commissioner had a staff of three clerks and a total of $18,600 to spend. From these humble beginnings, the department has grown to more than 4525 employees and annual expenditures of $57 billion in 2003. The department presently administers over 200 separate programs.[13] The original purpose of the department was to collect and disseminate statistics and facts and to promote the goals of education throughout the country. Even though it was known as the Department of Education, the commissioner was not a member of the president's cabinet. In fact, the department

---

[12] Daniel U. Levine and Allan C. Ornstein, "Assessment of Student Achievement: National and International Perspectives," *NASSP Bulletin,* 77 (1993): 46–59. *Digest of Education Statistics,* 2003 (Washington, DC: U.S. Government Printing Office, 2004), tables 171, 247, pp. 210–211, 402–403.

[13] *Digest of Education Statistics, 1989* (Washington, DC: U.S. Government Printing Office, 1989), fig. 20, p. 333; *Digest of Education Statistics, 1993,* table 351, p. 371; *Digest of Education Statistics, 2005,* table 367, p. 436.

was attached to the Department of the Interior in 1868 and given the status and name of a bureau.

In 1929, the title Office of Education was adopted; ten years later, the office was transferred to the Federal Security Agency. In 1953, the Office of Education was transferred again, this time to the newly formed Department of Health, Education, and Welfare (HEW). The Office of Education continued to perform its original functions, and additional responsibilities and program activities were added by various acts of Congress or by order of the president. In particular, it assumed new responsibilities of (1) administering grant funds and contracting with state departments of education, school districts, colleges, and universities; (2) engaging in educational innovation, research, and development; and (3) providing leadership, consultative, and clearinghouse services related to education.

In 1979, after much congressional debate, a Department of Education (DOE) was signed into law by President Carter who declared that education was the "biggest single national investment" and that the creation of the department was the "best move for the quality of life in America for the future." The president, at that time, was reflecting the growing concern among educational reformers that linked the development of human capital (an educated populace) with the prosperity and growth of the nation. A secretary of education, Shirley Hufstedler, was named with full cabinet-level status, and the department officially opened in 1980.

The establishment of a Department of Education with full cabinet status has long been a goal of many professional organizations, especially the American Association of School Administrators (AASA), National Association of Secondary School Principals (NASSP), National Association of Elementary Principals (NAEP), American Federation of Teachers (AFT), and National Education Association (NEA). In theory, there now exists a person (the Secretary of Education) with potentially widespread influence and with cabinet status, who can exert persuasion and pressure in political and educational circles and who is in charge of educational policy at the federal level and the promotion of programs to carry out these policies.

Although President Reagan almost eliminated the Department of Education and reduced its staff by one-third between 1980 and 1985,[14] it was during his administration that the department gained in stature and visibility because of the outspoken and controversial William Bennett, Secretary of Education between 1985 and 1988. Bennett stated forceful positions on several educational issues, including but not limited to academic standards, moral education, school discipline, computer literacy, school prayer, drug education and getting drugs out of schools, teacher accountability and teacher testing, and teaching essential knowledge for a democratic society and national pride. His critics, in fact, labeled Bennett as a "bully" and charged that he used his office as a "bully pulpit."

The secretary during the later Bush II administration, Margaret Spellings, was much less visible and controversial. Spellings focused on achieving the goals of No Child Left Behind, disseminating test information and tracking student progress, holding school districts accountable and using government leverage to demand results, and creating better partnerships among educators, parents, business people, labor, and the community. She initiated a move from negativism and political bickering in education to positive solutions, to ensure that educators are committed to school reform and that students will receive a challenging, world-class education.[15] Although few people can quarrel with such lofty goals, achieving them is another story. (See the Pro/Con Debate at the end of this chapter.)

## Congressional Influence on Education

Although the framers of the Constitution gave the states primary responsibility to maintain and operate schools through the Tenth Amendment, they also provided another important provision—that Congress could "provide for the . . . general welfare of the United States."

Congress remained in the background for the first 150 years, at least in terms of supporting and enacting educational legislation. But a sense of national need, starting in the mid-1930s with the Great Depression, moved Congress to strengthen school support and enact laws. Between 1787 and 1937, for example, Congress enacted only fourteen major educational laws. During the last seventy years, however, more than 175 major laws were passed.[16]

---

[14]Thomas Skelly, director of Budget Systems Division, Department of Education, personal communication, February 23, 1989.

[15]Seymour B. Sarason, *Letters to a Serious Education President* (Thousand Oaks, CA: Corwin, 2006).

[16]*Digest of Educational Statistics, 2006* (Washington, DC: U.S. Government Printing Office, 2006).

The federal government, particularly Congress, never completely ignored schools and colleges, but the fact they remained in the background was welcomed by most state legislatures, who wished to maintain control over education. Most administrative organizations, such as the National School Boards Association (NSBA), also welcomed federal indifference. The NSBA stated that "public education is a local function [and that] school boards are accountable directly to the communities which select them." Yet the federal government has a major role to play: to provide a clear mission and sufficient resources so that "local administrators and teachers [can link] the schoolhouse to broader national and global priorities."[17]

While the NSBA "recognizes that special assistance and general aid are appropriate federal activities," it urges that local schools "not be subject to federal regulation."[18] Similarly, the Council of Chief State School Officers (CCSSO) maintains that the federal government should ensure that the education serves the goals of the nation, but "the governance of education has been and should remain a matter of states to decide. The interests of children [and] youth . . . are best served when state and local agencies work together . . . [and when] federal funds are used in conjunction with state and local funds."[19]

The NSBA emphasizes the local level in terms of responsibility. The CCSSO, as representatives of state educational agencies, puts the emphasis at the state level. However, both groups are concerned with national priorities and would like to see the federal government play a more active role in improving and funding educational programs, while not subjecting the states or local school districts to federal requirements or regulations.

The No Child Left Behind law favors both positions, while also increasing federal leverage by connecting standards, time lines, and federal resources. In fact, the federal government will spend $400 million to assist states and school districts with the cost of developing assessment systems, followed by accountability plans. The new challenge is for the federal government to support its investment in human capital—that is, the education

of its people—for the nation to remain viable and compete internationally. State and local resources are insufficient to support high-quality investment in education; they need federal support and involvement but not control.

## Federal Programs and Activities in Education

Until the mid-twentieth century, the federal government gave very little financial assistance to the states (or local schools) for the education of students. This attitude was in line with the majority belief that the federal government should have little to do with education and that education is a state responsibility. Federal programs and activities might be characterized as passive and uncoordinated during this period. This is not to say that the federal government had no influence on education. National laws and federal programs had a significant impact on the way education developed in the United States. But we must remember that these programs and acts were not part of a broadly conceived national plan for education. After Sputnik in 1957, however, as national policy became more closely linked to education, federal funding dramatically increased, steadily involving specific educational targets. This growth was curbed in the 1980s (with the Reagan and Bush I administrations) but restored in the 1990s with Clinton. Although federal funding in real dollars has decreased with Bush II, federal involvement remains significant.

### Grants for Schools

The **Northwest Ordinances** of 1785 and 1787 were the first instances of federal assistance to education. The Northwest Ordinance of 1785 divided the Northwest Territory into townships and each township into thirty-six sections; it reserved the sixteenth section "of every township for the maintenance of public schools within the said township." The Ordinance of 1787 stated that "schools and the means of education shall forever be encouraged" by the states. The federal government thus demonstrated its commitment to education while ensuring the autonomy of state and local schools. As a result of these ordinances, thirty-nine states received over 154 million acres of land for schools from the federal government.[20]

[17]National School Boards Association, *A National Imperative: Educating for the 21st Century* (Washington, DC: NSBA, 1989), p. 3.

[18]National School Boards Association, *Resolutions of the National School Boards Association: 1988–89* (Washington, DC: NSBA, 1989), p. 1.

[19]Council of Chief State School Officers, *Council Policy Statements 1998* (Washington, DC: CCSSO, 1998), p. 49.

[20]Ellwood P. Cubberly, *Public Education in the United States*, rev. ed. (Boston: Houghton Mifflin, 1934).

## Grants for Colleges

Seventy-five years passed before another major federal educational program was enacted. This program involved institutions of higher learning, not elementary and secondary schools. In the **Morrill Act** of 1862, federally owned lands totaling 30,000 acres were set aside for each state, with the provision that the income from the sale or rental of these lands was to be used to establish colleges for the study of agriculture and mechanical arts. A total of 6 million acres of federal lands was given to the states. These "people's colleges," or land grant institutions, were to become the great multipurpose state universities that now enroll students from all segments of society. The Morrill Act demonstrated that the federal government would take action in education for the good and welfare of the nation; it also marked the beginning of meaningful federal influence on higher education.

## Vocational Education Acts

The third phase of federal activity in public education came with the conditional grants for highly specific purposes in public secondary schools. The **Smith-Hughes Act** of 1917 provided money grants for vocational education, home economics, and agricultural subjects. The original act called for federal appropriations to be matched by state or local educational agencies. It was extended by various acts between 1929 and 1984; the 1984 legislation, called the Perkins Vocational Education Act, extended funding into the 1990s by various job training amendments, and included people with handicaps, single parents, homemakers, and the incarcerated among its beneficiaries.

The 1917 federal vocational act marked the federal government's first annual appropriation for public secondary education. The 1963 federal vocational act appropriated $235 million for vocational training, quadruple the annual appropriations of the original Smith-Hughes Act;[21] by 1998, the annual federal funding for vocational programs had reached $1.5 billion, and the average vocational program (Carnegie) units completed by public high school students was 3.8 (including consumer and homemaker education and labor-market preparation) with rural students averaging 4.5

course units. By 2002, however, vocational funding dramatically decreased to $1.2 billion.[22]

Unquestionably, some educators are alarmed at this decrease in the vocational budget. They would not only increase monies but also establish a national apprenticeship program, as in Europe, that would encourage non-college-bound students to stay in school two years longer in order to get further training and be better prepared to move into the workforce. In fact, Clinton had once proposed that all employers invest up to 1.5 percent of their payroll in retraining their workforce so as to keep it competitive.[23]

In order for the U.S. to remain competitive on a global basis, some business pundits are urging that more funds be allocated to technology education (which is a federal component of vocational and adult education appropriations). Bill Gates addressed the National Governors Association education summit in 2003 and asserted, "When I compare our high schools to what I see when traveling, I am terrified for our work force of tomorrow."[24] Given the fact that approximately 90 percent of current engineers and scientists are being graduated from China, India, and Japan, Gates's observation about America's future is cause for concern.[25]

## Relief Acts

The fourth phase of federal activity emerged during the Great Depression. Federal interest in schools at that time was only incidental to greater concerns for the welfare of unemployed youth from ages sixteen to twenty-five. The Civilian Conservation Corps (CCC) was organized in 1933 for unemployed males ages seventeen to twenty-three. More than half of the youth who joined had never finished grade school, and a substantial number were practically illiterate. The act provided federal appropriations for the education and vocational training of more than 3 million youth until it was abolished in 1943. Almost a generation passed before the CCC idea was brought back as part of the Job Corps in the mid-1960s.

---

[21] *The Condition of Education, 1983* (Washington, DC: U.S. Government Printing Office, 1983), table 3.8, p. 152.

[22] *Digest of Education Statistics 2003,* Table 371, p. 445.

[23] Bill Clinton, "The Clinton Plan for Excellence in Education," *Phi Delta Kappan,* 74 (1992): 131–138.

[24] "Gates 'Appalled' by High Schools," *Seattle Times,* 27 February 2005, p. 27.

[25] Allan C. Ornstein, *Class Counts: Education, Inequality and the Shrinking Middle Class* (Lanham, MD: Rowman & Littlefield, 2007).

Other federal programs of the Depression era included the National Youth Administration (1933), which provided welfare and training programs for unemployed youth ages sixteen to twenty-five as well as financial aid for needy students attending secondary schools and colleges; the Federal Emergency Relief Administration (1933), which allocated funds for the employment of unemployed rural teachers; the Public Works Administration (1933) and Works Progress Administration (1935), both of which provided federal money for school construction and repairs, amounting to 30 to 45 percent of the national allocation of funding of new schools from 1933 to 1938. All federal relief agencies were terminated by the mid-1940s. Although some educators were concerned about possible federal domination of public schooling during the 1930s, these fears subsided; the communities that had participated in these programs were in a better position to meet the classroom shortage that occurred after World War II.[26]

## War Acts

The fifth phase of federal activity took place during World War II and the immediate postwar period. Three major bills were passed at this time.

1. The Lanham Act (1941) provided aid for construction and maintenance of local schools in areas where military personnel resided or where there were extensive federal projects.

2. The Occupational Rehabilitation Act (1943) provided educational and occupational assistance to disabled veterans.

3. The Serviceman's Readjustment Act (1944), commonly called the **GI bill,** provided funds for the education of veterans and enabled hundreds of thousands of Americans to attend institutions of higher learning or special training schools.

The benefits of the GI bill were extended to the Korean and Vietnam conflicts. Direct aid, totaling more than $10 billion, has helped more than 7.5 million veterans to attend institutions of higher learning or special training schools. The GI bill, along with the baby boom, was a major factor in the growth and expansion of American colleges, including community colleges.

Since 1990, the GI education benefits have been extended by four bills and amendments, including the "Veterans" Educational Assistance Amendments (PL 102-127), which restored benefits to reserve and active duty personnel, and amended Title 38, which increased veterans' education and employment programs. In 2003 as much as $2.6 billion in tuition assistance was granted to Iraq veterans, an increase of only 10 percent since 1980.[27]

## National Defense Education Act

The Cold War and the Soviet launching of Sputnik in 1957 increased pressure for better schools and federal funding. This led to the sixth phase of federal education legislation, particularly the **National Defense Education Act** (NDEA) of 1958. The act stressed the importance of education to the national defense, and funding was earmarked for educational programs that enhanced "the security of the nation . . . and [developed] the mental resources and technical skills of its young men and women."

This broad act emphasized improvement of instruction in science, mathematics, foreign languages, and other critical subjects; provided college and university students loans and scholarships; funded numerous teacher training programs, including those for teaching the disadvantaged; stimulated guidance and counseling programs; and promoted curriculum reform and programs in vocational and technical education. By 1960, the federal government was spending nearly $240 million annually on NDEA programs; in the mid-1960s, the act was extended to include history, geography, English, and reading as critical subjects.[28]

## Compensatory Education Acts

The 1960s and 1970s brought a new emphasis on equality in education and represents the seventh stage of federal programs. With the War on Poverty and the spread of the civil rights movement, national policy became linked to education, as the government targeted specific groups—namely, minorities and the poor—

---

[26]Roland S. Barth, *Lessons Learned* (Thousand Oaks, CA: Corwin, 2003); Marvin Lazerson and W. Norton Grubb, *The Education Gospel: The Economic Power of Schooling* (Cambridge, MA: Harvard University Press, 2004).

[27]*Digest of Education Statistics, 1989,* table 304, p. 337; *Digest of Education Statistics, 2003,* table 367, p. 436.

[28]Allan C. Ornstein, *Education and Social Inquiry* (Itasca, IL: Peacock, 1978); S. Alexander Rippa, *Education in a Free Society,* 8th ed. (New York: Longman, 1997).

and created specific policies to improve their educational opportunities. The federal government took on an active and coordinated posture with reference to education as it substantially increased its contributions to a variety of targeted programs and increased its regulations over specific policies.

The most important act of this period was the **Elementary and Secondary Education Act** (ESEA) of 1965, part of President Johnson's Great Society. It focused on compensatory programs for the disadvantaged student, immediately providing $1 billion for the first year. In 1980, at the height of its popularity, monies totaled $3.5 billion, or about $300 per disadvantaged child; from 1965 to 1980, $30 billion had been appropriated. (Appropriations for the disadvantaged fluctuated between $3.2 billion and $4.5 billion per year from 1980 to 1990.)[29] Considering inflation, this was a slight drop in real dollars that reflected the general cutbacks in education by the federal government during this period. However, by 2003 funding had increased to $11.2 billion or $900 per disadvantaged child, reflecting the nation's emphasis on social and educational spending.[30] This dollar amount was amid increased military and home security spending and consolidation of many federal programs, reflecting the elements of President George W. Bush's prized Reading First Program and Leave No Child Behind plan.[31]

During this thirty-eight-year period (1965–2003), the Consumer Price Index increased about four times, but compensatory funding soared 11.5 times. Funding for **Title I**, or disadvantaged students, has become big business—with a host of bureaucratic layers and jobs and subsequent advocates for compensatory funding. In the name of a variety of environmental and behavioral theories, as well as President Johnson's dream of the Great Society, compensatory programs proliferated as educators and social designers rushed to make claims to federal monies, spending billions of dollars based on hunches and sometimes sloppy program designs. Although compensatory programs from the Johnson era to the George W. Bush administration had a great deal in common, the latter was the first president to raise the difficult issue of how to define *failing schools;* how to resolve the problem, however, has always remained unclear during these four decades.

In the early years, one educator summarized compensatory funding as an "ineffective free for all . . . with few federal strings attached to the expenditures.[32] Program after program seemed to make little difference. Perhaps the only consistent thread running through the programs was the demand that more money be spent. Only gradually, after some fifteen or twenty years, did we come to the first stage of wisdom: confession of how little we know about improving the education of inner-city students—namely, poor and minority students. And, more than forty years later, after spending nearly half a trillion dollars on compensatory education, one educator concluded there was "no answer to the question of whether increases in school funding would change measured [student] achievement." Educators are still unable to determine "how economic circumstances affect educational outcomes." Obviously, there are a number of "other variables that ought to be considered," such as the characteristics of families, peer groups, and student population.[33]

It should also be noted that most grants for compensatory education are earmarked for urban disadvantaged students, now called at-risk students, and tend to fall in early childhood programs (such as Head Start and Follow-Through) and reading, language, and basic skills development (nearly half deal directly with the improvement of basic skills in reading, language, and communication).

## Title IX

Title IX (PL 92-318) of the 1972 Education Amendments to the **Civil Rights Act** prohibits discrimination against women in educational programs receiving federal assistance. Part of the movement toward equality of opportunity (and later acts such as the Women's

---

[29] *Digest of Education Statistics, 1983–84* (Washington, DC: U.S. Government Printing Office, 1983), table 144, p. 174; *Digest of Education Statistics, 1989,* table 307, p. 344.

[30] *Digest of Education Statistics, 1993,* tables 3, 21, 350, pp. 12, 29, 365–368; *Digest of Education Statistics, 2003,* table 368, p. 437.

[31] Erik W. Robelen, "Amid Crisis, Outlook for ESEA Overhaul Unclear," *Education Week* (September 26, 2001): 25–26; Robelen, "Congress Refocuses on ESEA," *Education Week* (October 3, 2001): 27, 31. Also see Stuart Yeh, *Raising Student Achievement through Test Reform* (New York: Teachers College Press, 2006).

[32] Howard A. Glickstein, "Federal Educational Programs and Minority Groups," *Journal of Negro Education,* 38 (1969): 305.

[33] Allan C. Ornstein, *Teaching and Schooling in America: Pre and Post September 11* (Boston: Allyn and Bacon, 2003). Also see Rothstein, *Class and Schools.*

Educational Equity Act of 1974) and a host of affirmative action rulings enforced by the Office of Civil Rights (which is also under the jurisdiction of the Department of Labor) evolved out of the Civil Rights Act of 1964 to include women's rights and concerns.

Federal control over these school matters is implicitly stated by the regulations governing Title IX and outline in detail what schools and colleges must do in terms of making available female sports programs and facilities and in the hiring of women to prevent sex discrimination and possible loss of federal funds. Individuals and organizations can challenge any discriminatory practice by contacting the local agency of the Office of Civil Rights or Department of Labor. Moreover, Title VII of the Civil Rights Act of 1964 covers all educational institutions regardless of whether they receive federal funds or not. The latter condition reflects the fact that the U.S. Supreme Court has ruled that education is a right, guaranteed by the Constitution, and therefore it extends federal influence over schools and colleges.[34]

The law, which marked its thirtieth anniversary in 2002, mandates gender equality at the K–12 and college levels not only in sports (the original goal) but also in math and science classes. Even as many proponents celebrate this law, opponents behind the scenes still exist and the George W. Bush administration is scrutinizing the law's mandates. The other side of the coin is that Title IX "robs Peter to pay for Pauline," and that a number of second-tier male sports such as wrestling, volleyball, gymnastics, and rowing have been dramatically cut, in some cases entirely eliminated.[35] The debate over Title IX remains highly political, often emotionally charged, and bolstered by personal experiences, pro and con.

## Bilingual Education

Bilingual education, which provides instruction in the native language of non-English-proficient students, has been expanding in U.S. public schools — in part due to federal policy. In 1968, Congress passed the **Bilingual Education Act** and amended it in 1974 to ensure that instruction be given in English or the native language of the child, whichever is more suitable, "to allow the child to progress effectively through the educational system."

Much of bilingual educational expansion is based on the 1974 U.S. Supreme Court ruling in *Lau v. Nichols* that requires schools to help students who "are certain to find their classroom experiences wholly incomprehensible" because they do not understand English. Congressional appropriations for bilingual education increased from $36.4 million in 1974 to $496 million in 1999.[36] Although the federal and state governments fund bilingual projects for more than sixty language groups speaking various Asian, Indo-European, and Native American languages, the large majority (about 70 percent) of children in these projects are Hispanic.

Although this country continues to attract hundreds of thousands of immigrants from around the world each year, Hispanics represent the fastest-growing ethnic population in the country. In 1980, 15 million was the legal Hispanic population. Based on current immigration and fertility trends as shown in Table 9–2, the Hispanic population reached 30 million in the year 2000 (10.8 percent of the total population) and is projected to be 47 million in 2020 (14.7 percent), surpassing the U.S. black population (14 percent) as the largest minority group. On the heels of the Hispanic population is the Asian group — the next fastest-growing minority group. It reached 12 million in 2000 (4.3 percent) and is expected to reach 20 million in 2020 (6.3 percent) compared to 4 million (2 percent) in 1980.[37] The composition of the United States is undergoing considerable ethnic change — largely because of immigration trends — and the federal government is responding in the schools by requiring that the states and local educational agencies meet the needs of these children.

---

[34]Kern Alexander and M. David Alexander, *American Public School Law,* 6th ed. (Belmont, CA: Wadsworth, 2005).

[35]Michelle R. Davis, "Title IX: Too Far, or Not Far Enough?" *Education Week* (June 19, 2002): 1, 29; Davis, "Diverse Title IX Panel Takes on Tough Task," *Education Week* (September 4, 2002): 37, 42. Also see Elizabeth H. De Bray, *Politics, Ideology and Education: Federal Policy During the Clinton and Bush Administrations* (New York: Teachers College Press, Columbia University, 2006).

---

[36]*Digest of Education Statistics, 1976* (Washington, DC: U.S. Government Printing Office, 1976), table 157, p. 173; *Digest of Education Statistics, 2000,* table 361, p. 407; *The Fiscal Year 2000 Budget,* appendix, p. 8.

[37]L. F. Bouvier and C. B. Davis, *The Future Racial Composition of the United States* (Washington, DC: Population Reference Bureau, 1982); Allan C. Ornstein, "Enrollment Trends in Big-City Schools," *Peabody Journal of Education,* 66 (1989): 64–71; Ornstein, "Curriculum Trends Revisited," *Peabody Journal of Education,* 69 (1994), pp. 4–20. Also see Harold Hodgkinson, "Educational Demographics: What Teachers Should Know," *Educational Leadership,* 58 (2000): 6–11.

**Table 9–2   Total U.S. and Minority Population, Based on Current Immigration Rates and Fertility, 1980–2020 (in millions)**

|  | 1980 | | 2000 | | 2020 (est.) | |
|---|---|---|---|---|---|---|
|  | **Number** | **%** | **Number** | **%** | **Number** | **%** |
| White (non-Hispanic) | 181.0 | 79.9 | 200.3 | 71.7 | 205.6 | 64.9 |
| Black | 26.5 | 11.7 | 36.4 | 13.0 | 44.4 | 14.0 |
| Hispanic | 14.6 | 6.5 | 30.3 | 10.8 | 46.6 | 14.7 |
| Asian | 4.4 | 2.0 | 12.1 | 4.3 | 20.3 | 6.3 |
| **Total:** | 226.5 | 100.0 | 279.1 | 100.0 | 316.9 | 100.0 |

Source: Adapted from Allan C. Ornstein, "Urban Demographics for the 1980s: Educational Implications," *Education and Urban Society*, 16 (1984), table 2, p. 486. Used by permission.

Bilingual education has been expanding partly because the federal Office of Civil Rights (OCR) has been insisting that special educational opportunities be improved for limited-English-proficient (LEP) and non-English-proficient (NEP) students. Controversies over bilingual education have become somewhat embittered as federal and state actions have led to the establishment of various bilingual programs. There are arguments between those who would "immerse" children in an English-language environment and those who believe initial instruction will be more effective in the native language. On one side are those who favor maintenance because they believe this would help build a constructive sense of identity, and on the other are those who believe that cultural maintenance is harmful because it separates groups from one another or discourages students from mastering English well enough to function successfully in the larger society.[38]

Adherents and opponents of bilingual education also differ on the related issues of whether bilingual programs sometimes or frequently are designed to provide teaching jobs for native-language speakers and whether individuals who fill these jobs are competent in English. Observers who favor bilingual and bicultural maintenance tend to believe that the schools need many adults who can teach LEP or NEP students in their own language, whereas observers who favor transitional programs feel that very few native-language or bilingual speakers are required to staff a legitimate program.

## Education for the Handicapped

Federal legislation focusing on the rights of handicapped people and governing much of the subsequent activity in educating handicapped students was spelled out in three major laws: the Rehabilitation Act of 1973, Public Law 93-380 in 1974, and **Public Law 94-142** (the **Education for All Handicapped Children Act**) in 1975.

The Rehabilitation Act provided that no "program" or "activity" receiving federal assistance can exclude or discriminate against persons solely because of their handicaps. Public Law 93-380 authorized increased levels of aid to states for the implementation of special education services and set forth due process requirements to protect the rights of affected children and their families. Public Law 94-142 set forth as national policy the goal that "free appropriate public education . . . must be extended to handicapped children as their fundamental right."

The 1975 Act has been rewritten several times and was renamed the Individuals with Disabilities Education Act (IDEA) in 1990. IDEA requires that states have "an approved plan meeting certain specified guidelines assuring all disabled children education benefits." The plan is known as the Individualized Education Plan (IEP) and requires a document explaining what and how education services will be provided to special needs students, particularly disabled ones, so they can benefit from their schooling.

---

[38]James A. Banks, *Cultural Diversity and Education,* 5th ed. (Needham Heights, MA: Allyn and Bacon, 2005); Nathan Glazer, *We Are All Multiculturalists* (Cambridge, MA: Harvard University Press, 1997).

**Table 9–3     Number of Students Receiving Public Educational Services by Type of Disability, 1980–2002**

| Handicap | 1980 | 1990 | 2000 | 2002 |
|---|---|---|---|---|
| Learning disabled | 1,462,000 | 2,129,000 | 2,789,000 | 2,846,000 |
| Speech impaired | 1,168,000 | 985,000 | 1,068,000 | 1,084,000 |
| Mentally retarded | 830,000 | 535,000 | 597,000 | 592,000 |
| Emotionally disturbed | 347,000 | 390,000 | 462,000 | 476,000 |
| Hard of hearing/deaf | 79,000 | 58,000 | 70,000 | 70,000 |
| Orthopedically impaired | 59,000 | 49,000 | 69,000 | 73,000 |
| Other health impaired | 98,000 | 55,000 | 221,000 | 337,000 |
| Visually impaired | 31,000 | 23,000 | 26,000 | 25,000 |
| Multiple disabilities | 68,000 | 96,000 | 106,000 | 127,000 |
| Deaf–blind | 3,000 | 1,000 | 2,000 | 2,000 |
| Autism | a | a | 67,000 | 118,000 |
| Developmentally delayed | a | a | 12,000 | 45,000 |
| Preschool disabled (three to five years old) | 231,000 | 441,000 | 568,000 | 612,000 |
| Total: (all conditions) | 4,144,000 | 4,761,000 | 6,055,000 | 6,407,000 |
| Percentage of public school enrollment | 10.1 | 11.4 | 13.0 | 13.4 |

Note: a = no information.

Source: *Digest of Education Statistics, 1987* (Washington, DC: U.S. Government Printing Office, 1987), table 38, p. 49; *Digest of Education Statistics, 2000* (Washington, DC: U.S. Government Printing Office, 2001), table 53, p. 65); *Digest of Education Statistics 2003* (Washington, DC: U.S. Government Printing Office, 2004), table 53, p. 73.

The IEP must include (1) an assessment of the student's present performance, (2) the effects of the disability on the student's involvement and progress in the school curriculum, (3) measurable annual goals related to meeting the student's needs and involvement in the school curriculum, (4) the provision for services and personnel to meet the student's needs, and (5) assurance that the disabled student will participate in curricular activities and other experiences with nondisabled students.

As indicated in Table 9–3, the total number of special education students served by public funds has increased over twenty-two years, from 4.1 million to 6.4 million (or 13.4 percent of the public school enrollment), with 47 percent being served in regular classes (part time or full time), 21 percent in self-contained classes, and the remaining in special schools or facilities.[39]

The rising number of handicapped students has been associated with the civil rights movement and its concern with making equal educational opportunity available to all students—not that more of our students have become handicapped. The numbers also include a somewhat large and fuzzy category, "learning disabled," in which many slow learners, underachievers, and precocious students are hastily slotted—in part because of an overemphasis on testing and labeling students and the influence of special education advocates as a lobby and advocate group. Although *Brown v. Board of Education* in 1954 addressed the segregation of black students, it also served as a precedent in establishing the rights of students with special needs to be provided with equal educational opportunity under the umbrella notion of **mainstreaming.**

In terms of costs, special education expenditures rose steadily in the 1970s and 1980s. The average cost of educating a child with handicaps is much higher than the national average for a nonhandicapped child— almost double the national average of $8100 in 2002.[40]

---

[39] *Digest of Education Statistics, 1994* (Washington, DC: U.S. Government Printing Office, 1994), table 53, p. 66; *Digest of Education Statistics, 2003*, table 53, p. 73.

[40] *Digest of Education Statistics, 2003*, figure 11, p. 53. *Twenty-fifth Annual Report to Congress on the Implementation of the Education of the Handicapped Act* (Washington, DC: U.S. Government Printing Office, 2005).

Although federal law requires local school districts to provide free appropriate education, the federal government, which originally contributed relatively few dollars to this effort, has dramatically increased its funding in the 1990s, largely corresponding with the Clinton administration. Federal expenditures for special education increased from $79 million in 1970 to $1.5 billion in 1980 to $3.5 billion in 1990 to $5.4 billion in 2000.[41] In real dollars, after inflation, this amounts to an increase of about 50 percent since 1980. Still, special education mandates place a heavy financial burden on the states and local educational agencies.

## Education Consolidation and Improvement Act (ECIA)

At the insistence of the Reagan administration, Congress changed the long-term direction and method of federal funding of education from categorical grants (funds for specific groups and designated purposes) to **block grants** (funds for general purposes without precise categories).

Categorical grants were an important feature of federal involvement in education during the mid-1960s and 1970s. But Chapter 2 of the federal ECIA of 1981 replaced categorical grants for twenty-eight separate educational programs (at which Title I funding, the most popular, was specifically aimed) with one block grant that state and local educational agencies could use for broadly defined educational purposes. (However, categorical grants for vocational, bilingual, and handicapped students were retained.) This move should be seen as part of the trend toward a new federalism, reflecting increased conservatism, reduced federal bureaucracy and centralization, and a shift in many social and educational programs from the national to the state governments.[42]

As a result of the act, funds have shifted from grants based on need, which mainly served disadvantaged students and urban school districts, to state-devised formulas based on student enrollments. The programs fall into one of three broad categories: (1) basic skills development in reading, writing, and math; (2) services for staff and school support such as staff training, instructional equipment, testing and evaluation, as well as desegregation; and (3) special projects, including those related to career education, parental involvement, and gifted and talented students. There is also a special provision for support of "secular" or "neutral services" of nonpublic schools such as transportation, school lunches, and instructional materials, media, and equipment.

Observers cite a number of advantages of the block grant approach for educational programs. It has reduced the amount of paperwork required to get a grant (from twenty to thirty pages for a $50,000 program to four to six pages), simplified the administration of grant monies, and enabled school districts to cut down the bureaucracy devoted to grants. Instead of submitting applications to several different federal agencies, a school district now has to deal only with its own state's educational agency. The block grant approach has also enhanced the role of local administrators in determining how resources will be used. (See Administrative Advice 9–1.) Finally, under the old system, some school districts were continually unsuccessful at competing for federal grants, whereas others became very skillful at the process. Block grants, according to their supporters, have reduced this kind of competition among districts.[43]

On the other hand, critics point out that the states have failed to pick up some of the programs formerly funded by the federal government. Many states have chosen to distribute funds to local schools on a per-child basis rather than on the basis of need. The "winners" under the block grant approach have included small-town and rural school districts; the "losers" have often been urban districts with high percentages of minority and disadvantaged students. Districts under court-ordered desegregation that previously received federal funds also have taken large cuts. Many critics contend that the federal government began providing its services and programs in the first place because states did not accept those responsibilities.

---

[41]*Digest of Education Statistics, 1993,* table 350, pp. 365–368; *Digest of Education Statistics, 2000,* table 361, p. 407.

[42]Denis P. Doyle and Bruce S. Cooper, *Federal Aid to the Disadvantaged* (New York: Falmer Press, 1988); Connie L. Fulmer and Frederick Dembrowski, *National Summit on School Leadership* (New York: Rowman & Littlefield, 2005); and Robert E. Slavin and Nancy A. Madden (eds.), *Success for All* (Mahwah, NJ: Erlbaum, 2001).

---

[43]Christopher T. Cross and S. Nathan Cross, "Will Congress Save Our Schools from the Tyranny of Red Tape?" *Phi Delta Kappan,* 74 (1993): 651–653; Andy Hargreaves and Dean Fink, "The Ripple Effect," *Educational Leadership,* 63 (2006): 16–21.

## ▪ Exemplary Educational Administrators in Action

**JOE A. HAIRSTON** Superintendent, Baltimore County Public Schools, Towson, Maryland.

**Previous Positions:** Superintendent, Clayton Public Schools, Jonesboro, Georgia; Assistant Superintendent, Prince George's County Public Schools, Upper Marlboro, Maryland; Principal, Prince George's County Public Schools, Upper Marlboro, Maryland.

**Latest Degree and Affiliation:** Ed.D., Virginia Polytechnic Institute and State University.

**Number One Influence on Career:** My parents impressed upon me during my youth the desire to help others and "save the world." (I am still trying to save the world.)

**Number One Achievement:** During my tenure as principal at Suitland High School in Forestville, Maryland, my school was named a National Exemplary Secondary School and cited as a national model for reform and innovation by then-President Ronald Reagan, Vice President George Bush, and Secretary of Education William Bennett.

**Number One Regret:** My number one regret is now one of my virtues: If I had been more assertive when I was younger, I would have spent more time debating issues. Today, I don't debate issues or get deeply involved in a full discourse on issues. I now expect my staff to do this before bringing their recommendations to me.

**Favorite Education-Related Book or Text:** *Effective Executive* by Peter F. Drucker and *Churchill on Leadership* by Steven F. Hayward.

**Additional Interests:** Adventure, travel, tinkering with computers, music, WWII history.

**Leadership Style:** Adaptive and reflective.

**Professional Vision:** All over America, parents, elected officials, and community members are watching educators manage the latest challenges presented by the No Child Left Behind legislation. They don't really believe that all children can learn. They see the "achievement gap," and they know that it is not new. Children of color and children of poverty in this country have never enjoyed the success rates of their majority and wealthy peers. Meanwhile, every day children come through our doors and sit in our classrooms, not to be selected and sorted, but to be taught the skills and content they will need to be successful in this world.

**Words of Advice:** We cannot waste any more time making yesterday better for children. There is an urgency that we cannot deny any longer for educators to embrace the phrase "quality education for all children," and I believe that if any school system in America can find the way to make a difference for children, my school district must be the one. If anyone can take the negative energy that is out there and turn it into opportunities for children to have a meaningful educational experience, my staff will be the ones to do it.

How do I know this? Because I have an uncompromising belief in the possibilities created when the right people are in the right positions that together we can bring dignity, caring, and integrity back to the business of teaching and learning.

No one has come forward yet to show a better way to improve student achievement than to focus on quality teaching and a commitment to excellence. With that focus, there is nothing complicated about it. This is not about stifling the human spirit; rather, it is about enabling teachers to be all they can be. It is about making their work and the students' work more engaging and therefore making both groups able to know more and do more. It is a simple fact that all children can learn more than they are currently learning if they are provided with schoolwork they find to be engaging.

## National Reform of Education

The rapid expansion of federal influence in education coincides with national reform, based on perceived problems of society and what is in the best interests of the nation. What educational policies the president puts on his agenda, what educational programs Congress establishes and funds, and how the Supreme Court interprets the Constitution on educational matters create a national policy in education.

National priorities in the 1960s and 1970s for the most part focused on educational equality, whereby the definition of minority status was expanded beyond traditional minority and disadvantaged groups to include bilingual and handicapped groups as well as women. The notion of equality was enlarged from its original meaning for the first 175 years of the nation's history—

## Administrative Advice 9–1

### Dealing with the Politics of Block Grants

A critical issue for school administrators is to deal with the reduction in federal funding and in other policy areas. Efforts to deregulate these programs pose new challenges to school districts in the way they deal with state agencies. The states tend to view the block grants as an opportunity to increase their policymaking role in education, and local school administrators must learn the new policies and procedures in order to obtain their share of funds. Here are some practical suggestions:

■ Determine which federal programs the federal government will continue to fund and which the states will fund.

■ Determine how local school programs have to be modified to reflect changes in federal guidelines.

■ Determine which local school programs have to be modified to reflect changes in state guidelines.

■ Decide how to modify those programs to meet state guidelines.

■ Decide what, if any, state guidelines conflict with federal mandates. For those that conflict, ask the state to clarify the specific guidelines.

■ Determine how block grants to local school districts will be distributed and monitored.

■ Determine what part of the local school program will receive greater scrutiny by the state. Make appropriate adjustments.

■ Reduce central personnel who had to be hired to process now obsolete categorical grants.

■ Organize a staff development program to enhance block grant funding for local school districts; collaborate with teachers, administrators, and community members.

■ Design your block grant program around the characteristics and needs of your school district; look at practical matters — budget, staff size, number of students, grade levels, and the like.

■ Maintain broad-based political pressure for continually increasing the funding of block grants in your school district.

■ Keep in contact with the state legislature and state department of education to determine policy or program shifts in block grants; hire a local ombudsman or consultant to build communication links with state agencies.

---

namely, equality of opportunity, that is, free and universal education for all groups.

The modern view of **equality of opportunity** now includes (1) equality based on spending additional monies for special programs and personnel, illustrated by compensatory funding; (2) equality based on racial composition, as suggested by school desegregation and integration; (3) equality based on outcomes for students with similar backgrounds, spearheaded by the accountability movement and school finance reform; and (4) equality based on equal outcomes for students (and adults) with unequal backgrounds and abilities, expressed by affirmative action and quotas.

Once we start to define inequality in terms of equal outcomes (both cognitive and economic), we eventually compare racial, ethnic, religious, and gender groups. In a heterogeneous society like the United States, this comparison results in some hotly contested issues — including how much to invest in human capital (and for how much gain), how to determine cost-effectiveness of

social and educational programs, who should be taxed and how much, how should money be redistributed, to what extent are we to restrict our brightest and most talented minds to enable those who are slow to finish at the same time, and whether our policies result in reverse discrimination or hinder excellence. Indeed, we cannot treat these issues lightly because they affect most of us in one way or another and lead to questions over which wars in the past have been fought.

All these issues involve balancing acts that affect individuals, groups, and society. On one hand, too much egalitarianism can lead to mediocrity, indifference, and economic decline within society. On the other hand, excellence carried too far can create wide social and economic gaps, hostilities among groups, and a stratified society with a permanent underclass. The idea is to search for the golden mean.

School administrators are compelled to carry out the law of the land and, more precisely, to carry out the policies of the school board. The best we can hope for are enlightened school boards whose members understand and abide by the law. Administrators are also compelled, by virtue of their job, to deal with pressure groups and community groups that often have their own agendas. Indeed, questions that deal with equality and excellence have no easy answers, and they will continue to plague anyone, including principals and superintendents, who must make school decisions that affect students, teachers, and other administrators.

## The Call for Excellence

Since the mid-1980s, the pendulum has swung from equality to excellence. National attention has turned to the need for higher academic standards: tougher subjects, rigorous testing, and stiffer high school graduation and college admission requirements. The educational dimensions of and reasons for this new movement were documented in a number of policy reports released between 1983 and 2003. Many of these (including the most famous, *A Nation at Risk*) were written and distributed by the federal government, and all called for reforms to improve the quality of education in the United States. The background data to these reports show a low performance standard that must be addressed:

1. Schools and colleges have shifted away from requiring students to take what had been the standard academic core curriculum for graduation thirty years ago: foreign language, mathematics, science, English, and history. Elective courses and remedial courses have replaced many standard academic courses.

2. Grade inflation is on the rise, and students are required to complete less homework (26 percent of twelfth-grade high school students completed less than one hour of homework a night, and 13 percent claim they have no homework).[44]

3. Although National Assessment of Educational Progress (NAEP) indicates math proficiency improved for all age groups between 1973 and 1999, with nine-year-olds making the greatest gains, among twelfth-grade students only 61 percent were capable of performing at grade level and only 8.4 percent were capable of advanced work such as calculus or statistics.[45]

4. The NAEP shows a large achievement gap in reading and math between white and black students: 35 points among nine-year-olds and 31 points among seventeen-year-olds in reading; 28 points among nine-year-olds and 32 points among seventeen-year-olds in math.[46] These trends persisted up to 1999 despite billions of dollars annually spent on compensatory and remedial programs. Between 1999 and 2004 black nine-year-olds gained 14 points in reading and thirteen-year-olds rose 6 points, but whites have also shown gains,[47] suggesting that the tests might have been adjusted to offset the changing demography, especially the growing number of minority students.

5. By the twelfth grade, the NAEP gap in math and science proficiency between black and white students had more than doubled in reading, was 4.5 times greater in math, and 6 times greater in science. The Hispanic–white gap is slightly narrower: 1.5 times in reading, 3 times greater in math, and 4 times greater in science. The minority-white gap remains constant in all social class levels or measured by parents' education.[48]

6. Between 1992 and 2003 reading and math proficiency scores remained flat for fourth and eight graders. In 2003, only 22 percent of fourth grade lower-income students were at or above proficient in reading and mathematics. By the eighth grade 19 percent of these students were at or above proficient in reading and mathematics.[49]

7. Average achievement scores on the **Scholastic Aptitude Test** (SAT) demonstrate a virtually unbroken decline from 1963 to 1994. Average verbal scores fell over 40 points (466 to 423), and mathematics scores dropped 13 points (492 to 479). In the next five years (1995–2000) there was an increase of 58 points total (verbal and math combined), mainly because the mean scores were adjusted downward in 1995, thus masking the continual decline.

[44]*The Condition of Education, 2001* (Washington, DC: U.S. Government Printing Office, 2001), Indicator 22, p. 42.

[45]*The Condition of Education, 2001,* Indicator 12, p. 24: *Digest of Education Statistics, 2000,* table 123, p. 140.

[46]*The Condition of Education, 2001,* Appendix I, Indicators 11–12, pp. 122–123.

[47]Gerald W. Bracey, "The 15th Bracey Report on the Condition of Public Education," *Phi Delta Kappan,* 87 (2005): 138–153.

[48]*The Condition of Education, 2001,* Indicator 13, pp. 22–25; *Reaching the Top: A Report of the National Task Force on Minority Achievement* (New York: The College Board, 1999), pp. 7, 9.

[49]*The Condition of Education, 2005* (Washington, DC: U.S. Government Printing Office, 2005), table 14-2, p. 142.

8. For white students compared to black students, the verbal score was 96 points higher in 1987 and 92 points higher in 1997. In math, white students scored 103 points higher than black students in both SAT tests. The Hispanic-white gap was about 60 points different in reading and 50 points different in math for both years.[50] All these differences in achievement scores (NAEP and SAT) cannot be fully explained by social class, and the inferences cover a wide and controversial spectrum.

9. International comparisons of student achievement, beginning in the 1970s, reveal that on nineteen academic tests U.S. students were never first or second and, in comparison with other industrialized nations, were last seven times. By 2003, international test comparisons in math and science were so bleak that score comparison was broadened to include all countries, which masked the performance of American students vis-à-vis their industrial counterparts by reporting U.S. math and science scores as above average.[51]

10. Some 23 to 25 million U.S. adults are functionally illiterate by the simplest tests of everyday reading and writing. Moreover, about 13 percent of all seventeen-year-olds in the United States are considered functionally illiterate, and this rate jumps to 35 percent among minority youth. The percentage of adults age 25 or older who reported reading any literature (novel, short story, poem, play, newsmagazine article) in the past year declined from 1982 and 2002, from 50 to 47 percent. It dropped to 40 percent among those with a high school diploma and 19 percent for those with less than a high school diploma.[52]

11. The high school dropout rate among sixteen- to twenty-four-year-olds is 11 percent, but for blacks and Hispanics it increases to 13 and 26 percent, respectively, and in some large cities like New York and Chicago it borders on 33 to 40 percent.[53]

12. Business and military leaders complain that they are required to spend millions of dollars annually on remedial education and training programs in the basic skills, or the Three Rs. Between 1975 and 2000 remedial mathematics courses in four-year colleges increased by 75 percent and constituted one-fourth of all mathematics courses taught in these institutions. As many as 24 percent of college students have taken a remedial reading course, and 16 percent have taken three or more remedial courses. As many as 25 percent of the recruits in the armed forces cannot read at the ninth-grade level.[54]

13. All these figures pile up and stare at us, despite the fact that our student-teacher ratios were 16.5:1 in 2000, which put us seventh lowest in the world (whereas such countries as Japan and Korea have higher student-teacher ratios—18:1 and 28:1, respectively). Yet our pupil expenditures for education K–12 were the second highest in the world (about $500 less than first-ranked Switzerland).[55]

## Racial and Class Implications

How we interpret these trends largely depends on our social lens and political motives, what side of the ideological aisle we sit on, and to what extent and how we balance issues related to excellence, equality, and equity. It also depends on whether we want to focus on class or caste. For example, we can talk about *cultural inversion,* a concept introduced by black social scientists such as John Ogbu or John McWhorter.[56] Their thesis is that poor academic achievement among blacks has more to do with their own negative attitudes than the effects of prejudice or poor schools; and that negativism is rooted in slave history and segregation, but dramatically worsened by a "cult of separation," which makes blacks think that whatever whites do, they should do the opposite. As well, they identify a "cult of anti-intellectualism," which holds that academic excellence is a white thing, and "cult of victimization" in which black youth adapt and act out the labels or stereotypes foisted on them by the majority population— "dumb," "lazy," or "delinquent."

[50]*Digest of Education Statistics 1998* (Washington, DC: Government Printing Office, 1998), table 131, p. 146.

[51]*The Condition of Education, 2005,* Indicators 11–13; pp. 45–47.

[52]*The Condition of Education, 2005,* Indicator 15, p. 49.

[53]*The Condition of Education, 2001,* Indicator 23, p. 43. Also, "Few Minorities Get Best High School Diplomas," *New York Times,* November 30, 2005, p. M3; "School Financing Case Plays Out in Court," *New York Times,* 10 October 2006, pp. B1, B8.

[54]*The Condition of Education, 2001,* Indicator 28, p. 49.

[55]*Digest of Education Statistics, 2000,* table 412, p. 469; *The Condition of Education, 2001,* Indicator 38, p. 65; Appendix I, Indicator 57, p. 178.

[56]John N. Ogbu, *Minority Education and Caste* (New York: Academic Press, 1978); John H. McWhorter, *Losing the Race* (New York: Simon & Schuster, 2000).

This negativism is also supported by prejudicial attitudes of teachers and their low expectations of minority students, compounded by years of unequal schooling and institutional racism. Roland Fryer, a black Harvard economist, looked at 90,000 minority students from grades 7 to 12 and concluded that acting white and getting good grades is a problem in integrated schools but not in all-black schools or private schools. He concludes that black and Hispanic students with good grades end up with fewer friends at integrated public schools, but it is more a *class* issue than a racial problem. In any society where inequality exists, members of the disadvantaged group have torn loyalties—wanting to excel in the larger society but maintaining kinship and loyalty to one's own subgroup.[57]

Class is an important idea, particularly now, when race and class vie for the reformer's eye and seem to be competing for popularity in the reform literature. There is a history of unequal schooling related to class which dates back to colonial America in terms of who dropped out of school (common student) and returned to the farm or became an apprentice in a craft or labor-related position, and who graduated (upper-class student) from the Latin School in Boston or a private school in Charlestown and went on to Harvard or Yale. Two hundred fifty years later, as we begin the twenty-first century, class issues persist at Harvard and Yale, with no more than 3 to 4 percent of the student body representing lower- and working-class white students.

In fact, President Roosevelt's New Deal and President Johnson's Great Society used a poverty index or economic need in lieu of race to determine how additional resources would be allocated. The concept of welfare rights, affirmative action, entitlements, and reparations have only been tied to race since the late 1960s, coinciding with the civil rights movement. Some scholars advocate a return to the poverty index and funneling resources and services based on need or *class*, not for a particular racial/ethnic group or *caste*. It's a matter of focusing on *all* low-performing students, not just minority students. Until recently most policymakers and educators have been afraid to publically discuss this issue, or to suggest that school integration or government funding be based on class and not race.[58]

---

[57]Roland Fryer, "Acting White" *Education Next*, Winter 2006: 52–59.

[58]See Richard D. Kahlenberg, "The New Integration," *Educational Leadership*, 63 (2006): 22–26; Ornstein, *Class Counts: Education, Inequality, and the Shrinking Middle Class*; and Rothstein, *Class and Schools*.

## General Implications

These deficiencies have come to light at a time when the demand for highly skilled military personnel and workers in labor and industry is accelerating rapidly and amidst growing concern that the United States is being overtaken by other nations in commerce, industry, science, and technology.

Table 9–4 summarizes the major policy reports. Seven of these twelve emphasize the need to strengthen the curriculum on the core subjects of English, math, science, social studies, and foreign language. The focus is thus on a common curriculum. Technology and computer courses are mentioned often, either as components of science or math or as a separate subject area (sometimes referred to as the Fourth R). High-level cognitive and thinking skills are also stressed. Most of the reports are also concerned with programs and personnel for disadvantaged students and students with learning disabilities, although this message is not always loud and clear.

Eleven reports emphasize tougher standards and tougher courses, and seven out of the twelve propose that colleges raise their admission requirements. Many of the reports also mention increasing homework, time for learning, and time in school, as well as instituting more rigorous grading, testing, homework, and discipline. They mention upgrading teacher certification, increasing teacher salaries, increasing the number of and paying higher salaries for science and math teachers, and providing merit pay for outstanding teachers. Overall, most stress academic achievement (not the whole child) and increased productivity (not valuing or humanism).

Most of the reports express concern that the schools are pressed to play too many social roles, that the schools cannot meet all these expectations, and that the schools are in danger of losing sight of their key role—teaching basic skills and core academic subjects, new skills for computer use, and higher-level cognitive skills for the world of work, technology, and military defense. Many of the recent reports, concerned not only with academic productivity but also with national productivity, link human capital with economic capital. Investment in schools, this argument runs, is an investment in the economy and in the nation's future stability. If education fails, so do our workforce and nation. Hence, it behooves business, labor, and government to work with educators to help educate and train the U.S. populace.

Despite criticisms by some members of the educational community that the reports are too idealistic and unrealistic, that they put too much emphasis on

**Table 9–4  Overview of Reports on Excellence in Education, 1983–2001**

| Report and Sponsor | Curriculum Objectives | Content Emphasis | School Organization | Government/ Business Role |
|---|---|---|---|---|
| 1. *Action for Excellence,* Education Commission of the States | Establish minimum competencies in reading, writing, speaking, listening, reasoning, and economics<br><br>Strengthen programs for gifted students<br><br>Raise college entrance standards | English, math, science, foreign language, history, computer literacy | Consider longer school day<br><br>Emphasize order and discipline<br><br>More homework<br><br>More rigorous grading with periodic testing<br><br>Independent learning | Foster partnerships between private sector and education<br><br>Increase federal funds for education |
| 2. *Educating Americans for the 21st Century,* National Science Foundation | Devote more time to math and science in elementary and secondary schools<br><br>Provide more advanced courses in science and math<br><br>Raise college entrance standards | Math, science, technology, computers | Consider longer school day, week, and/or year<br><br>Twelve-year plan for math and science | Federal input in establishing national goals for education<br><br>Increase NSF role in curriculum development and teacher training |
| 3. *High School,* Carnegie Foundation for Achievement in Teaching | Mastery of language, including reading, writing, speaking, and listening<br><br>Expand basic academic curriculum<br><br>Student transition to work and further education<br><br>Strengthen graduation requirements | Core of common learning, including English, history, civics, math, science, technology<br><br>Computer literacy | Improve working conditions for teachers<br><br>Utilize technology to enrich curriculum<br><br>Flexible schedules and time allotments<br><br>One track for students<br><br>School-community learning activities<br><br>Greater leadership role for principal | More connections between school and community, business, and universities<br><br>Increase parent and community coalitions with and service to schools<br><br>Utilize retired personnel from business and colleges<br><br>Federal scholarships for science and math teachers |
| 4. *A Nation at Risk,* National Commission on Excellence in Education (President Reagan, Secretary of Education Bell) | Improve textbooks and other instructional materials<br><br>Provide more rigorous courses in vocational education, arts, and science<br><br>Strengthen graduation requirements<br><br>Raise college entrance requirements | Five new basics: English, math, science, social studies, and computer science | Consider seven-hour school day<br><br>Tighten attendance and discipline<br><br>More homework<br><br>More rigorous grading and periodic testing<br><br>Group students by performance rather than age | Federal cooperation with states and localities<br><br>Meet needs of disadvantaged student populations as well as gifted and talented<br><br>National standardized tests in context with national interest in education |

(continued)

**Table 9–4   Overview of Reports on Excellence in Education (continued)**

| Report and Sponsor | Curriculum Objectives | Content Emphasis | School Organization | Government/ Business Role |
|---|---|---|---|---|
| **5.** *The First Lesson: A Report on Elementary Education in America,* Secretary of Education William Bennett | Improve basic skills for young children<br><br>Improve complex learning tasks and abilities for higher-grade children<br><br>Increase knowledge base essential for democratic society and national identity<br><br>Improve textbook and workbook writing and selection<br><br>Raise academic standards | Basic skills, especially reading through phonics<br><br>Problem-solving skills in mathematics and hands-on learning and discovery in science<br><br>Unified sequence stressing history, geography, and civics<br><br>Computer literacy and cultural literacy | Lengthen school day<br><br>More homework<br><br>More rigorous testing<br><br>Parental choice in children's schools<br><br>Reward teacher performance | Communitywide and parental responsibility in education<br><br>Teacher and school accountability<br><br>Improve training programs for elementary teachers; emphasis on arts and science rather than methods courses |
| **6.** *The Early Years,* Carnegie Foundation for the Advancement of Teaching | Focus on plight of at-risk children, the nation's underclass<br><br>Emphasis on basic skills<br><br>Priority on childhood education | Language development, including reading, writing, and listening skills | Flexible school schedules reflecting changing family and work patterns<br><br>Longer school day and school year<br><br>Reward teacher performance; attract better teachers<br><br>Parental choice for after-school and summer programs; end of traditional summer vacation | Increased federal aid for education of at-risk children<br><br>Increased role of business and industry<br><br>Greater involvement of teachers in decision making; increased pay |
| **7.** *Time for Results: The Governors' 1991 Report on Education,* National Governors' Association | Focus on teenage pregnancy, school dropouts, adult illiteracy, and drug abuse<br><br>Improve school leadership and management<br><br>Better use of technology in the classroom<br><br>Increase state role and responsibility in education<br><br>Higher academic standards at all grade levels | Basic skills, math, science, and technology<br><br>Research and development in education | Kindergarten for all children; early childhood programs for all at-risk children<br><br>Parental education programs<br><br>Parental choice in selecting children's school<br><br>Reliable and valid assessment of student performance<br><br>Year-round schooling<br><br>Reorganize and regulate schools and school districts that are "academically bankrupt" | National school board to certify teachers<br><br>Increased pay and accountability for teachers and principals<br><br>Improved teacher training and educational leadership programs<br><br>Greater involvement in education of local leaders, teachers, parents, citizens, and business people<br><br>Greater state role, regulation, and spending in education<br><br>Annual progress reports on what each state is doing to carry out educational reform |

**Table 9–4    Overview of Reports on Excellence in Education (continued)**

| Report and Sponsor | Curriculum Objectives | Content Emphasis | School Organization | Government/ Business Role |
|---|---|---|---|---|
| 8. *The Disappearing Quality of the Workforce: What Can We Do to Save It?* National Alliance of Business | Educate all youth in basic skills<br><br>Provide students with high-level skills required for our information and service economy<br><br>Face our educational problems<br><br>Restructure education; provide financial support<br><br>Increase the quality of the nation's workforce | Basic skills<br><br>Critical thinking skills<br><br>Tutoring programs<br><br>Raise academic standards and high school graduation requirements | Reduce school dropout rates<br><br>Increase attendance rates<br><br>Improve national test scores and achievement levels<br><br>Increase adopt-a-school programs<br><br>Teacher/ administrative accountability<br><br>Staff development/ mentor programs | Business leaders must take an active role in implementing educational reform<br><br>Collaborative efforts between business and educational groups<br><br>Reshape education at state and local levels<br><br>Involve citizen, parent, political and business groups |
| 9. *Investing in People: A Strategy to Address America's Workforce Crisis,* U.S. Department of Labor | Commitment to basic skills and literacy<br><br>Invest in human capital<br><br>Increase federal and business support in educational and human resource programs<br><br>Upgrade workforce quality<br><br>Upgrade high school graduation, college entry, and labor-market standards<br><br>Develop national goals and timetables to improve education training | Basic skill programs for dropouts<br><br>Literacy programs for illiterate adults<br><br>Lifetime education and training<br><br>Combine vocational and technical education | Reduce dropout rates<br><br>Increase attendance rates<br><br>Increase parent participation<br><br>Increase business community presence in schools<br><br>Reduce competitive learning; increase cooperative learning<br><br>More rigorous teacher training and testing of new teachers | Partnerships between business, labor, and government at all levels<br><br>Business to fund incentive programs to improve teacher/ school performance<br><br>Increase government and training programs to address needs of private sector and labor<br><br>Tax credits for educational and training programs for private sector |
| 10. *National Goals for Education,* U.S. Department of Education (President Bush I, Secretary of Education Bennett) | Focus on all students, with emphasis on at-risk students<br><br>Equip students with knowledge and skills necessary for responsible citizenship and world of work<br><br>Ensure readiness for school; upgrade school standards and student achievement<br><br>Improve adult literacy and lifelong education | Basic knowledge and skills<br><br>Reasoning and problem-solving skills<br><br>Math, science, English, history, and geography<br><br>Drug and alcohol prevention programs<br><br>Citizenship, community service, cultural literacy, and knowledge of the international community | Preschool programs for all disadvantaged learners<br><br>Parental training for child's early learning; parental choice in children's schools<br><br>Up-to-date instructional technology<br><br>Multilayer system of vocational, technical, and community colleges<br><br>More student loans, scholarships, and work study programs in higher education | Inspire reform at the federal, state, and local levels<br><br>Enlist assistance of parents, community, business, and civic groups; involve all parts of society<br><br>Create effective apprenticeships, job training, teacher–employee exchanges, and adopt-a-school programs<br><br>Increase flexibility, innovation, accountability, and results |

(*continued*)

## Table 9–4  Overview of Reports on Excellence in Education (continued)

| Report and Sponsor | Curriculum Objectives | Content Emphasis | School Organization | Government/ Business Role |
|---|---|---|---|---|
| 10. *National Goals for Education,* U.S. Department of Education (President Bush I, Secretary of Education Bennett) | Provide a safe and drug-free school environment | | Upgrade teacher preparation; reward teachers but hold them accountable | Target established for the year 2000 and beyond |
| 11. *Goals 2000,* U.S. Department of Education (President Clinton, Secretary of Education Riley) | Set in law the original six National Education Goals (established by the Bush–Bennett administration)<br><br>Develop national performance standards in the core subject areas of science, math, history, geography, English, and foreign languages<br><br>Improve teacher training, textbooks, instructional materials, and technologies so students will have the tools to achieve higher standards<br><br>Develop rigorous occupational skill standards to ensure that workers are better trained and internationally competitive | Core subject areas of science, math, history, geography, English, and foreign languages<br><br>Vocational and technical education<br><br>Upgrade academic standards to create a "world-class education" for *every* child<br><br>Produce better ways of testing and assessing student performance | Greater involvement of parents and better ways for measuring their children's progress<br><br>Teacher and administrative accountability<br><br>More opportunities for staff development<br><br>Provide schools with the tools and resources they need, in exchange for better results for students | Partnerships among educators, parents, business people, labor, and government<br><br>Provide seed capital and encourage school reform at local and state levels<br><br>Improve workforce skills, and thus reduce dollars spent on training new workers<br><br>Use national skill standards to build a training system that ties schools, colleges, training institutions, and employers together to create a high-skills, high-wage workforce<br><br>Use national academic standards as a benchmark for increasing school performance standards |
| 12. *No Child Left Behind* (President George W. Bush, Secretary of Education Paige) | All states and school districts must meet a state standard of academic proficiency<br><br>Consequences are provided for schools that are unable to meet state goals<br><br>States are allowed to have different academic goals | Basic reading, literacy, and math<br><br>Annual testing to show school and school district progress | Improve quality of teacher workforce<br><br>Greater leadership role of principals<br><br>Students have *choice* to transfer to another school within the district if school fails to show progress two years in a row[a]<br><br>Students must be provided additional services such as after-school (or private) tutoring if school fails to show progress three years in a row[b] | Improve connection between school, community, and parents<br><br>Transportation money and additional services are to come from the school district's Title I dollars |

[a]For 2003–04 some 8900 schools had to offer school choices. Nationwide, only about 2 percent of the students eligible exercised this option.

[b]To be removed from the "need of school improvement" list, a school must make adequate progress for two consecutive years. If so, the school choices and additional services would no longer be required.

Chapter 9 ■ The Federal and State Government and Education

excellence at the expense of equality and equity, and that they are enormously expensive to implement,[59] the reports have captured national attention, spotlighted nationwide concern for the quality of education, and upgraded nationwide school standards. The two most recent reports have come under severe criticism: *Goals 2002* as being unrealistic and *No Child Left Behind* as a "simple" and "stupid" phrase that has minimal monetary backing.[60] In addition, James Popham has raised many concerns about the testing process involved with NCLB, reporting on a monthly basis in *Educational Leadership* and writing a recent book dealing with reliability, validity, and useability problems of high-stake tests.[61] But publication and discussion of these and other national reports and studies have reinforced and accelerated many federal, state, and local activities designed to improve education. Despite the national spotlight school reform now commands, and despite all the reports and good intentions, huge learning gaps still exist between rich and poor schools and white and black students. The empirical data are persuasive: A sizeable percentage of at-risk students are "left behind" for their school lives.

### Need for Caution

Administrators must understand the broad cycles of change and improvement, which come and go like a pendulum, and the fact that schools have been burdened by the rest of society with roles and responsibilities that other agencies and institutions no longer do well or, for that matter, want to do.[62] The schools are seen as ideal agencies to solve the nation's problems and to reform or change what ails us. With this perspective many people refuse to admit their own responsibilities in helping children and youth develop their individual capacities and adjust to society. Similarly, parents and policymakers alike often expect administrators and teachers to be solely responsible for carrying out reform.

Seasoned administrators have learned that there are no "magic bullets" for reforming schools; there is no one policy or single combination of policies that will automatically lead to answers or transform ineffective schools into effective ones. School life, like human life itself, is much more complicated. Over and over, reform measures that have been imposed on school officials by the federal government and other groups have failed. As one author notes, "The freeway of American education is cluttered with the wrecks of famous bandwagons."[63]

In the 1950s, for example, the Ford Foundation invested $250 million in innovative programs before it asked for results—and then found out the projects did not work.[64] In the early 1970s, when the U.S. Office of Education evaluated more than 1200 of its own compensatory programs and after spending more than $1 billion in less than two years, only ten programs showed solid empirical data that demonstrated their success.[65]

Some critics conclude that we have been spending too much on school reform and compensatory programs and not getting enough in return. What often occurs is a marginal improvement in the beginning—then, gradually, diminishment until input (time and money) is wasted because there is virtually no increase in output.[66] A "flat area"—less output in relation to input—is reached eventually, or, even worse, there is no return. According to critics, demand for money has created a cottage industry for reformers and lawyers to exploit the legal system and to point the finger of blame at teachers and administrators, while ignoring students

[59]Carl D. Glickman, "Dichotomizing School Reform," *Phi Delta Kappan*, 83 (2001): 147–152; Allan Odden, "The New School Finance," *Phi Delta Kappan*, 83 (2001): 85–91; Robert Hess, *Excellence, Equity, and Efficiency* (New York: Rowman & Littlefield, 2005).

[60]M. Donald Thomas and William L. Bainridge, "No Child Left Behind: Facts and Fallacies," *Phi Delta Kappan*, 83 (2002): 781–782; Christopher A. Tracey et al., *Changing NCLB District Accountability Standards* (Cambridge, MA: Harvard University Press, 2005); Gerald W. Bracey, "No Child Left Behind: Where Does the Money Go?" Educational Policy Studies Laboratory, Arizona State University, Tempe, June 2005.

[61]See W. James Popham, *What Every Teacher Should Know about Educational Assessment,* 2nd ed. (Boston: Allyn and Bacon, 2007).

[62]John Chubb, *Within Our Reach* (New York: Rowman & Littlefield, 2005); Leithwood, *Making Schools Smarter;* and Diane Ravitch (ed.), *Brookings Papers on Education Policy: 2005* (Washington, DC: Brookings Institute, 2005).

[63]Ron Brandt, keynote address to Washington State Association for Curriculum Development and Supervision, Seattle, February 11, 1983.

[64]*A Foundation Goes to School* (New York: Ford Foundation, 1972).

[65]*Compensatory Education and Other Alternatives in Urban Schools* (Washington, DC: U.S. Government Printing Office, 1972); Richard L. Fairley, "Accountability's New Test," *American Education*, 5 (1972): 33–35.

[66]Allan C. Ornstein, "In Pursuit of Cost-Effective Schools," *Principal*, 70 (1990): 28–30; Herbert J. Walberg et al., "Productive Curriculum Time," *Peabody Journal of Education*, 69 (1994): 86–100; Walberg, "Productive Teachers," in A. C. Ornstein et al., *Contemporary Issues in Curriculum*, 4th ed. (Boston: Allyn and Bacon, 2007), pp. 99–112.

and parents—and their role in academic output.[67] The same kind of criticism has been leveled at school reform in general, although the reasons and responsibilities vary according to the critics' politics and view of the social world.

Administrators need to remember to go slow in the beginning of reform, to weigh the risks and rewards before making decisions, and to search for a balance—where there is no extreme emphasis on subject matter or students' sociopsychological needs, no extreme emphasis on one or two subjects at the expense of others, or no extreme emphasis on excellence or equality. What we need is a prudent social policy, one that is politically and economically feasible and that serves the needs of all students and society. Implicit in this view of education is that too much emphasis on any one policy, sometimes at the expense of another, may do harm and cause conflict. How much we emphasize one policy is critical because no society can give itself over to extreme "isms" or political views and still remain a democracy. The kind of society into which we evolve is in part reflected in our educational system, which is influenced by the policies that we eventually define and develop.

Schools reflect community norms, and administrators must learn the rules of the game and how the game is played in the local community. When local policy and ensuing programs are out of sync with state or national policies and programs, the administrator's decisions are more difficult, and the needs for balance and change are greater.

## State Government and Education

Every state, today, by constitution, statute, and practice, assumes that education is the function of the state, and federal and state courts have supported this interpretation. The federal government's powers related to education have been delegated to the states through the Tenth Amendment of the Constitution. This is a dramatic difference from what exists in most parts of the world, including almost every industrialized nation, where the schools are centralized and controlled by the federal government, usually through a ministry of education.

Each state in the United States has legal responsibility for the support and maintenance of the public schools within its borders. Local school boards, as we

will see in the next chapter, are considered creatures of the state and have been devised for the purpose of running a system of schools. Being responsible for the schools, the state enacts legislation; determines school taxes and financial aid to local school districts; sets minimum standards for training, certification, and salaries of personnel; decides on curriculum (some states establish minimum requirements, others establish recommendations); provides special services (such as transportation and free textbooks); and provides funding through monetary grants and various aid formulas.

The state school code is a collection of laws that establish ways and means of operating schools and conducting education in the state. The state, of course, cannot enact legislation that is contrary to or conflicts with the federal Constitution. State statutes can be divided into two groups: (1) mandatory laws that establish a minimum criterion or program of education and (2) permissive laws that define the functions that are delegated to the school district under appropriate conditions.

### State Hierarchy of Education

Although state constitutions and statutes provide for the establishment of a uniform system of schools, provisions in most states are detailed concerning state and local powers and authority and methods of school operation. The typical state hierarchy, as with the federal government, consists of three branches: (1) executive or governor, (2) legislative or state legislature, and (3) judicial or state courts.

The governor usually depends on a group of advisors and consultants to report on educational matters. The state legislatures have created a **state education agency** consisting of a state board of education, chief state officer, and state department of education. The relationship between the state education agency and local school districts has changed over time to reflect new problems and concerns. Since the 1980s, for example, with the new federalism, the state legislature and its education agency have taken on a more active role in educational reform. The state courts have also become increasingly active in educational matters.

### The Governor

Although the powers of governors vary widely, their authority on educational matters is spelled out in law. Usually, the governor is charged with the responsibility of formulating educational budget recommendations to the

---

[67]Eric A. Hanushek (ed.), *Courting Failure: How School Financing Lawsuits Exploit Judges' Good Intentions and Harm Our Children* (Stanford, CA: Education Next Books, 2006).

legislature. In many states, the governor has legal access to any accumulated balances in the state treasury, and these monies can be used for school or college purposes.

The governor (and state legislature) has available staff members and agencies to help analyze and interpret data and can obtain additional information on matters of educational concern as needed. The governor can appoint or remove administrative school personnel at the state level. These powers often carry restrictions, such as approval by the legislature. In a majority of states, the governor can appoint members to the state board of education and, in a few states, the chief state officer. Except in North Carolina, a governor can "kill" educational measures through his veto powers or threaten to use the veto to discourage the legislature from enacting laws he opposes — or at least encourage the legislature to modify a pending bill.

The governor in today's political arena will invariably have an educational platform during the election campaign. Thus, all candidates will make specific commitments and promises for education. These platforms vary widely — from a promise to reduce educational spending or to increase it, a pledge for increasing educational equality such as increased prekindergarten programs or college scholarships for minority and needy students on one hand to increased quality and productivity in math, science, and technical education on the other.

The successful gubernatorial candidate must listen to different lobby groups, and the various educational administrative associations recognize the importance of gaining the ear of each candidate. In recent years, the National School Boards Association, National Chief States School Organization, and American Association of School Administrators have increased their lobby efforts and funding to help elect candidates who support their political views on education.[68] In most states, however, the lobby efforts are focused on state legislative officials — at least once the governor is elected.

If the governor chooses to take a visible or outspoken position on educational matters, this influence will be felt. Some legislators may consider it interference; others may welcome it. Indeed, in a growing number of cases — especially dealing with money matters — education has been used as part of a political struggle between the governor and the legislature.[69]

**Time for Results** In the early 1990s, in a departure from tradition, the fifty governors issued a joint report that stated their willingness to act as "strong and eager partners in education reform."[70] Their influence is obvious, and never before have they so dramatically shown their willingness to work with educators. The report examines the relationship of education, jobs, and their states' economies. Governors consider a highly educated populace vital to economic development within their states (and for the nation); those states that have invested in education have also developed new industry and an enlarged tax base. All this background is essential for understanding the governors' readiness to take a firm stand on educational reform and to earmark increased spending for education.

At the same time, state governments that have invested large sums of money in education do not want well-educated students to leave their states for jobs elsewhere. This is especially the case in the Frostbelt (the regions of the Northeast and Midwest), which has witnessed a large outmigration of young adults (who were educated by state monies) to the Sunbelt (the Southeast, Southwest, and West) in the last thirty-five years.[71]

The governors point out the changes in the student population — a growing number of low-income, minority, and immigrant (limited-English-proficient) children as well as abused, homeless, and drug-addicted youngsters who have enormous problems that hinder learning. A related concern deals with changes in the family. Single-parent households, teenage mothers, divorced mothers, mothers who work outside the home, and low-income families have grown, along with a related decline in family structure and/or responsibility for raising and educating children. The report is also concerned

---

[68]Michael W. Apple, *The State and Politics of Knowledge* (New York: Routledge-Falmer, 2003); Ernest L. Boyer, *Selected Speeches* (San Francisco: Jossey-Bass, 1997); and Tom Shannon, executive director emeritus, National School Boards Association, personal communication, June 28, 1999; May 5, 2002.

[69]Kathy Christie, "Stateline: Exploring New Possibilities," *Phi Delta Kappan*, 87 (2006): 421–422; Dan French, "The State's Role in Shaping a Progressive Vision of Public Education," *Phi Delta Kappan*, 80 (1998): 185–194; Michael S. Trevisan, "The States' Role in Ensuring Assessment Competence," *Phi Delta Kappan*, 83 (2002): 766–771.

[70]*Time for Results: The Governors' 1991 Report on Education* (Washington, DC: National Governors' Association, 1992), p. 60.

[71]Allan C. Ornstein, "Decline of the Frostbelt," *Dissent*, 30 (1983): 366–374; Ornstein, "Regional and Urban Population and Student Enrollment Trends," *Journal of Research and Development in Education*, 18 (1985): 19–28; *Projections of Education Statistics to 2008*, table 64, p. 101.

with the decreasing proportions of families with school-age children and middle-class families with more than one child; these trends may lead to a decline in the level of support for education. The report acknowledges that there is no one best reform method and that different states will opt for different reform strategies. The governors agree, however, that students need more than a basic skills education. They must be good problem solvers and creative thinkers. Nothing less will permit our country to maintain its standard of living and solve its national problems.

The report notes public willingness to spend more money on education, but only if improvement is likely to follow. The governors are willing to work for increased spending for education, but they want educators to show results in student achievement, attendance, and retention of learning.

The criticisms leveled at the governors' report are similar to those leveled at the other national reports on reform—that is, the report is too idealistic and unrealistic, and calls for too many expensive reforms; moreover, it glosses over the resistance to and realities of change. For example, how do we get more students to be problem solvers and creative thinkers when an increasing number arrive at our school doors with basic cognitive deficits, unable to perform simple reading, writing, and computing exercises.

The governors now meet on a continuing basis to discuss vital education issues. In general, their concerns are economic with the belief that problems with education have put this country at a terrible competitive disadvantage. They reaffirm that the federal government's role in education is limited and should stay that way. However, within these limits, the federal government is now "defining for the governors which children are achieving 'proficiently,' commanding states to upgrade [curriculum and teaching], prying open suburban schools for kids fleeing the inner city, and the nation to start testing preschoolers." All this, as the governors battle pending state deficits and are forced to make cuts, including *education* rollbacks, or raise taxes.[72]

**Education Goals for the Nation** In their round-table discussions, the governors established a six-point plan for education that was basically adopted by pres-

idents Bush I, Clinton, and Bush II: (1) high school graduation rates will rise to 90 percent (presently at 75 percent); (2) U.S. students will be first worldwide in math and science (presently at the bottom of the industrialized rankings); (3) every adult will be literate (about 25 million are currently classified as illiterate); (4) every school will be drug free (probably the exact opposite is currently true for every middle, junior, and senior high school); (5) students will be tested nationwide in major subjects and in grades 4, 8, and 12, to be accompanied by stiffer graduation requirements (the majority of states currently assess most programs and have mandated minimal exit competency tests); and (6) preschool programs will include increased parental training and nutrition education (only 25 percent of disadvantaged students are enrolled in preschool programs because of cuts in federal and state funds in this category).

Clinton was a member of the governors' delegation that hammered out these six goals, and thus the goals were also incorporated in his administration's Goals 2000. Bush II needed committed governors to implement his school reforms, including the need to raise teacher proficiency and student performance. But the president was unwilling to foot the bill, putting the tab on the governors.

Many governors have taken a more proactive stance on education than most presidents, and have been willing to step up investment at the state level in human capital when convinced that investments were being made effectively and fairly. However, it was hard for the governors to get on the Bush II bandwagon, given Bush's tax policies that reduced taxes among the top 5 percent of all taxpayers and reduced state revenues. Then there was the problem of demonstrating the worth of educational policies, and programs—that is, what works—because of the complexity of the human condition and the many variables that influence our educational environment. Hence, the governors have been left with a good deal of fuzziness, faith, and testimonial views about "what works" as they prepare their educational investment strategy for the new millennium. "What works" has been adopted by the Bush II administration, as part of the philosophy that "all children can learn." The need was to establish a database, according to the No Child Left Behind Act, and for schools and school districts to provide programs, resources, and services in conjunction with what we know works (at least what researchers claim works).

An unintended consequence of NCLB is that effective programs that do not stress drill and test prepara-

---

[72]Gerald W. Bracey, *Setting the Record Straight* (Greenwich, CT: Heinemann, 2004); DeBray, *Politics, Ideology, and Education;* and Bruce Fuller, "Federalism on the Cheap! School Reform Edicts Grow Longer—as State Budgets Implode," *Education Week* (January 15, 2003): p. 44.

tion are now discarded because of the current shift in funding and evaluation which emphasize extra drill and testing. This is true even with highly effective programs such as "HOTS," "Success for All," and the "Junior Great Books" program, as well as factors associated with *effective school research* which have more to do with administrative leadership, school climate, teacher expectations, and teamwork than a direct instruction or measurement approach to learning.[73]

## State Legislatures

With the exception of Nebraska (which has a unicameral arrangement), every state has a two-house legislative body. There is much variation in size and resources, however. Membership in the state Senate ranges from a low of 21 in Nevada to a high of 67 in Minnesota, with most states electing 30 to 40 state senators. Membership in the state House ranges from 40 in Alaska to 400 in New Hampshire, with most states electing 100 to 125 state House members.[74] Nationwide, the state legislative staff size has grown from 27,000 state workers (average size of 519) in 1979 to 40,000 (average size of 800) in 2004, despite the fact that financial conditions of most states worsened during this period. Vermont and South Dakota are the only states with fewer than 100 staff members, whereas California and New York have 3000 or more staff members. The typical state legislator is a white male (about 30 percent are female and another 25 percent are minority) who is an attorney or businessperson by profession.[75]

In most states, the legislature is responsible for establishing and maintaining the public schools and has broad powers to enact laws pertaining to education. These powers are not unlimited; there are restrictions in the form of federal and state constitutions and court decisions. But within these parameters, the legislature

has the full power to decide basic school policy in the state. (See Administrative Advice 9–2.)

The state legislature usually determines how the state boards of education will be selected, what their responsibilities will be, how the chief state officer will be selected, what the duties of this office will be, what the functions of the state department of education will be, what types of local and regional school districts there will be, and what the methods of selection and powers of local school boards will be. The legislature usually decides on the nature of state taxes for schools, the level of financial support for education, and the taxing power for schools to be allocated on a local or municipal level. The legislature may determine what may or may not be taught, how many years of compulsory education will be required, the length of the school day and school year, and whether there will be state community colleges and adult and vocational schools. The legislature may also determine staff and student policies and testing and evaluation procedures, authorize school programs, set standards for building construction, and provide various auxiliary services (e.g., student transportation and school lunches). Where the legislature does not enact these policies, they are usually the responsibility of the state board of education.

The system tends to operate much more effectively when the legislature focuses on broad policies such as financing and organization of schools, thus delegating enforcement of specific criteria and operation of schools to the various state education agencies. The legislature only establishes the minimums in public education, with the proviso that local school districts may exceed these minimum yardsticks. There should be a partnership concept between those who establish legal requirements and basic policies for a state educational system—that is, the legislature—and those who are responsible for implementing the will of the legislature: the state agencies (state board of education, state department of education, and state chief officer).

**State Interest and Lobby Groups**   State legislative officials respect the prevailing political climate and wishes of the people with respect to education and other policy issues. In effect, the people elect state legislatures and speak through the laws enacted by the officials they have elected. All representatives in the state legislatures understand the necessity of listening and responding to the wishes of the people in their district if they wish to be reelected.

The role of educational groups in the state political process usually evolves into a basic form: **political**

---

[73]Daniel L. Duke, "What We Know About Improving Low-Performing Schools," *Phi Delta Kappan*, 87 (2006): 728–734; Stanley Pogrow, "Hots Revisited," *Phi Delta Kappan, 87* (2005): 64–75. Also see Gail Sunderman, James Kim, and Gary Orfield, *NCLB Meets School Realities* (Thousand Oaks, CA: Corwin, 2006).

[74]"2005 Elections," *State Legislature*, 31 (2005): 19.

[75]*Directory of Legislative Leaders 2005* (Denver: National Conference of State Legislatures, 2005); *State Legislative Directory 2006* (Denver: National Conference of State Legislatures, 2006).

## Administrative Advice 9–2

### Increasing Receptivity to Reform

Reform requires adjusting personal and professional habits, changing attitudes and behavior, modifying programs and processes, adopting new curricula and instructional practices, and providing ongoing staff development and technical assistance. The ease with which a school principal or district-wide administrator can trigger such reform depends in part on his or her understanding of the people involved and the organizational system—that is, how the school system operates. The recommendations below help us better understand the system and its players.

1. *School Reform Should Be Perceived as a Cooperative Effort.* Cooperation should evolve among teachers, supervisors, and administrators and to a lesser extent students, parents, and community residents. The sense of cooperation is achieved by involving people in the major aspects of planning and implementation.

2. *People Resist Change; People Accept Change.* Most people resist change before they accept it, especially if they are content with the existing program or organization. Administrators need to anticipate initial resistance to change and deal with concerns and questions about change: how people feel about change, conflicts that may surface, what can be done to lessen anxiety, and how to facilitate the change process.

3. *People, Programs, and Organizations Change.* Nothing lasts forever. School and society change, and reforms are modified to reflect changes. Change is constant, and educators need to realize that people and programs change, as well as the school as a whole. The need is to play a role in change, rather than be victimized by it or be made powerless by its forces.

4. *Innovations Change.* What is viewed as innovative today, if accepted as part of the school program or organization, will eventually become dated. As time passes, contexts change, and modifications are required. Educators should accept the continual need for change and innovation.

5. *Timing Is Crucial.* If people are satisfied with the status quo and there is little demand for change, then a major reform in the curriculum can rarely be implemented. If the local, state, or federal government perceives a need for change, then a new program addressing this need is likely to be implemented.

6. *Educators Need to Be Rewarded.* Right now, there is little pressure for reform among rank-and-file educators, much less reward for change. Because schools are not competitive, they see little need for improving their products or improving customer satisfaction. Rewards—in the form of either salary, promotion, or recognition—need to be part of the reform and innovative process of schools.

7. *An Internal Advocacy Group Improves the Chances for Change.* An internal advocacy group at the district office or community level increases the pressure and likelihood for change. When a particular group of educators or community members sees the benefit of a particular program, they will put pressure on the people and the organization for change. Sometimes, however, another group of educators or community residents who are threatened by the advocacy group surfaces. Conflict then arises, and negotiations or modifications are essential before change can be implemented.

8. *Training and Technical Assistance Are Essential.* Continual staff development within the organization and technical assistance from outside the organization (say, the state) are important. However, many teachers don't want to stay after school to receive training or technical assistance and may rely on their contracts for reasons why they don't have to stay late. If necessary, attitudes among the staff may also need to be changed first, before considering staff training or technical assistance.

9. *Administrators Must Understand Their Mission and Priorities.* Many supervisors and administrators lack a clear idea of their school mission and priorities. They see little need for reform or for making it a priority. Reform and innovation should be part of the leadership behaviors that are highlighted among all theoreticians and practitioners who administer our schools.

10. *Rewards and Risks Must Be Considered.* The political, social, and legal factors related to reform and innovation are important factors that cannot escape the thinking of a wise administrator. Educators must realize that when the rewards are substantial and the risk is minimal, it is worthwhile to pursue change. Most important, school leaders can reduce their risk by understanding the nature of their staff, school district, and community.

Source: Adapted from Allan C. Ornstein and Francis P. Hunkins, *Curriculum: Foundations, Principles, and Issues*, 4th ed. (Boston: Allyn and Bacon, 2004).

action committees (PACs) to financially support, volunteer time for, or endorse candidates for election and educational groups—including administrative associations, teacher associations, parent associations, and special interest groups (such as those concerned with bilingual education, special education, and vocational education). All recognize the need for coalition building and working toward as well as challenging or spearheading policies that affect education.

Another important function of interest groups is their lobbying efforts—both direct, face-to-face presentations and indirect contacts by mail and telephone.[76] Because education is a state responsibility, rather than a federal one, education lobbyists—whether groups of people or associations—focus on state legislatures. And because education is usually the largest expenditure item in the state budget (about 60 percent on a total state-by-state basis when transportation is omitted),[77] it makes the existence of educational interest groups and their lobby efforts an important element of the political arena and policymaking process at the state level.

The state legislature's time is often consumed by formal and informal meetings and conferences on educational matters held with staff, consultants, other government officials, and constituents. Many people do not recognize or realize just how much lobbying is done over educational issues; failure to understand this political process puts school administrators in a vulnerable position on matters that directly affect their school districts and the students they are responsible for educating.

To lobby effectively, an education interest group should (1) know what goals it wishes to emphasize, (2) have feasible goals, (3) designate a primary spokesperson to avoid conflicting signals or information, (4) be willing to consider compromise, (5) look to broaden its "friends" and "allies" to get certain bills passed, (6) know when to use the press or television and when to listen or quietly negotiate, and (7) not become too closely tied with one political party.[78]

Ideally, lobby groups should have an ongoing relationship with important government officials. If information, news releases, and reports on issues are provided on a regular basis by a pressure group (or an administrative association), government officials often request the input of the group when an issue becomes active or part of a pending bill. A cordial working relationship with the legislative staff also helps provide insight into how receptive the members of the group (or association) will be to particular policies or recommendations that might be advanced by the particular legislator or interest group. This is how political networks and relationships develop. The fact that administrative groups such as the National School Boards Association or American Association of School Administrators (as well as teacher groups such as the American Federation of Teachers and National Education Association) have had access to federal policymakers makes them sometimes overlook state officials; that is, national administrative groups need to develop access to policymakers at the state level, where the action is on school affairs.

## State Courts

All states have constitutional provisions pertaining to education but leave the details, policies, and provisions to legislative bodies. There is no national uniformity in the state court organization. At the lowest level, most states have a court of original jurisdiction, often referred to as a *municipal* or *superior court,* where cases are tried. Adverse decisions can be appealed to the next level, usually called the *appellate court,* by the losing side. This court reviews the trial record from the lower court and additional materials submitted by both sides; it assumes that appropriate laws were properly applied at the lower court level. Should any one side still not be satisfied, another appeal can be made to the state's highest court, often called the *state supreme court.* The decision of this court is final unless an issue involving the

---

[76]Susan H. Fuhrman, ed., *From the Capitol to the Classroom* (Chicago: National Society for the Study of Education, 2001); Charles De Pascale, *Education Reform Restructuring Network* (Quincy, MA: Department of Education, 1997); and Rita Schweitz et al., *Future Search in School District Change* (New York: Rowman & Littlefield, 2006).

[77]Julie Bell, director of education affairs, National Conference of State Legislatures, personal communication, May 17, 1994; Agnes G. Case, *How to Get the Most Reform for Your Reform Money* (New York: Rowman & Littlefield, 2004); Jacqueline P. Danzberger, Michael W. Kirst, and Michael P. Usdan, *Governing Public Schools* (Washington, DC: Institute for Educational Leadership, 1992); Susan Moore Johnson, *Leading to Change* (San Francisco: Jossey-Bass, 1996); and Schweitz et al., *Future Search in School District Change.*

[78]John R. Curley, "Education Interest Groups and the Lobbying Function in the Political Process," *Urban Education*, 23 (1988): 261–279; Phillip C. Schlechty, *Shaking Up the Schoolhouse* (San Francisco: Jossey-Bass, 2000); and Kenneth A. Strike, *Ethical Leadership in Schools* (Thousand Oaks, CA: Corwin, 2006).

U.S. Constitution has been raised. The U.S. Supreme Court can be petitioned to consider such an issue; this is a growing trend in issues involving education.

State court decisions have force only in the area served by that court. For this reason, it is possible to find conflicting rules in different circuits. Judges often look to previous law, and to surrounding court circuits, in rendering decisions. Similarly, a state supreme court decision in one state may conflict with a decision of the court in another state; decisions rendered in one state are not binding in another state. Nevertheless, there is a good deal of consistency among the states in matters dealing with education.

State courts have generally rendered decisions upholding the following.

1. Public education is a state function, and control and operation of the schools (and state colleges) are vested in the power and lawmaking agencies of the state.

2. The state controls education and operates schools for the general good of the people and society.

3. The legislative power extends to nonpublic schools, but it has limitations as expressed by the separation of state and religion and in the First Amendment, which protects religious expression.

4. The state legislature is the main body for exercising control over public schools and colleges and enacting educational laws.

5. This lawmaking body decides how it wishes to determine or distribute authority among the state education agencies (state board of education or state department of education) or local school districts (including local school boards).

6. Local school boards are creatures of the state and have no inherent powers of government other than those given to them by the legislature.

7. State agencies and state officers are also creatures of the state with no inherent powers of government other than those given to them by the legislature (or sometimes by the governor).

8. Legislative power extends to financial concerns, rooted in the **Kalamazoo decision** of 1874 (which determined that the state has the right to levy taxes for the support of public schools), and it has the power to define the method of allocation of state funds for schools.

9. States have the right (through one of their education agencies) to prescribe job qualifications and require certification and testing of personnel so long as they are not discriminatory.

10. Tenure and employment constitute a contract between the local school district (not the state) and the administrators and teachers.[79]

In all cases, the authority of the state to prescribe policies is upheld so long as these policies do not conflict with federal or state constitutional provisions.

In many relationships between officials of the state and those at the school district level, differences evolve that are carried into court—such as matters dealing with school desegregation, school finance, school prayer and Bible reading, teacher and student rights, affirmative action, and school safety. Often these cases have gone beyond the state supreme courts to the federal courts. Many other issues end up in state courts because they have little to do with the U.S. Constitution. These issues mainly deal with compulsory attendance, administrator or teacher fitness, teacher strikes, teacher gay rights, school negligence, child abuse, educational malpractice, copyright laws, computer ethics, and an AIDS school policy.

## State Education Agencies

All states recognize the importance of establishing a state education agency, or what is sometimes called a state system of education. The idea of a *state education agency* is based on the Northwest Ordinances of 1785 and 1787, which enabled territories to transform into states, subject to many conditions including a system of public education to be implemented through the state.

Until the mid-twentieth century, the role of the state education agency was limited and leadership in public education was mainly expressed at the local level. We illustrate this with two historical examples: (1) Horace Mann's idea of a system of public education supported by public money and controlled by the state was slow to be accepted beyond Massachusetts and Connecticut in the 1820s; (2) as late as 1930, only 17 percent of total

---

[79]William G. Cunningham and Paula A. Cordeiro, *Educational Leadership: A Problem-Based Approach,* 2nd ed. (Boston: Allyn and Bacon, 2003); Michael W. La Morte, *School Law: Cases and Concepts,* 6th ed. (Needham Heights, MA: Allyn and Bacon, 1999); Martha M. McCarthy, Nelda H. Cambron-McCabe, and Stephen B. Thomas, *Public School Law,* 4th ed. (Needham Heights, MA: Allyn and Bacon, 1998).

school revenues came from state sources compared with 83 percent from the local level.

The state education agency is a system comprising the state board of education, chief state school officer, and state department of education. In most cases, the governor appoints the state board of education, and the latter usually appoints the chief state school officer. In a few states, voters elect members of the state board of education and chief state school officer. The state department of education usually consists of career educators, and a few leadership and directorship posts are filled by the chief state school officer.

## The State Board of Education

The *state board of education* is usually the most influential and important state education agency. Almost all states have some sort of state board of education, which is dependent on the state legislature for appropriations and authority and serves an advisory function for the legislature. (New York's Board of Regents is perhaps the strongest and most respected state board of education.) In addition, most states have a separate governing board for the public schools grades K–12 and for state colleges and universities; thus, there are often two separate state boards, one for elementary and secondary education and another for higher education.

With the exception of Wisconsin, all states have boards of education. As of 1999, thirty-four were appointed by the governor of the state, fourteen were elected by popular vote (this method has increased during the last twenty years), two (New York and South Carolina) were appointed by state legislatures, and one (Washington) was elected by the local school board members. The number of members of state boards ranges from seven to seventeen, with a nine-member board occurring most frequently. (An odd number of members eliminates tie votes.) The term of appointment or election ranges from four to nine years, with most states at the four- to five-year range.[80]

There is some controversy involving the method by which the state board of education members acquire their position. The controversy centers on the merits of election versus gubernatorial appointment. The rationales for election are the following: It provides the people with a direct voice in educational policy; the governor tends to appoint people who agree with her views; it enhances political representation of the people; and gubernatorial appointments concentrate too much power in the hands of one official, whereas elections provide for a system of checks and balances.[81]

The major reasons for appointment are these: (1) Well-qualified people are more inclined to accept appointment than to be candidates in an election; (2) appointment tends to lessen controversy between the governor and board; (3) appointment tends to ensure that the governor will have a continued interest in education; and (4) an election provides the opportunity for interest groups to finance and influence candidates.[82]

Whereas state boards were originally dominated by white males, their composition has changed dramatically in the past few decades. A survey of board members conducted in 1967 showed that only 18 percent were women and 3 percent were minorities.[83] By 1993, 31 percent of board members were women, and 20 percent were minorities.[84] This trend toward greater heterogeneity is important; it broadens the perspectives of board members and ensures that boards reflect a wide range of political, social, and educational concerns.

One recent survey of state boards shows that most members tend to be older (88 percent were age forty or older) and well educated (99 percent have at least some postsecondary education, and 67 percent have a degree beyond the bachelor's). The voluntary nature of service on a state board means that the members must have the time and resources to participate. As a result, the survey found that most board members who were in the workforce described their occupation as managerial (24 percent) or professional (55 percent); those not in the paid

[80]*State Education Governance at a Glance* (Alexandria, VA: National Association of State Boards of Education, 1999); Andrew Stamp, director of public affairs, National Association of State Boards of Education, personal communication, May 3, 1999.

[81]Ralph W. Kimbrough and Michael U. Nunnery, *Educational Administration,* 5th ed. (New York: Macmillan, 1998); Joel Spring, *Political Agendas for Education,* 3rd ed. (Mahwah, NJ: Erlbaum, 2005).

[82]Frederick M. Hess, *Spinning Wheels: The Politics of School Reform* (Washington, DC: Brookings Institution, 1999); Thomas J. Sergiovanni, *Rethinking Leadership* (Thousand Oaks, CA: Corwin, 2006).

[83]Gerald Stroufe, "An Examination of the Relationship between Methods of Selection and the Characteristics and Self-Role Expectations of State School Board Members," doctoral dissertation, University of Chicago Press, 1970.

[84]*How State Board Members Are Selected* (Alexandria, VA: National Association of State Boards of Education, 1993).

workforce were either retired (16 percent) or homemakers (5 percent) with a history of voluntary service.[85]

The precise duties and functions of state boards of education vary, but generally the boards are charged with the following functions.

1. Setting statewide curriculum standards.

2. Establishing qualifications and appointing personnel to the state department of education.

3. Setting standards for teacher and administrative certificates.

4. Establishing standards for accrediting schools.

5. Managing federal and state funds earmarked for education.

6. Keeping records and collecting data needed for reporting and evaluating.

7. Adopting long-range plans for the development and improvement of schools.

8. Creating advisory bodies as required by law.

9. Advising the governor or legislature on educational matters.

10. Appointing the chief state school officer, setting minimum salary schedules for teachers and administrators, and adopting policies for the operation of institutions of higher learning.[86]

## Chief State School Officer

The *chief state school officer* (sometimes known as the *state superintendent* or commissioner of education) serves as the head of the state department of education and, in most cases, is also the chief executive of the state school board. He or she is usually a professional educator.

The first chief state officer's position was established in New York in 1812, with the title "superintendent of common schools," and the duties of this position re-

volved around coordination and management. Perhaps the two most famous chief state officers were Horace Mann, the first Massachusetts "commissioner of education," who spearheaded the common school movement in the mid-1820s, and Henry Barnard, the first Connecticut state commissioner in 1838, who adopted many of Mann's progressive ideas and later became the first U.S. commissioner of education from 1867 to 1870.[87] After Mann popularized the role of state commissioner, the position increased rapidly so that by 1859 this post was found in twenty-four states.[88] To be sure, the role of state school officer came into being many decades after local school districts within the states were in operation.

The office is filled in one of three ways: In 2002, nine states filled the position through appointment by the governor, twenty-six states through appointment by the state board of education, and thirteen states by popular election.[89] The duties of the chief state school officer and the relationship between that position and the state board and state department vary from state to state. They usually depend on whether the official was appointed or voted into office. When the chief officer is elected, he tends to have more independence.

As of 2002, seven chief state school officers were minority; moreover, there were seventeen female chief officers.[90] The increasing number of women as chief state school officers (two in 1985, nine in 1994) represents a noticeable change[91] and a departure from the "old boy network" that is common in school administration.

Because of differences in method of selection and in legal relationship between the state board of education and the chief state officer, the responsibilities of the chief state officer vary widely. However, the major re-

---

[85] *Membership Directory 2000* (Alexandria, VA: National Association of State Boards of Education, 2000).

[86] National Association of State Boards of Education, *Annual Report 1999* (Alexandria, VA: National Association of State Boards of Education, 1999); *State Boards of Education in an Era of Reform, Final Report of the National Association of State Boards of Education* (Alexandria, VA: National Association of State Boards of Education, 1987). Also see Allan C. Ornstein and Daniel U. Levine, *Foundations of Education*, 9th ed. (Boston: Houghton Mifflin, 2006).

[87] Lawrence A. Cremin, *The Republic and the School* (New York: Teachers College Press, 1957); E. P. Cubberly, *The History of Education* (Boston: Houghton Mifflin, 1920).

[88] Kimbrough and Nunnery, *Educational Administration*; Stephen J. Knezevich, *Administration of Public Education*, 4th ed. (New York: Harper & Row, 1984); Theodore J. Kowalski, *Contemporary School Administration*, 2nd ed. (Boston: Allyn and Bacon, 2003).

[89] *Chief State School Officers 2002* (Washington, DC: Council of Chief State School Officers, 2002). Two states did not report information.

[90] Ibid.

[91] Paula Dello, director of public information, National Chief States School Organization, personal communication, May 20, 1994.

sponsibilities associated with the office are likely to include the following duties:

1. Serving as the chief administrator of the state department of education.

2. Selecting personnel for the state department of education.

3. Recommending and administering an educational budget for the state department of education.

4. Ensuring compliance with state educational laws and regulations.

5. Explaining and interpreting the state's school laws.

6. Deciding controversies involving the administration of the schools within the state.

7. Arranging the studies, committees, and task forces necessary to identify problems and recommend solutions.

8. Reporting on the status of education within the state to the governor, legislature, state board of education, and public.

9. Recommending improvements in educational legislation and policies to the governor and state legislature.

10. Working with local school boards and administrators to improve education within the state.[92]

## State Departments of Education

Another major state education agency is the *state department of education,* which usually operates under the direction of the state board of education and is administered by the chief state school officer. Traditionally, the primary function of state departments of education was to collect and disseminate statistics about the status of education within the state. Since the 1950s, they have enlarged their services and functions to include (1) accrediting schools; (2) certifying teachers; (3) apportioning funds; (4) overseeing student transportation and safety; (5) monitoring state regulations; (6) conducting research, evaluating programs, and is-

suing reports; and (7) monitoring federally funded programs to ensure compliance with regulations.[93]

During recent decades, state departments have had to grapple with controversial issues such as desegregation, compensatory education, bilingual and special education, student rights and unrest, school finance reform and school choice, aid to minority groups, increasing enrollments, collective bargaining, accountability, assessment and standards, and certification for teachers and principals. The federal government, the courts, and active interest groups have joined in the fray and wrestled with many educational or school issues — forcing governors and legislators to increase the staff budget and functions of state departments of education.

State departments of education, once innocuous and invisible, have doubled and tripled in size and have assumed new responsibilities in administering complex programs. In 1900, there were a total of 177 staff department employees nationwide, and 47 were chief state school officers.[94] In 1962, ten states had departments of more than 100 professionals, and twenty-one had fewer than 50 staff members; in two states, the staff exceeded 1000.[95] By 1982, only six states (Delaware, Idaho, Nevada, South Dakota, North Dakota, and Wyoming) had professional staffs of fewer than 100, and six states (California, Connecticut, Michigan, New Jersey, New York, and Texas) had staffs of more than 1000. Twenty years later (2002), five states (omit Connecticut) had staffs of more than 1000.[96]

As a general rule, the more populated the state and/or the larger the number of local school districts in the state, the higher the degree of centralization and the larger the state department staff. Less populated states

---

[92] Campbell et al., *The Organization of American Schools;* Walter G. Hack, J. Carl Candoli, and John R. Ray, *School Business Administration,* 6th ed. (Needham Heights, MA: Allyn and Bacon, 1998); Jerome T. Murphy, *State Leadership in Education: On Being a Chief State Officer* (Washington, DC: Washington University Press, 1980); Allan C. Ornstein, *Education and Social Inquiry* (Itasca, IL: Peacock, 1978).

[93] James W. Guthrie and Rodney J. Reed, *Educational Administration and Policy,* 3rd ed. (Needham Heights, MA: Allyn and Bacon, 1998); Joseph Murphy and Karen Seashore Louis (eds.) *Handbook of Research on Educational Administration,* 2nd ed. (San Francisco: Jossey-Bass, 2000); Ornstein, *Education and Social Inquiry.*

[94] Fred F. Beach and Andrew H. Gibbs, *Personnel of State Department of Education* (Washington, DC: U.S. Government Printing Office, 1952); Knezevich, *Administration of Public Education;* Ronald W. Rebore, *Personnel Administration in Education,* 5th ed. (Needham Heights, MA: Allyn and Bacon, 1998).

[95] Ornstein, *Education and Social Inquiry.*

[96] Dinah Wiley, *State Boards of Education* (Arlington, VA: National Association of State Boards of Education, 1983). Telephone conversation with David Griffiths, Director of Public Affairs, National Association of State Boards of Education, February 5, 2003.

and states with fewer school districts have smaller and decentralized staffs. Although some divisional administrators of these departments change with changes of political party control or with a change in the chief officer, the professional staff—such as researchers and statisticians, curriculum and supervisory specialists, and clerks and secretaries—are usually career or civil service employees. By and large, staff members of the state departments of education are recruited from public school personnel and from local school districts and colleges of education.

The leadership role of the state departments of education expanded in the 1980s. The 1981 Education Consolidation and Improvement Act (ECIA) presented states with a broad number of options for spending federal monies allocated to the states. Not only did ECIA give the states more responsibility for determining how and where to spend federal money for education, but also it reduced federal funding and thus put more importance on state funding. This trend continued through the 1990s and into the twenty-first century.

Recent federal funding policies and mounting state deficits have put added pressure on state departments to spend educational money wisely, to administer the state programs effectively, and to think about the bottom line. Competition over school choice, voucher programs, and charter schools have increased this pressure on state departments. In addition, controversial issues in education will not go away, and public groups are becoming more aggressive and astute in making their demands felt at the state level including tougher academic standards, high-stake testing, and teacher/school accountability. In short, state departments of education must now provide increased leadership and technical assistance to local school districts as well as to state boards of education, state legislators, and governors.

## State Reform Movements

Not since the wave of school reform that followed Sputnik has education been so prominently on stage at the national and state level, on television, and in local newspapers. Presidential candidates, governors, state legislators, and chief state school officers have all gotten involved, indicating the high priority of education, the desire to reform it, and the need to allocate more resources for it. Businesses such as Microsoft, IBM, and Motorola have recently taken active roles in helping to shape education policy, in part because jobs are becoming more demanding and complex and the school products (students) are becoming "dumber." Teachers' unions have shifted their focus from the welfare of teacher members to the need to cooperate with school administrators and school board members for purposes of reform; in making this transition, they have shifted the image of union-based organizations to professional organizations and are now willing to work with (not against) administrative associations for institutional welfare.[97]

Nationwide, more than 1500 state statutes affecting some aspect of school reform were enacted between 1985 and 1990. During the next fifteen years, 1991 to 2005, approximately 3000 state statutes dealing with reform were enacted.[98] They came as "waves" with tremendous fanfare, publicity, and controversy attached to the reform measures. These waves can be classified into four reform-type packages: (1) academic standards, (2) professional policy, (3) curriculum development, and (4) assessment and accountability. In general, all four waves stressed productivity and efficiency as well as education excellence.

The first wave, dealing with student achievement, focused on *academic standards;* graduation and college admission requirements; more frequent exit tests; time on task, attendance, and homework; reduced class size; and early childhood education. The second wave, dealing with *professionalism,* focused on competency-based training, certification and testing requirements, accountability, salary increases, merit pay and career ladders, differential roles and salaries, evaluation, and staff development. The third wave focused on the *curriculum*—the need to emphasize the basics, computers, and technology; a common core (academic) high school curriculum, especially increased science, math, and foreign language; and business-university-school partnerships. The fourth wave focused on *school improvement;*

[97]Tom Loveless (ed.), *Conflicting Missions: Teacher Unions and Education Reform* (Washington, DC: Brookings Institution, 2000); Albert Shanker, "School Boards Are Being Massacred," *American School Board Journal,* 176 (1989), pp. 29–30. Also see James P. Spillane et al., *Distributed Leadership in Practice* (New York: Teachers College Press, Columbia University, 2008).

[98]Case, *How to Get the Most Reform for Your Reform Money;* Jay P. Greene, *Education Myths: What Special Interest Groups Want You to Believe About Our Schools* (New York: Rowman & Littlefield, 2006); Josephy Murphy and Amanda Datnow, *Leadership Lessons from Comprehensive School Reforms* (Thousand Oaks, CA: Corwin, 2003).

**Table 9–5    Average Number of Carnegie Units Earned by Public High School Graduates in Academic Subjects, 1982, 1994, 1998, and 2000**

|      | Total | English | Social Studies | Math | Science | Foreign Language | Computer Science |
|------|-------|---------|----------------|------|---------|------------------|------------------|
| 1982 | 21.6  | 3.9     | 3.2            | 2.6  | 2.2     | 1.0              | 0.14             |
| 1994 | 24.2  | 4.2     | 3.6            | 3.4  | 3.0     | 1.8              | 0.65             |
| 1998 | 25.1  | 4.3     | 3.7            | 3.4  | 3.1     | 1.9              | 0.74             |
| 2000 | 26.0  | 4.4     | 3.8            | 3.6  | 3.2     | 1.9              | 0.83             |

Source: *The Condition of Education 1993* (Washington, DC: U.S. Government Printing Office, 1993), tables 24-1, 26-1, pp. 266, 278; *The Condition of Education 1998* (Washington, DC: U.S. Government Printing Office, 1998), indicator 26, p. 88; *Digest of Education Statistics, 2000* (Washington, DC: U.S. Government Printing Office, 2001), table 138, p. 154; *Digest of Education Statistics, 2004* (Washington, DC: U.S. Government Printing Office, 2005), table 135, p. 152.

standard-based education; accountability and high-stake testing.

By 2005, a series of actions had been taken at the state level, largely to improve the quality of education. All states had undertaken academic and curriculum reform (categories 1 and 3), forty-seven states had undertaken items dealing with professional reform (category 2) and/or school improvement (category 4), and all states had implemented some form of standards, accountability, and/or testing, also category 4.[99]

Especially dramatic increases of students enrolled in academic programs, core academic subjects, and advanced placement examinations occurred after the 1983 publication of *A Nation at Risk* (Table 9–5). The concerns voiced today parallel those voiced after Sputnik and during the Cold War. Although military concerns have been replaced by economic concerns, the threat of foreign competition still forms the basis of our educational debates. What was unimaginable began to occur in the 1970s and 1980s—other nations were surpassing our educational attainments and industrial output. Even though our population is increasing, our human capital is being depleted. This decline is linked to the foundations of our educational institutions and a growing underclass, which is spilling over into the workplace and other sectors of society.

The states have responded. Between 1985 and 2000, forty-nine states increased or introduced student as-sessment programs, twenty-eight states required competency tests for high school graduation, all fifty introduced or raised requirements for high school graduation in terms of Carnegie units (see Table 9–5), and forty-three states raised college entrance requirements. Twelve states increased the length of the school year, and thirteen states introduced additional instructional time. Twenty states reduced class sizes, and twenty-four states started students at a younger age.[100] Surprisingly, however, the U.S. high school graduate rate slightly inched downward, from 72 percent in 1985 to 71 percent in 2000—suggesting a flat outcome or fade-out factor despite increased reform efforts.[101]

By 2000, all fifty states had introduced changes in teacher preparation, thirty-four required testing for admission to teacher-education programs, thirty-five required exit tests from teacher-education programs, thirty-nine required testing for initial certification of teachers, and twelve introduced career ladders for teachers.[102] In thirty-nine states, higher teacher salaries were attributed in part to the national reform movement. As

[99] Gerald W. Bracey, "The 15th Bruce Report on the Condition of Public Education," *Phi Delta Kappan,* 87 (2005): 138–153; William J. Gallagher, "The Contradictory Nature of Professional Teaching Standards," *Phi Delta Kappan,* 87 (2005): 112–115; and Paul Hill and James Harvey, *Making School Reform Work* (Washington, DC: Brookings Institution, 2005).

[100] Bruce J. Biddle and David C. Berliner, "Small Class Size and Its Effects," *Educational Leadership,* 59 (2002): 12–23; *The Condition of Education 2006* (Washington, DC: U.S. Government Printing Office, 2006). Indicators, 28, 35, pp. 65, 78; *Digest of Education Statistics 2003,* table 6, p. 17; and Marge Schreren, "How and Why Standards Can Improve Achievement," *Educational Leadership,* 59 (2001): 14–19.

[101] *Digest of Education Statistics, 2003,* table 102, p. 134.

[102] *The Condition of Education, 2006,* Indicator 37, p. 80; Linda Darling-Hammond, *Solving the Dilemmas of Teacher Supply and Demand* (New York: National Commission on Teaching and America's Future, 2000); and Linda Darling-Hammond and J. Bransford, *Preparing Teachers for a Changing World* (San Francisco: Jossey-Bass, 2005).

many as thirty-five states have upgraded the educational and testing requirements of principals between 1985 and 2000 and others have demanded stricter evaluation and accountability of principals.[103] More than twenty-five states have already introduced centers or academies for principals, to help them improve their leadership and managerial skills.

## Lessons to Be Learned

Recent efforts show that education reform, if it is to be successful, cannot come from only one group—politicians, state officials, taxpayers, administrators, or teachers—but needs cooperation among all groups. Moreover, responsibility is needed at all levels. For example, regardless of how much money is earmarked for increased salaries or merit pay, we need responsible teachers and administrators at the school level; no one can reform dedication and hard work. Regardless of number or type of student tests, or how much homework is assigned, students (and parents) must make a concerted effort in academic input and performance. Regardless of the motivation or incentives we provide, no student can be compelled to learn; enthusiasm for learning cannot be coerced. Learning involves delayed gratification and sweat; it does not come easy and cannot be regulated by a clause, resolution, or mandate.

The second lesson to be learned is that education reform—more precisely, the success of reform—depends in large measure on the features of the local school: the school organization, school culture, and school ethos. In effect, school as a whole and school as a process are interlinked, with a changing and dynamic environment. A broader construct in education that represents this concept of school organization, culture, and ethos is referred to as school climate (see Chapter 3). The idea of a corporation's culture as used by Thomas Peters and Robert Waterman's analysis of the best-run American companies comes near to capturing this concept.[104] A more

precise term is **subjective culture**—that is, the way the organizational environment or social system operates, its belief systems, structures, stereotype formations, norms, roles, values, rules, and task definitions.[105] The values, beliefs, and behaviors of the school's players—administrators, teachers, students (even parents)—all play a role in determining reform and what will be accomplished at the school level.

The third lesson, although somewhat over-simplified, is that the reform measures that states adopt are not likely to make a difference or lead to serious improvement unless the policies are responsive to local needs and pressures and unless the local school environment, including the people, are willing to adopt those measures. (See Administrative Advice 9–3.)

Although states generally control funding, curriculum requirements, teacher and administrative certification, high school graduation requirements, and even textbook selection (in twenty-two states), they still have limited control over the daily operation of schools. State efforts to reform education may be visible and vocal and take on many political and economic dimensions, but the dynamics of local schools and school administrators can torpedo authorized reform policies. State reform, then, must be sensitive to and include the local interpretation and responses to the official version of reform. Educational change must be played out in the classrooms and schools of America, and state-initiated reforms should conform—at least be modified—to local politics, processes, and perceptions.

## State–School District Relationship

Policymakers and educators must understand that in some states school reform has involved billions of dollars and millions of students, tens of thousands of teachers and administrators, and hundreds of programs. In California and New York, for example, $1 billion or more has been appropriated for reform each year since 1983.[106] Considering the proportion of students, similar financial and political investment in school reform

[103]John C. Daresh, *Beginning the Principalship* (Thousand Oaks, CA: Corwin Press, 2006); *Leading Learning Communities: Standards for What Principlas Should Know and Be Able to Do* (Alexandria, VA: National Association of Elementary School Principals, 2001); and Marc Tucker and Judy B. Codding, *The Principal Challenge* (San Francisco: Jossey-Bass, 2002).

[104]Thomas Peters and Robert Waterman, *In Search of Excellence: Lessons Learned from America's Best-Run Companies* (New York: Harper & Row, 1982).

[105]Terrance E. Deal and Kent D. Peterson, *Shaping School Culture* (San Francisco: Jossey-Bass, 1998); Michael Fullan, *The New Meaning of Educational Change*, 4th ed. (New York: Teachers College Press, Columbia University, 2007).

[106]*Digest of Education Statistics, 2000*, table 363, p. 414; Also see Gary Orfield and Elizabeth H. DeBray (eds.), *Hard Work for Good Schools: Facts, Not Fads, in Title I Reform* (Washington, DC: Brookings Institution, 2001).

## Administrative Advice 9–3

### Principles for Improving Schools

A number of important principles result in school effectiveness and excellence. Based on the recent state-initiative programs to improve local schools, as well as the school-reform managerial literature in general, many of the factors and variables are listed below. School leaders can adapt these principles to help improve their own schools.

■ The school has a clearly stated mission or set of goals.

■ Students are achieving at a level commensurate with their abilities.

■ School achievement is closely monitored.

■ Provisions are made for *all* students, including tutoring for low achievers and enrichment programs for the talented and gifted.

■ Teachers and administrators agree on what is "good" teaching and learning; a general philosophy and psychology of learning prevails, although it may not be clearly stated or labeled by the staff.

■ Emphasis on cognition is balanced with concerns for students' personal, social, and moral growth; students are taught to be responsible for their actions and behaviors; every student has a "home base" where teachers advise and provide guidance.

■ Teachers and administrators are up to date on the knowledge of teaching and learning, as well as knowledge in their specific area or specialty.

■ Teachers and administrators expect students to learn and convey their expectations to students and parents.

■ Teachers are expected to make significant contributions to school improvement.

■ Administrators provide ample support, information, and time for teacher enrichment.

■ A sense of teamwork prevails; the staff works together in teams, and there is interdisciplinary and interdepartmental communication.

■ Incentives, recognition, and rewards are conveyed to teachers and administrators for their efforts on behalf of the team and school mission.

■ The interests and needs of the individual staff members are matched with the expectations of the institution (or school).

■ New professional roles are created and others are redefined; the staff has the opportunity to be challenged and creative; there is a sense of professional enrichment and renewal.

■ Staff development programs provide teachers with the latest instructional techniques, including how to teach students how to learn so they can eventually learn without the teacher.

■ The school environment is safe and healthy; there is a sense of order (not control) in classrooms and hallways.

■ Parents and community members are supportive of the school and are involved in school activities.

■ The school has a structure and identity of its own that students, teachers, parents, and community members understand and share.

■ The school is a learning center for the larger community, for the young and old, for students and parents alike; it reflects the norms and values of the community, and the community sees the school as an extension of the community.

---

has characterized states such as Michigan, New Jersey, North Carolina, and Tennessee. Regardless of results, some advocates would like to declare state reform as a great success in order to justify more expenditures for public schools. Others would like to declare schools a failure, and use national and international achievement scores as the acid test. Some argue for alternative reform packages, often coinciding with the special interests of their own pressure group with whom they identify. Still others seek various school choice and voucher programs

for improving schools. To be sure, there are many unanswered questions, and it will take many years to determine if our state initiatives have made substantial change.

In one recent California study of seventeen secondary schools (twelve high schools and five middle/junior high schools) in ten different school districts, a number of successful reform-change strategies seem to show that district leadership is important but school sites (and teachers and school administrators) are crucial for implementation of school reform. Although commitment to reform and efforts to bring it about were under way in many districts before the state stepped in with its provisions and resources, the state reform legislation strengthened the local desire to focus on school improvement and effectiveness; moreover, the district reform policies became more comprehensive and expanded to include other areas of education and all students. Reforms were typically initiated from the top down (district to school), not a popular idea today among many critics, and tended to result in greater centralization, but principals, supervisors, and teachers played an active role in implementation. By the mid-1990s, reform had become driven by mandated testing and high-stake accountability.[107]

In New York, as part of the Comprehensive School Improvement Planning process, about 1500 schools in more than 100 school districts have seen five principles emerge among reform- and change-minded schools:

1. *Excellence and Equity.* With these two essential philosophical ingredients, emphasis is on both basic skills and advanced level courses.

2. *Research and Evaluation.* Highly prized, research and evaluation use instruments to assess needs, plan improvements, and evaluate results.

3. *Data.* Data are seriously considered, but the information is made clear, simple, and brief before presented.

4. *Site-Based Collaboration and Planning.* Emphasis is on site-based collaboration and planning; that is, the staff is involved in planning and making decisions to ensure their commitment to change.

5. *Instruction.* Emphasis is on instruction while avoiding the tendency to be driven by test data or statewide assessments.[108]

In short, these five principles can guide school districts in all parts of the country in their mission pursuits and reform processes.

In North Carolina, reform involved student achievement tests; a focus on reading, writing, and mathematics; and teacher and school accountability. The school's performance was assessed in context with state standards. Schools were labeled "exemplary," "meets expectations," "adequate performance," and "low performance." Among the high stakes attached to the test outcomes were incentives of $1500 for teachers if their school exceeded expectations. However, schools that failed to meet expectations were earmarked for assistance and the potential removal of teachers and principals. Test scores were made public, and many administrators were embarrassed if their schools were among the low performing.[109] The lesson in North Carolina is simple. Since the focus of the tests was on basic skill subjects, the sciences, social sciences, and arts were pushed aside and taught only if extra time was left in the schedule or if administrators were confident that their schools could meet expectations. Right answers counted more than thinking, and teaching toward the test counted more than teaching about ideas, values, and character development.

## Guidelines for Reform

The theory of school reform today recognizes that state-level policymakers, professional associations and people, and local administrative and teaching personnel play important roles in producing and maintaining reform measures. These players exist in a vague and uneasy harmony; the fragility of the relationship is increased from efforts to balance state and local policies. Reform measures at the state level require fundamental redefinition of organizational roles and relationships among state education agencies and between state agencies and local school districts. The need for cooperation, vision, and goal setting has become increasingly clear. Next are ten recommendations for enhancing today's reform efforts:

1. *Develop Comprehensive Reforms.* Reforms should focus on major areas of restructuring school organization, school finance, personnel, curriculum, and student policy. A comprehensive reform

[107]Kenneth A. Sirotnik, "Promoting Responsible Accountability in Schools and Education," *Phi Delta Kappan,* 83 (2002): 662–673; Richard Stiggins, "Assessment Crisis: The Absence of Assessment for Learning," *Phi Delta Kappan,* 83 (2002): 758–765.

[108]Gerald Benjamin and Richard P. Nathan, *Regionalism and Realism: A Study of Governments in the New York Metropolitan Area* (Washington, DC: Brookings Institution, 2001); Thomas Kelly, "Five Ways to Make Your Schools Effective," *School Administrator,* 56 (1999): 26–29.

[109]James B. Hunt, "Leadership in Education: A View from the State," *Phi Delta Kappan,* 83 (2002); 714–720; Gail Jones et al., "The Impact of High-Stakes Testing on Teachers and Students in North Carolina," *Phi Delta Kappan,* 81 (1999): 199–203.

package involves the coordinated efforts of several state education agencies and departments within each agency. Reform, to be comprehensive, cannot be based on demands of one internal advocacy group; it must include many diversified groups and agencies within the organization and as many of their services as possible.

2. *Plan Long-Range Reforms.* To have the greatest impact, long-range planning should be built into reform; short-range planning should be developed as part of the feedback process to make adjustment in long-range goals.

3. *Involve Many Agencies Other than Schools.* School cannot be expected to solve all the ills of society; business, universities, government, community, social and recreational agencies, the home, and mass media have a role to play in reform. Similarly, school administrators can learn from the examples of successful administrators in other organizations. (See Administrative Advice 9–3.)

4. *Consider the Unique Needs of City, Suburban, and Rural School Districts.* The problems facing schools are different in various geographic settings. Reform in big-city school districts needs to focus on basic problems that deal with student attendance, reading, and discipline. The suburbs often have problems of latchkey children, overstressed and overprogrammed students, and a narrow emphasis on grades and cognitive activities at the expense of socialization and personal development. Reform of rural schools needs to center on inadequate personnel and programs, transportation, and school district sharing plans.

5. *View State–City Problems as Mutual Problems.* Often big cities find themselves treated as stepchildren and at the short end of the funds when they have to depend on state agencies because the rural/suburban legislators often gang up against city interests. Reform measures need to involve cooperation among various state and city institutions and officials. Suburbs, adjacent to the cities, that fail to recognize that the problems and prospects of the city eventually affect their own municipalities are naive about metropolitan trends. By ignoring the inevitable, the suburbs make themselves more vulnerable to future consequences.

6. *Consider Research and Development as an Integral Part of Reform.* Relations among universities, state education agencies, and local school districts need to be improved in the areas of research and development. Professors have often engaged in research considered to be esoteric and of little value for practitioners. Research and development need to be applied to the realities of classrooms and schools—and what concerns practitioners should become the agenda. Research and development budgets, which often comprise less than 2 percent of a state educational agency or school district's budget, need to be tripled in order to make a real impact and produce change.

7. *Structure State Education Agencies to Provide Leadership.* Most state education agencies are increasingly becoming more active in reform; however, they are not organized to carry out missions and policies and programs that are regarded as ad hoc—temporary or transitory. Greater stability and institutionalization of departments and units in these agencies are required.

8. *Staff State Education Agencies with Highly Qualified Personnel.* Careers in state education agencies should be seen as important and challenging careers; yet little attention is given to these jobs by the educational establishment. Failure to recognize that these state educational jobs should be staffed by competent people, who can deal with administrative, supervisory, and technical problems, has created a void in some states; public policy goals that could be achieved often fail to materialize. Plans should provide for recruitment of personnel who are qualified to carry out the missions of the respective state organizations.

9. *Develop State Partnerships at the Regional Level in Six to Ten Different Areas of the Country.* By sharing personnel, programs, and research and development data, state education agencies can save money (instead of duplicating many efforts), resolve some problems that they have trouble dealing with on a separate basis, and engage in comprehensive, intrastate reform. The establishment of a loose regional structure in education, where the states still retain primary identity, provides nearby state education agencies with the opportunity to communicate and share ideas that work, draw on the abilities of key personnel, engage in comprehensive staff development and training, and conduct research and development deemed important.

10. *Improve Reform by Forming a Federal Partnership with State Education Agencies.* The federal government has recently shifted too many educa-

## PRO/CON Debate

### Abolishing the U.S. Department of Education

Two recent secretaries of education, William Bennett and Lamar Alexander, have called for the elimination of the U.S. Department of Education. Key congressional leaders indicated that they, too, will push to eliminate this cabinet-level federal agency.

**Question:** Would education be enhanced if the Department of Education were abolished?

**Arguments PRO**

1. American education was alive and well before the Department was formed and it can exist very well without it; critics point out that most federal education programs are unsuccessful and education research and development has had minimal worth and impact.

2. The Department of Education has proven to be a disappointment. Rather than enhancing school district self-sufficiency, it has spawned a proliferation of red tape that inhibits the work of educators.

3. The U.S. Constitution does not specifically state that education is a responsibility of the federal government. Therefore the states are the units that assume primary responsibility for education. State education departments, not a Department of Education, should assume the primary burden for education.

4. Deficit reduction is essential if the economy is to rebound. The cost of public education has risen beyond a level that taxpayers can be expected to support. The majority of educational resources should be diverted to states and localities, not to a federal bureaucracy.

**Arguments CON**

1. The Department was established over twenty years ago with the approval, which it still has, of the vast majority of educational and professional organizations; the DOE helps organize, coordinate, and administer federal educational programs, research, and development.

2. Officials within the Department of Education assert that U.S. public schools are "turning the corner." This is due, at least in part, to federal efforts to increase attention to, and divert resources to, education.

3. The vast differences between the states are nowhere as evident as in the educational arena. In some states, poor children are seriously deprived by receiving an inadequate education. This disparity can only be addressed at the federal level.

4. Nothing will ensure the nation's prosperity more than a strong and vital educational system. This cannot occur without consistent, clear voices supporting education at all levels: federal, state, and local.

tion responsibilities to the states. Many states have budget problems and cannot afford a comprehensive reform package that costs money; nor do some have the inclination to help out big-city school districts. Increased federal aid to strengthen state education agencies is required—paralleling action to improve educational opportunities of inner-city students. Although reform should be carried out by the state (and the state has that legal responsibility), the federal government must remain involved in and supportive of state efforts and provide supplementary funding to poorer school districts.

Finally, policies designed to reform education are no better than the school districts and schools that implement them. The target of reform must always be at

the local level, and it must always consider people, for they are the ones who must implement reform. Indeed, every individual who comes into a system or organization plays a multitude of roles; each professional brings to that role personality as well. Each person has certain needs to fulfill within the system—whether it is a business, school, hospital, or the like. Rarely is there absolute congruence between institutional roles and expectations and individual personality and needs.

Administrators must recognize that they cannot always avoid this conflict; they must manage it. The way they manage it is reflected in the social behavior of their staff and how these people react to change and reform. Right now, much of the emphasis on reform is related to high-stake testing, accountability, and "report cards" which show how schools perform in relation to prescribed standards and state benchmarks.

## Summary

1. The federal role in education dramatically increased through the twentieth century, especially between the Roosevelt and Carter years. Since the 1980s, however, federal involvement in education has been reduced, highlighted by the new federalism.

2. The Department of Education (DOE) was established in 1980 with full cabinet status. Secretary William Bennett added visibility and prestige to the department even though many of his views on education were considered controversial.

3. Federal programs and activities in education were uncoordinated until the enactment of the relief acts during the Depression and the War Act during World War II. After Sputnik and with the War on Poverty and civil rights movement, national policy became linked to education, and federal funding dramatically increased.

4. The growth in federal funding leveled off in the 1980s, and the Educational Consolidation and Improvement Act (ECIA) of 1981 shifted much of the federal responsibility for education programs to the states. Monies were mainly earmarked on the basis of student enrollment instead of basic need. Twenty years later, under the Bush II administration, federal funding increased in real dollars; however, monies were partially allocated on the basis of student test performance, not need.

5. The national reform movement in education shifted educational policy from equality to excellence. The current demand for excellence is highlighted by a series of policy reports for national consumption. Of all the reports, *A Nation at Risk,* the best-known one, started the movement.

6. The state hierarchy of education includes the governor, state legislature, and courts. In recent years, all three groups have taken a more active role in education.

7. With the exception of Wisconsin, all states have state boards of education. State departments of education operate under the direction of the state boards and are headed by the chief state school officer.

8. The chief state school officer, likely to be called a state superintendent of instruction or state commissioner of education, usually reports to the state department of education and advises the state legislature and governor.

9. The state reform movement in education gained momentum since the 1980s and can be categorized into four types of reform: student achievement, professionalism, curriculum, and high-stake testing and accountability.

10. Although Americans have high expenditures for public education, the results are not impressive when compared to the financial commitment to education and student achievement test scores of other nations.

## Key Terms

separation of powers
dual federalism
national federalism
new federalism
national standards movement
Northwest Ordinances
Morrill Act
Smith-Hughes Act
GI bill
National Defense Education Act
Elementary and Secondary Education Act
Title I
Title IX
Civil Rights Act
Bilingual Education Act
Education for All Handicapped Children Act
  (PL 94-142)
mainstreaming
block grants
equality of opportunity
Scholastic Aptitude Test
state education agency
political action committees
Kalamazoo decision
subjective culture

## Discussion Questions

1. What are the arguments for and against shifting educational responsibility from the federal government to the states?

2. What are the arguments for and against Title IX, special education legislation, bilingual education legislation, and No Child Left Behind?

3. What are the major responsibilities and functions of the state boards of education and state departments of education?

4. Explain the concept of state reform in education as it is presently evolving. How can state reform be improved?

5. What educational and social factors should be considered when comparing American students' performance with that of their international counterparts on like tests?

## Suggested Readings

Alexander, Kern, and M. David Alexander. *American Public School Law,* 6th ed. (Belmont, CA: Wadsworth, 2005). The authors provide a comprehensive overview of the laws governing the state and local school systems.

Bennis, Warren, et al. *The Future of Leadership* (San Francisco: Jossey-Bass, 2001). The book offers thoughts on leadership in an era of school reform and a new economy.

English, Fenwick, ed. *Encyclopedia of Educational Leadership and Administration* (Thousand Oaks, CA: Sage Publications, 2006). Up-to-date research review of supervision and administration.

Goodlad, John I. *In Praise of Education* (New York: Teachers College Press, Columbia University, 1997). This book offers an uplifting message of what is good about our schools and what we must do to reaffirm the schools' mission.

Murphy, Joseph and Amanda Datnow, *Leadership Lessons from Comprehensive School Reforms* (Thousand Oaks, CA: Corwin, 2003). The book discusses the roles and responsibilities of educational leaders involved in school reform.

Ornstein, Allan C. *Teaching and Schooling in America: Pre and Post September 11* (Boston: Allyn and Bacon, 2003). The author discusses inequality and equality, injustice and justice, immorality and morality, and a host of reform issues.

Sergiovanni, Thomas J. *Leadership for the Schoolhouse* (San Francisco: Jossey-Bass, 2000). The author examines the relationship between school improvement and moral leadership.

# 10. Local School Districts

FOCUSING QUESTIONS

1  What is the ideal size of a school district? Why?

2  What factors have stimulated the consolidation of local school districts in the last fifty years or so?

3  What factors have stimulated interest in school decentralization?

4  What is the best method of selecting school board members?

5  What are the major responsibilities of the school board?

6  How does the school board work with the district superintendent in formulating school policy?

7  What is a fair salary for a superintendent? Should district size and performance be factors?

8  Why are superintendents considered key personnel in the operation of school districts? What are the similarities and differences between the job of superintendent and the job of principal?

9  What are the major problem areas faced by superintendents? Principals?

In this chapter, we attempt to answer these questions by first examining school districts—in particular, their size and structure. Then we discuss the structure and duties of the local school board, the responsibilities of the superintendent, and the relationship between the board and the superintendent. Next, we explore the role of the central office staff and its obligations to the district and the superintendent. Finally, we discuss what makes an effective school principal.

## Local School Policy

The local school district is the basic administrative unit in the education hierarchy, which starts at the federal level and works its way to the state and then local level. For the greater part, the local school district consists of many schools. Most school districts comprise grades K to 12, with separate elementary and secondary schools; however, a small school district (in a rural or suburban area) may include only grades K to 8 (and consist of one or more elementary and/or middle-grade schools) and a neighboring school district will include grades 9 to 12 (with one or more high schools).

Regardless of the exact school structure within the district, every public school in the United States is part of a local school district. The district is created by the state. The state legislature, subject to the restrictions of the state constitution, can modify a local district's jurisdiction, change its boundaries and powers, or even eliminate it altogether. The local dis-

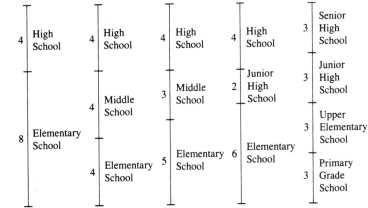

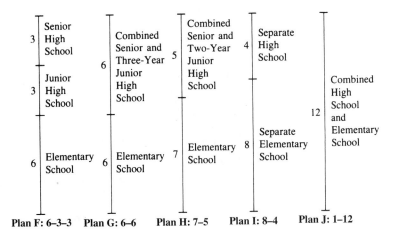

**Figure 10–1**

School District Organization by Grades

Source: Adapted from *Digest of Education Statistics, 2005* (Washington, DC: U.S. Government Printing Office, 2006, fig. 1, p. 9).

trict encompasses a relatively small geographic area and operates the schools for children within a specific community. It is the avenue through which local citizens act in establishing districtwide policies in education. However, because a school district operates to carry out a state function, not a local function, local policies must be consistent with policies set forth in the state school code. The local district can be compared to a limited corporation whose powers are granted by state laws; it has only those powers expressly granted to it and those discretionary powers essential to its operation.

## Organization of School Districts

The organization of school districts permits several grade plans and combinations of elementary and secondary schools. Figure 10–1 shows ten common organizational plans; a description for each follows.

1. Plan A shows the traditional 8–4 organizational plan consisting of an eight-year elementary school and a four-year high school.

2. Plan B exemplifies a 4–4–4 district plan, where the first four grades are elementary school, the next four are middle school, and the final four are high school.

3. Plan C illustrates the 5–3–4 plan, providing a five-year elementary school, a three-year middle school, and a four-year high school. Both Plans B and C are growing in popularity because of the middle-school movement.

4. Plan D shows a 6–2–4 district plan, where grades 1 to 6 comprise the elementary school, grades 7 to 8 comprise the junior high school, and grades 9 to 12 comprise the high school.

5. Plan E is the 3–3–3–3 plan, used in parts of the country that wish to promote school integration at

the elementary school level or in rural areas that need to consolidate school facilities. There are also a three-year junior high school and three-year senior high school.

6. Plan F represents a typical 6–3–3 elementary, junior high, and senior high school plan. Plans D, E, and F illustrate the junior high school in relation to elementary school and either high school or senior high school.

7. Plan G is the 6–6 organizational plan consisting of an elementary school for grades 1 to 6 and a combined three-year junior high school and three-year senior high school.

8. Plan H illustrates the 7–5 grade pattern, where the elementary school goes to grade 7, and there is a combined two-year junior high school and three-year senior high school. Plans G and H show the elementary school with a combined junior and senior high school, representative of a small number of U.S. schools.

9. Plan I shows two separate, usually adjacent, districts, where the elementary school grades K to 8 represent one district and the high school grades 9 to 12 represent the other district.

10. Plan J is the 1–12 plan, representative of even a smaller number of schools, usually special schools, alternative schools, one-room schoolhouses, or schools not classified by grade level.

It is difficult to say which plan is better or worse; it varies with educational philosophy and the conditions in the school district. Most progressive educators or communities prefer a middle-grade or junior high school, as a means of putting preadolescent students (who are usually undergoing rapid physical and social changes) under one roof for a number of years to facilitate their growth and development.

## Size of School Districts

What is the ideal size for a school district? In terms of minimum size, how many students must be enrolled to justify offering diversified programs, services, and personnel needed to meet modern educational requirements? The studies that suggest optimal size, over the last seventy years, have focused on cost analysis, curriculum offerings, staffing, and student achievement as the most important variables. During this period,

the minimum ideal size tends to be 10,000 to 12,000 students, and the maximum size tends to be 40,000 to 50,000 students.[1] One classic study considered the maximally effective school district to comprise 100,000 students.[2]

Today small is considered better; the idea is to scale down the school enterprise, whereas in the past big was considered better. Advocates of small school districts and rural schools point out that 5000-student maximums are more cost effective, have fewer student dropouts (in percentages), higher student SAT and ACT scores, and higher graduation and college entry rates than do school districts with more than 5000 students.[3] Although social class was not controlled in these studies, educational expenditures were. Small school districts, 5000 or fewer students, cluster in the 14th to 30th percentile in per-pupil expenditures but rank in the top 10 percent on nationwide achievement scores and other indicators of student performance (fewer dropouts, more high school graduates).[4]

---

[1] Howard A. Dawson, *Satisfactory Local School Units,* Field Study no. 7 (Nashville, TN: George Peabody College for Teachers, 1934); Mario D. Fantini, Marilyn Gittell, and Richard Magat, *Community Control and the Urban School* (New York: Praeger, 1970); A. Harry Passow, *Toward Creating a Model Urban School System* (New York: Teachers College Press, 1967); and *Summary of Research on Size of Schools and School Districts* (Arlington, VA: Educational Research Service, 1974).

[2] Paul R. Mort and Francis G. Cornell, *American Schools in Transition* (New York: Teachers College Press, 1941); Paul R. Mort, William S. Vincent, and Clarence Newell, *The Growing Edge: An Instrument for Measuring the Adaptability of School Systems,* 2 vols. (New York: Teachers College Press, 1955).

[3] *A Critique of North Carolina Department of Public Instruction's Plan to Mandate School District Mergers Throughout the State* (Raleigh: North Carolina Boards Association, 1986); Jacqueline P. Danzberger, Michael W. Kirst, and Michael P. Usdan, *Governing Public Schools: New Times, New Requirements* (Washington, DC: Institute for Educational Leadership, 1992); Susan Folleti Lusi, *The Role of State Departments of Education in Complex School Reform* (New York: Teachers College Press, Columbia University, 1997).

[4] Allan C. Ornstein, "School District and School Size: An Evolving Controversy," *High School Journal,* 76 (1993): 240–244; Ornstein, "School Size and Effectiveness: Policy Implications," *Urban Review,* 22 (1990): 239–245; and Diane M. Truscott and Stephen D. Truscott, "Differing Circumstances: Finding Common Ground Between Urban and Rural Schools," *Phi Delta Kappan,* 87 (2005): 123–130.

Other advocates maintain that school districts with 20,000 or fewer students have a significant positive relationship with SAT scores, high school graduation rates, and slightly more favorable pupil-teacher ratios than do districts with more than 20,000 students. Smaller school districts have significantly lower levels of parental income and spend about $250 less per student.[5] In short, "smaller districts . . . appear to achieve better results for students at equal [or less] cost."[6]

Studies of hundreds of school districts nationwide also confirm the relationship between inverse district size and student achievement, after controlling for per-pupil expenditures and social class.[7] Although larger school districts may be more efficient when it comes to spending—that is, per-unit costs decline with a greater number of students served because districts usually purchase more units cheaper and employ fewer teachers and administrators per student—the economies of scale enjoyed by large school districts come at the expense of educational outcomes. Moreover, there are some data to suggest that large school districts are actually inefficient and wasteful.[8] The dependence of costs seems U-shaped, with very small and very large school districts spending more per student than moderate-sized districts.

## Number of School Districts

Historically, 10,000 students is a large number for a school district. Our schools, we must remember, are an outgrowth of one-room schoolhouses and school districts in the rural United States. With the exception of a few urban areas, even as late as the turn of the twentieth century, most school districts consisted of three, four, or five schools and a few hundred students. As late as 1930, nearly 50 percent of U.S. school districts had fewer than 300 students. By 2003, as many as 21 percent of the school districts (enrolling only 1 percent of the nation's students) had fewer than 300 students. Inversely, 5.9 percent of public school districts contained 10,000 or more students. There were only 256, or 1.8 percent, school districts with 25,000 or more students, but they accounted for 16.2 million students, or 33 percent, of the nation's public school enrollment.[9] Table 10–1 shows how school districts today are distributed.

Most of the larger school districts (25,000 or more students) are in California, Florida, Texas, and Maryland, but the states with the largest district averages are, in descending order, Hawaii (183,600 students), Maryland (36,200), Florida (39,600), and Louisiana (10,700). The states with the smallest district averages—that is, less than 1000 students per district—are Maine, South Dakota, Vermont, Nebraska, and Montana.[10]

As many as twenty-six school districts have enrollments that exceed 100,000 students. In most cases, the larger school districts are located in or near cities, the largest being the New York City system with approximately 1,024,000 students, followed by Los Angeles with 747,000 students, Chicago with 434,000 students, and Dade County, Florida, with 372,000 students.[11] Reflecting both national enrollment trends and immigration trends to the larger cities, six of the ten largest school districts (in the Sunbelt) have experienced increased enrollments in the last ten years. The four (New York City, Baltimore, Detroit, and Philadelphia) that have experienced minus growth are located in the North (sometimes called the Frostbelt). The medium-sized and smaller school districts have followed metropolitan sprawl and tend to be located in the outer ring of the suburbs or in rural areas.

[5]Robert W. Jewell, "School and School District Size Relationships," *Education and Urban Society,* 21 (1989): 140–153; Jean Johnson, "Do Communities Want Smaller Schools?" *Educational Leadership,* 59 (2002): 42–46; Johnson "Will Parents and Teachers . . . Reduce School Size?" *Phi Delta Kappan,* 83 (2002): 353–356.

[6]Jewell, "School and School District Size Relationships," p. 151. Also see Kari Artstrom, "Overlooked Too Long, Small Schools Deserve Our Attention," *School Administrator,* 56 (1999): 50.

[7]Tom V. Ark, "The Case for Small High Schools," *Educational Leadership,* 59 (2002): 55–59; David H. Monk, "Secondary School Size and Curriculum Comprehensiveness," *Economics of Education Review,* 6 (1987): 137–150; William J. Fowler and Herbert J. Walberg, "School Size, Characteristics, and Outcomes," *Educational Evaluation and Policy Analysis,* 13 (1991): 189–202; and Joe Nathan and Karen Febey, *Smaller, Safer, Saner, Successful Schools* (Minneapolis: Center for School Change, 2001).

[8]Rick Allen, "Big Schools: The Way We Were," *Educational Leadership,* 59 (2002): 36–41; Donna Driscoll, Dennis Halcoussis, and Shirley Svorny, "School District Size and Student Performance," *Economics of Education Review,* 22 (2003): 193–201.

[9]*Digest of Education Statistics, 2005* (Washington, DC: U.S. Government Printing Office, 2006), table 85, p. 130.

[10]Ibid., tables 34, 86, pp. 63–64, 131.

[11]Ibid.

**Table 10–1**  **Distribution of School Districts by Size, 2003–2004**

| Size of District (Number of Pupils) | Public School Districts | | Public School Students | |
|---|---|---|---|---|
| | Number | Percent | Number[a] | Percent |
| Total operating districts | 14,383 | 100.0 | 48,354 | 100.0 |
| 25,000 or more | 256 | 1.8 | 16,150 | 33.4 |
| 10,000–24,999 | 594 | 4.1 | 9187 | 19.0 |
| 5000–9999 | 1058 | 7.4 | 7447 | 15.4 |
| 2500–4999 | 2031 | 14.1 | 7253 | 15.0 |
| 1000–2499 | 3421 | 23.8 | 5657 | 11.7 |
| 600–999 | 1728 | 12.0 | 1354 | 2.8 |
| 300–599 | 1981 | 13.8 | 870 | 1.8 |
| 1–299 | 2994 | 20.8 | 435 | 0.9 |
| Size not reported | 320 | 2.2 | — | — |

[a]in millions, based on Fall 2003.

Source: *Digest of Education Statistics, 2005* (Washington, DC: Department of Education, 2006), tables 85, 87, pp. 130, 133.

## Students and Schools

Across the nation, public school student enrollments show a 23 percent projected increase from 1989 to 2014, from 41 million to 50 million. The public elementary school enrollment (grades PK–8) is expected to exhibit a 5 percent increase from 2002 to 2014; the public high school enrollment (grades 9–12), a 2 percent increase.[12] The vast majority of enrollment increases will take place in the Sunbelt states (the South and West, 5 and 13 percent, respectively), while the Northeast will decrease 5 percent and the Midwest will decrease 2 percent from 2002 to 2014.[13]

The number of public elementary schools grew from 61,340 in 1990 to 71,195 in 2003. The number of public secondary schools grew from 23,460 in 1990 to 28,219 in 2003. In total, there were 82,475 public schools in 1990 and in 2003 there were 93,977—a 14 percent increase.[14]

The growth in student enrollments has affected school size in two ways: increasing the average school size at the elementary level from 449 in 1990 to 476

in 2003 and at the secondary level from 663 in 1990 to 722 in 2003. It also correlates with a reduction of small school districts (fewer than 300 students), from 3816 in 1990 to 2994 in 2003, a reduction of nearly 22 percent.[15]

**Demographics and Diversity**  In 1970, minority students comprised 20 percent of student enrollments. By 1995, it was 32 percent. In 2003, 42 percent of all students were minority. While the total number of school-aged children is expected to increase by 2.5 percent between 1998 and 2008, the number of white students is expected to decline by 3 percent. The number of black students will increase by 3 percent, Asian Americans by 5 percent, and Hispanics by 15 percent, making them the largest minority group in American schools.[16]

The U.S. Census predicts that by 2050 race in America will be turned upside down. There will be more minorities than whites living in America. Today's school enrollments exemplify the future; it is the most racial mix of students this country has experienced. Today's cities like New York, Miami, Houston, Dallas, Detroit, Chicago, and Los Angeles are already mostly minority,

---

[12]*Projections of Education Statistics to 2014* (Washington, DC: U.S. Government Printing Office, 2005), figures A, B, pp. 5–6.

[13]Ibid., table B, p. 7; Deidre A. Gaquin and Katherine A. DeBrandt (eds.), *The Almanac of American Education 2005* (Lanham, MD: Bernan Associates, 2005).

[14]*Digest of Education Statistics, 2005*, table 84, p. 129.

[15]Ibid., table 93, p. 165.

[16]*The Condition of Education, 2005* (Washington, DC: U.S. Government Printing Office, 2006), p. 33; *Projections of Education Statistics to 2008*, table 1, p. 8. Also see Harold Hodgkinson, "Educational Demographics: What Teachers Should Know," *Educational Leadership,* 58 (2000): 6–11.

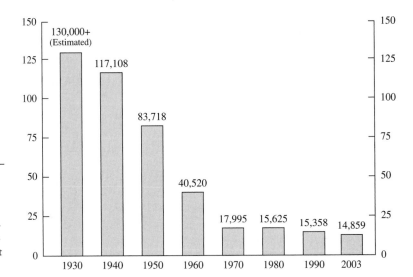

**Figure 10–2**

Declining Number of School Districts, 1930–2003

Source: *Digest of Education Statistics, 1972* (Washington, DC: U.S. Government Printing Office, 1973), fig. 7, p. 53; *Digest of Education Statistics, 2005* (Washington, DC: U.S. Government Printing Office, 2006), table 85, p. 130.

and the public school student population in these cities comprises 85 percent minority or more.

By 2010, whites will account for only 9 percent of the world's population, compared to 17 percent in 1997—making them the world's smallest ethnic minority. Only 12 percent of our current immigration is from Europe; almost all the remaining from Latin America and Asia.[17] The children of these immigrants represent the new immigrant students enrolling in schools across the nation. The successful administrator of the twenty-first century will have to deal with ethnic, religious, and linguistic diversity. The issue for schools is the same as it was one hundred years ago—to socialize immigrant children as soon as possible, but with understanding and respect for group and individual differences.

## Consolidation of School Districts

The number of school districts in the United States continues to decline. In 1930, there were more than 130,000 school districts. By 1950, the number had shrunk to 83,718; by 1980, to 15,625; and by 2003, to 14,859—suggesting a leveling process (see Figure 10–2).

The reduced number of school districts is a result of **consolidation,** the combination of a number of smaller school districts into one or two larger ones. Consolida-

tion is thought to bring about more effective schools by increasing the tax base, quality of professional personnel, breadth of educational programs, special services, and transportation facilities and by reducing overall educational costs per student.[18]

The data on consolidation, however, remain inconclusive. Moreover, consolidating districts usually means closing some schools, and this has proved to be a serious and emotional matter, especially in small and rural school districts where the local school may be a focal point of the community's identity. In many cases state school officials, operating under the assumption that consolidation is cost-effective and enhances student opportunity, have clashed with local townspeople who resent the interference of distant bureaucrats. The process can be demoralizing to students, parents, and the community at large. Local taxpayers, who might normally support plans for saving money, have often refused to endorse consolidation.[19]

Because of this opposition, officials in many states have begun looking for ways to obtain the benefits of consolidation without eliminating schools or districts.

---

[17]Hodgkinson, "Educational Demographics"; Allan C. Ornstein, *Teaching and Schooling in America: Pre- and Post-September 11* (Boston: Allyn and Bacon, 2003).

[18]William Howell (ed.), *Besieged: School Boards and the Future of Education Politics* (Washington, DC: Brookings Institution Press, 2005): 56–80. Jewell, "School and School District Size Relationships"; Deborah Meier, "Just Let Us Be: the Genesis of a Small Public School," *Educational Leadership,* 59 (2002): 76–80; Debra Viadero, "Small Is Better," *Education Week,* 13 November 2001, pp. 28–30.

[19]Ornstein, "School District and School Size."

One method is for neighboring districts to share programs and personnel. Minnesota, for example, encourages this trend by providing up to 75 percent of the cost of shared secondary school facilities and programs. Wisconsin provides additional Title I support for sharing facilities.[20] Iowa provides between 5 and 50 percent extra funding to local school districts that share course offerings, teachers, administrators, and school buildings.[21] In Illinois, Montana, and Nebraska, there is a hold on new consolidation plans, and there are school committees organized to restructure school district sizes.[22]

In many large school districts, such as Chicago and Philadelphia, no school can exceed a specific enrollment number. If so, there is pressure to create a "School within a School." In Chicago, a new reform effort called Renaissance 2010 involves changing 100 schools "into smaller institutions run under a variety of different arrangements." In Los Angeles, there is a reform effort to create a "shadow" school district, some 100 small charter schools serving some 50,000 students.[23] Hence larger school districts are trying to reduce unit sizes.

Some educators contend that consolidation has served its major purpose—eliminating many one-room schools and inefficient small districts—and that this trend will soon pass. But it remains a controversial issue that affects many school districts across the country.

## Decentralization of School Districts

Changes in the urban population after 1950 gave rise to changes in the composition of urban schools. As middle-class and white populations fled to the suburbs—in what became known as the "white flight movement"—the percentages of low-income and minority residents increased in the cities. As a result, city schools became multiethnic, and many schools in the suburbs became more homogeneous in terms of income and race. By the 1960s, many inner-city ethnic groups, especially blacks, began to feel that the schools did not serve their needs. They began to call for decentralization as a means to greater community involvement in the schools.

By definition, **decentralization** divides the school system into smaller units, but the focus of power and authority remains in a single central administration and board of education. There is usually little controversy over decentralization as long as jobs are not consolidated or expanded on the basis of racial or ethnic patterns. Even professional educators today see a need to reduce school bureaucracy and to accept decentralization because it allows the professional educators to retain power. At the same time, school critics and minority spokespersons believe that decentralization will give the people greater access to the schools.

Consequently, while many small and rural school districts have been consolidated in recent decades, many large urban districts have decentralized their schools. A nationwide survey on decentralization of school systems with 50,000 or more students was conducted in 1980.[24] Data on some sixty-six out of sixty-nine school districts in that group (96 percent return rate) were reported. Of the sixty-six districts, forty-two (67 percent) reported they were decentralized. Larger school districts (100,000 or more students) had decentralized more than smaller ones (50,000 to 99,999 students). For example, twenty out of twenty-two (91 percent) of the larger ones had decentralized, whereas only twenty-two out of forty-four (50 percent) enrolling fewer than 100,000 students were decentralized.

The decentralized unit names were largely confined to three terms. Twenty-eight referred to *areas* (67% adjusted percentage); seven referred to *districts* (17%), including community districts and subdistricts; and six referred to *regions* (14%). One district (2%) used the term *zone*. The number of decentralized units varied from as few as two areas in Oakland, California, and Portland, Oregon, to as many as thirty-two community districts in New York City, with four decentralized units the most frequent plan in fourteen school districts (33% adjusted percentage) and three units second most frequent in ten districts (24%). The number of

[20]Jeremy D. Finn, "Small Classes in American Schools," *Phi Delta Kappan,* 83, (2002): 551–560; Chris Pipho, "Rural Education," *Phi Delta Kappan,* 69 (1987): 6–7.

[21]*Annual School District Reorganization Report* (Des Moines: Iowa Department of Education, 1999).

[22]Evans Clinchy, "The Educationally Challenged American School District," *Phi Delta Kappan,* 80 (1998): 272–277; Allan C. Ornstein, "Controversy Over Size Continues," *School Administrator,* 46 (1989): 42–43; Pipho, "Rural Education."

[23]William Ayers and Michael Klonsky, "Chicago's Renaissance 2010," *Phi Delta Kappan,* 87 (2006): 453–456; Caroline Hendrie, "'Shadow' L.A. District Idea in the Works," *Education Week,* 27 November 2002, pp. 1, 13; Mary Anne Raywid, "The Policy of Small Schools and Schools-Within-Schools," *Educational Leadership,* 59 (2002): 47–51.

[24]Allan C. Ornstein, "Decentralization and Community Participation Policy of Big School Systems," *Phi Delta Kappan,* 62 (1980): 225–257.

decentralized units averaged 5.6, with larger districts (100,000 plus students) averaging 7.7 and smaller ones (fewer than 100,000 students) averaging 3.9.[25]

In a companion study, seventeen reasons were given for decentralization. The top eight reasons, in order of priority and representing 79 percent of the responses, are the following.

1. To enhance school-community relations.

2. To provide greater community input at the local level.

3. To provide local schools with more field and resource personnel.

4. To provide efficient maintenance and support for local schools.

5. To reduce administrative span of control.

6. To provide greater linkages between local schools and the central school board.

7. To redirect spending for local school needs.

8. To provide greater curriculum continuity from kindergarten through grade 12.[26]

Oddly enough, little evidence supported these reasons for decentralization. Very few of the school systems have conducted evaluations of their new organizational models or tested the assumptions, goals, and recommendations related to decentralization. Little hard evidence supports the assertion that school decentralization improves education.[27]

In 1988, the number of school districts with 50,000 or more students had decreased to sixty-two; in a follow-up study to the 1980 study, data were obtained from fifty-one districts (82 percent response rate). Only sixteen school districts (31 percent) reported being decentralized, although three others had recently moved from decentralization to centralization.[28] Even school districts that reported being decentralized were more centralized than decentralized in organizational hierarchy and administrative positions. Table 10–2 presents data concerning the sixteen large school districts that were decentralized in 1988. The table shows that four out of sixteen school districts claiming to be decentralized (Palm Beach, Florida; New Orleans; Jefferson County, Colorado; and Cleveland) were strongly committed to centralization. This is based on the fact that their central administrative staffs were each 10.8 to 21.5 times greater than their respective decentralized staffs. The majority of the school districts, ten out of sixteen, were moderately more centralized than decentralized. Their centralized administration was 1.5 to 4.0 times greater than their decentralized administration.

Only two school districts, New York City and St. Louis, were seemingly more committed to decentralization than centralization by virtue of their administrative positions being greater at the decentralized level than the centralized level. This fact is represented by the ratios of less than 1 of the two districts in the table. Hence, a school district planning to study decentralization might look at these two districts because in the past their commitment to decentralization seemed more evident from their administrative assignments. (See Administrative Advice 10–1.)

The concept of decentralization seems to be on the decline for two reasons: (1) there has been a drop in the percentage of decentralized school districts, from 67 percent (forty-two out of sixty-six) in 1980 to 31 percent (sixteen out of fifty-one) in 1988, and (2) the majority of districts currently claiming to be decentralized seems more committed to centralization. There is also research suggesting that increased administrative layers leads to bureaucracy, extra costs, and slower decision making from the central office. Thus, in an effort to enhance fiscal management and consolidate power and authority at the central office, the biggest governance change for New York City's schools in the last four decades was enacted in 2003: The thirty-two community school districts were abolished and replaced with 10 regional divisions, each headed by a superintendent, ranging in number of students from 67,700 to 137,200.[29]

---

[25]Ibid.

[26]Patrick B. Forsyth and Marilyn Tallerico (eds.), *City Schools: Leading the Way* (Thousand Oaks, CA: Corwin Press, 1993); Allan C. Ornstein, "Decentralization and Community Outlook," *Educational Forum,* 46 (1981): 45–54; John Simmons, *Breaking Through: Transforming Urban School Districts* (New York: Teachers College Press, 2006).

[27]Michael W. Kirst, "A Changing Context Means School Board Reform," *Phi Delta Kappan,* 75 (1994): 378–381; Allan C. Ornstein, "School Consolidation vs. Decentralization: Trends, Issues, and Questions," *Urban Review,* 25 (1993): 167–174; and John L. Rury (ed.), *Urban Education in the United States: A Historical Reader* (Gordonsville, VA: Palgrave, 2005).

[28]Allan C. Ornstein, "Centralization and Decentralization of Large Public School Districts," *Urban Education,* 24 (1989): 233–235.

[29]John Gehring, "New York: Schools Get New Aid," *Education Week,* 27 November 2002, p. 18. New York City Department of Education, Press Release, "Map of Instructional Divisions," 23 January 2003.

**Table 10-2**  **Centralization–Decentralization Ratios for School Districts Comprising 50,000 or More Students**

| | School Enrollment | Number of Central Administrators | Number of Decentralized Administrators | Ratio of Centralized to Decentralized Administrators |
|---|---|---|---|---|
| New York | 939,933 | 2100 | 3730 | 0.56 |
| Los Angeles | 592,273 | 340 | 101 | 3.37 |
| Chicago | 419,537 | 399 | 120 | 3.33 |
| Dade County, Florida | 254,235 | 270 | 66 | 4.09 |
| Philadelphia | 194,698 | 251 | 166 | 1.51 |
| Hawaii | 165,455 | 139 | 92 | 1.51 |
| Montgomery County, Maryland | 96,271 | 115 | 34 | 3.38 |
| Palm Beach, Florida | 90,235 | 359 | 25 | 14.36 |
| New Orleans | 83,188 | 127 | 9 | 14.41 |
| Jefferson County, Colorado | 75,337 | 140 | 13 | 10.77 |
| Charlotte–Mecklenburg, North Carolina | 74,146 | 99 | 25 | 3.96 |
| Cleveland | 72,639 | 258 | 12 | 21.50 |
| Atlanta | 65,458 | 160 | 60 | 2.67 |
| El Paso, Texas | 61,857 | 118 | 42 | 2.81 |
| Tucson | 56,475 | 45 | 24 | 1.88 |
| St. Louis | 50,000 | 84 | 159 | 0.53 |

Source: Allan C. Ornstein, "Centralization and Decentralization of Large Public School Districts," *Urban Education*, 24 (1989): 234. Used by permission.

Other data also suggest that, despite apparent decentralization, the large, urban school districts in fact remain highly centralized. Decisions regarding curriculum, instruction, staffing and teacher evaluation, student testing, graduation requirements, and budgeting are still made at the central level, or at what is sometimes referred to as the "downtown" office. Furthermore, the central office is increasingly involved in negotiations with teachers' unions, compliance with court-ordered busing requirements, affirmative action, and allocation of state monies and special programs for the local district. All these trends tend to expand the authority of the main district office and reduce the effect of decentralization.[30]

[30]Michael Fine and Janis Somerville (eds.), *Small Schools: Big Imaginations* (Chicago: Campaign for Urban School Reform, 1998); Frank W. Lutz and Carol Merz, *The Politics of School/Community Relations* (New York: Teachers College Press, Columbia University, 1992); Debra Viadero, "Big-City Majors' Control of Schools Yield Mixed Results," *Education Week,* 11 September 2002, p. 8.

According to some observers, however, the concept of decentralization is alive and well and associated with urban school reform and restructuring movements: to create small school communities and new school boards called **charters**. Instead of special interest groups dominating the agendas of school districts and school boards, through political pressure and/or school board elections, citizens put together a slate, state their views on schooling and how, if elected, they would govern schools. The charter becomes the basis for the school election of board members and administrative appointments within the school district. Administrators and board members are held accountable for their actions in context with the charter.

## Local School Boards

The local school boards of education have been delegated powers and duties by the state for the purpose of ensuring that their schools are operated properly. De-

## Administrative Advice 10–1

### Questions to Consider When Your School District Contemplates Consolidation or Decentralization

Both school consolidation and school decentralization often involve emotional issues—where some groups are perceived as "winners" and others are "losers." Often the issues become highly vocalized at school meetings and in the local press, and so-called solutions are often slogans rather than carefully worked-out concepts understood and accounted for in the rhetoric or press. We assume the "community voice" is the most visible or vocal, and yet we sometimes fail to consider the silent parents who have their own views of reform for their children's education. Thus, there is good reason to proceed with caution. As an administrator, ask yourself the questions below. Be candid and analytic in your answers.

- Who are the advocates?

- What are their motivations? What are their political-economic reasons? Do they have hidden agendas?

- Does the majority of the community want to consolidate (decentralize)? Or is a small, well-organized group behind the plan?

- Do students, parents, teachers, community residents gain under the plan? How?

- Which parents or community residents lose, or feel they lose, under the plan?

- How do various interest groups feel about the plan? Is there considerable conflict or emotion? Is it really worthwhile to proceed, given the conflict or emotion? Why?

- How do the various interest groups want to be represented under the plan? Are there differences among groups based on race, ethnicity, social class, or residents with and without children?

- How do community agencies and local business groups fit into the plan? Have their concerns or interests been considered?

- As a result of the plan, will teaching jobs or administrative positions be affected? Is there current concern among the professional staff?

- What administrative levels (central office, decentralized, or field office) should be consolidated (decentralized)? Why?

- How does the plan affect student performance? Are there data to indicate that the plan will have a positive impact on student performance?

- What unit size is most effective? Most efficient? Is there past history in adjacent (or similar) communities or school districts to verify these assumptions?

- When does bigness lead to increased bureaucracy? When does smallness lead to reduced range of educational services?

- What is the projected cost of the plan? Is it realistic? Is it worthwhile in terms of assumed outcomes?

- Does the plan consider future population growth? Student enrollments? School construction sites? School integration?

- Who really benefits from the plan? Do students? (Remember, they are the real consumers and the reason for the schools.)

spite the fact that their prerogatives are limited by the state, school boards have assumed significant decision-making responsibility. School boards have the power for the most part to raise money through taxes. They exercise power over personnel and school property. Some states leave curriculum and student policy in the hands of the school board, but others, by law, impose specific requirements. In general, the school board must conform to state guidelines to qualify for state aid, as well as conform to federal guidelines where federal monies are involved.

Methods of selecting board members are prescribed by state law. The two basic methods are election and appointment. Election is thought to make for greater accountability to the public, but some people argue that appointment leads to greater competence and less politics. (See the PRO/CON Debate at the end of this chapter.) Election is the most common practice. In 2001,

96 percent of school board members nationwide were elected and only 4 percent were appointed.[31]

Appointment is more common in large urban districts than in suburban or small-town districts; between 1988 and 1998, 11 to 13 percent of urban board members were appointed. A few states specify a standard number of board members, still others specify a permissible range, and a few have no requirements. Most school boards (80 percent) comprise a seven- to nine-member range, with the largest school board having nineteen members; the average size is seven members.[32]

A recent nationwide survey of school board members indicates that the percentage of women on school boards is 39 percent and minority representation is 14 percent. (Southern states show a higher minority representation on school boards: 16 percent black and 3 percent Hispanic.)[33] School board members tend to be older than the general population (94 percent are over age forty); more educated (67 percent have had four or more years of college); wealthier (59 percent have family incomes of $75,000 or more, and 37 percent earn more than $100,000 annually); and more likely to be professionals or businesspeople (45 percent) or homemakers or retired persons (26 percent).[34] Interestingly, 51 percent have no children in school right now, and 41 percent are relative neophytes, having served on the boards for five or fewer years.[35]

The largest school systems (those enrolling 50,000 or more students) tend to have more heterogeneous boards. One survey indicates that minority members constitute 29 percent of the school board in these systems; women make up 36 percent, but family income and educational levels are more diversified.[36] In another survey of the 100 largest school districts in the country, as many as 27.5 percent of the board members were classified as minority, including 21 percent who were black.[37] In 2001, 29 percent of large school district (25,000+ students) boards were 21 to 60 percent black and 44 percent female compared to small district (less than 5000 students) boards in which 15 percent comprised 21 to 60 percent black members and 37 percent female members.[38]

## School Board–Public Problems

The top five problems of school board members are school finance, student achievement, special education, educational technology, and teacher quality (see Table 10–3). Budget issues held the top spot on board members' worry lists for the last eighteen out of twenty years. Academic issues have been in the top five because of the media and state mandates.[39] Since 2000, the public ranked finances as a top concern. The second to fifth concerns of school board members reflect state and local pressures to improve what goes on in schools and classrooms. Infrastructure problems and student enrollments, which have often been among the top concerns of school boards, have now been replaced by drug, discipline, and gang problems, which have always been top concerns of the public.

In the eyes of the public, drug abuse, school violence, and lack of discipline consistently ranked as three of the five most important problems throughout the 1980s and 1990s.[40] These rankings were related to a perceived breakdown of student behavior, includ-

---

[31]Frederick M. Hess, *School Boards at the Dawn of the 21st Century* (Alexandria, VA: National School Boards Association, 2002): table 5, p. 5; Susan F. Shultz, "Landing the Best Trustees in Your Boardroom," *School Administrator*, 61 (2004): 6.

[32]Thomas A. Shannon, former executive publisher of the *American School Board Journal*, personal communication, July 14, 1999; "Twenty-first Annual Survey of School Board Members," *American School Board Journal*, 186 (1999): 34–37.

[33]"School Board Members," *American School Board Journal*, 185 (1998): A-15; Kathleen Vail, "The Changing Face of Education," *American School Board Journal*, 188 (2001): 39–42; Hess, *School Boards at the Dawn of the 21st Century*, tables 21–23, pp. 25–26.

[34]Hess, *School Boards at the Dawn of the 21st Century*, tables 24–27, pp. 26–28.

[35]Ibid., p. 28.

[36]Allan C. Ornstein, "Composition of Boards of Education of Public School Systems Enrolling 50,000 or More Students," *Urban Education*, 16 (1981): 232–234.

[37]Allan C. Ornstein, "School Superintendents and School Board Members: Who They Are," *Contemporary Education*, 63 (1992): 157–159.

[38]Hess, *School Boards at the Dawn of the 21st Century*, tables 22–23, pp. 25–26.

[39]Hess, *School Boards at the Dawn of the 21st Century*; "Money and Other Worries," *American School Board Journal*, 177 (1990): 34–35.

[40]"Board Members' Worries," *American School Board Journal*, 185 (1998): A-15; "Money and Other Worries"; "The Public's Attitude Toward Public Schools," *Phi Delta Kappan*, 80 (1998): 51.

**Table 10–3    Problems in Rank Order Facing Schools: Boards versus Public[a]**

| As Seen by the School Board | As Seen by the Public |
|---|---|
| School finance | Lack of financial support |
| Student achievement | Overcrowded schools |
| Special education | Lack of discipline |
| Educational technology | Use of drugs |
| Teacher quality | Pupils' lack of interest |
| Parental support | Parents' lack of support |
| Federal/state regulations | Fighting/violence/gangs |
| Drug/alcohol use | |
| Discipline | |

[a]Respondents to the school board survey were asked to indicate "significant" or "moderate" concerns. Respondents to the public poll, on the other hand, were asked to name the biggest problems facing their public schools. In both surveys, percentages total more than 100 because of multiple responses.

Source: Frederick M. Hess, *School Boards at the Dawn of the 21st Century* (Alexandria, VA: National School Boards Association, 2002); "38th Annual Phi Delta Kappan/Gallup Poll of Public Schools," *Phi Delta Kappan*, 88 (2006): 45.

**Table 10–4    Public's Attitude toward School, 2005–2006**

| | Grade the Public Schools in Your Community | | Grade the Public Schools Nationally | |
|---|---|---|---|---|
| | 2005 | 2006 | 2005 | 2006 |
| A, B | 48% | 49% | 24% | 21% |
| A | 12 | 13 | 2 | 2 |
| B | 36 | 36 | 22 | 19 |
| C | 29 | 32 | 46 | 51 |
| D | 9 | 9 | 13 | 14 |
| F | 5 | 5 | 4 | 3 |
| Don't know | 9 | 5 | 13 | 11 |

Source: "The 38th Annual Phi Delta Kappa/Gallup Poll of . . . Public Schools," *Phi Delta Kappan*, 88 (2006): 43–44.

ing their moral standards, lack of interest and truancy, drinking and alcoholism, crime and vandalism, disrespect for teachers, and fighting. Historically, school board members did not have such strong feelings about the breakdown of school discipline, moral standards, or the law. Interestingly, both school boards and the public are not too concerned about school integration or busing, which was one of the most controversial issues in the sixties and seventies. Since the year 2000, lack of financial support has topped the list of school problems as purported by the public, with overcrowded schools and lack of discipline mentioned second or third in the years 2000, 2001, and 2002 and tied for second place in 2002.

Since the mid-1970s, respondents to the Phi Delta Kappa/Gallup education polls have been asked to grade the public schools in their communities and the nation as a whole on a scale of A to F. Table 10–4 shows that when people are asked about the schools they know, the grades they assign go up. The percentage of respondents who award schools an A or B increases about 25 percent when respondents are asked about the schools in their own community rather than the nation's schools. However, based on a study conducted in Michigan in 2003, "African Americans and urban res-

idents are far less likely than other citizens to award their local schools an A or a B."[41]

When the public is asked how much confidence they have in American institutions, respondents give the highest ratings to churches (57%) and schools (42%). Local government, state government, big business, national government, the justice/legal system, and organized labor, in descending order, receive lower ratings.[42] In the nationwide Hart survey, 66 percent of adults believe we are asking our schools to do too many things that really should be handled by parents at home. When asked what counts more—the quality of teachers and schools or the involvement of parents—21 percent of the respondents claimed the first choice and 42 percent claimed the second choice. As many as 36 percent said both equally; 1 percent were unsure.[43] When asked what they prefer—improving

[41]"The 38th Annual Phi Delta Kappa/Gallup Poll of Public Schools," *Phi Delta Kappan*, 88 (2006): 41–53; David Plank, "Unsettling the State—How Demand Challenges the Education System in the U.S.," *European Journal of Education*, 41 (2006): 16–17.

[42]"The Public's Attitude Toward Public Schools."

[43]"News and Notes: Survey Roundup," *Thrust for Educational Leadership*, 28 (1998): 4. See Shell Oil Survey Conducted by Peter D. Hart Research Associates, 1998.

## ■ Exemplary Educational Administrators in Action

**DAVID A. KAZAKOFF** Principal, Terra Nova High School, Pacifica, California.

**Previous Positions:** Vice-Principal, Guidance; Vice-Principal; Attendance Supervisor, Auto Shop Teacher.

**Latest Degree and Affiliation:** Ed. D., Organization and Leadership, University of San Francisco; M.A., Educational Administration; B.A., Industrial Education.

**Number One Influence on Career:** Mother, brother, and uncle are all in education. Best influence was my high school auto shop teacher.

**Number One Achievement:** Personally, obtaining a doctoral degree while still being married to the same woman for 36 years. Professionally, guiding the re-emergence of Terra Nova High School into one of the top four public high schools in San Mateo County and rated 8 out of 10 throughout the state of California according to the state's latest API (Academic Performance Indicator) information.

**Number One Regret:** My parents died too early to see what they turned out.

**Favorite Education-Related Book or Text:** *Management* by Peter Drucker.

**Additional Interests:** Woodworking, minor construction, gardening, reading, and I eventually want to restore a real old car during my future retirement. I want to get back into the trades where I can see immediate results from individual work and labor.

**Leadership Style:** Hands on, letting people do their job and not interfering unless absolutely necessary. Not letting work pile up. I'm highly organized. Students come first, teachers and staff come second, administration comes third.

**Professional Vision:** As a principal and site manager, my major concern is to make the environment as safe and conducive as possible for teachers to teach and students to learn—no matter what it takes. Everything I do revolves around this issue. All my educational philosophies also revolve around this issue.

**Words of Advice:** Where do I see public education going in the next ten years? If the funding for education, federal and state, continues to dwindle, there will be no public education as we know it. A two-class education system will begin to exist. In some cases, it probably already exists. The Bush administration continued to push school vouchers and private education by increasing student accountability and trying to relax the church-school separation system that had been in place since the Founding Fathers had envisioned its necessity. Teacher and student accountability is a good thing, but it seems as though the federal government and the states are pushing accountability too fast and too soon without proper research and proper funding. As usual, the powers that be start the ball rolling, fund it, and then reduce funding but still expect schools to raise performance with less qualified teachers, loss of funding, and a system of testing that changes at the whim of the budget analyst of each state. You will never get quality teachers without giving them adequate compensation. Most states and counties (with very few exceptions) in this nation are compensating teachers at just above the subsistence level.

Anyone who wants to become an administrator needs to be trained as an intern in all areas of administration before being given a responsible position. Most administrators I know have all been put into a position and told "Go for it" without proper training. The colleges and universities cannot come close to real-life situations that administrators handle on a daily basis.

---

existing schools or finding alternatives (vouchers or charter schools)—71 percent opt for the first choice, 24 percent select the second choice, and 5 percent are unsure.[44]

---

[44] "The 38th Annual Phi Delta Kappa/Gallup Poll of . . . Public Schools."

## School Board Meetings

There are three general types of board meeting: regular, special, and executive. The first two are usually open meetings, and the public is invited. The third type is usually closed to the public and deals with managerial issues or serious problems. Open or **public board meetings** obviously enhance school-community relations and allow parents to understand the problems of education as well as air their concerns; however, they can also degenerate into gripe sessions or conflict if someone in charge is not skilled in guiding large-group discussions and building consensus.[45] If a skilled leader is not available, it is best to limit the number of public meetings.

Holding closed or **executive board meetings** to reach major policy decisions is generally discouraged, but school boards occasionally use this tactic if conflict and tension arise. Many school districts, however, have mandated open meetings except under certain specified conditions. However, the executive meeting, if properly organized, produces the best results in terms of time management and outcomes.[46]

School board meetings are actually control systems that bring school resources into line with school policies. One way to ensure that organizational work is directed toward the appropriate mission statements or goals is to make school board meetings more focused in terms of resources and policies. Board members spend about twenty-five hours a month on board business, and roughly one-third of that time in board meetings. In large school districts (25,000+ students), 35 percent of the members claim they spend more than fifty hours a month.[47]

School board meetings, just as with meetings involving school administrators, are rarely one-time events; they are usually part of an ongoing cycle. According to one administrator, "Effective board meetings are the first prerequisite for an effective board. There's no one pattern for effective board meetings. Boards have traditions. What works for one school board may not work for another."[48]

Managers in private industry contend they spend 25 to 60 percent of their time in meeting rooms, and much of that time is wasted. "Meetings are where you keep the minutes and throw away the hours."[49] Thousands of school administrators would most likely nod in agreement—school meetings are places where participants learn to doodle, look attentive, nod politely, and pinch themselves to keep awake. Most people agree that school meetings, including board meetings and staff meetings, should be trimmed, and that shorter meetings (no more than one to one and one-half hours) are more productive than longer meetings. Generally, one meeting a month is enough.[50] (See Administrative Advice 10–2.) Board meetings (or meetings in general) with too many people—or people from too many bureaucratic layers—with many different interests or agendas will cause bog-down. The use of a consent agenda "can help boards streamline meetings so they can spend more time on important matters." By using a consent agenda, boards are able to include routine items under a broad category (curriculum, personnel) and vote on each category with a single motion.[51] However, data suggest that strong superintendents conduct longer meetings (two to three hours per session), more meetings, and more board functions than do weak superintendents. In school districts controlled by the board, members make quick decisions and board meetings average less than one hour, with the superintendent simply carrying out board mandates.

## School Board Responsibilities

The administration and management of schools is big business, and school board members must have or acquire knowledge of good business practices. Overall, school boards have fiscal responsibility for more than $400 billion each year and employ over 5.9 million individuals; this makes them the largest nationwide employer.[52] Board members must also be fair and mindful of the law when dealing with students, teachers, administrators, parents, and other community residents. Board members are public servants and represent the community and are expected to govern the school system without encroaching on the authority of the su-

[45] James Bushman and Virginia Boris, "Listening to the Public," *American School Board Journal*, 185 (1998): 27–29; Joan Irvine, "Governance: Welcome to the Board," *American School Board Journal*, 185 (1998): 38–40.

[46] Joan P. Shapiro and Jacqueline A. Stefkovich, *Ethical Leadership and Decision Making in Education* (Mahwah, NJ: Erlbaum, 2001); Roger Soder, *The Language of Leadership* (San Francisco: Jossey-Bass, 2001).

[47] Hess, *School Boards at the Dawn of the 21st Century*, table 11, p. 17.

[48] Donald McAdams, "The Short, Productive Board Meeting," *School Administrator*, 62 (2005): 6.

[49] Lynn Oppenheim, "Why Meetings Sometimes Fail, *Executive Educator*, 11 (1989): 6.

[50] Michael R. Weber, "A Balancing Act of Demands and Needs," *School Administrator*, 56 (1999): 38–41.

[51] Judith A. Zimmerman, "Free to Focus," *American School Board Journal*, 191 (2004): 39–41.

[52] *Digest of Education Statistics, 2005*, table 79, pp. 3, 119–120.

## Administrative Advice 10–2

### Making Board Meetings More Meaningful

Most school board members spend too much time at meetings (usually without compensation) and are unable to devote sufficient time to important policy issues; alternately, they find the meetings mired in controversy. Here are some suggestions from two board presidents (Arcement and Rude) and two superintendents (Chopra and Kleinsmith) from different parts of the country (Louisiana, California, Pennsylvania, and Missouri) to make meetings more productive.

**A.** *Board members need to:*

1. *Understand* their own roles and duties, and especially understand the relationship of the superintendent and board president.

2. Understand the importance of *teamwork,* trust, and exchange of ideas at meetings.

3. Exhibit *positive attitudes* in the way they conduct themselves at meetings, including support for the district's programs, professional staff, and other members of the school board.

4. *Communicate* with lay and professional people at meetings in an honest and open way, *listening* to others when they are talking.

5. Learn *committee structure* — how to present information in committees, how to follow standard procedures, how to avoid airing dirty laundry at meetings, and how to avoid prolonged meetings that often result in conflict.

6. Exhibit *professional behavior* at meetings and control their emotions; if board members show up at meetings to demand action, they should do so as individual citizens.

7. Ask good *questions,* seek clarification of issues, and follow parliamentary procedures.

**B.** *Board presidents need to:*

1. Ask themselves whether the meeting is *necessary*— or can the task be accomplished without a meeting, say with a memo or a telephone call.

2. State the *purpose* or agenda of the meeting in advance, or at a previous meeting, in the form of written communication.

3. Be *punctual*—come on time to meetings and begin promptly. Others will get the message.

4. Direct the flow of *discussion,* ask *questions,* encourage democratic or balanced *participation,* and be aware of *time.*

5. *Summarize* frequently, follow parliamentary *procedures,* maintain necessary *control,* and bring discussions to a satisfactory *close.*

6. Keep and publish *minutes* to ensure follow-up, monitor progress, and use as a reference.

7. Make the *superintendent* feel comfortable at meetings by not surprising her or him, not undercutting the person, and not probing too much in front of others (the latter can be done in private).

Source: Adapted from Billy Arcement, "Taking a Sounding of Your School Board Leadership Skills," *American School Board Journal,* 181 (1994): 24; Raj K. Chopra, "Making Your Meetings Matter," *Executive Educator,* 11 (1989): 23; Ron Rude, "Administration: Lessons from the Top," *American School Board Journal,* 186 (1999): 41–42; Stephen L. Kleinsmith, "What Comprises an Award-Winning Board," *School Administrator,* 62 (2005): 8.

---

perintendent. Members have no legal authority except during a board meeting and while acting as a collective group or board.[53] Board members must be politically prudent because someone will eventually ask for a favor — a friend, a friend of a friend, or a special interest group — and this pressure should be resisted.

According to a survey of sixty-six Illinois school superintendents, school boards have become more political and divisive in recent years; board members are less willing to compromise on major issues and there is a greater tendency among candidates to represent coalitions or special interest groups when running for elec-

[53]Davis W. Campbell and Diane Greene, "Defining the Leadership Role of School Boards in the 21st Century," *Phi Delta Kappan,* 75 (1994): 391–395; Howard Good, "Governance: Then and Now," *American School Board Journal,* 185 (1998): 50–51.

tion.[54] In short, new board members seem more interested in the views of their electors than in the views of other board members or professional educators.

Some board members run because they have an ax to grind, a hidden agenda, or a specific educational view. Overall, fewer people want to serve on school boards. In 2005, on Long Island, New York, board members ran unopposed in about one-third of the elections. This is not uncommon in other areas.[55]

In addition, many board members do not attend training sessions. Part of the problem is that only eighteen states, mostly in the South, require training for new school board members. In these states, and in the others where training is voluntary, training sources include state school boards, state departments of education, regional service units, and universities. Superintendents feel the focus on training should be the following: (1) conducting a superintendent's search, (2) dealing with school sports, (3) dealing with members of the community, (4) resisting pressure to hire family members or firing employees they don't like, (5) understanding their roles and responsibilities, and (6) understanding legal and ethical obligations.[56]

In districts where the school board is elected, board members are subject to the same laws as other elected officials; in many states, each member must file a statement of ethics. In the final analysis, the quality of the local schools is an important factor in determining the community's reputation, the value of property, and the willingness of businesses to locate in the vicinity. Board members represent the public at large; and they must be willing to work with businesses, government, and community organizations to promote the community's schools and students' welfare.[57]

The powers and responsibilities of school boards may be classified into the following categories:

1. *Policy.* School boards set the general rules about what will be done in the schools, who will do it, and how it will be done.

2. *Staffing.* Technically, the board is responsible for hiring all employees of the school district. In practice, however, school boards usually confine themselves to recruitment and selection of the school superintendent (the district's chief executive office) and high-ranking members of the central office staff. Decisions on the hiring and retention of principals and teachers are usually made at lower levels of the hierarchy, after review by professional peers.

3. *Employee Relations.* School board members are responsible for all aspects of employee relations, including collective bargaining with teachers' unions. Large school districts rely on consultants or attorneys to negotiate with teachers; small school districts may use the superintendent or a school board committee to negotiate.

4. *Fiscal Matters.* The board must keep the school district solvent, effect savings when possible, and get the most out of every tax dollar. The school district usually has a larger budget than does any other local public agency; the school superintendent often makes more money than any other local official, including the mayor, fire chief, and police chief.

5. *Students.* The board addresses questions of student rights and responsibilities, extracurricular activities, attendance, and requirements for promotion and graduation.

6. *Curriculum.* The school board is in charge of developing curriculum—especially as it relates to state law and guidelines—and approving textbooks.

7. *Community Relations.* The school board must be responsive to parents and other members of the community.

8. *Intergovernment Requirements.* Federal and state agencies establish a variety of requirements for local

[54]David Elsner, "School Boards More Political," *Chicago Tribune,* 22 January 1990, section 2, p. 4. Also see Penny Bender Sebring and Anthony S. Bryk, "School Leadership and the Bottom Line in Chicago," *Phi Delta Kappan,* 81 (2000): 440–443.

[55]Carol Chmelynski, "In Some Communities, Fewer People Are Willing to Run for the School Board," *School Board News,* 23 (2003): 7; Mark Grossman, "Wanted—School Board Candidates," *American School Board Journal,* 192 (2005): 47–53; Jack McKay and Mark Peterson, "Recruiting Board Members: Should Superintendents Have a Role in the Process? A Survey Finds Divided Results," *School Administrator,* 61 (2004): 27–29.

[56]Nicholas D. Caruso, Jr., "Teach the Board Its Proper Role," *School Administrator,* 62 (2005): 8; Marilyn Grady and Bernita Krumm, "Learning to Serve," *American School Board Journal,* 185 (1998): 36, 43.

[57]Kathleen Vail, "The Changing Face of Education: Portrait of a School Board," *American School Board Journal,* 188 (2001): 39–42; Malia Villegas, "Leading in Difficult Times: Are Urban School Boards up to the Task?" *Policy Trends* (San Francisco, CA: WestEd, 2003).

schools, and the school board is responsible for seeing that these mandates are carried out.[58]

In general, the most efficient school boards pull together as a team and get along with the superintendent. They are characterized by effectively using the strengths of each other, having confidence in each other's abilities, giving one another honest feedback about each other's performance in board matters, and generally supporting one another, especially when the "chips are down."

## School Board Views on School Reform

These days it is hard to find anyone—inside or outside of education—who doesn't believe that schools need to be reformed.

Superintendents and principals are the most likely leaders of school reform, according to school board members, followed closely by school board members themselves and state departments of education. Most other players (teachers, professors, social reformers) or groups (federal agencies, community groups, or teacher associations) are not perceived as having much impact or interest in reform.

As many as 10 percent of board members characterize their own school district as "moderately" or "greatly" involved in reform—and on a grassroots basis or from local initiatives (superintendent or the board)—not from state or federal directives. More than half (58%) maintain that reform is improving the quality of education.[59]

Curriculum and instruction reforms are most prevalent in school districts: involving computer instruction (91%), programs for at-risk students (84%), foreign language instruction (84%), adoption of a common core curriculum (75%), and whole language instruction (73%). Given the current emphasis on standards and high-stake testing, we would expect more emphasis today on aligning the curriculum with state standards and tests. This is highlighted by the public's response to support a standardized national curriculum both in 1991 (69% in favor) and again when asked in 2002 (66% in favor).[60] In 2006, 47 percent of the public responded that the current curriculum should be changed in order to meet the challenges of today. As many as 40 percent of respondents believe that every high school student should take at least one course online while in school.[61]

Another common reform strategy among school districts, according to board members, involves school time. Two-thirds of the school districts have modified the school calendar or clock: offering summer school (68%), offering before and after school studying sessions (48%), extending the school day (42%), introducing flexible scheduling options (40%), and extending the school year (38%). Perhaps the only radical change is that 16 percent say their schools are on a year-round calendar.

When it comes to less traditional, more fashionable changes, only a small percentage of board members say they are embarking on reforms that involve (1) alternative assessment, (2) parental training programs, (3) student work apprenticeships, (4) school choices, (5) charter schools, (6) magnet schools, and (7) voucher systems.[62]

Budget limitations have proven to be the biggest obstacle to reform. Some 48 percent of school board members claim they don't have sufficient revenues to do what they think needs to be done. A second obstacle, as perceived by board members, are teachers and teacher associations. Not surprisingly, teacher associations perceive school board members as adversaries—hindering improved salaries and working conditions.[63]

---

[58]Eva K. Bascal, "On Being a Board Member," *American School Board Journal*, 174 (1987): 11–16; Stephen P. Heyneman, "America's Most Precious Export: the Local School Board," *American School Board Journal*, 182 (1995): 22–26. Also see Rene S. Townsend et al., *A Practical Guide to Effective School Board Meetings* (Thousand Oaks, CA: Corwin Press, 2005).

[59]Thomas H. Gaul, Kenneth E. Underwood, and Jim C. Fortune, "Reform at the Grass Roots," *American School Board Journal*, 181 (1994): 35–38, 40.

[60]"The 38th Annual Phi Delta Kappa/Gallup Poll of . . . Public Schools," 47. Also see Thomas R. Guskey, "Helping Standards Make the Grade," *Educational Leadership*, 59 (2001): 20–27; Deborah Meier, "Standardization Versus Standards," *Phi Delta Kappan*, 84 (2002): 190–198.

[61]Ibid. Also see "The 37th Annual Phi Delta/Gallup Poll of . . . Public Schools," 53.

[62]"The 37th [and 38th] Annual Phi Delta/Gallup Poll[s]."

[63]Lawrence Hardy, "Building Blocks of Reform," *American School Board Journal*, 186 (1999): 16–21; Donna Harrington-Lueker, "AFT Goes in Quest of School Reform," *American School Board Journal*, 178 (1991): 49; Jo Anna Natale, "NEA: Toward a More Perfect Union," *American School Board Journal*, 178 (1991): 49; Allan Odden, "The Costs of Sustaining Educational Change Through Comprehensive Reform," *Phi Delta Kappan*, 81 (2000): 433–439.

The irony is that while school board members perceive themselves, their superintendents, and state departments of education as vanguards of reform, they perceive teachers, scholars, and social reformers as having almost no role, responsibility, or influence in school reform. However, these latter people see school board members as an obstacle to school reform, especially in urban school districts where political and ethnic rivalries dominate board meetings and where serious questions about disbursement of funds and nepotism concerning contracts and jobs have surfaced.[64] Urban school boards are viewed as constantly being in flux and turmoil, exhibiting "a lack of skill among members in resolving conflicts and tensions both within the board and with superintendents."[65] They are also perceived as "reactive [and emotional] and for having poor relationships with state policy members" and units of general local government.[66]

Suburban, and especially rural and small-town, school boards are viewed as maintaining tradition and spending too much time dealing with administrative trivia. The suburban/rural boards generally operate in less contentious political environments and govern with more cohesive community values; and although the board members usually have leadership experience, they are seen as representing entrenched power groups or special interests and "defending the status quo"—sometimes having as much interest in athletic and social events as in academic outcomes—or more.

For school reform to take place, board members must exhibit consistency in goals, philosophy, and mission; fundamental reform requires several years of continual direction and involvement with the same policies and programs. According to a recent survey, 40 percent of urban board members have served between 2 and 5 years (the national mean is 6.7) and the urban superintendent has worked in the district for 4.6 years (the national average is 5.5).[67] Constant turnover of lay and professional leadership and turmoil between and among superintendents and board members in some urban settings make reform nearly impossible. Since 1970, the big-city school districts with the most superintendents' turnover have been Baltimore, Denver, Miami, New York City, St. Louis, and Washington, D.C.[68]

The outcome is that many school boards, especially in urban areas, are viewed as giving lip service to reform. Without consensus and saddled by gridlock and mistrust, school boards are perceived as focusing on short-term management problems, committee intrigue, and rules of order, and responding to special-interest factions. As Philip Schlechty remarks, "Perhaps the greatest barrier to revitalizing America's schools is that too many board members view themselves as educational leaders and too few [view] themselves as moral and cultural leaders."[69]

A variety of approaches to replace the existing school board governance are now under way: One plan (Danforth Foundation) argues that school boards should be elected but not certified unless more than 20 percent of registered voters turn out. A different approach is to allow the mayor (as in the case of Boston, Chicago, and now New York City) to take control of the schools and appoint and replace urban board members in an attempt to curtail politicization and polarization. In Michigan, the state took over the Detroit schools and replaced an elected board with an appointed board (in conjunction with the mayor). Another blueprint (shaping up in California) is for downsizing school boards around one high school and its feeding schools. A different downsizing idea (evolving in Arizona, Florida, and Minne-

---

[64] Larry Cuban and Michael Usdan (eds.), *Powerful Reforms With Shallow Roots* (New York: Teachers College Press, Columbia University, 2001); Frederick M. Hess, "The Urban Reform Paradox," *American School Board Journal*, 185 (1998): 24–29; Michael Usdan, "The Relationship Between School Boards and General Purpose Government," *Phi Delta Kappan*, 75 (1994): 374–377.

[65] Linda J. Dawson, "Coherent Governance: A Board-Superintendent Relationship Based on Defined Goals Can Raise Achievement," *School Administrator*, 61 (2004): 4; Villegas, *Leading in Difficult Times*.

[66] Frederick M. Hess, *Spinning Wheels: The Politics of Urban School Reform* (Washington, DC: Brookings Institution, 1999); Ron A. Zimbalist, *The Human Factor in Change* (Lanham, MD: Rowman & Littlefield, 2005).

[67] Hess, *School Boards at the Dawn of the 21st Century*, tables 16, 44, pp. 21–22, 38; *CUBE Survey Report, Superintendent Tenure* (Alexandria, VA: National School Board Association, 2002).

[68] Paul Houston, "Superintendents for the 21st Century: It's Not Just a Job, It's a Calling," *Phi Delta Kappan*, 82 (2001): 428–433; Gary Yee and Larry Cuban, "When Is Tenure Long Enough: A Historical Analysis of Superintendent Turnover and Tenure in Urban School Districts," *Educational Administration Quarterly*, 32 (1996): 615–641.

[69] Philip C. Schlechty, "Deciding the Fate of Local Control," *American School Board Journal*, 179 (1992): 28. Also see Philip C. Schlechty, *Shaking Up the Schoolhouse* (San Francisco: Jossey-Bass, 2000).

sota) is for individual schools to create a "charter" with its own school board and operate independently of the local school district. There are also proposals to up-size: to create regional school boards (evolving in Ohio) that deal with long-range planning, policies, and budgets; still another idea is to shift powers away from local school district boards to state education agencies, which then hold local school boards accountable to specific standards and may even dismantle the boards if they don't meet specific standards or benchmarks.

## State Standards: A National Movement

Unquestionably, the state standards movement, which involves curriculum reform and student assessment, has gained most of the attention over reform. As of 1997, thirty-nine states had developed new standards or revised old ones and ten were in the midst of developing or revising them. As many as twenty-nine states had developed comprehensive standards in at least three of four core subject areas; history has become the most difficult one because of political ideology and content controversies.[70] Talk of world-class standards right now is only talk because of different content coverage, thinking patterns of students, linguistic appropriateness and translations, and the different degrees of meaningfulness that students of various nations place on these tests. The best standards, so far, seem to combine in-depth content with specific proficiency levels such as expectations at specific grade levels.

State standards are being used to compare school districts and schools within districts. In most states, raising standards means the elimination of social promotion; a large percentage of inner-city students are being held back for academic reasons and/or are required to attend summer school. High school students are being told that if they don't meet the new expectations, they will not graduate or receive a standard academic diploma. Teachers and administrators are being told that where performance doesn't measure up, the school can be put under state review and possibly closed—jobs will be at stake. School districts have set up ex-

tended school days and six-day school weeks (like in Japan and Taiwan) for kids who need extra help (about three to four hours on Saturday). The assumption is that the more *instructional time* students have, assuming *instruction quality* is constant, the more likely that they will be successful.

The hard task is to move from the adoption of good state standards to actual changes in classroom practice. Because the standards have not considered inputs from instructional leaders or teachers, the new state rules and regulations may only lead to minimum commitment of principals and teachers; the state standards may result in teacher conformity and loss of teacher control. Others feel that teachers will merely teach toward the tests, at the expense of in-depth knowledge and critical thinking. Some administrators may even urge selected students to stay home or label them as learning disabled so they may have more time to complete the tests. In the real world of classrooms and schools, these are practical concerns to deal with.

## Effective School Reform

Reformers have developed a literature on **more effective schools** which purports that inner-city schools can successfully educate poor and minority students. Advocates in this camp pay attention to schools as an institution and the environment in which they operate, usually defined in terms of student achievement and usually focused on primary and elementary school. This emphasis corresponds with environmental research data indicating that intervention is most critical in the early stages of human development, because that is the period of most rapid cognitive growth (50 percent by age four, another 25 percent by age nine according to Bloom).[71]

Given that the early years are so formative, it would be wise for the nation to commit to the care and education of its young and to make it compulsory, especially for "at-risk" and poor children, in order to prepare them for or catch them up to grade level when they enter school. A few states such as Massachusetts, Vermont, and West Virginia are providing comprehensive programs for infants and toddlers, and the federal government in 2000 provided $3.5 billion in block grants to states to provide some child-care services and assist working women with children (73 percent of women

---

[70]Joint Committee on Standards for Educational Evaluation, *The Student Evaluation Standards* (Thousand Oaks, CA: Corwin Press, 2002); Rick Stiggins, "From Formative Assessment to Assessment for Learning: A Path to Success in Standards-Based Schools." *Phi Delta Kappan,* 87 (2005): 324–328. Marc S. Tucker and Judy B. Colding, *Standards for Our Schools* (San Francisco: Jossey-Bass, 1998).

---

[71]Benjamin S. Bloom, *Stability and Change in Human Characters* (New York: Wiley, 1964).

between ages 25 and 34 are in the workforce.)[72] The outcomes are piecemeal and inadequate; we need more like $12 billion, twice the appropriations for Head Start, to ensure that all our nation's poor or at-risk children are receiving appropriate services and education.

The advent of school nutrition programs; extended-day, weekend, and required preschool programs; required summer school for primary students (grades 1–3); to neutralize cognitive deficits as opposed to allowing them to increase; reading and tutoring programs, and parenting education, as well as making class size and schools smaller, are all considered crucial.[73] The instruction that is recommended is prescriptive and diagnostic; emphasis is on basic-skill acquisition, review and guided practice, monitoring of student programs, providing prompt feedback and reinforcement to students, and mastery-learning opportunities.[74] All of these instructional methods suggest a behaviorist, direct, convergent, systematic, and low cognitive level of instruction as opposed to a problem-solving, abstract, divergent, inquiry-based, and high level of instruction. (Some critics would argue this type of instruction is second-rate and reflects our low expectations of low-achieving students.)

The fact is that schools with high concentrations of poor students are usually overloaded with enormous problems, ranging from (1) inexperienced and uncertified teachers, poor morale, and working conditions; (2) children who cannot read at grade level or control themselves in class; (3) children deprived by lack of sleep, food, and basic health care; and (4) children victimized by drugs, gangs, crime, and teenage pregnancy. All that is needed is a critical mass of poor students, about 25 to 30 percent, and the values and behaviors of this group will take over and prevail in the school.[75] There is a threshold where the climate or ethos of a school deteriorates due to the attitudes and behavior of students. There is also a point when schools cannot have much positive impact (i.e., Coleman, Jencks, Duncan, Moynihan, Hanushek thesis), and other social or psychological factors (i.e., family, peer group, community, socioeconomic status, students' motivation, personality, and prior achievement) become more critical in determining academic outcomes. Indeed the "rags to riches" story has real significance for many immigrant groups, but it remains largely a fable for those immersed in the "culture of poverty."

The United States provides real potential for upward mobility that is unusual by international standards,[76] but the advantages to the middle class and upper class are more numerous and noticeable. This will always be the case unless we wish to socialize society and redistribute income. Depending on whose figures you accept, 21 to 25 percent of American students live in poverty[77]—most of them in a "culture of poverty," from one generation to the next. Writes one author, "We have put great faith in public schools to enhance social mobility and equality. Suggestions or evidence that this part of the American dream is at risk or in decline is at best dis-

[72]Elena Bodrova and Deborah J. Leong, "Uniquely Preschool," *Educational Leadership,* 63 (2005): 44–47; Sharon L. Kagan and Lynda G. Hallmark, "Early Care and Education Policies in Sweden: Implications for the United States," *Phi Delta Kappan,* 83 (2001): 237–245, 254; Sally Lubeck, "Early Childhood Education and Care in Cross National Perspective," *Phi Delta Kappan,* 83 (2001): 213–215.

[73]Lorin Anderson and Leonard O. Pellicer, "Synthesis of Research Compensatory and Remedial Education," *Education Leadership,* 48 (1990): 10–16; Allan C. Ornstein and Daniel U. Levine, "School Effectiveness and Reform: Guidelines for Action," *Clearing House,* 63 (1990): 115–118; William C. Symonds, "How to Fix America's Schools," *Business Week,* 19 March 2001, pp. 68–80. Also see Donald L. Rollie, *The Keys to Effective Schools* (Thousand Oaks, CA: Corwin Press, 2002). Georgia was the first state to require pre-K programs for all four-year-olds in the state. The authors would start with toddler programs at age three.

[74]Linda Darling-Hammond and Olivia Ifill-Lynch, "If They'd Only Do Their Work," *Educational Leadership,* 63 (2006): 8–13; Daniel U. Levine and Allan C. Ornstein, "Research on Classroom and School Effectiveness and Its Implications for Improving Big-City Schools," *Urban Review,* 21 (1989): 81–95; Allan C. Ornstein and Daniel U. Levine, "Urban School Effectiveness and Improvement," *Illinois School and Research Development,* 71 (1991): 111–117.

[75]This tipping point is rooted in the studies of social class by Allison Davis, Robert Havinghurst, and Lloyd Warner in the 1940s and 1950s; in the studies of equality by Samuel Bowles, Herbert Gans, and Frederick Mosteller in the 1960s and 1970s; and in the ethnographic studies of Phillip Cusick, Elizabeth Eddy, and Sara Lawrence Lightfoot in the 1980s and 1990s.

[76]Richard C. Leone, "Forward." In R.D. Kahlenberg (ed.), *A Nation at Risk: Preserving Public Education as an Engine for Social Mobility* (New York: Century Foundation, 2000), pp. v–viii.

[77]Harold Hodgkinson, "Educational Demographics: What Teachers Should Know," *Educational Leadership* (January 2001): pp. 6–11; Lynn Olson and Greg F. Orlofsky, "2000 and Beyond: The Changing Face of American Schools," *Education Week,* 28 September, 2000, pp. 30–38. Also see Richard Rothstein, *Class and Schools* (New York: Teachers College Press, 2004).

quieting to Americans and often produces controversial debates among intellectuals and policymakers. But those who live on the downside of advantage are more often destined to remain at the bottom of the heap."[78]

In order to neutralize skeptical and conservative attitudes about the minimal influence of schooling, reformers have developed a literature on more effective schools, which claims that inner-city schools successfully educate poor and minority students. Advocates in their camp pay attention to the school environment, teacher attitudes and behaviors, principal leadership—and usually define "success" in terms of student achievement and usually focus on preschool and elementary schools. In a review of six cities, for example, Paul Hill concludes that for schools to become more effective, they need to (1) define and use a consistent plan based on a particular philosophy or pedagogy so that teachers are clear on aims, goals, and strategies, (2) encourage parental and family engagement in their children's schooling, and (3) increase teacher responsibility for improving their own teaching practices and engagement in innovation. On a more theoretical level, Hill recommends that staff members from effective schools be permitted "to charge for help and advice given to other schools" in the district,[79] thus enhancing performance incentives and professionalism.

Casey Carter described twenty-one high-performing high-poverty schools across the country in his book *No Excuses*. The overall message of his research was to reject the ideology of victimization or discrimination that dominates most discussion about poverty, race, and low achievement. Carter contends that the schools (18 out of 21 are elementary schools) profiled in his book do not reject standardized tests as discriminating against poor or minority children, but use them for diagnostic and benchmark purposes. They show that children can master the core subjects, especially reading and math, but some children learn at different paces and need extra time or tutoring.[80] The key to the success of these schools is the principal, who establishes the

school climate—where there is an orderly environment and good teaching is expected. "Finding the right principals, who in turn [are given latitude to] find the right teachers, may be the most important variable for eliciting high performing, high poverty schools.[81, 82]

With the exception of **compensatory programs** such as reading or tutoring, the more effective school approach suggests very little additional cost and depends more on leadership of the principal, as well as the attitudes, motivation, and responsibility of the teachers, parents, and students. Money does not seem to be the answer; in fact, failure becomes a rationale to demand more money. The approach is not piecemeal, or perceived as part of the compensatory movement (which costs billions of dollars). The focus is on a macro level—the entire school, not a specific program or specific teacher. The need is to analyze, modify, and improve the roles, values, and beliefs of all those concerned with the teaching and learning process. The idea is to create a school culture, an ethos, that the principal and the majority of teachers believe in and that is based on expectations of success. (See Administrative Advice 10–3.)

What we need to do is to translate what we know works (common characteristics) to a larger scale and properly reward people (principals and teachers) for a job well done. Instead of paying inner-city teachers more money to attract quality, we pay them less money than suburban teachers—about 15 to 20 percent less in New York City than surrounding Nassau County suburbs, about 20 to 25 percent less in Chicago than adjacent Cook County suburbs. Furthermore, according to Arthur Wise, "we currently pay the same salary to qualified and unqualified teachers, a disincentive for individual teachers to prepare" and give their best efforts.[83] Why work hard when easier routes are available for the same compensation? Is everyone in education expected to be idealistic and dedicated? If we ignore the economics of the situation, or if we think the answer to

[78]Allan C. Ornstein, *Teaching and Schooling in America: Pre- and Post-September 11* (Boston: Allyn and Bacon, 2003): 459.

[79]Paul Hill, "Good Schools for Big-City Children," Research Paper published by the Brookings Institution, Washington, DC, November 2000.

[80]Samuel C. Carter, *No Excuses: Lessons from 21 High-Performing High Poverty Schools* (Washington, DC: Heritage Foundation, 2000).

[81]Allan Meyerson, "Forward," in Carter, *No Excuses*, p. 4.

[82]While the report is uplifting and provides needed hope, the book and Heritage Foundation have been criticized by one reporter and editor for its political agenda and false impressions, reporting of test scores, exclusion of students expected to score low in post-tests, and misrepresentation of poverty schools (some of which were middle class). See George Schmidt, "No Excuses for No Excuses," *Phi Delta Kappan*, 83 (2001): 194–195.

[83]Arthur E. Wise, "Creating a High-Quality Teaching Force," *Educational Leadership*, 58 (2001): 20.

## Administrative Advice 10–3

### Overview of Major Learning Theories and Principles

The major theories of learning of the last one hundred years can be divided into three classic schools of thought (behaviorism, cognition, and humanistic). The overview helps define, explain, and provide a yardstick for effective teaching and learning for all students, as well as forms the basis for discussion during staff development meetings.

| Psychologist | Major Theory or Principle | Definition or Explanation |
| --- | --- | --- |
| *Behaviorist* | | |
| Thorndike | Law of effect | When a connection between a situation and response is made, and it is accompanied by a satisfying state of affairs, that connection is strengthened; when accompanied by an annoying state of affairs, the connection is weakened. |
| Pavlov-Watson | Classical conditioning | Whenever a response is closely followed by the reduction of a drive, a tendency will result for the stimulus to evoke that reaction on subsequent occasions; association strength of the stimulus-response bond depends on the conditioning of the response and stimulus. |
| Skinner | Operant conditioning | In contrast to classical conditioning, no specific or identifiable stimulus consistently elicits operant behavior. If an operant response is followed by a reinforcing stimulus, the strength of the response is increased. |
| Bandura | Observational learning | Behavior is best learned through observing and modeling. Emphasis is placed on vicarious, symbolic, and self-regulatory processes. |
| *Cognitive* | | |
| Piaget | Cognitive stages of development | Four cognitive stages form a sequence of progressive mental operations; the stages are hierarchical and increasingly more complex. |
| | Assimilation, accommodation, and equilibration | The incorporation of new experiences, the method of modifying new experiences to derive meaning, and the process of blending new experiences into a systematic whole. |
| Dewey | Problem solving | Being in a situation, sensing a problem, clarifying it with information, working out suggested solutions, and testing the ideas by application. |
| Bruner-Phenix | Structure of a subject | The knowledge, concepts, and principles of a subject; learning how things are related is learning the structure of a subject. |
| Gardner | Multiple intelligences | A cross-culture, expanded concept of what is intelligence—such areas as linguistics, music, logical-mathematical, spatial, body-kinesthetic, and personal. |
| Lipman-Marzano-Sternberg | Critical thinking | Teaching students how to think, including forming concepts, generalizations, cause-effect relationships, inferences, consistencies and contradictions, assumptions, analogies, and the like. |
| *Humanistic* | | |
| Maslow | Human needs | Six human needs related to survival and psychological well-being; the needs are hierarchical and serve to direct behavior. |
| Rogers | Freedom to learn | Becoming a full person requires freedom to learn; the learner is encouraged to be open, self-trusting, and self-accepting. |
| Raths | Value clarification | Analysis of personal preferences and moral issues to reveal or clarify one's values—that is, beliefs, attitudes, and opinions. |
| Johnson-Slavin | Cooperative learning | Cooperative and group approaches to learning are considered more effective than competitive and individualistic learning situations. |

Source: Adapted from Allan C. Ornstein and Francis P. Hunkins, *Curriculum: Foundations, Principles and Issues*, 5th ed. (Boston: Allyn and Bacon, 2008).

the last question is yes, we might as well live in Sidney Poitier's world of teaching in *To Sir, With Love.*

The chain of events about salaries and qualifications has a greater negative impact with inner-city children than with suburban children, since the latter generally have better academic skills and support structures at home and therefore can learn on their own, sometimes even with unqualified or uncaring teachers. The fact is, effective teaching is more important in inner-city schools than elsewhere, and it is crucial if we are to build more effective school programs.[84] Morale is important, along with a sense of collegiality and cooperation, for teachers to give their best efforts. The school must be a place where the leadership is perceived as fair, where good teachers are recognized and developed into better teachers, where inexperienced teachers and average teachers are mentored by experienced and above-average teachers, where all teachers are treated as professionals and given extra support from their supervisors and administrators.

Achieving more-effective schools is about more-effective teaching. It means that we bring back our retired teachers as part-time mentors. It suggests that we pay "good" teachers more than "average" teachers, and we think about allowing teachers and principals either to receive bonuses for merit or to negotiate salary and assignments, thus allowing the labor market to take its natural course, for the sake of professionalism and school success. It means that we break the "isolationist culture" that exists in most schools, and that people involved in leadership positions recognize and reward teachers.

School people can influence children's development almost in the same way as competent parents. To be effective, schools need to create conditions supportive of, and encourage teachers to consider, students' cognitive and social development. Successful education starts at the early grade levels, builds on past and continuous ex-

periences, and combines various domains of learning—not only cognitive. As James Comer puts it, we need a "pool of teachers and administrators who, in addition to having thorough knowledge of their discipline," understand "how children develop generally and academically and how to support that development." (This is critical in high schools, where teachers are subject focused rather than student focused, and often ignore student developmental needs.)[85] Teachers must be able to engage parents of students and people in the community in ways that benefit student growth and development, and particularly their children's education. Providing vouchers, planning the curriculum, or imposing performance standards are infrastructure changes. What Comer advocates is a change in attitude. Teachers must become more professional and more collegial; likewise, they need to be adequately paid and recognized for their expertise and services.

Probably the most important factor in more effective schools is a strong *principal* with conviction, zeal, and a clear mission who can stretch budgets and get more out of people than might be expected. Second, there is need for hardworking and dedicated *teachers* who expect students to learn. Next, *parents* must accept their responsibilities in providing support structures and a home environment that is conducive to proper socialization, personal growth, and learning. Finally, *students* must be held responsible for their actions and accept that it takes self-control, self-reliance, no excuses, no laying blame on others, and no expecting a free ride to achieve academic success. It needs to be reemphasized that time-on-task, completing homework, review and practice, and studying are basic ingredients for academic success. This simply translates into Thomas Sowell's concept of hard work, or what Admiral Rickover, fifty years ago, and Thomas Edison, some seventy-five years ago, called "perspiration."

## The School Superintendent

One of the board's most important responsibilities is to appoint a competent superintendent of schools. The superintendent is the executive officer of the school system, whereas the board is the legislative policymaking body. Because the school board consists of laypeople who are not experts in school affairs, it is their responsibility to see that the work of the school is properly performed by professional personnel. The board of ed-

---

[84]The fact is, however, 17 percent of New York City teachers are uncertified; that is, they have not yet passed a simple general knowledge test and teaching-skills test or they lack the necessary credits for a teacher license. These percentages compare to less than 5 percent who are uncertified in the remaining parts of the state. As well, 29 percent of minority teachers (blacks and Hispanics) are uncertified in the City. See Carl Companile, "Racial Gap in Teacher Tests Brings Alarm," *New York Post,* 31 March 2002, p. 3.

Comparable percentages exist for nearly every large city such as Boston, Chicago, Dallas, Los Angeles, and Miami, and their respective states. See Allan Ornstein and Daniel U. Levine, *Foundations of Education,* 10th ed. (Boston: Houghton Mifflin, 2008).

[85]James P. Comer, "Schools That Develop Children," *American Prospect,* 23 April 2001, pp. 30–35.

ucation often delegates many of its own legal powers to the superintendent and his staff, although the superintendent's policies are subject to board approval.

## The Superintendent's Job

One of the major functions of the school superintendent is to gather and present data so that school board members can make intelligent policy decisions. Increasing board reliance on the superintendent and staff is evident as school districts grow. The superintendent advises the school board and keeps members abreast of problems; generally, the school board will refuse to make policy without the recommendation of the school superintendent. However, it is common knowledge that when there is continued disagreement or a major conflict over policy between the school board and the superintendent, the latter is usually replaced.

According to survey data, the average tenure of superintendents is approximately 5.5 years. The average tenure for a superintendent in a small district is 6 years, while the average tenure of a superintendent in a large district is 4 years;[86] for Great City Superintendents (56 big-city schools/districts), the average tenure increased from 2.5 years in 2001 to 2.75 years in 2003. According to school board members, the ideal superintendent's contract should last two to three years (and then be open for renewal). The majority of superintendents move around every few years seeking "greener pastures." More than 50 percent of the 13,800 superintendents were expected to retire between 1993 and 2003;[87] hence, the opportunity to become a chief school executive is increasing as we move forward into the twenty-first century. In fact, in a recent survey it was found that 24 percent of superintendents in the largest 100 school districts were freshmen superintendents.[88]

Although a wealth of data exists on what makes a school principal effective, there is little information on what makes a superintendent effective and to what extent, if any, the superintendent contributes to teacher effectiveness or student performance. This dearth of information is probably related to the fact that the superintendent is considered a manager of the entire district, not a direct leader of curriculum, instruction, teaching, or learning.

The superintendent's powers are broad and duties are many and varied. Besides being an advisor to the board of education, the superintendent is usually responsible for certain functions:

1. Serves as supervisor and organizer of professional and nonteaching personnel (e.g., janitors and engineers).

2. Makes recommendations regarding the employment, promotion, and dismissal of personnel.

3. Ensures compliance with directives of higher authority.

4. Prepares the school budget for board review and administers the adopted budget.

5. Serves as leader of long-range planning.

6. Develops and evaluates curriculum and instructional program.

7. Determines internal organization of the school district.

8. Makes recommendations regarding school building needs and maintenance.[89]

In addition, the superintendent is responsible for the day-to-day operation of the schools within the district and serves as the major public spokesperson for the schools.

Superintendents are often under strong pressure from various segments of the community, and much of the superintendent's effectiveness will depend on his ability to deal with such pressure groups. In large, urban school districts, for example, demands may be made for better facilities for students with handicaps or learning disabilities, more bilingual programs, improved vocational education, and school desegregation.

[86] "Highlights of Administrators' Survey," *Education Week*, 20 January 1988, p. 23; *Tenure of Urban School Superintendents Almost Five Years* (Alexandria, VA: National School Boards Association, 2002).

[87] Council of the Great City Schools, *Urban School Superintendents: Characteristics, Tenure, and Salary* (Washington, DC: The Council, 2002); *Professional Standards for the Superintendency* (Arlington, VA: American Association of School Administrators, 1999).

[88] Allan C. Ornstein, "School Superintendents and School Board Members: Who They Are," *Education Week*, November 1990, p. 5. Also see John R. Hoyle et al., *The Superintendent as CEO* (Thousand Oaks, CA: Corwin Press, 2005).

[89] William E. Eaton, *Shaping the Superintendency* (New York: Teachers College Press, Columbia University, 1990); Petra E. Snowden and Richard A. Gorton, *School Leadership and Administration*, 6th ed. (Boston: McGraw-Hill, 2002); and Rene S. Townsend et al., *Effective Superintendent-School Board Practices* (Thousand Oaks, CA: Corwin Press, 2006).

In middle-class suburbs, parents may be especially sensitive to student achievement scores, demanding upgraded academic programs if they feel the education is not as superior as their children deserve. Such students are often overprogrammed and overstressed, and a confident school leader is needed to balance the demands and expectations of the parents with the sociopsychological needs of the students. In small or rural districts where enrollments are declining, the superintendent may be pressured, on one hand, to save money by closing schools and, on the other hand, to keep all schools open to preserve the pride and identity of the community. Given the politics, policies, and pressures of the job at the community and state levels, "the superintendent must never lose sight that the ultimate client is the student," asserts former New York deputy superintendent Robert Brasco.[90] Educational administration courses fall short in this area because the emphasis is on leadership, management, organizational theory, school finance and law—not on the needs or interests of the students.

## Superintendents' Salary and Performance

According to a 2003 Business Week Survey of the top executives in private industry, the average CEO's salary, bonus, and long-term compensation increased 9.1 percent from the previous year to $8.1 million. In the past, CEO compensation has been more about wealth creation than pay for salaries. The key was stock options, and when exercised they tended to exceed salary, bonuses, and other perks. Leading the list of top executives was Colgate-Palmolive's Reuben Mark with $141 million in total pay ($136 million in long-term compensation), followed by Steven Jobs of Apple Computer with $75 million in long-term compensation. "The close alignment of pay and performance reflected in the 2003 Mercer survey numbers indicates that organizations are moving toward more responsible executive compensation."[91] Some people would call this "greed," others "corporate excess," and still others an example of increasing "inequality."

Inequality can be gauged another way. In 2001, the top CEOs of 365 companies earned 500 times the average factory worker's pay of $34,000.[92] Superintendents, on the other hand, averaged $118,811 for districts of all sizes, earning a little more than two and a half times a teacher's average pay of $44,000. The average pay for superintendents of school districts with 25,000 or more students averaged $170,024 in 2003 or more than three and a half times a teacher's average salary.[93]

In 2003, the average salary for Great City Superintendents was $189,000 up from $183,200 in 2001. The salary range was between $120,000 and $325,500 in 2003. The average superintendent's salary in districts with between 50,000 and 100,000 students was $193,700; in districts with more than 100,000 students the average was $222,500.[94] A few school superintendents in districts such as Syosset, Hewlett-Woodmere, Commack in New York and Miami-Dade County, Florida were earning over $300,000, with bonuses and perks, in 2003. Whereas the bonuses for top CEOs are in the millions, the bonuses for superintendents nationwide average about $25,000 to $50,000, not counting sabbaticals and pensions mostly linked to achieving prestated goals or raising student achievement within the school district. For the Great City Superintendents, pay-for-performance ranged from $4,050 to $100,000 in 2003. Their average benefits were worth $40,000.[95]

Howard Smucker, former superintendent of Lisle, Illinois, schools (3500 students), welcomes the idea of extra benefits such as travel and housing but feels that merit pay or bonuses for performance among educators lead to politics, dysfunctional behavior, and poor morale among "losers."[96] Jim Jenkins, former superintendent of Greshan, Oregon, schools (15,000 students), is even more critical of merit pay, arguing that "it is too subjective, that it creates competition, and that people start to work against each other—and at the ex-

---

[90]Robert Brasco, former Deputy Superintendent, Community District #32, New York City; personal communication, March 16, 2007.

[91]"Executive Pay," *Business Week*, 19 April 2004, pp. 106–120; "Adding it All Up," *Wall Street Journal*, 10 April 2006, R1–R3.

[92]"Executive Compensation Scoreboard," *Business Week*, 15 April 2002, pp. 87–100.

[93]Council of the Great City Schools, *Urban School Superintendents*, p. 2.

[94]Council of the Great City Schools, *Urban School Superintendents*; Ruth Sternberg, "Contracts and Compensation," *American School Board Journal*, 191 (2004): 44–47.

[95]Council of Great Schools, *Urban School Superintendents*; Scott Lafee, "Pay for Performance," *School Administrator*, 56 (1999): 18–23; John Hildebrand, "New Math for School Chiefs," *Newsday*, 30 October 2004, p. 3.

[96]Howard Smucker, former superintendent of Lisle (IL) School District, personal communication, March 11, 1999.

pense of cooperation."[97] This is similar to W. Edward Deming's view about evaluation of merit performance: "short-term thinking and short-time performance," whereby we sacrifice pride of performance and teamwork for easy-to-count measurements.[98]

Comparing level of responsibility, size of budget, number of personnel, and separate (school) sites where a superintendent oversees school districts of 50,000 to 100,000 students, a comparable position in private industry would reap an annual salary of $3 million to $5 million. There are no stock options available in the public sector. For the fifteen largest school districts comprising 100,000 or more students, the salary should be about $5 to $10 million. In 2003, Joel Klein, the New York City school superintendent, who oversees an annual budget of $12 billion, some 105,000 employees (including 80,000 teachers), and 1.1 million students, earned a "farcical" salary—some $250,000.

Former superintendent Jerry Cicchelli of Mahopac, New York (6000 students), maintains the problems and issues are different between the CEO of the corporate world and the school district, but he feels that "$500,000 per year is not unrealistic in the [near horizon] and not unfair given the responsibilities of a superintendent in a large school district of 100,000 or more students."[99] The difference is, of course, that private industry is for-profit and a money-producing unit and schools are not-for-profit and a cost-producing center. The private sector is about financial reward, supply and demand, and in some cases greed. Education is a helping profession—dominated by women who have traditionally earned less than men—where people are supposed to be dedicated and "not in it for the money."

To avoid being raided, corporate boards keep an eye on other firms in deciding on how much to pay top administrators. When directors give their chief executives a raise, they tend to lift salaries high above the industry average and thus create a new high or yardstick for other companies to match or exceed. When superintendents go before the school board for a raise, they have to contend with board members who frequently earn less money and are under pressure to keep down expenses

and resulting property taxes. Because most school superintendents earn more than their local government counterparts—fire chiefs, police chiefs, and mayors—it is difficult to argue before the community or taxpayers' group that higher salaries are warranted. When student performance exceeds projections, the argument can be made that it was the input, not the treatment, that made the difference. When student outcomes decline, criticism is often leveled at the teachers and administrators. Hence, it is a no-win situation for leaders in charge of schools.

It must be noted that schools are noncompetitive and do not deal in bottom lines or profit; they are not-for-profit organizations, and the kind of people that are selected to run the schools fill a political need, not an economic need. Often the idea is to hire a "safe" person, someone who will get along with the school board president, or hire a person from a particular minority, ethnic, or religious background. Schools are what Milton Friedman calls a "tampered marketplace," not a "free marketplace." Finally, superintendents are political animals, not necessarily business leaders or people expected to assert positions. Superintendents are expected to report and follow board policy. Given a tough-minded school board or a small community with an entrenched power structure, their expectations for leadership are further lessened; the idea is to get along with people, keep one's nose clean, and not embarrass important players on the board or in the community.

## Up the Professional Ladder

Although it takes a mixture of hard work, luck, and political savvy, moving from district to district is usually the quickest way to move up the career ladder—especially if the district is small and the superintendency is your goal. Otherwise, you will sit in the same place for years waiting for someone to retire or die, with the possibility of being passed over because of a new boss or school board. Of course, there are more openings in larger school districts, and in a recent report 39 percent of new superintendents in districts with more than 25,000 students said they had come up from within the district, compared to 29 percent in smaller districts.[100]

[97]Jim Jenkins, former superintendent of Greshan (OR) School District, personal communication, April 14, 1999.

[98]W. Edwards Deming, *Out of Crisis* (Cambridge, MA: MIT Press, 1986).

[99]Jerry Cicchelli, former superintendent of Mahopac (NY) School District, personal communication, January 8, 2003. The authors venture to guess that no later than 2010 the salaries for superintendents will reach the half million mark.

[100]Thomas E. Glass, et al., *The Study of American School Superintendents* (Arlington, VA: American Association of School Administrators, 2000); Hess, *School Boards at the Dawn of the 21st Century*, table 17, p. 22; Lance D. Fusarelli and Barbara L. Jackson, "How Do We Find and Retain Superintendents?" *School Administrator*, 61 (2004): 56.

## Table 10–5  Paths to the Superintendency

| | |
|---|---|
| 49% | Teacher, Principal, Central Office |
| 31% | Teacher, Principal |
| 9% | Teacher, Central Office |
| 2% | Teacher only |
| 2% | Principal, Central Office |
| 2% | Principal only |
| 1% | Central Office only |
| 4% | Not reported |

Source: Thomas E. Glass, et al., *The Study of the American School Superintendency* (Alexandria, VA: American Association of School Administrators, 2000), table 6.20, p. 86.

The path to the superintendency usually consists of two major roads: 49 percent take the teacher–principal–central office route and 31 percent travel the teacher-principal route (43 states require superintendents to have education training and be former educators). All other roads to the top are secondary, as shown in Table 10–5, although 61 percent stopped off at the central office for a while before becoming superintendents. Most associate superintendents or superintendents land their first administrative job before age thirty (assistant principal or principal), and most make the decision to become superintendent while serving as a school principal.[101]

The first superintendent job is considered the hardest. It involves many job searches, interviewing skills, and matching personal experience and style with school district needs and expectations, to compensate for lack of experience as a superintendent. The more mobility someone has, the better the chances. The number-one barrier limiting administrative opportunities relates to lack of mobility of family members (21% for males; 41% for females.)[102] Perhaps for this reason, 80 percent of the superintendents report remaining in one state for their entire career.[103] Female superintendents are making the most progress, up from 2.8 percent in 1984, 4.5 percent in 1990, and 16.5 percent in 1998. They still

have a way to go until they are equitably represented; estimated to account for 20 percent in 2006.[104]

Having a doctorate is important: 41 percent of the nation's superintendents possess this degree, and today there are more women than men enrolled in educational administration doctoral programs. Because of burnout, retirement, and the usual turnover among experienced superintendents, the demand for new superintendents is expected to increase. And because of the gender breakdown among administrative doctoral candidates, we expect a continued increase in female superintendents, especially black females in big-city school districts. As of 2003, 23 percent of big-city superintendents (Great City Schools) were female (13% were black, 10% were white, and none were Hispanic or Asian).[105]

For 2005, the projections are 35–40 percent female big-city superintendents. The "old boy network" has been eroding since the 1990s; just count the number of female superintendents being profiled by Jay Goldman, editor of *School Administrator*.[106] And although 7 percent of the nation's superintendents are minority, within the larger 100 school districts the percentage is more than 30 percent, and within the fifty-six Great City School districts the minority percentage is 52.[107]

Each school district is unique, as is each superintendent. But once you have landed the job, your challenges begin! Peter Negroni, former superintendent of the Springfield, Massachusetts, public schools, recommends several job strategies:

1. *Watch Your Image.* Be aware of how the board and the public perceive you. The image you create the

[101]Glass et al., *The Study of American School Superintendents,* tables 6.20, 6.23, pp. 85–86; Frederick M. Hess, *Common Sense School Reform* (Gordonville, VA: Palgrave, 2006).

[102]Glass et al., *The Study of American School Superintendents,* table 6.28, p. 88.

[103]Thomas E. Glass, "Superintendent Leaders Look at the Superintendency," Paper issued by the Education *Commission of the States,* Denver, July 2001.

[104]Joyce A. Dana and Diana M. Bourisaw, *Women in the Superintendency* (Lanham, MD: Rowman & Littlefield, 2006); "Memo to Women: You're Making Progress," *Executive Educator,* 14 (1992): 18; Hess, *School Boards at the Dawn of the 21st Century,* p. 22; Marilyn Tallerico and Joan N. Burstyn, "Retaining Women in the Superintendency," *Educational Administration Quarterly,* 56 (1999): 642–664.

[105]Council of the Great City Schools, *Urban School Superintendents,* p. 1.

[106]See Jay Goldman's "Profile" series. Between 2000 and 2002, 35 percent of the profiles were women superintendents. Also see Robert R. Spillane and Paul Regnier, *The Superintendent of the Future* (Annapolis, MD: Aspen, 1998).

[107]Jay Mathews, "On the Job Training of Nontraditional Superintendents," *School Administrator,* 56 (1999): 28–33; Rosemary Henze et al., *Leading for Diversity* (Thousand Oaks, CA: Corwin Press, 2002); Ornstein, "School Superintendents and School Board Members: Who They Are"; Council of the Great City Schools, *Urban School Superintendents.*

first three to six months will most likely stick with you.

2. *Find Out About Your Predecessor.* The former superintendent's attitudes and behaviors left a mark on the office. Find out what the people didn't like about him or her and make it a point not to repeat those mistakes.

3. *Don't Bite Off More Than You Can Chew.* Don't take the job if you find it is too stressful or full of political minefields that you feel you cannot navigate.

4. *Keep Focused.* Keep track of your progress towards certain goals.

5. *Build a Positive Relationship with the School Board.* This requires constant attention and communication, knowledge of changing issues and hidden agendas, and familiarity with the personalities of the board members.

6. *Improve Your Relations with the Public and the Media.* The local press can vilify or champion your cause. Learn to define an issue in public in 30 seconds or less.

7. *Don't Be a Loner.* You cannot run a school district locked in your office. Get out to the schools and community.[108]

One board member in Newbury, Massachusetts, links the superintendent's success with the school budget. Despite previous increases in state aid, board members everywhere are now struggling with spiraling costs, painful cutbacks, and the need to streamline programs and staff. As superintendent, you must deal with fiscal reality, and recommend cuts without major harm to the basic educational program. Cutting sports programs is an emotional issue; avoid it if possible. Trimming the transportation and maintenance budgets is easier and more common. Unessential programs such as elective courses, extracurricular activities, and special services are more acceptable than the academic basics. Rather than reducing or freezing teacher salaries, it is better to cut teacher preparation periods, classroom aides, and professional travel or in-service programs; to increase student-teacher ratios by 1-or 2; and to let attrition and retirement take its course without hiring as many teacher replacements. Most important,

involve the community in budget priorities and fundraising to pick up some of the slack.[109]

If your school board is in conflict, their problems will eventually become your problems. According to one administrative veteran, going public with your disagreements is "clearly counterproductive." When the votes are continually split 4–3 or 5–4, and the majority group decides simply to force its policies through without regard for the minority, that will result in further entrenchment. If there are two factions on the board, the new superintendent should not expect to play mediator or peacemaker—at least not until having earned the board's respect. "Undiscussable" issues confronting the new person can include race, gender, politics, or whatever else may be the root cause of conflict.[110] Here the safe course of action is to bring in an outsider or neutral observer. The board can also select a facilitator from its own members—someone perceived as fair—to keep the board on task. The goal as superintendent is to improve the board process before tackling the issues.

Politics influence the superintendent's leadership role. Some superintendents are hired to implement change: "reform," "restructure," "innovate." And others are hired to maintain the status quo. In still other cases, reform is "tolerated," such as responses to state or court mandates, but the underlining or private order is to go slow. The turnover rate among superintendents is high. In one study by Thomas Glass, 64 percent of school districts reported having three or more superintendents in the last ten years. And 23 percent of the districts indicated asking the previous superintendent to leave, not renewing or buying out the person's contract.[111] The turnover among big-city superintendents is well known and largely associated with politics and

---

[108]Peter J. Negroni, "Landing the Big Job," *Executive Educator,* 14 (1992): 21–23; Negroni, "The Right Badge of Courage," *School Administrator,* 56 (1999): 14–17; Priscilla Pardini, "Ethics in the Superintendency," *School Administrator,* 61 (2004): 10–19.

[109]Don Davies, "The 10th School Revisited: Are School/Family/Community Partnerships on the Reform Agenda Now?" *Phi Delta Kappan,* 83 (2002): 388–392; Joyce L. Epstein, "Creating School, Family, Community Partnerships," in A. C. Ornstein et al., *Contemporary Issues in Curriculum,* 3rd ed. (Boston: Allyn and Bacon, 2003): 354–373.

[110]Martha Bruckner, "Private Lives of Public Leaders," *School Administrator,* 55 (1998): 24–27; David Sadker, "An Educator's Primer on the Gender War," *Phi Delta Kappan,* 84 (2002): 235–240; L. Rabinowitz, "Difficult Conversations," *Wall Street Journal,* 18 November 2002, p. 21.

[111]Thomas E. Glass, "School Board Presidents and Their View of the Superintendency." Paper issued by the Education Commission of the States, Denver, CO: May 2002. Also see David E. Lee, "Landmines in the Pathway of the Superintendency," *School Administrator,* 63 (2006): 47.

ethnic controversy. As many as 54 percent of the superintendents in the largest school districts have held the job for less than five years, in comparison to 64 percent in 2001.[112] Not only must superintendents have administrative experience, they must also be politically savvy in their responses to board members and the public, as well as various pressure groups. You must understand the community and treat most educational issues in a political context.

Former successful urban superintendents offer the following advice: "(1) The main thing is to maintain student achievement as the primary objective, (2) if what you are doing does not improve what happens in classrooms between teachers and students, it is probably not worth doing, (3) conflict is the price you pay for leadership, (4) listen to the people around you, and (5) making permanent change means changing the things that are permanent."[113]

Robert Peterkin, the former Milwaukee superintendent, puts it this way: "The most important lesson an urban superintendent must learn has to do with power." The power you sought must be shared. You need "to figure out how to give away power" to obtain loyalty.[114] The concept here ties closely to Macchiavelli's *The Prince*, which might make useful bedtime reading for aspiring superintendents.

Probably the only saving grace of the job is that the superintendent has the luxury of time and the option to consult with others before making most critical decisions. This is quite different from the situation of the school principal, who is always on the firing line and must make decisions on the spot, often without consulting with the next level of the bureaucratic hierarchy.

Eventually, the job comes down to "management of our schools," asserts Franklin Smith, the former superintendent of the Washington, D.C., schools, and "learning from the experience of others, exploring various options," and integrating new ideas into a system of management. "We must look to the vast resources of community"—its people, businesses, and institutions—to contribute to the education of our students. The school cannot do the job alone. "We are out of tricks," adds Smith.[115] All superintendents, new and experienced, need to rethink education and to look for outside help and partnerships with groups that have a vested interest in education.

Tom Brown has been superintendent for thirty-two years (since he was twenty-seven years old) in six school districts, both rural and suburban. He relies on "common sense . . . working with and through people . . . allowing flexibility and trusting them to do their jobs." Shared decision making and "bringing people in as true participants" has been his style. He uses the metaphor of "planting . . . and cultivating crops" to describe how he implements change in his district so that when a superintendent leaves, the good ideas and programs may have permanency.[116]

Robert Brasco, who was deputy superintendent for eleven years, believes in teamwork, but the ultimate decision rests with the superintendent, "the person at the top is going to take the 'rap,' if the decision is wrong. Michael Corleone, of the *Godfather*, would agree with this perspective, and so would General Patton."[117] Shared decision making is nice, but it has its limitations for the person who is ultimately responsible for the school district.

## The Superintendent and the School Board

Today's superintendents not only must work with their staffs but also must have a good relationship with a demanding public that is more informed than ever about educational issues, as well as a school board that is increasingly scrutinizing the superintendent's performance and results. Board members, parents, the community, and the professional staff hear a great deal about reform and have their own set of expectations, political agendas, and ideas about how students should be educated (often pushing a particular program or subject area that will benefit their children, sometimes at the expense of others). Today's superintendent must deliver the goods ("standards" and "accountability" are the watchwords in education), withstand public scrutiny, and provide more services without increased

[112]Council of the Great City Schools, *The Urban School Superintendents*, p. 113.

[113]Council of the Great City Schools, *The Urban Superintendent: Creating Great Schools While Surviving on the Job* (Washington, DC: The Council, 2003).

[114]Robert Peterkin, "Bright Lights, Big City," *Executive Educator*, 14 (1992): 19.

[115]Franklin L. Smith, "The Outside Opinion," *American School Board Journal*, 181 (1994): 42.

[116]Jay P. Goldman, "Profile: Thomas A. Brown—Always Ready to Share Good Counsel," *School Administrator*, 55 (1998): 51.

[117]Robert Brasco, former Deputy Superintendent, Community District #32, New York City; personal communication, January 29, 2007.

funding. Personality and style are important, although not easy to measure or quantify.[118]

Although the public is better educated and has become more demanding in recent years, the superintendent's real concern should be with school board members who frequently do not understand how complex systems are managed and who, despite their dedication and hard work, often are politically motivated and themselves divided on many issues. Sometimes it is healthy to have a diverse school board (with members who have different views on life), but when the board fails to act together or sends mixed messages, this places great stress on the superintendent.

According to observers, when the school board and superintendent are out of sync, the superintendent often gets bogged down in trying to please the board or defending decisions, and thus is unable to lead. Boards that are divided among themselves or are continually challenging the superintendent invite the resignation of the superintendent and a succession of short-lived superintendents. It is the schools, staff, and students that often lose when board-superintendent power often tips the opposite way.[119]

As many as 90 percent of the superintendents from 100 of the nation's biggest school districts stated that "they need more power to hire and fire employees, reconfigure struggling schools, and make curriculum changes."[120] For the most part, however, school board–superintendent relations are better than critics might think. Nationwide school boards (2166 respondents) are happy with their superintendents. Although there may be grumblings among board members, 53 percent are "very satisfied" with their school chiefs, and another 30 percent are "satisfied." Only 12 percent are "dissatisfied" or "very dissatisfied."[121]

Specifically, with respect to superintendent–school board interactions, the behavior of board members tends to cluster along a continuum from passive-acquiescence to proactive-supportive to restive-vigilance. *Passive-acquiescent* board members tend to rely primarily on the information and interpretations provided by the superintendent (or the administrative staff) and refer to the superintendent for problem resolutions and professional judgment or recommendations. In contrast, *restive-vigilant* board members personally visit schools and central offices on a regular basis, cultivate a wide range of information sources, actively participate in local and state education committees, build support for their own goals and objectives, and provide a check for and challenge the superintendent. *Proactive-supportive* board members exhibit similar behaviors to restive-vigilants in their degree of active involvement in school affairs, but they are similar to passive-acquiescents in that they usually support the superintendent rather than scrutinize or challenge the person's stance.[122]

Based on a sample of twenty-six board members in six Arizona school districts, the variables of board member gender, occupation, and political viewpoint correlate with the three identifiable patterns. Female board members and those who are not employed outside the home (retirees or homemakers) tend to be restive or proactive. Males, nonretirees, and nonhomemakers are more often passive. Proactive and passive board members ascribe to a traditional interpretation of parliamentary democracy and reference to the executive leadership role in government. Restive board members assert the notion of participatory democracy, lay control, and the rights of the people.[123] Under most conditions and with most superintendents, especially the traditional type, restive-vigilant board members can be viewed as trouble, and superintendents can possibly lock horns with the board if the membership is predominantly restive.

[118]General Davie and Ernest A. Silva, "The Politics of Accountability," *Thrust for Educational Leadership,* 28 (1999): 6–9; Daniel Domenech, "Situational Governance: A Continuum of Board Types," *School Administrator,* 62 (2005): 6; Allan C. Ornstein, "Superintendents: Gauge Your Performance and Productivity," *Executive Educator,* 12 (1990): 22–25.

[119]Vincent T. Beni, Bruce S. Cooper, and Rodney Muth, "Boards and Superintendents: Balance the Power," *American School Board Journal,* 175 (1988): 24–25. Donna Harrington-Lueker, "An Olive Branch for Boards," *American School Board Journal,* 180 (1993): 40–41; Robert Reeves, *What Every Rookie Superintendent Should Know* (Lanham, MD: Rowman & Littlefield, 2006).

[120]Bruce Buchanan, *Turnover at the Top: Superintendent Vacancies and the Urban School* (New York: Rowman & Littlefield, 2006), p. 352.

[121]"Twelfth Annual Survey: Happily Ever After." Also see "Indicators of School Success," *American School Board Journal,* 185 (1998): A-16–A-20.

[122]Marilyn Tallerico, "The Dynamics of Superintendent–School Board Relations," *Urban Education,* 24 (1989): 215–232.

[123]Paul Chollet, "Governance: From Boardroom to Classroom," *American School Board Journal,* 185 (1998): 42–43; Tallerico, "The Dynamics of Superintendent–School Board Relations."

## Superintendents' Problems and Performance

Major reasons why superintendents ultimately come under attack or resign can be classified into ten problem areas:

1. Too many board members who want to run the show; that is, too many people think they are "presidents."

2. Budget cuts, accompanied by a shrinking tax base.

3. Increasing amounts of reports and paperwork to meet government or legal requirements.

4. Dissension among school board members.

5. Declining enrollments matched with increasing expenditures.

6. Taxpayers' resistance to supporting education.

7. Teacher strikes and militancy.

8. Special interest groups who persistently promote their own causes.

9. Student crime and vandalism as well as discipline problems.

10. News media reportage that is erroneous or controversial.[124]

Although only two reasons (1 and 4) are directly linked to the school board, two others are related to community factors (2 and 6), which in turn have a ripple effect on board members who represent the community.

The typical conflict between superintendents and school board members usually involves political agendas, and different philosophies or values. Typically, the stage is set when two or more school board incumbents are challenged and unseated; this is an indicator of community dissatisfaction that can be easily transferred to the superintendent's office.[125] Increasingly, new board members are being elected on a single-issue platform or by a special interest group—a situa-tion that is likely to cause conflict with the superintendent. When community demographics rapidly change and are accompanied by a new advocacy group or by demands for a change in the superintendent—one who is more relevant, more sensitive, or more in line with new demands—it's time to look at other options. The situation boils down to politics and has nothing to do with performance or ability.[126]

The idea is to control the conditions under which the superintendent leaves, not to fight a losing battle or try to enlist a special interest group and split the community. When a superintendent does battle with the school board, students, parents, and community members lose as frustrations, emotions, and charges run rampant. And when a superintendent leaves a district, whether by quitting or being fired, the school and community, the students, teachers, and staff lose considerable continuity and progress toward sustainable reform.[127]

Although school boards have stated procedures for evaluating superintendents, too often the procedure is not technically valid, reliable, or useful, and it may result in turning the evaluation process into whatever board members decide to make of it. In theory, the superintendent's evaluation is not complicated; it should be based on precise *criteria* (agreed-on behaviors or competencies) and a method of *measurement* (such as a rating scale, observations, letters, or self-appraisal reports).

Board members, working with or independent of the superintendent, can determine the priorities, behaviors, or responsibilities they wish to stress. Nine major areas of responsibility, with equal weight, were originally adopted by the American Association of School Administrators (AASA) in 1980. They were (1) board relations, (2) community relations, (3) staff personnel management, (4) fiscal management, (5) facilities management, (6) curriculum and instruction, (7) student services, (8) planning, and (9) professional development. The nine categories, each with several subcategories, re-

[124]Dale Brubaker, *The Charismatic Leader* (Thousand Oaks, CA: Corwin Press, 2005); Sidney A. Freund, "Superintendent: Here's How I Stay Friends with the Board President," *American School Board Journal,* 175 (1998), 39–40; Jack Kaufhold, "Lessons not Taught in Superintendents' School," *School Administrator,* 60 (2003): 36.

[125]Alan K. Gaynor, *Analyzing Problems in Schools and School Systems* (Mahwah, NJ: Erlbaum, 1998); Michael Kirst, *Who Controls Our Schools?* (New York: Freeman, 1994); Frank W. Lutz and Carol Merz, *The Politics of School/Community Relations* (New York: Teachers College Press, Columbia University, 1992).

[126]Andrew K. Davis, "The Politics of Barking and the State of Our Schools," *Phi Delta Kappan,* 82 (2001): 786–789; Priscilla Pardini, "When Termination's in the Air," *School Administrator,* 55 (1998): 6–12; Michael Rist, "Race and Politics Rip into the Urban Superintendency," *Executive Educator,* 47 (1990): 23–25. Also see Kenneth A. Strike, *Ethical Leadership in Schools* (Thousand Oaks, CA: Corwin Press, 2006).

[127]Negroni, "The Right Badge of Courage"; Larry Nyland, "The Shortcut Search: What to Do When You Need to Hire a Superintendent—Now," *American School Board Journal,* 185 (1998): 48–49.

mained major criteria for evaluating superintendents for twenty years. In fact, Marion Hunt, who was in charge of disseminating the instrument for the AASA, contended that the demand for the instrument was high among school board members and school superintendents throughout the 1990s.[128]

According to Hess, the relationship with the school board, the morale of system teachers and administrators, and the safety of district students are the top three factors that school boards examine in evaluating the superintendent.[129] School districts also have adopted superintendent evaluation systems that coincide with or include (1) state standards for improving student achievement, (2) the direction and goals of the school board, (3) the superintendent's personal/professional goals for the year, (4) a collaborative goal-setting arrangement between the superintendent and school board, and (5) merit pay or performance bonuses. Board members are divided almost evenly between whether pay for performance for superintendents is likely to increase student achievement.[130]

More recently, there has been an attempt to customize the superintendent's evaluation according to the goals and needs of a school district. Rooted in AASA thinking, the new standards examine seven domains of leadership and human skills behavior and suggest four sources of evaluating the superintendent's performance: (1) student performance, (2) document review, (3) staff and community surveys, and (4) self-assessments. The overall idea is to provide a practical, easy-to-implement, as well as informative, useful evaluation of the superintendent, based on performance standards.[131]

Issues involving the superintendent's evaluation include the following: (1) How often will the superintendent be evaluated? (2) What kind of evaluation instrument will be used? (3) Will the superintendent have input in determining the instrument? (4) How will the evaluation be related to the superintendent's job description? (5) Who will evaluate the superintendent—the board, a consultant group, the community, or some combination? (6) How will evaluation outcomes affect the renewal of the superintendent's contract?[132]

The key to the evaluation process is to collect data from several sources, including major client groups within the school district: board members, central administrators, community leaders, and parents (or parent groups). The advantage of a client-based or stakeholder-based evaluation instrument is that it has public relations value among board members, staff, and community members because they have been included in the process. Not only does it help head off potential problems because of its openness and inclusion, but also a hostile board would have difficulty building a case by itself for dismissal because the superintendent is being judged by many more people besides the board members.

Of course, when termination is around the corner, the evaluation instrument will most likely be used as a paper trail to accelerate the dismissal process. These days, being forced out as superintendent rarely carries a stigma or spells the end of a professional career, because dismissal is an occupational hazard of the position.[133] It is prudent, however, to leave on a voluntary basis, before the bell sounds: to move on to a larger or better-financed school district, with bigger challenges and a bigger salary and benefit package. Of course, happy endings do not always occur.

The main reasons that superintendents say boards evaluate them are for accountability, to establish performance goals, to assess performance, to identify areas needing improvement, and to comply with board policy, in that order.[134] As Dean Speicher, former president of AASA, asserts, school superintendents must learn to act as CEOs; they must exhibit courage and take risks "on behalf of students, staff, and commu-

[128]Marion Hunt, AASA Director of Membership Services, personal communication, June 24, 1999; December 1, 2002.

[129]Hess, *School Boards at the Dawn of the 21st Century*, p. 23.

[130]Larry Lashway, "Instruments for Evaluation," *School Administrator*, 55 (1998): 14–20; Scott Lafee, "Pay for Performance," *School Administrator*, 56 (1999); 18–23; Sharon Rallis et al. "Superintendents in Classrooms: From Collegial Conversation to Collaborative Action," *Phi Delta Kappan*, 87 (2006): 537–545; Don Senti and Linda A. Smith, "A Client-Based System for Superintendent Evaluations," *School Administrator*, 55 (1998): 44–45.

[131]Michael F. Dipoala and James H. Stronge, *Superintendent Evaluation Handbook* (Lanham, MD: Scarecrow Press, 2003).

[132]Lars G. Bjork and Theodore J. Kowalski, *The Contemporary Superintendent* (Thousand Oaks, CA: Corwin Press, 2005); Theodore J. Kowalski, "Critiquing the CEO," *American School Board Journal*, 185 (1998): 43–44.

[133]Gordon Ambach, "Leadership Education for the 'Fortune 300' of Education," *Phi Delta Kappan*, 87 (2006): 519–520; Linda Chion-Kenny, "The Perils of Pension Partiality," *School Administrator*, 55 (1998): 24–27; Pardini, "When Termination's in the Air."

[134]Glass et al., *The Study of American School Superintendents*.

nity." They must become "visionaries, strategists, and diplomats" as they put their plans in place and organize the key players around their educational goals.[135]

**Vision** has become a buzzword in educational circles: the act of seeing, anticipating, and imagining. Vision that reflects only the leader's view is bound to fail, since it lacks motivational appeal with which people can identify. Stakeholders, including teachers, administrators, board members, and community residents, must buy into the vision. Ideally, school districts and even schools should be defined by a vision, and changes within the district (or school) should reflect the vision.[136]

Based on a review of fifty years worth of research (and including the classic studies by Chester Barnard, Philip Selznick, and James McGregor Burns), Larry Cuban concludes that the superintendent must do the following to accomplish desired results:

1. Imagine what the organization can become; define the mission; set the goals.
2. Motivate people's energies toward achieving the organizational goals.
3. Link the mission to organizational routines and behaviors.
4. Promote certain values that give the organization a distinctive character.[137]

Cuban argues that leadership at one level in the school district influences what occurs at the next level below, a **top-down model** that most superintendents adopt. The superintendent's leadership style filters down from the central office to the school principal, affecting the behavior of lower-ranking administrators.[138] With this top-down model, if the superintendent is business or task oriented, then low-ranking administrators pick up these cues and modify their behavior accordingly.

But if the superintendent is humanistic or people oriented, then administrators will modify their behavior in the other direction. Indeed, most school administrators have sufficient common sense not to irritate people on top.

## Superintendents' Skill Areas

The AASA, working in conjunction with the University of Texas, conducted a nationwide survey of superintendents who ranked fifty-two skills in the order of their importance for effective performance. The ten most important skill areas were (1) leadership, (2) organizational management, (3) fiscal responsibility, (4) school-community relations, (5) teacher evaluation, (6) cost-effective budgeting, (7) motivational techniques, (8) conflict mediation, (9) testing and evaluation of student performance, and (10) curriculum development and instructional planning.[139] Three additional skill areas were recommended by a group of 100 business executives, state educational officers, superintendents, and professors of educational administration: (1) policy and governance, (2) instructional management, and (3) values and ethics.[140] These thirteen skill areas are now considered generic skills for effective superintendents.[141]

Joseph Murphy and colleagues have published a series of research studies associating twelve school districts (ranging in size from 2000 to 19,350 students and five to twenty-nine schools) whose student achievement scores exceeded expectations, as well as the scores of other districts, after controlling for the students' socioeconomic status over a three-year period. Nine superintendents' functions or areas of responsibility were defined and associated with these high-performing school districts:

1. *Selection.* Ten out of twelve districts had administrative internship programs to socialize potential principals. When hiring principals, five superintendents stressed technical skills in curricu-

[135]Dean Speicher, "Courage, Risks Essential to Leadership," *School Administration,* 56 (1999): 6j. Also see Roger Soder, *The Language of Leadership* (San Francisco: Jossey-Bass, 2001).

[136]Philip Hallinger and Kenneth Leithwood, "Unforeseen Forces: The Impact of Social Culture on School Leadership," *Peabody Journal of Education,* 73 (1998): 126–151; Jerome T. Murphy, "An Interview with Henry Mintzberg," *Phi Delta Kappan,* 87 (2006): 527–528; James Scoolis, "What Is Vision?" *Thrust for Educational Leadership,* 28 (1998): 20–21, 36.

[137]Larry Cuban, *The Managerial Imperative and the Practice of Leadership in Schools* (Albany: State University of New York Press, 1988).

[138]Ibid.

[139]John R. Hoyle, *Leadership and Futuring: Making Visions Happen* (Thousand Oaks, CA: Corwin Press, 2006); John R. Hoyle, Fenwick English, and Betty Steffy, *Skills for Successful School Leaders,* rev. ed. (Arlington, VA: American Association of School Administrators, 2000).

[140]*Professional Standards for the Superintendency.*

[141]Gary Marx, Associate Executive Director, American Association of School Administrators, personal communications, June 12, 1994; March 11, 1999.

lum, instruction, and teaching, and four stressed human relation skills and the ability to motivate people.

2. *Supervision.* In ten out of twelve districts, the superintendent was personally responsible for the supervision and evaluation of principals. Superintendents averaged twenty-one 8-hour days per year at school sites, between 8-and 10 percent of their total work year.

3. *Evaluation.* Principals in all districts were evaluated annually; procedures were clearly defined; the criteria and method of evaluation were known in advance.

4. *Staff Development.* Participation in administrative staff development was mandatory in all twelve districts, although it was sometimes voluntary for teachers in many of the same districts. The emphasis was on improving curriculum, instruction, teaching, and teacher evaluation.

5. *Rewards and Sanctions.* None of the twelve districts had a merit-pay program for principals, and salaries were not tied to evaluation results. A number of superintendents reported that they frequently promoted internally when filling a central office position, but the only major formal reward was continued employment.

6. *Goals.* All superintendents reported that the district had written goals; eight indicated they had specific objectives at the school level. All twelve superintendents used district goals as influencing budget allocations, and a comprehensive testing program.

7. *Resource Allocation.* Resource allocations in all twelve districts were determined by the central office and used to control and constrain school activities and spending. The schools received an extra-small allotment per student: These funds could be used at the principals' discretion.

8. *Monitoring.* Superintendents relied strongly on supervision and evaluation of the principals' behaviors. Frequent site visits and regular reviews of progress on school goals were the major monitoring activities used by the superintendents. Test scores were used to monitor school goals or objectives.

9. *Technical Specifications.* All superintendents attempted to influence technical activities related to curriculum, instruction, and evaluation. Nine of the twelve districts had a preferred method of teaching or instruction, which they expected principals to emphasize in their schools.[142]

What emerges in the research is a superintendent who establishes the direction and tone of the school system. This leader has a philosophy or mission, even a preferred teaching or instructional model, which is embedded at the district and school level. The superintendent is a no-nonsense person who controls, coordinates, and communicates the operation to the district and school-level staff. He or she monitors, reviews, and holds rank-and-file administrators accountable according to prescribed goals and procedures. The person is "hip deep" in school district and school activities — very much aware of what is going on within the system. Emphasis is on school matters dealing with curriculum, instruction, teaching, learning, and evaluation.[143]

Here the question arises of whether a superintendent in a larger school district, 25,000 or more students, could spend so much time on these technical matters and not have to delegate them to lower-ranking administrators and leave more discretion to the principal in deciding these matters. One might also conclude that the site visits and monitoring functions of the superintendent would be more limited in a larger school district.

Indeed, this type of superintendent tends to coincide more with our earlier definition of a manager, and not a leader. It is similar to a military model or taskmaster in which George Patton and Vince Lombardi would feel comfortable. The superintendent seems much more concerned with controlling and coordinating activities, doing things his or her way — end of discussion — or what James Thompson would refer to as the "technical" aspects of running an organization.[144] (For Thompson,

---

[142] Joseph Murphy and Philip Hallinger, "Characteristics of Instructionally Effective School Districts," *Journal of Educational Research*, 81 (1988): 175–180; Murphy et al., "The Administrative Control of Principals in Effective School Districts," *Journal of Educational Administration*, 25 (1987): 161–192. Also see Joseph Murphy and Karen Seashore Louis (eds.), *Handbook of Research on Educational Administration*, 2nd ed. (San Francisco: Jossey-Bass, 1999).

[143] Amy M. Hightower, *School Districts and Instructional Renewal* (New York: Teachers College Press, Columbia University, 2001); Joseph Murphy and Philip Hallinger, "The Superintendent as Instructional Leader: Findings from Effective School Districts," *Journal of Educational Administration*, 24 (1986): 213–236; Gary Schomburg, "Superintendent in the Classroom," *Phi Delta Kappan*, 87 (2006): 546–550.

[144] James D. Thompson, *Organizations in Action* (New York: McGraw-Hill, 1967).

the more the organization maneuvers, modifies, or compromises its behavior, the more disruptive and costly it is—a highly close-ended view of organizations.)

Leadership, according to our earlier definition, is still evidenced by the superintendents in the study; they possess vision and values and are able to establish direction and meaning for members of the district and schools. But the leadership style that emerges is not overwhelmingly humanistic or people oriented and provides minimal professional autonomy at the school level. The maverick school principal would have trouble lasting in such a school system.

The point to remember is, schools are democratic institutions and people can topple champions, gurus, and generals. The Lombardi/Patton leadership style is dated in educational settings, as is the John Wayne (leadership by muscle), Lone Ranger (loner, calm, unemotional type), or Napoleon–Boss Lady model.[145] Given the emphasis today on working together and communicating with people, on collaboration, collegiality, and consensus, yesterday's rough-and-tough style is a trap. The old idea to manipulate, monitor, or move people to act in certain ways may get people to do things, but it doesn't lead to sustained motivation and it usually results in minimal (but passing) performance.

## The Central Staff

The superintendent is assisted by a **central office staff.** In large districts of 25,000 or more students, there may be many levels in the staff hierarchy: a deputy superintendent, associate superintendents, assistant superintendents, directors, department heads, and a number of coordinators and supervisors, each with supporting staff members. The picture is further complicated when a large school district decentralizes its operation into several areas or subdistricts; there may be a "field" superintendent, with his or her own staff (as well as other administrators) in each area who in turn reports to an associate superintendent in the central office.[146]

Although the idea of decentralization and on-site management is to reform and streamline the system, what often happens is that the school district gets a new bureaucratic layer.

Most large school districts are highly centralized. The key issue is power and control. Central staff matrices are often built on top of other matrices, each with its own functions that are jealously guarded. (See Administrative Advice 10–4.) Decisions that should take days or weeks often take months or even years, as each department conducts its own review and adds its own recommendations to be considered by the next level. This phenomenon is typical not only of large school districts but also of large corporations, which have had to learn some tough lessons about inefficiency and have recently trimmed and streamlined top layers to save money.[147] In an era of retrenchment, school administrators may have to learn the same lesson. To be sure, there is a recent trend to push decisions closer to the school site and level of implementation.

### Large Districts: Increased Central Offices

Large, urban districts have tended to expand their centralized staff and activities over recent years in order to administer court-ordered policies and state and federal guidelines, programs, and funds and to cope with union-style teacher associations. All these trends, according to one recent study, lead to elaborate bureaucratic efforts, in which central office personnel are hired to oversee these efforts.[148] In addition, when there is a changing of the guard at the top level in large school districts, new managers are sometimes brought in from outside and/or others are promoted from within. The old guard or outgroup often are career administrators with tenure. They are not replaced but reassigned; thus, the central staff continues to grow. Similarly, school principals who are displaced because of community politics or pressures often find refuge at the central office in

[145]George A. Goens, "The John Wayne Model: A Leadership Trap," *Principal,* 77 (1998): 40–42; Elizabeth A. Herbert, *The Boss of the Whole School: Effective Leadership in Action* (New York: Teachers College Press, 2006).

[146]Donna Costello, "The Human Cost of Cuts," *American School Board Journal,* 178 (1991): 37–39; Ira W. Krinsky, "Getting Down to Business," *American School Board Journal,* 181 (1994): 26–29; Jerry Patterson, "Harsh Realities about Decentralized Decision Making," *School Administrator,* 55 (1998): 10–12.

[147]Dale L. Brubaker and Larry D. Coble, *The Hidden Leader* (Thousand Oaks, CA: Corwin Press, 2005); Thomas Moore, "Goodbye, Corporate Staff," *Fortune,* 21 December 1987, pp. 65, 68, 76; Robert R. Spillane and Paul Regnier, "A World Apart: Decision Making in the Public and Private Sectors," *School Administrator,* 55 (1998): 20–23.

[148]Peter Flynn, "Ready, Set, Decide!" *School Administrator,* 55 (1998): 14–18; Jack Frymier, "Bureaucracy and the Neutering of Teachers," *Phi Delta Kappan,* 69 (1987): 9–14.

---

## Administrative Advice 10-4

### Considering a Promotion to the Central Office?

Many successful principals are lured into central office positions and view the move as a promotion in terms of status and salary. Before considering the move, especially if you are successful and happy as principal, read between the lines in the job description, visit the central office, and speak to trusted central office colleagues. Some important questions to consider are the following:

- What does the word *coordinate* or *direct* actually mean?
- Does the word *supervise* ever appear in the job description? What are the ramifications?
- What is the superintendent's perception of my job?
- Will I have line authority for decision making or will I be only a facilitator?
- Will I provide a genuine professional service to the educational process, or is the job best defined as a district "gofer"?
- Will I be directly involved in budget preparation and budget allocations?
- What are my role and responsibilities involving the community, staff, curriculum, and planning?

- Will my leadership role make a difference in school improvement, reform, or restructuring of the schools within the district?
- What does the statement "other duties as assigned by the superintendent" really mean?
- What is the overall mission or objective of the position? Does it have ongoing tasks and responsibilities included, or are many of them short-term or terminal tasks?
- Are there other benefits beyond those enjoyed by the principalship in the new job?

---

a new quasi-administrative clerical position, and their seniority and tenure are protected.[149]

Economics or efficiency is not always the key issue in large, urban districts; rather, school politics and ethnic considerations often affect who gets hired or fired. To support the bloated bureaucracy, school districts sometimes waste money and hire consulting firms to claim that the bureaucracy is needed and that administrator-teacher or administrator-student ratios are within tolerant ranges, by selecting and comparing school districts elsewhere that are just as top heavy or more so at the central level. In short, the central administration gets the results they want, since they are paying the consultant; it's a matter of spelling out the particulars.[150]

Only when the money runs out, enrollments are drastically down, and the community is looking to put a lid on spending will school board officials look to topple school administrators or take other saving measures. However, many school districts will consolidate facilities, close down schools, and/or cut teaching positions before they trim down the central office staff.[151] New York City's budget trimming for 2003 represents the most dramatic reduction of central administrators in the nation's school history: in one year some 550 central administrators' jobs were eliminated as part of a $200 million budget cut for the school district. The 550 administrators who were laid off represent 21 percent of the district's central administrators.[152]

A centralized authority is characteristic of school districts that have a tall hierarchy and an increased specialization of professional tasks. In a centralized system, important decisions can be made quickly with few personnel involved. A decentralized authority suggests a

---

[149]Priscilla Ahlgren, "An Overabundance of Decision Makers?" *Milwaukee Journal*, 30 July 1990, pp. 1, 5; Fred Hess, "Who'll Replace Retiring School Leaders," *American School Board Journal*, 175 (1988): 43–48; John R. Hoyle and Robert O. Slater, "The Role of Educational Leadership in the 21st Century," *Phi Delta Kappan*, 82 (2001): 790–794.

[150]Vickie Bane and Kay Pride, "The $325 Million Bargain," *American School Board Journal*, 180 (1993): 24–28; Carol Peek and Dee Ann Spencer, "Getting the Results You Want," *School Administrator*, 55 (1998): 17–23; Garnett J. Smith, "The Consultant from Oz Syndrome," *School Administrator*, 55 (1998): 30–35.

[151]Allan C. Ornstein, "Trimming the Fat, Stretching the Meat for School Budgets," *School Administrator*, 46 (1989): 20–21; Ornstein, "School Budgets for the 1990s," *Educational Digest*, 55 (1990): 15–16.

[152]Abby Goodnough, "Jobs Are First of 550 Central Staff Will Lose," *New York Times*, 23 November 2002, p. B1.

flat hierarchy and/or several school sites that are considered part of a particular subdistrict or area. Upper management must be willing to work through subordinates in a decentralized system. However, subordinate power is only temporary, as long as the person has the title or until the job or task is completed. Many superintendents (as well as associates or assistants) are turf-conscious and are reluctant to part with their authority.

## Small Districts: Understaffed Central Offices

Small school districts, and especially rural ones, face almost the opposite dilemma. They tend to be understaffed at the central level to the extent that superintendents, and whatever assistant superintendents or directors there are, often seem overworked and involved in many areas of responsibility, which they lack time to adequately perform. As one superintendent (twenty years experience) of a small school district in Pennsylvania stated: "Owing to skimpy staffing in central offices, many school chiefs do the work of several administrators. Eventually, they are unable to distance themselves from day-to-day tasks [and lose sight of] the big picture." The problem of not enough time for small school superintendents and their central staff "is real," and some of these administrators become "isolated and frustrated" by all their chores.[153]

A former superintendent of a small suburban school district in Illinois asserted: "Most of my job was hands on, nonmanagerial work. I was involved in almost everything—from helping to select textbooks, visiting teachers in classrooms, and working with parents. Superintendents in large school districts are far removed from the 'nuts and bolts' of [working with individual or small groups of teachers and parents], and serve mainly in an executive capacity."[154]

Jack Lortz wound up at the end of the world—Fossil, Oregon, population 430, student enrollment 100. As superintendent, his tasks included grading English papers, proofreading the student newspaper, supervising the lunchroom and schoolyard, making coffee, putting up bulletin boards in the hall, and filling the soda machine. He classified some of his tasks as "menial, sometimes quirky," but as a good trooper he also felt they were "necessary . . . and bread and butter [for] running school districts in rural America."[155]

Some districts are so small (21 percent have fewer than 300 students and another 26 percent have between 300 and 1000 students)[156] that the superintendent is allotted only one or two assistants (sometimes on a part-time level). In still other cases, the superintendent is expected to manage two adjacent districts in an effort for both districts to save money.[157] Obviously, there is no central office to speak about in these small school districts, and the superintendent relies on the school principals (and teachers) to carry out many activities that are otherwise delegated to the central office personnel in large school districts.

It is common for school principals and teachers in large school districts (25,000 or more students) to be sometimes disfranchised from decisions involving specific areas such as curriculum, instruction, teaching, testing, and learning, and they become distant from the top administration.[158] In small school districts (1000 or fewer students), teachers and principals are often overburdened with these types of responsibilities. In large districts, teacher empowerment is the issue; in small districts, administrative and teacher overload is the issue.

## Organizational Hierarchy

In small school districts, the operation of the central office is less bureaucratic simply because there are fewer layers. Figure 10–3 illustrates a small (and "flat") district of more than 1000 and fewer than 5000 students, which represents 38 percent of all districts. Figure 10–4 shows a larger (and taller) **organizational chart** of a medium-sized school district with 5000 to 25,000 students; this represents almost 12 percent of

---

[153] Kathleen Grove, "The Invisible Role of the Central Office," *Educational Leadership*, 59 (2002): 45–47. Also see Kate Beem, "In the Name of Survival: The Dual Superintendency," *School Administrator*, 63 (2006): 18.

[154] Ken Kaufman, former superintendent of Bensonville (Illinois) School District, personal communication, April 27, 1999; May 12, 2006.

[155] Jack Lortz, "School Daze: The Life of a Rural Administrator," *School Administrator*, 55 (1998): 36.

[156] *Digest of Education Statistics*, 2005, tables 85, 87, pp. 130, 133.

[157] Guy Gahn, Research Consultant, Iowa Department of Education, personal communication, March 12, 1999.

[158] Roland S. Barth, "Improving Relationships Within the Schoolhouse," *Educational Leadership*, 63 (2006): 8–13; Tom Corcoran, Susan H. Fuhrman, and Catherine L. Belcher, "The District Role in Instructional Improvement," *Phi Delta Kappan*, 83 (2001): 78–84; Allan C. Ornstein, "Leaders and Losers," *Executive Educator*, 15 (1993): 28–30.

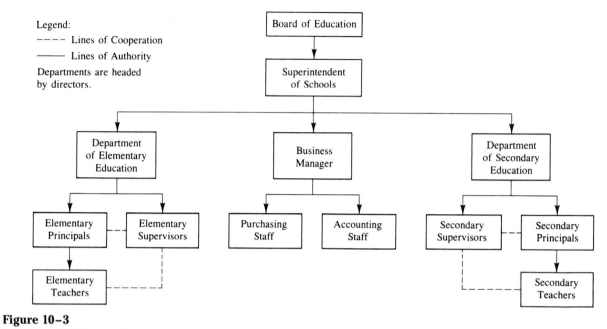

**Figure 10–3**

Typical Small-Sized School District (1000 to 5000 Students)

school districts nationwide.[159] The organizational hierarchy of larger school districts would be cumbersome, and those with 100,000 or more students (.02 percent of all school districts) would extend off the page. Most readers would have difficulty understanding these latter charts, not because they are incomprehensible but because of the nature of bureaucratic and hierarchical complexity in big school districts.

## Efficiency Ratios

Just because large school districts have more hierarchical layers at the central office, and their organizational charts are taller and more difficult to understand, does not mean they have better or worse manager-student ratios or are more or less efficient in running the schools within the district. For example, in a survey of fifty-one school districts with 50,000 or more students, the manager-student ratio at the central office averaged one manager per 569 students and the median was 578. The ranges were as high or efficient as one manager per

1650 students and as low or inefficient as one manager per 161 students.[160]

Eleven school districts out of fifty-one had one central administrator per 750 students. The researcher concluded that school districts should aim for one central manager per 1200 or more students. Only six of the fifty-one surveyed school districts achieved this level of efficiency (Los Angeles 1343:1, Indianapolis 1401:1, Mesa, AZ 1446:1, West Jordon, UT 1512:1, Clark County, NV 1539:1, and Granite, UT 1650:1).[161]

Nationwide, the average is one district administrator for 954 students, and for principals and assistant principals combined the ratio is 1 to 370 students, but for teachers the ratio is 1 to 16 students.[162] As budget-minded school officials look at administrative jobs, there probably will be improved manager-student ratios (what William Bennett, the former Secretary of Education, some fifteen years ago termed the "blob" — or

[159] *Digest of Education Statistics,* 2005, tables 85, 87, pp. 130, 133.

[160] Allan C. Ornstein, "Administrator/Student Ratios in Large School Districts," *Phi Delta Kappan,* 70 (1989): 806–808.

[161] Ibid.

[162] "News and Notes: Survey Round Up," *Thrust for Educational Leadership,* 29 (1998): 4; *Projections of Education Statistics to 2011,* table 32, p. 80.

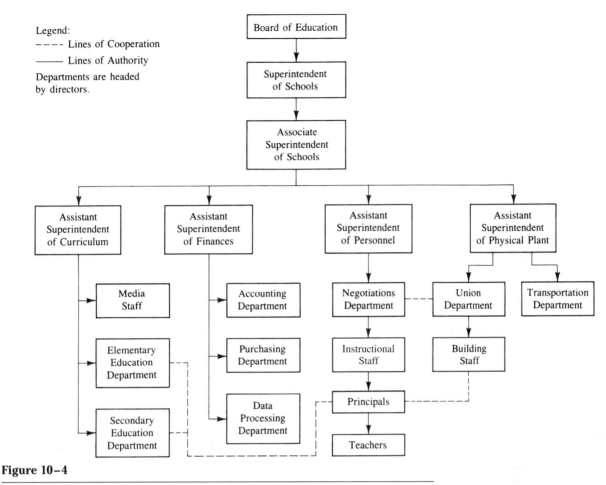

**Legend:**
---- Lines of Cooperation
——— Lines of Authority
Departments are headed by directors.

**Figure 10–4**

Typical Medium-Sized School District (5000 to 25,000 Students)

Source: Allan C. Ornstein and Daniel U. Levine, *Foundations of Education*, 10th ed., © 2008. Used by permission of Houghton Mifflin Company, Boston.

bloated bureaucracy). In school districts with declining student enrollments, the target of one manager to 1200 students will be difficult to achieve without changes at the central administrative level. It will be up to moderate voices and rational groups to prevent this degree of change. In school districts with increasing student enrollments, this target is feasible, and what may be needed is to wait for administrative attrition to take its effect.

Finally, we need to ask the following: To what extent do administrator-student ratios represent cost-effectiveness and efficiency, and to what extent to do the ratios connote budget restraints and limited education spending? At what point do administrative numbers become costly, laborious, and a drag on decision making? What

is the optimal number of school administrators in relation to the number of students? How many associate and assistant superintendents are necessary? How many directors and coordinators are needed? How big should be their support staffs? A reduction program may be directly related to economic factors—that is, budget problems (and not efficiency)—but who gets eliminated is a political consideration and can have legal implications.

It can also be argued, however, that the size and cost of school administration is a manufactured issue. The American Association of School Administrators (AASA) argues that central administrators represent 1.0 percent of the total staff and 4.5 percent of the total budget of public school districts nationwide. All principals and assistant principals add another 2.4 percent to the staff and 5.6 percent to the budget, whereas teaching and instructional services comprise about 70 percent.[163] Diverting *all* salaries of central administrators to teacher salaries would theoretically increase the average pay 5 percent; diverting it all to reducing class size would amount to a reduction of only one student per class. The AASA argues there is no "blob" or bloated bureaucracy at the central level; moreover, the percentage of overhead for central and school site administration has changed very little over the years—about 10 percent.[164] The popular assertion that school administrators are overpaid or have erected an overweight bureaucracy diverts attention from real educational issues.

## The Principal and the School

Usually, each school has a single administrative officer, a principal, who is responsible for the operation of the school. In small schools, the person may teach part-time as well. In large schools, there also may be one or more assistant or vice principals. The administrative hierarchy may also consist of a number of department chairpersons, a discipline officer (e.g., dean of boys, dean of girls), a director of guidance, and so on.

Although functions vary by locality and size, the principal is primarily responsible for administering all aspects of a school's operations. It is common practice for the principal to work with some type of community group for the improvement of the school; this group is often a PTA or advisory school community committee. Increased teacher militancy and the movement toward teacher empowerment have also led many principals to share decision-making responsibilities with teachers. This new role for teachers is seen by school authorities, including many principals, as essential if schools are to improve.

### Conditions, Employment, and Trends

On the average, grades K to 8 principals work 51 hours a week on school-related activities, while the number of hours a day ranges from 8 to 10 hours, including

an additional 8 hours at home.[165] High school principals average about 53 hours a week on the job and 11 hours in the evening.[166] In theory, the work of high school principals can be categorized into 149 specific tasks in which unscheduled meetings account for 27.5 percent of their time, scheduled meetings for 17.3 percent, desk work 16 percent, personal exchanges (and conversations) 14.1 percent, hallway-classroom tours 7.7 percent, and phone calls 5.8 percent.[167] In total, face-to-face contacts involve 59 percent of the principal's time on the job, and they tend to occur in their offices (usually in meetings); thus, skill in verbal communication is an important part of the principal's job. Similar percentages are reported in two separate studies of elementary principals' task performance by time.[168]

Bureaucracy and politics are at the top of the list of school administrators' complaints. Fifty-seven percent of the principals reported that "even good administrators in their district are so overwhelmed by day-to-day activities that their ability to provide vision and leadership is stymied."[169]

Researchers have asked principals to specify how they spend time and how they would prefer to spend time. Five general categories of work activities were developed: administrative operations, staff and curriculum development, community relationships, student services, and evaluation. Detailed logs were kept for several weeks. Discrepancies exist between actual and ideal use of time, where both elementary and secondary level principals would prefer to spend more time on staff and curriculum development and staff evaluation. On the other hand, they would prefer to spend less time on administrative operations (that is, daily tasks, meetings,

---

[163] Nancy Protheroe, "The Blob Revisited," *School Administrator,* 55 (1998): 26–29.

[164] Allan Odden and Sarah Archibald, *Reallocating Resources* (Thousand Oaks, CA: Corwin Press, 2001); Richard Rothstein, *Where's the Money Going?* (Washington, DC: Economic Policy Institute, 1997).

[165] James L. Doud, "The K–8 Principal in 1988," *Principal,* 68 (1989): 6–12; James L. Doud and Edward P. Keller, "The K–8 Principal in 1998," *Principal,* 78 (1998): 5–12. Also see Vincent Ferrandino, "Challenges for 21st-Century Elementary School Principals," *Phi Delta Kappan,* 82 (2001): 440–442.

[166] Gay Fawcett et al., "Principals and Beliefs-Driven Change," *Phi Delta Kappan,* 82 (2001): 405–410; Gerald C. Ubben, Larry W. Hughes, and Cynthia J. Norris, *The Principal: Creative Leadership for Effective Schools,* 5th ed. (Boston: Allyn and Bacon, 2006).

[167] Ibid.

[168] Doud and Keller, "The K–8 Principal in 1998"; Ronald H. Heck, "Conceptual Issues in Investigating Principal Leadership," *Peabody Journal of Education,* 73 (1998): 51–80.

[169] Jean Johnson, "Staying Ahead of the Game," *Educational Leadership,* 59 (2002): 26–30.

and paperwork) and student services (primarily discipline and record-keeping functions).[170]

Two independent views of principals suggest the principal occupies a role with contradictory demands. They are expected to work to transform, reform, and restructure schools while they hold positions historically committed to controlling change and maintaining stability.[171] Researchers from the University of Washington identified seven leadership functions that exist in schools: "instructional, cultural, managerial, human resources, strategic, external development, and micropolitical."[172]

A 1998 survey defines the most difficult aspects of the job as (1) high workload (up to 60–80 hours a week) and complexity of the job; (2) supervision of unending evening activities; (3) minimal pay difference between top teachers and principals; (4) the pressure of very high expectations of the parents and employer; (5) state and school district mandates; (6) mountains of paperwork; (7) increasingly complex society with attendant social and student problems; (8) difficulty in finding effective vice principals; and (9) difficulty in teachers' acting collaboratively.[173]

A joint nationwide survey by the elementary (NAESP) and secondary school (NASSP) principals associations maintains that the compensation is considered "inadequate when compared to the responsibilities of the position, the stress of the job," and the long hours required.[174] Teachers work an average of 187 days and earn $241 a day; elementary school principals work 223 days and earn $339 a day; middle school principals work 228 days and earn $356 a day; and senior high school principals earn $373 a day.[175] One principal compares the job to "being a mayor of a small city." Another principal contends "there is no slack and little forgiveness when things go wrong." A third principal asserts the public "insists on simple solutions" to problems that require "superhuman" characteristics of a principal.[176] (See Administrative Advice 10–5.)

Typically, superintendents interview three to six candidates from a pool of applicants for principal. In a recent study of 725 superintendents, the mean number of interviews was 4.6. Larger schools tend to draw the most applicants and the superintendents interview more candidates. In 5 percent of the cases, superintendents interviewed only one candidate, usually an insider. Ironically, however, 52 percent of the superintendents rated candidates to be "average" or "below average." On a five-point scale, the mean rating given to all applicants by the superintendents was average (2.6%).[177]

Nationwide, the pool of candidates for qualified principals (K to 12) is shrinking, and some estimates are the pool is only half of what it was ten years ago. Interestingly, more people are earning administrative certificates and doctorates in educational administration, but fewer are actually applying for available positions.[178] School districts, in response to the undersupply of qualified principals, are grooming their own teachers in university-sponsored programs.

The recent surge in the number of certified administrators can be explained by the increased number

---

[170]James L. Hager and L. E. Scarr, "Effective Schools—Effective Principals: How to Develop Both," *Educational Leadership,* 40 (1983), 37–41; Janice L. Herman and Jerry J. Herman, "Deferring Administrative Tasks, Escalating Performance," *NASSP Bulletin,* 79 (1995): 16–21; Peggie J. Robertson, "How Principals Manage Their Time," *Principal,* 86 (2006): 12–16.

[171]Michael Fullan, *What's Worth Fighting For in the Principalship* (New York: Teachers College Press, Columbia University, 1997); Lynda Lyman, *How Do They Know You Care? The Principal's Challenge* (New York: Teachers College Press, Columbia University, 2000).

[172]Bradley Portin, "The Roles That Principals Play," *Educational Leadership,* 61 (2004): 14–18.

[173]Dean Fink and Carol Brayman, "School Leadership Succession and the Challenges of Change," *Educational Administration Quarterly,* 42 (2006): 62–89; Diane M. Yerkes and Curtis L. Guaglianone, "Where Have All the High School Administrators Gone?" *Thrust for Educational Leadership,* 18 (1998): 10–14.

[174]*Is There a Shortage of Qualified Candidates for Openings in the Principalship?* (Washington, DC: National Association of Elementary and National Association of Secondary School Principals, 1998); Cheryl Riggins, "The Eight-Hour Principal: Learning to Say No," *Principal,* 86 (2006): 8.

[175]John Forsyth, "Administrator Pay Vs. Teacher Pay," *School Administrator,* 60 (2003): 6.

[176]*California School Principals* (Palo Alto, CA: Ed Source, 1998); Yerkes and Guaglianone, "Where Have All the High School Administrators Gone?" Also see Sheryl Boris–Schacter and Sondra Langer, *Balanced Leadership: How Effective Principals Manage Their Work* (New York: Teachers College Press, 2006).

[177]Thomas E. Glass and Amy L. Bearman, "Criteria and Processes Used By Superintendents to Select and Hire Secondary Principals." Paper commissioned by the Education Commission of the States. Denver, CO: 2001.

[178]Robin Ray Field and Thomas Diamantes, "Task Analysis of the Duties Performed in Secondary School Administration," *Education,* 124 (2004): 709–712; John H. Holloway, "A Defense of the Test for School Leaders," *Educational Leadership,* 59 (2002): 71–75; *Is There a Shortage of Qualified Candidates for Openings in the Principalship?*; Richard P. McAdams, "Who'll Run the Schools?" *American School Board Journal,* 185 (1998): 37–39.

## Administrative Advice 10–5

### Reducing Stress: Making Better Use of Your Time

The principal's job is packed full of daily stress, but it can be reduced by following the suggestions below, recommended by a seasoned administrator, which balance personal well-being and the priorities of work. Since the suggestions are generic, they apply to all administrators—not only principals. They deal with controlling time, planning your schedule, and dealing with people.

■ *Determine what's important to you.* If you found out you were going to die six months from now, would your life priorities be different? If they would be, you might be moving in the wrong direction. Why wait until you are about ready to die before doing what is important to you?

■ *Communicate politely yet firmly.* Everyone around you wants your attention. You cannot possibly satisfy that demand. Therefore, develop ways to respectfully communicate how you are going to manage your time. Consider this: "I'm sorry, I cannot add that into my schedule at this time. However, I can give it the attention it deserves if you can meet with me two weeks from Friday at 10 A.M."

■ *Learn to say no.* Sometimes the best solution is to say no at the outset. Used promptly and with courtesy, it can save a great deal of time.

■ *Do not permit interference.* You should not allow other people to fritter away your time, especially if it is interfering with your life priorities and effective service to others.

■ *Exercise regularly.* Build into your schedule regular, enjoyable physical exercise to release stress.

■ *Ensure you and the board are on the same wavelength.* You and your [superintendent] must be clear on the priorities and the vision for the district. Schedule your workday around these priorities and weave your own life priorities into your schedule.

■ *Build quiet time into your daily schedule.* It is during quiet time that your best ideas occur. This can significantly reduce stress and save time.

■ *Recognize the limits to efficiency.* Trying to be more efficient with your time when you are already at your maximum efficiency level creates tremendous stress, results in significant health problems, and decreases your effectiveness as a leader and a family member.

■ *Pay attention to the present.* You cannot live in the past, and you cannot live in the future. You can only live in the now. Cherish your moments and make certain you are doing what is important for you and your family.

■ *Consider time as a tool.* View time as a way to structure your vision for the children in your district and to pursue your overall mission and priorities in life.

■ *Grabbing your calendar is the last step.* First ask: "Why do I want to do this in the first place, and is it in line with my life priorities and/or the [superintendent's] priorities? If I take the time to do this, what will I need to drop out of my schedule?" Once you have asked these hard questions, then attend to your calendar, knowing you are in control.

Source: Michael R. Weber, "A Balancing Act of Demands and Needs," *School Administrator*, 56 (1999): 38–40.

---

of women completing certification and doctoral programs. In 1978, approximately 20 percent of elementary and middle school principal positions were held by women. By 1998, it had reached 42 percent. Of these principals with fewer than five years of experience, 65 percent were women.[179] By 2004, it had reached 50 percent at the elementary school level. Although both male and female principals were satisfied with their positions, "gender differences exist in how they obtained the position and in how they view the position."[180]

The decline in the supply of qualified candidates can be explained in terms of lack of financial incentives vis-à-vis the increased complexity of the job, time demands,

---

[179]Kathy L. Adams and W. Grant Hambright, "Encouraged or Discouraged? Women Teacher Leaders Becoming Principals," *Clearing House*, 77 (2004): 209–24; *The Elementary School Principal in 1998* (Washington, DC: National Association of Elementary School Principals, 1998).

[180]Ellen W. Eckman, "Does Gender Make a Difference? Voices of Male and Female High School Principals," *Planning and Changing*, 35 (2004): 192–208.

and accountability for results—which all amount to more stress. The added job commitment, compared to a typical teacher's job, also affects the decision of some women with children not to apply. Another factor is that twenty-five years ago, the principal was the master of the ship. Changes over the last decade have enhanced the power and influence of students, teachers, and parents. The legal issues are more complex, and demands for accountability for student performance by the states and public have dramatically increased. These trends lead some principals to frustration and burnout, and others not to apply because of quality of life and family concerns.

Despite all these concerns, principals feel positive about their career choice: 90 percent report high morale and 60 percent indicate that the principalship is their final professional goal. Job security is not an issue. About 85 percent report that they are pleased with their relationships with superintendents and school board members. Principals with fewer than five years of experience report more positive experiences working with their superintendent, probably because the boss selected them. The most pervasive concerns among principals are the fragmentation of their time (72%), the need for additional resources (56%), and students not performing to potential (32%).[181]

Reform is at the top of the principal's list of things to do, first involving statewide competency standards and assessment goals, followed by implementing new technology and new methodologies, staff development, class scheduling, and collegial and collaborative relationships among staff members. As many as 80 percent of principals report upgrading curriculum content in the last three years. Principals K–8 use a wide variety of resources to help implement reform practices: the top five are institutes/workshops (44%), other principals (38%), school district data (33%), professional journals (33%), and state/district conferences (31%). In describing barriers that impede reform, principals often cite teaching students of different ability levels (56%), unpractical or unrealistic assessments (45%), inadequate parental involvement (45%), outdated technology (41%), and high student mobility (40%).[182]

Nationwide, the general feeling is that we need to (1) examine salaries and benefits for principals (see

the salary projections of principals for 2007–2008 in Table 10–6); (2) better train and recognize principals for their leadership roles; (3) ensure more qualified assistant principals to reduce some of the principals' stress and allow time to do more than react to problems and crises; (4) restructure job responsibilities and reduce the number of evening activities of principals; (5) increase vacation time to six weeks rather than the typical three or four weeks; (6) increase support staff, especially in curriculum and student activities; and (7) introduce more professional support mechanisms (such as workshops and institutes) and resources for reflection and planning expected of most organizational leaders, as well as for forming professional networks and bonding.

To attract qualified principals, the authors believe that the average base salary should be $200,000 as of the year 2008. Based on years of experience, education, and the number of teachers they supervise, these leaders should have the potential to earn $250,000 to $300,000. Big-city principals have a tougher job than suburban and rural principals and an extra stipend (10 to 20 percent) should be provided—possibly linked to improving student achievement. Leadership needs to be properly recognized and rewarded. As the old axiom says: You get what you pay for.

## Leadership Role of the Principal

In recent decades, the terms *climate, ethos,* and *culture* have been used to capture or describe the norms, values, behaviors, and rituals of the school organization, what can simply be called the significant features or personality of the organization. Here we are talking about everything that goes on in school: how teachers interact and dress, what they talk about, what goes on at meetings, their expectations of students, how students behave, how parents interact with the staff, and what type of leadership behavior is exhibited by the principal.

Peterson and Deal contend that many schools have **toxic cultures**—that is, over time the staff becomes fragmented and demoralized. The purpose of serving students has been lost; negativism and criticism dominate. A disgruntled staff attacks new ideas, criticizes dedicated teachers, makes fun of colleagues who attend conferences or workshops, and recounts past failures. In contrast, other schools have **positive cultures,** where the staff shares a sense of purpose, and is dedicated to teaching and school improvement. Student successes are highlighted and collegiality permeates

---

[181]Doud and Keller, "The K–8 Principal in 1998"; "Education Vital Signs 1998," *American School Board Journal,* 185 (1998): A–15.

[182]Thomas D. Snyder, "Trends in Education," *Principal,* 78 (1998): 40–48.

**Table 10–6**   **Average Salaries for School Administrators,[a]
1987–88 and 1997–98, with Projected Figures for 2007–08**

| | 1987–88 | 1997–98 | Dollars Ahead of Inflation (33%)[b] | Projected Salary 2007–08[c] |
|---|---|---|---|---|
| Central Office Administrators—Superintendents | $68,147 | $101,519 | $+7203 | $150,081 |
| Associate Superintendents | 63,872 | 90,226 | +1827 | 127,301 |
| Assistant Superintendents | 56,894 | 82,239 | +3498 | 118,470 |
| Directors of Finance/Business | 47,330 | 67,724 | +2219 | 96,681 |
| Directors of Personnel | 51,421 | 71,073 | −94 | 98,240 |
| Subject Area Supervisors | 41,086 | 60,359 | +3496 | 88,197 |
| Principals | | | | |
|   Elementary School | 43,664 | 64,653 | +4610 | 95,625 |
|   Junior/Middle School | 47,078 | 68,740 | +3626 | 99,969 |
|   High School | 50,512 | 74,380 | +4471 | 108,901 |
| Assistant Principals | | | | |
|   Elementary School | 36,364 | 53,206 | +2878 | 77,473 |
|   Junior/Middle School | 40,093 | 57,768 | +2279 | 82,988 |
|   High School | 41,839 | 60,999 | +3094 | 88,547 |
| Counselors | 32,896 | 45,365 | −163 | 62,573 |
| Librarians | 30,046 | 44,310 | +2726 | 63,283 |
| Teachers | 28,230 | 40,133 | +1063 | 56,967 |

[a]Contract salary, no perks or bonuses included.

[b]Consumer Price Index average increase for previous ten-year period was 3.3%, or 33% for ten years. This yields a 1.384 multiplication factor for the 1987–88 base pay. For example, $68,147 × 1.384 = $94,316. Superintendents' actual salary average was $101,519, yielding plus $7203.

[c]Projections based on extrapolating previous ten-year (CPI 33%) increase for each position, then multiplying 1997–98 salary by 1.33 and adding the amount in the column "Dollars Ahead of Inflation."

the atmosphere. High morale, caring, and commitment abound.[183]

According to Peterson and Deal, the school leader is key in shaping school culture. Principals communicate core values, behaviors, and expectations in their everyday work and interaction with staff. Their actions, words, memos, and even nonverbal behavior send messages and over time shape culture. Either they encourage and reward effective teachers and accomplished students, or they ignore them and bury themselves in micromanagement or politics.

Leadership has been described as a balancing act between self and others. The effective leader recognizes

his or her personality and how operational factors or daily tasks affect his or her relationship with others. The effective leader comprehends how other people differ in temperament and expectations and how they may best be motivated.[184] The principal is like a coxswain, giving orders to eight oarsmen to row simultaneously forward and backward, faster and slower, left and right. The principal must learn to deal with eight different groups of people, like the eight oarsmen, and have them row in a unified, cohesive effort: (1) the superintendent and central administration, (2) the school board, (3) peers, (4) parents, (5) community residents/taxpayers, (6) teachers, (7) students, and (8) external

[183]Kent D. Peterson and Terrance E. Deal, "How Leaders Influence the Culture of the Schools," *Educational Leadership,* 56 (1998): 28–30. Also see Terrance Deal and Kent D. Peterson, *Shaping School Culture: The School Leader's Role* (San Francisco: Jossey-Bass, 1999).

[184]Warren G. Bennis, *On Becoming a Leader* (Upper Saddle River, NJ: Addison-Wesley, 1994); Gordon A. Donaldson, *Cultivating Leadership in Schools,* 2nd ed. (New York: Teachers College Press, 2006); Joyce Kaser et al., *Leading Every Day* (Thousand Oaks, CA: Corwin Press, 2002).

entities such as professors, consultants, accrediting groups, and state education groups.[185]

The principal stands at the confluence of all these systems and people and is affected by their competing and overlapping perceptions, expectations, and concerns. Not all leaders face this conflict well, and having technical skills is no substitute for the ability to deal with people and subsequently to lead. People skills are just as important as, possibly more important than, technical skills. Although there is agreement in the literature on the need to improve the leadership role of the principal, there is disagreement on what behaviors or practices principals should pursue—and to what extent a principal should be a **general manager** or **curriculum-instructional leader.**

When given the opportunity to categorize their professional colleagues into one of five leadership roles (principal/teacher, scientific manager, instructional leader, curriculum leader, or general manager), 60 percent of secondary school principals in a North Carolina sample of 370 choose general manager.[186] Female principals and principals with more formal education (doctorate degree), however, prefer the role of curriculum or instructional leader compared with male principals and principals with less education (masters degree, sixth-year certificate), who prefer the role of general manager.

In a study of 149 successful elementary school principals in Massachusetts, selected on the basis of being strong leaders and because of their schools' student achievement levels, more than 75 percent described themselves as "instructional leaders" who devoted most of their own professional development time and resources to curriculum, instruction, and school improvement.[187]

Other data suggest that suburban school principals and elementary school principals spend more time on curriculum and instructional matters than do urban and secondary school principals, but still not enough time, given the fact they must still deal with leaking roofs, shrinking budgets, and personnel squabbles. Secondary school principals, especially those in large schools, devote more time to managerial concerns. The latter group of principals rely on their assistant principals and chairpersons in various subject areas to deal with curriculum and instructional activities.[188]

Elementary schools are smaller than high schools and are often cornerstones of homogeneous neighborhoods, whereas secondary schools often cut across and include many neighborhoods. Because of neighborhood size and homogeneity, elementary principals must be more sensitive to the needs, views, and priorities of parents and community members, which often center around curriculum and instructional leadership. However, a point is reached, when a school is very small (fewer than 100 students) or rural, where the principal is given other duties that take away time from curriculum matters. These might deal with central office tasks, teaching, or the shared principalship of another site.[189]

## Managerial Role of the Principal

The role of manager is essential for the principal and is probably the most important aspect of school leadership. In their classic text on organizational behavior, Daniel Katz and Robert Kahn divide management skills into three major areas: *technical*, involving good planning, organizing, coordinating, supervising, and controlling techniques; *human*, dealing with human relations and people skills, good motivating and morale-building skills; and *conceptual*, emphasizing knowledge and technical skills related to the service (or product) of the organization.[190] (For principals,

[185] George A. Goens, "Too Many Coxswains: Leadership and the Principal," *NASSP Bulletin,* 82 (1998): 103–110; Patricia E. Holland, "Principals as Supervisors: A Balancing Act," *NASSP Bulletin,* 88 (2004): 3–14. Linda Lambert, "A Framework for Shared Leadership," *Educational Leadership,* 59 (2002): 37–40.

[186] Dale L. Brubaker and Lawrence H. Simon, "How Do Principals View Themselves, Others?" *NASSP Bulletin,* 71 (1987): 72–78. Also see Lee G. Bolman and Terrance E. Deal, *Reframing the Path to School Leadership* (Thousand Oaks, CA: Corwin Press, 2002).

[187] Laura A. Cooper, "The Professional Development of Principals: The Principal's Perspective," unpublished doctoral dissertation, Harvard University, 1988; Cooper, "The Principal as Instructional Leader," *Principal,* 68 (1989): 13–16. Also see Mary Neuman and Judith Pelchart, "The Challenge to Leadership: Focusing on Student Achievement," *Phi Delta Kappan,* 82 (2001): 732–736.

[188] William L. Boyd, "What School Administrators Do and Don't Do," *Canadian Administrator,* 22 (1983): 1–4; Brett D. Jones and Robert J. Egley, "Looking Through Different Lenses: Teachers' and Administrators' Views of Accountability," *Phi Delta Kappan,* 87 (2006): 767–771; Ernestine C. Riggs and Ana G. Serafin, "The Principal as Instructional Leader," *NASSP Bulletin,* 82 (1998): 78–85.

[189] Jonathan Hill, "The Rural School Principalship: Unique Challenges, Opportunities," *NASSP Bulletin,* 77 (1993): 77–81.

[190] Daniel Katz and Robert L. Kahn, *The Social Psychology of Organizations* (New York: Wiley, 1966).

conceptual leadership connotes knowledge or curriculum, instruction, teaching, and learning.) Thomas Sergiovanni has added three other areas of management for school administrators, including *symbolic leadership,* those actions the principal emphasizes and wishes to model to the staff; *cultural leadership,* those values and beliefs the principal believes are important;[191] and *moral leadership,* behavior built around purpose, ethics, and beliefs—which can help transform a school from a formal organization to a "community" and inspire commitment, loyalty, and service.[192] Michael Fullan and Seymour Sarason add a seventh dimension of school management—the principal as a *change agent* and facilitator.[193] Finally, Deal and Peterson refer to an eighth characteristic, based on *cooperative leadership,* that is, building collegiality, a sense of school identity, and a democratic and inspiring school culture.[194]

In all eight areas of leadership, the principal attempts to organize the school's mission or goals by reaching *consensus* with the teachers on the actions necessary to move the school forward. The idea is for the principal to persuade others to accept a particular vision of the school by (1) building *collegiality* among teachers, (2) forging *partnerships* with the parents, community residents, and community institutions, and (3) *manipulating* symbols, resources, and rewards toward common goals.[195]

It can all be summed up in Chester Barnard's theory of leadership and management linked to *cooperation,* which in turn results in purposeful organizational behavior. Leadership consists of technical and moral aspects, which lead to cooperation and responsibility among the rank and file. The technical and moral factors also produce conditions of *responsibility.* According to Barnard, "responsibility is the property of an individual by which whatever *morality* exists in him becomes effective in conduct." But one must also possess ability to cope with moral dilemmas, and coping requires clear understanding of one's beliefs and values. Moral values determine leadership and that leadership is crucial for developing cooperation.[196] (Sergiovanni was later influenced by Barnard's notion of moral leadership and responsibility.)

In general, there seems to be agreement that principals must "lead from the center," that is, be more democratic, delegate responsibilities, share decision-making powers, and develop collaborative efforts that bond students, teachers, and parents. In an era of reform and restructuring of schools, with increased legal consideration and government regulations, the principal's duties and tasks have increased to an overload level.[197] Principals are almost forced to share responsibilities with and empower others in order to manage schools on a day-to-day basis. But if they give away power selectively to individuals and groups, they can retain and enhance their span of control and subsequent influence.

James Lipham and his colleagues have developed a "four-factor theory" of leadership for principals. These four factors (or **leadership styles**) are (1) *structural leadership,* taking immediate action on important issues, delegating to staff members, stressing organizational goals, and monitoring implementation of decisions; (2) *facilitative leadership,* obtaining and providing requisite resources, minimizing bureaucratic paperwork, offering suggestions for solving problems, and scheduling activities; (3) *supportive leadership,* encouraging others' efforts, demonstrating friendliness and collegiality, trusting others with delegated responsibilities, and enhancing staff morale; and (4) *participative leadership,* seeking decisional input and advice, working

[191]Thomas J. Sergiovanni, *The Principalship: A Reflective Practice Perspective,* 3rd ed. (Needham Heights, MA: Allyn and Bacon, 1995); Sergiovanni, *Moral Leadership* (San Francisco: Jossey-Bass, 1996); Sergiovanni, *Rethinking Leadership,* 2nd ed. (Thousand Oaks, CA: Corwin Press, 2006).

[192]Thomas J. Sergiovanni, *Building Community in Schools* (San Francisco: Jossey-Bass, 1999); Sergiovanni, *Leadership for the Schoolhouse* (San Francisco: Jossey-Bass, 2000).

[193]Michael G. Fullan and Suzanne M. Stiegelbauer, *The New Meaning of Educational Change,* 3rd ed. (New York: Teachers College Press, Columbia University, 2001); Seymour B. Sarason, *Barometers of Social Change* (San Francisco: Jossey-Bass, 1996); Sarason, *Educational Reform* (New York: Teachers College Press, Columbia University, 2002).

[194]Terrance E. Deal and Kent D. Peterson, *Shaping School Culture* (San Francisco: Jossey-Bass, 1998); Deal and Peterson, *The Leadership Paradox* (San Francisco: Jossey-Bass, 2000).

[195]Paula Blake and Scott Pfeiffer, "School-Business Partnerships," *NASSP Bulletin,* 77 (1993): 28–33; John R. Hoyle, "Can the Principal Run the Show and Be a Democratic Leader?" *NASSP Bulletin,* 78 (1994): 33–39; Nancy Mohr and Alan Dichter, "Building a Learning Organization," *Phi Delta Kappan,* 82 (2001): 744–747.

[196]Chester I. Barnard, *The Functions of the Executive* (Cambridge, MA: Harvard University Press, 1964).

[197]Judith Chapman, *Creating and Managing the Democratic School* (New York: Falmer Press, 1995); Cheryl H. Wilhoyte, *Leadership Without Easy Answers* (Cambridge, MA: Harvard University Press, 1997).

actively with individuals and groups, involving others in decision making, and maintaining willingness to modify preconceived positions.[198]

Note that all these leadership factors emphasize administrative and managerial skills. Most authorities contend that not one of these leadership styles is best; rather, the successful principal is able to modify or adapt the four leadership factors to the demands of the school setting.[199] The persistent use of a single leadership factor often renders the principal ineffective. Nonetheless, all of us have particular strengths and weaknesses. A balanced leadership team—say, in which the principal is a strong participative and supportive leader and the assistant principal is strong on the other two dimensions—enhances the effective operation of the school.

## Curriculum-Instructional Role of the Principal

Although the literature generally agrees on the need for the principal to be a leader in the areas of curriculum and instruction, it sometimes disagrees on what specific roles and behaviors should be exhibited and how much time should be devoted to these twin areas of leadership. When principals are surveyed, they often report that the curriculum and instruction aspects of the job are top-priority work areas and that they need to spend more time on the job related to these two technical areas of development.[200]

Given the national and state standards movement, and the need to upgrade the curriculum to meet these standards, school principals' attention has increasingly focused on curriculum. Most national standards have been greeted with approval by business groups but not by all state education agencies or education administrative groups. The standards emphasize specific knowledge, modes of inquiry and thinking, and consider certain subjects more important than others. Through legislation and assessment, they impact school practice, leadership behavior, and teaching practices.[201]

But a significant discrepancy exists between statements and actions. Data suggest that teachers do not view curriculum-instructional leadership as a major responsibility of principals, do not see much evidence of such leadership on the part of principals, and are reluctant to accept principals in this leadership capacity.[202] Often teachers feel that principals are not capable of providing such leadership, and don't always want the principal's assistance in these technical areas that teachers consider to be more appropriate for peer coaching and collegial staff development.[203]

Principals have historically spent little time (15 to 20 percent)[204] coordinating activities in curriculum and instruction, and spend much less time (3 to 7 percent) observing teachers in the classroom, complaining that managerial activities take up most of their time.[205]

[198]James M. Lipham, Robb E. Rankin, and James A. Hoeh, *The Principalship: Concepts, Competencies, and Cases* (New York: Longman, 1985).

[199]Philip Hallinger, Kenneth Leithwood, and Joseph Murphy (eds.), *Cognitive Perspectives on Educational Leadership* (New York: Teachers College Press, 1993); Robert G. Owens, *Organizational Behavior in Education,* 9th ed. (Needham Heights, MA: Allyn and Bacon, 2006).

[200]Lynn Beck and Joseph Murphy, *Understanding the Principalship* (New York: Teachers College Press, Columbia University, 1992); L. Joseph Matthews and Gary M. Crow, *Being and Becoming a Principal* (Boston: Allyn and Bacon, 2003); Ubben, Hughes, and Norris, *The Principal: Creative Leadership for Effective Schools.*

[201]O. L. Davis, "National and State Curriculum Standards," *Journal of Curriculum and Supervision,* 13 (1998): 297–299; Allan A. Glatthorn, *Performance Assessment and Standards-Based Curricula* (Larchmont, NY: Eye on Education, 1998); Glatthorn, *The Principal as Curriculum Leader,* 2nd ed. (Thousand Oaks, CA: Corwin Press, 2000).

[202]Michael Fullan, Barrie Bennett, and Carol R. Bennett, "Linking Classroom and School Improvement," *Educational Leadership,* 47 (1990): 13–19; Robert Hess, *Excellence, Equity, and Efficiency* (Lanham, MD: Rowman & Littlefield, 2005); Anita Woolfolk-Hoy and Wayne K. Hoy, *Instructional Leadership: A Learner Centered Guide* (Boston: Allyn and Bacon, 2003).

[203]Bruce J. Biddle and Lawrence J. Saha, "How Principals Use Research," *Educational Leadership,* 63 (2006): 72–78; Robert J. Garmston, "How Administrators Support Peer Coaching," *Educational Leadership,* 44 (1987): 18–26; Leslie M. Inman and Joann Atkinson, "Evaluating School Administrator: Perceptions of Teachers, Principals," *NASSP Bulletin,* 77 (1993): 87–90; Norris et al., *Developing Educational Leaders.*

[204]Boyd, "What School Administrators Do and Don't Do"; James T. Scarnati, "Beyond Technical Competence: Nine Rules for Administrators," *NASSP Bulletin,* 78 (1994): 76–83.

[205]Lewis Cohen, "It's Not About Management," *Phi Delta Kappan,* 87 (2006): 459–461; Thelbert L. Drake and William H. Roe, *The Principalship,* 6th ed. (Columbus, OH: Merrill, 2003); Michael Fullan, *Leadership and Sustainability* (Thousand Oaks, CA; Corwin Press, 2005).

Dealing with the daily operation of the school and attending meetings tend to take up most of their time. Although the major principal associations (NAEP and NASSP) overwhelmingly envision the principal as a curriculum-instructional leader, and this theme continually appears in their respective journals (which principals read), the realities of the job do not permit emphasis in these twin leadership areas.

In this connection, Joseph Murphy has developed six curriculum and instructional roles for the principal:

1. *Promoting Quality Instruction.* Ensuring consistency and coordination of instructional programs and defining recommended methods of instruction.

2. *Supervising and Evaluating Instruction.* Ensuring that school goals are translated into practice at the classroom level and monitoring classroom instruction through numerous classroom observations.

3. *Allocating and Protecting Instructional Time.* Providing teachers with uninterrupted blocks of instructional time and ensuring that basic skills and academic subjects are taught.

4. *Coordinating the Curriculum.* Translating curriculum knowledge into meaningful curriculum programs, matching instructional objectives with curriculum materials and standardized tests, and ensuring curriculum continuity vertically and across grade levels.

5. *Promoting Content Coverage.* Ensuring that content of specific courses is covered in class and extended outside of class by developing and enforcing homework policies.

6. *Monitoring Student Progress.* Using both criterion- and standardized-reference tests to diagnose student problems and evaluate their progress, as well as using test results to set or modify school goals.[206]

Based on a review of the research, according to Murphy, the six major dimensions or roles exemplify an effective principal; moreover, Murphy's research supports the assumption that the distinguishing reason for effective schools is a school principal who exhibits strong curriculum-instructional leadership.

## Effective Principals

The basis for judging effective schools is largely based on student outcomes on standardized tests in reading and math. The findings are only correlational, meaning it is not clear whether the leadership characteristics of the principal produce effective schools or whether effective schools create effective principals.

In general, the characteristics of effective principals, as supported by a review of numerous research investigations, describe the effective K to 12 principal as one who evidences strong leadership in the areas of curriculum and instruction and who

1. Keeps the interests of the students at heart.

2. Is a leading learner.

3. Acts ethically.

4. Puts instructional leadership first.

5. Practices efficient management.

6. Builds strong relationships.

7. Knows what to expect.

8. Orchestrates school-community partnerships.

9. Is a lifelong learner.

10. Builds a positive school climate.[207]

What seems to be paramount in the effective schools literature is the need to change the organizational structure, as well as to emphasize the principal's leadership and the process of teaching and learning.

One approach to increasing the number of effective school principals in urban poverty schools focuses on selection and on-the-job training. The Urban Administrator Selection Interview is an instrument developed by Martin Haberman currently utilized in several big cities.[208] It assesses factors synthesized from two

---

[206]Joseph Murphy, "Principal Instructional Leadership," in P. W. Thurston and L. S. Lotto (eds.), *Advances in Educational Administration*, vol. 1B (Greenwich, CT: JAI Press, 1990), pp. 162–200; Murphy, "What's Ahead for Tomorrow's Principals," *Principal*, 78 (1998): 13–16. Also see Jerome Murphy, "Dancing Lessons for Elephants: Reforming Ed School Leadership Programs," *Phi Delta Kappan*, 87 (2006): 488–491.

[207]Harvey Alvy and Pam Robbins, "Growing into Leadership," *Educational Leadership*, 62 (2005): 50–54; Robert J. O'Donnell and George P. White, "Within the Accountability Era: Principals' Instructional Leadership Behaviors and Student Achievement," *NASSP Bulletin*, 89 (2005): 56–71.

[208]Martin Haberman, *The Urban Administrator Selection Interview* (Houston: The Haberman Educational Foundation, 1993); Martin Haberman, personal communication, June 19, 1999.

sources: the explanations of star urban principals as to what makes them effective, and the knowledge base of theory and research compiled by the professional associations. The eleven dimensions covered by this interview are leadership, commitment to student learning, theory into practice, the role of the school serving children in poverty, curriculum and instructional leadership, creating a positive school climate (fighting burnout), evaluation, decision making, fallibility, administrative style, and administrative relations with parents and community.[209]

Another approach examines three types of leadership (instructional, transformational, and balanced) and offers suggestions on how to retain strong leaders.[210]

**Evaluation of Principals** Principals generally lack expertise in assessment. They are not effective in conducting school-level assessment or classroom assessment (of their own teachers), according to authorities, because they lack evaluation and assessment training. Even when such courses are offered in their preparation programs, those courses are usually optional and bypassed because competence in assessment does not appear to affect certification or employability.[211] Nonetheless, principals are required to conduct formal assessments in their roles as instructional leaders, managers, and change agents—to obtain information for making decisions about the school, particularly with regard to students and staff.

Evaluation of principals' contractual obligations has taken on new importance, coinciding with the general frenzy of testing and evaluation; today, more and more superintendents are insisting on clarifying the evaluation process involving principals. According to the AASA, indicators of a good evaluation are that: (1) the evaluation is conducted in a positive climate; (2) the superintendent is familiar with the principal's goals and/or has communicated expectations to the principal early in the process; (3) the superintendent gives the principal frequent and timely feedback; (4) the superintendent's judgments are supported with specific examples; (5) the evaluation focuses on performance results, not personalities; (6) the principal is afforded an opportunity to respond to the evaluation; and (7) the evaluation is limited to those matters over which the principal has responsibility.[212]

Given the fact that the school principal has been cited as the most influential person in promoting school reform, change, and innovation, and given the public's concern about student achievement, the evaluation of principals has changed from a static or matter-of-fact process to a hot issue. Many administrators welcome new evaluation options because they believe traditional evaluation forms are outmoded and irrelevant to the performance of the school and the demands of the public.

**Accountability Plans** The reform movement in education, followed by the state standards movement and the public's interest in school choices and alternative education, has stimulated the age of accountability for all educational players—teachers, principals, and superintendents.

Whether we call it accountability to the public (as educators call it), better management (as business, government, and a few school administrators would say), or improving test scores (as parents and school boards would have it), the challenge is to get better results at no increase in cost.[213] Across the country, superintendents now receive annual bonuses for meeting new standards of learning and/or district goals. There is no reason why principals will not move in the same direction in the near future.

For example, New York City's contract in 2007 with school principals not only holds them accountable for students' progress, but also provides for them to be rated by teachers. Several district superintendent posi-

[209]Scott D. Thompson and Samuel Hill, eds., *Principals for Our Changing Schools: Knowledge and Skills Base* (Fairfax, VA: National Policy Board for Educational Administration, 1992); Robert D. Ramsey, *Lead, Follow, or Get Out of the Way* (Thousand Oaks, CA: Corwin Press, 1999).

[210]Cori Brewster and Jennifer Klump, *Leadership Practices of Successful Principals* (Portland, OR: Northwest Regional Educational Lab, 2005).

[211]Gary L. Anderson, "A Critique of the Test for School Leaders," *Educational Leadership,* 59 (2002): 67–70; Ronald W. Rebore, *A Human Relations Approach to the Practice of Education Leadership* (Boston: Allyn and Bacon, 2003); David Squires, *Aligning and Balancing the Standards-Based Curriculum* (Thousand Oaks, CA: Corwin Press, 2004).

[212]Jack McCurdy, *Building Better Board-Administrator Relations* (Arlington, VA: American Association of School Administrators, 1992).

[213]John L. Herman, "The State of Performance Assessments," *School Administrator,* 55 (1998): 17–23; Richard J. Stiggins, "Assessment Crisis: The Absence of Assessment for Learning," *Phi Delta Kappan,* 83 (2002): 758–765; Stiggins, "From Formative Assessment to Assessment For Learning," *Phi Delta Kappan,* 87 (2005): 324–328.

tions will be eliminated, and principals will gain power and become "field commanders."[214] To be sure, evaluation systems of school principals will be further developed to reward academic improvement, as well as other goals, and to penalize poor performance.

**Performance Assessment**   In 1997, the nation's second largest school system, Los Angeles, developed seven indicators of school improvement for determining pay increases for the superintendent and senior administrators: (1) increased student achievement as measured by standardized tests, (2) improved pass rates for students in college preparation classes, (3) increased percentage of third-grade students reaching third-grade literacy, (4) improved transition rate of non-English-speaking students to English, (5) increased number of students taking advanced placement courses, (6) higher student and staff attendance levels, and (7) lower dropout rates.[215] The evaluation system was subsequently used for principals in 100 of the lowest-performing schools. Support to those schools included instructional resource assistance, staff training, and funds for student tutoring. Within six months, more than two-thirds of the 100 schools demonstrated improvement in at least four of the seven areas.

In 1995, performance contracts were approved for all district superintendents and central administrators reporting to the superintendent in the Houston school district. The following year, these performance contracts were established for principals as well. Performance standards for each principal include measurable objectives related to the goals of the school improvement plan and goals of the district. Among the objectives principals can select are the following: (1) increase percentage of students passing state-mandated tests, (2) increase student attendance rates, (3) increase teacher/staff attendance rates, (4) reduce disciplinary incidents, (5) reduce dropout rates, (6) increase parental participation in school activities, and (7) align curriculum. The involvement of the district superintendent in reviewing the principal's performance is critical.[216]

**Peer Evaluation**   Several school districts have introduced peer reviews of principals, to assess strengths and weaknesses and to make recommendations for improvement. The process tends to be ongoing (in one district principals meet in cohorts of four to seven members on a monthly basis throughout the school year) and reflects honest communication, involving the sharing of common and uncommon problems, brainstorming, building support and assistance for dealing with difficult problems, and receiving critical feedback about performance.[217]

Peer group evaluations can be formed through self-selection with consideration for common grade levels, goals, geographical proximity, size, diversity, and professional relationships. More than one evaluation from more than one peer is common. Performance indicators or objectives are usually worked out with the superintendent or district superintendent, depending on the size of the school district. They can also be worked out by the principals according to some professional growth or school improvement plan. Peer groups or principals who conduct the evaluation should be rotated to avoid politics and the "error of leniency" (too easy or too hard) that affects all raters and evaluation instruments.

Theoretically, the peer evaluation system provides an effective and collegial system for continuous professional support and growth; it builds trust among principals if implemented properly, and it allows the superintendent or district superintendents to focus on individuals who need the most assistance.

**Portfolio Evaluation Systems**   Some school districts have introduced portfolio assessments in response to principals who have expressed concerns that principal evaluations are not tied to the overall performance of the school, that previous evaluation systems stress management issues, or they feel excluded from the evaluation process. Portfolios attempt to resolve these concerns and permit principals to participate in the evaluation system and be evaluated on agreed-upon standards.

Portfolios permit personal artifacts and reflective entries for purposes of exhibiting professional growth

[214]David M. Herszenhorn, "Respect Is Nice, But Principals Want A Raise," *New York Times,* 29 January 2007, p. B1.

[215]Douglas Trelfa, "How the Nation's Second Largest School District Holds Educators Accountable," *Thrust for Educational Leadership,* 28 (1999): 25.

[216]Rod Paige, Susan Sclafani, and Michael J. Jimenez, "Performance Contracts for Principals," *School Administrator,* 55 (1998): 32–33.

[217]Libia S. Gil, "Principals Evaluating Peers," *School Administrator,* 55 (1998): 28–30; Larry Lashway, "Instruments for Evaluation," *School Administrator,* 55 (1998): 14–19; Dennis Sparks, *Leading for Results* (Thousand Oaks, CA: Corwin Press, 2005).

and/or fulfillment of professional goals. The portfolio outcomes may also include mentoring and coaching situations. Portfolios tend to be less systematic and objective than other assessment tools, and usually require a considerable amount of time to prepare and assess.[218] They force supervisors to analyze a considerable amount of data, to provide feedback and enhance communication with principals. Although they are homegrown, they tend to be more meaningful to principals and foster more professional development than typical and so-called objective rating instruments.[219]

**School Leadership Assessment**   An important step in evaluation of principals is deciding what needs to be evaluated—that is, the behaviors, performances, goals, or skills most important for principals and the school district. An excellent starting point is to look at the standards established by the Interstate School Leaders Licensure Consortium, an umbrella group with membership in thirty-five states as of 2002. It has boiled down leadership to six standards, ranging from vision to school culture, and encourages individuals (principals and school districts) to either use predetermined success indicators (six to eight) for each standard or adopt their own to fit the leadership priorities of the particular school and district.[220] The latter approach increases professional standards and recognizes differences at the school and district level but reduces local input and relevancy.

The Educational Testing Service has developed a School Leadership License Test, already adopted in five states, which consists of three 2-hour modules that ask candidates to respond to practical problems that might be encountered in the principalship. Scores are assigned by evaluators with school leadership experience. The test is rooted in the well-known assessment centers established by NASSP and NAESP in which candidates go through leadership training and exercises designed to parallel real-world tasks in a principal's typical day.[221]

**Value-Added Assessment**   We know that student achievement generally correlates with demographic variables such as class, race, peer group, family size and structure, parents' education, and so on—all hard-to-change variables. Put another way, we can predict that high academic scores predominate in affluent schools, whereas lower scores tend to show up in less affluent schools.

But Tennessee has been the first state to introduce a value-added assessment system, a sophisticated statistical method developed by William Sanders for determining the effectiveness of schools and teachers in sustaining academic growth for each student each year.[222] The assessment system is easy to use and measures the effects of teachers at the elementary school level, where teachers work in self-contained classrooms, but it can be used at all grade levels to measure the effects of the school staff and principal. Over time, the school district sees a pattern in a positive or negative direction and knows which teachers and principals are performing above average. The test scores are not the only source of data for evaluating teachers and principals in Tennessee, but more than half of the school districts in 1998 used this information as part of the evaluation of principals.[223]

[218]Genevieve Brown, Beverly J. Irby, and Charles Neumeyer, "Taking the Lead: One District's Approach to Principal Evaluation," *NASSP Bulletin,* 82 (1998): 18–25; Kenneth A. Leithwood, "Using the Principal Profile to Assess Performance, *NASSP Bulletin,* 81 (1987): 63–66; Alexander Russo, "Evaluating Administrators with Portfolios," *School Administrator,* 61 (2004): 34–38.

[219]Tim Cuneo, "Planning for Accountability," *Thrust for Educational Leadership,* 28 (1999): 18–21; Larry Lashway, "What's Available in Assessment Instruments?" *School Administrator,* 55 (1998): 16; Mary Lou Yealts, "Before Turning Over the Keys to the New Principal," *School Administrator,* 62 (2005): 16.

[220]Leslie S. Kaplan, William A. Owings, and John Nunnery. "Principal Quality: A Virginia Study Connecting Interstate School Leaders Licensure Consortium Standards with Student Achievement," *NASSP Bulletin,* 89 (2005): 28–44; Larry Lashway, "Instruments for Evaluation," *School Administrator,* 55 (1998): 14–19; Deborah Perkins-Gough, "Defining Instructional Leadership," *Educational Leadership,* 59 (2002): 96; Tim Waters and Sally Kingston, "Standards We Need," *Leadership,* 35 (2005): 14, 16, 36–39.

[221]Fenwick W. English, *The Postmodern Challenge to the Theory and Practice of Educational Administration* (Springfield, IL: Thomas, 2003); Lashway, "What's Available in Assessment Instruments?"

[222]William L. Sanders, "Value-Added Assessment," *School Administrator,* 55 (1998): 24–27.

[223]Samuel E. Bratton, "How We're Using Value-Added Assessment," *School Administrator,* 55 (1998): 30–32; Ted Hershberg, Virginia Adams Simon, and Barbara Lea-Kruger, "The Revelations of Value-Added: An Assessment Model that Measures Student Growth in Ways that NCLB Fails to Do," *School Administrator,* 61, (2004): 10–14; William Sanders, Professor and Director of the Value-Added Research and Assessment Center, University of Tennessee, Knoxville, personal communication, March 15, 1999.

The data show that the single most important variable affecting student achievement is the individual teacher and the effect is cumulative, especially among early-grade teachers. Since there is dramatic variability among students year to year within schools (based primarily on teacher effectiveness), it can be assumed that school principals do not play a major role in effecting student achievement. Principal leadership is mainly at the managerial level, not at the instructional level, and the variance in student achievement related to teaching is much greater than the principal's impact.[224]

As we depart from this section, we outline policy considerations for superintendents and school boards as they seek to devise appropriate and relevant systems for evaluating principals. The evaluation system should (1) focus on school improvement; (2) be performance based; (3) include the principal's input; (4) be agreed upon by all stakeholders; (5) be relevant to the principal's functions and tasks; (6) correspond to local (and state) performance expectations or goals; (7) promote communication and collaboration among all administrators; (8) promote principal growth and improved leadership behaviors; (9) clearly define assessment procedures such as standards, criteria, scoring expectations, and meetings and conferences; (10) include mentoring and coaching time and time for reflection and self-evaluation; (11) ensure frequency of assessment and feedback; and (12) hold principals accountable and reward effective leaders.[225]

## Preparation and Planning for Principals

One aspect of professional development involves the training and preparation of principals. When school principals were surveyed to find out what sources of information were most helpful in learning about the latest reform strategies and instructional practices, among twenty sources they chose institutes/workshop as the best.[226] As many as 44 percent selected this training vehicle, followed by other principals (39%), school district information (33%), professional journals (33%), and state/district conferences (31%).

Most training and preparation of principals is conducted through university-based programs, although an increasing number include partnerships with professional administrative organizations. Licensing requirements are usually controlled by the state. Although a doctorate is not required, an increasing number of school districts prefer someone who possesses a doctorate or is enrolled in a doctorate program accredited by the state in which the university is based.

**The Management Profile**  Developed by the Texas A&M University Principal's Center, and initially adopted by several school districts in Texas in the mid-1980s and early 1990s, the **Management Profile** was later adopted by the National Association of Secondary School Principals' Commission on Standards for the Principalship as a framework to facilitate their performance and growth. The instrument provides assessment information for the principal as a *manager* and includes three basic or broad-based leadership *roles* (motivator, director, and evaluator) and six specific *functions* (administration, technical, influence, persuasion, training, and planning). The principal (or administrator) is assessed in these roles and functions for the purpose of self-improvement.[227]

Principals participating in the Management Profile begin with a videotaped interview; a trained interviewer queries the principal to elicit specific answers relevant to his or her unique work situation. The questions are also designed to elicit answers applicable to the three basic roles and six functions of the management profile. The tapes are then evaluated by one or more trained assessors, and a confidential report is prepared for each principal that addresses individual strengths and weaknesses as well as areas for improvement.

The plan provides a variety of opportunities for administrators to be evaluated and grow professionally over a thirty-six-month period. At the end of the period, the principal is interviewed again and a new thirty-six-month plan is developed. The idea of the Management Profile is to detail what goes on in school, and exactly

---

[224]Sanders, personal communication, March 15, 1999; December 4, 2002.

[225]Genevieve Brown and Beverly J. Irby, "Seven Policy Considerations for Principal Appraisal," *School Administrator,* 55 (1998): 10–11; Douglas B. Reeves, "Holding Principals Accountable," *School Administrator,* 55 (1998): 6–12; Marc S. Tucker and Charles S. Clark, "The New Accountability," *American School Board Journal,* 186 (1999): 26–29.

[226]Thomas D. Snyder, "Trends in Education," *Principal,* 78 (1998): 40–48.

[227]Elaine Wilmore, "The Management Profile and Site-Based Management," *NASSP Bulletin,* 77 (1993): 84–88; Elaine Wilmore and David A. Erlandson, "Planning for Professional Growth: A Process for Administrators," *NASSP Bulletin,* 77 (1993): 57–63. Also see Wilmore, *Principal Leadership* (Thousand Oaks, CA: Corwin Press, 2002).

what administrators do, so they can view themselves in context with their roles and functions within the organization. It is a safe way for principals to get to know themselves without their "boss" or teachers evaluating or criticizing them.

**Performance Domains**  The National Policy Board for Educational Administration (NPBEA) has developed twenty-one domains that represent critical knowledge, skills, and behaviors needed by effective principals. These domains reflect the principals' job requirements and address the changing nature of the position; the development of these domains is an attempt to bridge theory with practice, and it is also supported by the National Association of Secondary School Principals.[228]

A prescription for training principals cannot be easily agreed upon or predetermined for groups of principals, since training needs are based on situational and individual circumstances, and problems and issues change from year to year. A survey of 140 experienced principals in South Carolina rated experience and training in (1) curriculum design, (2) instruction, (3) learning, and (4) legal application as the most important domains needed for the job. However, the same principals reported the need for additional participation and training activities in eleven of the twenty-one domain areas: (1) resource allocation, (2) public and media relationships, (3) information collection, (4) problem analysis, (5) oral and nonverbal expression, (6) written expression, (7) philosophical and cultural values; (8) policy and political influence, (9) judgment, (10) implementation, and (11) delegation.[229] Concern for training on these topics suggests that traditional university programs may not sufficiently address many issues relevant to principals.

**PEP Program**  Located at the University of North Carolina at Chapel Hill, the Principals' Executive Program (PEP) is modeled after Harvard's leadership training program for business executives. Each year approximately 300 principals who are nominated by their superintendents come to the university for in-service training over a four-month period. Much more rigorous than standard courses in educational administration, the program gives principals feedback and assistance on their personality, leadership style, stress management ability, human relations skills, communication skills, and fiscal- or budget-related skills.[230]

Prior to the program, principals are briefed on what will be expected of them. The reading is intense, and some class sessions last for up to ten hours a day; participants also have to develop and implement a school improvement plan. A good deal of bonding takes place as principals discuss the similar problems they face back home and the books they are reading. As of 1997, some 2238 administrators out of approximately 5000 in North Carolina have graduated from PEP or one of three other administrative programs that have developed from it. In a recent PEP survey, 96 percent of the participants gave PEP an extremely high rating. PEP graduates attend biannual symposiums dealing with legal issues and timely curriculum and instructional issues.

**Site-Based Management (SBM)**  Site-based management—sometimes called *school-based management, school-based decision making,* or *collaborative decision making*—means different things to different people. It is often associated with some school reform or restructuring process that translates into modifying school governance, moving in some way from a top-down approach to a bottom-up approach. The belief is that by shifting decision-making authority to the school site and involving teachers (and also parents and the community) in setting goals, making decisions, and assuming accountability, the teaching and learning process will improve. It involves the principal in all three roles: instructional leader, manager, and change agent.

Approximately 75 percent of the more than 1300 K–8 principals in the 1998 NAESP study reported that within the previous three years (1995–98) they received increased authority to make decisions at the school site.[231] Advocates of SBM claim that most teachers welcome the increased involvement and eventually reach personal and professional maturity. Where such reforms are successful, teacher morale and the overall climate of

---

[228]*Building a Career: Fulfilling the Lifetime Professional Needs of Principals* (Fairfax, VA: National Policy Board for Educational Administration, 1994); Elaine L. Wilmore, *Principal Leadership: Applying the New ELCC Standards* (Thousand Oaks, CA: Corwin Press, 2002).

[229]Diane Ricciardi, "Sharpening Experienced Principals' Skills for Changing Schools," *NASSP Bulletin,* 81 (1997): 65–71.

[230]Robert E. Phay, "Learning to Be Effective CEOs: The Principal's Executive Program," *NASSP Bulletin,* 81 (1997): 151–157.

[231]Doud and Keller, "The K–8 Principal in 1998."

## PRO/CON Debate

### The Politics of School Elections

Although people in the United States value the democratic process, for many people the term *politics* carries a negative connotation. Politics implies tradeoff, compromise, less-than-perfect solutions, and, perhaps, secret deals that benefit those in power. Given this perception, the practice of electing to office those who set policy for schools is debatable.

**Question:** Considering the political ramifications of elections, should school board members be elected?

### Arguments PRO

1. Service on the school board requires little political experience. Concerned citizens can assume office and contribute to the general welfare in important and meaningful ways without major changes in their personal or professional lives. They need not be or become career politicians.

2. Election is effective and sacred. The electoral process guarantees that issues are discussed in an open forum. Voters choose candidates who are most conversant with the issues and most able to act upon them.

3. Single-issue candidates are rarely elected to office because their constituents are a small portion of the community. If elected, their perspective broadens as they learn about other issues and the board's responsibilities.

4. An appointed board vests power in the person making the appointments. It leads to rule by an elite or specific pressure group rather than rule by the people.

5. As chief executive officers, school superintendents are accountable to the community for the state of the schools. It is right and proper for local citizens to express their concerns to their elected board members and for board members to carry these concerns to the superintendent. Board members protect superintendents from capricious expectations.

### Arguments CON

1. A seat on the school board is sometimes an entry-level political office. Board members who are striving for more prestigious offices use the board seat to attract the attention of the media and the public, thereby bringing undue stress to the superintendent and the school district.

2. Election is inefficient. For example, many school board members are elected to three-year terms. It takes them at least two years to learn boardsmanship. Then they begin running for reelection.

3. Single-issue candidates may be elected to the board. Their narrow focus prevails, regardless of the needs of the community or the schools. They are more concerned about representing special interest groups than representing the larger community.

4. Appointed board members are selected on the basis of their unique skills at policy development. Those making appointments ensure that a board is balanced so that all interests are represented.

5. Some of the most competent school superintendents lose their positions because they are unable or unwilling to appease elected board members. This is especially apparent in small towns where local citizens often want to run the schools. They are more concerned about administrative details than large policy issues.

the school are dramatically enhanced.[232] In addition, many principals feel that their roles and responsibilities have become more complex as a result of recent (1) school restructuring efforts, (2) state and federal regulations, and (3) accountability trends and forces—and they need to delegate powers to other individuals and groups who can plan and work effectively.[233]

---

[232]Mary E. Driscoll, "Professionalism Versus Community: Themes from Recent School Reform Literature," *Peabody Journal of Education*, 73 (1998): 89–127; Carl D. Glickman, "The Courage to Lead," *Educational Leadership*, 59 (2002): 41–44; Starita Smith, "How Site-Based Management Is Transforming Education in Austin," *American School Board Journal*, 185 (1998): 22–25.

[233]Kenneth Leithwood and Daniel Duke, "Mapping the Conceptual Terrain of Leadership," *Peabody Journal of Education*, 73 (1998): 31–50; Joseph Murphy, "Redefining the Principalship in Restructuring Schools," *NASSP Bulletin*, 79 (1994): 94; Gerald N. Tirozzi, "The Artistry of Leadership," *Phi Delta Kappan*, 82 (2001): 434–439.

Critics contend that the result of collaboration is often not very useful. Considerable time devoted to discussing daily teaching problems such as classroom management, equipment needs, clerical routines, and working conditions means that little time remains for the larger governance and administrative issues. In addition, some administrators argue that many big-city teachers (and community members) are ill equipped for shared leadership because they are not trained for it. Instead of cooperating, teachers sometimes revert to a hostile collective bargaining stance, and the community often bickers and fights over spoils and jobs.[234] In most situations, the big-city teachers, community representatives, and others often have hidden agendas.[235] It is important to move away from seeing SBM as a goal, or an end, or a new wave of reform, and instead to view it as an administrative process for the principal and teachers that allows them to share power as well as accountability. Parents and community residents should be involved in a limited way, as consumers and citizens—and not as policymakers.

## Summary

1. There are several plans for organizing school districts. Most districts comprise elementary schools, middle-grade or junior high schools, and senior high or high schools.

2. Schools are organized into school districts, and there are today nearly 15,000 public school systems operating under a widely accepted system of laws, regulations, and customs.

3. Whereas most small and rural school districts have consolidated their schools since 1930, many large urban areas have decentralized since the 1960s. However, the number of decentralized school districts has declined in recent years.

[234]Michael A. Copeland, "The Myth of the Superprincipal," *Phi Delta Kappan*, 82 (2001): 528–533; Richard F. Elmore, "Hard Questions About Practice," *Educational Leadership*, 59 (2002): 22–25.

[235]Carl Glickman, "Educational Leadership: Failure to Use Our Imagination," *Phi Delta Kappan*, 87 (2006): 689–690; Jane Clark Lindle and James Shrock, "School Based Decision-Making Counsels and the Hiring Process," *NASSP Bulletin*, 77 (1993): 71–76; Carol Midgely and Stewart Wood, "Beyond Site-Based Management," *Phi Delta Kappan* (1993): 245–249.

4. School board members are agents of the state, chosen locally (and in most cases elected) to run the local schools.

5. Board members are the official link between the public and school administration. Board members reflect the public will and have managerial responsibilities that are crucial to the operation of schools.

6. The relationship between school boards and superintendents deserves continued attention; school board members and superintendents must work together and avoid overt conflict. When differences or tensions exist between board members and the superintendent for too long, most superintendents are forced to resign.

7. Superintendents spend most of their time as managers, not as leaders. The average workday is largely desk work, phone calls, and meetings. Superintendents interpret school board policy and carry it out in connection with contemporary events; there is little time for them to initiate reform.

8. The central administrative staff, usually consisting of an associate superintendent, a number of assistant superintendents, department heads, and coordinators, are given responsibility by the superintendent to help run the schools. The central staff is usually top heavy in large districts and streamlined in small districts.

9. Principals spend the most time as general managers but would prefer to spend more time as curriculum-instructional leaders and change agents. The realities of the principal's job often prevent emphasis on the latter two areas of leadership.

10. Evaluation of principals include various accountability, performance-based, peer evaluation, value-added, and portfolio plans.

11. Principals engage in various forms of planning and assessment, including but not limited to curriculum management audits, value-added assessment, and site-based management.

## Key Terms

consolidation
decentralization
charters

public board meeting
executive board meeting
more effective schools
compensatory programs
vision
top-down model
central office staff
organizational chart
toxic cultures
positive cultures
general manager
curriculum-instructional leader
leadership styles
Management Profile
site-based management

## Discussion Questions

1. What is the ideal school district size? Defend your number(s).

2. Why have school districts consolidated? Why have they decentralized? What are the advantages and disadvantages of each trend?

3. What are the advantages and disadvantages of an elected or appointed local board of education?

4. How would you describe an effective superintendent? How do you see the superintendent's role in context with effective schools?

5. How would you describe an effective principal? What differences or emphasis, in terms of leadership behavior, do you envision for an elementary vs. secondary principal?

## Suggested Readings

Bennis, Warren, Gretchen Spreitzer, and Thomas Cummings (eds.). *The Future of Leadership: Today's Top Leadership Thinkers Speak to To-morrow's Leaders* (New York: John Wiley, 2001). Based on interviews with leaders in academia and the private sector, this book provides practical advice on developing leadership behavior.

Cuban, Larry. *Why Is It So Hard to Get Good Schools?* (New York: Teachers College Press, Columbia University, 2002). The author discusses the relationship between school policy, school administration, and education bureaucracy.

Deal, Terrence E., and Kent D. Peterson. *Shaping School Culture* (New York: John Wiley, 2003). The book provides an action blueprint for school leaders.

English, Fenwick W. *Encyclopedia of Educational Leadership and Administration* (Thousand Oaks, CA: Sage Publications, 2006). The book contains over 600 entries on theories, research, and concepts in education.

Owens, Robert G. *Organizational Behavior in Education,* 9th ed. (Boston: Allyn and Bacon, 2006). The author emphasizes organization, behavior and culture, school leadership, and decision making.

Sarason, Seymour B. *Letters to a Serious Education President,* 2nd ed. (Thousand Oaks, CA: Corwin Press, 2006). The book is about fundamental changes that are needed for sustained school reform.

Sergiovanni, Thomas J. *Rethinking Leadership* (Thousand Oaks, CA: Corwin Press, 2006). The author examines the concept of leadership and its relation to learning.

# 11

## School Finance and Productivity

FOCUSING QUESTIONS

1  What proportion of school revenues do the local, state, and federal governments contribute?

2  Why are many local school authorities looking increasingly to the states for educational revenues?

3  What is wrong with solely relying on property taxes as revenue sources for schools?

4  What fiscal problems characterize urban schools?

5  Given the task to reduce your school budget 10 percent, what three or four items would you cut? Why?

6  How can school productivity be increased without changing expenditures?

7  What financial trends will most likely affect school management in the twenty-first century?

8  What is the average age of the schools in your district? What school infrastructure problems are most costly in your district?

9  Why is there such resistance to closing schools? What is the best economic solution to take in dealing with closed schools?

---

In this chapter, we attempt to answer these questions about financing and productivity by first examining the sources and distribution of funding. Next we explore the methods of school funding and the advantages and disadvantages of each. Then we discuss developing budgets and the correlation between expenditures and student productivity. We examine how aging school buildings and environmental hazards can affect expenditures. Finally, we explore international and U.S. spending for education.

---

### Education and Economics

Education is big business. In 2003 the operating school budget of grades K–12 was more than $440 billion, an increase from $247 billion expended ten years ago.[1] The estimated capital expenditures for education in America should increase another $100 billion by 2014.[2]

---

[1] *Digest of Education Statistics, 2005* (Washington, DC: U.S. Government Printing Office, 2006).

[2] *Projections of Education Statistics 2014* (Washington, DC: U.S. Government Printing Office, 2005), table 33.

The operating school budget of K–12 schools is equivalent to 3.6 percent of the gross domestic product. (The **gross domestic product,** GDP, is the market value of all goods and services produced within a specified period—in practice, one year.) When institutions of higher learning are included, that amount is increased to 4.9 percent of the gross domestic product.[3] In terms of people involved, about one of every four Americans is engaged in some aspect of education as student, teacher, administrator, counselor, aide, or support staff. The clientele served in 2005 included 54.7 million K–12 public and private students; 3.5 million teachers; and approximately another 3.2 million professionals, administrators, counselors, and support staff.[4] What we spend on human capital and services is likely to determine the quality of life of our children and grandchildren.

Because most school-related costs (including salaries) have increased more rapidly than inflation in recent years, the business of schooling is in trouble. In 2003, the states increased their K–12 school spending from the previous year by about 5 percent,[5] while the inflation rate was a mere 2.28 percent.[6] In 1998, state government budget surpluses were $40 billion among the states.[7] (The federal government surplus was $69 billion in the same year, with a projected surplus of $79 billion in fiscal year 1999).

Then came September 11, the stock market collapse, recession, war on terrorism, Afghanistan, Iraq, and homeland security. The economy was bleeding, and the states by 2003 and 2004 were facing a fiscal crisis not experienced in the last sixty-five years. Nearly every state was facing budget deficits, and politically sensitive taxes and/or drastic cuts were on the horizon. For example, New York State was facing an estimated $10 billion deficit in 2003 and the governor told state agencies to reduce spending by 5 percent. Oklahoma instructed all state agencies to reduce spending 6.5 percent. The prison system reacted by allowing thousands of prisoners their freedom in order to save money. In Illinois, after twenty-six years of uninterrupted growth, the state projected a $2.5 billion deficit and was forced to increase personal income taxes and reduce spending in education, medicine, and children's services. In California, the governor cut $5 billion from the budget.[8] State government budget deficits were estimated at $40 billion for fiscal 2003 and $60 billion for 2004. As many as thirty-eight states were forced to slash or freeze their budgets, although many tried to shield education cuts. But the shortfalls were huge and the states were forced to cut services.[9]

School construction, in 2004, was at a record high of $29 billion.[10] Just over half the money was spent on new schools, while about 25 percent went to additions for existing buildings and about 24 percent to renovation. By 2005, the situation had reversed. Schools were only completing previously budgeted construction of buildings, and state and local government agencies were looking at ways to save money: increasing tuition at state colleges, increasing classroom size, not filling vacancies and laying off employees, trimming textbook purchases, extracurricular activities, enrichment programs and summer programs, introducing additional student user fees, and even chopping off school days from the academic calendar.

Oregon was perhaps in the worst shape. The schools depend on the state for nearly 70 percent of their budget and consume 43 percent of the state's revenues. Because state revenues had declined dramatically, school officials were forced to consider cutting ten to fifteen days from the academic calendar in 2003.[11] Big-city school districts across the country were weighing the possibility of either eliminating teaching jobs or administrative jobs to plug up budget holes in fiscal 2004. Other districts such as Baltimore were contemplating unpaid days off for top school administrators, and Austin and Detroit were eliminating part-time teachers, substitute teachers, and teaching assistants. Still other districts (New York City, Buffalo and Albany) were being forced to trim prekindergarten programs, special

[3] *Digest of Education Statistics, 2005,* table 407, p. 666.

[4] Ibid., tables 1 & 2, p. 13.

[5] Ibid., table 32, p. 59 (calculations derived by authors).

[6] U.S. Bureau of Labor Statistics (http://data.bls.cqi-bin/cpicalc.pl).

[7] "NCSL Tracks Link Between State Surpluses, Education Spending," *Education Week,* 5 August 1998, p. 24.

[8] Robert Pear, "States Are Facing Big Fiscal Crises, Governors Report," *New York Times,* 26 November 2002, pp. 1, 22.

[9] Allan Richard and Joetta L. Sack, "States Brace for Tough New Year," *Education Week,* 8 January 2003, pp. 1, 16–19.

[10] http://asumag.com/mag/university_stalled_momentum/ retrieved on 19 December 2006.

[11] "To Balance Books, Oregon Districts Try Fewer Days," *New York Times,* 29 December 2002, p. 28.

education programs, and health-insurance benefits for teachers.[12]

Even though the states and the federal government are facing decreased revenues and surpluses, the funding issues for education always seem to be the same. Taxpayers want lower taxes, and social agencies have different perceptions on how taxes should be spent. Interest groups, such as those who are pursuing choice and/or voucher programs, complicate educational funding decisions and potentially draw money away from public schooling. Therefore, how to design and fund an educational system that provides for adequacy and equity in their educational finance models has been and will be an ongoing priority for educational leaders.

The result is that since the 1990s, and as we enter the twenty-first century, school board members, who are the people closest to the problem of school financing, have ranked "lack of financial support" as their number-one challenge.[13] School superintendents also consider school finance to be their number-one problem and the major reason (44 percent) why they would leave their job, either to look for another superintendency or to retire.[14]

These rankings come as no surprise; board members and superintendents have to watch the bottom line. In an era of budget balancing and taxpayer resistance to higher price tags for education, the people responsible for financial decisions are very sensitive to expenditures and capital outlays.

The three major sources of revenue or financial support for public schools are the local, state, and federal governments. State and local money remains the basic source of revenue for public education. Contributions by the states have increased from 16.9 percent in 1930 to a high of 48.7 percent in 2003. Local revenue sources have decreased from 82.7 percent in 1930

---

**Table 11–1   Revenues for Public Schools, Source of Government Funds, 1929–1930 to 2002–2003**

| School Year | Total (in millions) | Federal (%) | State (%) | Local (%) |
|---|---|---|---|---|
| 1929–1930 | 2,089 | 0.4 | 16.9 | 82.7 |
| 1939–1940 | 2,261 | 1.8 | 30.3 | 68.0 |
| 1949–1950 | 5,437 | 2.9 | 39.8 | 57.3 |
| 1959–1960 | 14,747 | 4.4 | 39.1 | 56.5 |
| 1969–1970 | 40,267 | 8.0 | 39.9 | 52.1 |
| 1979–1980 | 96,881 | 9.8 | 46.8 | 43.4 |
| 1989–1990 | 208,547 | 6.1 | 47.1 | 46.8 |
| 1999–2000 | 372,944 | 7.3 | 49.5 | 43.2 |
| 2002–2003 | 440,157 | 8.5 | 48.7 | 42.8 |

Source: *Digest of Education Statistics, 2005* (Washington DC: US Government Printing Office, 2006), table 152, p. 252.

---

to 42.8 percent in the same year.[15] It is expected that this trend will continue as more and more states recognize the value of providing equity among the school districts in their respective states. Table 11–1 shows the breakdown in revenues from 1929–30 to 2002–2003 with states and local governments providing 91.5 percent of the funds, and 8.5 percent from the federal government. At the extremes, a little more than 2 percent of school funding in Hawaii comes from local sources, while in New Hampshire local funds alone account for almost 90 percent of school funding. Those respective percentages were constant during the decades of the 1980s and 1990s—with the federal government providing limited support but often attempting considerable control.

## Tax Sources of School Revenues

The operation of public schools relies primarily on revenues generated from taxes, especially the property tax on the local level, sales and income taxes on the state level, and indirectly on individual income tax at the national level. (Lotteries, which by some are not considered a tax, are being used in thirty-six states and the District of Columbia to raise from 2 to 5 percent of their revenue.)

---

[12]John Gehring, "N.Y. Governor Proposes Deep Cut in School Aid . . .," *Education Week,* 5 February 2003, p. 16; Catherine Gewertz and Karla Scoon Reid, "Hard Choices: City Districts Making Cuts," *Education Week,* 5 February 2003, pp. 1, 14.

[13]"Sixth Annual Survey of School Board Members," *American School Board Journal,* 171 (1984): 24–27, 40; "Money Remains the Root of Your Problems," *American School Board Journal,* 176 (1989): 24; Larry Hedges, "Does Money Matter?" *Educational Researcher,* 23 (1994): 5–14; Frederick M. Hess, *School Boards at the Dawn of the 21st Century* (Alexandria, VA: National School Boards Association, 2002).

[14]Thomas E. Glass, *The Study of the American School Superintendency* (Arlington, VA: American Association of School Administrators, 2000), tables 5-24, 5-27, pp. 68, 70.

[15]*Digest of Education Statistics, 2005,* table 152, p. 252.

Some kinds of taxes are considered better than others. Most people today accept several criteria for evaluating various types of taxes. Some commonly mentioned are the following:

1. *A Tax Should Not Cause Unintended Economic Distortions.* It should not alter economic behavior, change consumer spending patterns in favor of one good or service over another, negatively affect a taxpayer's willingness to work, or cause the relocation of business, industry, or people.

2. *A Tax Should Be Equitable.* It should be based on the taxpayer's ability to pay. Those with greater incomes or with property worth more money should pay more taxes than those with less income or less desirable property. Taxes that are not equitable and that require lower-income groups to pay a higher proportion of their income than higher-income groups are called **regressive taxes.** In contrast, taxes that require high-income groups to pay higher percentages of their income are called **progressive taxes.**

3. *A Tax Should Be Collected Easily.* This requires that the tax be collected with minimum costs to the taxpayer or government; it also means that it should be difficult to evade and should have minimal or no loopholes.

4. *The Tax Should Be Responsive to Changing Economic Conditions.* During inflation (when government costs and expenditures rise), the tax revenue should also rise; in a recession, the tax revenue should decrease. Responsive taxes are **elastic;** those that are not responsive are **inelastic.**

5. *A Tax Should Provide Adequacy of Yield.* There is no logic in having a tax with little potential for yielding revenue in substantial amounts. Nuisance taxes that provide small amounts of money should be avoided; they often result in added bureaucracy and public frustration.[16]

## Local Financing of Public Schools

Although education is the responsibility of the states, they have traditionally delegated much of this responsibility to local school districts. As indicated earlier, the local contribution to school financing has decreased over the last several decades, whereas the state contribution has increased. Nevertheless, local funding remains a crucial part of public school financing.

### Property Tax

The **property tax** is the main source of revenue for local school districts. It is the most important tax supporting education, with a long history in this country. (The property tax has been used since the colonial period.)

Property taxes are determined by first arriving at the **market value** of a property—the amount the property would likely sell for if it were sold. Then the market value is usually converted to an **assessed value** using a predetermined index or ratio, such as one-fourth or one-third; for example, a property with a market value of $80,000 might have an assessed value of only $20,000. The assessed value is nearly always less than the market value in order to protect the owner and to avoid controversies and appeals. Finally, the local tax rate, expressed in mills, is applied to the assessed value. A **mill** represents one-thousandth of a dollar ($.001); thus, a tax rate of 25 mills amounts to $25 for each $1000 of assessed value.

The property tax does not rate well on the criterion for equity. Because of differing assessment practices and lack of uniform valuation, people owning equivalent properties may pay different taxes. This results in unequal treatment of equal property. The property tax does not always distribute the tax burden according to the ability to pay. A retired couple may have a home whose market value has increased substantially, along with their taxes, but because they live on a fixed income they cannot afford the increasing taxes. In this respect, it can be argued that the property tax may be regressive.

In addition, the property tax is not immediately responsive to changing economic conditions. In some states properties are reassessed every one or two years, but in others reassessments occur only every three to four years. Thus, a property's assessed value and actual tax are often based on old market conditions. If property values have risen since the last reassessment, then the school district is losing potential tax income; if property values have decreased, property taxes may be overburdensome, thereby causing a declining neighborhood to deteriorate further.

The property tax is not always easy to collect. Collection depends on the efficiency of the local tax collection department. Wealthy individuals and businesses

---

[16]Allan Odden and Sara Archibald, *Reallocating Resources* (Thousand Oaks, CA: Corwin Press, 2001); Allan C. Ornstein and Daniel U. Levine, *Foundations of Education*, 10th ed. (Boston: Houghton Mifflin, 2008).

## ▪ Exemplary Educational Administrators in Action

**WILLIAM G. MEUER** Principal, Norwood Park School, Chicago, Illinois.

**Previous Position:** Teacher, then Principal, Winnetka, Illinois.

**Latest Degree:** Ed. D., Administration and Leadership, Loyola University, Chicago.

**Number One Influence on Career:** My parents—my father, who saw the value of an education and never had the opportunity to go to high school, and my mother, who taught thirty years in the rural schools and later in two small communities in South Dakota. I am pleased that our son, William Becht Meuer, is the fourth generation of educators in my family.

**Number One Achievement:** 2002—Distinguished School Administrator's Award sponsored by American Association of School Librarians and SIRS, Inc. 1998—School Leadership Award for Outstanding Principals sponsored by the Chicago Principals and Administrators Association.

**Number One Regret:** As a young administrator, I felt that 100 percent of my time should be devoted to students and teachers. I soon realized the value and the necessity of involving the parent community and fostering the participation of the larger school community.

**Favorite Education-Related Book or Text:** *Leadership* by Rudolph W. Giuliani with Ken Kurson.

**Additional Interests:** Water sports, gardening, golf, and playing bridge.

**Leadership Style:** I believe it is imperative to seek professionals whose skills and talents are superior to mine; to develop strong beliefs and communicate those beliefs; to remove the roadblocks that interfere with the instructional process for staff; to support their contributions; and to recognize their accomplishments.

**Professional Vision:** To me, a leader is a person who is in a position to influence others to act and who has the moral, intellectual, and social skills required to take advantage of that position. If the leaders enlist the hearts and minds of those around them, there is commitment and dedication. When adults act like adults and when professionals act like professionals, the organization will have established an environment where all children can learn.

**Words of Advice:** While school administration can be stressful and exhausting, it can be enormously rewarding. I have enjoyed and continue to enjoy it every day.

First, determine the age range of students you wish to work with. Develop an expertise for specific areas of the curriculum and a thorough understanding of the psychology for the age group you select.

Seek out a school community that supports your philosophy or one that is open to or desires change. Communicate your philosophy, goals, and beliefs.

Limit the number of goals on the "front burner." Where are these goals coming from? Are they coming down from the central office? The parent community? How does each impact the teaching/learning process? Has the staff had input into the decisions and is there a feeling of ownership?

Celebrate your successes! Everyone needs to know when the task is completed—the goal met, the objective accomplished.

Recognize that children need some fun! Plan and celebrate student successes. Individual and group recognition is essential.

Recognize that staff have out-of-school responsibilities, needs, and interests. Some may be in a degree program that occupies untold hours of study and schoolwork. For another, it may be the responsibility of an aging parent, a health issue, or a second job. Listen! Listen! Listen! Don't be afraid to ask a question.

Finally, I communicate to the staff that I am not above doing what I am requesting of them. Model organization and hard work. Always keep a sense of humor! It has served me well!

---

that contest their property taxes often receive abatements. Most states specify the basic minimum property tax rate that local school districts can levy. An increase in the tax rate often requires voter approval at the local level. Since the mid-1970s, local school districts have had difficulty getting voter approval for raising taxes. As we march into the twenty-first century, there is movement from reliance on the local property taxes to reliance on other sources of revenues such as user fees, state sales taxes, and personal property taxes.

### User Fees

Besides the property tax, some school districts gather revenues through user fees, special income taxes, and revenue-sharing monies. **User fees**—that is, fees charged specifically to people who use a certain facility or service—are becoming increasingly popular (both with state and local governments) for supporting, partially or wholly, specific services or functions. Usually, income from user fees is earmarked for a particular agency fund supporting the activity that justifies the imposition of the fee. In instances where the fees do not cover the entire cost for the service, and they rarely do, the legislature may pick up the difference by appropriating general revenues.

User fees are attractive because the public helps pay for the service's provision and only people using it are taxed. We should expect greater increases in user fees, especially if state or local revenues fall short, because they can be assessed on almost any government service or function. A few school districts (mostly affluent) already levy user fees on bus service, textbooks, athletic and recreational activities, nursery classes, and after-school centers. To maintain balanced budgets, the schools will probably increase these fees, just as colleges and universities are increasing tuition fees. But, just as college and university tuitions are regressive, because they are not determined on ability to pay, so are user fees.

## Tobacco Settlement

Educators want their fair share of the $206 billion tobacco settlement that became available in 2000 from the states that won this amount from the five largest tobacco companies. Other state agencies raised concerns about the wisdom of shifting funds from health-related programs, maintaining that tobacco monies should be used for health-related needs.[17] For poor school districts, the opportunity to generate additional funds is considerably limited in comparison to wealthier districts. Hopefully, these poorer districts will receive a larger portion of the tobacco settlement money, as opposed to a proportional share or share based purely on student enrollments.

Since 2002, states and local governments across the country have been turning to tobacco money to plug their deficit gaps at a time when the states are experiencing the worst fiscal crisis in decades. By using billions of dollars from the industrywide tobacco settlement of 1998, they are generating revenue now, opting for a one-time infusion and borrowing against future revenues. As of the school year 2002–2003, eight states (California, Iowa, Missouri, New Jersey, Oregon, Rhode Island, Washington, and Wisconsin) were using proceeds from the settlement to reduce budget deficits and six were considering it for 2003–2004,[18] including New York, which was in very bad shape because of September 11, the recession in financial markets (and Wall Street), and the decline in tourism in New York City.

Most of these states have already had their credit ratings lowered by the major credit agencies or have been placed on alert. For the most part, the above eight states are rich states and/or states that have, in the past, funded education above the national norm. When ratings are lowered, states have to pay more when selling bonds to compensate investors for increased risk, raising their costs of capital by hundreds of millions for projects from schools to roads. The rating agencies are concerned that opting to use large sums of tobacco money to reduce budget deficits is a signal of fiscal crisis (although it is not the sole cause of the downgrades). Tobacco money is a one-time, nonrecurring revenue. If there is no plan to replenish the fund, then a red flag is raised among credit analysts.[19]

Credit agencies are also worried that money is now being borrowed over a long period, such as twenty years. In the past, state (and city) bonds have been sold for shorter periods. Borrowing over a longer period raises the potential that the state or local government will be under fiscal stress for longer than usual.

## Urban/Suburban Disparities

As helpful as state and federal aid is to most school districts (see Table 11–1), the differential ability of school districts to support education still persists. A school district located in a wealthy area or an area with a broad tax base obviously can generate more local revenue than can poor school districts. As a result, in many states total expenditures per student may be two to four times greater in the five wealthiest school districts than in the five poorest school districts.[20] These variations

---

[17]Eric Lichtblau, "U.S. Lawsuit Seeks Tobacco Profits," *New York Times*, 18 March 2003, pp. A1, A29; "States Covet Tobacco Bounty for Education," *Education Week*, 24 February 1999, p. 18.

[18]Jonathon Fuerbringer, "Tobacco Money Could Harm Credit Ratings of Some States," *New York Times*, 29 November 2002, pp. C1, C5.

[19]Ibid.

[20]Richard King, Austin D. Swanson, and Scott R. Sweetland, *School Finance: Achieving High Standards with Equity and Efficiency*, 3rd ed. (Boston: Allyn and Bacon, 2003); Allan C. Ornstein, *Teaching and Schooling in America: Pre- and Post-September 11* (Boston: Allyn and Bacon, 2003).

exist among communities in every state, and they tend to be growing wider between urban areas and suburban areas adjacent to them. This trend is more apparent in the Northeast and Midwest, owing to the flight of urban populations and businesses to the suburbs and Sunbelt states (which in turn causes further depletion of the tax base and increasing disparities between rich and poor school districts).

Most urban property taxes (as well as those of some poor suburbs) are alarmingly high, about 33 to 100 percent higher per capita than taxes in wealthy adjacent suburbs. High property taxes make it difficult to attract middle-income residents and new jobs to broaden the tax base. As the cities lose their middle-class population and businesses, their tax base is further undermined. They are forced to cut city services, including education, to balance their budgets; these cuts drive away more middle-class citizens and businesses and, in turn, more tax revenues. The cycle reinforces itself, and this is one reason for the decline of many urban schools. Financing has become the major problem for many city schools, and recommendations for cutting costs and reducing wasteful programs have become important issues.

This phenomenon exists despite attempts by the federal government to favor poorer school districts and urban schools through Title I and compensatory funding and despite the various states' attempts to redistribute school revenues through state funding methods and court-ordered reforms. For example, in 2003, federal revenues for schools averaged 8.5 percent nationwide. Among the largest school districts (with 50,000 or more students), those with highest poverty indices (percentage of students eligible for free lunch), the average federal share of revenues was 13.8 percent and the median was 14.0 percent. (See Table 11.2.) Fresno had the distinction of enrolling the most poor students, 37.4 percent, as defined by federal criteria. The fact remains, however, that U.S. school funding is largely based on a local community's ability to fund education through property taxes, in contrast to most other industrialized countries, where funding is relatively equal among students throughout the nation, state, province, or municipality.[21]

### Municipal and Educational Overburden

Cities are plagued by what is commonly called **municipal overburden,** or severe financing demands for public functions because of population density and the high

**Table 11–2** Large School Districts (50,000 or More Students) with Highest Poverty Rates (30% or More) and Federal Revenues as a Percent of the Total School District Budget, 2003

| School District | Poverty Rate | Federal Revenues Percent Total |
|---|---|---|
| Fresno Unified, CA | 37.4 | 13.1 |
| San Bernardino City Unified, CA | 35.7 | 11.5 |
| EL Paso ISD, TX | 35.3 | 14.0 |
| Orleans Parish, LA | 35.1 | 17.8 |
| San Antonio USD, TX | 34.8 | 15.7 |
| Atlanta City, GA | 32.3 | 9.6 |
| Ysleta ISD, TX | 31.7 | 14.2 |
| Detroit City, MI | 31.0 | 14.3 |
| Long Beach Unified, CA | 30.8 | 13.8 |
| Mean (of above) | 33.79 | 13.78 |

Note: Poverty rate is defined as the poverty rate of 5–17-year-olds below the poverty level.

Source: *Digest of Education Statistics, 2005* (Washington DC: US Government Printing Office, 2006), table 90, pp. 160–162.

proportion of disadvantaged and low-income groups. Therefore, large cities cannot devote as great a percentage of their total tax revenues to the schools as suburban and rural districts can. For example, in the early 1990s, Cleveland, Detroit, Gary (Indiana), Newark (New Jersey), and New York City spent less than 30 to 35 percent of all local tax revenues for school purposes, whereas the rest of their respective states were able to spend 45 to 50 percent of local taxes for schools.[22]

Then there is the issue of **educational overburden.** A large percentage of the student population in city schools is in technical and vocational programs, which cost more per student than the regular academic high school program. Similarly, there is a greater proportion of special needs students—namely, poor, bilingual, and learning disabled students—in the city schools

---

[21] Ornstein, *Teaching and Schooling in America: Pre- and Post-September 11;* Joel Spring, *Globalization and Educational Rights* (Mahwah, NJ: Erlbaum, 2001.)

[22] Allan C. Ornstein, "Regional Population Shifts: Implications for Educators," *Clearing House, 59* (1986): 284–290; George C. Galster and Ronald B. Mincy, "Poverty in Urban Neighborhoods," *Urban Institute, 23* (1993): 11–13. Also see Joseph Cordes, Robert D. Ebel, and Jane Gravelle, *Encyclopedia of Taxation and Tax Policy* (Washington, DC: Urban Institute, 1999).

than in suburban or rural schools. These students require remedial programs and services, which cost 50 to 100 percent more per student than basic programs. Moreover, the need for additional services tends to increase geometrically with the concentration of immigrant children and poverty.[23] City schools, therefore, have to spend more educational resources per student than a similar-size school district or group of school districts comprising middle-class students.

Finally, city schools tend to have a greater proportion of senior teachers at the top of the pay scale than do their suburban counterparts. Many suburban districts have as a matter of policy replaced many experienced teachers to save money. They have also experienced a high turnover of pregnant and experienced teachers who did not return to the teacher profession. Cities have higher vandalism costs, lunch costs, desegregation costs, insurance costs, and maintenance costs (their buildings are older than suburban schools) per school than do other districts within the state. Both city and rural school districts spend more than suburban districts on transportation.[24]

## Spending versus Outcomes

There is little agreement on whether a direct relationship exists between school spending and student performance. In a classic study, Paul Mort summarized his research by stating that "empirical study of the relationship between expenditure level and quality of education . . . is that the relationship is strong."[25] In other classic studies of equality and opportunity, Coleman[26]

and Jencks,[27] however, maintained that "costs . . . have only a minor effect on achievement of students when compared with the much larger effect of their local community's values, family background, peer group, and IQ scores." Jencks took the analysis one step further by arguing that "luck," or the unaccounted for variance related to economic outcomes, was more important than school achievement, which of course sent reformers into the trenches.

Coons, Clune, and Sugarman summed up the situation: "There are similar studies suggesting stronger positive consequences from dollar increments; there are others suggesting only trivial consequences and still others suggesting no effect."[28] Hanushek declared that "there is no strong or systematic relationship between school expenditures and student performance."[29]

A fifteen-year analysis of studies by the National Institute of Education noted that the school makes a difference if the school emphasizes (1) a safe, secure environment, (2) instructional leadership from its principal, (3) personnel who have high expectations of the students, (4) a careful monitoring system, (5) schoolwide emphasis on basic skill instruction, and (6) classroom time on task.[30] Another study indicated that the teacher plays a dramatic role in a student's academic success. Researchers found that "after three years with ineffective teachers, fifth-graders averaged 54 to 60 points lower on achievement test scores than students who had worked with highly effective teachers; and those students continued to have lower scores."[31] But it has also been found that higher per-pupil expenditures, new schools, smaller classes, higher teacher salaries, and increased curriculum/instructional expenditures have little to do with student performance.[32] Money might make a difference if it was spent properly and under the right circumstances.

[23]Michael Fix and Wendy Zimmerman, *Educating Immigrant Children: Chapter 1 in the Changing City* (Washington, DC: Urban Institute Press, 1993); Bruce Katz and Robert E. Lang, *Redefining Urban and Suburban America* (Washington, DC: Brookings Institution, 2003); Milton Schwebel, *Remaking America's Three School Systems: Now Separate and Unequal* (Lanham, MD: Rowman & Littlefield, 2003).

[24]David Brunori, *The Future of State Taxation* (Washington, DC: Urban Institute, 1988); Paul Hill, Christine Campbell, and James Harvey, *It Takes a City: Getting Serious About Urban School Reform* (Washington, DC: Brookings Institution, 2000); Joseph F. Murphy and Walter G. Hack, "Fiscal Problems in Central-City Schools," *Urban Review*, 15 (1983): 229–244.

[25]Paul Mort, *Problems and Issues in Public School Finance* (Washington, DC: National Conference on Professors of Educational Administration, 1952), p. 9.

[26]James S. Coleman et al., *Equality of Educational Opportunity* (Washington, DC: U.S. Government Printing Office, 1966).

[27]Christopher Jencks et al., *Inequality: A Reassessment of the Effect of Family and Schooling in America* (New York: Basic Books, 1972).

[28]John E. Coons et al., *Private Wealth and Public Education* (Cambridge, MA: Belknap Press of Harvard University Press, 1970), p. 36.

[29]Eric A. Hanushek, "The Impact of Differential Expenditures on School Performance," *Educational Researcher*, 18 (1989): 47.

[30]Michael Cohen, "Effective Schools: Accumulating Research Findings," *American Education* (January/February 1982): 13–16.

[31]*The Deseret News*, 8 March 1999, p. C1.

[32]Mano Singham, *The Achievement Gap in U.S. Education* (Lanham, MD: Rowman & Littlefield, 2005).

So there is a great deal of debate as to whether money matters. A more global approach to this issue might be that a *variety of factors* affect student performance—money, intelligence, student input (such as motivation and prior achievement), family background, school culture, and teachers. If we really want to increase student performance, then we have to look at some sensitive issues: financial adequacy and equity, student and family responsibilities, peer group influence in and out of school, teacher and administrative preparation programs, and evaluation procedures to ensure that competence is the norm for educators who deal with students.

## Learning and Earning

Recent analyses of education and earnings are by Mayer and Peterson (Mayer is actually a spinoff of the old Jencks team, and Peterson is a Harvard professor) and by David Grissmer and his colleagues at Rand—and in the publications of Brookings Institution, Rand, and the Urban Institute. In general, these reports do not repudiate Coleman, Jencks, the notion of luck, or the unaccounted variance related to economic outcomes. We are told that schools help promote intergenerational mobility, although they do not provide sufficient opportunity by themselves to break the general pattern of class structure. Given the information age we live in, where knowledge is crucial, formal education should increase social mobility in the future; however, we cannot dismiss growing economic inequality, especially in an era where students are completing more school years. Students at the bottom of the social order tend to be "frozen" into the status of their parents, but for those who are able to escape (the percentage is small), the schools are the chief route for success.

Mayer and Peterson fuel the debate by arguing that both aptitude and achievement result in adult success. But *aptitude,* they argue, is more important because people who learn more quickly are more useful to their employers than people who learn slowly or with difficulty. Their model also assumes that "the entire school curriculum is a prolonged aptitude test, and that the specific skills and knowledge taught in school have no economic value," because people who easily learn Latin are the same people who can easily learn algebra and computer skills or master finance and banking skills.[33]

Most educators and policymakers prefer the *achievement model,* arguing that academic outcomes and schooling count, and what you know counts more than how hard you need to study to learn it. The theory is that, for this group, outcomes count more than the process. Similarly, math or verbal scores count because employers seek people who are versed in math or verbal skills, not because the scores are indicators of the workers' ability to learn something else. But Mayer and Peterson ask us to imagine two groups of adults with similar math (or verbal) scores: one with less math training but high aptitude and the other with better math training but low aptitude.

The achievement model assumes that both groups have equal opportunity to earn the same wages. The aptitude model assumes that the high-aptitude/less-math-trained group can learn more math in the long run and can also function better in other content areas and thus earn substantially more than the low-aptitude/better-math-trained group.[34] Most people have no problem with this analysis until we come to the realization that aptitude connotes heredity. Then, the conversation slows down or is stifled.

Mayer and Peterson further maintain that schools can exert considerable influence on a child's experiences, and these experiences have an effect on educational achievement. Before we go around modifying the school environment—that is, altering the classroom and instructional experiences for students—we need to know how much achievement would vary if we treated all children alike, then how assigning children with different aptitudes to different environments would alter the variance of achievement.[35] In this way, we could determine which alterations have the most influence, and how our resources can be earmarked to get the best results for improving achievement.

David Grissmer takes us to the final step in the debate about family and school characteristics, and the effect on achievement. He argues there is such a thing as family capital and social capital. *Family capital* refers to characteristics within the family passed from parent to child, the quality and quantity of resources within the family, and the allocation of these resources toward the child's education and socialization. *Social capital* refers to long-term capacities existing within the community and school district that affect achievement,

[33] Susan E. Mayer and Paul E. Peterson, *Earning and Learning: How Schools Matter* (Washington, DC: Brookings Institution, 1999).

[34] Ibid.

[35] Cheri P. Yecke, *The War Against Excellence* (Lanham, MD: Rowman & Littlefield, 2005); Mayer & Peterson, *Earning and Learning.*

such as peer group, parental trust in the community, the safety and support structure of the community, and the ability to support and pay for schools and social institutions (community centers, theaters, athletic clubs, etc.) within the community.[36]

He infers that family capital is more important than social capital, and we would firmly agree since the family doesn't change but the school and community can change (simply by moving) and the child's earliest experiences (which are essential) are rooted in the family. However, Grissmer points out that family and social capital are not independent, or randomly distributed, but are grouped together because of economics. "More social capital arises in communities and states having higher income and more educated families. Thus achievement scores across schools, communities, and states differ partly because their families differ in their internal capacity to produce achievement and partly because families with similar characteristics are grouped in communities or states creating different levels of social capital."[37] To put it in different words, high-income families tend to cluster together in high-income communities, which spend more money on schooling and have smaller classes and better-paid, more experienced teachers.

Do school characteristics by themselves shape academic outcomes? Very little. It's family and social capital differences that lead to academic differences. For instance, a review of the National Assessment of Educational Progress (NAEP) results, which now test fourth and eighth graders in forty-four states and are considered the best indicators we have for assessing national achievement, clearly shows that achievement levels are directly related to family and social characteristics across states and only a tiny portion is related to what schools do. Moreover, it is difficult to discern which school policies are successful because so many of the measures concerning school spending, classroom size, teacher education levels, and so on, are related to family and social capital. There is some indication that changes in school spending and classroom size count, but these results are too "inconsistent and unstable . . . to guide policy" and sometimes even based on "noncredible estimates."[38]

And what do the recent scores in Texas tell us? It is worth noting because President George W. Bush ran on his education record and boasted about statewide test scores in Texas while he was governor. On the surface, these scores inform us that teachers and schools can improve student performance and reduce differences in average scores among minority groups in only four years, thus bolstering the achievement model.

The "Texas Miracle," as it's often referred to, reveals upon closer examination intense test preparation in low-performing schools, large-scale cheating, and large numbers of students held back so that on the posttest they show more improvement than comparable students who passed to the next grade. Most important, each school selected the students and classrooms that would be tested, thus screening out low-performing students on the posttests.[39] This situation is not unique. Other teachers, schools, and school districts involved in high-stakes testing, and showing large-scale or sudden gains, usually reveal similar findings, which distort inferences from test score gains.[40] In a nutshell, it is very difficult to put stock in the results of any standardized test where stakes are high and scores rapidly increase, when claims are being made for the purpose of promoting a policy or program, or when black, Hispanic, and white scores are being compared.

## State Financing of Public Schools

Over the years, the states have delegated many powers and responsibilities to local school districts; nevertheless, each state remains legally responsible for educating its children and youth. Because many local school districts now have trouble financing their own schools through property taxes, states are expected to assume

---

[36]David Grissmer et al., *Improving Student Achievement* (Santa Monica, CA: Rand, 2000).

[37]Ibid, p. 18.

[38]Ibid, pp. 29, 31.

[39]Debra Viadero, "Candidates Spar Over Test Gains in Texas," *Education Week,* 1 November 2000, pp. 1, 30; Stephen P. Klein et al., "What Do Test Scores in Texas Tell Us?" *Issue Paper* (Santa Monica, CA: Rand, 2000); and W. James Popham, "Those Fill-in-the Blank Tests," *Educational Leadership,* 63 (2006): 85–86.

[40]David J. Hoff, "As Stakes Rise, Definition of Cheating Blurs," *Education Week,* 21 June 2000, pp. 1, 14–15; R. C. Johnston, "Texas Presses Districts in Alleged Test-Tampering Cases," *Education Week,* 17 March 1999, p. 22, 28; Jessica Portner, "Pressure to Pass Tests Permeates VA Classrooms," *Education Week,* 6 December 2000, pp. 1, 20; Erik W. Robelen, "Parents Seek Civil Rights Probe of High Stake Tests in LA," *Education Week,* 11 October 2000, p. 14. Also see Kenneth A. Strike, Emil J. Haller, and Jonas F. Soltis, *The Ethics of School Administration* (New York: Teachers College Press, 2005).

greater financial responsibility for and control over the schools.

The sales tax and personal income tax are the two major sources of revenue for states. Because states currently pay 49 percent of the cost of education, these two taxes are important elements in the overall support of public education. Since sales and personal income tax receipts vary with economic conditions and localities, schools sometimes seem to ride a revenue roller coaster. In the 1990s, most states felt the "boom" of the economy and had healthy sales and personal income taxes. Since September 11, there has been a major downturn in the economy.

## Sales Tax

Forty-six states have statewide sales taxes, with such taxes making up approximately 32.7 percent of state revenues.[41] Although the sales tax is considered a viable means for raising tax money for education, it may cause some economic distortions; for example, the difference in the tax rates may make it worthwhile to travel to the low-tax or no-tax state to purchase expensive items, which has generated a *use tax* among states. For example, if an automobile were purchased out of state, in order to *use* it the owner must pay what the sales tax would have been to register and license the car.

The sales tax meets the criterion of equity if food and medical prescriptions are removed from the tax base. If the tax is placed on all goods, however, low-income groups are penalized because they spend a large portion of their incomes on basic goods such as food and drugs. This measure has been moderated to some degree by the fact that many low-income people receive supplementary aid in buying food through the federal and state food stamp programs and aid in buying drugs and other medical assistance through Medicaid.

The sales tax is elastic because the revenue derived from it tends to parallel the economy. The trouble is, when the state (or nation) is in a recession, sales tax revenues decrease sufficiently to reduce the state's income. The tax is useful because relatively small changes in the rate result in large amounts of revenue, which can reduce or eliminate deficits. Recently, for example, a sales tax increase of two cents in Louisiana accounted

for $320 million, or more than 10 percent of the total state tax revenue.[42]

In 1970, the median sales tax was 3 percent, and only one state had a rate as high as 6 percent. By 1987, the median rate was 4.75 percent, and seven states had rates of 6 percent or higher. By 1994, the median was 6.1 percent and eight states had rates of 7.5 percent or higher. In 2000, the median had inched to 6.3 percent.[43] Since 1985, and well into the 1990s, rate increases were enacted to offset both the erosion of the sales tax base (especially in farm and energy states) and the fact that states have increasingly exempted food (thirty-five states) and drug (forty-six states) purchases from the tax base.[44]

As mentioned earlier, nearly every state was in fiscal crisis until 2005, forcing governors to take unpopular trimming measures. Health benefits now account for 30 percent of state spending, second to education, and it is likely that the next cut in spending at state levels will focus on employee health benefits and a leveling of school spending, especially in teacher salaries. The last recession, between 2000 and 2002, reduced state revenues so that the amount of money states had on hand at the end of fiscal year 2003 was 2.9 percent, the smallest cushion since 1992. Total state collections declined 6 percent from 2000 to 2002 and declined every quarter, even as spending grew by 1.3 percent per year.[45]

One expert, Abe Lackman, uses the metaphor of a storm to describe what has happened to state revenues. The states' fiscal future looks like a version of the book and movie about three storm systems all converging at once off the coast of New England, creating a meteorological nightmare.[46] In the book, the storm comes out of nowhere and it comes with an enormous buildup of speed and power; those affected are unable to prepare for the mounting crisis. The storm hit just about every

---

[41] Federation of Tax Administrators, "2005 State Tax Collection by Source" (http://www.taxadmin.org/fta/rate/05 taxdis .html); accessed on 28 December 2006.

[42] *State Tax Actions 2002* (Denver: National Conference on State Legislatures, 2002).

[43] *Bad Breaks All Around,* the Report of the Century Foundation Working Group on Tax Expenditures (Washington, DC: Brookings Institution, 2001).

[44] David Brunori, *The Future of State Taxation; Financing State Government in the 1990s* (Denver: National Conference of State Legislatures, 1993); Allan C. Ornstein, "State Financing of Public Schools: Policies and Prospects," *Urban Education,* 23 (1989): 188–207.

[45] Pear, "States Are Facing Big Fiscal Crisis, Governors Report."

[46] Joyce Purnick, "The Perfect Storm, Seen Heading for the Budget," *New York Times,* 20 November 2002, p. 16.

state with a ferocity that has not been witnessed by any reader of this text. One has to go back to the Depression to fully understand the impact of this storm: The fiscal crisis the states are in and the need to increase taxes (including personal and corporate) and cut spending will probably impact all state (and local) education budgets across the nation.

Although short lived, the recession represented a dramatic shift from years of robust growth that produced revenue windfalls and appeared to accommodate permanent policy changes that reduced revenues and increased spending. While most of the recession officially occurred in 2001, state revenue shortfalls were not realized until the end of fiscal year 2002, and state budgets did not begin substantial attempts to address the shortfalls until 2003. By 2003, more than 50 percent of the states cut capital budgets to fund operating budgets.[47] In 2003 half of all states cut spending for elementary and secondary education. By 2005 the states' fiscal picture had begun to turn around; however, state budgets continue to face fiscal pressure because of aging populations and the opposing pressures of tax reductions and greater expenditures.

What makes matters worse is that the states are facing increased education expenses, related to court decisions, voter initiatives, and requirements of the No Child Left Behind Act of 2001. Some states had also previously approved reduced class sizes, increased teacher pay, school construction, new tests, and new computer data systems for high-stake tests—all now in the midst of pressure from reduced budgets.[48] Ironically, critics are claiming that the states will pay more to implement the new act than the federal government's contribution, especially among small states and states with fewer disadvantaged or poor students.

## Personal Income Tax

The personal income tax is the second-largest source of tax revenue for the states. Only ten states do not levy a personal state income tax. Just as the sales tax rate varies among the states, from 2 percent to 8.75 percent, the state income tax (based on a percentage of personal income) also varies.[49]

A properly designed income tax should cause no economic distortions. Assuming no loopholes, it rates very high in terms of equity. In theory, the personal income tax is supposed to reflect the taxpayer's income and ability to pay. The income tax is also more equitable than other taxes because it considers special circumstances of the taxpayer—such as dependents, medical expenses, moving expenses, and the like—and uses tax deductions or credits to take into account these variations among individuals. It becomes less equitable only if the taxpayer has many items that can be deducted to minimize his income tax.

The personal income tax is very elastic; it allows the state government to vary rates (if it wishes) according to the economy. On the other hand, the elasticity of the income tax makes it vulnerable to recession because the revenue derived from it declines at a faster rate than revenue from other tax sources.

As a result of the 1986 Tax Reform Act, personal state taxes have become more progressive than they were formerly, owing to decreased property write-offs, standard deductions, and personal exemptions. The following year, 1987, a total of eleven states that formerly imposed taxes on poor families eliminated those taxes,[50] and in the 1990s several other states lightened taxes on poor and middle-class families. However, by 2002 state personal income tax revenues ($87.7 billion) were down 12.8 percent because of the recession, and the states were looking at ways to increase taxes—which unintentionally would impact more on the working and middle class than the upper class.[51]

## Lotteries and Other State Taxes

Other state taxes contribute limited amounts to education. These taxes include excise taxes on liquor and tobacco products; motor vehicle license taxes; estate and gift taxes; real estate transfer taxes; insurance premium

---

[47]*Ensuring the Future Prosperity of America: Addressing the Fiscal Future,* a report of the National Academy of Public Administration (Washington, DC: NAPA, November 2005), p. 24.

[48]Richard and Sack, "States Brace for Tough New Year"; Sack, "'No Child' Law Vies for Scarce State Resources," *Education Week,* 8 January 2003, pp. 16–17; Winnie Hu, "In Budget Fury, School Officials Seek New Ways to Save," *New York Times,* 23 March 2003, pp. A31, A34.

[49]*The Performance Budget Revisited: A Report on State Budget Reform* (Denver: National Conference of State Legislatures, 2004).

[50]*State Deficit Management Strategies* (Denver: National Conference of State Legislatures, 1987).

[51]Frank Bruni, "Bush Pushes Rule of Private Sector in Aiding the Poor," *New York Times,* 21 May 2001, pp. A1, A15; Pear, "States Facing Big Fiscal Crisis, Governors Report."

taxes; hotel taxes (readers who visit New York City can expect to pay a whopping 13.3 percent for hotel tax); and severance taxes (on the output of minerals and oils).[52] As of 1998, thirty-seven states levied a severance tax with several of them receiving more than 10 percent of their total tax revenues from that source: Alaska received 63 percent, Wyoming 30 percent, North Dakota 12 percent, and New Mexico 10 percent.[53]

A growing trend seeks to establish state lotteries to support education. In most of the states where lotteries exist, the lottery contributes from 2 to 5 percent of the total revenue. In 1997, sixteen states had lottery revenues earmarked for education; in thirteen states and the District of Columbia, lottery revenues support the general fund, which may or may not be used for the education program. In total, forty-four states and the District of Columbia now use the lottery. In addition to education and the general fund, lottery revenues are used for transportation, parks, recreation, pensions, prisons, economic development, environment, senior citizens, and property tax relief.

Some people are critical of this trend to use lotteries. Many educators see the general fund for education being reduced because lottery funds are available, often with the result that the state receives a smaller amount than was intended.[54] Some report that bond issues and other traditional revenue sources for education are diminished because the electorate has been led to believe that the lottery is taking care of education. Also, after money for prizes, marketing, and administration of the program has been subtracted, the net proceeds to public schools are only 10 to 15 percent of the money generated[55]—a fraction of the billions that were promised to voters. Lotteries are regressive because a higher proportion of low-income people play the lottery and spend larger percentages of their annual income on it.

This concern prompted the National Gambling Impact Study Commission to investigate state-operated lotteries. In a 1999 report to the commission, it was found that "a small number of poorer, less-educated people provide the lion's share of money for state lot-

teries. And states prod them to spend more by using ads that are somewhat misleading" in that they rarely fully disclose the long- shot odds of winning and by using ploys to make lotteries appear more winnable than they truly are. In detailing the issue the report states:

> Lottery spenders come disproportionately from poorer, less educated groups. Lottery players who have never graduated from high school spend an average of $700 a year on lotteries; high school graduate players spend $408; those who attended some college spend $210; and college graduates spend $178. Also, those players whose house-hold income is less than $10,000 spend $597 on average annually on lotteries, those making between $10,000 and $24,999 spend $589; those between $25,000 and $49,999 spend $382; those between $50,000 and $99,999 spend $225; and those making more than $100,000 spend $289.[56]

### The States' Ability to Finance Education

Some students are more fortunate than others, simply by geographic accident. State residence has a lot to do with the quality of education received. In 2003, as Table 11–3 shows, three states spent more than

---

**Table 11–3  Current Expenditures per Student in Public Schools K–12 by State (Highest and Lowest, 2003)**

| State/Highest | Expenditure per Student |
|---|---|
| District of Columbia | $14,419 |
| New Jersey | $13,884 |
| New York | $13,316 |
| Connecticut | $12,653 |
| Alaska | $11,896 |
| Delaware | $11,382 |

| State/Lowest | Expenditure per Student |
|---|---|
| Kentucky | $7,012 |
| Idaho | $6,978 |
| Tennessee | $6,962 |
| Oklahoma | $6,611 |
| Mississippi | $6,356 |
| Utah | $5,969 |
| **U.S. Average** | **$9,299** |

Source: *Digest of Education Statistics, 2005* (Washington, DC: U.S. Government Printing Office, 2006), derived from table 164, pp. 268–269.

---

[52] *State Fiscal Outlook for 1994* (Denver: National Conference of State Legislatures, 1994).

[53] U.S. Department of Commerce, Bureau of Census (www.census.gov/govs/www/statetax.htm/scrollstatest-53).

[54] Erik Calonius, "The Big Payoff from Lotteries," *Fortune*, 25 March 1991, p. 109.

[55] *Earmarking State Taxes*, 3rd ed. (Denver: National Conference of State Legislatures, 1994); Kathleen Vail, "Eleven Ways to Make Money," *School Administrator*, 185 (1998): 30–33.

[56] Lee Davidson, "Poor, Less Educated Pay Most of Lottery Revenue," *The Deseret News*, 20 March 1999, pp. A1, A3.

**Table 11–4**   Current Expenditures per Student in Public Schools K–12 by State (Highest and Lowest, 2003) with Percent of Revenue from Federal, State, Local, and Private Source

| State/Highest | Expenditure | % Federal | % State | % Local | % Private |
|---|---|---|---|---|---|
| District of Columbia | $14,419 | 13.8 | NA | 85.5 | 0.8 |
| New Jersey | $13,884 | 4.3 | 43.5 | 50.1 | 2.1 |
| New York | $13,316 | 7.0 | 45.6 | 46.6 | 0.8 |
| Connecticut | $12,653 | 5.2 | 37.4 | 55.8 | 1.6 |
| Alaska | $11,896 | 17.7 | 56.8 | 23.3 | 2.2 |
| Delaware | $11,382 | 8.6 | 63.4 | 26.8 | 1.2 |
| Mean/Highest | $12,925 | 9.4 | 49.3 | 48.0 | 1.5 |
| **State/Lowest** | **Expenditure** | **% Federal** | **% State** | **% Local** | **% Private** |
| Kentucky | $7,012 | 10.6 | 58.8 | 28.5 | 2.1 |
| Idaho | $6,978 | 9.8 | 59.1 | 29.5 | 1.6 |
| Tennessee | $6,962 | 10.0 | 43.8 | 39.6 | 6.6 |
| Oklahoma | $6,611 | 12.7 | 54.7 | 27.6 | 5.0 |
| Mississippi | $6,356 | 15.4 | 53.8 | 27.8 | 3.0 |
| Utah | $5,969 | 9.3 | 56.4 | 32.3 | 2.0 |
| Mean/Lowest | $6,648 | 11.3 | 54.4 | 30.9 | 3.4 |
| U.S. Average | $9,299 | 8.5 | 48.7 | 40.5 | 2.3 |

Source: *Digest of Education Statistics, 2005* (Washington, DC: U.S. Government Printing Office, 2006), derived from table 164, pp. 268–269 and table 153, p. 253.

$12,500 per student, namely New Jersey ($13,884), New York ($13,316), and Connecticut ($12,653), while five states—Idaho ($6978), Tennessee ($6962), Oklahoma ($6611), Mississippi ($6356), and Utah ($5969)—spent less than $7000 per student.

It is incorrect to assume that, based on dollars only, the education priorities of some states are higher than are the priorities of other states. But we must ask what the states can afford, and this has a lot to do with the personal income of the states' inhabitants. Also, we must ask what the states spend on all other services and functions (such as social, housing, transportation, and medical outlays). In the first case, we are able to get a good idea of the states' financial ability to fund education; in the second case, we can determine the states' priorities.

For example, the six states with the lowest expenditures per student (Table 11–4) received on average 54.4 percent of its school revenues from the state, whereas the six states with the highest expenditures per student averaged 49.3 percent of its revenues from the state (also see Table 11–4), suggesting an inverse relationship between ability and priority to fund education at the state level.

The ability to finance education is also associated with regional attitudes toward education. For example, eleven out of twelve states in the Southeast, all four states in the Southwest, and six out of seven Mountain West states spent less money on education per student than the national average ($9299) in 2003. The states in the Southeast and Southwest comprise most of the Sunbelt region, which tends to be more politically conservative and spends less money per capita in human services than the Frostbelt region. In contrast, in the Northeast (which represents more than half the Frostbelt), all eleven states spent more money per student than the national average.[57]

Historically, the Northeast and Midwest (or Frostbelt region) have been net losers in the tax burden borne and monies received back from the federal government in terms of programs, contracts, and assistance.[58]

---

[57] *Digest of Education Statistics, 2005,* table 153, p. 253.

[58] Daphne A. Kenyon and John Kincaid, *Competition among States and Local Governments* (Washington, DC: Urban Institute, 1995); Allan C. Ornstein, "Decline of the Frostbelt," *Dissent,* 30 (1983): 366–374.

In order to help finance education and other public services, the states are embracing three different types of budget reforms. Some, such as Minnesota, Oregon, and Utah, are thinking beyond the present budget cycle and revising spending policy in terms of long-range planning. A second type of reform is more immediate, focusing on efficiency and effectiveness of current services. Texas is a prime example. A third type of reform is managerial, whereby lawmakers are reducing staff and also allowing administrators to reallocate appropriated sums as conditions merit. California, Massachusetts, and Mississippi are moving in this direction.[59]

## State Financial Responsibility

State funding of education is largely based on a mixture of **discretionary funding**—that is, subjective criteria based on need or eligibility requirements—and **formula funding**, whereby all recipients are treated equally and the role of the administrator is merely ministerial. Over the years, the several states have used a variety of funding patterns. Presently many states have established a policy that individual students will be given an *authorized amount* of financial support regardless of where they live within the state. States have different procedures by which that authorized amount is collected.

### State Funding Methods

States use six basic methods to finance public education. Some states combine more than one method.

1. *Flat-Grant Model.* This is the oldest, simplest, and most unequal method of financing schools. State aid to local school districts is based on a fixed amount multiplied by the number of students in attendance. It does not consider the special needs of students (bilingual students are more expensive to educate than native English-speaking students), special programs (vocational programs are more expensive than regular programs), or the wealth of the school districts (wealthy school districts have more money to spend on students or schools than do-less wealthy school districts).

   In most states, the distribution of education funds is based on some type of equalization plan designed to provide extra money for less wealthy

school districts. The remaining methods (except 6) each seek to bring about greater equality of educational opportunity by allocating more funds to the school districts in greatest need of assistance.

2. *Foundation Plan.* This is the most common approach, and its purpose is to guarantee a minimum annual expenditure per student for all school districts in the state, irrespective of local taxable wealth. However, the minimum level is usually considered too low by reformers, and wealthy school districts far exceed the minimum levels. School districts with a high percentage of low-income students suffer under this plan.

3. *Power-Equalizing Plan.* This is a more recent plan, and many of the states have adopted some form of it. Under this scheme, the state pays a percentage of the local school expenditures in inverse ratio to the wealth of the district. Although the school district has the right to establish its own expenditure levels, wealthier school districts are given fewer matching state dollars. The program is constrained by lower and upper limits, and the matching dollars are insufficient for poor school districts. In the end, the equalization effect is usually insufficient.

4. *Guaranteed-Tax Base Plan.* The guaranteed-tax plan has the same economic philosophy as the power-equalizing plan, that is, equalizing fiscal capacity and expenditures as much as possible. This is accomplished by determining an assessed valuation per student, which the state guarantees to the local school district. State aid becomes the difference between what the district raises per student and what the state guarantees per student.

5. *Weighted-Student Plan.* Students are weighted in proportion to their special characteristics (i.e., handicapped, disadvantaged, etc.) or special programs (e.g., vocational or bilingual) to determine the cost of instruction per student. For example, a state may provide $9000 for each student in a basic program, whereas the state contribution per student may be 1.3 times higher, or $11,700, for vocational education and 1.5 times higher, or $13,500, for a learning disabled student.

6. *Choice and Voucher Plans.* Some states allow parents more choice in selecting which school their children will attend, even using a financial voucher to attend a nonpublic school. The actions are controversial and court decisions are also varied but seem to allow the practice. Low-performing schools, especially those taken over by the state in the past, have become "guinea pigs" for the private

---

[59]Myron Orfield, *American Metropolitics: Social Separation and Sprawl* (Washington, DC: Brookings Institution, 2002); *The Performance Budget Revisited.*

## Administrative Advice 11–1

### Checklist for Developing a School Budget

A budget is a financial plan that reflects the local needs of the school (or school district), its history, and its fiscal health. A number of state and local factors such as past practices, state/local codes and regulations, and board policies influence the process, format, and contents. Below is a general checklist for administrators to adapt and use when organizing their own budget.

| Process: Conducting the Hearings | Yes | No |
| --- | --- | --- |
| 1. Roles of board and superintendent clearly defined | ☐ | ☐ |
| 2. Board financial policies updated regularly | ☐ | ☐ |
| 3. Accuracy and timeliness of all financial data | ☐ | ☐ |
| 4. Adequate staff involvement in budget request | ☐ | ☐ |
| 5. Adequate public hearings and citizen participation | ☐ | ☐ |
| 6. Budget document (or summary) widely distributed | ☐ | ☐ |
| 7. Compliance with legal requirements | ☐ | ☐ |
| 8. Community/political support generated for budget | ☐ | ☐ |
| 9. Contingency strategy for cuts (budget options) | ☐ | ☐ |
| 10. Efficient accounting/financial reporting system | ☐ | ☐ |

| Format: Organizing the Document | | |
| --- | --- | --- |
| 11. Attractive cover, title page, overall appearance | ☐ | ☐ |
| 12. Table of contents or index; numbered pages | ☐ | ☐ |
| 13. Names of board members, officers listed | ☐ | ☐ |
| 14. Table of organization, administrators listed | ☐ | ☐ |
| 15. Budget message or letter of transmittal | ☐ | ☐ |
| 16. Graphics-artwork charts, figures, tables | ☐ | ☐ |
| 17. Clarity of style; avoidance of technical jargon | ☐ | ☐ |
| 18. Manageable size and shape of document | ☐ | ☐ |
| 19. Glossary of key terms | ☐ | ☐ |
| 20. Concise executive summary ("budget-in-brief") | ☐ | ☐ |

*(continued)*

management of public education, with the Edison Company obtaining most of the contracts.[60]

## School Budgeting

Budgeting is both an executive and a legislative function. The executive entity (superintendent and staff at the district level, principal and/or assistant at the school level) proposes and the legislative entity (board of education) enacts. On formal adoption by the school board,

the budget becomes a legal document that serves as the basis for annual expenditures, accounting, and auditing. According to financial school experts, five major steps are involved in budgeting: preparation, submission, adoption, execution, and evaluation. The third step, adoption, involves the school board, through which it appropriates specific amounts for specific categories. The other four steps involve the superintendent, business manager, and/or principal.[61]

---

[60]Glenn Cook, "Searching for Miracles," *American School Board Journal,* 188 (2001): 18–23; Chester Finn and Marci Kanstoroom, "Do Charter Schools Do It Differently?" *Phi Delta Kappan,* 84 (2002): 59–62.

[61]Fenwick W. English (ed.), *Encyclopedia of Educational Leadership and Administration* (Thousand Oaks, CA: Sage, 2006), Vol. 1; Kenneth Leithwood et al., *Making Schools Smarter: Leading with Evidence* (Thousand Oaks, CA: Corwin Press, 2006).

---

## Administrative Advice 11–1 (continued)

| Contents: Compiling the Data | Yes | No |
|---|:---:|:---:|
| 21. Political feasibility of bottom-line request | ☐ | ☐ |
| 22. School system goals and objectives | ☐ | ☐ |
| 23. Budget assumptions, guidelines, or priorities | ☐ | ☐ |
| 24. Object budget summary (e.g., salaries, supplies) | ☐ | ☐ |
| 25. Program budget summary (e.g., reading, math) | ☐ | ☐ |
| 26. Site budget summary (e.g., individual schools) | ☐ | ☐ |
| 27. Budget history (expenditures for past five years) | ☐ | ☐ |
| 28. Unit-cost analysis (per-pupil expenditures) | ☐ | ☐ |
| 29. Summary of estimated revenues (all sources) | ☐ | ☐ |
| 30. Explanation of impact on tax rates | ☐ | ☐ |
| 31. Explanation of major cost factors (contracts, inflation) | ☐ | ☐ |
| 32. Budget coding system explained (chart of accounts) | ☐ | ☐ |
| 33. Performance measures program outcomes; test data | ☐ | ☐ |
| 34. Pupil enrollment projections by grade | ☐ | ☐ |
| 35. Staffing history and projections | ☐ | ☐ |
| 36. Long-range plans (five years) for the school system | ☐ | ☐ |
| 37. Justification for major decisions (layoffs, school closing) | ☐ | ☐ |
| 38. Comparisons with other districts (or with state averages) | ☐ | ☐ |
| 39. Capital budget summary (capital improvement projects) | ☐ | ☐ |
| 40. Budget detail (line-item expenditure data) | ☐ | ☐ |

Source: Adapted from Harry J. Hartley, "Checklist for Evaluating Local School Budgets," *American School Board Journal*, 46 (1989): 36. Copyright 1989, the National School Boards Association. Used by permission.

---

Typically, the annual budget is organized around four major categories: objects (e.g., salaries, supplies, travel), functions (e.g., instruction, transportation, plant), programs (e.g., English, math, gifted education), and location (school, group of schools, or district). The state usually mandates the items for objects and functions, whereas the school district usually develops the items for programs and locations. The budget may also include other features such as a list of goals, objectives, or criteria; projected revenues from all local, state, and federal sources; comparison of expenditures for last year by categories; the amount needed to pay the principal and interest for the school bonds maturing during the fiscal year; and a budget summary. (See Administrative Advice 11–1.)

Although the major responsibility for submitting a budget rests with superintendents and their staffs, depending on the superintendent's management style the school principal's role in budgeting may be limited or substantial. A superintendent who maintains a highly centralized administration will most likely limit the principal's input in budgeting to filling out requisitions, receipts, and disbursements. A superintendent who believes in a decentralized administration, site budgeting, or school-based management will probably delegate more budget responsibility to the principal.[62]

Regardless of the amount of professional empowerment, the school staff must understand that only 5 to 10 percent of the district's budget is available for modification: 60 to 70 percent is earmarked for salaries and benefits; 15 to 25 percent is for operating expenses such as utilities, water, insurance, repairs, and mainte-

---

[62]Lars G. Bjork and Theodore J. Kowalski (eds.), *The Contemporary Superintendent* (Thousand Oaks, CA: Corwin Press, 2005); Jerry Patterson, "Harsh Realities About Decentralized Decision Making," *School Administrator*, 55 (1998): 6–13.

nance; and another 5 to 10 percent should be committed to reserves and replacement. Although the school principal (and staff) may be permitted to make budget recommendations, the school board finalizes the budget.

The principal's budgeting roles can be classified into four major activities: (1) *budget planning,* assisting the superintendent in identifying budget priorities and focusing on school needs at the planning stage; (2) *budget analysis,* dealing with goals, objectives, and evaluative criteria, suggestions for curriculum materials and instructional equipment, and communicating concerns of the students, teachers, parents, and community about specific expenditures or special purposes; (3) *budget requesting,* involving a review of requests by different groups such as teachers or parents, establishing program priorities, submitting a total budget, and negotiating specific items; and (4) *budget controls,* dealing with inventory expenses, receipts and disbursements, monthly reporting, and balancing the books at the building level.[63] (The fourth activity deals with the regular operation of the school and involves ongoing paperwork and record keeping.)

In large elementary schools, a person (perhaps the assistant principal or a teacher) representing a program area or grade level, and in secondary schools a department head, is usually asked to list needs in order of priority. If it becomes necessary to reduce school budgets because of cutbacks, the trimming process usually begins with the low-priority programs or items. Ultimately the principal submits the budget to the central office, and it is either approved or modified, sometimes through negotiation with the principal and sometimes without negotiation. Eventually, an approved budget is returned to the principal. Each month a person at the program or department level may be required to fill out requisitions and purchase orders; each month a budget summary to date may be returned by the business manager or financial officer at the district level to the principal and/or department or program level, indicating the amount of money remaining in each account item.

The principal is usually required to submit a monthly budget to the central office, which includes several income and expense categories. Depending on the accounting system adopted by the school district, the budget items may include receipts, vouchers, bank statements, a method for authorizing expenditures, expenditures paid only by check, a regular audit, and monthly and annual reporting.[64]

A word of caution is needed. Whether the budget is being prepared on a school district or school level, school leaders must be responsible and guard against faddism and wasting money on unproven programs, methods, or other phenomena that have an inadequate research base or limited history of empirical success. Too many programs and concepts in education expand on the basis of testimonial data or on ideas that are considered "innovative" or "reform-oriented" after appearing in the popular educational journals.

Why some educational leaders jump onto popular bandwagons and spend large sums of money in the absence of hard data is difficult to answer. One possible explanation involves "popularism" and "pressure" as pendulums swing and impulses take on a life of their own. Common sense shows that, before administrators adopt a program on a large scale, pilot testing is needed and the program must be evaluated in school settings as if the district were thinking about investing money in the program or practice.[65] The emphasis must shift from what's new to *what works.*

## School Effectiveness and Productivity

There are few agreed-on indicators to determine the ideal (or most efficient) size of schools or to determine whether a school is effective. Just what is a productive, or well-run, school? When do decision makers at the local or state level know that they are getting their money's worth in a school? The indicators are extremely fuzzy, but we will take positions to help clarify the data.

[63]L. Joseph Matthews and Gary M. Crow, *Being and Becoming a Principal* (Boston: Allyn and Bacon, 2003); Anthony G. Picciano, *Data-Driven Decision Making for Effective School Leadership* (Columbus, OH: Merrill, 2006).

[64]Walter G. Hack, Carl Candoli, and John R. Ray, *School Business Administration,* 6th ed. (Needham Heights, MA: Allyn and Bacon, 1998); Richard D. Sorenson and Lloyd M. Goldsmith, *The Principal's Guide to School Budgeting* (Thousand Oaks, CA: Corwin Press, 2006).

[65]See Lee G. Bolman and Terrance E. Deal, *Reframing the Path to School Leadership* (Thousand Oaks, CA: Corwin Press, 2002); Michael Fullan, *What's Worth Fighting for in the Principalship* (New York: Teachers College Press, Columbia University, 1997).

## Size of Schools

Educators have long debated the optimal size for an individual school in terms of efficiency and student outcomes. A school is considered too small where underutilization of staff and curriculum occurs and when the operating unit cost per student exceeds the average cost in the state. A school is considered too large when a loss of personal or school identity among students occurs: They are unable to fully participate in social and athletic activities or have difficulty interacting among themselves or feel they do not belong to the student body or school in general.[66] An overlarge school causes a sense of aimlessness, isolation, even despair among a large number of students—which in turn causes other social and psychological problems (such as delinquency, drugs, and cults) that are more overt in nature.

In terms of numbers, 15 percent of public elementary schools are considered too small (fewer than 200 students), and 12 percent are too large (over 800 students). As many as 27 percent of the public secondary schools are too small (under 300 students) and as many as 14 percent are too large (over 1500 students); moreover, 1.2 percent of the secondary schools enroll 3000 or more students.[67]

Conventional wisdom has maintained that large schools were more efficient and offered more diversified opportunities for students. This thinking was derived from Raymond Callahan's "cult of efficiency," which associated bigness with growth and productive efficiency and greater opportunity to specialize. It is also based on James Conant's description of the American high school during a period of school consolidation, in which he promulgated the need for large "comprehensive" high schools (comprising graduating classes of 100 students or more) and considered small high schools problematic in terms of lack of special facilities and subjects as well as economically wasteful.[68]

Large schools were considered well organized and offering something for everyone, as well as a means for promoting integration and democratic values among students of varied backgrounds under one roof. Whatever strengths small schools had—a sense of community, minimum bureaucracy, and curriculum offerings that coincided with the "core curriculum" (four years of English and history; three years of science and math; and two or three years of a foreign language)—were overlooked.[69]

In sparsely populated areas, with small schools, educational opportunities in part can be equalized with technological innovations: two-way interactive television, cable and satellite networks, the Internet, and various regional networks involving course offerings over vast portions of a state. Data suggest that it takes three to five weeks for teachers to make the necessary adjustment in "electronic education" while it takes high school students two or three days. Some in-service training is needed for teachers.[70]

Sociological data strongly suggest that small schools (K–12) are often considered part, even the hub, of a homogeneous neighborhood where parental involvement and school-community relations are high. Parental pressure is often felt in the school, teacher expectations are felt in the home, and people in small, homogeneous communities tend to cooperate in school and civic activities; in fact, social life often centers on school and community activities.

As larger schools are divided into smaller and smaller unit sizes, students have the potential to play an increased role in school-community functions. Students in small schools have a better chance to participate in leadership roles and extracurricular activities, especially the high-status ones such as student government, student newspaper, school band, and numerous athletics. They also have a better chance for academic recognition, based on the fact that they are competing with fewer students on a districtwide or schoolwide

[66]Allan C. Ornstein, "Private and Public School Comparisons," *Education and Urban Society,* 21 (1989): 192–206; Ornstein, "School Size and Effectiveness: Policy Implications," *Urban Review,* 22 (1990): 239–245.

[67]*Digest of Education Statistics, 2005,* table 92, p. 164.

[68]Raymond Callahan, *Education and the Cult of Efficiency* (Chicago: University of Chicago Press, 1962); James B. Conant, *The American High School Today* (New York: McGraw-Hill, 1959).

[69]Deborah Meier, "As Though They Owned the Place: Small Schools as Membership Communities," *Phi Delta Kappan,* 87 (2006): 657–662; Nel Noddings, "What Does it Mean to Educate the Whole Child." *Educational Leadership,* 63 (2005): 8–13; Mary A. Raywid, "Small Schools: Themes That Serve Schools Well," *Phi Delta Kappan,* 87 (2006): 654–656.

[70]Kari Arfstrom, "Overlooked Too Long, Small Schools Deserve Our Attention," *School Administrator,* 56 (1999): 50; Mary Burns, "From Compliance to Commitment: Technology as a Catalyst for . . . Learning," *Phi Delta Kappan,* 84 (2002): 295–302.

basis.[71] Moreover, the sociopsychological benefits of recognition and affiliation, and the result in terms of self-concept and motivation for achievement, are well documented in the social and educational literature.

Large schools, according to the authors, exclude students, teachers, parents, and community members from curriculum development, and the curriculum becomes centralized and standardized by the administrative hierarchy. Large high schools win state championships in sports and national recognition in academic scholarships, and they also have impressive bands and student papers. Yet with the exception of a few talented ball players, scholars, and social elites, most students don't participate or receive recognition from their teachers or counselors; thus, the costs for these extra facilities and activities are high (and dysfunctional) per student.

In this connection, Thomas Gregory and Gerald Smith argue that school size, school structure, and community life are interrelated and should be seriously considered in the school reform literature. After a review of several studies, they recommend a high school size of no more than 250 students because larger enrollments mentally result in a counterproductive preoccupation with control and order, and anonymity works against the concept of sharing ideas and working together in cognitive and social learning. As for the *structure,* the authors are concerned with governance and how space, time, and people are organized—in small schools these kinds of arrangements are more supportive and positive to human functioning. By *community,* Gregory and Smith are concerned with the bonding of people—commitment and morale among students, teachers, and parents—and a feeling of a stake in the school and a place to live and find meaning in the community. This sense of community is more easily obtained in small schools that are located in the small towns and villages of America.[72]

With the exception of one study by Richard and Patricia Schmuck (they visited eighty small schools in twenty-five small districts) who claim to have observed small schools to be "regimented and authoritarian" and run by few well-educated board members, small schools in most other studies correlate with effective schools in terms of management, spending, and achievement. They get more results than big schools (and school districts) for less money.[73]

The characteristics of "large" appear to consistently connote negative descriptors, at least a "less satisfying" school experience.[74] Children, even adults, get lost in large organizations; they easily fall through the cracks, unless they are special. Because most students (and adults) are average but still prefer to make the team or excel in front of their peers, they have a better chance of being recognized (and feeling good about themselves) when the numbers are fewer and the surroundings are more familiar. Large schools tend to be more expensive per student than smaller ones because of increased bureaucracy, staff support, and extra curriculum and instructional offerings, but student outcomes (even when social class is held constant) appear to be higher in small schools.

Research now shows that oversized schools are actually a detriment to student achievement, especially for poor children. Even assuming that larger schools did equate to more fiscal efficiency, diverse curriculum, and extracurricular activities, those factors have rarely translated into better student achievement. In fact, the research is pretty clear on this point: Smaller schools help promote learning. And, contrary to the prevailing wisdom, research shows that small schools are able to offer a strong core curriculum and, except in extremely small schools, a nearly comparable level of academically advanced courses. Rotherham also states:

> Additional research has shown that students from smaller schools have better attendance, and that when students move from large schools to smaller ones their attendance improves. Smaller schools also have lower dropout rates and fewer discipline problems. Behavior problems are so much greater in larger schools that any possible virtue of

[71]Philip A. Cusick, *Inside High School* (New York: Holt, Rinehart, 1973); Sara Lawrence Lightfoot, *The Good High School* (New York: Basic Books, 1983); Andrew Rotherham, "When It Comes to School Size, Smaller Is Better," *Education Week,* 24 February 1999, p. 76. Also see Alfie Kohn, *The Schools Our Children Deserve* (Boston: Houghton Mifflin, 1999); Kohn, *Unconditioned Parenting* (New York: Atria Books, 2005).

[72]Thomas B. Gregory and Gerald R. Smith, *High Schools as Communities: The Small School Reconsidered* (Bloomington, IN: Phi Delta Kappan Educational Foundation, 1987).

[73]Richard A. Schmuck and Patricia A. Schmuck, *Small Districts, Big Problems* (Newbury, CA: Corwin Press, 1992).

[74]John I. Goodlad, *A Place Called School* (New York: McGraw-Hill, 1984); Goodlad, *Educational Renewal* (San Francisco: Jossey-Bass, 1998); Milbrey W. McLaughlin and Joan E. Talbert, *Building School-Based Teacher Learning Communities* (New York: Teachers College Press, 2006).

larger size is canceled out by the difficulties of maintaining an orderly learning environment.[75]

Not only are larger schools less safe, they are also less efficient and more expensive because their sheer size requires more administrative support. More important, additional bureaucracy translates into less flexibility and innovation.[76] Research shows that economically advantaged students can achieve in larger schools. Paradoxically, it is underprivileged students who are likely to be concentrated in oversized schools.

## Effective Schools

A powerful and long-term commitment is required to bring about substantial, widespread, and enduring gains in the performance of students. Attention must be paid to the school as an institution and, in the final analysis, to the larger context of the school district and the environment in which schools operate. The effectiveness of the school as a whole helps determine what happens in each classroom. In the words of one observer, "School performance is unlikely to be significantly improved by any measure or set of measures that fails to recognize that schools are institutions"— complex organizations composed of interdependent parts, "governed by well-established rules and norms of behavior, and adapted for stability."[77] Money does not seem to be the key or secret ingredient; rather, a number of intangible items that promote school effectiveness and productivity seem to coincide with school climate or culture.

Most of the recent research on **effective schools** has focused on elementary education. Authors of various studies generally have identified specific characteristics of effective elementary schools and have usually defined effectiveness at least partly in terms of outstanding student achievement. One of the best-known studies is that of Ronald Edmonds and his colleagues, who

defined an effective school as one in which lower-class students score as high as middle-class students on basic skills tests. Based on analysis of such schools, Edmonds identified an effective school as one in which there is strong leadership, an orderly, humane climate, frequent monitoring of students' progress, high expectations and requirements for all students, and focus on teaching important skills to all students.[78]

Other observers and groups frequently extend this type of list to include one or more additional characteristics. A good example is the analysis used by the Connecticut School Effectiveness Project, which describes an effective school as having the following characteristics:

1. *A safe and orderly environment* that is not oppressive and is conducive to teaching and learning.

2. *A clear school mission* through which the staff shares a commitment to instructional goals, priorities, assessment procedures, and accountability.

3. *Instructional leadership* by a principal who understands and applies the characteristics of instructional effectiveness.

4. *A climate of high expectations* in which the staff demonstrates that all students can attain mastery of basic skills.

5. *High time on task* brought about when a high percentage of students' time is spent "engaged" in planned activities to master basic skills.

6. *Frequent monitoring of student progress,* using the results to improve individual performance and the instructional program.

7. *Positive home-school relations* in which parents support the school's basic mission and play an important part in helping to achieve it.[79]

Several individuals and agencies have gone even further in refining and modifying research to identify characteristics of unusually effective schools. Besides the characteristics highlighted by earlier studies, Lawrence Stedman's research has emphasized several other key features of effective schools, including (1) attention

[75]Rotherham, "When It Comes to School Size, Smaller Is Better," p. 76.

[76]Tom Vander Ark, "The Case for Small High Schools," *Educational Leadership,* 59 (2002): 55–59; Mary Anne Raywid, "The Policy Environments of Small Schools and Schools-within-Schools," *Educational Leadership,* 59 (2002): 47–54.

[77]John E. Chubb, "Why the Current Wave of School Reform Will Fail," *Public Interest,* 90 (1988): 29. Also see John E. Chubb, *Within Our Reach: How America Can Educate Every Child* (Lanham, MD: Rowman & Littlefield, 2005).

[78]Ronald R. Edmonds, "Programs of School Improvement: An Overview," *Educational Leadership,* 40 (1982): 4–11; Edmonds, "Characteristics of Effective Schools," in U. Neiser (ed.), *The School Achievement of Minority Children* (Hillsdale, NJ: Erlbaum, 1986), pp. 89–111.

[79]Ornstein, *Teaching and Schooling in America: Pre- and Post-September 11.*

to goals involving cultural pluralism and multicultural education, and (2) emphasis on responding to students' personal problems and developing their social skills.[80] Other educators have stressed cooperation between educators and parents and parental participation in school decision making; their theories and policies are being used to guide projects in New Haven, Baltimore, and some other school districts.[81]

Among the actions and changes that appear to help at-risk students, according to still other researchers, are the following:

1. Emphasis on reading and language development programs, and willingness to remediate reading failure as soon as possible, since reading and academic success are linked together.

2. Remedial and tutoring programs in all subject areas — before school starts, after school, and even Saturday sessions.

3. Daily homework assignments that are monitored by teachers.

4. Strict discipline enforced.

5. Teachers required to participate in staff development programs that help them diagnose student problems and modify instruction according to student needs.

6. Teachers required to visit the home of absentees and students receiving a D or an F.

7. Teachers and schools that nurture character, encourage civility, foster responsibility, and build character — what some might call "old-fashioned" values.[82]

## Effective School Indicators

Criteria of effectiveness for schools emphasize student achievement scores. Some of the indicators commonly assessed include (1) a comparison of expected levels of student achievement with current levels of achievement; (2) analysis of levels of student achievement in a prior grade compared with that in the present grade; (3) a comparison of achievement scores between similar schools, sometimes after controlling for family income or social class; (4) a comparison of subgroups of students by gender, race, and social class; and (5) an analysis of grading inflation and how it skews achievement levels. High schools can also analyze or compare student participation and achievement in advanced placement courses or honors classes, student achievement by programs or courses, high school graduation, and college acceptance.[83]

Other indicators might include attitudes and levels of satisfaction among students, staff, parents, and community residents, as well as previously mentioned characteristics such as clear academic goals, order and discipline, focus on academic learning time, remedial and tutoring programs, teacher morale, staff development, administrative leadership, and community support.

Almost all these criteria involve little or no extra money; rather, they require changes in school climate or school culture that can be induced by school leadership and changes in school structure. Judgment or basis for success can be discussed on the school district, school, or grade level. Site visitors, superintendents, or school principals can use these comparisons as a yardstick for their own reporting.

Table 11–5 illustrates indicators for judging school effectiveness at the elementary, junior high school, and high school levels. The elementary indicators are based on the North Central Association's guide for self-study and team visits in evaluating successful schools. The junior high and high school indicators are based on the U.S. Department of Education's Secondary School Recognition Program, which identified 202 effective secondary schools. Whereas the elementary school indicators tend to mix cognitive and affective outcomes, the secondary school indicators are more achievement and social oriented. The elementary school indicators go beyond students and also look at staff, parents, and the community; the secondary school indicators focus on students and their performance.

[80] Lawrence Stedman, "The Effective Schools Formula Still Needs Changing," *Phi Delta Kappan,* 69 (1988): 439–442.

[81] James P. Comer et al., *Child By Child* (New York: Teachers College Press, Columbia University, 1999); Robert E. Slavin, "Putting the School Back in School Reform," *Educational Leadership,* 58 (2000): 22–27.

[82] Richard L. Allington and Patricia M. Cunningham, *Schools That Work* (Bloomington, IN: Phi Delta Kappan Educational Foundation, 2002); Roland S. Barth, *Lessons Learned* (Thousand Oaks, CA: Corwin Press, 2003); and Linda Darling-Hammond, *The Right to Learn* (San Francisco: Jossey-Bass, 2001).

[83] Larry Cuban, *How Can I Fix It?* (New York: Teachers College Press, Columbia University, 2001); Carl D. Glickman, *Renewing America's Schools* (San Francisco: Jossey-Bass, 1998); Harris Sokoloff, *School Reform and the Rebuilding of Social Capital* (New York: Doubleday, 1997).

## Table 11–5 Indicators for Judging School Effectiveness

| Elementary School Indicators | Junior High/Middle School Indicators | High School Indicators |
|---|---|---|
| 1. Scores on norm-reference tests | 1. Student performance on standard achievement tests | 1. Student performance on standard achievement tests |
| 2. Scores on criterion-reference tests | 2. Student performance on minimum-competency tests | 2. Student performance on minimum-competency tests |
| 3. Scores on teacher-made tests, writing samples, and other "nonobjective" measures | 3. Student success in high school | 3. Numbers of students who go on to postsecondary education, enlist in the military, or find employment |
| 4. Valid measures of affective outcomes such as self-concept | 4. Daily student and teacher attendance rates | 4. Daily student and teacher attendance rates |
| 5. Teacher (and administrator) opinions of student goal attainment | 5. Rates of student suspensions and other exclusions | 5. Rates of suspensions and other exclusions |
| 6. Opinions of students, parents, and community residents | 6. Awards for outstanding school programs and teaching | 6. Student awards in academic or vocational competition |
| 7. Participation of students in extracurricular activities | 7. Student awards in academic or vocational competitions | 7. Awards for outstanding school programs |
| 8. Student awards and distinctions | | 8. Percentage of students enrolled in advanced education subjects and/or scored above 3 on placement exams |
| 9. Attendance | | |
| 10. Amount of material borrowed from media center or library | | |
| 11. Quality of student performance in programs such as art, music, and drama | | |
| 12. Community support organizations devoted to school programs | | |

Source: Adapted from Allan C. Ornstein, *Teaching and Schooling in America: Pre- and Post-September 11* (Boston: Allyn and Bacon, 2003), p. 474.

## School Finance Trends

A number of monetary trends, which have direct meaning for administrators, are affecting schools. As we examine those trends, we should note that the notions of "equal educational opportunity" and "egalitarianism" are no longer the focus of attention as in the 1970s, 1980s, and early 1990s. Today, the focus is on "excellence," "efficiency," and "productivity." Budgets today are leaner and meaner, and less real money (after accounting for inflation) is earmarked for schools. Despite increased national productivity, there is less real money to split up among all public groups and sectors of the economy; moreover, the growing elderly population is demanding more of the economic pie—at the expense of children and youth. For example, since 1980 the economic well-being of the elderly has improved while the well-being of children has deteriorated. This is because of increased tax burdens to parents and tax transfers and Social Security and health benefits to the aging population.[84] It also results from the increasing school wars over religion and values, as well as over vouchers and school choice—in short, public disenchantment with our schools[85]—and the breakdown of the Ameri-

---

[84]Laurence J. Kotlikoff and Scott Burns, *The Coming Generation Storm* (Cambridge, MA: MIT Press, 2004); see also John L. Palmer, Timothy Smeeding, and Barbara B. Torrey, "America's Young and Old: Comparisons of Well-Being," *Urban Institute Policy and Research Report*, 8 (1988): 4–5.

[85]Andrew K. Davis, "The Politics of Barking and the State of Our Schools," *Phi Delta Kappan*, 82 (2001): 786–789; Richard F. Elmore, "Breaking the Cartel," *Phi Delta Kappan*, 87 (2006): 517–518.

can family. Fewer than 25 percent of U.S. families consist of a mom and dad, what some of us call a "nuclear family." The number of latchkey children now total 70 percent.[86]

## Streamlining Budgets

In an era of taxpayer wariness, school boards are being pressed to eliminate needless spending before recommending tax increases. Not only must school outcomes measure up to expected standards, but the budget must stand up to close scrutiny.

Although the taxpayer's resistance to increased property tax for schools crested in the 1990s, as we enter the twenty-first century we are experiencing a demand to prune school budgets and save money. Because of the competing demands for public money, especially from our "graying" population, coupled with the reduced percentage of households with children in school, and the current budget deficits, we are forced to downsize our school expenditures and do more with less money per student.[87]

Businesses and corporations have learned to slim down in many ways—by selling off unprofitable enterprises, closing old plants, cutting corporate and regional staff; in some respects, life in the "minimalist" corporation is tougher but simpler. With smaller staffs, decisions can be made more quickly, accountability is clearer, and many people seem to work harder. Not surprisingly, the same principles are being applied to the public schools. Corporate leaders often serve on school boards, and the gospels of "streamlining" and "cost efficiency" have spilled over to U.S. education. We should continue to see the following cost-reducing trends:

1. *Class size.* Class size, in the interest of economy, leveled off to 16 students per teacher in 2000. The data on class size and student achievement are somewhat complex and contradictory, and most studies show no significant differences between

achievement in small classes and in large classes—that is, other variables are more important.[88]

When differences are found, they are about as likely to favor large classes as small. Some recent reviews of the research have shown that class size is only related to pupil achievement when the size of classes is reduced (originally thought to be below fifteen students but in most cases below five students) to result in altered teaching methods.[89] Thus, educators should not be too quick to reduce class size without considering whether money is available or whether teachers can adopt appropriate methods for small classes.

2. *Modernization of Older Buildings.* In the era of declining enrollments, many older school buildings were closed. Often these facilities were rented to other social service agencies such as churches and community centers. In some cases, school buildings were sold to private developers, who converted them into shopping malls and condominiums.

In an era of increasing enrollments, for the last twenty-five years, more schools are clearly needed. But the funds to build them are hard to find. This is especially true in the major cities of the Frostbelt, where the costs of land and labor and the need to enclose and insulate space makes the total cost of new construction twice what it would be in the rural South or Southwest.[90]

To minimize costs, many districts will choose to maintain and modernize their old buildings, especially in the Northeast and Midwest, in the hope

---

[86]"Nearly 20.5 Million Children of Employed Parents in Child Care," *Urban Institute Policy and Research Report*, 15 (2002): 1–2; Ornstein, *Teaching and Schooling in America: Pre- and Post-September 11*.

[87]The proportion of people age sixty-five and over increased from 6 percent in 1950 to 11.3 percent in 1980; it is expected to increase to 20 percent or more by 2030. The number of households made up of married couples with children declined from 40 percent in 1970 to less than 30 percent in 1990; it was less than 25 percent as of 2000.

[88]William Ayers and Michael Klonsky, "The Small School Movement Meets the Ownership Society," *Phi Delta Kappan*, 87 (2006): 453–456; Eric A. Hanushek, "The Impact of Differential Expenditures on School Performance," *Educational Researcher*, 18 (1989): 45–51; Larry V. Hedges et al., "Does Money Matter?" *Educational Researcher*, 23 (1994): 5–14; Lawrence O. Picus, "How Much Is Enough," *American School Board Journal*, 188 (2001): 28–30.

[89]Kirk A. Johnson, "The Downside to Small Class Policies," *Educational Leadership*, 59 (2002): 27–29; Allan C. Ornstein, "In Pursuit of Cost-Effective Schools," *Principal*, 70 (1990): 28–30; Robert E. Slavin, "Class Size and Student Achievement: Small Effects of Small Classes," *Educational Psychologist*, 24 (1989): 99–110.

[90]William Brubaker, "Building for Tomorrow," *American School Board Journal*, 175 (1988): 31–33, 66; Allan C. Ornstein, "School Budgets in the 1990s," *Education Digest*, 55 (1990): 15–16; Ornstein, *Pushing the Envelope* (Columbus, OH: Merrill, 2003).

of avoiding extensive new construction. Although proper maintenance of older buildings is expensive, it is often less costly than starting from scratch. Older buildings frequently were better constructed than recent ones; moreover, older buildings per se are not detrimental to student learning. Nonetheless, by 1998, it would have taken $112 billion to repair or upgrade our schools to an overall good condition.[91] By the year 2005, the figure was more than $175 billion.

3. *Smaller Schools.* Emphasis will be placed on smaller schools because they are cheaper to operate (per square foot) than larger schools, especially if they are well insulated and stress optimal utilization of space. Big and expensive cafeterias, auditoriums, and gymnasiums may become expendable areas due to major fuel, lighting, insurance, and maintenance expenses associated with them. These facilities add to construction costs, remain unoccupied for a large portion of the day and year, and cost a great deal to operate and maintain. Smaller schools usually mean not only more efficient use of space but also fewer administrators, which results in lower costs.[92]

Rather than replace or build new schools, approximately 20 percent of the nation's public schools had plans to build permanent additions between 2000 and 2003. This was due more to overcrowded conditions (increasing enrollments) than to the need to repair or replace schools. As of 2000, 22 percent of the nation's public schools were considered overcrowded and another 26 percent were operating within 95 percent of capacity.[93]

4. *Energy Economies.* Between 1973 and 1980, the total bill for heating schools in the United States tripled, despite reduced fuel consumption.[94] School officials responded and discovered several ways to reduce energy use. Nevertheless, energy prices continued to rise, doubling again in most parts

of the country by 1984.[95] However, post-1984 consumption-cutting techniques paid off when coupled with sharply declining prices. For example, the bill for heating Midwest schools in 1988 returned to 1980 price levels. Between 1988 and 1996, the average Midwest school heating bill increased less than 5 percent per year.[96] Between 1996 and 2006, however, the heating bill (especially in the Northeast where oil is still used on a large scale) increased between 50 to 125 percent, depending on the region and energy source.[97]

The next energy crisis has arrived, however, as we take note of the volatility in the world! Some schools are forced to dial down temperatures, delay warming up the school before classes each morning, or reduce heat in the hallways. Other schools continue to save money by insulating pipes, walls, and windows and installing energy-saving devices. An increasing number of school districts are bypassing utility companies and buying directly from gas and oil distributors. Future-oriented school officials have invested money by upgrading equipment to more energy-efficient forms and by training personnel to operate in an energy-efficient manner. Those schools that were slow to take precautionary energy-related steps in the recent past, when time was available, are paying dearly as we progress through the new millennium. And, as auto gasoline heads for $3 to $4/gallon, there is serious talk about hydrogen-fueled cars and a gas-guzzler tax on SUVs.

As of 2003, utility bills (including gas, electric, and water) have become the second largest operating expense (next to salaries) for most school districts, and the cost of lighting and air conditioning accounts for 40 percent. Turning off lights in the hallway or dimming security lights after 10 P.M., using energy-efficient bulbs, and turning the cooling system up to 75 or 76°F yields enormous savings. Watch those utility bills, also: About one

[91] James C. Moulton et al., "Structurally Sound?" *American School Board Journal,* 186 (1999): 38–40.

[92] Rick Allen, "Big Schools: The Way We Were," *Educational Leadership,* 59 (2002): 36–41; Allan C. Ornstein, "Trimming the Fat, Stretching the Meat," *School Administrator,* 46 (1989): 20–21.

[93] *Digest of Education Statistics, 2005,* table 100, p. 177.

[94] John Mulholland, "How to Save in School Fuel," *Phi Delta Kappan,* 62 (1980): 639; Stephen F. Sloan et al., *Energy in School Costs Too Much* (Albany: New York State Senate Research Service, 1982).

[95] Allan C. Ornstein, "Frostbelt-Sunbelt Energy Policies," *High School Journal,* 67 (1984): 92–103.

[96] *Illinois State Building Energy Expense Study FY 1986 and Projected FY 1987–90* (Springfield: Illinois Department of Energy and Natural Resources, 1987); Brian Quirke, public affairs specialist, U.S. Department of Energy, personal communication, June 21, 1989, and May 15, 1997.

[97] Lou Dobbs, "Money Line," CNN News, February 17, 2003; Dobbs, "Money Line," CNN News, June 30, 2006.

out of twenty schools is overcharged $50,000 to $100,000 a year.[98]

5. *Administrative Layoffs.* The focus of streamlining has begun to shift away from teachers to nonteaching positions. When a school district faces the need to downsize, guidance counselors, curriculum specialists, coordinators, directors, managers, and assistant superintendents are released. When administrators are let go for budget reasons, there is much less outcry than when teachers are cut.

We might argue that an overly trimmed central staff office reflects strained budgets and is unable to perform all necessary tasks, but it is just as likely that a fat central office is inefficient and needs to slim down in an age of reform and retrenchment.

Administrators who sit in big central offices away from schools generate their own layers of bureaucracy within their departments—additional supervisors, consultants, and support staff—all of whom, no doubt, are good to have and are useful on frequent occasions. But they do bloat the school district payroll, and in tough times they are unneeded.

A school district's organizational chart should be something that a parent can understand, yet most of the charts depicting large school districts cannot be understood by many professional educators. In an age of downsizing, the time has come to clear out the crowd at central offices. Profitable corporations have learned this lesson, in some cases the hard way. Some large companies operate with as few as 1 headquarters manager to 5000 employees.[99] Now is the time for wise decision makers to slowly eliminate staff matrices built on top of other matrices; doing so through attrition will be far less painful than waiting for financial problems to force school officials to cut needed staff.

## Environmental Hazards

A number of environmental hazards, including asbestos, toxic waste, landfill and chemical dump sites, ground water contamination, lake and river pollution, air pollution, and ozone depletion, threaten America's health and economy and dominate the headlines. Moreover, in the 1990s these hazards moved indoors and now threaten the schools and workplace.

## Asbestos

The U.S. Environmental Protection Agency (EPA) has ordered government and commercial property owners to clean up **asbestos-laden buildings** that have been housing people at work and in school for the last twenty-five to fifty years. Estimated costs to clean up these buildings are hard to come by, although one estimate was $100 billion for government and commercial buildings and $3.5 billion for some 45,000 schools in 31,000 school districts.[100] Another nationwide study puts the estimate at $1.2 billion, or $22,858 per school and $31 per student. In 1990 the cost exceeded $150 per student in 10 percent of the schools, and the Oklahoma City School District had the greatest expenditures—or the dubious distinction of having a $65 million bill and $1688 cost per student.[101] These costs are based on an estimate of $15 to $20 a square foot to remove asbestos, depending on whether this once-acclaimed "wonder fiber" is located in the ceilings, walls, floors, or basements. In 1999, some 8 to 10 million children and 1.1 million school employees were subject to asbestos exposure, which is a marked improvement from ten years earlier, when some 15–20 million children and 1.5 million employees were exposed.[102]

The estimates of people on the job who will die from direct exposure to asbestos in buildings are extremely low (25 a year) compared to those who will die from workplace accidents (10,000 a year).[103] The ultimate question is, do we need to spend all this money on asbestos removal? At what level of exposure is asbestos unsafe? If asbestos is intact, not flaking, and out of reach of students and employees, should it be removed? Although airborne asbestos can be deadly (more than 1 percent in the air), the dangers of inert asbestos are

---

[98] Rebecca Jones, "Fourteen Ways to Save Money," *American School Board Journal,* 185 (1998): 26–29.

[99] Thomas Moore, "Goodbye, Corporate Staff," *Fortune,* 21 December 1987, pp. 65, 68, 76; Allan C. Ornstein, "School Finance in the '90s," *American School Board Journal,* 177 (1990): 36–39; Nancy Protheroe, "The Blob Revisited," *School Administrator,* 55 (1998): 26–29; Moulton, "Structurally Sound?"

[100] Louis S. Richman, "Why Throw Money at Asbestos?" *Fortune,* 6 June 1988, pp. 155–170.

[101] Allan C. Ornstein and Robert C. Cienkus, "The Nation's School Repair Bill," *American School Board Journal,* 177 (1990): 2A–4A.

[102] Rebecca Jones, "Waste Not, Want Not," *American School Board Journal,* 186 (1999): 16–19.

[103] James J. Florio, "Asbestos in the Schools: New Requirements Take Effect," *PTA Today,* 14 (1988): 31–32; Richman, "Why Throw Money at Asbestos?"

minimal in most buildings. Nonetheless, children are considered to be especially vulnerable because their longer life expectancy means that a latent asbestos-related disease has more time to develop.

During the 1980s and 1990s, the federal government imposed many environmental requirements and regulations on the schools but did not provide funds for compliance. Many school districts delayed removing the asbestos, while others used funds from their school maintenance budget to comply with federal regulations. However, one EPA study reports that as much as 75 percent of all school cleanup work was done improperly up to 1985.[104] Rather than mitigating the problem, it is likely that the problem was exacerbated in many cases; indeed, the "cure" may be worse than the "disease," especially with a lot of "rip and skip" companies.

It should be pointed out that removal is not the only form of abatement, although the great majority of school districts have chosen this option. Encapsulation, if done properly, can last for ten or more years, depending on what and how the materials are applied, at an average cost of 10 percent of the removal bill.[105] The savings is obvious, but in cases where asbestos is loose or crumbling, removal is the best solution. In still other cases, encapsulation is only a stopgap measure until a school district can raise sufficient money for removal (see Administrative Advice 11–2).

## Radon Gas

While schools are just getting over the shock of asbestos, **radon gas** arises as a cancer threat. (It is considered the second leading cause of lung cancer among adults.) EPA tests show dangerously high levels of this invisible, odorless gas in 54 percent of the 130 schools randomly checked; homes are also affected. In short, many of our children are exposed to a risk equivalent to smoking ½ to 1 ½ packs of cigarettes a day.[106]

The gas seeps into buildings through the foundation from soil and rock as radium-266 decays. In some cases, well water may be a source of radon. No EPA, federal, or state guidelines exist for containment or abatement of the gas; however, the situation is considered dangerous, and levels are too high in some schools to wait for the EPA. Basically, testing procedures include monitoring (1) all school rooms on and below ground level, (2) in the cold months of the year, and (3) for two days to four weeks, depending on the type of test. Screening test results over 4 pCi/L (picoCuries/liter, or one-trillionth of a unit of radon) are considered enough to warrant a lengthy retest (nine to twelve months); levels over 100 pCi/L are considered sufficiently dangerous to justify relocating children.[107]

Average corrective costs per school run from as low as $1000 if ventilation adjustment works to $10,000 if subventilation is needed. Some observers contend that the cost for decontaminating the nation's schools runs into billions of dollars, and since the connection between radon and illness has not been firmly proven, it may not be worth the cost to ventilate schools.

## Electromagnetic Fields

**Electromagnetic fields** (EMF) are everywhere; they are part of our complicated and growing technology: radio, television, computers, microwaves, fluorescent lights, and so on. The most controversial and visible electromagnetic fields are produced by the existence of transmission lines running through our communities—often near our schools, playgrounds, and homes. Only six states set limits on the strength of EMF around transmission lines. New York State, for example, requires a 350-yard corridor around their lines. The fear seems to coincide with growing research data: Children exposed to these power lines suffer from childhood cancer two to three times more (depending on years of exposure) than children who are not exposed.[108]

What about our home appliances and school machines? The higher the strength of the magnetic field (as in devices such as microwaves, ovens, stoves, and heaters), as well as the closer the object and the longer the exposure (as with electric blankets, computers, copy machines, televisions, and fluorescent lights), the greater the risk. Actually, objects with electric motors (such as air conditioners, electric clocks, hair dryers, and even telephones) present a possible risk to humans.

---

[104]Telephone conversation with Robert Garratt, Staff Specialist, Environmental Protection Agency, Region 5, personal communication, 7 June 1990.

[105]Tom Probst, "Case Study: Asbestos Encapsulation," *Executive Educator,* 12 (1990): 11A–12A.

[106]Radon in Schools, Bulletin No. 520 (Washington, DC: U.S. Government Printing Office, 1989); Hugh Wright, "Radon Gas New Threat in Schools," *USA Today,* 21 April 1989, p. 1A.

[107]Donna Harrington-Lueker, "Are Pesticides the Latest Peril Facing Your Schools," *Executive Educator,* 12 (1990): 21–23; Kurt Schneider, "Battling Radon: Changing Targets," *New York Times,* 24 March 1993, p. C19.

[108]Carl Burko, "Jury Out on Risk from Power Lines," *Chicago Tribune,* 26 May 1991, p. 19.

## Administrative Advice 11–2

### Dealing with Asbestos Abatement Contractors

Most school districts, especially the larger ones, are still involved in asbestos abatement. Some still need time extensions, some have an abatement plan in place, others are involved with contract bids, and others are in the process of removing or encapsulating this "wonder fiber." Here are some questions that school districts might consider when selecting an asbestos contractor.

- How many companies are bidding for the job? (Permit at least three to bid each job, especially if the cost is more than $3000.)

- Has the company performed other jobs for your district?

- How long has the company been in business? (There are many new asbestos abatement companies.)

- What are the company's assets? What jobs has the company performed? For whom? Is the company willing to provide references?

- Has someone in the district called the regional or state EPA and local regulatory agency to ensure that the company has not been cited for health or work violations?

- Are the contractor's workers fully certified? Is the company licensed or certified by the state or local regulatory agency?

- Is the company bonded for performance? Do the workers have adequate liability insurance?

- Does the company carry adequate liability insurance? From an A or A+ rated insurance company? At least a $5 million umbrella policy for each occurrence (not cumulative)?

- Does the company employ a state-licensed health (or air quality) engineer? If not, will an engineer supervise the health aspects of the job?

- Are the health safeguards clearly outlined in the proposal and contract? Will the contaminated areas be properly sealed off?

- Will the company test the air quality before the job, hourly on the job, and after the job? Who will ensure that the readings are accurate? (Preferably an independent or third party should inspect the quality of the air and conduct appropriate tests.)

- Is a timetable clearly established? Are penalties provided for unusual delays?

- Will the public be properly notified when the job is to commence? Will students be in the surrounding area? What about vacation or summer time?

- Besides removal, what other options has the asbestos company suggested? Will guarantees be included with the other options?

- How viable are the options? Have you considered the cost for removal versus the cost for the options?

- Does the district's contract with the company include a save harmless agreement? Does the district have an escape clause (and right to hire another company) in the event that legal, health, or governmental problems arise?

---

In theory, these household and school objects may be more dangerous than transmission lines because our bodies are often only inches away.

To get an idea of the emission effects of these household and school objects, copy machines give off 4.0 milligauss units, computers 10.0, and microwave ovens 15.0.[109] The problem is, some of us sit by a computer for hours. In general, the research on EMF is highly complex and tentative. Some scientists claim we are unsure what to measure to determine exposure. Right now the best precaution is to have children keep their distance from all EMF emitters at home and in school, especially televisions and computers. Schools need to enforce this notion of distance and purchase computers and electronic equipment with screens or filters. Since there is little public pressure to spend money on screens or filters, and no legislation requiring schools

---

[109] "Electromagnetic Fields: Are They a Cause of Concern?" *Winnetka Report*, 11 June 1991, pp. 1–2.

to take corrective steps, few schools are considering these precautions.

## School Lead

"Water, water everywhere, and not a good drop to drink" is a play on words reflecting reality. The water our children are drinking at home and school may be tainted with lead that accumulates in their blood and bones and eventually dulls the mind and causes severe behavior problems.

According to one U.S. government survey, 15 to 16 percent of the nation's children under fourteen years have lead levels in their blood high enough to cause academic and neurobehavioral problems in school, which eventually results in failure at school. The incidence of elevated lead levels is three times higher among poor white than middle-class white children, and seven times higher among inner-city blacks than suburban whites, largely because of the differences in air quality and the age of their housing.[110]

The federal Centers for Disease Control and Prevention (CDC) maintains that lead poisoning is the nation's number-one preventable child health problem and that proper lead abatement would eventually reduce the cost of child medical care and special education as much as $45 billion annually.[111] The CDC has revised its definition of lead poisoning, lowering the level at which lead is now considered dangerous, from 25 micrograms per deciliter in 1974 to 10 micrograms in 1991. The last revision resulted in a tenfold increase in the number of children now considered poisoned—about 1.5 percent (now affecting 15 percent of all U.S. preschoolers).[112] Moreover, there are at least twenty recent U.S. and international studies from industrialized nations showing that levels of lead in children are associated with measures of low IQ, language and reading incompetency, limited attention span, inability to follow instructions, behavioral impairment, and forty additional cognitive, social, psychological, and health problems.[113]

In a recent study one researcher found that first and second graders who had moderate quantities of lead (5 micrograms or less) in their systems were six times as likely to exhibit reading problems and seven times more likely to drop out of high school compared to children who were lead free.[114] Although the lead variable possibly interacts with a social-class variable, the fact remains that lead infects multiple organs of the body.

In short, childhood poisoning may be one of the most important and least acknowledged causes of school failure and learning disorders. Given all the rhetoric and funding for school reform, which focuses on curriculum, instruction, teaching, and testing, we may have been myopic and even foolhardy not to realize that part of school failure may be related to the adverse effects of lead.

The major source of lead poisoning is the old lead-based paint and the dust produced from it when windows are opened and closed or renovations take place. The problem exists in nearly all schools built before 1978, the year when lead-based paint was banned by Congress (and that's more than 65 percent of the nation's schools). Several layers down, because of cracking and flaking, the paint is not always sealed as we might believe, and it can be found in the air teachers and students breathe. Renovations cause bigger problems because these building areas are not properly sealed and monitored with sample air readings, as in the prescribed manner for asbestos removal.

Dangerous traces of lead are sometimes found in the municipal water we drink. Even worse, lead gets into water from lead lines in our older water coolers, faucets (unless made from plastic, which most people feel is inferior in quality), copper pipes (because of the lead solder on the joints), and the old plumbing in cities and

[110]U.S. Agency for Toxic Substances, *The Nature and Extent of Lead Poisoning in Children in the United States* (Washington, DC: U.S. Government Printing Office, 1988). Also see Kari Arfstrom, "Keeping the Feds Out of Your Airspace," *School Administrator,* 55 (1998): 39.

[111]Centers for Disease Control, *Strategic Plan for the Elimination of Childhood Lead Poisoning,* rev. ed. (Washington, DC: U.S. Government Printing Office, 2005).

[112]Russ Banham, "Lead Paint Poisoning: Who's Liable? Who Pays?" *Independent Agent,* 14 (1994): 22–30; Susan Black, "Heavy Metal," *American School Board Journal,* 188 (2001): 62.

[113]Donald Bellinger, "Longitudinal Analysis of Prenatal and Postnatal Lead Exposure and Early Cognitive Development," *New England Journal of Medicine,* 316 (1987): 1037–1043; Harry L. Needleman, "Childhood Exposure to Lead: A Common Case of School Failure," *Phi Delta Kappan,* 74 (1992): 35–37.

[114]Bruce P. Lanphear, "Blood Levels Below 'Acceptable' Value Linked with IQ Deficits," Paper presented at the Pediatric Academic Societies, Cincinnati, April 30, 2001. Also see *Lead Action News,* 8 (2001): 6–8.

villages that connects the water main to our schools and homes. Allowing water to run for a couple of minutes before drinking it or using it for cleaning foods can flush out the lead that has collected—but that idea does not always sit well with budget-minded people who pay utility bills.

It costs about $50 to $75 for a laboratory to test each water faucet and cooler in our schools; however, this is not going to happen on a large scale unless schools are forced to budget this item. The National Education Association estimates that $30 million per year is needed for paint and water testing in our schools, a tiny sum for such an important safety measure.[115] Since the problem is odorless and invisible, and since most parents are not aware the problem even exists, school officials are not under pressure to take appropriate measures.

No testing and reporting procedures are required for lead, and school authorities have been remiss in dealing with the problem. Furthermore, many school officials who are in the position to do something about it take the position that there is no problem (they believe it went away when lead was outlawed in paints and gasoline) or see the solutions as too expensive because eventually abatement and not testing is what has to be done in many schools (and other government buildings). The cost of lead abatement is estimated between $5000 and $15,000 per 1000 square feet of lead paint coverage. Most school boards (and owners of property) find the cost too expensive and just leave the problem as is, gambling that if a party files a lead-injury claim their insurance will pay for it. Verdicts run as high as $10 million, though most are settled in the range of $500,000.[116]

In order to ensure adequate compliance by schools, requirements need to be enacted by EPA or other health agency for lead abatement. But, as with the tobacco industry fighting facts about cigarette smoking and cancer, the lead industry has its spokespeople and lobbyists who obscure the health hazards of lead. The federal government, medical profession, and socially concerned groups need to come together to force cleanups of lead contamination.

## Indoor Air Quality

We are now becoming aware of the **sick building syndrome** (SBS) and other indoor air-quality shortcomings as a result of the trend to increase insulation and tighten schools (and office buildings) to save energy. The outcome, in extreme cases, is virtually no outside air infiltration.

Everything in a building has some form of toxic emission. The human body exhales carbon dioxide, and it emits body odors, gases, and other *bioeffluents.* Carbon monoxide, also colorless and highly poisonous, results from incomplete combustion of fuel. It can be a problem when auto engines are left running, say, in school parking lots near open windows when parents pick up or drop off their children. Diesel exhaust from parked buses is also common, as drivers wait for students or warm the bus in winter before students board. Carpets, plastics (most furniture and bathroom fixtures contain plastics), and pressed wood emit formaldehyde and other gases. Room dividers and window blinds emit a host of carbon chemicals. Copy machines give off ozone, spirit duplicators give off methyl alcohol, and fluorescent lights give off ultraviolet rays.

Then there is the dilemma of doing battle with pests—fleas, cockroaches, termites, wasps, and rodents. Although chemical pesticides are a critical component of successful pest control, there is the other side of the coin—our concern to limit or even rid schools of pesticides.[117] It's one thing to permit weeds to run amok on school playgrounds because of our concern to reduce pesticide exposure, but it's quite another to allow the aforementioned pests to run wild with the likelihood of increasing. Nonetheless, educators and parents are concerned that students are unknowingly breathing in various poisonous chemicals used to kill vermin. As of 2000, thirty-one out of fifty states had school pesticide management policies that were considered "inadequate" or "unsatisfactory" for protecting children from pesticides that are harmful to their central nervous system and have "very profound consequences for human beings."[118]

Even drywall, paints, and cleaning fluids have various fumes that are dangerous if sufficient quantities exist. Long-term exposure to chemicals and volatile

[115]Jean A. Natale, "Tainted Water, Poison Paint," *American School Board Journal,* 178 (1991): 24–28. Also see *Legislative Guidance for Comprehensive State Groundwater Protection Program* (Denver: National Conference of State Legislatures, 1999).

[116]Banham, "Lead Paint Poisoning: Who's Liable? Who Pays?"

[117]Robert Krieger, "Policing Pests," *American School Board Journal,* 187 (2000): 52–54.

[118]Kevin Bushweller, "Schools Curtail Pesticide Use," *American School Board Journal,* 187 (2000): 53.

compounds from art supplies, science labs, shop facilities, and indoor pools is potentially dangerous, and it affects all students because the vapors and dusts enter the heating and cooling systems. Excessive humidity—found in locker rooms, pool areas, and school basements—can lead to mold and fungus growths that multiply to potentially harmful levels—which they often do without school authorities recognizing it.

As schools become more insulated, the toxins from cigarette smoke, chalk dusts, science labs, art rooms, and shop facilities cannot escape and thus get circulated through the ventilation system. In addition, the entire duct system usually has dust or mold that spreads germs throughout the building. Few schools regularly clean their vents, and Legionnaires' disease is an example of illness caused by germs in the vents and return lines of the duct system.

Roughly one-third of the nation's schools (and offices) are considered to be afflicted with sick building syndrome. We need to follow the amended recommendations of the American Society for Heating, Refrigeration and Air Conditioning Engineers; they raised air circulation standards from 5 cubic feet per minute to 15.[119] Two problems arise: More energy is consumed, and in some big cities, such as Los Angeles, Houston, and New York, it is even more damaging to bring in outside air at certain times of the year.

The human symptoms of poor indoor air quality are eye, nose, throat, or lung irritations. Students (and teachers) are drowsy, exhibit shorter attention spans, or become out of breath when walking up the stairs or playing in the gym. In searching for problems, one important consideration is whether people's symptoms disappear in a few hours after school.[120] Parents whose children suffer from respiratory problems often feel their children are being infected by classmates—not considering the strong possibility that the school air may be the culprit.

Unless symptoms are apparent, educators usually believe the indoor air quality of the school is fine. But many air pollutants, including radon gas, carbon monoxide, asbestos particles, and lead dust, are not easily detectable by sight or smell. Other pollutants are obvious only in high concentrations. Formaldehyde, paint and cleaning fluid vapors, and mold and fungus, for example, have an odor only at harmful levels.

Obviously, schools need to test air quality regularly and not assume the best-case scenario. But when was the last time your neighborhood school, or the school your brother, sister, or children attend, tested the air to see whether it was "healthy"? Given the budget constraints of most school districts, the answer is probably, "Not since anyone can remember." So long as parental and public pressure is on improving the curriculum and teaching process, and minimal attention is directed at the air we breathe (being merely taken for granted), and so long as there is no legislation requiring the testing and improvement of our air, the problem will be ignored. With lack of funds as a common school problem, ventilation maintenance is not a top priority; in fact, the maintenance budget is often robbed to pay for curriculum and teaching reform—an unfortunate circumstance that threatens student health and learning conditions.

When the public becomes more aware of the hazards related to indoor pollutants, air quality within school buildings will become the focal point for student rights and litigation. Lack of responsiveness today by school officials can make a seemingly innocuous problem and noncontroversial issue into a serious one in the future.

## School Infrastructure Costs

The nation's **school infrastructure** is in a state of critical disrepair. By *infrastructure* we mean the physical facilities that underpin the school plant (plumbing, sewer, heat, electric, roof, masonry, carpentry). Schools seem to be deteriorating at a faster rate than they can be repaired, and faster than most other public facilities.[121] Plumbing, electrical wiring, and heating systems in many schools are dangerously out of date, roofing is below code, and exterior materials (brickwork, stone, and wood) are chipped or cracked. The cost of deferred expenditures currently runs to over $100 million in Los Angeles, Detroit, Chicago, Seattle, and Miami's Dade County, with an enormous bill of $680 million for the New York City schools. The accumulated cost to repair the nation's public schools, according to knowledgeable

---

[119]David Dunn, "Environmental Health Hazards Move Indoors," *Midwest Real Estate News*, 14 (1990): 1–5; *Legislative Requirements Under the Clean Air Act Amendment of 1990* (Denver: National Conference of State Legislatures, 1993).

[120]Charles Greim and William Turner, "Breathing Easy Over Air Quality," *American School Board Journal*, 178 (1991): 29–32.

[121]Allan C. Ornstein, "Prescriptions for Sick Schools," *Principal*, 73 (1993): 25–27.

sources, can now be conservatively placed at $50 billion and may run as high as $115 billion.[122] In the year 2000, government sources estimated the nation's school repair bill to be $2,900 per student, and the cost per student for schools needing to make the repairs was $3,800 per student. Approximately 76 percent of public schools needed major repair or renovation.[123]

Although experts maintain that schools need to allocate 5 percent a year for repairs and replacement, recent findings suggest that schools allocate only 3 percent. The investment in new construction is equally insufficient. Whereas colleges and universities allocate 7 percent annually for new construction and other public sectors allocate 8 percent, public schools allocate approximately 3.5 percent.

Schools in small towns and suburbs are in the best shape. A majority of these school board members report their school buildings are in either better than adequate (43%) or adequate (35%) condition. They say this despite the fact that their schools are aging. More than 60 percent report their schools are between twenty-five and fifty years old. Nearly 25 percent say their schools are between ten and twenty-five years old.[124]

Schools in cities and in the Frostbelt suffer the greatest infrastructure problems because they are the oldest and the most decayed. Nearly 35 percent of the schools in the older industrial cities of the Northeast and Midwest were built before 1930; a large number were constructed before 1900. For example, nearly half of Chicago's 597 school buildings were built before 1930, and as many as 80 schools still in existence in 1991 were built before 1900. In Akron, Buffalo, Houston, Kansas City (Missouri), Minneapolis, and Portland (Oregon), 50 percent or more of the schools were built before 1930 (see Table 11–6).

A school building has five stages. It has lived its normal life the first twenty years, especially in the Sunbelt where construction is cheaper. When it is twenty to thirty years old, frequent replacement of equipment is needed. When it is thirty to forty years old, most of the original equipment and materials should have been replaced—especially roofs, lighting fixtures, and heating

equipment. Accelerated deterioration takes place when it is forty to fifty years old. A fifty-year-old building is sometimes too new to abandon, especially in the Frostbelt, where construction is usually good; but after sixty years, a number of buildings are usually abandoned, reconstructed, or replaced.[125]

Nationwide, 29 percent of all public schools are considered in "inadequate condition," built before 1970. Sixty-one percent have been built after 1970, but renovated since 1980, and are considered in "adequate" condition. Ten percent are considered in "good" condition, built after 1984. A larger percentage of schools in the Midwest (36%) and Northeast (33%) are considered inadequate and in need of major repair or renovation, compared to the Southeast (21%) and West (25%). Only 6 percent of schools in the Midwest and 5 percent in the Northeast are in the "new" category ("good" condition) compared to 11 percent in the Southeast and 15 percent in the West.[126] The differences among regions reflect in part stagnant enrollments in the Midwest and Northeast and growing enrollments in the Southeast and West.

Small schools (fewer than 300 students) have an average age of forty-eight years compared to large schools (1000 or more students) with an average age of thirty-nine years. City schools have a mean age of forty-six years compared to suburban (40 years) and rural schools (42 years).[127] Nationwide, 26 percent of schools were built before 1950. Interestingly, schools in poorer areas have a greater percentage of newer schools than those in middle-class areas, which flies against the charges of reformers who often refer to most inner-city schools as dilapidated. For example, for schools with less than 20 percent of students eligible for free or reduced-price lunch, 48 percent were built before 1950. In contrast, of schools where 50 percent or more students are eligible for free or reduced-price lunch, 42 percent were built before 1950.[128]

Leading the list of inadequate buildings are Connecticut (60%), California (55%), Washington, D.C.

[122]Ornstein and Cienkus, "The Nation's School Repair Bill"; Telephone conversation with Michael Spring, [Editor, *American School and University Magazine*], May 13, 1990; "School Facilities Condition of American Schools," *Report to Congressional Requesters* (Washington, DC: U.S. Government Printing Office, 1995).

[123]*Digest of Education Statistics, 2005*, table 100, p. 176.

[124]Moulton, "Structurally Sound?"

[125]Ann Lewis, *Wolves at the Schoolhouse Door: An Investigation of the Condition of Public School Buildings* (Washington, DC: Education Writers Association, 1989); Allan C. Ornstein, "School Finance Trends for the Year 2000," *Educational Horizons*, 69 (1990): 59–64; and Paul Theobald, "Urban and Rural Schools: Lingering Obstacles," *Phi Delta Kappan*, 87 (2006): 116–122.

[126]*The Condition of Education, 2000* (Washington, DC: U.S. Government Printing Office, 2001), indicator 49, p. 75.

[127]Ibid, table 49-1, p. 168.

[128]Ibid.

## Table 11–6  School Districts with the Newest and Oldest Schools

| Ranking | School District | Number of Schools | Number of New Schools[a] | Percentage of New Schools |
|---|---|---|---|---|
| 1 | Gwinnett, GA | 60 | 32 | 53.3 |
| 2 | Jordan, UT | 70 | 36 | 51.4 |
| 3 | Cumberland, NC | 68 | 30 | 44.1 |
| 4 | Broward County, FL | 157 | 60 | 38.2 |
| 5 | San Antonio, TX | 50 | 18 | 36.0 |
| 6.5 | Chesterfield, VA | 48 | 17 | 35.4 |
| 6.5 | Arlington, VA | 48 | 17 | 35.4 |
| 8 | Mt. Diablo, CA | 54 | 19 | 35.2 |
| 9 | Cobb County, GA | 77 | 25 | 32.5 |
| 10 | Virginia Beach, VA | 69 | 22 | 31.8 |

| Ranking | School District | Number of Schools | Number of Old Schools[b] | Percentage of Old Schools |
|---|---|---|---|---|
| 65 | Chicago | 597 | 264 | 44.2 |
| 66 | Detroit | 287 | 130 | 45.3 |
| 67 | St. Louis | 134 | 65 | 48.5 |
| 68 | Minneapolis | 57 | 28 | 49.1 |
| 69 | Houston | 233 | 116 | 49.8 |
| 70 | Portland, OR | 108 | 54 | 50.0 |
| 71 | Akron, OH | 59 | 30 | 50.8 |
| 72 | Prince William County, GA | 82 | 47 | 57.3 |
| 73 | Buffalo, NY | 75 | 45 | 60.0 |
| 74 | Kansas City, MO | 79 | 48 | 60.8 |

[a]Fifteen years old or less, as of 1990.

[b]Sixty years old or more, as of 1990.

NOTE: School districts with the highest ratio of new schools (one to fifteen years old) are located in the South and West and suburban areas; school districts with the highest ratio of old schools (sixty years or more) are (with the exception of two) located in the Northwest and Midwest and (with the exception of one) big cities.

Source: Allan C. Ornstein and Robert C. Cienkus, "The Nation's School Repair Bill," *American School Board Journal,* 177 (1990): 4A. Copyright 1990, the National School Boards Association. Used by permission.

(50%), Illinois (50%), and Rhode Island (40%). Of the buildings that are inadequate, 61 percent need major repairs, 43 percent are obsolete, 25 percent are overcrowded, and 13 percent are structurally unsound.[129] Many, of course, have multiple problems.

In comparison with other public sectors, the construction and repair needs for schools rank among the most serious in the nation. Yet it is doubtful that the public is willing to spend sufficient money to meet these needs. A nationwide survey of the largest 100 school districts (74% responded) identified in rank order the top three repair items on which schools are spending money: (1) roofs, averaging $21,555 per school and $29 per student; (2) heating and air conditioning at $17,652 per school and $24 per student; and (3) painting at $15,101 per school and $22 per student. Other costly repair items in descending order were plumbing and sewer repairs, electric repairs, carpentry, brick and mortar, carpet and tile, and insulation.[130]

[129]Lewis, *Wolves at the Schoolhouse Door.*

[130]Allan C. Ornstein and Robert C. Cienkus, "Asbestos Removal from Schools: How Much Will It Cost?," *Transaction,* 28 (1991): 2–3; Ornstein and Cienkus, "The Nation's School Repair Bill."

Government estimates for the condition of the nation's schools are grim. The top items rated as "inadequate" and in need of repair or replacement in the year 2000 were as follows: (1) heating, air, and ventilation (29%), (2) plumbing (25%), (3) exterior walls, windows, or doors (24%), (4) roofs (22%), and electricity (22%). As much as 50 percent of the nation's schools had at least one inadequate feature.[131]

Several factors other than age contribute to the deterioration of school buildings and the costs for repairs and renovation.

1. *Energy Prices.* Although energy prices stabilized in the 1990s, they have dramatically increased since 2000. K–12 schools spend more than $7 billion a year on energy costs — or $125/student/year. Most schools, particularly in old, Frostbelt communities, continue to be heated by inefficient boilers. Electrical costs are higher because the school design rarely takes advantage of sunlight. The operating funds devoted to increased energy costs and energy-saving devices have robbed schools of money for repairs and maintenance.

2. *Weather Conditions.* The weather is severe in certain parts of the country, especially in the Frostbelt where the 100- to 120-degree annual temperature range causes considerable contraction and expansion of school buildings, roofs, and pavement. The intense cold makes the water and sewer systems, as well as exterior brick, vulnerable to cracks and leaks. In addition, acid rain, common in heavily industrialized or polluted areas, causes deterioration of all structural surfaces.

3. *Density and Vandalism.* Big-city schools are usually located in densely populated areas, resulting in concentrated use of and greater demand for facilities. Moreover, many of these schools are located in highly concentrated poverty areas and service youth populations that are more often involved in property destruction and theft than youth from more affluent areas. All this results not only in higher costs and more frequent repairs but also in higher budgets for security measures, which depletes a system's financial resources and operating funds for repairs and maintenance.

4. *Newer Buildings.* Many new schools were constructed during the last twenty-five years, especially in the Sunbelt and suburbs. Many of these schools were constructed with haste to accommodate expanding enrollments. Quality suffered, and these buildings are now approaching the end of their life spans. In contrast, the problems with older buildings involve not only their quality but also their energy efficiency, their failure to meet health and safety codes, and the results of accumulated neglect.

5. *A Ticking Time Bomb.* For the most part, educators and the public alike are unaware of the time bomb that is ticking in U.S. schools. What catches our attention is student test scores and the need to reform or upgrade the curriculum; the safety and operating efficiency of the schools are not on the minds of the public unless there is a call for new taxes.[132]

Many school board officials are aware of our schools' environmental and structural problems, but have left them for the next generation. Ignoring our inadequate school *facilities* has enormous costs and will potentially lead to inadequate schools. The longer we wait, the greater the cost for future educational services and the more difficult it becomes to sustain long-term educational growth and financial solvency among school districts. Either we devote, today, a greater share of local and state revenues to the repair and renovations of our educational facilities, or we burden our children and grandchildren with crippling educational expenses.

## Financing School Construction

Public school investment in new schools, compared to other public sectors, has been minimal in the last fifteen to twenty years because of previous taxpayer resistance and student-enrollment declines. Nationwide, 61 percent of the schools were constructed during the 1950s and 1960s, and only 6 percent were built in the 1980s; more than 20 percent were over fifty years old in 1990, and the percentage is growing about 0.5 percent each year.[133] As of 2000, the average age of the na-

---

[131] *Digest of Education Statistics, 2005*, table 100, p. 176.

[132] Allan C. Ornstein, "School Finance and the Condition of Schools," *Theory into Practice*, 33 (1994): 118–125. Also see William Howell, *Besieged School Boards and the Future of Education Politics* (Washington, D.C.: Brookings Institution Press, 2004).

[133] Lewis, *Wolves at the Schoolhouse Door*; Ornstein, "School Finance and the Condition of Schools."

tion's schools was forty years and the average age or year since the last renovation was eleven years.[134]

Where will the money come from to build new schools? Although the states fund about 50 percent of the revenues for the maintenance and operation of schools, they only contribute about 23 percent for construction. According to one study, twenty-seven states use grant programs (equalized, flat, or matching) to finance new schools, twelve states rely on state or local bonds, two states use fully funded capital programs, but sixteen states provide no state financial assistance.[135] (Based on these numbers, some states use more than one program.)

The big-spending region for building is the Southeast, comprising eight states (Alabama, Florida, Georgia, Kentucky, Mississippi, North Carolina, South Carolina, and Tennessee). These eight states spent more than $3.3 billion on education construction in 2002. Of that amount, 67 percent went for new buildings, 20 percent for additions, and 13 percent for modernizations. School officials predict that school construction will continue to rise (it has been rising since 1985).

Public school enrollments K–12 from 2002 to 2014 are expected to increase 13 percent in the West compared to the South (5%) and the Midwest (−2%) and Northeast (−5%). All thirteen states in the West are expected to show increases, with Idaho (13.8%), New Mexico (5.7%), Nevada (28%), Alaska (7.7%), Hawaii (5%), and Arizona (14.5%) expected to show the greatest amount.[136] In short, the western region of the country has replaced the South in K–12 student growth and construction. Nationwide school construction is expected to total approximately $30 to $40 billion per year from 2000 to 2011 and then level off, reflecting a need to replace and renovate old buildings on the one hand, and the slowdown of increasing public school enrollments (3.5 million students from 1993 to 2000 compared to 125,000 students from 2000 to 2011) on the other hand.[137]

Building a new school is no simple task. The rules are complex, the stakes are high, and the considera-

tions are political. Try these questions, for example: How many students will the school accommodate? Where will the building site be located? How will attendance boundaries be drawn? Have environmental concerns been fully addressed? How will the cost be funded? How will voters react? Which companies will get the contracts? How many minority contractors will be hired? The list of questions, with the potential for vague answers, is endless. See Administrative Advice 11–3.

Is it possible for one school serving the same number of students to be three or four times more expensive than another? You bet. Consider different building requirements (local construction codes, insulation factors, space requirements), building designs (open-air or enclosed, horizontal or vertical), land prices, professional fees, labor and material expenses.

As of the year 2005, a downtown Chicago or New York City attorney charges $250 to $500 an hour compared to $150 to $250 for an attorney in New Orleans or Tampa, Florida. A union plumber costs more than $75 an hour in the Northeast or Midwest urban areas; the cost is half in southern urban areas, and in rural areas it is even cheaper. The cost of land can be two to ten times as high in one city (New York, Chicago, or Los Angeles) as another (Baton Rouge, Louisiana, or El Paso, Texas). In short, *where* you build is important. The cost of a school building can run from $75 to $100 a square foot in rural southern areas to $150 to $200 per foot in the major cities (and adjacent metropolitan areas).[138]

Another factor to consider is square footage. High schools need more square footage per student (about 1½ times more) than do elementary schools to adequately serve their clientele. The reason is related to specialization and additional facilities for older students—larger auditoriums, pools, theaters, cafeterias, indoor gyms, outdoor ball fields, student parking lots. Also, schools in cold climates cannot use outdoor areas as effectively as schools in warm climates. A typical high school serving 1000 students might comprise 100 square feet per student (at $100 per square foot) in the rural South. Another high school serving the same number of students might comprise 200 square feet per student (at $200 per square foot) in the urban Northeast or Midwest. The school's total cost in the urban Northeast or Midwest can run three to four times as high as in the rural sites: One school costs $5000 per

---

[134] *Digest of Education Statistics, 2005*, table 100, p. 176.

[135] *Projection of Population by States, 1988–2010* (Washington, DC: National Association of State Directors of Education Plant Services, 1989).

[136] *Projections of Education Statistics to 2014*, p. 6.

[137] Ibid, table 1, p. 12. Also see *The Condition of Education, 2002* (Washington, DC: U.S. Government Printing Office, 2002), table 7, p. 12.

[138] Ornstein, "School Finance Trends for the Year 2000."

## Administrative Advice 11–3

### Borrowing with Bonds

Most states allow the local school district to borrow money from the citizens by floating a bond issue. In this way, the school board raises money for capital projects such as new buildings, remodeling programs, replacement or purchase of expensive equipment (e.g., boilers or buses) and facilities (e.g., pools or parking lots). Subject to state statutes and debt limitations (usually related to the assessed valuation of the district's property), bond issues must be passed in a local election to learn whether the people wish to incur additional debt for the district. If passed, the bonds are prepared, publicized, purchased, and traded. In this connection, school administrators should know the facts about bonds.

■ The amount to be repaid by the school district is the *principal amount, face value,* or *par value,* which is printed on the face of the bond.

■ The repayment date is the *maturity date.*

■ The period of time that the bond is outstanding is the *term.* Municipal bonds usually have a term of from one through twenty years.

■ Bond certificates must now be registered because of the 1983 Tax Equity and Fiscal Responsibilities Act (TEFRA).

■ Registered bonds require that all payments be made solely to the registered owners on record with the school district that issued them.

■ When the bonds are backed up by collateral, such as property, the bonds are referred to as *mortgage bonds.*

■ When the bond is issued on the full faith of the borrower, it is called a *debenture.*

■ *Municipal bonds* are issued by cities, states, and political subdivisions.

■ Municipal bonds differ from corporate bonds in that they are *tax exempt.*

■ There are three basic types of municipal bonds:

*General obligation bonds,* which are backed by the faith and taxing authority of the issuer.

*Revenue bonds,* which are backed by the earning power of the facility constructed. (A stadium would generate gate receipts that would be used to retire the bonds.)

*Special tax bonds,* which are backed by a special tax levied yearly to pay the principal and interest of a maturing series. This is the type usually issued by school districts.

■ Bonds are rated by the following two independent agencies, which measure the probability of a bond issuer being capable of repaying the principal amount at maturity and the interest schedule:

*Standard and Poor's Corporation* uses the first four letters of the alphabet—AAA, AA, A; BBB, BB, B; CCC, CC, C; through D (default)—in rating bonds, with AAA being the most secure.

*Moody's Investor Service Incorporated* also uses the alphabet but stops with C.

Source: Adapted and amended from Jeffrey B. Little and Lucien Rhodes, *Understanding Wall Street,* rev ed. (Cockeysville, MD: Liberty Publishing, 1994), pp. 126–128.

student, and the other costs $20,000 per student.[139] To be sure, these differences in school construction costs have ramifications for property tax assessments.

Schools in the future will cost more than current prices because the designs will be more complex and built for varied functions using more sophisticated components and materials. There will probably be more (1) technological equipment, such as computers, videos, and satellite dishes; (2) school laboratories; (3) places for small-group and independent study; (4) flexible spaces, module classrooms, and adaptable walls; (5) contrasting or great spaces such as common rooms, atriums, and open courtyards; (6) innovative spaces and materials such as underground structures and new plastic and prefabricated materials; (7) expensive lighting, heating, and communications equipment; (8) energy-conservation controls, solar features, heat pumps, and geothermal heating and cooling systems; (9) earth

[139] Ornstein, "School Finance Trends for the Year 2000." Also see Agnes G. Case, *How To Get the Most Reform For Your Reform Money* (Lanham, MD: Rowman & Littlefield, 2004).

berms and high clerestory windows; (10) curved corners and curved furniture; (11) pitched roofs and arches; and (12) centers or wings to house child-care, elderly, and community services.[140] Yesterday's "boxy" classrooms and rectangular buildings will increasingly be replaced by flexible spaces and a variety of exterior designs.

## International Comparisons of Education Spending

There is a growing interest in obtaining international comparisons of expenditures and other aspects of educational information. Because it is unreasonable to make comparisons with Third World or developing nations, most of the international comparisons are made with countries similar to ours. As shown in Figure 11–1, the United States spends 5.3 percent of its gross domestic product on education; that is, we rank tenth among the seventeen countries listed with data. Our expenditure in actual dollars per student is higher—second only to Switzerland.

One way to view these patterns is to conclude that the United States makes an average effort to finance education. Because its capacity for funding education is high, an average effort is insufficient. In America we also have very high academic expenditures. Our nation devotes resources to many different public areas, especially social security, health, and medicine; therefore, we are actually doing very well in our social and education funding patterns.[141]

When we look at what we spend and what we produce, we learn sadly that our output, as measured in the form of international achievement test scores, is very low compared to that of other industrialized nations. Japan and South Korea, for example, rank low in education spending, about one-third less per student for Japan and about 40 percent less for South Korea than in the United States, yet they have the highest math and science achievement test scores, while we have among the lowest.[142] One could infer that school expenditures do not correlate directly with academic output; other

variables (what some might call excuses) are more important (see Chapter 14).

Regardless of all the reasons, we are living in the midst of a workforce time bomb—growing illiteracy among U.S. workers will subsequently influence our economic output. Not only are our junior and senior high school students outperformed by their international counterparts, but the same holds true for American adults under age forty. For example, at the 55–65 age bracket, American adults rank fifth in literacy among seventeen industrialized nations; in the 36–45 age bracket, Americans rank eighth; in the 16–25 bracket, they rank fourteenth. Overall, U.S. adult literacy ranks tenth out of seventeen.[143] It appears, then, that we need to depend (and have depended) on "brain drain" from other countries, especially from Asia, to prop up American science and technology, and economic output in general.

As shown in Figure 11–1, examining the gross domestic product (GDP) is perhaps the best indicator of spending comparisons. GDP comparisons allow us to factor in expenditures relative to various nations' ability to finance education. According the Organization for Economic Cooperation and Development (OECD), a positive correlation exists between GDP per capita and levels of education. Wealthier countries tend to spend more per primary, secondary, and postsecondary students than do less wealthy countries. Annual expenditures at the primary level among OECD members ranged from $1467 in Mexico to $10,611 in Luxembourg, with the United States spending $8049 (a ranking of second among thirty nations). At the secondary level, expenditures ranged from $1768 in Mexico to $15,195 in Luxembourg. U.S. spending on secondary education was $9098, ranking fourth among thirty OECD nations with only Austria and Belgium spending more.[144]

Similarly, the United States averaged 15.5 students per class at the elementary school level, seventh lowest among nineteen industrialized countries, and 15.6 at the high school level, also fourteenth lowest among nineteen industrialized countries.[145] Nonetheless, U.S. achievement on international tests in reading, math, and science remains among the lowest compared to other industrialized nations; financial input does not correlate with academic output.

[140] Ornstein, "School Finance and the Condition of Schools"; Marla C. Rist, "Schools by Design," *American School Board Journal*, 176 (1989): 42–43, 48.

[141] Daniel U. Levine, "Educational Spending: International Comparisons," *Theory into Teaching*, 33 (1994): 126–131.

[142] *Digest of Education Statistics, 2005*, table 406, p. 665.

[143] Aaron Bernstein, "The Time Bomb in the Work Force: Illiteracy," *Business Week*, 25 February 2002, p. 122.

[144] *Digest of Education Statistics, 2005*, table 406, p. 665.

[145] Ibid, table 389, p. 642.

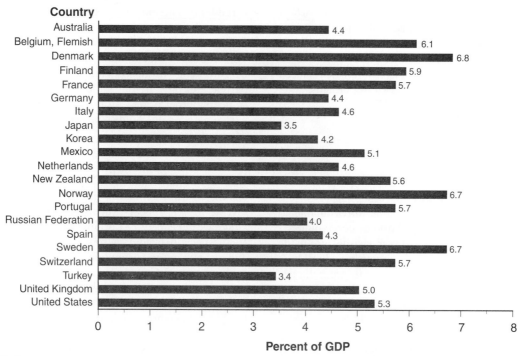

**Figure 11–1**

Education Expenditures as a Percentage of the Gross Domestic Product:
Selected Industrialized Countries, 2002

Source: *Digest of Education Statistics, 2005* (Washington, DC: U.S. Government Printing Office,
2006), fig. 28, p. 636.

NOTE: Includes all government expenditures for education institutions, plus public subsidies to
households for living costs which are not spent at educational institutions.

There are enough explanations to choose from to explain the input/output (money/achievement) factors for funding American schools. Although educators have improved their methods for analyzing and comparing international expenditures on education, it is still difficult to make precise comparisons that account for differences in operation of schools, money exchange rates, and social/political variables. At present, the data should be viewed with some reservations; however, it is difficult to have a frank discussion on policy issues involving different groups of students—and the cause-effect relations involving student achievement.

## Summary

1. Schools are supported by local, state, and federal revenues, with the greatest share derived from state sources and the smallest share from federal sources. Since the early twentieth century, state support has increased dramatically, and local support has been reduced; federal support grew until the early 1990s and then leveled off.

2. School finance is based on the principle of equality of opportunity; nevertheless, there is wide variation in the financial ability among states and within states (at the local school district level) to support education. Not all states or school districts can finance education equally well.

3. Poorer school districts tend to receive more money from their respective states than do wealthier school districts. Poorer states, especially those in the South and Southwest, tend to receive more money from the federal government than do wealthier states and states in the Northeast and Midwest. The additional amount of revenue received, however, rarely makes up for the total difference in expenditures.

# PRO/CON Debate

## Financing Education

Since colonial times, education in America has flourished at the local level. Over time most state governments have accepted primary responsibility. This acceptance is in accordance with the 10th Amendment to the U.S. Constitution, state constitutional obligations, and the U.S. Supreme Court's judicial review. Federal aid has affected the states' responsibility. Currently the generally accepted educational practice (GAEP) is one of federalism: a partnership of local control, state responsibility, federal interest.

**Question:** Should state government bear the primary responsibility for financing education?

### Arguments PRO

1. The Tenth Amendment to the U.S. Constitution implicitly suggests (since education is not mentioned in the Constitution) that education is the responsibility of individual states.

2. State constitutions, statutes, and practice affirm that education is the function of the state.

3. In *San Antonio Independent School District v. Rodriguez* (1973), the U.S. Supreme Court declared that "education was not among the rights protected by the U.S. Constitution."

4. The U.S. Supreme Court has refused to hear any case dealing with educational finance since the *Rodriguez* case. Since *Rodriguez,* forty-one states have been involved in litigation concerning the financing of education. Financing education is primarily a state responsibility.

5. State educational leaders know better the conditions in a state than people in Washington, DC; there are many differences between Pennsylvania and Montana, for example. Pennsylvanians and Montanans should be able to solve those educational differences as they see fit.

6. The practice of the federal government to spend about 7 percent of the educational funding has resulted in the federal government wanting significant control — instituting national standards, national tests, national promotion policies, national dress codes, etc. Based on their financial commitment, their controlling actions are far in excess of what they deserve or merit.

7. States still have the right, if they choose, to institute support programs for nonpublic schools.

### Arguments CON

1. Article 1, Section 8, of the U.S. Constitution gives Congress the power to "lay and collect taxes . . . to provide for the . . . general welfare of the United States." Education is part of the general welfare.

2. The U.S. Constitution's Fourteenth Amendment provides that "no state shall deny any person . . . equal protection of the law."

3. In *Brown v. Board of Education* (1954), the U.S. Supreme Court stated that "where the state has undertaken to provide it, [education] is a right which must be made available to all on equal terms."

4. The Supreme Court justices can change their collective mind. There are many examples of that in our history. Contrast, for example, the Dred Scott decision that stated "a slave was property" to the civil rights cases of the Warren and subsequent courts.

5. Because the federal government sends billions of dollars to states to solve nationwide needs, the federal government has the right to be assured that the money is being used efficiently, and for the purpose it was intended to be used.

6. Education is a national need and deserves national leadership. Almost all industrialized countries in the world have stronger central or federal control over schools than the United States. Implementing national standards and a national curriculum might very well improve our international test results.

7. There are serious constitutional questions generated when such aid is implemented. Prudence should be evidenced in such procedures.

4. There are six basic methods the states use to finance public education. The flat grant model is the oldest and most unequal method because it is based on a fixed amount multiplied by the number of students in attendance. The most common methods of finance are based on some type of equalization plan to supplement less wealthy school districts. The power-equalizing plan (which deals with inverse ratios of wealth) and weighted-student plan (which deals with special characteristics of students and special programs) are the most common methods. Another method is using choice as an option.

5. Developing a budget can be classified into four major activities: planning or identifying priorities; analysis, dealing with goals or evaluative criteria; requesting, that is, establishing priorities and negotiating; and controls, dealing with inventory, receipts, and disbursements.

6. Education costs per student tend to be higher in larger than smaller schools.

7. Most research indicates that specific items related to school effectiveness are not cost-related; rather, they deal with organizational climate and culture.

8. Because of the aftermath of September 11 and the current economy, there is still significant pressure to trim school budgets and save money. Competing demands for public revenues, especially from the aging population, and the fact there are fewer households with children attending school, are some of the reasons why taxpayers are not interested in spending more money for schools.

9. Controversy over school infrastructure costs and environmental hazards such as asbestos and radon gas are likely to affect school expenditures in the future.

10. Although Americans have high expenditures for public education, the results are not impressive when we make comparisons to other nations in our financial commitment to education and our academic achievement.

## Key Terms

gross domestic product
regressive taxes
progressive taxes
elastic taxes
inelastic taxes
property tax
market value
assessed value
mill
user fees
municipal overburden
educational overburden
discretionary funding
formula funding
effective schools
asbestos-laden buildings
radon gas
electromagnetic fields
sick building syndrome
school infrastructure

## Discussion Questions

1. Why do city schools have more fiscal problems than suburban or rural schools?

2. What state taxes are used to provide school revenues? Which ones are progressive? Regressive?

3. Why is it important to look at each budget item in terms of the percentage spent to date and the annual projected budget?

4. What are the primary reasons for closing schools? What options do school administrators have when they must close down schools?

5. What factors or financial considerations must school administrators deal with when building schools?

## Suggested Readings

Bracey, Gerald. *The War Against America's Public Schools: Privatizing Schools, Commercializing Education* (Boston: Allyn and Bacon, 2002). The author describes the influence of corporate America on education.

DeBray, Elizabeth. *Politics, Ideology, and Education* (New York: Teachers College Press, 2006). The author examines the politics of federal education policy and financing.

Finn, Chester. *We Must Take Charge* (New York: Free Press, 1993). The author presents some bold ideas for improving school outcomes—important for administrators and policymakers.

Moe, Terry M. *Schools, Vouchers, and the American Public* (Washington, DC: Brookings Institution, 2002). The author gives an analysis of school choice and public opinion.

Odden, Allan, and Sarah Archibald. *Reallocating Resources* (Thousand Oaks, CA: Corwin Press, 2001). The authors explain how schools can better plan and allocate resources to boost student achievement.

Owings, William, and Leslie Kaplan. *American Public School Finance* (Belmont, CA: Wadsworth, 2006). The authors provide a complete overview of school finance, including debunking myths about spending on public education.

Sergiovanni, Thomas J. *Rethinking Leadership*, 2nd ed. (Thousand Oaks, CA: Corwin Press, 2006). The focus is on moral leadership, school change, and financial policy.

# 12.

# Legal Consideratio and Education

*which provisions...*

## FOCUSING QUESTIONS

1  What are the sources of law under which school administrators operate?

2  How is the U.S. judicial system organized?

3  What are the legal issues related to professional school personnel?

4  What are the rights of students under the law?

5  What are the major legal issues pertaining to schools and the state?

6  Why is it important for school administrators to be knowledgeable about the law?

---

In this chapter, we attempt to answer these questions concerning the law as it applies to public schools. We begin our discussion by exploring the legal framework for public education. We examine the legal significance of federal and state constitutions and statutes, the major provisions of the U.S. Constitution affecting education, and the basic structure of the federal and state judicial systems. Then we discuss such personnel-related issues as certification, employment contracts, nonrenewal and dismissal, discrimination in employment, and torts. Next, we examine such student-related issues as school attendance, corporal punishment, suspension and expulsion, search and seizure, freedom of expression, and classification practices. Finally, we discuss such school-state issues as school desegregation, religion in the schools, and challenges to state finance schemes.

We emphasize decisions of the U.S. Supreme Court and those decisions of the highest state courts. The cases cited were selected for their precedent value on substantive legal principles of school law rather than their recency.

## Legal Framework for Public Education

All three units of government—federal, state, and local—exercise some degree of authority and control over U.S. public education. Educational governance of public schools is the result of constitutional and statutory provisions of the federal government, the fifty state governments, and case law. The degree of authority and control that local school boards have over school operations depends on the constitutional and statutory provisions of their state.

### Federal Role in Education

Education is not a function specifically delegated to the federal government. This is recognized in the Tenth Amendment to the U.S. Constitution, which provides that "the powers not delegated to the United States by the Constitution, nor prohibited by it to the States, are reserved to the States respectively, or to the people." Although education is not specifically delegated to the federal government, it has exercised considerable influence in educational matters, primarily through the provisions of the federal Constitution, decisions of the U.S. Supreme Court, and congressional acts.

**The Federal Constitution**    The Constitution established three separate branches of government: legislative, the Congress (Article I); executive, the president (Article II); and judicial, a Supreme Court and necessary inferior courts (Article III).[1] These three branches of government provide a system of checks and balances to ensure that the intent of the Constitution is upheld.

The federal Constitution is the supreme law of the land. All statutes passed by Congress, state constitutions and statutes, and policies of local boards of education are subject to the provisions of the U.S. Constitution. The provisions of the Constitution that have had the greatest impact on the operation of public schools are Article I, Section 10, and the First, Fourth, Fifth, and Fourteenth Amendments.

*Obligation of Contracts*    Article I, Section 10, provides in part that "no state shall . . . pass any . . . law impairing the obligation of contracts." This article guaranteeing the **obligation of contracts** has been litigated in numerous public school cases. Court decisions have verified that contracts entered into by school districts (including personnel contracts and other contracted services) are fully protected under Article I, Section 10. The provision also applies when a state legislature seeks to alter a teacher tenure or retirement statute in which contractual status prevails under the law.[2]

*First Amendment*    The **First Amendment** provides that "Congress shall make no law respecting the establishment of religion, or prohibiting the free exercise thereof; or abridging the freedom of speech, or of press; or of the right of the people peaceably to assemble, and to petition the Government for a redress of grievances." The first part of the amendment dealing with religious freedoms precipitated litigation challenging government aid to parochial schools and public school policies objected to on religious grounds. The *freedom of speech* portion has evoked numerous court cases involving students' and teachers' rights to freedom of expression. The *rights*

*of assembly* part has precipitated litigation involving students' organizations and employees' rights to organize and bargain collectively.

*Fourth Amendment*    The **Fourth Amendment** provides in part that "the right of the people to be secure . . . against unreasonable searches and seizures . . . and no Warrants shall issue, but upon probable cause. . . ." This amendment has been the subject of litigation involving searches of students' lockers and person and, in some cases, teachers' rights to privacy.

*Fifth Amendment*    The **Fifth Amendment** reads in part that "no person . . . shall be compelled in any criminal case to be a witness against himself, nor deprived of life, liberty, or property without due process of law; nor shall private property be taken for public use, without just compensation." The first clause is relevant to cases where teachers have been questioned by superiors about their alleged activities with subversive organizations. The **due process clause** pertains specifically to acts of the federal government. The last clause is germane in instances where states or school boards acquire property for school building purposes.

*Fourteenth Amendment*    The **Fourteenth Amendment** provides in part that no state shall "deprive any person of life, liberty or property without due process of law. . . ." Numerous education cases involving this provision have come to the courts. Compulsory school attendance laws give students a property right to attend school. Teachers with tenure have a property right to continued employment. Liberty rights include interests in one's reputation and the right to personal privacy.

The Fourteenth Amendment also provides that no state shall "deny to any person within its jurisdiction the equal protection of the law." The **equal protection clause** of the Fourteenth Amendment has been involved in a wide variety of education cases in recent years. Among them are cases involving alleged discrimination based on race, sex, ethnic background, age, and handicaps and state financing of public schools.

*Federal Statutes*    Article I, Section 8, grants Congress "the power . . . to lay and collect taxes . . . and provide for the Common Defense and general Welfare of the United States. . . ." This provision is based on the assumption that a high level of education is essential for the civic and economic prosperity of the nation. That is, to improve education is to provide for the general welfare of the United States. Congress acts under the "general welfare" clause when it passes federal statutes and

---

[1] U.S. Constitution, Articles I, II, III, ratified 1789.

[2] *Ball v. Board of Trustees of Teachers Retirement Fund,* 58 Atl. 111 (N.J. 1904).

provides federal tax dollars for school programs within the states. Federal statutes have provided extensive education programs in such areas as defense, vocational education, civil rights, elementary and secondary education, bilingual education, sex discrimination, special education, protecting the confidentiality of student records, and pregnancy bias.[3]

## State Role in Education

At no point does the federal Constitution refer to education. This, coupled with the language of the Tenth Amendment (". . . powers not delegated to the United States by the Constitution, nor prohibited by it to the States, are reserved to the States respectively, or to the people"), vested in state government the legal responsibility for the control and direction of public education. Thus, while federal authority is restrictive concerning education, the state has complete authority to provide a public education system.

**State Constitutions**    The United States is organized into two streams of government activity: a federal legal system and fifty separate state legal systems. Each state has its own constitution that forms its basic laws. The primary function of state constitutions is to restrict the powers of state legis— ance with federal l— tutions.[4] Generally — date for the establi— Frequently, state co— jects as the federal — sues, such as separ— stitutions may be n—

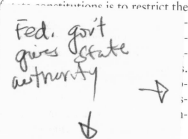

**State Statutes**    Every state legislature enacts, amends, and repeals laws. These laws affecting public schools form the statutes of the fifty U.S. states. Recall that the Tenth Amendment of the U.S. Constitution is a plenary, absolute, power grant to the state legislatures over public education. However, the laws enacted cannot contravene federal law or the state constitution.

For example, over the years, the federal government has limited state authority over public education as school operation matters have been challenged in the courts. Decisions on such state issues as racial desegre-

gation of public schools, teachers' free speech, students' symbolic protest, students' procedural due process, constitutionality of corporal punishment, search and seizure, and nontort liability of school board members have placed state authority over public school operations within the legal boundaries of the federal Constitution. Courts resolved these conflicts, and those decisions became part of **case law,** that is, principles of law derived from court decisions.

**Local Boards of Education**    Obviously, state legislatures cannot assume supervisory responsibility for public schools. In keeping with the framework of decentralization of educational operation, the general supervision and administration of each state's public school system is delegated to state and local boards of education who in turn are responsible for hiring school administrators and classroom teachers. These groups have the authority to enforce policies and procedures for the operation and management of public schools. Their actions must be within the legal boundaries of federal and state constitutions and statutes. For example, building principals and classroom teachers rely on this authority in dealing with such issues as administering student punishment, suspensions and expulsions, searching a student's locker, and the like.

## The Courts

The provisions of federal and state constitutions, statutes, and policies of local boards of education do not guarantee proper execution of the law. A mechanism exists in our legal system for allowing an individual or group whose constitutional rights may have been violated to seek adjudication in the courts. Courts, however, do not act on their own initiative. Instead, courts settle only those disputes referred to them for decision.[5]

The U.S. judicial system is complex and multifaceted. As noted earlier, it is organized into one federal court system and fifty state court systems.

**Federal Court System**    Article III, Section 1, of the U.S. Constitution provides that "(t)he judicial power of the United States shall be vested in one Supreme Court, and in such inferior courts as the Congress may from time to time ordain and establish."[6] These courts have the authority to adjudicate cases dealing with a provi-

[3] *Digest of Education Statistics* (Washington, DC: U.S. Government Printing Office, 2000).

[4] E. Edmund Reutter, *The Law of Public Education,* 5th ed. (Westbury, NY: Foundation Press, 1999).

[5] Ibid.

[6] U.S. Constitution, Art. III, Sec. 1, ratified 1789.

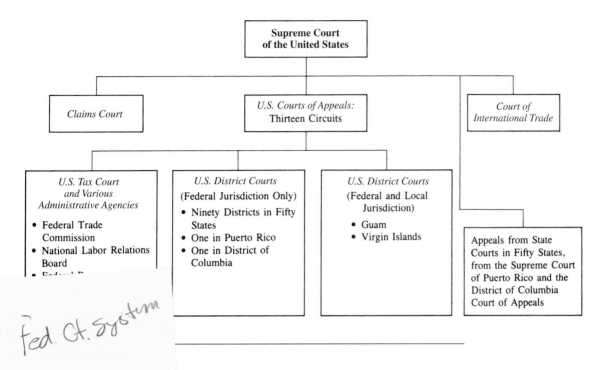

Fed. Ct. System

*ederal Courts,* rev. ed. (Washington, DC: WANT Publishing,

sion of the federal Constitution or a federal statute. For example, a federal court might decide an alleged breach of contract between a board of education and a private contractor under Article I, Section 10, of the U.S. Constitution or the nonrenewal of a tenured teacher's employment contract under the same article or the due process clause of the Fourteenth Amendment.

The federal court system contains three levels of general jurisdiction: district courts, courts of appeals, and the U.S. Supreme Court. In addition, there are some courts of special jurisdiction such as the claims court, tax court, and court of international trade. Figure 12–1 depicts the federal court system.

The federal court system contains ninety federal district courts. These are designated as courts of original jurisdiction or trial courts and serve as the first level in the federal court structure. Each state has at least one district court, and many states have between two and four districts. For example, California, New York, and Texas have four district courts each. In addition, separate districts exist with federal jurisdiction only in Puerto Rico and the District of Columbia and with federal and local jurisdictions in Guam and the Virgin Islands.

Appeals from the federal district courts can go to the U.S. Courts of Appeals, the next level in the federal court system. There are twelve federal circuits, with an appeals court for each. A thirteenth federal circuit court has jurisdiction to hear special claims such as customs, patents and copyrights, taxes, and international trade. (See the map in Figure 12–2.) Decisions rendered in appeals court are binding only in the states within uch decisions often influence other federal ealing with similar issues.

The e Court, the highest court in the system, is the cfinal appeal on federal law questions. Of the education-related questions that eventually reach the Court, petitioners claim that a states or the policies of a local board of educd their constitutional rights or sederal law. In cases directly involal matters, certain provisions of the U.S. Cion are involved more often than others. These provisions, noted previously, are Article I, Section 10, and the First, Fourth, Fifth, and Fourteenth Amendments, especially the due process and equal protection clauses of the Fourteenth Amendment.

14th

The 14th

**State Court Systems**  Because education is a state function, state courts decide most cases involving educational matters. Each state has its own unique court structure, but similarities exist. Many states have a three-level structure similar to the federal court sys-

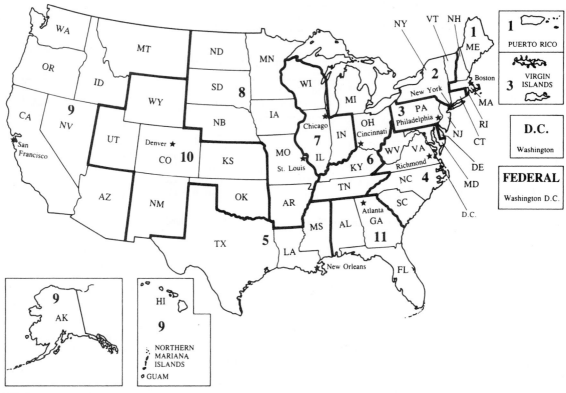

**Figure 12–2**

The Federal Judicial Circuits

tem. Typically, there are courts of original jurisdiction (trial courts), courts of appeal (appellate courts), and the state's highest court (Supreme Court), often referred to generally as the "court of last resort." Names assigned to these courts at each of the three levels are not uniform among the states. Decisions rendered by the state's highest court can be appealed to the U.S. Supreme Court only if a question of federal law is involved.

## The Law and Professional Personnel

The federal Constitution vested in state government the legal responsibility for the control and direction of public education through the fifty state legislatures. However, the actual administration of public school systems is delegated to state boards of education, state departments of education, and local boards of education. These agencies adopt and enforce reasonable rules and regulations emanating from statutes enacted by state legislatures for the operation of public school systems. In this section, we discuss the following issues related to professional personnel: certification, contracts, termination of employment, discrimination in employment, and tort liability.

### Certification

The schools employ several categories of professional personnel: superintendents, principals, curriculum specialists, business managers, school psychologists, social workers, counselors, classroom teachers, and the like. To be eligible for employment in a professional position, the individual should possess a valid certificate issued according to statutory provisions of a given state. These statutes, varying from state to state, concern requirements and procedures for obtaining the different certificates. Generally, the legislature delegates the legal authority to issue and process certification to state boards and departments of education. In some states, however, the legislature delegates that authority to a local school district as is the case in New York City and more recently in Chicago.

The preparation standards for each type of certificate are similar from state to state, with only a few exceptions. For example, every state requires applicants to have a college degree with a minimum number of credit hours in a prescribed curriculum. Besides educational requirements, other prerequisites may include evidence of good moral character, a minimum age, U.S. citizenship, and satisfactory performance on a state-administered examination.

The initial certification is usually issued for a specified period of time, including various designations such as temporary, emergency, conditional, standard, life, or permanent. It is the certificate holder's responsibility to keep it renewed. This may require evidence of additional coursework, professional experience in a public school, or passage of a standardized examination such as the National Teachers Examination (NTE). Certificates also include specific endorsements (e.g., superintendent, principal, counselor, teacher), subject areas (e.g., English, social studies, mathematics, sciences), and grade levels (e.g., elementary, middle or junior high school, high school). A school board's failure to assign professional personnel to positions for which they are certified can result in loss of state accreditation and federal funding.[7]

The state also has the power to revoke certification. Certification revocation is different from dismissal from employment by a local board of education. A local school board can legally dismiss a superintendent, principal, teacher, or other professional employee, but the state is generally the only government body that can revoke a certificate. Moreover, state statutes usually specify the grounds and procedures for certification revocation. For example, under the Kentucky statute, it is provided that "any certification . . . may be revoked by the Education Professional Standards Board for immorality, misconduct in office, incompetency or willful neglect of duty. . . . Before the certification is revoked the defendant shall be given a copy of the charges against him and given an opportunity, upon not less than twenty (20) days' notice, to be heard in person or by counsel."[8]

## Contracts

A certificate renders the holder eligible for employment in a state; it does not guarantee employment. Statutory law provides that local boards of education have the legal authority to enter into contracts with professional personnel. The relationship between a school board and its professional employees is contractual. The general legal principles governing contracts—offer and acceptance, competent parties, consideration, legal subject matter, and proper form—apply to this contractual relationship.

*Offer and acceptance* pertains to the job description, compensation level, and time of performance to which both parties have agreed. In most states, because only the board of education has the power to employ personnel, it must exercise that function itself. It cannot delegate the employment duty to the superintendent of schools or to individual members of the school board. Further, a local board of education is considered to be a legal body only as a corporate unit; therefore, for a board to enter into a valid contract with a teacher or other professional personnel, there must be a meeting of the board.

*Competent parties* means that, for a valid contract to exist, the parties must be authorized by law to enter into a contractual relationship. By law the school board possesses the legal authority to enter into contracts. A teacher or other professional employee is legally competent to contract providing she possesses the necessary certification and meets other state requirements. An application of this element of contracts is found in a Kentucky case. A teacher lacked a certificate when she began teaching and was ineligible for one because she was under the state's minimum-age requirement for certification. Consequently, the contract between the parties was void, and the teacher was not entitled to receive a salary for the work she performed while a minor.[9]

*Consideration* pertains to the promises bargained for and exchanged between the parties. Consideration is something of value—usually money or the equivalent. Promises to perform services gratuitously are not contracts because they are not supported by consideration. To have valid consideration, each party must give up something of value. In the case of an employment contract, consideration consists of the exchange of promises between the employee and the school district. The

[7]Martha M. McCarthy and Nelda H. Cambron-McCabe, *Public School Law*, 5th ed. (Needham Heights, MA: Allyn and Bacon, 2002).

[8]*Kentucky Rev. Stat.*, Ch. 161.120 (1992).

[9]*Floyd County Bd. of Educ. v. Slone,* 307 S.W. 2d 912 (Ky. 1957).

employee promises to perform specified services, and the school board promises to pay a specified salary.

*Legal subject matter* refers to mutual assurance between the parties that the job and its performance would not be a violation of the law. Finally, *proper form* means that all legal requirements, as stipulated in the state's statutes, must be followed in order for a contract to be valid. The precise form for contracts may vary from one state to another, but in most states, the statute requires that contracts with professional personnel be written.[10]

The policies and procedures of the local board of education, provisions of the state constitution and its statutes, and the collective bargaining agreement, if there is one, are considered part of the contract between the school district and the teacher or other professional employee. It is recommended therefore that the aforementioned inclusions to an employee's contract be referenced either in the body or on the face of the contract; they then become expressly part of the individual employment contract.

## Termination of Employment

Local boards of education possess the legal authority to terminate the employment of school personnel. The U.S. Supreme Court bestowed on school boards this authority when it held that ". . . school authorities have the right and the duty to screen the officials, teachers, and employees as to their fitness to maintain the integrity of the schools as part of ordered society. . . ."[11] However, despite the legal authority of a board of education to terminate the employment, it cannot arbitrarily discharge personnel at any time.

**Tenure Law**  Tenure statutes protect teachers (and other school district personnel specifically enumerated in state statutes) from arbitrary actions by local boards of education. The courts have sustained the constitutionality of such statutes. Teachers' Tenure Act cases[12] have concluded that tenure exists to protect competent teachers and other members of the teaching profession against unlawful and arbitrary board actions and to provide orderly procedures for the dismissal of unsatisfactory teachers and other professional personnel.

Tenure is attained by complying with specific provisions prescribed by state statutes. The nature of these provisions varies from state to state, but certain conditions are included in most legislation. Nearly all statutes require that teachers serve a probationary period before tenure becomes effective. Generally, the probationary period ranges from three to five years, during which time a teacher is employed on a term contract. On completion of the probation period, personnel acquire tenure either automatically or by school board action. Texas law is an exception and permits the local school board to choose between adopting continuing contracts and remaining under term contracts, in which case teachers do not have tenure.[13]

Which positions are to be covered under tenure laws is within the prerogative of state legislatures. In some jurisdictions, tenure legislation extends to selected administrative positions, but rarely to superintendents. Others afford tenure only to teachers. For example, in South Carolina, South Dakota, and Missouri, a school administrator possessing a teacher's certificate is a "teacher" within the meaning of tenure laws.[14] In Kentucky, "(t)he term 'administrator' for the purpose of (tenure) shall mean a certified employee, below the rank of superintendent. . . ."[15]

Although principals and certain other supervisory personnel can acquire tenure either as teachers or as principals in states having tenure laws, superintendents are not generally covered by tenure in that position unless the statute specifically indicates such inclusions. For example, the Illinois Supreme Court ruled that, because they are district employees who require certification, superintendents are covered by the tenure law, but that the tenure protection extended only to a teaching position and not to an administrative one.[16] On the other hand, tenure can be acquired by superintendents in New Jersey.[17]

In discussing the termination of employment of teachers and supervisory personnel, the terms *nonrenewal*

---

[10] *Gordon v. Board of Directors of West Side Area Vocational Tech. School,* 347 A. 2d 347 (Pa. 1975).

[11] *Adler v. Bd. of Educ.,* 342 U.S. 485 (1952).

[12] *Teachers' Tenure Act Cases,* 329 Pa. 213, 197 A. 344 (1938).

[13] *White v. South Park,* I.S.D., 693 F. 2d 1163 (5 Cir. 1983).

[14] *Snipes v. McAndrew,* 313 S.E. 2d 294 (S.C. 1984); *Waltz v. Bd. of Educ.,* 329 N.W. 2d 131 (S.D. 1983); *Fuller v. N. Kansas City,* S.D., 629 S.W. 2d 404 (Mo. 1982).

[15] *Ky. Rev. Stat.,* Ch. 161.720, Sec. 8 (1992).

[16] *Lester v. Bd. of Educ. of S.D.,* No. 119, 230 N.E. 2d 893 (Ill. 1967).

[17] *N.J. Stat. Ann.,* Sec. 18A:28–5(4) (1999).

and *dismissal* are often used interchangeably. There is a substantial difference, however, in the manner in which the termination operates in each case. If not protected by tenure, a school employee may be nonrenewed for no reason or for any reason whatsoever, providing it does not violate an employee's substantive constitutional rights (e.g., free speech, protection against racial discrimination). Courts have reasoned in these cases that the contract has simply terminated and there is no "expectancy of continued employment." Dismissal, on the other hand, whether under tenure status or during an unexpired contract, is permissible only "for cause." Consequently, a dismissal of a tenured employee or a nontenured professional during a contract year is entitled to a due process hearing embodying all the statutory and constitutional safeguards.

**Dismissal Procedures**   Most tenure laws provide specific procedures for dismissing tenured employees. The procedure typically includes three elements: notice by a specific date, specification of charges against the employee, and a hearing at which the charges are discussed. When state law describes a specific procedure for dismissal, it must be followed exactly to make the action legal.

Besides the procedures required under state law, tenure rights qualify for constitutional procedural protections encompassed within the concepts of **property** and **liberty interests** under the due process clause of the Fourteenth Amendment. The holding of a teaching position qualifies as a property right if the employee has an unexpired contract or has acquired tenure. The aforementioned protections of the Fourteenth Amendment do not normally extend to nontenured employees. The Supreme Court has affirmed the view of the courts that nontenured employees have no property or liberty interests in continued employment.[18] In exceptional situations, courts have recognized "de facto tenure" where there was no tenure law, but tenure was acquired by custom and precedent.[19] However, de facto tenure is not possible where there is a well-established statewide system.

A liberty interest would be an issue in dismissal, and due process required, when evidence exists that a charge has been made that places a stigma on an employee's reputation, thus foreclosing future employment opportunities or seriously damaging his standing in the community.[20] A liberty interest would not be a constitutional safeguard when school board members and school administrators refrain from making public statements or releasing information that is derogatory to the employee. Even when statements are made, if they simply describe unsatisfactory performance in general, normally they do not constitute a constitutional violation of the employee's Fourteenth Amendment rights.

Examples of charges against employees not involving stigma include ineffective teaching methods, inability to maintain classroom discipline, and inability to get along with administrators and colleagues. Failure to award tenure does not automatically create a stigma. Examples of stigmas that qualify for constitutional due process protection include manifest racism, immoral conduct, serious mental disorder, a drinking or drug problem, willful neglect of duty, and responsibility for the deterioration of a school.[21]

Causes for dismissal are generally specified in state statutes and differ from one state to another; however, there are similarities. For example, in Kentucky tenured employees can be dismissed for insubordination; immoral character or conduct; physical or mental disability; or inefficiency, incompetency, or neglect of duty.[22] In Illinois cause for dismissal is specified as incompetency, cruelty, negligence, immorality or other sufficient cause and whenever in the board's opinion a teacher is not qualified to teach or the best interests of the school require it.[23] In Connecticut cause is enumerated as inefficiency, incompetency, insubordination, moral misconduct, disability as shown by competent medical evidence, elimination of position, or for other due and sufficient cause.[24]

## Discrimination in Employment

Recent federal laws intended to remove discrimination in employment have had a direct impact on school board employment practices. Such legislation includes Title VII of the Civil Rights Act of 1964, Title IX of the Education Amendments of 1972, the Rehabilitation Act of 1973, the Equal Pay Act of 1963, the Age Discrimination Act of 1986, the Pregnancy Discrimination

---

[18] *Roth v. Bd. of Regents,* 408 U.S. 564 (1972).

[19] *Perry v. Sinderman,* 408 U.S. 593 (1972).

[20] *Roth v. Bd. of Regents.*

[21] Reutter, *The Law of Public Education.*

[22] *Ky. Rev. Stat.,* Ch. 161.790 (1998).

[23] *Ill. Ann. Stat.,* Ch. 122, Sec. 10–22.4 (1998).

[24] *Conn. Gen. Stat. Ann.,* Tit. 5A, Sec. 10–151 (1999).

Act of 1978, and the Americans with Disabilities Act of 1990 (ADA). In addition, guidelines and policies from such federal agencies as the Equal Employment Opportunity Commission (EEOC), the Office of Economic Opportunity (OEO), and 42 U.S.C. Section 1983, in particular, have been applied in claims of employment discrimination. This section briefly discusses race and gender discrimination, sexual harassment, discrimination based on disabilities, age, religious, and maternity discrimination.

**Race and Gender Discrimination**    Beginning in the early 1970s, the federal courts heard several cases challenging discrimination. In 1971 the U.S. Supreme Court, in *Griggs v. Duke Power Company,* determined that Title VII of the Civil Rights Act of 1964 (pertaining to hiring, promotion, salary, and retention) covered not only overt discrimination but also practices that are discriminatory in operation.[25] The Court held that an employment practice is prohibited if the exclusion of minorities cannot be shown to be related to job performance. The case involved requiring job applicants to possess a high school diploma and make a satisfactory score on a general intelligence test as criteria for employment. The practice was shown to discriminate against black applicants. During the same year, the Court, in *Phillips v. Martin Marietta Corporation,* handed down a decision relative to the disparate treatment of the sexes in the workplace. The Court ruled that discriminatory treatment of the sexes, by employment practices not necessary to the efficient and purposeful operation of an organization, is prohibited by the same federal legislation.[26]

The effect of these two landmark decisions was to force employers to remove "artificial, arbitrary, and unnecessary" barriers to employment that discriminate on the basis of race and gender classification. In 1972, the coverage of these provisions of Title VII, which previously had applied only to private employment, were extended to discriminatory employment practices in educational institutions. Subsequent to *Griggs* and *Phillips,* lower courts have applied these same legal standards to Fourteenth Amendment, Section 1983, and Title VII equal protection cases.

To establish a constitutional violation of equal protection, aggrieved individuals must prove that they have been victims of discrimination. In 1981, the Supreme Court set forth the procedural steps to file a Title VII suit.[27] The plaintiff has the initial burden of establishing a prima facie case of discrimination by showing the existence of five factors: (1) member in a protected group (e.g., minorities, women, aged, handicapped), (2) application for the position, (3) qualification for the position, (4) rejection for the position, and (5) employer's continued pursuit of applicants with the plaintiff's qualifications for the position. These factors constitute an initial, or prima facie, case of discrimination in any type of personnel decision. Once a prima facie case of discrimination is established, the defendant (employer) must articulate a nondiscriminatory reason for the action. If this is accomplished, the plaintiff (employee or applicant) then must prove that the explanation is a pretext for discrimination, the real reason for the personnel decision being based on the consideration of "impermissible factors" in employment.[28] In 1993, the Supreme Court reiterated that the ultimate burden of proof in a discrimination suit lies with the plaintiff.[29] The legal standards emanating from *Griggs, Phillips,* and *Hicks* in claims of discriminatory employment practices under Title VII have been applied also under civil rights legislation barring discrimination based on age. Title VII does not cover discrimination based on disabilities. Employees with disabilities in public schools must look to the Rehabilitation Act of 1973 (Section 504) and the Americans with Disabilities Act of 1990 (ADA).

**Sexual Harassment**    Charges of sexual harassment in the workplace have been litigated under Title VII of the Civil Rights Act of 1964 and Title IX of the Education Amendments of 1972. The regulations implementing Title VII define sexual harassment as follows:

> Unwelcome sexual advances, requests for sexual favors, and other verbal or physical conduct of a sexual nature constitute sexual harassment when (i) submission to such conduct is made either explicitly or implicitly a term or condition of an individual's employment, (ii) submission to or rejection of such conduct by an individual is used as the basis for employment decisions affecting such individual, or (iii) such conduct has the purpose or effect of unreasonably interfering with an individual's work performance or creating an intimidating, hostile, or offensive working environment.[30]

---

[25] *Griggs v. Duke Power Co.,* 401 U.S. 424 (1971).

[26] *Phillips v. Martin Marietta Corp.,* 400 U.S. 542 (1971).

[27] *Texas Department of Community Affairs v. Burdine,* 450 U.S. 248 (1981).

[28] *McDonnell Douglas Corp. v. Green,* 411 U.S. 792 (1973).

[29] *St. Mary's Honor Center v. Hicks,* 113 S. Ct. 2742, 125 L. Ed. 2d 407 (1993).

[30] 29 C.F.R., Sec. 1604.11(a) (1991).

In *Meritor Savings Bank v. Vinson,*[31] the Supreme Court initiated this definition by identifying two different forms of sexual harassment: *quid pro quo* harassment and hostile environment harassment. **Quid pro quo sexual harassment** involves conditioning tangible employment benefits (e.g., promotion, demotion, termination) on sexual favors. **Hostile environment sexual harassment** involves a pattern of unwelcome and offensive conduct that unreasonably interferes with an individual's work performance or creates an intimidating or offensive work environment. The Court warned that "for sexual harassment to be actionable, it must be sufficiently severe or pervasive to alter the conditions of (the victim's) employment and create an abusive working environment."[32] In 1993, the Supreme Court elaborated further on the concept of the hostile environment form of sexual harassment,[33] which creates a more difficult task for the courts to interpret than quid pro quo. In reaffirming the standard set in *Meritor,* the Court said that for sexual harassment to be actionable the conduct must cause "tangible psychological injury" rather than conduct that is "merely offensive." Courts determine this by examining such factors as frequency of the conduct, severity of the conduct, whether it is physically threatening or humiliating, and whether it unreasonably interferes with the employee's work performance.

Five kinds of sexual harassment include sexual bribery, sexual imposition, gender harassment, sexual coercion, and sexual behavior.

■ *Sexual Bribery.* **Sexual bribery** is solicitation of sexual activity or other sex-linked behaviors by promise of rewards; the proposition may be either overt or subtle.

■ *Sexual Imposition.* Examples of gross **sexual imposition** are forceful touching, feeling, grabbing, or sexual assault.

■ *Gender Harassment.* **Gender harassment** means generalized sexist statements and behaviors that convey insulting or degrading attitudes about the opposite sex. Examples include insulting remarks, offensive graffiti, obscene jokes, or humor about sex or women in general.

■ *Sexual Coercion.* **Sexual coercion** means coercion of sexual activity or other sex-linked behavior by

threat of punishment; examples include negative performance evaluations, withholding of promotions, threat of termination.

■ *Sexual Behavior.* **Sexual behavior** means unwanted, inappropriate, and offensive sexual advances. Examples include repeated unwanted sexual invitations, insistent requests for dinner, drinks, or dates, persistent letters, phone calls, and other invitations.[34]

School administrators are strictly liable for quid pro quo sexual harassment under both Title VII of the Civil Rights Act of 1964 and Title IX of the Education Amendments of 1972. Therefore, school leaders need to take positive steps to prevent sexual harassment in the workplace. (See Administrative Advice 12–1.)

**Discrimination Based on Disabilities** The principal federal statutes that affect people with disabilities are the Rehabilitation Act of 1973 (Section 504) and the Americans with Disabilities Act of 1990 (ADA). These statutes prohibit discrimination based on disabilities against persons who are "otherwise qualified" for employment. These laws extend to all stages of employment, from recruiting and screening to hiring, promotion, and dismissal.

Section 504 and the ADA define a disabled person as one who has a physical or mental impairment that substantially limits one or more of such person's major life activities, has a record of such impairment, or is regarded as having such an impairment.[35] The ADA and Section 504, as recently amended, specifically exclude from the coverage of either law persons currently using illegal drugs and alcoholics, whose use of alcohol interferes with job performance. But those in drug rehabilitation programs or who have successfully completed a program may be considered disabled.

The statutory definitions of a disabled person seem to include those with communicable diseases who are qualified to perform the job and whose condition does not threaten the health and safety of others. For example, the Supreme Court has ruled that the definition of a disabled person includes those with an infectious

---

[31]477 U.S. 57 (1986).

[32]*Meritor Savings Bank, id.* at 67.

[33]*Harris v. Forklift Systems, Inc.,* 114 S. Ct. 367, 126 L. Ed. 2d 295 (1993).

[34]Jerry Lowe and Kelly Strnadel, "Sexual Harassment: Approaches to a More Positive Work Environment," unpublished paper, Sam Houston State University, Huntsville, Texas, January 12, 1999.

[35]29 U.S.C. Sec. 706 (8) (B) (i) (1988); 42 U.S.C.A., Sec. 12102(2) (West Supp. 1992).

## ■ Exemplary Educational Administrators in Action

**JOANNA MILLER** Principal, E. M. Baker Elementary School, Great Neck, New York.

**Previous Positions:** Assistant Principal, E. M. Baker Elementary School, Great Neck, New York; Coordinator, Gifted Programs, Community School District 22, NYC Public Schools.

**Latest Degree and Affiliation:** Ed. D., Administration and Supervision, Teachers College, Columbia University.

**Number One Influence on Career:** President John F. Kennedy, Robert Kennedy—the idea of giving back, making a difference, and engaging in public service. Also, experiences at Teachers College, Columbia University, which introduced me to people who did not teach in New York City, thus motivating me to apply for a position in a suburban school district.

**Number One Achievement:** As an elementary school principal, I have been in the fortunate position of working closely with teachers, children, and parents on a daily basis. Together, we have created an educational environment that is warm, supportive, and committed to high academic and behavioral standards.

**Number One Regret:** Not understanding the importance of "politics" early enough in my career. Also, not having a professional career plan that would have motivated me to seek promotional positions earlier in my career.

**Favorite Education-Related Book or Text:** *Toward a Theory of Instruction* by Jerome Bruner and *Excellence* by John Gardner.

**Additional Interests:** Traveling, reading, physical fitness.

**Leadership Style:** I set high standards and follow through in an honest and direct manner; I am clear and specific in providing constructive suggestions, as well as praise. I work collaboratively with teachers to support their innovative ideas. I'm a "hands on" principal with respect for good teaching and appreciation that there is more than one way to be effective. I am a problem solver by nature and look for solutions rather than passive complaining.

**Professional Vision:** My vision is to provide leadership and to be a role model for excellence for all members of the school community. I want to encourage teachers to meet all students' needs by setting realistically high expectations and demonstrating sensitivity and understanding of individual differences. We all have to keep our eye on the ball and recognize that "kids come first."

**Words of Advice:** State standards and concomitant testing at specific grade levels have had a tremendous effect on education at the local level, positive as well as negative. Requiring youngsters as early as age 10 to communicate effectively in writing, to use data and information from documents, and to listen to a passage, take notes, and then respond to questions has raised the bar in New York State elementary schools and created great angst among children, teachers, administrators, and parents. Our teachers and children have risen to the occasion, and student writing has improved. Is there carryover after The Test? That remains to be seen. No one would argue that the skills being tested are not essential if one is to succeed as a student and productive adult. One might also argue that high-stakes testing for fourth graders is excessive and occurs too early in one's life.

What can you as an educational administrator do? You can set the tone for achieving state standards in a manner that is rational, grounded in good educational theory and practice, supportive of teachers, and cognizant of individual student needs. A tall order—and it can be done. Rely on your staff—you will probably have a lot of teacher talent. Use their ideas and expertise; support your teacher leaders. Encourage creativity, flexibility, and compassion. Don't become hysterical about results—if teachers have done their job in preparing children, then the results are what they are, and you can use them to help kids and improve instruction. Do your best to educate parents, which is not easy, as many parents are convinced that elementary school test results will affect college admission.

---

## Administrative Advice 12–1

### Positive Approaches to Sexual Harassment for the Workplace

There are several positive approaches to sexual harassment that school leaders can take to maintain a positive work environment.

■ *Establish a No Tolerance Policy.* Declare that the employer will not stand for sexual harassment, discrimination, or retaliation in the workplace. Under the law, the employer has the affirmative duty to rid the workplace of sexual harassment and discrimination. All employees should know their employer's policy that forbids sexual harassment, discrimination, and retaliation.

■ *Widely Disseminate the Policy.* Everyone should have the policy readily available. This is important for both employer and employee.

■ *Make It Easy for Employees to File Complaints.* Employees should be able to complain to someone other than their immediate superior. Someone outside the employee's chain of command, such as a human resource staff member, should be available to hear the complaint.

■ *Investigate Complaints Promptly and Objectively.* Promptness and objectivity should be the standard response. If management has knowledge of discrimination or sexual harassment happening, an investigation should be conducted. Prompt and objective investigation says to everyone that the complaint is serious.

■ *Take Appropriate Remedial Action to Prevent a Reoccurrence.* Actions might include informal resolution between parties and disciplinary action against harassers. Offer the victim free counseling, if appropriate. Most importantly, provide training to all employees periodically.

Source: Adapted from Jerry Lowe and Kelly Strnadel, "Sexual Harassment: Approaches to a More Positive Work Environment," unpublished paper, Sam Houston State University, Huntsville, Texas, January 12, 1999.

---

disease such as tuberculosis;[36] and a lower court has extended coverage to teachers with AIDS.[37]

The Supreme Court has said that an otherwise qualified disabled person is one who can meet all of the essential requirements of a job in spite of the disability. In determining whether a person with a disability is qualified to do a job, the central factors to consider are the nature of the disability in relation to the demands of the job. However, when a disabled person cannot meet all of the requirements of a job, an employer must provide "reasonable accommodation" that permit a qualified individual with a disability to perform the "essential functions" of a position.[38] Furthermore, courts have ruled that Section 504 and the ADA protect otherwise qualified disabled individuals but do not require accommodations for persons who are not qualified for the positions sought.[39]

**Age Discrimination**  The Age Discrimination in Employment Act (ADEA) was enacted to promote employment of older persons based on their ability and to prohibit arbitrary age discrimination in the terms and conditions of employment.[40] The law covers public employees, including teachers and school administrators. Thus mandatory retirement for teachers is prohibited by law.[41]

The act parallels Title VII in its application and operation. Thus, litigation under ADEA follows the disparate treatment standard used for race and gender discrimination cases. A school district charged with age discrimination may defend itself by articulating nondiscriminatory reasons for the adverse employment decision, such as inferior qualifications or poor performance rather than age.

**Religious Discrimination**  Citizens' free exercise of religion is protected under the religion clauses of the First Amendment and the Equal Protection Clause of the Fourteenth Amendment. These clauses prohibit discrimination against any public school employee on the basis of religious beliefs. In addition to constitu-

---

[36] *Sch. Bd. of Nassau Cty, FL v. Arline*, 480 U.S. 273 (1987).

[37] *Chalk v. U.S. District Court*, 840 F. 2d 701 (9th Cir., Cal., 1988).

[38] 42 U.S.C.A., Sec 12101 (West Supp. 1992).

[39] *Southeastern Community College v. Davis*, 442 U.S. 397 (1979); *Beck v. James*, 793 S.W. 2d 416 (MO Ct. App. 1990); *DeVargas v. Mason & Hanger-Silas Mason Co.*, 911 F. 2d 1377 (10th Circ. 1990, *cert. denied*, 111 S. Ct. 799 (1991).

[40] 29 U.S.C.A., Sec. 621–634 (1990) and (West Supp. 1992).

[41] 29 U.S.C.A., Sec. 631 (West Supp. 1992).

tional safeguards, public school employees are protected from religious discrimination under Title VII. In Title VII, as amended, Congress requires accommodation of "all aspects of religious observances and practices as well as belief, unless an employer demonstrates that he is unable to accommodate an employee's or prospective employee's religious observance or practice without undue hardship on the conduct of the employer's business."[42] The Equal Employment Opportunity Commission (EEOC) has developed guidelines with suggested accommodations for religious observance, such as assignment exchanges, flexible scheduling, job assignment changes, and using voluntary substitutes.

**Maternity Discrimination**    Mandatory maternity leave policies have been the subject of litigation. In *Cleveland Board of Education v. LaFleur*,[43] the Supreme Court held that a school board policy that required all pregnant teachers regardless of circumstances to take mandatory maternity leave for specified periods before and after childbirth was unconstitutional. The Court stated that it had long recognized that freedom of personal choice in matters of marriage and family life is one of the liberties protected under the due process clause of the Fourteenth Amendment. "By acting to penalize the pregnant teacher for deciding to bear a child…can constitute a heavy burden on the exercise of these protected freedoms."

The Constitution still permits school boards to implement maternity leave policies that are not arbitrary and fulfill a legitimate goal of maintaining continuity of instruction in a school system. For example, a mandatory maternity leave beginning date for teachers set at the beginning of the ninth month of pregnancy was upheld on "business necessity" grounds by the Court of Appeals, Ninth Circuit.[44] A New Jersey court has sustained a period of child-bearing disability of four weeks before expected birth and four weeks following the actual date of birth for purposes of sick leave benefits.[45] A court found a male teacher not entitled to paid maternity leave for the purpose of caring for his disabled pregnant wife.[46] However, child-rearing leave must not

be made available only to females. Such a provision in a collective bargaining agreement was declared to violate Title VII.[47]

A federal law, the Family and Medical Leave Act of 1993 (FMLA),[48] requires state and local government employers to provide up to twelve work weeks of unpaid leave during any twelve-month period for the birth or adoption of a child. Upon return from FMLA leave, an employee must be restored to his or her original job, or to an equivalent job with equivalent pay and benefits. Other provisions of the act are requirements to provide thirty days' notice of leave, medical certifications supporting the need for leave, and reports regarding the employee's intention to return to work. Employees can bring civil action for employer violations of the provisions of the act.

## Tort Liability

A **tort** is a civil wrong, not including contracts, for which a court will award damages. The three major categories of torts are intentional interference, strict liability, and negligence. Instances of intentional interference and strict liability in school-related injuries are rare and will not be pursued in this section. Accordingly, we examine the elements of negligence and the defenses against liability. Liability under Section 1983 of the Civil Rights Act is also addressed.

**Elements of Negligence**    To establish a legal cause for action in tort, four essential elements must exist: The individual has a duty to protect others against unreasonable risks; the individual failed to exercise an appropriate standard of care; the negligent act is the proximate cause of the injury; and a physical or mental injury, resulting in actual loss or damage to the person, exists.[49]

*Duty*    School employees have a **duty** to protect students entrusted to their care from being injured. Specifically, these duties include adequate supervision and instruction, maintenance of premises and equipment, and foreseeability. The test of foreseeability is whether under all circumstances the possibility of injury should have been reasonably foreseen and that supervision likely would

---

[42] 42 U.S.C., Sec 2000e (j) (1988).

[43] 414 U.S. 632 (1974).

[44] *deLaurier v. San Diego Unified Sch. Dist.*, 588 F. 2d 674 (9 Cir. 1978).

[45] *Hynes v. Bd. of Educ. of Tp. of Bloomfield, Essex County*, 190 NJ Super. 36, 461 A. 2d 1184 (1983).

[46] *Ackerman v. Bd. of Educ.*, 287 F. Supp. 76 (S.D. NY 1974).

[47] *Shafer v. Bd. of Educ. of Sch. Dist. of Pittsburgh, PA*, 903 F. 2d 243 (3 Cir. 1990).

[48] PL 103-3 (1993).

[49] William Prosser, John Wade, and Victor Schwartz, *Cases and Materials on Torts*, 7th ed. (St. Paul, MN: West, 1982).

have prevented the injury. For example, a teacher was found guilty of negligence when an eighth-grade pupil was injured from pebble throwing that continued for almost ten minutes during a morning recess.[50] Similarly, in a New Jersey suit, an elementary school principal was held liable for injuries suffered when a pupil was struck by paperclips shot from a rubber band by another child before the classrooms opened. The court found the principal had acted improperly by announcing no rules on the conduct of students before entering classrooms, by not assigning teachers to assist him in supervising the pupils before school, and by engaging in activities other than overseeing the activities of the pupils.[51]

*Standard of Care*   Failure of a school employee to act in a manner that conforms to an appropriate **standard of care** can render said employee negligent. The standard of care is that which a reasonable and prudent person would have exercised under similar circumstances. For example, the Oregon Supreme Court said "Negligence . . . is . . . the doing of that thing which a reasonably prudent person would not have done, in like or similar circumstances. . . ."[52] The model for the reasonable and prudent person has been described as one who possesses "(1) the physical attributes of the defendant himself, (2) normal intelligence, (3) normal perception and memory with a minimum level of information and experience common to the community, and (4) such superior skill and knowledge as the actor has or holds himself out to the public as having."[53]

The standard of care required would depend on such circumstances as the age, maturity, and experience of students; the type of activity; the environment; and the potential for danger. The amount of care owed to children increases with the immaturity of the child. A higher standard of care is required in shop, physical education, and laboratory classes and in situations and environments that pose a greater threat of danger (e.g., school field trips).

*Proximate Cause*   There must be a connection between the action of school personnel and the resultant injury sustained by the pupil. Courts will ask, Was the failure to exercise a reasonable standard of care the **proximate cause** of the injury? The cause of the injury first must be established. Then it must be shown that there was some connection between the injury and the employee's failure to exercise a reasonable standard of care.

As in determining whether an appropriate standard of care has been exercised, the test of foreseeability is used in establishing proximate cause. It is not necessary that a particular injury was foreseen for proximate cause to be established. If reasonable precautions are taken and an intervening injury not foreseen occurs, no negligence exists. Such was the case when a student returned to his desk and sat on a sharpened pencil placed there by another student. School authorities were not held liable for the injury.[54]

*Injury*   There must be proof of actual loss or damage to the plaintiff resulting from the **injury.** If the injury suffered is caused by more than one individual, damages will be apportioned among the defendants.[55] A school district may be required to compensate an injured party for negligent conduct of an officer, agent, or employee of the district. Individual school board members or employees (superintendents, principals, teachers) may also be liable personally for torts that they commit in the course of their duties. (See Administrative Advice 12–2.)

**Defenses against Negligence**   Several defenses can be invoked by a defendant (school board, superintendent, principal, teacher) in a tort action. These defenses include contributory negligence, assumption of risk, comparative negligence, and government immunity.

*Contributory Negligence*   If it is shown that a student's own negligence contributed to the injury, the law in many states would charge the student with **contributory negligence.** However, a student cannot be charged with contributory negligence if he is too immature to recognize the risks: A standard of care that is adequate when dealing with adults generally will not be adequate when dealing with children. For example, in about a dozen states, courts have ruled that students under seven years of age cannot be prohibited from recovery damages because of negligence. In other states, the age has been set at four, five, or six years. And for older children up to

---

[50] *Sheehan v. St. Peter's Catholic School,* 291 Minn. 1, 188 N.W. 2d 868 (1971).

[51] *Titus v. Lindberg,* 49 N.J. 66, A. 2d 65 (1967).

[52] *Biddle v. Mazzocco,* 284 P. 2d 364 (Ore. 1955).

[53] Kern Alexander and M. David Alexander, *American Public School Law,* 4th ed. (Belmont, CA: Wadsworth, 1998), p. 502.

[54] *Swaitkowski v. Bd. of Educ. of City of Buffalo,* 36 A.D. 2d 685 (N.Y. 1971).

[55] McCarthy and Cambron-McCabe, *Public School Law.*

---

### Administrative Advice 12–2

### Guidelines for Safer Playgrounds

You risk a lawsuit every time a child sets foot on your school playground. A child falls from a slide or ladder; a child is injured on the swings or seesaws. To protect students from injury—and schools from liability—the enlightened school administrator learns to identify and eliminate these dangers. To help make your playgrounds better and safer, the following principles of design, maintenance, and supervision are suggested:

- *Avoid Steep Slopes.* Ramps, slides, or climbing nets should not be installed at angles of greater than 45 degrees and preferably closer to 35 degrees. The steeper the slope, the greater the risk a child will suffer injury.

- *Limit Falls to 24 Inches.* A playground structure should follow a multilevel design—a series of constantly rising platforms. The distance between levels should vary from 18 to 24 inches, depending on the age of the children using the equipment. If a play structure is designed properly, no child should be able to fall more than two feet.

- *Consider Accessibility.* Playground design must take the "flow of play" into account. Injuries often occur when children who become impatient waiting their turn look for unsafe paths to their destination. The principle here: Give children room to play together and avoid waiting in line.

- *Provide Safe Clearances.* Place play equipment at least 20 feet away from trees, fences, or other playground structures.

- *Consider Exposure to the Sun.* Installing playground equipment under the shade of trees or buildings allows children to play longer and more actively. Shade also reduces the risk of sunburn or burns caused by hot metal slides.

- *Provide Enclosed Spaces.* Providing partially enclosed tube slides or tunnels makes playground equipment more versatile. Enclosures must be large enough for children to move freely through them and to permit teachers to supervise visually.

- *Use Interconnective Play Components.* An interconnective play structure connects ramps, climbing nets, stairs, slides, platforms, and pathways to provide easy movement throughout the play structure.

- *Use Good-Quality Materials.* Safe playground equipment requires strong, durable, and nontoxic material. The equipment must be structurally sound to support the weight of many children and adults at the same time. All edges must be rounded, smooth, and free of splinters.

- *Inspect Equipment Regularly.* Regular inspections are essential to ensure the safety of playground equipment.

Source: Adapted from Louis Bowers, "Follow These Guidelines for Better—and Safer—Playgrounds," *Executive Educator*, 11 (1989): 27–28.

---

the age of fourteen, there is a "rebuttable presumption" that they are incapable of contributory negligence.[56]

***Assumption of Risk*** Another commonly used defense in tort actions is the doctrine of **assumption of risk.** It is based on the theory that one who knowingly and willingly exposes oneself to a known danger may be denied tort recovery for injuries sustained. An essential requisite to invoking a defense of assumption of risk is that there be knowledge and appreciation of the danger. Thus, it was held that a child who was cut by submerged broken glass while playing in a high school sandpit did not assume the risk of injury because he did not know the glass was in the sandpit.[57] On the other hand, the Oregon Supreme Court found an assumption of risk in the injury of a high school football player when he was injured in a scheduled football game.[58] Like contributory negligence, courts will consider the age and maturity level of students when assessing a defense of assumption of risk in tort.

***Comparative Negligence*** Where the common law rule of contributory negligence and assumption of risk is followed, plaintiffs whose own negligence contributed to an injury are barred completely from recovery. This harsh rule has been modified. A number of states have adopted the doctrine of **comparative negligence.** Under the comparative negligence doctrine, a plaintiff can ob-

---

[56] Louis Fischer, David Schimmel, and Cynthia Kelly, *Teachers and the Law*, 5th ed. (New York: Longman, 1999).

[57] *Brown v. Oakland*, 124 P. 2d 369 (Cal. 1942).

[58] *Vandrell v. S.D. No. 26C Malheur Cty.*, 233 Ore. 1, 376 P. 2d 406 (1962).

tain a proportionate recovery for injury depending on the amount of negligence she contributed to the injury. Specific statutory provisions vary from state to state.[59]

*Government Immunity*　The origin of the doctrine of **government immunity** from tort liability can be traced to two early cases, one in England in 1788 and the other in Massachusetts in 1812.[60] The courts held that the government could not be sued for negligence. Thus, the precedent of the immunity of school districts from tort liability was established and remained in effect until the passage of the Federal Tort Claims Act of 1946. Subsequently, the doctrine of state immunity in tort has been abrogated or modified by state legislatures. However, tort law does extend certain immunity to teachers and administrators in the scope and performance of their duties. One example is administering corporal punishment in schools.[61]

School board members also have some degree of immunity in the scope and performance of their duties. However, Section 1983 of the Civil Rights Act rooted in 1871 changed the status of the immunity of school board members for their activities. This section provides that every person who subjects any citizen of the United States to the deprivation of any rights secured by the Constitution be liable to the (injured) party in an action at law.[62] A plethora of court cases have been litigated under the act, primarily dealing with First and Fourteenth Amendment rights. The tort liability of school board members was further extended under Section 1983 to students by the Supreme Court decision in *Wood v. Strickland*.[63] The Court held that school board members could be sued individually by students whose constitutional rights were denied. The case involved a denial of due process of students in a suspension hearing.

## The Law and Students

Schools exist for the purpose of educating the citizenry. Throughout its history, education has served as the backbone of the U.S. democratic system. This view is based on the premise that the country is best served by an educated, enlightened citizenry. With this mandate, the states have enacted legislation pertaining to the education of the nation's youth. These statutes provide regulations pertaining to school improvement, school attendance, student discipline, freedom of expression, and classification practices.

### School Improvement

Accountability for school improvement is a central theme of state policies. The No Child Left Behind Act of 2001 (Public Law 107–110) sets demanding accountability standards for schools, school districts, and states, including new state testing requirements designed to improve education. For example, the law requires that states develop both content standards in reading and mathematics and tests that are linked to the standards for grades 3 through 8, with science standards and assessments to follow. States must identify adequate yearly progress (AYP) objectives and disaggregate test results for all students and subgroups of students based on socioeconomic status, race/ethnicity, English language proficiency, and disability. Moreover, the law mandates that 100 percent of students must score at the proficient level on state tests by 2014. Furthermore, the No Child Left Behind Act requires states to participate every other year in the National Assessment of Educational Progress (NAEP) in reading and mathematics.[64]

### School Attendance

All fifty states have some form of compulsory school attendance law. These statutes provide the right of children residing in a district to receive a free public education up to a certain age and exact penalties for noncompliance on parents or guardians.

**Compulsory Attendance Laws**　The courts have sustained compulsory attendance laws on the basis of the legal doctrine of **parens patriae**. Under this doctrine, the state has the legal authority to provide for the welfare of its children. In turn, the welfare of the state is served by the development of an enlightened citizenry.

Attendance at a public school is not the only way to satisfy the compulsory attendance law. Over eighty

---

[59]William D. Valente, *Law in the Schools,* 5th ed. (Upper Saddle River, NJ: Prentice Hall, 2002).

[60]*Russell v. Men of Devon,* 100 Eng. Rep. 359, 2 T. R. 667 (1788); *Mower v. Leicester,* 9 Mass. 237 (1812).

[61]*Ingraham v. Wright,* 430 U.S. 651 (1977).

[62]42 U.S.C., Section 1983 (1871).

[63]420 U.S. 308 (1975).

[64]*No Child Left Behind Act of 2001* (www.ed.gov/legislation/ESEA02/).

years ago, the U.S. Supreme Court in *Pierce v. Society of Sisters* invalidated an Oregon statute requiring children between the ages of eight and sixteen to attend public schools.[65] The Court concluded that by restricting attendance to public schools, the state violated both the property rights of the school and the liberty interests of parents in choosing the place of education for their children, protected by the Fourteenth Amendment to the Constitution.

Subsequent to *Pierce,* states have expanded the options available to parents (guardians) for meeting the compulsory attendance law. For example, currently in the state of Kentucky, parents are in compliance with that state's statute by selecting from the following options: enrolling their children, who must regularly attend, in a private, parochial, or church-related day school; enrolling their children, who must regularly attend, in a private, parochial, church- or state-supported program for exceptional children; or providing home, hospital, institutional, or other regularly scheduled, suitable, equivalent instruction that meets standards of the state board of education.[66]

Parents or guardians who select one of the options to public school instruction must obtain equivalent instruction. For example, the Washington Supreme Court held that home instruction did not satisfy that state's compulsory attendance law, for the parents who were teaching the children did not hold a valid teaching certificate.[67] In its decision, the court described four essential elements of a school: a certified teacher, pupils of school age, an institution established to instruct school-age children, and a required program of studies (curriculum) engaged in for the full school term and approved by the state board of education. Subsequently, statutes establishing requirements for equivalent instruction (such as certified teachers, program of studies, time devoted to instruction, school-age children, and place or institution) generally have been sustained by the courts.[68]

**Exceptions to Compulsory Attendance**   The prevailing view of the courts is that religious beliefs cannot abrogate a state's compulsory attendance law. An exception is the U.S. Supreme Court ruling in *Wisconsin v. Yoder,* which prevented that state from requiring Amish children to submit to compulsory formal education requirements beyond the eighth grade.[69] The Court found that this was a violation of the free exercise of religion clause of the First Amendment. However, most other attempts to exempt students from school based on religious beliefs have failed.

It is commonly held that married pupils, regardless of age, are exempt from compulsory attendance laws. The rationale is that married persons assume adult status, and consequently the doctrine of parens patriae no longer applies. The precedent in this area is based on two Louisiana cases in which fifteen- and fourteen-year-old married women were considered not "children" under the compulsory attendance law.[70] A later New York case followed the rationale of the two Louisiana cases in declaring that the obligations of a married woman were inconsistent with school attendance.[71] It should be noted, however, that a state cannot deny married minors the right to attend school if they wish.

Some parents have used illness as an exemption from compulsory school attendance. In such situations, the school has the right to require proof of illness through medical certification of a physician. For example, in an Illinois case, parents were charged with truancy when their school-age child was absent from school for 339½ days during a two-year period. As a defense, the parents claimed illness of the child as a reason for nonschool attendance. The pupil's physician testified that the child suffered from allergies but not sufficient to warrant excessive absence from school. The charge of truancy against the parents was upheld by the Illinois court.[72]

**Vaccinations**   In an effort to protect the health and welfare of all students, states have required students to be vaccinated. The precedents in this area are derived from two U.S. Supreme Court cases decided nearly a century ago.[73] A more recent case struck down a challenge to a state's mandatory vaccination on religious grounds, even though there was no epidemic imminent.[74] Other courts have upheld religious exemptions against vaccination when such practices are prohibited

[65] *Pierce v. Society of Sisters,* 268 U.S. 510 (1925).

[66] *Ky. Rev. Stat.,* Ch. 159.030 (1992).

[67] *State ex. rel. Shoreline S.D. No. 412 v. Superior Court,* 55 Wash. 2d 177, 346 P. 2d 999 (1959).

[68] *State ex. rel. Douglas v. Faith Baptist Church of Louisville,* 454 U.S. 803 (1981).

[69] *Wisconsin v. Yoder,* 406 U.S. 205 (1972).

[70] *State v. Priest,* 210 La. 389, 27 So. 2d 173 (1946); *in re State,* 214 La. 1062, 39 So. 2d 731 (1949).

[71] *In re Rogers,* 36 Misc. 2d 680, 234 N.Y.S. 2d 179 (1962).

[72] *People v. Berger,* 65 Ill. Dec. 600, 441 N.E. 2d 915 (1982).

[73] *Jacobsen v. Commonwealth of Mass.,* 197 U.S. 11 (1905); *Zucht v. King,* 260 U.S. 174 (1922).

[74] *Bd. of Educ. of Mt. Lakes v. Maas,* 56 N.J. Super. 245, 152 A 2d 394 (1959).

---

## Administrative Advice 12–3

### CDC Guidelines for AIDS Education Programs

Guidelines for AIDS education have been developed to help school personnel and others plan, implement, and evaluate educational efforts to prevent unnecessary mortality associated with AIDS. The guidelines incorporate principles for AIDS education that were developed by the president's Domestic Policy Council and approved by the president in 1987. You can assess the extent to which your district program measures up with the guidelines by answering each question below:

■ To what extent are parents, teachers, students, and appropriate community representatives involved in developing, implementing, and assessing AIDS education policies and programs?

■ To what extent is the program included as an important part of a more comprehensive school health education program?

■ To what extent is the program taught by regular classroom teachers in elementary grades and by qualified health education teachers or other similarly trained personnel in secondary grades?

■ To what extent is the program designed to help students acquire essential knowledge to prevent HIV infection at each appropriate grade?

■ To what extent does the program describe the benefits of abstinence for young people and mutually monoga-

mous relationships within the context of marriage for adults?

■ To what extent is the program designed to help teenage students avoid specific types of behavior that increase the risk of becoming infected with HIV?

■ To what extent is adequate training about AIDS provided for school administrators, teachers, nurses, and counselors—especially those who teach about AIDS?

■ To what extent are sufficient program development time, classroom time, and educational materials provided for education about AIDS?

■ To what extent are the processes and outcomes of AIDS education being monitored and periodically assessed?

---

Source: Adapted from Centers for Disease Control, "Halt the AIDS Rampage," *School Administrator*, 10 (1988): 53–55. Used by permission.

---

in official church doctrine.[75] A Kentucky federal district court rejected a parent's attempt to use statutory religious exemptions merely because he was "philosophically opposed" to immunization.[76]

**Students with AIDS**  Recent controversy has focused on school attendance of pupils with acquired immunodeficiency syndrome (AIDS). Medical research indicates that AIDS cannot be transmitted through casual contact.[77] An AIDS-infected child poses negligible risk for transmission to classmates or to other school personnel and thus does not threaten their health and safety. Therefore, having AIDS is not grounds to exclude a child automatically from school. In fact, courts have ruled that children have a right to attend school, and, barring complications, AIDS does not diminish that right, pro-

vided that the AIDS-infected child is "not a significant health risk" to others.[78]

Some states have adopted policies governing school attendance of students with AIDS, modeled after guidelines issued by the National Centers for Disease Control and Prevention (CDC). The CDC stipulates that students with AIDS who are under medical care may continue regular school attendance unless they have skin eruptions, exhibit inappropriate behavior such as biting, or are unable to control bodily secretions. The CDC further suggests that decisions concerning school attendance for AIDS-infected students be made on a case-by-case basis. Continuing research on the nature and prevention of this dreaded disease will undoubtedly yield further legal guidelines for its prevention and control. (See Administrative Advice 12–3.)

---

[75] *State v. Miday*, 140 S.E. 2d 325 (N.C. 1965); *Maier v. Besser*, 341 N.Y.S. 2d 411 (N.Y. Sup. Ct. 1972).

[76] *Kleid v. Bd. of Educ. of Fulton, Kentucky Indep. Sch. Dist.*, 406 F. Supp. 902 (W.D.KY 1976).

[77] Rothstein, *Children with AIDS*, 12 Nova L. Rev. 1259 (1988).

[78] *Martinez v. Sch. Bd. of Hillsborough Cty*, 861 F. 2d 1502 (11th Cir. 1988); *Doe v. Dolton Elem. Sch. Dist.*, 694 F. Supp. 440 (N.D. IL 1988); *Phipps v. Saddleback Valley Unified Sch. Dist.*, 251 Cal. Rptr. 720 (Cal. Ct. App. 1988); *Parents of Child, Code No. 870901w v. Coker*, 676 F. Supp. 1072 (E.D. OK 1987).

**Curriculum**    The state legislature has the authority to prescribe the curriculum of the public schools. Such authority is based on the premise that the course of study in the public schools includes those subjects that are essential to good citizenship. All states require teaching of the federal Constitution, and most mandate instruction in U.S. history. Other subjects commonly required include English, mathematics, science, family life and sex education, drug education, and health and physical education.

All state-mandated courses must be offered, but local school boards have great latitude in supplementing the curriculum required by the state legislature. The precedent-setting case in this area was the landmark 1874 decision of the Michigan Supreme Court, which held that the local board of education had the authority to maintain a high school.[79] This landmark decision and subsequent cases established the implied powers of local school boards in curricular matters. These implied powers apply not only to additions of specific curricular elements, such as sex education, drug education, competitive sports, and vocational education programs, but also the determination of methods of carrying out state-mandated curriculum. Generally, the courts have sustained such local board activities, providing they do not contravene the state constitution and the federal Constitution.

The implied powers of local school boards in curriculum matters has led to the teaching of controversial topics such as abortion, contraception, venereal disease, and AIDS. In some situations, parents have objected that such instruction violates their privacy rights or their protected religious freedom. A New York appellate court asserted that the state had a compelling interest in the issue because the purpose of the educational requirement was the protection of the health and safety of students.[80] However, a decision by one state court, that compulsory courses in AIDS for all public school students does not violate parents' constitutionally protected religious freedom, does not require courts of other jurisdictions to arrive at the same conclusion.[81] As new courses dealing with controversial topics (e.g., abortion, contraception, venereal disease, AIDS) are de-

veloped, the legality of teaching them will be judged on their content, manner of delivery, and whether they are elective or compulsory in nature.[82]

**Residency Requirements**    Generally, eligibility to attend tuition free the public schools of a district is extended by statute to school-age children who have a **domicile** in the district or who are residents of the district. To understand the decision of the courts in this area, it is necessary to define the **residence** and domicile of pupils and their parents. These terms are legally defined as follows:[83]

- *Domicile* is a place where one intends to remain indefinitely, and each person may have only one domicile. A minor child's legal domicile is that of the father except in special circumstances, such as the father's death or parental separation or divorce where custody of the child has been awarded to the mother or another custodial guardian.

- *Residence* is the place where one is actually, physically living.

Generally, it is held that a child has the right to attend the public school of a district in which he or she is living—unless the child is living in that district solely for the purpose of attending school there, in which case the child is not entitled to education without the payment of tuition.[84]

*In loco Parentis*

## Student Discipline

It is expected that schools will be operated according to the rules and regulations of local boards of education. However, teachers and other school personnel are granted wide discretion in disciplining students. The legal doctrine that defines the relationship of educator to pupil is **in loco parentis** ("in place of the parent"). The doctrine is well stated in a precedent-setting Wisconsin case:

> While the principal or teacher in charge of a public school is subordinate to the school board . . . and must enforce rules and regulations adopted by the board . . . he does not derive all his power and authority in the school and

[79]*Stuart v. S.D. No. 1 of Village of Kalamazoo,* 30 Mich. 69 (1874).

[80]*Ware v. Valley Stream H.S. Dist.,* 545 N.Y.S. 316 (A.D. 1989).

[81]*Ware v. Valley Stream H.S. Dist.,* 550 N.E. 2d 420 (N.Y. 1989) (burden on the state to deny the exemption from AIDS course).

[82]Valente, *Law in the Schools.*

[83]Henry Black, *Black's Law Dictionary,* 8th ed. (Belmont, CA: Wadsworth, 1998).

[84]*Turner v. Bd. of Educ.,* N. Chicago Community H.S. Dist. 123, 54 Ill. 2d 68, 294 N.E. 2d 264 (1973).

over his pupils from affirmative action of the board. He stands for the time being in loco parentis to his pupils, and because of that relation he must necessarily exercise authority over them in many things concerning which the board may have remained silent.[85]

In this section, we examine students' rights pertaining to corporal punishment, expulsions and suspensions, and search and seizure.

**Corporal Punishment**    Under common law, teachers and other school personnel have the right to administer reasonable corporal punishment, which is the infliction of physical pain on a student for misconduct. State statutes deal with corporal punishment in different ways. Some states authorize it; others forbid it. Still others are silent on the matter but by implication allow it.[86] Massachusetts and New Jersey prohibit corporal punishment by statute. In Maryland state board of education policy bans corporal punishment. New York permits corporal punishment unless local boards of education prohibit it. Kentucky allows a teacher to use physical force to maintain reasonable discipline in a school, class, or other group.[87]

In the landmark Supreme Court decision *Ingraham v. Wright,* the Court held that corporal punishment of students does not violate the Eighth Amendment nor the due process guarantees of the Fourteenth Amendment. The Court said that the Eighth Amendment's prohibition of cruel and unusual punishment applies to criminals only and is not applicable to the disciplining of students in public schools. The Court noted that "at common law a single principle has governed the use of corporal punishment since before the American Revolution: Teachers may impose reasonable but not excessive force to discipline a child." Regarding due process, the Court held that a student is not entitled to notice and a hearing prior to the imposition of corporal punishment.[88]

Although the Supreme Court has held that the federal Constitution does not prohibit corporal punishment in schools, its use may conflict with state constitutions, state statutes, or local school board policies.

**Expulsions and Suspensions**    Expelling and suspending students from school are among the most widely used measures of disciplining students. From a practical standpoint, expulsion is the exclusion of a student from school for a period of time exceeding ten days or more. Under common law, the power of expulsion is vested exclusively in the board of education. Professional personnel may not expel students unless authorized by state statute.

Generally, courts have held that expulsion of students from school jeopardizes a student's property interests in an education. Thus, students are guaranteed at least minimum due process under the Fourteenth Amendment. The following list enumerates elements of recommended procedural due process in such cases:[89]

1. A speedy and full notification of the charges should be given to the accused.

2. The accused should be provided with an opportunity to answer the charges and to prepare an adequate defense.

3. The hearing should be conducted by an impartial tribunal.

4. The accused should be given the names of adverse witnesses, access to adverse evidence, and the right to introduce evidence.

5. The decision must be based on the evidence adduced at the hearing.

6. A prompt finding, giving the reasons for the decision and the evidence supporting it, should be delivered at the conclusion of the hearing.

7. The accused (or her counsel) should have the right to cross-examine adverse witnesses and introduce witnesses in her defense.

8. The accused has a right to representation by legal counsel.

9. A written record of the proceedings should be maintained.

10. The accused should have the right to appeal an adverse decision.

Suspensions generally involve exclusion of a student from school for a brief, definite period of time, usually not exceeding ten days. In contrast to detailed procedures related to expulsion, state statutes have been less specific regarding the procedures that should be followed when suspending students from schools. Prior

---

[85] *State ex. rel. Burpee v. Burton,* 45 Wis. 150, 30 Am. Rep. 706 (1878).

[86] H. C. Hudgins and Richard S. Vacca, *Law and Education,* 2nd ed. (Charlottesville, VA: Michie, 1985).

[87] *Ky. Rev. Stat.,* Ch. 503.110 (1992).

[88] *Ingraham v. Wright,* 430 U.S. 651 (1977).

[89] Valente, *Law in the Schools.*

to 1975, procedural due process accorded to suspended students was poorly defined. Lower courts differed widely in their interpretation of the Fourteenth Amendment guarantees in suspension cases. In 1975, in *Goss v. Lopez,* the U.S. Supreme Court prescribed the minimum constitutional requirements in cases involving student suspensions of ten days or less.[90] The Court concluded that oral notice to the student of the reason for short suspensions, followed by an immediate, informal hearing by a local school official, would fulfill the due process requirement in brief suspensions. The Court specifically rejected the usual trial-type format including the involvement of attorneys and the presentation and cross-examination of adverse witnesses typical in criminal cases.

The Rehabilitation Act (Section 504), the Individuals with Disabilities Education Act (IDEA), and the Americans with Disabilities Act (ADA) provide special safeguards in the suspension and expulsion of children with disabilities. IDEA, in particular, assures all children with disabilities a free appropriate public education in the least restrictive environment. Federal courts have regarded expulsion and long-term suspension as a change in placement when children with disabilities are involved.[91]

A crucial issue when suspending or expelling a disabled child is whether the misbehavior is related to the disability. Disabled students may be suspended for ten days or fewer without inquiry into whether the student's misbehavior was caused by the disability.[92] Courts reasoned that short-term suspension is not a change of placement and therefore does not trigger the procedures of IDEA. Expulsions and suspensions of more than ten days are changes of placement. They may not be used if there is a relationship between the misbehavior and the child's disability.[93] In these cases, transferring the child to a more restrictive environment is an option, after following change-of-placement procedures. If the misbehavior is not related to the disability, then expulsion and long-term suspension are permissible; but all educational services cannot be terminated.[94] These special safeguards for the disciplining of disabled children do

not apply to pupils w⸍        ⸍gs or alcohol as stipulated in the .[⸍

**Search and Seizu**    ⸍he Fourth Amendment provides that "the right of people to be secure in their persons, houses, papers, and effects, against unreasonable searches and seizures shall not be violated, and no warrants shall issue, but upon probable cause. . . ." The clause has been involved in numerous criminal cases. Evidence obtained in violation of the amendment is inadmissible in court.

The introduction of drugs and other contraband in schools has placed school officials in the position of searching students' person or lockers, and students claim that such acts are a violation of ⸍⸍ Fourth Amendment guarantees. A student'⸍       ⸍ourth Amendment's protection fr⸍            and seizure must be balance⸍       ⸍hool officials to maintain discip⸍      ⸍de a safe environment conducive to lear⸍   ⸍tate and federal courts generally have relied on the doctrine of in loco parentis, reasoning that school officials stand in the place of a parent and are not subject to the constraints of the Fourth Amendment. In 1985 in *New Jersey v. T.L.O.,* the U.S. Supreme Court held that searches by school officials in schools come within the constraints of the Fourteenth Amendment.[96] The Court concluded that the special needs of the school environment justified easing the warrant and probable cause requirement imposed in criminal cases, provided that school searches are based on "reasonable suspicion."

In 1995, the United States Supreme Court rendered its decision in *Vernonia School District 47J v. Acton,* holding that a school district's random suspicionless drug testing of student athletes as a condition for participation in interscholastic athletics did not violate the Fourth Amendment's prohibition against unreasonable searches and seizures. In this particular case, however, the Court noted specific features including student athletes' decreased expectations of privacy, the relative unobtrusiveness of the search procedures, and the seriousness of the need met by this search. Regardless of the procedures, however, this case clearly lowered schools' previous legal search standard of "reasonable suspicion," set forth by *New Jersey v. T.L.O.* in 1985.

The Supreme Court ruled on the issue of random suspicionless drug testing of students in June 2002 with its

---

[90]*Goss v. Lopez,* 419 U.S. 565 (1975).

[91]*S-1 v. Turlington,* 635 F. 2d 342 (5th Cir. 1981), *cert. denied,* 454 U.S. 1030 (1981); *Honig v. Doe,* 484 U.S. 305 (1988).

[92]*Bd. of Educ. of Peoria v. IL State Bd. of Educ.,* 531 F. Supp. 148 (C.D. IL 1982).

[93]*S-1 v. Turlington.*

[94]Ibid.

---

[95]29 U.S.C.A., Sec. 706 (8) (West Supp. 1992).

[96]*New Jersey v. T.L.O.* 469 U.S. 325 (1985).

decision in *Board of Education v. Earls,*[97] a 10th Circuit case from Oklahoma in which drug testing of students in any extracurricular activities was determined to be unconstitutional. In a 5–4 decision, the Supreme Court upheld the school district's policy of random suspicionless drug testing of all students who participated in any extracurricular activities, not just athletics. Using *Vernonia* as a guideline, the 10th Circuit in *Earls* held that "before imposing a suspicionless drug testing program a school must demonstrate some identifiable drug abuse problem among a sufficient number of those to be tested, such that testing that group will actually redress its drug problem." In overturning the 10th Circuit's decision, the Supreme Court's majority in *Earls* stated that "a demonstrated drug abuse problem is not always necessary to the validity of a testing regime." Furthermore, the Court defends this stance by adding that "the need to prevent and deter the substantial harm of childhood drug use provides the necessary immediacy for a school testing policy." Thus, based on the *Earls* decision, random suspicionless drug testing of students does not violate the Fourth Amendment's protection from unreasonable searches and seizures.

## Freedom of Expression

Of all the freedoms guaranteed in this country, none is more protected than the right of freedom of speech and the press and the right to peaceable assembly as set forth in the First Amendment. Specifically, it provides that "Congress shall make no law . . . abridging the freedom of speech, or of press; or the right of the people peaceably to assemble. . . ." The gamut of protected expression litigated in state and federal courts includes symbolic expression, dress and grooming, oral and written expression, and group associations and assembly. These categories of expression have received differential treatment in the courts.

**Personal Expression** Historically, students generally played a submissive role in relation to freedom of expression within the public schools. In 1969, the landmark case of the U.S. Supreme Court *Tinker v. Des Moines Independent School District*[98] marked the emergence

of a new era in students' protected expression in the public schools. The Court invalidated a rule prohibiting students from wearing black arm bands in school as a protest against the Vietnam War. The Court stated that "undifferentiated fear or apprehension of disturbance is not enough to overcome the right to freedom of expression." Furthermore, the Court declared that the prohibition of the wearing of symbols can be sustained only if such activity would "materially and substantially disrupt the work and discipline of the school."

Thus, the *Tinker* test of "material and substantial disruption" emerged as a determinant in subsequent student expression litigation. The Court made it clear that school authorities would not be permitted to deny a student her fundamental First Amendment rights simply because of a "mere desire to avoid discomfort and unpleasantness that always accompany an unpopular viewpoint."

**Freedom of Speech and Press** Courts commonly extend broad-based protection to freedom of speech and press. Nevertheless, they recognize that free expression rights can be restricted. For example, freedom of speech does not allow an individual to yell "Fire!" in a crowded theater when there is no fire because of the tremendous potential for harm to people and property.[99] Although public school students enjoy free speech rights, the Supreme Court has recognized that "the constitutional rights of students in public school are not automatically coextensive with the rights of adults in other settings."[100] In other words, the First Amendment rights of students may be restricted by the operational needs of the schools.

Not all student expression receives the same level of First Amendment protection. Obscene, defamatory, and inflammatory expression are not protected by the First Amendment. To be legally obscene, material must violate three tests developed by the U.S. Supreme Court: (1) It must appeal to the prurient or lustful interest of minors, (2) it must describe sexual conduct in a way that is "potently offensive" to community standards, and (3) taken as a whole, it "must lack serious literary, artistic, political, or scientific value."[101] *Defamation* may be defined as a false statement made to a third party that subjects a person to public shame or ridicule. *Inflamma-*

[97]*Bd. of Educ. of Independent School District No. 92 of Pottawatomie County et al. v. Linsay Earls et al. 122 S. Ct. 2559.*

[98]393 U.S. 503 (1969).

[99]*Schenck v. United States,* 249 U.S. 47, 52 (1919).

[100]*Bethel Sch. Dist. No. 403 v. Fraser,* 478 U.S. 675 (1986).

[101]*Miller v. California,* 413 U.S. 15 (1973).

*tory expression,* or "fighting words," refers to face-to-face communication that is likely to incite violence.[102]

Nonetheless, school authorities retain the burden of justifying restraints on student expression. In this regard, the Supreme Court has relied primarily on the "material and substantial disruption" standard derived from the *Tinker* decision. More recently, in *Bethel School District No. 403 v. Fraser,*[103] the Supreme Court expanded the rationale for schools to restrict students' freedom of speech when obscenity is involved. The case arose when Matthew Fraser delivered a speech at a required assembly of about 600 high school students that featured sexual innuendo. He was subsequently suspended from school and later brought suit on First and Fourteenth Amendment grounds. The U.S. Supreme Court ruled that no constitutional rights had been abrogated. In its decision the Court made a distinction between the silent political speech in *Tinker* and the lewd, vulgar, and offensive speech of Fraser. The Court said that ". . . the determination of what manner of speech in the classroom or in a school assembly is appropriate properly rests with the school board." The Court added that while students have the right to advocate controversial rules in school, ". . . that right must be balanced against the school's interest in teaching socially appropriate behavior."[104]

During the 1970s, a number of courts considered school-sponsored publications as forums for student expression. Accordingly, courts held that school newspaper articles on controversial topics such as abortion, the Vietnam War, and contraception could not be barred from these publications.[105] Courts scrutinized policies requiring prior administrative review and placed the burden on school officials to justify such review procedures.

In 1988, the U.S. Supreme Court heard the case of *Hazelwood School District v. Kyhlmeier*[106] involving a high school student newspaper. The case arose when a principal deleted certain stories that had been scheduled for release in the school newspaper. One story recounted personal experiences of three pregnant girls in the school. The other related personal accounts of siblings whose parents were going through a divorce proceeding and was strongly accusative of the father. The Court differentiated the case from *Tinker* in that here the issue was not personal speech, which is still protected by a strict scrutiny under the "material and substantial disruption" standard, but rather the right of school authorities not to promote particular speech. In other words, the Supreme Court drew a distinction between speech occurring in school-sponsored (curriculum-related) and nonschool-sponsored contexts. The Court reasoned that school authorities have much greater leeway in regulating speech that has the imprimatur of the school, provided that restrictions are based on "legitimate pedagogical concerns."

Based on the *Bethel* and *Hazelwood* decisions, the school's authority to [prohibit lewd, vulgar] and offensive" speech in these [school-sponsored] activities is well established. Recent courts followed these precedents by allowing censorship of student speeches at school assemblies provided that the decision was based on "legitimate pedagogical concerns."[107]

**Student Appearance**   School boards may enact reasonable regulations concerning student appearance in school. Appearance regulations have focused on male hairstyles and pupil attire. Student challenges to these regulations have relied on First Amendment constitutional freedoms to determine one's appearance. The U.S. Supreme Court has consistently refused to review the decisions of lower courts on these matters. In one case involving male hairstyle, Court Justice Hugo Black commented that he did not believe "the federal Constitution imposed on the United States courts the burden of supervising the length of hair that public school students should wear."[108]

*Pupil Hairstyle*   Five of the federal circuit courts of appeal (third, fifth, sixth, ninth, and tenth) have sustained the authority of public schools to regulate hairstyles of male students. Four federal circuit courts (first, fourth, seventh, and eighth) have overturned such regulations, finding that hair-length regulations impinge student's constitutional rights. Significantly, all circuit courts refused to treat hairstyle as a form of symbolic speech, which would implicate the test of the *Tinker* case.[109]

---

[102] *Chaplinsky v. New Hampshire,* 315 U.S. 568 (1942).

[103] 478 U.S. 675 (1986).

[104] Ibid.

[105] *Gambino v. Fairfax Cty. Sch. Bd.,* 564 F. 2d 157 (4th Cir. 1977); *Shanley v. Northeast Indep. Sch. Dist.,* 462 F 2d 960 (5th Cir. 1972); *Koppell v. Levine,* 347 F. Supp. 456 (E.D. NY 1972).

[106] 484 U.S. 260 (1988).

[107] *Poling v. Murphy,* 872 F. 2d 757 (6th Cir. 1989), *cert. denied,* 493 U.S. 1021 (1990).

[108] *Karr v. Schmidt,* 401 U.S. 1201 (1972).

[109] Valente, *Law in the Schools.*

*Pupil Attire*   Generally, courts tend to provide less protection to some forms of expression (e.g., pupil hairstyle and attire) than to others (e.g., symbolic expression and student publications). Nonetheless, awareness of constitutional freedoms places limits on school officials to regulate student dress, excluding special situations (e.g., graduation and physical education classes). Pupil attire can always be regulated to protect student health, safety, and school discipline. In short, the extent to which school officials may control student appearance depends more on different community mores and on "the times" than on strict principles of law.

## Freedom of Association and Assembly

Under the First Amendment, students have a constitutional right to freedom of association and to peaceable assembly. Public schools are places where student associations and clubs are part of the daily routine of the school, some of which have been formally designated as cocurricular activities. However, most schools prohibit secret societies, associations, clubs, fraternities and sororities, and satanic cults. Courts have reasoned that such organizations have a detrimental influence on schools by tending to perpetuate antidemocratic values such as elitism, discrimination, and divisiveness. Various pleas of an abrogation of students' First and Fourteenth Amendment rights in these situations have not prevailed.[110] An Oregon court ruled that any nonschool-affiliated organization could associate in any manner it wished.[111]

## Classification Practices

The courts have evaluated classification practices to determine their legitimacy under the equal protection clause of the Fourteenth Amendment, state constitutions, and state and federal statutes. In this section, we explore student classification practices based on gender, marriage and pregnancy, age, and ability.

**Gender**   Litigants claiming sex discrimination can seek relief under the equal protection clause of the Fourteenth Amendment, Title VII of the Civil Rights Act of 1964, Title IX of the Education Amendments of 1972, Section 1983, the Equal Educational Opportunities Act

of 1974, equal rights amendments to state constitutions, and new and evolving sex discrimination statutes.

To receive affirmation from the courts, defendants in sex discrimination cases must present a preponderance of evidence that gender-based classifications are completely related to a legitimate government purpose. One public school case to reach the Supreme Court, *Vorchheimer v. School District of Philadelphia*, involved a challenge brought by a female student who had been denied admission to an all-male academic high school. The school district maintained among its high schools two sex-segregated schools for high-achievement students. The Court, equally divided, affirmed an earlier Third Circuit Court of Appeals decision that had ruled in favor of the school district.[112]

On the other hand, sex discrimination was held to violate the equal protection clause in two public school districts in which the schools set higher standards for girls than for boys.[113] In another case, the exclusion of male students from participation in a sex-segregated girls' program in a coeducational public high school was held to violate the state constitution's provision against sex discrimination.[114] In a more recent and famous university case, the Court held that the denial of admission to a male registered nurse to a state-supported university for women was unconstitutional discrimination based on gender classification.[115]

An area that has received much publicity concerning gender-based classifications is high school athletics. A precedent-setting eighth circuit court case invalidated a school policy that restricted participation to only male athletes on several noncontact sports' teams.[116] Generally, most courts have followed suit. The general proposition that female athletes must be provided the opportunity to participate in contact sports either through single-sex or coeducational teams has been sustained in federal district courts in Wisconsin, Missouri, and New York and the Pennsylvania Supreme Court. The converse is not true, however; male athletes can be barred

---

[110]*Passel v. Fort Worth I.S.D.*, 453 S.W. 2d 888 (Tex. Civ. App. 1970); *Robinson v. Sacramento U.S.D.*, 53 Calif. Reptr. 781, 788–789 (1966).

[111]*Burkitt v. S.D. No. 1, Multnomah Cty.*, 195 Ore. 471, 246 P. 2d 566 (1952).

---

[112]*Vorchheimer v. S.D. of Philadelphia*, 532 F. 2d 880 (3 Cir. 1976), aff. 430 U.S. 703 (1977).

[113]*Bray v. Lee*, 337 F. Supp. 934 (D. Mass. 1972); *Berkelman v. San Francisco U.S.D.*, 501 F. 2d 1264 (9 Cir. 1974).

[114]*Opinion of the Justices to the Senate*, 373 Mass. 883, 366 N.E. 2d 733 (1977).

[115]*Mississippi University for Women v. Hogan*, 458 U.S. 718 (1982).

[116]*Brenden v. Independent School District*, 477 F. 2d 1292 (8 Cir. 1973).

from all-female teams if their participation impedes the athletic opportunities of the females.[117]

**Marriage and Pregnancy**   Historically, public school districts have generally discouraged, and in some cases even barred, students from school attendance or participation in school-sponsored activities for reason of marriage or pregnancy. In more recent years, courts have invalidated school district policies for differential treatment of married or pregnant students. Federal district courts in Massachusetts, Mississippi, Montana, Ohio, Tennessee, and Texas have held that exclusion from school attendance and from participation in various school-sponsored activities could not be made solely on the basis of marital status or pregnancy.[118]

It is apparent from federal district court decisions in various states that students within the age limits of statutorily permitted school attendance are entitled to a free public school education. As such, they may not be excluded because of marriage or pregnancy from school activities nor isolated from contact with other students within the school environment.

**Age**   School boards have used age as a criterion for public school admission, compulsory education, and participation in some cocurricular activities. Courts have generally sustained school board policy and state statutes specifying minimum age requirements used in operating school systems. For example, a Wisconsin court and a federal district court in Maine supported a local school board policy and the state's minimum-age law, respectively, as a valid criterion for admission to its public schools. And a New York court upheld a school board policy restricting entry into a special accelerated junior high school program solely on the basis of an age requirement.[119] The Age Discrimination Act of 1975 has had little effect on public school students.

**Ability**   Generally, courts have supported ability grouping in theory unless racial or cultural bias is shown. In a famous case, *Hobson v. Hansen*, a federal district court in Washington, D.C., invalidated an ability-grouping plan based on the use of standardized test scores because it was shown to discriminate against minority students.[120] Subsequently, the fifth and ninth circuit courts

struck down ability-grouping practices based on the use of standardized achievement tests for the same reason. Later, the eleventh, another fifth circuit court, and an Illinois federal district court upheld grouping as free of cultural bias and contributing to the instruction and achievement of minority students.[121]

## Students with Disabilities

Historically, the attitude that prevailed concerning the education of disabled students was that retarded, learning disabled, emotionally disturbed, deaf, blind, or otherwise disabled children were not the responsibility of the public schools. Consequently, many disabled children were exempted from compulsory school attendance laws either by parental choice or by school district design. Nationally, services for the disabled were either nonexistent or nonextensive. Very few school districts provided services; where such services existed, they were inadequate to meet even the minimal needs of this vulnerable minority group.

In recent years, substantial changes in the attitude toward the disabled have occurred. Although disabled students do not comprise any "protected group" (such as race or gender) that is entitled to constitutional guarantees, federal statutes and state special education statutes were enacted to satisfy their constitutional rights. Lower court decisions and federal and state legislative enactments of the past three decades have mandated that all children, including the disabled, are entitled to admission to a school and placement in a program that meets their special needs. As summarized in the landmark Supreme Court school desegregation case, *Brown v. Board of Education of Topeka*, "education . . . is a right which must be made available to all on equal terms."[122] Although the Brown decision dealt with the constitutional protections afforded minority children, its consent agreement implied a mandate that all students of legal school age must be provided with appropriate school and classroom placement.

Two key court decisions outlined the legal framework for the constitutional protections of disabled children. In *Pennsylvania Association for Retarded Children (PARC) v. Commonwealth*,[123] a federal district court held that retarded children in Pennsylvania were enti-

[117]McCarthy and Cambron-McCabe, *Public School Law.*

[118]Reutter, *The Law of Public Education.*

[119]McCarthy and Cambron-McCabe, *Public School Law.*

[120]*Hobson v. Hansen*, 269 F. Supp. 401 (D.C.C. 1967), aff. *Smuck v. Hobson*, 408 F. 2d 175 (D.C. Cir. 1969).

[121]McCarthy and Cambron-McCabe, *Public School Law.*

[122]347 U.S. 483 (1954).

[123]334 F. Supp. 279 (E.D. Pa. 1972).

tled to a free public education and that, whenever possible, disabled children must be educated in regular classrooms and not segregated from other students. In *Mills v. Board of Education of the District of Columbia*,[124] another federal district court expanded the PARC decision to include all school-age disabled children.

Subsequent to the *PARC* and *Mills* decisions, Congress passed two landmark pieces of legislation that led to the rapid development of comprehensive, nationwide educational programs for the disabled. Section 504 of the Rehabilitation Act of 1973 is a broad-based federal law that addresses discrimination against the disabled both in the workplace and in schools. The statute, as amended, stipulates:

> No otherwise qualified individual with handicaps . . . shall solely by reason of her or his handicap, be excluded from participation in, be denied the benefits of, or be subjected to discrimination under any programs or activity receiving Federal financial assistance.[125]

Thus Section 504 would cut off all federal funds from schools that discriminate against the disabled. The statute also provides that all newly constructed public facilities be equipped to allow free access by disabled individuals.

The Education for All Handicapped Children Act (EAHCA) of 1975 and the Individuals with Disabilities Education Act (IDEA) provide federal funds to school districts that comply with its requirements. The major thrust of these acts was to ensure the right of all disabled children to a public education. Major provisions include a free appropriate public education, an individualized education program, special education services, related services, due process procedures, and the least restrictive learning environment.[126]

According to IDEA, all disabled children have the right to a "free appropriate public education." An appropriate education for the disabled is defined as special education and related services. Special education refers to specially designed instruction at public expense, including a variety of opportunities on a spectrum from regular classroom instruction and special classes to placement in a private facility. Related services include transportation, physical and occupational therapy, recreation, and counseling and medical diagnosis. A written **individualized education program (IEP)** is another key element in a free appropriate public education. An

IEP includes an assessment of the child's needs, specification of annual goals, strategies (methods, materials, interventions) to achieve the goals, and periodic evaluations of the child's progress. And, finally, a disabled child must be educated in the least restrictive environment. That is, the placement must be tailored to the special needs of the disabled student. In combination with related state laws, these federal statutes provide the guidelines for the education of the disabled.

In addition to the Rehabilitation Act, the disabled are now protected by the Americans with Disabilities Act of 1990 (ADA).[127] This law prohibits discrimination in employment (and other situations) against any "qualified individual with a disability." Essentially it amplifies and extends prohibitions of Section 504 of the Rehabilitation Act of 1973. Coverage is not dependent on involvement of federal funds. A "reasonable accommodation" that would permit a qualified individual with a disability to perform the "essential functions" of a position (or other activity) must be provided.

The definition of a disabled person under the ADA is somewhat different from the Rehabilitation Act. Under the newer law, a "qualified individual with a disability" means "an individual with a disability who, with or without reasonable modifications . . . meets the essential eligibility requirements for the receipt of services or the participation in programs or activities provided by a public entity."[128] To prevent conflict between the Rehabilitation Act and ADA, legislation requires that ADA be interpreted consistently with the older law. Thus, court decisions interpreting Section 504 are not affected by the later law. Furthermore, the Rehabilitation Act looks to the terms of the IDEA for resolution of most disputes concerning the education of the disabled; and compliance with IDEA will usually meet the requirements of ADA. Of these three laws, IDEA has had the most significant impact on public schools.

**IDEA 2004**   On November 19, 2004, Congress passed legislation reauthorizing IDEA and replacing it with the Individuals with Disabilities Education Improvement Act (Public Law 108-446), known as IDEA 2004.[129]

---

[124] 348 F. Supp. 866 D.D.C. (1972).

[125] 29 U.S.C. Sec. 794 (a) (1988).

[126] 20 U.S.C.A. Sec. 1400 (a) (West Supp. 1992).

[127] 42 U.S.C.A., Secs. 12101-12213 (1990 & West Supp. 1992).

[128] 42 U.S.C.A., Sec. 12131 (2) (West Supp. 1992).

[129] Council for Exceptional Children, http://www.cec.sped.org/pp/IDEA_120204.pdf; Congressional Research Service, http://www.nasponline.org/advocacy/IDEACRSAnalysis.pdf.

**Table 12–1**    **Summary of Requirements to Be a Highly Qualified Special Education Teacher**

| Category of Special Education Teachers | Requirements Under P.L. 108-446 (IDEA) |
|---|---|
| All special education teachers | *General Requirements*<br>Hold at least a bachelor's degree<br>Must obtain full state special education certification or equivalent licensure<br>Cannot hold an emergency or temporary certificate |
| New or veteran *elementary school* teachers teaching one or more core academic subjects only to children with disabilities held to alternative academic standards (most severely cognitively disabled) | In addition to the General Requirements above, may demonstrate academic subject competence through "a high objective uniform State standard of evaluation" (HOUSSE) process |
| New or veteran *middle or high school* teachers teaching one or more core academic subjects only to children with disabilities held to alternative academic standards (most severely cognitively disabled) | In addition to the General Requirements above, may demonstrate "subject matter knowledge appropriate to the level of instruction being provided, as determined by the State, needed to effectively teach to those standards" |
| *New* teachers of *two or more academic subjects* who are highly qualified in either mathematics, language arts, or science | In addition to the General Requirements above, has two-year window in which to become highly qualified in the other core academic subjects and may do this through the HOUSSE process |
| *Veteran* teachers who teach *two or more core academic subjects* only to children with disabilities | In addition to the General Requirements above, may demonstrate academic subject competence through the HOUSSE process (including a single evaluation for all core academic subjects) |
| *Consultative teachers* and other special education teachers who do not teach core academic subjects | Must only meet the General Requirements above |
| Other special education teachers teaching core academic subjects | In addition to the General Requirements above, meet relevant NCLB requirements for new elementary school teachers, new middle/high school teachers, or veteran teachers |

President George W. Bush signed this bill into law on December 3, 2004. IDEA 2004 has significantly affected the professional lives of general education teachers and special educators as well as parents of children with disabilities, all of whom encountered new roles and responsibilities as a result of the law.

> The Individuals with Disabilities Education Improvement Act of 2004 (New IDEA) increased the focus of special education from simply ensuring access to education to improving the educational performance of students with disabilities and aligning special education services with the larger national school improvement efforts that include standards, assessments, and accountability.[130]

Following are highlights of some significant issues addressed in this historic document. These provisions provide a framework for individual states to develop their own standards and procedures.

---

[130] Victor Nolet and Margaret J. McLaughlin, *Accessing the General Curriculum: Including Students with Disabilities in Standards-Based Reform*, 2nd ed. (Thousand Oaks, CA: Corwin Press, 2005), pp. 2–3.

***Highly Qualified Special Education Teachers***   The language contained in IDEA 2004 concerning who is considered a "highly qualified" special educator is complementary to the standards promulgated in the No Child Left Behind Act (see Table 12–1).

***Individualized Education Program (IEP) Process***

- Short-term objectives and benchmarks will no longer be required except for those pupils who are evaluated via alternate assessments aligned to alternate achievement standards.

- Assessment of the progress that a student is making toward meeting annual goals, which must be written in measurable terms, is still required. Reference, however, to the current requirement of reporting the "extent to which progress is sufficient to enable the child to achieve goals by the end of the year" is eliminated. The IEP will now need to describe how the individual's progress toward achieving annual goals will be measured and when these progress reports will be made.

- A new provision of the legislation allows for members of the IEP team to be excused from participating in all or part of the meeting if the parents and school district agree that attendance is not necessary because the individual's area of curriculum or related service is not being reviewed or modified. The team member will be required, however, to submit written input into the development of the IEP prior to the meeting.

■ PL 108-446 allows for alternatives to physical IEP meetings such as video conferencing and conference telephone calls.

■ Once an IEP is established, IDEA 2004 will allow for changes to be made via a written plan to modify the document without convening the entire team and redrafting the whole IEP.

■ The new legislation deletes references to transition services beginning at age fourteen. Now, transition services are to begin no later than the first IEP in effect when the student turns sixteen (and updated annually). It also establishes a new requirement for postsecondary goals pertaining to appropriate education, training, employment, and independent living skills.

■ School districts will be allowed, with parental consent, to develop multiyear IEPs (not to exceed three years).

■ The U. S. Department of Education is charged with developing and disseminating model IEP forms and model IFSP (individualized family service plan) forms.

*Identifying Students with Specific Learning Disabilities* Under IDEA 1997, when identifying an individual for a possible learning disability, educators typically looked to see if the student exhibited a severe discrepancy between achievement and intellectual ability. This discrepancy provision was removed from IDEA 2004. School districts will now be able, if they so choose, to use a process that determines if the pupil responds to empirically validated, scientifically based interventions—a procedure known as Response-To-Intervention. Under the new guidelines, rather than comparing IQ with performance on standardized achievement tests, general education teachers can offer intensive programs of instructional interventions. If the child fails to make adequate progress, a learning disability is assumed to be present and additional assessment is warranted.

*Discipline*

■ PL 108-446 stipulates that when a student is removed from his current educational setting, the pupil is to continue to receive those services that enable partici-

pation in the general education curriculum and ensure progress toward meeting IEP goals.

■ IDEA 1997 allowed school authorities to unilaterally remove a student to an interim alternative educational setting (IASE) for up to forty-five days for offenses involving weapons or drugs. IDEA 2004 now permits school officials to remove any pupil (including those with and without disabilities) to an IASE for up to forty-five days for inflicting "serious bodily injury."

■ Removal to an IASE will now be for forty-five *school* days rather than forty-five calendar days.

■ Behavior resulting in disciplinary action still requires a manifestation review; however, language requiring the IEP team to consider whether the pupil's disability impaired his ability to control behavior or comprehend the consequences of his actions has been eliminated. IEP teams now need to ask only two questions: (1) Did the disability cause or have a direct and substantial relationship to the offense? (2) Was the violation a direct result of the school's failure to implement the IEP?

■ IDEA 2004 modifies the "stay put" provision enacted during an appeals process. When either the LEA (local education agency) or parent requests an appeal of a manifestation determination or placement decision, the pupil is required to remain in the current IASE until a decision is rendered by the hearing officer or until the time period for the disciplinary violation concludes. A hearing must be held within twenty school days of the date of the appeal.

*Due Process*

■ Parents will encounter a two-year statute of limitations for filing a due process complaint from the time they knew or should have known that a violation occurred. Alleged violations might involve identification, assessment, or placement issues or the failure to provide an appropriate education.

■ A mandatory "resolution session" is now required prior to proceeding with a due process hearing. (The parents and school district may waive this requirement and proceed to mediation.) School districts must convene a meeting with the parents and IEP team members within fifteen days of receiving a due process complaint. If the complaint is not satisfactorily resolved within thirty days of the filing date, the due process hearing may proceed.

■ Under provisions of IDEA 1997, parents who prevailed in due process hearings and/or court cases could seek attorney's fees from the school district. IDEA 2004 now permits school districts to seek attorney's fees from the parents' attorney (or the parents themselves) if the due process complaint or lawsuit is deemed frivolous, unreasonable, or without foundation or the attorney continues to litigate despite these circumstances. Reasonable attorney fees can also be awarded by the court if the complaint or lawsuit was filed for an improper purpose such as to harass, cause unnecessary delay, or needlessly increase the cost of litigation.

*Funding*   IDEA 2004 continues to be a discretionary program allowing Congress to fund it at whatever level it chooses. When IDEA was initially enacted in 1975 as PL 94-142, Congress authorized the federal government to pay 40 percent of the "excess cost" of educating pupils with disabilities (commonly referred to as "full funding"). Although mandatory full funding was not accomplished with this reauthorization, a six-year plan or "glide path" for achieving this goal was enacted. Interestingly, only two days after passing this law, Congress appropriated significantly less ($1.7 billion) than it had just promised. While considerable, the federal government currently provides only about 18 percent of the cost of educating students with disabilities.

### Evaluation of Students

- School districts will be required to determine the eligibility of a student to receive a special education and the educational needs of the child within a sixty-day time frame. (This provision does not apply if the state has already established a timeline for accomplishing this task.) The sixty-day rule commences upon receipt of parental permission for evaluation.

- Reevaluation of eligibility for a special education may not occur more than once per year (unless agreed to by the school district and parent); and it must occur at least once every three years unless the parent and school district agree that such a reevaluation is unnecessary.

- IDEA 2004 modifies the provision pertaining to native language and preferred mode of communication. New language in the bill requires that evaluations are to be "provided and administered in the language and form most likely to yield accurate information on what the child knows and can do academically, developmentally, and functionally, unless it is not feasible to so provide or administer."

- School districts are not allowed to seek dispute resolution when parents refuse to give their consent for

special education services. If parents refuse to give consent, then the school district is not responsible for providing a free and appropriate public education.

*Assessment Participation*   PL 108-446 requires that *all* students participate in all state- and district-wide assessments (including those required under the No Child Left Behind Act), with accommodations or alternative assessments, if necessary, as stipulated in the pupil's IEP. States are permitted to assess up to 1 percent of students with disabilities (generally those pupils with significant cognitive deficits) with alternative assessments aligned with alternative achievement standards. This legislation further requires that assessments adhere to the principles of universal design when feasible.

## The Law and State Issues

This section focuses on major legal issues pertaining to school desegregation, church-state relations, and school finance schemes.

### School Desegregation

A U.S. Supreme Court decision, *Plessy v. Ferguson*, established the **"separate but equal"** doctrine regarding the use of public railroad facilities by blacks and whites in 1896.[131] Subsequently, this doctrine was used as the basis for public school segregation of black and white students for the next fifty years in many states. Under dual school systems, black students attended all-black schools staffed predominantly by black teachers, and white children attended all-white schools. Such de jure segregation was rendered constitutional because the separate-but-equal rationale served as a national standard satisfying the equal protection clause of the Fourteenth Amendment.

In 1954 the landmark decision of *Brown v. Board of Education of Topeka* repudiated the Plessy doctrine.[132] The Court stated that "in the field of public education the doctrine of 'separate but equal' has no place. Separate educational facilities are inherently unequal." Because of the significant impact of this decision, the Court postponed for one year the issuance of an enforcement decree. The decision, known as *Brown II*, di-

---

[131] *Plessy v. Ferguson*, 163 U.S. 537 (1896).

[132] *Brown v. Bd. of Educ. of Topeka*, 347 U.S. 483 (1954).

rected lower federal courts to enforce remedies "with all deliberate speed." [133]

Following *Brown,* southern school districts attempted numerous strategies to avoid desegregation—including transfer provisions; closing the public schools and maintaining state-supported, private, segregated white schools; integrating schools on a one-grade-a-year plan and freedom-of-choice plans; rezoning school districts; and the like—all of which perpetuated segregated dual school systems. Fourteen years after *Brown II,* the Court discarded the "all deliberate speed" criterion for complying with its desegregation enforcement decree. It stated that ". . . every school district is to terminate dual school systems at once and to operate now and hereafter only unitary schools." [134]

This ultimatum affected only those states with **de jure segregation**—segregation that is derived from the influence of the law and is unconstitutional. Southern school districts were quick to point out that there was plenty of segregation in the North created by special forces (such as housing patterns), independent of state sponsorship, which is called **de facto segregation** and is not unconstitutional. For de jure segregation to exist, three factors must be present: (1) Segregation must be initiated and supported by government action; (2) the action must have been taken with the intent to segregate; and (3) the action must have created or increased segregation. [135]

After the *Alexander* decision, many types of remedies of de jure segregation were ordered by lower federal courts. The famous *Swann v. Charlotte-Mecklenburg Board of Education* busing case served as a model remedy for school desegregation. The Court concluded: "In these circumstances, we find no basis for holding that the local school authorities may not be required to employ bus transportation as a tool of school desegregation. Desegregation plans cannot be limited to the walk-in school." [136] This case launched busing as an effective tool to remedy school desegregation.

The courts have used interdistrict desegregation as another remedy for de jure segregation in some situations. In what has become known as the "Detroit case," the Supreme Court affirmed de jure segregation in Detroit because it was shown that racially discriminatory acts of one or more school districts caused racial segregation in an adjacent district and that district lines were deliberately drawn on the basis of race. [137] Three years later, the Detroit case was heard by the Supreme Court once again. [138]

The Court ordered several curriculum programs to eradicate the vestiges of de jure segregation, including remedial reading, teacher in-service training in human relations, expanded counseling and career guidance services for minority students, and a nondiscriminatory testing program. Also ordered was state support of one-half the cost to implement these programs. Subsequent interdistrict remedies were ordered in numerous school districts including Jefferson County, Kentucky, which has served as a model of interdistrict desegregation for many years. [139]

## Church-State Relations

Issues concerning church-state relations have provided a steady stream of litigation since World War II. No other area in school law, except school desegregation, has received more attention in the courts than issues involving religion in the public schools. In this section, we examine legal developments concerning church-state-education relationships. Our discussion is limited to school prayer and Bible reading, religion in the curriculum, released time for religious instruction, and use of facilities.

Contained in the U.S. Constitution is a separation of church and state provision, which guarantees religious freedom and forbids the establishment of religion by the government. The First Amendment provides in part that "Congress shall make no law respecting the establishment of religion, or prohibiting the free exercise thereof." These two religious clauses, the *establishment clause* and the *free exercise clause,* protect a person's religious liberty. The two combined prevent religious indoctrination in the public schools and prohibit the use of public funds to support religion.

It should be noted that this provision restricts only the federal government from making such laws. However, through numerous Supreme Court decisions, jus-

---

[133] *Brown v. Bd. of Educ. of Topeka,* 349 U.S. 294 (1955).

[134] *Alexander v. Holmes Cty. Bd. of Educ.,* 396 U.S. 19 (1969).

[135] Valente, *Law in the Schools.*

[136] *Swann v. Charlotte-Mecklenburg Bd. of Educ.,* 402 U.S. 1 (1971).

[137] *Milliken v. Bradley,* 418 U.S. 717 (1974).

[138] *Milliken v. Bradley,* 433 U.S. 267 (1977).

[139] *Newburg Area Council, Inc., v. Bd. of Educ. of Jefferson County, Ky.,* 510 F. 2d 1358 (6 Cir. 1974), cert. den. 421 U.S. 931 (1975).

tices have incorporated clauses in the U.S. Constitution as applicable to the states by means of the Fourteenth Amendment. This has been effected primarily through two Court cases. The free exercise clause was incorporated in *Cantwell v. Connecticut* and the establishment clause in *Everson v. Board of Education*.[140]

**Vouchers**   On June 27, 2002, the U.S. Supreme Court ruled in favor of a Cleveland program that allows public money to be used to send children to private schools, including religious schools. The 5–4 ruling, which overturned a lower court ruling, was seen as a victory for "school voucher" programs that have been established in some parts of the country with the goal of providing more options to students who would otherwise be sent to underperforming public schools. The decision sparked more debate in the controversy over separation of church and state, especially after an appeals court ruled the Pledge of Allegiance unconstitutional because it mentions "under God."[141]

**School Prayer and Bible Reading**   Historically, many public schools began each day with a prayer and/or Bible reading. Three significant Court decisions established the precedent concerning Bible reading in the public schools. In *Engel v. Vitale,* the Court struck down a New York statute requiring the recitation of a prayer as a violation of the establishment clause of the First Amendment.[142] One year later, in *School District of Abington v. Schempp,* the Court declared unconstitutional a Pennsylvania statute requiring Bible reading and recitation of the Lord's Prayer ". . . when it is part of the school curriculum and conducted under the supervision of teachers employed in the schools."[143] The *Lemon v. Kurtzman* decision established a three-factor test of constitutionality under the establishment clause. The Court declared that to withstand constitutional challenge, the statute must pass three tests: (1) It must have a secular purpose, (2) have a primary effect that neither advances nor inhibits religion, and (3) not foster excessive government entanglement with religion.[144] This three-factor test has been applied in most establishment clause cases.

Persistent litigation concerning prayer and Bible reading in the public schools continued in the lower courts, but it was not until 1985 that a similar challenge reached the Supreme Court in *Wallace v. Jaffree*.[145] In this case, the issue was whether setting aside class time for silent prayer was constitutional. The Court held that such activity was unconstitutional. Although the Court applied the three-factor **Lemon test,** a minority of justices objected to its rigidity in assessing individual situations.

In 1992, in *Lee v. Weisman,* the Supreme Court declared that opening prayers at graduation ceremonies are unconstitutional.[146] The question addressed by the Court was "whether including clerical members who offer prayers as part of the official school graduation ceremony is consistent with the Religions Clauses of the First Amendment." The Court followed the standard set in *Engel* and *Abington:* "The principle that government may accommodate the free exercise of religion does not supersede the fundamental limitations imposed by the Establishment Clause."

Three post–*Lee v. Weisman* decisions of the Fifth Circuit Court of Appeals illustrate distinctions that courts may make for different school events. After ruling that student-led prayer at commencements were valid under the *Lee* guidelines,[147] the court struck down as unconstitutional school practices that allowed school employees to participate in or supervise student-led prayers at athletic team games and practices, while upholding school permission for the school choir to adopt a Christian religious song as its theme song.[148] Still later, the same

---

[140]*Cantwell v. Connecticut,* 310 U.S. 296 (1940); *Everson v. Board of Education,* 330 U.S. 1 (1947).

[141]ABC News Internet Ventures, June 27, 2002. http://abcnews.go.com/section/us/DailyNews/scotus_vouchers020627.html

[142]*Engel v. Vitale,* 370 U.S. 421 (1962).

[143]*S.D. of Abington Twp., Pa. v. Schempp,* 374 U.S. 203 (1963).

[144]*Lemon v. Kurtzman,* 403 U.S. 602 (1971).

[145]472 U.S., 105 (1985).

[146]*Lee v. Weisman,* 60 U.S.L.W. 4723 (1992).

[147]*Jones v. Clear Creek Indep. School Dist.,* 977 F. 2d 963 (5th Cir. 1992). But see, *contra: ACLU v. Black Horse Pike Regional Bd. of Educ.,* 84 F. 3d 1471 (3d Cir. 1996) (refusing to follow Jones and overturning student-initiated prayers at high school graduation).

[148]*Doe v. Duncanville Ind. School Dist.,* 70 F. 3d 402 (5th Cir. 1995). See also *Bauchmann v. West High School,* 900 F. Supp. 254 (Utah 1995), which held that singing Christian songs at Christian places of worship by a high school choir did not violate the religious freedom of a Jewish choir member. A contrary view was taken by another court for a student-organized gospel choir that a school secretary supervised. *Sease v. School Dist. of Phila.,* 811 F. Supp. 183 (E.D. Pa. 1993).

court struck down a Mississippi statute that authorized student-initiated prayer at sporting events, student assemblies, and other school-related student events.[149]

**Released Time for Religious Instruction**  Two Supreme Court cases have addressed the issue of released time for religious instruction. In the first case, *McCollum v. Board of Education,* the Court invalidated a program in which religion classes were taught in the public schools.[150] The Court declared that the use of tax-supported school facilities to promote religious instruction was clearly a violation of the First Amendment. In the second case, *Zorach v. Clausen,* the Court upheld a program whereby students were permitted to leave the school premises during the school day to receive religious instruction at various religious centers.[151] The significant difference between *Zorach* and *McCollum* was that the latter program did not involve the use of public school buildings or the direct use of public funds. Such released-time religious instruction is used in many school communities throughout the country. The arrangement does not violate the federal Constitution as long as the established program is not held on school grounds and is not conducted by teachers or religion instructors affiliated with the school and as long as these instructors are not paid by the school district.

**Religion in the Curriculum**  The *Lemon* test was used in two cases to assess the permissibility of offering Bible study courses in the public schools. In earlier decisions dealing with the constitutionality of school-sponsored prayer and Bible reading, the courts noted that the teaching of the Bible and religion as an aspect of our culture and our history and as a nonbiased academic subject is permissible. In *Wiley v. Franklin* and four years later in *Crockett v. Sorenson,* the courts ruled such practices unconstitutional.[152] Study of the Bible in both jurisdictions when scrutinized by the courts failed one or more prongs of the *Lemon* tripartite test. In a related case, a third circuit court held that a course on Transcendental Meditation (TM) violated the First Amendment.[153] In applying the *Lemon* test, the court concluded that the

objectives of TM may have been secular but the means used were religious.

A recent development in this area involves state statutes requiring the teaching of creationism in courses that also teach about the theory of evolution. State statutes in Arkansas and Louisiana that required balanced treatment of the two perspectives were struck down as efforts to advance religion and in violation of the First Amendment.[154]

**Use of Facilities**  It is common practice in public schools to permit student organizations to use school buildings during noninstructional time. Local boards of education have implied powers to regulate such use. In such situations, the question arises concerning the constitutionality of meetings involving religious groups. In 1984, Congress passed the Equal Access Act (EAA), which has since been amended, in an attempt to clarify the unsettled area of law where students' free speech rights compete with the rights of public schools to control access to the school as a forum for public discourse. The EAA,[155] as amended, states in part that:

> It shall be unlawful for any public secondary school which receives Federal financial assistance and which has a limited open forum to deny equal access or a fair opportunity to, or discriminate against, any students who wish to conduct a meeting within that limited open forum on the basis of the religious, political, philosophical, or other content of the speech at such meetings.

A school has complied with the *fair opportunity* requirement if the meetings (1) are voluntary and student-initiated; (2) involve no school or government sponsorship; (3) allow the presence of school employees only in a nonparticipatory capacity; (4) do not materially and substantially interfere with the orderly conduct of educational activities within the school; and (5) are not directed, controlled, or regularly attended by nonschool persons; and the school cannot limit these groups to a specified size.[156]

The constitutionality of this federal statute is questionable. Three federal circuit courts (second, third, and fifth) have held that such meetings are unconstitutional and a violation of the establishment clause of the First

---

[149] *Ingebretson v. Jackson Public School Dist.*, 88 F. 3d 274 (5th Cir. 1996).

[150] 333 U.S. 203 (1948).

[151] *Zorach v. Clausen,* 343 U.S. 306 (1952).

[152] *Wiley v. Franklin,* 474 F. Supp. 525 (Tenn. 1979); *Crockett v. Sorenson,* 568 F. Supp. 1422 (Va. 1983).

[153] *Malnak v. Yogi,* 592 F. 2d 197 (3 Cir. 1979).

[154] *McLean v. Arkansas Board of Education,* 529 F. Supp. 1255 (Ak. 1982); *Aguillard v. Edwards,* 765 F. 2d 1251 (5 Cir. 1985).

[155] 20 U.S.C., Sec. 4071 (1988).

[156] Ibid.

Amendment.[157] The courts' view in these cases is that, if these meetings are sanctioned, students will believe that schools support religious groups and that this violates the posture of avoidance of excessive government entanglement with religion outlined in *Lemon*.

In 1990, the Supreme Court resolved some of the legal questions when it rendered a decision in *Board of Education of Westside Community Schools v. Mergens*.[158] The case arose when a group of high school students sought permission to form a club that would meet at the public school on noninstructional time and engage in Bible discussions, prayer, and fellowship. The Court held that the school could not bar the religious club from non-curriculum-related student group meetings during noninstructional time. The Court reasoned that denial of recognition to a student-initiated religious club by a public school that recognized a variety of other non-curriculum-related student groups violated the EAA.

## Financing Education

Throughout the history of public education in the United States the property tax has served as the major source of financing for public schools at the local level. The use of the property tax to finance public education has received much attention recently and has led to a steady stream of litigation in state and federal courts. Challenges have been advanced on the issue of equality of educational opportunity for all people. Dependence on local property tax revenues to support public education has caused wide inequities in interdistrict funding of educational programs in various states. The equal protection clause of the Fourteenth Amendment and specific state statutes have been the primary vehicles under which litigants have sought relief. This section focuses on levying taxes and challenges to state finance schemes.

**School Taxes**  The Tenth Amendment to the U.S. Constitution provides: "The powers not delegated to the United States by the Constitution nor prohibited by it to the states, are reserved to the states respectively, or to the people." This clause confers on the state the authority not only to regulate and control education but also to devise and implement its own system of taxation. Congress was reminded of the sovereignty of the state over public education in an early Supreme Court case. The Court concluded that "all powers not expressly granted to the United States by the Constitution or reasonably implied therefrom were reserved to the states."[159] This statement provided a case law basis for the state's power to tax and to appropriate funds for public schools.

The authority of school districts to raise and collect taxes for schools is a power that must be conferred on them by the legislature. Furthermore, not all districts have the same taxing power. The legislature can classify school districts and delegate varied financial powers to them depending on their classification.[160]

There are two broad classifications of school districts with respect to their power to tax and raise funds for public schools: fiscally independent and fiscally dependent school districts. The vast majority of the more than 15,000 public school districts in the nation are fiscally independent.

*Fiscally Independent School Districts*  These school districts are granted legal authority by the state legislature to set the tax rate on real property, within state constitutional and legislative limits; to levy and collect taxes for the support of local schools; and to approve the expenditure of the funds collected. States require local school boards to prepare budgets of proposed expenditures. In fiscally independent school districts, then, boards of education have a relatively free hand in determining how and where expenditures are to be made, subject to limitations on the total amount by the state's constitution or statute. For example, in Florida local school authorities levy and collect taxes for school purposes, independent of the local county or city governments. However, Florida state law sets a legal limit on the tax rates that can be established by local boards of education.[161] Similarly, in Kentucky state statutes grant local school boards authority to tax property for the support of public schools.[162]

[157]*Brandon v. Bd. of Educ.*, 635 F. 2d 971 (2 Cir. 1980), *cert. den.*, 454 U.S. 1123 (1981); *Bender v. Williamsport Area S.D.*, 741 F. 2d 538 (3 Cir. 1984), *cert. aff.* 1055 S. Ct. 1167, 54 L.W. 4307 (1986); *Lubbock Civil Liberties Union v. Lubbock I.S.D.*, 699 F. 2d 1038 (5 Cir. 1982).

[158]496 U.S. 226 (1990).

[159]*U.S. v. Butler*, 297 U.S. 1 (1936).

[160]*Pirrone v. City of Boston*, 364 Mass. 403, N.E. 2d 96 (1973).

[161]*Gulesian v. Dade Cty. School Board*, 281 So. 2d 325 (Fla. 1973).

[162]*Ky. Rev. Stat.*, Ch. 160.593 (1992).

*Fiscally Dependent School Districts* In this configuration, the board of education prepares and adopts a budget specifying the anticipated expenditures and projected revenue needs. Then a different municipal government may reduce the total budget or eliminate items not required by state law and apportion the school taxes. For example, in Chicago statutory language authorized the school tax levy to be a cooperative endeavor, joining the board of education and city officials. While the local board performed all the preliminary steps in the budget process—preparation, review, and adoption—no school taxes could be forthcoming without the adoption by the city council of an ordinance levying the tax.[163] In a more recent case in Chicago, a two-year collective bargaining agreement was held unenforceable regarding the second year's salary provisions. The state statute stipulated that the local board of education could not incur a contractual liability without an apportionment of funds, and apportionments were made annually by the city council.[164] Similarly in Alaska, Maryland, Massachusetts, New Hampshire, New York, and Pennsylvania, school districts are fiscally dependent on the municipal government to apportion taxes for school purposes.[165]

**Challenges to State Finance Schemes** Beginning in the late 1960s and continuing to the present, litigation has addressed the issue of inequality of educational opportunity resulting from public school finance schemes. Rooted in the famous landmark desegregation case, *Brown v. Board of Education of Topeka,* courts initially invoked equal protection rights as a means of forcing redistribution of state funds for public education. A key paragraph of *Brown,* often used by plaintiffs in school finance litigation, recognizes the importance of education in contemporary American society:

> Today, education is perhaps the most important function of state and local governments . . . [and] the great expenditures for education . . . demonstrate our recognition of the importance of education to our democratic society. . . . In these days, it is doubtful that any child may reasonably be expected to succeed in life if he is denied the opportunity of an education.

The Court went on to say, "Such an opportunity, where the state has undertaken to provide it, is a right which must be made available to all on equal terms."[166]

**Educational Needs Standard** Two 1968 Supreme Court cases challenged the constitutionality of state finance schemes in Illinois and Virginia under the equal protection clause of the Fourteenth Amendment. The first case, *McInnis v. Shapiro,* was a class action suit brought on behalf of elementary and secondary public school students and their parents in four Cook County school districts in Illinois.[167] The plaintiffs claimed that the Illinois system of public school finance violated the equal protection guarantees of the Fourteenth Amendment. Additionally, they claimed that there were markedly inequitable per-pupil expenditures among Illinois school districts.

In rejecting their contention, the court cited the following points: (1) The Fourteenth Amendment did not require that public school expenditures be made solely on the basis of "educational needs"; (2) "educational expenses" were not the "exclusive yardstick" for measuring the quality of a child's educational opportunity; and (3) there were no "judicially manageable standards" by which a federal court could determine if and when the equal protection clause is satisfied or violated. The court further stated, "The General Assembly's delegation of authority to school districts appears designed to allow individual localities to determine their own tax burden according to the importance which they place upon public schools." The U.S. Supreme Court affirmed the judgment. In the same year, the Court rejected a second challenge in Virginia, *Burruss v. Wilkerson,* advanced on the **educational needs standard.**[168]

**Fiscal Neutrality Standard** In 1971 the California Supreme Court, in *Serrano v. Priest (Serrano I),* contradicted the stance taken by the U.S. Supreme Court two years earlier.[169] In both *McInnis* and *Burruss,* the U.S. Supreme Court rejected the federal constitutional theory that education is a right under the Constitution. The Court left in the hands of state legislatures the responsi-

---

[163]*Latham v. Bd. of Educ. of the City of Chicago,* 31 Ill. 2d 178, 201 N.E. 2d 111 (1964).

[164]*Bd. of Educ. v. Chicago Teachers Union,* Local 1, A.F.T., 26 Ill. App. 3d 806 N.E. 2d 158 (1975).

[165]Hudgins and Vacca, *Law and Education.*

[166]*Brown v. Bd. of Educ. of Topeka,* 347 U.S. 483 (1954).

[167]*McInnis v. Shapiro,* 293 F. Supp. 327 (N.D. Ill. 1968), aff., *McInnis v. Ogilvie,* 394 U.S. 322 (1969).

[168]*Burruss v. Wilkerson,* 301 F. Supp. 1237 (W.D. Va. 1968), 310 F. Supp. 372 (W.D. Va. 1969), aff., 397 U.S. 44 (1970).

[169]*Serrano v. Priest,* 5 Calif. 3d 584, 96 Calif. Rptr. 601, 487 P. 2d 1241 (1971).

bility to remedy any existing inequities in state funding systems. *Serrano v. Priest,* then, represents an evolutionary step in judicial expansion of equal rights protection under the federal Constitution regarding public school finance. This case generated more reaction than any decision rendered in a state court, for it restricted the state's plenary power to devise and implement its own system of funding public schools.

The plaintiffs in *Serrano,* a group of elementary and high school pupils and their parents, brought a class action suit against the state of California and the county of Los Angeles pertaining to the financing of the public schools. The plaintiffs argued that the California school finance scheme, which relied heavily on local property taxes, caused wide interdistrict disparities in per-pupil expenditures. Such a system was not fiscally neutral, according to the court, because it made the quality of a child's education dependent on the wealth of the school district and therefore invidiously discriminated against the poor in violation of the equal protection clause of the Fourteenth Amendment and similar provisions in the California constitution. The California Supreme Court concluded that under the **fiscal neutrality standard,** the quality of a child's education could not be a function of the wealth of the child's local school district but rather must be based on the wealth of the state as a whole.

The California Supreme Court in *Serrano v. Priest (Serrano II)* reaffirmed its position in *Serrano I* and provided remedies available to the legislature to rectify the wide disparities in the state-funding formula in California. Included among the remedies were the following proposals: full state funding to be supported by a statewide property tax; district consolidation with boundary realignments to equalize assessed valuations of real property among school districts; retention of present school district boundaries with removal of commercial and industrial property from tax warrant rolls for school purposes and placement on state-tax warrant rolls for school purposes; and implementation of a voucher system.[170] One decade later, *Serrano v. Priest (Serrano III)* held that there had been full compliance with the original *Serrano* order to improve the inequities in state financing of public schools in California.[171]

**The Rodriguez Case**   Another major case that has had significant impact on public school finance is *San Antonio Independent School District v. Rodriguez.* The

U.S. Supreme Court altered the *Serrano* attitude that public education is a fundamental right protected by the Constitution. Further, it struck ___ the fiscal neutrality standard that the equali___ education cannot be a function of we___ ___ the wealth of the state as a whole. S___ . *Rodriguez* marked a return to the view ___ ___ion is a plenary power granted to the st___ ___irectly a federal matter.

*Rodriguez* wa___ ___y heard by a three-judge federal district court i___ ___as in which the state's school finance system was challenged. The plaintiffs alleged that the Texas system of financing its public schools, which relied heavily on the local property tax base, tolerated inequitable per-pupil expenditures among local school districts and discriminated against poor families. The rationale of fiscal neutrality and precedents of *Serrano* fashioned their plea. The district court concluded that the Texas system of financing public schools was a violation of the Fourteenth Amendment.[172]

Upon appeal of the state of Texas, the U.S. Supreme Court reversed the lower court.[173] The appellees' rationale was rejected on two fundamental points. First, the Court commented that the evidence did not support the contention that the Texas finance system was discriminatory against the poor. The Court stated that the suit involved "a large, diverse, and amorphous class, unified only by the common factor of residence in districts." Further, the fiscal neutrality standard was struck down by the Court because the Texas school finance system was based on a statewide minimum foundation program financed by state and local revenue. The program was designed to provide at least a basic education to each student in the state. Local school districts contributed a portion to the state's foundation program reflective of the assessed property valuation in the district. The Court concluded that no child was completely deprived of educational opportunity in Texas.

Second, concerning the issue of whether education is a "fundamental" constitutional right under the equal protection clause, the Court concluded that there was no such right "explicitly or implicitly guaranteed by the Constitution." In so ruling, the Court reverted to the traditional attitude of leaving the financing of public schools in the hands of state legislatures. The Court concluded: "The . . . complexity of the problems of financing . . . a state-wide public school system suggests that

[170]*Serrano v. Priest,* 18 Calif. 3d 728, 135 Calif. Rptr. 345 (1976), *cert. den.* 432 U.S. 907 (1977).

[171]*Serrano v. Priest,* 226 Calif. Rptr. 584 (1986).

[172]*Rodriguez v. San Antonio I.S.D.,* 337 F. Supp. 280 (W.D. Tex. 1971).

[173]*San Antonio I.S.D. v. Rodriguez,* 411 U.S. 1 (1973).

---

## PRO/CON Debate

### Equal Access

Congress passed the 1984 Equal Access Act in an attempt to clarify the unsettled area of law wherein the free-speech rights of students compete with the right of schools to control access to schools as a forum for public discourse. Since that time, lawsuits and court decisions have only added to the confusion and uncertainty.

**Question:**  Should student religious clubs be allowed to meet in public school facilities?

**Arguments PRO**

1. Young people should be encouraged to engage in wide-ranging discussions on any issue. The developmental stage of adolescence is one where young adults are interested in religion.

2. Students do not leave their constitutional rights to freedom of speech at the schoolhouse door. They have the right to express their views in the classroom during class time. Why should they not be allowed to express them in after-school activities that are tied to religious groups?

3. Student religious clubs should have the same access to school facilities as is routinely granted to secular groups. Frequently, religious clubs have church or synagogue sponsors, and adults are present to supervise the students.

4. Under the federal equal access law, it is unlawful for a public secondary school that has created a limited open forum to deny access to student-initiated groups on the basis of the religious, political, or philosophical content of the group's speech.

**Arguments CON**

1. The U.S. Constitution provides for the separation of church and state. No religious events of any kind should be allowed in public school buildings.

2. Opening the schools to one student-initiated group opens the doors to all student-initiated groups. School administrators need clear restraints on the use of school buildings so that they do not have to decide on the basis of the desirability of one religious group over another. Without a limitation, students may request that an undesirable club, such as a cult or paramilitary group, meet in the school.

3. The current law restricts the amount of supervision that can be exercised over religious clubs. For purposes of safety, school administrators must have the latitude to supervise any student group that meets in the building.

4. The right way to guarantee freedom of religion is to keep the state out of the religious process altogether. To require the schools to allow access to religious groups is to get the schools involved, not to keep church and state separate.

---

there will be more than one constitutionally permissible method of solving them, and that, within the limits of rationality, the legislature's efforts should be entitled to respect.[174]

**Post-*Rodriguez* Litigation**  Subsequent to *Rodriguez,* litigation in school finance issues continued to flourish. The federal courts were abandoned, however, as an arena for such litigation. The Supreme Court's position in *Rodriguez* made it clear that successful challenges to state finance systems must be pursued on state constitutional grounds rather than on the provisions of the U.S. Constitution. Plaintiffs continued to pattern their argu-

ments on the *Serrano* and *Rodriguez* cases. Because of individual differences in each state's constitution, decisions have been inconsistent.

The highest courts in eleven states (Arizona, Colorado, Georgia, Idaho, Illinois, Maryland, Michigan, New York, Oklahoma, Oregon, and Pennsylvania) have upheld the state's system of financing public schools as constitutional. Most of these decisions were rendered by the court using the *Rodriguez* rationale and precedents. On the other hand, decisions by the highest courts in other states (Arkansas, California, Connecticut, Kentucky, Montana, New Jersey, Texas, Washington, West Virginia, Wisconsin, and Wyoming) have struck down the constitutionality of the state's public school finance system. Most of these decisions were rejected primarily

---

[174]Ibid.

on the legal principles forwarded by the California Supreme Court in *Serrano*.[175]

## Summary

1. All three units of government—federal, state, and local—exercise some degree of authority and control over public education.

2. The state was given plenary power over public education through the Tenth Amendment to the U.S. Constitution.

3. Nevertheless, the federal government has exercised and continues to exercise profound influence in educational matters, primarily through the provisions of the federal Constitution, decisions of the U.S. Supreme Court, and congressional enactments.

4. The provisions of the Constitution that have had the greatest impact on the public schools are Article I, Section 10, and the First, Fourth, Fifth, and Fourteenth Amendments.

5. Litigation has reached both federal and state courts primarily in the areas of school desegregation, religion in the schools, and, more recently, challenges to state school finance schemes and sexual harassment.

6. U.S. Supreme Court decisions have been prevalent also in such student-related issues as corporal punishment, search and seizure, freedom of expression, and various classification practices related to sex, marriage and pregnancy, ability grouping, and handicaps.

## Key Terms

obligation of contracts
First Amendment
Fourth Amendment
Fifth Amendment
due process clause
Fourteenth Amendment
equal protection clause
case law
tenure
property interest
liberty interest

quid pro quo sexual harassment
hostile environment sexual harassment
sexual bribery
sexual imposition
gender harassment
sexual coercion
sexual behavior
tort
duty
standard of care
proximate cause
injury
contributory negligence
assumption of risk
comparative negligence
government immunity
parens patriae
domicile
residence
in loco parentis
individualized education program
"separate but equal"
de jure segregation
de facto segregation
*Lemon* test
educational needs standard
fiscal neutrality standard

## Discussion Questions

1. What are the roles of the federal, state, and local governments in the operation of schools?

2. What is the basic structure of the federal and state judicial systems?

3. Which provisions of the U.S. Constitution have had the greatest impact on litigation involving public schools? Discuss the major Supreme Court cases applicable to each provision enumerated, and evaluate the principles of law derived from these court decisions.

4. What can school administrators hope to gain from a knowledge of the sources of law that impact schools?

5. Which case (or cases) has had the greatest impact on your role as a professional educator, or which has changed your attitude toward the operation of schools?

---

[175]Michael Imber and Tyll Van Geel, *Education Law* (New York: McGraw-Hill, 1993).

## Suggested Readings

Alexander, Kern, and M. David Alexander. *American Public School Law,* 6th ed. (Belmont, CA: Thomson West, 2005). The text is designed to inform the practicing educator of the current and rapidly evolving nature of the law as it affects public schools.

Fischer, Louis, David Schimmel, and Cynthia Kelly. *Teachers and the Law,* 7th ed. (Boston: Allyn and Bacon, 2006). This book covers those issues most central to the daily lives of teachers, using a question-answer format.

Imber, Michael, and Tyll van Geel. *Education Law,* 3rd ed. (Mahwah, NJ: Lawrence Erlbaum, 2004). This textbook is approximately two-thirds cases, with the cases integrated throughout.

LaMorte, Michael W. *School Law: Cases and Concepts,* 6th ed. (Needham Heights, MA: Allyn and Bacon, 2001). The author examines the sources of law under which educators operate, the legal constraints to state action in the educational arena, the legal rights and restrictions applicable to students' behavior, the historical and legal foundations of both desegregation and recent school finance reform, and the application of tort law to public education.

McCarthy, Martha M., and Nelda H. Cambron-McCabe. *Public School Law: Teachers' and Students' Rights,* 5th ed. (Needham Heights, MA: Allyn and Bacon, 2003). The text provides a comprehensive treatment of the evolution and current status of the law governing public schools.

Reutter, E. Edmond. *The Law of Public Education,* 6th ed. (Westbury, NY: Foundation Press, 2003). This textbook-casebook is designed to provide basic knowledge of the law directly affecting public education in the United States, including hundreds of cases and judicial decisions.

Valente, William D. *Law in Schools,* 5th ed. (Englewood Cliffs, NJ: Prentice Hall, 2004). The text thoroughly addresses the legal principles governing American schools, discusses the origin and development of laws pertaining to schools, and explores the many ways in which laws influence specific educational policies, practices, and goals.

# 13. Curriculum Development and Implementation

FOCUSING QUESTIONS

1 How can we define curriculum?

2 What approach to curriculum do most administrators adopt?

3 How do philosophy of education and psychology of learning influence curriculum and instruction?

4 Why are curriculum development models usually behaviorist in nature? Can humanistic educators rely on such models?

5 What are good criteria to use in selecting content and experiences for planning curriculum?

6 How are content, experiences, and environment related in the planning of curriculum?

7 Why is change difficult to implement in schools?

8 What strategies or methods of change are important for a school environment?

---

In this chapter, we attempt to answer these questions about curriculum development and implementation by first defining curriculum and examining the four basic approaches to develop it. Then we list the criteria for and define the administrator's role in planning and implementation. Finally, we look at ways to implement a new curriculum and to urge staff to accept the change it may bring about.

Much of the professional literature currently stresses the need for supervisors and administrators to become more involved in curriculum development and implementation. The need to plan effective curricula is obvious because curriculum is often considered the heart of schooling. The difficulty, however, is there are various definitions of curriculum development and implementation. Not everyone agrees what curriculum is or what is involved in curriculum development and implementation. We present a definition that allows different views and interpretations to exist—and which permits school administrators to become more involved in curriculum matters.

## Curriculum Definitions and Approaches

What is curriculum? What is its purpose? How does it affect students, teachers, and administrators? The way we define curriculum in part reflects our approach to it. A curriculum can be defined as a *plan* for action, or a written document, which includes strategies for achieving desired goals or ends. Most educators agree with this definition, as do most administrators who approach curriculum in terms of a behavioral or managerial outlook.

Curriculum can also be defined broadly, as dealing with the *experiences* of the learner. This view considers almost anything in school, even outside of school (as long as it is planned) as part of the curriculum. It is rooted in John Dewey's definition of experience and education, as well as Hollis Caswell and Doak Campbell's view, from the 1930s, that curriculum was "all the experiences children have under the guidance of the teacher."[1] Humanistic curricularists and elementary school administrators subscribe to this definition, at least more so than traditional curricularists and secondary school administrators.

Curriculum can be viewed as a *field of study*, that is, as an intellectual or an academic subject that attempts to analyze and synthesize major positions, trends, and concepts of curriculum. The approach tends to be historical and philosophical and, to a lesser extent, social and psychological in nature. The discussion of curriculum making is usually scholarly and theoretical, not practical, and concerned with broad issues of curriculum. Many administrators would reject this approach as lacking in practical value; administrators who might appreciate this approach as providing a worthwhile framework to help explain curriculum are those with advanced degrees and/or with several courses in curriculum. Those who might have faith in curriculum as a field of study would appreciate the functions of theory and theory building. They might also view curriculum as a *system* with its own definitions, operational constructs, assumptions, postulates, generalizations, laws, and specialists to interpret this knowledge.[2]

Finally, curriculum can be viewed in terms of specific *subject matter* (mathematics, science, English, history, etc.) and *grade levels*. This viewpoint emphasizes knowledge, concepts, and generalizations of a particular subject or group of subjects (such as the core curriculum, which combines two separate subjects such as history and English, or the broad fields curriculum, which combines many similar subjects into new courses such as social studies, language arts, or general science). All classroom and school approaches have elements of this definition—that is, there is recognition of subjects and grades.

## Behavioral Approach

Rooted in the University of Chicago school, the behavioral approach is the oldest and most popular approach to curriculum. As a means-ends approach, it is logical and prescriptive. It relies on technical and scientific principles and includes models, prescriptions, and step-by-step strategies for formulating curriculum.[3] Usually based on a plan, sometimes called a *blueprint*, it specifies goals and objectives, sequences content and experiences to coincide with the objectives, and evaluates learning outcomes in relation to the goals and objectives.

This curriculum approach, which has been applied to all subjects for the last 90 years (since the Bobbitt era), constitutes a frame of reference against which other approaches to curriculum are compared and criticized.[4] Other names have been used to identify this approach— including logical/positivist, conceptual/empiricist, experimentalist, rational/scientific, and technocrat.[5]

The behavioral approach started with the idea of efficiency, promoted by business and industry, and the scientific management theories of Frederick Taylor, who analyzed factory efficiency in terms of time-and-motion studies and concluded that each worker should be paid on the basis of individual output, as measured by the number of units produced in a specified period of time. Efficient operation of the schools (and other

---

[1] John Dewey, *Experience and Education* (New York: Macmillan, 1938); Hollis L. Caswell and Doak S. Campbell, *Curriculum Development* (New York: American Books, 1935), p. 69.

[2] Herbert M. Kliebard, "What Is a Knowledge Base?" *Review of Educational Research*, 63 (1993): 295–304; Allan C. Ornstein and Francis P. Hunkins, "Theorizing about Curriculum Theory," *High School Journal*, 72 (1989): 77–82; James T. Sears and Dan Marshall, "General Influences on Contemporary Curriculum," *Journal of Curriculum Studies*, 32 (2000): 199–214.

[3] Linda Behar and Allan C. Ornstein, "An Overview of Curriculum: The Theory and Practice," *NASSP Bulletin*, 76 (1992): 1–10; Allan C. Ornstein, "The Field of Curriculum: What Approach? What Definition?" *High School Journal*, 70 (1987): 208–216; Allan C. Ornstein, Edward Pajak, and Stacey B. Ornstein, *Contemporary Issues in Curriculum*, 4th ed. (Needham Heights, MA: Allyn and Bacon, 2007).

[4] Herbert M. Kliebard, *The Struggle of the American Curriculum: 1893–1958* (New York: Routledge & Kegan Paul, 1987); Kliebard, *Changing Course: American Curriculum Reform in the 20th Century* (New York: Teachers College Press, Columbia University, 2002); William H. Schubert, *Curriculum Books: The First Eighty Years* (Lanham, MD: University Press of America, 1980).

[5] Michael W. Apple, *Official Knowledge* (New York: Routledge, 1993); Elliot Eisner, *The Educational Imagination*, 3rd ed. (Columbus, OH: Merrill, 2002).

social systems), sometimes called **machine theory** by its critics, became a major goal in the 1920s and 1930s.

Often, ensuring efficiency in schools meant eliminating small classes, increasing student-teacher ratios, hiring few administrators, cutting costs in teacher salaries, maintaining or reducing operational costs, and so on, and then preparing charts and graphs to show the resultant lower costs. Raymond Callahan later branded this idea the "cult of efficiency."[6] The effects were to make administration in general and curriculum making more scientific, at least more precise, and to reduce teaching and learning to precise behaviors with corresponding activities that could be measured.

Franklin Bobbitt described the problems as he set out to organize a course of studies for the elementary grades. "We need principles of curriculum making. We did not know that we should first determine objectives from a study of social needs . . . [and] we had not learned that [plans] are means, not ends."[7]

Bobbitt further developed his objectives and activities approach in the early 1920s in *How to Make a Curriculum*. He outlined more than 800 objectives and related activities to coincide with student needs. These activities ranged from the "ability to care for [one's] teeth . . . eyes . . . nose, and throat; . . . to keep home appliances in good working condition; . . . to spelling and grammar."[8] Bobbitt's methods were sophisticated for the day; but taken out of context, his list of hundreds of objectives and activities, along with the machine or factory analogy that he advocated, was easy to criticize.

It was left to Ralph Tyler, a graduate student of Bobbitt's, to recognize the need for behavioral objectives that were not as tiny or lockstep, whereby basic techniques of curriculum, instruction, and evaluation were combined in a simple plan. He outlined four broad questions that he believed should be answered by anyone involved in planning or writing a curriculum for any subject or grade level:

1. What educational purposes should the school seek to attain?

2. What educational experiences can be provided that are likely to attain these purposes?

3. How can these educational experiences be effectively organized?

4. How can we determine whether these principles are being attained?[9]

Although Tyler's questions were not new when he wrote them, rather a condensed version of the *Twenty-Sixth Yearbook* of the National Society for the Study of Education (NSSE), he put forth the ideas in easy-to-read and brief form (128 pages). His approach, considered today a classic method and read by curriculum specialists and school administrators, combines behaviorism (objectives are an important consideration) with progressivism (the emphasis is on the needs of the learner); the procedures outlined are still applicable in varying school situations today.

## Managerial Approach

The managerial approach considers the school as a social system, reminiscent of organizational theory, in which groups of people such as students, teachers, curriculum specialists, and administrators interact according to certain norms and behaviors. Administrators who rely on this approach plan the curriculum in terms of programs, schedules, space, resources and equipment, and personnel and departments. This approach advocates, among other things, the need for selecting, organizing, communicating with, and supervising people involved in curriculum decisions. It considers committee and group processes, human relations, leadership styles and methods, and decision making.

An offshoot of the behavioral approach, the managerial approach also relies on a plan, rational principles, and logical steps, but not necessarily behavioral approaches. The managerial aspect tends to zero in on supervisory and administrative aspects of curriculum, especially the organizational and implementation process.[10]

Advocates of this approach are interested in change and innovation and in how curriculum specialists, su-

---

[6]Raymond Callahan, *Education and the Cult of Efficiency* (Chicago: University of Chicago Press, 1962).

[7]Franklin Bobbitt, *The Curriculum* (Boston: Houghton Mifflin, 1918), p. 283.

[8]Franklin Bobbitt, *How to Make a Curriculum* (Boston: Houghton Mifflin, 1924), pp. 14, 28.

[9]Ralph W. Tyler, *Basic Principles of Curriculum and Instruction* (Chicago: University of Chicago Press, 1949), p. 1.

[10]Michael Fullan, *Leadership and Sustainability: System Thinkers in Action* (Thousand Oaks, CA: Corwin Press, 2005); Josh Radinsky et al., "Mutual Benefit Partnership: A Curricular Design for Authenticity," *Journal of Curriculum Studies*, 33 (2001): 405–430; Jon Wiles and Joseph Bondi, *Curriculum Development: A Guide to Practice* (Columbus, OH: Merrill, 2002).

pervisors, and administrators can facilitate these processes. The curriculum specialist and supervisor are considered to be practitioners—change agents, resource people, and facilitators—not theoreticians. They report to an administrator and follow the mission and goals of the school. If the school does not appreciate change, then the change role of the job is minimized. If the school is progressive, then changes are expected to be child centered. If the school emphasizes the three Rs, then the curriculum specialist introduces plans accordingly.

The managerial approach is rooted in the organizational and administrative school models of the early 1900s—a period that combined a host of innovative plans involving curriculum and instruction that centered on individualization, departmentalization, nongrading, classroom grouping, homeroom, and work-study activities. It was an era when various school district plans were introduced by their respective superintendents in an attempt to modify the horizontal and/or vertical organization of the schools. The names of the plans were usually based on either the school district's name or organizational concept—such as the Batavia (New York) Plan, Denver Plan, Elizabeth (New Jersey) Plan, Pueblo (Colorado) Plan, Platoon (Gary, Indiana) Plan, Portland (Oregon) Plan, Santa Barbara (California) Plan, Study Hall (New York City) Plan, and Winnetka (Illinois) Plan. Superintendents and associate superintendents were very much involved in curriculum leadership, often developing a plan in one school district and being hired by another one to implement the plan there. Hence, there was a good deal of hopscotching around of administrators, based on a combination of their managerial and curriculum skills.

The managerial approach became dominant in the 1950s and 1960s among school principals and superintendents. During this era, Midwest school administrators and professors (with administrative backgrounds) dominated the field of curriculum in terms of setting policies and priorities, establishing the direction of change and innovation, and planning and organizing curriculum and instruction.

The pacesetters for this era were such school superintendents as Robert Anderson (Park Forest, Illinois), Leslee Bishop (Livonia, Michigan), William Cornog (New Trier Township, Winnetka, Illinois), Robert Gilchrist (University City, Missouri), Arthur Lewis (Minneapolis), Sidney Marland (Winnetka, Illinois), Lloyd Michael (Evanston, Illinois), Stuart Rankin (Detroit), and J. Lloyd Trump (Waukegan, Illinois). Other superintendents (or associate superintendents) from outside the Midwest were also influential, such as Ches-

ter Babcock (Seattle), Muriel Crosby (Wilmington, Delaware), Gerald Firth (Roslyn, New York), and John McNeil (San Diego).[11]

These superintendents were very active politically, at both the local and national levels. They used the professional associations and their respective journals and yearbooks as platforms to publicize their ideas. In particular, they were frequently published by the Association for Supervision and Curriculum Development, American Association of School Administrators, and National Association of Secondary School Principals. Many like Anderson (Harvard), Firth (University of Georgia), Lewis (University of Florida), McNeil (UCLA), and Trump (University of Illinois, Urbana) became professors at major universities; others became active as board directors and executive committee members of professional and administrative organizations that have had major impact on curriculum, supervision, and administration.

Most of these administrators tended to be less concerned about teaching and learning than about organization and implementation. Similarly, they were less concerned about subject matter, methods, or materials than improving curriculum in light of policies, plans, and people on a school-wide or school district basis. They envisioned curriculum change and innovation as they administered the resources and restructured the schools. Most of their innovative practices can be grouped into five categories—personnel, instructional media, instructional groups, grading, and schools—according to how they were to be organized or modified:

1. Personnel changes focused on the way staff was to be used in the classroom, involving team teaching, differential staffing, and teacher aides (or paraprofessionals).

2. Media changes focused on instructional technology, including programmed instruction, language laboratories, and educational television.

3. Grouping practices involved individualized instruction, independent instruction, small-group instruction, and various homogeneous and heterogeneous groups.

4. Grading practices included nongraded plans, continuous progress plans, and pass-fail.

---

[11]Allan C. Ornstein and Francis P. Hunkins, *Curriculum: Foundations, Principles, and Issues,* 5th ed. (Boston: Allyn and Bacon, 2008).

5. School plans were numerous and included various options such as flexible scheduling and module scheduling, as well as open schools, schools without walls, community schools, street academies, special service schools (for the emotionally disturbed or mentally retarded), and specialized schools (music, art, engineering, science, etc.).

Most of the curriculum innovations developed during this period are still considered viable today and often discussed in the literature and implemented as new or innovative. Indeed, these administrators had good theoretical insight, and their practices would prove to last; their plans were usually well thought out and developed.

### Systems Approach

It was not far to leap from organizing people and policies, a managerial view, to organizing curriculum into a system. The systems aspect tends to view various units and subunits of the organization in relation to the whole, and organizational units, flowcharts, and committee structures are often diagrammed as the curriculum plan is introduced and monitored.[12]

Sometimes referred to as **curriculum engineering**, the approach includes processes necessary to plan the curriculum by *engineers*—superintendents, directors, coordinators, and principals; *stages*—development, design, implementation, and evaluation; and *structures*—subjects, courses, unit plans, and lesson plans. The systems approach to curriculum was influenced by systems theory, systems analysis, and systems engineering. These principles, originally developed by social scientists in the 1950s and 1960s, continue to be used or at least discussed widely by school managers as part of administrative and organizational theory.

In the systems approach to curriculum, the "parts" of the total school district or school are closely examined in terms of their interrelatedness and influence on each other. Components like departments, personnel, equipment, and schedules are planned to create changes in people's behavior and expectations. In general, information is communicated to administrators who consider alternatives and choices.

One application of the systems approach was developed by the Rand Corporation and has rapidly spread from government to business and school agencies. It is called a *planning, programming, budgeting system* (PPBS), and it brings together those components with the system's structure, functions, and capabilities. In this case, the system is the curriculum.

Another well-known systems approach is the *program evaluation and review technique* (PERT), which was introduced by the Department of Defense and subsequently spread to business and industry in the 1960s; like PPBS, it has been introduced into education. Progress and interruptions of various facets of the program, in this case the curriculum, are computed, analyzed, and made available to administrators. Progress reports are continually updated, reflecting changes in schedule, possible difficulties, and achievement rates. In both systems' approaches, the curriculum is closely monitored by administrators; revisions and corrective action are introduced on a continual basis.

It was George Beauchamp (a former school administrator and professor of curriculum) who developed the first systems theory of curriculum. He divided theories of education into five major theories of equal importance: administrative, counseling, curriculum, instructional, and evaluation.[13] Many school administrators do not accept this notion of equal theories, for they view administration as their major system or field of study and curriculum as a component or subsystem of the major system. In fact, they often delegate supervisors to take care of curriculum matters, especially if they view their leadership role chiefly in terms of management. On the other hand, curriculum specialists usually view curriculum as the major system and related fields such as supervision, teaching, instruction, and evaluation as subsystems, which help implement the curriculum.[14]

However, what Beauchamp was trying to convey is that the five theories of education are applied realms of knowledge that draw their ideas from the foundations

---

[12] Allan C. Ornstein, "Analyzing the Curriculum," *NASSP Bulletin*, 77 (1993): 58–64; Ornstein, "The Field of Curriculum: What Approach? What Definition?"

[13] George A. Beauchamp, *Curriculum Theory*, 4th ed. (Itasca, IL: Peacock, 1981).

[14] Allan C. Ornstein, "Curriculum, Instruction, and Supervision—Their Relationship and the Role of the Principal," *NASSP Bulletin*, 70 (1986): 74–81; Robert Lister, "Integrative Curriculum: Developing Interdisciplinary Teaching and Learning Teams," *Curriculum Report*, 28 (1998): 1–4; Edward Pajak, "Clinical Supervision and Psychological Functions," *Journal of Curriculum and Supervision*, 17 (2002): 189–205.

---

## Table 13–1   Fundamental Questions of Curriculum

### Eighteen Questions (1930)

1.  What period of life does schooling primarily contemplate as its end?

2.  How can the curriculum prepare one for effective participation in adult life?

3.  Are the curriculum makers of the schools obliged to formulate a point of view concerning the merits or deficiencies of American civilization?

4.  Should the school be regarded as a conscious agency for social improvement?

5.  How shall the content of the curriculum be conceived and stated?

6.  What is the place and function of subject matter in the education process?

7.  What portion of education should be classified as "general" and what portions as "specialized" or "vocational" or purely "optional"? To what extent is general education to run parallel with vocational education and to what extent is the latter to follow on the completion of the former?

8.  Is the curriculum to be made in advance?

9.  To what extent is the "organization" of subject matter a matter of pupil thinking and construction of, or planning by, the professional curriculum maker as a result of experimentation?

10. From the point of view of the educator, when has "learning" taken place?

11. To what extent should traits be learned in their "natural" setting (i.e., in a "life situation")?

12. To what degree should the curriculum provide for individual differences?

13. To what degree is the concept of "minimal essentials" to be used in curriculum construction?

14. What should be the form of organization of the curriculum? Shall it be one of the following or will you adopt others?

    (a) A flexibly graded series of suggested activities with reference to subject matter that may be used in connection with the activities? Or,

    (b) A rigidly graded series of activities with subject matter included with each respective activity? Or,

    (c) A graded sequence of subject matter with suggestion for activities to which the subject matter is related? Or,

    (d) A statement of achievements expected for each grade, a list of suggested activities, and an outline of related subject matter, through the use of which the grade object may be achieved? Or,

    (e) A statement of grade objectives in terms of subject matter and textual and reference materials?

15. What use, if any, shall be made of the spontaneous interests of children?

16. What types of materials [or activities] should the curriculum maker [provide] for students?

17. How far shall methods of learning be standardized?

18. For what time units [and] what geographic units shall the curriculum be made [national, state, school district, local school]? What is the optimal form in which to publish the course of study?

---

Source: Adapted from Harold Rugg et al., "List of Fundamental Questions on Curriculum Making," in G. M. Whipple (ed.), *The Foundations of Curriculum Making,* Twenty-Sixth Yearbook of the National Society for the Study of Education, Part II (Bloomington, IL: Public School Publishing, 1930), p. 8.

---

of education: psychology, sociology, history, philosophy, and so on. Rather than disputing what the major systems or subsystems are, it is more important to design procedures that are applicable to the real world and use whatever theory that can be helpful.

Administrators who value the systems approach take a macro, or broad, view of curriculum and are concerned with curriculum issues and questions that relate to the entire school or school system, not only in terms of subjects or grades. They ask theoretical questions, often referred to as the "fundamental" or "basic"

questions of curriculum, listed in Table 13–1. These questions do not have simple or linear answers, and they evoke philosophical and political debates among respondents.

These types of questions were first raised in 1930, when a famous twelve-person committee on curriculum, headed by Harold Rugg, presented a general statement on curriculum making and raised eighteen "fundamental questions" for the National Society for the Study of Education (see Table 13–1). They were raised again in the 1983 Yearbook of the Association for Supervision and Curriculum Development,[15] and still later on by other curriculum specialists.[16] They are generic questions that have stood the test of time.

The posture one takes in answering the questions in Table 13–1 will greatly influence the planning of curriculum; the place and function of subject matter; the types of subjects offered; the methods and materials for facilitating instruction; the role of curriculum specialists and supervisors, as well as teachers; and how the school (or school district) is organized to carry out curricula functions. It will determine in part how curriculum is to be developed and implemented, as well as the policies and processes involved in administering the curriculum.

## Humanistic Approach

Some administrators and curriculum leaders reflect on the field and contend that the above approaches are too technocratic and rigid. They contend that in our attempt to be scientific and rational, administrators (or supervisors) in charge of curriculum miss the personal and social aspects of curriculum and instruction; ignore the artistic, physical, and cultural aspects of subject matter; rarely consider the need for self-reflection and self-actualization among learners; and, finally, overlook the sociopsychological dynamics of classrooms and schools.

This view is rooted in progressive philosophy and the child-centered movement of the early 1900s (first spearheaded at the University of Chicago when John Dewey, Charles Judd, and Francis Parker developed progressive methods of teaching, based on the student's natural development and curiosity). In the 1920s and 1930s, the progressive movement moved east and was dominated by Teachers College, Columbia University, and by such professors as Frederick Bosner, Hollis Caswell, L. Thomas Hopkins, William Kilpatrick, Harold Rugg, and John Dewey (who had changed professional affiliations to Columbia). This progressive view gained further impetus in the 1940s and 1950s with the growth of child psychology (which deals with the needs and interests of

children) and humanistic psychology (which deals with valuing, ego identity, psychological health, freedom to learn, and personal fulfillment).

From this approach, a host of curriculum activities have emerged, mainly at the elementary school level, including lessons based on life experiences, group games, group projects, artistic endeavors, dramatizations, field trips, social enterprises, learning and interest centers, and child and adolescent needs. These activities include creative problem solving and active student participation; they emphasize socialization and life adjustment for students, as well as stronger family and school-community ties. They are representative of Parker, Dewey, and Washburne's (Parker and Washburne were superintendents) ideal school, and the kinds of curriculum activities they put into practice are still practiced in many private and university lab schools and suburban school districts across the United States.

The humanistic curriculum seems more suitable for middle- and upper middle-class students, as well as high achievers. Evidence suggests that these students exhibit high independence in learning and are better off in low-structured situations in which they can exercise their own initiative. Lower-class students often lack inner controls necessary for self-discipline, and low-achieving students often lack cognitive skills necessary for independent learning. These students need stricter rules and highly structured activities in class.[17]

This does not necessarily mean that inner-city schools cannot be humanistic. What counts is that teachers and administrators have faith in and high expectations for students, attempt to form meaningful and honest relationships between teachers and students (not coercive or controlling relationships), and that teachers try to foster individuality, self-direction, and self-confidence. Without a humanistic principal, a person who is more concerned about people than tasks, it is almost impossible for inner-city schools (or for that matter suburban or rural schools) to exhibit a humanistic atmosphere.[18] Inner-city schools tend to be char-

---

[15]Elizabeth Vallence, "Curriculum as a Field of Practice," in F. W. English (ed.), *Fundamental Curriculum Decisions,* 1983 Yearbook (Washington, DC: Association for Supervision and Curriculum Development, 1983), pp. 154–164.

[16]Jon W. Wiles, *Curriculum Essentials: A Resource for Educators,* 2nd ed. (Boston: Allyn and Bacon, 2005); Decker F. Walker and Jonas F. Soltis, *Curriculum and Aims* (New York: Teachers College Press, Columbia University, 1998).

[17]Larry Cuban, *How Can I Fix It?* (New York: Teachers College Press, Columbia University, 2001); Carolyn Evertson, et al., *Classroom Management for Elementary Teachers,* 7th ed. (Boston: Allyn and Bacon, 2006); Milbrey W. McLaughlin, *Urban Sanctuaries* (San Francisco: Jossey-Bass, 2000).

[18]Richard F. Elmore, "Breaking the Cartel," *Phi Delta Kappan,* 87 (2006): 517–518; Andy Hargreaves and Dean Fink, "The Ripple Effect," *Educational Leadership,* 63 (2006): 16–21; and Mary Anne Raywid, "Themes That Serve Schools Well," *Phi Delta Kappan,* 87 (2006): 654–656.

acterized not only by the regular bureaucratic tasks (which many schools exhibit) but also by basic tasks dealing with classroom discipline, reading and language problems, and lack of parental support for learning. Without involved parents and better childhoods, we will never see lasting reform or humanistic programs, on a large scale, that work.

Curriculum leaders who believe in the humanistic approach tend to put faith in cooperative learning, independent learning, small-group learning, and social activities, as opposed to competitive, teacher-dominated, large-group learning, and only cognitive instruction. Each child, according to the humanistic approach, has some input in curriculum and shares responsibility with teachers in planning classroom instruction. Administrators tend to permit teachers more input in curriculum decisions. Curriculum committees are bottom up instead of top down, and students are often invited into curriculum meetings to express their views on content and experiences related to curriculum development.

The humanistic approach became popular again in the 1970s, as relevancy, radical school reform, open education, and alternative education became part of the reform movement in education. Today, demands for educational excellence and academic productivity have resulted in emphasis on cognition, not humanism, and on subjects such as science and math, not art or music. The humanistic approach has always represented a minority view among administrators, who are usually more concerned with the "nuts and bolts" of curriculum—that is, the three Rs in elementary school and the basic academic subjects in secondary school. The humanistic approach has now been relegated almost to a fringe view, overshadowed by a return to "back to basics" and tougher academic standards.

## Curriculum Development

The need to develop curriculum is obvious; however, there are various ways to define and proceed with **curriculum development.** Ideally, those who are affected by curriculum should be involved in the process of *planning* and then in the process of *implementation* and *evaluation*. Table 13–2 raises important questions pertaining to these three phases of curriculum. Administrators and

---

**Table 13–2  Steps in Curriculum Development**

### I. Planning the Curriculum

1. Who assigns committee members?
2. What groups are represented within the committee?
3. Who determines priorities, standards, competencies, etc.?
4. How do we identify needs, problems, issues, etc.?
5. Who formulates goals and objectives? What type of goals, objectives?

### II. Implementing the Curriculum

1. Who defines what knowledge is most important?
2. Who decides on instructional materials and media?
3. Who evaluates teachers? What measurement criteria are used?
4. Who decides how teachers will be prepared and trained for the program?
5. Who determines how much money/resources will be made available?

### III. Evaluating the Curriculum

1. Who decides how the curriculum will be evaluated?
2. Who decides on assessment procedures? tests? and how are they to be used?
3. Have our goals and objectives been addressed in the evaluation?
4. Does the program work? To what extent? How can it be improved?
5. Who is responsible for reporting the results? To whom?
6. Do we wish to make comparisons or judgments about the program? Why? Why not?

## Administrative Advice 13–1

### Guidelines for Curriculum Development

Below are some guiding statements to help clarify the steps involved in curriculum development. These statements are based on school practice and apply to all curriculum models.

- The curriculum-design committee should include teachers, parents, and administrators; some schools might include students, too.

- The committee should establish a sense of mission or purpose in the early stages or meetings.

- Needs and priorities should be addressed in relation to students and society.

- School goals and objectives should be reviewed, but they should not serve as the only guiding criteria on which to develop the curriculum. Such criteria should connote a broad educational philosophy to guide curriculum development.

- Alternative curriculum designs should be contrasted in terms of advantages and disadvantages such as cost, scheduling, class size, facilities and personnel required, existing relationship to present programs, and so on.

- To help teachers gain insight into a new or modified design, it should reveal expected cognitive and affective skills, concepts, and outcomes.

- Principals have significant impact on curriculum development through their influence on school climate and their support of the curriculum process.

- District administrators, especially the superintendent, have only a peripheral impact on curriculum development because their outlook and concerns center on managerial activities. Their curriculum role is minor, but their support and approval are essential.

- State education officials have even less impact on curriculum development, although various departments publish guides, bulletins, and reports that can be informative. However, these educators establish policies, rules, and regulations that affect curriculum and instruction.

- The influence of special interest groups and local politics should not be underestimated. Polarization or conflict has frequently obscured reasonable efforts for reform and meaningful dialogue between educators and parents in regard to educational matters.

supervisors involved in curriculum making should be willing to discuss these questions with their respective board members and professional staff. But like many aspects of education, there is some debate about the formula to follow in order to achieve the particular educational goal. Although there are many developmental models of curriculum to choose from, we focus on one representative model for each approach previously mentioned. (See Administrative Advice 13–1.)

### Tyler: Behavioral Model

Ralph Tyler is often considered the bridge between the first and second half-century of the field of curriculum, whereby he fused the best ideas of curriculum making during the early period and set the stage for the modern period.[19] Tyler proposed a number of steps in planning

a curriculum, outlined in Figure 13–1, starting with the goals of the school. These goals would be selected on the basis of what he called **sources of information** about important aspects of contemporary life, subject matter, and the needs and interests of learners. By analyzing changing society, at the local, state, or national level, it could be determined what goals (and also what subject matter) were most important. By consulting with subject specialists (as well as teachers), helpful decisions could be determined about concepts, skills, and tasks to be taught in the various subjects (reading, math, science, etc.). By identifying the needs and interests of students, a beginning point in content, methods, and materials could be determined. (Hence, Tyler helped popularize the concept of a needs assessment study.)

Tyler then suggested that the school staff, possibly organized as a curriculum committee, **screen** the recommended **goals** according to the school's (or school district's) philosophy and beliefs about psychology of learning (or what some might call learning theory). What resulted from this screening process would be *in-*

---

[19]Tyler, *Basic Principles of Curriculum and Instruction.*

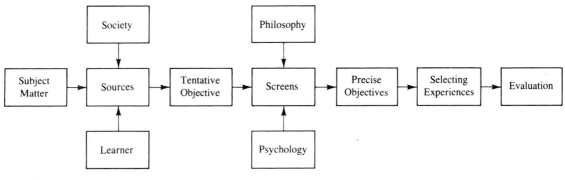

**Figure 13–1**

Organizing the Curriculum—A Behavioral Approach, Based on the Tyler Model

*structional objectives,* more specific than the school's goals and designed for classroom use.

Tyler then proceeded to the *selection of learning experiences* that would allow the attainment of objectives. Learning experiences would take into account the developmental stage of the learners, such as their age and abilities, and consider the learners' background (present attainments), external environment (classroom and school), and what the learners did (their behavior) when learning. Tyler next talked about *organizing learning experiences* in a systematic way to produce a maximum, positive effect. Here he elaborated on the vertical (recurring subject matter such as social studies from grade to grade) relationship and horizontal (integration of different subjects at the same grade level) relationship of curriculum.

Tyler elaborated on the need for *evaluation* to determine whether the objectives were achieved or the learning experiences actually produced the intended results. Also, it was necessary to determine whether the curriculum was effective or ineffective and whether changes should be made or a new curriculum was warranted.

Although Tyler never introduced his model of curriculum development in a graphic manner, Figure 13–1 helps interpret what he was hoping to achieve. Because Tyler did not clarify at what level his model could be used, school district or school level, or whether it was a top-down (line staff) model or bottom-up (teacher empowerment) model, it can be applied to both orientations. However, at the period of his writings, the top-down model prevailed in schools: Curriculum experts usually presented ideas for teachers to develop, and administrators either supervised or delegated supervision to ensure that the ideas were implemented in the classroom.

## Saylor, Alexander, and Lewis: Managerial Model

Galen Saylor and his colleagues belong to the managerial school. As former administrators, they were very clear about the lines of authority and the need for supervisors and administrators to be in charge of the curriculum at the state and local district levels, in terms of curriculum guidelines and textbook selection, as well as at the school level, in terms of subjects for study on the basis of grade levels.[20] Saylor saw curriculum as a general plan, through which particular plans for individual programs of studies, courses of study, syllabi, unit plans, policy statements, handbooks, and learning packages were used in different parts of the school and school district by many groups of people and individuals. Curriculum had to be put together or incorporated as a total package, or *curriculum plan,* by those in charge of running the schools.

As Figure 13–2 indicates, a number of considerations enter into the development of curriculum. *Goals and objectives* are largely influenced (1) by external forces such as legal requirements, current research, professional knowledge, interest groups, and state agencies and (2) by the bases of curriculum such as society, learners, and knowledge. (These bases were similar to Tyler's sources, which had originally been elaborated on by Boyd Bode and John Dewey.)

Agreed on goals and objectives then provide a basis for **curriculum design,** that is, a view of teaching and learning. Five different designs are examined: (1) subject

[20]J. Galen Saylor, William M. Alexander, and Arthur J. Lewis, *Curriculum Planning for Better Teaching and Learning,* 4th ed. (New York: Holt, Rinehart & Winston, 1981).

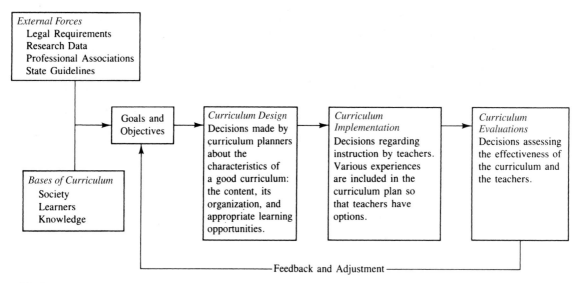

**Figure 13–2**

Managing the Curriculum

Source: Adapted from J. Galen Saylor, William M. Alexander, and Arthur J. Lewis, *Curriculum Planning for Better Teaching and Learning*, 4th ed.; © 1981, pp. 29–30.

matter/disciplines, (2) competencies, (3) human traits and processes, (4) social functions and activities, and (5) individual needs and interests. A subject matter design emphasizes the role of knowledge and problem-solving activities. Specific competencies emphasize performance objectives, task analysis, and measurable outcomes. Human traits and processes are concerned with the learners' feelings, emotions, and values, as well as the affective domain of learning. A design that focuses on social functions and activities emphasizes the needs of society and, to a lesser extent, the needs of students. The individual needs and interests design is concerned with what is relevant to and motivates learners and what learning experiences lead to their full potential. Depending on the nature of management, the design can be optional and chosen by the classroom teacher, or it can be recommended by a school curriculum committee (administrators, supervisors, and/or teachers) or recommended by the central school district. School authorities, however, rarely require a particular design because curriculum matters involve teachers as well as possibly students and parents.

*Curriculum implementation* is mainly concerned with instructional activities that facilitate or put in practice the design. It includes instructional methods, materials, and resources, often listed in courses of study,

unit plans, and lesson plans and often observed in classrooms as the teaching and learning process unfolds. Curriculum implementation includes supervision of instruction, teacher-supervisor planning and meetings, as well as staff development programs. The help teachers receive from resource personnel, supervisors, and administrators is the basis of implementation.

*Curriculum evaluation* involves the procedures for evaluating student outcomes and the curriculum plan. Evaluative data become the basis for decision making and planning among administrators. Administrators rarely engage in this type of evaluation; rather, they often delegate it to supervisors or outside consultants who report their findings to administrators, who in turn have the option of communicating the findings to teachers, parents, or the community.

### Macdonald: Systems Model

Theory development prior to the 1960s tended to separate curriculum and instruction from teaching and learning. The classic model by James Macdonald showed the relationship between these four systems, as illustrated in Figure 13–3. He defined curriculum as a plan *for* action and instruction as the plan *put into* ac-

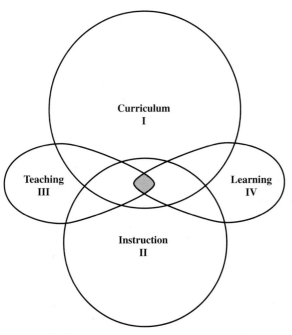

**Figure 13–3**

Systematizing the Curriculum

Source: Adapted from James B. Macdonald, "Educational Models for Instruction," in J. B. Macdonald (ed.), *Theories of Instruction* (Washington, DC: Association for Supervision and Curriculum Development, 1965), p. 5.

tion. Teaching was defined as the *broad behavior* of the teacher and learning as the *change* in learner.

Another way of explaining the Macdonald model is the following: *Curriculum* is planning endeavors that take place prior to instruction; *instruction* deals with teacher-student interaction (usually taking place in the classroom, library, or laboratory); *teaching* is the act of presenting stimuli or cues; and *learning* involves student responses. When appropriate instruction and teaching take place, desired responses will occur. When instruction or teaching is inappropriate, dysfunctional or unintended responses will take place.

Most curriculum leaders today agree with the Macdonald model: Curriculum is viewed as planning; instruction is seen as implementation; teaching involves behavior, methods, and/or pedagogy; and learning connotes desired responses or student actions. Macdonald's view was easy to understand, a reason for the classic status of the model, and it helped show the relationship among the four systems. Breaking from the previous generation of linear models by interrelating

his systems, Macdonald contended that curriculum was the heart of the educational enterprise (note that it represents the largest component in his system, as per Figure 13–3) in part because everything that followed was based on this plan and in part because he was a curriculum theorist—not a professor of pedagogy or philosophy. Had he been a professor of educational psychology, Macdonald probably would have seen teaching and learning as the most important component. Similarly, had he been a professor of supervision or administration, he might have viewed supervision (or supervision of instruction) as more important than curriculum, or curriculum as a subcomponent or one aspect of the larger field of educational leadership. Indeed, a person's professional background and knowledge base determines his or her view of what is essential or secondary in education, what is a macrosystem and a microsystem.

## Weinstein and Fantini: Humanistic Model

Gerald Weinstein and Mario Fantini link sociopsychological factors with cognition so learners can deal with their problems and concerns. For this reason, these authors consider their model a "curriculum of affect." In viewing the model, some readers might consider it part of the behavioral or managerial approach, but the model shifts from a deductive organization of curriculum to an inductive orientation and from traditional content to relevant content.[21]

The first step, shown in Figure 13–4, is to identify the *learners,* their age, grade level, and common cultural and ethnic characteristics. Weinstein and Fantini are concerned with the group, as opposed to individuals, because most students are taught in groups. Therefore, knowledge of common characteristics and interests is considered prerequisite to differentiating and diagnosing individual problems.

In the second step, the school determines the learners' *concerns* and assesses the reasons for these concerns. Student concerns include the needs and interests of the learners, self-concept, and self-image. Because concerns center on broad and persistent issues, they give the curriculum some consistency over time. Through *diagnosis,* the teacher attempts to develop strategies for instruction to meet learners' concerns. Emphasis is on how students

---

[21]Gerald Weinstein and Mario D. Fantini, *Toward Humanistic Education* (New York: Praeger, 1970).

**Figure 13–4**

Curriculum of Affect

Source: Gerald Weinstein and Mario D. Fantini, *Toward Humanistic Education*, p. 35. Copyright © 1970 by the Ford Foundation.

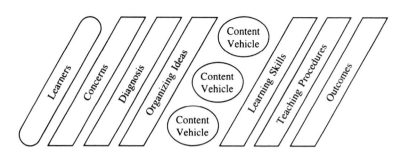

can gain greater control over their lives and feel more at ease with themselves. In *organizing ideas,* the next step, the teacher should select themes and topics around learners' concerns rather than on the demands of subject matter. The concepts and skills to be taught should help the learners cope with their concerns.

The *content* is organized around three major principles, or what Weinstein and Fantini call *vehicles:* life experiences of the learners, attitudes and feelings of the learners, and the social context in which they live. These three types of content influence the concepts, skills, and values that are taught in the classroom, and they form the basis of the "curriculum of affect."

According to the authors, *learning skills* include the basic skill of learning how to learn which in turn increases learners' coping activity and power over their environment. Learning skills also help students deal with the content vehicles and problem solve in different subject areas. Self-awareness skills and personal skills are recommended, too, to help students deal with their own feelings and how they relate to other people.

*Teaching procedures* are developed for learning skills, content vehicles, and organizing ideas. Teaching procedures should match the learning styles of students, which in turn are partially based on their common characteristics and concerns (the first two steps). In the last step, the teacher evaluates the *outcomes* of the curriculum: cognitive and affective objectives. This evaluation component is similar to the evaluation components of the previous models (Tyler and Saylor); however, there is more emphasis on the needs, interests, and self-concept of learners—that is, affective outcomes.

## Scientific-Aesthetic Model

Elliot Eisner combines scientific and behavioral principles with aesthetic components to form a curriculum planning model. It is more rational and measurable than one might expect from Eisner who tends to stress

artistic and qualitative forms of education. His model comprises four major areas of planning: (1) aims and objectives, (2) curriculum planning, (3) teaching, and (4) evaluation. Each contains numerous categories, as shown in Figure 13–5.

*Aims and Objectives* (Category 1) include (a) behavioral objectives that can be easily observed and measured; (b) problem-solving objectives that involve broader concepts and various forms and solutions that cannot be easily measured; and (c) expressive outcomes—that is, results or qualities (intended or unintended, attitudinal or artistic) that are not always rational, predictable, or easy to measure.

*Curriculum Planning* (Category 2) includes the input and influence of the (a) federal and (b) state agencies, which provide direction, policies, and money; (c) the school district, which appoints curriculum committees and personnel for planning content and developing materials; (d) the teacher's role in planning, such as choosing topics, textbooks, and other materials to meet objectives; (e) research centers, which develop materials, methods, and pilot programs; (f) commercial publishers, which provide textbooks, materials, and (if the authors may add) tests; and (g) curriculum developers, groups, and associations, which prescribe content in particular subject areas.

*Teaching* (Category 3) involves (a) the art of teaching as expressive and qualitative forms and behaviors; (b) the difference between teaching and instruction, the latter of which is more technical and controls content and classroom activities; and (c) the difference between teaching and curriculum—in simple Eisner terms, "curriculum is the content that is taught and teaching is how the content is taught."

*Evaluation* (Category 4) is divided into five areas: (a) diagnose student learning and prescribe treatment; (b) revise, that is, modify and/or improve the curriculum; (c) compare programs to determine which is more effective for specific students; (d) identify education needs by employing interviews, questionnaires,

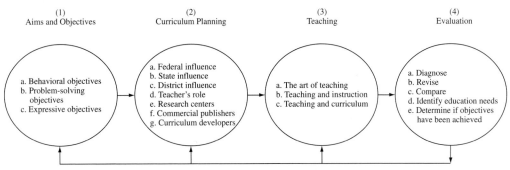

Figure 13–5

Eisner's Curriculum Planning Model

Source: Adapted from Elliot W. Eisner, *The Educational Imagination,* 3rd ed. (Columbus, OH: Merrill, 2002), chaps 6–7, 9–10. Diagram and sequencing have been interpreted by the authors.

and tests in order to justify programs and content; and (e) determine if objectives have been achieved—to what extent and whether revisions are needed, or possibly new objectives are needed.

## Curriculum Overview

Figure 13–6 presents an overview of the procedures and steps to consider for planning, developing, and evaluating the curriculum. The model is based on a behavioral/managerial model, rooted in the Tyler-Taba (behavioral) and Saylor-Alexander (managerial) approaches.

Overall, the model reflects a *traditional* approach because decisions and actions take place within a formal organization that has a prescribed and expected way of doing things. In joining the school (or school district), participants accept an authority relation and understand certain roles, limits, and expectations of behavior, and certain policies and procedures for communication, collegiality, and change (the three Cs).

As part of *curriculum planning,* the political forces (category 1) are considered, the situation as it "really is"—or, more precisely, as it appears to the participants. National, state, and local issues and opinion in general will reflect in the aims, goals,[22] and objectives of the curriculum, but they will change over time. Standards are expressed at the federal and state level—and

imposed on the local or district/school level. Specialists, consultants, and experts can provide knowledge or expertise (category 2) for modifying the school district's or school's goals and objectives. These people will most likely be subject, learning, technological, or testing specialists. In determining what to teach, external groups (category 3) play a major role in influencing curriculum participants, organizational norms and policies, and criteria for the selection of content. Major external groups are from the testing industry, textbook companies, professional associations, and colleges. The connection between the external forces and individual participants is virtually "one way"; that is, external groups influence participants' decisions and actions, but the reverse influence is almost nonexistent or slight. Viewed as "experts," those involved in determining the content of tests (and now standards), the content of textbooks, college requirements (or Carnegie units), and/or establishing standards and policies of professional associations transmit, from one generation to the next, many of the major ideas of objectives and subsequent content.

"Experts" from external groups may see the world quite differently than teachers and administrators, but the latter have little influence in determining the content domain (category 4); basically, their job is to implement the curriculum. *Curriculum implementation* involves the what and how of curriculum. The content is the *what*, sometimes called the heart of the curriculum, and the instructional activities represent the *how*. Content is divided into knowledge, skills, concepts, research methods, ideas, and values. (Knowledge and skills have been delineated elsewhere by Adler, Taba,

---

[22]Aims and goals are sometimes used interchangeably at the federal and state level. Ralph Tyler also used them interchangeably, in his book *Basic Principles of Curriculum and Instruction,* referring to them as "purposes."

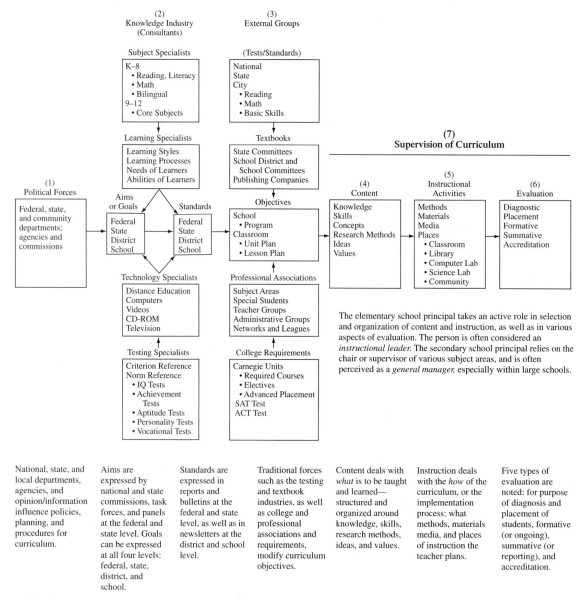

**Figure 13–6**

Planning and Developing the Curriculum

Source: Allan C. Ornstein, "Curriculum Planning and Development," in Fred Lunenburg and Allan Ornstein, *Educational Administration: Concepts and Practices,* 4th ed. (Belmont, CA: Wadsworth, 2004). Copyright © by Allan Ornstein, 2003. Revised by Allan Ornstein, 2007.

and Tyler; concepts and relationships are best represented by the theories of Bruner, Dewey, and Ausubel; research methods are expressed by Bruner, Dewey, and Tyler; ideas are described by Adler, Bruner, and Taba; and values are delineated by Adler, Dewey, and Tyler).

Instructional activities (category 5)—methods, materials and media—usually take place in the classroom (although they can take place in the local and larger community) and represent the processes through which the teacher delivers the content. Activities are part of the implementation process. Although most activities are well entrenched by tradition, different methods, materials, and media evolve and replace traditional modes of instruction. The tension between traditional and progressive ideas of education is clearly depicted in Dewey's compact book, *Education and Experience* (1938). The term *instructional activities* (category 5) closely resembles what Dewey called "techniques and practices," what Kilpatrick called "purposeful methods," what Taba and Tyler referred to as "experiences," and what Bruner termed "processes." In short, instruction deals with ways in which content (subject matter) is taught by the teacher and learned by the student—that is the *how* of implementation.

*Curriculum evaluation* provides information for the purpose of making judgments and decisions about students, teachers, and programs—or whether to postpone, modify, continue, or maintain the curriculum. Such decisions can be made at the classroom, school, and school district level. The role of the curriculum leader—resource teacher, program director, supervisor or chair, principal or superintendent in charge of curriculum—is crucial at this stage. The person in charge, the curriculum leader, provides direction, oversees content and instruction, and then based on some form of evaluation makes recommendations and decisions for maintaining, improving, or terminating the program. Five purposes and forms of evaluation (category 6) are listed: diagnosing problems; placement of students; formative, that is, during the implementation stage; summative, or at the end of the program; and accreditation, the whole program is assessed.

Finally, curriculum leaders at the school level include program directors, coordinators, chairs, and principals. They are responsible for overseeing curriculum, instruction, and evaluation. In Figure 13–6, this is represented by the term *supervision of curriculum* (category 7). At the district level, the curriculum leader is usually called a director or an assistant or associate superintendent.

## Nontechnical Model

The danger in noting that one model is systematic, rational, or technical and another is nonsystematic, irrational, or nontechnical is that the latter will be considered as fluff, watered down, or disorderly by most administrators, who rely on an orderly and rational world. Advocates of the latter model take issue with the assumption and consequences of traditional models.

They reject the high degree of objectivity, order, and logic; they also reject the assumption that reality can be defined and represented by symbolic forms—by boxes, arrows, or graphs. Finally, they feel that aims and goals of education cannot always be known in advance, stated precisely, or addressed in a linear or step-by-step approach.

It may not make practical sense for administrators who need to plan and who have only so much time in the day, but the world is much more complex, involving subjective, personal, aesthetic, heuristic, transactional, and intuitive forms of thinking and behavior. The argument is that curriculum cannot be precisely planned—it evolves as a living organism as opposed to a machine which is precise and orderly.

Common among advocates of the **nontechnical model,** sometimes called naturalistics, conversationalists, critical pedagogists, and postpositivists, is the belief that the focus should be on the student, not the content or subject matter. Subject matter has importance only to the degree that students can find meaning in it for themselves. Subject matter should provide opportunities for reflection and personal growth.[23]

In contrast to the majority of teachers and administrators who consider curriculum as a plan, blueprint, or product consisting of a series of rational steps and outcomes, people in the nontechnical camp often view curriculum more as a drama or conversation. People don't develop conversation or plan it; they create opportunities for it to evolve. If we accept that curriculum involves conversation, then it makes sense to reflect on the social, political, and moral thoughts and voices involved in curriculum making. Such consideration brings into focus concepts that are ignored in technical approaches, such as ideology, values, beliefs, and power. Communication, collegiality, and consensus are necessary processes or social activities to consider. Creating curricula through conversation relies on dialogue, debate, and deliberation—the ebb and flow of ideas and ideology.

The contemporary, nontraditional paradigm of curriculum questions the scientific paradigm of sound logical thought that rests on Newtonian logic. In a theoretical sense, these nontraditional people advocate that we detach ourselves from rational or scientific mod-

---

[23]Herbert Kohl, *Beyond the Silence* (Westport, CT: Heinemann, 1998); Nel Noddings, *The Challenge to Care,* 2nd ed. (New York: Teachers College Press, Columbia University, 2005).

els of accepted procedures that follow preestablished rules. They suggest that our actions in creating curricula cannot be judged according to predetermined criteria, generalized findings, or rational or empirical judgment; moreover, what appears objective or rational is frequently selective, incomplete, or reflective of a political agenda.[24]

According to this model, old criteria cannot be used to critique new curricula. It challenges the technical rationality of viewing the world as a machine that we can study, observe, and objectively evaluate as bystanders. It questions assumptions about facts as well as about cause and effect. The data we obtain through tests and evaluative procedures are also questioned. In short, all the old assumptions about curriculum development that administrators rely on are challenged by many who call themselves postmodern thinkers.

Nontechnical contemporary educators believe that curriculum making represents an uncertain system and an uncertain set of procedures. People like James Macdonald, Elliot Eisner, Peter McLaren, and William Pinar argue that aesthetic rationality and artistic forms complement our technical rationality. What we are asked to do as education leaders is to transform images and aspirations about education into curriculum programs.[25]

The nontechnical process evolves in an open, unexpected, free-flowing way. It even permits chaos to occur so that some unplanned system may result. In the same vein, artistry is considered a special way of knowing and constructing reality. Reality, according to Peter Senge, exists in circles and is constructed of overlapping and interacting systems, not neat little boxes or flowcharts. Reality involves circularity, confusion, and interrelatedness of decisions and actions.[26] Goals (objectives) and outcomes (products) are no longer perceived so much as ends but as beginnings, a view advocated by Dewey that is now part of the new literature on change and curriculum reform. Of course, all this new dialogue is hard to sell to a school principal or superintendent who is responsible for meeting goals and achieving certain products and must deal with social, political, and educational reality—high-stake tests, state standards, and students who are entering the workforce or applying to college.

The nontechnical model maintains that curriculum specialists have lost their visionary, moral, and social purposes, their sense of reform and innovation. This argument dates back to George Counts, in his famous speech to the Progressive Education Association published a year later under the title *Dare the Schools Build a New Social Order?*[27] Actually, Joseph Schwab's concern with theory and practice represents a benchmark or transition period between the traditional and new models. An advocate of scientific methods and rational planning, a person who appreciated the need for technical experts, Schwab also had a clear moral vision of schooling, an awareness of social and cultural forces influencing curriculum, and a concern for relations of people involved in curriculum making. He argued that "the field of curriculum [had become] moribund,"[28] that it had ceased to flourish and offer anything new, and that it needed to be "resurrected to include alternative perspectives and systems as viable solutions to varying problems."[29] This rejection of the traditional curriculum by a traditionalist, and the need to revise or remake the curriculum in terms of alternative ways, is a prelude to the nontechnical interpretation of the field of curriculum today.[30]

A wider conception of curriculum—nontechnical and more philosophical, personal, and interesting meth-

---

[24]Tom Barone, "Science, Art, and the Predispositions of Educational Researchers," *Educational Researcher,* 30 (2001): 24–28; Gerald W. Bracey, "How to Avoid Statistical Traps," *Phi Delta Kappan,* 63 (2006): 78–82; Elliot Eisner, "Back to Whole," *Educational Leadership,* 63 (2005): 14–19; and William A. Reid, "Reconceptualist and Dominant Perspectives in Curriculum Theory," *Journal of Curriculum and Supervision,* 13 (1998): 287–298.

[25]Elliot W. Eisner, *The Kind of School We Need* (Westport, CT: Heinemann, 1998); Peter McLaren, *Life in Schools,* 5th ed. (Boston: Allyn and Bacon, 2007); William F. Pinar, *Contemporary Curriculum Discourses* (New York: Peter Lang, 1999).

[26]Peter M. Senge, *The Fifth Discipline* (New York: Doubleday, 1990).

[27]George S. Counts, *Dare the Schools Build a New Social Order?* (New York: John Day, 1932).

[28]Joseph J. Schwab, "Education and the State: Learning Community," in R. M. Hutchins and M. J. Adler (eds.), *The Great Ideas Today* (Chicago: Encyclopedia Britannica, 1976), p. 238.

[29]Ibid, p. 271.

[30]See William F. Pinar (ed.), *Contemporary Curriculum Discourses* (New York: Peter Lang, 1999); William A. Reid, "Rethinking Schwab: Curriculum Theorizing as a Visionary Activity," *Journal of Curriculum and Supervision,* 17 (2001): 29–41; Leonard J. Waks, "Reid's Theory of Curriculum as Institutionalized Practice," *Journal of Curriculum Studies,* 32 (2000): 589–598.

## ■ Exemplary Educational Administrators in Action

**LONNIE E. PALMER**  Superintendent, City School District of Albany, New York.

**Previous Positions:**  Assistant Superintendent, New Rochelle School District; High School Principal, in Averill Park; Science Department Chair and Assistant Principal, Spackenkill High School, Poughkeepsie, New York; Teacher of ninth grade science, at Hackett Junior High School, Albany, New York.

**Latest Degree and Affiliation:**  Certificate of Advanced Study, Educational Administration, State University College at New Paltz.

**Number One Influence on Career:**  With military draft waiting, I decided to teach as an uncertified teacher in the Albany City School District. After one short month teaching ninth-grade science, I knew that my career was to work in education.

**Number One Achievement:**  Being a relatively successful urban school superintendent for six years in the same job. It has been extremely rewarding to have seen improved test scores, balanced budgets that have been supported through public votes, and the passage of a $175 million school facilities improvement plan.

**Number One Regret:**  As a principal and central office administrator, I have been more removed from students than I would like. I have always enjoyed what students bring to making our professional lives rewarding and fulfilling.

**Favorite Education-Related Book or Text:**
*Seven Habits of Highly Effective People* by Stephen Covey.

**Additional Interests:**  I'm an avid amateur golfer (handicap 2). I paint watercolor paintings, play the guitar, and sing. I love gardening, and I've become more versatile with the computer.

**Leadership Style:**  I try to see each problem that comes my way as an opportunity. I also believe in giving to others ownership for problems and successes. My job is to coach them, support them, provide resources, and encourage them, but not to tell them how to resolve the issues, which they own.

**Professional Vision:**  I believe that educators who tackle the most difficult of tasks of trying to help urban students with great needs and limited family support need to be recognized, encouraged, and supported.

**Words of Advice:**  One of the current trends in education in the United States is to test students extensively and to use these results to drive decision making. While the analytical part of my background agrees that such an approach will provide the best research for measured, productive, positive change, I'm also concerned that in the process we'll lose what truly makes learning a lifelong, exciting quest for knowledge and opportunity. The assumption that somehow we can teacher-proof the curriculum with research-tested, instructional methods and thereby help children from poverty to achieve test success, ignores some basic facts.

Teaching is as much an art as a science. And while the science can help us with strategies and tactics to overcome the obstacles that children face as they learn, nothing can replace the love of learning, the love of children, and the understanding of those factors in children's backgrounds that inhibit their success.

While the pendulum swings far to the right with federal (No Child Left Behind) mandates and New York State–mandated testing and prescriptive academic intervention services, little attention is being paid to the hearts, souls, and values of those entering the education profession. Educators must not only be smarter, more attuned to research and data, and cognizant of the best research-based strategies for student learning; they must also care deeply for their students, their parents, and their communities.

ods—includes numerous theories and ideas that are artistic and aesthetic (Elliot Eisner), gay (James Sears) and feminist (Madeline Grumet), pluralistic and diverse (James Banks), political/ social (Henry Giroux and Peter McLaren), moral/ethical (William Reid), visionary and imaginative (Maxine Greene), and even spiritual (William Pinar). These new theories and ideas repre-

sent a rejection of traditional curriculum planning, a rethinking of curriculum, but not necessarily a "practical" interpretation (a term used by Schwab and later Reid) that assists teachers and curriculum leaders (directors, chairs, supervisors, principals, etc.) in the organization and operation of classrooms and schools. Although some of these new concepts may be considered dysfunctional and divisive, as well as impractical for practitioners, among theorists and academics they are considered relevant—or at least interesting. Much of the new "new" curriculum is considered more speculative, expressive, emotional, argumentative, and political—based on heated controversy and crisis, far different from the rational, logical, behaviorist, and technocratic ideas that have characterized mainstream curriculum making.

## Components of Curriculum Development

Curriculum leaders must always be concerned with *what* should be included and *how* to present or arrange what is selected. In other words, they must first deal with content or subject matter and then learning experiences. Regardless of the curriculum approach or development model used, curriculum leaders cannot ignore these two components.

Groups charged with curriculum planning have options in selection of **content and experiences**—to be determined in part by the philosophical and psychological views of the committee members and school. Unquestionably, there are too much content and too many learning experiences to include, and committee members (or those in charge of curriculum) must decide what content and experiences to include.

### Criteria for Selecting Content

Curriculum planners should apply criteria in choosing curriculum content. Although the following criteria are neutral and can fit into any curriculum approach or model, various philosophical camps might place greater emphasis on particular criteria. For example, Hilda Taba, in a classic text on curriculum, maintains that content should include the following functions.

1. *Four Levels of Knowledge.* These include specific facts, skills, and processes; basic ideas such as generalizations, principles, and causal relationships within the subject matter; concepts dealing with abstract ideas, complex systems, multiple causations, and interdependence; and thought systems or methods of problem solving, inquiry, and discovery.

2. *New Fundamentals to Master.* The content in many subjects becomes increasingly obsolete, especially in light of the explosion of knowledge. The curriculum must be periodically updated to include new content to be learned.

3. *Scope.* Scope is the breadth, depth, and variety of the content and includes the coverage of boundaries of the subject.

4. *Sequence.* By sequencing, there is recognition of and need for differentiating levels of knowledge, that learning is based on prior knowledge, and that the curriculum should be cumulative and continuous.[31]

5. *Integration.* Integration emphasizes the relationships among various content themes, topics, or units; it helps explain how content in one subject is related to content in another subject.[32]

A more recent text established seven additional criteria to consider when selecting and organizing content. Whereas Taba stresses cognitive learning theory for her five criteria, these seven combine cognitive and humanistic psychology:

1. *Self-Sufficiency.* A guiding principle for content selection is that it helps learners attain learning skills and self-sufficiency in learning (economy of the teacher's effort and time in instruction and economy of students' efforts and time in learning).

2. *Significance.* Content should contribute to learning particular concepts, skills, or values; it should be significant in terms of what knowledge needs to be transmitted to students.

3. *Validity.* As new knowledge is discovered, old knowledge that is less relevant, misleading, or incorrect must be pruned. Only relevant and accurate knowledge should be a part of the curriculum content. The content should also be sound in relation to stated goals and objectives.

4. *Interest.* Content is easier to learn when it is meaningful. The interest criterion is a progressive concept, but all content should be selected in part on the basis of students' interests.

5. *Utility.* Content should be useful in and out of school. What is considered useful will also reflect philosophy.

---

[31]This concept is similar to Jerome Bruner's idea of a "spiral curriculum": Previous learning is the basis of subsequent learning; learning should be continuous, and the content (or subject matter) is built on a foundation (from grade to grade).

[32]Hilda Taba, *Curriculum Development: Theory and Practice* (New York: Harcourt, Brace & World, 1962).

6. *Learnability.* The content must be within the experiences and understanding of the learner; content should be selected and arranged on the basis that it makes learning easy, at least less difficult, for students.

7. *Feasibility.* The content must be considered in terms of time allotted, personnel and resources available, and sometimes existing legislation, political climate, and money. Although some educators may like to think that they have an entire world of content from which to choose, they do have limitations on their actions. (Consider content related to sex education, race relations, morality, and religion, for starters.)[33]

## Criteria for Selecting Learning Experiences

Tyler, in his classic text on curriculum, outlined five general principles in selecting learning experiences. These experiences can take place in the classroom, outside the classroom (say, in the schoolyard, auditorium, or laboratory), or outside the school (on a field trip, in the library or a museum, etc.).

1. *Learners Must Have Experiences That Give Them Opportunity to Practice the Behavior(s) Implied by the Objective(s).* If the objective is to develop problem-solving skills, then students must have ample opportunity to solve problems. In other words, there must be experiences for students to practice what they are required to learn.

2. *Students Must Obtain Satisfaction in Carrying Out or Performing the Learning Experiences.* Students need satisfying experiences to develop and maintain interest in learning; unsatisfying experiences hinder learning.

3. *Learning Experiences Must Be Appropriate to the Student's Present Attainments.* This basically means that the teacher must begin where the student is and that prior knowledge is the starting point in learning new knowledge.

4. *Several Experiences Can Attain the Same Objective.* There are many ways for learning the same thing; as long as they are effective and meaningful, a wide range of experiences is better for learning than a limited range. Capitalize on the various interests of students.

5. *The Same Learning Experience Usually Results in Several Outcomes.* While students are acquiring knowledge of one subject or idea, they often develop ideas and attitudes in other subjects and certain attitudes toward the original subject.[34]

More recently, the criteria for selecting experiences have been stated in the form of a question: Will the learning experience do what we wish it to do in light of the overall aims and goals of the program and specific objectives of the curriculum? The following are specific extensions of this questions. Are the experiences

1. Valid in light of the ways in which knowledge and skills will be applied in out-of-school situations?

2. Feasible in terms of time, staff expertise, facilities available within and outside of the school, and community expectations?

3. Optimal in terms of students' learning the content?

4. Capable of allowing students to develop their thinking and problem-solving skills?

5. Capable of stimulating in students greater understanding of their own existence as individuals and as members of groups?

6. Capable of fostering an openness to new experiences and a tolerance for diversity?

7. Such that they will facilitate learning and motivate students to continue learning?

8. Capable of allowing students to address their needs?

9. Such that students can broaden their interests?

10. Such that they will foster the total development of students in cognitive, affective, psychomotor, social, and spiritual domains?[35]

What educators need to remember is that content and experiences are interrelated. If students are engaged in some experience in classrooms, such as reading a book, they are combining that experience with content. Students cannot engage in learning without

[33]Ornstein and Hunkins, *Curriculum: Foundations, Principles, and Issues;* Allan C. Ornstein and Richard Sinatra, *K-8 Instructional Methods* (Boston: Allyn and Bacon, 2005).

[34]Tyler, *Basic Principles of Curriculum and Instruction.*

[35]Ronald C. Doll, *Curriculum Improvement: Decision Making and Process,* 9th ed. (Needham Heights, MA: Allyn and Bacon, 1996).

experiencing some activity and content. Likewise, students cannot deal with content without being engaged in some experience or some activity. Content and experience comprise curriculum unity.

## Balance in Determining the Curriculum

The need for a **balanced curriculum** with appropriate emphasis on content and experiences to ensure a proper weight and broad range to each aspect of the curriculum is obvious, but not easy to achieve given competing philosophies, ideologies, and views of teaching and learning. John Goodlad maintains that the curriculum should be balanced in terms of subject matter and learner; however, he comments that "the interested observer has little difficulty finding school practices emphasizing one component to the impoverishment of the other." He further points out that balance needs to be incorporated into the curriculum to "impose floors and ceilings," a proper range of required knowledge, skills, concepts, and learning experiences that considers the "interests, abilities, and backgrounds" of students,[36] as well as the educational space and environment. (See Administrative Advice 13–2.)

For Doll, a balanced curriculum fits the learner in terms of educational needs, abilities, and growth pertaining to the learner's development. Within the classroom and school, the student should receive content and experiences of two sorts: those suitable for the whole group and those specifically designed for the individual student—his or her personal needs and abilities.[37] This is easier said than done, since it takes a highly effective teacher to meet the needs, abilities, and interests of the whole group while serving the needs, abilities, and interests of individuals. It is much easier to teach toward the average, some "mystical mean"; sadly, high-achieving students are often bored, and low-achieving students are often frustrated as the teacher teaches toward the "average" student in the class.

Adding to the complexity of attaining balance in the curriculum is that what might be considered balanced today might be considered imbalanced tomorrow. What might be considered balanced in one school district might not be considered balanced in an adjacent school district. The times in which schools find themselves are always changing. As we strive for balanced content and experiences, we must always consider the pulls and tugs of traditional and contemporary philosophies, conservative and liberal politics, and changing state standards. It behooves curriculum leaders to consider the elements of balance—the mix of philosophy and politics, as well as the various schools of thought on teaching and learning—in developing curriculum. The question arises, what should be an appropriate emphasis? To be sure, the concept of balance invokes several competing forces and variables, and a great deal of controversy in some schools and very little controversy in other schools. On a practical level, supervisors and administrators need to compromise on differences and reach consensus on the following political concerns, philosophical and social issues, and moral questions:

1. Needs of society vs. learner
2. Excellence vs. equality
3. Standard-based vs. individualized education
4. Cognitive, affective, psychomotor, and moral domains of learning
5. Behavioral vs. nonbehavioral objectives
6. Technological/computerized vs. humanistic/artistic focus
7. Subject-centered vs. student-centered curriculum
8. General vs. specialized content
9. Breadth vs. depth in content
10. Content vs. process
11. Essential (core) knowledge vs. abstract (problem-solving) methods
12. Traditional vs. progressive ideas (and authors)
13. National vs. global and Western vs. non-Western history and culture
14. Academic, business, vocational, and technical tracks
15. Gifted, talented, average, and slow learners
16. Advanced placement, required, and elective courses
17. Whole language vs. phonetics
18. Classroom, lab activities vs. community, field-based activities
19. Homogenous vs. heterogeneous grouping
20. Whole-group, small-group, and individualized instruction

---

[36]John I. Goodlad, *Planning and Organizing for Teaching* (Washington, DC: National Education Association, 1963), p. 29.

[37]Doll, *Curriculum Improvement: Decision Making and Process.*

## Administrative Advice 13–2

### Dealing with the Physical and Health Factors of the Environment

Until recently curriculum leaders did not give much attention to the curriculum environment. One way of viewing this environment is to look at the physical and health factors that affect student learning. The factors considered below represent a "nuts and bolts" view, typical of a supervisor or practitioner who deals in the real world of classrooms and schools as opposed to the theoretical world.

■ **Arrangements.** Identify the activities that will take place and the best way to combine or arrange the physical layout or setting. Different configurations must be evaluated on the basis of how they will accommodate lectures, demonstrations, experiments, etc. Other factors include storage space, electrical/telephone outlets, teacher work space, student learning space (open/closed) and grouping patterns (whole group, small group, and independent learning) or spaces.

■ **Floors, Ceilings, Windows.** Consider carpeting versus tile in terms of cost, durability, and esthetics. Electrostatic charges are important, too, in terms of human sensitivity and technical equipment (especially computers). Ceiling materials and window treatments affect acoustics and lighting.

■ **Temperature.** The research data suggest that students learn best when the temperature is 70° to 74° Fahrenheit, since they are seated and somewhat inactive in most classroom situations. They also learn best when the relative humidity is between 40 and 60 percent.

■ **Electrical.** Electrical wires should run parallel to the walls, and when they run across floors they should be taped down to prevent accidents. Equipment and adapter plugs should be stored when not in use, and in no one's way when in use. There should be more than one circuit in a classroom to guard against possible line failure, and surge suppressers need to be installed in schools/classrooms that cannot risk data loss in the event of a power surge.

■ **Lighting.** In most cases windows are suitable for providing adequate light, coupled with the standard fluorescent lighting to save money. In small learning areas, recessed lighting is more effective than fluorescent light.

■ **Acoustics.** Room noise can be a problem, especially when students are active or involved in an open classroom setting and are permitted to talk or engage in multiple activities at the same time. Neutralizing noise with appropriate floor, ceiling, and window treatments are basic considerations; some schools are experimenting with soft background music, and in other schools special window panes have been installed to reduce outside noise.

■ **Security.** Physical security is a consideration in entryways, hallways, and schoolyards, especially in terms of unwarranted intruders. It is also a factor when storing office and instructional equipment, as well as with student lockers and teacher closets. Schools are increasingly installing special locks and bolts, steel plates with locking cables, electronic trackers, closed circuit television, and alarm systems connected to police departments.

■ **Dust.** Elimination of dust has always been a concern. When remodeling or designing a new school, all chalkboards should be replaced with dry marker boards. Special consideration should also be given to paper and disk storage.

■ **Safety.** To protect students (or teachers) from injury and the school from liability, the smart administrator learns to identify and eliminate as many hazards as possible. Science labs, gyms, cafeterias, and schoolyards are major places where accidents take place, but injuries also occur in classrooms, hallways, and auditoriums.

*Source:* Allan C. Ornstein, "Components of Curriculum Development," *Illinois School Research and Development,* 26 (1990): 208–209. Used by permission.

## Leadership Considerations

Regardless of how we view the relationship among content, experience, and environment, the center of curriculum development continues to be the local school, which in turn is related to the abilities and performance of the school principal and her assistants. The key to curriculum leadership is not the school superintendent, who should be more concerned about managerial decisions; it is the school principal.

The problem is, however, that many school superintendents are not clear about delegating authority over curriculum matters to the school principal. The superintendent is usually much clearer about delegating responsibility at the centralized level—say, to the business manager or director of public information—than about delegating it to the principal. In these cases, it seems that the superintendent is more concerned about business or community affairs—that is, how the school district appears—than curriculum for students the district serves.

Another problem seems to involve a conflict between local school personnel (teachers, chairpersons, and principals) and supervisors from the central office—and that the latter sometimes bypass or ignore the prerogatives of curriculum leaders in their own schools. On the other hand, principals who are zealots are sometimes known to operate their schools as little fiefdoms or empires, ignoring the advice and help of the supervisors from the central office. Certainly, the roles and responsibilities of the various school personnel, as they relate to curriculum matters, need to be clear to avoid conflict.

In large school districts (50,000 or more students), the central office usually houses a curriculum department whose responsibility is to develop curriculum materials and guides while minimizing the role of the teacher and school principal. Curriculum development is centralized and usually rubber-stamped at the school level; what ideas people have at the local level are passed upward but often lost in the paper shuffle at the centralized level.

In small school districts, however, teachers, principals, and even parents are expected to spend substantial time and effort in curriculum making. Under the leadership of the principal, schools are often expected to develop mission statements, a clear understanding of what constitutes learning, the content and experiences to be included in the curriculum, how the curriculum is to be implemented and evaluated, and how the community is to be included.[38] Many teachers and principals become involved in curriculum development as a matter of professional routine; but they are rarely, if ever, paid for their time after 3 P.M.

Differences also exist between elementary and secondary school principals. Most elementary principals devote more time to curriculum and instructional mat-

ters than do their secondary counterparts, and they view themselves more often as curriculum or instructional leaders rather than managers. Secondary school principals usually complain they have little time for curriculum and instruction (although they recognize the importance of such matters) and see themselves more often as general managers.[39] Most school principals have been taught to accept some bureaucratic, scientific, or rational model of management, but elementary principals have been forced to throw away their managerial theories and deal with the needs and concerns of the students at the school door, as well as their parents and the community.

Part of the difference is related to school size. Within the same school district, high schools are usually two to four times the size of elementary schools. In high schools that house more than 1000 students (24 percent of U.S. high schools), principals are often engaged with a continual stream of problems that make it difficult for them to leave the office, and they are more concerned about administrative detail and formal structures than with people.[40] Another reason for the difference is that in medium-sized secondary schools (750 to 1000 students) and large secondary schools (1000+ students), there are usually chairpersons responsible for particular subject areas who plan with teachers and supervise curriculum and instruction. Elementary schools do not have chairpersons as part of their staff, and the focus is on the three Rs (not particular subjects). The principal is supposed to provide the curriculum and instructional leadership in this general area of study.

Some balance is needed. In large school districts, curriculum leaders at the central level should make it easier for school personnel to become involved in curriculum opportunities. In small school districts, teachers involved in curriculum should be paid for their services or relieved from other duties, so they can devote time to curriculum. Without being made to feel guilty, school authorities should recognize that teachers are already performing important responsibilities other than

[38]Jeffrey Glanz, *What Every Principal Should Know About School-Community Leadership* (Thousand Oaks, CA: Corwin Press, 2006); Thomas J. Sergiovanni, *The Principalship, A Reflective Practice Perspective*, 6th ed. (Needham Heights, MA: Allyn and Bacon, 2006).

[39]Dale L. Brubaker and Lawrence H. Simon, "How Do Principals View Themselves, Others?" *NASSP Bulletin,* 71 (1987): 72–78; Fenwick W. English, "The Battle for the Principalship," *NASSP Bulletin,* 78 (1994): 18–25; and Frederick M. Hess, "Looking Beyond the Schoolhouse Door," *Phi Delta Kappan,* 87 (2006): 513–514.

[40]Deborah Meier, "As Though They Owned the Place: Small Schools as Membership Communities," *Phi Delta Kappan,* 87 (2006): 657–662; Allan C. Ornstein, "School Size and Effectiveness: Policy Implications," *Urban Review,* 22 (1990): 34–45.

curriculum development and teachers should have the option to reject new responsibilities.

## What Knowledge Is of Most Worth?

Some 150 years ago, Herbert Spencer in his famous essay, "What Knowledge Is of Most Worth?" argued that science was the most practical subject for the survival of the individual and society, yet it occupied minimal space in the curriculum because impractical and ignorant traditions prevailed. Spencer also maintained that students should be taught how to think (and problem solve) and not what to think.[41] Spencer's ideas were to influence John Dewey some fifty years later.

Although many of Spencer's ideas about evolution and social progress (less intelligent, lazy, and weak people would slowly disappear, and heredity was the key to intelligence) created a furor—and they still do among observers today—his ideas fit well with many thinkers of the second half of the nineteenth century, a period that was characterized by industrial growth, manifest destiny, and colonial expansion of European countries and the United States.

Spencer's original question about the worth of subject matter is more relevant today because of the increased complexity of society. Actually, the question dates back to ancient Greece, when Plato and Aristotle questioned the value of knowledge in relation to citizenship and government affairs, and to ancient Rome, when Quintilian (influenced by Plato)[42] set forth the seven liberal arts—grammar, rhetoric, logic, arithmetic, geometry, astronomy, and music—as the ideal curriculum for educated citizens of public life: senators, lawyers, teachers, civil servants, and politicians. During the modern school period, these seven liberal arts have expanded to include many other subjects.

One must understand that Greek and Roman education (the latter influenced by the Greeks) cultivated contemplative knowledge, metaphysics, and rationality for the purpose of nurturing the mind, body, and soul. The truly educated person had the power to think, to exercise reason, and to judge moral and ethical behavior. (This separates us from lower animals.) The good life was one of balance and moderation. This interpretation of knowledge and intellectual thought, promoted by Aristotle and Plato, was adopted by the medieval universities and by humanistic philosophers. It is the opposite type of knowledge—concerned with utility, function, vocational education, and relevant education—that is trendy and becomes obsolete in a few years.

### Knowledge as Facts

Spencer also advocated a curriculum appropriate for an industrialized and scientific society, characterized by problem solving and specialized professions. But facts, more facts, and still more facts was the ideal method of teaching and learning, keenly expressed by Charles Dickens in his novel *Hard Times*. Mr. Gradgrind, the school patron, demonstrates model teaching for the school-teacher: "Now what I want is Facts. Facts alone are wanted in life. Plant nothing else, and root out everything else, this is the principle on which I bring up children. Stick to the facts, Sir!!"[43]

There is little difference between facts and some aspects of knowledge, but more than one hundred years after the publication of *Hard Times* the issues are still being discussed. In a well-accepted classification of thinking and problem solving by Benjamin Bloom, knowledge was ranked as the lowest form of cognitive learning. However, he pointed out that the acquisition of knowledge is the most common educational objective, that teachers tend to emphasize it in the classroom, and test makers tend to emphasize it on tests.[44] To help clarify Bloom: knowledge by itself has limited value and should be used as a basis or foundation for more advanced thinking, what he calls "problem solving." Of course, basic knowledge has some practical or functional value, but it only serves as the rudiment of more theoretical or abstract thinking.[45]

---

[41]Herbert Spencer, *Education: Intellectual, Moral, and Physical* (New York, Appleton, 1860).

[42]Plato also advocated several subject areas in his *Republic*, although there was greater emphasis on mastering reading, being involved in gymnastics, and displaying good rules of diet and hygiene.

[43]Charles Dickens, *Hard Times* (New York: Dutton, 1894), p. 1.

[44]Benjamin S. Bloom et al., *Taxonomy of Educational Objectives, Handbook I: Cognitive Domain* (New York: McKay, 1956).

[45]The goal is to encourage advanced thinking—what the Greeks called "contemplation," John Dewey called "rational" and "reflective thinking," what Jerome Bruner and Joseph Schwab called "structure," what Mortimer Adler and Ted Sizer called "ideas," what Jeanne Chall and E. D. Hirsch called "deep understanding," what learning theorists today call "critical thinking" and "high-order thinking," and what the authors simply call old-fashioned, "analysis and problem solving."

Knowledge is often construed as an index of intelligence and level of education attained by a person: Witness the popularity of the "$64,000 Question" and forty years later "Who Wants to Be a Millionaire?" Facts drive the shows, and listeners often comment how "smart" someone is who answers several fact-oriented or knowledge-based questions. The point is, however, that knowledge of facts is of little value if it cannot be used in new situations and for more complex learning; the learner (and teacher) need to make use of knowledge—as a base or tool for the pursuit of higher forms of cognition—often called problem solving by progressive educators (Dewey and Tyler), inquiry-based or discovery learning (Ausubel and Bruner), formal operations (Piaget and Vygotsky), and/or critical thinking (Marzano or Sternberg).

## Explosion of Knowledge

Since the 1950s, many educators have continued to call attention to the explosion of knowledge. Every fifteen years or so, our significant knowledge doubles. Although it cannot continue indefinitely to double in the future, the explosion of knowledge—especially in health, science, and technology—makes it important to continuously reappraise and revise existing curricula. "It can be affirmed unequivocally," says Bently Glass, "that the amount of scientific knowledge available at the end of one's life will be almost one hundred times what it was when he was born." Moreover, 95 percent of all scientists who ever lived are alive today.[46]

Although Glass published these remarks more than twenty-five years ago, they still ring true; in fact, it can be inferred that half of what a graduate engineer or computer specialist studies today will be obsolete in ten years; half the pills dispensed today at your local pharmacist will also be replaced or improved. The authors venture to guess that half or more of what we need to know to function in scientific or technical jobs by the year 2020 is not even known today, by anyone.

The idea that knowledge is increasing exponentially or geometrically obscures the fact that the development of knowledge in many fields—especially science, technology and medicine—is more typically related to "branching"—that is, the creation of several subdivisions or specialties within fields, not just simple growth. Each advance in a particular field has the potential for creating another branch. (In education, one can find some indicators of proliferation of several fields of study or branches sometimes identified by departments, programs, and core courses or minors), and within each field or branch several specializations of knowledge and job titles. With this increase of knowledge come new professional journals, papers, and speeches, all adding to the proliferation of knowledge. The almost incredible explosion of knowledge threatens to overwhelm us unless we can find ways to deal with the new and growing wealth of information; new knowledge must be constantly introduced into each field of study while less important material is pruned away. In assessing the ongoing rush of knowledge, Alvin Toffler asserts that knowledge taught should be related to the future. "Nothing should be included in the required curriculum unless it can be strongly justified in terms of the future. If this means scrapping a substantial part of the formal curriculum, so be it."[47]

The question arises whether teachers are readily keeping up with the explosion of knowledge, at least the knowledge in pedagogy or the content they teach. A harsh portrait of the teacher was made by one of the authors as it relates to change and the explosion of knowledge when he was younger and more feisty: "Had Rip Van Winkle been a teacher and slept for *fifty years* he could return to the classroom and perform relatively well; the chalk, eraser, blackboard, textbook, and pen and paper are still the main tools for most teachers, as they were a half a century ago—or longer. If Mr. Van Winkle's occupation had been related to one of three fields . . . science, technology, and medicine . . . and had he dozed off for five years, he would be unable to function effectively, for his knowledge and skills would be drastically dated."[48]

The above statement was made over *thirty-five years* ago, before the proliferation of the computer. No question, the computer represents a significant change in the classroom, and is essential for teachers to be com-

[46] Bentley Glass, *The Timely and Timeless* (New York: Basic Books, 1980). Also see Edward Teller, *A Twentieth-Century Journey in Science and Politics* (Cambridge, MA: Perseus Press, 2001). Cornering scientific knowledge, not sharing it with others, was a crucial factor in the outcomes of World War II and the Cold War.

[47] Alvin Toffler, *Future Shock* (New York: Random House, 1970), p. 132. Also see Alvin Toffler, *The Third Wave* (New York: Morrow, 1980).

[48] Allan C. Ornstein, *Urban Education* (Columbus, OH: Merrill, 1972), p. 50.

petent. Yet, we all know that most classrooms don't have computers; the pen or pencil still makes the point, and a goodly percentage of older teachers (forty years or more) are computer illiterate. To update matters, had Rip Van Winkle gone to sleep for eighty-five years (the original 50 + 35), he would still be able to bluff his way in the classroom. If he taught at the middle school or high school level, he would most likely need to do some last-minute preparation in his content area. But we all know teachers who teach out of license, and others who lack depth of knowledge in their content area, and prepare by reading the homework assignment or textbook the night before teaching the lesson.

## Essential Knowledge

If you will welcome or support E. D. Hirsch's idea of **cultural literacy,** then Mr. Van Winkle's content or subject preparation is basically intact because more than 80 percent of the 5000 items Hirsch recommends as important refer to events, people, or places in use for more than a hundred years; about 25 percent of his essential knowledge deals with the classics. The inference is that Hirsch is against large-scale pruning and updating of the curriculum; as a modern-day essentialist, he maintains there is a body of knowledge essential to learn for cultural literacy (what he calls "functional literacy") and "effective communication for our nation's populace. . . . Shared information is necessary for true literacy," and it has nothing to do with white or middle-class culture (or the metaphors of domination) nor specific job-related tasks, but with the imperatives of a broad grasp and understanding of mainstream culture.[49] This argument, of course, omits pop culture and the contributions of media that influence our changing culture, as well as all ethnic and folk references.

Complementing his narrative is a compilation of "essential items from history, geography, literature, and science," not to be memorized as Mr. Gradgrind might have us do, but for students to know something about in context with their thoughts and discussion. We don't have to know the fine details, but there should be some minimum level of understanding and competence, depending on the subject area and topic, for effective communication. Hirsch maintains that students who are unable to master the common knowledge can-

not become intelligent readers and cannot speak properly (or formally).[50] He also stresses the importance of scientific information at all levels of schooling; moreover, he has written a series of follow-up books on essential knowledge for every grade level. Knowing the facts, for him and a growing number of present-day essentialists (Lynne Cheney, William Bennett, Chester Finn, Diane Ravitch, et al.) increases the students' capacity to comprehend what they read, see, hear, and discuss. The need for background knowledge is judged important for future communication and specialization. Finally, Hirsch argues that we have overlooked content and have stressed process—or thinking skills—with little regard for subject matter. The outcome has been a decline in national literacy.

The need is to transmit the shared knowledge and values of adult society to youth. Without the transmission of a shared cultural core to the young, conservative educators argue, our society will become fragmented and our ability to accumulate and communicate information across the nation and to various segments of the populace will diminish, especially among immigrants and ethnic groups. We may all subscribe to multicultural education and recognize we are a nation of many nations, but this only increases the need for a knowledge base and an academic core, to be taught to all students.

## Returning to the Liberal Arts

A few years ago, Allan Bloom, in *The Closing of the American Mind,* voiced concern about education being relative to particular times and places instead of being consistent with universal standards and subjects.[51] Like other perennialists, Bloom asserts that cultural relativism—with its emphasis on trivial pursuits, quick fixes, relevancy, and self-esteem—has eroded the quality of American education. Our media and educational institutions are marked by an easygoing, flippant indifference to critical thought. Deprived of a serious liberal arts and science education, avoiding an engagement with great works and great ideas of the past, our youth lack educational depth.

Indeed, if we want to ask ourselves how and where we went wrong, why we are in social and moral decline, Bloom offers a conservative analysis and sense of

---

[49]E. D. Hirsch, *Cultural Literacy: What Every American Needs to Know,* rev. ed. (Boston: Houghton Mifflin, 1987), p. 10.

[50]E. D. Hirsch, *The Knowledge Deficit* (Boston: Houghton Mifflin, 2006).

[51]Allan Bloom, *The Closing of the American Mind* (New York: Simon and Schuster, 1987).

fundamental reform and what is crucial to the well-being of the nation. To remedy American education and to neutralize the problems caused by cultural relativism, Bloom, as did Robert Hutchins and Mortimer Adler over twenty-five years ago, seeks to reestablish the idea of an educated person along the line of the great books and great thinkers and to reestablish the virtues of a liberal education.

Now it is somewhat mind-boggling, even foolhardy, to downplay the importance of Western culture (our own civilization) or the **great books** that purport our heritage and illustrate the great ideas, principles, and values that have evolved and shaped our culture over the last 2500 to 5700 years. (Where we trace our historical roots and culture depends largely on whether we start with the Hebrews or the Greeks.) It is fashionable to criticize the great books as white, male, and Eurocentric, but Western civilization is rooted in European history, philosophy, and literature—and with the exception of the ancient Greeks, past civilizations rarely gave women equal education or equal status. (Athena is perched at the top of the Acropolis as a reminder that the ancient Greeks believed in equal opportunity. "Imagine" all the civilizations believing in equality among people. I guess you can say John Lennon was not the only dreamer.)

The great-book approach, along with serious thinking and meritocracy, is disfavored partially because of matters of political correctness. Many educators would like to stress what Robert Hutchins (former president of the University of Chicago) called the *liberal arts,* what Jeanne Chall (Harvard reading specialist) calls *world knowledge,* what E. D. Hirsch calls *essential knowledge* and *cultural literacy,* and what Allan Bloom (and also Mortimer Adler) call the *great books.* But educators are afraid of being labeled as antiminority and not sensitive to multiculturalism and diversity. It is this fear that makes it easy to substitute works by women, minority and Third World authors for Plato, Locke, Kant, or Ibsen.[52]

Western civilization as perceived by postmodernists has come at a price, according to Shelby Steele, that is, the exploitation and victimization of people of color[53]

(and, if we may add, women). Therefore, a revisionary list of great books and liberal arts courses is needed to balance the literature of the dominant group. The cultural capital of women and minorities, their voices and stories, must be heard to "educate" those who need to be educated and to learn the "truth." It is this war in academia that holds hostage many educators and prevents them from advancing the great ideas and great literature of Western civilization, and leads, we are sad to say, to cultural relativism and the decline of liberal arts, reiterated by Bloom and Hutchins.

## Modern Languages

Once more—what knowledge is worth learning? The number-one primary language in the world is Mandarin, followed by English, Hindi, and Spanish. Japanese ranks tenth and German and French rank lower. Nearly all foreign language programs in American schools offer Spanish, French, and Italian, and some offer German and Latin. Only 41 percent (or 5 million) of all high school students (grades 9–12) are enrolled in foreign language courses. As many as 58 percent of secondary students enrolled in a foreign language study Spanish, but only 0.3 percent of U.S. high school students enrolled in a foreign language course study Japanese, and about 0.1 percent attempt Mandarin.[54]

Failure to train students in Mandarin, the official language of China, is representative of our attitude toward the non-Western world, a dysfunctional foreign policy, and the closed-mindedness of ignoring the largest country in the world—stemming from the Cold War thinking of the Eisenhower-Dulles administration. What percentage of American high school students study Hindi, the official language of the second-largest country? None. What percentage of American high school students, except those in Islamic private schools, study Arabic and Farsi, the two major languages of the Muslim world? Next to none (less than 0.05 percent for Arabic and zero for Farsi).[55] Do high schools offer these languages? Yes. About one-half of one percent in the coun-

---

[52] Allan C. Ornstein, *Teaching and Schooling in America: Pre- and Post-September 11* (Boston: Allyn and Bacon, 2003). The gender/race/class argument is keenly depicted in the writings of Michael Apple, James Banks, and especially Henry Giroux and Peter McLaren (the latter two often labeled as neomarxists).

[53] Shelby Steele, "War of the Worlds," *Wall Street Journal,* 17 September 2001, p. 18.

[54] Ornstein, Pajak, and Ornstein, *Contemporary Issues in Curriculum;* Ornstein, *Teaching and Schooling in America: Pre- and Post-September 11.*

[55] Dora Johnson of the Center for Applied Linguistics in Washington, D.C., claims that only two public high schools—one in Dearborn, Michigan, and the other in Houston—offer two or more years in Arabic. None offer Farsi. Personal conversation, July 23, 2002.

try have a community education program, usually meeting once or twice a week in the evening, serving adults and not children or youth.

During the Cold War, there were increased enrollments in Russian language courses and other "security related" courses such as math, science, and engineering at the college level. A sense of relaxation surfaced, coinciding with the reduced threat of war with the Soviet Union. Thus, over the last decade many schools of international relations shifted their emphasis from security to human rights, global economics, and environmental issues.[56]

As we begin the twenty-first century, it would be a shame if any modifications in foreign language courses—from European or Western languages to Mandarin, Hindi, Arabic, or Farsi—were to be based on an international crisis, a reaction to the new economic enemy being China or India, or the Muslim world. This type of thinking only creates new polarities: the United States versus China or the West versus Islam. Instead of modifying the curriculum because of a new understanding of economic markets, respect for other cultures and people, or the fact that the world is more interconnected, the curriculum may be changed because of perceived threats or fear. If so, that would be counterproductive—almost as counterproductive as framing the Chinese, Indian, or Islamic world in sweeping generalizations. One billion Chinese, one billion Indians, and one billion Muslims are very diverse. Although history does not change (it only gets revised or rewritten), political leaders and economic conditions do change, and, subsequently, so do foreign policy and the need to communicate with, understand, and respect other cultures.

In an age of multiculturalism, pluralism, and diversity, why is it that foreign language requirements for four-year college graduation have decreased from 34 percent in 1965 to less than 20 percent today?[57] Is it simply because of the increasing worldwide use of English dictates that we no longer have to learn other languages? Is it because the Cold War spurred the growth of foreign languages and now there is no Soviet threat? (If so, why didn't we offer Russian classes in high school when the Cold War was hot?) Is it based on difficulty of the language or lack of willingness to break from Western tradition? Why is it that in a world in which Western countries represent less than 10 percent of the population, Spanish, French, Italian, German, and Latin (Western and European languages) dominate almost 99 percent of all high school foreign language study? Given a shrinking Western world and the declining role of Spain, France, Italy, and Germany on the world stage, why do we cling to an outdated Western view of the world?

Many Americans have no interest in learning difficult languages and languages other than those of Western nations. We seem to need some foreign stimulant, some vague feeling that we should expand our horizons—something like a wartime concern, an economic imperative, or even some missionary calling. "Multiculturalism may not have prodded us to study cultures fundamentally different from our own," writes one observer, but the "war on terrorism" may be the catalyst.[58] For the last 100 years or more, the door has been closed to studying other cultures, despite the fact that about 700,000 immigrants from non-Western countries have come to our shores each year since 1970. Given the shrinking global village we live in, and the need to understand the world's inhabitants (so we won't kill each other or blow ourselves off the map), we need to expand global education and foreign language studies.

## Computer Knowledge and Technology

Certainly, technology has changed the curriculum in terms of new skills and ideas to learn, but many students and teachers have superficial knowledge and some have limited exposure due to lack of opportunity or choice. A number of states are now requiring proficiency in using technology in order to be certified to teach, and several school districts are offering online courses for middle school and high school students. At the college level the day has come when it is now easier to sit in bed or on a couch at home than to go to class, as reading assignments and notes become available online. The biggest problem is the lack of socialization, and creating a passive recipient knowledge that does little to improve problem-solving skills.

Do students learn more with computers? Of hundreds of studies involving computers and students, grades K–12, few have focused on learning outcomes. Several problems have been reported, however, including dropped computers and broken monitors; misplaced accessories such as cards, disks, and batteries; technical

---

[56]Eyal Press, "It's a Volatile, Complex World," *New York Times Education Life,* 11 November 2001, pp. 20–22, 35.

[57]Telephone conversation with Laura Siaya, American Council on Education, July 24, 2002.

[58]Margaret Talbot, "Other Woes," *New York Times Magazine,* 18 November 2001, p. 24.

problems like freezing, crashing, and misaligned printing (requiring the addition of an extra technician); physical strains among laptop users (back and neck); and the lack of proper teacher training.[59] Thus, one child's great new organizational learning tool can be another child's electronic headache. Being wired up and having access to unlimited information doesn't necessarily improve students' thinking or increasing their reading of important books or their understanding of important ideas.

After wading through the hype about the potential of computers, the research suggests there is no academic improvement among most students who use computers.[60] A computer can make it easier for students to retrieve information, process words for a report, and communicate with people around the world, but it doesn't motivate them to learn or improve their learning. Increased time on the computer often means spending time e-mailing, chatting, or browsing at the expense of schoolwork and reading books.

Actually, there are too many students nestled in their respective time zones chatting with people online in Boston, Chicago, and LA, exchanging intimacies and ideologies and spending hours of "E-life" time that otherwise might be spent engaged in homework and related academics. It is a world of instant messaging, a world that inadvertently pulls children into a web of people, boys and girls, men and women, whom they don't know; yet, they converse sometimes for hours with these "virtual" strangers. Increasingly, parents will have to take responsibility and free their children from this escapism, from this world of squares and rectangles, and help them rejoin the world of reality—even if it means communicating occasionally with Luddites. Teachers and schools will have to find ways to (1) help parents restrict the use of computers for children so they stay in touch with friends and family, (2) adopt age-appropriate guidelines for children's computer use, (3) educate children to make good choices about their computer use, and (4) equalize access to computers for rich and poor students.

## Moral Knowledge

It is possible to give instruction in *moral knowledge* and ethics. We can discuss philosophers such as Socrates, Plato, and Aristotle who examined the good soci-

ety and the good person; the more controversial works of Immanuel Kant, Franz Kafka, and Jean-Paul Sartre; religious leaders such as Moses, Jesus, and Confucius; and political leaders such as Abraham Lincoln, Mohandas Gandhi, and Martin Luther King. Through the study of the writings and principles of these moral people, students can learn about moral knowledge. Teaching Johnny or Jane to read by assigning "Dick and Jane" workbooks or "cat and mouse" readers alone is inadequate; the idea is to encourage good reading (which has social and moral messages) at an early age—and which teaches self-respect, tolerance of others, and social good.

The teaching of morality starts at the first grade with folktales such as "Aesop's Fables," "Jack and the Beanstalk," "Guinea Fowl and Rabbit Get Justice," and the stories and fables of the Grimm Brothers, Robert Louis Stevenson, and Langston Hughes. For older children, there are *Sadako and the Thousand Paper Cranes, Up from Slavery,* and *The Diary of a Young Girl.* And for adolescents, there are *Of Mice and Men, A Man for all Seasons, Lord of the Flies,* and *Death of a Salesman.* By the eighth grade, assuming average or above average reading ability, students should be up to reading the authors (and books) listed in Table 13–3. This list of twenty-five recommended titles exemplifies literature rich in social and moral messages.

As students move up the grade levels and their reading improves, greater variety and options among authors are available to them. Of course, community mores will influence the book selection process. Here we are dealing with issues of whose morality? Whose values? The assumption is that there are agreed-upon virtues such as hard work, honesty, patriotism, integrity, civility, and caring that represent local consensus, if not an American consensus. All we as educators need is sufficient conviction to find core commonalities.

The works suggested in Table 13–3 can be read in traditional history and English courses or in an integrated course such as Junior Great Books, World Studies, or American Studies. Harry Broudy refers to this type of content as a *broad fields approach* to curriculum; he organizes the high school curriculum into five categories, including "moral problems" that address social and moral issues.[61] Florence Stratemeyer and her coauthors developed a curriculum based on ten "life situations," comprising the ability to deal with social,

---

[59]Daniel J. Rocha, "The Emperor's New Laptop," *Education Week,* 27 September, 2001, pp. 42, 46–47.

[60]William M. Bulkeley, "Hard Lessons," *Wall Street Journal,* Technology section, 17 November 1997, pp. 1, 4, 6; Rocha, "The Emperor's New Laptop."

[61]Harry S. Broudy, B.O. Smith, and Joe R. Bunnett, *Democracy and Excellence in American Secondary Education* (Chicago: Rand McNally, 1964).

## Table 13–3   Twenty-five Recommended Works to Be Read by Eighth Grade

1. Maya Angelou, "The Graduation"
2. Pearl Buck, *The Good Earth*
3. Truman Capote, "Miriam"
4. James Fenimore Cooper, *The Last of the Mohicans*
5. Charles Dickens, *Great Expectations*
6. Anne Frank, *The Diary of a Young Girl*
7. William Faulkner, *Brer Tiger and the Big Wind*
8. William Golding, *Lord of the Flies*
9. John Kennedy, *Profiles in Courage*
10. Martin Luther King, *Why We Can't Wait*
11. Rudyard Kipling, "Letting in the Jungle"
12. Harper Lee, *To Kill a Mockingbird*
13. Jack London, *The Call of the Wild*
14. Herman Melville, *Billy Budd*
15. George Orwell, *Animal Farm*
16. Tomas Rivera, "Zoo Island"
17. William Saroyan, "The Summer of the Beautiful White Horse"
18. John Steinbeck, *Of Mice and Men*
19. Robert Louis Stevenson, *Dr. Jekyll and Mr. Hyde*
20. William Still, *The Underground Railroad*
21. Ivan Turgenev, *The Watch*
22. Mark Twain, *The Adventures of Huckleberry Finn*
23. John Updike, *The Alligators*
24. H. G. Wells, *The Time Machine*
25. Elie Wiesel, *Night*

Note: List, compiled by Allan Ornstein, of works that address moral and social issues. Originally published in Allan C. Ornstein, *Teaching and Schooling in America* (Boston: Allyn and Bacon, 2003).

political, and economic forces.[62] Mortimer Adler divided the curriculum into organized knowledge, intellectual skills, and understanding of ideas and values. The latter deals with discussion of "good books" (his term), and not textbooks, and the Socratic method of questioning.[63] Ted Sizer has organized the high school curriculum into four broad areas, including "History and Philosophy" and "Literature and the Arts."[64]

The content of moral knowledge, according to Phillip Phenix, covers five main areas: (1) *human rights,*

[62] Florence B. Stratemeyer et al., *Developing a Curriculum for Modern Living* (New York: Teachers College Press, Columbia University, 1947).

[63] Mortimer J. Adler, *The Paideia Program* (New York: Macmillan, 1984).

[64] Theodore Sizer, *Horace's Compromise* (Boston: Houghton Mifflin, 1987).

involving conditions of life that ought to prevail, (2) *ethics* concerning family relations and sex, (3) *social relationships,* dealing with class, racial, ethnic, and religious groups, (4) *economic life,* involving wealth and poverty, and (5) *political life,* involving justice, equity, and power.[65] The way we translate moral content into moral conduct defines the kind of people we are. It is not our moral knowledge that counts; rather, it is our moral behavior in everyday affairs that is important.

The different courses of study by these authors represent a way of organizing and combining history and English into an interdisciplinary area; great books and great authors can be added to this approach. In general, the content of the courses deal with moral and social issues; ideas that deal with life and how to live it; thoughts that are elegant, witty, and weighty, and make us think and reflect; and dilemmas that help us understand ourselves, our society, our universe, and our realities. By engaging in purposeful discussion agreeing and disagreeing with the ideas expressed, synthesizing and building on ideas through conversation and consensus, questioning and testing arguments, and supporting evidence to bolster opinions, students can gain immense insight into making personal decisions and choices. The content should also help students accept personal responsibility for their behavior, and appreciate religious and political freedom and economic opportunities that exist in this country. Ultimately, the idea is to respect and promote human rights and social justice among all people and nations, as well as to attain a global perspective and appreciation.

### Moral Character

A person can have moral knowledge and obey secular and religious laws but still lack moral character. *Moral character* is difficult to teach because it involves patterns of attitudes and behavior that result from stages of growth, distinctive qualities of personality, and experiences. It involves a coherent philosophy and the will to act in a way consistent with that philosophy; it also means to help people, to accept their weaknesses without exploiting them, to see the best in people and to build on their strengths, to act civilly and courteously in relations with classmates, friends, or colleagues, to express humility, and to act as an individual (and accept individual responsibility) even if it means being different from the crowd.

[65] Phillip Phenix, *Realms of Meaning* (New York: McGraw-Hill, 1964).

Perhaps the real test of moral character is to cope with crisis or setback, deal with adversity, and be willing to take risks (that is, possible loss of a job, even life itself) because of one's convictions. Courage, conviction, and compassion are the ingredients of character. What kind of person do we want to emerge as a result of our efforts as teachers or principals? We can engage in moral education and teach moral knowledge, but can we teach moral character? In general, the morally mature person understands moral principles and accepts responsibility for applying these principles in real-life situations.

The world is full of people who understand the notion of morality but take the expedient way out or follow the crowd. Who among us possesses moral character? Who among the students in our schools will develop into morally mature individuals? To be sure, moral character cannot be taught by one teacher; rather, it involves the leadership of the principal and takes a concerted effort by the entire school, cooperation among a critical mass of supervisors and teachers within the school, and the nurturing of children and youth over many years. Ted and Nancy Sizer ask teachers to confront students with moral questions and moral issues about their own actions or inactions in ways that may be unsettling or difficult; teachers need to address things that threaten the self-concept and self-esteem of students. We need to deal with issues of inequity and social injustice, while promoting cooperative behaviors and intergroup relations among children and youth.[66]

The Sizers want teachers to "grapple" with ideas, to "dig deep," to ask why things are so, what evidence there is, what thoughts and actions mean. They hope that teachers will stop "bluffing," that is, taking short cuts in their preparation, homework, or testing and evaluation practices. They hope that schools will reduce the "sorting" practice in ways that sometimes correspond with social (class or caste) groupings. Although some sorting of students is necessary, it should be flexible enough to respect students' and parents' wishes and to avoid stereotyping. In the end, the Sizers argue, students should not experience hypocrisy in classrooms and schools that claim all students are equal or all students can be what they can be, while at the same time discriminating against students of class, caste, or low ability.

The authors believe that schools should adopt moral character as priority or policy, adopted in turn by all teachers. One or two teachers by themselves cannot have real impact—relevant and long term. It takes the leadership of the principal, as well as a school-community, to implement a program cultivating moral character, through which students are taught responsibility for their actions and the worth of values such as honesty, respect, tolerance, compassion, and a sense of justice.

As education leaders, we have an obligation to promote character development while recognizing that there is a broad range of opinion on what this means or whether it is even possible. Amy Gutman represents one extreme in her belief that moral issues are inappropriate in public schools because of the diverse backgrounds and biases of students. At the other extreme is Nel Nodding's notion that caring for strangers is more important than shaping minds and attitudes of students.[67]

In spite of the controversy, school leaders must not be afraid to take moral positions. There are certain events that are horrifying and represent the most evil aspects of human behavior. Students who laugh at pictures of the rape of Nanking, the Holocaust, the Killing Fields—or incineration of the World Trade Center—should not be excused because of their ignorance, or religious, racial, or ethnic background; nor should they be permitted to voice their "justification" or to get into a historical debate about racial superiority or the decadent values of Western civilization. They are wrong on all moral grounds. Here the schools are not being asked to impose Western or Christian values on the nation's student population. Rather, schools can help teach the understanding that accentuating visible differences under the banner of religious freedom, or tolerating hate groups under the guise of free speech or free press, does not prepare students for a diverse world.

## The Roles of the Curriculum Worker

Much has been written about the roles and responsibilities of the curriculum worker. *Curriculum worker* is a general term that includes a variety of educators from teacher to superintendent. Any person involved in some

---

[66]Theodore R. Sizer and Nancy Faust Sizer, *The Students Are Watching: Schools and the Moral Context* (Boston: Beacon Press, 1999).

[67]Amy Gutman, *Democratic Education,* rev ed. (Princeton: Princeton University Press, 1999); Nel Noddings, *Educating Moral People: A Caring Alternative to Character Education* (New York: Teachers College Press, Columbia University, 2002).

form of curriculum development, implementation, or evaluation is a curriculum worker. A *curriculum supervisor* is usually a chairperson, assistant principal, or principal; he or she usually works at the school level. A *curriculum leader* can be a supervisor or administrator — not only a chairperson or principal but also a director or associate superintendent of curriculum. A *curriculum coordinator* usually heads a program at the school district, regional, or state level; it may be a special government-funded program or a traditional subject area involving math or English. A *curriculum specialist* is a technical consultant from the district level, regional or state department of education, or university. The person provides advice or in-service assistance, sometimes in the classroom but usually at meetings, conferences, or staff sessions. Most of the terms, as well as the related responsibilities and functions of these people, depend on the philosophy and organization of the school district (or state education agency) and the personal preferences and views of the administration.

Confusion exists about whether curriculum planning or development should take place at the local, state, or national level. In the past, emphasis on curriculum development was at the school or school district level. (Bear in mind that most other nations have a national ministry of education with major curriculum responsibilities.)

Curriculum roles in the past were defined at the local level, and decisions were made to develop curriculum leaders at the chair and principal's level. The majority of school districts depend on school people (teachers and supervisors) to develop curriculum — and usually without pay, unless they meet in the summer; parents are also included in many curriculum committees at the school level. Staff limitations make unlikely the provision of curriculum specialists from the central office, and if such a person exists it is one person (possibly two) whose time is limited because of other responsibilities. Only large school districts can afford to have a curriculum department with a full staff of specialists. In such school districts, most curriculum development takes place at the central level and teachers often complain that their professional input is minimal, relegated to implementing predetermined and prepackaged materials from the district office.

## Responsibilities of the Curriculum Worker

What are the responsibilities of the curriculum worker? Assigned responsibilities within the school structure are important but unclear, because a variety of people (teachers, supervisors, principals, district personnel, and others) are expected to serve in the role of curriculum worker. Each position holder has different professional responsibilities, needs, and expectations. Adjustments must be made by each holder of a position. For example, teachers are usually expected (among other things) to provide instruction, but principals are expected to manage a school and provide assistance to teachers.

The curriculum worker has many different titles; nonetheless, the teacher is a member of the curriculum team and works with supervisors and administrators as part the team. Early identification of teachers to serve in the capacity of curriculum workers is essential for the growth of teachers and the vitality of a school (and school district). Where there is need or attention for clarifying the responsibilities of curriculum workers, consider the following:

1. Develop technical methods and tools to carry out curriculum planning in the school (or school district or state agency).

2. Blend theory building with practice; obtain curriculum knowledge and apply it to the real world of classrooms and schools.

3. Agree on what is involved in curriculum development and design, including the relationships that exist among the elements of curriculum.

4. Agree on the relationship among curriculum, instruction, and supervision, including the explicit language of each area and how each aids the work of the other.

5. Act as a change agent who considers schools in context with society; balance the demands and views of the local community with state and national goals and interests.

6. Create a mission or goal statement to provide direction and focused behavior within the organization.

7. Be open to new curriculum trends and thoughts; examine various proposals and suggest modifications, while not falling victim to fads and frills of a particular pressure group.

8. Confer with various parental, community, and professional groups; have skills in human relations and in working with groups and individuals.

9. Encourage colleagues and other professionals to innovate, solve professional problems, and adopt new programs and ideas.

10. Develop a program for continual curriculum development, implementation, and evaluation.

11. Balance and integrate subject areas and grade levels into the total curriculum; pay close attention to scope and sequence by subject and grade level.

12. Understand current research in teaching and learning, as well as new programs that are relevant to target students for teaching and learning.

Other theorists identify other responsibilities and duties of curriculum leaders. For example, Ronald Doll tends to see the curriculum leader involved in coordinating instructional activities, facilities, materials, and special personnel (such as librarians, resource personnel, and program coordinators) and working with and interpreting the curriculum to the public. The focus is on *process*.[68] Allan Glatthorn is more task oriented and *product based*. He envisions the curriculum leader aligning school goals with curricular subjects, organizing and monitoring curriculum committees and projects, and using assessment data to implement and improve curriculum.[69] Finally, John McNeil focuses on the teacher's role in developing curriculum and encourages teachers to develop postmodernist ideas and see the implications of these ideas for their own practice. His recommendation for the curriculum leader is to adapt to and foment social change.[70]

The authors' list of responsibilities tends to be more theoretical than the responsibilities advocated by Doll and Glatthorn—the latter of which tend to be more practical. However, McNeil is the most theoretical of all of us. Our view implies that curriculum workers may be teachers, supervisors (chairs or assistant principals), coordinators, or directors employed at the school, school district, or state level. Doll and Glatthorn examine the activities of curriculum leaders and connote a narrower view, which suggests a chair or principal operating at the school level. McNeil is even more restrictive and views the curriculum leader as a teacher who makes decisions in consultation with the assistant principal or principal. Finally, the authors' concept of the curriculum worker frames the person in terms of broad responsibilities and the whole organization. The others focus on explicit responsibilities or activities that are considered important for the curriculum leader—and explicit personnel, such as the school principal with Doll and Glatthorn or the teacher with McNeil—and thus consider a limited part of the school organization.

## The Teacher and the Curriculum

Although Doll views the curriculum expert primarily as a chair or principal, he is concerned with the teacher's role in planning and implementing the curriculum at three levels: classroom, school, and district. In his opinion, the teacher should be involved "in every phase" of curriculum making, including the planning of "specific goals . . . materials, content, and methods." Teachers should have a curriculum "coordinating body" to unify their work and develop relationships with "supervisors [and] other teachers" involved in the curriculum.[71]

Peter Oliva adopts a broader and ideal view of the teacher's role. For him, teachers are the "primary group in curriculum development." They constitute the "majority or the totality of the membership of curriculum committees and councils." Their role is to develop, implement, and evaluate curriculum. In his words, teachers work in committees and "initiate proposals . . . review proposals, gather data, conduct research, make contact with parents and other lay people, write and create curriculum materials . . . obtain feedback from learners and evaluation programs."[72]

The views of Doll and Oliva, along with those of McNeil, suggest a **bottom-up approach** to curriculum, in which the teacher has a major role to perform. This view was popularized by Taba in her classic text on curriculum development, but actually first introduced and elaborated by Harold Rugg in 1930. Rugg argued that teachers needed to be released from all classroom duties "to prepare courses of study, and assemble materials, and develop outlines of the entire curriculum." Later Caswell and Campbell, in 1935, envisioned teachers participating in curriculum committees at the school,

[68] Doll, *Curriculum Improvement: Decision Making and Process.*

[69] Allan A. Glatthorn, *Curriculum Leadership* (Glenview, IL: Scott, Foresman, 1987); Glatthorn, *The Principal as Curriculum Leader,* 2nd ed. (Thousand Oaks, CA: Corwin Press, 2000).

[70] John D. McNeil, *Curriculum: The Teacher's Initiative,* 2nd ed. (Needham Heights, MA: Allyn and Bacon, 1999).

[71] Doll, *Curriculum Improvement: Decision Making and Process,* p. 334.

[72] Peter Oliva, *Developing the Curriculum,* 6th ed. (Boston: Allyn and Bacon, 2005), p. 128.

district, and state levels during the summers and sometimes as a special assignment during the school year.[73]

## The Central (District) Office

On the other end of the continuum, Glatthorn makes little provision for teacher input, a view similar to Tyler's, which few people recognize of Tyler because of his overall popularity. Glatthorn discusses the role of the "coordinators" at the district level and the roles of the principal, assistant principal, and chair at the school level. Only in elementary schools is he willing to recognize the role of a "teacher specialist" as a member of a subject or grade-level team and mainly confined to "reading and mathematics."[74]

Lester Golden presents an even more **top-down approach,** outlining a bureaucratic, big-city model in which the teacher is given the curriculum by the assistant principal or principal and is expected to teach that curriculum. Those teachers who are "master teachers" and capable of "mentoring other teachers" will climb a career ladder, become assistant principals or principals, and then serve as curriculum leaders in their school.[75]

According to Bolman and Deal, and other administrators,[76] the influence and contributions of the central office show up everywhere, although often they go unnoticed. In many school districts, the central office is crucial to curriculum development, instructional improvement, and assessment and evaluation. In fact, the central office administrators are expected to exhibit leadership and improve schools, although they are not always given credit. Not only does the central office provide support and foster leadership among teachers, supervisors, and principals, but also "central office leaders are effective, in part, because they are invisible, much as the skeleton in the body is invisible."[77]

Based on contemporary theories of social organization and open systems, and the latest we know about effective schools, we regard the teachers' role in curriculum making as central. They are part of a professional team, working with supervisors and administrators (and other colleagues) at all levels—school, district, and state. In small and medium-sized school districts, teachers also work with parents. Big-city and large school districts usually have centralized curriculum committees—a top-down model with minimal teacher input.

## The Team Collaborative Approach

In our view, the teacher sees the curriculum as a whole and, at several points, serves as a resource and change agent: developing it in committees, implementing it in classrooms, and evaluating it as part of a technical team. To guarantee continuity and integration of the curriculum within and among subjects and grade levels, teachers must be actively involved in the curriculum, ideally as part of a curriculum team. An experienced teacher has a broad and deep understanding of teaching and learning; the needs and interests of students; and the content, methods, and materials that are realistic. Therefore, it is the teachers (not the supervisors or administrators) who have the best chance of taking curriculum making out of the realm of theory or judgment and translating it into practice and utility.

Accordingly, the school administration must see to it that every teacher is assigned to a *team* of teachers who share the same assignment (e.g., all fourth-grade elementary school teachers, all math teachers in high school). This team should meet on a regular basis to plan goals and objectives, prune and update content, review instructional materials and media and methods of assessment, and evaluate curriculum outcomes. Similarly, teachers need to engage in *peer observation* and receive feedback from peers (not only from supervisors). This would include new and experienced *study groups* on a regular basis, whereby they can share ideas, raise questions, discuss problems, and experiment. The administration needs to encourage teachers to become

---

[73]Harold Rugg, "The Foundations of Curriculum Making," in W. G. Whipple (ed.), *The Foundations of Curriculum Making,* Twenty-Sixth Yearbook of the NSSE, Part II (Bloomington, IL: Public School Publishers, 1930), pp. 439–440; Hollis L. Caswell and Doak S. Campbell, *Curriculum Development* (New York: American Book, 1935).

[74]Glatthorn, *Curriculum Leadership,* pp. 148–149.

[75]Lester Golden, "The Secondary School Assistant Principal," *NASSP Bulletin,* 79 (1995): 68–74. Also see John C. Daresh, *Beginning the Assistant Principalship* (Thousand Oaks, CA: Corwin Press, 2004).

[76]Lee G. Bolman and Terrance Deal, "Leading with Soul and Spirit," *School Administrator,* 59 (2002): 21–26; Kathleen F. Grove, "The Invisible Role of the Central Office," *Educational Leadership,* 59 (2002): 45–47.

[77]Grove, "The Invisible Role of the Central Office," p. 46.

part of *action research*—committed to the improvement of curriculum and instruction.[78]

This team **collaborative** or **approach** can take shape with a nearby college of education willing to move from "data extraction"—that is, traditional research arrangements in which schools are viewed as resources and teachers/students as subjects—to real partnerships or co-learning arrangements between researchers and educational practitioners. All teachers and supervisors should be expected to participate, on a regular basis throughout their professional careers, in curriculum committees, staff development/mentoring groups, *school improvement* (dealing with the school operation) and *school reform* (dealing with school change) task forces. The focus is on collaboration, collegiality, and teacher involvement—short and simple—in order to enhance school climate, professional growth, and student learning.

Finally, Fullan and Sergiovanni both contend that the notion of collaboration has reached bandwagon status among educators involved in school reform and change processes. The evolving roles of supervisors and administrators now include collaborative-based terms such as *change agents, problem solvers,* and *educational leaders.*[79] Collaboration reflects the idea that the school is organized as a *community* that values professional interaction and provides opportunities for *colleagues* to meet and work together.

But throughout the literature there is the false assumption that educators know what collaboration means, how it is practiced, and what actually happens. **Collaboration** requires that professional teams and/or committee members interact with mutual respect and open communication; and jointly consider issues or problems, shared decision making, and joint ownership of purposes or programs. Collaboration among teachers, supervisors, and curriculum leaders involves sharing information or resources to meet a common goal—

in our case, to implement change and innovation.[80] The collaborative exchange within a school should cut across grades, departments, and programs to involve a greater amount of communication and collegiality among staff members and to avoid departmentalization or turf problems.

## Implementation as a Change Process

Whenever the curriculum leader attempts to implement the curriculum, the principles of change come into play. Much that is planned and developed often does not get implemented, much of what is new or innovative rarely gets off the ground, and what gets reported often gathers dust on shelves. Many charged with **curriculum implementation** neither have a good macro view of the change process nor realize that it occurs at different levels or in stages and must be monitored continually.

Although experienced leaders of curriculum realize that implementation is an essential aspect of curriculum development, only in recent years has implementation become a major concern—largely due to the nature of change and not curriculum. As two authors maintain in their review of change and innovation, "If there is one finding that stands out in our review, it is that effective implementation of . . . innovations required time, personal interaction and contacts, inservice training, and other forms of people-based support." Their research shows that the leadership style, personal relations, and personal contacts of implementers and planners are crucial to effect change and "implement most innovations."[81]

### Incrementalism for Change

People want to change; yet they are also afraid of change, especially if it comes quickly or if they feel they have little control or influence over it. People become

[78]William A. Firestone and Carolyn Riehl, *A New Agenda for Research in Educational Leadership* (New York: Teachers College Press, Columbia University, 2005); John I. Goodlad, *In Praise of Education* (New York: Teachers College Press, Columbia University, 1998); Seymour B. Sarason, *How Schools Might Be Governed and Why* (New York: Teachers College Press, Columbia University, 1997).

[79]Michael Fullan, *The New Meaning of Educational Change,* 3rd ed. (New York: Teachers College Press, Columbia University, 2001); Thomas J. Sergiovanni, *Building Communities in Schools* (San Francisco: Jossey-Bass, 1994).

[80]Marilyn Friend and Lynne Cook, *Interactions: Collaboration Skills for School Professionals,* 2nd ed. (New York: Longman, 1996); James G. Henderson, et al., *Transformative Curriculum Leadership,* 3rd ed. (Columbus, OH: Merrill, 2007).

[81]Michael Fullan and Alan Pomfret, "Research on Curriculum and Instruction Implementation," *Review of Educational Research,* 47 (1977): 391–392. Also see Elliot Washor and Charles Mojkowski, "Creating New Steps: Innovating from the Edge to the Middle," *Phi Delta Kappan,* 87 (2006): 735–739.

accustomed to the status quo and prefer to make modifications in behavior in small and gradual steps.

The professional world of the teacher does not allow for much receptivity to change. Many educators have described the teacher's daily routine as presenting little opportunity for interaction with colleagues. This isolation results partly from the school's organization into self-contained classrooms and partly from the teaching schedules. According to Seymour Sarason, the reality of the school has made teachers feel that professionally they are on their own: It is their responsibility, and theirs alone, to solve their own problems. This posture causes teachers to view change introduced into the program as an individual activity. Viewing their struggles as solitary, teachers often develop a psychological loneliness that results in hostility to administrators and outside change agents who seem insensitive to the teachers' plight.[82] Dan Lortie has noted that, in fact, many factors detrimentally affect teachers' receptivity to change: "Teachers have a built-in resistance to change because they believe that their work environment has never permitted them to show what they can really do." Many proposals for change strike them as "frivolous and wasteful"—not addressing the real issues that deal with student disruptions or discipline, student reading problems, administrative support, and so on.[83]

Curriculum leaders must create an environment that encourages openness and trust and gives feedback so that teachers realize that their contributions are appreciated and their talents considered worthwhile. Teachers need time to "try" the new program to be implemented. They need time to reflect on new goals and objectives; to consider new content, learning experiences, and environments; and to try out new tasks. They need time to map out their tactics for meeting the challenges of the new program, and they need time to talk to their colleagues. Teachers can handle new programs if the changes demanded in their attitudes, behaviors, and knowledge are to be attained in manageable increments.

Curriculum implementation does not occur all at once with all teachers. Ideally, an implementation process allows sufficient time for certain groups of teachers to try out the new curriculum in "pieces." Researchers have found that teachers go through levels of use with a new curriculum. First, they orient themselves to the materials and engage in actions that will prepare them to deliver the curriculum. Their beginning use of the new curriculum is mechanical, and they follow the guide with little deviation. Their delivery of the curriculum becomes rather routine, and they take little initiative to make any changes in it. As they become more comfortable with the curriculum, they may begin to modify it, either to adjust it to their own educational philosophies or to better meet students' needs.[84]

Successful implementers appreciate that it takes time for teachers to "buy into" a new curriculum and to become skilled in delivering the new program. Curriculum leaders should anticipate teachers' questions and concerns and plan potential strategies for addressing them.

In planning **change** or **innovation,** those who will be affected by it experience various levels of concerns or anxieties: first, concern about self; second, concern about the mechanics or operation of the new program or curriculum; and third, concern about students (and others such as colleagues or the community).[85] These stages of concern are important for school leaders to recognize, especially those in charge of implementation of curriculum change. Effective administrators should be prepared first to deal with personal issues, then professional or technical issues, and finally client issues.

## Resistance to Change

A curriculum leader who accepts that people are the key to successful curriculum activity and implementation is cognizant of the barriers that people place between themselves and change efforts. Perhaps the biggest barrier is inertia among the staff, the administration, or the community. Many people think that it is just easier to keep things as they are. If we think of our-

---

[82]Seymour B. Sarason, *The Case for a Change* (San Francisco: Jossey-Bass, 1994); Sarason, *Political Leadership and Educational Failure* (San Francisco: Jossey-Bass, 1998).

[83]Dan Lortie, *Schoolteacher: A Sociological Study* (Chicago: University of Chicago Press, 1975), p. 235.

[84]Linda Darling–Hammond, *Professional Development Schools* (New York: Teachers College Press, Columbia University, 2005); Grant Wiggins and Jay McTighe, *Understanding by Design* (Columbus, OH: Merrill, 2006).

[85]Philip W. Jackson (ed.), *Contributing to Educational Change* (Berkeley, CA: McCutchan, 1988); Linda Lambert et al., *The Constructivist Leader,* 2nd ed. (New York: Teachers College Press, Columbia University, 2002); and Robert G. Owens and Thomas C. Valesky, *Organizational Behavior in Education: Adaptive Leadership and School Reform,* 9th ed. (Boston: Allyn and Bacon, 2007).

selves as systems, we realize that we like to maintain steady states. We have traditions to which we adhere and institutions that we cherish—and we do not wish to change them. Many people are happy with the current school setup as a bureaucracy.

Wanting to keep things as they are is often mixed with believing that things do not need to be changed or that the change being suggested is unwise and will thus be unproductive in meeting school objectives. Educators themselves argue this point. Some say that the schools are fine and just need to be maintained, whereas others claim that the schools are not responsive to the times and require major modification. The status quo tends to be maintained if those suggesting change have not presented precise goals for the new program being suggested—that is, they have not planned adequately what the new program will look like or indicated ways in which the new program will be superior to the existing one.

Often, teachers have not been able or willing to keep up with scholarly development. They have not stayed abreast of the knowledge explosion that would allow them to feel committed to curriculum change and the implementation of new programs. Teachers frequently view change as just signaling more work—something else to add on to an already overloaded schedule for which little or no time is allotted. Usually, no extra money or reward is earmarked for the extra work either. Often they view new curricular programs as requiring them to learn new teaching skills, develop new competencies in curriculum development and the management of learning resources, or acquire new skills in interpersonal relations. In some instances, even staff development programs fail to develop those competencies necessary for teachers to become active participants in innovation.

Another reason administrators have difficulty getting teachers to accept innovation is, according to Edgar Friedenberg, people who go into teaching tend to be conformist in nature, not innovative. These people have succeeded in the school system as it has existed. They have learned to play it safe and to keep a low profile in a bureaucratic system run by administrators who do not like "waves" created.[86] They have found success and fulfillment first as students and now as teachers in this system, and for this reason many see no reason to change it. To many beginning teachers, the bureauc-

racy in place is a welcome and familiar support system, and they are often slow to change it.

Can educators cope with the demand for more change or for assuming change agent roles? Uncertainty fosters insecurity. Often educators who feel comfortable with the present are reluctant to change for a future they cannot comprehend or see clearly. People often prefer to stay with certain known deficiencies rather than venture forth to uncertain futures, even if the changes most likely would be improvements. Bringing new students or parents into the curriculum realm or organizing the program in new ways makes many teachers uneasy.

Another factor that causes people to resist change is the rapidity of change. Many people feel that if something is implemented this year, it will most likely be abandoned when another innovation appears and will thus make most of their efforts useless. There have, in fact, been enough bandwagons in education to make educators innovation-shy.

Sometimes people resist innovation and its implementation because they are ignorant. They either do not know about the innovation or have little information about it. Curriculum leaders must furnish all affected parties—teachers, pupils, parents, community members—with information about the nature of the program and its rationale. Ideally, all affected parties should be informed either directly or indirectly by school representatives of the reasons for the new program.

People often resist change, too, if no financial support or additional time is given for the effort. A project for which no monies are budgeted is rarely destined to be implemented. School districts often budget monies for materials but fail to allocate funds for the creation of the curriculum plan, its delivery within the classroom, or necessary in-service training. Also, we raise the question of whether a person who earns $40,000 to $80,000 is supposed to be a **change agent.** Teachers are not paid enough to innovate; that is the role of a leader, not of a teacher. Teachers are required to implement change, but the school leader (principal) or school district leader (superintendent) should be the one to initiate change and provide the ingredients and processes for constructive change.

Conversely, teachers are an untapped source of energy and insight, capable of profoundly changing the schools if they act as a group and direct their energies to local and state policy matters. Many teachers desire to do something different or innovative, but have few ideas of what it is they wish to do or how to implement it. Most teachers have a deep sense of caring and desire

[86]Edgar A. Friedenberg, *Coming of Age in America* (New York: Random House, 1965).

to help the children. They prefer to teach; they are motivated in helping young people, embedded in the ideas of "feminist" pedagogy, rather than serving as bureaucrats or technocrats.[87]

It may seem that administrators face insurmountable problems. But resistance to change is good because it requires change agents to think carefully about the innovations and to consider the human dynamics involved in implementing programs. Having to fight for change protects the organization from becoming proponents of just random change and educational bandwagonism.

## Improving Receptivity to Change

Curriculum activity involves people thinking and acting. Leaders of curriculum development, and especially implementation, realize that the human equation is of paramount importance and that they must therefore understand how people react to change. Often people say they are willing to change but act as though they are unwilling to adjust. A successful change agent knows how people react to change and how to encourage them to be receptive to change.[88] A wise administrator understands that teachers often are reluctant to change their own behavior, because of habit, tradition, or laziness, but often feel that their colleagues need changing. A smart administrator understands that people often say they want change, but not for themselves, and she must separate lip service from action. The change agent must listen carefully and move slowly in these situations in order to incorporate into the change process those who really prefer no change.

Curriculum innovation and implementation require face-to-face interaction—person-to-person contact. People charged with implementation must understand the interpersonal dimension of leadership. Curriculum innovation and implementation is a group process involving individuals working together. The group not only enables certain actions to occur but also serves to change its individual members.

Of course, if a group is to change individuals, it must be attractive to its members. The ideas and values the group expresses must be acceptable to the individuals within the group. This is why curriculum leaders need to make sure that the members of the group are clear about the platform on which they are to build the curriculum. As groups talk about the need to change and the strategies for implementation, they create a pressure for change within the educational system. Creating a well-formed group, with a clear sense of mission and confidence that it can bring about change, is one way to make individuals receptive to the notion of change.

Analysis of efforts over the past decade to improve schools has resulted in a much better understanding of the steps that must be taken to ensure that change and innovation efforts have a significant and lasting impact. Among the lessons learned from past change efforts are the following:

1. *Adaptive Problem Solving.* Change or innovation must be introduced in such a way that the staff can reasonably implement it.

2. *School-Level Focus.* The focus in bringing about change must be at the school level where the problems occur; teaching and learning take place at the school level, not the district level.

3. *Compatibility.* Successful reform depends on whether changes introduced are implementable, that is, if teachers perceive that they can use the reforms.

4. *Principal's Leadership.* Successful implementation requires change in institutional arrangements and structures; the building principal is the key person for making such decisions.

5. *Teacher Involvement.* To fully cooperate, teachers must have a voice in designing and implementing change. They must be given time, resources, and opportunity to collaborate and make decisions.

6. *Top-Down/Bottom-Up Approaches.* Both approaches have been underscored as important for change. The bottom-up approach encourages a sense of ownership among teachers. The top-down approach communicates to teachers: "We are trying a new approach, we are going to implement it, and we are going to help each other."

7. *Staff Development.* Staff development in terms of continuous participation, feedback, and support of the staff is essential for school improvement.

---

[87]Margaret Smith Crocco, Petra Munro, and Kathleen Weiler, *Pedagogies of Resistance: Women Educator Activists* (New York: Teachers College Press, Columbia University, 1999); Madeleine Grumet, *Bitter Milk: Women and Teaching* (Amherst, MA: University of Massachusetts Press, 1988); Noddings, *Educating Moral People: A Caring Alternative to Character Education.*

[88]Michael Fullan, "The Change Leader," *Educational Leadership*, 59 (2002): 16–21; Carl D. Glickman, "Educational Leadership: Failure to Use Our Imagination," *Phi Delta Kappan*, 87 (2006): 689–690.

8. *School-Business Cooperation.* Some of the most promising reforms and innovations include partnerships between schools and business—sort of a revitalization or rediscovery of the old stewardship concept of the private sector.[89]

Curriculum leaders can also increase educators' willingness to change by linking the needs and expectations of the individuals with those of the organization. Each person has certain needs and interests that she expects to fulfill within the school organization. Every individual who comes into a system plays a multitude of roles; each professional brings to her role a personality as well. Rarely, however, are institutional expectations absolutely compatible with individual needs. Misalignment can cause conflict. Administrators need to recognize that they cannot always avoid this conflict; they must manage it. The way they manage it is reflected in their own personality and leadership behavior.

At the school level, the principal is the key person for matching individual needs and institutional expectations; she is crucial to creating school spirit and receptivity to change by promoting trust and teamwork. However, the principal can dampen spirit and change by promoting distrust and demoralization. What matters most to principals—values and attitudes—gets articulated (directly and indirectly) to the school staff. At the school district level, the same is true, only then the key person is the superintendent. What the superintendent values gets filtered down to the central administration, principals, and school staff. (See Administrative Advice 13–3.)

## Guidelines for Change

Much has been written about the nature of change and the best methods to promote it. Based on the research of Fortune 500 companies, ten principles influence most organizations, including schools. Leaders do make a difference, and those who wish to implement change should

1. Move groups of people in the same direction through mostly noncoercive means.

2. Move people in a direction that is genuinely in their own long-term interests.

3. Establish a set of processes or strategies that aligns the needs and values of individuals and groups with the mission and goals of the organization.

4. Develop a set of strategies that will move the organization toward achieving its mission or goals.

5. Instill cooperation and teamwork within the organization, aimed at achieving shared goals.

6. Allow for input and participation in decision making among participants, as opposed to directing or dictating.

7. Motivate a group of key people who are committed to the mission and goals of the organization.

8. Be consistent and practice what is preached.

9. Deliver what is promised and promise only what is feasible and within one's authority to follow through.

10. Create and maintain professional work conditions, attractive work environment, challenging work opportunities, and opportunity for career development.[90]

Two important characteristics seem to sum up the qualities of this kind of leader. First, the leader is viewed as trustworthy and tends to obtain the best work from employees in terms of quantity and quality. When administrators are trusted, workers tend to exhibit more emotional stability, satisfaction in working, improvement in originality, willingness to take risks, and adaptability to change. Second, the leader is more people oriented than task oriented. When administrators are concerned about people, people tend to put more effort into achieving the goals of the organization. The bottom line is still important, and it improves because people are willing to extend effort and complete tasks, not because they are being directed or coerced. Positive comments, praise when it is honest, and subtle manipulation are much more effective than merely delegating tasks and expecting them to be completed on time. The latter is representative of a military or machine model that does not work well in a professional organization

[89]Daniel U. Levine and Allan C. Ornstein, "Effective Schools: What Research Says About Success," *High School Magazine,* 1 (1993): 32–34; Allan C. Ornstein and Daniel U. Levine, *Foundations of Education*, 10th ed. (Boston, Houghton Mifflin, 2008).

[90]Dean Speicher, "Leadership with Vision," *School Administrator,* 46 (1989): 6. Also see Lee G. Bolman and Terrance Deal, *Leading with Soul* (San Francisco: Jossey-Bass, 2001).

---

**Administrative Advice 13–3**

## Information Checklist for Implementing Curriculum Change and Innovation

Administrators involved in curriculum implementation will have concerns about change and how teachers will react to it. People prefer the status quo when they are familiar and satisfied with it. This checklist consists of a number of questions that deal with the organization of information that school leaders might wish to include in a presentation to the staff. Their emphasis is mainly on teachers' personal and technical concerns.

- How will a teacher's personal day be changed by the innovation?
- How much additional preparation time will the innovation require?
- How much paperwork will be involved in implementing and monitoring the innovation?
- How will the innovation fit in to the content to which learners have already been exposed?
- What kinds of teacher resource materials will be provided?
- Will resource materials be in each teacher's room, in a separate room in the building, or at some other location?
- What kinds of new materials will be provided for learners?
- Are reading levels and other characteristics of these materials clearly appropriate for the learners to be served?

- Will any required instructional procedures demand teaching techniques teachers have not already mastered?
- What kinds of in-service training will be provided?
- What is the relationship of the innovation to standardized tests learners must take?
- What are the implications of the new program for classroom management?
- How strong is the central district administration's commitment to the support of the new program?
- Who, specifically, can be called on for help if there are problems regarding implementation of the innovation?
- What school library and media resources can support the new program?
- To what extent do parents know about and support the new program?

*Source:* Adapted from David G. Armstrong, *Developing and Documenting the Curriculum*, 2nd ed. (Needham Heights, MA: Allyn and Bacon, 1995).

---

or a modern era, especially with the growth in rights of labor and the education of professionals.

## Summary

1. Curriculum can be defined in many ways: as a plan, in terms of experiences, as a field of study, and in terms of subject matter and grade levels. Most curriculum leaders in schools are comfortable with three out of four definitions, except the one about a field of study, with which theoreticians and professors tend to feel comfortable.

2. There are four basic approaches to developing curriculum: behavioral, managerial, systems, and humanistic. Most school administrators adhere to the first two approaches. The systems approach is a little more theoretical, and the humanistic approach tends to coincide with progressive thought. The nontechnical model relies on personal, philosophical, and reflective ideas; most administrators would consider the model to be impractical.

3. The classic method of curriculum development is based on the Tyler model, which is behaviorist in nature.

4. There are a number of fundamental questions that help determine the planning and implementation of curriculum, the function of subject matter, and the role of curriculum leaders and specialists.

5. Regardless of definition or approach, curriculum can be organized into three major components: content, experiences, and environment. Content basically answers the *what* of curriculum, and experiences and environment answer the *how*.

## PRO/CON Debate

### Teaching Values

The crux of the issue can be simply stated: Should schools teach a set of values as a framework for determining, or at least influencing, subject content and its organization, broad issues and tasks, or what belief systems and attitudes should guide students' actions?

**Question:** Should schools implement a values-centered curriculum?

### Arguments PRO

1. There are certain basic core values (or American values) that we should be able to agree upon and incorporate into curriculum.

2. Schools and classrooms are appropriate places for students to discuss values and share a diversity of opinions.

3. Organizing our values according to a generalized framework or set of criteria results in personal commitment, self-confidence, and social responsibility.

4. Schools have a responsibility to teach valuing.

5. Valuing is part of citizenship and national pride. Given our growing diverse population, agreed-to values can be the cement that holds the nation together.

6. A set of core values helps children and youth express themselves, make wise choices, and be responsible for their behavior. It also helps in the self-actualization and potential development of students.

### Arguments CON

1. Values are subjective, not neutral, and therefore we cannot agree upon them. It boils down to whose values? Who speaks for the community?

2. Discussion of values results in peer pressure and school pressure—whatever is the dominant or prevailing attitude of the group.

3. Organizing our values according to a generalized framework or set of criteria results in group thinking and group behavior.

4. Valuing is the responsibility of the home and/or church.

5. Valuing is not part of citizenship, but it can lead to an "ism"—some form of indoctrination—such as nationalism, ethnocentrism, fascism, communism, and so forth.

6. Learning to make wise choices and take responsibility for one's actions is based on learning essential knowledge, which has enabled humankind to advance civilization; learning how to think, not feel, is the basis for self-actualization.

6. Curriculum implementation is largely a function of leadership style and involves personal interaction, program development, and organizational structures.

7. Successful change involves collaboration, collegiality, and communication—what the authors call the three Cs.

8. In implementing curriculum, administrators need to consider the principles of change and how they can influence change among staff members.

9. Ideally, curriculum leaders must understand how professional people can plan, implement, and evaluate change.

10. People often resist change, as well as accept it. An effective administrator can work with and

convince the staff to be more receptive than resistant to change. A number of leadership characteristics improve receptivity to change among staff participants.

### Key Terms

machine theory
curriculum engineering
curriculum development
sources of information
screening goals
curriculum design
nontechnical model
content and experiences

balanced curriculum
cultural literacy
great books
bottom-up approach
top-down approach
collaborative approach
collaboration
curriculum implementation
change or innovation
change agent

## Discussion Questions

1. What definition of curriculum do you prefer? Why?
2. What approach to curriculum do you prefer? Why?
3. In developing curriculum, what criteria for selecting content do you feel are important? What criteria not mentioned in the chapter would you add? In developing curriculum, what criteria for selecting experiences do you feel are important? What criteria not mentioned in the chapter would you add?
4. How can curriculum implementation be improved in your school? As a curriculum leader, how do you involve teachers and students, if at all, in curriculum making?
5. How can the change process in schools be improved? As a curriculum leader, what specific steps would you take to improve the receptivity to change in your school?

## Suggested Readings

Deal, Terrence, E., and Kent D. Peterson. *The Leadership Paradox* (San Francisco: Jossey-Bass, 2000). The authors explain how leadership and management serve as complements for school improvement and curriculum reform.

Drucker, Peter. *The Leader of the Future* (San Francisco: Jossey-Bass, 1998). The author offers unique perspectives on management and leadership and how organizations and their leaders must evolve.

Fullan, Michael and Clif St. Germain, *Learning Places: A Field Guide for Improving Schools.* (Thousand Oaks, CA: Corwin Press, 2007). A practical guide to inspiring school change and reform.

Glickman, Carl D., et al. *Supervision and Instruction*, 4th ed. (Needham Heights, MA: Allyn and Bacon, 1998). The book describes a "bottom-up" administrative approach to supervising and evaluating instruction.

Ornstein, Allan C., Edward F. Pajak, and Stacey B. Ornstein, *Contemporary Issues in Curriculum*, 4th ed. (Boston: Allyn and Bacon, 2007). A comprehensive book that focuses on contemporary and controversial issues in curriculum.

Sarason, Seymour B. *Educational Reform: A Self-Scrutinizing Memoir* (New York: Teachers College Press, Columbia University, 2002). The author shares his thoughts about the future of school reform.

Tyler, Ralph W. *Basic Principles of Curriculum and Instruction* (Chicago: University of Chicago Press, 1949). This classic curriculum book largely exemplifies a behavioral and rational approach.

# 14. Analyzing and Improving Teaching

## FOCUSING QUESTIONS

1 What is the difference between teacher processes and teacher products?

2 How can the interaction between the teacher and students in the classroom be measured?

3 What are the characteristics of a good teacher?

4 How can we determine teacher effectiveness?

5 How would you define an expert teacher and a novice teacher? How do experts and novices differ in the role they assume in classroom instruction and classroom management?

6 What are some current methods for understanding how teachers teach and what they are thinking about when they are teaching?

7 Should public school teachers be committed to teaching moral values? Why? Why not?

8 Should teachers be primarily evaluated on improving student test outcomes?

9 For what reasons do students from industrialized countries outperform U.S. students on math and science tests?

---

In this chapter, we present an overview of the research on effective teaching and five basic ways of analyzing teaching: teacher styles, teacher interactions, teacher characteristics, teacher effects, and teacher contexts. In the early stages of research, up to the mid-1970s, theorists were concerned with **teacher processes**—that is, what the teacher was doing while teaching. They attempted to define and explain good teaching by focusing on teacher styles, teacher interactions, and teacher characteristics. From about 1975 to 1990, researchers shifted their concerns to **teacher products**—that is, student outcomes—and the assessment focused on teacher effects. More recently, theorists have attempted to analyze the culture, language, and thoughts of teachers, combine (rather than separate) teaching and learning processes, and use qualitative methods to assess what they call **teacher contexts.** We intend to move the discussion one step further, as we reconceptualize teaching, and examine the need for **humanistic teaching.**

The second part of the chapter deals with teaching and testing. Beginning teachers in particular should expect to encounter some problems and frustrations, but with proper supervisory and administrative assistance they should be able to improve their technical skills and student test scores. International test comparisons, with emphasis on math and science, are reported and analyzed.

## Review of the Research on Teaching

Over the years thousands of studies have been conducted to identify the behaviors of successful and unsuccessful teachers. However, teaching is a complex act; what works in some situations with some teachers may not work in different school settings with different subjects, students, and goals. There will always be teachers who break many of the rules of procedures and methods and yet are profoundly successful. There will always be teachers who follow the rules and are unsuccessful.

Some educational researchers maintain that we cannot distinguish between "good" and "poor" or "effective" and "ineffective" teachers, that no one knows for sure or agrees on what the competent teacher is, that few authorities can "define, prepare for, or measure teacher competence."[1] They point out that disagreement over terms, problems in measurement, and the complexity of the teaching act are major reasons for the negligible results in judging teacher behavior. The result is that much of the data have been confusing, contradictory, or confirmations of common sense (a cheerful teacher is a good teacher), and that so-called acceptable findings have often been repudiated.[2] The more complex or unpredictable one views teaching as being, the more one is compelled to conclude that it is difficult to agree upon generalizations about successful teaching.[3]

Other researchers assert that appropriate teaching behaviors can be defined (and learned by teachers), that good or effective teachers can be distinguished from poor or ineffective teachers, and that the magnitude of the effect of these differences on students can be determined.[4] They conclude that the kinds of questions teachers ask, the ways they respond to students, their expectations of and attitudes toward students, their classroom management techniques, their teaching methods, and their general teaching behaviors (sometimes referred to as "classroom climate") all make a difference. However, in some cases the positive effects of teachers upon student performance may be masked or washed out by the relative negative effects of other teachers in the same school.[5] The teachers may not be the only variable, or even the major one, in the teaching-learning equation, but they can make a difference, either positive or negative. Here it should be noted that negative teacher influences have greater impact than positive ones, in that students can be turned into nonlearners and experience loss of self-concept in a matter of weeks as a result of a hostile or intimidating teacher.

If teachers do not make a difference, then the profession has problems. If teachers do not make a difference, the notions of teacher evaluation, teacher accountability, and teacher performance are nonworkable; sound educational policy cannot be formulated, and there is little hope for many students and little value in trying to learn how to teach. However, even if we are convinced that teachers have an effect, it is still true that we are unable to assess with confidence the influence a teacher has on student performance because the learning variables are numerous and the teaching interactions are complex.

## Teacher Styles

Teacher style is viewed as a broad dimension or personality type that encompasses teacher stance, pattern of behavior, mode of performance, and attitude toward

[1]Bruce J. Biddle and William J. Ellena, "The Integration of Teacher Effectiveness," in B. J. Biddle and W. J. Ellena (eds.), *Contemporary Research on Teacher Effectiveness* (New York: Holt, Rinehart and Winston, 1964), p. 3.

[2]Allan C. Ornstein, "Successful Teachers: Who They Are," *American School Board Journal,* 180 (1993): 24–27; Ralph T. Putnam and Hilda Borko, "What Do New Views of Knowledge . . . Say About Research on Teaching?" *Educational Researcher,* 29 (2000), pp. 4–16.

[3]Homer Coker, Donald M. Medley, and Robert S. Soar, "How Valid Are Expert Opinions about Effective Teachers?" *Phi Delta Kappan,* 62 (1980): 131–134, 149; Lee S. Schulman, "A Union of Insufficiencies: Strategies for Teacher Assessment," *Educational Leadership,* 46 (1988): 35–41; Arthur E. Wise and Jane A. Leibbrand, "Standards and Teacher Quality," *Phi Delta Kappan,* 81 (2000): 612–621.

[4]Jere E. Brophy, "Classroom Management Techniques," *Education and Urban Society,* 18 (1986): 182–194; N. L. Gage and Margaret C. Needels, "Process-Product Research on Teaching," *Elementary School Journal,* 89 (1989): 253–300; Catherine E. Snow, "Knowing What We Know: Children, Teachers, Researchers," *Educational Researcher,* 30 (2001): 3–4.

[5]Thomas L. Good, Bruce J. Biddle, and Jere E. Brophy, *Teachers Make a Difference* (New York: Holt, Rinehart and Winston, 1975); Allan C. Ornstein, "A Look at Teacher Effectiveness Research: Theory and Practice," *NASSP Bulletin,* 74 (1990): 78–88; Pamela Tucker, "Helping Struggling Teachers," *Educational Leadership,* 58 (2001): 52–56.

self and others. Penelope Peterson defines teacher style in terms of how teachers utilize space in the classroom, their choice of instructional activities and materials, and their method of student grouping.[6] Still others describe teacher style as an *expressive* aspect of teaching (characterizing the emotional relationship between students and teachers, such as warm or businesslike) and as an *instrumental* aspect (how teachers carry out the task of instruction, organize learning, and set classroom standards).[7]

Regardless of which definition of teacher style you prefer, the notion of stability or pattern is central. Certain behaviors and methods are stable over time, even with different students and different classroom situations. There is a purpose of rationale—a predictable teacher pattern even in different classroom contexts. Aspects of teaching style dictated by personality can be modified by early experiences and perceptions and by appropriate training as a beginning teacher. As years pass, a teacher's style becomes more ingrained and it takes a more powerful set of stimuli and more intense feedback to make changes. If you watch teachers at work, including teachers in your school, you can sense that each one has a personal style for teaching, for structuring the classroom, and for delivering the lesson.

### Research on Teacher Styles

Lippitt and White laid the groundwork for a more formal classification of what a teacher does in the classroom. Initially, they developed an instrument for describing the "social atmosphere" of children's clubs and for quantifying the effects of group and individual behavior. The results have been generalized in numerous research studies and textbooks on teaching. The classic study used classifications of authoritarian, democratic, and laissez-faire styles.[8]

The *authoritarian* teacher directs all the activities of the program. This style shares some characteristics with what is now called the *direct teacher*. The *democratic* teacher encourages group participation and is willing to let students share in the decision-making process. This behavior is typical of what is now called the *indirect teacher*. The *laissez-faire* teacher (now often considered to be an unorganized or ineffective teacher) provides no (or few) goals and directions for group or individual behavior.

One of the most ambitious research studies on teacher styles was conducted by Ned Flanders and his associates between 1954 and 1970. Flanders focused on developing an instrument for quantifying verbal communication in the classroom.[9] Every three seconds observers sorted teacher talk into one of four categories of *indirect* behavior or one of three categories of *direct* behavior. Student talk was categorized as response or initiation, and there was a final category representing silence or when the observer could not determine who was talking. The ten categories are shown in Table 14–1.

Flanders's indirect teacher tended to overlap with Lippitt and White's democratic teaching style, and the direct teacher tended to exhibit behaviors similar to their authoritarian teacher. Flanders found that students in the indirect classrooms learned more and exhibited more constructive and independent attitudes than students in the direct classrooms. All types of students in all types of subject classes learned more working with the indirect (more flexible) teachers. In an interesting side note, Flanders found that as much as 80 percent of the classroom time is generally consumed in teacher talk. We will return to this point later.

The following questions, developed by Amidon and Flanders, represent a possible direction for organizing and analyzing observations.

[6]Penelope L. Peterson, "Direct Instruction Reconsidered," in P. L. Peterson and H. J. Walberg (eds.), *Research on Teaching: Concepts, Findings, and Implications* (Berkeley, CA: McCutchan, 1979), pp. 57–69. Also see Richard F. Elmore, Penelope L. Peterson, and Sarah J. McCarthy, *Restructuring in the Classroom* (San Francisco: Jossey-Bass, 1996).

[7]Donald R. Cruickshank and Donald Haefele, "Good Teachers, Plural," *Educational Leadership*, 58 (2001): 26–30; Susan L. Lytle and Marilyn Cochran-Smith, "Teacher Research as a Way of Knowing," *Harvard Educational Review*, 62 (1992): 447–474; Karen Zumwalt, "Alternate Routes to Teaching," *Journal of Teacher Education*, 43 (1992): 83–92.

[8]Ronald Lippitt and Ralph K. White, "The Social Climate of Children's Groups," in R. G. Barker, J. S. Kounin, and H. F. Wright (eds.), *Child Behavior and Development* (New York: McGraw-Hill, 1943), pp. 485–508. Also see Kurt Lewin, Ronald Lippitt, and Ralph K. White, "Patterns of Aggressive Behavior in Experimentally Created Social Climates," *Journal of Social Psychology*, 20 (1939): 271–299.

[9]Ned A. Flanders, *Teacher Influence, Pupil Attitudes, and Achievement* (Washington, DC: U.S. Government Printing Office, 1965); Flanders, *Analyzing Teaching Behavior* (Reading, MA: Addison-Wesley, 1970).

---

**Table 14–1   Flanders's Classroom Interaction Analysis Scale**

---

I. Teacher Talk

  A. Indirect Influence

    1. *Accepts Feelings.* Accepts and clarifies the tone of feeling of the students in an unthreatening manner. Feelings may be positive or negative. Predicting or recalling feelings is included.

    2. *Praises or Encourages.* Praises or encourages student action or behavior. Jokes that release tension, but not at the expense of another individual, nodding head or saying "Um hm?" or "Go on" are included.

    3. *Accepts or Uses Ideas of Student.* Clarifying, building, or developing ideas suggested by a student. As teacher brings more of his own ideas into play, shift to category 5.

    4. *Asks Questions.* Asking a question about content or procedure with the intent that a student answer.

  B. Direct Influence

    5. *Lecturing.* Giving facts or opinions about content or procedure; expressing her own ideas, asking rhetorical questions.

    6. *Giving Directions.* Directions, commands, or orders which students are expected to comply with.

    7. *Criticizing or Justifying Authority.* Statements intended to change student behavior from unacceptable to acceptable pattern; bawling someone out; stating why the teacher is doing what he is doing; extreme self-reference.

II. Student Talk

    8. *Student Talk: Response.* Talk by students in response to teacher. Teacher initiates the contact or solicits student statement.

    9. *Student Talk: Initiation.* Talk initiated by students. If "calling on" student is only to indicate who may talk next, observer must decide whether student wanted to talk.

III. Silence

    10. *Silence or Confusion.* Pauses, short periods of silence, and periods of confusion in which communication cannot be understood by the observer.

---

Source: Ned A. Flanders, *Teacher Influence, Pupil Attitudes, and Achievement* (Washington, DC: U.S. Government Printing Office, 1965), p. 20.

1. What is the relationship of teacher talk to student talk? This can be answered by comparing the total number of observations in categories 1 to 7 with categories 8 and 9.

2. Is the teacher more direct or indirect? This can be answered by comparing categories 1 to 4 (indirect) with categories 5 to 7 (direct).

3. How much class time does the teacher spend lecturing? This can be answered by comparing category 5 with the total number of observations in categories 1 to 4 and 6 to 7.

4. Does the teacher ask divergent or convergent questions? This can be answered by comparing category 4 to categories 8 and 9.[10]

The data obtained from this system do not show when, why, or in what context teacher-student interaction occurs, only how often particular types of interaction occur. Nonetheless, the system is useful for making teachers aware of their interaction behaviors in the classroom.

The Flanders system can be used to examine teacher-student verbal behaviors in any classroom, regardless of grade level or subject. Someone can observe the verbal behavior of a prospective, beginning, or even experienced teacher and show how direct or indirect the teacher is. (Most prospective and beginning teachers tend to exhibit direct behavior, since they talk too much. Professors also usually lecture and thus exhibit many direct behaviors while teaching.) In fact, education students and student teachers often associate good teaching with some form of lecturing, since most of their recent teaching models are professors who often do a lot of talking—the wrong method for younger students who lack the maturity, attentiveness, and focus to cope with a passive learning situation for any length of time. Beginning teachers, therefore, must often unlearn what

---

[10]Edmund J. Amidon and Ned A. Flanders, *The Role of the Teacher in the Classroom* (St. Paul, MN: Amidon & Associates, 1971). Also see Robert F. McNergney and Carol A. Carrier, *Teacher Development,* 2nd ed. (New York: Macmillan, 1991).

## Administrative Advice 14–1

### Observing Other Teachers to Improve Teaching Patterns

The statement "Teachers are born, not made" fails to take into account the wealth of knowledge we have about good teaching and how children learn. Teachers can supplement their pedagogical knowledge and practices by observing other good teachers. Supervisors or administrators are in a position to ensure that their school has a policy for inexperienced teachers or for those who need assistance, and to see how other teachers organize their classrooms and instruct their students. Here are some of the things teachers can observe.

**Student-Teacher Interaction**

- What evidence was there that the teacher truly understood the needs of the students?
- What techniques were used to encourage students' respect for each other's turn to talk?
- What student behaviors in class were acceptable and unacceptable?
- How did the teacher motivate students?
- How did the teacher encourage student discussion?
- In what way did the teacher see things from the students' point of view?
- What evidence was there that the teacher responded to students' individual differences?
- What evidence was there that the teacher responded to students' affective development?

**Teaching-Learning Processes**

- Which instructional methods interested the students?
- How did the teacher provide for transitions between instructional activities?

- What practical life experiences (or activities) were used by the teacher to integrate concepts being learned?
- How did the teacher minimize student frustration or confusion concerning the skills or concepts being taught?
- In what way did the teacher encourage creative, imaginative work from students?
- What instructional methods were used to make students think about ideas, opinions, or answers?
- How did the teacher arrange the groups? What social factors were evident within the groups?
- How did the teacher encourage independent (or individualized) student learning?
- How did the teacher integrate the subject matter with other subjects?

**Classroom Environment**

- How did the teacher utilize classroom space/equipment effectively?
- What did you like and dislike about the physical environment of the classroom?

---

they have learned from their experiences with their own professors. (See Administrative Advice 14–1.)

## Teacher Interaction

An approach to the study of teacher behavior is based on systematic observation of **teacher-student interaction** in the classroom as, for example, in the work of Flanders, which we have already described. The analysis of interaction often deals with a specific teacher behavior and a series of these behaviors constituting a larger behavior, described and recorded by an abstract unit of measurement that may vary in size and time (for example, every 3 seconds a recording is made).

## Verbal Communication

In a classic study of teacher-student interaction, Arno Bellack and colleagues analyzed the linguistic behavior of teachers and students in the classroom.[11] Classroom activities are carried out in large part by verbal interaction between students and teachers; few classroom activities can be carried out without the use of language. The research, therefore, focused on language as the main instrument of communication in teaching. Four basic verbal behaviors or "moves" were labeled.

---

[11] Arno A. Bellack et al., *The Language of the Classroom* (New York: Teachers College Press, Columbia University, 1966).

1. *Structuring moves* serve the function of focusing attention on subject matter or classroom procedures and beginning interaction between students and teachers. They set the context for subsequent behavior. For example, beginning a class by announcing the topic to be discussed is a structuring move.

2. *Soliciting moves* are designed to elicit a verbal or physical response. For example, the teacher asks a question about the topic with the hope of encouraging a response from the students.

3. *Responding moves* occur in relation to and after the soliciting behaviors. Their ideal function is to fulfill the expectations of the soliciting behaviors.

4. *Reacting moves* are sometimes occasioned by one or more of the above behaviors, but are not directly elicited by them. Reacting behaviors serve to modify, clarify, or judge the structuring, soliciting, or responding behavior.[12]

According to Bellack, these pedagogical moves occur in combinations he called **teaching cycles.** A cycle usually begins with a structuring or soliciting move by the teacher, both of which are initiative behaviors; continues with a responding move from a student; and ends with some kind of reacting move by the teacher. In most cases the cycle begins and ends with the teacher. The investigators' analysis of the classroom also produced several insights.

1. Teachers dominate verbal activities. The teacher-student ratio in words spoken is 3:1. (This evidence corresponds with Flanders's finding that teachers' talk is 80 percent of classroom activity.)

2. Teacher and student moves are clearly defined. The teacher engages in structuring, soliciting, and reacting behaviors, while the student is usually limited to responding. (This also corresponds with Flanders's finding that most teachers dominate classrooms in such a way as to make students dependent.)

3. Teachers initiate about 85 percent of the cycles. The basic unit of verbal interaction is the soliciting-responding pattern. Verbal interchanges occur at a rate of slightly less than two cycles per minute.

4. In approximately two-thirds of the behaviors and three-fourths of the verbal interplay, talk is content oriented.

5. About 60 percent of the total discourse is fact oriented.

In summary, the data suggest that the classroom is teacher dominated, subject centered, and fact oriented. The student's primary responsibility seems to be to respond to the teacher's soliciting behaviors. As an instructional leader, you need to help teachers break this cycle of teaching.

## Nonverbal Communication

According to Miles Patterson, nonverbal behavior in the classroom serves five teacher functions: (1) *providing information,* or elaborating upon a verbal statement; (2) *regulating interactions,* such as pointing to someone; (3) *expressing intimacy or liking,* such as smiling or touching a student on the shoulder; (4) *exercising social control,* reinforcing a classroom rule, say, by proximity or distance, and (5) *facilitating goals,* as when demonstrating a skill that requires motor activity or gesturing.[13] These categories are not mutually exclusive; there is some overlap, and nonverbal cues may serve more than one function depending on how they are used.

Although the teaching-learning process is ordinarily associated with verbal interaction, **nonverbal communication** operates as a silent language that influences the process. What makes the study of nonverbal communication so important and fascinating is that some researchers contend that it comprises about 65 percent of the social meaning of the classroom communication system.[14] As the old saying goes, "Actions speak louder than words."

In another study of 225 teachers (and school principals) in forty-five schools, Stephens and Valentine observed ten specific nonverbal behaviors: (1) smiles or frowns, (2) eye contact, (3) head nods, (4) gestures, (5) dress, (6) interaction distance, (7) touch, (8) body movement, (9) posture, and (10) seating arrangements.[15] In general, the first four behaviors are easily interpreted by the observer; some smiles, eye contact, head nods, and gestures are expected, but too many make students suspicious or uneasy. Dress is a matter of professional code and expectation. Distance, touch, body move-

---

[12]Ibid.

[13]Miles L. Patterson, *Nonverbal Behavior: A Functional Perspective* (New York: Springer, 1983).

[14]Sonia Nieto, *Language, Culture, and Teaching* (Mahwah, NJ: Erlbaum, 2002); Albert Oosterhof, *Developing and Using Classroom Assessments,* 2nd ed. (Columbus, OH: Merrill, 1999).

[15]Pat Stephens and Jerry Valentine, "Assessing Principal Nonverbal Communication," *Educational Research Quarterly,* 11 (1986): 60–68.

ment, posture, and seating are open to more interpretation, are likely to have personal meaning between communicators, and are based on personalities and social and cultural relationships.[16] Different types of these five behaviors, especially distance, touch, and body movement, can be taken as indications of the degree of formality in the relationship between the communicators, from intimate and personal to social and public. Teachers should maintain a social or public relationship— that is, a formal relationship—with their students. Behaviors that are inappropriate or could be interpreted as indicating intimate and personal relations must be avoided. It is difficult to define the point in a student-teacher relationship where friendliness can be misconstrued. To some extent that point differs for different students and teachers. It is fine to be warm, friendly, and caring—but too much warmth or friendliness in your interaction (distance, touch, body movement, posture) can get you in trouble as a teacher. Teachers need to be aware of the messages they are sending to students, especially if the students are teenagers and teachers are in their twenties.

When the teacher's verbal and nonverbal cues contradict one another, according to Charles Galloway, the students tend to read the nonverbal cues as a true reflection of the teacher's feelings. Galloway developed global guidelines for observing nonverbal communication of teachers, which he referred to as the "silent behavior of space, time, and body."[17]

1. *Space.* A teacher's use of space conveys meaning to students. For example, teachers who spend most of their time by the chalkboard or at their desk may convey insecurity, a reluctance to venture into student territory.

2. *Time.* How teachers utilize classroom time is an indication of how they value certain instructional activities. The elementary teacher who devotes a great deal of time to reading but little to mathematics is conveying a message to the students.

3. *Body Maneuvers.* Nonverbal cues are used by teachers to control students. The raised eyebrow, the pointed finger, the silent stare all communicate meaning.

Galloway suggests that various nonverbal behaviors of the teacher can be viewed as encouraging or restricting. By their facial expressions, gestures, and body movements, teachers affect student participation and performance in the classroom. These nonverbal behaviors—ranging from highly focused to minimal eye contact, a pat on the back to a frown, a supporting to an angry look—all add up to suggest approval and support or irritability and discouragement. In sum, these nonverbal behaviors influence teacher-student interactions. What teachers should do, both in their personal and professional pursuits, is to become aware of how their mannerisms influence their communication and relations with others.

## Teacher Expectations

Teachers communicate their expectations of students through verbal and nonverbal cues. It is well established that these expectations affect the interaction between teachers and students and, eventually, the performance of students. In many cases teacher expectations become **self-fulfilling prophecies**; that is, if the teacher expects students to be slow or exhibit deviant behavior, the teacher treats them accordingly, and in response they adopt such behaviors.

The research on teacher expectations is rooted in the legal briefs and arguments of Kenneth Clark prepared during his fight for desegregated schools in the 1950s and in his subsequent description of the problem in New York City's Harlem schools.[18] He pointed out that prophesying low achievement for black students not only provides teachers with an excuse for their students' failure but also communicates a sense of inevitable failure to the students.

Clark's thesis was given empirical support a few years later by Rosenthal and Jacobsen's *Pygmalion in the Classroom*, a study of students in the San Francisco schools.[19] After controlling for the ability of students, experimenters told teachers there was reason to expect

---

[16]D. Jean Claudinin and F. Michael Connelly, *Narrative Inquiry* (San Francisco: Jossey-Bass, 1999); Jane Roland Martin, *Cultural Miseducation* (New York: Teachers College Press, Columbia University, 2002).

[17]Charles M. Galloway, "Nonverbal Communication," *Theory into Practice* (December 1968): 172–175; Galloway, "Nonverbal Behavior and Teacher Student Relationships: An Intercultural Perspective," in A. Wolfgang (ed.), *Nonverbal Behavior: Perspectives, Applications, Intercultural Insights* (Toronto: Hogrefe, 1984), pp. 411–430.

[18]Kenneth B. Clark, *Dark Ghetto* (New York: Harper & Row, 1965).

[19]Robert Rosenthal and Lenore Jacobson, *Pygmalion in the Classroom* (New York: Holt, Rinehart and Winston, 1968).

that certain students would perform better—and that expectancy was fulfilled. However, confidence in *Pygmalion* diminished when Robert Thorndike, one of the most respected measurement experts, pointed out that there were several flaws in the methodology and that the tests were unreliable.[20]

Interest in teacher expectations and the self-fulfilling prophecy reappeared in the 1970s and 1980s. Cooper, and then Good and Brophy, outlined how teachers communicate expectations to students and in turn influence student behavior.

1. The teacher expects specific achievement and behavior from particular students.

2. Because of these different expectations, the teacher behaves differently toward various students.

3. This interaction suggests to students what achievement and behavior the teacher expects from them, which affects their self-concepts, motivation, and performance.

4. If the teacher's interaction is consistent over time, it will shape the students' achievement and behavior. High expectations for students will influence achievement at high levels, and low expectations will produce lower achievement.

5. With time, student achievement and behavior will conform more and more to the original expectations of the teacher.[21]

The most effective teacher is realistic about the differences between high and low achievers. The teacher who develops a rigid or stereotyped perception of students is likely to have a harmful effect on them. The teacher who understands that differences exist and adapts realistic methods and content accordingly will have the most positive effect on students.

## Teacher Characteristics

Of the reams of research published on teacher behavior, the greatest amount concerns **teacher characteristics**. The problem is that researchers disagree on which teacher characteristics constitute successful teaching, on how to categorize characteristics, and on how to define them. In addition, researchers use a variety of terms to name what they are trying to describe, such as *teacher traits, teacher personality, teacher performance,* or *teacher methods.* Descriptors or characteristics have different meanings to different people. "Warm" behavior for one investigator often means something different for another, just as the effects of such behavior may be seen differently. For example, it can be assumed that a warm teacher would have a different effect on students according to age, sex, achievement level, socioeconomic class, ethnic group, subject, and classroom context.[22]

Such differences tend to operate for every teacher characteristic and to affect every study on teacher behavior. Although a list of teacher characteristics may be suitable for a particular study, the characteristics (as well as the results) cannot always be compared with another study.

Yet as Lee Shulman points out, teacher behavior researchers often disregard factors such as the time of day, school year, and content, and combine data from an early observation with data from a later occasion. Data from the early part of the term may be combined with data from the later part of the term; data from one unit of content (which may require different teacher behaviors or techniques) are combined with those from other units of content.[23] All these aggregations assume that instances of teaching over time can be summed to have equal weights, which is rarely the case. The accuracy issue is further clouded when such studies are compared, integrated, and built upon each other to

[20]Robert Thorndike, "Review of Pygmalion in the Classroom," *American Educational Research Journal,* 5 (1968): 708–711.

[21]Jere E. Brophy and Thomas L. Good, *Teacher-Student Relationships* (New York: Holt, Rinehart and Winston, 1974); Harris M. Cooper, "Pygmalion Grows Up: A Model for Teacher Expectation Communication and Performance Influence," *Review of Educational Research,* 49 (1979): 389–410; Cooper and Good, *Pygmalion Grows Up* (New York: Longman, 1983); Thomas L. Good and Rhona G. Weinstein, "Teacher Expectations: A Framework for Exploring Classrooms," in K. Zumwalt (ed.), *Improving Teaching* (Alexandria, VA: Association for Supervision and Curriculum Development, 1986), pp. 63–85. Also see Iris C. Rotberg, "A Self-Fulfilling Prophecy," *Phi Delta Kappan,* 83 (2001): 170–171.

[22]N. L. Gage, "Confronting Counsels of Despair for the Behavioral Sciences," *Educational Researcher,* 25 (1996): 5–16; Allan C. Ornstein, "A Look at Teacher Effectiveness Research," *NASSP Bulletin,* 73 (1990), 78–88; W. James Popham, "Why Standardized Tests Don't Measure Educational Quality," *Educational Leadership,* 56 (1999): 8–16.

[23]Lee S. Shulman, "Paradigms and Research Programs in the Study of Teaching," in M. C. Wittrock (ed.), *Handbook of Research on Teaching,* 3rd ed. (New York: Macmillan, 1986), pp. 3–36; Shulman, "Ways of Seeing, Ways of Knowing: Ways of Teaching, Ways of Learning About Teaching," *Journal of Curriculum Studies,* 23 (1991): 393–396.

form a theory or viewpoint about which teacher characteristics are most effective.

Despite such cautions, many researchers feel that certain teacher characteristics can be defined, validated, and generalized from one study to another. In turn, recommendations can be made from such generalizations for use in a practical way in the classroom and elsewhere.

## Research on Teacher Characteristics

Although researchers have named literally thousands of teacher characteristics over the years, A. S. Barr organized recommended behaviors into a manageable list.[24] Reviewing some fifty years of research, he listed and defined twelve successful characteristics, including resourcefulness, intelligence, emotional stability, buoyancy (or enthusiasm), and considerateness (or friendliness). Other authorities have made other summaries of teacher characteristics, but Barr's work is considered most comprehensive.

While Barr presented an overview of hundreds of studies of teacher characteristics, the single most comprehensive study was conducted by David Ryans.[25] More than 6000 teachers in 1700 schools were involved in the study over a six-year period. The objective was to identify through observations and self-ratings the most desirable teacher characteristics. Ryans developed a bipolar list of eighteen teacher characteristics (for example, original vs. conventional, patient vs. impatient, hostile vs. warm). Respondents were asked to identify the approximate position of teachers for each pair of characteristics on a seven-point scale. (A seven-point scale makes it easier for raters to avoid midpoint responses and nonpositions.)

The eighteen teacher characteristics were defined in detail and further grouped into three "patterns" of successful versus unsuccessful teachers:

1. *Pattern X:* understanding, friendly, responsive, versus aloof, egocentric.
2. *Pattern Y:* responsible, businesslike, systematic, versus evading, unplanned, slipshod.
3. *Pattern Z:* stimulating, imaginative, original, versus dull, routine.

These three primary teacher patterns were the major qualities singled out for further attention. Elementary teachers scored higher than secondary teachers on the scales of understanding and friendly classroom behavior (Pattern X). Differences between women and men teachers were insignificant in the elementary schools, but in the secondary schools women consistently scored higher in Pattern X and in stimulating and imaginative classroom behavior (Pattern Z), and men tended to exhibit businesslike and systematic behaviors (Pattern Y). Younger teachers (under 45 years) scored higher than older teachers in patterns X and Z; older teachers scored higher in Pattern Y.

A similar but more recent list of teacher characteristics was compiled by Bruce Tuckman, who has developed a feedback system for stimulating change in teacher behavior.[26] His instrument originally contained twenty-eight bipolar items and was expanded to thirty items (for example, creative vs. routinized; cautious vs. outspoken; assertive vs. passive; quiet vs. bubbly) on which teachers were also rated on a seven-point scale.

## Teacher Effects

Teacher behavior research has shown that teacher behaviors, as well as specific teaching principles and methods, make a difference with regard to student achievement. Rosenshine and Furst analyzed some forty-two correlational studies in their often-quoted review of process-product research. They concluded that there were eleven teacher processes (behaviors or variables) strongly and consistently related to products (outcomes or student achievement). The first five teacher processes showed the strongest correlation to positive outcomes:

1. *Clarity* of teacher's presentation and ability to organize classroom activities.
2. *Variability* of media, materials, and activities used by the teacher.
3. *Enthusiasm,* defined in terms of the teacher's movement, voice inflection, and the like.
4. *Task orientation* or businesslike teacher behaviors, structured routines, and an academic focus.

[24]A. S. Barr, "Characteristics of Successful Teachers," *Phi Delta Kappan,* 39 (1958): 282–284.

[25]David G. Ryans, *Characteristics of Teachers* (Washington, DC: American Council of Education, 1960).

[26]Bruce W. Tuckman, "Feedback and the Change Process," *Phi Delta Kappan,* 67 (1986): 341–344; Tuckman, "The Interpersonal Teacher Model," *Educational Forum,* 59 (1995): 177–185.

5. *Student opportunity to learn,* that is, the teacher's coverage of the material or content in class on which students are later tested.[27]

The six remaining processes were classified as promising: use of student ideas, justified criticism, use of structuring comments, appropriate questions in terms of lower and higher cognitive level, probing or encouraging student elaboration, and challenging instructional materials.

Rosenshine himself later reviewed his conclusions; his subsequent analysis showed that only two behaviors or processes consistently correlated with student achievement: (1) task orientation (later referred to as *direct instruction*), and (2) opportunity to learn (later referred to as *academic time, academic engaged time,* and *content covered*). On a third behavior, clarity, he wavered, pointing out that it seemed to be a correlate of student achievement for students above the fifth grade. The other eight processes appeared to be less important and varied in importance not only according to grade level but also according to subject matter, instructional groups and activities, and students' social class and abilities.[28] Nevertheless, the original review remains a valuable study on how teacher processes relate to student products.

### The Gage Model

Nate Gage analyzed forty-nine process-product studies. He identified four clusters of behaviors that show a strong relationship to student outcomes: (1) *teacher indirectness,* the willingness to accept student ideas and feelings, and the ability to provide a healthy emotional climate; (2) *teacher praise,* support and encouragement, use of humor to release tensions (but not at the expense of others), and attention to students' needs; (3) *teacher acceptance,* clarifying, building, and developing students' ideas; and (4) *teacher criticism,* reprimanding students and justifying authority. The relationship between

the last cluster and outcome was negative — where criticism occurred, student achievement was low.[29] In effect, the four clusters suggest the traditional notion of a democratic or warm teacher (a model emphasized for several decades).

From the evidence on teacher effects upon student achievement in reading and mathematics in the elementary grades, Gage presented successful teaching principles and methods that seem relevant for other grades as well. These strategies are summarized below. Bear in mind that they are commonsense strategies. They apply to many grade levels, and most experienced teachers are familiar with them. Nonetheless, they provide guidelines for education students or beginning teachers who say, "Just tell me how to teach."

1. Teachers should have a system of rules that allow students to attend to their personal and procedural needs without having to check with the teacher.

2. A teacher should move around the room, monitoring students' work and communicating an awareness of their behavior while also attending to their academic needs.

3. To ensure productive independent work by students, teachers should be sure that the assignments are interesting and worthwhile, yet still easy enough to be completed by each student without teacher direction.

4. Teachers should keep to a minimum such activities as giving directions and organizing the class for instruction. Teachers can do this by writing the daily schedule on the board and establishing general procedures so students know where to go and what to do.

5. In selecting students to respond to questions, teachers should call on volunteers and nonvolunteers by name before asking questions to give all students a chance to answer and to alert the student to be called upon.

6. Teachers should always aim at getting less academically oriented students to give some kind of response to a question. Rephrasing, giving cues, or asking leading questions can be useful techniques for bringing forth some answer from a silent student, one who says "I don't know," or one who answers incorrectly.

[27]Barak V. Rosenshine and Norma F. Furst, "Research in Teacher Performance Criteria," in B. O. Smith (ed.), *Research on Teacher Education* (Englewood Cliffs, NJ: Prentice Hall, 1971), pp. 37–42; Rosenshine and Furst, "The Use of Direct Observation to Study Teaching," in R. M. Travers (ed.), *Second Handbook of Research on Teaching* (Chicago: Rand McNally, 1973), pp. 122–183.

[28]Barak V. Rosenshine, "Content, Time and Direct Instruction," in Peterson and Walberg (eds.), *Research on Teaching: Concepts, Findings, and Implications,* pp. 28–56.

[29]N. L. Gage, *The Scientific Basis of the Art of Teaching* (New York: Teachers College Press, Columbia University, 1978).

7. During reading group instruction, teachers should give a maximum amount of brief feedback and provide fast-paced activities of the drill type.[30]

## The Good and Brophy Model

Over the last twenty years, Good and Brophy have identified several factors related to effective teaching and student learning. They focus on basic principles of teaching, but not teacher behaviors or characteristics, since both researchers contend that teachers today are looking more for principles of teaching than for prescriptions.

1. *Clarity* about instructional goals (objectives).
2. Knowledge about *content* and ways for teaching it.
3. *Variety* in the use of teaching methods and media.
4. "*With-it-ness,*" awareness of what is going on, alertness in monitoring classroom activities.
5. "*Overlapping,*" sustaining an activity while doing something else at the same time.
6. "*Smoothness,*" sustaining proper lesson pacing and group momentum, not dwelling on minor points or wasting time dealing with individuals, and focusing on all the students.
7. *Seatwork* instructions and management that initiate and focus on productive task engagement.
8. Holding students *accountable* for learning; accepting responsibility for student learning.
9. *Realistic expectations* in line with student abilities and behaviors.
10. *Realistic praise,* not praise for its own sake.
11. *Flexibility* in planning and adapting classroom activities.
12. *Task orientation* and businesslike behavior in the teacher.
13. *Monitoring* of students' understanding; providing appropriate feedback, giving praise, asking questions.
14. Providing student *opportunity to learn* what is to be tested.

15. Making comments that help *structure learning* of knowledge and concepts for students; helping students learn how to learn.[31]

The fact that many of these behaviors are classroom management techniques and structured learning strategies suggests that good discipline is a prerequisite for good teaching.

## The Evertson-Emmer Model

The Evertson and Emmer model is similar to that of Good and Brophy (in fact, Evertson has written several texts and articles with Brophy). The models are similar in three ways: (1) Teacher effectiveness is associated with specific teaching principles and methods, (2) organization and management of instructional activities is stressed, and (3) findings and conclusions are based primarily on process-product studies.

Nine basic teaching principles represent the core of Evertson's work with Emmer (and, to a lesser extent, with Brophy). Effectiveness is identified in terms of raising student achievement scores.

1. *Rules and Procedures.* Rules and procedures are established and enforced and students are monitored for compliance.
2. *Consistency.* Similar expectations are maintained for activities and behavior at all times for all students. Inconsistency causes confusion in students about what is acceptable.
3. *Prompt Management of Inappropriate Behavior.* Inappropriate behavior is attended to quickly to stop it and prevent its spread.
4. *Checking Student Work.* All student work, including seatwork, homework, and papers, is corrected, errors are discussed, and feedback is provided promptly.
5. *Interactive Teaching.* This takes several forms and includes presenting and explaining new materials, question sessions, discussions, checking for student understanding, actively moving among students to correct work, providing feedback, and, if necessary, reteaching materials.

---

[30]Ibid. The authors disagree with item 5. Most good teachers first ask the question, then call on a student so everyone in the class is required to listen; hence, no one knows who the teacher will call on.

[31]Thomas L. Good and Jere E. Brophy, "Teacher Behavior and Student Achievement," in M. C. Wittrock (ed.), *Handbook of Research on Teaching,* 3rd ed. (New York: Macmillan, 1986), pp. 328–375; Good and Brophy, *Looking into Classrooms,* 9th ed. (Boston: Allyn and Bacon, 2003).

6. *Academic Instruction,* sometimes referred to as "academic learning time" or "academic engaged time." Attention is focused on the management of student work.

7. *Pacing.* Information is presented at a rate appropriate to the students' ability to comprehend it, not too rapidly or too slowly.

8. *Transitions.* Transitions from one activity to another are made rapidly, with minimal confusion about what to do next.

9. *Clarity.* Lessons are presented logically and sequentially. Clarity is enhanced by the use of instructional objectives and adequate illustrations and by keeping in touch with students.[32]

## The Master Teacher

The national interest in education reform and excellence in teaching has focused considerable attention on teachers and the notion of the **master teacher.** The direct behaviors suggested by Rosenshine, and the Good, Brophy, and Evertson models, correspond with Walter Doyle's task-oriented and businesslike description of a master teacher. Such teachers "focus on academic goals, are careful and explicit in structuring activities . . . , promote high levels of student academic involvement and content coverage, furnish opportunities for controlled practice with feedback, hold students accountable for work, . . . have expectations that they will be successful in helping students learn, [and are] active in explaining concepts and procedures, promoting meaning and purpose for academic work, and monitoring comprehension."[33]

When 641 elementary and secondary teachers were asked to "rate criteria for recognition of a master teacher," they listed in rank order: (1) knowledge of subject matter, (2) encourages student achievement through positive reinforcement, (3) uses a variety of strategies and materials to meet the needs of all students, (4) maintains an organized and disciplined classroom, (5) stimulates students' active participation in classroom activities, (6) maximizes student instruction time, (7) has high expectations of student performance, and (8) frequently monitors student progress and provides feedback regarding performance.[34]

Although the sample of teachers was predominantly female (71 percent), so that it can be argued that the recommended behaviors reflect female norms, it must be noted that the teaching profession is predominantly female (67 percent, according to NEA survey data). Most important, the teachers surveyed were experienced (77 percent had been teaching for at least eleven years) and their rank order list of criteria corresponds closely to the principals' rank order list and to Doyle's notion of a master teacher.

Based on a study of several hundred teachers who teach in multiracial and multilinguistic schools, Martin Haberman's portrait of what he termed "star" urban teachers revealed a host of behaviors and attitudes that dismiss what many educators say makes master or effective teachers.[35] Star teachers develop an ideology—that is, a pervasive way of believing and acting. These teachers do not use theory to guide their practice; they do not refer to the axioms or principles of Piaget, Skinner, or the like. Star teachers do not consider the research on teacher effectiveness or school effectiveness. They are generally oblivious to and unconcerned with how researchers or experts in various subjects organize the content in their disciplines. Rather, they have internalized their own view of teaching, their own organization of subject matter, and their own practices through experience and self-discovery. Their behaviors and methods are not forms of knowledge learned in university courses. "Almost everything star teachers do that they regard as important," according to Haberman, "is something they believe they learned on

[32]Edmund T. Emmer, Carolyn M. Evertson, and Jere E. Brophy, "Stability of Teacher Effects in Junior High Classrooms," *American Educational Research Journal,* 6 (1979): 71–75; Emmer et al., *Classroom Management for Middle and High School Teachers,* 7th ed. (Boston: Allyn and Bacon, 2006); Evertson, "Do Teachers Make a Difference?" *Education and Urban Society,* 18 (1986): 195–210; and Evertson et al., *Classroom Management for Elementary Teachers,* 7th ed. (Boston: Allyn and Bacon, 2006).

[33]Walter Doyle, "Effective Teaching and the Concept of Master Teacher," *Elementary School Journal,* 86 (1985): 30; Doyle, "Curriculum and Pedagogy," in P. W. Jackson (ed.), *Handbook of Research on Curriculum* (New York: Macmillan, 1992), pp. 486–516.

[34]Jann E. Azumi and James L. Lerman, "Selecting and Rewarding Master Teachers," *Elementary School Journal,* 88 (1987): 197.

[35]Martin Haberman, "The Pedagogy of Poverty versus Good Teaching," *Phi Delta Kappan,* 72 (1991): 290–294; Haberman, "The Ideology of Star Teachers of Children of Poverty," *Educational Horizons,* 70 (1992): 125–129; and Haberman, "The Dimensions of Excellence," *Peabody Journal of Education,* 70 (1995): 24–43.

---

### Administrative Advice 14-2

### Improving Support for Beginning Teachers

Whatever the existing policies regarding the induction period for entry teachers, there is the need to improve provisions for their continued professional development, to make the job easier, to make them feel more confident in the classroom and school, to reduce the isolation of their work settings, and to enhance interaction with colleagues. Here are some recommendations that administrators can implement for achieving these goals.

- Schedule beginning teacher orientation in addition to regular teacher orientation. Beginning teachers need to attend both sessions.

- Appoint someone to help beginning teachers set up their rooms.

- Provide beginning teachers with a proper mix of courses, students, and facilities (not all leftovers). If possible, lighten their load for the first year.

- Assign extraclass duties of moderate difficulty and requiring moderate amounts of time, duties that will not become too demanding for the beginning teacher.

- Pair beginning teachers with master teachers to meet regularly to identify general problems before they become serious.

- Provide coaching groups, tutor groups, or collaborative problem-solving groups for all beginning teachers to attend. Encourage beginning teachers to teach each other.

- Provide for joint planning, team teaching, committee assignments, and other cooperative arrangements between new and experienced teachers.

- Issue newsletters that report on accomplishments of all teachers, especially beginning teachers.

- Schedule reinforcing events, involving beginning and experienced teachers, such as tutor-tutoree luncheons, parties, and awards.

- Provide regular (say, monthly) meetings between the beginning teacher and supervisor to identify problems as soon as possible and to make recommendations for improvement.

- Plan special and continuing in-service activities with topics directly related to the needs and interests of beginning teachers. Eventually, integrate beginning staff development activities with regular staff development activities.

- Carry on regular evaluation of beginning teachers; evaluate strengths and weaknesses, present new information, demonstrate new skills, and provide opportunities for practice and feedback with master teachers and/or supervisors.

---

the job after they started teaching."[36] Star teachers reflect on what they are doing in the classroom, why they are doing it, and the best way to do it. These teachers are also guided by the expectations that inner-city and poor children can learn, think, and reflect.

For the casual observer it may seem that teachers generally perform the same way. Going beyond the data, the inference is that star teachers or master teachers are different from the average; they have a well thought-out ideology that gives their performance a different meaning. They appear to be mavericks (or at least atypical) and confident in the way they organize and operate their own classrooms. They are sensitive to their students

and teach in ways that make sense to their students, not necessarily according to what researchers or administrators and colleagues have to say about teaching. These teachers seem to be driven by their own convictions of what is right and not by how others interpret the teacher's role or teacher's pedagogy. See Administrative Advice 14-2.

### Cautions and Criticisms

Although the notions of teacher competencies or teacher effectiveness are often identified as something new in research efforts to identify good teaching, they are nothing more than a combination of teaching principles and methods that good teachers have been using for many years prior to this recent wave of research. What these

---

[36] Martin Haberman and Linda Post, "Teachers for Multicultural Schools: The Power of Selection," *Theory Into Practice*, 37 (1998): 99.

product-oriented researchers have accomplished is to summarize what we have known for a long time, but often passed on in the form of "tips for teachers" or practical suggestions that were once criticized by researchers as being recipe oriented. These researchers confirm the basic principles and methods of experienced teachers. They give credibility to teaching practices by correlating teacher behaviors (processes) with student achievement (products). Product-oriented researchers also dispel the notion that teachers have little or no measurable effect on student achievement.

However, there is some danger in this product-oriented research. The conclusions overwhelmingly portray the effective teacher as task oriented, organized, and structured (nothing more than Ryans's Pattern Y teacher). But the teacher competency and teacher effectiveness models tend to overlook the friendly, warm, and democratic teacher; the creative teacher who is stimulating and imaginative; the dramatic teacher who bubbles with energy and enthusiasm; the philosophical teacher who encourages students to play with ideas and concepts; and the problem-solving teacher who requires that students think out the answers. In the product-oriented researchers' desire to identify and prescribe behaviors that are measurable and quantifiable, they overlook the emotional, qualitative, and interpretive descriptions of classrooms, and the joys of teaching; they tend to be driven by high-stake tests and the need for teachers to show evidence of student learning and progress on achievement tests.[37] Most of their research has been conducted at the elementary grade levels, where one would expect more social, psychological, and humanistic factors to be observed, recorded, and recommended as effective. A good portion of their work also deals with low achievers and at-risk students — perhaps the reason many of their generalizations or principles coincide with classroom management and structured and controlling techniques.[38]

[37] See Gerald W. Bracey, "How to Avoid Statistical Traps," *Educational Leadership,* 63 (2006): 78–82; Elliot W. Eisner, "Opening a Shuttered Window: A Special Section on the Arts and Intellect," *Phi Delta Kappan,* 87 (2005): 8–10; and W. James Popham, "Branded by a Test," *Educational Leadership,* 63 (2006): 86–87.

[38] Allan C. Ornstein, "Teacher Effectiveness Research: Theoretical Considerations," in H. C. Waxman and H. J. Walberg (eds.), *Effective Teaching* (Berkeley, CA: McCutchan, 1991), pp. 63–80; Allan C. Ornstein and Richard C. Sinatra, *K–8 Instructional Methods: A Literacy Perspective* (Boston: Allyn and Bacon, 2005).

## Teacher Contexts: New Research, New Paradigms

For the last fifty years or more, research on teacher behavior has been linear and category-based, focused on specific teacher styles, interactions, characteristics, or effects. It focused on either the *process* of teaching (how the teacher was behaving in the classroom) or the *products* of teaching (student outcomes). As the 1990s unfolded, the research on teaching examined the multifaceted nature and context of teaching; it examined the relationship of teaching and learning, the subject-matter knowledge of the teacher, how knowledge was taught, and how it related to pedagogy.

The new emphasis on teaching goes beyond what the teacher is doing and explores teacher thinking from the perspective of teachers themselves. The teacher is depicted as one who copes with a complex environment and simplifies it, mainly through experience, by attending to a small number of important tasks, and synthesizing various kinds of information that continually evolve. The impact of professional knowledge (that is, both subject matter and pedagogical knowledge—knowing *what* you know, and how well you know it) is now considered important for defining how teachers and students construct meaning for their respective academic roles and perform tasks related to those roles.

An alternative for understanding the nature of teaching has evolved—one that combines teaching and learning processes, incorporates holistic practices, and goes beyond what teachers and students appear to be doing to inquire about what they are thinking. This model relies on language and dialogue, and not mathematical or statistical symbols, to provide the conceptual categories and organize the data. It uses the approaches that reformers, reconceptualists, and postliberal theoreticians have advocated: metaphors, stories, biographies and autobiographies, conversations (with experts), and voices (or narratives). Such research, which has surfaced within the last two decades, looks at teaching "from the inside." It focuses on the personal and practical knowledge of teachers, the culture of teaching, and the language and thoughts of teachers.

### Metaphors

Teachers' knowledge, including the way they speak about teaching, not only exists in propositional form but also includes figurative language or **metaphors.** The thinking of teachers consists of personal experiences, images, and jargon, and therefore figurative language is central to the expression and understanding of the teachers' knowledge of pedagogy.[39]

Metaphors of space and time figure in the teachers' descriptions of their work ("pacing a lesson," "covering the content," "moving on to the next part of the lesson").[40] The studies on teacher style, examined in the earlier part of the chapter, represent concepts and beliefs about teachers that can be considered as metaphors: the teacher as a "boss," "coach," "comedian," or "maverick." The notions of a "master" teacher, "lead" teacher, "star" teacher, or "expert" teacher are also metaphors, or descriptors, used by current researchers to describe outstanding or effective teachers.

Metaphors are used to explain or interpret reality. In traditional literature, this process of understanding evolves through experience and study—without the influence of researchers' personal or cultural biases. But the use of metaphors can also be conceptualized in the literature of sociology to include ideas, values, and behaviors that derive in part from a person's position within the political and economic order. Similarly, critical pedagogists and liberal theorists argue that personal and cultural factors such as gender, class, and caste influence the formation of knowledge, especially metaphors as well as behavior.[41]

## Stories

Increasingly, researchers are telling stories about teachers—their work and how they teach—and teachers are telling stories about their own teaching experiences. Most **stories** are narrative and descriptive in nature; they are rich and voluminous in language, and those about teachers make a point about teaching that would otherwise be difficult to convey with traditional research methods. The stories told reflect the belief that there is much to learn from "authentic" teachers who tell their stories about experiences they might otherwise keep to themselves or fail to convey to others.[42]

Stories have an important social or psychological meaning. Stories of teachers allow us to see connections between the practice of teaching and the human side of teaching. The stories of individual teachers allow us to see their knowledge and skills enacted in the real world of classrooms, and lead us to appreciate their emotional and moral encounters with the lives of the people they teach.

Stories by teachers such as Bel Kaufman, Herbert Kohl, Jonathan Kozol, and Sylvia Ashton-Warner have become best-sellers because of their rich descriptions, personal narratives, and the way they describe the very stuff of teaching. These stories are aesthetic and emotional landscapes of teaching and learning that would be missed by clinically based process-product research studies of teacher effectiveness. Still others criticize such personal teacher stories for lacking scholarly reliability and accuracy—flaws they see as grounded in egoism or exaggeration.

Stories of teachers by researchers are less descriptive, less emotional, and less well known. Nevertheless, they are still personal and rich encounters with teachers, and they provide us with teachers' knowledge and experiences not quite on their own terms, but in a deep way that helps us understand what teaching is all about. These stories provide unusual opportunities to get to know and respect teachers as people, on an emotional as well as intellectual level. Most important, these stories represent a shift in the way researchers are willing to convey teachers' pedagogy and understanding of teaching. However, some researchers point out that observers and authors construct different realities, so that different storytellers could write very different versions of the same teacher. But the author is only one variable. Subject matter, students, and school settings could lead

[39]Christopher Clark, "Real Lessons from Imaginary Teachers," *Journal of Curriculum Studies,* 23 (1991): 429–434; Cindy Dooley, "Teaching as a Two-Way Street: Discontinuities Among Metaphors, Images, and Classroom Realities," *Journal of Teacher Education,* 49 (1998): 97–107; Joy S. Richie and David E. Wilson, *Teacher Narrative as Critical Inquiry* (New York: Teachers College Press, Columbia University, 2000).

[40]Tom Barone, "Science, Art, and the Predispositions of Educational Researchers," *Educational Researcher,* 30 (2001): 24–28; Kathy L. Carter, "The Place of Story in the Study of Teaching," *Educational Researcher,* 22 (1993): 5–12.

[41]Michael W. Apple, *Cultural Politics and Education* (New York: Teachers College Press, Columbia University, 1996); James A. Banks, *Cultural Diversity and Education,* 5th ed. (Needham Heights, MA: Allyn and Bacon, 2006).

[42]Sandra Golden et al., "A Teacher's Words Are Tremendously Powerful: Stories from the GED Scholars Initiative," *Phi Delta Kappan,* 87 (2005): 311–315; Allan C. Ornstein, "Beyond Effective Teaching," *Peabody Journal of Education,* 70 (1995): 2–23; John K. Smith, "The Stories Educational Researchers Tell About Themselves," *Educational Researcher,* 26 (1997): 4–1.

## ■ Exemplary Educational Administrators in Action

**ART RAINWATER** Superintendent, Madison Metropolitan School District, Wisconsin.

**Previous Positions:** Deputy Superintendent, Madison, Wisconsin; Special Assistant to Superintendent, Kansas City, Missouri; Associate Superintendent, Kansas City, Missouri; Assistant Superintendent, Kansas City, Missouri; Principal, Kansas City, Missouri.

**Latest Degree:** Ed.S., University of Missouri, Kansas City.

**Number One Influence on Career:** Br. Adrian Gaudin, S.C.

**Number One Achievement:** Creating a research-based, data-driven organization in Madison.

**Number One Regret:** I will retire without having solved the minority achievement gap problem.

**Favorite Education-Related Book or Text:** *The Black-White Test Score Gap* by Christopher Jencks and Meredith Phillips (Editors).

**Additional Interests:** Reading and travel.

**Leadership Style:** I try to build a collaborative team that works closely with everyone in the organization.

**Professional Vision:** Creating public schools that serve all children effectively in an inclusive environment. Every child is important and valued by every adult.

**Words of Advice:** The complexity and expectations of modern public education make it impossible to be an effective "lone wolf" administrator. A team of talented and committed people focused and working with a common vision can accomplish things that no one of us could accomplish alone. Several key points are essential in creating a successful collaborative team approach to administration:

- The children always, always, always come first!

- The leader must have a thorough understanding of his or her own personal nonnegotiable core beliefs and values about children and the learning process. These nonnegotiables must be communicated clearly to the team both initially and as the vision grows and changes.

- Common vision must be developed through ongoing discussion and negotiation between the leader and the team around all of the values and beliefs that make up the culture and working relationship of the team.

- Trust between the leader and the rest of the team is critical. There can never be an effective collaborative team in which members feel they have to look over their shoulder at the leader or at each other.

- The leader must establish trust, and it must be apparent that he or she: believes the team members will make quality, competent decisions; accepts the decisions team members make; never publicly rebukes a member, and is constantly guiding and developing team members' skills.

- To operate effectively, all team members must have the authority to act within their own area. Although authority can be delegated, responsibility always remains with the leader.

- Leadership is creating positive change. It only takes a manager to maintain the status quo. Every organization has a culture that is developed over many years. To lead change you must stay within the culture and ethos of the organization.

Educational leadership today is a challenging profession. It requires people with dedication, courage, and resilience. The rewards of seeing success in the eyes of a child are worth it all.

---

to a striking contrast in portrayal and interpretation of the same teacher.[43]

---

[43] Antoinette Errante, "But Sometimes You're Not Part of the Story," *Educational Researcher,* 24 (2000): 16–27; Shulman, "Ways of Seeing, Ways of Knowing"; Grant Wiggins and Jay McTighe, *Understanding By Design,* 2nd ed. (Columbus, OH: Merrill, 2006).

### Biographies and Autobiographies

Stories written by researchers about teachers tend to be biographical and stories written by teachers about themselves tend to be autobiographical. Both **biography** and **autobiography** encompass a "whole story" and represent the full depth and breadth of a person's experiences, as opposed to commentary or fragments. Unity and wholeness emerge as a person brings past experience to make present action meaningful—to make experiences understandable in terms of what a person has undergone.[44]

The essence of an autobiography is that it provides an opportunity for people to convey what they know and have been doing for years, and what is inside their heads, unshaped by others. Whereas the biography is ultimately filtered and interpreted by a second party, the autobiography permits the author (in this case the teacher) to present the information in a personal way on his or her own terms.

As human beings, we all have stories to tell. Each person has a distinctive biography or autobiography in which is shaped a host of experiences, practices, and a particular standpoint or way of looking at the world. For teachers, this suggests a particular set of teaching experiences and practices, as well as a particular style of teaching and pedagogy.

A biography or an autobiography of a teacher may be described as the life story of one teacher who is the central character based in a particular classroom or school, and of the classroom dynamics and school drama that unfolds around the individual. These types of stories are concerned with longitudinal aspects of personal and professional experiences that can bring much detailed and insightful information to the reader. They help us reconstruct teachers' and students' experiences that would not be available to use by reading typical professional literature on teaching.[45]

The accounts in biographies and autobiographies suggest that the author is in a position of "authority" with respect to the particular segment of the life being described—hence the thoughts and experiences of the author take on a sense of reality and objectivity not always assumed in other stories.[46] However, when teachers write an autobiography (as opposed to someone else writing the story in biography form), they run the risk of being considered partial or writing self-serving descriptions of their teaching prowess.

Thus Madeleine Grumet suggests that researchers publish multiple accounts of teachers' knowledge and pedagogy, instead of a single narrative. The problem is that this approach suggests taking stories out of the hands of teachers.[47] Joint publications between teachers and researchers may be appropriate in some situations and a method for resolving this problem.[48]

## The Expert Teacher

The **expert teacher** concept involves new research procedures—such as simulations, videotapes, and case studies—and a new language to describe the work, prestige, and authority of teachers.[49] The research usually consists of small samples and in-depth studies (the notion of complete lessons and analysis of what transpired), in which expert (sometimes experienced) teachers are distinguished from novice (sometimes beginning) teachers. Experts usually are identified through administrator nominations, student achievement scores, or teacher awards (e.g., Teacher of the Year). **Novice teachers** commonly are selected from groups of student teachers or first-year teachers.

Dreyfus and Dreyfus delineate five stages from novice to expert across fields of study. In stage 1, the novice

[44]William Ayers, *To Teach: The Journey of a Teacher* (New York: Teachers College Press, Columbia University, 2001); Donna Kagan, "Research on Teacher Cognition," in A. C. Ornstein (ed.), *Teaching: Theory and Practice* (Needham Heights, MA: Allyn and Bacon, 1995), pp. 226–238; and Selma Wassermann, *This Teaching Life: How I Taught Myself to Teach* (New York: Teachers College Press, Columbia University, 2004).

[45]Robert V. Bullough and Stefinee Pinnegar, "Guidelines for Quality in Autobiographical Forms of Self-Study," *Educational Researcher*, 30 (2001): 13–22; Robert Donmoyer, "Research as Advocacy and Storytelling," *Educational Researcher*, 26 (1997): 2–3; John Solas, "Investigating Teacher and Student Thinking About the Process of Teaching and Learning Using Autobiography and Repertory Grid," *Review of Educational Research*, 62 (1992): 205–225.

[46]Sara Day Hatton, *Teaching By Heart: The Fox-fire Interviews* (New York: Teachers College Press, Columbia University, 2005); Myles Horton, Judith Kohl, and Herbert Kohl, *The Long Overhaul: An Autobiography* (New York: Teachers College Press, Columbia University, 1998); Betsy Rymes, *Conversational Borderlands* (New York: Teachers College Press, Columbia University, 2001).

[47]Madeleine R. Grumet, "The Politics of Personal Knowledge," *Curriculum Inquiry*, 17 (1987): 319–329.

[48]Donna Kagan and Deborah J. Tippins, "The Genesis of a School-University Partnership," *Educational Forum*, 60 (1995): 48–62; Allan C. Ornstein, "Critical Issues in Teaching" in A. C. Ornstein, E. Pajak, and S. B. Ornstein (eds.), *Contemporary Issues in Education*, 4th ed. (Boston: Allyn and Bacon, 2007), pp. 82–98.

[49]Robert J. Garmston, "Expert Teachers Carry a Satchel of Skills," *Journal of Staff Development*, 19 (1998): 54–56; Donald C. Wesley, "Eleven Ways to Be a Great Teacher," *Educational Leadership*, 55 (1998): 80–81; Scott Willis, "Creating a Knowledge Base for Teaching," *Educational Leadership*, 59 (2002): 6–11.

is inflexible and follows principles and procedures the way they were learned; the advanced beginner, stage 2, begins to combine theory with on-the-job experiences. By stage 3, the competent performer becomes more flexible and modifies principles and procedures to fit reality. At stage 4, the proficient performer recognizes patterns and relationships and has a holistic understanding of the processes involved. Experts, stage 5, have the same big picture in mind but respond effortlessly and fluidly in various situations.[50] Cushing and others point out that "expert teachers make classroom management and instruction look easy," although we know that teaching is a complex act, requiring the teacher "to do many many things at the same time."[51]

Data derived from recent studies suggest that expert and novice teachers teach, as well as perceive and analyze information about teaching, in different ways. Whereas experts are able to explain and interpret classroom events, novices provide detailed descriptions of what they did or saw and refrain from making interpretations. Experts recall or see multiple interactions and explain interactions in terms of prior information and events, whereas novices recall specific facts about students or what happened in the classroom.

The data derived from experts are rich in conversational and qualitative information, but limited in statistical analysis and quantifiable information. What experts (or experienced teachers) say or do about teaching is now considered important for building a science of teaching. Studies of expert and novice teachers show they differ in many specific areas of teaching and instruction.

1. *Experts are likely to refrain from making quick judgments about their students and tend to rely on their own experiences and gut feelings, whereas novices tend to lack confidence in their own judgments and are not sure where to start when they begin teaching.* For example, experts look at student profiles left by previous teachers as reference material but don't place too much stock in them. Novices consider the previous teachers' comments on student information cards to be good starting points, even valid indicators of what to expect.

---

[50]Hubert L. Dreyfus and Stuart E. Dreyfus, *Mind over Machine* (New York: Free Press, 1986).

[51]Katherine S. Cushing, Donna S. Sabers, and David C. Berliner, "Investigations of Expertise in Teaching," *Educational Horizons*, 70 (1992): 109.

2. *Experts tend to analyze student cues in terms of instruction, whereas novices analyze them in terms of classroom management.* Expert teachers assess student responses in terms of monitoring student learning, providing feedback or assistance, and identifying ways instruction can be improved. Novices fear loss of control in the classroom. When given the opportunity to reassess their teaching on videotape, they focus on cues they missed that deal with students' inattentiveness or misbehavior. Although negative student cues appear to be of equal importance to experts and novices, positive cues figure more prominently in the discussion of expert teachers.

3. *Experts make the classroom their own, often changing the instructional focus and methods of the previous teacher.* Novices tend to follow the previous teacher's footsteps. Experts talk about starting over and breaking old routines; they tell us about how to get students going and how to determine where the students are in terms of understanding content. Novices, on the other hand, tend to begin where the previous teacher left off. They have trouble assessing where the students are, what their capabilities are, and how and where they are going.

4. *Experts engage in a good deal of intuitive and improvisational teaching.* They begin with a simple plan or outline and fill in the details as the teaching-learning process unfolds, and as they respond to students. Novices spend much more time planning, stay glued to the content, and are less inclined to deviate or respond to students' needs or interests while the lesson is in progress. Experts are able to adjust and teach to standards and focus on improving test scores; novices experience stress and frustration in the first years of teaching and need practical guidance to stay afloat—not workshops on raising proficiency scores on state exams.

5. *Experts seem to have a clear understanding of the types of students they are teaching and how to teach them.* In a sense, they seem to "know" their students before they meet them. Novices do not have a well-developed idea of the students they are teaching. Whereas novices have trouble beginning the new term, experts routinely find out just what it is the students already know and proceed accordingly.

6. *Expert teachers are less egocentric and more confident about their teaching.* Novices pay more

attention to themselves, worrying about their effectiveness as teachers and about potential discipline problems. Experts are willing to reflect on what they were doing, admit what they did wrong, and comment about changes they would make. Although novices recognize mistakes and contradictions in their teaching, they are defensive about their mistakes and seem to have many self-concerns and doubts about where and how to improve.[52]

In short, expert teachers see the big picture, understand human behavior and relationships, perform in an easy and fluid manner, have their own style or way of doing things, and set up routines or take precautionary steps to avoid trouble or potential problems in their classrooms.

## Voice

The notion of **voice** sums up the new linguistic tools for describing what teachers do, how they do it, and what they think when they are teaching. Voice corresponds with such terms as the *teacher's perspective, teacher's frame of reference,* or *getting into the teacher's head.* The concern with voice permeates the teacher empowerment movement and the work of researchers who collaborate with teachers in teacher effectiveness projects. The idea of voice should be considered against the backdrop of previous teacher silence and impotence in deciding on issues and practices that affect their lives as teachers. The fact that researchers are now willing to give credibility to teachers' knowledge, teachers' practices, and teachers' experiences helps redress an imbalance that in the past gave little recognition to teachers. Now teachers have a right and a role in speaking for themselves and about teaching.[53]

Although there are some serious attempts to include teachers' voices, the key issue is to what extent these new methods permit the "authentic" expression of teachers to influence the field of teacher effectiveness research and teacher preparation programs. In the past, it has been difficult for teachers to establish a voice, especially one that commanded respect and authority, in the professional literature. The reason is simple: The researchers and theoreticians have dominated the field of inquiry and decided on what should be published.

With the exception of autobiographies and stories written by teachers, teachers' voices generally are filtered through and categorized by researchers' writings and publications. For decades, firsthand expressions of teacher experiences and wisdom (sometimes conveyed in the form of advice or recommendations) were considered nothing more than "recipes" or lists of "dos and don'ts"—irrelevant to the world of research on teaching. Recently, however, under umbrella terms such as *teacher thinking, teacher processes, teacher cognition, teacher practices,* and *practical knowledge,* it has become acceptable and even fashionable to take what teachers have to say, adapt it, and turn it into *professional knowledge, pedagogical knowledge,* or *teacher knowledge.* Yet, although researchers are now collaborating with practitioners, taking teacher views seriously, and accepting teachers on equal terms as part of teacher-training programs, teachers still do not always receive credit where it is due. Whereas in scholarly publications researchers and practitioners are named as co-authors, practitioners may be acknowledged only by pseudonyms such as "Nancy" or "Thomas." The culture of schools and universities, and of teachers and professors, should be compatible enough to bridge this gap in the near future.

## Reconceptualizing Teaching

To argue that good teaching boils down to a set of prescriptive behaviors, methods, or proficiency levels, that teachers must follow a "new" research-based teaching plan or evaluation system, or that decisions about teacher accountability can be assessed in terms of students passing some standardized or multiple-choice test is to miss the human aspect of teaching—the "essence" of what teaching is all about.

The stress on standards (or outcomes), assessments, and evaluation systems today illustrates that behaviorism has won at the expense of humanistic psychology. The ideas of Thorndike and Skinner have prevailed over the ideas of Dewey and Kilpatrick. It also suggests that

[52]David C. Berliner et al., "The Vision Thing," *Educational Researcher,* 26 (1997): 12–20; Kathy Carter, Walter Doyle, and Mark Riney, "Expert-Novice Differences in Teaching," in A. C. Ornstein (ed.), *Teaching: Theory and Practice* (Needham Heights, MA: Allyn and Bacon, 1995), pp. 259–272; Kathleen Fulton, Mary Burns, and Lauren Goldberg, "Teachers Learning in Networked Communities," *Phi Delta Kappan,* 87 (2005): 298–301, 305; Scott Mandel, "What New Teachers Really Need," *Educational Leadership,* 63 (2006): 66–69.

[53]Barnett Berry, "Recruiting and Retaining Board-Certified Teachers for Hard-to-Staff Schools," *Phi Delta Kappan,* 87 (2005): 290–297; Andy Hargreaves, "Revisiting Voice," *Educational Researcher,* 25 (1996): 12–19. Also see Thomas Hatch et al., *Going Public with Our Teaching* (New York: Teachers College Press, Columbia University, 2005).

school administrators, policymakers, and researchers focus on the *science* of teaching—behaviors and outcomes that can be observed, counted, or measured—rather than on the *art* of teaching with its humanistic and hard-to-measure variables.

Researchers contend that assessment of teachers and students can be easily mandated, implemented, and reported, and thus has wide appeal under the guise of "reform." Although these assessment systems are supposed to improve education, they don't necessarily do so.[54] Real reform is complex and costly (for example, reducing class size, raising teacher salaries, introducing special reading and tutoring programs, extending the school day and year), and it takes time before the results are evident. People, such as politicians and business leaders, who seem to be leading this latest wave of reform want a quick, easy, and cheap fix. Thus, they will always opt for assessment since it is simple and inexpensive to implement. It creates heightened media visibility, the feeling that something is being done, and the "Hawthorne effect" (novelty tends to elevate short-term gains). This assessment focus (which is a form of behaviorism) also provides a rationale for teacher education programs, because it suggests that we can separate the effects of teachers from other variables and identify good teaching. Yet it is questionable, given our current knowledge of teaching and teacher education and the human factor that goes with teaching and learning, whether new teachers can be properly prepared in terms of both pedagogical rigor and practical reality.

For those in the business of preparing teachers, there is need to provide a research base and rationale showing that teachers who enroll and complete a teacher education program are more likely to be effective teachers than those who lack such training. The fact that there are several alternative certification programs for teachers in more than forty states, in which nearly 5 percent (as high as 16 percent in Texas and 22 percent in New Jersey) of the nationwide teaching force entered teaching,[55] makes teachers of teachers (professors of education) take notice and try to demonstrate that their teacher preparation programs work and that they can

prepare effective teachers. Indeed, there is need to identify teacher behaviors and methods that work under certain conditions—leading many educators to favor behaviorism (or prescriptive ideas and specific tasks) and assessment systems (close-ended, tiny, measurable variables) that correlate teaching behaviors (or methods) and learning outcomes.

The reason is, there is a growing body of literature informing us that traditional certification programs and education courses make little difference in teacher effectiveness; therefore, they should be curtailed to allow alternative certification programs to expand. For the time being, Linda Darling-Hammond assures us that the bulk of the research suggests that teachers who are versed in both pedagogical knowledge and subject knowledge are more successful in the classroom than teachers who are versed only in subject matter. It is also true that teachers who hold standard certificates are more successful than teachers who hold emergency licenses, or who attend "crash" programs in the summer and are then temporarily licensed.[56]

Being able to describe detailed methods of teaching and how and why teachers do what they do should improve the performance of teachers. But all the new research hardly tells the whole story of teaching—what leads to teacher effectiveness and student learning: Being able to describe teachers' thinking or decision making, analyzing their stories and reflective practices, suggests that we understand and can improve teaching. The new research on teaching—with its stories, biographies, reflective practices, and qualitative methods—provides a platform and publication outlet for researchers. It promotes their expertise (which in turn continues to separate them from practitioners) and permits them to continue to subordinate teaching to research. It also provides a new paradigm for analyzing teaching since the older models (teacher styles, teacher personality, teacher characteristics, teacher effectiveness, etc.) have become exhausted and repetitive. The issues and questions related to the new paradigm create new educational wars and controversy between traditional and nontraditional researchers, between quantitative and qualitative advocates. It is questionable whether this new knowledge base about teaching really improves teaching and learning or leads to substantial and sustained improvement.

---

[54]W. James Popham, "The Age of Compliance," *Educational Leadership*, 63 (2005): 84–86; Popham, "Those [Fill-in-Blank] Tests," *Educational Leadership*, 63 (2006): 85–88; and Richard J. Stiggins, "From Formative Assessment to Assessment for Learning: A Path to Success in Standards-Based Schools," *Phi Delta Kappan*, 87 (2005): 324–328.

[55]Abby Goodnough, "Regents Create a New Path to Teaching," *New York Times*, 15 July 2000, pp. B4, B7.

[56]Linda Darling-Hammond, "The Challenge of Staffing Our Schools," *Educational Leadership*, 58 (2001): 12–17; Darling-Hammond, "Keeping Good Teachers," in A. C. Ornstein et al. *Contemporary Issues in Curriculum*, 4th ed. (Boston: Allyn and Bacon, 2007), pp. 139–146.

## The Need for Humanistic Teaching

The focus of teacher research should be on the learner, not the teacher; on the feelings and attitudes of the students, not on knowledge and information (since feelings and attitudes will eventually determine what knowledge and information are sought and acquired); and on long-term development and growth of the students, not on short-term objectives or specific teacher tasks. But if teachers spend more time with the learners' feelings and attitudes, as well as on social and personal growth, teachers may be penalized when cognitive student outcomes (little pieces of information) are correlated with their behaviors and methods in class.

Students need to be encouraged and nurtured by their teachers, especially when they are young. They are too dependent on approval from significant adults—first their parents, then their teachers. Parents and teachers need to help young children and adolescents establish a source for self-esteem by focusing on their strengths, supporting them, discouraging negative self-talk, and helping them take control of their lives in context with their own culture and values.

People (including children) with high self-esteem achieve at high levels, and the more one achieves, the better one feels about oneself. The opposite is also true: Students who fail to master the subject matter get down on themselves and eventually give up. Students with low self-esteem give up quickly. In short, student self-esteem and achievement are directly related. If we can nurture students' self-esteem, almost everything else will fall into place, including achievement scores and academic outcomes. Regardless of how smart or talented a child is, if he or she has personal problems, then cognition will be detrimentally effected.

This builds a strong argument for creating success experiences for students to help them feel good about themselves. The long-term benefits are obvious: The more students learn to like themselves, the more they will achieve; and the more they achieve, the more they will like themselves. But that takes time, involves a lot of nurturing, and does not show up on a standardized test within a semester or school year, moreover, it doesn't help the teacher who is being evaluated by a content- or test-driven school administrator who is looking for results now. It certainly does not benefit the teacher who is being evaluated by a behaviorist instrument that measures how many times he or she attended departmental meetings, whether the shades in the classroom were even, whether his or her instructional objectives were clearly stated, or whether homework was assigned or the computer was used on a regular basis.

It is obvious that certain behaviors contribute to good teaching. The trouble is that there is little agreement on exactly what behaviors or methods are most important. There are some teachers who gain theoretical knowledge of "what works" but are unable to put the ideas into practice. Some teachers act effortlessly in the classroom, while others with similar preparation consider teaching a chore. All this suggests that teaching cannot be described in terms of a checklist or a precise model. It also suggests that teaching is a humanistic activity that deals with people (not tiny behaviors or competencies) and how people (teachers and students) behave in a variety of classroom and school settings.

While the research on teacher effectiveness provides a vocabulary and a system for improving our insight into good teaching, there is a danger that it may lead some of us to become too rigid in our view of teaching. Following only one teacher model or evaluation system can lead to too much emphasis on specific behaviors that can be easily measured or prescribed in advance—at the expense of ignoring humanistic behaviors that cannot be easily measured or prescribed in advance such as aesthetic appreciation, emotions, values, and moral responsibility.

Although some educators recognize that humanistic factors influence teaching, we continue to define most teacher performance in terms of behaviorist and cognitive factors. Most teacher evaluation instruments tend to de-emphasize the human side of teaching because it is difficult to observe or measure. In an attempt to be scientific, to predict and control behavior, we sometimes lose sight of the attitudes and feelings of teachers and their relations with students. As Maxine Greene asserts, good teaching and learning involve feelings, insights, imagination, creative inquires—an existential and philosophical encounter—which cannot be readily quantified. By overlooking hard-to-measure aspects of teaching, we miss a substantial part of teaching, what Greene calls the "stuff" of teaching, what Eisner calls the "artful elements" of teaching, and what others refer to as drama, tones, and flavor.[57]

Teacher behaviors that correlate with measurable outcomes often lead to rote learning, "learning bits"

[57]Maxine Greene, *The Dialectic of Teaching* (New York: Teachers College Press, Columbia University, 1998); Greene, *Variations on a Blue Guitar* (New York: Teachers College Press, Columbia University, 2001); Elliot W. Eisner, *The Educational Imagination*, 3rd ed. (Columbus, OH: Merrill, 2002).

and not the whole picture, to memorization and automatic responses, not high-order thinking. These evaluation models seem to miss moral and ethical outcomes, as well as social, personal, and self-actualizing factors related to learning and life—in effect, the affective domain of learning and the psychology of being human. In their attempt to observe and measure what teachers do, and detail whether students improve their performance on reading or math tests, current models ignore the learner's imagination, fantasy, and intuitive thinking, their dreams, hopes, and aspirations, and how teachers have an impact on these hard-to-define-and-measure but very important aspects of students' lives.

In providing feedback and evaluation for teachers, many factors must be considered so the advice or information does not fall on deaf ears. Teachers appreciate feedback processes whereby they can improve their teaching, so long as the processes are honest and professionally planned and administered, so long as teachers are permitted to make mistakes, and so long as more than one model of effectiveness is considered so that they can adopt recommended behaviors and methods to fit their own personality and philosophy of teaching.

Teachers must be permitted to incorporate specific behaviors and methods according to their own unique personality and philosophy, to pick and choose from a wide range of research and theory, and to discard other teacher behaviors that conflict with their own style without the fear of being considered ineffective. Many school districts, even state departments of education, have developed evaluation instruments and salary plans based exclusively on prescriptive and product-oriented behaviors. Even worse, teachers who do not exhibit these behaviors are often penalized or labeled as "marginal" or "incompetent."[58] There is an increased danger that many more school districts and states will continue to jump on this bandwagon and make decisions based on prescriptive behaviors research without recognizing or giving credence to other teacher behaviors or methods that might deal with feelings, emotions, and personal connections with people—what some educators label as fuzzy or vague criteria.

## Examples of Humanistic Teaching

In traditional terms, humanism is rooted in the fourteenth- and fifteenth-century Renaissance period of Europe, where there was a revival of classical humanism expressed by the ancient Greek and Latin culture. The philosophers and educators of the Renaissance, like the medieval Scholastics before them (who were governed and protected by the church), found wisdom in the past and stressed classical manuscripts. Unlike the Scholastics, they were often independent of the church, and were concerned with the experiences of *humans* and not God-like or religious issues.[59]

In the early twentieth century, humanistic principles of teaching and learning were envisioned in the theories of progressive education: in the *child-centered* lab school directed by John Dewey at the University of Chicago from 1896 to 1904; the *play-centered* methods and materials introduced by Maria Montessori that were designed to develop the practical, sensory, and formal skills of prekindergarten and kindergarten children in the slums of Italy starting in 1908; and the *activity-centered* practices of William Kilpatrick who in the 1920s and 1930s urged the elementary teachers to organize classrooms around social activities, group enterprises, and group projects, and allow children to say what they think.

All of these progressive theories were highly humanistic and stressed the child's interests, individuality, and creativity—in short, the child's freedom to develop naturally, freedom from teacher domination, and freedom from the weight of rote learning. But progressivism failed because, in the view of Lawrence Cremin, there weren't enough good teachers to implement progressive thought in classrooms and schools.[60] To be sure, it is much easier to stress knowledge, rote learning, and right answers than it is to teach about ideas, to consider the interests and needs of students, and to give them freedom to explore and interact with each other without teacher constraints.

---

[58]Gary D. Borich, *Effective Teaching Methods,* 6th ed. (Columbus, OH: Merrill, 2007); Allan C. Ornstein, *Teaching and Schooling in America: Pre- and Post-September 11* (Boston: Allyn and Bacon, 2003); and Allan C. Ornstein and Thomas J. Lasley, *Strategies for Effective Teaching,* 4th ed. (Boston: McGraw-Hill, 2004).

[59]The religious scholar of the medieval period, versed in scriptures and theological logic, was no longer the preferred model; rather, it was the Courtier—man of style, wit, and elegance, liberally educated, a diplomat, politician, or successful merchant. See Baldesar Catiglione, *The Book of the Courtier,* rev. ed. (Garden City, NY: Doubleday, 1959). Niccolò Machiavelli's *The Prince* is a perfect example of the preferred philosophy, advice, and behavior for this Renaissance period.

[60]Lawrence A. Cremin, *The Transformation of the School* (New York: Random House, 1961).

By the end of the twentieth century, the humanistic teacher was depicted by William Glasser's "positive" and "supportive" teacher who could manage students without coercion and teach without failure.[61] It was also illustrated by Robert Fried's "passionate" teachers and Vito Perrone's "teacher with a heart"—teachers who live to teach young children and refuse to submit to apathy or criticism that may infect the school in which they work.[62] These teachers are dedicated and caring; they actively engage students in their classrooms, and they affirm their identities. The students do not have to ask whether their teacher is interested in them, thinks of them, or knows their interests or concerns. The answer is definitely "yes."

Good teaching, according to Alfie Kohn, requires that we accept students for who they are rather than what they do or how much they achieve. All children and youth need to know that their parents will accept them unconditionally, but Kohn goes one step further and maintains that unconditional teaching is also important.[63] For their own self-esteem and ego identity, all children and youth need to feel loved, understood, and valued; this idea is based on Carl Rogers' classic notion of effective teaching and learning, William Glasser's concept of a successful school, and Abraham Maslow's notion of personal healthy growth and development.[64] These are basic sociopsychological principles that date back more than a half century—and they are still relevant today. Now all students need support and encouragement from teachers, but lower-achieving students and disadvantaged learners are more in need of support and positive reinforcement from their teachers. "Unconditional teachers are not afraid to be themselves with students—to act like real human beings rather than controlling authority figures." These are the kind of teachers who act informally—"write notes to students, have lunch with them [and] . . . listen carefully to what kids say and remember details about their lives."[65]

The humanistic teacher is also portrayed by Ted Sizer's mythical teacher called "Horace," who is dedicated and enjoys teaching, treats learning as a humane enterprise, inspires his students to learn, and encourages them to develop their powers of thought, taste, and character.[66] Yet, the system forces Horace to make a number of compromises in planning, teaching, and grading that he knows he would not make if we lived in an ideal world (with more than twenty-four hours in a day). Horace is a trouper; he hides his frustration. Critics of teachers don't really want to hear him or face facts; they don't even know what it is like to teach. Sizer simply states: "Most jobs in the real world have a gap between what would be nice and what is possible. One adjusts."[67] Hence, most caring, dedicated teachers are forced to make some compromises and accommodations and take some shortcuts. So long as no one gets upset and no one complains, the system permits a chasm between rhetoric (the rosy picture) and reality (slow burnout).

There is also a humanistic element in Nel Noddings's ideal teacher who focuses on the nurturing of "competent, caring, loving, and lovable persons." To that end, she describes teaching as a caring profession in which teachers should convey to students the caring way in thinking about one's self, siblings, and strangers, and about animals, plants, and the physical environment. She stresses the affective aspect of teaching: the need to focus on the child's strengths and interests, the need for an individualized curriculum built around the child's abilities and needs, and the need to develop sound character.[68]

Caring, according to Noddings, cannot be achieved by a formula or checklist. It calls for different behaviors for different situations—from tenderness to tough love. Good teaching, like good parenting, requires continuous effort, trusting relationships, and continuity of purpose—the purpose of caring, appreciating human connections, and respecting people and ideas from a historical, multicultural, and diverse perspective. The teacher is not only concerned about educating students

[61]William Glasser, *Schools Without Failure* (New York: Harper & Row, 1969); Glasser, *The Quality School* (New York: HarperCollins, 1990).

[62]Fried, *The Passionate Teacher;* Vito Perrone, *Teacher with a Heart* (New York: Teachers College Press, Columbia University 1998).

[63]Alfie Kohn, *Unconditional Parenting: Moving from Rewards and Punishments to Love and Reason* (New York: Atria Books, 2005).

[64]Glasser, *Schools Without Failure;* Abraham Maslow, *Motivation and Personality* (New York: Harper & Row, 1954); and Carl Rogers, *On Becoming a Person* (Boston: Houghton Mifflin, 1961).

[65]Alfie Kohn, "Unconditional Teaching," *Educational Leadership,* 63 (2005): 20–24.

[66]Theodore R. Sizer, *Horace's Compromise* (Boston: Houghton Mifflin, 1985).

[67]Ibid, p. 20.

[68]Nel Noddings, *The Challenge to Care in Schools,* 2nd ed. (New York: Teachers College Press, Columbia University, 2005).

to be proficient in reading and mathematics but also about making classrooms happy places and helping students become happy with life.[69]

Actually, the humanistic teacher is someone who highlights the personal and social dimension in teaching and learning, as opposed to the behavioral, scientific, or technological aspects. We might argue that everything the teacher does is "human" and the expression "humanistic teaching" is a cliché. However, the authors also use the term in a loose sense to describe the teacher who emphasizes the arts as opposed to the sciences, and people instead of numbers. Although the teacher understands the value of many subjects, including the sciences and social sciences, he or she feels there is the need for students to understand certain *ideas* and *values*, some rooted in 3000 years of philosophy, literature, art, music, theater, etc. Without certain agreed-on content, what Arthur Bestor and Allan Bloom would call the "liberal arts," what E. D. Hirsch and Diane Ravitch would call "essential knowledge," and what Robert Hutchins and Mortimer Adler would call "the Great Books," our heritage would crumble and we would be at the mercy of chance and ignorance; moreover, our education enterprise would be subject to the whim and fancy of local fringe groups.

**Humanistic education,** according to Jacques Barzun, the elegant and eloquent writer of history and humanism, leads to a form of knowledge that helps us deal with the nature of life, but it does not guarantee us a more gracious or noble life. "The humanities will not sort out the world's evils and were never meant to cure [our] troubles. . . . They will not heal diseased minds or broken hearts any more than they will foster political democracy or settle international disputes." The so-called humanities (and if we may add, the humanistic teacher) "have meaning," according to Barzun, "because of the inhumanity of life; what they depict is strife and disaster";[70] and, if we may add, by example, they help us deal with the human condition and provide guidelines for moral behavior, good taste, and the improvement of civilization.

On a schoolwide level, the authors would argue that humanism (what Fried calls "passion," Perrone calls "heart," Sizer calls "dedication," Noddings calls "caring," and Barzun calls "the well-rounded person") means that we eliminate the notion that everyone should go to college since it creates frustration, anger, and unrealistic expectations among large numbers of children and youth. According to Paul Goodman, it requires that society find viable occupational options for non–college graduates, and jobs that have decent salaries, respect, and social status.[71] It suggests, according to John Gardner, that we recognize various forms of excellence— the excellent teacher, the excellent artist, the excellent plumber, the excellent bus driver—otherwise, we create a myopic view of talent and subsequent tension that will threaten a democratic society.[72] It also means that we appreciate and nurture different student abilities, aptitudes, and skills, what Howard Gardner calls "multiple intelligences."[73]

We need to provide more options and opportunities for children and youth, not only preparation for jobs related to verbal and math skills or aptitudes (the ones usually emphasized in schools and tested on tests) but also skills and aptitudes that produce poets, painters, musicians, actors, athletes, mechanics, and public speakers or politicians. Both Gardners believe in performance and merit, although John calls it "talent" and Howard calls it "intelligence" (we call it "skills and aptitude"). John Gardner is more concerned about the social consequences if we only emphasize academic performance as a criterion for success and status. Similarly, Howard Gardner feels that emphasis on verbal-logical-mathematical learning is rooted in classic Piagetian theory, which ignores a pluralistic approach to cognition and a wider range of domains conducive to different cultures.

## Moral and Civic Virtues

Teaching should be committed to a higher purpose, not just teaching knowledge for passing a standardized test; rather, a humanistic-moral purpose designed for academic excellence as well as personal and social responsibility. It should be built around people and community, around respecting, caring for, and having compassion

[69] Nel Noddings, *Educating Moral People* (New York: Teachers College Press, Columbia University, 2001); Noddings, *The Challenge to Care in Schools;* and Noddings, *Happiness and Education* (Cambridge, MA: Cambridge University Press, 2003).

[70] Jacques Barzun, *Teachers in America,* rev ed. (Lanham, MD: University Press of America, 1972).

[71] Paul Goodman, *Compulsory Mis-Education* (New York: Horizon Press, 1964).

[72] John Gardner, *Excellence: Can We Be Equal Too?* (New York: Harper & Row, 1962).

[73] Howard Gardner, *Frames of Mind: The Theory of Multiple Intelligences* (New York: Basic Books, 1983).

towards others. This means that teachers in the classroom would deal with social and moral issues—with the human condition and good and evil. Such teaching encourages students to ask "why?" as opposed to merely giving the "right" answer. The question should start with family conversation and then be nurtured in school during the formative years of learning so that students develop a sense of social and moral consciousness. But our teachers and schools register a disturbing deficit on this score, originally because morality was thought to tread on the spiritual domain and now because there is little time to inquire about and discuss important ideas and issues. Today's curriculum is test driven by items of knowledge and short-answer outcomes.

"Why?" is the existential question that every individual must be permitted to ask and must receive an appropriate and meaningful answer to from those in power or who mete out of justice. Denial of the question means the individual has no basic rights. This ultimately creates a totalitarianism in which the individual is trivialized, as in the Roman empire, where the ruling classes' main amusement was watching humans being eaten by animals or fighting each other to the death; as in the cattle cars to the concentration camps of Auschwitz and Maidenek, where the individual was reduced to a serial number and human remains were often retrofitted into soap products, lamp shades, and gold rings; as in the Serbian ethnic cleansing and rape of Bosnia and Kosovo, and the cleansing and rape of Rwanda and Darfur, as well as many other tragic slaughters through history.

How many of us can locate Rwanda or Darfur on the map?, asks one of the authors. Does anyone among us know where Auschwitz and Maidenek are located? How many among us, except for a few elderly statesmen, scholars, and descendants of the victims, care? Given the "luxury of late birth" and "geographical distance," recent and current generations are expected to do little more than cite a few numbers or statements to put the horrors of humanity into some context or understanding. Few students learn to care about the sufferings of all the folk groups, tribes, and nations since humanity emerged from the caves. Do any students any more know the names of one or two people who died in Nanking, at Pearl Harbor, in the Holocaust, at Juno or Utah Beach, in the killing fields of Cambodia, or in Croatia or Kosovo? Can they cite one name that appears on the Arc de Triomphe or the Vietnam Memorial?

How many of today's students know the name of the pilot (Paul Tibbets) who dropped the atomic bomb on Hiroshima—what his thoughts were as he approached the target or after the carnage and cloud of dust? Who

among us cares to know or can explain what happened or why it happened that more than 100 million soldiers and civilians died in war (or related civilian activities) in the last century, in what one of the authors has called the most ruthless century—consisting of the most vile deeds and crimes against people? Can today's children weigh the value of Western technology and industry against the millions who died beside railroad tracks and in battle trenches using the most advanced killing machines?[74]

Note here that Louis Raths some thirty years ago talked about valuing as part of the teaching and learning, choosing, prizing, cherishing, affirming, and acting upon choices. Similarly, Carl Rogers sought ways for teachers to understand what goes on inside students' minds—their needs, wants, desires, feelings, and their ways of perceiving, appreciating, and valuing. Today, Nel Noddings talks about multiple aims—social, emotional, and spiritual—not just promoting reading and math skills. Similarly, Ted Sizer is worried about our democratic future and insists that we take time out from cognitive processes and educate for sound character and personal responsibility; to teach students to grapple with ideas, as well as enable them to understand the big picture and become active citizens in a democratic society.[75]

Moral practices start with the family and continue with the church and community, but teachers must also play an active role if our society is to become more compassionate, caring, and just. Teachers need to encourage open debate concerning the thorniest issues of the present and past, to welcome discussions without ad hominem attacks or stereotypes, and to build a sense of community (what the French call *civisme*) and character. For the educational system itself to be moral, teachers must be allowed to go beyond facts, raise thoughtful questions that stem from meaningful readings, and transcend the cognitive domain into the moral universe—at all grade levels.

As educational leaders, we have twenty-five or thirty years to make an imprint on the next generation, to remember the millions who are not in the encyclopedias

---

[74] Allan C. Ornstein, *Teaching and Schooling in America: Pre- and Post-September 11* (Boston: Allyn and Bacon, 2003).

[75] Nel Noddings, "What Does It Mean to Educate the Whole Child?" *Educational Leadership*, 63 (2005): 8–13; Louis E. Raths, Merrill Harmin, and Sidney B. Simon, *Values and Teaching*, 2nd ed. (Columbus: Merrill, 1978); Carl Rogers, *Freedom to Learn*, 2nd ed. (Columbus OH: Merrill, 1983); Ted Sizer and Nancy Sizer, "Grappling," *Phi Delta Kappan*, 81 (1999): 184–190.

and who no longer exist, to pass on their thoughts and deeds to the next generations. Our work requires that we understand what is at stake: Improving and enriching society by making our children, and their children, care about what is morally right. We are obliged to motivate students to accomplish great things that exhibit the good side of humanity.

Active teaching and learning means that students be encouraged and rewarded for moral and community action, for helping others and volunteering their time and service. Therefore, character development and civic service should receive the same attention and recognition that we give to A students and star quarterbacks. Active teaching and learning call for special assemblies, special scholarships, and special staff development programs that promote character development, the desire to help others, and the expectation of social and civic involvement. It means giving character development—helping and caring for others, contributing back to the school and community—as much attention as we give academics and sports in school.

This does not require a special course or program to meet some "service-learning" mandate, but rather a school ethos or a common philosophy that teachers and administrators support. The idea must permeate the entire school and be expected of all students. One or two teachers attempting to teach moral responsibilities or civic participation cannot effect long-term change; it takes a team effort and schoolwide policy, demanding nothing less than a reconceptualization of the roles, expectations, and activities of students and teachers involved in the life of schools and communities. The idea flows back to the early philosophy and cardinal principles of progressive education of the 1910s and 1920s and the core curriculum of the 1930s and 1940s, which promoted the study of moral and social issues, social responsibility, and civic education and youth service for the community and nation.

In an era of high-stake testing and cognitive outcomes, school reform has become fixated on raising reading and math test scores. Such an approach has narrowed the curriculum and teaching emphasis. Elliot Eisner asks that we return to John Dewey's philosophy of teaching the "whole child." He warns that "children respond to educational situations not only intellectually, but emotionally and socially as well."[76] The contemporary stress on cognition is based on an Essentialist philosophy that reached its height of influence during the Cold War and has been propelled by a technical and competitive orientation to teaching, influenced by globalization and big business and big government.

In answer to the question, "What are schools for?" John Goodlad says they are established to develop individual potential and serve the needs of society. Both purposes call for a holistic process of teaching, embracing both the arts and sciences, and total development (not just cognitive) of children and youth.[77] Aristotle examined this idea in a clear, concise way more than 2000 years ago: "The habits we form from childhood make no small difference, but rather they make all the difference."

A humanistic, civic, and holistic view of education also means that we consider the basic school, conceived by Ernest Boyer and the Carnegie Foundation. Boyer focuses on the child (or adolescent) and community, where schools are kept small so that people work together and feel connected and empowered; and the school provides emotional and social support for children, beyond academics and test scores, to concentrate on the whole child and teach the importance of values, ethics, and moral responsibility. Boyer's view suggests that a moral and civil society is a requirement for democracy to work, as so keenly described over 150 years ago in Alexis de Tocqueville's classic treatise *Democracy in America* and reaffirmed by John Dewey nearly 100 years ago in his book *Democracy and Education*. Humanism emphasizes teaching the importance of connecting with nature and the ecology of our planet, to preserve our resources and ensure our future. This philosophy requires that we bring competitiveness and social cohesion, excellence and equality, as well as material wealth and poverty, into harmony—not an easy task compared to squaring a circle. Ideally, we need to focus on the whole child, keenly expressed in the 1918 Cardinal Principles of Secondary Education, and not just cognitive outcomes. Educating the whole child includes health, leisure and recreation, civic participation, work, family life, ethics, and the fundamentals, as well.

## Teaching, Testing, and the Achievement Gap

Today the focus on testing dominates the teaching process—a return to the era of World War I, when large-scale testing was first introduced and used to sort indi-

---

[76]Elliot W. Eisner, "Back to the Whole," *Educational Leadership*, 63 (2005): 16.

[77]John I. Goodlad, *What Schools Are For*, 2nd ed. (Bloomington, IN: Phi Delta Kappan Educational Foundation, 1994); John I. Goodlad and Timothy J. McMannon (eds.), *The Public Purpose of Education and Schooling* (San Francisco: Jossey-Bass, 1997).

viduals into qualified and less qualified for schools and colleges, employment, and the armed forces. The same testing and teaching ethos resurfaced during the post–Sputnik/Cold War era, a reaction to the Soviet military threat, which led to the proliferation of standardized testing; advanced placement high school courses; and, as well, as a focus on talented and gifted students, reforming or upgrading the curriculum (more academic courses, more homework, etc.) and emphasis on science and math.

The current threat perceived by Americans centers around economics, particularly with globalization, and the impact of tens of millions of skilled workers and technicians in Asia and Europe competing with American workers. One source claims that 40 to 50 million jobs can potentially be eliminated (as has happened with GM or Ford Motors) or outsourced to other countries (as with IBM, Cisco, and Hewlett-Packard) for 25 to 33 percent of the American wage. The need is to provide American students with scientific and technical skills so they can compete in the twenty-first century. In 2007, according to Marge Schever, the editor-in-chief of the Association for Supervision and Curriculum Development, U.S. students will take nearly 70 million standardized tests to meet the requirements of the No Child Left Behind Act alone, and possibly another 70 million involving international tests, National Assessment of Educational Progress (NAEP), and the SATs and ACTs.[78]

Even when testing measures achievement, using assessment for feedback and learning has become secondary. The schools are more interested in measuring student results and rankings, improving proficiency levels, holding teachers and administrators accountable, and ensuring that everyone has complied with state and federal guidelines.[79] In this high-stake testing era, the scoreboard officially indicates whether a school has been successful or unsuccessful in showing test score improvement that state and federal assessment requires.

Teaching has become geared toward improving student test outcomes and getting measurable results, not whether students are really learning. Tests are driving curriculum in the form of content standards, and teachers are expected to teach toward those standards. There is little concern about whether students can critically think or solve problems, or whether their social, personal, and emotional needs are being met. Given the concern for compliance with state and federal testing programs, teachers and administrators have been depersonalized and deprofessionalized, reduced to technicians who are now told from the top down what strategies are needed to raise proficiency scores and what content should be scheduled. Increasingly, school administrators are planning workshops on "Teaching Toward Tests," "Raising Student Test Scores," and "Getting Results," while traditional staff development themes such as classroom management, lesson planning, and team teaching—the "nuts and bolts" of teaching—get forced to the wayside.

## International Educational Achievement (IEA) Studies

The first IEA study evolved from an international conference in the 1950s at which researchers from a dozen countries agreed to assess children's achievement on a cross-national basis; it is the largest cross-cultural study on academic achievement. The first major survey, in the area of mathematics, involved 133,000 elementary and secondary students, 13,500 teachers, and 5,450 schools in twelve technological countries including the United States. After this study the researchers embarked on a six-subject survey of science, literature, reading comprehension, English and French as foreign languages, and civic education. Together with mathematics, these subjects cover practically all the principal subjects in the secondary curriculum. This survey involved 258,000 secondary students and 50,000 teachers from 9,700 schools in nineteen countries (four of them less developed).

The data analysis in the math survey was complicated but tended to show that the teacher and school characteristics are relatively unimportant in determining math achievement. Student characteristics highly correlated with achievement, and the child's social class accounted for the greatest share of variation in learning. The study also showed that, at every age level and in most countries, boys outperformed girls in math.[80]

[78]Marge Schever, "Reclaiming Testing," *Educational Leadership*, 63 (2005): 9.

[79]Thomas R. Guskey, "Mapping the Road to Proficiency," *Educational Leadership*, 63 (2005): 32–38; Laura Lefkowits and Kristen Miller, "Fulfilling the Promise of the Standards Movement," *Phi Delta Kappan*, 87 (2006): 401–407; and W. James Popham, "The Age of Compliance," *Educational Leadership*, 63 (2005): 84–85.

[80]Torsten Husen, *International Study of Achievement in Mathematics: A Comparison of Twelve Countries*, 2 vols. (New York: John Wiley & Sons, 1967).

The six-subject survey was reported in nine volumes beginning in 1973. The reading survey is especially pertinent to Americans, in that it shows that the conventional view of the relation of socioeconomic level to reading scores apparently holds true internationally. The general belief in the superiority of girls' reading ability holds up only in the early grades; at the secondary school level, reading scores of teenage boys and girls are similar. The relatively low scores of American compared to European students supports the view that many students in the United States are disadvantaged and have fundamental reading problems.[81]

The data from all six areas tend to confirm the influence of the students' culture, and particularly the home, on achievement. The total effect of home background is considerably greater than the direct effect of school variables. At age four the overall average is 0.42 for home factors but only 0.26 for school (including the teacher); at age ten, it is 0.35 for home factors and 0.22 for school.[82] The data are also sufficiently detailed to conclude, as the science report does, "that learning is a continuous and cumulative process over generations."[83]

Put in different terms, human beings learn during all their waking hours, most of which are spent at home and not in school; moreover, each generation provides and affects the intellectual capital for the next generation to rise to higher educational achievements. Not only is the child's family or home environment important, but so is his culture, which is rooted in generations of environmental (and genetic) change; and previous geographic isolation. Significantly, the impact of schooling in context with culture is shown to be more important in science and foreign language than in other areas.[84] Since the Coleman and Jencks data are based on reading and mathematics scores in the United States, the suggestion that certain subjects might be more amenable to school influences (0.26) is taken as an encouraging sign for those who feel that schools make a difference and educators should be held accountable.

Of course, there are many limitations to such a large-scale study. For instance, there is the question of common content across countries. (All thirteen-year-olds have not had or are supposed to have had the same amount of schooling cross-nationally.) Translation of content may be accurate, but it is difficult to assure that the vocabulary and resulting speed passages are similar. There is the sheer magnitude of the data; and because of the size of the tested population, there are numerous variables possibly not accounted for which may have affected the scores. With all of these problems, still, the studies constitute probably the best models in existence for cross-national research on social institutions and social behavior. This fact should not be lost in the critique or criticism of these studies by secondary analysis.[85]

The revolutionary conclusions of the 1966 Coleman report, followed by the Jencks report six years later,[86] and the first IEA studies challenge the notion of the benefits of universal education and the concept of equal educational opportunity. The research of the mid-1960s and early 1970s shows that school reform has little effect on reducing social or economic inequality and differences in educational outcomes. Moreover, the notion of *culture*, touched on lightly by the IEA studies, is an interesting and thorny topic rarely mentioned in the literature. Culture, here, is being distinguished from environment in that it has a historical and geographical component. Culture is also divorced from social class—formed over generations and exhibited by general attitudes, motivations, and behaviors. It helps explain, for example, why Asian American students study so hard—to please mom and dad, and because of family honor. It suggests that a family's climb from low income to middle income may not be enough to affect a child's achievement scores. For example, there are significant achievement and test-score gaps between middle-class black and white students that cannot be fully explained by race or class. On a typical standardized test, the gap between blacks and whites is 75 percent, and the "gap shrinks only a little when black and white families have the same amount of schooling, the same income, and the same wealth."[87]

[81]Robert L. Thorndike, *Reading Comprehension Education in Fifteen Countries* (New York: John Wiley & Sons, 1973).

[82]James S. Coleman, "Methods and Results in the IEA Studies of Effects of School on Learning," *Review of Educational Research* (Summer 1975), pp. 335–386.

[83]L. C. Comber and J. P. Keeves, *Science Education in Nineteen Countries* (New York: John Wiley & Sons, 1973), p. 298.

[84]William E. Coffman and Lai-min P. Lee, "Cross-National Assessment of Educational Achievement: A Review," *Educational Researcher* (June 1974), pp. 13–16.

[85]Allan C. Ornstein, *Educational and Social Inquiry* (Itasca, IL: Peacock, 1978).

[86]Christopher Jencks et al., *Inequality: A Reassessment of the Effect of Family and Schooling in America* (New York: Basic Books, 1972); Jencks, *Who Gets Ahead?* (New York: Basic Books, 1979).

[87]Christopher Jencks and Meredith Phillips (eds.), *The Black-White Test Score Gap* (Washington, DC: Brookings Institution, 1998), p.2.

## Recent International Comparisons in Science and Math

What knowledge is of most worth? The demands of the information age and technology have brought increased demands for education standards and an emphasis on science and mathematics. Since the mid-1900s there has been a slight average increase in science and mathematics coursework among graduating high school students, ranging from 0.2 to 0.4 of one year (for example 2.5 to 2.9 years).[88] But the data are not impressive when comparisons are made with high school seniors in other advanced, technological countries. Japanese, South Korean, and Hong Kong high school students, for example, average 1¼ science courses per year and 1½ math courses per year, including calculus and statistics.[89]

One result is that Japanese, South Korean, and Hong Kong students consistently outperform American students on international tests in science and mathematics, and the gaps increase in the higher grades[90] in part because of the cumulative effects of more courses and more hours in science and math. In the last thirty years there have been three international mathematics and science studies (TIMSS) comparing industrialized countries in grades four, eight and twelve. The conclusion for all three studies is clear: The longer American students stay in school, the further they fall behind their counterparts in most industrialized nations. In the last TIMSS report, published between 1998 and 2001, U.S. fourth grade students in math ranked eighth out of eighteen among industrialized countries that participated, and in science tied for third place. In eighth grade, U.S. students ranked slightly below average in math (twenty-three out of thirty-eight industrialized countries) and slightly above average in science (below fourteen countries). By the twelfth grade, American students scored last in math among twenty industrialized countries, and

in science they scored below sixteen countries. While the international average math/science scores were 500, the U.S. average in math was 461 and in science 480.[91]

The picture worsens when education spending is compared on an international level. Among industrialized countries reporting education spending, the United States spends only 3.5 percent of its GDP on education, ranking eighth among twenty industrialized countries. But our expenditure per student is higher—second only to Switzerland.[92] In other words, other countries do not have same resources as we do, yet they make a greater effort by spending more of their GDP on education.

## Excuses and More Excuses

Among the common reasons or excuses given for the consistently low scores of American students are:

1. American twelfth-grade students average almost one year younger (18.0 compared to 18.7) than their international counterparts.[93]

2. Measuring the cumulative achievement on a short test may not sufficiently cover what students have learned. About 25 percent of the test items in math and science reflect topics not studied by American test takers.[94]

3. About 20 to 33 percent of American middle school and high school science and math teachers are teaching out of license; furthermore, nearly half of those certified to teach science and math teach

---

[88]Government sources conflict and depend on the precise date and volume of *The Condition of Education.*

[89]Kay M. Troost, "What Accounts for Japan's Success in Science Education," *Education Leadership* (December–January 1984), pp. 26–29; Herbert J. Walberg, "Improving School Science in Advanced and Developing Counties," *Review of Education Research* (Spring 1991), pp. 25–70. Also see *The Educational System in Japan* (Washington, DC: U.S. Government Printing Office, 1998); Marcia C. Linn et al., "Beyond Fourth-Grade Science: Why Do U.S. and Japanese Students Diverge?" *Educational Researcher* (April 2000), pp. 4–14.

[90]*The Condition of Education 2002* (Washington, DC: U.S. Government Printing Office, 2002), table 13.

[91]Gerald W. Bracey, "The TIMSS Final Year Study and Report," *Educational Research* (May 2000), pp. 4–10; E. Bronner, "U.S. 12th Grades Rank Poorly in Math and Science, Study Says," *New York Times,* 21 February 1998, p. A1; *Digest of Education Statistics* 1998 (Washington, DC: U.S. Government Printing Office, 1998), tables 404–406, pp. 462–464; TIMSS Video Mathematics Research Group, "Understanding and Improving Mathematics Teaching," *Phi Delta Kappan* (June 2003): 768–775; and Arthur Eisenkraft, "Rating Science and Math," *Education Week,* 14 February 2001, pp. 46, 48.

[92]*The Condition of Education 2004* (Washington, DC: U.S. Government Printing Office, 2004), table 36, p. 180; *Education at a Glance* (Paris: Organization for Economic Cooperation and Development, 2003), table B2, p. 1b.

[93]Bracey, "The TIMSS Final Year Study and Report."

[94]Ibid; Jianjun Wang, "TIMSS Primary and Middle School Data: Some Technical Concerns," *Educational Researcher* (August-September 2001): 17–21.

subjects they are not qualified to teach.[95] For example, a science teacher may not be qualified to teach physics (only biology and chemistry) and a math teacher may not be qualified to teach calculus (only algebra and geometry).

4. American science and math textbooks are numerous—some above average, some average, some below average in quality—whereas textbooks in other countries are approved by the ministry of education so there is consistency of coverage. Our textbooks emphasize *breadth* of topics, to please a wide audience (15,000 different school districts) as the expense of *depth* of topics. As a result, American textbooks (and teachers who rely on these textbooks) foster superficial learning of a large body of information, while teachers of countries with a ministry have more time to teach students to think about procedures, to help students frame hypotheses, make predictions, and acquire skills to conduct experiments and contrast ideas and findings.[96]

5. American students have less homework (23 percent of eleventh graders report no assigned homework, 14 percent do not do their homework, and 26 percent do less than one hour per day of homework), and engage in more social activities, out-of-school activities, and part-time jobs than their international counterparts.[97]

6. American students average 3.5 hours per day of TV viewing, not to mention Internet surfing, and we know there is an inverse relationship between TV viewing and student achievement, especially after the second or third grade. (The positive effects of watching *Sesame Street* and other language skill programs become increasingly irrelevant after age seven or eight.)[98]

7. European and Asian students have a longer school day and school year, with European countries averaging 200 days and Asian countries averaging 220 days, compared to the United States which has about a 180-day school calendar.[99]

8. Student poverty among American students is the highest, about 21 to 25 percent. It is nearly 50 percent higher than in any other industrialized country; next is Australia with 14 percent and Canada with 13.5 percent.[100] Moreover, we know poverty clearly correlates in an inverse relationship with student achievement. In addition, the United States has among the highest or highest student drug addiction, student violence, gang activity and teenage pregnancy among industrialized nations.

9. Finally, the breakdown of the American family is well documented. More than 50 percent of American students live with a single head of household; it approaches 75 percent in our big cities, where student achievement is the lowest compared in other parts of the country.[101]

10. It should not be assumed that the students taking the test in all countries are drawn from an estimated normal bell curve or ability distribution. Some countries—such as China, Japan, and Russia—may have certain political agendas, or sensitivity about "saving face," and be more selective in determining which students will take the test. Moreover, if you eliminate black and Hispanic students from the test pool, American white students compare favorably with European nations and Asian American students compare favorably with

[95]Richard M. Ingersoll, "The Problem of Underqualified Teachers in American Secondary Schools," *Educational Researcher* (March 1999): 26–37; Stephen J. Friedman, "How Much of a Problem: A Reply to Ingersoll, 'The Problem of Underqualified Teachers,'" *Educational Researcher* (June-July 2000): 18–24.

[96]Eisenkraft, "Rating Science and Math"; Sandra H. Fradd and Okhee Lee, "Teachers' Roles in Promoting Science Inquiry," *Educational Researcher* (August-September 1999): 14–20; William Hook, "A World-Class K–7 Math Curriculum," Paper presented for the California State Department of Education, 2004; and Linn, "Beyond Fourth Grade Science."

[97]*The Condition of Education 1998*, table 37, p. 118; *Outcomes of Learning: Results from 2000 Program for International Student Assessment in Reading, Mathematics and Science Literacy* (Washington, DC: U.S. Government Printing Office, 2002).

[98]Allan C. Ornstein and Thomas J. Lasley, *Strategies for Effective Teaching*, 4th ed. (Boston: McGraw-Hill, 2004).

[99]Ibid.

[100]*The Condition of Education 2003* (Washington, DC: U.S. Government Printing Office, 2003), Appendix, p. 13; Kevin J. Payne and Bruce J. Biddle, "Poor School Funding, Child Poverty, and Mathematics," *Educational Researcher*, 28 (1999): 4–13.

[101]Allan C. Ornstein and Daniel U. Levine, *Foundations of Education*, 9th ed. (Boston: Houghton Mifflin, 2006); William J. Wilson, et al. *The Roots of Racial Tension* (New York: Knopf, 2003).

Asian nations which score the highest in math and science.[102]

Although all of these reasons help explain the low scores in math and science achievement among American students on international tests, part of the problem lies in the limited amount of course work in these twin subjects areas. By way of example, if you want to learn how to drive a car, play tennis or chess, or read, you need to devote time to the endeavor—the more *instructional time*, the more proficient you should become. Thus, if Americans are concerned about math and science (and we should because of the information-technology age we live in), then we need to modify the general curriculum and instructional time to allow for proficiency in these subjects. This consideration must be weighed against a belief among many educators that schools need to emphasize the whole child and the liberal arts, and that teachers should be paid on the basis of qualifications and experience (with no differential for specific subjects such as math or science). Based on supply and demand, as well as the needs of the nation, free marketers would support higher pay for math and science teachers. In fact, with most school districts focusing on reading and literacy achievement, there is concern among policymakers that science is getting shortchanged in the elementary and junior high schools.

Similarly, classroom size, or instructional ratios of a group, contributes to students' learning capacity and, ultimately, American competitiveness in the international arena. Obviously, one-to-one learning (a coach and student) is more effective than a five-to-one ratio of students to teacher; and this small group is more beneficial than a class of twenty-five or thirty students. Potential and limitations are driven by money and social policy. Also, inequality, as caused by social class differences, cannot be ignored because it contributes to attitudes and behaviors that affect students' ability or willingness to learn.

About the only realistic thing schools can do in the midst of the high-stake tests priority is to redesign the curriculum to coincide with the tests that policymakers determine are important. This has resulted in many schools across the country, especially low-income schools whose students test below grade level, emphasizing reading and math at the expense of all other subjects. Some of the lowest-performing schools have gone

so far as to ban students from taking anything except reading and math. This assures conservative educators that schools are focusing on required basic skills and seriously responding to the No Child Left Behind Law.[103]

Most of the workforce problems are reflected in our minority and immigrant populations. Hispanics scored 75 points lower than whites, and blacks scored 63 points lower. Native-born whites and Asian Americans were tied for second place in the international ranking in literacy. Immigrants account for 40 percent of the U.S. labor force, but they rank 74 points behind native-born Americans.[104] In short, American productivity is partially based on the GI Bill and pre-1950 immigrants who (90 percent) were largely from Europe and more skilled than today's immigrants, who hail from non-European and Third World countries. Soon these workers will be retiring and replaced by a less literate workforce.

### Learning and Earning: 1990s and 2000+

Throughout the 1980s and 1990s, a debate focused on whether schooling improved cognitive test scores and whether these outcomes affected economic earnings. Schooling explained only a modest amount of the variations related to academic achievement, highlighted by Jerome Coleman; and academic achievement explained a modest amount of the variation related to wages, highlighted by Christopher Jencks. Although employers value what students learn in school and are willing to pay for it, they also value other skills.

Most of the variation in economic outcomes can be attributed to noncognitive factors such as physical characteristics, personality, motivation, reliability, honesty, and creativity. Since social scientists have spent little effort analyzing these characteristics, the cognitive factors remain masked (by noncognitive factors) and for the time being appear to be less than what educators would like to hear.

The negligible impact of schooling was bolstered in the 1980s and 1990s by Erik Hanushek's review of the research, which confirmed—like the Coleman and Jencks reports—that schools have no measurable effect

---

[102]Deborah I. Nelson, "What Explains Differences in International Performance," *CPRE Policy Briefs* (September 2003): 1–4; Wang, "TIMSS Primary and Middle School Data."

[103]See Sam Dillon, "Schools Cut Back Subjects to Push Reading and Math," *New York Times*, 26 March, 2006, p. 1.

[104]Aaron Bernstein, "The Time Bomb in the Work Force: Illiteracy," *Business Week*, 25 February 2002, p. 122. The 17 industrialized countries were from Western Europe, plus Canada, and Australia. Test data is reported in a study, conducted between 1994 and 1998, by the Educational Testing Service.

on students' test scores or future earnings, and there is no strong relationship between school spending and student performance.[105] Where research did show that school characteristics or school spending had positive effects, the relationship was small or shown to be contaminated by (1) methodological assumptions, (2) weighting procedures of school characteristics, and (3) unlike comparisons across schools, school districts, or states.[106] Despite these flaws in the research, student expenditures, smaller classrooms, and teacher experience (not salaries or education) demonstrated the most consistent effects. Nonetheless, other studies showed contradictory or inconsistent results among these factors.[107]

The 1990s also revived the argument of hereditary, with Herrnstein and Murray's 1994 publication of *The Bell Curve*, which claimed that cognitive tests that predict life chances and economic earnings were measuring a collection of stable abilities. Psychologists, since Charles Spearman's research in 1904 often called this ability set *g*, for general intelligence.[108] The most important characteristic of *g* is the general ability to learn new skills and knowledge quickly and easily—exactly the type of "human capital" that employers seek and reward. It

just so happens that "smart" people with a high *g* factor tend to go to school longer and get higher grades; it is not the amount of schooling or high test scores that are primarily associated with future earnings, but the *g* factor which leads to more schooling and better test scores. The *Bell Curve* authors argued that this trait was biological or genetic, not environmentally based.

## NAEP/State Standards and Test Scores

Thousands of publications exist showing relationships between social class and achievement and race/ethnicity and achievement. Since 1990, the National Assessment of Educational Progress (NAEP), known as the nation's "Report Card," has reported fourth-, eighth-, and twelfth-grade performance scores in reading and math, as well as other subject areas. It is considered perhaps the most comprehensive and reliable set of data, although some critics have questioned the instructional validity of the test items. Consistently, over the last fifteen years, lower-class students (eligible for free or reduced-priced lunch) and minority students (blacks and Hispanics) perform three to four grade levels below their middle-class and white counterparts by grade eight and this continues in grade twelve despite all the remediation, tutoring, and compensatory programs that have been introduced.[109]

In 2003, the average *reading* NAEP score at grade four was 218. For black students it was 198, for Hispanic students 200, and for white students 229. By grade eight the reading gap had increased. The average reading score was 263. For black students it was 244, Hispanic students 245, and white students 272. Using class as an indicator: in grade four, in schools where 76 to 100 percent of the students were eligible for free or reduced-price lunch, the average score was 194, compared to schools where 0 to 10 percent of the students participated in the lunch program, the average score was 238. By grade eight the scores were 239 for the low-income students and 280 for the middle- and upper-middle class students.[110]

In *math*, the average NAEP gap in scores were similar by race and class. For example, at grade four, white students scored 27 points higher than blacks and 21

[105] Eric A. Hanushek, "The Economics of Schooling." *Journal of Economic Literature*, 2 (1986): 1141–1176; Hanushek, "The Impact of Differential Expenditures on School Performance," *Educational Researcher* (May 1989): 45–51; and Hanushek, *Making Schools Work* (Washington, DC: Brookings Institute, 1994).

[106] Ronald F. Ferguson, "Teachers' Perceptions and Expectations and the Black-White Score Gap," in C. Jencks and M. Phillips (eds.), *The Black White Score Gap* (Washington, DC: Brookings Institute, 1998); Helen F. Ladd (ed.), *Holding Schools Accountable* (Washington DC: Brookings Institute, 1996); and Larry Hedges, Richard D. Laine, and Rob Greenwald, "Does Money Matter: Meta-Analysis of . . . School Inputs on Student Outcomes," *Educational Researcher* (April 1994): 5–14.

[107] Gary Burtless (ed.), *Does Money Matter? The Effect of School Resources on Student Achievement and Advent Success* (Washington, DC: Brookings Institute, 1996); Eric A. Hanushek, "Assessing the Empirical Evidence on Class Size Reductions from Tennessee and Non-experimental Research," *Education Evolution and Policy Analysis* (Summer 1999): 123–144; and Helen F. Ladd (ed.), *Holding Schools Accountable: Performance-Based Reform in Education* (Washington, DC: Brookings Institution, 1996).

[108] Richard J. Herrnstein and Charles Murray, *The Bell Curve: Intelligence and Class Structures in American Life* (New York: Free Press, 1994). Also see Charles E. Spearman, "General Intelligence Objectivity Determined and Measured," *American Journal of Psychology* (April 1904): 201–293.

[109] There was minimal reduction in the achievement gap between 1996 and 2000, which then leveled off between 2001 and 2004.

[110] *The Condition of Education 2004* (Washington, DC: U.S. Government Printing Office, 2004), table 9–2, p. 120.

**Table 14–2**    **Percent of Eighth Grade Reading and Math Scores of States at or Above Proficient, 2003**

| | NAEP | | State Test | | Difference Total |
| | Reading | Math | Reading | Math | Reading + Math |
|---|---|---|---|---|---|
| Tennessee | 26 | 21 | 80 | 79 | 54 + 58 = 112 |
| Texas | 26 | 25 | 88 | 72 | 62 + 47 = 109 |
| N. Carolina | 29 | 32 | 86 | 82 | 57 + 50 = 107 |
| W. Virginia | 25 | 20 | 80 | 69 | 55 + 49 = 104 |
| Oklahoma | 30 | 20 | 79 | 73 | 49 + 53 = 102 |
| Georgia | 26 | 22 | 81 | 67 | 55 + 45 = 100 |
| Ohio | 34 | 30 | 87 | 71 | 53 + 41 = 94 |
| Wisconsin | 37 | 35 | 84 | 76 | 47 + 41 = 88 |
| Colorado | 36 | 34 | 86 | 68 | 50 + 34 = 84 |
| Connecticut | 37 | 35 | 77 | 77 | 40 + 42 = 82 |

Source: Adapted from "Quality Counts 2005: No Small Change," *Education Week*, 6 January 2005: 1–5.

points higher than Hispanics. By grade eight, the white-black math gap was 36 points and white-Hispanic math gap was 29 points. In terms of class, in grade four the math gap between lower-class students and middle-class students was 34 points, and by grade eight it was 49 points.[111] In short, the NAEP achievement gap between minority and white students and between lower- and middle-class students increased by grade level, as originally pointed out in the Coleman Report in 1966.

Under the No Child Left Behind Act (NCLB), fourth-grade and eighth-grade students in every state are required to participate in NAEP reading and math tests every other year, in part to verify state assessments. Such comparisons on state and national tests have never been possible or required before. The test content and benchmarks for passing vary dramatically by state, resulting in a variable definition of "proficiency." For example, in 2003, the highest proficiency rates were reported in Colorado and Mississippi: 87 percent of fourth graders passed their exams. But the Colorado proficiency rate fell a dramatic 50 points to 37 percent on the NAEP, and Mississippi fell 69 points to 18 percent, placing last among all the states. The comparisons were similar among fourth graders in math. Colorado showed a proficiency level of 86 percent, whereas the NAEP revealed it to be 34 percent—a 52-point difference. In Mississippi, 74 percent scored at or above proficient, but on the NAEP the score was 17 percent—a difference of 57

points. The same pattern existed at the eighth-grade level. Table 14–2 reports ten states with the greatest NAEP difference in scores of proficiency in reading and math at the eighth grade. All these states, in short, are misrepresenting their results and thus evading the real issues of student achievement and education reform.

According to NCLB, all students are required to reach proficiency on state reading and math tests by 2014. States are judged on yearly progress and penalized, including the loss of federal funds, if proficiency levels decline. Yet states continue to use their own definition of proficiency. Those "states that have the bar lower will have an easier time meeting the mark and avoiding federal sanctions,"[112] but it can be expected that eventually state officials and education policy makers will address these different standards.

In 2003 no state performed better on the NAEP in fourth-grade reading than on the state's own exam, and only two did better at the eighth-grade level (Vermont, 3 percent difference; Missouri, 2 percent). Two states scored better on the NAEP fourth-grade math test than on their own state exams (Vermont, 2 percent; Massachusetts, 1 percent) and three states did better on the NAEP eighth-grade math test (Massachusetts by 1 percent, South Carolina by 7, and Missouri by 14).

More than three-fourths of the states require state proficiency tests to determine whether students will

---

[111]Ibid, table 11–2, p. 128.

[112]Susan Saulny, "State to State, Varied Ideas of 'Proficient,'" *New York Times*, 19 January 2005, p. B8.

pass to the next grade or graduate from high school.[113] Minority students and low-income students fail these tests at rates of 50 to 90 percent, depending on the state and year. In Louisiana, for example, nearly 50 percent of the poor and minority students failed the state tests, even after taking them a second time. In Georgia, two-thirds of low-income students failed the math and reading sections of the state competency tests. Almost half the students of Ohio from families with incomes below $20,000 failed the state exams, while 80 percent of students from families earning more than $30,000 passed.[114]

In Minnesota, the overall mean difference between lunch and non-lunch program students was 6.9 raw points in the third grade, equivalent to more than one grade level. By the fifth grade the achievement gap by income was nearly two grade levels apart.[115] After matching pre- and posttest scores, it was rare to find any member of the disadvantaged group who made equal progress from grade three to five, never mind more progress; so the trend repeated itself for more than 95 percent of the students. The only low-income group to keep up with their more-advantaged group peers were the Asian disadvantaged, as their limited English proficiency declined.

The Minnesota assessment program consisted of 47,300 students, and the size of the sample suggested minimal statistical error. The data implies that once the achievement gap begins, it worsens over time. Students do not make up lost ground. Moreover, longitudinal data from the NAEP show similar gaps increasing in reading, math, and other subject areas from grade four, the earliest grade for which the tests are given. "Once [NAEP] achievement gaps between students group emerge, they tend to persist over time."[116] The groups most effected by declining achievement test scores are racial, ethnic, and low socio-economic groups.[117] Whether the problem results from poverty, or inadequacies of students and their families, or teachers, or underlying racism, the solution is to prevent the gaps from emerging in the first place by focusing on infant and preschool education, and family conditions. But as critics point out, early childhood programs are diffuse, uncoordinated, and underfunded[118], and family differences and issues lead to controversial and heated debates and politically complicated solutions.

In general, student achievement has remained flat based on the results of the NAEP tests in reading, math, and science for minority (black and Hispanic) students. Of the fifty states, the majority received a D, that is, minimal or limited progress, on the 2005 annual report card for closing achievement gaps between black and Hispanic students and their white and Asian counterparts.[119] The results, published by Fordham Foundation, a conservative education think tank, advised that progress has been negligible since the 1983 release of *A Nation at Risk*, which warned of the "rising tide of mediocrity" in American schools and the inability of the U.S. to economically compete on a global basis because of its workforce. The same trend has held true since 2002, when NCLB went into effect, despite government insistence that by 2014 the performance of white and minority students must be indistinguishable. In 2002, for example, 13 percent of the nation's black eighth-grade students were proficient in reading. By 2005 (the latest available data) the figure had dropped to 12 percent. In other words, the performance of black students had slightly declined.

The report contradicts the rhetoric of reform among education leaders. State educators and school superintendents reject the report as unusually "harsh" and not reflecting the problems encountered by the schools in educating low-income and minority students. Family background remains a reliable predictor of student performance. According to recent research, a public school

[113]Martin Carnoy and Susanna Loeb, "Does External Accountability Affect Student Outcomes?" *Educational Evaluation and Policy Analysis* (Winter 2002), pp. 305–332.

[114]Jay Heubert, "First, Do No Harm," *Educational Leadership* (January 2003): 26–30; David Sadker and Karen Zittleman, "Test Anxiety: Are Students Failing Tests—Or Are Tests Failing Students?" *Phi Delta Kappan* (June 2004): 740–744, 751.

[115]Mark L. Davidson et al., "When Do Children Fall Behind?" *Phi Delta Kappan* (June 2004): 752–761.

[116]Mano Singham, "The Achievement Gap: Myths and Reality," *Phi Delta Kappan* (April, 2003): 586.

[117]Davidson, "When Do Children Fall Behind?"; Ruth S. Johnson, *Using Data to Close the Achievement Gap* (Thousand Oaks, CA: Corwin Press, 2002).

[118]Gerald Bracey and Arthur Stellar, "Long-Term Studies of Preschool: Lasting Benefits Far Outweigh Costs," *Phi Delta Kappan* (June 2003): 780–783, 797.

[119]*Quality Counts* (Washington, DC: Thomas B. Fordham, 2006). Also see Linda Jacobson, "States Get Poor Grades on Closing Achievement Gaps," *Education Week*, 8 November 2006, pp. 18–19.

that enrolls middle-class white children has a 25 percent (or 1 in 4) chance of earning high test scores on the NAEP two years in a row, whereas a school with mostly poor minority children has a 0.33 percent (or 1 in 300) chance.[120]

## Race and Class

Explanations for the achievement gap run the gamut from differences in family and health conditions, to teacher expectations and experience, to school spending and changing student exclusion rates, to television viewing and "hip-hop" culture. Research by Paul Barton of the Educational Testing Service summarizes fourteen factors related to home and school conditions and student achievement for low-income and minority students for which they are disadvantaged. Home conditions include (1) low birth weights, (2) exposure to lead poisoning found in old houses, (3) hunger and malnutrition, (4) parents or adults who rarely read to young children, (5) watching lots of television, (6) significant percentages of one-family households (2.5 times higher among black children compared to white children), (7) high student mobility rates, (8) and minimal parent participation in school matters. School conditions include (9) easier courses, (10) teachers with fewer years of experience and larger absentee rates, (11) teachers with less preparation and more of them out of license, (12) fewer computers available in school and less Internet use at home, (13) larger class sizes, and (14) more unsafe schools.[121]

There was no mention in the report about school spending as a factor. The data about it are consistent, however. In wealthy states, average school spending between big-city school districts and nearby affluent suburbs runs 2 to 2.5 times as high, say, $10,000 versus $20,000 per student. Over a twelve-year period, the impact of $120,000 per student is substantial. Furthermore, the student poverty index in the majority of big-city school systems run 25 percent or more, and in ten big cities it runs 40 to 50 percent, with Atlanta (51 percent) and Detroit (48 percent) having the highest poverty rates.[122] Clearly, poor and minority students have more

social, psychological, and educational problems than do affluent students, and therefore need more money (not less) to attempt to diminish achievement disparities. A conservative interpretation is that money and whatever the school attempts are not the main contributing factors—a reaffirmation of Coleman and Jencks. Once students begin to fall behind most will never catch up, which is the reason why the achievement gap has persisted so long.[123] This fact is unacceptable to liberal and minority reformers, and is considered a form of class and race bias.

For the nation as a whole, the disparity in school performance tied to race and class has become a major issue because of the social and economic implications of the continuous failure of schools to prepare tens of millions of children for the technological and information age, and to compete in the global economy. The inability of schools to close the achievement gap has led business and parent groups to lose faith in public schools, to insist on higher standards and more testing as an overall "solution" to the problem, and to insist on a variety of school alternatives. The concern is further heightened upon recognition that black and Hispanic students accounted for about one-third of the 54 million children in the nation's public schools in 2000 and are expected to increase to two-thirds by 2015.[124]

## Another Option

There are no agreed-upon solutions to the education crisis afflicting U.S. society. After forty-five years of compensatory funding and some $20 billion invested, the results are at best mixed; the programs and money spent have not had much impact on the achievement gap between low-income students and middle-income students and minority and white students. In order to neutralize the skepticism of the education establishment, reformers have developed a literature on *more effective schools* which purports that inner-city schools can successfully educate poor and minority students.

Advocates of this approach pay attention to schools as institutions (focusing on preschool and elementary

[120]Paul Tough, "Can Teaching Poor Children to Act More Like Middle-Class Children Help Close the Education Gap?" *New York Times Magazine,* 26 November 2006, pp. 44–51, ff.

[121]Paul E. Barton, *Passing the Achievement Gap* (Princeton, NJ: Educational Testing Service, 2003).

[122]*Digest of Education Statistics 2003* (Washington, DC: U.S. Government Printing Office, 2004), table 91, pp. 124–125.

[123]Davidson, "When Do Children Fall Behind?" Julian Weissglass, "Racism and the Achievement Gap," *Education Week,* 8 August 2001, p. 8.

[124]Robert C. Johnston and Debra Viadero, "Unmet Promises: Raising Minority Achievement," *Education Week,* 5 March 2000, p. 19; *The Condition of Education,* 2004, table 4–1, p. 112.

schools), the environment in which they operate, and usually define success in terms of student achievement. This emphasis corresponds with environmental research data indicating that intervention is most critical in the early stages of human development, which is the most rapid period of cognitive growth (50 percent by age four, another 25 percent by age nine, according to Ben Bloom).[125]

Given the public concern for young children, and the fact that Americans have sufficient wealth as a nation to meet the education and special needs of all young children, it is surprising that we lack a national and sustainable program that supports a public investment in infant and toddler education. The research is consistent about the value of early childhood education for children who are "at risk" and coincides with the developmental theories of Jean Piaget and Ben Bloom. In several European countries, there has been a trend toward nationalization of education services for all children from as early as eighteen months in Sweden, two years in Belgium, and three years in Italy.[126] To date, most federal and state initiatives in the United States focus on Head Start education for children four to five years old. However, only 36 percent of eligible children receive Head Start services,[127] which borders on a national embarrassment.

The industrialized countries of Europe, Australia, and New Zealand spend on average 0.5 percent of their GNP on education for early childhood.[128] Given the education benefits (exemplified by a longitudal preschool study through age 27 by David Weikart of the University of Michigan, the early childhood education studies in Europe, and the benefits to working mothers and ultimate savings to society),[129] it would seem to our advantage to expand prekindergarten education in the United States downward to age three; to upgrade training in personnel and provide for certification; to ensure a consensus on philosophy and pedagogy; to monitor the participation of parents and staff; and to pay sufficient wages to attract qualified personnel and reduce turnover. This combination could counteract the negative influence of a deprived environment and family discord.

As of 2000, about 2.6 million U.S. infants and toddlers were in some form of child care full time, or thirty-five hours a week, distributed among child-care centers (39 percent), relatives (27 percent), neighbors (27 percent), and nannies or babysitters (7 percent).[130] The Dependent Care Assistance Program allows families to deduct up to $5,000 per year for child-care expenses for children age fourteen and under. But again, who benefits? Certainly not the poor, who rely on relatives and neighbors to provide care.

Because a child's early years are so formative, it would be wise for the United States to commit to the care and education of its young and to make those compulsory, especially for "at risk" and poor children, in order to prepare or catch them up to grade level by the time they enter school. A few states, such as Massachusetts, Vermont, and West Virginia, do provide comprehensive programs for infants and toddlers, and the federal government in 2000 provided $3.5 billion in block grants to states for providing child-care services to assist working women with children (73 percent of women between ages twenty-five and thirty-four are in the workforce).[131] The outcomes of this, however, are piecemeal and inadequate. More like $12 billion is needed—twice the appropriations for Head Start—to ensure that all our nation's poor or at-risk children receive appropriate services and education.

School nutrition programs; extended day, weekend, and required preschool programs; required summer school for primary students (grades one through three) to neutralize cognitive deficits as opposed to allowing them to increase; reading and tutoring programs; parenting education; and reducing class and school

---

[125] Benjamin S. Bloom, *Stability and Change in Human Characters* (New York: Wiley, 1964).

[126] Michelle J. Neuman and John Bennett, "Starting Strong: Policy Implications for Early Childhood Education and Care in the U.S.," *Phi Delta Kappan* (November 2001): 246–254.

[127] Pauline B. Gough, "The Best Place to Start," *Phi Delta Kappan* (November 2001): 182.

[128] *A Caring World: The New Social Policy Agenda* (Paris: OECD, 1999); *Starting Strong: Early Childhood Education and Care* (Paris: OCED, 2001).

[129] Ibid. Also see David Weikart, *Significant Benefits: The High/Scope Perry Preschool Study Through Age 27* (Ypsilanti, MI: High/Scope Press, 1993).

[130] "Nearly 5 million Infants and Toddlers in Child Care," *New Federalism* (June 2001): 2.

[131] Sharon L. Kagan and Lynda G. Hallmark, "Early Care and Education Policies in Sweden: Implications for the United States," *Phi Delta Kappan* (November 2001): 237–245, 254; Sally Lubeck, "Early Childhood Education and Care in Cross National Perspective," *Phi Delta Kappan* (November 2001): 213–215; and *Starting Strong: Early Childhood Education and Care.*

## PRO/CON Debate

### Teacher Accountability

Parents and communities want what is best for children, and for many, high scholastic performance is the goal. In some communities, when the goal is not reached, school board members and/or administrators are replaced. But teachers have tenure and are exempt from such actions.

**Question:** Should teachers be accountable for high student performance?

**Arguments PRO**

1. It is important to relate dollars spent to student accomplishment, since 65 to 70 percent of the school budget is related to teacher/administrative salaries. Holding educational professionals accountable is wise policy, especially if we wish to focus on results. Failure to hold teachers accountable; lets them off the hook.

2. The heart of the educational system is the classroom. It is here that teaching occurs and learning results. If anyone should be accountable for scholastic achievement, it should be the teacher.

3. Stringent teacher accountability would ensure that marginal teachers do not remain in the classroom. Why do we pay high salaries to teachers who can't get the job done?

4. All professionals are accountable for performing their work well. If teaching is a profession, then once standards have been identified, it is the responsibility of teachers to meet them.

**Arguments CON**

1. Many variables impact on student accomplishment. Student achievement is a joint responsibility among students, parents, teachers, administrators, board members, and taxpayers (or the community). The idea of holding teachers and administrators accountable, without considering family and student responsibility, is highly political and unwise.

2. The teacher works with many children, each of whom has different talents, different potential, and a different home life. It would be unfair to expect teachers to meet high standards when the raw material is so variable and complex.

3. If teachers are likely to be fired when students do not perform well, then teachers will concentrate on teaching to the tests that measure student performance. Our tests are not reliable enough to make or break careers.

4. As a rule, professionals see the immediate results of their work. Doctors know if an operation is successful. Lawyers know if the case is won. Engineers see bridges built. The results of teaching are not evident in the short term: The truly educated person takes years to evolve.

size—all are crucial.[132] The instruction recommended is prescriptive and diagnostic, emphasizing basic skill

acquisition, review and guided practice, monitoring of student programs, prompt feedback and reinforcement to students, and mastery-learning opportunities. These actions point to a behaviorist, direct, convergent, systematic, and low cognitive level of instruction, as opposed to a problem-solving, abstract, divergent, inquiry-based, and high level of instruction. (Some critics would argue that this type of instruction is second rate and reflects our low expectations of low-achieving students. Perhaps. But the critics have had their opportunities and failed to close the achievement gap.) Plato may have been right: The state needs to intervene, if not to nationalize education then to provide the resources needed to educate children starting at a very young age.

[132]Lorin Anderson and Leonard O. Pellicer, "Synthesis of Research on Compensatory and Remedial Education," *Educational Leadership* (September 1990): 10–16; Allan C. Ornstein and Daniel U. Levine, "School Effectiveness and Reform: Guidelines for Action," *Clearing House* (November-December 1990): 115–118; and William C. Symonds, "How to Fix America's Schools," *Business Week,* 19 March 2001, pp. 68–80. Also see Ronald Kotulak, "Teaching Them Early," *Chicago Tribune,* 3 June 2001, pp. 1, 9. Georgia was the first state to require pre-K programs for all four-year-olds in the state. We recommend starting toddler programs at age three.

## Summary

1. Research on teacher behavior has looked at teacher styles, teacher-student interactions, teacher characteristics, teacher effects, and teacher contexts.

2. Although much remains to be learned about successful teaching, research has identified some teacher behaviors that seem to be effective and influence student performance.

3. Recent research on effective teaching has shifted from the process of teaching to the products of teaching and, most recently the context of teaching.

4. The classic, important research on teaching prior to the 1970s was the work of A. S. Barr, Arno Bellack, Ned Flanders, and David Ryans. These researchers focused on teacher styles, teacher-student interactions, and teacher characteristics—that is, the process, what was happening in the classroom or the behavior of the teacher.

5. In the 1970s and 1980s, the research on teaching was based on the work of Jere Brophy, Walter Doyle, Carolyn Evertson, N. L. Gage, Thomas Good, and Barak Rosenshine. Their research focused on teacher effectiveness and on the products or results of teaching.

6. Since the 1990s, two trends influenced research on teaching. One was the nature of expertise in teaching, and how expert and novice teachers differ in approach and in seeing and analyzing classroom events. The other promoted different forms of investigating teaching, based on language and dialogue: metaphors, stories, biographies, autobiographies, expert opinions, and voice. All these methods dismiss traditional qualitative methods of examining teacher behavior.

7. The need for humanistic teachers is highlighted in context with the history of effective teaching for the new century.

8. Evaluation of teachers is becoming increasingly linked to student test outcomes, at the expense of humanistic, inquiry-based, and creative instruction.

9. Data analysis shows that U.S. students are consistently outperformed by their foreign counterparts on international tests of science and mathematics, and older U.S. students fall further behind foreign students. Several reasons for this achievement gap are discussed.

10. Data analysis also shows that U.S. students consistently score higher on state reading and mathematic tests than on national tests, indicating that the states are dumbing down their tests in order to appease the public by making it appear that the local schools are doing an adequate job.

## Key Terms

teacher processes
teacher products
teacher contexts
humanistic teaching
teacher style
teacher-student interaction
teaching cycles
nonverbal communication
self-fulfilling prophecies
teacher characteristics
master teacher
metaphors
stories
biography
autobiography
expert teacher
novice teachers
voice
humanistic education
human capital
National Assessment of Educational Progress (NAEP)
Nation's "Report Card"

## Discussion Questions

1. How would you use the Flanders interaction analysis scale to provide feedback for a beginning teacher?

2. What teacher characteristics and competencies described in this chapter seem important for effective teaching in your school district? Why?

3. What behaviors listed by Gage, Good and Brophy, and Evertson coincide with the ideal teacher behavior in your school district?

4. To what extent does your school district provide peer coaching and technical coaching for teachers? Which do you prefer? Why?

5. How do you personally expect to use videos, computers, and the Internet with your teaching practice? Explain.

## Suggested Readings

Darling-Hammond, Linda, Arthur E. Wise, and Stephen P. Klein. *A License to Teach* (San Francisco: Jossey-Bass, 1999). The authors discuss how to improve teacher education and staff development.

Freire, Paulo. *Pedagogy of the Oppressed,* rev ed. (New York: Continuum, 2005). A radical interpretation of teaching and learning.

Glatthorn, Allan A. *The Principal as Curriculum Leader,* 2nd ed. (Thousand Oaks, CA: Corwin Press, 2000). The author explains how the principal should work with teachers and provide leadership for schools.

Good, Thomas L., and Jere E. Brophy. *Looking into Classrooms,* 9th ed. (Boston: Allyn and Bacon, 2003). This important book helped move the field from the study of teacher processes to teacher products and presents a convincing argument that teachers do make a difference.

Goodlad, John I. *Teachers for Our Nation's Schools* (San Francisco: Jossey-Bass, 1994). As many as twenty-nine teacher training institutions are examined and nineteen postulates are set forth for reforming teacher education.

Ornstein, Allan C. *Teaching: Theory into Practice* (Needham Heights, MA: Allyn and Bacon, 1995). The author discusses the thoughts and behaviors of teachers, as well as the social and political contexts of teaching.

Popham, W. James. *America's Failing Schools* (New York: Routledge-Falmer, 2004). The book examines the implications of teaching toward standardized tests, particularly *No Child Left Behind.*

# 15. Human Resources Administration

FOCUSING QUESTIONS

1 How does the personnel function support the overall strategy of an organization?

2 What are the steps in personnel planning?

3 How do organizations go about recruiting personnel?

4 What is the process used in selecting personnel?

5 Why are professional development programs needed? What are the most commonly used professional development methods?

6 Why is performance appraisal important? How can employee performance be measured and improved?

7 What are the forms of intrinsic and extrinsic compensation, and how are they used to motivate and reward personnel?

8 What is the impact of union demands on the day-to-day operation of schools? How is a collective bargaining agreement negotiated and administered? Is there a new unionism emerging in the schools?

In this chapter, we attempt to answer these questions concerning human resource management in school organizations. We begin our discussion with an overview of the personnel process. Then we look at recruiting, selecting, and professional development of personnel. Performance appraisal and compensation are discussed next, and last we explore union-management relations, including the negotiation and administration of the collective bargaining agreement, and new thinking concerning union-management relations.

## The Human Resource Management Process

The human resource management process comprises six programs: human resource planning, recruitment, selection, professional development, performance appraisal, and compensation.[1] Figure 15–1 outlines the personnel management steps, which are affected by legislative constraints and union demands.

1. *Human Resource Planning.* Good **human resource planning** involves meeting current and future personnel needs. The school administrator ensures that personnel needs are

---

[1]L. Dean Webb and M. Scott Norton, *Human Resources Administration: Personnel Issues and Needs in Education,* 5th ed. (Upper Saddle River, NJ: Prentice Hall, 2007).

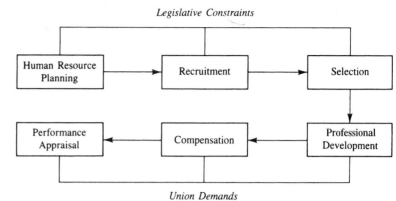

**Figure 15–1**

The Human Resource
Management Process

met through ongoing analysis of performance objectives, job requirements, and available personnel, coupled with a knowledge of employment laws.

2. *Recruitment.* Once personnel needs have been identified, **recruitment** involves locating qualified applicants to satisfy the organization's personnel plans.

3. *Selection.* After carefully evaluating applicants in the recruiting pool, the organization makes a **selection** of candidates who meet the job requirements.

4. *Professional Development.* **Professional development** involves improving employees' present skills and preparing them for additional responsibilities or advancement in the organization.

5. *Performance Appraisal.* **Performance appraisal** involves rating personnel performance in relationship to the organization's standards and goals. This step involves rewarding personnel, providing feedback, and maintaining communications between administrators and subordinates.

6. *Compensation.* **Compensation** involves decisions concerning salary, fringe benefits, and merit.

## Human Resource Planning

School organizations typically plan their future needs for supplies, equipment, building capacity, and financing. School organizations must also plan to ensure that their human resource needs are satisfied. Human resource planning involves identifying staffing needs, forecasting available personnel, and determining what additions or replacements are required to maintain a staff of the desired quantity and quality to achieve the organization's mission.

The human resource planning function involves at least three different elements: job analysis, forecasting demand and supply, and legal constraints.

### Job Analysis

Superintendent, assistant superintendent, director of personnel, curriculum coordinator, legal counsel, labor relations specialist, principal, assistant principal, college president, dean, and professor are all jobs. To recruit and select the appropriate personnel for specific jobs, it is necessary to know what the jobs entail. **Job analysis** is the process of obtaining information about jobs through a systematic examination of job content.[2] A job analysis usually consists of two parts: a job description and a job specification. The **job description** is a written statement that outlines the duties and responsibilities expected of a job incumbent. It usually includes a job title, the title of the incumbent's immediate supervisor, a brief statement of the job goal, and a list of duties and responsibilities (see Table 15–1).[3] The **job specification** is a written document that outlines the qualifications that a person needs in order to accomplish the duties and responsibilities set forth in the job description.

Job analysis provides valuable information for forecasting future staffing needs and other personnel management functions. For example, the data produced by the job analysis can be used to develop appropriate recruitment and selection methods, to determine dimensions on which personnel should be evaluated, to deter-

---

[2]U.S. Department of Labor, *Handbook for Job Analysis* (Washington, DC: U.S. Government Printing Office, 2008).

[3]The sample job description was provided by the New Orleans Public Schools.

## Table 15–1 Job Description

| | |
|---|---|
| *Job Title:* | School Principal |
| *Job Goal:* | To administer and supervise all activities and personnel within an assigned school, toward the fullest possible development of the skills and motivations of each pupil for fulfillment as a responsible and significant human being. |
| *Reports to:* | District Superintendent |
| *Supervises:* | All professional and nonprofessional staff assigned. |

*Job Responsibilities:*

1. Supervises the school's instructional and extracurricular programs and all activities within the school.
2. Works toward the improvement of the instructional program within the school through faculty study groups and other evaluation processes.
3. Implements all board policies and administrative rules and regulations.
4. Develops and encourages programs of orientation and self-improvement of teachers and others within the school.
5. Determines the work assignment of all professional personnel.
6. Plans and conducts faculty meetings.
7. Observes and reviews the performance of all personnel to provide a basis for effective counseling and for encouraging optimum performance.
8. Assists in the selection of teaching personnel and recommends to the assistant superintendent personnel candidates for positions.
9. Provides for the health, safety, and welfare of students and staff within the school.
10. Maintains standards of student discipline designed to command the respect of students and parents and to minimize school and classroom interruptions.
11. Coordinates the use of student transportation services provided for the school.
12. Develops working relationships among school staff and school system resource personnel available to the school.
13. Makes regular and thorough inspections of the school plant and school properties.
14. Supervises the preparation of all school reports, student records, and the school's internal accounts, and maintains a record-keeping system.
15. Approves or initiates requisitions for supplies, equipment, and materials necessary for the operation of the school.
16. Interprets activities and policies of the school to the community and encourages community participation in school life.
17. Makes recommendations to the district superintendent and the superintendent concerning policy, practice, or personnel for the purposes of improving the quality of the school system.

mine the worth of jobs for compensation purposes, and to develop training programs for personnel.

**Job Analysis Techniques** A variety of techniques are available for conducting a job analysis. The technique most appropriate for a given situation depends on a number of factors, such as the type of job being analyzed, the resources available for doing a job analysis, the scope of the job, and the size of the organization. Some of the most commonly used techniques for conducting a job analysis include observation, work sampling, critical incidents, interviews, and questionnaires.[4]

*Observation* The most straightforward method of job analysis is **observation** of people performing the job. Observation can be a good way of examining jobs that consist mainly of observable physical activity. Jobs such as school custodian, groundskeeper, and machine operator are examples. Analyzing a job through observation is not appropriate where the job requires much abstract thinking, planning, or decision making (e.g., superintendent, labor relations specialist, college dean).

*Work Sampling* A variation of the observation technique is the **work sampling** approach. The job analyst periodically samples employees' activities and behavior on jobs that have long cycles, that have irregular patterns of activity, or that require a variety of different tasks. For example, research on the administrative demands of school principals consistently shows that they are fragmented and rapid fire.[5]

---

[4]U.S. Department of Labor, *Handbook for Job Analysis.*

[5]Fred C. Lunenburg and Beverly J. Irby, *The Principalship: Vision to Action* (Belmont, CA: Thomson Wadsworth, 2006).

A personnel administrator could examine the job activities of twenty-five or thirty high school principals on a given day or randomly select twenty-five or thirty days of the school year and observe the job activities of one or two principals during those days. This approach is similar to the one used by Henry Mintzberg in his analysis of a school superintendent and that of Harry Wolcott in his study of school principals.[6] Both researchers, however, went well beyond the work sampling approach in their analysis of school principals and superintendents. They used a combination of ethnographic techniques including observation, interviews, document analysis, and structured questionnaires to obtain their data.[7]

*Critical Incidents*    Another variation of the observation technique, known as **critical incidents,** examines only those job activities leading to successful or unsuccessful performance. This approach is similar to the trait approach used to identify effective and ineffective leaders. An outside consultant, an immediate supervisor, or a job incumbent can conduct this technique. Direct observation and the two variations thereof are frequently used in conjunction with interviewing.

*Interviews*    Probably the most widely used technique for determining what a job entails is the **interview** technique, and its wide use attests to its advantages. Observation of a school district's labor relations specialist, for example, would only reveal that the district's chief negotiator conducts research, prepares proposals and counterproposals, confers with management's bargaining team, and negotiates at the bargaining table. This method fails to identify other important aspects of the job, such as analytic thinking and problem solving. Interviewing the labor relations specialist allows that person to describe important activities of the job that might not be revealed through direct observation.

*Questionnaires*    Many organizations use job analysis **questionnaires** to elicit information concerning what a job entails. Such questionnaires have at least two advantages. First, they can pool the responses of numerous job incumbents and compare job activities across many jobs, using a standard set of common dimensions. Second, questionnaires can generate much information quickly and inexpensively. For example, a job analyst could administer a questionnaire to 100 job incumbents in less time than it would take to observe a single job or interview one job occupant.

The U.S. Air Force has developed the Comprehensive Occupational Data Analysis Program (CODAP).[8] It elicits data about hundreds of job tasks. Another popular, structured job analysis questionnaire is the Position Analysis Questionnaire (PAQ) developed at Purdue University. It consists of 194 items designed to assess six broad categories of work activity: information input, mental processes, work output, relationships with others, job context, and other job characteristics such as working irregular hours.[9] The PAQ is inadequate for analyzing upper-level administrative or professional jobs (superintendent, college dean) because it fails to address higher-level cognitive processes such as abstract thinking and strategic planning. Well-known instruments designed to elicit information about upper-level administrative jobs include the Management Position Description Questionnaire (MPDQ) and the Professional and Managerial Position Questionnaire (PMPQ).[10]

## Forecasting Demand and Supply

The second phase of human resource planning, **forecasting** demand and supply, involves using any number of sophisticated statistical procedures based on analysis and projections. Such forecasting techniques are beyond the scope of this discussion.

At a more practical level, forecasting demand involves determining the numbers and kinds of person-

[6]Henry Mintzberg, *The Nature of Managerial Work* (Reading, MA: Addison-Wesley, 1997); Harry F. Wolcott, *The Man in the Principal's Office* (New York: Altamira Press, 2003).

[7]Robert C. Bogdan and Sari Knopp Biklen, *Qualitative Research for Education: An Introduction to Theories and Methods,* 5th ed. (Boston: Allyn and Bacon, 2007).

[8]Raymond E. Christal and John J. Weissmuller, "New Comprehensive Data Analysis Programs (CODAP) for Analyzing Task Factor Information," *JSAS Catalog of Selected Documents in Psychology,* 7 (1977): 24–25.

[9]Ernest J. McCormick, Robert C. Mecham, and Paul R. Jeanneret, *Technical Manual for the Position Analysis Questionnaire (PAQ)* (West Lafayette, IN: Department of Psychological Services, Purdue University, 1972).

[10]Walter W. Tornow and Patrick R. Pinto, "The Development of a Managerial Job Taxonomy: A System for Describing, Classifying, and Evaluating Executive Positions," *Journal of Applied Psychology,* 61 (1976): 410–418; John L. Mitchell and Ernest J. McCormick, *Development of PMPQ: A Structured Job Analysis Questionnaire for the Study of Professional and Managerial Positions* (West Lafayette, IN: Department of Psychological Sciences, Purdue University, 1979).

nel that the organization will need at some point in the future. Most school administrators consider several factors when forecasting future personnel needs. The demand for the organization's product or service is paramount. Thus, in a school district, student enrollments are projected first. Then the personnel needed to serve the projected enrollment is estimated. Other factors typically considered when forecasting the demand for personnel include budget constraints; turnover due to resignations, terminations, transfers, and retirement; new technology in the field; decisions to upgrade the quality of services provided; and minority hiring goals.[11]

Forecasting supply involves determining what personnel will be available. The two sources are internal and external: people already employed by the organization and those outside the organization. Factors school administrators typically consider when forecasting the supply of personnel include promoting employees from within the organization; identifying employees willing and able to be trained; availability of required talent in local, regional, and national labor markets; competition for talent within the field; population trends (such as movement of families in the United States from the Northeast to the Southwest); and college and university enrollment trends in the needed field.[12]

Internal sources of employees to fill projected vacancies must be monitored. This is facilitated by the use of the human resource audit, or the systematic inventory of the qualifications of existing personnel. A **human resource audit** is simply an organizational chart of a unit or entire organization with all positions (usually administrative) indicated and keyed as to the promotability of each role incumbent.

Figure 15–2 depicts a human resource audit, or inventory chart, for a hypothetical school district. As Figure 15–2 shows, the superintendent can see where she stands with respect to future staff actions. The superintendent's successor is probably the assistant superintendent for instruction. This person has a successor, the director of elementary education, ready for promotion. Subordinates to the director of elementary education are two principals who are promotable now, three who will be ready for promotion in one or two years, two who are not promotable, and one who should be dismissed.

The other subordinate to the assistant superintendent of instruction, the director of secondary education, is satisfactory but not promotable. That person has two principals who are promotable now, one who will be promotable with further training, and one who is satisfactory but not promotable.

The assistant superintendent of business requires further training before being ready for promotion. Here is a person who knows the job of business management extremely well but lacks training in other aspects of the superintendency, such as curriculum development, personnel administration, public relations, and the like. Some of the accountants reporting to the assistant superintendent of business are promotable now, while others either are nonpromotable or require additional training before being ready for promotion.

The assistant superintendent of personnel, while occupying a very specialized function, is promotable now. Subordinates to that person occupy such specialized jobs that, although performing these roles satisfactorily, they require additional training before being ready for promotion to assistant superintendent of personnel.

The assistant superintendent of research and development was a newly created position in this hypothetical school district. Because of the specialized nature of the position, that person requires considerable training before being ready for promotion. Subordinates to that position are designated similarly.

The analysis provided in Figure 15–2 is very valuable to the school administrator. Future needs and the potential of the existing administrative staff have been identified, and weaknesses have been uncovered. These data can help administrators plan immediate promotions for personnel from within the organization who are promotable, plan for appropriate training and development of others, or dismiss those who are unsatisfactory. If there are an insufficient number of candidates inside the organization to fill vacancies, staffing specialists typically analyze labor markets.

### Legal Constraints

Legislation designed to regulate hiring practices affects nearly every aspect of employment—from human resource planning to compensation. Our intent is not to make school administrators into attorneys but to examine the basic laws that relate to employment decisions. School administrators must avoid possible charges of discrimination on the basis of race, color, gender, national

---

[11]John T. Seyforth, *Human Resource Management for Effective Schools* (Boston: Allyn and Bacon, 2007).

[12]Ronald W. Rebore, *Human Resources Administration: A Management Approach* (Boston: Allyn and Bacon, 2006).

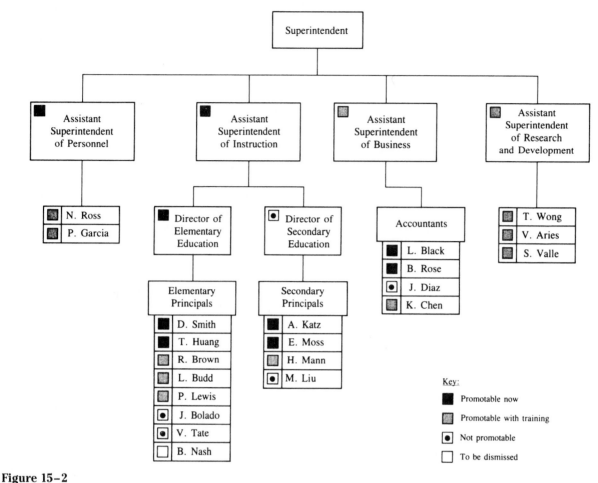

**Figure 15–2**

Human Resource Audit for Administrative Personnel

origin, age, or disability.[13] Table 15–2 summarizes some of the major laws pertaining to the personnel process.

**Women and Minorities**   The landmark legislation designed to ensure equal employment opportunity is the Civil Rights Act of 1964. In 1965, President Lyndon B. Johnson issued Executive Order 11246 (amended by Executive Order 11375 in 1967). These executive orders obligated employers to go beyond the provisions of nondiscrimination of the Civil Rights Act and to actively seek out women and minorities and hire, train, develop, and promote them. In 1972, Congress estab-

lished the **Equal Employment Opportunity Commission** (EEOC) and passed the Equal Employment Opportunity Act. This amendment to the Civil Rights Act of 1964 extended the jurisdiction of the EEOC and gave it the power to initiate court action against noncomplying organizations.

**Older Workers**   Congress passed the Age Discrimination in Employment Act in 1967. The act originally prohibited discrimination in employment of those people forty to sixty-five years of age; the act was amended in 1978 to move the top age from sixty-five to seventy years; and in 1986, the upper age limit was removed. In essence, the law prohibits discrimination in hiring, firing, compensating, or any other conditions of work of any person forty years of age or over. Exceptions to the leg-

[13]Patrick J. Cihon and James O. Castagnera, *Employment and Labor Law*, 5th ed. (Belmont, CA: Thomson South-Western 2005).

## Table 15–2   Major Laws Affecting Hiring Practices

| Law | Basic Requirements |
| --- | --- |
| Title VII of the Civil Rights Act of 1964 (as amended) | Prohibits discrimination in employment on the basis of race, color, religion, gender, or national origin. |
| Age Discrimination in Employment Act of 1968 (as amended) | Prohibits discrimination in employment against any person forty years of age or over. |
| Equal Pay Act of 1963 | Prohibits wage discrimination on the basis of gender; requires equal pay for equal work regardless of gender. |
| Rehabilitation Act of 1973 | Requires employers to take affirmative action to employ and promote qualified handicapped persons. |
| Pregnancy Discrimination Act of 1978 | Requires employers to treat pregnant women and new mothers the same as other employees for all employment-related purposes. |
| Vietnam Era Veterans' Readjustment Act of 1974 | Requires employers to take affirmative action to employ disabled Vietnam War veterans. |
| Occupational Safety and Health Act (OSHA) of 1970 | Establishes mandatory safety and health standards in organizations |

islation include tenured faculty and some high-salaried executives or for documented health- or performance-related reasons.

**The Handicapped**   The Vocational Rehabilitation Act was passed in 1973 and amended in 1978. The act requires employers who have a contract with the federal government worth $2500 or more to take affirmative action to hire and promote qualified handicapped persons. A handicapped person is defined as any individual with a physical or mental disability that limits normal activities such as walking, seeing, speaking, or learning. The law stipulates that the handicapped individual must be capable of performing the particular job for which she is being considered.

**Veterans**   The Vietnam Era Veterans' Readjustment Act of 1974 requires employers with federal contracts to take affirmative action to employ disabled veterans. The act also provides job assistance for Vietnam-era veterans in the form of job counseling, training, and placement.

**Equal Employment Opportunity**   Equal employment opportunity (EEO) is the right of all persons to work and to advance on the basis of merit, ability, and potential without regard to race, color, religion, gender, or national origin. Table 15–2 summarizes the primary legal base for EEO and supporting legal activities. The provisions of these acts generally apply to all public and private organizations employing fifteen or more people. The EEOC administers and federally enforces the various equal employment opportunity acts. The EEOC provides assistance to employers in developing affirmative action programs and in resolving discrimination complaints brought against employers.

### Affirmative Action Programs

Whereas EEO legislation prohibits discrimination in recruitment, hiring, promotion, compensation, and discharge, **affirmative action programs** are designed to increase employment opportunities for women and other minorities including veterans, the aged, and the handicapped. Based on two executive orders, originally issued by President Johnson, affirmative action requirements apply to public and private employers and educational institutions that either have contracts with or receive monies from the federal government. The intent of the program is to ensure that women and other minorities are represented in the organization in percentages similar to their percentage in the labor market from which the organization draws personnel. For example, if the labor pool in a community is 15 percent black and 5 percent Hispanic, then 15 percent and 5 percent of the labor force of an organization operating in that community should be black and Hispanic, respectively.

In general, affirmative action programs should include the following:[14] (1) making concerted efforts to recruit and promote women, minorities, the handicapped, and veterans, including recruiting through state employment services and at minority and women's colleges; (2) limiting the questions that can be asked in employment applications and interviews; (3) determining available percentages of women, minorities, and the handicapped in the labor market; (4) setting up goals and timetables for recruiting women, minorities, the handicapped, and veterans; and (5) avoiding testing unless it meets established guidelines.

## Recruitment

Whether recruitment of personnel should precede or follow selection is an interesting question. College athletics is a case in point. Coaches in major universities who run successful athletic programs determine their staffing needs (players), scan selected high schools and junior colleges, select the players they want, and then recruit them.

The University of Louisville basketball program has become one of the most successful in the country. For example, the team won two NCAA Championships in the 1980s (1980 and 1986), and the team made it to the final four playoffs in the NCAA tournament seven times between 1980 and 1995. To what can this success be attributed? Obviously, Louisville has an outstanding coaching staff. However, part of the explanation lies in the method of recruiting personnel (players) for the team.

Denny Crum, the University of Louisville's former men's basketball coach, had computerized information on the qualifications of basketball players from across the country. This procedure facilitated identifying, tracking, and screening personnel (players) for his basketball program. The plotting was done in what he referred to as the "War Room."[15] Crum selected his

personnel (basketball players) first, monitored their progress in high schools or junior colleges, and then recruited them. School organizations typically work in reverse order. Recruiting potential employees first, they then select the personnel they want from among the pool of recruits. Using this method, there is no guarantee that the pool of recruits from which selections are ultimately made are competent.

School districts can take lessons from the top college athletic coaches, who consistently acquire talented personnel to fill strategic slots in their organization. Just as a weak-to-mediocre athlete cannot be miraculously transformed into an All American, neither can weak faculty members and administrators be "trained and developed" out of their mediocrity. The key to the quality of an instructional program is the competency of its professional staff. Thus, recruitment and selection of competent personnel is an extremely important function of school administrators.

All school organizations, at one time or another, engage in recruiting to replace or expand their supply of personnel. Some organizations recruit better personnel than others, which is later reflected in the quality of their instructional programs. Recruitment refers to the process of generating a pool of competent applicants needed to fill the available positions in an organization. Emphasis on the word *competent* is important. No matter how personnel are later selected, developed, and compensated, it is important to begin with a group of high-caliber job applicants. Overall, sources of personnel available to fill vacant positions can be categorized as sources inside the organization and sources outside the organization.

### Internal Sources

The existing pool of employees within the school system is one source of recruiting personnel. Individuals already employed by the district might possess excellent qualifications for a vacant position. There are some advantages to using **internal recruitment**. First, it allows administrators to observe an employee over a period of time and to evaluate that person's potential and job behavior. These factors cannot be easily observed off the job. Second, when employees see that competence is rewarded with promotion, their morale and performance will likely be enhanced. Third, employees are likely to identify their long-term interests with an organization that provides them with a chance for promotion and hence are less likely to leave. Fourth, employees can

[14] Stephen D. Bruce, *The Federal Affirmative Action Regulation* (Mystic, CT: Ransom & Benjamin, 2001).

[15] Billy Reed, *Born to Coach: How Denny Crum Built the University of Louisville into a Basketball Powerhouse* (Louisville, KY: *Courier Journal* and *Louisville Times*, 1986).

be better qualified than outside candidates: Even positions that do not appear unique require familiarity with the people, policies, procedures, and special characteristics of the organization. Finally, when carefully planned, promoting from within can act as a training device for developing middle- and top-level administrators such as principals, central office administrators, and superintendents.[16]

Internal recruiting sources include inventory charts, informal search, talent search, and job posting.[17]

**Inventory Chart**   In filling administrative vacancies, a human resource audit of the type discussed earlier is helpful (see Figure 15–2). Many large school districts have computerized information on their administrators' qualifications and promotability. When a vacancy occurs at the administrative level, the computer can search the list of administrators having the qualifications that match the requirements of the position.

**Informal Search**   In large school districts with a personnel department, the administrator of the division or school having a vacancy consults the personnel director, and together they consider one or more possible candidates for the position. The administrator or the director may interview one or more employees who appear to have the necessary qualifications for the position. After the interview, the position may be offered to one of the candidates.

While the informal search was commonly used in the past, it represents a **closed recruitment system;** that is, it tends to exclude most employees who might be interested in the position from applying. Legislation to ensure equal employment opportunity and affirmative action (see Table 15–2) has resulted in a more **open recruitment system,** which increases in the in-house advertisement of all job vacancies.

**Talent Search**   A closely related procedure that represents an open recruitment system is the *talent search.* The school district uses this method when it anticipates vacancies at the administrative level and wishes to promote from within the system. Contrary to the informal search, a talent search is widely advertised throughout the school district. Training programs are offered

that will qualify personnel for promotion. Employees are asked to notify the personnel department or their building or division administrator if they are interested in participating in the training program. Some training programs are administered independently by the school district or collaboratively with a local university or consulting firm. Those who indicate an interest are administered a battery of cognitive or psychological tests and assessed in other ways. Employees who are selected are given appropriate training and then placed in a talent pool. They continue in their current jobs until an appropriate position for which they are qualified becomes vacant.

**Job Posting**   Another procedure to facilitate implementation of a promotion-from-within policy is job posting. A job posting system gives every employee an opportunity to apply for a vacant position within the school district. The posting notification may be communicated on bulletin boards throughout the district, in the weekly or monthly school district newsletter, or in a special posting sheet from the personnel department, outlining all positions currently available. The job posting usually contains information regarding job title, a brief job description, salary range, and school or division location. Collective bargaining agreements may contain a provision for job posting. In such instances, job posting can be formal. Unions generally prefer that promotions be based on seniority, whereas administration prefers that decisions be based on merit.

Internal sources of recruitment, involving talent searches and job posting, have received attention recently because of equal employment opportunity and affirmative action programs. Government agencies monitoring employment practices frequently require school districts that previously did not practice open recruitment and solicit inside candidates to do so. The ultimate goal of such procedures is to prevent women and minorities from being kept in lower-paying, entry-level jobs.

## External Sources

Internal sources do not always produce enough qualified applicants to fill vacant positions in the school district. Several **external recruitment** sources are available and include educational institutions, employment agencies, executive search firms, temporary help agencies, advertising, and unsolicited applicants.[18]

[16]David A. DeCenzo et al., *Fundamentals of Human Resource Management* (New York: John Wiley, 2006).

[17]John B. Miner, *Organizational Behavior 3: Historical Origins, Theoretical Foundations, and the Future* (New York: M. E. Sharpe, 2006).

[18]Ibid.

**Educational Institutions** Universities, colleges, vocational schools, technical schools, and high schools are all important sources of recruits for most school districts. High schools or vocational schools can provide service applicants such as plant-maintenance workers; business or secretarial schools can provide office staff such as bookkeepers and clerical personnel; colleges and universities can provide professional staff such as teachers, counselors, social workers, and school psychologists; and graduate schools can often provide administrative personnel such as superintendents and principals.

Most universities and colleges operate placement services. Potential employers can review credentials submitted by applicants. For professional positions in great demand, school districts may send recruiters to campuses for the purpose of interviewing job applicants. On-campus recruiting can be an expensive and time-consuming process. However, because there is a great deal of competition for the top graduating students in professional-type jobs, the recruiting visit may be worth the time and expense if a high-quality applicant is hired. Like the top business firms and athletic programs, school organizations need to do more active recruiting of top students graduating from universities and colleges.

**Employment Agencies** Every state in the United States operates a state employment agency under the umbrella of the U.S. Training and Employment Service (USTES) of the U.S. Department of Labor. There are 2400 such offices, which are staffed by state employees and funded by the federal government.[19] The service is free to all job applicants. These agencies have a poor image, which is no reflection on their competence or service. State employment agencies are perceived by job applicants as having few high-skilled jobs, and employers tend to view such agencies as having few high-quality applicants.

There are thousands of private employment agencies in the United States. Private agencies provide more services to an employer and are perceived to offer employers higher-quality applicants than public agencies do. For example, some private employment agencies advertise the position sought, screen applicants, and sometimes even provide a guarantee of satisfactory service to the hiring organization. For these services, a fee is charged, which is absorbed by the organization or the employee, or shared between the two. Such fees are usually set by state law. Private agencies can be sources of service, clerical, professional, and administrative personnel.

**Executive Search Firms** Many major corporations, hospitals, universities, and large school districts now use executive search firms (or "headhunters," as they are commonly called) to recruit middle-level and top-level executives. In searching for a superintendent of schools, for example, whose compensation package may be in excess of $225,000 a year, the school district is often willing to pay a very high fee to locate precisely the right person to fill the vacant position. A fee of 25 to 35 percent of the superintendent's first year's salary, plus $500 a day for expenses is not uncommon. These firms have contacts throughout the United States and are especially well trained in contacting highly qualified candidates who are already employed. In fact, executive search firms will not accept unsolicited applications from persons seeking employment. This procedure, often referred to as "pirating," is a common practice today among the larger, more successful organizations.

**Temporary Help Agencies** Organizations such as Kelly Services and Manpower can provide school organizations with temporary help. Traditionally developed to supply secretarial, clerical, and semiskilled labor, the temporary help agencies have expanded to include skilled and technical areas. One such agency is Account Temps, which provides temporary help in the accounting and computer fields. School districts can rent on a day-rate basis people with a broad range of skills, such as engineers, computer technicians, or accountants. Employing temporary help may be more efficient than employing permanent staff during peak periods. Temporary employees do not receive the fringe benefit package required for permanent employees; and costly layoffs (paying unemployment compensation) during less active periods can be avoided.

**Advertising** Advertising in newspapers, trade magazines, and professional journals is a widely used method of external recruiting. A local newspaper can be a good source of service workers, clerical staff, and lower-level administrative personnel. Trade and professional journals enable school organizations to aim at more specialized employees. For example, the *Chronicle of Higher Education* is commonly used to recruit personnel in higher education. Administrative positions in the public schools can be advertised in the *School Administrator, Executive Educator, NASSP Bulletin, Principal,*

---

[19]U.S. Department of Labor, *Employment and Training Report of the President* (Washington, DC: U.S. Government Printing Office, 2008).

*Educational Leadership, Educational Researcher,* or *Phi Delta Kappan.*

In contrast to print advertising in publications such as newspapers and trade and professional journals, other forms of recruitment advertising are used less frequently. These include television, radio, billboards, and the Internet. Advertising usually generates a large pool of applicants who then must be screened carefully to determine those who are qualified.

**Unsolicited Applicants**  Another source of prospective job applicants is the file, maintained at the school district office, of unsolicited candidates. Unsolicited applicants communicate with the school district by letter, by telephone, or in person. The qualifications of unsolicited applicants depend on several factors: the condition of the labor market, the school district's reputation, and the types of jobs available. Regardless of these factors, there will always be some unsolicited applicants in most school districts—people entering the labor force for the first time, women returning to work after a period of child rearing, or individuals improving their employment situation. Generally, the use of unsolicited applicants is prevalent in staffing clerical and plant-maintenance jobs. A school district with a good reputation can also rely on this source to fill professional positions including teachers and other support personnel.

## Internal versus External Recruitment

Both internal recruitment and external recruitment have advantages and disadvantages to the school district (see Figure 15–3).

Promoting from within can work to the school district's advantage. Applicants are already familiar with the organization, have a known performance record within the district that can be examined, and may be less expensive to recruit than external candidates.

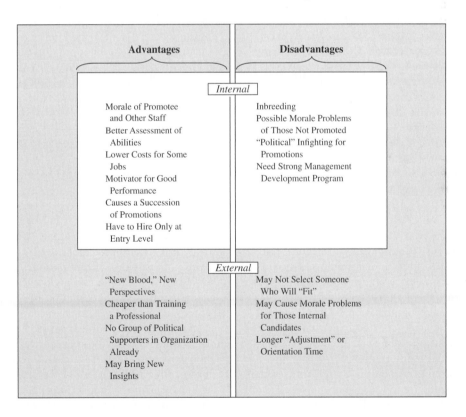

**Figure 15–3**

Internal and External Recruitment

Source: Adapted from Robert L. Mathis and John H. Jackson, *Personnel: Human Resource Management,* 5th ed., p. 229. Copyright © 1988. Reprinted with permission of South-Western College Publishing, a division of Thomson Learning.

## Administrative Advice 15–1

### Recruiting the Next Generation of Teachers

Here are some tips for improving teacher recruitment for the next generation of teachers in your school or school district.

■ *Retrain the best teachers to fill critical needs.* Offer retraining and recredentialing opportunities to teachers with proven track records. This can be accomplished by having teachers enroll in university courses at the district's expense plus a $2000 incentive if teachers agree to remain for two years after retraining.

■ *Institute a job-sharing or flex-time program.* Job sharing offers dedicated teachers an opportunity to remain professionally active while raising a family. Flex time allows two or more teachers to divide the workload during time intervals suitable to each.

■ *Recruit and train professionals from other career fields.* Two sources provide access to personnel from other career fields: alternative certification programs offered in some states, and businesses that pay their employee salaries and tuition while they retrain for a career in teaching.

■ *Tap the reservoir of retired people.* Many retired people look for ways to get involved in meaningful work activities. Schools can use senior citizens in paraprofessional and support roles.

■ *Grow your own.* Teacher cadet programs and future teacher clubs, Future Teachers of America (FTA), can inject enthusiasm for the teaching profession among young people.

■ *Capitalize on the talents of college students.* College students will respond to requests to work with troubled youth. Examples include VISTA, "Teach for America," and Madison House, voluntary tutoring programs staffed by collegians.

■ *Try part-time approaches.* Teaching part time, serving as a consultant, or as a mentor to new teachers might entice teachers who are near retirement to remain in the profession.

■ *Initiate cooperative programs with business.* Business-education partnerships have the potential to strengthen the teacher workforce. Examples include college loan and scholarship programs for high school graduates interested in teaching; and summer internships, teacher enrichment programs, research grants, company-sponsored management training made available to faculty might aid in recruiting quality teachers.

Source: Adapted from Sara Snyder Crumpacker, "Recruiting the Next Generation of Teachers," *School Administrator*, 11 (1992): 38–39. Used by permission.

As indicated previously, internal recruitment also improves morale and loyalty among employees because they believe that competence is rewarded with promotion. However, there are at least two disadvantages of internal recruitment: organizational inbreeding—a "but we've always done it that way" mentality—and increased political behavior if it is perceived that such behavior may result in a promotion.

External recruiting, on the other hand, infuses the organization with "new blood," which may broaden present ideas and knowledge and question traditional ways of doing things. The abundance of external sources almost guarantees that the school district will find an adequate number of candidates from which to choose. Promoting from outside the organization also provides an opportunity to recruit women and minorities at all levels in the school district. Exclusive reliance on promotions from within may further inhibit the entry of these groups into higher-level positions in the school district, assuming that past underrepresentation of these groups exists. On the negative side, using external sources can be quite costly, particularly the hiring of middle-level and top executives. In general, most school districts use a mixture of internal and external sources of recruitment.

One of the most important instructional decisions a principal or superintendent makes is hiring his teaching personnel. School administrators share one of the same concerns faced by top-level managers everywhere: how to find great employees and keep them productive and satisfied while they're at work. (See Administrative Advice 15–1.)

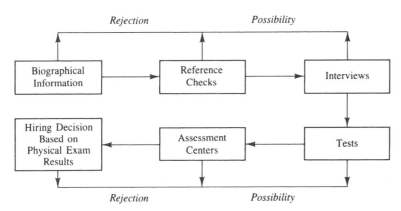

**Figure 15–4**

Steps in the Selection Process

## Selection

Once applicants have been recruited, the school district must select the most qualified people to fill existing vacancies. A comprehensive discussion of selection techniques can be found in personnel administration texts. The most common procedure involves a series of steps including biographical information, reference checks, interviews, tests, and assessment centers[20] (see Figure 15–4).

### Biographical Information

The first step in the selection process is searching for evidence of past performance in a candidate's record. This information can be secured from an application blank, a résumé, a letter of application, writing samples, school records or college transcripts, and similar biographical data. Research shows that **biographical information** can predict future job performance because a person's behavior is consistent over time.[21] The use of such information in making selection decisions is based on the idea that an effective predictor of future performance is past performance.

An approach that can be used to analyze biographical data is the *weighted method*. Statistically weighted biographical data can further enhance the predictability of job performance. The weighting procedure consists of identifying background factors on which high-performing employees tend to differ from low-

performing employees. Differential weights are then assigned to these background factors. The weightings are based on a statistical analysis that has shown, over time, that there is a high correlation between some background factors or categories of information and high or low performance.[22] Each candidate for a job receives a final score based on this analysis. The administrator then hires personnel who obtain a high score when their biographical information is weighted using this method. Thus, school employers increase the likelihood of employing high-performing personnel.

In practice, most school districts use different background factors, depending on the job level. For professional and administrative personnel, for example, biographical data may include an application blank, a letter of application, a résumé, a writing sample, and undergraduate and graduate transcripts. For building maintenance, clerical, and other noncertificated staff, background factors might consist of a different application blank, school records, military records, and other biographical sources.

### Reference Checks

**Reference checks** fall into two categories: letters of recommendation and subsequent telephone follow-up inquiries of the final candidates for a position. Letters of recommendation can be considered part of the biographical information or screening process and usually precede the interview. Telephone follow-up inquiries typically are made after all other steps in the selec-

[20]Webb and Norton, *Human Resources Administration: Personnel Issues and Needs in Education.*

[21]Ralph D. Thomas, *Pre Employment Investigation* (Austin, TX: Thomas Publications, 1992).

[22]Stephen D. Bruce, *Better Interviews Better Hires: The Clean and Simple Guide to Revealing Interviews That Impress the Best Candidates* (Mystic: CT: Ransom & Benjamin, 2004).

tion process are completed and just prior to making the hiring decision. For example, the administrator may wish to contact by telephone the present employer or student-teaching supervisor of each of the three leading candidates for a teaching position. Some school organizations mistakenly omit this vital step.

Letters of recommendation are generally of little value in the selection process, for at least four reasons. First, job applicants usually ask for references from persons who are likely to write complimentary letters. As a result, letters of recommendation are biased in the applicant's favor. Second, the recommender may possess only limited knowledge of the applicant. Third, under the Privacy Act of 1974, people have the right to examine letters of reference concerning them unless they waive that right. Because of this privacy legislation, recommenders are reluctant to provide negative information about an applicant in writing for fear of being sued. Fourth, occasionally, recommenders will write a favorable letter of recommendation for an incompetent applicant in order to facilitate their leaving their current employment. In one actual situation, the board of education of a suburban school district dismissed a teacher on the recommendation of the superintendent of schools. Later, the teacher sued the board and superintendent for damages. To avoid the legal costs of a trial, the superintendent was instructed by his board of education, at the urging of the dismissed teacher's attorney, to write a favorable letter of recommendation for the alleged incompetent teacher. The superintendent did so, and the lawsuit was dropped.

Despite their questionable value, school organizations typically require letters of recommendation as part of the selection process. There are ways to improve the validity of reference checks. First, telephone the references and ask for an oral recommendation. Most people are more likely to provide complete and frank statements orally than they would in writing. Second, contact people other than those referred by the job applicant. This increases the pool of information available about the candidate. Third, allow more credence to references provided by previous employers than those provided by other nonemployment sources such as colleagues, friends, ministers, and the like. Fourth, give more weight to references of those candidates who have waived their right to view their letters of recommendation. Fifth, contact the applicant's two previous employers. This provides wider coverage of previous employment. These techniques will strengthen the validity of reference checks. The rationale underlying reference checks,

like biographical information, is that past performance will to a great extent predict future performance.

## Interviews

The interview is perhaps the most widely used personnel technique in the selection process. It serves as a two-way exchange that allows both the school district and the applicant to gather information that would otherwise be difficult to secure. Unfortunately, despite its widespread use, the interview is a poor predictor of job performance.

**Interviewing Problems**   Six major interviewing problems should be avoided:[23]

1. *Unfamiliarity with the Job.* Interviewers frequently are unfamiliar with the job. When interviewers do not know what the job entails, they do not ask the right questions, interpret the obtained information differently, have faulty impressions of the information supplied, and spend time discussing matters irrelevant to the job.

2. *Premature Decisions.* Interviewers tend to make a decision about an applicant in the first few minutes of the interview before all relevant information has been gathered. Then they spend the rest of the interview seeking information that confirms their initial impression.

3. *Emphasis on Negative Information.* Interviewers tend to weight negative information supplied by the applicant more heavily than positive information. On occasion, the interviewer may change his or her mind, but the change tends to be from positive to negative rather than vice versa. In fact, in most cases, interviews tend to be a search for negative information.

4. *Personal Biases.* Some interviewers tend to have preconceptions and prejudices about people. Some examples follow: "fat people are lazy"; "people from the East are unfriendly and arrogant"; "people from the South are slow"; "people with low foreheads are stupid." Other biases may reflect negatively against some minority groups or in favor of those candidates who have backgrounds similar

---

[23]Gary Dessler, *Human Resource Management*, 9th ed. (Upper Saddle River, NJ: Prentice Hall, 2006).

to the interviewer(s). As ridiculous as these prejudices may seem, many of these personal biases still exist. Furthermore, some interviewers are overly impressed with surface signs of composure, manner of speech, and physical appearance.

5. *Applicant Order.* Interviewers' ratings of an applicant are influenced by the order in which candidates are interviewed. For example, when an average applicant is interviewed immediately following one or more below-average applicants, the average applicant tends to be evaluated well above average. A similar process works in reverse. If an average applicant follows an outstanding applicant, the former is rated below average.

6. *Hiring Quotas.* Interviewers who have been given hiring quotas tend to rate applicants higher than interviewers who have not been given quotas. Thus, pressure to hire influences the interviewer's judgments of the applicant and thereby diminishes the usefulness of the interview as a selection technique.

**Improving the Interview Process** School organizations will continue to use interviews regardless of the problems. Thus, researchers have identified several techniques for improving the interview process:[24]

1. *Use a Structured Interview Format.* Interviews should be more structured. In a structured interview, questions are written in advance, scaled on a standardized rating scale, and asked of all job applicants. The structured interview has three major advantages. It brings consistency to the interview process; it provides an opportunity to develop questions that are relevant to the job; and it allows screening and refinement of questions that may be discriminatory. In addition, the structured interview is more defensible in court. A less-structured method can be used when interviewing administrative personnel. That is, the interview is still carefully planned in terms of content areas covered, but it allows more flexibility by the interviewer.

2. *Train Interviewers.* One way to improve the validity and reliability of the interview is to train interviewers. Effective interviewing requires specific skills including asking questions, probing, listening, observing, recording unbiased information, rating,

and the like. Specifically designed workshops can teach these skills. A cadre of trained interviewers can then interview job applicants.

3. *Keep a Written Record of Each Interview.* Keeping a written record of each interview facilitates a comparison of the applicants interviewed. To make accurate comparisons among the candidates, maintain and preserve the details of their responses and impressions. Without such information, later deliberations and decision making will be less accurate and valid.

4. *Use Multiple Interviewers.* Using multiple interviewers facilitates a comparison of evaluations and perceptions. Specifically, it allows the school district to place greater confidence in areas where consensus of opinion exists. And it opens up discussion in specific areas where disagreement occurs, with the purpose of arriving at an equitable hiring decision. Personnel who have specific knowledge of the job and the candidate's immediate supervisor-to-be would provide a well-balanced interview team. Or the district may wish to use a cadre of trained interviewers in every interview situation.

5. *Get the Applicant to Talk.* The main purpose of an interview is to learn as much as possible about a job applicant. This can be accomplished by getting the applicant to talk. Establish a friendly, open rapport with the applicant early in the interview, with some brief comments about the organization and the job. Then shift to a preplanned question format. Listen carefully to content. Probe for answers to all questions and check for inconsistencies. Relate responses given to questions during the interview to written biographical information supplied earlier. Pay attention to nonverbal cues such as tone of voice, general personality, and emotional characteristics of the applicant. For example, failure of a candidate to maintain eye contact may be a danger sign. Thus, observation during an interview is as important as listening.

6. *Use the Interview as One Aspect of the Selection Process.* Avoid using the interview as the sole criterion for selecting applicants. By the same token, the interviewer(s) should not be the sole decision maker for who is or is not hired. Supplement the interview with data from other sources, including biographical information, results of tests, written references, and telephone inquiries. Interviewers may not be privy to the telephone reference checks, which may

---

[24]William L. Gagnon, *Complete Interview Procedures for Hiring School Personnel* (Lanham, MD: Scarecrow-Press, 2003).

---

## Administrative Advice 15–2

### Tips for Interviewing

Here are some tips for conducting a successful interview, including interviewing steps, the role of the interviewer, interviewing techniques, and questioning.

### Interviewing Steps

- *Step 1: Establish an atmosphere of interest in the interviewee.* Establishing an atmosphere of interest can be accomplished in three ways: by showing friendliness, by maintaining eye contact, and by using a firm handshake.

- *Step 2: Become an active listener.* It is the interviewer's responsibility to listen carefully to the spoken words of the interviewee, to direct the communication toward the final goal, and to remember key words that may add discussion or clarification.

- *Step 3: Make the purpose known.* Typically, the school administrator's purpose is to approve or recommend an interviewee for a professional or paraprofessional position. Once the purpose of the interview is known, the interviewer directs the questions and focuses the interview toward that purpose.

### Role of the Interviewer

- *Maximize the forces that lead to communication.* These include a relaxed atmosphere, focus on the interview purpose, and indication of listening by both parties.

- *Measure the data collected.* To measure the adequateness of a response, the interviewer must decide if the question was truly answered. If not, ask additional questions. If yes, reward the interviewee with a nod or murmur of understanding.

### How to Interview

- *The interviewer should have a strong background in all aspects of the job.*

- *The interview begins with observation.* The interviewer must note what the interviewee says and what the interviewee does not say.

- *Question with a purpose.* The purpose of every interview is to determine if the interviewee has the qualifications to do the job and fit in with the faculty and staff.

- *Pace your questions to the answers of the interviewee.* Proceeding too rapidly can cause confusion or a missed response and may give the interviewee the appearance of being uninterested.

### Questions

- *What if?* Hypothetical situation questions allow the interviewer to determine values, and to determine if the interviewee has orderly thought processes.

- *Describe your philosophy of education.* This helps the interviewer hear what the interviewee hopes his students will learn and how she has integrated the philosophy into teaching.

- *How would you set up a program (such as reading)?* Look for one-to-one student-teacher communication, a set of checks and balances for assessing mastery, a plan to monitor the plan, where to seek resources, how to accommodate individual differences in students.

- *What are your weaknesses?* Look for an admission that anyone can learn and an indication that the interviewee does not think she knows everything.

- *Define the principal's role.* Look for those applicants who perceive the principal as fulfilling multiple roles: a resource for research, a facilitator and supporter, a mentor, an instructional leader.

- *Describe yourself.* Look for enthusiasm, warmth, caring, emotional maturity, leadership skills, and a willingness to learn.

---

Source: Adapted from Cynthia Martin, "Hiring the Right Person: Techniques for Principals," *NASSP Bulletin,* 77, no. 550 (1993): 79–83. Copyright © 1993 National Association of Secondary School Principals. www.principals.org Reprinted with permission.

---

rest exclusively in the hands of the top-executive officer. When the aforementioned suggestions are implemented, the interview can be a useful source of information in the selection process.

An effective interview requires adequate preparation, a comfortable setting, and clear communication between interviewer and interviewee. (See Administrative Advice 15–2.)

## Tests

A comprehensive survey of 2500 corporations revealed that 64.5 percent use **testing** as a device in hiring and promotion decisions.[25] Most U.S. firms give an hour-long test for entry level, service workers, and applicants for top management positions take personality tests requiring a day or less. In contrast, the Toyota Motor Corporation in Georgetown, Kentucky, puts candidates for entry-level, shop-floor jobs through fourteen hours of testing.[26] School districts, however, infrequently use tests as an employment device. Perhaps school organizations should change that practice based on the evidence from business firms.

Many human resource experts believe that testing is the single best selection device. Tests yield more information about an applicant than do biographical information and letters of recommendation, and they are less subject to bias than are interviews. The primary advantages of testing include finding the right person for the job, obtaining a high degree of job satisfaction for the applicant because of a good fit between the organization and the person, and reducing absenteeism and turnover.[27]

Although there are many kinds of tests available for school district use, they can be classified into four major groups: achievement and performance tests, aptitude tests, personality tests, and interest tests.[28]

**Achievement and Performance Tests** These tests measure the applicant's ability to perform the tasks required in a job. Examples include typing and dictaphone tests for secretaries, speed and accuracy tests for computer operators, and a driving test for driver education teachers. The National Teacher Examinations (NTE) is an achievement test. Candidates for administrative positions are often given "in-basket tests," designed to examine their judgment. The applicant is given an in-basket of letters, memoranda, telephone messages,

and the like dealing with various school situations that might arise on the job and asked what she would do under the circumstances. (This is one of several exercises typically used in assessment centers, discussed later.)

**Aptitude Tests** These tests measure the potential of an applicant to perform some task. They are diversified in that some measure cognitive aptitudes, while others measure special aptitudes such as mechanical, clerical, or creativity. The Graduate Record Exam (GRE) and Miller Analogies Test (MAT), used by colleges and universities as a criterion for graduate school admission, are examples of cognitive aptitude tests. The Wechsler Adult Intelligence Scale is an aptitude test that measures general intelligence.

**Personality Tests** These tests attempt to measure personality characteristics that might be important on the job, such as emotional stability, introversion and extroversion, self-confidence, aggressiveness or submissiveness, neurotic tendencies, and many other characteristics and traits. Proponents claim that projective-type tests, such as the Rorschach (ink blot) test, the Thematic Apperception Test (TAT), and the Sentence Completion Test are less subject to "faking" than other personality tests.

**Interest Tests** These tests attempt to measure an applicant's interest in performing various kinds of activities. The notion underlying the administration of interest tests to job applicants is that certain people perform jobs well because the job activities are interesting. The purpose of this type of test is to create a better "fit" between the applicant and the specific job. Two popular interest tests are the Kuder Preference Record and the Strong-Campbell Interest Inventory.

The three major problems with using tests as an employment selection device are that they are time-consuming to administer, often require training to administer and score, and discriminate against minorities. Ethnic minorities, such as blacks and Mexican Americans, may score lower on certain paper-and-pencil tests because of cultural bias. EEOC guidelines and amendments to the Civil Rights Act prohibit employment practices that artificially discriminate against individuals on the basis of test scores.[29] That is, the test must relate to actual performance on the job, the test

---

[25]Irving E. Alexander, *Personology: Method and Content of Personality-Assessment and Psychobiography* (Durham, NC: Duke University Press, 1990).

[26]Fred Luthans, *Organizational Behavior,* 10th ed. (New York: McGraw-Hill, 2006).

[27]Raymond A. Noe, *Fundamentals of Human Resource Management* (New York: McGraw-Hill, 2005).

[28]Robert A. Spies et al., *The Sixteenth Mental Measurements Yearbook* (Lincoln, NE: Buros Institute of Mental Measurements, 2005).

[29]Dewey Publications, Inc., *Federal Sector EEO, Civil Service, and Labor Relations Reference Materials 2006* (Author, 2006).

## ▪ Exemplary Educational Administrators in Action

**RON SAUNDERS** Superintendent, Barrow County Schools, Winder, Georgia.

**Previous Positions:** Superintendent, Huntsville City Schools, Huntsville, Alabama.

**Latest Degree and Affiliation:** Ed.D., Administration and Leadership, University of Alabama.

**Number One Influence on Career:** My parents (both educators).

**Number One Achievement:** Developing a plan that enabled teachers and administrators to increase student learning and achievement according to state standards.

**Number One Regret:** Not aggressively relieving inadequate personnel of their positions. I of course did some, but looking back on my career, many more needed to be relieved of their positions.

**Favorite Education-Related Book or Text:** *Preparing Schools and School Systems for the 21st Century* by John Glenn.

**Additional Interests:** Travel, photography, golf.

**Leadership Style:** I try to hire excellent people and let them do their job. I am a "behind the scenes" person that respects the dignity of people.

**Professional Vision:** An educational leader must not only "talk the walk" but also "walk the walk." He or she must be seen in the community in which they

work and also be proactive, practical, caring, and knowledgeable. Your community (whether it be students, parents, teachers, administrators, business leaders, or taxpayers) must feel that you are approachable and a hard worker who cares for the betterment of everyone.

**Words of Advice:** Education will not get easier. The more diverse we become, the more that schools will be asked to do. Administrators must view this as an "opportunity to succeed" and not a "challenge to fail." An example is when I was a principal of a high school. I had a student who was a member of a gang and did some very foolish things that led him to be expelled from the school system three times. After every expulsion he would return to my office at the end of his expulsion and ask for a second chance. After long discussions, I would let him back into the school and watch him closely. He had a teacher who also looked after him. As long as he came back asking for another chance, I was willing to go the distance with him. He finally did graduate from high school and is a successful citizen today. He contributes much of his success to me and his teacher for not giving up on him. I contribute it mostly to his "no quit" attitude and the chance that two adults did not lose hope. Try to see the good in each student no matter how hard it is. Find a teacher to work along with you in your mission to guide the troubled student. Good luck.

---

must be valid (measures what it purports to measure), and the test must be reliable (scores of the test taker are repeatable over time).

### Assessment Centers

The National Association of Secondary School Principals (NASSP) Assessment Center is an approach to the selection of school principals that is rapidly gaining in popularity.[30] It is particularly good for selecting present school district employees for promotion to principal or assistant principal positions. A typical NASSP Assessment Center lasts two days, with groups of six to twelve

assessees participating in a variety of administrative exercises. Most **assessment centers** include two in-basket tests, two leaderless-group exercises, a fact-finding exercise, and a personal interview. A panel of NAASP-trained assessors evaluate candidates individually on a number of dimensions, using a standardized scale. Later, by consensus, a profile of each candidate is devised.

Assessment centers are valid predictors of administrative success, and some business firms now use them for hiring technical workers. Assessment centers are also used to help design training and development programs for the purpose of improving the leadership skills of pre-service principals and in-service principals.[31]

[30]National Association of Secondary School Principals, *Leaders for the Future: Assessment and Development Programs* (Reston, VA: NASSP, n.d.).

[31]National Association of Secondary School Principals, *Professional Development and Assessment Programs* (Reston, VA: NASSP, n.d.).

| | Blacks | Females | Elderly | Handicapped |
|---|---|---|---|---|
| Intelligence and Verbal Tests | ✓✓ | + | ✓ | ? |
| Work-Sampling Tests | + | NE | NE | NE |
| Interview | + | ✓✓ | ✓ | ✓ |
| Educational Requirements | ✓✓ | + | ✓ | ? |
| Physical Tests (height, weight, etc.) | + | ✓✓ | ? | ✓✓ |

Key:
✓✓  Fairly established evidence of adverse impact
✓   Some evidence of adverse impact
?   No data that bears direct evidence of adverse impact but seem likely depending on type of handicap or type of test
NE  No or little evidence to indicate one way or the other
+   Evidence indicates that particular minority group does as well as or even better than majority members

**Figure 15–5**

Adverse Effect of Selection Devices on Minorities

Source: Adapted from Richard D. Arvey and Robert H. Faley, *Fairness in Selecting Employees,* 2nd ed., © 1988. Reprinted by permission of Pearson Education, Inc., Upper Saddle River, NJ.

Some universities use the assessment center to pinpoint areas of strengths and weaknesses on which graduate students can then focus during their doctoral studies in educational administration. For example, The University of Texas Executive Leadership Program puts each of its doctoral candidates in educational administration through a variation of a standardized NASSP Assessment Center during their first semester of study. Faculty and students then work together to develop the latter's skills based on the results of their assessment profile.

### Hiring Decision

The final step in the selection process is the hiring decision. The person who has successfully passed through the steps in the process is offered employment. The offer may be subject to the successful completion of a physical examination.

There is no perfect selection procedure. As Figure 15–5 indicates, each step in the selection process can have a potentially adverse effect on one or more protected minorities. Discriminatory practices in the past were the catalyst for much of the recent legislation prohibiting discrimination against minority groups. Most school organizations make an effort not to discriminate in their hiring practices.

## Professional Development

After recruiting and selecting new personnel, the next step is professional development. Professional development refers to teaching administrators and professionals the skills needed for both present and future positions.[32] School administrators need to help all personnel fulfill their potential by learning new skills and developing their abilities to the fullest. The three basic

[32] Michael Di Pasla et al., *Supervision, Evaluation and Professional Development* (Boston: Allyn and Bacon, 2007).

**Table 15–3   Common Professional Development Techniques**

| Methods | Comments |
| --- | --- |
| Assigned readings | Readings may or may not be specially prepared for training purposes. |
| Behavior modeling | Use of a videotaped model displaying the correct behavior, then trainee role playing and discussion of the correct behavior. Used extensively for supervisor training in human relations. |
| Simulation | Both paper simulations (such as in-basket exercises) and computer-based games teach management skills. |
| Case discussion | Small-group discussion of real or fictitious cases or incidents. |
| Conference | Small-group discussion of selected topics, usually with the trainer as leader. |
| Lecture | Oral presentation by the trainer, with limited audience participation. |
| On the job | Ranges from no instruction, to casual coaching by more experienced employees, to carefully structured explanation, demonstration, and supervised practice by a qualified trainer. |
| Programmed instruction | Self-paced method using text followed by questions and answers; expensive to develop. |
| Role playing | Trainees act out roles with other trainees, such as "boss giving performance appraisal" and "subordinate reacting to appraisal" to gain experience in human relations. |
| Sensitivity training | Called T-group and laboratory training, this is an intensive experience in a small group; individuals try new behaviors and give feedback; promotes trust, open communication, and understanding of group dynamics. |
| Vestibule training | Supervised practice on manual tasks in a separate work area with emphasis on safety, learning, and feedback. |

Source: Adapted from Ricky W. Griffin, *Management*, 3rd ed., p. 363. Copyright © 1990 by Houghton Mifflin Company. Used by permission.

steps or phases in any professional development program are assessment, training, and evaluation.

## Assessment of Professional Development Needs

A *needs analysis* should precede the planning and execution of a training program. In a needs analysis, the school administrator or personnel department determines exactly what the staff training needs are before designing a program to meet them. A needs analysis typically has a threefold focus: *organizational analysis* (analyzing the needs of the entire school district now and in the future), *operational analysis* (analyzing the needs of a specific group of jobs or positions), and *individual analysis* (analyzing the needs of the specific individual).[33] A needs analysis helps specify training objectives, the criteria for training activities, and the criteria against which the programs will be evaluated.

There are several methods of determining which needs to focus on in the training programs. The first method is to evaluate the school district's output variables (see Figure 1–2). Such variables include performance levels and growth levels of students and employees, student dropout rates, employee turnover, student

and employee absenteeism, school-community relations, employee-management relations, student attitudes toward school, employee job satisfaction, and the like. Another method for determining training needs is direct feedback from school district employees regarding what they feel are the organization's development needs. A final method of determining training needs involves projecting. If new programs, procedures, or equipment are predicted, some type of corresponding training will be needed.

## Professional Development Techniques

Numerous techniques used for professional development are available. Table 15–3 presents the most common methods. The key is to match the technique with the objectives of the professional development program. For example, if the objective is for employees to learn school district policies and procedures, then assigned readings, lecture, and programmed learning might be an effective approach. If the objective is developing better human relations, group decision making, or communications, then case discussion, conference, role playing, and sensitivity training might work well. If the objective is to teach a skill, then behavior modeling, on-the-job training, and vestibule training might

[33]Ibid.

be the most appropriate techniques. Other considerations in selecting a staff development technique include cost, time constraints, number of employees, type of employee (maintenance, clerical, professional, or administrative), and who will do the training.

## Evaluating the Professional Development Program

Evaluating the effectiveness of a professional development program is the final phase of a professional development effort. Evaluation generally occurs during four stages: before professional development begins, during professional development, immediately after the professional development experience, and after a length of time on the job. Several validated instruments are available to evaluate professional development programs.[34]

Ideally, the best method to use in evaluating the effectiveness of professional development is the controlled experiment. In a controlled experiment, one or more groups that receive training (experimental groups) and a group that does not receive training (control group) are used. Relevant data (e.g., some output variable[s]) are secured before and after the training for both the experimental group(s) and the control group. Then a comparison of the performance of the groups is made to determine to what extent any change in the relevant variable(s) occurred as a result of training. One study, which used a quasi-experimental design, found no change in principals' leadership effectiveness before and immediately following situational leadership training but did discover a change in effectiveness three years after training.[35]

## Performance Appraisal

Once employees are trained and in place in their jobs, school administrators usually begin to appraise their performance. There are many reasons to appraise how well employees are performing. First, the school district needs a check on the effectiveness of its personnel-selection procedures, by comparing scores on various selection devices used with later performance on the job. Second, administrators use the evaluations to make decisions about compensation, promotions, transfers, and sometimes demotions or terminations. Third, performance appraisals show the school district where professional development programs are needed and later gauge whether these have been effective. Finally, if employees are to perform their jobs better in the future, they need to know how well they have performed them in the past. School administrators also use feedback about employees' performance to recognize them for a job well done and to motivate them.[36]

### Performance Appraisal Methods

Organizations currently use several methods to appraise performance. For the sake of simplicity, we can group them into three categories: the judgmental approach, the absolute standards approach, and the results-oriented approach.

**Judgmental Approach**   Under this approach, a school administrator or performance appraiser is asked to compare an employee with other employees and rate the person on a number of traits or behavioral dimensions. These appraisal systems are based on the exercise of judgment by the superior. Four widely used judgmental approaches are graphic rating scales, ranking, paired comparison, and forced distribution.[37]

*Graphic Rating Scales*   A popular, simple technique for evaluating employees is to use a **graphic rating scale.** Table 15–4 shows a typical rating scale for a school administrator. Note that the scale lists a number of important work dimensions (such as leadership and management) and a performance range for each one. For each work dimension, the evaluator circles the numerical value that best describes the employee's performance. A five-point evaluation scheme is typically used to assess the important work dimensions: (1) unacceptable, (2) needs improvement, (3) acceptable, (4) commendable, and (5) outstanding. The assigned values for each dimension are then added up and totaled.

*Ranking*   An alternative method to graphic rating scales involves administrators ranking their subordi-

[34]Thomas R. Guskey, *Evaluating Professional Development* (Thousand Oaks, CA: Corwin Press, 2000).

[35]Salvatore V. Pascarella and Fred C. Lunenburg, "A Field Test of Hersey and Blanchard's Situational Leadership Theory in a School Setting," *College Student Journal,* 21 (1988): 33–37.

[36]Rebore, *Human Resources Administration: A Management Approach.*

[37]John Ivancevich, *Human Resource Management,* 8th ed. (New York: McGraw-Hill, 2006).

**Table 15–4   Abbreviated Graphic Rating Scale for School Administrators**

| Work Dimension | Rating | | | | |
| --- | --- | --- | --- | --- | --- |
| | Unacceptable | Needs Improvement | Acceptable | Commendable | Outstanding |
| Leadership | 1 | 2 | ③ | 4 | 5 |
| Management | 1 | 2 | 3 | 4 | ⑤ |
| Personnel administration | 1 | 2 | ③ | 4 | 5 |
| Administrative teaming | 1 | ② | 3 | 4 | 5 |
| Budgeting | 1 | 2 | ③ | 4 | 5 |
| Total: 16 | | | | | |

Source: Fred C. Lunenburg, "One Method of Determining Administrative Salaries," *New York State School Board Association Journal* (January 1986), p. 20. Used by permission.

nates in order of their performance effectiveness from best to worst. The usual procedure requires the rater to write the name of the best subordinate on the top of a list, then the name of the worst at the bottom and continue this sequential procedure until all subordinates are listed. **Ranking** is most frequently used for making personnel decisions such as promotions or the merit salary increase each employee will receive.

*Paired Comparison*   A modification of the ranking procedure is the **paired comparison** technique. The method overcomes the problem associated with differentiating between subordinates in the middle range of the distribution. Under paired comparisons, raters compare only two subordinates at a time until all two-way comparisons have been made among all employees. After rating all pairs, the administrator can put the subordinates into a rank order by counting up the number of times each employee has been judged superior.

*Forced Distribution*   "Grading on a curve" is a good example of the **forced distribution** method of performance appraisal. With this technique, the rater places a predetermined percentage of ratees into four or five performance categories. For example, if a five-point scale is used, the school administrator might decide to distribute employees as follows: 5 percent in the "unacceptable" category, 25 percent in the "needs improvement" category, 40 percent in the "acceptable" category, 25 percent in the "commendable" category, and 5 percent in the "outstanding" category. The usual procedure for accomplishing such a distribution is to

record each employee's name on a separate index card. Then, for each dimension being appraised (leadership, management, etc.), the employee's index card is placed in one of the five categories.

**Absolute Standards Approach**   Most appraisal measures that employ an absolute standards approach are based on job analysis. As discussed earlier, this type of analysis can provide a more detailed description of the actual behavior necessary for effective performance. School administrators compare the performance of each employee to a certain standard instead of to the performance of other employees; thus, they rate the degree to which performance meets the standard. The most common performance appraisal processes in this group are checklists, essays, critical incidents, and behaviorally anchored rating scales.[38]

*Checklists*   The most common technique in the absolute standards group is some sort of **checklist**. Checklists tend to be more behaviorally based  than either graphic rating scales or other employee-comparison methods. Table 15–5 presents a humorous example of a checklist that might be used to appraise school administrators' performance. More elaborate procedures, such as weighted and forced choice checklists, are also available. Specific weights are assigned to a list of work behaviors in the *weighted checklist*. A *forced choice checklist* consists of job-behavior statements with two

---

[38]Ibid.

**Table 15–5  A Guide to Appraising School Administrators' Performance**

| Performance Factor | Outstanding | High Satisfactory | Satisfactory | Low Satisfactory | Unsatisfactory |
|---|---|---|---|---|---|
| Quality | Leaps tall buildings with a single bound | Needs running start to jump tall buildings | Can only leap small buildings | Crashes into buildings | Cannot recognize buildings |
| Timeliness | Is faster than a speeding bullet | Only as fast as a speeding bullet | Somewhat slower than a bullet | Can only shoot bullets | Wounds self with bullets |
| Initiative | Is stronger than a locomotive | Is stronger than a bull elephant | Is stronger than a bull | Shoots the bull | Smells like a bull |
| Adaptability | Walks on water consistently | Walks on water in emergencies | Washes with water | Drinks water | Passes water in emergencies |
| Communication | Talks with God | Talks with angels | Talks to himself | Argues with himself | Loses those arguments |
| Relationship | Belongs in general management | Belongs in executive ranks | Belongs in rank and file | Belongs behind a broom | Belongs with competitor |
| Planning | Too bright to worry | Worries about future | Worries about present | Worries about past | Too dumb to worry |

Source: Anonymous.

to five response items in each set that correlate with high- and low-performing employees. The end result is a single numerical rating that is useful for personnel decisions such as salary and promotion.

*Essays* The **essay** method requires the rater to describe in writing each employee's strengths and weaknesses, along with suggestions for ways to improve performance. Some school districts require every rater to respond to specific open-ended questions, whereas others allow more flexibility. Compared to employee comparison methods, the essay method is time-consuming and difficult to quantify. Variations in writing skills of raters is another limitation. Some school districts have combined the graphic and essay methods by providing space for comments on the graphic rating scale.

*Critical Incidents* The **critical incidents** technique begins by identifying job requirements for successful performance. Job requirements are those behaviors that determine whether the job is being done effectively or ineffectively. The school administrator keeps a log, for each subordinate, of both effective and ineffective "incidents" of on-the-job behaviors. The incidents are then analyzed and refined into a composite picture of the required essentials in a particular job. From this a checklist is developed, which constitutes the framework against which the subordinate is evaluated. During the evaluation conference, the administrator can refer to the critical incidents to correct work deficiencies, identify training needs, or praise successful performance.

*Behaviorally Anchored Rating Scales* A newer and somewhat related approach to the critical incidents technique is the **behaviorally anchored rating scale** (BARS). It was developed to cope with the problem of identifying scale anchor points. Specifically, the scale points such as unacceptable, needs improvement, acceptable, commendable, and outstanding (as shown in Table 15–4) may be difficult to define and may lead to unreliable or invalid appraisal results. Hence, the BARS defines scale points with specific behavior statements that describe varying degrees of performance. The form for a BARS generally covers six to eight specifically defined performance dimensions. A BARS should be developed for each dimension.

Figure 15–6 shows an example of a BARS for the testing competence-performance dimension for school psychologists. The scale anchors define the particular response categories for the evaluator. The response

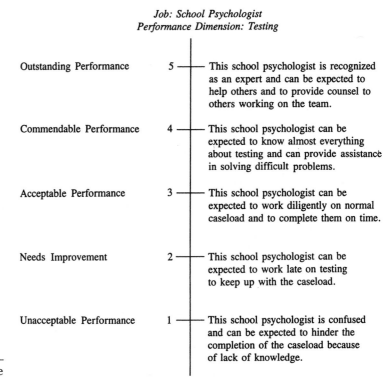

*Job: School Psychologist*
*Performance Dimension: Testing*

Outstanding Performance    5 ——— This school psychologist is recognized as an expert and can be expected to help others and to provide counsel to others working on the team.

Commendable Performance    4 ——— This school psychologist can be expected to know almost everything about testing and can provide assistance in solving difficult problems.

Acceptable Performance    3 ——— This school psychologist can be expected to work diligently on normal caseload and to complete them on time.

Needs Improvement    2 ——— This school psychologist can be expected to work late on testing to keep up with the caseload.

Unacceptable Performance    1 ——— This school psychologist is confused and can be expected to hinder the completion of the caseload because of lack of knowledge.

**Figure 15–6**

Behaviorally Anchored Rating Scale

made by the evaluator is specific enough to be used as feedback in an appraisal interview with the school psychologists and is meaningful to the subordinate. For example, if the school psychologist were given a 3 on this dimension, the subordinate would be given the specific performance indicators that led to the evaluator's rating.

**Results-Oriented Approaches**    In recent years, results-oriented approaches to performance appraisal have been suggested as an alternative to the judgmental and absolute standards approaches. As the name implies, the emphasis of results-oriented approaches is on the evaluation of results—both quantitative and qualitative. Put another way, the focus is on what the subordinate is supposed to accomplish on the job rather than a consideration of the subordinate's traits or on-the-job behaviors.

*Goal Setting*    One popular results-oriented approach is **goal setting.** We discussed goal-setting theory[39] in Chapter 4 and, more specifically, as a motivational

technique. Goal setting can also serve as the foundation for a school district's performance appraisal system. It is particularly well suited to high-level administrative positions for which methods such as BARS may be inappropriate.

This program typically includes two major elements. First, the supervisor and the subordinate meet to discuss goals, which are established by the supervisor alone or jointly by the supervisor and the subordinate. Second, the supervisor and the subordinate meet to appraise the subordinate's performance in relation to the previously established goals. For example, suppose a high school principal sets a goal of increasing average daily attendance (ADA) in the building next year by 15 percent. At the end of the school year, this goal provides a framework for performance appraisal. If attendance has increased by 15 percent or more, a positive performance appraisal is likely. However, if ADA has increased by only 5 percent and if the principal is directly responsible for the results, a more negative evaluation may be in order. Then suggestions for improvement can be specified.

*Other Results-Oriented Measures*    Besides goal setting, school administrators can use a variety of other results-

---

[39]Edwin A. Locke and Gary P. Latham, *A Theory of Goal Setting and Task Performance,* 2nd ed. (Englewood Cliffs, NJ: Prentice Hall, 1994).

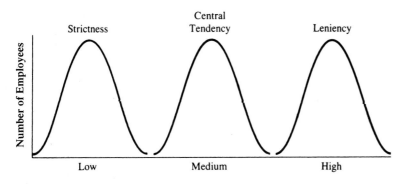

**Figure 15–7**

Strictness, Central Tendency, and Leniency Performance Ratings

oriented measures to assess subordinate performance. Some suggestions include measures of quantity of output, such as number of articles published, words typed, or items produced; measures of quality, such as reputation of the journal, typographical errors, or items rejected; measures of lost time, such as absenteeism or tardiness; or measures involving education, training, or experience, such as time in the field or time in a particular position. Although these measures tend to be nonjudgmental, they measure only one dimension of job performance. Such measures can also be tied to a goal-setting program.

### Rating Errors

In conducting performance appraisals, school administrators must be careful to avoid making rating errors. Four of the more common rating errors are strictness or leniency, central tendency, halo effect, and recency of events.[40]

**Strictness or Leniency**   Some supervisors tend to rate all their subordinates consistently low or high. These are referred to as **strictness and leniency errors.** The strict rater gives ratings lower than the subordinate deserves. This strictness error penalizes superior subordinates. The lenient rater tends to give higher ratings than the subordinate deserves. Just as the strictness error punishes exceptional subordinates, so does the leniency error. Strictness-leniency bias presents less of a problem when absolute standards and results-oriented approaches to performance appraisal are used.

---

[40]Michael Deblieux, *Performance Appraisal Source Book: A Collection of Practical Samples* (Alpharetta, GA: Society for Human Resource Management, 2003).

**Central Tendency**   Some raters are reluctant to rate subordinates as very high or very low. They dislike being too strict with anyone by giving them an extremely low rating, and they may believe that no one ever deserves to get the highest possible rating. The result of this type of attitude is that everyone is rated around average. Figure 15–7 depicts examples of strictness, leniency, and **central tendency biases.** The distribution of ratings on the left of the figure indicates a strictness error; those in the middle indicate a central tendency error; and the cluster on the right indicates a leniency error.

**Halo Effect**   When a single positive or negative dimension of a subordinate's performance is allowed to influence the supervisor's rating of that subordinate on other dimensions, a **halo effect** is operating. For example, the supervisor likes Tom because he is so cooperative. The halo effect leads Tom's supervisor to automatically rate him high on all appraisal dimensions, including leadership, management, personnel administration, administrative teaming, and even budgeting. The result is that subordinates are rated consistently high, medium, or low on all performance appraisal dimensions.

**Recency of Events**   Ideally, performance appraisals should be based on data collected about a subordinate's performance over an entire evaluation period (usually six months to a year). However, as is often the case, the supervisor is likely to consider recent performance more strongly than performance behaviors that occurred earlier. This is called the **recency of events error.** Failure to include all performance behaviors in the performance appraisal of a subordinate can bias the ratings.

Strictness or leniency, central tendency, halo effect, and recency of events all result in inaccurate performance appraisals of employees. The absolute standards and results-oriented approaches to performance appraisal, particularly BARS and goal setting, attempt to minimize such rating errors.

## Compensation

The compensation of employees is another important component of the personnel evaluation process.[41] A sound compensation program can help organizations attract qualified applicants, retain desirable employees, and motivate and reward high employee performance. The formal compensation system takes the form of wages and salaries and fringe benefits.

### Wages and Salaries

Because wages and salaries affect every member of the organization, they are one of the most important parts of a compensation program. A successful compensation program involves three major decisions: wage level decisions, wage structure decisions, and individual wage decisions.

**Wage Level Decisions**   To develop an equitable compensation program, personnel administrators determine wage and salary levels that are comparable for the industry and geographic area. *Wage leaders* are those organizations that pay employees more than the average paid for similar jobs in the industry and geographic area. One example of a wage leader is the Rochester (New York) Public Schools, known as the Rochester Experiment, which paid its teachers among the highest salaries in the nation—some at $70,000 a year almost twenty years ago.[42]

*Wage followers* pay less than the average for the industry and area. Most organizations make an effort to pay what the competition is paying. A **wage survey** can be used to determine what other organizations pay employees. Then personnel administrators can adjust wage levels to meet or exceed the comparable rates.

The salaries that a school district pays its certified employees vary by geographic area. There is published information on nonsupervisory jobs from which school organizations can draw. The Bureau of Labor Statistics has conducted a number of surveys covering various blue-collar and white-collar jobs in different regions of the country. Many professional associations also conduct surveys focused on specific jobs. For example, the National Association of Elementary School Principals (NAESP), National Association of Secondary School Principals (NASSP), American Association of School Administrators (AASA), and Association for School Business Officials (ASBO) survey wage levels, respectively, for elementary, middle, and high school principals, school superintendents, and school business officials. The American Association of University Professors (AAUP) annually surveys wage levels for college and university professors.

**Wage Structure Decisions**   Whereas wage level involves the comparison of wages and salaries paid in comparable organizations, wage structure describes the relative worth of particular jobs within the organization. To determine what jobs are worth, many organizations use a technique called **job evaluation.** The basic information necessary for a job evaluation is obtained during job analyses, discussed earlier. The results of job analyses describing such items as responsibilities, education, skill requirements, and physical requirements of the job are used to evaluate the job. The higher the evaluation, the higher the wages or salaries associated with the job.

The four principal systems of job evaluation are job ranking, the classification system, the point system, and the factor comparison method.[43]

*Job Ranking*   Job ranking is the simplest form of job evaluation. Responsibilities and other characteristics associated with each job are examined, and the jobs are ranked from most demanding to least demanding. To facilitate this ranking, benchmark jobs are selected, and others are inserted between them. For example, the most highly skilled nonsupervisory job in a school district is computer programmer, and the lowest is that

---

[41]WorldatWork, *The WorldatWork Handbook of Compensation, Benefits and Total Rewards* (New York: John Wiley, 2007); Bruce R. Ellig, *The Complete Guide to Executive Compensation* (New York: McGraw-Hill, 2007).

[42]Jerry Buckley, "The Rochester Experiment: A Blueprint for Better Schools," *U.S. News and World Report,* 104, no. 2 (1988): 60–65; Buckley, "The Rochester Experiment: School Reform, School Reality," *U.S. News and World Report,* 104, no. 24 (1988): 58–63.

[43]Michael Armstrong et al. *The Job Evaluation Handbook: A Guide to Achieving Equal Pay* (London: Kogan Page, 2004).

of maintenance worker. In between are numerous gradations of jobs. When a few of these nonsupervisory jobs are analyzed and placed on the scale, the remaining jobs can be ranked by comparing them with those already on the scale.

*Classification System*   A **classification system** places jobs and salaries in levels. The U.S. Civil Service has eighteen classification levels (L1 through L18) that are used to determine salary ranges for its employees. These classification levels are assigned to jobs from most to least difficult and important. For example, school organizations typically have classification levels for clerical employees: Receptionists may be classified as level 1 (L1), secretaries L2, private secretaries L3, office managers L4, and the like. If such a job evaluation is districtwide, it ensures that there is some internal equity in the ranking of jobs based on hierarchical positions.

*Point System*   One of the most widely used methods of job evaluation today is the **point system.** Under the point system, various factors are designated—for example, mental requirements, skill requirements, physical requirements, responsibilities, and supervision—and the maximum number of points allowable for each is determined. A computer programmer will then receive the maximum number of points for mental requirements, and other jobs proportionately less according to the number of mental requirements they require. Wage rates are then linked to the number of points assigned to the job.

*Factor Comparison Method*   Like the point system, the **factor comparison method** also makes use of job factors. However, the factor comparison method creates a key scale for measuring jobs. This is the basic difference between it and the point system. Typically, twenty or thirty jobs in the organization are analyzed to form the key comparison scale. Each job is ranked by each factor in turn, and the portion of the total salary paid for this factor is determined. This in turn determines the weight to be given to each factor in arriving at a final ranking. Table 15–6 presents the factors used in a hypothetical school district's job-evaluation system and the percentage of total wages that determines each one.

The major advantage of the factor comparison method over the point system is that higher-level jobs can be added to an original system. The point system, for example, requires developing separate systems to handle maintenance, professional, and administrative

**Table 15–6   Key Comparison Scale**

| Factor | Percentage |
| --- | --- |
| Mental requirements | 20 |
| Skill requirements | 30 |
| Physical requirements | 5 |
| Responsibilities | 20 |
| Supervision requirements | 25 |
| TOTAL | 100 |

tasks, whereas the factor comparison method can take care of each of these levels within a single system.

**Individual Wage Decisions**   Once wage ranges are developed for jobs, how does an administrator determine what to pay an employee? The easiest decision is to pay a single rate for each wage classification. More typically, decisions about individual wages generally are based on a combination of factors. Employees are paid according to qualification level, that is, their prior work experience and their skill level. For example, a secretary (L2) with five years of experience is likely to earn more than a beginner, because of superior skill development. Employees are also paid based on **seniority,** that is, the length of time they have worked for an organization or in their current job. For instance, most school districts use a lockstep salary schedule for determining pay increases for teachers based solely on job seniority. Finally, employees may be paid for their performance on the job, that is, their **merit.**

## Benefits

Wages and salaries make up the major part of an organization's compensation package. Equally important are the benefits paid to employees. A recent survey reveals that benefits constitute nearly 40 percent of the cash compensation paid to employees, and in some industries, employee benefits represent two-thirds of payroll costs.[44] Some of these benefits are legally required. For example, the Social Security Act requires retirement pay, disability pay, and survivor's benefits. Unemployment compensation, also required by the act,

---

[44]U.S. Chamber of Commerce, *Employee Benefits 2007* (Washington, DC: U.S. Chamber of Commerce, 2008).

provides subsistence payments to employees who have been laid off. All states have workers' compensation laws, which provide for those who suffer job-related illnesses and injuries. Voluntary benefits include health and dental insurance, life insurance, retirement benefits, paid vacations and holidays, sick-leave pay, credit unions, recreational programs, and payment for graduate courses completed.

## Union-Management Relations

A **union** is an organization of employees formed for the purpose of influencing an employer's decisions concerning conditions of employment. **Union-management relations** is the ongoing relationship between a group of employees represented by a union and management in the employing organization. The basis for any union-management relationship is **collective bargaining,** the process of negotiating and administering a collective bargaining agreement or negotiated contract between a union and the employing organization. Collective bargaining agreements specify the rights and duties of employees and management with respect to wages, hours, working conditions, and other terms of employment. They constitute a major influence on the day-to-day operation of a school as well as the long-term administrative activities of the school district.[45]

### Union Membership

The labor union movement in the United States began in response to undesirable management practices in industry. It has spread to include employees in the public sector, such as teachers and government workers. Teachers represent the largest group of employees in an educational institution. Today, all but nine states have enacted statutes specifically establishing some rights of employees in public schools to bargain collectively with boards of education. Over 80 percent of the nation's teachers belong to either the National Education Association (NEA), which has over 1.5 million members, or the American Federation of Teachers (AFT), which has about half a million members.[46]

### Collective Bargaining

Collective bargaining is the process of negotiating between management and employees on the terms and conditions of employment. It is collective in the sense that the employees, as a unit, select representatives from their membership to meet with management to discuss issues that need to be resolved. The union bargains on items that represent the concerns of its membership. Management tries to advance the interests of the organization.

**Bargaining Issues**   Collective bargaining agreements are complex and often lengthy, written contracts that are legally binding on both management and the union(s) representing its employees. A recent agreement between the Chicago Board of Education and the Chicago Teachers' Association is over 250 pages long.[47] It is more streamlined than most. Although the specific provisions of collective bargaining agreements vary from one school district to another, the collective bargaining process and negotiated agreement generally address the following issues.[48] (Because teachers make up the largest group of employees in schools, we will limit our discussion to teachers' collective bargaining agreements. It should be noted, however, that school administrators collectively bargain with other employee unions as well.)

*Management Rights*   During collective bargaining, unions strive to increase wages, protect job security, and improve the work conditions of employees. On the other hand, management tries to protect and clarify its rights as employer. Any rights not given to the union in the collective agreement are assumed to belong to management. These are called **management rights.** A strong management rights clause in the contract reinforces statutory rights of the board of education and aids in limiting the authority of an arbitrator in the grievance process. A common management rights clause is a lengthy list of specific management prerogatives, such as the right to supervise all operations; control all property and equipment; determine the size of the workforce; assign work to be done; introduce new methods,

---

[45]William L. Sharp, *Winning at Collective Bargaining: Strategies Everyone Can Live With* (Lanham, MD: Scarecrow Press, 2003).

[46]U.S. Department of Labor, Bureau of Labor Statistics, *Employment and Earnings* (Washington, DC: U.S. Government Printing Office, 2008).

[47]Chicago Board of Education, *Chicago Board of Education–Chicago Teachers' Association (CBA-CTA Agreement 1997–2000* (Chicago Board of Education, Chicago, 2000).

[48]Michael R. Carrell et al., *Labor Relations and Collective Bargaining: Cases, Practice and Law* (Englewood Cliffs, NJ: Prentice Hall, 2006).

programs, or procedures; hire and fire employees; promote, demote, and transfer employees; and in general maintain an orderly, effective, and efficient operation.

*Narrow Grievance Definition*　A grievance procedure is a formal system by which contract disputes are expressed, processed, and judged. The definition of a grievance in a written collective bargaining agreement determines which employee complaints are subject to binding grievance arbitration. A **narrow grievance definition** that limits employee complaints to the specific written agreement is recommended. Such an approach does not preclude other complaint procedures. It does limit what a grievance arbitrator can decide during the written terms of the negotiated agreement in force.

*No-Strike Provision*　Federal law prohibits strikes by teachers. Most states have passed similar laws. Because teacher strikes occur despite the laws against them, additional protection can be gained through a **no-strike provision** in the collective bargaining agreement. Such a provision puts the union on record against strikes and involves the union in the enforcement of the laws prohibiting them. In addition, a no-strike provision usually permits management to impose monetary damages on teachers who engage in an illegal strike.

*Zipper Clause*　A **zipper clause,** or waiver provision, stipulates that the written agreement is the complete and full contract between the parties and that neither party is required to bargain on other items during the term of the agreement. The purpose of such a provision is to avoid continuing negotiations after the contract has been ratified; when coupled with a strong management rights clause, it limits the role of past practice used by grievance arbitrators.

Such a provision, however, does not preclude the parties from negotiating further if both agree. New bargaining strategies, including collaborative or win-win bargaining, would be an exception to the use of a zipper clause. The idea of collaborative bargaining is that union and management negotiate continually during the year as problems arise.

*Maintenance of Standards*　Management should avoid a **maintenance of standards** provision. Such a provision is routinely included in most union proposals and incorporates the school district's current practices on a wide range of items, many of which are not mandatory subjects of bargaining. Furthermore, a maintenance of standards provision leaves the district vulnerable to the role of past practice used by grievance arbitrators in settling contract disputes. It is the antithesis of a management rights provision and a zipper clause.

An example of a maintenance of standards provision is the following:

> All conditions of employment, including teaching hours, extra compensation for work outside regular teaching hours, relief periods, leaves and general working conditions shall be maintained at not less than the highest minimum standards, provided that such conditions shall be improved for the benefit of teachers, as required by the express provisions of this agreement. The agreement shall not be interpreted or applied to deprive teachers of professional advantages heretofore enjoyed, unless expressly stated herein.[49]

Management should avoid such a provision.

*Just Cause*　The term **just cause** is found in numerous collective bargaining agreements in public education and is routinely included in most union proposals. There is a danger in using such a term, from management's standpoint, because *just cause* has no clear definition. If a collective bargaining agreement has binding arbitration as the last step in the grievance procedure, then an arbitrator will decide what the term means. The arbitrator's interpretation of the term may be different from what management had intended. For example, suppose a collective bargaining agreement contained the following provision: "No teacher will be disciplined without *just cause*." What does *just cause* mean in this case? It will likely mean something different to management than to employees. The point is that the meaning of *just cause* must be spelled out clearly somewhere in the contract or eliminated entirely.

*Reduction in Force*　Most all collective bargaining agreements have some form of **reduction in force** (RIF) provision. Seniority, or length of continuous service within a certificated field, is the key factor used in employee layoff and recall. Some agreements allow for **bumping,** which means that teachers laid off in one certificated field may replace another teacher in another certificated area who has less seniority in the field than the bumping teacher. A few RIF provisions stress other factors such as affirmative action and teacher merit. Such provisions are more favorable to management but are opposed by most teachers' unions.

---

[49]Peggy Odell Gander, *Collective Bargaining* (Arlington, VA: American Association of School Administrators, 1981), p. 22.

*Wages and Benefits*   Much time at the bargaining table is devoted to wage increases and fringe-benefit improvements. Wage and salary increases are often stated as across-the-board salary increases for steps on a lockstep salary schedule and **cost-of-living adjustments** (COLA) based on the Consumer Price Index in a designated geographic area. Besides salary increases, unions often demand improvements in various fringe benefits such as insurance programs (life, health, and dental); pension plans; merit pay; and sick leave, personal days, and paid religious holidays. Compensation costs in today's school districts often range from 75 to 85 percent of the total budget.

*Other Issues*   Among other important bargaining issues are grievance arbitration, teacher evaluation, class size, school calendar, and the like. Binding grievance arbitration is not a problem providing the rest of the agreement protects management prerogatives. Likewise, teacher evaluation, class size, and school calendar should not be overly restrictive on the school district.

**The Bargaining Process**   To bargain for these issues, management and the union each select a negotiating team. Opinions vary widely on who should conduct management negotiations. In small school districts, the superintendent or a board member often conducts negotiations with the teachers' union. Experts advise against this practice, however.[50] In large districts, a full-time administrator (director of employee relations, assistant superintendent, or director of personnel) usually serves as chief negotiator. Still other districts employ an outside negotiator—an attorney or labor relations specialist.

One of a superintendent's basic personnel decisions concerning collective bargaining is whether to have a labor relations specialist at the bargaining table to advise the school district or perhaps even represent the district during negotiations. When hiring a labor relations specialist, the superintendent must decide how much authority to give him or her.

One or more building administrators often are included on management's negotiating team. These people live with the contract day to day; they know its weak and strong points; they will administer the new agreement; and they will likely give the contract greater support if they can participate in the changes made in it. The union team generally consists of the local union

president and other members of the local membership. Its team may also include an attorney or a labor relations specialist from a regional unit who negotiates for other teachers' unions in the region.

Once each side has selected its negotiating teams, the bargaining process begins. The bargaining takes place in face-to-face meetings between management and union representatives during which numerous proposals and counterproposals are exchanged. Several rounds of negotiations may be needed to reach agreement on all issues. When the two parties agree on the issues, a new negotiated contract is presented to the union membership and the board for a **ratification vote.** If both parties approve the agreement, it goes into effect. If they reject the agreement, each goes back to the bargaining table for another round of negotiations.

An **impasse** is said to exist when both parties are unable to reach agreement on a contract. State procedures vary when the union and the school board are deadlocked in negotiations. Most states have some provision for resolving impasses. Some states, like Wisconsin, have developed a procedure for resolving impasses. The procedure involves the following three steps:

1. **Mediation.** The two contending parties meet with a neutral third person who attempts to persuade them to settle the remaining issues through discussion and by proposing compromise provisions to the contract. The mediator acts as a facilitator, however, and has no legal authority to force the parties to accept the suggestions offered.

2. **Fact Finding.** The state appoints a group or committee to investigate and report the facts that are presented by each party. The fact-finding committee's recommendations are generally made public, which places additional pressure on the parties to come to agreement.

3. **Arbitration.** If the parties are still at an impasse, state law may require the union and the school board to submit to arbitration or binding arbitration. Guidelines for teachers' contracts in Wisconsin, for example, stipulate that arbitrators must choose the proposal of either the school board or the teachers' union, but not a compromise solution. This forces the two contending parties to bring their contract proposals closer together. The result has been a decrease in teacher strikes in Wisconsin.[51]

[50]Ronald R. Booth, *Collective Bargaining and the School Board Member* (Springfield, IL: Illinois Association of School Boards, 1993).

[51]American Arbitration Association, *An Inside Look at Collective Bargaining* (New York: Author, 2003).

**Bargaining Tactics** Negotiators use a number of tactics to improve their bargaining. Four tactics that are typically used are counterproposals, trade-offs, the caucus, and costing proposals.[52]

*Counterproposals* Collective bargaining consists of the exchange of proposals and counterproposals in an effort to reach settlement between the negotiating parties. A proposal is an offer presented by one party in negotiations for consideration by the other party. A **counterproposal**, which is designed to bring the parties closer together on an issue, is an offer suggested as an alternative to the previous proposal by the other party. Because it is the union that is seeking improved conditions of employment, it introduces the majority of proposals. Generally, management responds to the union's demands through counterproposals. Actually, there are at least two advantages to this approach for management: (1) The party that moves first on an issue is usually at a disadvantage, for it invariably reveals some information helpful to the other negotiator; and (2) the union, as the initiating party, is forced to work for every concession it gets.

*Tradeoffs* Another bargaining tactic is the **tradeoff**, which is giving one issue in return for another. For example, a teachers' union will make a number of proposals, such as (1) fair share, (2) salary increase, (3) increased sick leave, (4) increased personal days, (5) extra holiday(s), (6) hospitalization, (7) life insurance, (8) dental insurance, (9) maternity leave, (10) binding arbitration of grievances, (11) past practice provision, (12) reduction in force procedures, (13) teacher evaluations, (14) class size, (15) school calendar, and the like. Management then responds by stating that it will grant a 5 percent salary increase if the union withdraws its proposals for increased sick leave and personal days, hospitalization, life insurance, and dental insurance. Further, management will grant the past practice clause if the union drops its request for binding arbitration of grievances. All proposals are "packaged" in this manner until the teacher's union and the school board reach a settlement. While neither party wants to give up its item, each may perceive the exchange as a reasonable compromise.

*Caucus* A basic principle of negotiating is that only one person speaks at the bargaining table—the chief negotiator. The other members of the bargaining team must remain quiet. Remaining quiet at the bargaining table can be a frustrating demand for the other members of the bargaining team. A **caucus** is a private meeting of a bargaining team to decide what action to take on a particular phase of negotiations. It provides an opportunity to get needed input from other team members and to release built-up tensions that arise during stressful negotiations.

*Costing Proposals* All proposals in collective bargaining have direct, hidden, and administrative costs. Management must know the cost of all union proposals. Therefore, **costing proposals** is another important bargaining tactic.

Preparation for this phase of bargaining should be a continual process throughout the school year. Such an approach will avoid errors made in costing proposals hastily during the heat of negotiations. The logical department in a school district to maintain a data bank and generate data for costing proposals is the business office. This office can then provide a database to the board's negotiating team at the beginning of the bargaining process.

The following guidelines for costing proposals are recommended:[53]

1. *Cost Proposals Accurately.* Typically, the union will request copies of all cost data that management prepares. Management can expect distribution of part or all of the data supplied. Therefore, prepare cost data carefully. All calculations must withstand the scrutiny of the public, a mediator, a fact-finding committee, or an arbitrator.

2. *Cost Proposals Separately.* Cost each union proposal separately. For example, the estimated cost of increasing the number of personal leave days must be costed independently of a proposal for increasing the number of sick days. Each must be based on historical data and cost projections.

3. *Cost Proposals from Management's Viewpoint.* Prepare costings from management's point of view. For example, proposals to reduce services must consider either the cost of replacing those services or the economic loss resulting from not having those services performed. In one school district in

[52]Richard G. Neal, *Bargaining Tactics* (Manassas, VA: Richard Neal Associates, 1982); Joyce M. Najita et al., *Collective Bargaining in the Public Sector: The Experience of Eight States* (New York: Sharpe, 2001).

[53]Neal, *Bargaining Tactics*, pp. 77–81.

a midwestern state, a teachers' collective bargaining agreement stipulated that high school English teachers were required to teach only four classes a day (not exceeding twenty-five students in a class) in order to alleviate the heavy load of correcting daily written assignments. All other high school teachers in the district taught five classes a day. Because there were twenty-four high school English teachers in the district at an average salary of $35,000 a year, this provision in the contract cost the school district $168,000 a year ($7000 × 24).

4. *Cost Proposals as of a Common Date.* Base all costings on data gathered as of a common date. The usual cycle used in school districts is the fiscal year beginning July 1.

5. *Analyze Comparable Data from Neighboring Organizations.* The board's chief negotiator must be able to analyze comparable data from neighboring school districts. For instance, cost data from neighboring school districts must not be considered in isolation. Public school financing is tricky business and comprises numerous factors. The personnel practices and curriculum of each situation are different. While the salary schedule in one district may be better than that in another, the work load in the latter district may be less demanding (e.g., see number 3). Or the salaries in the neighboring district may be distributed differently—higher at the top of the scale but lower at the bottom, for example. Therefore, the board's chief negotiator must be thoroughly familiar with the collective bargaining agreements in neighboring districts. It is a natural tendency for the teachers' union to seek the best of both worlds.

6. *Supply Specifically Requested Information Only.* Cost data should be pertinent to each proposal. Only management's chief negotiator should be provided with the raw data that was used to prepare summaries. Related data may suggest counterproposals. Never distribute raw data to the union and supply only specifically requested information.

7. *Provide Management's Negotiating Team with a Budget Projection.* Provide management's negotiating team with a budget projection at the start of bargaining. The document can be used to set the tentative limits on the chief negotiator. The budget projections must provide a minimum and several alternatives, including factors that might influence the final budget.

The following are some important factors that influence a school district's final budget.[54] This information should be part of a school district's data bank. Such cost data can assist management's bargaining team in costing proposals.

▪ *Salary*
  Salary schedules and placement of teachers (see Table 15–7)
  Average salary of newly hired teachers
  Average base salary of teachers, by school, level, department
  Contract salaries distribution
  Past record of salary schedule improvements (dollar amount and percentage)
  Total cost of past schedule improvements
  Past record of change in the salary schedule (steps and lanes)
  Projected cost: normal increment, $100 on base schedule, 1 percent schedule increase

▪ *Fringe Benefits*
  Fringe benefits as percentage of salaries paid
  Cost of fringe benefits per new position
  Leave history: policy and record
  Separation pay: number of individuals, per diem rate, annual rate, average pay
  Sabbatical leave: granted, denials, costs, subsequent separations
  Retirements: mandatory versus actual, reason for retirement

▪ *Staffing*
  Number of employees
  Staffing ratios by school, level, department
  Recruitment history: applicants, offers, acceptances
  Separation history: number, reason, scale placement, turnover experience
  General statistics: age, gender, race, marital status of employees
  Scale placement: academic advancement record, payment for graduate credits, merit pay

▪ *Administration*
  Cost of recruitment
  Cost of selection
  Cost of training
  Cost of basic supplies and equipment for new employees
  Cost of negotiations

---

[54]Ibid., pp. 79–81.

**Table 15–7** **Salary Schedule Scattergram for a Hypothetical School District**

| Step | B.A. | No. of Staff | Cost | Step | M.A. | No. of Staff | Cost | Step | Ph.D. | No. of Staff | Cost |
|---|---|---|---|---|---|---|---|---|---|---|---|
| 1 | $43,000 | 2 | $86,000 | 1 | $45,000 | 1 | $45,000 | 1 | $47,000 | | |
| 2 | 45,000 | | | 2 | 48,000 | 2 | 96,000 | 2 | 51,000 | | |
| 3 | 47,000 | | | 3 | 51,000 | 2 | 102,000 | 3 | 55,000 | | |
| 4 | 49,000 | 2 | 98,000 | 4 | 54,000 | 4 | 216,000 | 4 | 59,000 | | |
| 5 | 51,000 | | | 5 | 57,000 | 2 | 114,000 | 5 | 63,000 | | |
| 6 | 53,000 | | | 6 | 60,000 | 3 | 180,000 | 6 | 67,000 | 1 | 67,000 |
| 7 | 55,000 | 2 | 110,000 | 7 | 63,000 | | | 7 | 71,000 | | |
| 8 | 57,000 | 3 | 171,000 | 8 | 66,000 | 2 | 132,000 | 8 | 75,000 | | |
| 9 | 59,000 | 1 | 59,000 | 9 | 69,000 | 1 | 69,000 | 9 | 79,000 | | |
| 10 | 61,000 | 2 | 122,000 | 10 | 72,000 | | | 10 | 83,000 | | |
| 11 | 63,000 | 2 | 126,000 | 11 | 75,000 | 3 | 225,000 | 11 | 87,000 | | |
| 12 | 65,000 | 8 | 520,000 | 12 | 78,000 | 17 | 1,326,000 | 12 | 91,000 | 1 | 91,000 |
| Totals | | 22 | $1,292,000 | | | 37 | $2,505,000 | | | 2 | $158,000 |

Total number of teachers: 61

Total of teachers' salaries: $3,955,000

Average teacher salary: $64,836

Budget history/forecasting
Expenditure history
Enrollment history and projections
Per-pupil cost history
Reserve trends/forecasting
Building factors affecting conditions of employment

*New Bargaining Strategies* Currently, forty-one of the fifty states permit teachers to bargain collectively with school boards. Where such bargaining is allowed, almost all school districts employ traditional or adversarial bargaining. In recent years, a new unionism, one that connects teacher participation in educational decisions to taking responsibility for outcomes, has become apparent. Studies of a number of collaborative efforts in union-management relations describe reform initiatives in Rochester, Pittsburgh, Cincinnati, Glenview, IL, Greece, NY, Jefferson County, KY, and other cities.[55] This research describes professional unionism and how it con-

trasts sharply with the beliefs and practices of traditional industrial unionism. (See Administrative Advice 15–3.)

One consequence of professional unionism is the emergence of a new mode of principal leadership. While they vary in personal style, gender, and ethnicity, professional unions share similar management styles. They empower the people with whom they work. They use a hands-on approach. They are entrepreneurs; they gather and redistribute resources and encourage others to do so. They abide by a common realization that one leads best by developing the talent of others and gaining commitment rather than compliance with organizational rules.

Consistent with professional unionism is collaborative bargaining (also known as win-win bargaining). Typically, collaborative bargaining focuses on ongoing problem solving rather than dealing with a buildup of issues presented at the bargaining table. Both management and union keep a "tickler file" of problems encountered in administering the current contract. Joint committees deal with the problems encountered. Then when contract language is finally discussed the parties present specific notes to support their positions. Both parties establish agreed-on ground rules and specific time limits for negotiations, and write trust agreements and memoranda of understanding, and carefully select respected, credible members of negotiating teams.

[55]Charles T. Kerchner, Julia Koppich, and Joseph G. Weeres, *Taking Charge of Quality, How Teachers and Unions Can Revitalize Schools: An Introduction and Companion to United Mind Workers* (San Francisco: Jossey-Bass, 1998); Jane Hannaway et al., *Collective Bargaining in Education: Negotiating Change in Today's Schools* (Cambridge, MA: Harvard Education Publishing Group, 2006).

## Administrative Advice 15–3

### Contrasts Between Industrial and Professional Unionism

Here industrial-style teacher unionism is contrasted with professional-style teacher unionism in three areas: responsibilities, relationships, and protection.

### Industrial-Style Teacher Unionism

**Emphasizes the separateness of labor and management:**

- Separation of managerial and teaching work
- Separation between job design and its execution
- Strong hierarchical divisions

*Motto: "Boards make policy, managers manage, teachers teach."*

**Emphasizes adversarial relationships:**

- Organized around teacher discontent
- Mutual deprecation—lazy teachers, incompetent managers
- Win/lose distributive bargaining
- Limited scope contract

*Motto: "It's us versus them."*

**Emphasizes protection of teachers:**

- Self-interest
- External quality control

*Motto: "Any grievant is right."*

### The Emerging Union of Professionals

**Emphasizes the collective aspect of work in schools:**

- Blurring the line between teaching and managerial work through joint committees and lead teacher positions
- Designing and carrying out school programs in teams
- Flattened hierarchies, decentralization

*Motto: "All of us are smarter than any of us."*

**Emphasizes the interdependency of workers and managers:**

- Organized around the need for educational improvement
- Mutual legitimation of skill and capacity of management and union
- Interest-based bargaining
- Broad scope contract and other agreements

*Motto: "Be hard on the problem, not on each other."*

**Emphasizes protection of teachers:**

- Combination of self-interest and public interest
- Internal quality control

*Motto: "The purpose of the union is not to defend its least competent members."*

Source: Adapted from Charles T. Kerchner, "Building the Airplane as It Rolls Down the Runway," *School Administrator*, 10 (1993): 10. Used by permission.

---

These procedures can help establish trust and a sense of collaboration to solve mutual problems throughout the school year and at the bargaining table.

## Summary

1. The personnel process consists of the following steps: human resource planning, recruitment, selection, professional development, performance appraisal, and compensation. Of particular concern for today's administrators is the growing body of laws regulating the personnel process.

2. Human resource planning begins with a forecast of the number and types of employees needed to achieve the organization's objectives. Planning also includes preparation of job descriptions and specifications.

3. Recruitment involves the initial screening of prospective employees. Sources of prospective employees can be located inside or outside the organization.

## PRO/CON Debate

### Superintendent Searches

One of the most important decisions a school board can make is the appointment of a superintendent of schools. Some boards conduct a search on their own. Some work with their local intermediate unit or district superintendent. Minimal expense is incurred with either of these options. Other boards employ executive search firms or superintendent search consultants (generally, educational administration professors who specialize in this service). Search firms and search consultants charge large fees.

**Question:** Does the involvement of an executive search firm or a superintendent search consultant justify the expense?

### Arguments PRO

1. Boards rarely have the expertise to conduct a legal search. Candidates' civil rights are protected by law and regulation. Without the guidance of experts, boards have been known to make serious errors in these areas.

2. Consultants and search firms can get inside information about candidates because they know the network and have the credibility to tap into the network. They are more likely to learn sensitive information about candidates from references and other sources.

3. Consultants and search firms are constantly on the alert for good candidates. They follow the careers of promising administrators and share perceptions with each other. They have an expert's knowledge of the candidates.

4. Aspiring superintendents know who the search consultants are and can strive to attract their attention.

5. The intermediate unit heads or district superintendents are expert at conducting searches. However, because the superintendent works in a dependent relationship to them, the intermediate unit or district superintendent has a vested interest in the identification of candidates who fit their profile, not the school district board's profile.

6. The use of professional researchers depoliticizes the process of identifying a superintendent. The consultant is an outside person without ties in the district who can be disinterested about the identification of candidates.

### Arguments CON

1. Boards can learn how to conduct an appropriate search by consulting the state school board association and reviewing the literature.

2. Board members can learn what they need to know about candidates from a careful reading of résumés, telephone contact with references, thoughtful interviews, and site visits to candidates' workplaces.

3. Consultants and search firms are notorious for nurturing and recommending white males whom they perceive to be the best candidates in their network. Their network is the "old-boy" network.

4. The search experts become king makers. They gain power because aspiring administrators must stay in their good graces. Candidates call search consultants' interviews at national conferences "meat markets."

5. Intermediate unit heads or district superintendents are as expert at search consulting as the firms that charge for the service. In addition, they know the school district well and therefore can help the board find a candidate who will meet its unique needs.

6. The school board makes the final selection of the superintendent whether or not a search consultant is involved.

4. Selection involves choosing an individual to hire from among the pool of applicants who have been recruited. Biographical information, testing, interviews, reference checks, and assessment centers are often used as aids in the selection process.

5. Professional development helps employees perform their jobs better and prepares them for future jobs. The professional development process involves determining development needs, designing and implementing the development program, and evaluating the development program.

6. Performance appraisal is the systematic observation and evaluation of employee behavior. Some of the most commonly used methods of appraisal include the judgmental approach, the absolute standards approach, and the results-oriented approach.

7. Compensation includes wages and salaries and fringe benefits. Wage and salary levels are usually tied to what other organizations in the field pay. Legally required benefits are Social Security, workers' compensation, and unemployment insurance. Other benefits include pension plans, insurance programs, leaves, educational benefits, and the like.

8. Most states permit teachers to bargain collectively with boards of education. Labor relations refers to dealing with employees when they are organized into a union. Management must engage in collective bargaining with the union in an effort to reach agreement on a contract. The most recent approaches to collective bargaining are referred to as "win-win bargaining."

## Key Terms

human resource planning
recruitment
selection
professional development
performance appraisal
compensation
job analysis
job description
job specification
observation
work sampling
critical incident
interview
questionnaire
forecasting

human resource audit
Equal Employment Opportunity Commission
equal employment opportunity
affirmative action program
internal recruitment
closed recruitment system
open recruitment system
external recruitment
biographical information
reference checks
testing
assessment center
graphic rating scale
ranking
paired comparison
forced distribution
checklist
essay
critical incidents
behaviorally anchored rating scale
goal setting
strictness and leniency errors
central tendency bias
halo effect
recency of events error
wage survey
job evaluation
job ranking
classification system
point system
factor comparison method
seniority
merit
union
union-management relations
collective bargaining
management rights
narrow grievance definition
no-strike provision
zipper clause
maintenance of standards
just cause
reduction in force
bumping
cost-of-living adjustments
ratification vote
impasse
mediation
fact finding
arbitration
counterproposal

tradeoff
caucus
costing proposal

## Discussion Questions

1. What steps does your school/school district use in selecting personnel?

2. Discuss the advantages and disadvantages of internal and external recruiting. What techniques can administrators use to improve their recruiting and selection practices?

3. What are some of the federal laws and agencies that affect recruitment and selection of personnel?

4. Describe the procedure used to develop a wage and salary structure for a school district. What system does your school/school district use to compensate personnel?

5. What are the major issues that are negotiated at the bargaining table between the board of education and the teachers' union? Discuss some bargaining tactics that management can use to improve its position in the collective bargaining process. Discuss some of the new bargaining approaches that have emerged over the last decade.

## Suggested Readings

David A. DeCenzo et al. *Fundamentals of Human Resource Management* (New York: John Wiley, 2006). This text provides the most practical, most comprehensive treatment available of the personnel function as it applies to educational administration.

Harris, Ben M. *Human Resource Management,* 3rd ed. (Fort Worth, TX: Harcourt Brace, 2003). The author looks to the future and addresses specialized aspects of personnel practice including the legal and financial, as well as collective bargaining and salary administration.

Nigro, Felix A., and Lloyd G. Nigro. *The New Public Personnel Administration,* 6th ed. (Itasca, IL:

Peacock, 2002). The authors provide an excellent introduction to all aspects of personnel administration, including human resource planning, recruitment, selection, appraisal, development, compensation, and bargaining.

Rebore, Ronald W. *Human Resources Administration: A Management Approach,* 7th ed. (Boston, MA: Allyn and Bacon, 2006). The author provides a practical, comprehensive treatment of the personnel function as it operates from a central office perspective. The text emphasizes the management approach, which is organized around the processes and procedures necessary for effective personnel administration.

Sanders, James R. *Program Evaluation Standards,* 4th ed. (Thousand Oaks, CA: Sage, 2003). Aimed at providing a guide for evaluating educational and training programs, projects, and materials in a variety of settings, these thirty standards were compiled by the Joint Committee on Standards for Educational Evaluation from knowledge gained from the professional literature as well as from years of experience by educators and evaluation specialists.

Seyfarth, John T. *Personnel Management for Effective Schools,* 4th ed. (Needham Heights, MA: Allyn and Bacon, 2007). The book emphasizes the relationship of personnel management to student learning. It also emphasizes personnel practice in schools with site-based management and shows practical applications for research related to personnel practice.

Webb, L. Dean, and M. Scott Norton. *Human Resources Administration: Personnel Issues and Needs in Education,* 5th ed. (Upper Saddle River, NJ: Prentice Hall, 2007). The authors address all traditional topics in personnel administration, with care taken throughout to provide a strong human resources perspective. They underscore the realization that the human element is central to an organization's progress, and that the human resources function encompasses utilization, development, and the teaching environment.

# Name Index

*Italic page numbers indicate material in tables or figures.*

# Subject Index

*Italic page numbers indicate material in tables or figures.*

# Case Index